AA

The
Pub Guide
2002

AA **Lifestyle Guides**

Produced by AA Publishing
Ordnance Survey® This product includes mapping data licensed from Ordnance Survey® with the permission of the Controller of Her Majesty's Stationery Office. © Crown copyright 2001. All rights reserved. License number 399221

Maps prepared by the Cartographic Department of The Automobile Association
Maps © The Automobile Association 2001
Directory generated by the AA Establishment Database, Information Research, AA Hotel Services
Design by Nautilus Design UK Ltd, Basingstoke, Hampshire

Editor: David Hancock
Editorial Contributors: Nick Channer, David Foster, Martin Greaves, Julia Hynard

Cover photograph The Angel, Hetton, North Yorkshire

Advertisement Sales advertisingsales@theAA.com

Lifestyle Guides Editorial:
lifestyleguides@theAA.com

Typeset/Repro by Avonset, 11 Kelso Place, Bath BA1 3AU

Printed in Italy by Rotolito Lombarda SpA

The contents of this book are believed correct at the time of printing. Nevertheless, the Publisher cannot be held responsible for any errors or omissions, or for changes in the details given in this guide, or for the consequences of any reliance on the information provided in the same. We have tried to ensure accuracy in this guide but things do change and we would be grateful if readers would advise us of any inaccuracies they may encounter.

Published in the USA by AAA

A CIP catalogue record for this book is available from the British Library

Published by AA Publishing, which is a trading name of Automobile Association Developments Limited whose registered office is Millstream, Maidenhead Road, Windsor, Berkshire, SL4 5GD Registered number 1878835.

ISBN 0749531096

Contents

PUBS

Welcome to
The Guide

Welcome to the 2002 edition of The AA Pub Guide

We aim to bring you the country's best pubs, selected for their great food and authentic atmosphere. Ours is the only major pub guide to feature colour photographs, and to highlight the 'Pick of the Pubs', uncovering Britain's finest hostelries. Fully updated, this year you will find an additional 200 pages including lots of old favourites as well as plenty of new destinations for eating and drinking and great places to stay across the country.

Who's in the guide?

Recommended pubs are carefully researched, pubs make no payment for their inclusion and selection is based on two main criteria, fine food and 'destination' pubs.

Fine Food

In addition to traditional pub favourites, we look for menus showing a commitment to home-cooking, in particular a daily-changing range of freshly prepared dishes. In keeping with recent trends in pub food, particular emphasis is placed on those offering imaginative, innovative, modern bar food and specialising in fresh fish or local produce. Around 150 pubs and inns in the guide are awarded AA Rosette Awards for food quality, these places also feature in The AA Restaurant Guide 2002.

Destination Pubs

We look for attractive and appealing pubs that are really worth going out of your way to visit. Interesting towns and villages, unusual or historic buildings and unique settings can all be found within this guide.

Pick of the Pubs & Full Page Entries

Over 500 pubs have highlighted 'Pick of the Pubs' entries. Chosen by AA Restaurant Guide inspectors and from the editor's personal knowledge, these are the best pubs in each county and feature more detailed descriptions. Ultimately, these pubs stand out and should not be missed! In the 2002 edition, 53 of our selected 'Pick of the Pubs' have opted to enhance their entry with two photographs as part of a full-page entry.

New for 2002
Get out and walk!

Why not take the whole family and the dog, work up an appetite for lunch or walk off that satisfying meal with a country ramble? Try some of the 48 new circular walks across England, Scotland and Wales, ranging from 3 to 6 miles in length and each starting from the pub car park. Walk directions and details are supplied by the pubs featured on these pages.

Tell us what you think...

We welcome your feedback about the pubs included and about the guide itself. Reader's Report forms appear at the back of the book, please write in or e-mail lifestyleguides@theaa.com to tell us about pubs you have visited and to help us improve future editions. Pubs, restaurants, hotels and bed & breakfast accommodation all feature on the AA internet site www.theAA.com.

Who's Cooking in the Pub Kitchen?

Eating out in British pubs has never been more exciting with a choice of gastro-pubs turning out delicacies from top chefs escaped from the rat race. Pub expert, Martin Greaves, explores this trend in his feature on page 12.

Pick of the Beers

Martin Greaves takes a light-hearted look at how the micro-breweries have challenged the multi-nationals and won the approval of the beer-drinking pub-goer by offering quality and choice to Britain's free houses, on page 20.

New AA Pub of the Year Award

The 2002 edition sees the introduction of a prestigious Pub of the Year Award for England, Scotland and Wales. Selected with the help of the Restaurant Guide inspectors, the chosen winners (and runners-up in England) stand out for being great all-round pubs or inns, combining excellent food, comfortable accommodation, a great pub atmosphere and a warm welcome from friendly, efficient staff, with a high standard of management from hands-on owners. The winning entries appear at the front of each country section in the guide.

Pub of the Year for England

The Drunken Duck, Ambleside, Cumbria
(see entry on page 93)

Runners-Up:

The Village Pub, Barnsley, Gloucestershire
(see entry on page 180)
The Rose and Crown, Romaldkirk, Co. Durham
(see entry on page 169)

Pub of the Year for Scotland

The Wheatsheaf Inn, Swinton, Scottish Borders
(see entry on page 561)

Pub of the Year for Wales

The Bear Hotel, Crickhowell, Powys
(see entry on page 594)

About The Editor

David Hancock has edited The AA Pub Guide for four years. Over the past decade he has inspected and written about pubs for several pub food guides, including Egon Ronay's Pubs & Inns Guide and the Which? Guide to Country Pubs, as well as writing and editing various walking, cycling and general leisure guides for the AA and other leading publishers.

How to Use the Guide

ANY TOWN   Map 04 SU53

The Any Town Arms ◉ ♦♦♦♦ ♀
Any Lane RT26 1XE ☎ 05562 662764
▤ 05562 662769
Dir: *Village signed off A31 Winchester to Alton road, 6m E of Winchester*
Tucked away down a winding, wooded lane off the B52 is the

Any Town Arms, a delightful rose-covered pub in a charming setting by the tranquil River Puddle. Enjoy a riverside stroll then relax with a bar meal, perhaps mussel and prawn chowder or pork on mustard mash with juniper and fennel sauce.
OPEN: 11-3, 6-11 Sun 12-3, 7-10.30. Closed Sun eve **BAR MEALS:** L served all week 12-2.30, D served Mon-Fri 6.30-9.30 Sat 10. Av main course £8.10. **BREWERY/COMPANY:** Wadworth. **PRINCIPAL BEERS:** Wadworth 6X, Henrys IPA, & Farmers Glory, Badger Tanglefoot, guest ales. **FACILITIES:** Children welcome; Children licence; Garden, terrace, patio, pond, outdoor eating. No dogs in bar. **NOTES:** Parking 30. **ROOMS:** 4 bedrooms 4 en suite s£35 d £75

SYMBOLS AND ABBREVIATIONS

☎ Telephone number ▤ Fax number

◉ Rosettes - The AA's food award. Explanation of awards on page 9

★ Stars - The AA's rating for Hotel accommodation. Explanation of ratings on page 8

♦ Diamonds - The AA's rating for Bed and Breakfast accommodation. Explanation on page 8

🐟 Shown where a pub serves a minimum of four main course dishes where sea fish is the main ingredient. The Sea Fish Industry Authority (see page 16) have chosen seven regional winners and one overall national winner which have their entries highlighted in blue. For a list of winners see pages 18-19.

♀ 6 or more wines available by the glass

LISTING ORDER

Pubs are listed by name within their town, towns are listed within their county (a county map appears at the back of the guide). The Guide has listings for England, Scotland and Wales, in that order.

PICK OF THE PUBS

Around 500 of the best pubs in Britain have been selected by the editor and inspectors and highlighted with longer descriptions and a tinted background. 53 have a full page entry and two photographs.

PUB LISTINGS

Short pub entries. Pubs that have been recommended to us but general statistics were not available at the time of going to press.

MAP REFERENCE

The reference number denotes the map page number in the atlas section at the back of the book and the National Grid reference. Some pub listings and pubs in the Greater London area do not have a map reference.

DIRECTIONS

Directions are given wherever they have been supplied by the proprietor.

ENTRY STATISTICS

OPEN Open indicates the hours when the establishment is open and closed. Sunday hours are generally 12-3 7-10.30 unless stated.

BAR MEALS Bar Meals indicates the times and days when bar food is available, and the average price of a main course as supplied by the proprietor. Last orders may be approximately 30 minutes before the times stated.

RESTAURANT Restaurant indicates the times and days when restaurant food is available. The average cost of a 3 course à la carte meal and a 3 or 4 course fixed price menu are shown as supplied by the proprietor. Last orders may be approximately 30 minutes before the times stated.

BREWERY/COMPANY This indicates the name of the Brewery the pub is tied to or the Company the pub is owned by.

FREE HOUSE Free House indicates that the pub is independently owned and run.

ROOMS

Accommodation prices indicate the minimum single and double room prices per night. Family rooms (FR) and en suite bedrooms are also listed, and breakfast is generally included in the price, but guests should check when making a reservation. Circumstances and prices may vary during the currency of the Guide. Only accommodation with stars or diamonds has been inspected by the AA.

PRINCIPAL BEERS

Only up to five cask or hand-pulled beers served by each pub are listed.

FACILITIES

This section includes information on children (i.e. whether or not the pub welcomes children, childrens' licence etc) and gardens (e.g. outdoor eating, floral displays or barbecue area).

NOTES

Includes information on dogs and parking.

CREDIT CARDS NOT TAKEN

As so many establishments take one or more of the major credit cards, only those which take no cards are indicated.

All AA-recognised accommodation has been assessed under quality standards agreed between the AA, the English Tourism Council and the RAC and given a classification that is based on an overnight 'mystery guest' visit by one of our highly qualified inspectors. This means that whether you choose to stay in a country farmhouse or a luxury five-star hotel, you can be sure of its quality and service.

For hotels, star ratings from one to five symbolise the level of service, range of facilities and quality of guest care that you can expect. Hotels are required to meet progressively higher standards as they move up the scale from one to five stars. A small number of hotels are awarded the AA Red Star Award for outstanding quality. These hotels are indicated with red instead of black stars. For Bed & Breakfast accommodation (guest houses, farmhouses and inns), ratings from one to five diamonds reflect visitors' expectations where quality is seen as more important than facilities and services.

Detailed information on both star and diamond ratings is available at www.theAA.com/hotels.

AA Rosette Awards

How the AA assesses restaurants for Rosette Awards

The AA's rosette award scheme was the first nation-wide scheme for assessing the quality of food served by restaurants and hotels. The rosette scheme is an award scheme, not a classification scheme and although there is necessarily an element of subjectivity when it comes to assessing taste, we aim for a consistent approach to our awards throughout the UK. It is important, however, to remember that many places serve enjoyable food but do not qualify for an AA award.

Our awards are made solely on the basis of a meal visit or visits by one or more of our hotel and restaurant inspectors who have an unrivalled breadth and depth of experience in assessing quality. They award rosettes annually on a rising scale of one to five.

So what makes a restaurant worthy of a Rosette Award?

For our inspectors the top and bottom line is the food. The taste of the food is what counts for them, and whether the dish successfully delivers to the diner what the menu promises. A restaurant is only as good as its worst meal. Although presentation and competent service should be appropriate to the style of the restaurant and the quality of the food, they cannot affect the rosette assessment as such, either up or down.

The following summaries attempt to explain what our inspectors look for, but are intended only as guidelines. The AA is constantly reviewing its award criteria and competition usually results in an all-round improvement in standards, so it becomes increasingly difficult for restaurants to reach award level.

One rosette

At the simplest level, one rosette, the chef should display a mastery of basic techniques and be able to produce dishes of sound quality and clarity of flavours, using good, fresh ingredients.

Two rosettes

To gain two rosettes, the chef must show greater technical skill, more consistency and judgement in combining and balancing ingredients and a clear ambition to achieve high standards. Inspectors will look for evidence of innovation to test the dedication of the kitchen brigade, and the use of

seasonal ingredients sourced from quality suppliers.

Three rosettes

This award takes a restaurant into the big league, and, in a typical year, fewer than 10 per cent of restaurants in our scheme achieve this distinction. Expectations of the kitchen are high, and inspectors find little room for inconsistencies. Exact technique, flair and imagination will come through in every dish, and balance and depth of flavour are all-important.

Four rosettes

This is an exciting award because, at this level, not only should all technical skills be exemplary, but there should also be daring ideas, and they must work. There is no room for disappointment. Flavours should be accurate and vibrant.

Five rosettes

This award is the ultimate awarded only when the cooking is at the pinnacle of achievement. Technique should be of such perfection that flavours, combinations and textures show a faultless sense of balance, giving each dish an extra dimension. The sort of cooking that never falters and always strives to give diners a truly memorable taste experience.

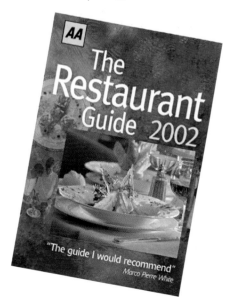

The Restaurant Guide 2002

"The guide I would recommend"
Marco Pierre White

AA ROSETTE AWARDS FOR FOOD

Pubs with
AA Rosette Awards

The pubs listed below are those which have been assessed by the AA's team of highly qualified restaurant inspectors and have been awarded one or more rosettes (the scale runs from one to five) for the notable quality of their food. A full explanation of what the Rosette award means can be found on page 9.

England

BEDFORDSHIRE
Knife & Cleaver, BEDFORD ⍟

BERKSHIRE
Inn on the Green, COOKHAM DEAN ⍟
The Red House, MARSH BENHAM ⍟
Rose & Crown, WINKFIELD ⍟
Royal Oak Hotel, YATTENDON ⍟⍟

BUCKINGHAMSHIRE
Green Dragon, HADDENHAM ⍟⍟
The Angel, LONG CRENDON ⍟⍟

CAMBRIDGESHIRE
The Chequers Inn Restaurant FOWLMERE ⍟
The Old Bridge Hotel, HUNTINGDON ⍟⍟
Pheasant Inn, KEYSTON ⍟⍟
Three Horseshoes Restaurant, MADINGLEY ⍟
Bell Inn Hotel, STILTON ⍟⍟

CORNWALL & ISLES OF SCILLY
Trengilly Wartha Inn, CONSTANTINE ⍟⍟
Old Coastguard Inn, MOUSEHOLE ⍟
Port Gaverne Hotel, PORT GAVERNE ⍟
Rising Sun Hotel, ST MAWES ⍟
New Inn, TRESCO ⍟

CUMBRIA
Drunken Duck Inn, AMBLESIDE ⍟
Tufton Arms Hotel, APPLEBY-IN-WESTMORLAND ⍟
Punch Bowl Inn, CROSTHWAITE ⍟⍟
Kings Head Hotel, THIRLSPOT ⍟⍟
Queens Head Hotel, TROUTBECK ⍟⍟

DERBYSHIRE
Rutland Arms Hotel, BAKEWELL ⍟

DEVON
The Masons Arms, BRANSCOMBE ⍟
Drewe Arms, BROADHEMBURY ⍟
Rock Inn, HAYTOR VALE ⍟
Arundell Arms, LIFTON ⍟⍟⍟
Dartmoor Inn, LYDFORD ⍟⍟
Rising Sun Hotel, LYNMOUTH ⍟⍟
The Jack In The Green Inn, ROCKBEARE ⍟
Sea Trout Inn, STAVERTON ⍟⍟
The Durant Arms Restaurant, TOTNES ⍟

DORSET
The Fox Inn, Corscombe ⍟

CO DURHAM
Rose & Crown Hotel, ROMALDKIRK ⍟⍟

ESSEX
White Hart, GREAT YELDHAM ⍟

GLOUCESTERSHIRE
Churchill Arms. CHIPPING CAMPDEN ⍟⍟
Noel Arms Hotel, CHIPPING CAMPDEN ⍟⍟
The Crown Of Crucis, CIRENCESTER ⍟
The New Inn at Coln, COLN ST-ALDWYNS ⍟⍟
Wild Duck Inn, EWEN ⍟
Fossebridge Inn, FOSSEBRIDGE ⍟
Egypt Mill Hote,l NAILSWORTH ⍟
Halfway Inn, STROUD ⍟
Trouble House Inn, TETBURY ⍟⍟

GREATER MANCHESTER
The White Hart Inn, OLDHAM ⍟⍟

HAMPSHIRE
Bell Inn, BROOK ⍟
Master Builders House Hotel, BUCKLERS HARD ⍟⍟
Star Inn, EAST TYTHERLEY ⍟
The Three Lions, FORDINGBRIDGE ⍟⍟⍟
Wykeham Arms, WINCHESTER ⍟

HEREFORDSHIRE
Roebuck Inn, BRIMFIELD ⍟⍟
The Feathers, LEDBURY ⍟
The Stag Inn, KINGTON ⍟⍟
Ye Olde Salutation Inn, WEOBLEY ⍟⍟

KENT
Dove Inn, DARGATE ⍟⍟
Royal Wells Inn, ROYAL TUNBRIDGE WELLS ⍟⍟

LANCASHIRE
Millstone Hotel, BLACKBURN ⍟
Mulberry Tree, WRIGHTINGTON ⍟

LINCOLNSHIRE
Black Horse Inn, BOURNE ⍟⍟
Wig & Mitre, LINCOLN ⍟
The George of Stamford, STAMFORD ⍟

LONDON POSTAL DISTRICTS
The Salt House, LONDON NW8 ⍟
The Fire Station, LONDON SE1 ⍟
Swag & Tails, LONDON SW7 ⍟
Anglesea Arms, LONDON W6 ⍟

NORFOLK
Hoste Arms Hotel, BURNHAM MARKET ⍟⍟
The Kings Head, COLTISHALL ⍟
Lifeboat Inn, THORNHAM ⍟
Titchwell Manor Hotel TITCHWELL ⍟

NORTHAMPTONSHIRE
The Falcon, FOTHERINGHAY ⍟⍟
The Sun Inn, MARSTON TRUSSELL ⍟

NORTHUMBERLAND
Victoria Hotel, BAMBURGH ⍟
Blue Bell Hotel, BELFORD ⍟

OXFORDSHIRE

The Blewbury Inn, BLEWBURY
The Goose, BRITWELL SALOME
The Inn For All Seasons, BURFORD
The Lamb Inn, BURFORD
Red Lion Inn, CHALGROVE
The Sir Charles Napier, CHINNOR
George Hotel, DORCHESTER-ON-THAMES
White Hart Hotel, DORCHESTER-ON-THAMES
The Lamb at Buckland, FARINGDON
Jersey Arms Hotel, MIDDLETON STONEY
The Crazy Bear, STADHAMPTON
Kings Head Inn & Restaurant, WOODSTOCK

RUTLAND

Barnsdale Lodge Hotel, OAKHAM
Ram Jam Inn, STRETTON

SHROPSHIRE

Crown Inn, Cleobury Mortimer
Hundred House Hotel, NORTON

SOMERSET

Woolpack Inn, BECKINGTON
Crown Hotel, EXFORD
The Talbot Inn, FROME
Royal Oak Inn, WITHYPOOL

STAFFORDSHIRE

The Moat House ACTON TRUSSELL

SUFFOLK

Cornwallis Country Hotel, BROME
St Peter's Hall, BUNGAY
Angel Hotel, LAVENHAM
The Cock Inn, POLSTEAD
The Crown, SOUTHWOLD
The Crown at Westleton, WESTLETON

SURREY

Bryce's Seafood Restaurant & Country Pub, OCKLEY

EAST SUSSEX

Mermaid Inn, RYE

WEST SUSSEX

George & Dragon, BURPHAM
White Horse Inn, CHILGROVE
Lickfold Inn, LICKFOLD
The Chequers Inn, ROWHOOK

WARWICKSHIRE

Howard Arms, ILMINGTON
Fox & Goose, STRATFORD

WEST MIDLANDS

The Malt Shovel at Barston, BARSTON

ISLE OF WIGHT

Seaview Hotel & Restaurant, SEAVIEW

WILTSHIRE

White Hart, FORD
The Linnet, GREAT HINTON
The Grosvenor Arms, HINDON
Lamb at Hindon Hotel, HINDON
The Harrow Inn, LITTLE BEDWYN
The Horse & Groom, MALMESBURY
George & Dragon, ROWDE
The Angel Inn, WARMINSTER
The Pear Tree, WHITLEY

WORCESTERSHIRE

Peacock Inn, TENBURY WELLS

NORTH YORKSHIRE

Crab and Lobster, ASENBY
Three Hares Inn, BILBROUGH
The Buck Inn, BUCKDEN
Red Lion Hotel, BURNSALL
The Boar's Head Hotel, HARROGATE
Feversham Arms Hotel, HELMSLEY
The Star Inn, HELMSLEY
The Angel, HETTON
The Worsley Arms Hotel, HOVINGHAM
General Tarleton Inn, KNARESBOROUGH
Fox & Hounds Country Inn, PICKERING
White Swan, PICKERING
Yorke Arms, RAMSGILL
Milburn Arms Hotel, ROSEDALE ABBEY
Wensleydale Heifer Inn, WEST WITTON

WEST YORKSHIRE

Shibden Mill Inn, HALIFAX

Scotland

Loch Melfort Hotel, ARDUAINE, ARGYLL & BUTE
Harbour Inn, BOWMORE, ARGYLL & BUTE
Cairnbaan Hotel, LOCHGILPHEAD, ARGYLL & BUTE

Creggans Inn, STRACHUR, ARGYLL & BUTE
Ubiquitous Chip, GLASGOW,
The Seafood Restaurant, ST MONANS, FIFE
Dundonnell Hotel, DUNDONNELL, HIGHLAND
Moorings Hotel, FORT WILLIAM, HIGHLAND
Hotel Eilean Iarmain, ISLE ORNSAY, HIGHLAND
Onich Hotel, ONICH, HIGHLAND
Killiecrankie Hotel, KILLIECRANKIE, PERTH & KINROSS
Lomond Country Inn, KINNESSWOOD, PERTH & KINROSS
Burt's Hotel, MELROSE, SCOTTISH BORDERS
Wheatsheaf, SWINTON, SCOTTISH BORDERS
Champany Inn, LINLITHGOW, WEST LOTHIAN

Wales

Ye Olde Bulls Head Inn, BEAUMARIS, ISLE OF ANGLESEY
Caesars Arms, CREIGIAU, CARDIFF
Kinmel Arms, ABERGELE, CONWY
Penhelig Arms Hotel Restaurant, ABERDYFI, GWYNEDD
Pantrhiwgoch Hotel, ABERGAVENNY, MONMOUTHSHIRE
Walnut Tree Inn, ABERGAVENNY MONMOUTHSHIRE
Bricklayers Arms, MONTGOMERY, POWYS
Seland Newydd, PWLLGLOYW, POWYS
Bear Hotel, CRICKHOWELL, POWYS
Gliffaes Country House Hotel, CRICKHOWELL, POWYS
Nantyffin Cider Mill Inn, CRICKHOWELL, POWYS
Dragon Hotel, MONTGOMERY, POWYS
West Arms Hotel, LLANARMON DYFFRYN CEIRIOG, WREXHAM

PUBS WITH AA ROSETTE AWARDS FOR FOOD

Who's Cooking in *the Pub Kitchen*.

by Martin Greave

The word is out in the nation's pub kitchens: produce counts.
The importance of good shopping, fresh ingredients and food
that tastes of its proper origins has entered public awareness
and fuelled debate over the last few years as never before.

So where did it all begin? One theory is that it is much longer ago than many may be aware. He was Italian, a native of Le Marche in north east Italy, a gifted cook and, as much as anything, a brilliant communicator. He married a Welsh girl, a daughter of our own Marches, dedicated, devoted and professional; and then for reasons best known only to themselves they went into business together. They bought a pub. The year was 1964 and their names were Franco and Ann Taruschio.

Interviewed some 12 years ago, Franco summed up his first quarter century in the business as follows: 'I have been so lucky to spend my working life doing what I do best - and being paid for doing it. It is a gift, a talent that is naturally ours for others to enjoy, and using this to become some sort of media idol is uncalled for'. Prophetic words, indeed.

Memories flood back of fine Italian wines purchased from the 'pub' bar and served in something akin to tooth-mugs; bowls of salad perched on bar stools adjacent to a far-too-small Britannia table; the 'boys from the back' tucking into home-made Bolognese in the half hour they had to spare between finishing the evening's preparations and the doors' re-opening; and Franco, immaculate in grey slacks untouched by gravy stains, conducting an unforgettable master-class.

Total dedication to a cause; but in so many ways a unique exception to the perceptions of the day. Those were still the days when the impression was that fine dining belonged to the city centre and dinner 'chez' whoever that would leave little change from a prince's, if not a king's, ransom. And the chef: over-worked and underpaid? Think again!

Imperceptibly at first, today's generation of cooks has come a long way in emulating Ann and Franco's basic philosophy that for so long stood virtually alone. If you can cook and do so to the best of your ability, what is wrong with plying your trade out of town and taking advantage of what our glorious countryside has to offer? This, after all, is where the finest produce can be found right on the doorstep and where the appreciation of a food-conscious public is at its most sincere - jeans, Burberrys, walking boots and all.

Even 20 years ago, one would have been hard put to find more than a handful of such places. Dennis Watkins at The Angel at Hetton (this edition's Sea Fish Industry Authority Seafood Pub of the Year), Ray Carter at The Sportsman's Arms at Pateley Bridge and the Oliver family whose Cricketers Inn at Clavering demonstrates their love of

all things Italian on menus that have evolved over the years, probably top the list of exceptions.

A little later along came Alan Reid at the Wheatsheaf at Swinton in the Scottish Borders (our Scottish Pub of the Year for 2002) whose regular hunting and fishing trips keep the kitchen in constant supply, and the incomparable Carol Evans whose breakfasts at The Roebuck in Brimfield, Shropshire, were unforgettable - from the dry-cured bacon, hand-made sausages and free-range eggs to her home-made breads, preserves and chutneys. Carol's legacy lives on there today with a blackboard selection of some dozen or more British cheeses, such as Hereford Hop, Ragstone (from Dorstone in the Golden Valley) and unpasteurised Malvern ewes' milk cheese, that is as good as anywhere in the land.

Such true dedication is the first pre-requisite, taking the time and showing the interest to find where the best fresh produce - much of it organic these days - is available; where meats of the finest provenance, from identifiable single herds, can be found and where fresh wet fish and seafoods seem to beg 'eat me now' from every ice-packed delivery box.

Perhaps they have been encouraged into this path by sheer default of so many others - and there have always been those who refer to the value of their pub outing by volume: 'I had a steak this big, and more chips than I could eat'. Wow! Backed in many cases by corporate investment it equates 'Traditional British Pub Food' with American-style burgers, beef Madras, baked lasagne and - famously it seems - chicken tikka masala; followed of course by Mississippi mud pie and Death by Chocolate delivered in moribund condition by some not-so-local food factory. Phoney foods, washed down with unliving lagers and designed to enfeeble the palate and benumb the brain.

Why then, and where-from this sudden apparent sea-change? A deep-seated and longer standing tradition probably lies at the root of it. From Nottingham's Olde Trip to Jerusalem, whence the 12th-century crusaders departed for the Holy Land to the Old Bell at Stilton, where Dick Turpin is said to have evaded the law for a full fortnight, the British have always nurtured a particular pride in their ale houses, as quintessentially British as pie-and-mash. Some of the country's more enlightened brewers and an increasing number of our best young cooks have at last hit upon a mutually beneficial solution. Any village becomes a sadder place without its local, whilst in these times if it cannot provide at least half-way acceptable food, the pub itself will die anyway.

Enter a new breed of landlord and cook where once the term chef/patron was almost de haut en bas: a man or woman of dedication and desire whose ambition to provide good food at affordable prices is ever more frustrated by the high rents, business rates and staffing costs of the Country House hotel or town-centre restaurant. And why not? A self-motivated person in the kitchen who can cook, who knows about good food and enjoys the simple pleasures of cooking unpretentiously draws in new custom, deservedly, from far and wide to the benefit of all.

Encouraged by these innovators and aware of the legitimacy of their endeavours, our dining public has opted for a new, alternative culture - and it is beginning to

> " *if my customers wish to take the time and trouble to experiment, then so will I* "

show in spades. A pint of good - and often local - real ale or a glass of carefully selected house wine on arrival; a blackboard or daily menu of fresh local produce; neither fancily-folded napkins nor ostentatious ice-buckets; an informal atmosphere for the enjoyment of good, fresh-flavoured food for its own sake are all the stuff of the new pub gourmand.

Where once fish choices might have been limited to skate wings with black butter and sole meunière, one might expect instead to find sea bream with orange and chilli and seared tuna with tomato and lentil salsa. Indeed, incomparably fresh fish features as far apart as Argyll's Tayvallich Inn, the Penhelig Arms in Aberdyfi and London's Cow Saloon Bar in Westbourne Park Road. Cream-laden Stroganoff and roux-based beef carbonade cedes to teriyaki stir-fry simply chargrilled beef rib-eye with pink peppercorns in its own jus. Similarly, pubs and inns whose fruit, salad leaves and herbs come from their own gardens are legion compared even to a decade ago.

In recent years some notable converts to the cause have included Michael Hirst who in 1996 abandoned the stoves at Green's in Duke Street to revitalise The King's Arms in Fernhurst in West Sussex and now regularly drives to Portsmouth in the early hours to collect his market produce. After Turners, Kensington Place and 755 Fulham Road, Alan and Georgina Thompson have totally transformed the historic Royalist Hotel in Stow-on-the-Wold into an up-market bistro and dining venue. Paul Hackett, whose impressive CV lists employment at The Waterside, Gavroche and La Tante Claire now runs, with his wife Anna, The Yew Tree at Clifford Mesne, near Newent in Gloucestershire, that has brought them almost instant acclaim. And one of Scotland's top chefs, Scott Chance - who comes from Warwickshire - 'emigrated' to the Isle of Islay where his Harbour Inn in the picturesque capital, Bowmore, was so admired by one visitor that a replica of the entire inn has been constructed in Japan!

Three AA Rosettes have followed Jane and Michael Wormersley to their unpretentious, converted 17th-century farmhouse in Fordingbridge, Hampshire, where they still stick to what they do best - real food on the plate: while Ken Adams has forsaken his three-starred restaurant in Ludlow - arguably the gastronomic capital of the heart of

England - to open The Waterdine (formerly The Red Lion) in Llanfair Waterdine, just on the English side of the Welsh border deep in the Teme Valley.

The response to any question as to what relevance such quality of cooking has in a Guide to recommended pubs and inns addresses the core of our argument. All-comers are welcome to enjoy the ambience;

The Village Pub, Barnsley, Gloucestershire.

real ales and quality wines; informal lunches of no more than a generously priced single dish if desired; a garden to air and water the dog in; overnight accommodation (just three en suite bedrooms in each case) in tranquil surroundings; a terrific breakfast to send you on your way and simply no inflated egos or standing on ceremony. The new millennium's Pub has come of age.

It is not hard to understand the motivation. Licensees have become the masters of their own destiny. They buy what they want to cook in quantities that ensure the total freshness of their produce; they are no longer constrained by the strictures of banqueting and corporate events and, in so doing, they pass on the sheer pleasure of their art to a clientele that appreciates, as they do, good food for good food's sake.

Little else remains but to let these chefs air their own aspirations into words. Jonathan Furby, who cut his teeth at the award-winning Pear Tree at Whitley, near Melksham, was tempted by the freedom of it all. Having now moved into The Linnet at nearby Great Hinton, a tiny hamlet hidden down narrow lanes, he has immediately doubled local trade by sensible, unflashy redecoration of the interior and by providing sensibly short daily menus based on whatever he can best obtain at market. 'It sounds so simple', he says, 'but running the pub has become a way of life where the pleasure and sheer appreciation of my customers makes it all worthwhile'.

South African Simon Leese, spurred on by the birth of a daughter some two years ago, made the conscious decision with his wife Gillian to forsake the bright lights and frenetic pace of London for the peace and relative quiet of Norfolk, at the Railway Tavern in Reedham. He now has time for the quality of life that the countryside offers, free from the pressures of heading a large brigade on the Fulham Road. Here he can reflect on the quality of his ingredients, the virtues of careful presentation and the opportunity to experiment with ideas culled from his travels around the Middle East, Thailand and Australia. 'If my customers wish to take the time and trouble to experiment, then so will I. I am still learning too, after all!'.

Another young lion in Gloucestershire, Dominic Blake, came to the Village Pub in Barnsley near Cirencester from one of the county's most celebrated Country House hotels. Yet here he has the freedom to change his menus twice daily, reduce the over-elaboration expected of his former life and let the flavours of organic, single breed meats and vegetables garnered practically within sight of the kitchen door speak for themselves;- 'amazingly different' he avers. He balances traditional village pub food (what an inspired name!) with thoroughly up-to-date variations on salmon - served with potato, cauliflower and spinach curry - and English veal, perhaps with Parma ham and mushroom risotto.

Newly arrived in nearby Tetbury, at the Trouble House Inn, is Michael Bedford who, after stints at Raymond Blanc's Manoir and Pierre Koffmann's La Tante Claire, turned his back on London's acclaimed City Rhodes to 'do his own thing' to the extent that even the washing-up is a part of his daily routine. 'Love it? We can all cook - but it is the satisfaction of producing all the food myself that is both a challenge and an inspiration'. To Wadworth, the Wiltshire brewers from Devizes, should go many plaudits for their enlightened

it is a gift, a talent that is naturally ours for others to enjoy

foresight that has allowed so many chefs of Bedford's ilk a step on the ladder to success in the pub trade.

To expand the argument further would become more of a repetitive news item than an acknowledgement of the increasing numbers of talented cooks who have taken a plunge which the country dining public is proving in ever-increasing numbers to appreciate. Herefordians Steve and Nicola Reynolds have performed wonders since returning home from London to The Stagg Inn at Titley. Nigel Morris confesses to a love affair with The Dove Inn at Dargate in Kent - leased from brewers Shepherd Neame - since his arrival from One Sixteen in Knightsbridge, finding his new job satisfaction eminently more satisfying than rosettes and stars. Sellack, near Ross-on-Wye, has recently celebrated the arrival at The Loughpool Inn of Stephen Bull, who has left behind his two eponymous London restaurants.

And finally, an already celebrated protégé of none other than Marco Pierre White, Stephen Terry has returned to his native Brecon Beacons to provide new cooking inspiration at The Walnut Tree at Llandewi Skirrid near Abergavenny. If the name sounds familiar this is in no way surprising. It is, of course, the same pub at which Franco Taruschio and Ann set out their stall those four decades ago. To this day, as we go to press, the gents' toilet remains out-of-doors in an adjacent privy - and who cares? Plus ça change

The Drunken Duck, Ambleside, Cumbria.

WHO'S COOKING IN THE PUB KITCHEN?

Seafood is deliciou
the perfect choic

Whether you're looking for a light and nutritious meal or a hearty but healthy dish - seafood is the perfect choice when eating out.

With over 60 different species of seafood available in the UK - seafood is a versatile, healthy option with dishes to suit everyone's taste. From Cullen Skink to Tuna Nicoise or steamed mussels with garlic and white wine - you can find a wide range of succulent and tasty seafood meals in pubs around Great Britain.

Best Seafood Pub in Britain 2002

To help you find the pubs that serve the finest seafood dishes, the Sea Fish Industry Authority (Seafish) has sponsored the 'Best Seafood Pub in Britain' 2002 competition. As well as presenting the first prize to the top seafood pub in Britain, seven regional winners up and down the country are awarded an accolade from Seafish.

nd nutritious - when eating out

Good Seafood Served Here

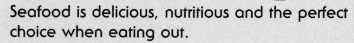

This guide provides you with information on all the competition winners, together with details of around 500 British pubs that serve the best seafood dishes. Finding them in the guide is easy; your nearest pub is marked with the symbol stating 'Good Seafood Served Here' and have all been visited by AA inspectors to ensure that the menu features a wide range of seafood dishes. Look out too for the competition winners, they are highlighted with a light blue background.

Seafood is delicious, nutritious and the perfect choice when eating out.

Sea Fish Industry Authority, 18 Logie Mill, Logie Green Road, Edinburgh EH7 4HG
Tel: 0131 558 3331 Fax: 0131 558 1442
E-mail: marketing@seafish.co.uk Website: www.seafish.co.uk

The Best Seafood
Pubs of the Year

The Angel

best

Hetton
Skipton
North Yorkshire
See entry on page 505

THE ANGEL INN

REGIONAL WINNERS

West Country

The Victory
St Mawes
Cornwall
See entry on page 85

South & South East

The Dering Arms
Pluckley
Kent
See entry on page 252

THE BEST SEAFOOD PUBS

Sponsored by the Sea Fish Industry Authority

London

St John's
91 Junction Road
London N19
See entry on page 287

Wales

Ye Bull's Head
Beaumaris
Isle of Anglesey
See entry on page 580

Central & East Anglia

The White Horse
Brancaster Staithe
Norfolk
See entry on page 305

Scotland

The Plockton Hotel
Plockton
Highland
See entry on page 554

Pick of the
Beers
by Martin Greaves

Old Spot Bitter - named after a rare-breed Gloucestershire pig; Hog's Back Rip Snorter; Pig's Ear Strong Beer; Ye Olde Pig's Swill; - even Pigs Might Fly and a Piddle in the Wind: we have every reason these days to ask what it is we are being served in the country local. It can only be said that following exhaustive research - much of it at their own expense -our tasting team has concluded 'Jolly good beer, that is what'!

Highlighted throughout the 'Pick of the Pubs' pages of this year's edition is a new breed of landlord who is both a good cook and a dedicated mover of the new force for good in our peculiarly British pub fraternity. As the conglomerates expand into menus-by-numbers, cooking-by-rote and, frankly, Euro-brewing by any other name, so have they left behind the traditions that once made our pubs - and the food they serve - unique.

Over the last ten years, since government Beer Orders were introduced as an artificial means (it was hoped) of limiting the power of the 'Big Five' major brewers, the entire set of ground rules has changed beyond recognition. Some three dozen breweries, many of them household names in their respective regions, have been absorbed by larger competitors and simply closed - as though market forces can compensate for the singular quality of the upper Thames, say, being reproduced unnoticed when their beers end up being brewed with down-stream, dirty Wandsworth water! The brewing arms of Bass and Whitbread (how the old Colonel must be turning in his grave) have been hived off to Interbrew of Belgium, with less than 20 per cent of the Bass empire's profits nowadays coming from the one single product on which it built its name. And that was beer.

Out of the ashes, however, of Theakstons (swallowed up by Scottish neighbours) and Buckleys (absorbed by their 'Brainy' Welsh ones) arose not so long ago two young independents who have made a significant statement that smaller can be - and often is - better. It might be surprising to the uninitiated to know that their

> *refreshing the parts other beers daren't mention*

founders were already household names. Paul Theakston's Black Sheep Brewery at Masham, set up in 1992 and Simon Buckley, who founded the Tomos Watkin micro-brewery at Llandeilo, south west Wales, in 1995 (recently moved to larger premises in Swansea) have raised the profile nation-wide of those smaller, yet expanding independents who have refused to let their individuality be swallowed up or otherwise put down by conglomerate take-overs.

As so many breweries of not so insignificant size, whose names were once household names, have been swallowed up by their wealthier peers and in too many cases their historic premises, once

Below: The distinctive bottles of St Peter's Brewe

worthy in their own right, converted to faceless brand names with homogenised 'nitro-keg' beers imposed upon them, so have dedicated real ale brewers set up a host of often tiny businesses that are to all intents and purposes the new cottage industry of rural Britain. 'There is life in the old cask yet' enthuses one expert in recording the growth of micro-breweries at a rate of up to 20 per year. A new generation of master brewers

Above: St Peter's Hall Suffolk

is on the move - and God forbid that they should be denied the pleasure of indulging in that favourite of all British characteristics - a vigorous sense of humour.

Northumbria's Mordue Workie Ticket; Cheriton Pots Ale and Diggers Gold from Hampshire; the Grainstore's Steaming Billy Bitter from Oakham; and The Red McGregor from the Orkney Brewery are cases in point. What's in a name? It is what is in the brew that counts. And it is in the single unit, stand-alone food pubs that they are finding their market. Good beer and wines-by-glass, chosen primarily for their quality and flavour, are the natural accompaniments to good pub food that this year's AA Pub Guide seeks to highlight.

To the rare-breed, single-herd beef and lamb, locally-landed sea-foods, new found interest in organic produce and the unashamed enthusiasm of today's young lions in the kitchen, can be added the simple pleasure now on offer of enjoyment by real ale enthusiasts of a burgeoning and ever-less rare breed of micro-brewers. Surviving household names such as Wadworth of Devizes - commendable estate holders of some of the South West's best dining pubs - Adnams in Southwold - steadfast for years as wine merchants of impeccable quality - and the Hook Norton Brewery in Oxfordshire - whose beers were once quoted as 'refreshing the parts other beers daren't even mention' - share their notoriety these days with such quality independents as the St Peter's Brewery of St Peter South Elham in Suffolk (whose bottled beer range is arguably without equal) and Traquair House of Innerleithen, whose Jacobite ale is brewed to this day in the

oldest inhabited house in Scotland (brewing only suspended here from 1566 until 1965!).

In tandem with the seasonal produce that marks out the Pick of the Pubs are micro-brews that also reflect changing tastes and flavours that follow any sporting or drinking calendar from Day One to year's end. Bowler Bitter at the 17th-century Bell Inn, Langton, celebrates the cricket season on the village green opposite, while some ten years on at the Old Crown at Hesket Newmarket in Cumbria they still brew the 90th Birthday Ale named in honour of old Aunt Doris. Anyone for Dorothy Goodbody's Wonderful Springtime Bitter, Hobson's Town Crier, a drop of Boot Loosener or Santa's Wobble?

Fresh and locally available, brewed with care and a proper understanding of the process involved, these ales parallel the philosophy of the small food-minded country publican. Willingness to deliver in the smallest quantities and at the shortest notice works in favour of brewer, licensee and consumer alike. To the conglomerates, 'downsizing' has come to be viewed with the greatest suspicion, yet in this context thinking 'small' has become anything but a dirty word. Thus a final word might appositely go to Butts Brewery of Great Shefford in Berkshire whose plant, set up in converted farm buildings back in 1994, today supplies some ninety outlets with Jester, Blackguard and Barbus Barbus real ales. 'We're just two guys in a shed: and when we run out we brew some more. We've even been known to deliver on a motorcycle and sidecar'. Is this the future of a new cottage industry, or are they simply out to lunch? In either case, move over the two fat firkins!

PICK OF THE BEERS

AA Hotel Booking Service

Telephone: 0870 5050505
e-mail: accommodation@aabookings.com
24 hours a day 7 days a week

www.theAA.com/hotels

Tell us where you want to go and we'll help you find a place to stay.

From a rustic farm cottage to a smart city centre hotel even a cosy weekend for two – we can accommodate you.

www.theAA.com/latebeds

Latebeds, a new online service that offers you reduced-price late deals on hotels and B&Bs.

You can find a last-minute place to stay and then book it online in an instant.

Choose from 8,000 quality-rated hotels and B&Bs in the UK and Ireland.
Why not book on-line at www.theAA.com/hotels

England

Pub of the Year for England

The Drunken Duck,
Ambleside, Cumbria

England

ENGLAND

BEDFORDSHIRE

BEDFORD   Map 06 TL04

Pick of the Pubs

Knife & Cleaver ◉ ♦♦♦♦ 🍴 ♀
The Grove, Houghton Conquest MK45 3LA
☎ 01234 740387 ▤ 01234 740900
e-mail: info@knifeandcleaver.com
Dir: from A6 south of Bedford follow signs on R for Houghton
Conquest. Hotel in village on L opposite the church.
Opposite the largest parish church in the county, on a
quiet village lane, this uniquely-named inn of 17th-century
origins was once a butcher's shop and slaughterhouse.
Self-styled as a 'restaurant with rooms', both the relaxing,
Jacobean oak-panelled bar, complete with open fire and
daily papers, and the airy, plant-festooned conservatory
dining-room are geared to serious dining. Good bar food
delivers Thai-style mussel soup, chicken and pancetta
ciabatta, salmon and shrimp fishcake with tarragon beurre
blanc, and 'dishes of the day' like steamed minted lamb
pudding and spiced chicken risotto with Parmesan crisps.
In addition the daily fish board may offer king scallops
with creamy pesto sauce, Loch Fyne rock oysters and
supreme of wild sea bass with Pernod and fish velouté.
Separate restaurant menu, fixed-price Sunday lunch and
an impressive list of wines; 26 by the glass. Comfortably
appointed and well-equipped bedrooms surround an
enclosed garden and orchard.
OPEN: 12-2.30 7-11. **BAR MEALS:** L served all week.
D served Mon-Sat 12-2.30 7-9.30. Av main course £6.25.
RESTAURANT: L served Sun-Fri. D served Mon-Sat 12-2.30
7-11. Av 3 course à la carte £27. Av 3 course fixed price £20.
BREWERY/COMPANY: Free House.
PRINCIPAL BEERS: Batemans XB, Bass.
FACILITIES: Children welcome Garden: Food served
outside. **NOTES:** Parking 40. **ROOMS:** 9 bedrooms 9 en
suite s£49 d£64

The Three Tuns
57 Main Rd, Biddenham MK40 4BD ☎ 01234 354847
Friendly, thatched village pub with large garden and play area
and dovecote. Very popular bar menu.

BROOM   Map 06 TL14

The Cock
23 High St SG18 9NA ☎ 01767 314411
Dir: Off B658 SW of Biggleswade
Part of a row of 17th-century cottages, this unspoilt ale house
has several intimate, quarry-tiled rooms with latch doors and
panelled walls. There is no bar. The beer is served straight
from the cask by the cellar steps. Homely bar food ranges
from vegetarian lasagne or sirloin steak, to cajun chicken or
home-made casseroles. Light bites include sandwiches,
ploughmans' and jacket potatoes.
OPEN: 12-3 (Sun 12-4, 7-10.30) 6-11. **BAR MEALS:** L served all
week. D served Mon-Sat 12-2.30 7-9. Av main course £4.
RESTAURANT: L served all week. D served Mon-Sat 12-2.30
7-9.30. Av 3 course à la carte £13.
BREWERY/COMPANY: Greene King.
PRINCIPAL BEERS: Greene King Triumph, Abbot Ale & IPA.
FACILITIES: Children welcome Children's licence Garden: Beer
garden, outdoor eating Dogs allowed. **NOTES:** Parking 30

EATON BRAY   Map 06 SP92

The White Horse ♀
Market Square LU6 2DG ☎ 01525 220231
▤ 01525 222485
Dir: Take A5 N of Dunstable then A5050, 1m turn L & follow signs
Splendid 18th-century pub on the village green, with low
beams, brasses and a garden for summer drinking. The bar
menu offers salads, home-made pies and international dishes,
particularly from India. The restaurant carte has a range of
steaks, chicken stuffed with pate with red wine and port sauce,
and half a traditional roast duck.
OPEN: 11.30-3 (Sun 12-3, 7-11) 6.30-11. **BAR MEALS:** L served
all week. D served all week 12-2.15 7-9.30. Av main course £6.50.
RESTAURANT: . D served Sat 7.30-9.30. Av 3 course à la carte
£18.50. **BREWERY/COMPANY:** Punch Taverns.
PRINCIPAL BEERS: Courage Best, Greene King IPA.
NOTES: Parking 40

KEYSOE   Map 06 TL06

The Chequers
Pertenhall Rd, Brook End MK44 2HR ☎ 01234 708678
e-mail: Chequers@bigfoot.com
Dir: On B660 N of Bedford
15th century inn with a quiet village setting, characterised by
beams and an open stone fireplace. Food served in the bar
might include Swedish fish casserole, chicken stuffed with
Stilton in a chive sauce, or pan-fried steak with a green
peppercorn and brandy cream sauce.
OPEN: 11.30-2.30 (Sun 12-2.30) 6.30-11 (Sun 7-11).
BAR MEALS: L served Wed-Mon. D served Wed-Mon 12-2 7-
9.45. Av main course £6. **BREWERY/COMPANY:** Free House.
PRINCIPAL BEERS: Hook Norton Best, Fullers London Pride.
FACILITIES: Children welcome Garden: Patio and outdoor
eating. **NOTES:** Parking 50

See Pub Walk on page 25

LINSLADE   Map 06 SP92

The Globe Inn
Globe Ln, Old Linslade LU7 7TA ☎ 01525 373338
▤ 01525 850551
Dir: A5 S to Dunstable, follow signs to Leighton Buzzard (A4146)
Attractive 19th-century whitewashed pub standing beside the
towpath of the Grand Union Canal, close to the River Ouzel,
Linslade Wood and the Greensand Ridge. Character bars, good
range of ales; great walking country. Old English Inns.

MILTON BRYAN   Map 06 SP93

The Red Lion
MK17 9HS ☎ 01525 210044
Nestling in a pretty village close to Woburn Abbey, this
attractive, brick-built pub is festooned with colourful hanging
baskets in the summer. Relaxing, neatly maintained interior,
with beams, rugs on wooden floors, and well-kept ales. Wide-
ranging menu offering grills, casseroles and pies, along with
paella, whole plaice, and nursery puddings.
OPEN: 11-3 6-11. **BAR MEALS:** L served all week. D served all
week 11-3 6-11. Av main course £7. **RESTAURANT:** L served all
week. D served all week 11-3 6-11. Av 3 course à la carte £16.50.
BREWERY/COMPANY: Free House.
PRINCIPAL BEERS: Greene King IPA & Old Speckled Hen,
Ruddles County, Bass. **FACILITIES:** Children welcome Garden:
Dogs allowed. **NOTES:** Parking 40

CHEQUERS INN, KEYSOE
Pertenhall Road, Brook End
MK44 2HR
Tel: 01234 708678
Directions: on B660 north
of Bedford
Relaxed and friendly 15th-century inn enjoying a quiet village setting close to Graffham Water and the Cambridgeshire border. Beamed interior and a good range of bar food.
Open: 11.30-2.30, 6.30-11
(Sun 12-2.30, 7-10.30). Closed
Tue. Bar Meals: 12-2, 7-9.45.
Children welcome. Garden
and terrace. Parking.
(telephone to ensure car park
gates are open)

(see page 24 for full entry)

*Pub*WALK

Chequers Inn, Keysoe

An interesting ridge top walk affording pleasant rural views across North Bedfordshire and Cambridgeshire. Take a pair of binoculars.

Turn left out of the pub car park and walk along the pavement. Where it ends, keep ahead along the wide verge for 200 yards (182m) to the waymarked bridleway on your left (partly hidden by a tree). Take this path, alongside The Grange and through a cherry orchard to the bottom of a large field. Proceed straight across the field (can be muddy) to reach the next footpath marker, then keep ahead to reach a wooden bridge (signpost). Cross the bridge and proceed along the edge of a small copse, cross a further wooden footbridge and turn right along the top edge of the copse.

Follow the path across a large field to reach a concrete farm track. Turn left along the track and continue past farm buildings (Middle Lodge Buildings) to the next footpath marker. From this lofty position on a clear day you can see four church spires and one church tower. Ignore the path left and continue along the top of the ridge, enjoying good views over Swineshead and Keysoe. Eventually, pass through a copse (Willow Spinney) and turn left along a bridleway. Keep the hedge on your right to reach a track, then proceed straight ahead across the field. Go through some trees and cross a wooden bridge to join the Riseley road. Turn left and reach the junction with the B660 in 1/2 mile (0.8km). Turn left for 100yards (91m) back to the Chequers Inn.

Distance: 3.5 miles (5.6km)
Map: OS Landranger 153
Terrain: farmland and country lanes
Paths: field and woodland path; bridleways
Gradient: one gentle climb

Walk submitted by The Chequers Inn

NORTHILL Map 06 TL14

The Crown
2 Ickwell Rd SG18 9AA ☎ 01767 627337
New owners are settling in at this delightful 16th-century pub, in its three-acre garden between Northill church and the village duck pond. This is a popular area with walkers, and the Shuttleworth Collection of vintage aircraft is just down the road. Freshly prepared meals include lasagne, cottage pie, and salmon supreme, as well as main course salads and chargrilled steaks.
OPEN: 11.30-3 (Summer all day Sat-Sun) 6-11.30. Closed 25 Dec. **BAR MEALS:** L served all week. D served all week 12-2.30 7-9.30. Av main course £7.95. **RESTAURANT:** L served all week. D served all week 12-2.30 7-9.30. Av 3 course à la carte £11. Av 3 course fixed price £10.95. **BREWERY/COMPANY:** Greene King. **PRINCIPAL BEERS:** Greene King IPA, Abbot Ale, Bass. **FACILITIES:** Children welcome Garden: Food served outside Dogs allowed. **NOTES:** Parking 30

ODELL Map 06 SP95

The Bell ♀
Horsefair Ln MK43 7BB ☎ 01234 720254
Set in a large garden with an aviary and plenty of room for picnics, the Bell is a 16th-century thatched pub with five cosy bars. Low beams, old furniture and real fires lend character and charm. Nearby attractions include the River Ouse, Harrold and Odell country parks, and lots of walks and wildlife. Look to the specials board for dishes such as braised lamb shank, asparagus and mushroom pasta, poached salmon and fish pie.
OPEN: 11-2.30 6-11 (Sun 12-2.30,7-10.30). **BAR MEALS:** L served all week. D served Mon-Sat (Sun in summer)12-2 7-9.30. Av main course £6.75. **BREWERY/COMPANY:** Greene King. **PRINCIPAL BEERS:** Greene King IPA & Abbot Ale, Ruddles County & seasonal beers. **FACILITIES:** Children welcome Garden: patio, Food served outside. **NOTES:** Parking 14

RADWELL Map 06 TL05

The Swan Inn ♀
Felmersham Rd MK43 7HS ☎ 01234 781351
🖹 01234 783004
e-mail: Forge.inns@AOL.com
Dir: Off A6 N of Bedford

Stone and thatched listed pub in a quiet country setting overlooking the River Ouse. The large garden to the rear is ideal for families. Menu may include salmon fillet, turkey Roquefort, seafood risotto, beef casserole, crayfish or red snapper.
continued

OPEN: 12-2.30 6-11. **BAR MEALS:** . D served all week 12-2 6.30-10.00. Av main course £6. **RESTAURANT:** L served Tue-Sun. D served Tue-Sat 12-2 6.30-10.00. Av 3 course à la carte £20. **BREWERY/COMPANY:** Charles Wells. **PRINCIPAL BEERS:** Wells Eagle. **FACILITIES:** Garden: Food served outside. **NOTES:** Parking 25

RISLEY

The Fox & Hounds
High St MK44 1DT ☎ 01234 708240
Busy pub with low beams, a new terrace and comfortable lounge. Regularly changing guest beers.

SILSOE

The Old George Hotel ♦♦
High St MK45 4EP ☎ 01525 860218 🖹 01525 860218
17th-century coaching inn retaining many original features, situated in the heart of the village. Simply appointed bedrooms and traditional bar meals. Regular live music, including jazz every month, and an organist every Saturday.

STANBRIDGE Map 06 SP92

Pick of the Pubs

The Five Bells 🍴 ♀ NEW
Station Rd LU7 9JF ☎ 01525 210224 🖹 01525 211164
Dir: M1 10 M via Woburn A5 from Dunstable 5M on A5 onto A505 signposted Stambridge Leighton Buzzard 5M
Rescued from the brink and totally refurbished by Corrine Bell and Carl May in Summer 2000, this white-painted, 400-year-old village inn now offers a stylish and relaxing dining atmosphere, and high-quality, freshly prepared food. Exposed stripped beams, rug-strewn polished floors and comfortable armchairs characterise the spacious, well designed bar area, while the modern decor extends to the light and airy dining-room extension. Fresh produce is the key to the imaginative menus that draw discerning diners out from Milton Keynes, Aylesbury and Luton. Fish and game feature prominently, but favourites on the seasonal menu and daily specials include Moroccan braised lamb shank with saffron and mint couscous, roast cod on pea mash with red pepper butter, and chargrilled ribeye steak on rösti with chilli and tomato salsa. Begin with Thai mussel, crab and coconut broth and round off with plum and ginger tatin with caramel sauce and ice cream. Lighter lunchtime meals - roast beef and red onion marmalade sandwich. Good cask ales, decent coffee and well chosen wines; 6 by the glass.
OPEN: 12-3 (open all day Sat-Sun) 5-11. **BAR MEALS:** L served all week. D served all week 12-2.30 7-9. Av main course £10. **RESTAURANT:** L served all week. D served all week 12-2.30 7-9. Av 3 course à la carte £19. **BREWERY/COMPANY:** Free House. **PRINCIPAL BEERS:** Bass, Fullers London Pride. **FACILITIES:** Children welcome Garden: Food served outside. **NOTES:** Parking 100

England

TURVEY
Map 06 SP95

The Three Cranes ♀
High St Loop MK43 8EP ☎ 01234 881305
📠 01234 881305
Dir: Through Olney, R at rdbt onto A428, then R towards Bedford
Ivy-clad, stone-built inn dating from the 17th century, in a pretty village setting next to the church. It is renowned for its friendly atmosphere and good food.

BERKSHIRE

ALDERMASTON
Map 04 SU56

The Hinds Head
Wasing Ln RG7 4LX ☎ 0118 9712194 📠 0118 9712194
Dir: A4 towards Newbury, then L on A340 towards Basingstoke, 2m to village
With its distinctive clock and belltower, this 16th-century inn still has the village lock-up which was last used in 1865. The old brewery has recently been refurbished to provide a new restaurant. Typical dishes are pan-fried breast of chicken with a fricassee of smoked bacon and mushroom, or grilled salmon on bubble and squeak glazed with a Béarnaise sauce.
OPEN: 11-2.30 5-11 (Sat 11-2.30, 6-11; Sun 12-3, 7-10.30).
BAR MEALS: L served all week. D served all week 12-2 6.30-9.30.
Av main course £11.95. **BREWERY/COMPANY:** Gales.
PRINCIPAL BEERS: Gales Best, HSB & Guest ale.
FACILITIES: Garden: Walled garden Dogs allowed Guide dogs only. **NOTES:** Parking 50. **ROOMS:** 16 bedrooms 16 en suite

ALDWORTH
Map 04 SU57

Pick of the Pubs

The Bell Inn
RG8 9SE ☎ 01635 578272
Dir: Just off B4009 (Newbury-Streatley rd)
Perfectly capturing the atmosphere of a traditional classic local, the Bell's simple format and lack of modern day luxury create the feeling that you could be stepping back in time to a world where piped music, mobile phones and games machines don't exist. The only real way to appreciate it is to go and have a pint or perhaps something to eat there. Once inside, you'll see that the interior of this 14th-century cruck-built inn is fascinating. Among its most striking features are a glass panelled hatch and a shiny ochre ceiling. Outside are geese, guinea fowl and donkeys and not far away lies the spectacular Ridgeway National Trail. Plain, simple but appetising food includes hot crusty rolls, baguettes, ploughman's lunches, and pasta bolognase with meaty sauce. A range of hot and cold puddings, including whole lemon sorbet and home-made jam sponge, is also available.
OPEN: 11-3 6-11 (closed Mon ex BHs). Closed Dec 25.
BAR MEALS: L served Tue-Sun. D served Tue-Sun 11-2.50 6-10.50. Av main course £3.95.
BREWERY/COMPANY: Free House.
PRINCIPAL BEERS: Arkell's Kingsdown.
FACILITIES: Children welcome Garden: outdoor eating Dogs allowed must be kept on leads. **NOTES:** Parking 12 No credit cards

ASCOT
Map 04 SU96

The Thatched Tavern ♀
Cheapside Rd SL5 7QG ☎ 01344 620874
📠 01344 623043
Dir: Follow signs for Ascot Racecourse drive through Ascot 1st L (Cheapside) drive 1.5 M and pub is on the L
Not actually thatched but very attractive nonetheless, this 500-year-old inn features low ceilings, standing timbers, flagstone floors and an inglenook fireplace. Good range of real ales and a choice of interesting bar food - shoulder of lamb, home-made fishcakes, calves' liver with crispy bacon and red onion confit, and red mullet with sun-dried tomato risotto. Sheltered garden.
OPEN: 12-3 7-10. **BAR MEALS:** L served all week. D served all week 12 7. Av main course £6. **RESTAURANT:** L served all week. D served all week 12 7. Av 3 course à la carte £22.
BREWERY/COMPANY: PRINCIPAL BEERS: Greene King Abbot Ale, Brakspears, Fullers London Pride, John Smiths.
FACILITIES: Garden: Food served outside Dogs allowed Water. **NOTES:** Parking 30

ASHMORE GREEN
Map 04 SU56

The Sun in the Wood ♀
Stoney Ln RG18 9HF ☎ 01635 42377 📠 01635 528392
Dir: A34 Robin Hood rndbt, L to Shaw, at mini rndbt R then 7th L into Stoney Lane, 1.5m, pub on L
Standing in the shadow of tall trees, this popular, extensively refurbished pub occupies a delightful woodland setting and yet is only a stone's throw from the centre of Newbury. Stone floors, plenty of wood panelling and various prints by Renoir and Monet add to the appeal. Try the braised lambs' liver and sausages, the salmon fishcakes or perhaps pork in an orange and fresh basil sauce. Extensive range of starters and a good choice of Sunday lunch dishes.
OPEN: 12-2.30 6-11 (closed Mon). **BAR MEALS:** L served Tue-Sun. D served Tue-Sat 12-2 6.30-9.30. Av main course £11.
RESTAURANT: L served Tue-Sun. D served Tue-Sat 12-2 6.30-9.30. Av 3 course à la carte £20.
BREWERY/COMPANY: Wadworth.
PRINCIPAL BEERS: Wadworth 6X, Farmers Glory & Henrys IPA, Badger Tanglefoot. **FACILITIES:** Children welcome Garden: patio, outdoor eating. **NOTES:** Parking 60

BINFIELD

Stag & Hounds
Forest Rd RH12 4HA ☎ 01344 483553
Historic old pub, with a collection of sporting prints and a restaurant. Low beams, log fires, front terrace and a legend about Elizabeth I and some Morris dancers.

BOXFORD
Map 04 SU47

The Bell at Boxford ♀
Lambourn Rd RG20 8DD ☎ 01488 608721
📠 01488 608749
e-mail: bell.boxford@dial.pipex.com
Dir: A338 toward Wantage, R onto B4000, take 3rd L to Boxford
Mock Tudor country pub at the heart of the glorious Lambourn Valley, renowned for its picturesque river and downland scenery. The 22-mile Lambourn Valley Way runs through the village. Relax in the cosy bar with its choice of real

continued

England

ales and peruse the impressive wine list (champagne by the glass!) before selecting something from the bistro-style blackboard menu. Dishes include Thai red fish curry, roast cod wrapped in Parma ham, grilled lemon sole, chicken a la Bell and beef Stroganoff on a pilau rice. Heated terraces for al fresco dining.

OPEN: 11-3 6-11 (Sat 6.30-11, Sun 7-10.30). **BAR MEALS:** L served all week. D served all week 12-2 7-10. Av main course £7. **RESTAURANT:** L served all week. D served all week 12-2 7-10. Av 3 course à la carte £22. Av 2 course fixed price £7.95. **BREWERY/COMPANY:** Free House. **PRINCIPAL BEERS:** Morrells Oxford, Badger Tanglefoot, Badger Best, Courage Best. **FACILITIES:** Children welcome Garden: Cosy, used for dining Dogs allowed. **NOTES:** Parking 36. **ROOMS:** 10 bedrooms 10 en suite s£45 d£55

BURCHETT'S GREEN Map 04 SU88

Pick of the Pubs

The Crown
SL6 6QZ ☎ 01628 822844
Dir: From M4 take A404(M), then 3rd exit
Good ales and an interesting daily-changing menu are among the attractions at this village pub close to Ashley Hill Woods, a haven for naturalists and country walkers. Inside, the whitewashed walls and low, beamed ceilings help to create a pleasant, welcoming ambience. The intimate restaurant has dining tables decorated with vases and fresh flowers. The short menu may list smoked salmon platter or Thai style curried mushrooms with garlic bread among the starters, while main courses range from poached chicken breast topped with walnut crumble, or poached salmon with prawn and herb cream, to escalope of veal stuffed with parma ham and Swiss cheese. Try the vanilla cheesecake with caramel ripple or the bread pudding for dessert.
OPEN: 12-3 6-11. **BAR MEALS:** L served Sun-Fri. D served all week 12-2.30 7-9.30. **RESTAURANT:** L served Sun-Fri. D served all week 12-2.30 7-9.30. Av 3 course à la carte £25. **BREWERY/COMPANY:** Greene King. **PRINCIPAL BEERS:** Ruddles Best, Wadworth 6X. **FACILITIES:** Children welcome Garden: outdoor eating. **NOTES:** Parking 18

CHADDLEWORTH Map 04 SU47

The Ibex
Main St RG20 7ER ☎ 01488 638311
Dir: A338 towards Wantage, through Great Shefford then R, then 2nd L, pub is on R in village
Grade II listed building which was originally a bakery and then an off-licence before finally becoming a pub. Frequented by the horse-racing fraternity, with many famous stables close by.

CHIEVELEY Map 04 SU47

The Blue Boar Inn
North Heath, Wantage Rd RG20 8UE ☎ 01635 248236
▤ 01635 248506
Dir: Off B4494 S of Wantage
Oliver Cromwell stayed here before the Battle of Newbury in 1644. His troops left a statue of a wild boar, from which the inn takes its name. It is an attractive thatched property offering the likes of poached salmon, char grilled chicken, local sausages, or lamb and mint pie.
OPEN: 11-3 6-11 (Sun 12-3, 7-10.30). Closed 25, 26 Dec. **BAR MEALS:** L served all week. D served all week 12-1.45 7-9.30. Av main course £7. **BREWERY/COMPANY:** Free House. **PRINCIPAL BEERS:** Wadworth 6X, Fullers London Pride, Boddingtons. **FACILITIES:** Children welcome Garden: patio, outdoor eating. **NOTES:** Parking 60. **ROOMS:** 17 bedrooms 17 en suite s£57 d£69 FR£75.00

COOKHAM Map 04 SU88

Pick of the Pubs

Bel and The Dragon
High St SL6 9SQ ☎ 01628 521263 ▤ 01628 851008
One of the oldest licensed houses in England, built of wattle and daub in the 15th century, the unusually named Bel and Dragon takes its name from one of the books of the Apocrypha and stands opposite the Stanley Spencer Gallery. Smartly refurbished by Michael and Andrea Mortimer in 1998. the rambling interior features a series of low-ceilinged rooms, with rustic wooden tables on board floors, open fires and an interesting decor, leading through to a fascinating galleried barn. Served throughout, the interesting bistro-style menu offers modern European dishes. From rustic breads served with roast garlic, olive oil and olives, the menu may list crispy duck Caesar salad, smoked cod, salmon and spinach fishcake with saffron butter sauce, lamb shank on chive mash with rosemary citrus jus, and chargrilled calves' liver with red wine jus and dauphinoise potatoes. Good lunch sandwiches; Brakspear Bitter; decent list of wines.
OPEN: 11.30-11 (Sun 12-10.30). **BAR MEALS:** L served all week. D served all week 12-2.30 7-10. Av main course £15. **BREWERY/COMPANY:** Free House. **PRINCIPAL BEERS:** Brakspear, Marstons Pedigree. **FACILITIES:** Children welcome Garden: Dogs allowed

Swan Inn, Inkpen

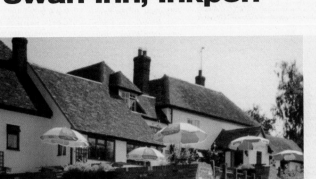

SWAN INN, INKPEN ♦♦♦♦
Craven Road, Lower Green
RG17 9DX. Tel: 01488 668326
Directions: From A4, left
down Hungerford High St, L to
common, then R, pub 3m
*Tastefully refurbished and
extended village inn with
beamed restaurant and
relaxing bars. Interesting
menus featuring organic meats
and produce from
the owners organic farm shop
next door. Accommodation.*
Open: 12-3 7-11 (all day
weekends). Bar Meals: 12-2.30
7-9.30. Children welcome.
Garden. Parking.
(see page 33 for full entry)

A gentle and varied ramble through mixed woodland and across the lush common land and rolling farmland that surround the scattered settlement of Inkpen.

Turn left and walk along to junction by telephone box. Keep right here and after a few paces take the drive on left. Bear left onto footpath, following it around field, down over footbridge and then up through kissing gates to Manor Farm. Turn left through gates, then right to road. Turn left, pass farmyard and then swing right onto footpath. Cross field diagonally to hedge corner and go through kissing gate to edge of garden. Follow footpath to bridleway and keep right.

Walk along to next junction, turn right and then bear immediately left to join footpath. At field edge turn half right to track. Bear left through woods, follow track over bridge and keep left at fork. Turn left at road, then immediately right through kissing gate. Cross field to another gate and bear left to third kissing gate. Cross Inkpen Great Common, following power lines, to meet track. Pass through kissing gate and turn left. Approaching some houses, turn left onto footpath. Cross common to road, cross over and follow bridleway past Willow Farm.

Go down into woods, over footbridge, turn left at top and follow bridleway to road. Cross into Folly Road and when it swings left, veer right onto byway through Folly Woods. Woodpeckers, muntjac deer and jays may be seen along here. Continue on bridleway to path junction at Balsdon Farm. Turn left over stile, go half-left across field to another stile, over footbridge and up bank. Follow path over fields to Northcroft Farm. Keep on path between fences, then turn right onto track running to road. Bear right, then right again over bridge and stile, then keep right to path beside stream.

Cross stile, walk over field to second stile, then beyond second bridge go up bank to third stile. Turn left to follow field edge to gravel track and road. Bear left, back to the Swan.

Distance: 5 miles (8km)
Map: OS Landranger 174
Paths: field and wood paths
Terrain: farmland, woodland, common, village lanes
Gradient: gently undulating

Walk submitted by:
West Berkshire Ramblers

COOKHAM DEAN   Map 04 SU88

Pick of the Pubs

Chequers Inn Brasserie 🕸 ⚲
Dean Ln SL6 9BQ ☎ 01628 481232 📠 01628 850124
e-mail: info@chequers-inn.com
Dir: From A4094 in Crookham High St take R fork after r'way bridge into Dean Lane. Pub in 1m

Kenneth Grahame, who wrote 'The Wind in the Willows,' lived at Cookham Dean as a child and then later with his wife and family. With its wooded hills and dales, it's not surprising that this delightful village has often been described as a miniature Switzerland. The green, with its striking Edwardian and Victorian villas, lends an air of charm to the place and at the heart of the village lies the Chequers Inn Brasserie, a charming old pub with oak beams and an open fire. A popular and well-established meeting point, the Chequers offers a daily-changing blackboard menu and carefully chosen wines and ales. Try the lamb shank with mint jus and vegetable purée or the Mediterranean prawn risotto with lemon and chives. Roast cod with smoked bacon and cauliflower purée, baked skate wing and marinated pork chop with mustard mash and apple chutney also feature among the perennial favourites. **OPEN:** 11-3 5.30-11. Closed Dec 25. **BAR MEALS:** L served all week. D served all week 12-2.30 6-9.30. Av main course £10.95. **BREWERY/COMPANY:** Free House. **PRINCIPAL BEERS:** Wadworth 6X, Morland Original. **FACILITIES:** Children welcome Children's licence Garden: Beer garden, patio with food served outdoors Dogs allowed garden Only. **NOTES:** Parking 50

TWO BLOKES IN A SHED
Dave Price and Chris Butt of the Butts Brewery live by the following maxim: "we are two blokes in a shed, we brew beer because we like beer, other people drink the beer because they like it too, and when we run out we brew some more." This ethos has led to the production of ales that include Jester (3.5%), Butts Traditional (4.6%), Barbus Barbus (4.6%), and Golden Brown (5%), named after a song by The Stranglers. Visitors are welcome provided they make an appointment with one of the two blokes.

Pick of the Pubs

The Inn on the Green 🏵 ♦♦♦♦ 🕸 ⚲
The Old Cricket Common SL6 9NZ ☎ 01628 482638
📠 01628 487474
e-mail: enquiries@theinnonthegreen.com

Traditional English country inn situated in a pretty Berkshire village with a delightful green overlooked by handsome Victorian and Edwardian villas. Kenneth Grahame, who wrote The Wind in the Willows, lived here as a child and then later with his wife and family. The Inn on the Green has been refurbished and modernised in recent times, though thankfully the building retains many traditional features, including a panelled dining room and an old English bar with a log fire. Run by a young, enthusiastic team, this 300-year-old inn offers imaginative dishes served in the intimate dining room with its cosy, inviting atmosphere. Main courses might include braised rump of lamb, roast mallard, pan-fried medallions of monkfish, griddled scallops, chicken liver salad, fish and chips and beef casserole.
OPEN: 12-3 5.30-11 (Sun 7-10.30). **BAR MEALS:** L served all week. D served all week 12-2.30. **RESTAURANT:** L served all week. D served all week 12-2.30 7-10. Av 3 course à la carte £17.98. **BREWERY/COMPANY:** Free House. **PRINCIPAL BEERS:** Brakspear Bitter, Fullers London Pride. **FACILITIES:** Children welcome Children's licence Garden: patio, BBQ Dogs allowed. **NOTES:** Parking 100. **ROOMS:** 8 bedrooms 8 en suite s£75 d£100 FR£120-£150

Uncle Tom's Cabin
Hills Ln SL6 9NT ☎ 01628 483339
Dir: A4 towards Maidenhead, over bridge, R on to Cookham High St, through town, over r'way, past Whyteladies Ln, pub on L
Pretty cottage, 300-years-old, with a lovely rear garden and a relaxing atmosphere throughout its series of little rooms. A good range of home-cooked dishes is prepared from fresh ingredients, including chicken and bacon in a Stilton sauce, seafood crêpes, and a prawn and vegetable balti.
OPEN: 11-3 5.30-11. **BAR MEALS:** L served all week. D served all week 12-2 7.30-10. Av main course £6.25. **RESTAURANT:** L served all week. D served all week 12-2 7.30-10. Av 3 course à la carte £13. **BREWERY/COMPANY:** Carlsberg Tetley. **PRINCIPAL BEERS:** Benskins, Fullers London Pride + Guest. **FACILITIES:** Children welcome Garden: BBQ, outdoor eating Dogs allowed. **NOTES:** Parking 20

England

CRAZIES HILL　　　　　　　　　　Map 04 SU78

Pick of the Pubs

The Horns 🏚 ♈
RG10 8LY ☎ 0118 9401416　🖹 0118 9404849
Dir: Off A321 NE of Wargrave
Set beside a narrow lane in a small hamlet, this whitewashed timbered cottage started life in Tudor times as a hunting lodge to which a barn (now the dining area) was added some 200 years ago. Sympathetically refurbished by Brakspear's brewery, it remains a delightful country pub complete with three interconnecting rooms, furnished with old pine tables and sporting exposed beams, open fires, rugby memorabilia and a peaceful, music- and game-free atmosphere. Dishes listed on the daily-changing blackboard menus range potato and onion soup, warmed goats' cheese on ciabatta with salad and pork and leek sausages with mash and onion gravy, to gammon hock with cider, honey and mustard gravy, stir-fried beef with black bean sauce, and fresh fish from Billingsgate, perhaps red snapper with lemon and chive butter or oven-baked cod with tomatoes, pepper and garlic. Decent filled baguettes (Mon-Fri lunchtime only).
OPEN: 11.30-2.30 (Sun 12-6, 7-10.30) 6-11. Closed 25-26 Dec. **BAR MEALS:** L served all week. D served Mon-Sat 12-2 7-9.30. Av main course £8. **RESTAURANT:** L served all week. D served Mon-Sat 12-2 7-9.30. Av 3 course à la carte £18.20. **BREWERY/COMPANY:** Brakspear. **PRINCIPAL BEERS:** Brakspear. **FACILITIES:** Children welcome Garden: Beer garden, outdoor eating Dogs allowed garden only, Please ask staff. **NOTES:** Parking 45

CURRIDGE　　　　　　　　　　　Map 04 SU47

The Bunk Traditional Inn
RG18 9DS ☎ 01635 200400
Dir: M4 J13/A34 N towards Oxford then 1st slip Rd then R for 1m. R at T-jnct, 1st R signposted Curridge
A traditional inn dating back about 150 years, with beams, brasses and a log fire in the attractive bar. The approach to food is very flexible, the main menu can be taken in the restaurant, bar, conservatory or patio, and vice versa with the bar menu. The food is largely traditional British.
OPEN: 11-11. Closed 26 Dec, 1 Jan. **BAR MEALS:** L served all week. D served all week 12-2.30 7-10. Av main course £9.50. **RESTAURANT:** L served all week. D served all week 12-2.30 7-10. Av 3 course à la carte £25. **BREWERY/COMPANY:** Free House. **PRINCIPAL BEERS:** Arkell's 3B, Wadworth 6X, Fullers London Pride. **FACILITIES:** Children welcome Garden: Dogs allowed. **NOTES:** Parking 38

DORNEY　　　　　　　　　　　　Map 04 SU97

The Palmer Arms
Village Rd SL4 6QW ☎ 01628 666612　🖹 01628 661116
Dir: From A4 take B3026, over M4 to Dorney
An 18th-century pub in a rural location close to Dorney Court and the River Thames. After a riverside stroll enjoy a pint of Rebellion IPA and your choice from a wide ranging menu serving both the bar and the restaurant. Options include mussels with saffron, tomato and coriander sauce, and breast of chicken marinated in Cajun spices and set on a spicy sweet potato, pepper and coconut gumbo.
OPEN: 12-3 6-11 (Sun 12-3, 7-10.30). **BAR MEALS:** L served all week. D served Mon-Sat 12-2.30 6-9.30. Av main course £8.

RESTAURANT: L served all week. D served Mon-Sat 12-2.30 6-9.30. Av 3 course à la carte £20. **BREWERY/COMPANY:** Old English Pub Co. **PRINCIPAL BEERS:** Rebellion IPA, Theakston Old Peculier, Courage Best. **FACILITIES:** Children welcome Garden: Dogs allowed. **NOTES:** Parking 50

EAST ILSLEY　　　　　　　　　　Map 04 SU48

The Swan
RG20 7LF ☎ 01635 281238　🖹 01635 281791
e-mail: theswan@east-isley.demon.co.uk
Dir: 5m N of J13 on A34. 18m S of Oxford on A34
16th-century coaching inn nestling in a peaceful downland village close to the long-distance Ridgeway national trail. Enclosed terraced gardens ideal for a drink or lunch. Traditional pub fare includes a selection of pies and cod and chips.
OPEN: 11-2.30 (Sun 12-3, 7-10.30) 6-11. Closed Dec 25. **BAR MEALS:** L served all week. D served all week 12-2 6-10. Av main course £7. **BREWERY/COMPANY:** Greene King. **PRINCIPAL BEERS:** Greene King, Abbot Ale & IPA. **FACILITIES:** Children welcome Garden: beer garden with seating, outdoor eating Dogs allowed. **NOTES:** Parking 40. **ROOMS:** 5 bedrooms 5 en suite s£50 d£60 FR£65

FRILSHAM　　　　　　　　　　　Map 04 SU57

Pick of the Pubs

The Pot Kiln
RG18 0XX ☎ 01635 201366
Dir: A34 towards Oxford, 1st L to Chieveley, then 1st R to Hermitage. 2nd L onto B4009, 2nd R to Yattendon, R on sharp L bend, on for 1m

With relaxing views across open fields to woodland from its peaceful garden, this timeless 400-year-old brick pub is justifiably popular among walkers, cyclists and real ale enthusiasts. Takes its name from being on the site of old brick kilns and the outbuildings now house the West Berkshire Brewery who brew the Brick Kiln Bitter exclusively for the pub. Delightfully old fashioned interior with lobby bar, simple wooden furnishings and warming open fires. Spotlessly kept by long-serving landlords, who also offer well kept Morlands Original and Arkell's 3B on tap. In keeping, food is simple and hearty, including filled rolls, salmon and broccoli fishcakes with fresh vegetables, liver and bacon casserole, and vegetable chilli.
OPEN: 12-3 (Tues 6.30-11 only) 6.30-11. Closed 25 Dec. **BAR MEALS:** L served Wed-Mon. D served Wed-Mon 12-2 7-9.30. Av main course £7. **BREWERY/COMPANY:** Free House. **PRINCIPAL BEERS:** West Berkshire Brick Kiln, Morlands Original, Arkells 3B, West Berkshire Goldstar. **FACILITIES:** Garden: outdoor eating, patio. **NOTES:** Parking 30 No credit cards

continued

GREAT SHEFFORD
Map 04 SU37

The Swan Inn ♀
Newbury Rd RG17 7DS ☎ 01488 648271 ▤ 01488 648175
Dir: 1.5m north of M4 J14 on A338
Early 19th-century coaching inn located on the banks of the River Lambourn, with its own circular walk, beginning and ending at the pub. In addition to the standard menu, daily specials might include crab au gratin, chargrilled Cajun rump, and country chicken stuffed with mushrooms and smoked bacon in a Stilton sauce.
OPEN: 11-3 (Sun 12-3, 7-10.30) 6-11. **BAR MEALS:** L served all week. D served all week 12-2.30 6.30-9.15. Av main course £8.80. **RESTAURANT:** L served all week. D served all week 12-2.30 6.30-9.15. Av 3 course à la carte £14.50.
BREWERY/COMPANY: Eldridge Pope.
PRINCIPAL BEERS: Courage Best & Directors, Bass.
FACILITIES: Children welcome Garden: patio, BBQ, food served outside. **NOTES:** Parking 25

HARE HATCH
Map 04 SU87

The Queen Victoria ♀
The Holt RG10 9TA ☎ 0118 9402477
Dir: On A4 between Reading & Maidenhead
Set between Reading and Maidenhead, and dating back over 300 years, this country cottage-style inn offers well-kept draught ales, good pub food and an interesting selection of wines. The blackboard menu changes daily, but may include cheese and chilli beef tortillas, slow roasted hock of lamb, venison and red wine sausages, or butterfish steak with seafood sauce.
OPEN: 11-3 5.30-11 (Sun 12-10.30). Closed Dec 25 & 26.
BAR MEALS: L served all week. D served all week 12-2.30 6.30-10.30. Av main course £6. **BREWERY/COMPANY:** Brakspear.
PRINCIPAL BEERS: Brakspear Bitter, Old, Special & Mild.
FACILITIES: Children welcome patio, outdoor eating.
NOTES: Parking 20

HURLEY
Map 04 SU88

The Rising Sun 🛏 ♀
High St SL6 5LT ☎ 01628 824274
Dir: Off the A4130 from Maidenhead
Traditional style pub and restaurant with black beams and a real log fire. Fresh fish and chips on Friday.

Ye Olde Bell Inn
High St SL6 5LX ☎ 01628 825881
Historic half-timbered inn with restaurant and rooms. Features a Norman window and doorway. A short stroll from the River Thames.

INKPEN
Map 04 SU36

Pick of the Pubs

The Swan Inn ♦♦♦♦
Craven Rd, Lower Green RG17 9DX ☎ 01488 668326
▤ 01488 668306
e-mail: enquiries@theswaninn-organics.co.uk
See Pub Walk on page 29
See Pick of the Pubs on page 33

KINTBURY
Map 04 SU36

Pick of the Pubs

The Dundas Arms 🛏
53 Station Rd RG17 9UT ☎ 01488 658263
▤ 01488 658568
e-mail: info@dundasarms.co.uk
Dir: M4 J13 take A34 to Newbury, then A4 to Hungerford, L to Kintbury. Pub 1m next to canal and river by railway station
The stretch of canal between Newbury and Hungerford is one of the loveliest on the Kennet & Avon, so take a stroll along the towpath before heading for the pub, named after the first chairman of the canal company. The Dundas occupies a lovely, unspoilt setting beside the water and is both a popular village local and a country pub/restaurant of distinction. Interesting selection of blackboard specials might feature ribeye steak, cod and chips, venison casserole and tagine and chicken with chilli and oranges. Extensive wine list.
OPEN: 11-2.30 6-11 (no food all Sun, & Mon eve). Closed 25 Dec, Dec 31. **BAR MEALS:** L served Mon-Sat. D served Tue-Sat 12-2 7-9. Av main course £9. **RESTAURANT:** D served Tue-Sat 7-9. Av 3 course à la carte £25.
BREWERY/COMPANY: Free House.
PRINCIPAL BEERS: Greene King IPA, Ringwood Best, Butts Barbus Barbus, Ruddles Best. **FACILITIES:** Children welcome Garden: patio, outdoor eating. **NOTES:** Parking 70. **ROOMS:** 5 bedrooms 5 en suite d£75

Pubs in Unusual Buildings
The classic image of a traditional country pub is surely a charming thatched building overlooking a picturesque village green and boasting cosy log fires and quaint beams adorned with horse brasses. In reality, many inns are like that, but throughout the country there are also many pubs that began life as something entirely different. For example, the Castle Inn at Edgehill in Warwickshire was originally built as a battlemented folly, while the Old Bank in England in London's Fleet Street was once, as the name suggests, a branch of the Bank of England. Opened to service the nearby Law Courts, it became a pub in 1995. The unspoilt Ring O'Bells at Thornton in West Yorkshire began as a Wesleyan chapel, the Cholmondeley Arms in Cheshire was a village school before being converted to a pub in the late 1980s, and the West Riding Licensed Refreshment Rooms at Dewsbury near Wakefield is a converted 19th-century railway station building on the Trans-Pennine route. Right down at the other end of the country, the Chequers at Rookley on the Isle of Wight used to be a customs and excise house.

OPEN: 12-3 7-11 (all day wknds).
Closed 25-26 Dec.
BAR MEALS: L served Sun-Fri.
D served all week 12-2.30 7-9.30.
Av main course £6.50
RESTAURANT: L served Wed-Sun.
D served Wed-Sat 12-2.30 7-9.30.
Av 3 course a la carte £24.95.
BREWERY/COMPANY:
Free House.
PRINCIPAL BEERS: Butts
Traditional & Blackguard, Hook
Norton Bitter & Mild.
FACILITIES: Children welcome.
Garden: terrace, outdoor eating.
NOTES: Parking 50.
ROOMS: 10 bedrooms 10 en suite
s£40 d£70-£90 FR£90-£110.

The Swan Inn

🍴 ♀ ♦♦♦♦
Craven Rd, Lower Green RG17 9DX
☎ 01488 668326 📠 01488 668396
e-mail: enquiries@theswan-
organics.co.uk
Dir: S down Hungerford High St, L to
common, R on common, pub 3m.

Heavily-beamed 17th-century village inn situated in unspoiled countryside between the Berkshire towns of Newbury and Hungerford. A short distance away to the south lie Combe Gibbet and Walbury Hill, the highest points in this corner of the south and a wonderful area for exploring on foot.

The Swan has undergone major refurbishment and restoration work in recent years, to give it a homely feel and a cosy, welcoming atmosphere. Inside are lots of exposed beams, open fires and photographs of the village and surrounding area in days gone by. Look out for unusual stained glass windows of wildlife scenes on several interior doors, as well as leaflets about local walks and places to visit. Outside at the front is a pleasant sunny brick terrace with tables and chairs where you can relax and eat on a summer's day.

There's a strong organic theme at the Swan which is hardly surprising as the inn is owned by local organic beef farmers. The menus for the restaurant and bar use mainly fresh organic produce as well as beef from the farm, and an extensive range of matured and traditionally butchered organic meats is available from the adjoining farm shop. Typical well presented, quality dishes on the bar menu include beef, leek and ale sausages with mash and onion gravy, organic beefburgers, rib-eye steak, chicken, leek and mushroom pie and salmon, cod and smoked haddock fishcakes. Restaurant dishes may include shoulder of lamb with rosemary, garlic and redcurrant jus and guinea fowl with Burgandy sauce.

For pudding, try the excellent hazelnut carrot cake or bread and butter pudding with cream or custard. Beers come from local breweries and include the popular Hook Norton and Butts ales.

England

Pick of the Pubs

Bird In Hand Country Inn 🐾 ♀
Bath Rd RG10 9UP ☎ 01628 826622 & 822781
📠 01628 826748
Dir: On A4, 5 Miles W of Maidenhead, 7 Miles E of Reading

The original oak-panelled bar and working inglenook fireplace have been retained in this 14th-century coaching inn, which has been in the same family for three generations. Steak and kidney pudding, crispy duck pancake, and guinea fowl hotpot are typical bar dishes, while the restaurant carte offers Loch Fyne shellfish, wild mushroom ravioli, and confit of duck leg.
OPEN: 11-3 (Sun 12-4) 6-11 (Sun 7-10:30). **BAR MEALS:** L served all week. D served all week 12-2.30 6.30-10.
RESTAURANT: L served all week. D served all week 12-2.30 7-10. Av 3 course à la carte £20. Av 3 course fixed price £17.50. **BREWERY/COMPANY:** Free House.
PRINCIPAL BEERS: Brakspear Bitter, Fullers London Pride.
FACILITIES: Children welcome Garden: Beer Garden: Outdoor eating. **NOTES:** Parking 86. **ROOMS:** 15 bedrooms 15 en suite s£55 d£70 FR£80-£130

The Hare & Hounds
Ermin St RG17 7SD ☎ 01488 71386 📠 01488 71386
Notable for its individual décor and good food, this 17th-century coaching inn is located in the beautiful Lambourn Valley and is a favourite with the horse racing fraternity. Dishes on offer include brill fillet with chargrilled potatoes, rocket salad and a lime and coriander dressing, and pan-fried duck breast with potato rösti and baby vegetables with a vanilla flavoured jus.
OPEN: 11-3.30 6-11. **BAR MEALS:** L served Mon-Sat. D served Mon-Fri 12-2.30 7-9.30. Av main course £7.50. **RESTAURANT:** L served all week. D served Mon-Sat 12-2.30 7-9.30. Av 3 course à la carte £23. **BREWERY/COMPANY:** Free House.
PRINCIPAL BEERS: Wadworth 6X, Flowers IPA, Boddingtons.
FACILITIES: Children welcome Garden: Dogs allowed.
NOTES: Parking 35

The Cricketers
Coronation Rd SL6 3RA ☎ 01628 822888
📠 01628 822888
Dir: 5m W of Maidenhead on A4 toward Reading. From M4 J8/9 take A404(M) to A4 junction
Standing in the shadow of a lovely walnut tree and

continued

overlooking the vast village cricket ground spread out opposite, this late-19th-century inn has an intriguing clocking-in-clock inside, possibly once owned by the Great Western Railway.

The Belgian Arms
Holyport SL6 2JR ☎ 01628 634468
Dir: 0.75m from Maidenhead
The former "Eagle" - unusually renamed to salute our World War I allies - sports a 200-year-old wisteria and a long, colourful history. A selection of meals from the menu may include various curries, poached salmon fillets, lamb noisettes, and a variety of chicken dishes.
OPEN: 11-3 (Fri All day) 5.30-11 (Sat 12-3, 6-11 Sun 12-3, 7-10.30). **BAR MEALS:** L served all week. D served all week 12-2 7-9.30. Av main course £7.95.
BREWERY/COMPANY: Brakspear.
PRINCIPAL BEERS: Brakspear Best. **FACILITIES:** Garden: outdoor eating, pond with ducks Dogs allowed.
NOTES: Parking 45

Pick of the Pubs

The Red House 🌐 🐾 ♀
RG20 8LY ☎ 01635 582017 📠 01635 581621
e-mail: redhouse@ukonline.co.uk
Dir: 5m from Hungerford, 3m from Newbury & 400yds off the A4
Just a quarter mile from the A4 between Hungerford and Newbury (3 miles), this handsome brick-and-thatch pub nestles in a tiny hamlet by the Kennet and Avon Canal - deep in Wind in the Willows countryside. Formerly known as The Water Rat, kitchen output has taken a new direction under its new owners and reports are very positive. A single menu, served throughout, is supplemented by a range of real ales and some favourably-priced wines by the glass. Whilst not cheap, the choice in the bar and re-styled restaurant has a broad appeal, encompassing fresh crabmeat spring rolls on stir-fried vegetables with sweet-and-sour sauce, followed by roast sea bass fillets with sauce vierge, or beef fillet with gratin dauphinoise and Madeira sauce; rounding off with apple and blackberry compote in a marshmallow case. A fairly adult approach to food production excludes children under six years of age. Splendid alfresco terrace with upmarket teak furniture overlooking the sloping lawns and watermeadows.
OPEN: 11.30-3 6-11. **BAR MEALS:** L served Tue-Sat. D served Tue-Sat 12-2.30 7-10. Av main course £8.50.
RESTAURANT: L served Tue-Sat. D served Tue-Sat 12-2.30 7-10. Av 3 course à la carte £20.
BREWERY/COMPANY: Free House.
PRINCIPAL BEERS: Fullers London Pride, Ruddles County.
FACILITIES: Children welcome Garden: patio, outdoor eating. **NOTES:** Parking 40

The Blackbird Inn
Bagnor RG20 8AQ ☎ 01635 40638
Unpretentious country pub close to Virginia Water. A good range of ales and a pre-theatre menu. Handy for the Watermill Theatre.

NEWBURY continued

The White Hart Inn
Kintbury Rd, Hamstead Marshall RG20 0HW
☎ 01488 658201 📠 01488 657192
Dir: A4, 2m after Speen, L at x-roads, cross railway & canal, L at jct, R at next jct, inn 300yds on R

16th-century coaching inn where tenants of the nearby Craven estate came to pay their rent. Decorating the specials board are unusual chalk drawings, a charming feature in the bar. Examples of the enterprising Italian-based blackboard specials and restaurant menu include pan-fried lambs' kidneys, Barbary duck, organic beef meatballs and pasta. Rhubarb crème brûlée and Italian chocolate bread-and-butter pudding feature among the appetising desserts.
OPEN: 12-2.30 6-11 (closed Sun, 2 wks summer). Closed 25-26 Dec, 1 Jan, 2 weeks in summer. **BAR MEALS:** L served Mon-Sat. D served Mon-Sat 12-2 6.30-9.30. Av main course £10.
RESTAURANT: L served Mon-Sat. D served Mon-Sat 12-2 6.30-9.30. **BREWERY/COMPANY:** Free House.
PRINCIPAL BEERS: Wadworth 6X, Hardy Country, Eldridge Pope. **FACILITIES:** Garden: patio, Beer garden.
NOTES: Parking 30. **ROOMS:** 6 bedrooms 6 en suite

Pick of the Pubs

The Yew Tree Inn ♀
Hollington Cross, Andover Rd, Highclere RG20 9SE
☎ 01635 253360 📠 01635 255035
Dir: A34 toward Southampton, 2nd exit bypass Highclere, onto A343 at rdbt, thru village, pub on R
350-year-old character inn situated in lovely rolling countryside close to Highclere Castle. Scrubbed pine tables, low beams and an inglenook fireplace characterise the main bar; rambling series of interconnecting rooms comprise the restaurant area. Imaginative menu and daily blackboard specials are served throughout the inn. Look for salmon fishcakes with parsley sauce, chicken with smoked bacon and mushroom sauce, beef Stroganoff and Yew Tree kedgeree. Test Valley trout, fresh fish and Cornish crabs feature in summer, while steak and kidney pudding and local pheasant are among the winter favourites. Puddings include crème brûlée and sticky toffee pudding. Comfortable bedrooms.
OPEN: 12-3 6-11. **BAR MEALS:** L served all week. D served all week 12-2.30 6-9.30. **RESTAURANT:** L served all week. D served all week 12-2.30 6-9.30. Av 3 course à la carte £25.
BREWERY/COMPANY: Old Monk Company.
PRINCIPAL BEERS: Ringwood True Glory, Hampshire King Alfred. **FACILITIES:** Children welcome Garden: patio/terrace, outdoor eating, herb garden. **ROOMS:** 6 bedrooms 6 en suite s£55 d£75

PEASEMORE Map 04 SU47

Fox & Hounds
Pleasmore RG20 7JN ☎ 01635 248252
e-mail: lori.fox.hound@tinyworld.co.uk
Originally the premises of a wheelwright and a carpenter, the Fox & Hounds has been a pub for more than 100 years. Situated next door to the cricket ground and affording fine views to the downland ridge of the Berkshire/Hampshire border, the atmosphere inside is warm and friendly. The two bars have wall settles and shiny wooden tables and a row of flat-capped fox masks is one of the more unusual features. Enterprising menu offers prawn Creole, spicy chicken with pasta and a herb sauce, mixed grill platter and speciality sausages.
OPEN: 11.30-3 6.30-11. **BAR MEALS:** L served all week. D served all week 11.30-2 6.30-10. Av main course £7.50.
RESTAURANT: L served all week. D served all week 11.30-2 6.30-10. Av 3 course à la carte £12. **PRINCIPAL BEERS:** Wadworth 6X, Fullers London Pride, Greene King IPA. **FACILITIES:** Children welcome Garden: Food served outside Dogs allowed.
NOTES: Parking 40

READING Map 04 SU77

Fishermans Cottage
224 Kennet Side RG1 3DW ☎ 0118 9571553
📠 0118 9610062
Dir: L from Kings Rd into Orts Rd then Canal Way
Popular Fullers pub set beside the towpath of the Kennet and Avon Canal, with a bar shaped like a canal barge, an airy conservatory, a warm, relaxed atmosphere and a great summer garden.

Sweeney & Todd
10 Castle St ☎ 0118 9586466
Town centre pie shop with well-stocked bar. The selection of pies is excellent, as are the pies themselves. A great stop after a hard day's shopping.

SONNING Map 04 SU77

Bull Inn ♀
High St RG4 6UP ☎ 01189 693901 📠 01189 691057
e-mail: dennis1925@aol.com
Enjoying a picture-postcard setting opposite the village church, this 400-year-old timbered inn boasts sturdy old beams, tiled floors, winter log fires, and a mention in Jerome K. Jerome's comic novel 'Three Men in a Boat'. Bar food includes Thai crab cakes, lamb shank on garlic mash, Moroccan lamb with couscous, grilled salmon with herb butter, and red snapper on roasted vegetables with a chilli glaze.
OPEN: 11-3 5.30-11. **BAR MEALS:** L served all week. D served all week 12-2 6.30-9. Av main course £10.95.
BREWERY/COMPANY: Gales. **PRINCIPAL BEERS:** Gales HSB & Gales Best. **FACILITIES:** Children welcome Garden: Patio, Food served outside Dogs allowed Dog Bowls.
NOTES: Parking 20. **ROOMS:** 7 bedrooms 6 en suite s£70 d£80 FR£105.00-£125.00

 ★ AA inspected hotel accommodation

THE THAMES PATH

The Oxfordshire stretch of the Thames Path boasts many pubs and inns. The Plough at Kelmscott, a short walk from the riverbank, is a popular watering hole; alternatively, you could continue downstream to the Trout at Tadpole Bridge or the White Hart at nearby Fyfield, south of the river. Another Trout, this time at Lower Wolvercote, offers the chance to sit outside and enjoy the timeless river, while historic Oxford has scores of character inns, including the charming Turf Tavern, splendidly hidden down a winding alleyway in the heart of the city. Beyond Abingdon, the trail's next stop is Dorchester, home to the 15th-century George and the White Hart. Suitably refreshed, continue downstream to the Perch and Pike at South Stoke and the ivy-clad Miller of Mansfield at Goring.

STANFORD DINGLEY Map 04 SU57

The Bull Inn ♀

RG7 6LS ☎ 0118 9744409 📄 0118 9744409
e-mail: robert.Archard@btinternet.com
Dir: *A4/A340 to Pangbourne. 1st L to Bradfield.Thru Bradfield, 0.3m L into Back Lane. At end L, pub 0.25m on L*
Traditional 15th-century inn featuring a wealth of timbers and even the remains of an original wattle and daub wall. Don't be surprised to see locals behind the Bull's bar. They liked it so much, they bought the pub. Classic cars, with Jaguars in particular, is the landlord's lifetime hobby and one of the bars is themed in this vein. Ancient pub game known as 'ring-the-bull' is sometimes played in the next door tap room. Irish stew, stuffed pork medallions, burger and fries, cod goujons, and bacon and cabbage are among the interesting specials.
OPEN: 12-3 Mar-Oct 11-3 6-11 Sun 7-10.30. **BAR MEALS:** L served all week. D served all week 12-2.30 6.30-10. Av main course £6.95. **BREWERY/COMPANY:** Free House.
PRINCIPAL BEERS: West Berkshire Brewery Ales, Brakspear Bitter. **FACILITIES:** Children welcome Garden: outdoor eating, patio Dogs allowed on a lead. **NOTES:** Parking 20

The Old Boot Inn ♀

RG7 6LT ☎ 01189 744292 📄 01189 744292
Dir: *M4 J12, A4/A340 to Pangbourne. 1st L to Bradfield. Through Bradfield & follow signs for Stanford Dingley*
Enjoy a walk in the glorious countryside of the Pang Valley before dining at this well-known 18th-century pub in one of the county's loveliest villages. The recently added conservatory is proving very popular and the extensive choice of freshly prepared dishes on the menu might include smoked salmon and baked avocado among the starters, while lamb fillet, roast duck breast and pork fillet en croute with herb and apple stuffing may feature among the main courses. Good selection of fresh fish on the daily-changing chalkboard.
OPEN: 11-3 (Sun 12-3) 6-11 (Sun 7-10.30). **BAR MEALS:** L served all week. D served all week 12-2.15 7-9.30. Av main course £7.95. **RESTAURANT:** L served all week. D served all week 12-2.15 7-9.30. Av 3 course à la carte £20.
BREWERY/COMPANY: Free House.
PRINCIPAL BEERS: Brakspear, Bass, West Berkshire Dr Hexters, Archers. **FACILITIES:** Children welcome Garden: Food served outside Dogs allowed. **NOTES:** Parking 40

SWALLOWFIELD

Pick of the Pubs

The George & Dragon ♀

Church Rd RG7 1TJ ☎ 0118 9884 432
📄 0118 9886474
Behind the unassuming façade of this old inn, set close to the River Blackwater on the village edge, is a smart and cosy interior featuring stripped low beams, terracotta-painted walls, log fires and rug-strewn floors. Very much a dining pub - booking essential. Look for Club sandwiches (goats' cheese, roasted pepper and rocket leaves), seafood bouillabaise, salmon on vegetable noodles with citrus butter sauce, and Cumberland sausage on bubble-and-squeak on the lunch menu; imaginative evening specials may feature seared Thai scallops with marinated cucumber, smoked salmon and pesto linguini, roast rack of lamb with whole garlic cloves and burnt onion mash, and pan-fried sea bream with Puy lentil purée with salsa verde. Round off with caramelised apple tart tatin, chocolate and roast hazelnut terrine with coffee sauce, or cheese with home-made chutney. Seasonal fish and game specials; interesting wines.
OPEN: 12 All day. **BAR MEALS:** 12-2.30. **RESTAURANT:** L served all week. D served all week 12-2.30 6.30-10. Av 3 course à la carte £22. **BREWERY/COMPANY:** Free House.
PRINCIPAL BEERS: Fullers London Pride, Adnams, Wadworth 6X. **FACILITIES:** Garden: Food served outside Dogs allowed. **NOTES:** Parking 50

THATCHAM Map 04 SU56

Pick of the Pubs

The Bladebone Inn 🍴 ♀ NEW

Chapel Row, Bucklebury RG7 6PD ☎ 0118 9712326
e-mail: bladebone@berkshirerestaurants.co.uk
Dir: *5m from Newbury and the A4, 2m from the A4 at Thatcham*
Standing at the end of a stately avenue of oak trees, planted to commemorate a visit by Elizabeth I, this popular inn takes its name from the bladebone hanging over the entrance. The scapula of a whale found sometime around the beginning of the 17th century, the bladebone has its own legend which suggests that the bone came from a mammoth which stalked the area until eventually the locals slew it and buried it on the riverbank. Originally the bladebone hung outside to indicate that whale oil, once used in lamps, was sold here. The inn has changed from a traditional village local to a sophisticated dining pub with the emphasis on modern pub food, comfortable furnishings and a relaxed atmosphere. Expect steamed mussels in a Chablis cream and Caesar salad with smoked bacon and Parmesan crackling among the starters, while Moroccan spiced lamb shoulder and Parma ham wrapped sea bass on wild mushroom risotto with basil oil and asparagus feature among the imaginatively presented main courses.
OPEN: 12-3 6.30-11. **BAR MEALS:** L served all week. D served all week 12-3 7-9. Av main course £10.
RESTAURANT: L served all week. D served all week 12-3 7-9. Av 3 course à la carte £20.
BREWERY/COMPANY: Whitbread.
PRINCIPAL BEERS: Fullers London Pride, Flowers IPA, West Berks Dr Hexters Healer. **FACILITIES:** Garden: outdoor eating. **NOTES:** Parking 20

UPPER BASILDON
Map 04 SU57

The Red Lion ☶
Aldworth Rd RG8 8NG ☎ 01491 671234 🖷 01491 671390
Dir: from M4 follow signs to Pangbourne, then L at 1st main jct
signed Upper Basildon, thru village, pub on R
Rural pub in the scenic Thames Valley, handy for the Thames
Path and the Ridgeway. One menu serves all in the spacious
bar and restaurant, with the likes of seafood bouillabaisse,
swordfish steak in spicy thyme marinade served on curried
egg noodles, and braised half shoulder of lamb set on bubble
and squeak with a rich port jus.
OPEN: 12-11 (Sun 12-10.30). **BAR MEALS:** L served all week.
D served all week 12-2 6.30-9.30. Av main course £5.
RESTAURANT: L served all week. D served all week 12-2 6.30-
9.30. Av 3 course à la carte £20. Av 2 course fixed price £8.
BREWERY/COMPANY: Free House.
PRINCIPAL BEERS: Adnams 6X, Fullers London Pride.
FACILITIES: Children's licence Garden: outdoor eating, patio
Dogs allowed. **NOTES:** Parking 25

WALTHAM ST LAWRENCE
Map 04 SU87

The Bell
The Street RG10 0JJ ☎ 0118 9341788 🖷 0118 9341782
e-mail: bellwsl@ukonline.co.uk
Dir: on B3024 E of Twyford (from A4 turn at Hare Hatch)
Since 1608, when it was left to the village in trust, the rent
from this 14th-century inn has been donated to local charities.
The same menu operates throughout, offering a variety of
meat pies and puddings, chilli, enchiladas, lamb and pork
shanks, chicken tikka, and fresh fish on Fridays.
OPEN: 11-3 (Sun 12-7) 6-11. **BAR MEALS:** L served all week. D
served Tue-Sat 12-2 7-9.30. Av main course £7. **RESTAURANT:** L
served all week. D served Tue-Sat 12-2 7-9.30.
BREWERY/COMPANY: Free House.
PRINCIPAL BEERS: Brakspear Dark Rose, Bass, Greene King
Abbot Ale. **FACILITIES:** Children welcome Garden: patio, BBQ,
beer garden with seating. **NOTES:** Parking 5

WARREN ROW
Map 04 SU88

The Crooked Inn
RG10 8QS ☎ 01628 825861 🖷 01628 825861
Dir: From M4 take A4 to Knowl Hill, 1st R down Warren Row Rd, inn
3m on R
Built in the 1920s, this attractive red-brick building with leaded
windows and polished wood floors is a popular village
restaurant with a modern European theme, and a small
welcoming bar.

WEST ILSLEY
Map 04 SU48

Pick of the Pubs

Harrow Inn ☶
RG20 7AR ☎ 01635 281260 🖷 01635 281139
This historic inn where the brewers Morland founded their
operation in 1711 lies in a peaceful settlement on the edge
of the Berkshire Downs, close to the Ridgeway Path and
surrounded by horse racing country. The open plan bar
with its creamy yellow décor and distinctive wall hangings
follows the racing line without over-elaboration, the tenor
of food on offer well grounded in thoroughbred English
tradition. Filled baguettes and flawless ham, egg and chips
vie for attention with daily blackboard specials such as
goats' cheese and walnut salad and lambs' liver with
bacon and caramelised onion gravy at lunchtime. Stepping
up a gear by night choices extend to double-baked
Roquefort cheese soufflé on watercress and pear salad,
Cornish king scallops with pesto mash and braised lamb
shank with honey roast parsnips. Award-winning cheeses
such as smoked Wedmore and Tornegus are acceptable
alternatives to home-made puddings - perhaps warm pear
and custard tart or hot chocolate fondant pudding.
OPEN: 11-3 (open Sun eve, Mon in summer) 6-11.
BAR MEALS: L served all week. D served all week 12-2 7-9.
Av main course £9.50. **BREWERY/COMPANY:** Greene
King. **PRINCIPAL BEERS:** Morland Original, Old Speckled
Hen, Abbot Ale. **FACILITIES:** Children welcome Garden:
Food served outside Dogs allowed. **NOTES:** Parking 10

WINKFIELD
Map 04 SU97

Pick of the Pubs

Rose & Crown ◉
Woodside, Windsor Forest SL4 2DP ☎ 01344 882051
🖷 01344 885346
Dir: M3 J3 from Ascot racecourse on A332 take 2nd exit from
Heatherwood Hosp r'about,then 2nd L
Totally refurbished over the last year, this is a 200-year-old,
family-run pub that has established a firm reputation for
good food, wine and ale in a relaxed and informal setting.
Simple home-cooked food is prepared with proper care
with results that appeal to a broad cross-section of clientele.
Interesting fillings of lunchtime panini and jacket potatoes
include seafood casserole and Mediterranean vegetables
with Mozzarella and various ploughman's choices. Specials
encompass chicken and seafood paella, tagliatelli with wild
mushrooms and pesto, Toulouse sausages with warm
potato salad and Greek salad with stuffed sardines. Evening
options then include aubergine alla Parmigiana, tagliatelli
Arrabbiata and lemon sole Florentine style. Alongside are
baked lamb shank with juniper berry sauce and Scottish
sirloin steak with peppercorn sauce, followed by lemon
meringue pie and decent coffee.
OPEN: 11-11 (Sun 12-7). **BAR MEALS:** L served Mon-Sat. D
served Tue-Sat 12-2.30 7-9.30. Av main course £6.95.
RESTAURANT: L served all week. D served Tue-Sat 12-2.30
7-9.30. Av 3 course à la carte £21 9.30.
BREWERY/COMPANY: Greene King.
PRINCIPAL BEERS: Adnams Broadside, Charles Wells
Bombardier, Morland Original, Ruddles Best.
FACILITIES: Children welcome Garden: beer garden, food
served outdoors. **NOTES:** Parking 24. **ROOMS:** 2
bedrooms d£45

WINTERBOURNE   Map 04 SU47

Pick of the Pubs

The Winterbourne Arms ♀
RG20 8BB ☎ 01635 248200 📠 01635 248824
Dir: *From M4 S on A34, 1st slip road*

The epitome of a quality country inn, this black and white timber-framed free house nestles below the tree-lined slopes of Snelsmore Common. Besides extensive local walks across West Berkshire's only country park, there's also a footpath link from this sleepy little village to the nearby manor house and church. The outdoor theme continues with picnic sets on the pub's tree-shaded lawn, and attractive views across rolling countryside.

Inside, you'll find well kept ales, winter fires, dried flowers, and a collection of old fire extinguishers. Evenings bring mellow candlelight to the intimate restaurant, where the new owners are continuing the Winterbourne Arms' tradition of offering imaginative dishes created from fresh ingredients.

Stilton, red onion and peppered beef salad or Tayside salmon roses might precede Scotch fillet on potato rösti, roast duckling with stir-fried peppers, or a wide selection of fresh fish dishes. Vegetarians are catered for and, with notice, the chef will offer individually tailored recipes.
OPEN: 11.30-3 6-11 (closed Sun eve). **BAR MEALS:** L served Tue-Sun. D served Tue-Sat 12-2.30 7-9.30. Av main course £6.50. **RESTAURANT:** L served Tue-Sun. D served Tue-Sat 12-2 7-9.30. Av 3 course à la carte £25.
BREWERY/COMPANY: Free House.
PRINCIPAL BEERS: Bass, Badger, Green King Old Speckled Hen. **FACILITIES:** Garden: stream, outdoor eating.
NOTES: Parking 30

WOKINGHAM

The Crooked Billet ♀
Honey Hill ☎ 0118 978 0438
Bustling 16th century country pub with a good garden, black beams and brick bar. Very busy in summer.

♀   Pubs offering six or more wines by the glass

YATTENDON   Map 04 SU57

Pick of the Pubs

The Royal Oak Hotel ◉ ◉ ★ ★
The Square RG18 0UG ☎ 01635 201325
📠 01635 201926
Dir: *From M4 J12, A4 to Newbury, R at 2nd rndbt to Pangbourne then 1st L. From J13, A34 N 1st L, R at T-jnct. L then 2nd R to Yattendon*
Thought to have been built en the 16th century of timber and thatch, the inn was subsequently re-faced in brick about 1700 when The Oak, as it was then known, was a well-known coaching inn. Recorded visitors have included Oliver Cromwell, King Charles I and several 20th-century Royals. Today it remains the quintessential English country inn by a village green whose noisiest interruption is that of horse-people hacking by. Whilst welcoming villagers to partake of a pint or two, the brasserie-style menu these days is rich in enticement to spend time over lunch and dinner at leisure and be relieved of a bob or three. Two or three daily specials supplement a seasonal menu that tempts with ham hock terrine with pistachios and horseradish or mussels with mild curried spices, followed by lemon sole on buttered spinach, breast of chicken with tomato risotto or calves' liver, onion marmalade and mash; followed by lemon posset with strawberry salad or baked chocolate fondant and banana ice cream. Side dishes, beers and house wines by the glass also come at a price.
OPEN: 11-3 6-11. **BAR MEALS:** L served all week. D served all week 12-2 7-9. Av main course £10. **RESTAURANT:** L served all week. D served Mon-Sat 12-2.30 7-9. Av 3 course à la carte £35. Av 3 course fixed price £35.
BREWERY/COMPANY: Regal. **PRINCIPAL BEERS:** Fullers London Pride. **FACILITIES:** Garden: patio, outdoor eating.
NOTES: Parking 15. **ROOMS:** 5 bedrooms s£100 d£120

BRISTOL

BRISTOL   Map 03 ST57

Brewery Tap
Upper Maudlin St BS1 5BD ☎ 0117 921 3668
Smiles Brewery tap (and shop). Small, unpretentious and bustling with real ale aficionados seeking an excellent pint of Smiles Bitter.

Highbury Vaults
164 St Michaels Hill, Cotham BS2 8DE ☎ 0117 9733203
📠 0117 9744828
e-mail: highburyvaults@smiles.co.uk
Dir: *Take main road to Cotham from inner ring dual carriageway*
This popular hostelry, close to the university, was once the lock-up for condemned prisoners. The original owner came from Highbury, London, hence the name. It is a traditional pub, with a cluster of small rooms and a heated garden terrace, serving real ales and good-value food. Dishes range through ploughman's, chilli, Spanish pork casserole, vegetable curry and beef in beer pie.
OPEN: 12-11 (Sun 12-10.30). **BAR MEALS:** L served all week. D served Mon-Fri 12-2 5.30-8.30. Av main course £3.65. **BREWERY/COMPANY:** Youngs. **PRINCIPAL BEERS:** Smiles, Best & Heritage, Brains SA, Youngs Special. **FACILITIES:** Children welcome Garden: patio, Food served outside No credit cards

CLUTTON
Map 03 ST65

The Hunters Rest ♀ NEW
King Ln, Clutton Hill BS39 5QL ☎ 01761 452303
📠 01761 452308
e-mail: info@huntersrest.co.uk
Dir: *Follow signs for Wells A37 go through village of Pensford untill large Rdbt turn L towards Bath after 100 yrds turn R into country lane pub 1M up hill*
A real rural retreat, this former 18th-century hunting lodge became a miner's tavern in 1892. Now a smart country inn with open fires and commanding views, plus well-furnished bedrooms and stunning en suite bathrooms. In summer, a miniature railway carries passengers around the pub garden. The varied international menu includes home-made 'oggies', pork steak and mango sauce, lamb balti, halibut and prawn sauce, or Stilton and broccoli pie.
OPEN: 11.30-3 6.30-11. **BAR MEALS:** L served all week. D served all week 12-2 6.30-9.45. Av main course £6.25.
BREWERY/COMPANY: Free House. **PRINCIPAL BEERS:** Bass, Smiles. **FACILITIES:** Children welcome Garden: Food served outside Dogs allowed Water. **NOTES:** Parking 80.
ROOMS: 4 bedrooms 4 en suite s£45 d£65

BUCKINGHAMSHIRE

AMERSHAM
Map 04 SU99

The Hit or Miss 🐾 ♀
Penn St Village HP7 0PX ☎ 01494 713109
📠 01494 718010

A lovely 14th-century country inn opposite the village cricket pitch, with a cricket-themed no smoking dining area. One menu operates throughout offering freshly prepared dishes running from snacks, pies and fish and chips, through to rack of lamb with wild berry jus, and fillet of salmon on crushed new potatoes with fine beans and tarragon sauce.
OPEN: 11-3 5.30-11 (Sat 11-3, 6-11 Sun 12-3, 7-10.30).
BAR MEALS: L served all week. D served all week 12-2.30 6-9.30. Av main course £10. **RESTAURANT:** L served all week. D served all week 12-2.30 6-9.30. Av 3 course à la carte £18.
BREWERY/COMPANY: Hall & Woodhouse.
PRINCIPAL BEERS: Badger Tanglefoot, Best & IPA.
FACILITIES: Garden: outdoor eating, patio/terrace, BBQ Dogs allowed. **NOTES:** Parking 40

The Kings Arms ♀
30 The High St, Old Amersham HP7 0DJ ☎ 01494 726333
📠 01494 433480

Historic atmosphere fills the bars of this 15th-century, black and white timbered inn. There are always four real ales on offer, two drawn directly from the cask behind the counter. Food options range from sandwiches in the bar to an impressive seafood platter in the restaurant. Popular blackboard specials include cassoulet with confit of duck, and game casserole.
OPEN: 11-11 (Sun 12-10.30). **BAR MEALS:** L served all week 12-2.30. Av main course £6.50. **RESTAURANT:** L served Tue-Sun. D served Tue-Sat 12-2 7-9.30. Av 3 course à la carte £25. Av 3 course fixed price £17. **BREWERY/COMPANY:** Free House.
PRINCIPAL BEERS: Rebellion IPA, Burton Ale, Benskins Best.
FACILITIES: Children welcome Children's licence Garden: Patio/terrace, outdoor eating, BBQ. **NOTES:** Parking 25

ASTON CLINTON
Map 06 SP81

The Oak 🐾 ♀
119 Green End St HP22 5EU ☎ 01296 630466
📠 01296 631796
e-mail: the-oak@tesco.net
Dir: *entry via Brook St, off the A41*

Thatched, 500-year-old coaching inn with flagstone floors, inglenook fireplace and bags of old-world charm. Set in the old part of the village, it offers a good family garden and a wide-ranging menu. Summer events include a beer festival and a charity fete. Expect traditional pub favourites, alongside beef Stroganoff, pan-fried salmon, and sweet and sour chicken with sweet peppers.
OPEN: 11.30-2.30 6-11.30 (open all day Sat-Sun in summer).
BAR MEALS: L served all week. D served all week 12-2 6-9.30. Av main course £4.75. **RESTAURANT:** L served all week. D served all week 12-2.30 6-9.30. Av 3 course à la carte £14.75.
BREWERY/COMPANY: Fullers. **PRINCIPAL BEERS:** Fullers London Pride, Fullers ESB. **FACILITIES:** Garden: patio/terrace, outdoor eating Dogs allowed Water. **NOTES:** Parking 30

AYLESBURY   Map 06 SP81

Pick of the Pubs

Bottle & Glass
Gibraltar, Nr Dinton HP17 8TY ☎ 01296 748488
📠 01296 747673
Dir: On A418 between Thame & Aylesbury

In a peaceful rural setting close to the Chiltern Hills, this 17th-century thatched inn with low ceilings, flagstone floors, intimate alcoves, open fires and an appealing decor has an immediately warm and welcoming ambience. Fresh fish and seafood, delivered daily, is a real strength: simply cooked to enhance their best flavours may be tuna on garlic mash with thyme cream and vinaigrette, chargrilled cod with sweet pepper coulis and balsamic reduction, and salmon on Asian noodles with orange dressing, basil oil and mango salsa. Meat dishes cover duck breast with wild mushroom sauce, beef fillet on rösti with Dijon mustard and tarragon sauce, and steak and kidney pie; excellent Sunday roasts with all the trimmings. With lunch in mind are open ciabatta sandwiches or a bowl of mussels served with fresh bread; follow with a home-made pudding, perhaps a tangy citron tart. Superb front terrace seating festooned with flowering hanging baskets and tubs.
OPEN: 11-3 6-11 (closed Sun eve). **BAR MEALS:** L served all week. D served Mon-Sat 12-2.30 7-9.30. Av main course £6. **RESTAURANT:** L served all week. D served Mon-Sat 12-2 7-9.30. Av 3 course à la carte £25.
BREWERY/COMPANY: Morrells.
PRINCIPAL BEERS: Morrells Oxford, Varsity & Mild.
FACILITIES: Children welcome. **NOTES:** Parking 50

BEACONSFIELD   Map 04 SU99

The Greyhound
33 Windsor End HP9 2JN ☎ 01494 673823
📠 01494 673379
e-mail: greyhound.windsorend@eldridge-pope.co.uk
Dir: Follow signs to Beaconsfield Old Town, left at central roundabout
Comfortable 16th-century drovers' tavern enjoying a secluded location opposite the parish church. Traditional, home-cooked pub food is served, including smoked haddock pie and home-made burgers, and there is an extensive specials board with plenty of fresh fish - strawberry grouper with Pernod sauce, tuna and escolard roulade, and shark supreme with herb dressing.
OPEN: 11-3 5.30-11. Closed May 10. **BAR MEALS:** L served all week. D served Mon-Sat 12-2 7-9.45. Av main course £9. **RESTAURANT:** L served all week. D served Mon-Sat 12-2 7-9.45. Av 3 course à la carte £18. **BREWERY/COMPANY:** Free House.
PRINCIPAL BEERS: Courage Best, Fullers London Pride, Wadworth 6X. **FACILITIES:** Garden: Dogs allowed

The Royal Standard of England
Brindle Ln, Forty Green HP9 1XT ☎ 01494 673382
📠 01494 523332
Dir: A40 to Beaconsfield. R at Church roundabout onto B474 towards Penn. L onto Forty Green Rd, then 1m

Country inn dating from the 12th century with lovely stained glass windows, beams, flagstone floors, and a large inglenook fireplace. During the Civil War the inn was a Royalist headquarters, after which it got its fine name. It's a great base for walking, and you can stoke up with speciality sandwiches, home-made pies and puddings, and specials such as fillet of lamb with herb crust.
OPEN: 11-3 5.30-11. **BAR MEALS:** L served all week. D served all week 12-2.15 6.30-9.30. Av main course £8.
BREWERY/COMPANY: Free House.
PRINCIPAL BEERS: Marstons Pedigree, Brakspear, Greene King Old Speckled Hen, Fullers London Pride. **FACILITIES:** Children welcome Children's licence Garden: outdoor eating, Dogs allowed garden only. **NOTES:** Parking 90
See Pub Walk on page 41

BLEDLOW   Map 06 SP70

The Lions of Bledlow
Church End HP27 9PE ☎ 01844 343345
Dir: M40 J6 take B4009 to Princes Risborough, through Chinnor into Bledlow
Grade II listed building in the heart of the Chiltern Hills and retaining the atmosphere of a traditional old-style country pub. Unchanged since the early 20th century, the rambling, low-beamed bar has a wealth of character and plenty of antique furniture. Popular patio and large garden for summer imbibing and good walks nearby. Apart from filled baguettes, salads and ploughman's lunches, dishes might include beef lasagne, steak and Guinness pie and spinach cannelloni.
OPEN: 11.30-3 6-11 (Sun 12-3,7-10.30). **BAR MEALS:** L served all week. D served all week 12-2.30 7-9.30. Av main course £6.50. **RESTAURANT:** L served all week. D served all week 12-2.30 7-9.30. Av 3 course à la carte £14. **BREWERY/COMPANY:** Free House. **PRINCIPAL BEERS:** Wadworth 6X, Courage Best, Marstons Pedigree, Brakspear Bitter. **FACILITIES:** Garden: beer garden , food served outdoors Dogs allowed Water, Biscuits, Toys, Towles. **NOTES:** Parking 60

 Pubs offering a good choice of seafood on the menu.

ROYAL STANDARD OF ENGLAND, BEACONSFIELD

Brindle Lane, Forty Green
HP9 1XT. Tel: 01494 673382
Directions: off B474 out of
Beaconsfield, turn L at Red
Lion in Knotty Green
*Historic inn dating from the
12th century and named by
the decree of Charles II
after it served as Royalist
headquarters during the Civil
War. Wealth of interesting
original features, good
choice of ales and a wide-
ranging menu.*
Open: 11-3 5.30-11 (Sun 12-4
7-10.30 Bar Meals: 12-2.15
6.30-9.30. Children welcome.
Garden & patio. Parking.
(see page 40 for full entry)

*Pub*WALK

Royal Standard of England, Beaconsfield

A peaceful and varied walk linking two pretty villages with Civil War history and surrounded by delightful Chiltern views.

Leave the pub car park and turn left down the lane. In 100 yards (91m), turn right over the stile and follow the path through a former orchard, heading diagonally right downhill to a stile by an electric pylon. Continue downhill along the right-hand field edge, with good Chilterns views .

Climb a stile and follow the path through mixed woodland to a stile and sloping field. Head across the field, the path leading to a track and turn right towards the farm. Cross a stile and walk to the lane outside the farmhouse. Turn right, pass barns on left, then climb the stile immediately beyond them.

Cross the field to the stile in the opposite corner and proceed ahead through the coniferous wood. Keep ahead at a fork to a stile. At next stile turn sharp left and shortly cross another stile on the left. Turn sharp right alongside the tall hedge to reach a wide fenced track (farm ahead). Turn right, then where the track curves left, keep ahead and bear half-left across the field to a stile and track. Walk up the track to a lane and turn right.

At Gnome's Cottage, on the right in 150 yards (136m), turn right then left at fork, passing between hedges to a stile. Cross the field to the stile opposite, turn right, then right again to follow a bridleway downhill between trees. Turn sharply left downhill on reaching the metalled lane, then turn right along a narrow road.

In 100 yards (91m), take the footpath left up to a barn and turn right through Corkers Wood. Exit via a stile on the right and follow the right-hand hedge down through the field to Brindle Lane and the pub.

Distance: 3 1/2 miles (5.6km)
Map: OS Landranger 175
Terrain: farmland, patches of woodland
Paths: field and woodland paths, bridleways
Gradient: undulating; three short medium climbs

*Walk submitted by:
The Royal Standard of England*

England

BLETCHLEY — Map 06 SP83

Pick of the Pubs

Crooked Billet ♀ **NEW**
2 Westbrook End, Newton Longville MK17 0DF
☎ 01908 373936 📠 01908 631979
e-mail: johngilchrist@the-crooked-billet-pub.co.uk
See Pick of the Pubs on page 43

BOLTER END — Map 04 SU79

The Peacock ♀
HP14 3LU ☎ 01494 881417
Dir: *A40 through Stokenchurch, then B482*
The oldest part of this pub dates from 1620, featuring original beams and a fireplace dating from the early 1800s. It is situated on top of the Chiltern Hills overlooking the common. A typical menu features Lincolnshire pork sausages, Aberdeen Angus steaks, cheesy mushroom pancakes, and spicy beef and bean chilli. Don't forget the daily specials.
OPEN: 11.45-2.30 6-11 (closed Sun eve). Closed 26 Dec.
BAR MEALS: L served all week. D served Mon-Sat 12-2 6.30-9.15. Av main course £7.25. **BREWERY/COMPANY:** Punch Taverns.
PRINCIPAL BEERS: Tetley, Brakspear Bitter, Fullers London Pride. **FACILITIES:** Garden: Beer Garden: Food served outside Dogs allowed none. **NOTES:** Parking 30

BRILL — Map 06 SP61

The Pheasant Inn ♀
Windmill St HP18 9TG ☎ 01844 237104
e-mail: mrcarr@btinternet.com
Occupying a fine hilltop position 603ft above sea level, with impressive views over the Vale of Aylesbury and the Chilterns, this 17th-century beamed inn is immediately adjacent to Brill Windmill, one of the oldest postmills in the country. The pub used to be a village shop and the en suite bedrooms are housed in the old bakehouse. The popular blackboard menu offers the likes of lamb with redcurrant and rosemary jus, vegetable curry, home-made steak and mushroom pie and halibut with wine, cream and mushroom sauce. Annual music festival.
OPEN: 11-3 5.30-11 (Sun 12-10.30). Closed Dec 25-26.
BAR MEALS: L served all week. D served all week 12-2 7-9. Av main course £8.95. **RESTAURANT:** L served all week. D served all week 12-2 7-9. Av 3 course à la carte £20.
BREWERY/COMPANY: Free House.
PRINCIPAL BEERS: Tetley, Youngs Special.
FACILITIES: Children welcome Garden: outdoor eating Dogs allowed Garden: Only. **ROOMS:** 3 bedrooms 3 en suite s£35 d£65

CHARLES WELLS

Many breweries are started for love, but usually this is a love of beer. Charles Wells (born in 1842) started his brewery for love of a woman. Mr Grimbley, the father of Charles' sweetheart, Josephine, insisted that no daughter of his would marry a seafaring man, and as Wells was Chief Officer of a frigate he decided to forsake the sea, and turn to drink. The Charles Wells Family Brewery began in 1876, and has given us Bombardier English Premium Bitter (4.3%), and Eagle Bitter (3.6%). Wells also produces the Japanese lager Kirin, and the powerful Jamaican brew, Red Stripe. Tours are available.

BUCKINGHAM — Map 06 SP63

The Wheatsheaf ♀
Main St, Maids Moreton MK18 1QR ☎ 01280 815433
📠 01280 814631
Dir: *From M1 J13 take A421 to Buckingham, then take A413*

Old world village pub serving real ales, quality bar snacks and an à la carte menu in the spacious conservatory overlooking the secluded beer garden. Options range from home-made burgers or battered cod and chips at lunchtime, to chicken with lemon and garlic or 16 oz T-bone steak from the evening menu. Fish specialities include smoked haddock topped with prawns and cheese, and hickory smoked tuna steak.
OPEN: 12-3 6-11 (Sun 7-10.30). **BAR MEALS:** L served all week. D served Tue-Sat 12-2.15 7-9.30. Av main course £5.
RESTAURANT: L served all week. D served Tue-Sat 12-2.15 7-9.30. Av 3 course à la carte £20. **BREWERY/COMPANY:** Free House. **PRINCIPAL BEERS:** Hook Norton Best, Wychwood Shires, Courage Directors, Rodwells Roddy's Best.
FACILITIES: Children welcome Garden: patio, outside eating. **NOTES:** Parking 15

AA Hotel Booking Service on 0870 5050505 to book at AA recognised hotels and B & Bs in the UK and Ireland, or through our Internet site:
www.theAA.com

OPEN: 12-2.30 5.30-11.
Closed Mon lunch
BAR MEALS: L served all week.
D served all week 12-2 7-10
Av main course £9.50.
RESTAURANT: L served all week
D served all week 12-2 7-10
Av 3 course a la carte £22.
Av 3 course Sun lunch £16.
BREWERY/COMPANY:
Greene King
PRINCIPLE BEERS: Greene King
Triumph, Abbot Ale & Old
Speckled Hen, Badger Tanglefoot.
FACILITIES: No children under 5
. Garden: terrace, outdoor eating.
Dogs allowed (garden only).
NOTES: Parking 25.

The Crooked Billet

♀ NEW

Newton Longville MK17 0DF
☎ 01908 373936 ▤ 01908 631979
e-mail: johngilchrist@the-crooked-
billet-pub.co.uk
Dir: M1 (J13) take A421for Buckingham.
At Bottledump Roundabout turn L into
Newton Longville. Pub on L

In a sleepy village on the edge of the Aylesbury Vale, just minutes from Milton Keynes, the 16th-century Crooked Billet has been given a new lease of life by Greene King, who have had the foresight to let a talented chef and an experienced sommelier take the helm of this pretty thatched pub.

Set in attractive gardens and with a tastefully refurbished interior, replete with original oak beams, open log fires, a modern feel to the bar, and a wine themed restaurant, the Crooked Billet has quickly established itself as a dining destination of repute since re-opening its doors just over a year ago. The combination of ex-London chef Emma Sexton and John Gilchrist a, former UK Sommelier of the Year, has proved a great success, attracting discerning pub-goers from miles around for innovative, modern British food served in informal pub surroundings, and a sublime wine list, of which a staggering 250 are served by the glass.

Well balanced weekly-changing menus make good use of first-rate local produce, including fresh seasonal herbs and vegetables from both the pub and neighbouring villager's gardens. Begin with fish soup, wild rabbit and leek terrine with spicy peach relish, or a plate of smoked salmon served with beetroot and horseradish cream. For main course, either choose an interesting fish dish - brill with lobster mash, wilted spinach and red wine reduction, crispy sea bass with chorizo sausage - or try perhaps lamb fillet and black pudding with caramelised shallots and red wine jus, or calves liver and bacon with mash and onion gravy. Finish with a rich dark chocolate pot, caramel and praline cheesecake or cheese from Neal's Yard. Good value Sunday lunch menu - booking essential.

CHALFONT ST GILES   Map 04 SU99

Pick of the Pubs

Ivy House ♀
London Rd HP8 4RS ☎ 01494 872184
🖳 01494 872840
Dir: *On A413 2m S of Amersham & 1.5m N of Chalfont St Giles*

A lovely owner-managed free house in the heart of the Chilterns, with flint and brick walls, a warm atmosphere of old beams and open fires and a colourful 200 years of local history. Very much customer-driven, Jane Mears and her team create an interestingly eclectic menu that is not simply food for thought. Home-made guacamole with tortilla chips and Parmesan mushrooms with peppered cream sauce, followed by chicken enchiladas with spicy tomato salsa and seared tuna steak with a sauce 'of the moment' are challenging variations on a modern theme. Special signature dishes include moules marinière in season, chargrilled duck breast with plum and port sauce and pan-fried calves' liver and garlic mash with onion and bacon gravy. Anthony Mears contributes a lifetime's experience in providing top-rated real ales and house wines of firm pedigree served by the glass. Interesting salads, children's choices and home-made desserts typified by classic bread-and-butter pudding.
OPEN: 12-3.30 6-11.30 (Sat 12-11, Sun 12-10.30). Closed 25-26 Dec. **BAR MEALS:** L served all week. D served all week 12-2.30 6.30-9.30. Av main course £10.
RESTAURANT: L served all week. D served all week 12-2.30 6.30-9.30. Av 3 course à la carte £22.50.
BREWERY/COMPANY: Free House.
PRINCIPAL BEERS: Fullers London Pride, Brakspear Bitter, Wadworth 6X, Hook Norton Old Hooky.
FACILITIES: Children welcome Garden: patio, outdoor eating Dogs allowed not in restaurant. **NOTES:** Parking 35

The White Hart ♀
Three Households HP8 4LP ☎ 01494 872441
🖳 01494 876375
Dir: *Off A413 (Denham/Amersham)*
Interesting food and a decent wine list are the hallmarks of this recently refurbished 100-year-old pub, located in a pretty village near Milton's Cottage. It's sensible to book for the new restaurant and lodge-style bedrooms, which are especially popular at weekends. Start with chilled salmon soufflé, or grilled peppered goat's cheese, followed by roast lamb, pan-fried Barbary duck, or red snapper with roasted vegetables.

continued

OPEN: 11.30-2.30 6-11 (Sun 12-3,7-10.30). **BAR MEALS:** L served all week. D served all week 12-2 6.30-9.30. Av main course £8. **RESTAURANT:** L served all week. D served Mon-Sat 12-2 6.30-9.00. Av 3 course à la carte £18.
BREWERY/COMPANY: Greene King.
PRINCIPAL BEERS: Morland Original, Greene King IPA, Wadworth 6X. **FACILITIES:** Children welcome Garden: Food served outside Dogs allowed Water. **NOTES:** Parking 40.
ROOMS: 11 bedrooms 11 en suite s£62.50 d£82.50

CHENIES   Map 06 TQ09

The Red Lion
WD3 6ED ☎ 01923 282722 🖳 01923 283797
Dir: *Between Rickmansworth & Amersham on A404, Sign posted to Chenies and Latimer*

Pub situated near historic Chenies Manor and the River Chess. Home-made pies are a speciality: perhaps cod in a creamed spinach and nutmeg sauce, vegetable and bean, or steak, stout and orange. Other options include French bread sticks or wholemeal baps, jacket potatoes, ploughmans' or salads.
OPEN: 11-2.30 (Sun 12-3) 5.30-11 (Sun 6.30-10.30). Closed 25 Dec. **BAR MEALS:** L served all week. D served all week 12-2 7-10. Av main course £7. **BREWERY/COMPANY:** Free House.
PRINCIPAL BEERS: Benskins Best, Vale Notley Ale, Wadworth 6X, Rebellion Lion Pride. **FACILITIES:** Garden: Beer garden, Outdoor Eating, Dogs allowed Water. **NOTES:** Parking 14

CHESHAM   Map 06 SP90

The Black Horse Inn 🐑
Chesham Vale HP5 3NS ☎ 01494 784656
Dir: *A41 from Berkhamstead, A416 through Ashley Green, 0.75m before Chesham R to Vale Rd, btm of Mashleigh Hill follow rd for 1m, inn on L*
A 16th-century listed building constructed from ship's timbers with a huge garden pond and active ghost. There is a massive barbeque for summer weekends, weather permitting.

The Swan ♀
Ley Hill HP5 1UT ☎ 01494 783075
e-mail: swan@publand.com
Dir: *E of Chesham by golf course*
400-year-old listed pub with many classic features, including large inglenook fireplace, leaded lights and original ship's timbers. Allegedly where condemned highwaymen had their final drink prior to execution. Good for numerous Chiltern walks. New owners have devised an interesting menu characterised by locally sourced meat, vegetables and dairy produce and including smoked fish and other specialities from Cornwall and Dorset. Specials range from lamb casserole and grilled sardines to halibut steak and wild boar sausages.

continued

OPEN: 12-3 (Sun 12-3) 5.30-11 (Sun 7-10.30). **BAR MEALS:** L served all week. D served all week 12-2 7-9. Av main course £6.95. **RESTAURANT:** L served all week. D served all week 12-2 7-9. Av 3 course à la carte £20. **BREWERY/COMPANY:** Free House. **PRINCIPAL BEERS:** Adnams, Fullers London Pride, Timothy Taylor Landlord, Marston Pedigree, Greene King Abbot Ale. **FACILITIES:** Garden: Patio, BBQ, Beer garden

CHICHELEY   Map 06 SP94

The Chester Arms
MK16 9JE ☎ 01234 391214   📠 01234 391214
Dir: On A422, 2m NE of Newport Pagnell. 4m from M1 J14
Top quality produce in home-cooked dishes at this comfortable roadside pub, situated near Chicheley Hall (NT), the former home of the Chester family after whom the pub takes its name. Under new management.

CHOLESBURY   Map 06 SP90

The Full Moon ♀
Hawridge Common HP5 2UH ☎ 01494 758959
📠 01494 758797
Dir: At Tring on A41 take turn for Wiggington & Cholesbury

A 16th-century coaching inn, known as the Half Moon in the 1800s. It has a wealth of low beams, and three real fires create a cosy atmosphere in winter. Food includes daily specials as well as favourites like ham and eggs, scampi, gammon steak or chilli con carne.
OPEN: 12-3 (Sat open all day) 5.30-11 (Sun12-4, 7-10.30). **BAR MEALS:** L served all week. D served Mon-Sat 12-2 6.15-9. Av main course £6. **BREWERY/COMPANY:** Enterprise Inns. **PRINCIPAL BEERS:** Bass, Fullers London Pride, Brakspear Special. **FACILITIES:** Children welcome Garden: Patio, food served outside Dogs allowed Water. **NOTES:** Parking 24

THE CHILTERN BREWERY

Among the first wave of micro-breweries in England, the Chiltern Brewery was formed in 1980 and ironically, is now the oldest working brewery in Buckinghamshire. Tours can be arranged by appointment and would take in the Buckinghamshire Breweries Museum. Opened in 1994, this collection of 'breweriana' was the first small brewers museum in the UK. Major brews are Chiltern Ale (3.7%), Beechwood Bitter (4.3%), and Three Hundred Old Ale (4.9%).

CUDDINGTON   Map 06 SP71

Pick of the Pubs

The Crown ♀
Spurt St HP18 0BB ☎ 01844 292222
e-mail: david@thecrowncuddington.co.uk
Having successfully run Annie Bailey's, a bar-cum-brasserie, in the village for some years, the Berrys have turned their attention to restoring the fortunes of The Crown, a pretty, Grade II listed thatched pub just around the corner. With Fuller's beers on tap, an extensive wine list, and an eclectic menu business has thrived since acquiring the lease two years ago. Full of character inside, with a popular locals' bar and a series low-beamed dining areas filled with attractive prints and evening candlelight. A short menu may list salads and open sandwiches (hot duck and bacon), starters like black pudding with baked red cabbage and main dishes such as cushion of lamb on sweet potato and cardamom mash, green Thai seafood curry, monkfish with smoked bacon in red wine sauce, seared tuna Niçoise, daily pasta dishes, real fish and chips, and ribeye steak with pink peppercorn sauce.
OPEN: 12-3 6-11. **BAR MEALS:** L served all week. D served all week 12-2.30 6.30-10. **RESTAURANT:** L served all week. D served all week 12-2.30 6.30-10. Av 3 course à la carte £20. **BREWERY/COMPANY:** Fullers. **PRINCIPAL BEERS:** Fullers London Pride, **FACILITIES:** Children welcome Garden: patio, outdoor eating. **NOTES:** Parking 12

DINTON

Seven Stars
Stars Ln HP17 8UL ☎ 01296 748241
Quiet village local with snugs and inglenook fireplace. Handy for Quainton Steam Centre. Large restaurant area.

FAWLEY   Map 04 SU78

Pick of the Pubs

The Walnut Tree ♀
RG9 6JE ☎ 01491 638360   📠 01491 532615
Dir: From Henley on A4155 towards Marlow, L at 2nd sign for Fawley. R at village green
Set in the Chiltern Hills with wonderful views some 400ft above Henley-on-Thames, the pub retains two gnarled walnut trees in a fine garden that boasts a barbecue, rustic swings and an original hitching-post: there is also walnut furniture in the restaurant reputedly made from a tree felled on the site. An up-to-date feel on the latest menus produces lunchtime fare such as seared sea bass fillets on smoked bacon mash, turkey escalope in a brioche crumb with red onion and celery sauce, Tuscan chicken wrapped in charred leeks with Parma ham, and grilled king scallops in cucumber and lemon butter. Also watch the blackboard menus for daily specials.
OPEN: 12-3 (All day w/end) 6-11 (Sat-Sun & Bhs 11-11). **BAR MEALS:** L served all week. D served all week 12-3 6.30-9.30. Av main course £7. **RESTAURANT:** L served all week. D served all week 12-3 6.30-9.30. Av 3 course à la carte £20. Av 3 course fixed price £13.95.
BREWERY/COMPANY: Brakspear.
PRINCIPAL BEERS: Brakspear. **FACILITIES:** Children welcome Garden: patio, outdoor eating, BBQ Dogs allowed. **NOTES:** Parking 50. **ROOMS:** 2 bedrooms 2 en suite s£35 d£50

England

FINGEST
Map 04 SU79

The Chequers Inn ♀
RG9 6QD ☎ 01491 638335
Dir: From M40 L towards Ibstone, L at T junc at end of rd, stay L, pub on R
Set deep in the Chiltern Hills, opposite a splendid Norman church, the Chequers is a 15th-century redbrick pub with log fires in the winter, and a delightful sun-trap garden with rural views for summer imbibing.

FORD
Map 06 SP70

The Dinton Hermit 🐑
Water Ln HP17 8XH ☎ 01296 747473
Dir: Off A418 between Aylesbury & Thame
In an isolated hamlet and set back from the lane, this 15th-century stone pub is named after John Briggs, clerk to one of the judges who condemned Charles I to death. So ashamed was he of his part in the execution that he became a hermit, and subsequently became a local legend. Another John - John Bingham-Chick - has recently taken over the pub and now offers hearty, freshly prepared food throughout the two beamed and warmly decorated bars. Typical dishes include blinis with gravadlax, baked avocado with goats' cheese, king prawn piri piri, calves' liver, Dover sole and beef Stroganoff. Lighter meals include pasta dishes and open sandwiches. Large pretty garden with rural views.
OPEN: 11-2.30 (From Easter open 7 days a Wk) 6-11.
BAR MEALS: L served Tue-Sun. D served Tue-Sat 12-2 7-9.30. Av main course £10. **RESTAURANT:** L served Tue-Sun. D served Tue-Sat 12-2 7-9.30. Av 3 course à la carte £20.
BREWERY/COMPANY: Free House.
PRINCIPAL BEERS: Hook Norton, Adnams.
FACILITIES: Garden: large, Food served outside.
NOTES: Parking 30

FRIETH
Map 04 SU79

The Prince Albert
RG9 6PY ☎ 01494 881683
Old fashioned country local ideal for a stop-off after walking in the Chilterns. Not suitable for children. Brakspear ales.

The Yew Tree
RG9 6PJ ☎ 01494 882330 ≣ 01494 882927
e-mail: theyewtree@hotmail.com
Dir: from M40 towards Stokenchurch, thru Cadmore End, Lane End R to Frieth
A huge yew tree spirals majestically outside this 16th-century red-brick pub in this truly rural Chilterns village. Sit in the pretty flower garden, or in the original-beamed bar with its inglenook and tip-top ales, and enjoy a hot chicken sandwich, traditional fish and chips, smoked salmon tagliatelle, or grilled plaice. New restaurant operation sounds interesting.
OPEN: 11-11. **BAR MEALS:** L served all week. D served all week 11-3 6.30-10.30. Av main course £7. **RESTAURANT:** L served all week. D served Tue-Sun 11-3 6.30-10.30. Av 3 course à la carte £18. **BREWERY/COMPANY:** Free House.
PRINCIPAL BEERS: Brakspear Bitter, Fullers London Pride, Rebellion IPA. **FACILITIES:** Children welcome Garden: Dogs allowed. **NOTES:** Parking 60

GREAT BRICKHILL
Map 06 SP93

The Old Red Lion ♀
Ivy Ln MK17 9AH ☎ 01525 261715 ≣ 01525 261716
Dir: Signposted off A5, 10m S of Milton Keynes
Believed to have the best view in Buckinghamshire, over the Vale of Aylesbury, the Old Red Lion was first established as a public house in 1771. New owners are introducing a new wine list and a menu of traditional home-cooked food, freshly prepared from locally sourced produce. There are filled baguettes at lunchtime, home-made pies, mixed grills and Sunday roasts.
OPEN: 11-1 (Sun 12-10.30). **BAR MEALS:** L served all week. D served all week 12-2 7-9. Av main course £10. **RESTAURANT:** L served all week. D served all week 12-2 7-9. Av 3 course à la carte £18. **BREWERY/COMPANY:** Whitbread. **PRINCIPAL BEERS:** Flowers Original, Greene King IPA & guest beer. **FACILITIES:** Garden: outdoor eating, children's play area Dogs allowed garden only. **NOTES:** Parking 12

GREAT HAMPDEN
Map 06 SP70

The Hampden Arms
HP16 9RQ ☎ 01494 488255
Dir: From M40 take A4010, R before Princes Risborough, Great Hampden signposted
Mock Tudor building dating in parts from the 17th century, situated on the Hampden Estate close to many popular wooded walks in the Chilterns. An extensive menu ranges through seafood lasagne, zingy salmon, steak Romanov, chicken curry and vegetarian dishes, finishing with a good choice of traditional puddings.
OPEN: 12-3 6.30-11 (Sun 6.30-10.30). **BAR MEALS:** L served all week. D served all week 12-2 6.30-9.30. Av main course £8.95. **RESTAURANT:** L served all week. D served all week 12-2 6.30-9.30. Av 3 course à la carte £17. **BREWERY/COMPANY:** Free House. **PRINCIPAL BEERS:** Adnams, Fullers London Pride, Brakspear. **FACILITIES:** Children welcome Garden: Beer garden, Outdoor Eating, Dogs allowed Allowed at owners discretion. **NOTES:** Parking 30

GREAT MISSENDEN
Map 06 SP80

The George Inn ♀
94 High St HP16 0BG ☎ 01494 862084 ≣ 01494 865622
Dir: off A413 between Aylesbury & Amersham
Ideally located for exploring the lovely Chiltern Hills, the George is a 15th-century coaching inn with many original oak beams and fireplaces. Bar snacks and English dishes are available at lunchtime, while in the evening the restaurant is given over to authentic Thai cooking provided under separate management.
OPEN: 11-11 (Sun 12-3, 7-10.30). **BAR MEALS:** L served all week 12.30-2.30. Av main course £6. **RESTAURANT:** D served Tue-Sat 6-10. Av 3 course à la carte £18. Av 3 course fixed price £12. **BREWERY/COMPANY:** Greenalls. **PRINCIPAL BEERS:** Adnams Bitter, Youngs Special, Flowers Original. **FACILITIES:** Children welcome Garden: Outside Eating, Patio Dogs allowed. **NOTES:** Parking 25. **ROOMS:** 6 bedrooms 6 en suite s£65 d£65 FR£70-£90

GREAT MISSENDEN continued

Pick of the Pubs

The Polecat Inn 🐾 ♀
170 Wycombe Rd, Prestwood HP16 0HJ
☎ 01494 862253 📠 01494 868393
e-mail: polecatinn@prestwood90.freeserve.co.uk
Dir: On the A4128 between Great Missenden and High Wycombe
A charming 17th-century inn situated in the heart of the
Chiltern Hills, with a three-acre garden and plenty of
tables for summer alfresco eating. A rambling series of
small, low-beamed rooms radiate off the central bar, each
with rug-strewn wooden or tiled floors and a comfortable
mix of furnishings. Good open fires and cabinets full of
stuffed birds. Everything listed on the wide-ranging menu
and interesting specials boards is prepared on the
premises from local ingredients and herbs from the
garden. Plenty of pub favourites can be found on the main
menu, alongside spiced lamb terrine with mint jelly, daube
of wild boar with red cabbage and honey-glazed
chestnuts, while seasonal dishes on the board may include
duck with rhubarb and sweet ginger sauce and monkfish
in saffron cream with crayfish risotto. Good puddings and
snacks like filled jacket potatoes and sandwiches.
OPEN: 11.30-2.30 6-11 (Sun 12-3 only). Closed Dec 25-26, Jan
1. **BAR MEALS:** L served all week. D served Mon-Sat 12-2
6.30-9. Av main course £7.90. **BREWERY/ COMPANY:** Free
House. **PRINCIPAL BEERS:** Theakston Best, Marstons
Pedigree, Wadworth 6X, Ruddles County. **FACILITIES:** Children welcome Garden: outdoor eating Dogs allowed.
NOTES: Parking 40 No credit cards

Pick of the Pubs

The Rising Sun 🐾 ♀
Little Hampden HP16 9PS
☎ 01494 488393 & 488360 📠 01494 488788
e-mail: sunrising@rising-sun.demon.co.uk
Dir: From A413 N of Gt Missenden take Rignall Rd on L (signed
Princes Risborough) 2.5m turn R signed 'Little Hampden only'
You'll find this award-winning, 250 year-old free house
tucked away amongst high beech woods on the Chiltern
Hills, with delightful walks right on the doorstep. There's a
friendly and relaxed atmosphere, with open fires and hot
mulled wine or spiced cider in winter time. The quiet location and comfortable en suite rooms makes this an ideal
venue for a getaway break, free from piped music or noisy
electronic games. Constantly changing blackboard menus
feature interesting and imaginative home cooked dishes;
typical choices might include grilled goat's cheese on garlic
bread, roast duck with mango and orange sauce, or asparagus and almond filo parcel. Seafood lovers have plenty of
choice; expect baked dressed crab, halibut with prawn and
mushroom sauce, poached salmon, and deep-fried plaice or
scampi. Chocolate roulade, caramel fruit tart or bitter-sweet
flummery with raspberries appear on the pudding board.
Walkers are welcome - although muddy boots are not!
OPEN: 11.30-2.30 6.30-11. **BAR MEALS:** L served Tue-Sun.
D served Tue-Sat 12-2 7-9. Av main course £8.95.
RESTAURANT: L served Tue-Sun. D served Tue-Sat 12-2 7-9.
Av 3 course à la carte £18. **BREWERY/COMPANY:** Free
House. **PRINCIPAL BEERS:** Adnams, Brakspear Bitter,
Marstons Pedigree. **FACILITIES:** Children welcome Garden:
Food served outside Dogs allowed Water. **NOTES:** Parking
20. **ROOMS:** 2 bedrooms 2 en suite s£30 d£58

HADDENHAM   Map 06 SP70

Pick of the Pubs

The Green Dragon 🏵 🏵 🐾 ♀
8 Churchway HP17 8AA ☎ 01844 291403
e-mail: paul.berry4@virgin.net
See Pick of the Pubs on page 49

HAMBLEDEN   Map 06 SP78

Pick of the Pubs

The Stag & Huntsman Inn
RG9 6RP ☎ 01491 571227 📠 01491 413810
Dir: 5m from Henley-on-Thames on A4155 toward Marlow, L at
Mill End towards Hambleden
Close to the glorious beech-clad Chilterns, this 400-year-
old brick and flint village pub has featured in countless
films and television series, including 101 Dalmatians,
Poirot and Midsomer Murders. After an exhilarating
ramble in the hills, savour the bustling atmosphere of the
L-shaped, half-panelled bar with its low ceilings and
upholstered seating. Two other bars, including a cosy
snug, add to the charm of the place. Try the fresh salmon
fishcakes, aubergine and courgette macaroni cheese or
steak topped with caramelised sugar and mustard. Game
features in season.
OPEN: 11-2.30 6-11 (Sun 12-3, 7-10.30, Sat 11-3, 6-11).
Closed Dec 25. **BAR MEALS:** L served all week. D served
Mon-Sat 12-2 7-9.30. Av main course £7.50.
BREWERY/COMPANY: Free House.
PRINCIPAL BEERS: Brakspear Bitter, Wadworth 6X, guest
ales. **FACILITIES:** Children welcome Garden: Food served
outside. **NOTES:** Parking 60. **ROOMS:** 3 bedrooms 3 en
suite s£58 d£68

Country Matters

Country occupations and pursuits
provide many inns with their names. The
Wheatsheaf, the Barley Mow, the Haywain, the
Dun Cow, the Heifer, the Plough (sometimes the
constellation) and the Harrow recall the farming
year's immemorial round. Horses, long essential
to agriculture, communications and sport, figure
frequently - the Black Horse, the Nag's Head, the
Grey Mare and many more. The Bull and the
Bear are often related to the once popular sport
of baiting the animals with dogs. The dog is
usually a sporting dog and hunting has supplied
many names, from the Fox and Hounds and the
Hare and Hounds to numerous deer (also from
heraldry), including the Stag and Hounds, the
White Hart and the Roebuck. There are signs
related to angling, too, such as the Angler and
the Trout, and there are Jolly Cricketers
and even Jolly Farmers.

Skittles

Skittles is a far older game than darts or dominoes, on record in London since the 15th century, when it was banned. Henry VIII enjoyed it and had his own skittle alley, but governments kept vainly trying to stop ordinary people playing, because they ought to have been practising their archery and because they gambled so heavily. Even so, the game became popular enough to make 'beer and skittles' proverbial. Basically, three wooden balls are propelled at nine pins to knock them down, but there are sharp variations in the rules between different areas and pubs. Varieties include London or Old English Skittles, West Country Skittles, Long Alley and Aunt Sally, as well as several types of table skittles.

HIGH WYCOMBE   Map 04 SU89

The Chequers
Bullocks Farm Ln, Wheeler End HP14 3NH
☎ 01494 883070
Dir: From M4 J5, B482 towards Marlow, L to Wheeler End. Or M4 J5 A40 towards H Wycombe, R to Wheeler End
The Chequers, situated on the edge of Wheeler Common, dates back 300 years and retains many original features. It is known locally for its quality real ale and bar food, with evening meals available Wednesday to Saturday, including fish night on Wednesday, and traditional Sunday lunch.
OPEN: 11-3 5.30-11 (Mon 11-2.30, 6-11 Sun 12-3, 7-10.30).
BAR MEALS: L served all week. D served Wed-Sat 12-2 7-9.
Av main course £7.95. **BREWERY/COMPANY:** Fullers.
PRINCIPAL BEERS: Fullers ESB, London Pride & Chiswick, Brakspear. **FACILITIES:** Garden: Dogs allowed.
NOTES: Parking 12

KINGSWOOD

Crooked Billet
Ham Green HP18 0QJ ☎ 01296 770239 🖹 01296 770094
Dir: On A41 between Aylesbury & Bicester
Located in peaceful Buckinghamshire countryside, The Crooked Billet has been a pub for about 200 years and is believed to be haunted by Fair Rosamund, a girlfriend of Charles I.

LACEY GREEN   Map 06 SP80

Pink & Lily
Pink Rd HP27 0RJ ☎ 01494 488308 🖹 01494 488013
Dir: Off A4010 S of Princes Risborough
The pub is named after a local butler (Mr Lily), who had a liaison with a chambermaid (Miss Pink). On being dismissed from service they set themselves up as innkeepers. The inn has several newly refurbished eating and drinking areas serving the likes of home-made pies, fresh cod in beer batter, and favourite sweets such as apple pie and sticky toffee pudding.
OPEN: 11.30-11 (Sat 11-11, Sun 12-10.30). **BAR MEALS:** L served all week. D served Mon-Sat 12-2 7-9.30. Av main course £8. **BREWERY/COMPANY:** Free House.
PRINCIPAL BEERS: Brakspear Bitter & Special, Fullers London Pride, Vale Notley Ale, Courage Best. **FACILITIES:** Children welcome Garden: beer garden with seating, patio Dogs allowed garden only. **NOTES:** Parking 40

LONG CRENDON   Map 06 SP60

Pick of the Pubs

The Angel Inn 🌐 🌐 🍸
47 Bicester Rd HP18 9EE ☎ 01844 208268
🖹 01844 202497
Dir: A418 to Thame, B4011 to L Crendon, Inn on B4011

Upgraded 16th-century coaching inn featuring wattle and daub walls, a warm, pastel yellow decor, an eclectic mix of furnishings from scrubbed pine tables and sturdy oak tables on light wooden floors, to Chesterfield sofas fronting the bar and inglenook fireplace. Air-conditioned rear conservatory, patio and sun terrace for alfresco dining. Real ales at the bar but the emphasis here is distinctly on first-class pub dining. The Angel is right-up-to-date in gastronomic terms, serving a broad range of modern dishes with a Mediterranean influence, with daily blackboards listing imaginative fish and seafood dishes. Choices range from Scottish rope mussels with saffron and garden herbs and provençale shellfish soup to seared sea bass on chargrilled vegetables with Thai sweet chilli dressing and whole lemon sole in caper butter. Alternative dishes may include Angel baguettes, open sandwiches and chargrilled seafood and antipasto salad for lunchtime snacks, to partridge on confit of wild mushrooms and root vegetables with port and redcurrant sauce, and warm apple and toffee brioche butter pudding. Extensive list of wines and efficient service.
OPEN: 12-3 7-10 (Closed Sun night). **BAR MEALS:** L served all week. D served Mon-Sat 12-3 7-10. Av main course £12.75. **RESTAURANT:** L served all week. D served Mon-Sat 12-3 7-10. Av 3 course à la carte £25.
BREWERY/COMPANY: Free House.
PRINCIPAL BEERS: Hook Norton Best, Adnams Broadside, Ridleys Rumpus. **FACILITIES:** Children welcome Garden: patio, outdoor eating. **NOTES:** Parking 25. **ROOMS:** 3 bedrooms 3 en suite s£55 d£65 FRE75.00

OPEN: 11.30-3 6.30-11.
Closed Sun eve
BAR MEALS: L served all week.
D served Mon-Sat 12-2 7-9.30.
Av main course £9.14.
RESTAURANT: L served all week.
D served Mon-Sat 12-2 7-9.30.
Av 3 course a la carte £22.
Av 3 course fixed price £17.95.
BREWERY/COMPANY:
Whitbread.
PRINCIPAL BEERS: Vale Notley
Ale, Fullers London Pride.
FACILITIES: Children welcome.
Garden: patio, outdoor eating
NOTES: Parking 18.

The Green Dragon

8 Churchway HP17 8AA
☎ 01844 291403
e-mail: paul.berry4@virgin.net
Dir: From M40 A329 to Thame, then
A418, 1st R after entering Haddenham

The Green Dragon enjoys a pretty location in the old part of Haddenham close to the 12th-century church and village green. Head chef Paul Berry has taken this manorial 17th-century former courthouse by the horns, with gratifying results for an ever-increasing following of discerning diners.

Most of the character interior is given over to a food operation that services a pair of stylish dining areas, with an enclosed gravel terrace handling the summer overflow. Fine ingredients and execution shine throughout a wide-ranging selection of daily menus that give precious little cause for complaint. Start off perhaps with real ale in the bar, turn off the mobile and then enjoy a compendium of options that begins with the day's soup and toasted snippets, duck liver parfait with orange dressing and a brochette of scallops, langoustine, halibut and salmon on a lime and pine-nut dressing.

Main dishes, inclusively served with potato and fresh vegetables, encompass Cornish sea bass with vanilla and Chablis beurre blanc, Gressingham duck on green cabbage with marjoram and Scottish sirloin steak with a sauce of Cashel Blue and walnuts. Dictated by careful daily shopping, specials might include a trio of local pork sausage with mash, gravy and crispy fried onions, pan-seared lambs' liver with onion marmalade and fillet steak flamed in brandy with wild mushroom sauce.

A varied selection of puddings is likely to include lemon tart and citrus sorbet, chocolate parfait with cappuccino sabayon and fruit rum toft with home-made Agen ice cream.

England

Pick of the Pubs

Mole & Chicken 🐄 ♀
Easington Ter HP18 9EY ☎ 01844 208387
🖂 01844 208250
e-mail: themoleandchicken@hotmail.com
Dir: Off B4011 N of Thame

Built in 1831 in a fold of the Chiltern Hills as a beer and cider house and formerly known as The Rising Sun, this fashionable dining pub was re-named after two latter day proprietors, Mr Mole and Mr Chicken: of such stuff are legends made. A tastefully decorated interior features cosy fireplaces, rag-washed walls and flagstone floors in the oak beamed bar, while the tiered and terraced garden enjoys outstanding views across three counties. Suggested menu specialities, posted on boards over the fireplace's oak lintel, include secret recipe fishcakes with mild curry sauce and skewers of satay chicken and shell-on prawns enticingly entitled Horses Douvay. Follow then with marinated and slow roast rack of pork ribs, salmon filled with prawn and dill mousse in filo pastry or penne pasta tossed in sun-dried tomato pesto. Roast lamb shoulder with honey and rosemary sauce and local pheasant with shallots, red wine, bacon and sage provide further variations on traditional themes.
OPEN: 12-3.30 6-12. Closed 25 Dec. **BAR MEALS:** L served all week. D served all week 12-2 6-10. Av main course £10.50. **RESTAURANT:** L served all week. D served all week 12-2 6-10. Av 3 course à la carte £20.
BREWERY/COMPANY: Free House.
PRINCIPAL BEERS: Hook Norton, Ruddles Best, Greene King IPA & Old Speckled Hen. **FACILITIES:** Children welcome Garden: outdoor eating, patio, beer garden.
NOTES: Parking 40

MARLOW   Map 04 SU88

The Kings Head ♀
Church Rd, Little Marlow SL7 3RZ ☎ 01628 484407
🖂 01628 484407
Dir: M40 J4 take A4040 S 1st A4155
Only 10 minutes from the Thames footpath, this 17th-century, flower-adorned pub offers a varied menu within its cosy, open-plan interior. From sandwiches and jacket potatoes, the menu may extend to pheasant casserole, Thai fishcakes with noodles and stir-fried vegetables, and steak and kidney pie.

continued

OPEN: 11-3 5-11 (Sat 11-11, Sun 12-10.30). **BAR MEALS:** L served all week. D served all week 12-2 7-10. Av main course £7.50. **RESTAURANT:** L served all week. D served all week 12-2 7-10. Av 3 course à la carte £12.50.
BREWERY/COMPANY: Whitbread.
PRINCIPAL BEERS: Brakspear Bitter, Fuller's London Pride, Wadworth 6X, Morrells Varsity. **FACILITIES:** Children welcome Garden: outdoor eating, **NOTES:** Parking 50

MILTON KEYNES   Map 06 SP83

The Old Thatched Inn ♀ NEW
Adstock MK18 2JN ☎ 01296 712584 🖂 01296 715375
This attractive old 17th-century inn was known as the Chandos Arms until it was renamed in the 1970s. New owner Jeremy Baker has kept the traditional atmosphere, with a roaring winter fire in the inglenook and a nice selection of real ales and fine wines. The good quality menu ranges from hand-cut sandwiches and ciabattas to speciality sausages with leek mash, rib eye beef and watercress sauce, and grilled red mullet.
OPEN: 12-3 6. **BAR MEALS:** L served all week. D served all week 12-2.30 6-9.30. Av main course £10. **RESTAURANT:** L served all week. D served all week 12-2.30 6-9.30. Av 3 course à la carte £18. **PRINCIPAL BEERS:** Hook Norton Best, Old Hooky, Bass, Fullers London Pride. **FACILITIES:** Children welcome Garden: Patio, Food served outside Dogs allowed.
NOTES: Parking 20

MOULSOE   Map 06 SP94

The Carrington Arms 🐄
Cranfield Rd MK16 0HB ☎ 01908 218050
🖂 01908 217850
e-mail: carringtonarms@btinternet.com
Dir: M1 J14 take rd signed 'Cranfield & Moulsoe'. Pub 1m on R
Before becoming a pub, this Grade II listed building was the home of Lord Carrington's estate manager. Orders are taken directly by the chef who cooks on a range in full view of his expectant customers. Food includes excellent steaks and fish, various Thai dishes, beef and ale cobbler and smoked chicken salad.
OPEN: 11-3 6-11. **BAR MEALS:** L served all week 12-2. Av main course £6. **RESTAURANT:** L served all week. D served all week 12-2 6.30-10. Av 3 course à la carte £20.
BREWERY/COMPANY: Free House.
PRINCIPAL BEERS: Brakspear Special & Best, Courage Directors.
FACILITIES: Children welcome Garden: Orchard Dogs allowed.
NOTES: Parking 100. **ROOMS:** 8 bedrooms 8 en suite d£40

PRESTON BISSETT   Map 06 SP62

Pick of the Pubs

The White Hart ♀ NEW
Pond Ln MK18 4LX ☎ 01280 847969
Dir: *5m South of Buckingham via Cowcott*
Tiny 18th-century thatched and timbered pub, which, with its charm and character, captures the essence of the traditional village inn. Inside are three small rooms with low ceilings, red banquettes, beams and a welcoming open fire, while the delightful enclosed garden and patio are the obvious choice on warm days and summer evenings.

Good quality menu prepared by the licensee, including roasted red peppers with black olive dressing and Parmesan crisps, lamb, apricot and rosemary pie, cod and chips, and cheese and spinach crêpe.

Wide selection of malt whiskies, country fruit wines and non-alcoholic drinks, including home-made lemonade and elderflower spritzer in the summer. Home-produced mulled wine is also a speciality.
OPEN: 12-2.30 6.30-11 (Sun 12-2.30, 7-10.30).
BAR MEALS: L served all week. D served all week 12-1.45 7-9. Av main course £8.50. **RESTAURANT:** L served all week. D served all week 12-1.45 7-9. Av 3 course à la carte £16. **PRINCIPAL BEERS:** Adnams + Guest Ale.
FACILITIES: Garden: Food served outside Dogs allowed Water, bonios. **NOTES:** Parking 9

PRINCES RISBOROUGH   Map 06 SP80

Red Lion
Upper Icknield Way, Whiteleaf HP27 0LL ☎ 01844 344476
🖷 01844 273124
e-mail: tim.hibbert@lineone.net
Dir: *A4010 thru Princes Risbro', then R into 'Holloway', go to end of road, R, pub on L*
Family-owned 17th-century inn in the heart of the Chilterns, surrounded by National Trust land and situated close to the Ridgeway national trail. Plenty of good local walks with wonderful views. A cosy fire in winter and a secluded summer beer garden add to the appeal. Hearty pub fare includes steak and kidney pudding, fresh fish and chips, salmon béarnaise, fresh pasta and various curry and chilli dishes.
OPEN: 11.30-3 (Sun 12-3, 7-10.30) 5.30-11 (All day Wkds May-Sept). **BAR MEALS:** L served all week. D served Mon-Sat 12-2 7-9. Av main course £7. **RESTAURANT:** L served all week. D served Mon-Sat 12-2 7-9. Av 3 course à la carte £14.
BREWERY/COMPANY: Free House.
PRINCIPAL BEERS: Brakspear Bitter, Hook Norton Best, Rebellion IPA. **FACILITIES:** Children welcome Garden: beer garden, patio, food served outdoors Dogs allowed Water.
NOTES: Parking 10. **ROOMS:** 4 bedrooms 4 en suite s£40 d£50 FR£60

For pubs with AA rosette awards for food see page 10

SKIRMETT   Map 04 SU79

Pick of the Pubs

The Frog 🏠 ♀
RG9 6TG ☎ 01491 638996 🖷 01491 638045
From its pretty, clay-tiled dormer windows to its overflowing flower tubs, this eye-catching whitewashed free house exudes warmth and tranquillity. Set deep in one of the loveliest valleys in the Chiltern Hills, The Frog lies close to the heart of 'Vicar of Dibley' country. There are attractive rural views from the delightful, tree-shaded garden, and you may be tempted to enjoy one of the recommended local walks. Once inside, this family-run pub does not disappoint though in wintertime you may have to queue for a place on the unusual wooden bench that encircles the fireplace. There are five comfortably furnished en suite bedrooms, and a reassuringly civilised non-smoking restaurant. The wide ranging international menu is changed monthly, and daily specials are featured on the blackboard. Fresh ingredients and confident cooking produce home-made soups, Irish fry-up, and braised lamb shank. There's always a good selection of fish, too; expect haddock in beer batter, red mullet, sea bass, or bream.

OPEN: 11-3 6-11. **BAR MEALS:** L served all week. D served all week 12-2.30 6.30-9.30. Av main course £8.50.
RESTAURANT: L served all week. D served all week 12-2.30 6.30-9.30. Av 3 course à la carte £12.50.
BREWERY/COMPANY: Free House.
PRINCIPAL BEERS: Adnams Best, Brakspear Bitter, Fullers London Pride. **FACILITIES:** Children welcome Garden: patio, outdoor eating Dogs allowed. **NOTES:** Parking 15.
ROOMS: 5 bedrooms 5 en suite

SPEEN   Map 04 SU89

King William IV 🏠
Hampden Rd HP27 0RU ☎ 01494 488329
🖷 01494 488301
Dir: *Through Hughenden Valley, off A4128 N of High Wycombe*
Nestling in the Chiltern Hills, this 17th-century, family run pub and restaurant boasts log fires in winter and a popular terrace and garden ideal for summer drinking. Choose from an interesting range of blackboard specials that might include Thai green chicken curry, grilled red snapper and trio of Welsh lamb cutlets.
OPEN: 12-3 6.30-11. **RESTAURANT:** L served Tue-Sun. D served Tue-Sat 12-2 7-9.30. Av 3 course à la carte £22.50.
BREWERY/COMPANY: Free House.
PRINCIPAL BEERS: Wadworth 6X, Boddingtons.
FACILITIES: Children welcome Garden: lawned area with cast iron feature, patio. **NOTES:** Parking 50

Royal State

The Crown is one of the commonest inn names, for patriotic reasons and sometimes because the inn stood on royal land. The Rose and Crown celebrates Henry VII's achievement in ending civil war by reconciling the rival roses of York and Lancaster in the crown. The King's Head, King's Arms and Queen's Arms are equally familiar, often with Henry VIII on the sign, roughly after Holbein. Elizabeth I, the Georges, Queen Victoria and Prince Albert make their appearances, too, and many pubs are named after childen of George III or Queen Victoria (the Duke of York, Duke of Clarence, Duke of Edinburgh, etc). Others honour the Prince of Wales or his badge of the Feathers, while the Fleur de Lys recalls the fact that down to 1801 the kings of England claimed to be kings of France as well.

THORNBOROUGH

The Lone Tree

Bletchley Rd MK18 2DZ ☎ 01280 812334
New landlords have taken over this rather isolated, 17th-century pub set beside the A421 between Buckingham and Milton Keynes. Expect regularly changing guest beers, traditional pub meals and hearty daily specials. Reports welcome.

TURVILLE   Map 04 SU79

Pick of the Pubs

The Bull & Butcher 🐾 🍷

RG9 6QU ☎ 01491 638283 📠 638283
e-mail: nick@bull&butcher.com
Dir: *M40 J5 follow signs for Ibstone. Turn R T-junc. Pub 0.25m on L*
Lovely, black and white timbered 16th-century pub tucked away in a secluded valley in a classic Chiltern's village that is regularly used as a film set, including The Vicar of Dibley. Two unspoilt, low-ceilinged bars with open fires, a welcoming atmosphere, and good restaurant-style food in a traditional pub setting. Daily menus, served throughout, show imagination and flair and make good use of fresh local produce, including local estate game and fish bought direct from Billingsgate. Don't expect traditional pub food, light meals include salads - grilled goats' cheese salad with tapenade, warm salad of king scallops and wild mushrooms - or starters like hot home-smoked beef pastrami on rye and smoked haddock, spinach and potato terrine. Hearty, rustic main dishes may feature Toulouse sausages with mash, roast shallots and gravy and calves' liver with peccorino mash and smoked bacon. Tip-top Brakspear ales on tap, 37 wines by the glass and excellent local walks; delightful summer garden.
OPEN: 11-3 (Sun 12-5, 7-10.30) 6-11 (Sat 6.30-11).
BAR MEALS: L served Mon-Sun. D served Mon-Sat 12-2 6-11. Av main course £10.95. **RESTAURANT:** L served Mon-Sun. D served Mon-Sat 12-2 6-11. Av 3 course à la carte £17.
BREWERY/COMPANY: Brakspear.
PRINCIPAL BEERS: Brakspear Mild, Bitter, Special & Old.
FACILITIES: Garden: BBQ, outdoor eating, beer garden Dogs allowed. **NOTES:** Parking 20

WADDESDON   Map 06 SP71

Pick of the Pubs

The Five Arrows Hotel 🐾 🍷

High St HP18 0JE ☎ 01296 651727 📠 01296 658596
e-mail: thefivearrows@netscapeonline.co.uk
Dir: *on A41 6m NW of Aylesbury*
Part of the National Trust's Waddesdon Estate, originally built in 1887 to house Baron Ferdinand de Rothschild's extensive art collection, the Grade II listed mansion features today some handsome overnight accommodation in individually decorated en suite bedrooms. Its fine chimneys, William Morris decor, fascinating photographic collection and wrought ironwork give the house a particularly striking appearance. Food can best be described as a culinary mix of Mediterranean and traditional English, with liberal use of fresh local produce. Daily lunch specials may thus include toasted mackerel open sandwiches, honey-roast ham with fried free-range egg and fries and butchers' pork sausages with mash and onion gravy. More elaborate dishes take in spaghetti with pancetta and Gorgonzola sauce, salmon fishcakes with coriander jam and Thai marinated red mullet with soy noodles, all offered as a starter or main course. Graduate then to confit duck with raspberry and red wine jus or fillet steak with red shallot butter and round off with treacle tart and clotted cream.
OPEN: 11-3 5.30-11 (Sun 12-3, 7-10.30). **BAR MEALS:** L served Mon-Sat 12-2.30 7-9.30. Av main course £10.95.
RESTAURANT: L served all week. D served all week 12-2.30 7-9.30. Av 3 course à la carte £25.
BREWERY/COMPANY: Free House.
PRINCIPAL BEERS: Fullers London Pride.
FACILITIES: Children welcome Garden: Food served outside. **NOTES:** Parking 35. **ROOMS:** 11 bedrooms 11 en suite s£60 d£80

WENDOVER   Map 06 SP80

Red Lion Hotel 🍷 NEW

High St ☎ 01296 622266 📠 01296 625077
e-mail: redlion@regentinns.plc.uk
A 17th-century coaching inn located in the heart of the Chilterns, popular with regulars and providing a welcome break for cyclists and walkers. One menu is served throughout offering the likes of grilled fillet of sea bass with lime, ginger and coriander marinade on linguine pasta, or slow cooked shoulder of lamb with cheddar mash and redcurrant, rosemary and red wine gravy.
OPEN: 7-11 (Sun 8-11). **BAR MEALS:** L served all week. D served all week 12-2 6-10. **RESTAURANT:** L served all week. D served all week 12-2 6-10. Av 3 course à la carte £19.
BREWERY/COMPANY: Free House **FACILITIES:** Children welcome Garden: Food served outside Dogs allowed Not during meal times. **NOTES:** Parking 60. **ROOMS:** 24 bedrooms 24 en suite s£55 d£65

WEST WYCOMBE   Map 04 SU89

The George and Dragon Hotel 🍷

High St HP14 3AB ☎ 01494 464414 📠 01494 462432
e-mail: enq@george-and-dragon.co.uk
Dir: *M40 North, J5, L onto A40, 4m into village. M40 South, J4, A4010 to T-jct, L onto A40, village 0.5m*
Set in a National Trust village in the heart of the Chilterns, this
continued

striking coaching inn (reputedly haunted) dates from 1402 and was extended and modernised in 1720. A varied menu of home-made food is supplemented by daily specials such as Thai green lamb curry, and chargrilled catfish marinated in lime and coriander.

OPEN: 11-2.30 5.30-11. **BAR MEALS:** L served all week. D served all week 12-2 6-9.30. Av main course £7.50.
BREWERY/COMPANY: Inntrepreneur.
PRINCIPAL BEERS: Fullers London Pride, Wells Bombardier, Greene King Abbot Ale, Wadworth 6X. **FACILITIES:** Children welcome Garden: BBQ, outdoor eating Dogs allowed Water.
NOTES: Parking 35. **ROOMS:** 11 bedrooms 11 en suite d£70 FR£80-£90

WHITCHURCH Map 06 SP82

The White Horse Inn
60 High St HP22 4JS ☎ 01296 641377 📠 01296 640454
Dir: A413 4 M N of Aylesbury
In a picturesque village setting, this 17th-century inn boasts an open fire and a resident ghost. The kitchen uses best local produce and has a good reputation in the area.

PINS & FIRKINS

Brewing has a rich store of technical terms and old-fashioned measures. The conventional container for draught beer - for centuries made of wood, but nowadays of metal - is called a cask. A barrel in brewing terminology is a 36-gallon cask, and a keg is a sealed metal container for beer that has been filtered, sterilised and pressurised before leaving the brewery. British beer in pubs still comes in pints or half-pints and pubs still order their beer using the old-style cask measures, which follow a scale of nine

pin - 4.5 gallons
firkin - 9 gallons
kilderkin - 18 gallons
barrel - 36 gallons
hogshead - 54 gallons

Two obsolete cask sizes are the butt of 108 gallons and the tun, which held varying quantities above 200 gallons. A yard of ale is a glass tube 3ft long and containing up to 3 pints, now only used in drinking contests.

WOOBURN COMMON Map 04 SU98

Pick of the Pubs

Chequers Inn ★ ★ 🐷
Kiln Ln HP10 0JQ ☎ 01628 529575 📠 01628 850124
e-mail: info@chequers-inn.com
Dir: M40 J2 through Beaconsfield towards H Wycombe. 1m turn L into Broad Lane. Inn 2.5m

Just two miles from the M40 at junction 2, it is hard to believe that this deeply rural inn is only 24 miles by road from central London. Built in the 17th century, with a massive oak post and beam bar, it is a splendidly snug spot on a cold winter's night and delightful when sitting out with a drink on balmy summer evenings. Bedroom accommodation is convenient, up-to-date and thoroughly comfortable.

Menus offer plenty of options, from a fixed-price dinner menu to daily fare in the bar that offers imaginative alternatives. From the first, choices include marinated sardines with mixed herbs and lemon oil dressing, roast rump of lamb with pancetta and thyme jus and marscapone and champagne cheesecake with fresh strawberries. Pricier additions could be terrine of foie gras and confit duck with fig and apple compote, followed by roast scallop and langoustine feuillete with tomato and salsa verde.

More simply, plump for calves' liver with red onion gravy or cod baked in olive oil with chive and mussel jus, and sleep well on refined real ales and notable malt whiskies by the score.
OPEN: 10-11. **BAR MEALS:** L served all week. D served all week 12-2.30 6.30-9.30. Av main course £8.95.
RESTAURANT: L served all week. D served all week 12-2.30 7-9.30. Av 3 course à la carte £30. Av 3 course fixed price £21.95. **BREWERY/COMPANY:** Free House.
PRINCIPAL BEERS: Wadworth 6X, Greene King IPA & Abbot Ale. **FACILITIES:** Children welcome Children's licence Garden: food served outdoors Dogs allowed Water.
NOTES: Parking 60. **ROOMS:** 17 bedrooms 17 en suite s£72.50 d£77.50 FR£130

CAMBRIDGESHIRE

BARRINGTON

The Royal Oak
West Green CB2 5RZ ☎ 01223 870791 📠 01223 871845
e-mail: chef289@netscapeonline.co.uk
Rambling timbered and thatched 14th-century pub. Overlooks village green and provides a wide range of fish and Italian dishes.

CAMBRIDGE
Map 07 TL45

The Anchor
Silver St CB3 9EL ☎ 01223 353554 📠 01223 327275
e-mail: anchor@whitbread.com
Waterside pub frequented by students from Queen's College opposite. There's a good selection of real ale, and the opportunity to hire a punt to go on the River Cam. Lots of bric-a-brac and a good atmosphere.

The Cambridge Blue
85 Gwydir St CB1 2LG ☎ 01223 361382 📠 01223 505110
e-mail: cambridgeblue@fsbdial.co.uk
Dir: Town centre
Purpose-built Victorian pub constructed as part of a development to house railway workers. Fascinating memorabilia on the theme of the University Boat Race, including the bow of the 1984 boat which hit a barge and sank. For cricket fans there is a bat used and signed by the legendary Jack Hobbs. Typical dishes might include sausage, mash and gravy, parsnip bake with salad, salmon fishcake, chilli con carne and smoked mackerel. Carrot cake, raspberry cheesecake and cherry and almond tart feature among the popular puddings.
OPEN: 12-2.30 6-11 (Sun till 10.30). **BAR MEALS:** L served all week. D served all week 12-2 6-9.30. Av main course £4.50.
BREWERY/COMPANY: Free House **FACILITIES:** Children welcome Children's licence Garden: outdoor eating, patio, BBQ Dogs allowed Water

The Eagle
Benet St CB2 3QN ☎ 01223 505020
Splendidly atmospheric city-centre pub with a fascinating history, first recorded in 1667, and retaining many original features - mullioned windows, fireplaces, wall paintings and pine panelling. Good Greene King ales and a wide-ranging pub menu.

Free Press
Prospect Row CB1 1DU ☎ 01223 368337
A small, highly atmospheric pub filled with rowing and cricketing memorabilia and located in a picturesque back street close to the city centre. Very traditional with no gaming machines, piped music and a popular no smoking throughout policy! Expect Greene King ales and simple, home-made bar food. New landlords offer sausage and mash, freshly-made soups, toasted filled ciabattas and raised pies with crisp salads.
OPEN: 12-2.30 6-11 (Sat-Sun 12-3, Sun 7-10.30). **BAR MEALS:** L served all week. D served all week 12-2 6-9. Av main course £5.95.
BREWERY/COMPANY: Greene King.
PRINCIPAL BEERS: Greene King - IPA, Abbot Ale, Dark Mild.
FACILITIES: Children welcome Garden: Food served outside, Dogs allowed

Live & Let Live NEW
40 Mawson Rd CB1 2EA ☎ 01223 460261 📠 01223 460261
e-mail: liveandletliveph@aol.com
A backstreet traditional pub with no electronic entertainment,
continued

---

only a few minutes from the bus and train stations. Theme nights are a regular event, as are performances by Dave, a local solo singer-guitarist.
OPEN: 11.30-2.30 5.30-11. **BAR MEALS:** L served all week. D served all week 12-2 6-9. Av main course £3.95.
BREWERY/COMPANY: Free House.
PRINCIPAL BEERS: Everards Tiger, Adnams Bitter, Nethergates Umbel, Batemans Mild & Shefford IPA. **FACILITIES:** Children welcome

The Tram Depot
5 The Tram Yard, Dover St CB7 4JF
A range of vegetarian meals is a feature of this unusual pub located in an old tramway stable building. The large terrace is the ideal place to relax and enjoy a pint.

CASTOR
Map 06 TL19

Pick of the Pubs

The Fitzwilliam Arms 🛏 ♀
34 Peterborough Rd PE5 7AX ☎ 01733 380251
📠 01733 380116
Dir: Off A47 Leicester to Peterborough rd, take Castor/Ailsworth turning (5m from A1)
Pretty long and low thatched pub situated just off the A47 and now owned by Edwin Cheeseman who masterminded the 'cooking in view' concept at his previous pub, the Carrington Arms at Moulsoe in Bedfordshire. Here, at this informal dining pub, his serious approach to cooking food is proving very popular. Aberdeen Angus steaks and fresh seafood - perhaps, sea bass, halibut, soles, tuna, tiger prawns - are all impressively laid out in display cabinets for you to make your choice, and there's a live lobster in a tank and, unusually, an oyster bar. Both fish and meat are sold by the ounce, so you can choose your cut and portion size as well as style of cooking, which is either flame-grilling, steaming or smoking, and seafood may be napped with garlic, ginger and soy sauce or a Thai jus. More traditional tastes are not forgotten as the bar menu does take in beef and ale cobbler, leek and bacon omelette and baked avocado with goats' cheese. Puddings range from caramelised rice pudding to chocolate and lime cheesecake. Good range of real ales and an interesting list of wines.

OPEN: 11-2.30 (Sun12-3, 7-10.30) 6-11. **BAR MEALS:** L served all week. D served Mon-Fri 12-2 6.30-10. Av main course £10. **RESTAURANT:** L served all week. D served all week 12-2 6.30-10. Av 3 course à la carte £20.
BREWERY/COMPANY: Free House.
PRINCIPAL BEERS: Adnams, Marstons Pedigree, Wadworth 6X. **FACILITIES:** Children welcome Garden: Food served outside. **NOTES:** Parking 50

England

CHITTERING   Map 07 TL46

The Travellers Rest
Ely Rd CB5 9PH ☎ 01223 860751 ▤ 01223 863362
A friendly welcome and a good choice of wholesome,
appetising dishes await at this recently refurbished
pub/restaurant whose hosts also own the George & Dragon at
Elsworth. Regular theme evenings featuring international
cuisine and perennial favourites. Prime beef from Scotland is
used here and the fish is bought at Lowestoft. Expect
lunchtime curries, pies and pasta dishes, as well as lamb
cutlets, swordfish steak and vegetable Stroganoff.
OPEN: 11-2.30 6-11. **BAR MEALS:** L served all week. D served
Mon-Sat 12-2 6-9.30. Av main course £6. **RESTAURANT:** L
served all week. D served Mon-Sat 12-2 6-9.30. Av 3 course à la
carte £15. **BREWERY/COMPANY:** Free House.
PRINCIPAL BEERS: Greene King IPA, Old Speckled Hen.
FACILITIES: Children welcome Garden: Food served outside.
NOTES: Parking 30

COTTENHAM   Map 07 TL46

The White Horse
215 High St CB4 5QG ☎ 01954 250257 ▤ 01954 206180
Dir: Exit A14 at Histon, on to Cottenham
Friendly old family-run pub with large open bar areas and a
restaurant.

DRY DRAYTON   Map 07 TL36

The Black Horse
Park St CB3 8DA ☎ 01954 781055 ▤ 01954 782628
Dir: Just outside Cambridge between A14 & A428
Characterised by exposed wooden beams and open fires, this
350-year-old village pub offers a warm welcome and an
extensive menu of traditional pub dishes. These range from
ploughman's and baguettes to steak and mushroom pie,
chicken curry, deep-fried battered haddock, and a choice of
steaks and burgers.
OPEN: 11.30-3 6.30-11 (Sun 12-3, 7-10.30). Closed Dec 25/26.
BAR MEALS: L served all week. D served Mon-Sat 12-2 7-9. Av
main course £6. **RESTAURANT:** L served all week. D served
Mon-Sat 12-2 7-9. Av 3 course à la carte £16.
BREWERY/COMPANY: Free House.
PRINCIPAL BEERS: Greene King IPA, Adnams, Bass & Guests.
FACILITIES: Garden: outdoor eating, Dogs allowed.
NOTES: Parking 40

DUXFORD   Map 07 TL44

The John Barleycorn
3 Moorfield Rd CB2 4PP ☎ 01223 832699
▤ 01223 832699
Dir: Turn off A505 into Duxford
Traditional thatched and beamed English country pub situated
close to Cambridge. The same menu is served throughout and
ranges from a cheese sandwich to tournedos Rossini. Typical
dishes are large leg of lamb in mint gravy and chicken breast
with garlic and herbs.
OPEN: 11-11 (Sun 12-10.30). **BAR MEALS:** L served all week.
D served all week 12-2.30 6.30-11. Av main course £7.50.
BREWERY/COMPANY: Greene King.
PRINCIPAL BEERS: Greene King IPA & Abbot Ale.
FACILITIES: Garden: BBQ, garden tables Dogs allowed.
NOTES: Parking 25

ELSWORTH   Map 06 TL36

The George & Dragon 🐑
41 Boxworth Rd CB3 8JQ ☎ 01954 267236
▤ 01954 267080
Dir: SE of A14 between Cambridge & Huntingdon
Set in a pretty village just outside Cambridge, this pub, which
originally was a row of shops, has one menu and three
separate dining areas, each with its own appeal. Dishes
feature smoked peppered mackerel, mushroom and spinach
lasagne, a variety of steaks, sandwiches, ploughmans' and
steak and kidney pudding.
OPEN: 11-3 6-11 (Sun 12-3). **BAR MEALS:** L served all week.
D served Mon-Sat 12-2 6-9.30. Av main course £8.50.
RESTAURANT: L served all week. D served Mon-Sat 12-2 6-9.30.
Av 3 course à la carte £15. Av 3 course fixed price £13.
BREWERY/COMPANY: Free House.
PRINCIPAL BEERS: Greene King IPA, Ruddles County, Greene
King Old Speckled Hen. **FACILITIES:** Children welcome Garden:
Food served outside Dogs allowed Guide dogs only.
NOTES: Parking 40

ELTISLEY   Map 06 TL25

The Leeds Arms
The Green PE19 4TG ☎ 01480 880283 ▤ 01480 880283
Dir: On A428 between Cambridge & St Neots
Named after local landowners, the Leeds Arms is located
opposite the village green where the local cricket team play in
season. Sizzling dishes are a speciality.

WHICH IS THE OLDEST PUB?
The question has no sure answer.
Records are fragmentary and a building,
or part of it, may be far older than its use
as a drinking house. The Old Ferry Boat
Inn at Holywell in the Cambridgeshire
fens is claimed to go back to the 6th
century as a monastic ferry station and
the Olde Fighting Cocks in St Albans to
the 8th century as an abbey fishing lodge
by the River Ver. A more believable
contender is the Bingley Arms at Bardsey,
West Yorkshire, recorded as the 'priest's
inn' in 905, but it was completely rebuilt
in 1738. The Ostrich at Colnbrook,
Buckinghamshire, is apparently on the
site of a monastic hospice recorded in
1106 (and its odd name is a pun on
'hospice'). Others claiming a 12th-century
origin include the wonderfully named
Olde Trip to Jerusalem in Nottingham, the
Cromwell-linked Royal Oak at Whatcote
in Warwickshire, the venerable Oxenham
Arms at South Zeal in Devon, the half-
timbered Pandy Inn at Dorstone,
Herefordshire, the Olde House Inn at
Llangynwyd in South Wales and the
Oldes Boar's Head at Middleton, Greater
Manchester. All of them, of course, have
been repeatedly rebuilt and altered over
the centuries.

ELTON   Map 06 TL09

Pick of the Pubs

The Black Horse ♀
14 Overend PE8 6RU ☎ 01832 280240
🗎 01832 280875

See Pick of the Pubs on page 57

ELY   Map 07 TL58

Pick of the Pubs

The Anchor Inn ♦♦♦♦ 👜 ♀
Sutton Gault CB6 2BD ☎ 01353 778537
🗎 01353 776180
e-mail: anchor@sutton-gault.freeserve.co.uk
Dir: From A14, B1050 to Earith, take B1381 to Sutton. Sutton Gault on L
Over some 350 years the Anchor has evolved to become an inn of immense character on the new Bedford River that offers every modern facility in its own special way. Evocative and stylishly furnished interior with log fires, scrubbed pine tables and attractive pictures; enhanced by gas mantles and evening candlelight. Daily-changing menus rely in large part on local produce that is put to good use in dishes such as grilled dates wrapped in bacon, venison carpaccio with shaved Parmesan, chicken, leek and bacon crumble and noisettes of Norfolk horn lamb with a warm Puy lentil salad. Lunch specials might include olive and caper salad with red pepper pesto, chargrilled pork rib laid over Savoy cabbage and creamy banoffee pie; whilst dinner may add grilled sea bass with salsa verde and rib-eye steaks topped with snails in garlic. Round off with organic Jersey ice creams or the selection of cheeses that travel the land from Cornish Yarg to Perthshire's Bishop Kennedy.
OPEN: 12-3 (Sat 6.30-11) 7-11. Closed Dec 25-26.
BAR MEALS: L served all week. D served all week 12-2 7-9. Av main course £11.50. **RESTAURANT:** L served all week. D served all week 12-2 7-9. Av 3 course à la carte £20. Av 2 course fixed price £7.50. **BREWERY/COMPANY:** Free House. **PRINCIPAL BEERS:** Nethergate IPA, Wolf Best, Batemans XB, Adnams. **FACILITIES:** Children welcome Garden: riverside terrace, outdoor eating. **NOTES:** Parking 16. **ROOMS:** 2 bedrooms 2 en suite s£30 d£66

The Fountain
1 Silver St CB7 4JF ☎ 01353 663122
Town centre pub close to the Cathedral. Open lunchtimes at weekends only, but no food served. Lots of bric-a-brac and memorabilia from the next door King's School.

FEN DITTON   Map 07 TL46

Ancient Shepherds
High St CB5 8ST ☎ 01223 293280 🗎 01223 294007
Dir: From A14 take B1047 signed Cambridge/Airport
Named after the ancient order of Shepherders who used to meet here, this pretty, 16th-century pub offers a friendly atmosphere and freshly-cooked food.

FEN DRAYTON

The Three Tuns ♀
High St CB4 5SJ ☎ 01954 230242 🗎 01954 230242
e-mail: mail@timspub.com
Dir: between Cambridge and Huntingdon

Originally the Guildhall of Fen Drayton, this thatched building is over 400 years old and there is some wonderfully ornate detail on the original oak beams.
The pub offers a good choice of beers and some imaginative bar food. House favourites are braised lamb shank served in its own jus, and duck breast with egg noodles and sizzling stir-fried vegetables.
OPEN: 12-2.30 6-11. **BAR MEALS:** L served all week. D served all week 12-2 7-9. Av main course £7. **RESTAURANT:** L served all week. D served all week 12-2 7-9. Av 3 course à la carte £15. **BREWERY/COMPANY:** Greene King. **PRINCIPAL BEERS:** Greene King IPA, Black Sheep, Greene King Abbott Ale, Badger Tanglefoot. **FACILITIES:** Children welcome Garden: patio, outdoor eating. **NOTES:** Parking 20

FENSTANTON   Map 07 TL36

King William IV 👜 ♀
High St PE28 9JF ☎ 01480 462467 🗎 01480 498205
e-mail: jerry@kingbill.co.uk
Dir: Off A14 between Cambridge & Huntingdon
Formerly three 17th-century cottages, this rambling, cream-painted inn enjoys a village centre location next to the old clock tower. The series of low-beamed rooms, including a lively bar area and plant-festooned Garden Room, attract A14 travellers, business people and local diners for reliable pub food.
Choices range from pub favourites (ploughman's and sandwiches lunchtime only) to grilled sardines with garlic lemon butter, herb-crusted lamb with red wine and rosemary sauce, and chargrilled sea bass with olive oil. Sticky toffee pudding or caramelised lemon tart for the sweet toothed.
OPEN: 11-3.30 6-11 (Sun 12-11). **BAR MEALS:** L served all week. D served Mon-Sat 12-2.15 7-10. Av main course £5.50. **RESTAURANT:** L served all week. D served Mon-Sat 12-2.15 7-10. Av 3 course à la carte £15. **BREWERY/COMPANY:** Greene King. **PRINCIPAL BEERS:** Greene King Abbot Ale & IPA, Ruddles County, Badger Tanglefoot. **FACILITIES:** Children welcome Dogs allowed Water. **NOTES:** Parking 14. **ROOMS:** 5 bedrooms 5 en suite s£45 d£50 FR£70

PICK OF THE PUBS

OPEN: 12-3 6-11.
Closed Sun eve in winter
BAR MEALS: L served all week.
D served all week 12-2 6-10.
Av main course £12.
RESTAURANT: L served all week
D served all week 12-2 6-10.
Av 3 course a la carte £25.
Av 3 course fixed price Sun lunch
£10.95. **BREWERY/COMPANY:**
Free House.
PRINCIPLE BEERS: Bass,
Deuchars IPA, Badger Best, Fullers
London Pride, Nethergate Ales.
FACILITIES: Children welcome.
Garden: patio, outdoor eating
dogs allowed.
NOTES: Parking 30.

The Black Horse

14 Overend PE8 6RU
☎ 01832 280240 📠 01832 280875
Dir: Elton is located just off the A605
Peterborough to Northampton road

Stone-built 17th-century dining pub enjoying a picturesque village setting and well worth the short detour off the A605 for its welcoming atmosphere and interesting food. Combine a satisfying summer lunch with a visit to elegant Elton Hall, noted for its paintings by Gainsborough and Reynolds.

In the late 1940s this plain-looking stone pub was owned by an English hangman named Harry Kirk who had to deal with some very sinister characters in his time. It is also said that it used to be the village morgue and that a dungeon exists below the bar! Just a stone's throw from the beautiful Saxon parish church, the Black Horse is decidedly more civilised nowadays, it's rustic interior is full of old-world charm with hop-strung oak beams, wooden and stone-tiled floors, antique furnishings, roaring log fires and interesting old artefacts.

Pop in for a pint of Deuchars IPA or a seasonal Nethergate brew and a decent bar snack (lunchtime only), perhaps a rare roast beef and horseradish sandwich, a plate of smoked salmon with lemon and black pepper, or home-baked gammon, egg and chips. More substantial meals include local game dishes such as venison with juniper berry and port sauce, rabbit with mustard and marjoram and partridge pot-roasted with shallots, red wine and herbs. Look to the chalk board for daily fish specials - monkfish with orange and limes in a ginger and scallion sauce, red snapper with saffron and minted fennel - and organic meat dishes like rack of lamb with a walnut and herb crust. Good puddings; traditional set Sunday lunch menu.

Delightful rear garden overlooking Elton's famous church and rolling open countryside.

England

FORDHAM
Map 07 TL67

Pick of the Pubs

White Pheasant 🐾 ♀
CB7 5LQ ☎ 01638 720414 📠 01638 720447
Part of the select Excalibur Inns group, this attractive,
white-painted 17th-century inn is set beside the A43 in a
Fenland village between Newmarket and Ely. Tasteful
simplicity characterises the front bar and adjacent rear
dining-rooms, with their rug-strewn wooden floors, tartan
check fabrics, soft wall lighting, interesting paintings and
candle-topped scrubbed tables. Piped classical/opera
music and winter log fires enhance the cosy atmosphere.
Ever-changing blackboard menus list a good range of
home-cooked food. Typical choices may include smoked
salmon and prawn mousse, spicy Jamaican chicken,
Suffolk ham hock with parsley sauce, and duck breast on
Chinese noodles with spring onion and plum sauce. Daily
fish board and good bar snacks.
OPEN: 12-3 6-11. **BAR MEALS:** L served all week. D served
all week 12-2.30 6-10.30. Av main course £10.
RESTAURANT: L served all week. D served all week 12-2.30
6-10.30. Av 3 course à la carte £25.
BREWERY/COMPANY: Free House **FACILITIES:** Children
welcome Garden: Food served outside. **NOTES:** Parking 30

FOWLMERE
Map 07 TL44

Pick of the Pubs

The Chequers ◎ 🐾 ♀
High St SG8 7SR ☎ 01763 208369 📠 01763 208944
Dir: From M11 A505, 2nd R to Fowlmere
There's a strong sense of history at this bustling inn with
its smart gallery restaurant. William Thrist renovated the
building in 1675 after a fire had devastated much of the
village, and you can still see his initials over the main door.
Samuel Pepys once stayed here, but the pub's sign betrays
its more recent past with intriguing blue and red chequers
in honour of the British and American squadrons based at
Fowlmere during the Second World War. Nowadays, the
pub's Mediterranean-style menu and decent wine list are
popular with business people, tourists and locals; eat
beside crackling log fires in winter or, on warmer days, sit
out in the attractive garden. Expect red lentil soup or warm
pancetta and prawn salad to start, with griddled salmon
and cod fishcakes, sautéed pheasant or vegetable kebabs
for the main event. Finish with chocolate mousse, pan-
fried apples, or a selection of Irish farmhouse cheeses.
OPEN: 12-2.30 6-11. Closed 25 Dec. **BAR MEALS:** L served
all week. D served all week 12-2 7-10. Av main course £8.60.
RESTAURANT: L served all week. D served all week 12-2
7-10. Av 3 course à la carte £17.10.
BREWERY/COMPANY: Free House.
PRINCIPAL BEERS: Adnams Bitter, Timothy Taylor Landlord.
FACILITIES: Garden: patio, outdoor eating.
NOTES: Parking 30

GODMANCHESTER
Map 06 TL27

Black Bull
32 Post St PE29 2AQ ☎ 01480 453310 📠 01480 435623
Dir: Off A1198 S of Huntington
Just yards from the Great River Ouse and the parish church,
this 17th-century coaching inn sports beams and a large
inglenook fireplace. Standard bar menu, interesting daily
specials.

GOREFIELD
Map 09 TF41

Woodmans Cottage
90 High Rd PE13 4NB ☎ 01945 870669 📠 01945 870631
Dir: A47 to Peterborough, ring road to A1M
The incoming brother and sister team who run this popular
pub have spent the best part of two years putting their own
stamp on the place.
   Their efforts have paid off and Woodmans Cottage remains
a welcoming local with live music, regular functions, well-kept
beers and a good choice of bar food. Sweet chicken curry,
lasagne and lamb shank in mint gravy feature among other
dishes.
OPEN: 11-2.30 7-11. **BAR MEALS:** L served all week. D served
all week 12-2.30 7-10. Av main course £6.50. **RESTAURANT:** L
served all week. D served all week 12-2.30 7-10. Av 3 course à la
carte £17. **BREWERY/COMPANY:** Free House.
PRINCIPAL BEERS: Greene King IPA, Greene King Abbot Ale.
FACILITIES: Children welcome Garden. **NOTES:** Parking 40

GRANTCHESTER

The Green Man
High St, Grantchester CB3 9NF ☎ 01223 841178
📠 01223 847940
Located close to Cambridge in the village of Grantchester,
once home to Rupert Brooke, this delightful old pub has many
original beams, and offers a traditional English pub welcome.

HILDERSHAM
Map 07 TL54

The Pear Tree
CB1 6BU ☎ 01223 891680 📠 01223 891970
e-mail: dgj-@excite.com
Dir: Just off A1307
Traditional village pub facing the village green, with oak beams
and a stone floor. It enjoys a good local trade, and is
particularly well known for its home-cooked food.
   Bar meals include soups, Lincolnshire sausages and chips,
local ham, battered haddock, and old-fashioned puddings.
OPEN: 11.45-2 (Sun 12-2, 7-10.30) 6.30-11. **BAR MEALS:** L
served all week. D served all week 12-2 6.30-9.30.
BREWERY/COMPANY: Greene King.
PRINCIPAL BEERS: Greene King IPA & Abbot Ale.
FACILITIES: Garden: rabbits, outdoor eating Dogs allowed.
NOTES: Parking 6

England

HILTON

The Prince of Wales
Potton Rd PE18 9NG ☎ 01480 830257 📠 01480 830257
e-mail: Princeofwales.hilton@tack21.com
Dir: on B1040 between A14 and A428 S of St Ives

Traditional two-bar village inn at the heart of rural Cambridgeshire, just a short drive from Cambridge, Peterborough and Huntingdon. Relax in the comfortable lounge and sample a freshly prepared meal or a simple bar snack from the varied menu. Dishes may include chicken korma, sirloin steak with mushrooms, lamb casserole or jumbo haddock. Well equipped bedrooms with modern facilities.
OPEN: 11-2.30 6-11 (Sun 12-3, 7-10.30). Closed Dec 25.
BAR MEALS: L served Tue-Sun. D served Mon lunch, Tue-Sun 12-2 7-9. Av main course £6. **BREWERY/COMPANY:** Free House. **PRINCIPAL BEERS:** Adnams Southwold, Elgoods Black Dog. **FACILITIES:** Children welcome Children's licence Garden: Beer garden, Outdoor Eating Dogs allowed in bar but not lounge. **NOTES:** Parking 9. **ROOMS:** 4 bedrooms 4 en suite s£42.50 d£60

HINXTON   Map 07 TL44

The Red Lion
High St CB10 1QY ☎ 01799 530601 📠 01799 531201
e-mail: lynjim@online.net
Dir: 1m from M11 J9, 2m from M11 J10
Sympathetically extended 16th-century inn with lots of clocks and other memorabilia. Fresh local produce is featured in an extensive menu, including light meals available at lunchtime only. Malaysian chicken curry, Moroccan lamb tagine, and oven-roasted sea bass are examples of the range.
OPEN: 11-2.30 6-11 (Sun 12-2.30, 7-10.30). Closed Dec 25-26.
BAR MEALS: L served all week. D served all week 12-2 7-9.30.
BREWERY/COMPANY: Free House.
PRINCIPAL BEERS: Adnams, Greene King IPA, Woodforde's Wherry. **FACILITIES:** Garden: patio, outdoor eating Dogs allowed garden only. **NOTES:** Parking 40

HOLYWELL   Map 06 TL37

The Old Ferryboat Inn ♀
PE27 4TG ☎ 01480 463227 📠 01480 463245
e-mail: the-old-ferryboat-inn@tinyworld.co.uk
Dir: A14 then R onto A1096 then A1123 R to Holywell
Claiming to be England's oldest inn, the Ferryboat is a most attractive thatched hostelry overlooking the Ouse. A ferry carried casks of ale across the river until it was killed off by the railways. The inn, now owned by Greene King, is reputedly haunted by the ghost of a young girl who, allegedly, is seen on March 17th, the anniversary of her death. Traditional menu
continued

might include salmon fishcakes, lamb shank and aubergine and Mozzarella bake.

OPEN: 11.30-11 (Sun 12-10.30). **BAR MEALS:** L served all week. D served all week 12-9.30. Av main course £7. **RESTAURANT:** L served all week. D served all week 12-9.30. Av 3 course à la carte £15. **BREWERY/COMPANY:** Greene King.
PRINCIPAL BEERS: Greene King Abbot Ale/IPA, Old Speckled Hen, Ruddles County. **FACILITIES:** Children welcome Garden: patio, outdoor eating Dogs allowed Water. **NOTES:** Parking 100.
ROOMS: 7 bedrooms 7 en suite s£50 d£60

HORNINGSEA   Map 07 TL46

Pick of the Pubs

Crown & Punchbowl 🛏️ ♀
CB5 9JG ☎ 01223 860643 📠 01223 441814
e-mail: lizard2020@supanet.com

Less than four miles from the centre of Cambridge, this five-bedroom, 17th-century inn stands in unspoilt countryside, offering fresh bar food at reasonable prices and candle-lit dinners in a beamed dining-room lent character by classical music, rugs and antique curios. In the bar, start with warm bacon and mushroom salad or spicy cheese balls with tomato chutney, followed by pork chops with peppercorn sauce, sausages and mash and daily specials such as cottage pie. Man-sized alternatives with an Italian accent take in antipasti with chilli, ginger and tomato relish, chicken fettuccine and beef olives with basil, celery and Parmesan on a bed of tagliatelle.
OPEN: 12-3 6-11. Closed 25 Dec. **BAR MEALS:** L served all week. D served all week 12-2.30 6-10. Av main course £9.
RESTAURANT: L served all week. D served all week 12-2.30 6-10. Av 3 course à la carte £19. **BREWERY/COMPANY:** Free House. **PRINCIPAL BEERS:** Adnams Broadside. **FACILITIES:** Children welcome Garden: outdoor eating, patio. **NOTES:** Parking 50. **ROOMS:** 5 bedrooms 5 en suite s£45 d£70

HORNINGSEA continued

The Plough & Fleece
High St CB5 9JG ☎ 01223 860795 ▤ 01223 860795
Dir: *E from A14 take B1047. Top of slip rd turn L. Pub opp garden centre*
Extended late 18th-century building, in the Dutch style so popular at that time. The bar features ancient settles, a tiled floor and an unusual open fire. Menus offer good regional cooking including a comforting hotpot of Suffolk ham, Welsh fish pie, and home-made steak, kidney and mushroom pie.
OPEN: 11.30-2.30 7-11 (Sun 12-2). **BAR MEALS:** L served all week. D served Tue-Sat 12-2 7-9.30. Av main course £6.95.
RESTAURANT: L served all week. D served Tue-Sat 12-2 7-9.30. Av 3 course à la carte £15. **BREWERY/COMPANY:** Greene King. **PRINCIPAL BEERS:** Greene King IPA & Abbott Ale.
FACILITIES: Children welcome Garden: outdoor eating, patio Dogs allowed in the garden. **NOTES:** Parking 20

HUNTINGDON   Map 06 TL27

Pick of the Pubs

The Old Bridge House ◉ ◉ ★ ★ ★ 🛏
1 High St PE29 3TQ ☎ 01480 424300
▤ 01480 411017
e-mail: oldbridge@huntsbridge.co.uk
Dir: *Signposted from A1 & A14*
Right on the edge of town, this handsome 18th-century house - once a private bank - stands on the banks of the River Ouse: much extended today, it houses bedroom accommodation of singular style and charm that include the luxury of air conditioning, satellite TV and CD players.
 Diners, both resident and casual, benefit from the choice of restaurant or terrace menus served throughout, with the addition of businessmen's specials and buffets from Monday to Friday and traditional Sunday lunch. One of a well-known partnership of chef-managed dining pubs in the area, menus strike the upper end of the market in style and price. Mix'n'match starters and light meals in the terrace and lounge encompass duck liver pâté with juniper, kumquat and orange marmalade, deep-fried cod with hand-cut chips and pease pudding and classic lemon tart.
 Further restaurant choices add crab and ginger bisque with crab ravioli, roast John Dory with orange and thyme, spinach and baby onions, pot-roast Goosnargh chicken with morels, sweet potato and leeks and beef fillet with potato and truffle gratin. Further facilities include a business centre, conferences and private dining with designer menus.
OPEN: 11-11 (Sun 12-10.30). **BAR MEALS:** L served all week. D served all week 11-11. Av main course £15.
RESTAURANT: L served all week. D served all week 12-3 6.30-10.30. Av 3 course à la carte £25.
BREWERY/COMPANY: Huntsbridge Inns.
PRINCIPAL BEERS: Adnams Best, Hobsons Choice, Bateman XXXB. **FACILITIES:** Children welcome Garden: Patio Dogs allowed In the garden, allowed overnight.
NOTES: Parking 60. **ROOMS:** 24 bedrooms 24 en suite s£80 d£95

KEYSTON   Map 06 TL07

Pick of the Pubs

The Pheasant Inn ◉ ♀
Village Loop Rd PE28 0RE ☎ 01832 710241
▤ 01832 710340
Dir: *Signposted from A14, W of Huntingdon*
Yet another of a small group of chef-managed dining pubs in the area with an admirably egalitarian attitude to eating out and continuing dedication to the provision of fine wines and East Anglian ales. Housed in a fine 15th-century thatched building of oak beams, open fires and simple wooden furniture, The Pheasant offers a single menu throughout in a modern eclectic style that recognises the quality and value of freshly available local produce. Imagin ative and unfussy snacks and simple dishes include warm goats' cheese or classic Caesar salads, Gloucester Old Spot sausages and mash in grain mustard sauce and tagliatelle with wild mushrooms, Jerusalem artichokes and truffle oil. Main dishes are exemplified by rare char-grilled tuna loin with Moroccan spiced quinoa, slow-braised Aberdeenshire beef blade with foie gras sauce and pan-roast duck breast on spiced barley with braised bok choi. Caramelised apple tart with Calvados ice cream and unpasteurised farmhouse cheeses; traditional roast beef on Sunday and fixed-price mid-week lunches are models of consistency.
OPEN: 12-2 6-11. **BAR MEALS:** L served all week. D served all week 12-2 6.30-10. Av main course £9. **RESTAURANT:** L served all week. D served all week 12-2 6.30-10. Av 3 course à la carte £25. **BREWERY/COMPANY:** Huntsbridge Inns.
PRINCIPAL BEERS: Adnams. **FACILITIES:** Children welcome herb garden, patio. **NOTES:** Parking 40

KIMBOLTON   Map 06 TL16

The New Sun Inn 🛏
20-22 High St PE28 0HA ☎ 01480 860052
▤ 01480 869353
Dir: *From A1 N, B645 for 7m, From A1 S B661 for 7m, From A14 B660 for 5m*

An impressive display of flowers greets visitors to this 16th-century inn near Kimbolton Castle. Enjoy a pint of Bombardier with a decent meal. The extensive menu ranges from doorstep sandwiches or steak and kidney pudding in the bar, to skate wing, or rack of lamb in the restaurant.
OPEN: 11-2.30 6-11 (all day Sun). **BAR MEALS:** L served all week 12-2.15 7-9.30. Av main course £5.50. **RESTAURANT:** L served all week. D served Tues-Sat 12-2 7-9.30.
BREWERY/COMPANY: Charles Wells.
PRINCIPAL BEERS: Wells Bombardier, Greene King Old Speckled Hen. **FACILITIES:** Children welcome Garden: patio, outdoor eating Dogs allowed

MADINGLEY	Map 07 TL36

Pick of the Pubs

The Three Horseshoes ⊛ 🐾 ⍭
High St CB3 8AB ☎ 01954 210221   🖺 01954 212043
Dir: M11 J13. 1.5m from A14
One of the well-known group of Huntsbridge Inns that dot the Cambridge, Huntingdon and Northampton county borders, this picturesque old thatched inn has a small, bustling bar adjoining the pretty conservatory dining room and a large garden that extends towards the local cricket pitch. An abiding philosophy is that you may choose as much or as little as your heart desires - wherever you want to be - although the menu is little short of sinfully seductive. Imaginative yet never outrageous dishes, accompanied by a range of real ales and outstanding wines, are hard to resist when faced with marinated salmon and dill terrine with fried oyster or sugar-cured venison with pink grapefruit salad, before venturing forth to chargrilled rump of lamb with courgettes and fried artichokes or roast cod fillet with lentils, pancetta and mushy peas. Puddings then add tangy caramelised lemon tart and an unusual fried custard and rhubarb compote, with unpasteurised British and French cheeses, Scotch oatcakes, celery and grapes as a more than acceptable alternative.
OPEN: 12-2 6-11. **BAR MEALS:** L served all week. D served all week 12-2 6.30-9.30. Av main course £10.
RESTAURANT: L served all week. D served Mon-Sat 12-2 6.30-9.30. Av 3 course à la carte £25. Av 5 course fixed price £35. **BREWERY/COMPANY:** Huntsbridge Inns.
PRINCIPAL BEERS: Adnams, Hook Norton Old Hooky, Smiles Best. **FACILITIES:** Garden: large, Food served outside. **NOTES:** Parking 70

NEWTON	Map 07 TL44

Pick of the Pubs

The Queen's Head
CB2 5PG ☎ 01223 870436
Dir: 6m S of Cambridge on B1368, 1.5m off A10 at Harston, 4m from A505
'An eternally English pub', dating back to 1680 (though the cellar is much older), that stands at the heart of the village by the green. There is no fruit machine or piped music to interrupt the lively conversation in the two small bars; nor for 40 years has there been a menu - or Specials, 'whatever that may mean'! Daily home-made soup is best described by its colour, while the cut-to-order sandwiches - beef, smoked ham and salmon and cheeses with pickle or salad items - are made with ehe freshest bread. Hot alternatives are limited to Aga-baked potatoes and toast with beef dripping. Adnams' ales are dispensed direct from the barrel in studious avoidance of modernisation.
OPEN: 11.30-2.30 6-11 (Sun 12-2.30,7-10.30). Closed 25 Dec.
BAR MEALS: L served all week. D served all week 11.30-2.15 6-9.30. Av main course £2.40. **BREWERY/COMPANY:** Free House. **PRINCIPAL BEERS:** Adnams Southwold, Broadside & Fisherman (winter only). **FACILITIES:** Children welcome outdoor eating, patio Dogs allowed none. **NOTES:** Parking 15 No credit cards

PETERBOROUGH	Map 06 TL19

The Brewery Tap ⍭
80 Westgate PE1 2AA ☎ 01733 358500   🖺 01733 310022
Visitors to this unusual American-style pub can view the operations of the Oakham brewery through a glass wall. The Tap has a capacity of over 500, specialises in real Thai food, and runs a nightclub Friday and Saturday.

Charters Café-Bar
Town Bridge PE1 1FP ☎ 01733 315700   🖺 01733 315700
Dir: A1/A47 Wisbech, 2m for city centre & town bridge (River Nene). Barge is moored at Town Bridge
Charters is a floating pub on the River Nene, right in the centre of Peterborough. The base is reputedly the biggest converted barge in Great Britain. Bistro-style menu.

ST IVES	Map 06 TL37

Pike & Eel Hotel ⍭
Overcote Ln, Needingworth PE27 4TW ☎ 01480 463336
🖺 01480 465467
e-mail: pikeandeelinn@classic.msn.com
17th-century listed inn with marina moorings on the River Ouse where the ferry once crossed: formerly well-known also for its fine pike fishing. Good fish includes crevettes flambees and seafood platter. In the bar enjoy Welsh rarebit and steak and kidney pudding. Restaurant carte and Sunday lunch.
OPEN: 11-11 (Sun 12-10.30). **BAR MEALS:** L served all week. D served all week 12-2.30 7-10.30. Av main course £5.75.
RESTAURANT: L served all week. D served all week 12-2.30 7-10.30. Av 3 course à la carte £17.50.
BREWERY/COMPANY: Free House.
PRINCIPAL BEERS: Greene King IPA, Bass, Greene King Old Speckled Hen. **FACILITIES:** Children welcome Garden: outdoor eating, BBQ, Marina adjacent Dogs allowed (except in garden). **NOTES:** Parking 75. **ROOMS:** 11 bedrooms 11 en suite s£35 d£50 1 family room £67-£87

ELGOODS OF WISBECH

Situated on the bank of the River Nene, this brewery is nearly 220 years old. Between 1714, when Matthew Gosling bought the site for £120, and 1877, when the current family owners Elgood bought it for £38,965, the North Brink Brewery passed through many hands and many changes of fortune (In 1809 a man fell into a vat and apparently died). The Elgoods have fulfilled the potential of the site and in 1985 were pioneers of low alcohol brewing using the 'reverse osmosis' process. Visitors can view traditional brewing methods and sup quality ales, as well as spend some time in the delightful garden behind which are herbaceous borders, a lake, water features and a maze.

England

STILTON Map 06 TL18

Pick of the Pubs

The Bell Inn ◎ ◎ ★ ★ ★
Great North Rd PE7 3RA ☎ 01733 241066
▤ 01733 245173
e-mail: reception@thebellstilton.co.uk
Dir: *from A1 follow signs for Stilton, hotel is situated on the main road in the centre of the village.*

Stories abound of the famous cheese, first sold to travellers around 1720, famous highwaymen (Dick Turpin hid here for nine weeks) and numerous other historic visitors from the Duke of Marlborough to Lord Byron. Completed in 1990 restoration added high quality bedrooms and conference facilities blended into the ageless inn's stonework around a central courtyard. Beamed ceilings and open fires imbue the Village Bar with great character, enhanced by fine real ales and an extensive monthly menu and daily specials. Broccoli soup, enriched of course with Stilton, and roast asparagus with pancetta and shaved Parmesan typically come before adventurous offerings of braised beef with Stilton dumplings, confit duck with black pudding and zesty orange sauce and glazed herb pancakes filled with ratatouille. Fixed-price restaurant menus make best use of local Fen Country produce in pigeon and pork faggots, boiled collar bacon with spring greens and pan-fried brill on caper mash and spinach. Finish with glazed lemon tart - or Long Cawson Stilton with plum bread.
OPEN: 12-2.30 6.30-11 (Sun 12-3, 7-10.30). Closed Dec 25.
BAR MEALS: L served all week. D served all week 12-2 6.30-9.30. **RESTAURANT:** L served Sun-Fri. D served all week 12-2 7-9.30. Av 3 course fixed price £21.50.
BREWERY/COMPANY: Free House.
PRINCIPAL BEERS: Marstons Pedigree, Greene King Abbot Ale, Oakham JHB, Boddingtons. **FACILITIES:** Garden: patio, outdoor eating. **NOTES:** Parking 30. **ROOMS:** 19 bedrooms 19 en suite s£69.50 d£89.50 FR£89.50-£99.50

STRETHAM

The Lazy Otter
Cambridge Rd CB6 3LU ☎ 01353 649780
▤ 01442 876893
Set alongside the River Great Ouse, this bar, restaurant and marina is between Ely and Cambridge. The marina houses around forty narrow boats. New landlord.

CHESHIRE

ALDFORD Map 08 SJ45

Pick of the Pubs

The Grosvenor Arms 🍴 ⓨ
Chester Rd CH3 6HJ ☎ 01244 620228
▤ 01244 620247
e-mail: grosvenor.arms@brunningandprice.co.uk
Dir: *on B5130 S of Chester*
Comfortably refurbished and relaxing Victorian inn with a bustling atmosphere throughout its spacious, open-plan interior, which includes a panelled library filled with books, and an airy conservatory adorned with hanging baskets; suntrap terrace and lawn for summer imbibing. Interesting bistro-style food, decent wines, a range of cognacs, armagnacs and ports, and good ales attract a discerning clientele.

Daily menus may offer medallions of beef fillet in a mustard, brandy and mushroom sauce, Cumberland sausage on creamy mashed potatoes, braised shoulder of lamb with an apricot and rosemary sauce, or duck breast served on creamed savoy cabbage with green peppercorn potato cake. Decent puddings to round off; granary bread sandwiches also available.
OPEN: 11-11 (Sun 12-10.30). **BAR MEALS:** L served all week. D served all week 12-10. Av main course £9.
BREWERY/COMPANY: Free House.
PRINCIPAL BEERS: Boddingtons, Flowers IPA, Beartown Bearskinful, Hanby. **FACILITIES:** Children welcome Garden: patio, outdoor eating Dogs allowed. **NOTES:** Parking 150

ALSAGER Map 08 SJ75

Wilbraham Arms
Sandbach Rd North ST7 2AX ☎ 01270 877970
▤ 01270 877970
e-mail: wilbrahamarms@freeserve.co.uk
Set in well-manicured grounds on the edge of town, this busy dining pub is opposite an equestrian centre, and offers a friendly welcome and appetising food. It has a conservatory restaurant, and has been home to Willy's Jazz Club for 20 years.

Expect such fine dishes as steak and kidney pie, lamb Henry, farmhouse chicken with leek and cheddar mash, stuffed ducks legs with red wine and fresh thyme gravy, and ham hock in honey and mustard sauce.
OPEN: 12-3 6-11 (Sun 7-10.30). **BAR MEALS:** L served all week. D served all week 12-2 6.30-9.30. Av main course £6.95.
RESTAURANT: L served Wed-Sun. D served Wed-Sun 12-2 6.30-9.30. Av 3 course à la carte £13. Av 4 course fixed price £16.
BREWERY/COMPANY: PRINCIPAL BEERS: Robinsons Best, Robinson's Frederics, Hartleys XB. **FACILITIES:** Children's licence Garden: patio, outdoor eating. **NOTES:** Parking 76

ASTON
Map 08 SJ64

Pick of the Pubs

The Bhurtpore Inn ♈
Wrenbury Rd CW5 8DQ ☎ 01270 780917
🖳 01270 780170
Dir: between Nantwich & Whitchurch on the A530
Unassuming and unpretentious stone-built village pub
whose unusual name originates from a town in India
where Lord Combermere, a local landowner, was involved
in a fierce battle in 1825. Landlord Simon George has
family links with the pub extending back some 150 years
when his great grandfather owned it in 1852.

Renowned locally for its superb range of nine changing
real ales, most from small, independent micro-breweries,
and the impressive collection of malt whiskies and foreign
bottled beers. Comfortable interior with traditional
furnishings, various interesting Indian artefacts, piped jazz,
a relaxing atmosphere, and home-cooked specials that
enhance a varied printed menu.

Alongside hot crusty baguettes, ploughman's lunches
and steak, kidney and ale pie you may find authentic
curries and baltis, venison casserole, pork fillet with
cream, apple and mustard sauce, and ribeye steak with
Madeira sauce.
OPEN: 12-2.30 (Sun 12-3, 7-10.30) 6.30-11. Closed Dec 25,
1 Jan. **BAR MEALS:** L served all week. D served all week
12-2 7-9.30. Av main course £7.95. **RESTAURANT:** L served
all week. D served all week 12-2 7-9.30. Av 3 course à la carte
£13. **BREWERY/COMPANY:** Free House.
PRINCIPAL BEERS: Hanbys Drawwell.
FACILITIES: Garden: patio, outdoor eating Dogs allowed
Water. **NOTES:** Parking 40 No credit cards

AUDLEM

The Shroppie Fly
The Wharf CW3 0DX ☎ 01270 811772
Lockside pub by the Shropshire Union Canal. One bar is a
converted barge and contains plenty of canal-themed articles.
Seating on canalside terrace.

BARTHOMLEY
Map 08 SJ75

The White Lion Inn
CW2 5PG ☎ 01270 882242 🖳 01270 873348
Historic half-timbered and thatched inn with character bars
and a lovely rural setting. It offers bar food ranging from hot
beef Ibanjol, tuna mayonnaise, and pâté with toast, to more
substantial dishes such as pie with peas, mash and gravy, and
a daily roast with creamed potatoes and vegetables.
OPEN: 11.30-11 (Thurs 5-11, Sun 12-10.30). **BAR MEALS:** L
served Fri-Wed 12-2. Av main course £3.50.
BREWERY/COMPANY: Burtonwood.
PRINCIPAL BEERS: Burtonwood Bitter, Top Hat & Guest ale.
FACILITIES: Children welcome Garden: patio, outdoor eating,
BBQ Dogs allowed. **NOTES:** Parking 20

BOLLINGTON
Map 09 SJ97

The Church House Inn
Church St SK10 5PY ☎ 01625 574014 🖳 01625 576424
Dir: Macclesfield turnoff on A34, thru Prestbury, follow
Bollington signs.
Convenient for both the natural landscape of the Peak District
National Park and the bright lights of Manchester, this village
inn has a varied menu. Diners may enjoy lunchtime specials
such as casseroles and home-made pies. Fresh fish dishes
feature on the evening menu.
OPEN: 12-3 5.30-11. **BAR MEALS:** L served all week. D served
all week 12-2 6.30-9.30. Av main course £6.
BREWERY/COMPANY: Free House.
PRINCIPAL BEERS: Timothy Taylors, Greene King IPA, Jennings,
Theakstons Black Bull. **FACILITIES:** Children welcome.
NOTES: Parking 4. **ROOMS:** 5 bedrooms 5 en suite

BROXTON
Map 08 SJ45

The Copper Mine
Nantwich Rd CH3 9JH ☎ 01829 782293 🖳 01829 782183
Dir: A41 from Chester, L at rdbt onto A534, pub 0.5m on R
Convenient for the Candle Factory at Cheshire Workshops,
Cheshire Ice Cream Farm, and the 14th-century Beeston
Castle, this pub has a conservatory with fine views of the
surrounding countryside. Favourite dishes include cod in
crispy batter, T-bone steaks and duck breast in port, damson
and blueberry sauce.
OPEN: 12-3 6-11. **BAR MEALS:** L served all week. D served all
week 12-2.30 6-9. Av main course £6.95. **RESTAURANT:** L
served all week. D served all week 12-2.30 6-9. Av 3 course à la
carte £15. Av 3 course fixed price £12.95.
BREWERY/COMPANY: Free House.
PRINCIPAL BEERS: Boddingtons, Bass. **FACILITIES:** Children
welcome Garden: patio, outdoor eating, BBQ.
NOTES: Parking 80

Jugs
Toby jugs grin cheerfully from
their vantage points in many a pub
interior. They were first made in the
Staffordshire Potteries in the 18th century and
the standard figure wears a black tricorn hat,
holds a foaming jug of beer and sits in a chair
whose sides are covered by the skirts of his
ample topcoat. This is the Ordinary Toby, but
connoisseurs distinguish between the Long
Face, the Sharp Face and the Roman Nose
variations. Numerous variants include the
Sailor, the Squire, the Tipsy Man and the
Drunken Parson. Other jugs represent famous
figures of history or literature, from Nelson and
Mr Gladstone to Falstaff and John Bull, while
modern examples include Winston Churchill
and Clark Gable. There are a few female
Tobies, but essentially the jugs depict the
jovial male toper, benevolent and
beery.

ROBINSON'S

Founded in 1838 by Frederic Robinson at his father's pub in Stockport, this long-lived brewery is today run by the fifth generation of brewing Robinsons. After the Unicorn Brewery proved too small at the end of the 1960s, work on the Bredbury plant was initiated in 1971. After two years of planning, site work began in 1973, and the building was ready for use in 1975. The site was declared open in October 1976. Among the brewery's current output of ales are Old Tom (8.5%), Hatters Mild (3.3%) and Frederics (5.0%). Brewery tours are available.

BUNBURY   Map 08 SJ55

Pick of the Pubs

The Dysart Arms ♀
Bowes Gate Rd CW6 9PH ☎ 01829 260183
📠 01829 261286
e-mail: dysart.arms@brunningandprice.co.uk
Dir: Between A49 & A51, by Shropshire Union Canal, and opposite church
At the top end of a typically rural Cheshire village this Grade II listed farmhouse, converted into a pub in Victorian times, underwent major extensions just five years ago. Within it remains a treasure trove of antique furniture and old prints in a succession of airy rooms with open fires set around the central bar servery. From the terrace tables and attractive garden are fine views of Peckforton and Beeston castles to one side and the splendid parish church to the other. Careful attention to food includes the use of home-grown garden herbs on an enticingly modern menu that is served throughout. Sate king prawns with prawn crackers and stir-fried bok choi with wild mushrooms and water chestnuts on a crisp noodle cake typify this approach and come in starter or large portions. Main dishes come precisely as described, as in "half a roast duck on braised red cabbage and apples with red wine sauce" and "grilled sea bass with spinach and green beans served with new potatoes and warm salsa". For enjoyable drinking there are changing guest ales and a dozen house wines by the glass.
OPEN: 11.30-11 (Sun 12-10.30). **BAR MEALS:** L served all week. D served all week 12-2.15 6-9.30. Av main course £9.25.
BREWERY/COMPANY: Free House.
PRINCIPAL BEERS: Timothy Taylor Landlord, Wood Shropshire Lad, Boddingtons, Hanby. **FACILITIES:** Children welcome Garden: outdoor eating, patio/terrace, Dogs allowed. **NOTES:** Parking 30

BURWARDSLEY   Map 08 SJ55

Pick of the Pubs

The Pheasant Inn ★ ★ 🐑 ♀
CH3 9PF ☎ 01829 770434   📠 01829 771097
Dir: From Chester A41 to Whitchurch, after 4m L to Burwardsley. Follow signs 'Cheshire Workshops'
A beautiful setting tucked into the Peckforton hills frames this sandstone, half-timbered former farmhouse that surprisingly has an unbroken history as an ale-house since the 17th century. The old outbuildings and barn house most of the bedrooms, recently up-graded and furnished in individual contemporary styles, while the interior of the main farmhouse makes the perfect setting for a bar that allegedly houses the largest log fire in the county. New chef/patron Lee McKone has retained the identity of a fine country inn where no-one need stand on ceremony. Fine real ales and wines by the glass accompany casserole of local mussels with Thai spices and buttered noodles - offered as a starter or main dish - an alternative starter taking in sautéed chicken livers with beetroot relish. Steamed native salmon on wilted spinach with a soft-poached egg and slow-roast lamb shank with a bubble-and-squeak potato cake may follow, with seafood and pasta showing strongly, as in fresh crab cannelloni with a lemon and vine tomato tian. The Bolesworth Restaurant, housed in the remodelled conservatory, goes up a gear in complexity and flair utilising local produce to good effect.
OPEN: 11-11. **BAR MEALS:** L served all week. D served all week 12-2.30 6.30-9.30. Av main course £7.
RESTAURANT: L served all week. D served all week 12-2.30 7-9.30. Av 3 course à la carte £27.
BREWERY/COMPANY: Free House.
PRINCIPAL BEERS: Bass, Weetwood Old Dog, Timothy Taylors Landlord. **FACILITIES:** Children welcome Garden: patio, outdoor eating. **NOTES:** Parking 40. **ROOMS:** 10 bedrooms 10 en suite s£55 d£80

CHESTER   Map 08 SJ46

Albion Inn
Park St CH1 1RN ☎ 01244 340345
Dir: In Chester City centre adjacent to Citywalls and Newgate overlooking the River Dee
The home fires still burn on cold winter nights at this living memorial to the 1914-18 war. Just around the corner from a former army recruiting centre, the traditional three room layout of this unspoilt Victorian pub is packed with period artefacts, and the popular Great War piano evenings are by ticket only. Trench rations include Great British butties, liver and bacon, haggis, and corned beef hash.
OPEN: 11.30-3 5.30-11. Closed 25 Dec, 1 Jan. **BAR MEALS:** L served all week. D served Tue-Sun 12-2 5-8. Av main course £6.
BREWERY/COMPANY: Inn Partnership.
PRINCIPAL BEERS: Timothy Taylor Landlord, Cains.
FACILITIES: Dogs allowed Water No credit cards

Old Harkers Arms ♀
1 Russell St CH1 5AL ☎ 01244 344525   📠 01244 344526
Tall windows, lofty ceilings and wooden floors make this former Victorian warehouse one of Chester's more unusual pubs. Even from the bar was made from salvaged doors. An ideal spot for watching boating activity, this popular city watering hole offers an interesting menu, with dishes ranging from

continued

grilled bream and ribeye steak to chicken supreme filled with thyme and goats' cheese and steak, mushroom and bacon pie.
OPEN: 11-11. Closed Dec 26 & Jan 1. **BAR MEALS:** L served all week. D served all week 11.30-2.30 5.30-9.30. Av main course £8.
RESTAURANT: L served Same as bar.
PRINCIPAL BEERS: Thwaites, Caledonian, Derwents.

CHOLMONDELEY — Map 08 SJ55

Pick of the Pubs

The Cholmondeley Arms ♦♦♦ 🐄 ♀
SY14 8HN ☎ 01829 720300 🖹 01829 720123
e-mail: cholmondeleyarms@cwcom.net
Dir: on A49, between Whitchurch & Tarporley

In a converted village schoolhouse by the A49, with separate guest accommodation across the spacious paddock, this has been a firm Cheshire favourite since 1988. Nearby, the Cholmondeley family has occupied the fine castle and gardens since Domesday, and this became the first licensed premises on their land for over 150 years. Daily menus, written up on the blackboard naturally, are an education in themselves providing food for thought and thoughtfully prepared fresh food. Roast local asparagus in season with olive oil, sea salt and Parmesan and baby smoked haddock fishcakes with devilled tomato sauce focus the mind initially, followed by Gressingham duck breast with red-currant sauce and sea bass fillets on buttered samphire with light veloute sauce that are essays in good taste: nor does attention to detail lapse in the hot chocolate fudge pudding or popular fruit crumbles that follow. Pay particular attention to the range of real ales and carefully chosen wines, or tarry after class over copious cups of strong coffee.
OPEN: 11-3 7-11. Closed 25 Dec. **BAR MEALS:** L served all week. D served all week 12-2.30 7-10. Av main course £8.50.
BREWERY/COMPANY: Free House.
PRINCIPAL BEERS: Marstons, Adnams, Weetwood Old Dod. **FACILITIES:** Children welcome Garden: outdoor eating Dogs allowed. **NOTES:** Parking 60. **ROOMS:** 6 bedrooms 6 en suite s£45 d£60 FR£70

CHURCH MINSHULL

The Badger Inn 🐄 ♀
Over Rd CW5 6DY ☎ 01270 522607 🖹 01270 522607
Originally known as the Brookes Arms, the inn later changed its name to the Badger Inn and became a coach stop on the route between Nantwich and Middlewich. The badger was part of the Brookes's family crest and has been used as the inn sign for many years. Live music once a fortnight and an interesting range of Mediterranean-style dishes, including tapas, paella and pasta.

OPEN: 12-12. **BAR MEALS:** L served all week. D served all week 12-2.15 6-9. Av main course £10. **RESTAURANT:** L served all week. D served all week 12-2.15 6-9. Av 3 course à la carte £15.
BREWERY/COMPANY: PRINCIPAL BEERS: Wadworth 6X, Boddington. **FACILITIES:** Children welcome Children's licence Garden: outdoor eating Dogs allowed. **NOTES:** Parking 30

CONGLETON — Map 08 SJ86

The Egerton Arms Hotel ♦♦♦ ♀
Astbury Village CW12 4RQ ☎ 01260 273946
🖹 01260 277273
e-mail: egertonastbury@bun.com
Named after Lord Egerton of Tatton, the local lord of the manor, this 16th-century village inn is situated in the picturesque village of Astbury, adjacent to the 11th-century church. Extensive menu ranges from roast topside of beef or chicken kiev, to a choice of fish including swordfish steak, smoked cod and shellfish cheese bake, and seabass with ginger and soy. Recently refurbished bedrooms are attractive and well equipped.
OPEN: 11.15-11 (Sun 11-3, 7-10.30). **BAR MEALS:** L served all week. D served all week 11.30-9 6.30-9. Av main course £6.
RESTAURANT: L served all week. D served all week 11.30-2 7-9. Av 3 course à la carte £11. **BREWERY/COMPANY:** Robinsons.
PRINCIPAL BEERS: Robinsons Old Stockport & Fredericks.
FACILITIES: Children welcome Garden: outdoor eating.
NOTES: Parking 100. **ROOMS:** 6 bedrooms 2 en suite s£24 d£32.50

BOTTOMS UP

As a customer in a 17th-century inn or alehouse, you might find yourself with a pint or quart pot made of wood, horn or leather in your hand. They all had the advantage of not breaking if dropped, though the effect on the beer's taste might not suit today's palates. A cut above these utensils were mugs and tankards of pewter, which some pubs still supply and some drinkers still swear by them. In 19th-century hostelries, however, pewter gradually gave way to china and glass, with the occasional joky china mug made with a frog crouching at the bottom, to give the unwary toper a nasty shock.

England

CONGLETON continued

Pick of the Pubs

Plough Inn Hotel
Macclesfield Rd, Eaton CW12 2NR ☎ 01260 280207
▤ 01260 280207
Dir: on A536 (Congleton to Macclesfield road)
A combination of small alcoves, comfortable corners and
blazing open hearth fires makes this nicely restored 17th-
century coaching inn an attractive place to meet, eat and
drink. One popular menu, which changes regularly, is
served throughout the bar and the wonderful Old Barn
restaurant. With its high beamed roof, intimate gallery and
wealth of gnarled old timbers, the Barn provides a
memorable venue for informal fine dining. The menu
begins with freshly made sandwiches and Cheshire
ploughman's, and moves on through lighter plates such as
chicken stir-fry or Mediterranean vegetable tagliatelle.
Imaginative, original starters like ham terrine with winter
vegetables and fresh duck, or white onion tarte Tatin are
followed by a nice selection of freshly cooked main
courses. Seared brill fillet, braised Welsh lamb shank, or
steamed beef and oyster pudding are typical choices,
followed by apple charlotte, mango and claret terrine, or
baked vanilla soufflé.

OPEN: 11.30-11. Closed 26 Dec, 1 Jan. **BAR MEALS:** L
served all week. D served all week 12-2 6-9.30. Av main
course £8.95. **RESTAURANT:** L served Sun. D served
Tue-Sat 12-2 6-9.30. Av 3 course à la carte £16.95.
BREWERY/COMPANY: Free House.
PRINCIPAL BEERS: Boddington Cask, Marstons Pedigree,
Bass. **FACILITIES:** Children welcome Garden: Food served
outside. **NOTES:** Parking 50. **ROOMS:** 8 bedrooms 8 en
suite s£45 d£55

AA Bed & Breakfast 2002

Britain's best-selling B&B
guide featuring over 3500
great places to stay

www.theAA.com

AA **Lifestyle Guides**

COTEBROOK   Map 08 SJ56

Alvanley Arms Hotel
Forest Rd CW6 9DS ☎ 01829 760200 ▤ 01829 760696
Dir: On the A49, 10m from Chester, 18m from M6 J16
Friendly, family-run inn which dates back to the 17th century
or even earlier, when the then landlord was fined for
permitting rogues, whores and general undesirables to lodge
on the premises. Ruth Ellis, the last woman to be hanged in
England, once stayed at the inn with her lover. The pub utilises
local produce and fresh fish is a speciality here, delivered
directly from coastal ports up to five times a week. Popular
specials board and a wide range of cask ales, wines and malt
whiskies.

OPEN: 11.30-3 5.30-11. **BAR MEALS:** L served all week. D
served all week 12-2.15 6-9.30. Av main course £7.50.
RESTAURANT: L served all week. D served all week 12-2.15 6-
9.30. Av 3 course à la carte £14.95.
BREWERY/COMPANY: PRINCIPAL BEERS: Robinsons Best,
Hatter Mild. **FACILITIES:** Children welcome Garden: Food
served outside. **NOTES:** Parking 75. **ROOMS:** 7 bedrooms 7 en
suite s£35 d£60

HANDLEY   Map 08 SJ45

The Calveley Arms 🐷 🍴
Whitchurch Rd CH3 9DT ☎ 01829 770619
▤ 01829 770619
Dir: 5m S of Chester, sign posted from A41
Old coaching inn first licensed in 1636 and still retaining plenty
of old-world charm. Beamed ceilings and open fires add to the
atmosphere and among the classic pub games found here are
cribbage, dominoes and bar skittles. An extensive menu offers
fresh fish, a traditional Sunday roast and a good choice of
starters. Sample stir-fried Oriental beef, grilled lemon sole or
pan-fried pheasant from the daily-changing specials board.
OPEN: 12-3 6-11 (Sun eve 7-10.30). Closed 25 Dec.
BAR MEALS: L served all week. D served all week 12-2.15 6-9.30.
Av main course £6.95. **RESTAURANT:** D served Same as bar.
BREWERY/COMPANY: Enterprise Inns.
PRINCIPAL BEERS: Boddingtons, Castle Eden, Wadworth 6X,
Marstons Pedigree. **FACILITIES:** Garden: Food served outside,
Beer garden Dogs allowed Water. **NOTES:** Parking 20

🐷 Pubs offering a good choice of
seafood on the menu.

England

Pick of the Pubs

The Dog Inn ♦♦♦♦ 🐑
Well Bank Ln, Over Peover WA16 8UP ☎ 01625 861421
🖹 01625 864800
*Dir: From Knutsford take A50 S. Turn L at 'The Whipping Stocks'.
Pub in 2m*
A traditional timbered 18th-century inn situated in the heart of the Cheshire countryside between Knutsford and Holmes Chapel, enhanced in summer by dazzling flowerbeds, tubs and hanging baskets. Wide use of fresh local produce - and guest ales from local micro-breweries - attracts a faithful following for its traditional style of pub fare. Starters such as duck-and-port pâté and black pudding served hot with English mustard are followed by boiled ham shank with parsley sauce, rack of lamb with apricot and ginger sauce, and roast topside of Cheshire beef with Yorkshire pudding. Halibut steak with spinach, and leek, Stilton and mushroom pancakes satisfy alternative persuasions.
OPEN: 11.30-3 5.30-11.30 (Sun all day, except Mar-Oct 12-4, 7-11). **BAR MEALS:** L served all week. D served all week 12-2.30 7-9.30. Av main course £9.95.
BREWERY/COMPANY: Free House.
PRINCIPAL BEERS: Tetley, Moorhouse Black Cat, Weetwood Old Dog & Best Bitter, Hydes Best.
FACILITIES: Children welcome Garden: large patio area.
NOTES: Parking 100. **ROOMS:** 6 bedrooms 6 en suite s£55 d£75

LANGLEY

Leathers Smithy
Clarke Ln SK11 0NE ☎ 01260 252313 🖹 01260 253460
Popular with walkers, this lovely old pub is close to Macclesfield Forest and enjoys good views of Ridgegate Reservoir. Lots of motoring memorabilia. The pub gets its name from a combination of William Leather, a local farrier who bought a license in 1821, and the history of the building as a blacksmiths. Good stock of malt whiskies.

LOWER WHITLEY   Map 08 SJ67

Chetwoode Arms ♀ NEW
St Lane WA4 4EN ☎ 01925 730203
e-mail: gfidler6@netscapeonline.co.uk
Dir: Chetwode Arms is on the A49 2 M S from J 10 M55, 6M S of Warrington
Country inn with buckets of character, believed to be over 300 years old. It has its own crown green bowling facilities and runs a bowls competition each August. Dishes are prepared to order from fresh produce sourced from small local suppliers. Specials include grilled sea bass with roasted vegetable and salsa verde, and saddle of venison with roast shallot tartlet and port and chestnut sauce.
OPEN: 12-11. **RESTAURANT:** L served all week. D served all week 12-3 6-9. Av 3 course à la carte £18.95.
BREWERY/COMPANY: Inn Partnership.
PRINCIPAL BEERS: Greenalls Bitter, Cains Bitter Marstons Pedigree. **FACILITIES:** Garden: Food served outside Dogs allowed Managers discretion. **NOTES:** Parking 60

The Windmill Inn ♀
Holehouse Ln, Whitely Green, Adlington SK10 5SJ
☎ 01625 574222
Dir: A523 to Adlington turn off to Holemouse Cane
On the fringe of the Peak District - just by the Macclesfield Canal - stands this heavily-beamed former farmhouse that dates back to 1684. Rustic specials boards promise pepper-pot mushrooms, monkfish in Pernod, duck breast in wild berry sauce. More traditional roast middle leg of lamb and fish in Speckled Hen batter happily co-exist.
OPEN: 12-11. **BAR MEALS:** D served all week 12-3. Av main course £7. **RESTAURANT:** D served all week 6.30-9. Av 3 course à la carte £12. **BREWERY/COMPANY:** Bass.
PRINCIPAL BEERS: Greene King Old Speckled Hen, Bass.
FACILITIES: Children welcome Garden: patio/terrace, outdoor eating, Dogs allowed Water. **NOTES:** Parking 100

MARBURY

The Swan Inn
SY13 4LS ☎ 01948 663715
Within walking distance of the beautiful Llangollen canal, this picturesque pub is set in an award-winning village. Panelled lounge, open fires.

MOBBERLEY

Plough & Flail
Paddock Hill WA16 7DB ☎ 01565 873537
🖹 01565 873902
Quaint, white-painted stone cottages with plenty of floral decoration. Became a pub after the inhabitants of the cottages found themselves locally famous for their home brew.

NANTWICH   Map 08 SJ65

The Thatch Inn ♀
Wrexham Rd, Faddiley CW5 8JE ☎ 01270 524223
Dir: follow signs for Wrexham from Nantwich, inn is 4m from Nantwich
Homely comfort and good food are the hallmarks of this pretty, 15th-century black and white inn. There's a lovely summer garden, and beneath the old thatched roof you'll find oak beams, traditional pub games, and winter fires. The menu features plenty of pub favourites like grilled gammon, steak and kidney pie or vegetarian lasagne, and the ever popular cod, chips and mushy peas.
OPEN: 12-3 6-10 (Sun all day). **BAR MEALS:** L served all week. D served all week 12-2 6.30-9.30. Av main course £7.50.
RESTAURANT: L served all week. D served all week 12-2 6.30-9.30. Av 3 course à la carte £12. Av 2 course fixed price £7.50.
BREWERY/COMPANY: Free House.
PRINCIPAL BEERS: Websters Yorkshire, Theakstons Best, Courage Directors. **FACILITIES:** Children welcome Garden: outdoor eating, patio/terrace Dogs allowed. **NOTES:** Parking 60

OVER PEOVER   Map 08 SJ77

Ye Olde Parkgate Inn ♀
Stocks Ln WA16 8TU ☎ 01625 861455
Dir: A50 from Knutsford. Inn 3m on L after Radbroke Hall
Ivy-covered village pub surrounded by fields and woodland. Attractively furnished beamed bars and comfortable lounge where home-cooked food is served. Expect a traditional setting offering a friendly welcome and good conversation. *continued*

Blackboard daily specials supplement the traditional pub menu, the latter listing wholetail scampi, fresh salmon fillet, tomato and mozzarella crumble, and chicken curry.
OPEN: 11.30-11 (Sun 12-3.30, 7-10.30). **BAR MEALS:** L served all week. D served all week 12-2 6.30-9. Av main course £7.95.
BREWERY/COMPANY: Samuel Smith.
PRINCIPAL BEERS: Samuel Smith Old Brewery Bitter.
FACILITIES: Dogs allowed Water Provided. **NOTES:** Parking 45

PENKETH · Map 08 SJ58

The Ferry Tavern ♀
Station Rd WA5 2UJ ☎ 01925 791117 · 01925 791116
e-mail: ferrytavern@talk21.com
Dir: A57 - A562, Fiddler's Ferry signposted
Tucked away on its own island, this 12th-century ale house welcomes walkers and cyclists from the trans-Pennine Way. Beneath the low beams in the stone-flagged bar you'll find a range of unusual guest beers, and over 300 different whiskies. The extensive bar menu includes burgers, baguettes and speciality sausages, with grills, oven-roasted lamb and Mexican dishes on offer in the upstairs dining room.
OPEN: 12-3 5.30-11 (open all day wknd). **BAR MEALS:** L served Mon-Sat. D served Mon-Sat 12-2 6-7.30. Av main course £5. **RESTAURANT:** L served Mon-Sat. D served Mon-Sat 12-2 6-9. Av 3 course à la carte £15. **BREWERY/COMPANY:** Free House. **PRINCIPAL BEERS:** Courage Directors, Boddingtons, Greene King Abbot Ale & Old Speckled Hen. **FACILITIES:** Children welcome Garden: outdoor eating, Dogs allowed Toys, Water. **NOTES:** Parking 46

PLUMLEY · Map 08 SJ77

The Smoker ⬡ ♀
WA16 0TY ☎ 01565 722338 · 01565 722093
Dir: from M6 J19 take A556 W. Pub is 1.75m on L
The outside of this thatched, Elizabethan coaching inn has changed little since Edwardian times, and you'll still find log fires burning in the panelled interior. Named after the Prince Regent's favourite racehorse, the pub nevertheless offers non-smoking areas in the bar and brasserie-style restaurant! The appetising menu includes seafood tagliatelle and sea bass, as well as grills, beef Stroganoff, hake with prawn and mushroom sauce and daily vegetarian dishes. Expect good Robinson's ales on tap.
OPEN: 11-3 6-11 (all day Sun). **BAR MEALS:** L served all week. D served all week 11.30-2.30 6.30-9.30. Av main course £7.95. **RESTAURANT:** L served all week. D served all week 11.30-2.30 6.30-9.30. Av 3 course à la carte £15.
BREWERY/COMPANY: PRINCIPAL BEERS: Robinsons Best & Mild. **FACILITIES:** Children welcome Garden: Food Served Outdoors. **NOTES:** Parking 100

PRESTBURY · Map 09 SJ87

The Legh Arms & Black Boy Restaurant ♀
Prestbury Village Centre SK10 4DG ☎ 01625 829130
· 01625 827833
Dir: From M6 thru Knutsford to Macclesfield, turn to Prestbury at Broken Cross. Pub in village centre
There is a weekly bar food menu and an extensive carte in the restaurant at this 15th-century pub, centrally located in historic Prestbury village. Fish specialities include paupiettes of lemon sole, filled with langoustine and fresh salmon mousse and served with fresh asparagus, and roast tail of monkfish, marinated with limes, coriander and chilli, carved into

continued

---

medallions and set on an orange, herb and frisée salad with roasted pine nuts.
OPEN: 11.30-3.30 (All day Fri-Sun in summer) 5.30-11.
BAR MEALS: L served all week. D served all week 12-2 7-9.30. Av main course £7. **RESTAURANT:** L served all week 12-2 7-9.30. Av 3 course à la carte £30. Av 3 course fixed price £15. **BREWERY/COMPANY:** Frederic Robinson **FACILITIES:** Children welcome Garden: Food served outside. **NOTES:** Parking 40

SMALLWOOD

Salamanca Inn
London Rd CW11 2TX ☎ 01477 500238
Deep in Cheshire countryside, this nicely maintained black and white roadside tavern has a homely feel and serves traditional pub grub.

SWETTENHAM · Map 08 SJ86

Pick of the Pubs

The Swettenham Arms ⬡ ♀
Swettenham Ln CW12 2LF ☎ 01477 571284
· 01477 571284
Dir: M6 J18 to Holmes Chapel, then A535 towards Jodrell Bank. 3m take rd on R (Forty Acre Lane) to Swettenham
This charming, white painted village inn is tucked away behind a 13th-century church in the lovely Dane valley. Formerly a nunnery, the pub once boasted an underground passage where bodies were stored before burial. Ghost stories abound, but there's nothing chilling about the large open fireplaces that warm the pub's heavily beamed interior. In summer, this tranquil spot is deservedly popular with walkers and country lovers. Owners Frances and Jim Cunningham have planted a two-acre wildflower meadow, and customers are welcome to walk in the adjoining Quinta Arboretum. A select wine list supplements the extensive range of unusual real ales and draught cider, and the imaginative menu features home-made dishes prepared from fresh local produce. Expect sautéed pigeon breasts in a filo pastry basket, pan-fried venison steak, game pie, roast trout with smoked salmon and asparagus, smoked halibut, or vegetable strudel with mixed cheeses and toasted pine kernels.
OPEN: 12-3 (Wknd 12-4) 6.30-11 (Sun 12-4, 7-11).
BAR MEALS: L served all week. D served all week 12-2.30 7-9.30. Av main course £9.95. **BREWERY/COMPANY:** Free House. **PRINCIPAL BEERS:** Jennings, Beartown. **FACILITIES:** Children welcome Garden: Large patio, outdoor eating. **NOTES:** Parking 150

TARPORLEY · Map 08 SJ56

The Boot Inn ⬡
Boothsdale, Willington CW6 0NH ☎ 01829 751375
Dir: off the A54 Kelsall By-pass
Originally a small beer house, the pub has expanded into a charming row of warm red brick and sandstone cottages in Cat Lane. Quarry tiled floors, old beams and open fires give this traditional country pub a style and character of its own. Local walks prepare you for well kept ales and appetising, freshly cooked food, served in the bar, restaurant or garden. Lunchtime brings hot panini sandwiches and filled baguettes, whilst the popular menu and evening specials include pan-

continued

England

fried chicken and bacon, Barnsley chops, or rarebit-topped smoked haddock on tomato and chive sauce.
OPEN: 11-3 6-11 (All day Sat-Sun & BHs). Closed Dec 25.
BAR MEALS: L served all week. D served all week 11-2.30 6-9.30. Av main course £7.95. **RESTAURANT:** L served all week. D served all week 11-2.30 6-9.30. Av 3 course à la carte £15.
BREWERY/COMPANY: Inn Partnership.
PRINCIPAL BEERS: Weetwood Oasthouse Gold, Ambush Old Dog & Eastgate, Cains. **FACILITIES:** Children welcome Garden: outdoor eating, Dogs allowed garden only, Water.
NOTES: Parking 60

The Fox & Barrel NEW ♀
Forest Rd, Cotebrook CW6 9DZ ☎ 01829 760529
▤ 01829 760529
Dir: On the A49 just outside Tarporley, very close to Oulton Park Race Circuit

Award-winning pub, renowned for its food, in the heart of the Cheshire countryside. There's a cosy bar offering cask ales and a good choice of wine by the glass, and a no-smoking restaurant extending onto an enclosed patio area. A seasonal menu includes the likes of fish stew with crusty bread, tuna and crab fishcakes, and pan-fried venison on braised sweet and sour red cabbage with blackberry and orange sauce.
OPEN: 12-3 (Sat 12-11, Sun 12-10.30) 5.30-11. Closed 25 Dec.
BAR MEALS: L served all week. D served all week 12-2.30 6.30-9. Av main course £10.50. **RESTAURANT:** L served all week. D served all week 12-2.30 6.30-9. Av 3 course à la carte £20.
BREWERY/COMPANY: Inn Partnership.
PRINCIPAL BEERS: Marstons Pedigree, Guest Beers.
FACILITIES: Garden: Food served outside

TUSHINGHAM CUM GRINDLEY   Map 08 SJ54

Blue Bell Inn
SY13 4QS ☎ 01948 662172
e-mail: pagage@aol.com
Dir: On the A41 N of Whitchurch
Exceptionally friendly black-and-white pub with a warm welcome. The building dates from the 17th century and has an abundance of beams, open fires, horse brasses, and an unknown but friendly spirit.

Room prices minimum single and minimum double rates are shown. FR indicates family room

---

WINCLE   Map 09 SJ96

The Ship Inn 🏠
SK11 0QE ☎ 01260 227217
Dir: Leave A54 at Fourways Motel x-rds, towards Danebridge, Inn 0.5m before bridge on L
Quaint 16th-century red sandstone pub with fascinating historical associations. A previous owner was held at gunpoint during the Jacobean uprising. Reputedly the oldest inn in Cheshire, the Ship is situated in the lower Pennines, close to some of the finest walking country in the north-west of England. Interesting choice of real ales while the blackboard menu changes at least twice a week. Typical examples include home-made steak and ale pie, Brie and leek parcels, and halibut with sweet pepper sauce.
OPEN: 12-3 7-11 (Sun 12-3, 7-10.30). **BAR MEALS:** L served Tue-Sun. D served Tue-Sun 12-2 7-9. Av main course £8.
RESTAURANT: L served Tue-Sun. D served Tue-Sun 12-2 7-9. Av 3 course à la carte £15. **BREWERY/COMPANY:** Free House.
PRINCIPAL BEERS: Wye Valley, Timothy Taylor Landlord, York, Beartown. **FACILITIES:** Children welcome Children's licence Garden: patio/terrace, outdoor eating. **NOTES:** Parking 15

WRENBURY   Map 08 SJ54

The Dusty Miller ♀
CW5 8HG ☎ 01270 780537
e-mail: dustymiller2@compuserve.com
A typical black and white lift bridge completes the picture postcard setting for this beautifully converted 19th-century mill building beside the Llangollen canal. The River Weaver flows through the pub garden, with its rose-covered terrace being the ideal spot to enjoy a pint of Robinsons Best or an alfresco meal in summer. The menu features freshly cooked dishes like Clewlows black pudding with bacon, chargrilled chicken, and blackened salmon. Watch the blackboard for daily vegetarian and fish dishes.
OPEN: 11.30-3.00 (closed winter Mon lunchtime) 6.30-11. Closed 2nd 2 weeks in Jan. **BAR MEALS:** L served all week. D served all week 12-2.00 6.30-9.30. Av main course £9. **RESTAURANT:** L served all week. D served all week 12-2.00 6.30-9.30. Av 3 course à la carte £17.
BREWERY/COMPANY: PRINCIPAL BEERS: Robinsons: Best, Frederics, Old Tom, Hatters Mild; Hartleys XB.
FACILITIES: Children welcome Garden: outdoor eating Dogs allowed, Water, Kennel. **NOTES:** Parking 60

WYBUNBURY   Map 08 SJ64

The Swan ♀
Main Rd CW5 7NA ☎ 01270 841820
Dir: M6 J16 towards Chester / Nantwich. Turn L at traffic lights in Wybunbury
The Swan, registered as an alehouse in 1580, is situated next to the church in the village centre. All the food is freshly prepared on the premises and includes home-made soups, braised shoulder of lamb, home made bangers and mash, or grilled fillet of swordfish or tuna.
OPEN: 12-11. **BAR MEALS:** L served all week. D served all week 12-2 6.30-9.30. **BREWERY/COMPANY:** Jennings.
PRINCIPAL BEERS: Jennings Bitter & Cumberland Ale.
FACILITIES: Children welcome Children's licence Garden: outdoor eating,. **NOTES:** Parking 40. **ROOMS:** 7 bedrooms 7 en suite s£25 d£45 FR£60-£75

CORNWALL & ISLES OF SCILLY

BODINNICK

Old Ferry Inn
PL23 1LX ☎ 01726 870237
Overlooking the ferry crossing to Fowey, this charming pub understandably has a nautical theme. Some of the bedrooms enjoy fine views.

BOSCASTLE   Map 02 SX09

The Wellington Hotel ★ ★
The Harbour PL35 0AQ ☎ 01840 250202
🖹 01840 250621
e-mail: vtobutt@enterprise.net
Dir: A30 onto A395, then A39, R onto B3314, R onto B3266

Fine 16th-century coaching inn located in glorious National Trust countryside and within easy reach of an Elizabethan harbour and heritage coastal footpath. The popular 'Welly Longbar,' with its log fires and original beams, is a comfortable and cosy retreat on a cold winter's day.
   Real ales and malts are served and traditional folk music is a regular fixture. Wild Boar sausages with mash and onion gravy, moules marinière are typical bar dishes, while the restaurant might offer calves' liver with sage and apple, and ham Bayonaise.
OPEN: 11-3 (Easter-Oct & BHs all day) 5.30-11. **BAR MEALS:** L served all week. D served all week 12-2 6-9.30. **RESTAURANT:** . D served all week 7-9.30. Av 3 course à la carte £16.
BREWERY/COMPANY: Free House.
PRINCIPAL BEERS: Flowers IPA, St Austell HSD & Daylight Robbery, Wadworth 6X, Greene King Abbot Ale.
FACILITIES: Children welcome Garden: Terrace, outdoor eating Dogs allowed. **NOTES:** Parking 20. **ROOMS:** 17 bedrooms 16 en suite s£31 d£54

CADGWITH   Map 02 SW71

Cadgwith Cove Inn NEW
TR12 7JX ☎ 01326 290513 🖹 01326 291018
e-mail: enquiries@cadgwithcoveinn.com
Prominently situated overlooking a lovely cove on the Lizard peninsula, the inn is right at the centre of this fishing and farming community. As might be expected, seafood is a
continued

speciality, with popular options of home-made crab soup, moules marinière, and traditional fish and chips with local white fish fillet. The inn lies on the Lizard Coastal walk, and live music, particularly folk, is a regular feature.

OPEN: 12-3 (Xmas Wk & Easter-end Sept 12-11) 7-11.
BAR MEALS: L served all week. D served all week 12 6. Av main course £7.95. **RESTAURANT:** L served all week. D served all week. Av 3 course à la carte £21. **BREWERY/COMPANY:** Inn Partnership. **PRINCIPAL BEERS:** Flowers IPA, Wadworth 6X, Marstons Pedigree, Sharps. **FACILITIES:** Garden: Patio, food served outside Dogs allowed. **NOTES:** Parking 4.
ROOMS: d£19.75

CALLINGTON   Map 02 SX36

The Coachmakers Arms NEW 🍸
6 Newport Square PL17 7AS ☎ 01579 382567
🖹 01579 384679
A wide range of customers - families, old and young - enjoy a drink or meal in comfortable surroundings at this traditional stone-built pub. Antique furniture, clocks, horse brasses and displays of foreign currency all contribute to the atmosphere. Home-made fare, from doorstep sandwiches, through fisherman's crumble, to T-bone steaks, is offered and there's a popular Sunday roast.
OPEN: 11-3 (Sun 12-3, 7-10.30) 6-11. **BAR MEALS:** L served all week. D served all week 12-2 7-9.30. Av main course £4.75.
RESTAURANT: L served all week. D served all week 12-2 7-9.30. Av 3 course à la carte £12. **BREWERY/COMPANY:** Free House. **PRINCIPAL BEERS:** Bass. **FACILITIES:** Children welcome Dogs allowed. **NOTES:** Parking 10. **ROOMS:** 4 bedrooms 4 en suite s£30 d£45

Manor House Inn ♦ ♦ ♦
Rilla Mill PL17 7NT ☎ 01579 362354 🖹 01579 363305
Dir: leave A30 and join B3254, L onto B3257 for 3m. R signed Rilla Mill
At the heart of a designated Cornish conservation area, the pub stands in its own mature gardens and orchard on the banks of the River Lynher. An extensive menu of daily home-made dishes and grills operates throughout; the steak and kidney pie, meat curry and vegetable lasagnes all prepared to the landlady's own recipes.
OPEN: 11-3 6-11. **BAR MEALS:** L served all week. D served all week 12-2 7-9.30. Av main course £6.50. **RESTAURANT:** L served all week. D served all week 12-2 7-9.30. Av 3 course à la carte £17. **BREWERY/COMPANY:** Free House.
PRINCIPAL BEERS: Bass, Whitbread Ales.
FACILITIES: Children welcome Children's licence Garden: patio, outdoor eating, BBQ Dogs allowed. **NOTES:** Parking 41. **ROOMS:** 12 bedrooms 12 en suite s£27.50 d£50

Tradition, charm, character...

...STYLE, QUALITY, COMFORT.

St Austell Brewery - **brewing great traditional beer for 150 years and renowned for the warm hospitality found in its Small and Friendly Inns. The Inns can be found throughout Cornwall and Devon, from Exeter to the Isles of Scilly, Padstow to the beautiful Helford river.**

Small and Friendly
TRADITIONAL INNS

Wherever you are, and whatever your taste you will find the ideal Inn to suit you - ranging from traditional village pubs to lively, modern establishments, many providing live entertainment. St Austell Brewery's Inns are all about variety and versatility and good home-cooked food.

Many offer comfortable, homely accommodation in scenic locations including fishing villages, sleepy country hamlets and bustling towns. Ideal for short breaks, family and touring holidays.

Brochureline: 01726 627299
For enquiries and bookings: 01726 627208
www.westcountryhotelrooms.co.uk

ST. AUSTELL BREWERY

St Austell Brewery, 63 Trevarthian Road, St Austell, Cornwall PL25 4BY

England

Pick of the Pubs

The Maltsters Arms 🏠 ♀
PL27 6EU ☎ 01208 812473
Dir: *From Wadebridge take A39 then 1st L, B3314. Village on R*

Rambling, whitewashed 16th-century village pub located a short drive from the dramatic north coast. Now a well established dining destination, the Maltsters has a character main bar with half-panelled walls, large log fire, heavy oak beams, in addition to spacious, simply decorated side rooms, all of which have a relaxing pub atmosphere. Talented young chefs Daniel and Libbe Latham source fresh local produce and menus place a particular emphasis on Cornish fish and seafood. The daily-changing fish board may list whole megrim sole baked with garlic mushrooms and Cheddar cheese, turbot with crab, brandy and cream sauce, and wild sea bass on samphire with Thai curry sauce. Carnivores aren't neglected though; try the roast duck breast with mulled wine and winter fruit sauce or roast lamb shank with Madeira sauce. Wholesome bar meals include speciality open sandwiches. Good home-made puddings; impressive West Country cheeses; Sunday roast carvery (booking advisable). Four real ales, an impressive list of 22 wines by the glass and 18 malt whiskies.
OPEN: 11-2.30 6-11 (Sun 12-2.30,7-10.30). **BAR MEALS:** L served all week. D served all week 12-1.45 6.30-9.30. Av main course £6. **RESTAURANT:** L served Sun. D served all week 12-2 6.30-9.30. Av 3 course à la carte £20.
BREWERY/COMPANY: Free House.
PRINCIPAL BEERS: Sharp's Cornish Coaster, Bass, Ruddles County. **FACILITIES:** Children welcome patio, outdoor eating. **NOTES:** Parking 9

Sharp's Brewery

Now available in some 350 free and tied houses throughout the Devon and Cornwall area, Sharp's only put out its first brew in August 1994. Sharp's beers include Cornish Coaster (3.6%), Doom Bar (4%), Sharp's Own (4.4%), and Will's Resolve (4.6%). The most recent addition is Eden Ale, brewed to commemorate the exciting Eden Project, it was recently voted Supreme Champion Ale of the Festival at the Cornwall Beer Festival.

Pick of the Pubs

Trengilly Wartha Inn ◎ ◎ ★ ★ 🏠 ♀
Nancenoy TR11 5RP ☎ 01326 340332
📠 01326 340332
e-mail: trengilly@compuserve.com
Dir: *SW of Falmouth*
Situated in a wooded valley close to the Helford River, a friendly and unstuffy family-run inn that appeals to a diverse group of customers including cricket lovers (they even have their own pitch). Bedroom accommodation is divided between six bedrooms in the main house and newer garden rooms, overlooking the inn's own lake, that are suitable for families. The bar menu includes both traditional and more unusual dishes with an emphasis on use of produce sought out by a chef/patron who founded the Food in Cornwall Association. Regularly featured are Cornish pasty, Trengilly sausages, crab cakes and stir-fried Thai pork with hot orange sauce: and seasonal additions include the likes of Cornish fish ceviche topped with crème fraiche, followed by pork fillet with braised black-eyed beans, chicken breast stuffed with sun-dried tomato and Parmesan pesto and Jerusalem artichoke gratin and butternut squash on creamed spinach. Good ale and fine wines; over 50 malt whiskies and a memorable breakfast.
OPEN: 11-3 6.30-11. **BAR MEALS:** L served all week. D served all week 12-2.15 6.30-9.30. Av main course £8.
RESTAURANT: . D served all week 7.30-9.30. Av 3 course à la carte £27. Av 3 course fixed price £27.
BREWERY/COMPANY: Free House.
PRINCIPAL BEERS: Sharps Cornish Coaster, St Austell HSD, Skinners, Exmoor Gold. **FACILITIES:** Children welcome Garden: patio, outdoor eating Dogs allowed.
NOTES: Parking 50. **ROOMS:** 8 bedrooms 7 en suite

Coombe Barton Inn ♦♦♦ ♀
EX23 0JG ☎ 01840 230345 📠 01840 230788
Dir: *S from Bude on A39, turn off at Wainhouse Corner, then down lane to beach*

Historic, family-run free house magnificently situated overlooking a beautiful Cornish bay. Originally built for the 'Captain' of the now-defunct slate quarry. Noted for its char-grilled steaks, Sunday carvery and home-made chef's specials. Home-baked Cornish pasties are a speciality and fresh local crab salad is one of many popular dishes.
OPEN: 11-11. **BAR MEALS:** L served all week. D served all week 11-2.30 6-10. Av main course £6.50. **RESTAURANT:** L served all
continued

week. D served all week 11-2.30 6-10. Av 3 course à la carte £14.
BREWERY/COMPANY: Free House.
PRINCIPAL BEERS: Dartmoor Best, Doom Bar, and 4 guest beers. **FACILITIES:** Children welcome Dogs allowed.
NOTES: Parking 40. **ROOMS:** 6 bedrooms 3 en suite s£30 d£50

CUBERT
Map 02 SW75

The Smuggler's Den Inn
Trebellan TR8 5PY ☎ 01637 830209 ▤ 01637 830580
e-mail: hankers@aol.com
Dir: From Newquay take A3075 to Cubert crossroads, then R, then L signed Trebellan, 0.5m

Nestling in a lovely valley in the heart of the countryside, this 16th-century stone and thatched pub is characterised by its long bar, barrel seats and inglenook woodburner. Family room, beer garden and well-kept ales tapped from the cask are among the many other attractions. Wide range of appetising seafood and prime quality steaks. Options include local butchers' sausages with horseradish mash and onion gravy, cheese and bacon burger and a selection of pasta and hot savoury dishes.
OPEN: 11-3 (Winter 12-2) 6-11. **BAR MEALS:** L served all week. D served all week 12-2 6-9.30. Av main course £8.50.
RESTAURANT: L served all week. D served all week 12-2 6-9.30. Av 3 course à la carte £15. **BREWERY/COMPANY:** Free House.
PRINCIPAL BEERS: Greene King Abbot Ale, Skinners Cornish Knocker, Sharp's Doom Bar, Cotleigh. **FACILITIES:** Children welcome Garden: patio, outdoor eating Dogs allowed Water.
NOTES: Parking 50

DULOE
Map 02 SX25

Ye Olde Plough House Inn
PL14 4PN ☎ 01503 262050 ▤ 01503 264089
e-mail: alison@theploughinn.freeserve.co.uk
Dir: A38 to Dobwalls, take turning signed Looe
Welcoming 18th-century pub with slate floors, wood-burning stoves, settles and old pews. Located in an unspoilt village, the inn is very handy for visiting the coast and exploring the Cornish countryside. Two Jack Russell dogs offer a friendly greeting and four chefs produce a tempting choice of freshly prepared dishes which might include beef Wellington, pheasant with mushroom, tomato and tarragon sauce and fresh scallops in saffron and ginger. Steak can be cooked at the table with your own pre-heated grillstone. Wide choice of starters.
OPEN: 12-2.30 6.30-11 (Sun 7.00-10.30). Closed Dec 25-26.
BAR MEALS: L served all week. D served all week 12-2 6.30-9.30. Av main course £4.95. **RESTAURANT:** L served all week. D served all week 12-2 6.30-9.30. Av 3 course à la carte £15.
continued

BREWERY/COMPANY: Free House.
PRINCIPAL BEERS: Sharps Doom Bar, Butcombe, Bass, Worthington. **FACILITIES:** Children welcome Garden: Food served outside Dogs allowed Water if requested.
NOTES: Parking 20
See Pub Walk on page 75

DUNMERE
Map 02 SX06

The Borough Arms
PL31 2RD ☎ 01208 73118 ▤ 01208 76788
e-mail: Borougharms@aol.com
Dir: From A30 take A389 to Wadebridge, pub approx 1m from Bodmin

The pub is set in stunning countryside, with trout and salmon fishing available close by, directly on the Camel Trail, giving access to over 20 miles of safe off-road cycling, horse-riding and walking. Food options range from steak and ale pie to jacket potatoes, or from hot rolls to amorini and stilton bake. There is a carvery every evening and Sunday lunchtime.
OPEN: 11-11 (Sun 12-10.30). **BAR MEALS:** L served all week. D served all week 12-2.15 6.30-9.15. Av main course £5.50.
RESTAURANT: L served all week. D served all week 12-2.15 6.30-9.15. Av 3 course à la carte £15.
BREWERY/COMPANY: Scottish & Newcastle.
PRINCIPAL BEERS: Bass, Sharps, Boddingtons.
FACILITIES: Children welcome Garden: outdoor eating Dogs allowed Water. **NOTES:** Parking 150

EGLOSHAYLE
Map 02 SX07

The Earl of St Vincent
PL27 6HT ☎ 01208 814807 ▤ 01208 814448
Originally built to house the masons who built the nearby church, this pub dates from the Middle Ages, and has colourful floral displays and a collection of old clocks. The current name comes from Sir John Jervis, the Earl of St Vincent and Nelsons superior officer.

FALMOUTH

Quayside Inn & Old Ale House
Fore St TR11 3JQ ☎ 01326 312113
Offering more than thirty real ales and hosting regular beer festivals, this is a real drinkers pub. Fresh-baked hot rolls in the bar.

FEOCK

The Punch Bowl & Ladle
Penelwey TR3 6QY ☎ 01872 862237
Thatched roadside inn, handy for Trelissick Gardens. Children welcome in restaurant. Open all day in summer.

England

FOWEY
Map 02 SX15

The Ship Inn ♀
Trafalgar Square PL23 1AZ ☎ 01726 832230
▤ 01726 832230
Dir: From A30,take B3269 & A390.
Dating from 1570, the Ship was originally the home of John Rashleigh, who helped defeat the Spanish Armada and brought great riches to Fowey. It is a traditional inn, with a real fire and well kept ales, centrally located in the lovely old seaport. All the food is home-made, featuring Cornish mussels, beer-battered fresh cod, and Fowey Coddle - locally made herb sausages with mash and an ale, leek and mushroom gravy.
OPEN: 11-11 Winter times vary - please telephone.
BAR MEALS: L served all week. D served all week 12-2 6-9.
Av main course £5. **BREWERY/COMPANY:** St Austell Brewery.
PRINCIPAL BEERS: St Austell Tinners Ale, Daylight Robbery.
FACILITIES: Children welcome Dogs allowed. **ROOMS:** 6 bedrooms 1 en suite s£17.50 d£35

GUNNISLAKE
Map 02 SX47

The Rising Sun Inn
Calstock Rd PL18 9BX ☎ 01822 832201 ▤ 01822 832201
Dir: From Tavistock take A390 to Gunnislake, pub is through village and quarter mile on L
Quaint 17th-century pub with glorious gardens and fine views over the Tamar Valley. Cottagey interior featuring a fascinating collection of china, a wide range of real ales, and home-cooked food. Soon to be under new management.

SOUTH WEST COAST PATH
The Cornish coastline has some of the most stunning coastal scenery in Europe. By exploring it on foot you can appreciate its beauty and isolation. Follow the South West Coast Path through Cornwall and you make a journey past wide river estuaries, busy seaside resorts and secret coves. Your walk along the South West Coast Path will pass by many pubs and inns, most of them too tempting to resist! Heading east to west you will find the Ship Inn at Fowey and the Rising Sun at Mevagissey before moving on to St Mawes where you'll find the Rising Sun and the Victory Inn. Continue along the coast to the Ferryboat Inn at Helford Passage and the Shipwrights Arms at Helford, then follow the trail further still to the Cadgwith Cove Inn, the Top House at the Lizard and the Halzephron Inn at Gunwalloe. The Ship at Portleven and the Victoria Inn at Perranuthnoe are worth a visit, as are the Old Coastguard Hotel and the Ship Inn at Mousehole. By the time you reach Treen, near Zennor, you may feel in need of a little sustenance. Try the Gurnards Head Hotel. St Ives is the setting for the historic Sloop, and nearby is Lelant where you'll find the Badger and the Watermill. Heading along the county's northern coast brings you to the Port William at Tintagel and the 16th-century Wellington Hotel at Boscastle.

GUNWALLOE
Map 02 SW62

Pick of the Pubs

The Halzephron Inn ◔
TR12 7QB ☎ 01326 240406 ▤ 01326 241442
Dir: 3m S of Helston on A3083, R to Gunwalloe. Then through village, inn is on L overlooking Mount's Bay.

Quintessentially Cornish, this 500-year old free house is spectacularly situated on the south-west coastal footpath overlooking Mount's Bay. Formerly known as The Ship, the pub remained 'dry' for half a century until 1958, when the licence was restored. Its unusual name comes from the old Cornish Als Yfferin, or Cliffs of Hell, a name borne out by the numerous wrecks along this rugged coast. A shaft still connects the pub to an underground tunnel, thought to have been used by smugglers in years gone by. Modern visitors will find a warm welcome, with real ales and a large selection of malt whiskies. Good quality food is freshly prepared from local ingredients, and served in both the bar areas and the bistro-style restaurant. Expect sea bass or seared scallops, duck leg confit, ratatouille au gratin, or braised lamb with port and redcurrents. Home-made desserts range from meringues with clotted cream to treacle sponge pudding. Overnight accommodation in two delightful en suite, each with stripped pine furniture, tasteful fabrics and decor, and hand-made quilts.
OPEN: 11-2.30 Summer & BHs Open at 6pm 6.30-11 (Sun 12-2.30, 6.30-10.30). Closed 25 Dec. **BAR MEALS:** L served all week. D served all week 12-2 7-9. Av main course £10.
RESTAURANT: L served all week. D served all week 12-2 7-9. Av 3 course à la carte £18.
BREWERY/COMPANY: Free House.
PRINCIPAL BEERS: Sharp's Own & Doom Bar, Tetley.
FACILITIES: Children welcome Garden: patio, outdoor eating, Dogs allowed Water garden only. **NOTES:** Parking 14. **ROOMS:** 2 bedrooms 2 en suite s£38 d£68

GWEEK
Map 02 SW72

The Gweek Inn
TR12 6TU ☎ 01326 221502 ▤ 01326 221502
Dir: 2m E of Helston near Seal Sanctuary
Traditional family run village pub and restaurant, situated at the mouth of the Helford River close to the National Seal Sanctuary. Quiz night every Tuesday all year.

**YE OLDE PLOUGH HOUSE,
DULOE**
PL14 4PN
Tel: 01503 262050
Directions: A38 to Dobwalls,
taking turning signed to Looe.
*Woodburning stoves,
polished Delabole slate
floors, high-backed settles
and interesting, home-
cooked food characterise this
18th-century village pub,
situated within easy reach of
Looe and the coast path.*
Open: 12-2.30, 6.30-11 (Sun
12-3, 7-10.30). Bar Meals:
12-2, 6.30-9.30. Children and
dogs welcome. Garden.
Parking.

(see page 73 for full entry)

*Pub*WALK

Ye Olde Plough
House, Duloe

This peaceful walk explores beautiful woodland and open countryside close to the West Looe River.

On leaving the pub turn left and follow the pavement towards the church. If you wish to visit the ancient stone circle on your left take the short path into the field. At the church, walk across the green to the far end, passing the entrance to Colhender Farm on your left. Walk along the metalled lane and soon descend a steep hill (known locally as 'cardiac hill') into woodland. Bear right at the bottom of the hill and continue along the track to a bridge (Coldrinnick Bridge) over the West Looe River. Just before the bridge, turn right over a small ford and gradually ascend a short incline.

At the top, keep to the main forest track, bearing left to keep the river on your left-hand side. Remain on this track for a mile (1.6km) to a stile and gate. Turn right along the road and walk uphill, passing Tremadart Farm on your right and, in 200 yards (182m), a road junction. Continue back into Duloe and return to the pub.

Distance: 3.5 miles (5.6km)
Map: OS Landranger 201
Terrain: farm lanes, forest.
Paths: woodland paths and metalled lanes
Gradient: one steep descent (pitted track)

*Walk submitted by
Ye Olde Plough House*

HAYLE
Map 02 SW53

The Watermill Inn NEW ♀
Old Coach Rd, Lelant Downs TR27 6LQ ☎ 01736 757912
e-mail: robandnikki@watermill1999.freeserve.co.uk
Dir: From the A30 take the A3074 towards St Ives take L turns at the next two mini Rdbts

This old mill, latterly a restaurant, was converted into a traditional 'local' by new owners in 1999, offering a wide range of real ales, world wines, malt whiskies and good pub food. New for this year is an extension to the bar to provide for live jazz events, and the refurbishment of the upstairs restaurant. Interesting dishes include king prawn and coconut curry, venison haunch steak, and smoked chicken strudel.
OPEN: 11-3 (Jul-Aug 11-11) 6.30-11. **BAR MEALS:** L served all week. D served all week 12-2.45 6.30-9.30. Av main course £6.
RESTAURANT: L served all week. D served all week 12-2.30 6.30-9.30. Av 3 course à la carte £15.
BREWERY/COMPANY: Free House.
PRINCIPAL BEERS: Sharps Doombar. **FACILITIES:** Children welcome Garden: Food served outside Dogs allowed Water.
NOTES: Parking 35

HELFORD
Map 02 SW72

Pick of the Pubs

Shipwright Arms
TR12 6JX ☎ 01326 231235
Dir: A390 through Truro then A39 to Mabe Burnthouse, A394 to Helston, before Goonhilly Down L for Helford
Superbly situated on the banks of the Helford River in an idyllic village, this small thatched pub is especially popular in summer when customers relax on the three delightful terraces, complete with palm trees and glorious flowers, which lead down to the water's edge. Heavy nautical theme inside. Summer buffet offers crab and lobster subject to availablity, alongside various ploughman's lunches, salads, home-made pies, steaks and a wide range of international dishes. Barbecues in summer on the terrace.
OPEN: 11-2.30 6-11. **BAR MEALS:** L served all week. D served all week 12-2 7-9. Av main course £4.75.
RESTAURANT: L served Sun. D served Sun 12-2 7-9. Av 3 course à la carte £14.50. **BREWERY/COMPANY:** Free House. **PRINCIPAL BEERS:** Castle Eden, Greene King IPA. **FACILITIES:** Children welcome Garden: barbecue Dogs allowed

HELFORD PASSAGE
Map 02 SW72

Ferryboat Inn
TR11 5LB ☎ 01326 250625 🖥 01326 250916
e-mail: gav13@tinyworld.co.uk
Dir: From A39 at Falmouth, head toward River Helford
Historic pub and eating house on the Helford River, opposite the ferry that runs daily across the river to Helford village. Used by Montgomery of Alamein as an HQ during the war. St Austell ales and scenic alfresco tables beside the river.

HELSTON
Map 02 SW62

Blue Anchor Inn
50 Coinagehall St TR13 8EX ☎ 01326 562821
🖥 01326 565765
Dir: A30 to Penzance, then Helston signposted
One of the oldest pubs in Britain to brew its own beer, this unpretentious, thatched pub dates from the 15th century when it was a monks' rest home. The inn has also been the haunt of Victorian tin miners, who collected their wages here. Sample excellent 'Spingo' ales in the low-ceilinged bars, tour the brewery, and tuck into a home-made pasty, fish pie, lamb hotpot, or a crusty filled roll. Specials may include braised steak, pork and bean casserole, or lasagne.
OPEN: 11-11 (Sun 12-10.30). **BAR MEALS:** L served all week 12-4. Av main course £2.95. **BREWERY/COMPANY:** Free House. **PRINCIPAL BEERS:** Blue Anchor Middle, Best, Special & Extra Special. **FACILITIES:** Children welcome Garden: Beer Garden: Outdoor Eating Dogs allowed. **ROOMS:** 4 bedrooms 4 en suite s£40 d£44 No credit cards

---

Strange Games
Competition and ingenuity have thrown up a rich variety of pub games besides the best-known ones, from lawn billiards to maggot racing to clay pipe smoking contests, where the object is to keep a pipeful of tobacco alight longest. Cribbage and other once popular card games are not seen so often nowadays, but bagatelle is alive and well in Chester and Coventry. In Knur and Spell up North the players hit a small ball (the knur) as far as possible with a bat. Bat and Trap, an odd variety of cricket, has a long history going back at least to the 16th century in Kent. In Sussex the game of Toad in the Hole involves pitching flat discs into a hole in a table and in Lincolnshire they throw pennies into a hole and call it gnurdling. For all the video games and one-arm bandits, older and more convivial pastimes are still alive in British pubs.

KINGSAND — Map 02 SX45

Pick of the Pubs

The Halfway House Inn
Fore St PL10 1NA ☎ 01752 822279 📠 01752 823146
e-mail: halfway@eggconnect.net
Dir: from either Torpoint Ferry or Tamar Bridge follow signs to Mount Edgcombe

Situated on the coast path and tucked among the narrow lanes and colour-washed house of this quaint fishing village, is the family-run Halfway House Inn, so named as it used to represent the border between Devon and Cornwall and now signifies the dividing line between the conservation villages of Kingsand and Cawsand. The inn, licensed since 1850, has a pleasant stone-walled bar and a small but intimate restaurant, where locally caught seafood is a speciality on the daily blackboard menus, perhaps including grilled bass on seafood rice and chive butter, crab cakes with a Mediterranean-style tomato sauce, and John Dory with Moroccan herbs and spices. Alternatives may feature devilled crab or Caesar salad to start, followed by wild boar and mushroom casserole, pork tenderloin with apples and Calvados and lamb shank with tomatoes and balsamic dressing. Finish with apricot and almond frangipane tart. Modern pine-furnished en suite bedrooms.
OPEN: 12-3 7-11. **BAR MEALS:** L served all week. D served all week 12-2 7-9. Av main course £4.25. **RESTAURANT:** L served all week. D served all week 12-2 7-9. Av 3 course à la carte £12.50. **BREWERY/COMPANY:** Free House.
PRINCIPAL BEERS: Sharp's Doom Bar, Timothy Taylor Landlord. **FACILITIES:** Children welcome Dogs allowed. **NOTES:** Parking 120. **ROOMS:** 6 bedrooms 6 en suite s£27.50 d£55

LAMORNA — Map 02 SW42

Lamorna Wink
TR19 6XH ☎ 01736 731566
Dir: 4m along B3315 towards Lands End, then 0.5m to turning on L
This oddly named pub was one of the original Kiddleywinks, a product of the 1830 Beer Act that enabled any householder to buy a liquor license. Popular with walkers and not far from the Merry Maidens standing stones, the Wink provides a selection of local beers and a simple menu that includes sandwiches, jacket potatoes and fresh local crab.
OPEN: 11-11 (evening food summer only). **BAR MEALS:** L served all week. D served all week 11-3 6-9. Av main course £5.50. **BREWERY/COMPANY:** Greenalls.
PRINCIPAL BEERS: Sharp's Doom Bar, Skinners, Cornish Knocker Ale. **FACILITIES:** Garden: beer garden, Dogs allowed In garden only. **NOTES:** Parking 40 No credit cards

LANLIVERY — Map 02 SX05

The Crown Inn
PL30 5BT ☎ 01208 872707
Dir: From Bodmin take A30 S, follow signs 'Lanhydrock', L at mini r'about .3m take A390, Lanlivery 2nd R
12th-century longhouse with three-foot thick exterior walls, large inglenook fireplace and a priest hole. The Crown was built to accommodate the masons who were building the church opposite, which in turn was frequented by the Black Prince. Food includes fresh fish from the quay.

LELANT

The Badger Inn ♦♦♦♦
Fore St TR26 3JT ☎ 01736 752181 📠 01736 759398
Dir: from rdbt at end of Hayle Bypass take A3074 to St Ives & Carbis Bay
Virginia Woolf stayed at this village inn near Hayle estuary, writing letters in her bedroom. The Badger, built on the site of a blacksmith's shop, is close to St Ives, as well as beaches and protected RSPB tidal flats. The menu offers the best of Cornish produce, with an impressive supply of fresh fish, shellfish and game.

OPEN: 11-2.30 6-11. **BAR MEALS:** L served all week. D served all week 12-2.00 6.30-10. Av main course £8.50.
RESTAURANT: L served all week. D served all week 12-2.00 6.30-10. Av 3 course à la carte £20.
BREWERY/COMPANY: Free House. **PRINCIPAL BEERS:** St Austell HSD. **NOTES:** Parking 30.
ROOMS: 5 bedrooms 5 en suite s£30 d£50

LIZARD — Map 02 SW71

The Top House ♈ NEW
TR12 7NQ ☎ 01326 290974
Dir: From Helston take A3083 to the Lizard
Close to the spectacular granite cliffs bordering Britain's most southerly village, this traditional Cornish local has been run by the Greenslade family for half a century. A fine collection of lifeboat and shipwreck ephemera reinforce the area's maritime heritage. Expect home-made soups and pies, local crab, steaks and grills, followed by Cornish farm ice creams and hot sponge puddings.
OPEN: 11-11 (Sun 12-10.30). **BAR MEALS:** L served all week. D served all week 12-2.30 6.30-9. Av main course £7.
BREWERY/COMPANY: Inn Partnership.
PRINCIPAL BEERS: Flowers IPA, Sharps Doom Bar.
FACILITIES: Children welcome Garden: Food served outside Dogs allowed Water. **NOTES:** Parking 20

England

LOSTWITHIEL
Map 02 SX15

Pick of the Pubs

Royal Oak Inn 🛏 ♀
Duke St PL22 0AQ ☎ 01208 872552 📧 01208 872552
Dir: *From Exeter take A30 to Bodmin then onto Lostwithiel or from Plymouth take A38 towards Bodmin then L onto A390 to Lostwithiel*
In Cornwall's old capital, the 13th-century Royal Oak stands close to the River Fowey. The inn has an underground tunnel reputed to connect the cellar with the dungeons in the courtyard of Restormel Castle. Inside the locals' saloon bar of the Royal Oak you can savour the friendly atmosphere of the place in front of the open log fire. Alternatively, the lounge bar serves as a venue for quieter dining, offering a full à la carte service with a wide selection of wines and real ales. Straightforward lunchtime snacks might feature Cheddar ploughman's, turkey sandwich and deep-fried plaice: main dishes include pork chop, Mrs Hine's curry and fillets of sole stuffed with prawns served with asparagus and white wine sauce.
OPEN: 11-11 (Sun 12-10.30). **BAR MEALS:** L served all week. D served all week 12-2 6.30-9.15. Av main course £7.50. **RESTAURANT:** L served all week. D served all week 12-2 6.30-9.15. Av 3 course à la carte £12.
BREWERY/COMPANY: Free House.
PRINCIPAL BEERS: Bass, Fuller's London Pride, Marston's Pedigree, Sharp's Own. **FACILITIES:** Children welcome Garden: patio, outdoor eating Dogs allowed.
NOTES: Parking 15. **ROOMS:** 6 bedrooms 5 en suite s£37.50 d£63

Ship Inn ♦♦♦♦ 🛏 ♀
Lerryn PL22 0PT ☎ 01208 872374 📧 01208 872614
e-mail: shiplerryn@aol.com
Dir: *3m S of A390 at Lostwithiel*

Dating back to the early 17th century, the Ship has an attractive riverside setting close to some lovely woodland, which makes it ideal for walkers. These riverbanks provided Kenneth Graham with much of the inspiration for 'The Wind in the Willows.' A sample menu includes a variety of pies, fresh fish, a vegetarian selection, steaks and pasta. Rooms are tastefully furnished and all have colour TV.
OPEN: 11.30-3 (Sun 12-3, 7-10.30) 6-11. **BAR MEALS:** L served all week. D served all week 12-2 6.30-9. Av main course £6.50.
RESTAURANT: L served all week. D served all week 12-2 6.30-9. Av 3 course à la carte £13. **BREWERY/COMPANY:** Free House.
PRINCIPAL BEERS: Bass, Sharp's, Skinners, Otter Ale.
FACILITIES: Children welcome Garden: outdoor eating Dogs allowed. **NOTES:** Parking 36. **ROOMS:** 4 bedrooms 4 en suite s£30 d£45

 ★ AA inspected hotel accommodation

LUDGVAN
Map 02 SW53

White Hart
Churchtown TR20 8EY ☎ 01736 740574
Dir: *From A30 take B3309 at Crowlas*
Early 14th-century pub with splendid views across St. Michael's Mount and Bay. An old-fashioned atmosphere means no fruit machines or jukeboxes. A typical menu includes toad-in-the-hole, lasagne, rabbit casserole, and a selection of steaks.
OPEN: 11-2.30 6-11. **BAR MEALS:** L served all week. D served all week 12-2 7-9. Av main course £4.50. **RESTAURANT:** L served all week. D served all week 12-2 7-9. Av 3 course à la carte £8.50. **BREWERY/COMPANY:** Inn Partnership.
PRINCIPAL BEERS: Marston's Pedigree, Flowers, Bass.
FACILITIES: Garden: Food served outside Dogs allowed.
NOTES: Parking 12 No credit cards

MANACCAN
Map 02 SW72

The New Inn NEW ♀
TR12 6HA ☎ 01326 231323
Thatched, cottagey pub deep in Daphne du Maurier country (the original Frenchman's Creek is nearby) that dates back to Cromwellian times when it was known to be 'out of bounds' to his soldiers. Enjoy the peaceful village setting, the large, flower-filled garden, and the homely and traditional bars. Worth finding for fresh fish - monkfish with creamy Pernod sauce, crab cakes with tomato sauce, cod and chips - the wide-ranging sandwich menu and evening favourites like pot-roasted oxtail, lasagne and fillet steak au poivre.
OPEN: 12-3 (Sat-Sun all day in summer) 6-11. **BAR MEALS:** L served all week 12-2.30. Av main course £7.50. **RESTAURANT:** L served all week. D served Mon-Sat 12-2.30 6.30-9.30. Av 3 course à la carte £15. **BREWERY/COMPANY:** Inn Partnership.
PRINCIPAL BEERS: Wadworth 6X, Flowers IPA.
FACILITIES: Children welcome Garden: Food served outside Dogs allowed Very welcome, Water. **NOTES:** Parking 14

METHERELL
Map 02 SX46

Carpenters Arms
PL17 8BJ ☎ 01579 350242
Dir: *From Saltash take A338 to Callington, then A390 to Tavistock, follow signs to pub*
A 15th-century building, originally the carpenter's workshop for Cotehele House, with slate floors, an internal well, original beams and fireplace.

MEVAGISSEY
Map 02 SX04

Rising Sun Inn
Portmellon Cove PL26 6PL ☎ 01726 843235
Superbly situated 17th-century inn next to the beach at Portmellon. The friendly bar has an open fire and the restaurant serves the same choice of home-made dishes, including daily specials such as smoked fish platter, beef in Guinness, and vegetable balti. An unusual facility here is a slipway for launching boats. *continued*

OPEN: 11.30-3 6-11 (closed Oct-Easter). Closed 1 Oct-16 Mar.
BAR MEALS: L served all week. D served all week 12-2 6.30-9.
RESTAURANT: L served all week. D served all week 12-2 6.30-9.
BREWERY/COMPANY: Free House.
PRINCIPAL BEERS: Wadworth 6X, Marston's Pedigree, St Austell
Daylight Robbery. **FACILITIES:** Children welcome patio Dogs
allowed. **NOTES:** Parking 60. **ROOMS:** 7 bedrooms 7 en suite
No credit cards

MITHIAN   Map 02 SW75

Miners Arms
TR5 0QF ☎ 01872 552375
Dir: From A30 take B3277 to St Agnes. Take 1st R to Mithian
Character pub with slate floors, wall paintings, exposed beams
and ornate plasterwork ceilings. Previously used as a
courtroom and a pay house for local miners. Straightforward
bar food includes steak, kidney and oyster pie, chicken
passanda, Sunday roasts, smoked pork sausages and wholetail
scampi.
OPEN: 12-3 6-11. **BAR MEALS:** L served all week. D served all
week 12-2.30 7-9.30. Av main course £6.50.
BREWERY/COMPANY: Greenalls.
PRINCIPAL BEERS: Sharp's Doom Bar & Special, Bass, Courage.
FACILITIES: Children welcome Garden: outdoor eating, patio,
Dogs allowed. **NOTES:** Parking 40

MORWENSTOW   Map 02 SS21

Pick of the Pubs

The Bush Inn
EX23 9SR ☎ 01288 331242
Ancient, historic country inn situated in a isolated cliff-top
hamlet close to bracing coastal path walks. Once a
monastic resting place on the pilgrim route between
Wales and Spain, and later the haunt of local
shipwreckers, the Bush is reputedly one of Britain's oldest
pubs, having been built as a chapel in 950 and becoming
a pub some 700 years later. Unspoilt and traditional
interior, with stone-flagged floors, old stone fireplaces and
a Celtic piscina carved from serpentine and set into one
wall behind the bar. Hearty lunchtime food includes
generously filled sandwiches, pasties and pasta dishes,
and thick soup and home-made stews in winter.
OPEN: 12-3 7-11 (closed Mon). **BAR MEALS:** L served
Mon-Sat 12-2. Av main course £4.
BREWERY/COMPANY: Free House.
PRINCIPAL BEERS: St Austell HSD. **NOTES:** Parking 30
No credit cards

MOUSEHOLE   Map 02 SW42

Pick of the Pubs

The Old Coastguard Hotel ◉ ★ ★ 🛏 ♀
The Parade TR19 6PR ☎ 01736 731222
🖨 01736 731720
e-mail: bookings@oldcoastguardhotel.co.uk
*Dir: A30 to Penzance, take coast road through Newlyn to
Mousehole, pub is 1st building on L*

The 'perfect base to discover Cornwall', with its stylish bar,
restaurant, sun lounge and each of its (non-smoking)
bedrooms sharing spectacular views of Mounts Bay across
the sub-tropical gardens, this is a venue for those in the
know to enjoy some of the county's finest seafood. Market
availability dictates choices such as crab soup with
Parmesan, rouille and toasted ciabatta, followed perhaps
by a mixed fish grill with warm potato, rocket and walnut
salad. Well-tried specialities include mussels and scallops
on herb spaghetti with salsa verde and Thai chicken curry
with a tomato and chilli pickle. Daily specials might add
Nanterrow cheese and olive salad with roast garlic
dressing and braised veal with tomato and thyme, while
some rationalisation of brasserie and dining menus has
produced consistently good dishes such as smoked
haddock fishcakes in lemon butter sauce, butternut
squash and Parmesan risotto with sunflower seeds and a
punchy, nicely-glazed lemon tart.
OPEN: 12-11. **BAR MEALS:** L served all week. D served all
week 12-3 6-9.30. Av main course £8.
BREWERY/COMPANY: Free House.
PRINCIPAL BEERS: Sharp's Doom Bar, Bass.
FACILITIES: Children welcome Garden: outdoor eating
Dogs allowed. **NOTES:** Parking 15. **ROOMS:** 23 bedrooms
22 en suite s£35 d£70 FR£100

Ship Inn ♦♦♦ 🛏
TR19 6QX ☎ 01736 731234
An old-world inn, with low beams and granite floors,
overlooking the harbour. Seafood landed at nearby Newlyn
figures prominently, with dishes such as crab bisque, seafood
platter and fisherman's lunch (smoked mackerel with salad
and brown bread). Other options might be monkfish, John
Dory, or traditional meat specials.
OPEN: 11-11 (Sun 12-10.30). **BAR MEALS:** L served all week.
D served all week 12-2.15 6-9. Av main course £5.
RESTAURANT: L served none. D served all week 6-9. Av 3
course à la carte £16. **BREWERY/COMPANY:** St Austell
Brewery. **PRINCIPAL BEERS:** St Austell's HSD & Tinners Ale,
Tribute. **FACILITIES:** Children welcome Dogs allowed.
ROOMS: 2 bedrooms 2 en suite s£35 d£50

MYLOR BRIDGE   Map 02 SW83

Pick of the Pubs

Pandora Inn ♀
Restronguet Creek TR11 5ST ☎ 01326 372678
▤ 01326 372678
Dir: North of Falmouth off the A39

This medieval thatched pub on the shore of Restronguet
Creek is especially popular with visiting yachtsmen who
call here at high tide. The idyllic location is handy for
Truro, Falmouth and the Lizard, and within easy reach of
some of Britain's most beautiful coastal scenery. Low
wooden ceilings and flagstone floors add to the charm of
the pub's quaint old interconnecting rooms, and intimate
alcoves are just the place for a quiet game of dominoes or
crib. Solid fuel stoves and open log fires drive out the
winter cold, and in summer you can sit out on the
attractive riverside patio or floating pontoon. You'll find
plenty of good home cooking; expect Club sandwiches, as
well as soups, pâté, and beef, pork or game pies. Other
dishes include filled savoury pancakes, Mediterranean fish
stew, plus fresh local crab and mussels. Finish off with
Bakewell tart, apple and raspberry pee or bread-and-
butter
pudding.
OPEN: 11-11 (Sun 12-10.30) Winter 11.30-2.30, 7-11.
BAR MEALS: L served all week. D served all week 12-2.00
7-9.00. **RESTAURANT:** L served none. D served all week
7-9.00. Av 3 course à la carte £20.
BREWERY/COMPANY: St Austell Brewery.
PRINCIPAL BEERS: St Austell Tinners Ale, HSD, Bass.
FACILITIES: Children welcome Patio, food served outside
Dogs allowed Water. **NOTES:** Parking 30

PELYNT   Map 02 SX25

Jubilee Inn ★ ★
PL13 2JZ ☎ 01503 220312 ▤ 01503 220920
e-mail: rickard@jubileeinn.freeserve.co.uk
*Dir: take A390 signpsted St Austell at village of East Taphouse, turn L
onto B3359 signposted Looe & Polperro. Jubilee Inn on left on leaving
Pelynt*
Originally known as the Axe, this 16th-century inn changed its
name in 1887 to celebrate Queen Victoria's Golden Jubilee.
Inside are oak beamed ceilings, blazing winter log fires and
Staffordshire figurines of the Queen and her consort, giving
the place a homely, welcoming feel. Accommodation includes
eleven well appointed en suite bedrooms and a bridal suite.
Local seafood is a popular favourite on both bar and
restaurant menus; alternatives might include steak and Stilton
pie, steak and kidney pudding, and home-made curry.*continued*

OPEN: 12-3 5.30-11. **BAR MEALS:** L served all week. D served
all week 12-2.30 5.30-9.30. Av main course £6.90.
RESTAURANT: L served all week. D served all week 12-2.30
7-9.30. Av 3 course à la carte £15. **BREWERY/COMPANY:** Free
House. **PRINCIPAL BEERS:** Bass. **FACILITIES:** Children
welcome Garden: patio, outdoor eating, BBQ Dogs allowed.
NOTES: Parking 70. **ROOMS:** 11 bedrooms 11 en suite s£32
d£52

PENDOGGETT   Map 02 SX07

The Cornish Arms ♀
PL30 3HH ☎ 01208 880263 ▤ 01208 880335
e-mail: cornisharm@aol.com
*Dir: From A30 Launceston, R onto A395, then L on to A39, then R
onto B3314. pub 7m along this road.*

Atmospheric 16th-century coaching inn a mile or so from the
beautiful and unspoiled Cornish coast. Hidden beaches and
secret coves are just a short walk away and nearby is the
fishing village of Port Isaac where you can watch the catch
being landed.
  Solid beams and stone-flagged floors characterise the pub's
interior and bar food might include sirloin steak, prime beef-
burger and butterfly chicken. Expect honey roast duck breast,
Thai vegetable curry and fillet of sea bass on the daily-
changing restaurant menu.
OPEN: 11-11 (Sun 12-10.30). **BAR MEALS:** L served all week.
D served all week 12-2 6.30-9.00. Av main course £5.
RESTAURANT: L served Sun. D served all week 12-2 7-9. Av 3
course fixed price £19.95. **BREWERY/COMPANY:** Free House.
PRINCIPAL BEERS: Bass, Sharp's Doom Bar.
FACILITIES: Children welcome Garden: outdoor eating Dogs
allowed Water. **NOTES:** Parking 50. **ROOMS:** 8 bedrooms 7 en
suite s£39 d£59

PENZANCE   Map 02 SW43

The Turks Head Inn 🍸
Chapel St TR18 4AF ☎ 01736 363093 📄 01736 363093
e-mail: turkshead@penzance4.fsnet.co.uk
There's a timeless feeling to this historic pub. Much of the
original building was destroyed by a Spanish raiding party in
the 16th century. Charming character interior features old flat
irons, jugs and beams. Sunny flower-filled garden at the rear.
Interesting selection of bar food includes such dishes as beef
and game pie, lamb chops, pheasant and rabbit casserole with
dumplings, lasagne and seafood platter.
OPEN: 11-3 (Sun 12-3) 5.30-11 (Sun 5.30-1030). Closed Dec 25.
BAR MEALS: L served all week. D served all week 11-2.30 6-10.
Av main course £5.50. **RESTAURANT:** L served all week. D
served all week 11-2.30 6-10. Av 3 course à la carte £13. Av 2
course fixed price £6.50. **BREWERY/COMPANY:** Inn
Partnership. **PRINCIPAL BEERS:** Boddingtons, Sharps Cornish
Coaster, Youngs Special. **FACILITIES:** Children welcome
Garden: Beer garden, Food served outside Dogs allowed except
in garden

PERRANUTHNOE   Map 02 SW52

The Victoria Inn NEW ♦♦♦ 🍸
TR20 9NP ☎ 01736 710309 📄 01736 710309
Dir: Take the A394 Helston- Penzance road and turn down to the
village following all the signs for Perranuthnoe
Reputedly the oldest recorded inn in Cornwall, dating back to
the 12th century, this ancient hostelry offers easy access to the
sandy beach and coastal footpath. Inside the pub's wine of the
month is chalked up on a board behind the bar, while the
restaurant exhibits paintings by local artists. A heated patio is
among the attractive garden features. Beef and game pie,
salmon with green bean and avocado salad, and duck breast
with a blueberry jus, are typical examples of the imaginative,
enterprising menu.
OPEN: 12-3 (Jul-Aug open all day) 7-11 (From May Open from
6.30). **BAR MEALS:** L served all week. D served all week 12-2 7-
9. Av main course £10. **RESTAURANT:** L served all week. D
served all week 12-2 7-9. Av 3 course à la carte £18.
BREWERY/COMPANY: PRINCIPAL BEERS: Courage Best,
Bass. **FACILITIES:** Children welcome Garden: Food served
outside Dogs allowed Water. **NOTES:** Parking 10. **ROOMS:** 3
bedrooms 2 en suite s£30 d£45

The George and Dragon

As England's patron saint, St George
figures frequently on inn signs, often with the
dragon whose defeat was his most celebrated
exploit. According to the legend, he killed it to
save a beauiful princess who would otherwise
have been given to the monster. Alternatively,
the George is the jewel of the Order of the
Garter, England's premier order of knighthood,
which was founded by King Edward III in the
14th century. An allied name is the Star and
Garter, which also refers to the order's insignia.
Or again, the George can mean any of the six
kings of that name since the
Hanoverian dynasty succeeded to
the throne.

PHILLEIGH   Map 02 SW83

Pick of the Pubs

The Roseland Inn 🍸
TR2 5NB ☎ 01872 580254 📄 01872 501528
The rural setting in a tiny Cornish village is a delightful one
for this unspoilt, 16th-century cob-built 'gem' peacefully
positioned beside the parish church, 2 miles from the King
Harry Ferry that crosses the River Fal. Outside you will find
a splendid, rose-adorned front terrace - perfect for
summer alfresco meals, while the cottagey interior offers
worn slate floors, lovely old settles, low beams, a roaring
log fire, and a warm welcome. The menu and blackboard
specials cover a range from decent sandwiches,
ploughman's lunches and light snacks or starters like
chicken liver pâté and chargrilled goats' cheese with mixed
leaves and tapenade dressing, to beef and Stilton suet
pudding, shank of lamb braised with cranberry and red
wine, whole Dover sole, cod in beer batter, and Philleigh
crab cakes with tomato and basil dressing. Well worth the
drive from St Mawes or Truro.
OPEN: 11-3 6-11. **BAR MEALS:** L served all week. D served
all week 12-2.15 6-9.30. Av main course £5.95.
RESTAURANT: L served all week. D served all week 12-2.15
6-9. Av 3 course à la carte £15.
BREWERY/COMPANY: Greenalls.
PRINCIPAL BEERS: Sharp's Doom Bar, Ringwood Best,
Bass, Marston's Pedigree. **FACILITIES:** Children welcome
Garden: rose garden, outdoor eating Dogs allowed.
NOTES: Parking 15

POLKERRIS   Map 02 SX05

The Rashleigh Inn 🍸
PL24 2TL ☎ 01726 813991
Dir: off the A3082 outside Fowey
Set in the harbour of a delightful old fishing village, the
Rashleigh is over 250 years old and is on the coastal path
known as 'the Saint's Way'. Daphne du Maurier lived nearby,
and set most of her novels in this area. The bar specialises in
real ale, and may offer over 300 in one year. Specials include
chicken lasagne in a brandy sauce, lamb rosemary or Fowey-
farmed sea trout.
OPEN: 11-3 6-11 (Winter 11.30-2.30, 6.30-10.00).
BAR MEALS: L served all week. D served all week 11-2.30 6-10.
Av main course £6. **RESTAURANT:** L served all week. D served
all week 11-2.30 6.30-10. Av 3 course à la carte £15.
BREWERY/COMPANY: Free House. **PRINCIPAL BEERS:** Bass,
Sharp's Doom Bar, Badger Tanglefoot, Fuller's London Pride.
FACILITIES: Children welcome Garden: outdoor eating Dogs
allowed garden only. **NOTES:** Parking 22

POLPERRO   Map 02 SX25

Old Mill House
Mill Hill PL13 2RP ☎ 01503 272362 📄 01503 272362
e-mail: info@oldmillhouse.i12.com
Stroll through the picturesque streets of Polperro and take a
look at the colourful harbour before relaxing at this delightful
old inn where log fires and a riverside garden enhance the
character of the place, and good home-cooked food and well
kept ales attract diners and drinkers alike. With the emphasis
on fresh fish, the menu offers the likes of local scallops,
smoked mackerel and swordfish steaks, as well as traditional
Cornish pasty, lasagne and steak and kidney pie. *continued*

81

OPEN: 11-11 (Winter open at 12). **BAR MEALS:** L served all week. D served all week 12 12-7. Av main course £6.95. **PRINCIPAL BEERS:** Sharps Eden Ale, Bass, Sharps Special. **FACILITIES:** Children welcome Garden: Food served outside Dogs allowed Water & Bonio. **NOTES:** Parking 8. **ROOMS:** 8 bedrooms 8 en suite s£27.50 d£55

POLRUAN

The Lugger
PL12 6QS ☎ 01726 870007
Waterside pub by Fowey foot-ferry. Great for walkers. St Austell Ales. Open all day.

PORT GAVERNE   Map 02 SX08

Pick of the Pubs

Port Gaverne Hotel 🏨 ★ ★
PL29 3SQ ☎ 01208 880244 📠 01208 880151
e-mail: pghotel@telinco.co.uk
Dir: Signed from B3314, S of Delabole via B3267 on E of Port Isaac

Set back from a spectacular small cove just down the coast from Port Isaac stands the small, family-run hotel that has established a popular following for over 30 years. The flagged floors, beamed ceilings and steep stairways, typical of an old fishing inn, evoke pictures of pirates and contraband. Yet the bar menus, in today's terms, remain a steal - with half-pint pots of prawns and deep-fried fillets of local plaice leading the way on the backboards' daily selections. Bangers and mash with onion gravy, home-made Cornish beef cottage pie and tagliatelle with leeks, mushrooms and Cheddar cheese are hearty enough to satisfy appetites of the many walkers who pass along the Heritage Coast Path: residents are more likely to dine in style on fresh shellfish salad, roast rack of lamb with redcurrant and rosemary gravy and freshly-made desserts such as chocolate torte with blackcurrant sauce and some of 'the clotted stuff'
OPEN: 11-2.30 (Bar open all day in Summer) 6.00-11. Closed Early Jan - Mid Feb. **BAR MEALS:** L served all week. D served all week 12-2.30 6.30-9.30. Av main course £5. **RESTAURANT:** L served Sun only. D served all week 12-2.30 7-9.30. Av 3 course à la carte £24.
BREWERY/COMPANY: Free House.
PRINCIPAL BEERS: Sharp's Doom Bar, Bass, Greene King Abbot Ale. **FACILITIES:** Children welcome Children's licence Garden: patio, outdoor eating Dogs allowed. **NOTES:** Parking 15. **ROOMS:** 16 bedrooms 16 en suite s£35 d£70

PORTHLEVEN   Map 02 SW62

The Ship Inn
TR13 9JS ☎ 01326 564204
17th-century inn built into steep cliffs and approached via a flight of stone steps. Wonderful views over the harbour, especially at night when it is floodlit. Inside is a knocked-through bar with log fires and a family room which has been converted from an old smithy. Popular dishes on the specials board tend to include beef in red wine, sea bass served with fresh vegetables and goats' cheese on pesto toast with gooseberry sauce and salad garnish.
OPEN: 11.30-3 6.30-11 (summer hols 11-11). **BAR MEALS:** L served all week. D served all week 12-2 7-9. Av main course £8.
BREWERY/COMPANY: Free House.
PRINCIPAL BEERS: Courage Best & Directors, Greene King Abbot Ale, Sharp's Doom Bar. **FACILITIES:** Children welcome Garden: Food served outside Dogs allowed

PORTREATH   Map 02 SW64

Basset Arms
Tregea Ter TR16 4NG ☎ 01209 842077 📠 01209 843936
Dir: From Redruth take B3300 to Portreath
Typical Cornish stone cottage, built as a pub in the early 19th century to serve the harbour workers, with plenty of tin mining and shipwreck memorabilia adorning the low-beamed interior.

ST AGNES   Map 02 SW75

Driftwood Spars Hotel ♦ ♦ ♦ ♦ 🏨
Trevaunance Cove TR5 0RT
☎ 01872 552428 / 553323 & 553323 📠 01872 553701
e-mail: driftwoodspars@hotmail.co.uk
Dir: A30 onto B3285, thru St Agnes, down steep hill, L at Peterville Inn, onto rd signed Trevaunance Cove
Atmospheric 17th-century smugglers' inn situated a stone's throw from a superb beach. Stone walls, shipwreck photographs and granite fireplaces characterise the bars, which have many ceiling beams made from the spars of ships wrecked in the Cove. Here you can enjoy home-made pies, smoked fish platter, steak and ale pie, and salmon with dill sauce. Some bedrooms are in the main building, while others are in the annexe across the road.

OPEN: 11-11 (Fri-Sat 11-12, Sun 12-10.30). **BAR MEALS:** L served all week. D served all week 12-2.30 6.30-9.30. Av main course £7. **RESTAURANT:** L served all week. D served all week 12-2.30 6.30-9.30. Av 3 course à la carte £12.
BREWERY/COMPANY: Free House.
PRINCIPAL BEERS: Tetley, Bass, Sharp's Own, St Austell HSD. **FACILITIES:** Children welcome Garden: outdoor eating Dogs allowed. **NOTES:** Parking 80. **ROOMS:** 15 bedrooms 15 en suite s£32 d£64

ST MAWES   Map 02 SW83

Pick of the Pubs

The Rising Sun ◉ ★ ★ 🐷 ♀
The Square TR2 5DJ ☎ 01326 270233
🖳 01326 270198
e-mail: therisingsun@bt.click.com
A magnetic draw to yachtsmen who moor by its quaint 19th-century harbour, St Mawes's central pub on the square is a deservedly popular meeting-place. The hotel is charming and convivial while the all-day bars form a focal-point of village life. Unsurprisingly, locally landed fish plays a major part in the kitchen's daily output, with qualified praise for seared scallops with warm pea purée and mixed sea-foods poached in celery, fennel and saffron broth. Other dishes include roast duck 'nestling' on potato gratin, fish crumble and white crabmeat sandwiches served in the bistro and cellar bar - and in summer on the cobbled patio. Afters, we're informed, have included wonderful coconut ice cream with a hot pudding. Most of the comfortable, recently refurbished bedrooms enjoy lovely views across the harbour and Fal estuary.
OPEN: 11-11 (Sun 12-10.30). **BAR MEALS:** L served all week. D served all week 12-2.30 6.30-9.30. Av main course £6. **RESTAURANT:** D served all week 7-9.30. Av 3 course à la carte £25. **BREWERY/COMPANY:** St Austell Brewery. **PRINCIPAL BEERS:** Hicks Special Draught, St Austell Tinners Ale. **FACILITIES:** Children welcome Garden: patio, BBQ, food served in garden Dogs allowed Water. **NOTES:** Parking 6. **ROOMS:** 8 bedrooms 8 en suite s£30 d£60 FR£90-£180

Pick of the Pubs

The Victory Inn 🐷 ♀ NEW
Victory Hill TR2 5PQ ☎ 01326 270324
🖳 01326 270238
Dir: In centre of village close to the harbour
AA/Sea Fish Industry Authority
Seafood Pub of the Year for the West Country 2002
'Keep it fresh, keep it simple' is chef Rob Dawson's motto at this friendly fishermen's local, situated a stone's throw from St Mawes's bustling harbour, which successfully combines the traditional virtues of a lively village inn with those of a modern dining pub offering the freshest of local seafood. Quality produce is sourced from the best suppliers; scallops, crabs and mackerel come straight from the boats in the harbour, oyster from beds on the Helford River, smoked fish cured in Penryn, samphire and seaweed is gathered from around the coast, and vegetable and cheeses come from Cornish producers. In the bar, tuck into crab bisque with clotted cream and chive, Spanish-style cod with chorizo, potatoes and peppers, grilled sand soles with roasted cumin and lemon butter, and red Thai curry of monkfish and tiger prawns with lime-scented rice. Alternatively, try the treacle-glazed ham with bubble-and-squeak. Good puddings; fixed-price 3-course seafood menu in the upstairs restaurant.
OPEN: 10.30-11 (Sun 12-10.30). **BAR MEALS:** L served all week. D served all week 12-2 7-9. Av main course £7.50. **RESTAURANT:** . D served Sun-Wed 7-9.30. Av 3 course fixed price £29.95. **BREWERY/COMPANY:** Inn Partnership. **PRINCIPAL BEERS:** Marstons Pedigree, Smiles Bitter. **FACILITIES:** Children welcome Garden: Food served outside Dogs allowed

ST MAWGAN   Map 02 SW86

The Falcon Inn ♦♦♦♦ ♀
TR8 4EP ☎ 01637 860225   🖳 01637 860884
e-mail: abanks@cwcom.net
Dir: From A30 8m W of Bodmin, follow signs to Newquay St Mawgan Airport. After 2m turn R into village, pub at bottom of hill

Taking its name from a falcon which, at the time of the Reformation, flew over the village to indicate a secret Catholic church service was being held, this 15th-century pub lies in the sheltered Vale of Lanherne. The dazzling gardens have won many awards and there are attractive terraces and wisteria-covered walls. Comprehensive menu and daily specials range from lemon sole and chilli con carne to lamb steak cooked in its own juices and venison medallions with a port and mushroom sauce. Well equipped bedrooms are individual in style and size.
OPEN: 11-3 6-11. **BAR MEALS:** L served all week. D served all week 12-2 6.30-9.30. Av main course £5. **RESTAURANT:** L served all week. D served all week 12-2 6.30-9.30. Av 3 course à la carte £14. **BREWERY/COMPANY:** St Austell Brewery. **PRINCIPAL BEERS:** St Austell HSD, Trelawneys Pride, & Tinners Ale. **FACILITIES:** Children welcome Garden: Food served outside Dogs allowed Water. **NOTES:** Parking 25. **ROOMS:** 3 bedrooms 2 en suite s£19 d£50

ST MERRYN

The Farmers Arms ♦♦♦ ♀
PL28 8NP ☎ 01841 520303   🖳 01841 520643
Lively pub dating from the 17th century, close to the fishing village of Padstow, in an area popular with holiday-makers and renowned for its beautiful beaches, golf courses and coastal walks. One menu is offered throughout, supported by daily specials, and accommodation is available in four en suite bedrooms.
OPEN: 11-11 (Winter 11-3, 6-11). **BAR MEALS:** L served all week. D served all week 12-2.30 6-9.30. Av main course £6. **RESTAURANT:** L served all week. D served all week 12-2.30 6-9.30. Av 3 course à la carte £9. **BREWERY/COMPANY:** St Austell Brewery. **PRINCIPAL BEERS:** Tinners. **FACILITIES:** Children welcome Children's licence Garden: Food served outside Dogs allowed. **NOTES:** Parking 80. **ROOMS:** 4 bedrooms 4 en suite s£30 d£20

SALTASH   Map 02 SX45

The Crooked Inn ♦♦♦♦ ♀
Stoketon Cottage, Trematon PL12 4RZ ☎ 01752 848177
🖳 01752 843203 e-mail: crookedinn@hotmail.com
16th-century, family-run inn set in 20 acres of gardens and grounds overlooking the lush Lynher Valley. Handy for many

continued

England

of Cornwall's attractions, including Plymouth, St Mellion golf course, wide open moorlands, and secluded beaches. Guests can use the heated pool. The picturesque bar serves steaks, home-made pies, lamb, beef and fish. Rooms are well-equipped, as well as being available all year.

OPEN: 11-3 6-11 (Sat 11-11, Sun 11-10.30). **BAR MEALS:** L served all week. D served all week 12-2.30 6-10.00. Av main course £6. **RESTAURANT:** L served all week. D served all week 12-2.30 6-10. **BREWERY/COMPANY:** Free House. **PRINCIPAL BEERS:** Hicks, Sharp's Eden Ale. **FACILITIES:** Children welcome Garden: outdoor eating, Dogs allowed. **NOTES:** Parking 60. **ROOMS:** 15 bedrooms 15 en suite s£39 d£65 5 family rooms £75-£85

The Weary Friar Inn ◆◆◆
Pillaton PL12 6QS ☎ 01579 350238 📄 01579 350238
Dir: 2m W of A388 between Callington & Saltash
Whitewashed inn with oak-beamed ceilings, an abundance of brass and blazing fires. It is believed to have accommodated the monks who built the 12th-century church next door, before it became a smugglers' hideaway. Typical dishes include pheasant rillets stuffed with chestnut and orange, nut roast with red wine and rosemary sauce, and grilled haddock with capers and lemon butter.

OPEN: 11.30-3 6.30-11 (Sun 12-3, 6-10.30). **BAR MEALS:** L served all week. D served Tue-Sat 7-9. Av 3 course à la carte £15.20. **RESTAURANT:** D served Tue-Sat 7-9. Av 3 course à la carte £15.20. **BREWERY/COMPANY:** Free House. **PRINCIPAL BEERS:** Wadworth 6X, Greene King Abbot Ale, Sharp's Doom Bar, St Austell Dartmoor Best. **FACILITIES:** Garden: patio, outdoor eating, Dogs allowed garden Only. **NOTES:** Parking 30. **ROOMS:** 12 bedrooms 12 en suite d£40 d£50 FR£50.00 (£10.00 extra per child)

Who'd Have Thought It Inn ♀
St Dominic PL12 6TG ☎ 01579 350214
Village free house with beam, open fire, antique furnishings, and lovely views across the Tamar Valley to Plymouth. Handy for Cotehele House (NT). The village of St Dominic is well-known for its strawberries and daffodils.

SENNEN

The Old Success Inn ★ ★
Sennen Cove TR19 7DG ☎ 01736 871232 📄 01736 871232
e-mail: oldsuccess@hotmail.com
Glorious location with tremendous views across Whitesand Bay. Modern, open-plan bar adorned with local seafaring photographs. Popular with the local lifeboat crew. Good area for walking, golf and wildlife. Bedrooms.

TINTAGEL   Map 02 SX08

The Port William ◆◆◆◆ 🍴
Trebarwith Strand PL34 0HB ☎ 01840 770230
📄 01840 770936
Dir: Off B3263 between Camelford & Tintagel
Former harbourmaster's house directly on the coastal path and occupying one of the best locations in Cornwall. Overlooking the beach and glorious coastal scenery at Trebarwith Strand, the building dates back over 300 years to a time when coal was brought ashore here and slate was shipped from Port William, an adjacent cove. Focus on the blackboard for fresh fish, including local crab and lobster, and dishes such as monkfish in tomato and garlic and halibut in cream and mustard. Extensive range of home-made specials varies from beef lasagne and leek and potato pie, to vegetable and lentil bake and ostrich fillet with Dijon mustard, cream and white wine sauce.

OPEN: 11-11 (Sun 12-10.30) 12 opening in winter. **BAR MEALS:** L served all week. D served all week 12-2.30 6-9.30. Av main course £8.50. **RESTAURANT:** L served all week. D served all week 12-2.30 6-9.30. Av 3 course à la carte £15. **BREWERY/COMPANY:** Free House. **PRINCIPAL BEERS:** St Austell Tinners, Hicks, Bass, Boddingtons. **FACILITIES:** Garden: patio overlooking sea, Food served outside Dogs allowed Water. **NOTES:** Parking 75. **ROOMS:** 6 bedrooms 6 en suite s£52 d£69

Tintagel Arms Hotel ◆◆◆◆
Fore St PL34 0DB ☎ 01840 770780
Dir: From M5 take A30- by pass Okehampton & Launceston turn L onto dual Rdbt B395 for North Cornwall follow signs Camelford, hotel opposite Lloyds Bank
250-year-old inn with quaint beamed bedrooms and a Cornish slate roof. Located in one of Britain's most famous villages, close to the remains of the famous castle associated with

continued

legends of King Arthur. The menu in Zorba's Taverna obviously has a Greek influence and includes kebabs and moussaka **OPEN:** 11-2.30 6-11 (Sun 12-2.30, 7-10.30). Closed Jan. **BAR MEALS:** L served all week. D served all week 11.30-2 6-9.30. Av main course £6. **RESTAURANT:** L served ALL. D served ALL 11.30-2 6-9.30. Av 3 course à la carte £12.50. **BREWERY/COMPANY:** Free House. **PRINCIPAL BEERS:** Bass, Sharp's Doom Bar, John Smiths, Courage Directors. **FACILITIES:** Patio, food outside Dogs allowed except guide dogs. **NOTES:** Parking 7. **ROOMS:** 7 bedrooms 7 en suite s£21 d£20

TORPOINT   Map 02 SX45

The Edgcumbe Arms ◆◆◆
Cremyll PL10 1HX ☎ 01752 822294 ▤ 01752 822014
Dir: Please phone for directions
Fine views of the Tamar can be enjoyed from the tables or bow window seats at this refurbished waterside inn situated by the foot ferry from Plymouth. Slate flagstones and plenty of panelling inside. Fresh local seafood, prime beef steaks and home-made pies feature on the varied menu.

TREBURLEY   Map 02 SX37

Pick of the Pubs

The Springer Spaniel 🐕 ♈
PL15 9NS ☎ 01579 370424 ▤ 01579 370113
Dir: On the A388 halfway between Launceston & Callington
Unassuming roadside hostelry set hard beside the A388, recently taken over Colin Phillips who runs The Roseland Inn at Philleigh (qv). Little has changed, this comfortable, warm and friendly pub is still a major attraction to local discerning diners for the above average bar food. The neat parquet-floored main bar has a high-backed settle and two farmhouse-style chairs nestling around a wood-burning stove, rustic tables and a relaxing chatty atmosphere. Separate, civilised beamed dining-room. Blackboards in the bar list the lighter snacks available, namely freshly-filled sandwiches and rolls, decent soups (vegetable and pearl barley broth), salads, pasta dishes, and daily specials like mullet with Moroccan fish stew. Main menu fare includes imaginative and well-presented dishes like venison and game pie, shank of lamb braised with orange, red wine, garlic and rosemary, and decent fishy options - herb-crusted cod with sweet pepper sauce, whole megrim sole with chilli butter. For pudding try the light bread-and-butter pudding.
OPEN: 11-3 5.30-11. **BAR MEALS:** L served all week 12-2 6.30. Av main course £6. **RESTAURANT:** L served all week. D served all week 12-2 7-9. Av 3 course à la carte £15.
BREWERY/COMPANY: Free House.
PRINCIPAL BEERS: St Austell Dartmoor Best & HSD.
FACILITIES: Children welcome Garden: outdoor eating Dogs allowed. **NOTES:** Parking 30

TREGADILLET   Map 02 SX38

Eliot Arms (Square & Compass) ♈
PL15 7EU ☎ 01566 772051
Dir: Turn of A30 for Tregadillett, Bodmin side of Launceston
Granite creeper-clad coaching inn, established 1625 and modernised 1840. An amazing collection of clocks, horsebrasses, cigarette cards and local photographs add interest to the rambling series of rooms. Favourite dishes
continued

---

include seafood pancake mornay, fillet steak Medici, and Eliot pie. A wide range of wines and champagnes by the glass is a popular feature.
OPEN: 11-3.00 6-11. **BAR MEALS:** L served all week. D served all week 12-2 7-9. **RESTAURANT:** L served all week 12-2 7-9. Av 3 course à la carte £15.
BREWERY/COMPANY: Free House.
PRINCIPAL BEERS: Sharp's Eden & Doom Bar, Courage Best & Directors. **FACILITIES:** Children welcome Dogs allowed.
NOTES: Parking 20. **ROOMS:** 3 bedrooms 2 en suite s£45 d£50

TRESCO   Map 02 SW17

Pick of the Pubs

The New Inn ◉ ★ ★ 🐕 ♈
New Grimsby TR24 0QQ ☎ 01720 422844
▤ 01720 423200
e-mail: newinn@tresco.co.uk
Dir: by New Grimsby Quay
At the Heart of England's Island of Flowers, the Tresco Estate's lovely quayside hotel and inn continues to blossom. Of the beautifully appointed bedrooms, fully half have fine ocean views out to the Atlantic, while the beer gardens and slate-roofed pavilion overlooking New Grimsby harbour are both a vital part of island life and a perennial summer draw. Bar lunch and evening bistro menus are a model of consistency with fresh fish at the fore, caught locally or landed at Newlyn. Blackboard specials list, in turn, local monkfish with Oriental noodles, wild Cornish sea bass with warm potato salad and John Dory fillets with Puy lentils and seasonal vegetables. The simplest lunches combine sandwich choices with home-made fresh soup, hand-made pasties from St Martins bakery and New Inn burgers of Tresco beef. Evening chargrills include five spice tuna steak, halibut with aïoli and steaks with chosen accompaniments. A special treat remains the peerless seafood platter for one or two people. A family team prides itself on high quality service and products, with the motto 'Arrive as a customer; return as a friend'.
OPEN: 11-11 (Nov-Feb 12-2.30, 7-11). **BAR MEALS:** L served all week. D served all week 12-2 7-9.
RESTAURANT: . D served all week 7-9. Av 4 course fixed price £26.50. **BREWERY/COMPANY:** Free House.
PRINCIPAL BEERS: St Austell Cornish IPA, Daylight Robbery. **FACILITIES:** Children welcome Garden: patio, outdoor eating. **ROOMS:** 14 bedrooms 14 en suite s£80.60 d£124

TRURO   Map 02 SW84

Old Ale House
7 Quay St TR1 2HD ☎ 01872 271122 ▤ 01872 223257
Dir: A30, Truro City centre
Olde-worlde establishment with a large selection of real ales on display. Lots of attractions, including live music and various quiz and games nights. Food includes huge hands of hot bread, oven-baked jacket potatoes, ploughman's lunches and daily specials. Spice Island chicken, seafood paella and Cantonese prawns feature among the sizzling skillets.
OPEN: 11-11 (Sun 12-10.30). Closed Dec 25. **BAR MEALS:** L served all week. D served Mon-Fri 12-3 7-9. Av main course £5.
BREWERY/COMPANY: PRINCIPAL BEERS: Skinners Kiddlywink, Courage Directors, Bass, Wychwood The Dog's Bollocks. **FACILITIES:** Children welcome

England

TRURO continued

The Wig & Pen Inn & Olivers Restaurant 🐑 ♀
Frances St TR1 3DP ☎ 01872 273028 📠 01872 273028
Dir: City centre nr Law Courts
City centre listed pub, originally known as the Star. It became the Wig & Pen when the county court moved to Truro. Good quality food is offered, with dishes ranging from grilled fillets of plaice and West Country saddle of lamb to pan-fried breast of duck and puff pastry case filled with stir-fried vegetables and tomato and garlic essence.
OPEN: 11-11 (Sun 12-10.30). **BAR MEALS:** L served all week. D served all week 12-3 6-9. Av main course £5.95. **RESTAURANT:** L served Tue-Sat. D served Tue-Sat 12-2 7-9. Av 3 course à la carte £22. Av 3 course fixed price £22. **BREWERY/COMPANY:** St Austell Brewery. **PRINCIPAL BEERS:** St Austell Tinners Ale & HSD. **FACILITIES:** Children welcome Garden: patio, BBQ, outdoor eating

VERYAN   Map 02 SW93

The New Inn ♀
TR2 5QA ☎ 01872 501362 📠 01872 501078
e-mail: jgayton@btclick.com
Dir: Off A3078 towards Portloe
Unspoilt village pub, based on a pair of 16th-century cottages, with a single bar, open fires and a beamed ceiling. The emphasis is on home cooking, with dishes such as casserole of duck with forest mushrooms, supreme of baked salmon with hollandaise sauce, coq au vin or braised beef and walnuts, all served with fresh local vegetables.
OPEN: 12-3 (Winter Mornings 12-2.30) 6.30-11. **BAR MEALS:** L served all week. D served Mon-Sat 12-2 7-9. Av main course £8. **BREWERY/COMPANY:** St Austell Brewery.
PRINCIPAL BEERS: St Austell HSD & Tinners Ale.
FACILITIES: Children's licence Garden: patio, outdoor eating.
ROOMS: 3 bedrooms 2 en suite s£22.50 d£45

WADEBRIDGE   Map 02 sw97

The Quarryman Inn 🐑
Edmonton PL27 7JA ☎ 01208 816444 📠 01208 815674
Dir: off A39 opp Royal Cornwall Showground

Friendly 18th-century inn that evolved from a courtyard of quarrymen's cottages. Handy for the Royal Cornwall Showground and the Camel Trail. Among the many features at this unusual pub are a small health club and several bow windows, one of which includes a delightful stained-glass quarry-man panel. Expect prime Aberdeen Angus steaks, fresh locally-caught fish, home-made pies, curries and pasta on the menu.
OPEN: 12-11. **BAR MEALS:** L served all week. D served all week 12-3 6-9. Av main course £6.50. **RESTAURANT:** L served all week. D served all week 12-3 6-9. Av 3 course à la carte £15. **BREWERY/COMPANY:** Free House. *continued*

PRINCIPAL BEERS: Sharps, Skinners, Timothy Taylor Landlord. **FACILITIES:** Garden: outdoor eating, Patio Dogs allowed Water. **NOTES:** Parking 100

Swan Hotel ♦♦♦♦
9 Molesworth St PL27 7DD ☎ 01208 812526
📠 01208 812526
Recently refurbished town centre hotel, where an antique fair is held every Monday in the function room. The beer garden is the venue for both barbecues and afternoon snacks, while the bar menu offers an extensive range of home-cooked dishes prepared from locally sourced ingredients - fish and chips, steaks, and liver and bacon.
OPEN: 11-11. **BAR MEALS:** L served all week. D served all week 12-2 6.30-8. Av main course £5. **BREWERY/COMPANY:** St Austell Brewery. **PRINCIPAL BEERS:** St Austell: Hicks, Tinners, Tribute & guest ale. **FACILITIES:** Children welcome. **NOTES:** Parking 4. **ROOMS:** 6 bedrooms 6 en suite s£32 d£45 1 family room £50-£71

ZENNOR   Map 02 SW43

Pick of the Pubs

The Gurnards Head Hotel ♀ NEW
Treen, Zennor TR26 3DE ☎ 01736 796928
📠 01736 795313
e-mail: enquiries@gurnardshead.free-online.co.uk
An imposing, colour-washed building that dominates the coastal landscape above Gurnard's Head, this traditional Cornish pub with its stone-flagged bar and open fires is just the place to get stranded on a wind-swept winter's night! This can be Cornwall at its harshest and most brutal; but, on warmer days, there are some great walks along the coast path or the rugged Penwith Moors, studded with wild flowers and ancient Celtic remains. As you'd expect, there's plenty of local seafood on the menu, from smoked fish medley or Cornish seafood broth, to grilled fillets of Gurnard on leek and potato galette with a white wine sauce. Other options include chorizo sausages on basil mash, local salami, or special bread-and-butter pudding with clotted cream. The vegetarian selection also offers a regular dish of the day, and there's a decent wine list featuring wines of the month by the bottle or glass.

OPEN: 12-3 (all day in Aug 12-11) 6-11. **BAR MEALS:** L served all week. D served all week 12-2.30 6.30-9.15. Av main course £9. **RESTAURANT:** L served all week. D served all week 12-2.30 6.30-9.15. Av 3 course à la carte £17. **BREWERY/COMPANY:** Free House.
PRINCIPAL BEERS: Flowers Original & IPA, Skinners Knocker Ale, Fullers London Pride. **FACILITIES:** Garden: Food served outside Dogs allowed Water. **NOTES:** Parking 60. **ROOMS:** 6 bedrooms 6 en suite d£50

England

CUMBRIA

AMBLESIDE   Map 11 NY30

Pick of the Pubs

Drunken Duck Inn 🏵 ◆◆◆◆ 🍽 ♀
Barngates LA22 0NG ☎ 015394 36347
📷 015394 36781
e-mail: info@drunkenduckinn.co.uk
AA Pub of the Year for England 2002.
See Pick of the Pubs on page 93

White Lion Hotel ◆◆◆ ♀
Market Place LA22 9DB ☎ 015394 39901
📷 015394 39902
Right in the heart of town, this Lakeland inn is superbly placed for both the tourist and business traveller. Spacious bedrooms; varied bar menu.
OPEN: 11-11. **BAR MEALS:** L served all week. D served all week 12-9. Av main course £7.50. **BREWERY/COMPANY:** Bass. **PRINCIPAL BEERS:** Bass, Worthington. **FACILITIES:** Children welcome Garden: outdoor eating, BBQ Dogs allowed. **NOTES:** Parking 9. **ROOMS:** 7 bedrooms 5 en suite s£25 d£45 FR£55.00-£65.00

APPLEBY-IN-WESTMORLAND   Map 11 NY62

The New Inn
Brampton Village CA16 6JS ☎ 017683 51231
At the heart of Brampton village with splendid Pennine views, a charming 18th-century inn with oak beams and an original range. One menu serves the bar and dining room with all home-cooked fare, from regulars like steak and ale pie and Cumberland sausage to specials of battered squid, and salmon and mushroom tagliatelle. Tempting sweets include steamed chocolate pudding with a chocolate cream sauce.
BAR MEALS: L served all week. D served all week 12-1.45 7-8.45. Av main course £7. **RESTAURANT:** L served all week. D served all week 12-2.30 7-8.45. Av 3 course à la carte £12.
BREWERY/COMPANY: Free House.
PRINCIPAL BEERS: Black Sheep, Charles Wells Bombardier, John Smiths. **FACILITIES:** Children welcome Children's licence Garden: outdoor garden, BBQ Dogs allowed. **NOTES:** Parking 16. **ROOMS:** 3 bedrooms s£23.50 d£22.50 No credit cards

Pick of the Pubs

The Royal Oak Inn ★ ★ ♀
Bongate CA16 6UN ☎ 017683 51463   📷 017683 52300
e-mail: m.m.royaloak@btinternet.com
Dir: *M6 J38 take A66 east .Village on B6542 on R.*
A modernised coaching inn, dating in parts back to 1100, that is popular with locals and tourists alike; bedroom accommodation renders it especially popular as a touring base for the Yorkshire Dales and the Lake District. Its well maintained character interior comprises a classic tap-room with blackened beams, oak panelling and an open fire, a comfortable beamed lounge and two dining rooms. Specials served throughout on a daily basis include home-made soups and desserts, Sunday lunches and vegetarian options. Items on the monthly menus are likely to include creamed smoked haddock pancake and Black Isle mussels to start, followed by Mrs Ewbank's secret-recipe sausages, baked cod with pancetta and garlic oil, lentil, red pepper and mushroom lasagne and Bongate beef and ale pie. The beer choice is, in fact, extensive as is the choice from some 50 malt whiskies.

OPEN: 11-11 (Sun 12-10.30). **BAR MEALS:** L served all week. D served all week 12-2.30 6-9. **RESTAURANT:** L served all week. D served all week 12-2.30 6-9.
BREWERY/COMPANY: Free House.
PRINCIPAL BEERS: Bates Biter, Black Sheep Bitter, Theakston Best Bitter, John Smiths. **FACILITIES:** Children welcome Garden: Terrace at front, outdoor eating Dogs allowed only allowed in bedrooms. **NOTES:** Parking 12. **ROOMS:** 9 bedrooms 9 en suite s£33 d£72 FR£105

THE DALES WAY

Heading for Ribblehead, the 84-mile Dales Way crosses windswept hills and tracts of rugged moorland deep in Pennine adventure country. This is a harsh environment of wild summits and high, breathtaking fells that seems a world away from the softer, more intimate surroundings of the lower Dales. After the long haul, savour a rewarding pint and something to eat perhaps at the Sun Inn in historic Dent, the only village in Dentdale. Next, make for the Dalesman Country Inn in the busy little town of Sedbergh, acknowledged as the western gateway to the Yorkshire Dales. Beyond the M6, the walk skirts Kendal, but you might like to visit the town and take a break at the aptly-named Gateway Inn in Crook Road. Continuing across country, the Dales Way finally comes to a halt at Bowness on the shores of Lake Windermere.

England

APPLEBY-IN-WESTMORLAND continued

Pick of the Pubs

Tufton Arms Hotel ⊛ ★ ★ ★ ♀
Market Square CA16 6XA ☎ 017683 51593
▤ 017683 52761
e-mail: info@tuftonarmshotel.co.uk
Solidly-built Victorian coaching inn at the heart of the old county town of Appleby-in-Westmorland - 'the place of the apple tree' - and now a popular base for tourists, anglers and ramblers. The glorious Eden valley boasts a complex network of walks in idyllic countryside and the Lake District and Yorkshire Dales National Parks are within easy reach. The family-run Tufton Arms is stylishly furnished with a smart conservatory restaurant overlooking a cobbled mews courtyard, and the impressive menu uses fresh local produce, including meat, game, fish and seafood. Expect fish pie, ham salad, rump steak and traditional lasagne in the bar, while the imaginative dinner menu offers hot pot of chicken livers and smoky bacon flamed in brandy with mustard and cream, followed by sea bass with braised fennel and a tomato and basil sauce, and rack of lamb with duchesse potatoes flavoured with red onion marmalade. Smart, well appointed en suite bedrooms.
OPEN: 11-3 6-11. **BAR MEALS:** L served all week. D served all week 12-2 7-9. Av main course £5. **RESTAURANT:** L served all week. D served all week 12-2 7-9. Av 3 course à la carte £22.50. **BREWERY/COMPANY:** Free House. **PRINCIPAL BEERS:** Tufton Arms Ale, Tetley. **FACILITIES:** Children welcome Dogs allowed. **NOTES:** Parking 15. **ROOMS:** 21 bedrooms 21 en suite s£55 d£90 FR£125-£145

ARMATHWAITE
Map 11 NY54

The Dukes Head Hotel ♀
Front St CA4 9PB ☎ 016974 72226
e-mail: HH@hlynch.freeserve.co.uk
Dir: A6, turn at Armathwaite turning
First used as a pub during the building of the Settle to Carlisle Railway, the establishment is named after Queen Victoria's son, the dissolute Duke of Clarence. The Lynch family has run it for 13 years, and they welcome walkers, climbers, anglers, and all who appreciate comfort and courtesy. Cumbrian produce is a feature of the menu, including roast duck, baked salmon with leeks and vermouth, and fell-bred sirloin steak.
OPEN: 12-3 5.30-11. Closed 25th dec. **BAR MEALS:** L served all week. D served all week 12-2 6.15-9. Av main course £7. **RESTAURANT:** L served all week. D served all week12-2 6.15-9. Av 3 course à la carte £14. **BREWERY/COMPANY:** Pubmaster. **PRINCIPAL BEERS:** Marston's Pedigree. **FACILITIES:** Children welcome Garden: Outdoor eating Dogs allowed Back bar only, Water. **NOTES:** Parking 30. **ROOMS:** 5 bedrooms 3 en suite s£28.50 d£48.50
See Pub Walk on page 91

ASKHAM
Map 11 NY52

The Punchbowl Inn
CA10 2PF ☎ 01931 712443 ▤ 01931 712374
Dir: From M6 N on A6 for 7m
An-easy-to-find haven in a beautiful Cumbrian village, this 16th-century coaching inn offers the best in old world charm and hospitality. There is a good choice of starters and light lunches, while more substantial dishes include marinated local pheasant,
continued

grilled tuna steak, wild duck breast or rabbit casserole.
OPEN: 12-3 5.30-11. **BAR MEALS:** L served all week. D served all week 12-2 6-9. **RESTAURANT:** L served all week. D served all week 12-2 6-9. Av 3 course fixed price £12. **PRINCIPAL BEERS:** Whitbread Castle Eden Ale, Wadworth 6X, Flowers IPA, Greene King Old Speckled Hen. **FACILITIES:** Children welcome Children's licence Garden: Dogs allowed. **NOTES:** Parking 30. **ROOMS:** 6 bedrooms 6 en suite s£28.50 d£53 FR£68.00

The Queen's Head
Lower Green CA10 2PF ☎ 01931 712225
Built in 1682, this welcoming village inn has neat lounges and open fires. Children welcome, games room, good garden, bedrooms. Daily changing specials board. This pub is a good base for walking, golf and birdwatching.

BARBON
Map 08 SD68

The Barbon Inn
LA6 2LJ ☎ 015242 76233 ▤ 015242 76233
Dir: 3.5m N of Kirkby Lonsdale on A683
A 17th-century coaching inn with oak beams and open fires, situated in a quiet village between the lakes and dales. Popular bar meals are smoked salmon baguette and Morecambe Bay shrimps; more substantial dishes include Lakeland lamb casserole, roast breast of duck, and halibut steak.
OPEN: 12-3 6.30-11. **BAR MEALS:** L served all week. D served all week 12-2 6.30-9. Av main course £5.50. **RESTAURANT:** L served all week. D served all week 12.30-2 7.30-9. Av 3 course à la carte £16.50. **BREWERY/COMPANY:** Free House. **PRINCIPAL BEERS:** Theakston. **FACILITIES:** Children welcome Garden: outdoor eating, Dogs allowed. **NOTES:** Parking 6. **ROOMS:** 10 bedrooms 10 en suite s£35 d£60 FR£75

BASSENTHWAITE
Map 11 NY23

The Pheasant ♀
CA13 9YE ☎ 017687 76234 ▤ 017687 76002
e-mail: Pheasant@easynet.co.uk
Dir: A66 to Cockermouth, 8m N of Keswick on L

Old coaching inn close to Bassenthwaite Lake, with an inglenook fireplace in the lounge. There is a light lunch menu available throughout the inn, and a fixed-price menu for lunch and dinner in the restaurant. Typical offerings are Cumberland smoked ham and local rainbow trout.
OPEN: 11.30-2.30 5.30-10.30. Closed Dec 25. **BAR MEALS:** L served all week 12-2. Av main course £6.50. **RESTAURANT:** L served all week. D served all week 12.30-2 7-9. Av 3 course à la carte £25. Av 3 course fixed price £21.95. **BREWERY/COMPANY:** Free House. **PRINCIPAL BEERS:** Theakston, Bass, Jennings Cumberland. **FACILITIES:** Garden: Food served outside Dogs allowed. **NOTES:** Parking 50. **ROOMS:** 16 bedrooms 16 en suite s£60 d£90

Pub**WALK**

Dukes Head Hotel, Armathwaite

DUKES HEAD, ARMATHWAITE
Front Street CA4 9PB
Tel: 016974 72226
Directions: A6, turn at Armathwaite turning
First used as a pub during the building of the Settle to Carlisle Railway, this unpretentious and welcoming village pub enjoys a beautiful setting in the Eden Valley. Good menu featuring local produce. Bedrooms.
Open: 12-3, 5.30-11. Bar Meals: 12-2, 6.15-9. Children and dogs welcome. Garden. Parking
(see page 90 for full entry)

From peaceful riverbank paths to gently undulating bridleways, this beautiful walk explores the serene, rolling landscape of the Eden Valley, and offers extensive views to the Pennines.

Turn right on leaving the pub and cross the bridge over the River Eden. Immediately across the bridge, descend steps on your left to a stile and follow the footpath under the bridge. Walk along the riverbank and continue through an avenue of mature beech and oak trees. At some rapids, turn left then right to follow a higher path. On reaching a fence on your left, follow the path uphill (Optional - for a fine view along the river keep ahead at the fence for 55 yards (50m) and return). Bear right on reaching a stile in the fence, the path soon widens and heads towards one of the Eden sandstone sculptures (ideal picnic spot and beautiful views). Continue on the wide forest track through Coombs Wood and ascend to a stile and road.

Turn left for 164 yards (150m), then turn right (telephone box), signed to Longdales. Shortly, just past Longdale Cottages, take the bridleway on the right and continue with extensive Pennine views to a road. Turn right and bear right at the next junction, keeping the Methodist Chapel on your right. Continue into Ainstable. Turn left at the crossroads and soon take the road on your left leading to Ainstable Church. Climb steeply and go through the kissing-gate into the churchyard. Follow the churchyard wall to a further kissing-gate and turn left. Head downhill, keeping the fence on your left, climb two stiles and go through a gate to a road.

Cross straight over to join a footpath beside a cottage. Beyond a metal gate, keep straight on beside a fence, then a wall on your right to a stile. Maintain direction beside the wall to a gate and continue ahead to reach a stile to the left of a gate. Turn left along a track, then left again on reaching a road. At the far side of a bridge over a stream, take the path on your right and walk along the riverbank to the bridge in Armathwaite. Retrace steps back to the pub.

Distance: 6 miles (10km)
Map: OS Landranger 86
Terrain: riverbank, fields and woodland; can be muddy in winter
Paths: footpaths, bridleways; some road walking
Gradient: Easy. Few steep climbs; suitable for familes

Walk submitted by:
Brian & Pat Porter

England

BEETHAM

Map 08 SD47

Pick of the Pubs

The Wheatsheaf Hotel ⛼
LA7 7AL ☎ 015395 62123 ▤ 015395 64840
e-mail: munrowheatsheaf@compuserve.com

See Pick of the Pubs on page 95

BLENCOGO

Map 11 NY14

The New Inn
CA7 0BZ ☎ 016973 61091 ▤ 016973 61091
e-mail: jez132@ukonline.co.uk
Dir: *From Carlisle, take A596 towards Wigton, then B5302 towards Silloth. After 4M Blencogo signed on L*
A late Victorian sandstone pub in a farming hamlet with superb views of the north Cumbrian fells and Solway Plain. Popular dinner menu ranges from roast duckling, grilled Cumberland sausage, rainbow trout with black butter, topside of Cumbrian beef, to scampi and mixed grills.
BAR MEALS: L served Sun. D served Thu-Tue 12-1.30 7-9. Av main course £10. **RESTAURANT:** L served Sun. D served Thu-Tue 7-9. **BREWERY/COMPANY:** Free House.
PRINCIPAL BEERS: Black Sheep, Yates, Timothy Taylor Landlord. **FACILITIES:** Garden: Beer garden, Patio. **NOTES:** Parking 50

BOOT

Map 11 NY10

The Burnmoor Inn ⛼
CA19 1TG ☎ 019467 23224 ▤ 019467 23337
e-mail: stay@burnmoor.co.uk
A traditional 16th-century inn which, not suprisingly, given its position at the foot of Scafell Pike, attracts many hill walkers. Also handy for the popular Ravenglass and Eskdale Steam Railway. Sheltered front lawn for summer days, while in the beamed bar a fire burns all day. The extensive menu features local produce, with meat from the valley and fish from the lakes. Expect salmon fillet parcel, three bean chilli, game pie cooked in brandy, red wine and herb sauce, and chicken and bacon salad. Good choice of local beers and a well-stocked wine cellar.
OPEN: 11am-11pm. **BAR MEALS:** L served all week. D served all week 11-5 6-9. Av main course £6. **RESTAURANT:** . D served all week 6-9. Av 3 course à la carte £17.50. Av 3 course fixed price £17.50. **BREWERY/COMPANY:** Free House.
PRINCIPAL BEERS: Jennings Cumberland, Black Sheep Bitter, Barngates Cracker Ale & Taglag. **FACILITIES:** Children welcome Children's licence Garden: patio, outdoor eating Dogs allowed dog blankets, water. **NOTES:** Parking 50. **ROOMS:** 9 bedrooms 9 en suite s£26 d£52 FR£60.00-£80.00

BOUTH

Map 08 SD38

The White Hart Inn
LA12 8JB ☎ 01229 861229
17th-century former coaching inn located in a quiet village at the heart of South Lakeland and surrounded by woods, fields and fells. Look out for plenty of bric-à-brac, including farm tools and long-stemmed clay pipes. Six cask real ales are available and the menu offers fresh food made to order. A typical menu might include Cumberland sausage, rare breed sirloin steaks, lamb Henry and chicken Balti.
OPEN: 12-2 (12-11 Sat & Sun) 6-11 (Mon & Tue 6-11 only).
BAR MEALS: L served Wed-Sun. D served all week 12-2 6-8.45.

continued

Av main course £7.95. **RESTAURANT:** L served Wed-Sun. D served all week 12-2 6-8.45. Av 3 course à la carte £15.
BREWERY/COMPANY: Free House.
PRINCIPAL BEERS: Black Sheep, Jennings Cumberland Ale, Barnsley, Boddingtons. **FACILITIES:** Children welcome Garden: Food served outside. **NOTES:** Parking 30. **ROOMS:** 4 bedrooms 2 en suite s£26 d£36 No credit cards

BRAITHWAITE

Coledale Inn ⛼
CA12 5TN ☎ 017687 78272
Dir: *From M6 J50 take A66 towards Cockermouth for 18 miles. Turn to Braithwaite then on towards Whinlatter Pass, follow sign on L, over bridge leading to hotel*
Set in a fine spot at the foot of Whinlatter Pass, this traditional pub is very popular with walkers. Terrace, garden and play area. Bedrooms.

BRAMPTON

Map 11 NY56

The Abbey Bridge
Lanercost CA8 2HG ☎ 016977 2224
17th-century riverside inn close to Lanercost Abbey. Selection of guest ales. Bedrooms.

Blacksmiths Arms ◆◆◆ ⛼
Talkin Village CA8 1LE ☎ 016977 3452 ▤ 016977 3396
Dir: *from M6 take A69 E, after 7m straight over rdbt, follow signs to Talkin Tarn*

Close to Talkin Tarn country park and handy for visiting Hadrian's Wall, the Borders and the Lake District. Attractive village inn, originally the local blacksmith's forge. Good, well-balanced menu and blackboard specials offer a variety of dishes. Try chicken and mushroom pie, fresh local trout, medallions of beef or salmon steak. Comfortable, attractive bedrooms have been thoughtfully equipped and furnished.
OPEN: 12-3 6-11 (Sun 12-3, 6-10.30). **BAR MEALS:** L served all week. D served all week 12-2 6.30-9. Av main course £7.50.
RESTAURANT: L served all week. D served all week 12-2 6.30-9. Av 3 course à la carte £12.50. **BREWERY/COMPANY:** Free House. **PRINCIPAL BEERS:** Black Sheep, John Smiths, Boddingtons. **FACILITIES:** Children welcome Children's licence Garden: outdoor eating Dogs allowed except in garden. **NOTES:** Parking 20. **ROOMS:** 5 bedrooms 5 en suite s£30 d£22.50 family room £50

We endeavour to be as accurate as possible but changes in personnel and data can occur in establishments after the guide has gone to press

AA PUB OF THE YEAR 2002

OPEN: 11.30-11 (Sun 12-10.30).
BAR MEALS: L served all week.
D served all week 12-2.30 6-9.
Av main course £9.25
RESTAURANT: D served all week
6-9. Av 3 course a la carte £22.
BREWERY/COMPANY:
Free House.
PRINCIPAL BEERS: Jennings
Bitter, Barngates Cracker Ale, Tag
Lag & Chesters Strong & Ugly.
FACILITIES: Garden: terrace
outdoor eating Dogs allowed
NOTES: Parking 40.
ROOMS: 11 bedrooms 11 en suite
d£85-£140.

The Drunken Duck Inn

⌖ ◆◆◆◆ 🦆 ♀
Barngates LA22 0NG
☎ 015394 36347 📄 015394 36781
e-mail: info@drunkenduckinn.co.uk
Dir: A592 from Kendal, follow signs for
Hawkshead, 2.5m sign for inn on R, 1m
up the hill.

With its own fishing tarn, micro-brewery and some of the best
Lakeland views to be enjoyed from a pub, this 17th-century
inn stands high in the hills at a country crossroads close to the
famous beauty spot of Tarn Hows, and looks across distant
Lake Windermere to its backdrop of craggy fells.

Memorable summer evenings can be spent enjoying a pint on the
front verandah which makes the most of the stunning view. Its unusual
name dates back to when a Victorian landlady found her ducks lying in
the road, presumably dead. As she started to pluck them she soon realised that they were drunk not dead, having
consumed beer that had seeped from a barrel to their feeding ditch. Ducks dabbling on the tarn behind the pub
may well meet a similar fate today, as the inn's own brewery - Barngates Brewery - produces some fine ales, notably
Cracker Ale and the more heady Chester's Strong & Ugly.

Good food ranges from interesting ciabatta sandwiches, pâtés,
pasta dishes and steak and red wine pie at lunchtime, to more
imaginative and adventurous evening fare, served throughout the
bar and the informal candlelit restaurant. Expect stir-fried prawns
marinaded in lime, chervil and chilli, herb-crusted noisettes of lamb
with broad bean purée and chilli-roasted sweet potatoes, and fresh
cod with prosciutto potatoes, chicory and sauce Maltaise.

For pudding try the melting dark chocolate and orange tart with
crème fraiche or toffee grilled figs and butterscotch ice cream.
Stylish, individually designed en suite bedrooms are well appointed
and smartly furnished with antiques. Two elegant and spacious
suites feature video players, bathrobes and quality toiletries, and
stunning views. Afternoon tea is served free to residents.

England

BROUGHTON IN FURNESS

Blacksmiths Arms
Broughton Mills LA20 6AX ☎ 01229 716824
🖥 01229 716824 e-mail: blacksmithsarm@aol.com
*Dir: A593 from Ambleside to Coniston then on to B-in-F, minor rd
2.5m from B-in-F*

Dating back to the 16th century, this historic pub is a Grade II
listed building with panelled walls, flagged floors, a cosy bar
and three small dining areas. Occasional Irish music makes for
a enjoyable evening. Making the most of local suppliers, the
intention is to offer the best Lakeland produce and the real ale
is also provided by nearby micro-breweries. The menu lists the
likes of haddock in beer batter, chicken with mushroom sauce,
spicy prawns in a Cajun sauce, and Stilton, broccoli and apple
lasagne.
OPEN: 12-11 (Sun 12-10.30) (Oct-Mar 12-2.30, 5-11 Sun 5-10.30).
Closed Dec 25. **RESTAURANT:** L served all week. D served all
week 12-2 6-9. Av 3 course à la carte £11.
BREWERY/COMPANY: Free House.
PRINCIPAL BEERS: Jennings Cumberland, Dent Aviator,
Barngates Tag Lag. **FACILITIES:** Children welcome Garden:
outdoor eating Dogs allowed Water. **NOTES:** Parking 30

BUTTERMERE   Map 11 NY11

Bridge Hotel ★ ★
CA13 9UZ ☎ 017687 70252 🖥 017687 70215
e-mail: enquiries@bridge-hotel.com
Dir: Take B5289 from Keswick
Spend a weekend at this traditional 18th-century former
coaching inn and enjoy its stunning setting. Located between
Buttermere and Crummock Water, the Bridge Hotel lies in an
area of outstanding natural beauty. Miles of spectacular
Lakeland walks await discovery and after an energetic hike in
the hills, it's very pleasant to return to the hotel for civilised
afternoon tea in the sitting room. Excellent ales in the bar,
hearty food and peaceful accommodation.
OPEN: 10.30-11 (food 12-2.30, 3-5.30, 6-9.30 in summer) (open
all day in summer). **BAR MEALS:** L served all week. D served all
week 12-2.30 6-9.30. **RESTAURANT:** D served all week 7-8.30.
Av 5 course fixed price £21. **BREWERY/COMPANY:** Free House.
PRINCIPAL BEERS: Theakston's Old Peculier, Black Sheep,
Flowers IPA. **FACILITIES:** Children welcome Garden: Food
Served Outside Dogs allowed garden: only. **NOTES:** Parking 60.
ROOMS: 21 bedrooms 21 en suite s£65 d£65

CALDBECK
See entry under Wigton

DENT BREWERY
Nestling in picturesque Dentadle, in that corner of
the Yorkshire Dales national Park that is actually in
Cumbria, is one of the most remote breweries in
the country. Martin Stafford, having bought the
Sun Inn at Dent in 1987, established the Dent
Brewery in a converted barn at Cowgill in 1990
with little knowledge about brewery, except that
he liked a good pint! Ten years on, the brewery
continues to prosper, serving the Sun Inn and the
free trade across the country, and, due to popular
demand the Ramsbottom, Kamikaze and T'Owd
Tup ales are now available in bottles.

CARTMEL   Map 08 SD37

Pick of the Pubs

The Cavendish 🐦
LA11 6QA ☎ 015395 36240 🖥 015395 36620
e-mail: thecavendish@compuserve.com
*Dir: M6 J36 take A590 follow signs for Barrow Furness, Cartmel is
signposted. In village take 1st R.*
Cartmel's oldest hostelry, dating from the 15th century,
with oak beams and log fires creating a cosy atmosphere.
Bar food ranges from soup and sandwiches to lamb Henry
or bangers and mash. Typical restaurant dishes might be
stuffed fillet steak, sea bass and local ostrich. Top quality
real ales and a good selection of wines by glass or bottle.
OPEN: 11.30-11. **BAR MEALS:** L served all week. D served
all week 12-2.15 6-9.30. Av main course £6.95.
RESTAURANT: L served all week. D served all week 12-2.15
6-9.30. Av 3 course à la carte £15.50. Av 3 course fixed price
£15.50. **BREWERY/COMPANY:** Free House.
PRINCIPAL BEERS: Jennings Cumberland, Marston's
Pedigree, Theakston's. **NOTES:** Parking 25. **ROOMS:** 10
bedrooms 10 en suite s£30 d£36

Pick of the Pubs

Masons Arms ♀
Strawberry Bank LA11 6HW ☎ 015395 68486 & 68686
🖥 01539 568780
Walkers and tourists alike flock here for the views across
Cartmel Fell from its elevated position, but those in the
know recognise the Masons as home to the Strawberry
Bank micro-brewery, which these days concentrates on
the production of the hugely popular damson beer and
damson gin. As well as a regularly changing choice of real
ales, pub food is an increasing draw. Considerable care is
taken over the use of local fresh produce in some
imaginative and unusual cooking. The kitchen awards its
own Oscar to the daily blackboards that typically feature
spinach and mushroom moussaka, leek and butter bean
pie salad and chicken breast in Cajun mushroom sauce in
supporting roles.
OPEN: 11.30-3 6-11 (Fri-Sat 11.30-11, Sun 12-10.30). Closed
Dec 25-26. **BAR MEALS:** L served all week. D served all
week 12-2 6-8.45. **BREWERY/COMPANY:** Free House.
PRINCIPAL BEERS: Damson Beer, and 4 guests.
FACILITIES: Children welcome Children's licence Garden:

OPEN: 11-3 6-11
(Sun 12-3 7-10.30).
BAR MEALS: L served all week.
D served all week 12-2 6-9.
Av main course £8.25.
RESTAURANT: L served all week
D served all week 12-2 6-9.
Av 3 course a la carte £16.
BREWERY/COMPANY:
Free House.
PRINCIPAL BEERS: Jennings
Bitter & Cumberland Ale.
FACILITIES: Children welcome
Garden: patio, Dogs allowed.
NOTES: Parking 40.
ROOMS: 4 bedrooms 4 en suite
s£45 d£60

The Wheatsheaf at Beetham

LA7 7AL
☎ 015395 62123 ▤ 015395 64840
email: wheatsheaf@beetham.plus.com
Dir: on A6 5m N of J35

Hard by the 12th-century St Michael's church in this historic village close to the A6, great enthusiasm has been injected into the local pub since its rejuvenation and refurbishment by the current licensees. It is now a civilised dining pub and a comfortable base for visiting the Lake District.

Pop in for a pint in the traditional bar or relax over a pre-prandial drink in the beamed lounge bar, prior to venturing upstairs into the warmly decorated and candlelit dining room. Throughout this family owned and run inn, quaint touches such as fresh flowers and crisp linen napkins abound, and residents feel at home perusing the local press, daily papers and magazines at leisure.

Similar attention to detail and, wherever possible, reliance on fresh local produce marks out this hospitable 16th-century inn for special mention. The talents of an ever-eager young chef are admirably demonstrated in all-encompassing menus that start with Morecambe Bay shrimps and goats' cheese bruschetta, leading on to braised local game and redcurrant pie, Cajun monkfish and vegetable kebabs and perhaps a wild mushroom and fennel risotto dressed with shaved Parmesan. Afters include lemon and almond tart and white chocolate bread-and-butter pudding, with a farmhouse cheese selection of note as an alternative.

House wines major in the New World while the bar dispenses a noteworthy range of Jennings' real ales. Rise early for traditional Cumbrian breakfasts. The Wheatsheaf is also handy for Leighton Moss Nature Reserve and the old railway station at Carnforth, used in the filming of Noel Coward's classic Brief Encounter.

COCKERMOUTH

Map 10 NY13

The Trout Hotel ★ ★ ★ ♀

Crown St CA13 0EJ ☎ 01900 823591   📠 01900 827514
e-mail: enquiries@trouthotel.co.uk
Dating from about 1670 and originally built as a private residence, the Trout became an hotel in e934. Hand-carved oak staircase and marble fireplaces are among the many striking features and the bedrooms are comfortable and well equipped. Choose from the evening bar snack menu, which includes lasagne bolognase, cold platters and scampi tails, or dine in the restaurant and perhaps try red onion tart, Dover sole or corn fed chicken supreme with saffron and pine nut mousseline on a Marsala jus.
OPEN: 11-3 5.30-11. **BAR MEALS:** L served all week. D served Sun-Fri 12-2 6.30-8.30. Av main course £7.95. **RESTAURANT:** L served all week. D served all week 12-2 7-9.30. Av 3 course à la carte £20.45. Av 4 course fixed price £22.45.
BREWERY/COMPANY: Free House.
PRINCIPAL BEERS: Jennings Cumberland, Theakston's, John Smiths, Marston's Pedigree. **FACILITIES:** Children welcome Garden: outdoor eating Dogs allowed Not in bar.
NOTES: Parking 70. **ROOMS:** 29 bedrooms 29 en suite s£59.95 d£89.95 FR£109.00-£140.00

CONISTON

Map 11 SD39

Black Bull Inn & Hotel ♀

1 Yewdale Rd LA21 8DU ☎ 015394 41335 41668
📠 015394 41168
Character 400-year-old coaching inn situated in the picturesque village of Coniston. Turner, Coleridge and Donald Campbell all enjoyed the inn's hospitality, the latter while attempting to break the water speed record on Lake Coniston. Sample a pint of Bluebird Bitter or Old Man Ale from the brewery behind the pub and tuck into a good meal from the extensive menu. From favourite snacks and Cumbria farmhouse grills, the choice includes steak and ale pie, haddock in beer batter, crispy duckling and spicy chilli with rice and pitta bread.
OPEN: 11-11 (Sun 12-10.30). Closed Dec 25. **BAR MEALS:** L served all week. D served all week 12-9.30. **RESTAURANT:** L served By appointment. D served all week 6-9. Av 3 course à la carte £18. **BREWERY/COMPANY:** Free House.
PRINCIPAL BEERS: Coniston Blue Bird, Old Man Ale, & Opium, Coniston Blacksmith. **FACILITIES:** Children welcome Garden: Outdoor eating Dogs allowed Walker, Dog beds and meals.
NOTES: Parking 12. **ROOMS:** 16 bedrooms 16 en suite s£35 d£60

CROOK

Map 08 SD49

The Sun Inn ♀

LA8 8LA ☎ 01539 821351   📠 01539 821351
Dir: off the B5284
Olde worlde wayside inn with winter fires and summer terrace overlooking rolling countryside. Imaginative hot bar meals include Welsh goats' cheese with apricot chutney and trout wrapped in bacon with lime and almond sauce. Main dishes such as Herdwick lamb shank, pot-roast pheasant and seared salmon fillets are tastily sauced.

OPEN: 11-2.30 5.30-11. **BAR MEALS:** L served all week. D served all week 12-2.30 6-9. **RESTAURANT:** L served all week. D served all week 12-2.30 6-9. **BREWERY/COMPANY:** Scottish & Newcastle. **PRINCIPAL BEERS:** Boddingtons, Theakston, John Smiths & guest. **FACILITIES:** Children welcome Garden: outdoor eating, patio Dogs allowed garden only.
NOTES: Parking 40

DOWN ON THE FARM

Cider has been drunk in Britain since before Roman times and was originally made of fermented crab apple juice. Farmers made their own, especially in the West Country, and by the 17th century about 350 varieties of cider apple tree were cultivated, with names like Redstreak and Kingston Black, Sweet Coppin and Handsome Maud. The basic process of cider-making is to crush apples in a press, run off the juice and leave it to ferment narurally in casks for four months or so. The Industrial Revolution, however, transferred cider from the farm to the factory and by the 1960s the major producers were following the same path as the brewers and efficiently turning out a standardised product - weak, sweet and fizzy - that had only a distant resemblance to the powerful ' rough cider' or 'scrumpy' of earlier days. Fortunately, a draught cider renaissance has followed in the wake of the real ale revival, and one of the Campaign for Real Ale's aim is to prevent the disappearance of rough cider and perry.

AA The Restaurant Guide 2002

The right choice every time with this invaluable guide for gourmets

AA Lifestyle Guides

www.theAA.com

CROSTHWAITE Map 08 SD49

Pick of the Pubs

The Punch Bowl Inn 🏵 🏵 🐑 ♀
LA8 8HR ☎ 015395 68237 🖺 015395 68875
e-mail: enquiries@punchbowl.fsnet.co.uk
Dir: *From M6 J36 take A590 towards Barrow, then A5074 &
follow signs for Crosthwaite. Pub next to church on L*

A traditional Lakeland pub with original beams and low
ceilings, open fires and a warm, friendly and informal
atmosphere. Although a serious dining destination,
walkers and casual visitors will find excellent Theakston
and Black Sheep ales on tap and imaginative sandwiches
for light bites. In fine weather food is also served on a
terrace that enjoys unsurpassed rural views across the
Lyth Valley. Two lunchtime menus served throughout
show a serious yet assured touch, as in mixed-leaf Caesar
salad, baked salmon fillet with curried leek sauce and
pears poached in red wine syrup. In the evening, ex-
Gavroche chef Steven Doherty, may well add specials like
crispy duck leg confit, followed by chicken breast roulade
with Cumbrian air-dried ham and chargrilled tuna loin
steak. His creative à la carte options may take in smoked
salmon blinis, braised oxtails with red wine sauce and
gratin of mash and a well-balanced vegetarian hors
d'oeuvre platter. Those with room will then indulge in
warm chocolate Nemesis or a selection of British
farmhouse cheeses.
OPEN: 11-11 (Sun 12-10.30. Closed 3 wks in Nov, 25 Dec.)
BAR MEALS: L served Mon-Sun. D served Mon-Sun 12-2
6-9. Av main course £10. **RESTAURANT:** L served Mon-Sun.
D served Mon-Sun 12-2 6-9. Av 3 course à la carte £17.50.
BREWERY/COMPANY: Free House.
PRINCIPAL BEERS: Black Sheep, Barngates Cracker Ale,
Greene King Old Speckled Hen. **FACILITIES:** Children
welcome Garden: patio, BBQ. **NOTES:** Parking 60.
ROOMS: 3 bedrooms 3 en suite s£37.50 d£55

DENT Map 08 SD78

Sun Inn
Main St LA10 5QL ☎ 015396 25208
Dir: *From M6 through Sedburgh, Dent signed, 4.5m*
Traditional character pub with sturdy oak timbers and beams
in a delightful Yorkshire village full of quaint whitewashed
cottages and winding cobbled streets and an ideal base for
breathtaking Pennine walking. Dent has the highest main line
railway station in England. The Sun Inn benefits from its own
brewery which supplies a variety of real ales to the pub.
Wholesome fare ranges from chicken curry and breaded
continued

haddock to Cumberland sausage and steak and kidney pie.
OPEN: 11-2.30 6.30-11 (Jul/Aug 11-11, no food Mon-Thu Jan-
Mar). Closed Dec 25. **BAR MEALS:** L served all week. D served
all week 12-2 6.30-8.30. Av main course £5.25.
BREWERY/COMPANY: Free House.
PRINCIPAL BEERS: Dent. **FACILITIES:** Children welcome
Garden: Food served outisde Dogs allowed Water.
NOTES: Parking 15. **ROOMS:** 4 bedrooms s£25 d£37

DOCKRAY Map 11 NY32

The Royal Hotel
CA11 0JY ☎ 017684 82356 🖺 017684 82033
Dir: *A66 towards Keswick for 8m, turn L onto A5091 signposted
Dockray*
Wordsworth and Mary Queen of Scots both visited this 16th-
century family-run inn, a mile from the shores of Ullswater. A
blazing log fire and flagstone floor help to create a cosy,
inviting atmosphere. Typical examples from the menu include
Cumberland sausage with egg, deep fried haddock fillet,
farmhouse omelette and chicken Mediterranean. Salads, grills,
soups, jacket potatoes and 'Hoagies' are also available.
OPEN: 11-11. **BAR MEALS:** L served all week. D served all week
12-2.30 6-9. Av main course £6.75. **RESTAURANT:** L served all
week. D served all week 12-2.30 6-9. Av 3 course à la carte £14.
BREWERY/COMPANY: Free House.
PRINCIPAL BEERS: Castle Eden Ale, Black Sheep, Jennings
Cumberland, Greene King Old Speckled Hen.
FACILITIES: Children welcome Children's licence Garden: Beer
garden, Food served outside, Stream Dogs allowed By
arrangement. **NOTES:** Parking 30. **ROOMS:** 10 bedrooms 10 en
suite s£36 d£62 FR£70.00

ELTERWATER Map 11 NY30

Pick of the Pubs

The Britannia Inn 🏵 ★ ♀
LA22 9HP ☎ 015394 37210 🖺 015394 37311
e-mail: info@britinn.co.uk
Dir: *A593 from Ambleside, then B5343 to Elterwater*
Overlooking the village green in a famous scenic valley,
the Britannia captures the essence of a traditional family-
run Lakeland inn. Originally a farmhouse and the
premises of a local cobbler, the Britannia really comes to
life in summer when colourful hanging baskets dazzle the
eye and the garden fills up with customers and Morris
dancers. Further away is the opportunity for energetic
hikes and leisurely strolls amid Lakeland's glorious
scenery. Lunches, afternoon snacks and dinner are served
daily, with an extensive range of food and daily specials,
and the emphasis is very much on freshly prepared home-
made food. Steak and mushroom pie and bacon-wrapped
chicken stuffed with cream cheese and asparagus in citrus
sauce are typical examples of the interesting dishes. With
its thirteen attractively furnished bedrooms, the Britannia
is an ideal base for a relaxing holiday or a weekend break.
OPEN: 11-11 (Sun 12-10.30). Closed 25/26 Dec.
BAR MEALS: L served all week. D served all week 12-2
6.30-9.30. Av main course £8.75.
BREWERY/COMPANY: Free House.
PRINCIPAL BEERS: Jennings, Coniston Bluebird, Dent
Aviator. **FACILITIES:** Children's licence patio, Dogs allowed
Water bowls. **NOTES:** Parking 10. **ROOMS:** 13 bedrooms 9
en suite s£27 d£54

England

ESKDALE GREEN　　　　　　　　　　Map 10 NY10

Pick of the Pubs

Bower House Inn ★ ★
CA19 1TD ☎ 019467 23244　▤ 019467 23308
e-mail: info@bowerhouseinn.freeserve.co.uk
Dir: 4m off A595 1/2m W of Eskdale Green

Fine 17th-century stone-built former farmhouse with welcoming log fire and sheltered, well established gardens overlooking Muncaster Fell. Oak beamed bar and alcoves enhance the character of the place and a charming candlelit restaurant plays host to a varied selection of hearty, imaginative dishes. Cumberland wild duck, local pheasant in whisky, salmon with red pesto crust and spinach and mushroom roulade may feature on the specials board, while the dinner menu may offer goats' cheese with hazelnut dressing and snails in garlic butter, followed by shoulder of lamb with mint sauce, roast duck with red wine and plum sauce, halibut with spring onion and Dijon mustard and ostrich fillet with Stilton sauce. Twenty four en suite rooms, including three family rooms, make the Bower House an ideal holiday retreat throughout the year.
OPEN: 11-11. **BAR MEALS:** L served all week. D served all week 12-2 6.30-9.30. Av main course £7. **RESTAURANT:** D served all week 7-8.30. Av 3 course à la carte £25.
BREWERY/COMPANY: Free House.
PRINCIPAL BEERS: Theakston Bitter, Jennings Bitter, Greene King Old Speckled Hen, Dent Ales.
FACILITIES: Children welcome Garden: outdoor eating Dogs allowed. **NOTES:** Parking 50. **ROOMS:** 24 bedrooms 24 en suite s£54 d£77.50

King George IV Inn ♀
CA19 1TS ☎ 019467 23262　▤ 019467 23334
Dir: A590 to Greenodd, A5092 to Broughton-in-Furness then over Ulpha Fell towards Eskdale
Centuries-old Lakeland inn situated at the heart of the delightful Eskdale Valley. Cosy bars feature open fires, low, oak-beamed ceilings and over 150 malt whiskies. Fresh home-cooked fare includes Cumberland sausage, gammon, peppered ostrich fillet steak or baked mussels with bacon and cheese.
OPEN: 11-3 (Sun 12-3) 6-11. Closed 25 Dec. **BAR MEALS:** L served all week. D served all week 12-2 6-9. Av main course £5.95. **RESTAURANT:** L served all week. D served all week 12-2 6-9. Av 3 course à la carte £12.50. **BREWERY/COMPANY:** Free House. **PRINCIPAL BEERS:** Theakston - Best, Old Peculier.
FACILITIES: Children welcome Garden: patio, food served outside Dogs allowed. **NOTES:** Parking 12. **ROOMS:** 4 bedrooms 4 en suite s£27 d£50

For pubs with AA rosette awards for food see page 10

GARRIGILL　　　　　　　　　　Map 11 NY74

The George & Dragon
☎ 01434 381293　▤ 01434 382839
Once serving the local zinc and lead mining communities, this 17th-century coaching inn is now popular with walkers, who enjoy log fires that stave off that brisk North Pennine weather.

GRANGE-OVER-SANDS　　　　　　　　　　Map 08 SD47

Hare & Hounds Country Inn
Bowland Bridge LA11 6NN ☎ 015395 68333
▤ 015395 68993
e-mail: innthelakes@supanet.com
Dir: M6 onto A591, L after 3m onto A590, R after 3m onto A5074, after 4m sharp L & next L after 1m

Beautifully located in the Winster Valley surrounded by the Cartmell Fells, this 17th-century coaching inn is close to many of the Lake District's attractions. The traditional atmosphere is maintained under new ownership, with oak beams and log fires, and meals include popular options of braised lamb shank with minted gravy, chilli and Cajun chicken.
OPEN: 11-11 (Sun 12-10.30). **BAR MEALS:** L served all week. D served all week 12-2 6-9. Av main course £6. **RESTAURANT:** L served all week. D served all week 12-2 6-9. Av 3 course à la carte £12.95. Av 3 course fixed price £12.95.
BREWERY/COMPANY: Free House.
PRINCIPAL BEERS: Tetleys, Shepherd Neame Bishops Finger.
FACILITIES: Garden: Food served outside Dogs allowed Not in bar. **NOTES:** Parking 80. **ROOMS:** 15 bedrooms 12 en suite s£35 d£40

GRASMERE　　　　　　　　　　Map 11 NY30

The Travellers Rest Inn
Keswick Rd LA22 9RR ☎ 015394 35604　▤ 017687 72309
e-mail: travellers@lakelandsheart.demon.co.uk
Dir: From M6 take A591 to Grasmere, pub 1/2m N of Grasmere
Some of the finest scenery in the country surrounds this 16th-century former coaching inn, which offers a good range of beers and and an extensive menu of home-cooked traditional fare. Typical dishes are moules marinière, pot-roasted lamb shank, and sticky date pudding. continued

OPEN: 12-11 (Sun 12-10.30). **BAR MEALS:** L served all week. D served all week 12-3 6-9.30. Av main course £5.95. **RESTAURANT:** L served all week. D served all week 12-3 6-9.30. **BREWERY/COMPANY:** Free House. **PRINCIPAL BEERS:** Jennings Bitter, Cumberland Ale, & Sneck Lifter, Greene King Abbot Ale. **FACILITIES:** Children welcome Children's licence Garden: patio, outdoor eating, BBQ Dogs allowed. **NOTES:** Parking 60. **ROOMS:** 9 bedrooms 9 en suite s£30 d£60

GREAT LANGDALE   Map 11 NY20

The New Dungeon Ghyll Hotel
LA22 9JY ☎ 015394 37213   015394 37666
Dir: From M6 into Kendal then A591 into Ambleside onto A593 to B5343, hotel 6m on R
The hotel enjoys a spectacular location at the foot of the Langdale Pikes and Pavey Ark. Adjacent bar with tiled floor and rustic furnishings - very popular with walkers returning from the fells.

GRIZEBECK   Map 08 SD28

The Greyhound Inn
LA17 7XJ ☎ 01229 889224   01229 889224
e-mail: greyhound@grizebeck.fsbusiness.co.uk
Situated on the edge of the Lake District National Park, this late 17th-century slate-roofed inn is set at the bottom of a long deep incline, and is an ideal location for walkers to gather their strength. The regularly changing specials blackboard may feature jumbo king-sized mixed grill, Welsh chicken, Barbary duck breast, or fillet of salmon in lemon and dill sauce. A steak selection is also available.

OPEN: 12-3 6-11. **BAR MEALS:** L served all week. D served all week 12-2 6-9. Av main course £5. **RESTAURANT:** L served all week. D served all week 12-2 6-9. **BREWERY/COMPANY:** Free House. **PRINCIPAL BEERS:** Jennings Bitter & Cumberland Ale. **FACILITIES:** Garden: Food served outside Dogs allowed. **NOTES:** Parking 20. **ROOMS:** 3 bedrooms 3 en suite s£20 d£35

HAVERTHWAITE   Map 08 SD38

Rusland Pool ♀
LA12 8AA ☎ 01229 861384   01229 861425
e-mail: enquires@rusland-pool.ndirect.co.uk
Dir: M6 J36 take A590 towards Barrow-in-Furness for 17m the hotel is on the R hand side of the A590 Westbound
Situated in open countryside at the foot of the Rusland Valley, this 18th-century coaching inn is named after the nearby river. The cosy bar has a log fire, and service is informal. Varied menus offer a good range of snacks and meals, including breast of duck in a cherry sauce, fillet steak with Stilton in a red wine sauce, and wild salmon with a hollandaise sauce. **OPEN:** 11-11 (food served all day, 12-9.15). **BAR MEALS:** L served all week. D served all week 12-9. Av main course £7.50. **RESTAURANT:** L served all week. D served all week 12-9. Av 3 course à la carte £7.50 . **BREWERY/COMPANY:** Free House. **PRINCIPAL BEERS:** Tetleys, Boddingtons. **FACILITIES:** Children welcome Children's licence Garden: outdoor eating,. **NOTES:** Parking 35. **ROOMS:** 18 bedrooms 18 en suite s£42 d£59 FR£70-£85

HAWKSHEAD   Map 11 SD39

Kings Arms Hotel
The Square LA22 ONZ ☎ 015394 36372   015394 36006
Low beamed ceilings and a winter log fire are among the charming features at this 16th century pub which overlooks the village square and is popular with locals and visitors. Beatrix Potter lived nearby and Wordsworth went to school here. Good choice of starters might include spicy chicken dippers or vegetable spring rolls, while main courses take in Cumberland sausage, home made steak and kidney pie, grilled lamb chops and game casserole. Bedrooms are cosy and traditionally furnished.

OPEN: 11-11 (Sun 12-10.30). **BAR MEALS:** L served all week. D served all week 12-2.30 6-9.30. Av main course £7.50. **RESTAURANT:** L served all week. D served all week 12-2.30 6-9.30. Av 3 course à la carte £14. **BREWERY/COMPANY:** Free House. **PRINCIPAL BEERS:** Tetley, Black Sheep, Yates, Jennings Cumberland Ale. **FACILITIES:** Children welcome Children's licence Garden: patio/terrace, outdoor eating Dogs allowed Water. **ROOMS:** 9 bedrooms 8 en suite s£29 d£24

Queens Head Hotel ★ ★ 🍸
Main St LA22 0NS ☎ 015394 36271   015394 36722
e-mail: enquiries@queensheadhotel.co.uk
Dir: M6 J36 A590 to Newby Bridge. Take 1st R, 8m to Hawkshead
Oak beamed ceilings, flagstone floors and winter fires make a warm and inviting blend at this traditional country inn. The 16th-century black and white building stands near the traffic-free centre of one of Lakeland's prettiest villages. Both lunch-

continued

England

England

time and evening menus feature an abundance of seasonal local produce. Options range from Cumberland sausage and mash or Westmorland pie, to Herdwick lamb steak, pheasant casserole, oven-baked hake, or aubergine and tomato soufflé.

OPEN: 11-11 (Sun 12-10.30). BAR MEALS: L served all week. D served all week 12-2.30 6.15-9.30. Av main course £6.
RESTAURANT: L served all week. D served all week 12-2.30 6.15-8.45. Av 3 course à la carte £15.
BREWERY/COMPANY: Frederic Robinson.
PRINCIPAL BEERS: Robinsons Hartleys XB & Frederics.
FACILITIES: Children welcome Children's licence patio.
NOTES: Parking 13. ROOMS: 13 bedrooms 10 en suite

The Sun Inn ♦♦♦♦
Main St LA22 0NT ☎ 015394 36236 ▤ 015394 36155
Listed 17th-century coaching inn at the heart of the village where Wordsworth went to school. Bar dishes range from baguette with bacon and melted Brie to Cumbrian lamb cutlets seasoned with coriander and chilli and served with a mixed fruit couscous. The monthly changing restaurant carte might have trio of local sausages on a creamed celeriac mash or fishcakes of Esthwaite water trout served with sweet chilli and tomato crème fraiche.

OPEN: 11-11. BAR MEALS: L served all week. D served all week 12-2.30 6.15-9.30. Av main course £6. RESTAURANT: D served all week. Av 3 course fixed price £17.50.
BREWERY/COMPANY: Free House.
PRINCIPAL BEERS: Black Sheep, Barn Gates Cracker.
FACILITIES: Children welcome Children's licence Garden: outdoor eating, patio Dogs allowed. NOTES: Parking 8.
ROOMS: 8 bedrooms 8 en suite s£30 d£70 FR£52-£80

HESKET NEWMARKET   Map 11 NY33

The Old Crown
CA7 8JG ☎ 016974 78288 ▤ 016974 78288
Dir: from M6 take B5305, L after 6m toward Hesket Newmarket
Delightful Cumbrian pub in a tiny fellside village, very popular with climbers, cyclists and hill-walkers. Handy for visiting

Carlisle, Penrith and the coast. Excellent home-brewed ales are provided by the small community-owed brewery at the top of the garden and the welcoming atmosphere in the bar is created by a nice blend of locals and visitors.
    Food is sourced locally and cooked on the premises. Expect chicken and mushroom casserole, steak and ale stew, ratatouille, and Cumberland sausage.

OPEN: 12-3 5.30-11 (Sun 12-3, 7-10.30, Mon 5.30-11 only).
BAR MEALS: L served Tue-Sun. D served none12-2. Av main course £5.50. RESTAURANT: L served Tues-Sun. D served Tues-Sat 12-2 6.30-8.30. Av 3 course à la carte £10.
BREWERY/COMPANY: Free House.
PRINCIPAL BEERS: Hesket Newmarket Brewery beers.
FACILITIES: Children welcome Garden: outdoor eating Dogs allowed Water No credit cards

HEVERSHAM   Map 08 SD48

Blue Bell Hotel ★ ★ ★ ♀
Princes Way LA7 7EE ☎ 015395 62018 ▤ 015395 62455
e-mail: bluebellhotel@aol.com
Dir: On A6 between Kendal & Milnthorpe
Once a vicarage, this welcoming inn exudes plenty of charm and period character. An ideal base for touring the Lake District and the Yorkshire Dales, the Blue Bell offers well-equipped modern bedrooms with pleasant country views, while downstairs meals are served in the comfortable lounge bar and attractive restaurant, where log fires and low beams add to the appeal.
    Food ranges from local game and lamb casserole, to freshly-battered haddock and steak and mushroom pudding. Seared sea bass and chicken breast with leek, mash and mushroom cream sauce are among the dinner menu favourites.
OPEN: 11-11. BAR MEALS: L served all week. D served all week 11-9 6. Av main course £6.95. RESTAURANT: L served all week. D served all week 11-9 7. Av 3 course à la carte £18.50. Av 5 course fixed price £19.95. BREWERY/COMPANY: Samuel Smith. PRINCIPAL BEERS: Samuel Smith Old Brewery Bitter.
FACILITIES: Children welcome Garden: patio, BBQ Dogs allowed Not in Garden. NOTES: Parking 100. ROOMS: 21 bedrooms 21 en suite s£49.50 d£66

HOWTOWN

Howtown Hotel
CA10 2ND ☎ 01768 486514
Pub and hotel right on the shores of Ullswater, very popular with walkers. Bedrooms.

continued

KENDAL   Map 10 SD59

Gateway Inn
Crook Rd LA8 8LX ☎ 01539 720605 & 724187
📠 01539 720581
Dir: From M6 J36 take A590/A591, follow signs for Windermere,
pub on L after 9m

Warm and welcoming Victorian country inn located within the
Lake District National Park. Delightful views, attractive gardens
and log fires add to the charm. Good range of appetising pub
food and traditional English dishes. Try shin of beef braised in
ale, smoked mackerel fishcakes or pancakes filled with ham,
mushrooms and Cheddar, finishing off perhaps with meringue
glace or chocolate and banana sundae.
OPEN: 11-11 (all day wknds). **BAR MEALS:** L served all week.
D served all week 12-2 6-9. Av main course £7.50.
RESTAURANT: L served all week. D served all week 12-2 6-9.
Av 3 course à la carte £15. **BREWERY/COMPANY:** Thwaites.
PRINCIPAL BEERS: Thwaites Bitter, Thwaites Smooth.
FACILITIES: Children welcome Garden: Food served outside
Dogs allowed Water, dog food available. **NOTES:** Parking 50.
ROOMS: 6 bedrooms 6 en suite s£35 d£25.50

KESWICK   Map 11 NY22

Pick of the Pubs

The Horse & Farrier Inn 🏵 ★ ★ ♀
Threlkeld Village CA12 4SQ ☎ 017687 79688
Situated below Blencathra and popular with hosts of fell
walkers this 300-year-old stone inn is home to
comfortable en suite bedrooms with space for all the
family plus the dog, imaginative home cooking and the
host brewer, Jennings's, real ales. In traditional style its
bars and dining-room are warmly welcoming, hung with
hunting prints and cheered by a roaring log fire. Available
for lunch are cold and hot open sandwiches, seasonal
salads and main dishes such as Lamb Jennings, slowly
braised in bitter and served with spinach mash, and
poached Scottish salmon on a mussel, leek and bacon
ragout. Rather more structured dinner menus begin with
duck liver and green peppercorn pate and prosciutto, feta
cheese and black olive salad, moving on to chicken breast
with mushroom, bacon and sherry cream sauce on herb
risotto, roast Mediterranean vegetable lasagne, red mullet
fillets with Thai green curry sauce and choice cuts of beef
steak sauced perhaps with onions and port and topped
with Stilton and thyme butter.
OPEN: 11-11 (Sun 12-10.30). **BAR MEALS:** L served all
week. D served all week 12-2 6.30-9.30. Av main course £10.
RESTAURANT: L served all week. D served all week 12-2
6.30-9.30. Av 3 course à la carte £18. **BREWERY/
COMPANY:** Jennings. **PRINCIPAL BEERS:** Jennings: Bitter,
Cocker Hoop, Sneck Lifter & Cumberland Ale. **FACILITIES:**
Children welcome Patio, Food served outside.
NOTES: Parking 60. **ROOMS:** 9 bedrooms 9 en suite
s£30 d£60

Pubs in the Park

There are eleven national parks in Britain, with the South Downs in
Sussex scheduled to become the twelfth in 2002. Walking is one of the
most popular pursuits within our national parks and so it's hardly
surprising that local pubs and inns draw a great many hikers and ramblers
throughout the year. One of Britain's most popular national parks is, of
course, the Lake District. Covering 866 square miles, this magical corner of
England retains a special place in the hearts of all those who love the great
outdoors. Within the region lies a varied assortment of pubs, including the
400-year-old Kirkstile Inn at Loweswater, the Blacksmiths Arms at Talkin,
the 17th-century Drunken Duck Inn at Ambleside, boasting its own fishing
lake and micro-brewery, the Wasdale Head Inn, which shelters beneath
England's tallest mountain, and the Three Shires at the foot of
Wrynose Pass in the valley of Little Langdale.

England

KESWICK continued

Pick of the Pubs

The Kings Head 🏨 🏨 ★ ★ ★ 🛏️
Thirlspot, Thirlmere CA12 4TN ☎ 017687 72393
🖨 017687 72309
Dir: From M6 take A66 to Keswick then A591, pub 4m
S of Keswick

Oak beams and inglenook fireplaces are features of this
17th-century coaching inn set in the heart of the Lake
District National Park. Good-value bar food is served, and
a four-course evening meal, with dishes such as baked
Borrowdale trout and slow-cooked pork roast.
OPEN: 12-11 (Sun 12-10.30). **BAR MEALS:** L served all
week. D served all week 12-3 6-9.30. Av main course £7.
RESTAURANT: L served Sun. D served all week 12-3 7-9. Av
3 course à la carte £20. Av 4 course fixed price £20.
BREWERY/COMPANY: Free House.
PRINCIPAL BEERS: Theakston XB, Best & Old Peculier,
Jennings. **FACILITIES:** Children welcome Children's licence
Garden: patio, BBQ, outdoor eating Dogs allowed.
NOTES: Parking 60. **ROOMS:** 17 bedrooms 17 en suite
s£32 d£64

The Swinside Inn ◆◆◆
Newlands Valley CA12 5UE ☎ 017687 78253
🖨 017687 78253
e-mail: theswinsideinn@btinternet.com
Set in a quiet valley this peaceful pub enjoys some stunning
views of the fells. Bedrooms.

KIRKBY LONSDALE   Map 08 SD67

Pick of the Pubs

Pheasant Inn ★ ★ 🛏️ 🍷
Casterton LA6 2RX ☎ 015242 71230 🖨 015242 71230
e-mail: Pheasant.casterton@eggconnect.net
See Pick of the Pubs on page 103

AA Hotel Booking Service on 0870 5050505 to book
at AA recognised hotels and B & Bs in the
UK and Ireland, or through our Internet site:
www.theAA.com

Pick of the Pubs

Snooty Fox Tavern 🍷
Main St LA6 2AH ☎ 015242 71308 🖨 72642
e-mail: Snootyfox84@freeserve.co.uk
Dir: M6 J36 take A65, tavern 6m
One of a trio of privately-owned, well-run Cumbrian inns
(viz Troutbeck's Mortal Man and the Royal Oak in
Appleby), the Snooty Fox is a listed Jacobean coaching inn
at the centre of town, the 'capital' of the scenic Lune
Valley. Inside are roaring fires in rambling bars full of eye-
catching artefacts, while adjacent to a quaint cobbled
courtyard is the pub's own herb garden. Expect therefore
a fairly serious approach to good food and well-balanced
flavours on the plate. Warm chicken liver salad, ham
shank with mustard mash, steak and kidney pudding and
a sticky toffee dessert are the stuff of fishermen and fell-
walkers, who will equally enjoy the prime condition of real
ales and guest beers. Game terrine with Cumberland
sauce and duck breast with glazed apricots and orange
sauce, followed by chocolate tiramisu, are supplemented
by daily-featured meat and fish dishes according to
market availability. The surroundings are comfortably
convivial and well-appointed bedrooms suitably conducive
to a good night's sleep.
OPEN: 11-11 (Sun 12-10.30). **BAR MEALS:** L served all
week 12-2.30. Av main course £10. **RESTAURANT:** L served
all week. D served all week 12-2.30 6.30-9. Av 3 course à la
carte £18. **BREWERY/COMPANY:** Free House.
PRINCIPAL BEERS: Theakston's Best, Greene King IPA,
Timothy Taylor Landlord. **FACILITIES:** Children welcome
Children's licence Garden: patio/terrace, outdoor eating,
Dogs allowed. **NOTES:** Parking 12. **ROOMS:** 9 bedrooms
9 en suite s£30 d£50

The Sun Inn
Market St LA6 2AU ☎ 015242 71965 🖨 015242 72489
Dir: From M6 J36 take A65
The same menu is offeredethroughout this 16th-century inn, in
the bar or 30's style restaurant (called Mad Carew's after the
poem by J Milton Hayes). People come a long way for the
house steak and ale pie, and another regular dish is bubble
and squeak with a real bacon chop. A full range of specials
might include mussels or honey roasted gammon.
OPEN: 11-11 (Sun 12-10.30). **BAR MEALS:** L served all week. D
served all week 11-3 6-9.30. Av main course £5.95. **RESTAURANT:** L
served all week. D served all week 11-3 6-9.30. Av 3 course à la carte
£13. **BREWERY/COMPANY:** Free House.
PRINCIPAL BEERS: Black Sheep, Dent, Boddingtons, Flowers IPA.
FACILITIES: Children welcome Dogs allowed.
ROOMS: 9 bedrooms 5 en suite s£29.50 d£54

Whoop Hall Inn 🍷
Skipton Rd LA6 2HP ☎ 015242 71284 🖨 015242 72154
e-mail: info@whoophall.co.uk
Dir: A65 from M6, pub 1m SE of Kirkby Lonsdale
Over 350 years old, Whoop Hall was once the kennels for local
fox hounds, and gets its name from the huntsman's call. In an
imaginatively converted barn you can sample Yorkshire ales
and a good menu of dishes based on local produce. There is a
popular carvery every Sunday lunchtime with live jazz.
OPEN: 7am-11.30pm. **BAR MEALS:** L served all week. D served
all week 11.30-2.30 6-10. Av main course £5.95.
RESTAURANT: L served all week. D served all week 12-2.30 6-10.
Av 3 course à la carte £17. Av 3 course fixed price £12.50.
BREWERY/COMPANY: Free House. *continued on p104.*

OPEN: 11-3 6-11 (Sun 12-3 7-10.30). Closed 25 & 26 Dec.
BAR MEALS: L served all week. D served all week 12-2 6.30-9.30.
RESTAURANT: D served Tue-Sun 7-9. Closed Sun & Mon Nov-Mar Av 3 course a la carte £15.
BREWERY/COMPANY: Free House.
PRINCIPAL BEERS: Theakston Best, Black Sheep Bitter, Dent Bitter, Wye Valley Bitter, Thwaites.
FACILITIES: Children welcome Children's licence. Garden: patio, outdoor eating. Dogs allowed.
NOTES: Parking 40.
ROOMS: 11 bedrooms 11 ensuite s£36 d72.

The Pheasant Inn

★★ 🛏 ♀

Casterton LA6 2RX
☎ 015242 71230 📠 015242 71230
e-mail: pheasant.casterton@eggconnect.net
Dir: M6 J6 onto A65 for 7m. L A683 at Devil's Bridge, 1m to Casterton

Idyllically situated at the edge of the Lune valley, only a short drive from both the Forest of Bowland and the Yorkshire Dales National Park, the civilised Pheasant Inn enjoys fine views over the nearby fells, and is just a mile away from the pretty market town of Kirkby Lonsdale.

But what a mile, to happen upon a traditional, family-run country inn that offers restful accommodation just ten minutes' drive from the M6 and a charm all its own. A fair dozen well-chosen wines by the glass and real ales from breweries as diverse as Dent and the Wye Valley indicate dedication to the house's individuality, demonstrated equally in their lunch and dining options that are served throughout the cosy bar and adjoining modernised beamed rooms.

Locally-sourced mussels, crevettes, haddock, hake and halibut share pride of place with Angus sirloin and fillet steaks served with seasonal vegetables. Yet there is more: salads of Bombay rice (with carrot, pineapple and sultanas) or fresh crab with aïoli preceding oven-baked red snapper with goats' cheese, casserole of rabbit and fresh vegetables, chorizo sausage and mixed bean casserole or chargrills like sail fish with olive oil and lemon juice and a trencherman's platter of venison, duck breast, wild boar and guinea fowl breast that is certainly not for the faint-hearted.

For those with lighter stuff in mind there are lunchtime sandwiches of honey-roast ham and coronation chicken and hearty soups like thick beef broth and cream of mushroom: and yet a certain temptation remains in the form of some wicked sticky toffee pudding topped with clotted cream.

Bedrooms are individually furnished and offer a high standard of comfort; a twin-bedded room for disabled guests is conveniently situated on the ground floor.

PRINCIPAL BEERS: Dent, Black Sheep, Timothy Taylor Landlord. **FACILITIES:** Children welcome Garden: Food served outside Dogs allowed. **NOTES:** Parking 120. **ROOMS:** 23 bedrooms 23 en suite s£40 d£60

KIRKBY STEPHEN

The Bay Horse
Winton CA17 4HS ☎ 01768 371451
Standing in a moorland hamlet off the A685, the Bay Horse offers home-cooked food and bedrooms.

LAZONBY   Map 11 NY53

Joiners Arms
Townfoot CA10 1BL ☎ 01768 898728
Dir: Take A6 N to Plumpton, R to Lazonby
18th-century village inn, formerly a farmhouse and barn. Close to the River Eden, with fine Pennine views.

LITTLE LANGDALE   Map 11 NY30

Pick of the Pubs

Three Shires Inn ★ ★
LA22 9NZ ☎ 015394 37215
e-mail: enquiries@threeshiresinn.co.uk
Dir: Turn off A593, 2.3m from Ambleside at 2nd junct signposted for The Langdales. 1st L 0.5m, Hotel 1m up lane
Traditional 19th-century hotel personally run by the same family since 1983. Close by is the Three Shires Stone which represents the meeting point for Lancashire and the old counties of Cumberland and Westmorland. During the 1880s and 90s the inn would have been a much-needed resting place and watering hole for travellers on the journey to or from the high passes of Hardknott and Wrynose. More than 100 years later, the Three Shires is still playing host to winter walkers and weekend break visitors to this majestic mountain country. Snacks, meals and an à la carte menu are available in the bar, while the restaurant offers an evening table d'hote menu. Typical dishes might include pan-fried salmon with a leek fondue and red wine sauce, roast leg of Lakeland lamb with a sweet port and redcurrant reduction, and onion and goats' cheese tart with french beans and a beetroot and fig salad.

OPEN: 11-11 (Sun 12-10.30) (Dec-Jan 12-3, 8-10.30). Closed Dec 25. **BAR MEALS:** L served all week. D served all week 12-2 6-8.45. Av main course £8. **RESTAURANT:** L served none. D served all week 6.30-8. Av 4 course fixed price £19.95. **BREWERY/COMPANY:** Free House.
PRINCIPAL BEERS: Jennings Best & Cumberland, Ruddles County. **FACILITIES:** Children welcome Children's licence Garden: Food served outside Dogs allowed. **NOTES:** Parking 20. **ROOMS:** 10 bedrooms 10 en suite s£29.50 d£59

> **Room prices** minimum single and minimum double rates are shown. FR indicates family room

---

LOWESWATER   Map 10 NY12

Kirkstile Inn
CA13 0RU ☎ 01900 85219 ▤ 01900 85239
e-mail: info@kirkstile.com
This beautifully situated 16th-century Lakeland inn still retains the low beams, open fires and warm hospitality that has welcomed travellers for centuries. But new owners have refitted the bedrooms, and completed major improvements to create an ideal base for walkers and climbers. The home-cooked menu features lamb cobbler with herb scone, chicken and mushroom pie, and cheese, spinach and broccoli bake. Finish with Bakewell tart or cinnamon-scented rice pudding.
OPEN: 11-11. **BAR MEALS:** L served all week. D served all week 12-2 6-9. Av main course £6. **RESTAURANT:** . D served all week 7. Av 3 course à la carte £16. **BREWERY/COMPANY:** Free House. **PRINCIPAL BEERS:** Jennings Bitter & Cumberland Ale. **FACILITIES:** Children welcome Children's licence Garden: patio, outdoor eating Dogs allowed. **NOTES:** Parking 40. **ROOMS:** 11 bedrooms 7 en suite s£35 d£56 FR£90-£112

MELMERBY   Map 11 NY63

The Shepherds Inn 🐑 ♇
CA10 1HF ☎ 01768 881217 ▤ 01768 881977
e-mail: eat@shepardsinn.net
Dir: On A686 NE of Penrith
Well-known in the North Pennines, this unpretentious sandstone pub overlooks the village green towards remote moorland country. Close to miles of spectacular walks. Renowned for its extensive choice of country cheeses, including Lanark Blue (ewe's milk similar to Roquefort), Westmorland Smoked (oak smoked Cheddar) and Tasty Lancashire (double curd cheese with a sharp bite).
Diners are drawn from far and wide to sample the interesting lunchtime snack menu or the daily specials, which might include beef in Guinness, tuna and sweetcorn quiche and beef and mushroom pie. Interesting mix of well-kept real ales.
OPEN: 10.30-3 6-11 (Sun 12-3, 7-10.30). Closed 25 Dec. **BAR MEALS:** L served all week. D served all week 10.30-2.30 6-9.45. Av main course £6. **BREWERY/COMPANY:** Free House. **PRINCIPAL BEERS:** Jennings Cumberland Ale, Holts, Greene King Abbot Ale, Flowers IPA. **FACILITIES:** Children welcome Children's licence patio Dogs allowed bottom bar only. **NOTES:** Parking 20

MUNGRISDALE   Map 11 NY33

The Mill Inn ♦♦♦
CA11 0XR ☎ 017687 79632
Dir: From Penrith A66 to Keswick, after 10m R to Mungrisdale, pub 2m on L
Set in a peaceful village, this 16th-century coaching inn is handy for spectacular fell walks. Charles Dickens and John Peel once stayed here. The inn has a cask marque for its beer, and the food is also an attraction, with specials such as game casserole, fresh fish, and fillet steak with haggis and whisky sauce.   *continued*

OPEN: 12-11 (Sun 12-10.30). **BAR MEALS:** L served all week. D served all week 12-2.30 6-8.30. Av main course £6.95. **RESTAURANT:** L served all week. D served all week 12-2.30 6-8.30. Av 3 course à la carte £12. Av 3 course fixed price £10.95. **BREWERY/COMPANY:** Free House. **PRINCIPAL BEERS:** Jennings Bitter & Cumberland + guest ale. **FACILITIES:** Children welcome Garden: Dogs allowed. **NOTES:** Parking 40. **ROOMS:** 9 bedrooms 7 en suite s£35 d£55

NEAR SAWREY   Map 08 SD39

Tower Banks Hotel ♀
LA22 0LF ☎ 015394 36334   ☐ 015394 36334
Dir: On B5285 SW of Windermere
17th-century Lakeland cottage pub next door to the former home of Mrs Heelis, better known as the writer and illustrator Beatrix Potter. A drawing of the inn appears in her book, 'Jemima Puddle-Duck.' With its comfortable bedrooms and good facilities, this makes an ideal base from which to explore the Lake District. Plenty of walking and sailing opportunities nearby. Traditional, wholesome bar menu offers hot and cold dishes such as Lakeland venison, lamb Henry, battered cod and home-made cheese flan. Good choice of beers and weekly-changing guest ales.
OPEN: 11-3 6-11 (Summer 6-10.30). Closed 25 Dec.
BAR MEALS: L served all week. D served all week 12-2 6.30-9. Av main course £6.50. **RESTAURANT:** D served all week 12-2 6.30-9. Av 3 course à la carte £13. **BREWERY/COMPANY:** Free House. **PRINCIPAL BEERS:** Theakston - Best, XB, & Old Peculier, Marston's Pedigree. **FACILITIES:** Children welcome Garden: outdoor eating Dogs allowed none. **NOTES:** Parking 8. **ROOMS:** 3 bedrooms 3 en suite s£37 d£52

NETHER WASDALE   Map 10 NY10

The Screes Hotel
CA20 1ET ☎ 019467 26262   ☐ 26262
Dir: E of A595 between Whitehaven & Ravenglass
300-year-old inn situated in a quiet valley amid majestic mountain scenery. Once a Temperance House after the local vicar in the 1800s revoked its license due to drunken goings-on. Accommodation.

NEWBY BRIDGE   Map 08 SD38

Eagle & Child Inn ♀
Kendal Rd, Staveley LA8 9LP ☎ 01539 821320
e-mail: eagleandc@g.wizz.net
Dir: Follow M6 to Jct 36 then A590 towards kendal join A591 towards Windermere Staveley approx 2 M
Currently undergoing major refurbishment, the name of this inn at the foot of the Kentmere valley refers to the crest of arms of the Lonsdale family who were local landowners in the area.

continued

Excellent walking country on the doorstep, as well as scope for cycling and fishing. Appetising range of dishes might include beef and ale pie, local trout stuffed with prawns and Cumberland sausage and mash. Well-kept local beers also feature.
OPEN: 11-11. **BAR MEALS:** L served all week. D served all week 12-3 6-9. Av main course £6.95. **RESTAURANT:** L served all week. D served all week 12-3 6-9. Av 3 course à la carte £17. **PRINCIPAL BEERS:** Black Sheep, Coniston Blue Bird, Dent Ales. **FACILITIES:** Children welcome Garden: Food served outside. **NOTES:** Parking 16. **ROOMS:** 5 bedrooms 5 en suite s£35 d£39.95

OUTGATE   Map 11 SD39

Outgate Inn
LA22 0NQ ☎ 015394 36413
Dir: From M6, A684 to Kendal, A591 towards Ambleside. At Plumgarths take B5284 to Hawkshead then Outgate
Once a toll house, this 18th-century Lakeland pub became licensed as the Outgate Mineral Water Manufacturer in 1903. Many of the original features have been retained and food can be enjoyed in the cosy dining room or the bar area.

RAVENSTONEDALE   Map 11 NY70

Pick of the Pubs

Black Swan Hotel ★ ★ 🐷 ♀
CA17 4NG ☎ 015396 23204 & 0800 0741394
☐ 015396 23604
e-mail: reservations@blackswanhotel.com
Dir: M6 J38 take A685 E towards Brough
In a peaceful village in the foothills of the Eden Valley, in the old county of Westmorland, this comfortable Lakeland stone hotel dates from 1899. The larger of two bars, with a comfortable air afforded by its bright copper-topped tables is well placed for good value portions of steak pie in shortcrust pastry, Cumberland sausage with caramelised apples and salmon marinated in lime and honey. The owners spend much of their day preparing dinner for their restaurant guests, with an emphasis on delights such as local beef, lamb and game and traditionally made cheeses. Flavours are a strong point in scallops with sweet potato purée and tartare of mussels, grilled sea bass with lobster tail and green pea mousse and chocolate torte with peppermint mousse. A perfect place to escape the pressures of the modern day world, there is tennis and fishing nearby, and a sheltered garden approached by way of a footbridge across the stream.
OPEN: 8.30-3 6-11 Wkds 08:00-24:00. **BAR MEALS:** L served all week. D served all week 12-2.15 6-9. Av main course £6.50. **RESTAURANT:** L served all week. D served all week 12-2.15 7-9. Av 3 course à la carte £18. **BREWERY/COMPANY:** Free House. **PRINCIPAL BEERS:** Black Sheep, Timothy Taylor Landlord, Greene King IPA. **FACILITIES:** Children welcome Children's licence Garden: outdoor eating Dogs allowed. **NOTES:** Parking 40. **ROOMS:** 20 bedrooms 18 en suite s£45 d£70

The Fat Lamb Country Inn ★ ★ ♀
Crossbank CA17 4LL ☎ 015396 23242   ☐ 015396 23285
e-mail: fatlamb@cumbria.com
Dir: On A683 between Sedbergh and Kirkby Stephen
Solid stone walls and open fires help to create a friendly welcome at this historic pub dating back to the 1600s. Situated between the Yorkshire Dales and the Lake District, the inn acts as a useful base for exploring some of the finest scenery in the

continued

North of England. Food is prepared in-house by the Fat Lamb's own chefs, using local produce whenever possible. Extensive and varied bar snack menu offers Cumberland sausage, scampi, lasagne, and various baguettes. Baked trout, vegetable carbonara and rack of lamb with a mint crust and honey jus are among the restaurant dishes.

The Fat Lamb Country Inn

OPEN: 11-2 6-11. **BAR MEALS:** L served all week. D served all week 12-2 6-10. Av main course £8. **RESTAURANT:** L served all week. D served all week 12-2 6-10. Av 3 course à la carte £15. Av 4 course fixed price £12. **BREWERY/COMPANY:** Free House. **PRINCIPAL BEERS:** Boddingtons.
FACILITIES: Children welcome Children's licence Garden: Outdoor eating Dogs allowed. **NOTES:** Parking 60.
ROOMS: 12 bedrooms 12 en suite s£46 d£72 FR£60

SCALES
Map 11 NY32

White Horse Inn
CA12 4SY ☎ 017687 79241 ▤ 017687 79241
e-mail: thewhitehouseinn.net
Dir: *Off A66 between Keswick & Penrith*
Traditional Lakeland inn, built in 1610, with beamed ceilings, an open fire and antique furnishings. It is situated on the slopes of Blencathra, offering outstanding mountain scenery and making a good base for walkers. The good-value Sunday lunch goes down well with families, while popular options from the carte or specials board include Cumberland sausage, salmon fillet with garlic prawns, and Borrowdale trout.
OPEN: 12-2.30 Summer open until 4pm 6.30-10.30.
BAR MEALS: L served all week. D served all week 12-2 6.45-9. Av main course £8. **BREWERY/COMPANY:** Free House.
PRINCIPAL BEERS: Bass, Jennings, Black Sheep, Worthington.
FACILITIES: Children welcome. **NOTES:** Parking 6

SEATHWAITE
Map 08 SD29

Newfield Inn ♀
LA20 6ED ☎ 01229 716208
e-mail: paul@seathwaite.freeserve.co.uk
Dir: *A590 toward Barrow, then R onto A5092, becomes A595, follow for 1m, R at Duddon Bridge, 6m to Seathwaite*
17th-century inn set in Wordsworth's favourite valley, popular with walkers and climbers. A typical menu includes half roasted chicken, breaded haddock, lasagne, large gammon steaks, vegetarian chilli, Lancashire salad and a choice of steaks. Check the blackboard for regularly changing specials.
OPEN: 11-11. **BAR MEALS:** L served all week. D served all week 12-9 12-9. Av main course £6. **RESTAURANT:** L served all week. D served all week 12-9 12-9. **BREWERY/COMPANY:** Free House. **PRINCIPAL BEERS:** Theakston Best, XB & Old Peculier.
FACILITIES: Children welcome Garden: Food served outside.
NOTES: Parking 30 No credit cards

SEDBERGH

The Dalesman Country Inn
Main St LA10 5BN ☎ 015396 21183 ▤ 015396 21311
Dir: *J37 on M6, follow signs to Sedbergh, 1st pub in town on L.*
This 16th-century, central coaching inn, renowned for its summer floral displays, is handy for walks along the Dee or up on Howgill Fells. Lunchtime food concentrates on home-made pies, Angus beefburgers and Dalesman club sandwiches; evening choices extend to Lamb Henry on the bone, prime steaks and local sausages. One of the growing number of establishments that is using ostrich as an ingredient.

OPEN: 11-11. **BAR MEALS:** L served all week. D served all week 12-2.30 6-9.30. Av main course £8. **RESTAURANT:** L served all week. D served all week 12-2.30 6-9.30.
BREWERY/COMPANY: Free House.
PRINCIPAL BEERS: Tetleys, Theakston. **FACILITIES:** Children welcome Children's licence Garden: patio, Food served outside.
NOTES: Parking 8. **ROOMS:** 7 bedrooms 7 en suite s£25 d£50

SHAP

Greyhound Hotel
Main St CA10 3PW ☎ 01931 716305 ▤ 01931 716905
e-mail: postmaster@greyhoundshap.demon.co.uk
Built as a coaching inn in 1684, the Greyhound is the first hostelry available to walkers crossing over the notorious Shap Fell. Bonnie Prince Charlie is thought to have stayed here in 1745. Good pub grub and real ales.

THORNTHWAITE
Map 11 NY22

Swan Hotel & Country Inn
CA12 5SQ ☎ 017687 78256 ▤ 017687 78080
e-mail: bestswan@aol.com
Dir: *3m out of Keswick off A66, through Thornthwaite village*

Family-run 17th-century coaching inn set in stunning Lakeland scenery, complete with fell views and nearby lakeside walks. Lookout for the nearby 'Bishop's Rock', which caused great

continued on p108.

OPEN: 11-11 (Sun 12-10.30).
Closed 25 Dec.
BAR MEALS: L served all week.
D served all week 12-2 6.30-9.
Av main course £9.95
RESTAURANT: L served all week.
D served all week 12-2 6.30-9.
Av 3 course a la carte £20.
Av 4 course fixed price £15.50.
BREWERY/COMPANY:
Free House.
PRINCIPAL BEERS: Boddingtons,
Coniston Bluebird & Old Man,
Jennings Cumberland Ale.
FACILITIES: Children welcome.
Children's licence. Garden: patio
outdoor eating. Dogs allowed.
NOTES: Parking 100.
ROOMS: 9 bedrooms 9 en suite
s£47.50 d£70-75.

The Queens Head

Townhead LA23 1PW
☎ 015394 32174 📠 015394 31938
Dir: M6 J36, A590/591 westbound
towards Windermere, R at mini-rdbt
onto A592 signed Penrith/Ullswater, pub
2m on R.

Classic Lakeland hostelry nestling in the shelter of the Troutbeck Valley with stunning views across the Garburn Pass to Applethwaite Moors. For over 400 years it has given shelter and sustenance to travellers journeying across the Kirkstone Pass between Penrith and Windermere.

Little has changed inside since the inn's heyday as a thriving coaching inn. The rambling series of rooms are full of character and atmosphere, featuring picturesque oak beams, open fires, ancient carved settles, stone-flagged floors, and interesting old prints. Relax over a drink at the bar, which used to be an impressive Elizabethan four-poster bed belonging to Appleby Castle, then find a table by the crackling log fire and enjoy an excellent pub meal.

Menus are varied and imaginative, and although cooking is generally rustic and unfussy, quality raw ingredients and flair in the kitchen combine well to produce some stylish dishes. From filled baguettes and hearty one-dish specials at lunchtime - spiced fishcake with tomato compôte, venison braised in red wine) - the inventive evening menu may offer pork and smoked duck terrine with beetroot chutney, braised lamb shank on herb and garlic mash with red wine and rosemary, pork medallions with grain mustard and black pudding cream, or smoked haddock poached in coriander cream with braised leeks. Puddings may include chocolate tart and the traditional sticky toffee pudding. Excellent choice of real ales, including beers from local micro-breweries, and a good value list of wines.

Modern-day comforts extend upstairs to the nine en suite bedrooms; all are tastefully furnished and enjoy breathtaking Lakeland views.

distress to the Bishop of Derry in 1783, and is now regularly whitewashed in a traditional ceremony. The varied menu may list Cajun chicken with peanut butter sauce, seafood risotto with saffron and tiger prawns, lamb cobbler, and sirloin steak with green peppercorn sauce.
OPEN: 12-11. **BAR MEALS:** L served all week. D served all week 12-2.00 6-9. Av main course £7. **RESTAURANT:** . D served all week 6-8.30. Av 3 course à la carte £12. Av 4 course fixed price £16. **BREWERY/COMPANY:** Free House.
PRINCIPAL BEERS: Theakston, Tetleys, Youngers.
FACILITIES: Children welcome Children's licence Garden: outdoor eating, patio Dogs allowed. **NOTES:** Parking 40.
ROOMS: 20 bedrooms 20 en suite s£29 d£58 FR£68.00-£78.00

TIRRIL   Map 11 NY52

Pick of the Pubs

Queens Head Inn 🐶 ♈
CA10 2JF ☎ 01768 863219 🖹 01768 863243
e-mail: bookings@queensheadinn.co.uk
Dir: A66 towards Penrith then A6 S toward Shap. In Eamont Bridge take R just after Crown Hotel. Tirril 1m on B5320.

Owned by the Wordsworth family in the early 1800s, with a rental document in the bar signed by the great William himself, this is a typical Cumbrian stone-built pub - Grade II listed - with a long and colourful history. Not least, its own Tirril beers ceased production in 1899 only to be revived exactly a century later by the current owners. Up to three own-brew beers are on tap in the bar, renowned also for its blazing log fires in a spectacular inglenook. Modest, good value accommodation and traditional English pub food are a bonus for appreciative locals, visiting tourists and walkers alike. Soup with fresh local bread, grilled black pudding and goats' cheese croutes are the curtain raisers to steak suet pudding cooked in Tirril ale, shoulder of Lakeland lamb with red-currant gravy and cobbler of wild mushrooms in a thick stew topped with herb scones. Blackboards offer fresh seasonal fish such as red snapper with Caribbean ginger, tomato and Cointreau sauce. Follow with home-made puddings, Lake District ice creams and selected north country cheeses.
OPEN: 12-3 6-11 (Sat 12-11, Sun 12-10.30). **BAR MEALS:** L served all week. D served all week 12-2 6-9.30. Av main course £6. **RESTAURANT:** L served all week. D served all week 12-2 6-9.30. Av 3 course à la carte £13.
BREWERY/COMPANY: Free House.
PRINCIPAL BEERS: Jennings Cumberland, Boddingtons, Tirril Bewshers Best, Dent Aviator. **FACILITIES:** Children welcome Children's licence Dogs allowed Water.
NOTES: Parking 60. **ROOMS:** 7 bedrooms 4 en suite s£30 d£45

TROUTBECK   Map 11 NY40

Mortal Man Hotel ★ ★ ♈
Upper Rd LA23 1PL ☎ 015394 33193 🖹 015394 31261
e-mail: the-mortalman@btinternet.com
Dir: 2 1/2m N of jct between A591 & A592, L at Troutbeck sign the R at T jct, Hotel 800yrds on R
Tucked away in the hamlet of Troutbeck beneath the fells, and commanding wonderful views towards Lake Windermere, this 300-year-old inn acquired its name from the legendary giant buried in its foundations. Bedrooms are attractively decorated. Home-cooked food ranges from steak and kidney pudding in the bar to a restaurant dish like salmon steak wrapped in bacon and served with a mustard sauce.
OPEN: 12-11. **BAR MEALS:** L served all week. D served all week 12-9.30. Av main course £7.50. **RESTAURANT:** L served all week. D served all week 12-3 7-9.30. Av 3 course à la carte £18.
BREWERY/COMPANY: Free House.
PRINCIPAL BEERS: Theakston Best. **FACILITIES:** Garden: Food served outside Dogs allowed. **NOTES:** Parking 15.
ROOMS: 12 bedrooms 12 en suite s£50 d£60

Pick of the Pubs

Queens Head Hotel 🏵 🏵 ♦♦♦♦ ♈
Townhead LA23 1PW ☎ 015394 32174
🖹 015394 31938

See Pick of the Pubs on page 107

Coniston Brewing Co.

Connected to The Black Bull Inn & Hotel, the Coniston Brewing Co. was launched to brew beer for the pub. Local mountain water is a vital ingredient of brews such as Blacksmiths Ale (5%), Old Man Ale (4.4%) and Opium (4%). Bluebird Bitter (3.6%) is brewed in memory of Donald Campbell who was killed on nearby Coniston Water in 1967 while attempting to break the water speed record.

OPEN: 12-11 (Sun 12-10.30). May close 3-5pm during winter.
BAR MEALS: L served all week. D served all week 12-2.30 6.30-9. Av main course £8.50.
RESTAURANT: L served all week. D served all week 12-2.30 6.30-9. Av 3 course a la carte £15. Av 3 course fixed price £14.95.
BREWERY/COMPANY: Free House.
PRINCIPAL BEERS: Theakston Best, Jennings Cumberland, Black Sheep Best & Special.
FACILITIES: No under 14s after 4pm. Garden: terrace, outdoor eating. Dogs allowed.
NOTES: Parking 40.
ROOMS: 11 bedrooms 11 en suite s£32-£37 d£54-£62 FR£54-£105.

The Brackenrigg Inn

◆◆◆ 🐾 ♀
CA11 0LP
☎ 017684 86206 📄 017684 86945
e-mail: enquiries@brackenrigginn.co.uk
Dir: A66 to Keswick, A592 for 6m to Watermillock

Enjoying sweeping views across Lake Ullswater and surrounding fells from its elevated terrace and fine gardens, this traditional 18th-century coaching inn majors on good quality food and comfortable modern accommodation in en suite bedrooms and self-catering in converted stable cottages.

The Brackenrigg Inn is an unpretentious, white-painted roadside hostelry that makes the most of its elevated position, offering casual visitors and overnight guests stunnings views of Ullswater and distant peaks, including Helvellyn, from its traditional bar lounge and, no-smoking dining room. Add Black Sheep and Jennings ales, an imaginative choice of modern pub food and varied styles of accommodation to suit all needs and you have the ideal base from which to explore the delights of the Northern Lakes, whether it be walking, climbing, watersports, golfing, or just touring this area.

Tuck into a traditional bar snack (hearty soups, filled baguettes) in the homely bar or out on the terrace on warm summer days, or sample modern British dishes in the restaurant. In the latter a weekly-changing menu may offer jumbo shrimps deep-fried in chilli and lime batter with avocado salad and sweet chilli dressing and warm mussel and leek tart infused with saffron with a lemon butter sauce to start, followed by salmon and crab risotto with Parmesan shavings and a white wine, mussel and dill sauce, oven-baked halibut with tomato, olive and herb crust, roast breast of duck with leg confit, grilled sweet potatoes and a cassis sauce, or Cumberland sausage braised with Puy lentils, smoked bacon and thyme and served with red cabbage. Round off with caramelised rice pudding.

Retire to one of the eleven, practically furnished en suite bedrooms, each with breathtaking lake and fell views.

ULVERSTON Map 08 SD27

Royal Oak
Spark Bridge LA12 8BS ☎ 01229 861006
Dir: From Ulverston take A590 N.Village off A5092
Set in a small village, this large, 18th-century pub offers a varied menu. Dishes include fresh fish, home-made pies and puddings, and regularly changing specials such as steak Harrington and braised lamb shank.
OPEN: 12-3 6-11 (Sun all day). **BAR MEALS:** L served all week. D served all week 12-2 6-9. Av main course £6.25.
BREWERY/COMPANY: Enterprise Inns.
PRINCIPAL BEERS: Tetley, Boddingtons, Marston Pedigree, Black Sheep. **FACILITIES:** Children welcome Garden: Food served outside Dogs allowed Water. **NOTES:** Parking 30

WASDALE HEAD Map 11 NY10

Wasdale Head Inn ♀
CA20 1EX ☎ 019467 26229 ▤ 019467 26334
e-mail: wasdaleheadinn@msn.com
Dir: Follow signs 'Wasdale' from A595, the inn is at the head of the valley
Dramatically surrounded by England's tallest mountains and superbly situated at the head of remote Wasdale, this welcoming Lakeland inn is a perfect base for walking and climbing. Inside you'll find a rustic, slate-floored bar and oak-panelled walls adorned with photographs recalling man's love affair with mountains.
Sample one of the local micro-brewery ales while you peruse the appealing menus. Expect goats' cheese and seafood pancake for starters, then halibut with hollandaise sauce and rack of local lamb with rosemary and mint jus among the main courses.
OPEN: 11-11 (Sun 12-10.30). **BAR MEALS:** L served all week. D served all week 11-9 11-9. Av main course £6.50.
RESTAURANT: . D served all week 7-8. Av 4 course fixed price £22. **BREWERY/COMPANY:** Free House.
PRINCIPAL BEERS: Wasd Ale, Jennings Cumberland, Heskett Newmarket, Kern Knott's Cracking Stout. **FACILITIES:** Children welcome Garden: beer garden Dogs allowed on lead, water. **NOTES:** Parking 50. **ROOMS:** 15 bedrooms 15 en suite s£35 d£70 FR£70-£90

WATERMILLOCK Map 11 NY42

Pick of the Pubs

Brackenrigg Inn ♦♦♦ 🕭 ♀
CA11 0LP ☎ 017684 86206 ▤ 017684 86945
e-mail: enquiries@brackenrigginn.co.uk
See Pick of the Pubs on page 109

WIGTON Map 11 NY24

Oddfellows Arms
Caldbeck CA7 8EA ☎ 016974 78227 ▤ 016974 78134
Situated in a scenic conservation village, this traditional country pub-restaurant is ideally placed for exploring the Lake District and the Eden Valley. Its spectacular location among the northern fells makes it a popular haunt of walkers on the Cumbrian Way and cyclists on the Coast to Coast route. A single menu throughout offers popular dishes such as chargrilled sirloin steak, deep-fried Whitby scampi, steak and ale pie and chicken curry.
OPEN: 12-3 6-11 (open all day during summer). **BAR MEALS:** L served all week. D served all week 12-2 6.00-8.30. Av main course £7.95. **RESTAURANT:** L served all week. D served all week 12-2 6.30-8.30. Av 3 course à la carte £14.45.
BREWERY/COMPANY: Jennings.
PRINCIPAL BEERS: Jennings Bitter. **FACILITIES:** Children welcome Garden: outdoor eating, Dogs allowed Water. **NOTES:** Parking 10. **ROOMS:** 8 bedrooms 8 en suite s£28 d£48

WINDERMERE

The Watermill
Ings LA8 9PY ☎ 01539 821309
This traditional, creeper-clad inn is very popular with walkers, not least because it is locally renowned for its impressive selection of real ales.

PUBS ON SCREEN
Next time you go to a pub, take a close look at your surroundings but don't be surprised if you can't remember exactly where you've seen the place before. It's more than likely that you've spotted it on the large or small screen as many of Britain's hostelries have been used as locations for film and television productions over the years. More often than not the company chooses a classic inn in a picturesque English village and sometimes a few minor cosmetic changes had to be met the demands of the script. For example, modern photographs and electric lighting had to be removed from the Fleece at Bretforton in Worcestershire before this historic pub could appear as the Blue Dragon in the 1994 version of 'Martin Chuzzlewit.' Elsewhere, the back parlour of the Kings Arms at Askrigg in North Yorkshire was converted into the Drovers Arms for the television version of James Herriot's 'All Creatures Great and Small.' The Jolly Sailor at Bursledon near Southampton featured in the sailing soap 'Howards Way' and the George at Norton St Philip in Somerset has appeared in 'Moll Flanders,' 'Tom Jones' and 'The Remains of the Day.' You might also recognise the Castle Inn at Chiddingstone in Kent from 'The Wind in the Willows,' 'The Wicked Lady' and 'Room with a View.' One of the most frequently used hostelries is the Stag & Huntsmen at Hambleden in Buckinghamshire. 'Chitty, Chitty, Bang, Bang,' 'Poirot,' 'A Village Affair' and '101 Dalmatians' were filmed here - among many other productions.

YANWATH   Map 11 NY52

Pick of the Pubs

The Yanwath Gate Inn
CA10 2LF ☎ 01768 862386 ▤ 01768 864006
e-mail: ian.rhind@virgin.net
Unassuming 17th-century village pub located two miles
from M6 (J40) and an ideal base for touring the Lake
District. Weary travellers can relax by the log fire in the
beamed bar and enjoy a pint of Hesket Newmarket
Skiddaw Special and good, imaginatively prepared food.
Alternatively, relax in the separate restaurant overlooking
a pleasant garden. Bar snacks range from smoked salmon
soufflé and baked stuffed mushrooms to steak baguette
and salmon fishcakes with tomato and basil sauce, while
Yanwath fish pie, chicken and leek pie and mustard and
garlic marinaded rump steak feature as main courses. Try
deep-fried Mozzarella with tomato and black olive salsa,
lamb steak with Parmesan and parsley topping or Barbary
duck with redcurrant and cream sauce from the
blackboard menu.
OPEN: 12-2.30 (Sun 12-3, 6-10.30) 6-11 (Winter 6.30-11).
Closed 2nd 2 weeks of Jan. **BAR MEALS:** L served all week.
D served all week 12-2 6-9.30. Av main course £6.25.
RESTAURANT: L served all week. D served all week 12-2.00
6-9.30. Av 3 course à la carte £16.
BREWERY/COMPANY: Free House.
PRINCIPAL BEERS: Theakston, Hesket Newmarket Skiddaw
Special. **FACILITIES:** Children welcome Children's licence
Garden: outdoor eating, patio. **NOTES:** Parking 20

DERBYSHIRE

ALFRETON   Map 09 SK45

White Horse Inn ♇
Badger Ln, Woolley Moor DE55 6FG ☎ 01246 590319
Dir: From A632 (Matlock/Chesterfield rd) take B6036. Pub 1m after
Ashover. From A61 take B6036 to Woolley Moor
Situated on an old toll road, close to Ogston Reservoir, this
18th-century inn has outstanding views over the Amber Valley.
Dishes from the bar menu or restaurant carte can be taken
anywhere in the pub, and options range from sandwiches,
paninis and traditional fish and chips to pan-fried tuna on
niçoise salad, and steak on tomato and mushroom ragout with
watercress butter.
OPEN: 12-2 6-11 (Sun 12-10.30, all day summer wknds). Closed
26 Dec. **BAR MEALS:** L served all week. D served all week 12-2
6-9. Av main course £5.50. **RESTAURANT:** L served all week.
D served all week 12-2 6-9. Av 3 course à la carte £13.
BREWERY/COMPANY: Free House. **PRINCIPAL BEERS:** Bass
& three regularly changing guest ales. **FACILITIES:** Children
welcome Garden: patio, BBQ, outdoor eating Dogs allowed.
NOTES: Parking 50

ASHBOURNE   Map 09 SK14

Barley Mow Inn
Kirk Ireton DE6 3JP ☎ 01335 370306
On the edge of the Peak District National Park, this imposing
inn at the head of the village street dates from 1683, and has
remained largely unchanged over the years. Close to
Carsington Water, ideal for sailing, fishing and bird watching.
Ales from the cask and traditional cider; fresh granary rolls at
lunchtime and evening meals for residents only.

OPEN: 12-2 7-11. Closed Dec 25 & Dec 31.
BREWERY/COMPANY: Free House.
PRINCIPAL BEERS: Marston's Pedigree, Hook Norton, Burton
Bridge, Whim Hartington. **FACILITIES:** Children welcome
Garden: beer garden, Dogs allowed. **ROOMS:** 5 bedrooms
5 en suite s£25 d£45 FR£50 No credit cards

Dog & Partridge Country Inn ★ ★
Swinscoe DE6 2HS ☎ 01335 343158 ▤ 01335 342742
17th-century coaching inn within easy reach of Alton Towers.
Variety of accommodation; welcoming bar; extensive pub
menu.

The Green Man ♦♦♦♦
St Johns St DE6 1GH ☎ 01335 345783 ▤ 01335 346613
Dir: In town centre off A52
Located in the heart of Ashbourne, this 17th-century coaching
inn has two bars, the Johnson and the Boswell. On the specials
board you'll find fresh fish and shellfish, local game, and
traditional favourites like beef in Guinness and home made
pies. The comfortable en suite bedrooms are attractively
decorated.
OPEN: 11-11 (Sun 12-10.30). Closed Dec 25. **BAR MEALS:** L
served all week. D served all week 12-2.30 6-8.30. Av main course
£5. **BREWERY/COMPANY:** Free House.
PRINCIPAL BEERS: Marston's Pedigree, Bass.
FACILITIES: Children welcome Dogs allowed Not during Meal
times. **NOTES:** Parking 12. **ROOMS:** 18 bedrooms 18 en suite
s£40 d£60 FR£80.00

BAKEWELL   Map 09 SK26

Pick of the Pubs

The Chequers Inn ▨ ♇
Froggatt Edge, Calver S32 3ZJ ☎ 01433 630231
▤ 01433 631072
On the steep banks of Froggatt Edge high above Calver
Bridge and close to many Peak District attractions, this
Grade II listed building was converted from 18th-century
cottages and now offers imaginative food and comfortable
en suite accommodation. The smart interior has a distinct
bistro feel with rag-washed yellow walls, bare board
floors, attractive prints and comfortable furnishings.
   A daily-changing blackboard menu might offer salmon
and langoustine terrine with lemon mascarpone, warm
salad of quail with grape chutney, Thai red pork curry and
whole grilled Dover sole.
   The regular 'Innkeeper's Fare' lists hearty sandwiches,
Greek salad and smoked haddock fishcakes. To follow, try
chocolate and nut pot or apple and almond crumble.
Behind the pub, a landscaped beer garden gives way to
some ten acres of steep, wild woodland.
OPEN: 12-3 (Sat 12-11, Sun 12-10.30) 6-11. **BAR MEALS:** L
served all week. D served all week 12-2 6-9.30. Av main
course £7.25. **BREWERY/COMPANY:** Free House.
PRINCIPAL BEERS: Theakstons, Marstons Pedigree, John
Smiths,. **FACILITIES:** Children welcome Garden: Food
served outside Dogs allowed. **NOTES:** Parking 45.
ROOMS: 6 bedrooms 6 en suite s£48 d£48

BAKEWELL continued

George Hotel ◆◆
Church St, Youlgreave DE45 1VW ☎ 01629 636292
Family-run pub close to many popular attractions, including
Haddon Hall and Chatsworth House, and a handy base for
walking and rock climbing in the Peak District and Derbyshire
Dales. Try one of the game dishes - pheasant, rabbit or hare -
or home-made pies. Alternatively, there are home-made
sausages, fresh cod, or giant Yorkshire puddings.

OPEN: open all day. **BAR MEALS:** L served all week.
D served all week 12-2 6.30-9. Av main course £6.50.
BREWERY/COMPANY: PRINCIPAL BEERS: Courage
Directors, Bateman XB, John Smiths, Theakston.
FACILITIES: Children welcome Dogs allowed Water.
NOTES: Parking 20. **ROOMS:** 3 bedrooms 2 en suite d£17 No
credit cards

Pick of the Pubs

The Lathkil Hotel
Over Haddon DE45 1JE ☎ 01629 812501
▤ 01629 812501
e-mail: info@lathkil.co.uk
Formerly 'The Miners Arms', named from the old lead
mines that date back to Roman times, an overnight stay
here remains in the memory for its panoramic views from
the Victorian-style bar of the hills and dales of the Peak
District.
    Home-cooked food has an enviable reputation locally
with a lunchtime hot and cold buffet in summer and more
extensive evening choices supplemented by cooked-to-
order pizzas. Following onion bhajis with cucumber raita
or tiger prawns in filo, indulge perhaps in a fruit sorbet
before tackling sea bass with garlic and rosemary,
Wootton Farm venison steak with Stilton sauce or Barbary
duck breast with blackcurrant coulis.
    More conventional steaks with optional seuces and
steak, kidney and oyster pie, along with a daily vegetarian
dish, are regular alternatives. To follow perhaps treacle
tart or toffee and apple crumble from the home-made
puddings list or cheese with biscuits.
OPEN: 11.30-3 (Summer open all day Sat-Sun) 7-11.
BAR MEALS: L served all week 12-2. Av main course £5.95.
RESTAURANT: . D served all week 7-9. Av 3 course à la carte
£12 9. **BREWERY/COMPANY: PRINCIPAL BEERS:** Whim
Hartington, Timothy Taylor Landlord, Wells Bombardier,
Marston's Pedigree. **FACILITIES:** Children welcome
Garden: outdoor eating Dogs allowed Water.
NOTES: Parking 28. **ROOMS:** 4 bedrooms 4 en suite
s£37.50 d£55

Pick of the Pubs

The Monsal Head Hotel ★ ★ ☜ ♀
Monsal Head DE45 1NL ☎ 01629 640250
▤ 01629 640815
e-mail: Christine@monsalhead.com
Dir: A6 from Bakewell towards Buxton. 1.5m to Ashford. Follow
Monsal Head signs, B6465 for 1m

Set against a spectacular backdrop of hills and dales, the
disused viaduct at Monsal Head has long been a familiar
landmark in the glorious Peak District. It even crops up on
television from time to time, most notably in the drama
series 'Peak Practice' which is filmed locally. Long before
the era of TV, horses dragged guests and their luggage
from the railway station up the steep incline to the hotel.
The old stable that once housed the horses is now a cosy
bar and part of the hotel. One menu operates throughout
the restaurant, bar and eating area, with such dishes as
venison steak with Kilkenny mash and redcurrant sauce,
game pie, pork loin steak glazed with smoked cheese on a
bed of caramelised apple, and cod and chips with mushy
peas. Small plates, grills and snacks are also available.
OPEN: 12-11. Closed 25 Dec. **BAR MEALS:** L served all
week. D served all week 12-9.30 7-9.30. Av main course £7.
RESTAURANT: L served all week. D served all week
7-9.30. Av 3 course à la carte £12.
BREWERY/COMPANY: Free House.
PRINCIPAL BEERS: Theakston Best & Old Peculier, Timothy
Taylor Landlord, Courage Directors, Whim Hartington.
FACILITIES: Children welcome Garden: Dogs allowed.
NOTES: Parking 20. **ROOMS:** 8 bedrooms 6 en suite s£30
d£35 FR£55.00-£65.00

The Rutland Arms Hotel ◉ ★ ★ ★
The Square DE45 1BT ☎ 01629 812812 ▤ 01629 812309
e-mail: rutland@bakewell.demon.co.uk
Dir: Town centre
Historic 18th-century former coaching inn, famous for being
where Jane Austen wrote her novel 'Pride and Prejudice'.
Popular food is served in both the Tavern Bar and Four
Seasons restaurant, the former offering classic dishes like
tagliatelle carbonara, oven baked fillet of salmon, grilled
chicken breast, fish and chips, and steak and kidney pudding.
Salads, baguettes, jacket potatoes and rolls are also available.
OPEN: 11-11. **BAR MEALS:** L served all week. D served all week
12-2 6.30-9. Av main course £6.50. **RESTAURANT:** L served all
week. D served all week 12-2 7-9. Av 3 course à la carte £19.50.
Av 2 course fixed price £16.50. **BREWERY/COMPANY:** Free
House. **PRINCIPAL BEERS:** Theakstons Best, Greene King
Morland Old Speckled Hen,. **FACILITIES:** Children welcome
Dogs allowed. **NOTES:** Parking 35. **ROOMS:** 35 bedrooms 35
en suite s£47 d£79

**YORKSHIRE BRIDGE INN,
BAMFORD ★ ★**
Ashopton Road S33 0AZ.
Tel: 01433 651361
Directions: A57 from M1, L
onto A6013, pub 1m on R
*Overlooking the Ladybower
Reservoir and the Derwent
Valley, this charming inn is
located in the heart of Peak
National Park - prime
walking country. Generous
bar food, good real ales and
a warm welcome in the well
refurbished bars. Bedrooms*
Open: 11-11. Bar Meals: 12-2,
6-9 (Sun 12-8.30). Children
welcome. Garden. Parking.
No muddy boots. No dogs
inside when food is being
served.
(see page 114 for full entry)

*Pub*WALK

Yorkshire Bridge Inn, Bamford

An exhilarating walk to the top of Win Hill, with its stunning Peak District views, and to Ladybower Reservoir and its magnificent dam.

On leaving the inn, turn right and follow the main road (A6013) for 110 yards (100m). Turn right, signed Thornhill, and follow the road downhill to cross the bridge (Yorkshire Bridge) over the River Derwent. Once over the bridge, bear left for 10m, then pass through the gate on your right and climb the track to a junction of paths. Proceed straight across and follow the track gently uphill for about 1/2m (0.8km) to the next footpath waymarker.

Take the track on the right and proceed along the side of the hill to a wooded area. Follow the waymarked path to the top of Win Hill. Pause to take in the magnificent view, then carry on down the opposite side and follow the track along the ridge for

approximately a mile (1.6km) to where a stone wall crosses your path. Bear right and head for the gate giving access to woodland. Enter the woodland and follow the road downhill to Ladybower Reservoir.

Turn right and follow the access road to the dam. Cross the dam, enjoying the fine views up and down the valley, then turn right along the main road (A6013) back to the inn.

Distance: 6 miles (10km)
Map: OS Landranger 110
Terrain: woodland and heather covered moorland
Paths: moorland paths, field and woodland tracks
Gradient: undulating; one fairly short steep climb

*Walk submitted by:
Nigel Palmer*

England

Pick of the Pubs

Yorkshire Bridge Inn ★ ★
Ashopton Rd S33 0AZ ☎ 01433 651361
▤ 01433 651361
e-mail: mr@ybridge.force9.co.uk
Dir: A57 from M1, L onto A6013, pub 1m on R

A classic 19th-century inn surrounded by majestic Peak District scenery and immortalised by the Dambusters' wartime training over the nearby Ladybower reservoir. Its newly refurbished accommodation is particularly useful to know in the area, with a slightly up-market feel pervading the bars and dining-room.

Cumberland sausages with crispy bacon, red snapper baked with crabmeat and chicken en croute with tarragon and spinach typify the daily specials, along with regular main dishes such as pot-roast lamb with minted gravy and crisply roast half duckling with chef's recipe sauce. Grills, salads, vegetarian dishes and children's options make up the numbers.
OPEN: 11-11. **BAR MEALS:** L served all week. D served all week 12-2 6-9. Av main course £6.50. **RESTAURANT:** L served all week. D served all week 12-2 6-9. Av 3 course à la carte £14. **BREWERY/COMPANY:** Free House.
PRINCIPAL BEERS: Theakston Best & Old Peculier, Stones, Bass, Tetley. **FACILITIES:** Children welcome Garden: Food served outside Dogs allowed residents only.
NOTES: Parking 40. **ROOMS:** 14 bedrooms 14 en suite s£39 d£54   *See Pub Walk on page 113*

Pick of the Pubs

The Devonshire Arms 🐑
The Square DE4 2NR ☎ 01629 733259
▤ 01629 733259
Dir: From A6 onto B6012 at Rowsley
Built of honey coloured stone, this civilised dining pub nestles in a picturesque village near Chatsworth Park. The pub originated as three separate cottages, and was converted into a popular coaching inn in 1747. John Grosvenor, the present landlord, keeps a list of all the innkeepers since that date. Charles Dickens was a frequent visitor, and it's rumoured that King Edward VII met here with his mistress, Alice Keppel. Today, visitors are welcomed by oak beams, stone flagged floors and winter fires.

Meals are freshly cooked to order, and the extensive menu is also served on the patio in warm weather. Come for home-made soup and a baguette if you must - but starters like devilled whitebait, or smoked chicken and bacon salad, herald a selection of main courses that includes beef and horseradish pudding, gammon hock with white bean sauce, or kiln roasted salmon.

OPEN: 11-11 (Sun 12-10.30). Closed 25 Dec.
BAR MEALS: L served all week. D served all week 12-9.30.
Av main course £5.95. **RESTAURANT:** L served all week.
D served all week 12-9.30. Av 3 course à la carte £10.
BREWERY/COMPANY: Free House.
PRINCIPAL BEERS: Black Sheep Best & Special, Theakston Old Peculier & XB. **FACILITIES:** Children welcome Garden: Patio area, Food served outside. **NOTES:** Parking 120

THE MAKING OF BEER

The traditional ingredients of beer are water, barley malt, hops, yeast and ripe judgement. One traditional brewery's product will taste different from another's due to variations in the blending of ingredients and the timing of processes. It all starts with barley, malted in a kiln at the maltings: the higher the temperature, the darker the beer. The powdered malt is mixed with hot water to make a mash. How hot the mash is and how long it is allowed to stand will affect the taste and in the old days local spring water gave beer a distinctive local flavour. Burton upon Trent's reputation rested on the gypsum in the town's water. The liquid from the mash is boiled up with the hops - the more hops, the bitterer - and sugar is often added. Next the liquid is cooled and yeast is added to make it ferment. The 'green beer' was eventually run into casks to mature, but nowadays most beer is filtered, sterilised and carbonated. This is keg beer, stored in sealed containers and tasting more like bottled beers, which are put through the same processes.

The Church's Sway

Inn signs reflecting the past importance of the Church include the Cross, the Mitre, the Adam and Eve, the Angel. The Salutation commemorates the Annunciation to the Virgin Mary. The Anchor is not always a nautical sign, but can be a Christian symbol of hope. The Star may be the one the three kings followed to Bethlehem and the Seven Stars are the Virgin Mary's crown. The Bell is a church bell and names like the Eight Bells are generally related to a notable local peal. Inns near a church dedicated to St Peter may be called the Cross Keys, which are the saint's keys of heaven and hell, or the Cock, for the one that crowed twice. The Lamb and Flag was the badge of the crusading Knights Templar (and was later adopted by the Merchant Tailors). The Catherine Wheel is the Emblem of St Catherine of Alexandria, who was much venerated in the crusading period and according to legend was martyred by being broken on a spiked wheel.

BIRCHOVER   Map 09 SK26

Pick of the Pubs

The Druid Inn
Main St DE4 2BL ☎ 01629 650302 📠 01629 650559
Dir: From A6 between Matlock & Bakewell take B5056, signed Ashbourne.Take 2nd L to Birchover

This ivy-covered free house stands in a quiet village above Darley Dale, close to the edge of the Peak District National Park. The nearby caves, canopies and terracing at Row Tor Rocks were supposedly once inhabited by Druids. In fact, most of these curious carvings date from the 19th century, and were carried out by an eccentric vicar, the Rev Thomas Eyres. A large two-storey extension supplements the narrow bar with its open fire and blackboard menus, and there's a terrace garden for al fresco summer dining. The eclectic menu has long been popular with the pub's faithful clientele. You might start with New Zealand mussels, deep-fried Buxton blue cheese, or crispy prawns with garlic and soy dip. Next comes marinated rack of lamb, Derbyshire pheasant and venison casserole, pan-fried swordfish, or Siam chicken. Puddings include treacle tart, brandy snap baskets, or apple and marzipan torte.
OPEN: 12-3 7-11. Closed 25/26 Dec. **BAR MEALS:** L served all week. D served all week 12-2 7-9.00. **RESTAURANT:** L served all week. D served all week 12-2 7-9.00. Av 3 course à la carte £15.
BREWERY/COMPANY: Free House.
PRINCIPAL BEERS: Mansfield Bitter, Marstons Pedigree.
FACILITIES: Children welcome Garden: terrace, outdoor eating Dogs allowed Guide dogs only inside, Water.
NOTES: Parking 36

BIRCH VALE   Map 09 SK08

Pick of the Pubs

The Waltzing Weasel Inn
New Mills Rd SK22 1BT ☎ 01663 743402
📠 01663 743402
e-mail: w-weazel@zen.co.uk
Dir: W from M1 at Chesterfield

Set within the heart of the Peak District Hills, a popular traditional English country inn beloved of walkers and business people alike, where there is no music nor machines - and mobile phones are not permitted. Country antiques are a feature of the bedrooms and bar, while from the garden and mullion-windowed restaurant there are dramatic views of Kinder Scout nearby.

Solidly English bar menus are supplemented by specialities influenced by the long-standing owners' love of Italy. Thus sirloin steak and onion baguettes rub shoulders with sardine tapenade; seafood tart and meat and game Peak Pie ('back to vieille cuisine') with a Fantasia Italiana large enough to be shared by two people and devised to delight - not just feed - vegetarians.

Marked alongside soups and pâtés on the chalk board are esoteric daily casseroles such as Greek stifado and Middle Eastern tagine. On Sunday only, traditional roast beef with Yorkshire pudding; and à la carte dining nightly in the restaurant.
OPEN: 12-3 6-11 (Sun 12-3, 6-10.30). **BAR MEALS:** L served all week. D served all week 12-2 7-9.30. Av main course £10. **RESTAURANT:** L served all week. D served all week 12-2 7-9. Av 3 course à la carte £26.50. Av 3 course fixed price £26.50. **BREWERY/COMPANY:** Free House.
PRINCIPAL BEERS: Marston's Best & Pedigree, Timothy Taylor Landlord, Camerons Strongarm. **FACILITIES:** Garden: outdoor eating, patio Dogs allowed. **NOTES:** Parking 42.
ROOMS: 8 bedrooms 8 en suite s£45 d£75

BRADWELL   Map 09 SK18

The Bowling Green
Smalldale S33 9JQ ☎ 01433 620450
The Bowling Green is an attractive 16th-century, white village inn decorated with colourful hanging baskets. Bedrooms.

BRASSINGTON   Map 09 SK25

Ye Olde Gate Inne
Well St DE4 4HJ ☎ 01629 540448
Dir: 3m NW of Carsington Water
The inn was built in 1616 of local stone and salvaged Armada timbers, and has one or two supernatural residents. There is a huge inglenook fireplace with a range, and a smaller one in the snug. Soon to come under new management.

BUXTON   Map 09 SK07

Bull i' th' Horn
Flagg SK17 9QQ ☎ 01298 83348
Part medieval hall and part roadhouse, this charming pub has a family room, a terrace and a garden play area. Close to High Peak Trail. Bedrooms.

BUXTON continued

The Queen Anne ♀
Great Hucklow, nr Tideswell SK17 8RF ☎ 01298 871246
e-mail: paul.alderson@talk21.com
Dir: A623 turn off at Anchor pub toward Bradwell, 2nd R to
Great Hucklow
Situated at the heart of the Peak District National Park, this
traditional country inn dates back to 1621 and is reputedly
haunted by the friendly ghost of a previous licensee. Ideally
located for walking, fishing and climbing. Expect steak and
kidney pie, venison sausages, chicken and Stilton sauce, and
rump steak - among other dishes.
OPEN: 11.30-3 (except Mon & Wed) 5-11 (Sat 11.30-11, Sun 12-
10.30). **BAR MEALS:** L served Tue, Thu-Sun. D served Tue-Sun
12-2 6.30-9. Av main course £5.95. **BREWERY/COMPANY:** Free
House. **PRINCIPAL BEERS:** Mansfield Cask Pedigree, Oakwell
Barnsley Bitter. **FACILITIES:** Children welcome Garden:
patio/terrace, outdoor eating, BBQ Dogs allowed.
NOTES: Parking 30. **ROOMS:** 2 bedrooms 2 en suite

The Sun Inn
33 High St SK17 6HA ☎ 01298 23452
Traditional town pub full of beams, boards, open fires and a
wealth of memorabilia. Unusual real ales, regular beer
festivals. Also a good choice of local cheeses.

CASTLETON	Map 09 SK18

The George
Castle St S33 8QG ☎ 01433 620238   ▤ 01433 620886
The earliest known reference to this pub comes from the
Domesday Book, and the building has been used as an
alehouse since at least 1577. This distinguished heritage is
guarded and extended by the current team who serve an
imaginative international menu.

The Olde Nag's Head
Cross St S33 8WH ☎ 01433 620248   ▤ 01433 621604
Grey-stone 17th-century coaching inn situated in the heart of
the Peak District National Park, close to Chatsworth House,
Haddon Hall and miles of wonderful walks. Cosy lounge bar
with open fire and antiques and a Victorian restaurant. Stylish
bedrooms. New owners, interesting menus - more reports
please!

DARLEY ABBEY	Map 09 SK33

The Abbey
Darley St DE22 1DX ☎ 01332 558297
Dir: A38 onto A6 to Duffield Rd
Dating from 1147, this simple medieval hall house is the only
remaining building of an Augustinian Abbey and makes a
striking pub. With beamed ceilings, church pews and a spiral
stone staircase, it is worth the riverside walk from Derby city
centre.

DERBY	

The Alexandra Hotel
203 Siddals Rd DE1 2QE ☎ 01332 293993
▤ 01332 293993
Two-roomed hotel filled with railway memorabilia. Noted for
its real ale (450 different brews on tap each year), range of
malt whiskies, and friendly atmosphere. Traditional pub food.

DOE LEA	Map 09 SK46

Hardwick Inn ♀
Hardwick Park S44 5QJ ☎ 01246 850245
▤ 01246 856365
e-mail: Batty@hardwickinn.co.uk
Dir: M1 J29 take A6175. 0.5m L (signed Stainsby/Hardwick Hall). After
Stainsby, 2m L at staggered jnctn

Dating from 1607 and built of locally quarried sandstone, this
historic inn was originally the lodge to the National Trust's
Hardwick Hall. Home-made pies feature on the menu and
there's a carvery restaurant offering traditional home-cooked
joints.
  The specials board includes daily delivered fresh fish. Also
available are ploughmans, salads, sandwiches, jacket potatoes
and a choice of steaks.
OPEN: 11.30-11 (Sun 12-10.30, food 12-9). **BAR MEALS:** L
served all week. D served all week 11.30-9.30. Av main course
£5.50. **RESTAURANT:** 12-2 7-9. Av 3 course à la carte £11.75. Av
3 course fixed price £11.75. **BREWERY/COMPANY:** Free House.
PRINCIPAL BEERS: Theakston Old Peculier & XB, Greene King
Old Speckled Hen, Ruddles County, Courage Directors.
FACILITIES: Children welcome Children's licence Garden:
patio, outdoor eating Dogs allowed outside only

DRONFIELD	Map 09 SK37

The Old Sidings
91 Chesterfield Rd DE8 2XE
☎ 01246 410023   ▤ 01246 292202
e-mail: bill@theoldsidings.demon.co.uk
Unpretentious, stone-built tavern, situated just 30 feet from
the main Sheffield railway line. A must for railway buffs, it's
full of railway paraphernalia.

EYAM	Map 09 SK27

Miners Arms ♦♦♦
Water Ln S32 5RG ☎ 01433 630853
Dir: Off B6521, 5m S of Bakewell
Expect a warm welcome from the new licensee at this 17th-
century inn and restaurant in the famous plague village of
Eyam, which developed during the Roman occupation as an
important centre for lead mining.
  Excellent walks close by in the glorious Peak District. Food is
freshly prepared with the use of local produce and the
seasonally changing dining-room menu is traditional English in
style with some French influences. Good bar meals include
steak and ale pie, Cumberland sausages and haddock in beer
batter.
continued

OPEN: 12-11. **BAR MEALS:** L served all week 12-9. Av main course £8. **RESTAURANT:** . D served Tue-Sat 7-9. Av 3 course à la carte £18.50. **BREWERY/COMPANY:** Free House. **PRINCIPAL BEERS:** Fuller's London Pride,. **FACILITIES:** Garden: patio, food served outdoors Dogs allowed. **NOTES:** Parking 50. **ROOMS:** 7 bedrooms 7 en suite s£30 d£50

FENNY BENTLEY   Map 09 SK14

The Coach and Horses Inn ♀ NEW
DE6 1LB ☎ 01335 350246
Beautifully located on the edge of the Peak District National Park, this warm, family-run 17th century coaching inn is handy for Dovedale and the Tissington Trail. Well kept ales and good home cooking are the watchwords; the daily-changing menu might include game casserole, steak and Stilton pie, salmon in wine and asparagus sauce, or vegetable Stroganoff. **BAR MEALS:** L served all week. D served all week 12-2.30 6.30-9. Av main course £6.50. **RESTAURANT:** L served all week. D served all week 12-2.30 6.30-9. Av 3 course à la carte £13. **BREWERY/COMPANY:** Free House. **PRINCIPAL BEERS:** Marstons Pedigree, Timothy Taylor Landlord, Black Sheep Best Bitter, Titanic Full Steam Ahead. **FACILITIES:** Children welcome Garden: Food served outside. **NOTES:** Parking 24

FOOLOW   Map 09 SK17

The Bulls Head Inn ♦♦♦♦ 🐄
S32 5QR ☎ 01433 630873   🖷 01433 631738
Dir: Just off A623, N of Stoney Middleton
Open fires, oak beams, great views and good food are among the attractions at this family-run inn, in a conservation village high up in the Peak District. Sample home-made pies, deep-fried cod in batter, local game, freshwater and seafish, plus a choice of home-made puddings. Comfortable, well-equipped bedrooms. **OPEN:** 12-3 5.30-11. **BAR MEALS:** L served all week. D served all week 12-2 7-9. **RESTAURANT:** L served all week. D served all week 12-2 7-9. **BREWERY/COMPANY:** Free House. **PRINCIPAL BEERS:** Black Sheep Bitter, Marstons Pedigree, Tetley Bitter. **FACILITIES:** Children welcome Garden: patio, outdoor eating. **NOTES:** Parking 20. **ROOMS:** 3 bedrooms 3 en suite

---

SHADES & GRADES OF BEER

A distinction between beer and ale used to be drawn centuries ago. Ale was the old British brew made without hops. In the 15th century the use of hops spread to Britain from the Continent and this bitterer drink was called beer. Ale is no longer made and the two words are now used indiscriminately. Bottled beer is distinguished from draught beer from a cask or keg, but a better dividing line is the one between real ale, which matures in the cask, and keg or bottled beer that doesn't. Bitter is the British draught beer, with plenty of hops. Mild, less hops and less sharp in taste, is often found in the Midlands and the North West. Old ale usually means stronger mild, matured longer. Light ale or pale ale is bottled beer of a lightish colour. Lager is lighter and blander. Brown ale is darker, richer bottled beer, and porter is richer still. Stout is the blackest and richest of all.
🐝

GRINDLEFORD   Map 09 SK27

Pick of the Pubs

The Maynard Arms ★ ★ ★ 🐄 ♀
Main Rd S32 2HE ☎ 01433 630321   🖷 01433 630445
e-mail: info@maynardarms.co.uk
Dir: From M1 take A619 into Chesterfield, then onto Baslow. A623 to Calver, R into Grindleford
This fine 1898 coaching inn overlooks the village and Derwent Valley beyond, and is situated at the heart of the Peak National Park. During the 1950s and 60s it often accommodated touring Australian cricket teams. The evocative interior is thoroughly up-to-date and the Longshaw Bar and Padley Restaurant menus have many confident modern touches. Thai style crab cakes, chicken liver parfait, or roast butternut squash risotto indicate the style of cooking here. Follow with grilled marinated chicken breast, traditional beer-battered fresh cod, roast fillet of sea bass, or trio of Yorkshire puddings with chicken liver, mushroom, and shallot casserole in Madeira gravy. Individual Bakewell pudding, the local speciality, is served with hot custard: good farmhouse cheeses. Fixed-price restaurant menu. Attractive bedrooms include some larger 'superior' rooms and two suites.
OPEN: 11-3 5.30-11 (Sun 12-10.30). **BAR MEALS:** L served all week. D served all week 12-2 6-9.30. Av main course £9. **RESTAURANT:** L served all week. D served all week 12-2 7-9.30. Av 4 course fixed price £23.50. **BREWERY/COMPANY:** Free House. **PRINCIPAL BEERS:** Boddingtons, Greene King Old Speckled Hen, Marston's Pedigree, Timothy Taylor Landlord. **FACILITIES:** Children's licence Garden: **NOTES:** Parking 60. **ROOMS:** 10 bedrooms 10 en suite s£69 d£79

HASSOP   Map 09 SK27

Eyre Arms ♀
DE45 1NS ☎ 01629 640390
Dir: Take the A6 to Bakewell, then the A619 towards Sheffield, after 0.5M turn onto the B6001 to Hathersage & Hassop
Just a short drive north of Bakewell, this 17th-century coaching inn is associated with the Civil War and boasts its own Cavalier ghost. Unaltered since the 1950s and featuring original oak pews, beams, old photographs and maps, this traditional pub has a warm, cosy atmosphere. Wide-ranging menu encompasses lemon sole with prawns, dill and white wine sauce, steak and kidney pie, tuna and pasta bake, grilled double lamb chop and chicken Kiev. Lovely garden overlooking rolling Peak District countryside. Excellent local walks. **OPEN:** 11.30-3 6.30-11 (Nov-March eve open from 7pm). Closed 25 Dec. **BAR MEALS:** L served all week. D served all week 12-2 6.30-9. Av main course £6.95. **BREWERY/COMPANY:** Free House. **PRINCIPAL BEERS:** Marston Pedigree, John Smiths, Black Sheep Special. **FACILITIES:** Garden: outdoor eating. **NOTES:** Parking 20

HATHERSAGE   Map 09 SK28

Millstone Inn ♦♦♦ ♀
Sheffield Rd S32 1DA ☎ 01433 650258   🖷 01433 651664
e-mail: jerry@millstone.f.s.business.co.uk
With its superb views over the unspoiled Hope Valley, this tastefully furnished former coaching inn has been reinvented for the twenty-first century. There's an open fire in the bar,

continued

England

HATHERSAGE continued

and the relaxed, civilised restaurant makes extensive use of fresh local produce. Start with mussel and saffron risotto or chilled gazpacho soup, before moving on to lamb and asparagus with couscous, baked gnocchi with Wensleydale, or monkfish and pernod. Comfortable well equipped bedrooms are suitable for both the business and leisure guest.
BAR MEALS: L served all week. D served all week 12-2 6-9. Av main course £7. **RESTAURANT:** . D served all week 6.30-9.30. Av 3 course à la carte £18. **BREWERY/COMPANY:** Free House.
PRINCIPAL BEERS: Taylor Landlord, Black Sheep, Adnams, Flowers. **FACILITIES:** Children welcome Children's licence Garden: outdoor eating, patio, historic well Dogs allowed Water.
NOTES: Parking 50. **ROOMS:** 7 bedrooms 7 en suite s£35 d£55 FR£65-£80

The Plough Inn ◆◆◆◆ ♀
Leadmill Bridge S32 1BA ☎ 01433 650319 650180

Situated on the B6001, one mile south of Hathersage, this 17th-century stone-built inn was originally a farm, standing in nine acres of land and bounded by the River Derwent. Charming public rooms with exposed beams and brickwork. A choice of dishes is offered in the bar, or from an interesting restaurant menu. Bedrooms are individually decorated and well equipped.
OPEN: 11-11. Closed Dec 25. **BAR MEALS:** L served all week. D served all week 11.30-2.30 6.30-9.30. Av main course £10.
RESTAURANT: L served all week. D served all week 11.30-2.30 6.30-9.30. Av 3 course à la carte £20.
BREWERY/COMPANY: Free House.
PRINCIPAL BEERS: Theakstons Old Peculier, Tetley, Adnams, Smiles. **FACILITIES:** Children welcome Garden: Food served outside. **NOTES:** Parking 50. **ROOMS:** 3 bedrooms 2 en suite s£45 d£60

Scotsmans Pack Inn ◆◆◆◆ 🍴
School Ln S32 1BZ ☎ 01433 650253 📠 01433 650253
Dir: Hathersage is on the A625 8 miles from Sheffield
Historic inn on one of the old packhorse trails used by Scottish 'packmen' or travelling drapers, who sold their tweeds to the local farmers. The village is also reputed to have connections with Robin Hood's right hand man, Little John. Ideally placed for touring the beautiful Derbyshire Dales. Interesting range of popular dishes and blackboard specials might include braised lamb knuckle, turkey escalope cordon bleu, salmon florentine, tagliatelle carbonara, or broccoli and Brie lasagne. The inn's five bedrooms are individually designed and well equipped.

OPEN: 11.30-3 5.30-11. (Sat and Sun 11.30-11) **BAR MEALS:** L served all week. D served all week 12-2 6-9. Av main course £7.
RESTAURANT: L served all week. D served all week 12-2 6-9. Av 3 course à la carte £18. **BREWERY/COMPANY:** Burtonwood.
PRINCIPAL BEERS: Burtonwood. **FACILITIES:** Children welcome Garden: Beer garden, outdoor eating.
NOTES: Parking 13. **ROOMS:** 5 bedrooms 5 en suite s£32 d£61

HAYFIELD   Map 09 SK08

The Sportsman
Kinder Rd SK22 2LE ☎ 01663 741565
Dir: Hayfield is 5m S of Glossop on A624
Standing in the glorious Peak District, this comfortable, family-run inn is an obvious watering hole for those tackling the popular Kinder Trail which runs out of Hayfield village centre towards Kinder Scout. Wholesome home-cooked food and hand-pulled beers are available in the traditional bar, with its warming log fires and welcoming atmosphere. Expect nut and lentil loaf with tomato sauce, salmon steak poached in white wine, home-made casserole and fresh Whitby cod among the imaginative blackboard dishes.
OPEN: 12-3 7-11. Closed 1Wk Mar/ Oct. **BAR MEALS:** L served Tue-Sun. D served Mon-Sat 12-2 7-9. Av main course £8.75.
RESTAURANT: L served all week. D served all week 12-2 7-9. Av 3 course à la carte £15. **BREWERY/COMPANY:** Thwaites.
PRINCIPAL BEERS: Thwaites Bitter & Reward, Daniels Hammer.
FACILITIES: Garden: Food served outside Dogs allowed Water bowl. **NOTES:** Parking 3. **ROOMS:** 6 bedrooms 4 en suite

---

Skills and Crafts

Inns with names like the Bricklayers Arms and the Masons Arms hark back to the days when groups of craftsmen and tradesmen met regularly in the local hostelry. The trade union movement originally grew up in pubs in this way and a 'local' can mean either a pub or a union branch. Itinerant craftsmen would expect a welcome at these houses, too, and pick up news of work. The Axe and Compasses is a carpenters' badge, the Three (or more) Horseshoes a device of smiths, the Wheatsheaf of bakers and the Beetle and Wedge of builders, while quite a few pubs display the Oddfellows Arms. The Shoulder of Mutton could signify that the landlord doubled as a butcher.

HOGNASTON
Map 09 SK25

Pick of the Pubs

The Red Lion Inn
Main St DE6 1PR ☎ 01335 370396 ▤ 01335 370961
e-mail: lionrouge@msn.com
Dir: M1 J25 take A52 towards Derby & Ashbourne. Hognaston on B5035
Traditional, 17th-century country inn with quaint beamed ceilings, open fireplaces and attractive, tastefully furnished bedrooms. Tucked away in the main street of a small village, the Red lion is a comfortable base for a weekend break spent walking in the beautiful Peak District National Park or visiting Kedleston Hall, Carsington Reservoir and the Crich Tramway Museum.

Local drinkers fill the bar early and late in the evening; at other times a dining ambience pervades this candlelit room and the intimate back room - ideal for families or parties. Blackboards list the imaginative choice of modern pub food on offer.

Competently cooked dishes, served on enormous white plates, range from crispy bacon and warm Brie baguette with mixed dressed salad, smoked salmon salad, and warm smoked chicken on seasonal leaves with Dijon mustard and honey dressing, to herb-stuffed pork fillet wrapped in Parma ham on polenta with a Stilton cream, or fresh fish dishes like deep-fried whole gurnard and fillet of Queen fish. Good home-made nursery puddings.
OPEN: 12-3 6-11 (Mon 6-11 only, Sun 12-3, 6-10.30).
BAR MEALS: L served all week. D served all week 12-2 7-9. Av main course £12.50. **RESTAURANT:** L served Tue-Sun. D served Mon-Sat 12-2 7-9. Av 3 course à la carte £22.50.
BREWERY/COMPANY: Free House.
PRINCIPAL BEERS: Marstons Pedigree, Greene King Morland Old Speckled Hen, **NOTES:** Parking 30.
ROOMS: 3 bedrooms 3 en suite s£45 d£75

HOPE
Map 09 SK18

Cheshire Cheese Inn ▽
Edale Rd S33 6ZF ☎ 01433 620381 ▤ 01433 620411
e-mail: cheshire.cheese@barbox.net
Dir: On A6187 between Sheffield & Chapel-en-le-Fri th
In the heart of the Peak District, close to the Pennine Way, this 16th-century inn offers a traditional pub experience in wonderful surroundings. It's on the old salt route, and payment for lodgings in those days was made in cheese - hence the name.

Real ales and home-cooked food are further attractions, including a mammoth mixed grill, grilled cod with lime and ginger butter, and a daily curry.
OPEN: 12-3 (all day Sat) 6.30-11. **BAR MEALS:** L served all week. D served all week 12-2 6.30-9. Av main course £6.95.
RESTAURANT: L served all week. D served all week 12-2 6.30-9. Av 3 course à la carte £14. **BREWERY/COMPANY:** Free House.
PRINCIPAL BEERS: Coach House Innkeeper's Special Reserve, Vaux Moonlight Mouse, Ward's Boxing Hare.
FACILITIES: Children welcome Garden: Food served outside.
NOTES: Parking 8. **ROOMS:** 2 bedrooms 2 en suite d£60

ILKESTON

Stanhope Arms
Stanhope St DE7 4QA ☎ 0115 9322603
Handy for the M1, yet set in an unspoilt village, this friendly local serves excellent home-made pies.

LITTON
Map 09 SK17

Red Lion Inn
SK17 8QU ☎ 01298 871458 ▤ 01298 871458
e-mail: forwarding@btinternet.com
Dir: just off the A623 Chesterfield to Stockport rd 1m E of Tideswell
This 17th-century pub overlooks the village green, where in summer customers can enjoy a drink and a bite to eat under the trees. It is an ideal spot for starting, or finishing, one of the many local walks. Beams and log fires are a feature of the cosy rooms, where favourite dishes include garlic and rosemary lamb, rabbit casserole, and pheasant in cider.
OPEN: 11-3 6-11 (Open all day Sat-Sun 11-11). **BAR MEALS:** L served all week. D served Mon-Sat 12-2 6-8.30. Av main course £6. **BREWERY/COMPANY:** Free House.
PRINCIPAL BEERS: Jennings Bitter, Barnsley Bitter, Black Dog.
FACILITIES: Dogs allowed

MATLOCK
Map 09 SK35

The White Lion Inn
195 Starkholmes Rd DE4 5JA ☎ 01629 582511
With spectacular views over Matlock Bath, and its proximity to many beautiful dales and valleys, this 18th-century inn is the ideal venue for a relaxing break. Typical dishes are rack of lamb with garlic mash, swordfish supreme, or pan seared medallions of venison.
OPEN: 12-3 5-11 (All day Sat-Sun & BHs). **BAR MEALS:** L served all week. D served Mon-Sat 12-2 7-9.30. Av main course £6.50. **RESTAURANT:** L served Sun. D served Tue-Sat 12-2 7-9.30. Av 3 course à la carte £18.50.
BREWERY/COMPANY: PRINCIPAL BEERS: John Smiths, Marston's Pedigree. **FACILITIES:** Garden: patio, outdoor eating Dogs allowed bar and garden only. **NOTES:** Parking 50.
ROOMS: 3 bedrooms 3 en suite d£48

MELBOURNE

Hardinge Arms
54-56 Main St, Kings Newton DE73 1BX ☎ 01332 863808
Handy for Donnington and Midlands Airports. Smart lounge area, children welcome, chalet-style bedrooms.

RIPLEY
Map 09 SK35

The Moss Cottage
Nottingham Rd DE5 3JT ☎ 01773 742555 ▤ 01773 741063
Specialising in carvery dishes, and offering four roast joints each day, the Moss Cottage also offers blackboard specials, and a selection of home-made puddings.

ROWSLEY

The Grouse & Claret
Station Rd DE4 2EB ☎ 01629 733233 ▤ 01629 733010
Dir: On A6 between Matlock & Bakewell
Recently refurbished pub close to Chatsworth and good walking country. Modern bedrooms and a varied menu of pub favourites. The name comes from a kind of fishing fly, and the pub is popular with local fly fisherman.

England

SHARDLOW   Map 09 SK43

The Old Crown
Cavendish Bridge DE72 2HL ☎ 01332 792392
Dir: *M1 J24 take A6 towards Derby turn L before river bridge into Shardlow*
Bustling 17th-century village pub situated next to the River Trent in the heart of Derbyshire. Besides an impressive choice of Shardlow's real ales, customers can tuck into a good choice of starters and light meals.

TIDESWELL   Map 09 SK17

Three Stags' Heads NEW
Wardlow Mires SK17 8RW ☎ 01298 872268
Dir: *Junct of the A623 & B6465 on the Chesterfield/Stockport road*
An unspoilt, basic old pub high on the limestone wolds in renowned walking country that provides hearty home-cooked food for ramblers, cyclists and locals alike. Some fascinating and unusual real ales accompany the steak and kidney pie, chicken and aubergine curry and fresh pasta with tomato and mushroom sauce, all cooked to order. In season, extra game specialities might be baked pigeon breasts and game or rabbit casserole. No children under 8.
OPEN: (open public holidays) 7 (Sat-Sun 12-11).
BAR MEALS: L served Sat-Sun. D served Fri-Sun 12.30-3 7.30-9.30. Av main course £7.50. **BREWERY/COMPANY:** Free House. **PRINCIPAL BEERS:** Broadstone Charter Ale, Abbeydale Martins. **FACILITIES:** Dogs allowed. **NOTES:** Parking 14 No credit cards

WARDLOW   Map 09 SK35

The Bull's Head at Wardlow
SK17 8RP ☎ 01298 871431
The inn is situated in the heart of the Peak District National Park, close to Monsal Head. Unaltered for many years, it is adorned with antique pictures, clocks, coach lamps, brass and copperware. Locally famous for its char-grilled steaks.

TEIGNWORTHY AT TUCKERS
The Teignworthy Brewery is a micro-brewery located in the historic Tuckers Maltings at Newton Abbot. The maltings is an impressive operation that has been supplying malt to breweries all over the West Country since 1900. The brewery has been around since 1994, and takes advantage of the maltings' traditional methods to brew many styles of beer including Reel Ale (4%), Maltsters (5%) and seasonal ales.

DEVON

ASHBURTON   Map 03 SX77

Pick of the Pubs

The Rising Sun
Woodland TQ13 7JT ☎ 01364 652544
🖷 01364 654202
e-mail: mail@risingsunwoodland.co.uk
See Pick of the Pubs on page 123

AVONWICK   Map 03 SX75

The Avon Inn
TQ10 9NB ☎ 01364 73475
Dir: *From A38 take South Brent turning, Avonwick signed on B3210*
Unassuming, cream-painted pub beside the River Avon, with a popular locals bar and a restaurant with a strong Italian theme influenced by the chef/owner. From authentic pasta dishes - maybe penne with broccoli, sun-dried tomatoes and anchovies - the menu extends to crab risotto, swordfish with hot salsa, and turbot in lobster bisque with prawns and asparagus.
OPEN: 11.30-2.30 6-11 (Sun 7-10.30). **BAR MEALS:** L served Mon-Sat. D served Mon-Sat 12-2 6.30-9.30. Av main course £5.95. **RESTAURANT:** L served Mon-Sat. D served Mon-Sat 12-2 6.45-9.30. Av 3 course à la carte £19. **BREWERY/COMPANY:** Free House. **PRINCIPAL BEERS:** Bass, Badger Best. **FACILITIES:** Children welcome Garden: outdoor eating. **NOTES:** Parking 30

AXMOUTH   Map 03 SY29

The Ship Inn
EX12 4AF ☎ 01297 21838
e-mail: theshipinn@axmouth.com
Dir: *From Lyme Regis takeA3052 W towards Seaton/Sidmouth, then L onto B3172 to Axmouth*
Built soon after the original 'Ship' burnt down on Christmas Day 1879, this creeper-clad inn can trace its landlords from 1769. Now run by Christopher Chapman - son of TV cook Fanny Craddock - and his family, the pub boasts over 700 items of Guinness memorabilia, and a fine collection of international dolls. Home-cooked dishes range from Devon pasties and all day breakfasts, to deep sea surprise, or half a local pheasant. Good fresh fish dishes.
OPEN: 11-2.30 6-11 (Sun 12-3, 6-10.30). **BAR MEALS:** L served all week. D served all week 12-2 7-9. Av main course £5. **RESTAURANT:** L served all week. D served all week 12-2 7-9. 3 course à la carte £12. **BREWERY/COMPANY:** Inn Partnership. **PRINCIPAL BEERS:** Bass, Otter Ale, Otter Bitter. **FACILITIES:** Children welcome Garden: Beer garden, outdoor eating Dogs allowed on leads Water. **NOTES:** Parking 20

The Hoops Inn, Horns Cross

DEVON

THE HOOPS INN, HORNS CROSS
Nr Clovelly EX39 5DL.
Tel: 01237 451222
Directions: A39 W of Bideford
Thatched-roofed and cob-walled 13th-century longhouse set in 16 acres close to the coast path. Successfully combines old-world charm with modern pub food, in particular fresh local fish and game dishes. Bedrooms.
Open: 8am-11 (Sun 8.30am-10.30). Bar Meals: 12-3 5.30-9.30 (all day weekends, July & Aug). Children welcome. Garden/patio. Parking.
(see page 135 for full entry)

A delightful rural walk combining bluebell woods, streams and a cliff-top stroll through ancient oak woods, with views across Bideford Bay to Wales and the option of two visits to the sea shore.

From the rear car park, take the short track on right and go through gate on left. Walk ahead through the paddock, bearing slightly left to a stile. Follow the footpath left along field edge, pass a gate and gently uphill towards farm buildings. Cross a stile and turn right along the lane to Northway Farm cottages. Turn sharp left down a lane, signed Unsuitable to Motors, then soon take the arrowed footpath right. Descend steeply on a rough path into Peppercombe Woods.

Veer left to junction with track and turn left down the valley (stream right). Pass cottages and cross bridge to join another track. Continue downhill to cross stream via bridge, with a ruined mill right, and go through the gate ahead. (Option - to reach the shore, take the lower track to a gate and continue downhill on a winding path to the beach). Just beyond the gate, take the Coast Path right and climb steps, then ascend (fairly steeply at first) through Sloo Woods for about a mile (1.6km).

(Short walk - turn left, signed 'footpath', uphill over three stiles to lane and turn left. Just beyond Sloo Farm, cross stile on right and retrace steps back to the inn).

Remain on Coast Path and eventually descend shaley path (can be slippery) into Bucks Mills village. (Option - turn right downhill to reach shore, waterfall and café). Turn left up the road to first right-hand bend and take the first of three paths here, over a footbridge and past Rose Cottage. Follow path round back of house and climb through wood, keeping stream right. Where stream divides, cross footbridge and continue through woods to field. Cross stile to the right of farm building ahead and proceed through Lower Worthygate Farm. Follow drive to the lane. Turn left and keep to lane past Higher Worthygate then, just beyond Sloo Farm, cross stile on right and retrace steps back to the inn.

Distance: 2.5 miles (4km) or 6 miles (10km)
Map: OS Landranger 190
Terrain: farmland, cliff-top woodland
Paths: field and woodland paths, coast path, lanes
Gradient: undulating; some fairly steep sections

Walk submitted by:
Dr Kit Mayers

BANTHAM
Map 03 SX64

Sloop Inn ♦♦♦ ⚲
TQ7 3AJ ☎ 01548 560489 560215 📠 01548 561940
Dir: *From Kingsbridge take A379. At roundabout after Churchstow follow signs for Bantham*
With its oak beams and flagstone floor, this 16th century smugglers' inn is only a short stroll from the beach. Fresh local produce features on the menu, with its emphasis on seafood dishes like grilled bass with watercress and avocado sauce, or pan-fried scallops with red onion and streaky bacon salad. The strong vegetarian selection includes thatched vegetable and lentil pie, and Mediterranean hotpot. Well equipped bedrooms provide comfortable accommodation and en suite bedrooms.
OPEN: 11-2.30 6-11 (Sun 12-2.30, 7-10.30). **BAR MEALS:** L served all week. D served all week 12-2 7-10. Av main course £9. **RESTAURANT:** L served all week. D served all week 12-2 7-10. Av 3 course à la carte £14. **BREWERY/COMPANY:** Free House. **PRINCIPAL BEERS:** Palmers IPA, Princetown Dartmoor IPA, Bass. **FACILITIES:** Children welcome Garden: outdoor eating Dogs allowed. **NOTES:** Parking 10. **ROOMS:** 5 bedrooms 5 en suite s£32 d£64 FR£64-£68

BEER
Map 03 SY28

The Anchor Inn
Fore St EX12 3ET ☎ 01297 20386 📠 01297 24474
Dir: *Turn off A3052 following signs for Beer, continue through the village to slip road for Beach Anchor Inn on the R.*
One of Britain's best sited inns, the Anchor overlooks the tiny working harbour and beach in this popular little resort. Good summer cliff-top garden and an open-plan bar where you can enjoy pub snacks and excellent fresh fish. From mussels and oysters, the choice extends to red mullet with crab and herb crust and white wine sauce, and sea bass with creamy tarragon and orange sauce.
OPEN: 11-11. **BAR MEALS:** L served all week. D served all week 12-2 7-9.30. Av main course £6. **RESTAURANT:** L served all week. D served all week 12-2 7-9.30. Av 3 course à la carte £20. **BREWERY/COMPANY:** Old English Inns. **PRINCIPAL BEERS:** Otter Bitter, Courage Directors, John Smiths. **FACILITIES:** Children welcome Garden:. **ROOMS:** 8 bedrooms 5 en suite s£55 d£75

BERE FERRERS
Map 02 SX46

Old Plough Inn
PL20 7JL ☎ 01822 840358
Dir: *A386 from Plymouth, A390 from Tavistock*
Originally three 16th-century cottages, the inn exudes character with its timbers and flagstones, which on closer inspection are revealed to be headstones. Lovely rear patio overlooking the River Tavy.

★   AA inspected hotel accommodation

BICKLEIGH

Fisherman's Cot
EX16 8RW ☎ 01884 855237 📠 01884 855241
e-mail: fishermanscot.bickleigh@eldridgepope.com
Well-appointed inn by Bickleigh Bridge over the River Exe with food all day and large beer garden: just a short drive from Tiverton and Exmoor. The Waterside Bar is the place for snacks and afternoon tea; restaurant incorporates carvery and à la carte menus: Sunday lunch: champagne and smoked salmon breakfast optional. The cosy bedrooms are comfortable and well equipped.

OPEN: 11-11 (Sun 12-10.30). **BAR MEALS:** L served all week. D served all week 12-10 12-10. **RESTAURANT:** L served all week. D served all week 12-10 12-10 10. **BREWERY/COMPANY: PRINCIPAL BEERS:** Bass, Theakston, Courage Best. **FACILITIES:** Children welcome Children's licence Garden: outdoor eating, patio/terrace, riverside Dogs allowed. **NOTES:** Parking 100. **ROOMS:** 21 bedrooms 21 en suite s£54 d£69 family room £79

BIGBURY-ON-SEA
Map 02 SX46

Pilchard Inn
Burgh Island TQ7 4BG ☎ 01548 810514 📠 01548 810514
e-mail: reception@burghisland.ndirect.co.uk
Dir: *From A38 turn off to Modbury then follow signs to Bigbury & Burgh Island*
Atmospheric 14th-century white-walled pub located on a tiny tidal island reached only by giant sea tractor when the tide is in. The main catch off the island was pilchard - hence the name.

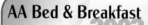

PICK OF THE PUBS

Open: 11-3 6-11(Mon 6-11, Sun
11-3 7-10.30. Closed all Mon Oct-
Apr ex BHs & 25 Dec.
Bar Meals: L served Tue-Sun.
D served all week 12-2.15 (3 Sun)
6-9.15. Av main course £8
RESTAURANT: L served Tue-Sun
D served all week 12-2.15 (3 Sun)
6-9.15. Av 3 course à la carte £15
BREWERY/COMPANY:
Free House.
PRINCIPLE BEERS: Princetown
IPA & Jail Ale, Teignworthy Reel
Ale.
FACILITIES: Children welcome.
Garden: patio outdoor eating.
NOTES: Parking 30.
ROOMS: 2 bedrooms 2 en suite
s£25 d£50 FR£75

The Rising Sun

Woodland TQ13 7JT
☎ 01364 652544 📠 01364 654202
e-mail: mail@risingsunwoodland.co.uk
Dir: E of Ashburton from A38 signed
Woodland & Denbury. Pub 11/2m on L

Conveniently situated just over a mile from the A38 between
Exeter and Plymouth, the pub stands in a splendid, isolated
position overlooking glorious Devon countryside. Its position
on the old drovers' route to Newton Abbot makes this a good
base for touring Dartmoor and the South Devon coast.

The sun rises directly in front of the main house - hence its name -
and the south-facing terrace and garden, and the views across rolling,
unspoilt South Hams countryside, are a delight in summer. Following a disastrous fire in 1986, the pub was
completely re-built to include two cosy en-suite bedrooms, whilst the spacious, open-plan interior was lovingly
restored to incorporate rough plaster walls and exposed beams, hung with a vast collection of door-keys.

Provision of fresh market food marks the philosophy of landlady Heather Humphries, with bread from the local
baker, a selection of four or five pies baked daily and Devon clotted
cream and ice creams from Langage Farm. Though snacks,
ploughman's and sandwich platters are readily available, the accent
is on home-cooked fresh produce on menus that are up-dated on a
daily basis. Leek and Devon Blue cheese tart and Dartmouth oak-
smoked salmon feature among overtures to cassoulet of Devon
pork with locally-made Toulouse sausages, guinea fowl with black
beans, garlic and apple and hazelnut and courgette bake with
tomato sauce. Roast cod with spring onion mash and butter sauce
and salmon fillet with tarragon cream typify fishy alternatives: then
round off with apricot and almond tart or spiced poached pears
with that superb cream, or select a plateful of fine West Country
cheeses, perhaps Ticklemore goat, Sharpham Rustic and Abbey
Gold, served with walnut bread.

BLACKAWTON
Map 03 SX85

Normandy Arms
Chapel St TQ9 7BN ☎ 01803 712316 📠 01803 712191
Dir: *A381 from Totnes, L onto A3122, 1st R to Blackawton after Kingsbridge turning*
Venture off the beaten track to find this 15th-century inn, re-named in honour of the Normandy Landings, for which training exercises took place on nearby Slapton Beach. The pub has interesting memorabilia from that period. Mussels and Torbay sole feature along with grilled steaks and meat pies.
OPEN: 12-2.30 7-11. **BAR MEALS:** L served all week. D served all week 12-1.45 7-9. Av main course £3.95. **RESTAURANT:** L served all week. D served all week 12-1.45 7-9. Av 3 course à la carte £12. **BREWERY/COMPANY:** Free House.
PRINCIPAL BEERS: Blackawton Bitter, Youngs Special.
FACILITIES: Children welcome Garden: outdoor eating Dogs allowed. **NOTES:** Parking 10. **ROOMS:** 5 bedrooms 5 en suite s£35 d£40

BRANSCOMBE
Map 03 SY18

Pick of the Pubs

The Masons Arms ◉ ★ ★ 🍷 ♀
EX12 3DJ ☎ 01297 680300 📠 01297 680500
e-mail: reception@masonarms.com.uk
Dir: *Turn off A3052 towards Branscombe, head down hill, hotel in the valey at the bottom of the hill*
Picturesque Branscombe lies in a steep valley, deep in National Trust land and only a ten-minute stroll from the sea. In the centre of the village is this delightful 14th-century, creeper-clad inn, formerly a cider house and well known smugglers' haunt.

Beyond the pretty front terrace lies a charming bar with stone walls, ancient ships beams, slate floors and a splendid open fireplace, used for spit-roasts on a weekly basis and including Sunday lunch.

Popular bar food ranges from a tried-and-tested selection of sandwiches, ploughman's lunches and hot filled baguettes to beer-battered cod, duck and bacon pie, pasta with pesto, and interesting daily dishes like Mediterranean fish soup, chargrilled red mullet with fennel compote and a coriander and cream sauce, and braised pork with root vegetables, Calvados and prunes. Separate fixed-price restaurant menu.

Newly refurbished bedrooms are split between the main building and neighbouring terraces of cottages; all are attractive and tastefully decorated. Conference/function room.
OPEN: 11-11 (winter 11-3, 6-11) Times vary please phone.
BAR MEALS: L served all week. D served all week 12-2 7-9. Av main course £10. **RESTAURANT:** . D served all week 7-8.45. Av 3 course à la carte £24. Av 3 course fixed price £24.
BREWERY/COMPANY: Free House.
PRINCIPAL BEERS: Otter Ale, Masons Ale, Bass, guest ale.
FACILITIES: Children welcome Garden: patio, BBQ, outdoor eating Dogs allowed Water. **NOTES:** Parking 30.
ROOMS: 22 bedrooms 19 en suite s£24 d£44 FR£82-£106

BRENDON

Rockford Inn ♀
EX35 6PT ☎ 01598 741214 📠 01598 741265
e-mail: enquiries@therockfordinn.com
A walker's paradise in the Exmoor National Park on the banks of the East Lyn River, with the National Trust's Watersmeet only 1.5 miles downstream, and the legendary Doone Valley four miles upstream. It's a traditional Exmoor pub, circa 1700, serving real ales and freshly prepared bar food including snacks, steaks, home-made pies and hot pot.
OPEN: 12-3 (Summer open all day) 6-11. **BAR MEALS:** L served all week. D served all week 12-2.30 7-9. Av main course £5.50. **PRINCIPAL BEERS:** Cotleigh Barn Owl, Tawny, Greene King Old Speckled Hen. **FACILITIES:** Garden: Food served outside Dogs allowed Water. **NOTES:** Parking 12. **ROOMS:** 6 bedrooms s£20 d£40

BROADHEMBURY
Map 03 ST10

Pick of the Pubs

Drewe Arms ◉ 🍷
EX14 3NF ☎ 01404 841267
e-mail: nigleburge@btconnect.co.uk
Dir: *A373 halfway between Cullompton and Honiton*
Set in an archetypal thatched Devon village in sprawling unspoiled countryside handy for Dartmoor and the spectacular Devon coast, its striking mullioned windows and quaint old furniture lend the Drewe Arms its particular tasteful character. The best available West Country produce form the basis of the daily menus that major in fresh fish.

Expect on any one day to feast on pollack baked with Cheddar and cream or sea bream with orange and chilli. Steamed mussels with garlic and herbs, griddled sardines and smoked haddock and Stilton rarebit are all offered in two portion sizes - large and very large. Alongside seared scallops with rouille and turbot fillet with hollandaise, on the fixed-price dining menu might be venison tenderloin with wild mushroom sauce, followed by chocolate St Emilion. For more dedicated meat-eaters are rare beef and hot chicken baguettes and a Bookmaker's fillet steak with anchovy butter. Good house wines from around the world are all offered by the glass.
OPEN: 11-3 6-11 (Sun 12-3 only). Closed Dec 25 & Dec 31.
BAR MEALS: L served all week. D served Mon-Sat 12-2 7-10. Av main course £10.50. **RESTAURANT:** L served all week. D served Mon-Sat 12-2 7-10. Av 3 course à la carte £25.25.
BREWERY/COMPANY: Free House.
PRINCIPAL BEERS: Otter Ale, Otter Bitter, Otter Head, Otter Bright. **FACILITIES:** Children welcome Garden: outdoor eating, patio Dogs allowed Water

For pubs with AA rosette awards for food see page 10

BUCKFASTLEIGH
Map 03 SX76

Dartbridge Inn
Totnes Rd TQ11 0JR ☎ 01364 642214 ▤ 01364 643839
Dir: Turn off A38 onto A384, the Dartbridge Inn is 200yrds on the L
Beamed inn, renowned for its colourful floral displays, situated close to the banks of the River Dart.

A good range of food is available, from sandwiches to steaks, and fresh local fish and seafood, perhaps grilled whole Brixham plaice, and salmon and broccoli bake.
OPEN: 11-2.30 6.30-11 (wknds all day). **BAR MEALS:** L served all week. D served all week 12-2 6.30-9. Av main course £7.
RESTAURANT: L served all week. D served all week 12-2 7-9.30. Av 3 course à la carte £16. **BREWERY/COMPANY:** Old English Inns. **PRINCIPAL BEERS:** Courage Best & Directors, Wadworth 6X. **FACILITIES:** Children welcome Garden: terrace Dogs allowed garden only. **NOTES:** Parking 100. **ROOMS:** 11 bedrooms 11 en suite s£55 d£70

BUCKLAND BREWER
Map 03 SS42

The Coach & Horses
EX39 5LU ☎ 01237 451395
Formerly the village courthouse, this popular 13th-century thatched free house is set in lovely countryside three miles from the Tarka Trail. Beneath its heavily beamed ceilings, locals and holidaymakers gather around the inglenook fireplaces, or spill out onto the terrace and garden.

Good, fresh food includes home-cooked pasties and pies, duck in redcurrant sauce, and cod fillet on spinach with cheese sauce.
OPEN: 12-3 6-11 (Sun 7-10.30). **BAR MEALS:** L served all week. D served all week 12-2 7-9.30. Av main course £6.50.
RESTAURANT: L served all week. D served all week 12-2 7-9.30. Av 3 course à la carte £15. **BREWERY/COMPANY:** Free House. **PRINCIPAL BEERS:** Fullers London Prise, Flowers Original, IPA, Whitbread Bitter. **NOTES:** Parking 12

BUCKLAND MONACHORUM
Map 02 SX46

Drake Manor Inn
The Village PL20 7NA ☎ 01822 853892 ▤ 01822 853892
Dir: Off A386 near Yelverton
Nestling between the church and the stream, this mainly 16th-century inn was built by the masons who constructed the local church. Renowned for its pretty garden and colourful, award-winning floral displays, the pub boasts quaint old beams and large fireplaces with wood-burning stoves.

There is an extensive wine list and over 100 malt whiskies. The menu includes beef in ale pie, medallions of pork fillet with wholegrain mustard, brandy and cream, and garlic mushrooms with chilli and prawns.
OPEN: 11.30-2.30 6.30-11 (Sun 12-3, 7-10.30). **BAR MEALS:** L served all week. D served all week 12-2 7-10. Av main course £6.
RESTAURANT: L served all week. D served all week 12-2 7-10. Av 3 course à la carte £15.
BREWERY/COMPANY: PRINCIPAL BEERS: Ushers Founders Ale, John Smiths, Courage Best, Bass. **FACILITIES:** Children welcome Garden: Beer garden, food served outdoors Dogs allowed. **NOTES:** Parking 4

BUTTERLEIGH
Map 03 SS90

The Butterleigh Inn NEW
EX15 1PN ☎ 01884 855407 ▤ 01884 855600
Dir: 3M from J 28 on the M5 turn R by The Manor Hotel in Cullompton and follow Butterleigh signs
Tucked away in a sleepy village amid glorious countryside south of Tiverton, this 400-year-old pub remains delightfully unpretentious and worth seeking out for its relaxed, traditional atmosphere and excellent Cotleigh Brewery ales. Homely and comfortably furnished bars with open fires and time-honoured pub games. Food ranges from ploughman's lunches and filled rolls to grilled tuna steak with hot tomato salsa and daily, home-cooked specials.
OPEN: 12-2.30 (Sun 12-3, 7-10.30) 6-11. **BAR MEALS:** L served all week. D served all week 12-2 7-9.45. Av main course £5.50.
BREWERY/COMPANY: Free House.
PRINCIPAL BEERS: Cotleigh Brewery, Tawny, Barn Owl, Old Buzzard. **FACILITIES:** Children welcome Garden: Food served outside Dogs allowed

CADELEIGH
Map 02 SS90

Cadeleigh Arms NEW
Cadeleigh EH16 8HP ☎ 01884 855238 ▤ 01884 855385
Plain, very relaxed and informal, 200-year-old pub tucked away in a small community high in the rolling hills above the Exe Valley. Rambling interior with a comfortably rustic feel, complete with flagged-stone bar and pine-furnished rear dining room with rural views. Good food ranges from sardines marinated in basil and duck rilletes with home-made chutney to guinea fowl supreme with roast garlic sauce, braised lamb shank with mustard mash and red wine sauce, and prawn gumbo on tagliatelle. For pudding try the home-made pear and white chocolate flan.
OPEN: 11-3.30 (Sun 12-3.30, 7-10.30) 5.30-11 (All day Sat).
BAR MEALS: L served all week. D served all week 12-2.30 7-9.30. Av main course £7.50. **RESTAURANT:** L served all week. D served all week 12-2.30 7-9.30. Av 3 course à la carte £15.
BREWERY/COMPANY: Free House.
PRINCIPAL BEERS: Tawny Bitter, John Smiths.
FACILITIES: Children welcome Garden: Food served outside Dogs allowed. **NOTES:** Parking 30

CHAGFORD
Map 03 SX78

Ring O'Bells ♀
44 The Square TQ13 8AH ☎ 01647 432466
Dir: From Exeter take A30 to Whiddon Down Rdbt, take 1st L onto A382 to Mortonhampstead. After3.5M to Easton Cross Turn R Signed to Chagford
Traditional, much-extended inn in a picturesque old stannary town. Chagford is also particularly popular as a base for walking expeditions and tours of Dartmoor's antiquities. The original inn sign still hangs in the dining room and behind the pub is a sunny walled garden. Daily changing menus use locally-bought produce as much as possible, including fresh fish and seafood - Devonshire mussels - meat, seasonal game and home-made vegetarian dishes.
OPEN: 9-3 (Times vary please ring for details) 5-11 (Sun 12-3, 5-10.30). **BAR MEALS:** L served all week. D served all week 12-2 6-9. Av main course £7. **BREWERY/COMPANY:** Free House.
PRINCIPAL BEERS: Butcombe Bitter & Gold, Exmoor Ale.
FACILITIES: Children welcome Garden: outdoor eating, patio Dogs allowed Very dog friendly Water and biscuits Provided. **ROOMS:** 4 bedrooms 2 en suite s£20 d£40

CHAGFORD continued

The Sandy Park Inn ♀
Sandy Park TQ13 8JW ☎ 01647 432236 🖹 01647 432236
Dir: on A382 between Moretonhampstead and Whiddon Down
Situated in a small, picturesque Teign Valley hamlet, a 16th-century thatched inn unspoilt by progress. Local fresh ingredients widely used in dishes such as monkfish, Parma ham and pesto and pheasant with wild mushrooms. Start with marinated salmon and round off with plum and orange crumble with Devon ice cream.

OPEN: 12-2.30 6.30-11 (Sun 12-2.30, 7-10.30). **BAR MEALS:** L served Tue-Sun. D served Tue-Sun 12-2 7-9.30. Av main course £5. **RESTAURANT:** L served Tue-Sun. D served Tue-Sun 12-2 7-9.30. Av 3 course à la carte £16. **BREWERY/COMPANY:** Free House. **PRINCIPAL BEERS:** Banks, Morland Old Speckled Hen, Wadworth 6X, Marstons Pedigree. **FACILITIES:** Children welcome Garden: outdoor eating, patio Dogs allowed. **NOTES:** Parking 6

CHARDSTOCK

The George Inn 🕮
EX13 7BX ☎ 01460 220241
Dir: A358 to Chard, then A358 toward Axminster, R at Tytherleigh
Picturesque thatched 13th-century inn supposedly haunted by the ghost of a parson. Original stonework, mullioned windows and hanging baskets add to the charm. Fresh, home-cooked food.

CHERITON BISHOP   Map 03 SX79

The Old Thatch Inn ♀
EX6 6HJ ☎ 01647 24204 🖹 01647 24584
e-mail: theoldthatchinn@aol.com
Dir: Take A30 from M5, about 10m turning on L signed Cheriton Bishop
Old world charm and modern comforts are effectively combined at this listed inn, originally built as a coaching house and licensed as a public house as recently as 1974.
Meals range from freshly baked baguettes to a 16oz mixed grill and include old favourites like fish and chips and home-made steak and kidney pudding.
OPEN: 11.30-3 6-11. Closed 25 Dec. **BAR MEALS:** L served all week. D served all week 12-2 7-9.30. Av main course £7.95. **BREWERY/COMPANY:** Free House. **PRINCIPAL BEERS:** Branscombe Vale Branoc, Sharp's Own Otter Ale, Skinners Figgy's Brew + guest beers. **FACILITIES:** Children welcome Garden: food served outdoors. **NOTES:** Parking 30. **ROOMS:** 3 bedrooms 3 en suite s£34.50 d£46

CHUDLEIGH KNIGHTON   Map 03 SX87

The Claycutters Arms
TQ13 0EY ☎ 01626 853345 🖹 01626 852219
Dir: Turn off the Devon Expressway at Chudleigh Knighton
Thatched village pub, originally three Quaker cottages, on the flanks of Dartmoor, complete with beams, an open fire and an abundance of hanging baskets in summer. Dishes range from home-made pigeon pie, wild boar sausages and cider apple sauce, to duck with leeks and port, and venison with honey and juniper.
OPEN: 11-3 6-11. **BAR MEALS:** L served all week. D served all week 12-2.30 6.30-10.00. Av main course £5.95. **RESTAURANT:** L served all week. D served all week 12-2.30 6.30-10. Av 3 course à la carte £20. **BREWERY/COMPANY:** Heavitree. **PRINCIPAL BEERS:** Bass, Morland Old Speckled Hen, Marston's Pedigree, Wadworth 6X. **FACILITIES:** Children welcome Garden: Dogs allowed. **NOTES:** Parking 60

CLYST HYDON   Map 03 ST00

Pick of the Pubs

The Five Bells Inn 🕮 ♀
EX15 2NT ☎ 01884 277288 🖹 01884 277693
Dir: B3181 3M out of Cullompton, L to Clyst Hydon then R to Clyst St Lawrence. Pub on R
Originally located by the church, the Five Bells was moved to the present 16th-century Devon longhouse during the early 20th century, when the then rector objected to the close proximity of the two buildings. With its front terrace and raised side garden, both enjoying far-reaching country views, this attractive thatched pub has been modernised inside over the years. Main menu and specials board meals are available in the carpeted open-plan bar, adjacent long barn and garden and fresh local produce, notably fish and game, is used in preparing such home-cooked dishes as broccoli and Stilton soup, smoked fish platter, steak and kidney pudding, rack of lamb with mint and honey glaze, Duck breast with black cherries and cherry brandy, whole sea bass stuffed with lime, ginger and shallots, and prime steaks grilled to your liking. Famous butterscotch gooey meringues with clotted cream or bread-and-butter pudding to finish.
OPEN: 11.30-3 (Sun 12-2.30, 6.30-10.30) 6.30-11. Closed Dec 26 & Jan 1. **BAR MEALS:** L served all week. D served all week. Av main course £7.95. **RESTAURANT:** L served all week. D served all week 12-2 7-10. Av 3 course à la carte £25. **BREWERY/COMPANY:** Free House. **PRINCIPAL BEERS:** Wadworth 6X, Cotleigh Tawny, Otter Bitter. **FACILITIES:** Garden: patio, outdoor eating Dogs allowed Water. **NOTES:** Parking 40

COCKWOOD   Map 03 SX98

The Anchor Inn 🕮 ♀
EX6 8RA ☎ 01626 890203 🖹 01626 890355
Dir: Off A379 between Dawlish & Starcross
With its splendid setting on the broad estuary of the River Exe, overlooking a landlocked harbour, it's hardly surprising this historic inn attracts a fascinating, wide-ranging mix of smart diners, local fishermen, birdwatchers, cyclists and walkers. Rustic, unspoilt main bar with low ceilings, black panelling and intimate little alcoves, one with an open fire. Extensive fish and seafood menu, including lobster, brill, skate, Dover sole, and a

continued

mind-boggling range of sauces for scallops, oysters and scallops. Non fish-fanciers can choose from home-made steak and kidney pudding, garlic lamb, 8oz sirloin steak and pork escalopes stuffed with Brie.
OPEN: 11-11 (Sun 12-10.30). **BAR MEALS:** L served all week. D served all week 12-3 6.30-10. Av main course £4.95.
RESTAURANT: L served all week. D served all week 12-3 6.30-10. Av 3 course à la carte £20. **BREWERY/COMPANY:** Heavitree.
PRINCIPAL BEERS: Bass, Flowers Original, Wadworth 6X, Hardy Royal Oak. **FACILITIES:** Garden: patio, food served outside Dogs allowed Water. **NOTES:** Parking 15

CORNWORTHY   Map 03 SX85

Hunters Lodge Inn
TQ9 7ES ☎ 01803 732204 ▤ 01803 732056
Dir: Off A381 S of Totnes
Simply furnished country local, dating from the early 18th century, tucked away in a sleepy village close to the River Dart. Eat in the low-ceilinged bar or in the cosy dining room by the open fire. Ever-changing blackboard menus.

CREDITON   Map 03 SS80

Pick of the Pubs

The New Inn 🛏 🍷
Coleford EX17 5BZ ☎ 01363 84242 ▤ 01363 85044
e-mail: new-inn@reallyreal-group.com
See Pick of the Pubs on page 129

Pubs with literary connections

Many of Britain's pubs are associated with some of the country's leading literary figures. One or two were regular customers, while others were occasional callers. Charles Dickens writes about the Waggon & Horses at Beckhampton in Wiltshire in 'Pickwick Papers', one of Scotland's most famous sons, Robert Burns, was a frequent visitor to the Black Bull at Moffat in Dumfries and Galloway, while Thomas Hardy refers to the Turf Tavern in Oxford in 'Jude the Obscure.' In London the Jerusalem Tavern, the Centre Page and Ye Olde Cheshire Cheese are associated with such luminaries as Samuel Johnson, Ernest Hemingway, GK Chesterton and Arthur Conan Doyle. James Herriot and his wife celebrated their second wedding anniversary at the Wensleydale Heifer at West Witton in the Yorkshire Dales, and JB Priestley's favourite pub was the George Inn at nearby Hubberholme. One of Britain's more adventurous literary figures was the French-born writer Hilaire Belloc who spent much of his life in Sussex. In the autumn of 1902 Belloc walked from Robertsbridge in the east of the county to South Harting in the west, later writing about his odyssey and his visits to various country inns along the way. Among other pubs in Sussex, he refers to the 14th-century Blackboys Inn near Uckfield and the Grade II listed Bridge Inn near Amberley.

DALWOOD   Map 03 ST20

Pick of the Pubs

The Tuckers Arms 🛏
EX13 7EG ☎ 01404 881342 ▤ 01404 881802
e-mail: tuckers.arms@cwcom.net
Dir: off A35 between Honiton & Axminster
Historic, part-thatched 13th-century pub, decked with colourful hanging baskets in summer, set in a delightful Axe Valley village in a quiet corner of East Devon. The classic, low-ceilinged bar with flagstone floor and inglenook fireplace, is the pleasantly rustic setting in which to sample reliable bar food, notably fresh fish and seafood and game. Typical dishes on the daily-changing menu may include oysters, Lyme Bay crab, roast monkfish with Mediterranean vegetables, smoked haddock with rosemary cream, vermouth and prawns, venison steak, ribeye steak with pepper sauce, and a good range of traditional pub snacks.

OPEN: 12-3 6.30-11. **BAR MEALS:** L served all week. D served all week 12-2 6.30-8. Av main course £5.
RESTAURANT: L served all week. D served all week 12-2 6.30-8. Av 3 course fixed price £16.50.
BREWERY/COMPANY: Free House.
PRINCIPAL BEERS: Otter Bitter, Otter Ale, Courage Directors & Best. **FACILITIES:** Garden: patio, outdoor eating Dogs allowed garden only. **NOTES:** Parking 5.
ROOMS: 5 bedrooms 5 en suite

DARTINGTON   Map 03 SX76

Cott Inn 🛏 🍷
TQ9 6HE ☎ 01803 863777 ▤ 01803 866629
Dir: On A384 between Totnes & Buckfastleigh
Picture-postcard pretty, 14th-century stone and cob-built inn, continuously licensed since 1320, with a wonderful 183ft thatched roof - one of the longest in England. Carpeted bar with open fires, a wealth of beams and a comfortable collection of antique and older-style furnishings. Popular buffet-style lunchtime menu; more elaborate evening dishes like wild sea bass dressed with dill and sweet pepper, and beef filler stuffed with pâté with a rich game jus. Pine-furnished upstairs bedrooms. Old English Pub Company.
OPEN: 11am-11pm. **BAR MEALS:** L served all week. D served all week 12-2.30 6.30-9.30. Av main course £9. **RESTAURANT:** L served all week. D served all week 12-2.30 6.30-9.30. Av 3 course à la carte £20. **BREWERY/COMPANY:** Old English Inns.
PRINCIPAL BEERS: Bass, Courage Directors & Best, Wadworth 6X , Greene King Old Speckled Hen. **FACILITIES:** Children welcome Garden: Food served outside Dogs allowed.
NOTES: Parking 40. **ROOMS:** 6 bedrooms 6 en suite s£55 d£65

DARTMOUTH	Map 03 SX85

The Cherub Inn 🛏 ♈
13 Higher St TQ6 9RB ☎ 01803 832571 ▤ 01803 832762
e-mail: enquiries@the-cherub.co.uk
Dartmouth's oldest building, dating from circa 1380, survived
World War II bombing and 1950s dereliction to achieve
authentic restoration and its current status as a Grade II listed
building. Bar meals are available at lunchtime and in the
evening, and the restaurant is open every night for dinner.
Fresh fish is a speciality, alongside steak, poultry and game
dishes.
OPEN: 11-11 (Sun 12-10.30) Dec-Mar Closed Mon-Thurs
Afternoons. **BAR MEALS:** L served all week. D served all week
12-2 7-10. Av main course £7. **RESTAURANT:** D served all week
7-9.30. Av 3 course à la carte £18. **BREWERY/COMPANY:** Free
House. **PRINCIPAL BEERS:** Wadworth 6X, Cherub Best Bitter.
FACILITIES: Children welcome Dogs allowed

Pick of the Pubs

Royal Castle Hotel ★ ★ ★ 🛏 ♈
11 The Quay TQ6 9PS ☎ 01803 833033
▤ 01803 835445
e-mail: enquiry@royalcastle.co.uk
See Pick of the Pubs on page 131

DITTISHAM

The Ferry Boat
Manor St TQ6 0EX ☎ 01803 722368
Picture windows make the most of the charming waterside
location at this homely pub. Popular with walkers and Dart
boatmen.

DODDISCOMBSLEIGH	Map 03 SX88

Pick of the Pubs

The Nobody Inn ♈
EX6 7PS ☎ 01647 252394   ▤ 01647 252978
e-mail: inn.nobody@virgin.net
*Dir: From A38 follow signs for Dunchideock and
Doddiscombeleigh*
A charming 16th-century inn just off the old Plymouth to
Exeter road where weary travellers were once reputedly
greeted with calls from indoors of 'Nobody in'! Its
reputation today is based on the unsurpassed selection of
West Country cheeses that regulars wash down with some
unique ales, wines and whiskies in the character bar, with
it wealth of old beams, ancient settles, antique tables, and
huge inglenook fireplace. This is not, however, to belittle a
bar menu that includes steak and kidney suet pudding and
a bake of polenta and Devon feta cheese; or more formal
restaurant meals that run to chicken, wild mushroom and
tarragon terrine, braised lamb sweetbreads with creamy
white wine sauce and white chocolate and Grand Marnier
mousse.
   Great pride is taken in the sourcing of fresh local
ingredients, including herbs from their own vegetable
garden. The globe-trotting wine list is impressive, featuring
over 700 bins. Comfortable en suite accommodation
upstairs and in a small 17th-century manor house next to
the church.
OPEN: 12-2.30 6-11. Closed 25/26 31 Dec. **BAR MEALS:** L
served all week. D served all week 12-2 7-10. Av main course
£7. **RESTAURANT:** D served Tue-Sat 7.30-9. Av 3 course à
la carte £16. **BREWERY/COMPANY:** Free House.
PRINCIPAL BEERS: Bass, Nobody's Bitter, Otter Ale.
FACILITIES: Garden: Paved patio area, outdoor eating.
NOTES: Parking 50. **ROOMS:** 7 bedrooms 5 en suite s£23
d£33

THE TWO MOORS WAY

Officially opened in 1976, the Two Moors Way crosses two of Britain's most
popular National Parks - Dartmoor and Exmoor. Though largely set against a
spectacular backdrop of remote moorland and wide horizons, the route offers plenty of
alternatives to the open country by exploring unspoilt valleys and peaceful stretches of
shaded riverbank. Early on in the walk, you reach the village of Holne, birthplace of the
writer Charles Kingsley. The Church House Inn was once a resting place for pilgrims.
Today, it's a welcome watering hole and overnight stop for walkers on the Two Moors
Way. Continue to Widecombe-in-the-Moor, famous for the song Widecombe Fair, and
perhaps break for a pint at the Rugglestone Inn. The delightful Drewe Arms at
Drewsteignton, on the northern edge of Dartmoor, the thatched Masons Arms at
Knowstone and the 300-year-old Crown at Exford are either directly on the route or
near it. On completing the walk, in glorious Lynmouth, you'll want to savour that
precious moment when you know all the hard work is over. Choose the Rising
Sun, a 14th-century smugglers inn, to celebrate.

OPEN: 12-3 6-11.
Closed 25-26 Dec.
BAR MEALS: L served all week.
D served all week 12-2 7-10.
Av main course £6.95.
RESTAURANT: D served all week
7-10. Av 3 course a la carte £18.
Av 3 course fixed price £13.95.
BREWERY/COMPANY:
Free House.
PRINCIPAL BEERS: Otter Ale,
Badger Best, Shepherd Neame
Spitfire.
FACILITIES: Children welcome.
Garden: patio outdoor eating.
Dogs allowed (not in bedrooms).
NOTES: Parking 50.
ROOMS: 6 bedrooms 6 en suite
s£50-£65 d£65-£75 FR£85-£95.

The New Inn

Coleford EX17 5BZ
☎ 01363 84242 📠 01363 85044
e-mail: new-inn@reallyreal-group.com
Dir: from Exeter take A377, 1.5m after
Crediton turn L for Coleford. Pub 1.5m

Original beams under an historic cob-and-thatch roof are particular features of this 13th-century listed building in a conservation village alongside Cole Brook, a tributary of the River Yeo, with comfortable en suite accommodation in an interesting variety of styles.

'Captain', the chatty resident parrot, welcomes folk into the rambling interior, with the ancient bar blending successfully with extensions created from the old barns. The latter accommodate dining areas that enjoy a rare balance of local and tourist clientele, attracted by conservative food choices that score highly in freshness and value. Best choices will be found on daily blackboards offering West Country dishes from local suppliers, in particular fresh fish from Brixham.

Typical are liver and smoked bacon with passata, creamy fish pie and root vegetable and herb casserole with cheese scones, then spicy bread pudding or the unexplained 'Wemborthy cream' to follow. Restaurant options include warm duck breast with orange salad, beef fillet on a pâté crouton with Madeira sauce, and apple Bakewell tart with cinnamon ice cream.

A varied Sunday lunch menu lists garlic mushrooms, sausages with caramelised onion sauce and a mixed seafood platter alongside generous portions of roast Devon beef rib or leg of lamb with appropriate accompaniments. There remain restaurant options at night that might include a Stilton and port pot with walnut oil, salmon fillet with sweet red pepper sauce and a Devon cream meringue with ice cream and raspberry coulis.

There's accommodation in six spacious, light and airy bedrooms, a good choice of ale on tap and decent wine by the glass, and the stream-side patio is perfect for quiet alfresco summer drinking.

England

DOLTON   Map 02 SS51

Pick of the Pubs

The Union Inn ♦♦♦♦ 🛏
Fore St EX19 8QH ☎ 01805 804633   🖹 01805 804633
e-mail: union.inn@eclipse.co.uk
Dir: *From A361 take B3227 to S Molton, then Atherington. L onto B3217 then 6m to Dolton. Pub on R*

Traditional cob-built Devon longhouse that was converted into a hotel in Georgian times to serve the growing market that was held behind the inn. Very traditional pub interior, with a homely beamed bar with open fire, oak settles and sturdy wooden tables. Personally-run by Irene and Ian Fisher who offer a warm welcome and good bar food.

Locally supplied meat and fish from Bideford figure prominently on the specials boards, perhaps including fish soup, Devon mussels steamed with shallots, wine and cream, seared salmon with fennel and garlic, lamb shank braised with red wine, garlic and vegetables, and turbot with mussels, saffron and cream. Lighter bites include ploughman's and home-made burgers. Comfortably furnished bedrooms.
OPEN: 12-2 6-11 (closed Wed & 1st 2wks Feb). Closed 1st 2 wks Feb. **BAR MEALS:** L served Thu-Tue. D served Thu-Tue 12-2 7-9. Av main course £5. **RESTAURANT:** D served Thu-Tue 7-9. Av 3 course à la carte £16.
BREWERY/COMPANY: Free House.
PRINCIPAL BEERS: Sharp's Doom Bar, St Austell HSD, Barum Original, St Austell Tinners Ale. **FACILITIES:** Garden: outdoor eating Dogs allowed. **NOTES:** Parking 15.
ROOMS: 3 bedrooms 3 en suite d£50

AA Hotel Booking Service on 0870 5050505 to book
at AA recognised hotels and B & Bs in the
UK and Ireland, or through our Internet site:
www.theAA.com

DREWSTEIGNTON   Map 03 SX79

Pick of the Pubs

The Drewe Arms 🛏 ♀
The Square EX6 6GN ☎ 01647 281224
Dir: *W of Exeter on A30 for 12 Miles L at Woodleigh junction follow signs for 3 Miles to Drewsteignton*
Picture-postcard, long and low thatched inn tucked away in a sleepy village square high above the wooded slopes of the Teign Valley, close to Castle Drogo (NT), Dartmoor and beautiful walks. A rural gem, once totally in a time warp when Britain's longest-serving landlady Mabel Mudge (75 years) was at the helm until she officially retired in 1996 aged 99.

Although the pub has been sympathetically refurbished by Whitbread, ales are still drawn from the cask and served through two hatchways, one in a classic, unspoilt and simply adorned bar, and a pine-furnished room with roaring log can also be found off the flagged passageway. 'Mabels Kitchen', now the dining-room, retains her old black range and original dresser.

Good food, listed on a short blackboard menu, ranges from decent ploughman's lunches, crispy belly pork with neeps and tatties, home-made steak pudding, hock of ham with mash and cabbage and Devonshire junket, to scallops with pesto, trio of grilled fish and grilled bass on gratin leeks.
OPEN: 11-2.30 6-11. **BAR MEALS:** L served all week. D served all week 12-2 6.30-9.30. Av main course £6.95.
RESTAURANT: D served all week 6.30-9.30. Av 3 course à la carte £20. **BREWERY/COMPANY:** Whitbread.
PRINCIPAL BEERS: Flowers IPA, Bass ,Greene King, Greene King Old Speckled Hen. **FACILITIES:** Children welcome patio, outdoor eating, Dogs allowed. **NOTES:** Parking 12.
ROOMS: 3 bedrooms 1 en suite d£50

EAST PRAWLE   Map 03 SX73

The Freebooter Inn ♀ NEW
TQ7 2BU ☎ 01548 511208
Dir: *From Kingsbridge take road to Dartmouth turn R at Frogmore, over Frogmore bridge follow signs to East Prawle past duck pond first on L*
Formerly known as The Providence, this unspoilt, 18th-century inn nestles in the southernmost village in Devon, just off the coast path west of Start Point. Simple, open-plan bar with rug-strewn wooden floors, a rustic mix of furnishings, two open fires and a relaxing 'local' atmosphere.

Famished walkers will not find chips on the menu, instead, expect home-made pasties, and organic meats and vegetables in such dishes as beef in ale, seafood au gratin and chicken cacciatore. Local Dartmoor ales and farm ciders, and organic fruit juices.
OPEN: 12-2.30 (Winter 12-2.30, 6.30-11) 6-11. **BAR MEALS:** L served all week 12-2.30. **RESTAURANT:** D served all week 7-9. Av 3 course à la carte £15. **BREWERY/COMPANY:** Free House.
PRINCIPAL BEERS: Greene King Abbot Ale, Dartmoor Princetown IPA, Jail Ale. **FACILITIES:** Children welcome Garden: Food served outside Dogs allowed Water No credit cards

OPEN: 11-11 (Sun 12-10.30).
BAR MEALS: L served all week.
D served all week 11.30-10.
Av main course £6.
RESTAURANT: L served all week.
D served all week 12-2 7-9.
Av 3 course a la carte £21.50.
Av 3 course fixed price £18.45.
BREWERY/COMPANY:
Free House.
PRINCIPAL BEERS: Wadworth 6X,
Courage Directors, Exe Valley
Dob's Best Bitter.
FACILITIES: Children welcome.
Dogs allowed. Civil Weddings
ROOMS: 25 bedrooms 25 en suite
s£45-£75 d£90-£120

Royal Castle Hotel

★★★ 🐷 🍸
11 The Quay TQ6 9PS
☎ 01803 833033 📠 01803 835445
e-mail: enquiry@royalcastle.co.uk
Dir: In the town centre overlooking
inner harbour and the river

Handsome former 17th-century coaching inn commanding the best site overlooking the Dart estuary and the small harbour in this historic small port. A great all-round inn with lively bars and attractive bedrooms, it is the perfect base from which to explore the magnificent South Hams coastline.

Originally four Tudor houses built on either side of a narrow lane that now forms the fine hallway and foyer, complete with original open staircase and an impressive Bell Board full of room-call bells, this established small hotel boasts a welcoming and very individual interior of period antiques and maritime memorabilia. A distinct pubby atmosphere prevails in the lively Harbour Bar with its nautical decor, whereas the more refined and spacious Galleon Bar is a popular destination for morning coffee and a decent pub meal (served all day). A wide-ranging menu should please all tastes, from good ploughman's lunches, home-made fish soup and filled jacket potatoes to chargrilled steaks, fish casserole, beef Stroganoff, and daily specials listing seafood specialities, fresh from the boats - battered cod, dressed crab salad - and braised lamb shank.

In winter months an added attraction are the spit-roast lunches cooked over a 300-year-old range. At the bar you'll find local farm cider, cask Devon ales, numerous malt whiskies and 12 wines by the glass. More imaginative restaurant food is available in the upstairs dining room.

Individual bedrooms are decorated with stylish fabrics, wallcoverings and antiques. If yours is one of the few without a stunning river view, make sure you bag one of the sought-after windows seats at breakfast and enjoy a leisurely start to the day.

England

EXETER
Map 03 EX99

Double Locks Hotel
Canal Bank EX2 6LT ☎ 01392 256947 📄 01392 250247
Dir: *From M5 follow signs for Marsh Barton Trading Est, R at 2nd rdbt, then onto slip rd to L of incinerator, R after bridge across canal*
Difficult to find but well worth the effort involved for the real ale connoisseur, this red-brick Georgian pub enjoys a peaceful canalside setting within sight of Exeter Cathedral. A splendid summer destination (ideal for families), it also offers appetising bar food, including sandwiches, salads, jacket potatoes, toasties, ploughmans' and curries.
OPEN: 11-11 (Sun 12-10.30) (bar food 11-10.30, Sun 12-10).
BAR MEALS: L served all week. D served all week 11-10.30.
Av main course £5.45. **BREWERY/COMPANY:** Smiles.
PRINCIPAL BEERS: Adnams Broadside, Everard's Original, Smiles Best, Branscombe Vale Branoc. **FACILITIES:** Children welcome Garden: Outdoor eating Dogs allowed.
NOTES: Parking 100

Red Lion Inn
Broadclyst EX5 3EL ☎ 01392 461271
e-mail: redlion@broadclyst.fsbusiness.co.uk
Dir: *on the B3181 Exeter to Cullompton.*
Situated at the centre of a National Trust village, close to Killerton House and Gardens, this renowned 15th-century inn features original beams and antique furniture inside and a cobbled courtyard outside.
The daily specials board includes fresh fish from Brixham, vegetarian options, spicy dishes and game in season. There is a bar menu with traditional snacks and a full carte in the restaurant.
OPEN: 11-2.30 5.30-11 (Sun 12-3, 7-10.30). **BAR MEALS:** L served all week. D served all week 12-2 6-9.30. **RESTAURANT:** L served all week. D served all week 12-2 6-9.30.
BREWERY/COMPANY: Free House. **PRINCIPAL BEERS:** Bass, Fullers London Pride, Hardy Royal Oak, Worthington Best.
FACILITIES: Children welcome Garden: outdoor eating, patio, BBQ Dogs allowed. **NOTES:** Parking 70

EXMINSTER
Map 03 SX98

Swans Nest ♀
Station Rd EX6 8DZ ☎ 01392 832371
e-mail: swans-nest.co.uk
Dir: *From M5 follow A379 Dawlish Rd*

Formerly the Railway Inn, this much extended pub dates from 1854 and enjoys a pleasant rural location close to the Exeter Canal. One unusual feature of this pub is the ballroom dance floor and stage, which are used at weekends and for line dancing on Thursdays. Sunday lunchtime is the time for children's entertainment. *continued*

Pub menu offers wild boar steak with caramelised cider sauce, golden Exmoor trout, plant pot pudding, a turkey carvery and lamb rump steak with minted gravy.
OPEN: 10.30-2.30 6-11. Closed Dec 26. **BAR MEALS:** L served all week. D served all week 12-2 6-10. Av main course £6.
BREWERY/COMPANY: Free House. **PRINCIPAL BEERS:** Bass, Wadworth 6X. **FACILITIES:** Children welcome Garden: patio, outdoor eating. **NOTES:** Parking 102

Turf Hotel
Turf Lock EX6 8EE ☎ 01392 833128 📄 01392 832545
Dir: *Off A379 turn L at end of Exminster by-pass/over rail bridge. Park by canal (pub is 0.75m on foot)*
Remotely situated on the Exeter Canal, this is one of only a few pubs in the country that cannot be reached by car. Follow the paths or travel there on the inn's own boat. Bedrooms.

HARBERTON
Map 03 SX75

The Church House Inn ♀
TQ9 7SF ☎ 01803 863707
Dir: *From Totnes take A381 S. Take turn for Harberton on R, adjacent to church in centre of village*
Originally built to house the stonemasons working on the church next door around 1100, this charming inn has also been used as a chantry house for monks. Inside there are a medieval oak screen, the original oak beams, and a latticed window containing 13th-century glass.
The specials board changes regularly, but may include roast lamb, Thai duck curry, pork tenderloin in apple sauce or Portuguese steak Picado. Light bites are also available.
OPEN: 12-3 6-11 (Sat 12-4,6-11 Sun 12-3,7-10.30).
BAR MEALS: L served all week. D served all week 12-1.45 7-9.30. Av main course £7. **RESTAURANT:** L served all week. D served all week 12-1.45 7-9.30. Av 3 course à la carte £15.
BREWERY/COMPANY: Free House. **PRINCIPAL BEERS:** Bass, Wells Bombardier. **FACILITIES:** Children welcome Dogs allowed Water, dog Biscuits. **NOTES:** Parking 20. **ROOMS:** 3 bedrooms s£25 d£40

HATHERLEIGH
Map 02 SS50

Tally Ho Inn & Brewery
14 Market St EX20 3JN ☎ 01837 810306 📄 01837 811079
e-mail: tally.ho@virgin.net
A 15th-century pub, located in the heart of the historic town, with a beamed bar and cosy dining room. It brews its own ales on site, and the product is featured in the prize-winning Tally Ho sausages and the popular steak and ale pie.
OPEN: 11-3 6-11.30. **BAR MEALS:** L served all week. D served all week 11-2.30 6-9.30. Av main course £5.50. **RESTAURANT:** L served all week. D served all week 11-2.30 6-9.30.
BREWERY/COMPANY: Free House. **PRINCIPAL BEERS:** Tally Ho! Tarka's Tipple & Nutters Ale. **FACILITIES:** Children welcome Children's licence Garden: outdoor eating, BBQ Dogs allowed.
ROOMS: 3 bedrooms 3 en suite s£25 d£50 FR£60

> We endeavour to be as accurate as possible but changes in personnel and data can occur in establishments after the guide has gone to press

HAYTOR VALE　　　　　　　　　Map 03 SX77

Pick of the Pubs

The Rock Inn ⊛ ★ ★ 🏠 ♈
TQ13 9XP ☎ 01364 661305　🖺 01364 661242
e-mail: inn@rock-inn.co.uk
Dir: A38 from Exeter, at Drum Bridges rdbt take A382 for Bovey Tracey, 1st ex at 2nd rdbt (B3387), 3m L to Haytor Vale.
A coaching inn from around 1750, with much evidence of an earlier past, The Rock stands in a pretty village on the fringe of Dartmoor National Park.

The rambling traditional bars, characterised by open fires, antique tables and sturdy furnishings, are peaceful with an old world feel, where menu options can include open field mushrooms in garlic butter, local gamekeeper's pie and long-standing favourites such as tossed warm salmon salad and mild chicken or hot beef curries.

To start in the restaurant are also fresh mussels and king prawns, English sirloin and fillet steaks and vegetarian options such as roast red pepper and spinach lasagne. Round off the meal with a Rock Inn chocolate pot or the famous cappuccino cup-and-saucer (don't ask!) and relax overnight with champagne and roses in the four-poster or garden view bedrooms named since 1920 after former Grand National winners.
OPEN: 11-11. Closed Dec 25-26. **BAR MEALS:** L served all week. D served all week 12-2.30 6.30-9.30. **RESTAURANT:** L served all week. D served all week 12-2.30 7-9.
BREWERY/COMPANY: Free House.
PRINCIPAL BEERS: Hardy Royal Oak, St Austell Dartmoor Best, Bass. **FACILITIES:** Children welcome Garden: patio, food served outdoors. **NOTES:** Parking 35. **ROOMS:** 9 bedrooms 9 en suite s£50.50 d£70

HOLBETON　　　　　　　　　Map 03 SX65

Mildmay Colours Inn
PL8 1NA ☎ 01752 830248　🖺 01752 830432
Dir: S from Exeter on A38, ex at Nat Shire Horse Centre, S past Ugborough & Ermington R onto A379. After 1.5m
Close to the coast and Dartmoor, this 17th-century village pub is named after a famous jockey, Lord Anthony Mildmay, whose portrait is hung in the pub along with his racing colours. The pub is set in a typical English village, surrounded by thatched cottages and rolling hills, and close to Mothecombe Beach.

The food choices include steak and Stilton pie, salmon darne with garlic butter, pork chops with apple sauce, and vegetable nut and fruit roast. Light meals include salads, triple sandwiches, ploughmans', and jacket potatoes.
OPEN: 11-3 6-11 (Sun 12-3, 7-10.30). **BAR MEALS:** L served all week. D served all week 12-2 6-9. Av main course £7.
RESTAURANT: L served Sun. D served Sat-Sun 12-2 7-9. Av 3 course à la carte £10.95. Av 3 course fixed price £10.95.
BREWERY/COMPANY: Free House.
PRINCIPAL BEERS: Mildmay Colours Bitter & Mildmay SP, Gale's HSB. **FACILITIES:** Children welcome Garden: Patio, Beer Garden: Food served outside Dogs allowed Water.
NOTES: Parking 20. **ROOMS:** 8 bedrooms 8 en suite s£30 d£50

All AA listed accommodation can also be found on the AA's internet site **www.theAA.com**

HOLNE　　　　　　　　　Map 03 SX76

Church House Inn ♈
TQ13 7SJ ☎ 01364 631208　🖺 01364 631525
Dir: Turn off A38 at Buckfast, take road signed for Two Bridges & Princetown
Tucked away in the tranquil south Devon countryside, this traditional 14th-century free house offers a warm welcome and old-fashioned service. This is a paradise for outdoor enthusiasts, and the new owners are building a reputation for quality local fare. Bar lunches include sandwiches, salads and Dartmoor rabbit pie, whilst evening brings good fresh soups, scallops, venison casserole, or West Country fish pie.
OPEN: 11.30-3 6.30-11. **BAR MEALS:** L served all week. D served all week 12-2.30 7-9.30. Av main course £9.
RESTAURANT: L served Sun. D served all week 12.00-2.30 7-8.30. Av 3 course à la carte £17.50. **BREWERY/COMPANY:** Free House. **PRINCIPAL BEERS:** Butcombe, Butcome Gold, Badger Tanglefoot, guest beers. **FACILITIES:** Children welcome Garden: Food served outside Dogs allowed. **NOTES:** Parking 6. **ROOMS:** 6 bedrooms 4 en suite s£25 d£22.50

HONITON　　　　　　　　　Map 03 ST10

The Otter Inn ♈
Weston EX14 3NZ ☎ 01404 42594　🖺 01404 549070
Dir: Just off A30 W of Honiton
On the banks of the idyllic River Otter, this ancient 14th-century inn is set in over two acres of grounds and was once a cider house. Enjoy one of the traditional real ales, try your hand at scrabble, dominoes or cards, or peruse the inn's extensive book collection. A wide-ranging menu caters for all tastes and includes fresh fish, game, steak, vegetarian dishes, bar meals and Sunday lunch.
OPEN: 12-2.30 (Fri-Sun 12-3) 6-11.30. **BAR MEALS:** L served all week. D served all week 12-2 7-9. Av main course £5.95.
RESTAURANT: L served all week. D served all week 12-2 7-9.30. Av 3 course à la carte £15.95. Av 2 course fixed price £12.95.
BREWERY/COMPANY: Free House. **PRINCIPAL BEERS:** Bass, Wadworth 6X, Flowers IPA. **FACILITIES:** Children welcome Garden: Food served outside Dogs allowed Water.
NOTES: Parking 60

HORNDON　　　　　　　　　Map 02 SX58

The Elephant's Nest Inn
PL19 9NQ ☎ 01822 810273
e-mail: elephant@globalnet.co.uk
Dir: Off A386 N of Tavistock

Isolated 16th-century inn located on the flanks of Dartmoor and reached via narrow lanes from the A386 at Mary Tavy. A welcome sight after a bracing moorland ramble, it features

continued

rustic furnishings, old beams, rugs on flagstone floors, a large collection of elephants, and roaring log fires to relax in front of. The pub takes its name from a earlier portly landlord with a bushy beard. Traditional pub food ranges from filled granary cobs and ploughman's lunches to local game pie, beef curry, grilled Tavy trout and Aberdeen Angus steaks. Lovely front garden with open views across the moor.
OPEN: 11.30-2.30 (Sun 12-2.30, 7-10.30) 6.30-11.
BAR MEALS: L served all week. D served all week 11.30-2 6.30-10. Av main course £5.50. **BREWERY/COMPANY:** Free House.
PRINCIPAL BEERS: Boddingtons, Palmers IPA, St Austells HSD.
FACILITIES: Children welcome Garden: Large food served outside Dogs allowed dogs must be on leads.
NOTES: Parking 30

HORN'S CROSS   Map 02 SS32

Pick of the Pubs

The Hoops Inn 🐑 ♀
Clovelly EX39 5DL ☎ 01237 451222
📠 01237 451247
e-mail: sales@hoopsinn.co.uk
See Pub Walk on page 121
See Pick of the Pubs on page 135

HORSEBRIDGE   Map 02 SX47

The Royal Inn
PL19 8PJ ☎ 01822 870214
e-mail: paul@royalinn.co.uk
Dir: South of B3362 Launceston/Tavistock road
15th-century inn visited by Charles I - hence the name. Originally a nunnery, the Royal is situated on the banks of the Tamar in a wooded river valley location. Plenty of good local walks to be enjoyed. No jukeboxes or electronic games. Varied choice of wholesome food might include shank of lamb, curry, chilli, duck breast, ham, egg and chips or baguettes.
OPEN: 12-3 7-11 (Summer Open 6.30pm). **BAR MEALS:** L served all week. D served all week 12-2 7-9. Av main course £5.50.
RESTAURANT: L served all week. D served all week 12-2 7-9.
BREWERY/COMPANY: Free House.
PRINCIPAL BEERS: Sharp's Doom Bar, Bass, Wadworth 6X, Ash Vine Hop & Glory. **FACILITIES:** Garden: outdoor eating, patio, Dogs allowed bar and garden only. **NOTES:** Parking 30

IVYBRIDGE

Anchor Inn
Lutterburn St, Ugborough PL21 0NG ☎ 01752 892283
Open all day, this charming pub is just off the A38 and has a small patio, an oak beam bar with log fire, and real ale from the cask. Bedrooms.

For pubs with AA rosette awards for food
see page 10

KENTON   Map 03 SX98

Devon Arms ♦♦♦
Fore St EX6 8LD ☎ 01626 890213 📠 01626 891678
e-mail: devon.arms@ukgateway.net
Dir: A379 between Exeter & Dawlish 7M from Exeter, 5M from Dawlish, adjacent to powderham castle
Mid-way between Exeter and Dawlish, a family-run freehouse that dates back to 1592 and once housed its own brewery. Freshly prepared bar food incorporating daily curries and pies is supplemented at night by steaks and mixed grills. Daily blackboard specials: garden with aviary and fish pond; childrens' menus and Sunday lunch.

KINGSBRIDGE   Map 03 SX74

Church House Inn
Churchstow TQ7 3QW ☎ 01548 852237
Dir: On A379 1 1/2m W of Kingsbridge
Rebuilt in the 15th century, this historic inn originated as a rest house for Cistercian monks in the 13th century. Very popular hot carvery.

The Crabshell Inn
Embankment Rd TQ7 1JZ ☎ 01548 852345
Free mooring at the quay and a splendid waterside terrace are just two draws at this family-run hostelry. An extensive menu includes a wide range of seafood dishes, vegetarian options, salads, jacket potatoes and sandwiches.

KINGSKERSWELL   Map 03 SX86

Barn Owl Inn ♀
Aller Mills TQ12 5AN ☎ 01803 872130
Located at the heart of an area of sleepy Devon hamlets, this 16th-century longhouse boasts many charming features, including flagged floors, a black leaded range and oak beams in a high-vaulted converted barn with a minstrel's gallery. Handy for Dartmoor and the English Riviera towns of Torquay, Brixham and Paignton. The menu offers hearty wholesome fare such as hog roast, mixed grill, half-shoulder of lamb and steak and kidney pie with Guinness.
OPEN: 11-11 (Sun 12-10.30). **BAR MEALS:** L served all week. D served all week 12-2.30 6-9.30. Av main course £4.75.
RESTAURANT: L served all week. D served all week 12-2.30 6-9.30. Av 3 course à la carte £15.
BREWERY/COMPANY: Eldridge Pope.
PRINCIPAL BEERS: Bass, Courage Best. **FACILITIES:** Children welcome Garden: Food served outside. **NOTES:** Parking 30.
ROOMS: 6 bedrooms s£49 d£64 FR£74

AA The Hotel Guide
2002 The Hotel Guide 2002
Britain's best-selling hotel guide for all your business and leisure needs
www.theAA.com
AA Lifestyle Guides

OPEN: 8am-11pm (Sun 8.30am-10.30pm). Closed Dec 25.
BAR MEALS: L served all week. D served all week 12-3 5.30-9.30. Food all day Sat & Sun, daily July-Sep. Av main course £8.50
RESTAURANT: L served all week D served all week 12-3 7-9.30. Av 3 course a la carte £16.50.
BREWERY/COMPANY: Free House.
PRINCIPAL BEERS: Jollyboat Mainbrace, Cottage, Exe Valley, Cotleigh Barn Owl, Bass, Barum.
FACILITIES: Children welcome. Garden: patio, BBQ, outdoor eating, herb garden. Dogs allowed
NOTES: Parking 150.
ROOMS: 12 bedrooms 12 en suite s£50-£75 d£75-£130 FR80.

The Hoops Inn

Clovelly EX39 5DL
☎ 01237 451222 📠 01237 451247
e-mail: sales@hoopsinn.co.uk
Dir: Horns Cross is on the A39 between Bideford and Clovelly.

Set in 16 acres of garden and meadow close to the North Devon coast path, this thatch-roofed, cob-walled 13th-century smugglers' inn combines old-world charm with up-to-date fine cuisine and comfortable accommodation. Ideally placed for touring Exmoor, Dartmoor and the rugged coastline.

Picture-postcard pretty with its long thatch and whitewashed walls, The Hoops takes its name from a type of bullfinch known in Devon as the Hoopspink. Two-hundred-years ago the bird was the curse of local farmers and the going rate for killing one was one old penny. The inn was also a regular haunt of highwaymen and the second home to notorious smugglers and seafarers from Clovelly and Westward Ho!. Historic charm is maintained in the attractive rambling interior, with oak beams and panelling, thick cob walls, log fires in huge fireplaces, and period furniture characterising the bar.

Fresh West Country produce from local suppliers, including fish and seafood landed at Bideford and organic meats, features strongly on the extensive menu served throughout the bar and candlelit dining room. Grilled chicken livers wrapped in bacon and wild mushroom risotto precede solidly traditional main dishes like chargrilled rump steak with home-made 'chunky' chips, steak and kidney pudding, Hoops crackly pork knuckle and wild rabbit braised in ale and mustard. Pride of place goes to the fish blackboards with daily-changing options of Clovelly mackerel on garlic mash with mustard sauce, mixed fish grill and whole grilled sole. Good Sunday roasts, ploughman's lunches and home-made pudding specials.

Blackboards also list the local ales - Jolly Boat Mainbrace - tapped from the barrel and around 22 wines by the glass. En suite bedrooms are split between the pub and rear Coach House.

See Pub Walk on page 121

135

England

KINGSTEIGNTON Map 03 SX87

Old Rydon Inn
Rydon Rd TQ12 3QG ☎ 01626 354626 📠 01626 356980
e-mail: martinweb@lineone.net
Dir: From A380 take B3193 into Kingsteignton
A feature of this Grade II listed former farmhouse is its large
family dining conservatory filled with flowering tropical plants
and grape vines. Adjacent, the pub area is housed in the old
stables with a cider apple loft above it.

A typical menu features Old Rydon seafood salad, grilled
salmon on vegetable spaghetti, venison and wild boar steaks,
and Nasi Goreng. Light bites include salads, jacket potatoes,
toasted muffins, and ploughmans.
OPEN: 11-3 6-11. Closed 25 Dec. **BAR MEALS:** L served all
week. D served all week 12-1.30 6.30-9.30. Av main course £6.50.
RESTAURANT: D served Mon-Sat 7-9.30. Av 3 course à la carte
£25. **BREWERY/COMPANY:** Heavitree.
PRINCIPAL BEERS: Bass, Fullers London Pride.
FACILITIES: Children welcome Garden: patio, outdoor eating
Dogs allowed Water, toys in garden. **NOTES:** Parking 40

KINGSTON Map 03 SX64

The Dolphin Inn
TQ7 4QE ☎ 01548 810314 📠 01548 810314
Historic 16th-century beamed inn situated in a delightful South
Hams village. Bigbury Bay and Burgh Island are nearby and
the pub is handy for rambling by the tranquil River Erme or
strolling by the coast.

Relax by the inglenook fireplace and enjoy a pint of real ale
or perhaps something from the appetising menu which uses
locally-grown produce. Typical dishes include steak in ale
casserole, pan-fried scallops with bacon in garlic butter and
spinach and Stilton bake with garlic bread.
OPEN: 11-2.30 6-11 (Sun 12-3,7-10.30). **BAR MEALS:** L served
all week. D served all week 12-2 6-9.30. Av main course £5.95.
BREWERY/COMPANY: Ushers. **PRINCIPAL BEERS:** Ushers -
Founders & Four Seasons Ale, Courage Best.
FACILITIES: Children welcome Garden: Beer garden, outdoor
eating Dogs allowed garden only, water. **NOTES:** Parking 40.
ROOMS: 3 bedrooms 3 en suite s£39.50 d£55

KINGSWEAR Map 03 SX85

The Ship
Higher St TQ6 0AG ☎ 01803 752348
Historic village pub overlooking the scenic River Dart towards
Dartmouth and Dittisham. Located in one of South Devon's
most picturesque corners, this tall, character inn is very much
a village local with a friendly, welcoming atmosphere inside.
Well-prepared fresh food is the hallmark of the menu.
Sandwiches, baguettes and pies are available in the bar, while
the restaurant menu offers duck, venison, sea bass, and crab
wrapped in a salmon parcel.
OPEN: 11-3 6-11. **BAR MEALS:** L served all week. D served all
week 12.30-2 7-9.30. Av main course £5.95. **RESTAURANT:** D
served all week 7-9.30. Av 3 course à la carte £8.95. Av 4 course
fixed price £18.95. **BREWERY/COMPANY:** Heavitree.
PRINCIPAL BEERS: Flowers IPA, Bass. **FACILITIES:** Children
welcome Garden: outdoor eating, patio/terrace Dogs allowed
Water No credit cards

KNOWSTONE Map 03 SS82

Pick of the Pubs

Masons Arms Inn
EX36 4RY ☎ 01398 341231
e-mail: masonarmsinn@aol.com
Dir: M5 J27 Off A361 between Tiverton & S Molton

Having celebrated its 800th birthday in 2001, this
quintessential thatched Devon inn, nestling in a sleepy
village in the foothills of Exmoor, received a much needed
facelift from new, enthusiastic owners and perfect hosts,
Paul and Jo Stretton-Downes.

With a new thatch, new kitchen, new dining area, new
landscaped garden and new menus, the Masons has
realised its potential and is the place to go for atmosphere
and excellent food. Untouched, thankfully, is the classic
main bar with its inglenook fireplace, old bread oven,
heavy medieval beams and rustic pine tables. Refurbished
is the now cosy lower dining area, with polished
darkwood dining tables, tasteful prints and warming log
fires and, like the garden, the new dining extension enjoys
excellent Exmoor views.

Blackboard menus are right up-to-date, offering prawn
and red pepper pâté, salmon and dill fishcakes with lemon
dressing, lamb shank casserole with root vegetables,
beans and lentils and pan-fried duck with red onion confit
and port and honey sauce. More traditional puddings
include sticky toffee pudding and treacle tart. Delightful,
self-contained one-bedroomed cottage a short stroll from
the pub.
OPEN: 12-3 6-11 (Sun 12-3, 7-10.30). Closed Dec 25.
BAR MEALS: L served all week. D served all week 12-2 7-9.
Av main course £6.50. **BREWERY/COMPANY:** Free House.
PRINCIPAL BEERS: Cotleigh Tawny. **FACILITIES:** Garden:
outdoor eating, patio Dogs allowed On lead.
NOTES: Parking 10. **ROOMS:** 1 bedrooms 1 en suite s£35
d£50

 AA inspected guest accommodation

DEVON

**DARTMOOR INN,
LYDFORD**
EX20 4AY.
Tel: 01822 820221
Directions: on A386 south
of Okehampton
*Refurbished 16th-century
roadside inn set on the edge
of Dartmoor close to Lydford
Gorge (NT). Fresh flowers
adorn the well decorated bar
and restaurant. Expect
upmarket pub food, decent
wines and a warm welcome;
value for money winter set
lunch.*
Open: 11.30-3 6.30-11 (from
6 in summer). Closed Mon.
Bar Meals: 12-2.15, 6.30-10.
Children and dogs welcome.
Garden. Parking.
(see page 139 for full entry)

*Pub*WALK

Dartmoor Inn, Lydford

An enjoyable and beautiful walk on the western flanks of Dartmoor, following the course of a moorland river valley and returning via a high disused railway line, affording excellent moorland views.

Turn right out of the pub car park, then immediately right onto a track alongside the pub to reach a gate leading on to Dartmoor. Continue straight ahead, keeping the wall on your left, for 1/2m (0.8km) to the footbridge and stepping stones across the River Lyd. Cross the bridge, turn left and follow one of the numerous tracks parallel with the river. Continue past two fords within 1/2m (0.8km), and proceed beside the river, soon to walk beside an old dry leat close to the river (keep to right side). Head towards a large steep hill on the left side of the river, the valley sides gradually becoming much steeper.

Walk round Great Nodden and pass a large old tree on the left bank of the river. Shortly, where the river bends sharp right, cross the river (now no more than a stream) and walk straight ahead.

Ascend to an old railway embankment with a small bridge. This is the old peat railway that connected valley peat workings with Bridestowe station. Turn left along the railway and savour the superb views into Cornwall. Follow the track bed for 1 1/2 miles (2km) to Nodden Gate. Go through the gate, turn left and left again through a second gate and follow the footpath sign. At a junction of three paths, take the left-hand fork across the field, following the markers to a wall stile close to the footbridge and stepping stones negotiated earlier. Turn right along the track and retrace steps back to the inn.

Distance: 5 miles (8km)
Map: OS Landranger 191
Terrain: moorland; can be wet underfoot in places
Paths: bridleways, tracks and a disused railway line
Gradient: Fairly easy; one long gradual incline

*Walk submitted by:
Ian Hardy*

LEWDOWN

Map 02 SX48

The Harris Arms NEW
Portgate EX20 4PZ ☎ 01566 783331 🖹 01566 783161
e-mail: grant-p@btconnect
Dir: From A30 take Lifton turning, halfway between Lifton and Lewdown
In the past this comfortable inn has served as a corn merchants and a church brewery. Set on the West Devon Drive this is a good location for walkers, and enjoys some spectacular views of Dartmoor.
OPEN: 11-3 (Sun 12-3, 7-10.30) 5.30-11. **BAR MEALS:** L served all week. D served all week 12-2.30 6.30-9.15. Av main course £7.50. **RESTAURANT:** L served all week. D served all week 12-2.30 6.30-9.15. Av 3 course à la carte £15.
BREWERY/COMPANY: Free House. **PRINCIPAL BEERS:** Bass, St Austell Tinners. **FACILITIES:** Garden: Food served outside. **NOTES:** Parking 30

LIFTON

Map 02 SX38

Pick of the Pubs

The Arundell Arms 🏵 🏵 🏵 ★ ★ ★ ♀
PL16 0AA ☎ 01566 784666 🖹 01566 784494
e-mail: ArundellArms@btinternet.com
Dir: 2/3m off the A30 dual carriageway, 3m E of Launceston
Some forty years in the same ownership, this creeper-clad 18th-century coaching inn at the heart of a delightful Devon village draws discerning guests to its comfortable rooms and relaxing atmosphere, spurred on by 20 miles of private fishing and numerous country pursuits. The Courthouse Bar (originally the magistrates' court) has a year-round local appeal, while the Arundell Bar is a focal point of the hotel proper.
   Starters and light meals run from baked goats' cheese salad with avocado, through toasted fillet steak with Dijon mustard to sweet pepper salad with pickled anchovies, pesto and Parmesan shavings. There are salads of smoked salmon, home-cured gammon and roast Devon beef with horseradish cream. Daily hot dishes might be Spanish omelette with deep-fried onions or sole fritters in beer batter with curried mayonnaise. A la carte dining of considerable class features locally-sourced meat, fish, vegetables and cheeses.
OPEN: 11.30-3 6-11. **BAR MEALS:** L served all week. D served all week 12-2.30 6-9.30. Av main course £10. **RESTAURANT:** L served all week. D served all week 12.30-2 7.30-9.30. Av 5 course fixed price £31.
BREWERY/COMPANY: Free House **FACILITIES:** Children welcome Garden: Food served outside Dogs allowed. **NOTES:** Parking 70. **ROOMS:** 27 bedrooms 27 en suite s£46 d£93

LITTLEHEMPSTON

Map 03 SX86

Tally Ho Inn 🍺
TQ9 6NF ☎ 01803 862316 🖹 01803 862316
Dir: off the A38 at Duckfastleigh
Old pub very much at the centre of community life, catering for locals and the many visitors to the Devon countryside. In summer the hanging baskets and flower-filled patios are a delight, and in winter there are roaring fires and cosy corners. A varied menu features fresh fish alongside local game and home-made desserts. Typical dishes are Brixham fisherman's
continued

pie and grilled Torbay sole filled with prawns and mushrooms.
OPEN: 12-3 (Winter close lunch at 2.30) 6-11. Closed Dec 25.
BAR MEALS: L served all week. D served all week 12-2 7.00-9.
Av main course £8.95. **BREWERY/COMPANY:** Free House.
PRINCIPAL BEERS: Bass. **FACILITIES:** Children welcome
Garden: Patio, food served outdoors Dogs allowed.
NOTES: Parking 20. **ROOMS:** 4 bedrooms 4 en suite d£55

LOWER ASHTON

Map 03 SX88

Manor Inn 🍺 ♀
EX6 7QL ☎ 01647 252304
e-mail: manor_ashton@compuserve.com
Dir: A38, Teign Valley turning, follow signs for B3193, pub 5m on R, Just over the stome bridge
Traditional and authentic country pub situated in a picturesque village in the lovely Teign Valley. A sheltered garden and scenic views enhance the setting. Expect a friendly welcome and plenty of atmosphere in the two homely and simply furnished bars which are warmed in winter by log fires.
   Good range of sandwiches, jacket potatoes and ploughman's lunches. Home-cooked specials might include a hearty beef and red wine casserole, chicken curry, lamb goulash and lasagne. Over 1500 guest ales have been sold and the inn is the venue for an annual beer festival in September.
OPEN: 12-2.00 (2.30 Wkds 6.30-11 (Sat & Sun 7-11; closed Mon ex BHS). **BAR MEALS:** L served Tue-Sun. D served Tue-Sun 12-1.30 7-9.30. Av main course £6.50. **BREWERY/COMPANY:** Free House. **PRINCIPAL BEERS:** Teignworthy Reel Ale, Wadworth 6X, Princetown Jail Ale, RCH Pitchfork. **FACILITIES:** Garden: outdoor eating Dogs allowed. **NOTES:** Parking 20

LUSTLEIGH

Map 03 SX78

The Cleave ♀
TQ13 9TJ ☎ 01647 277223 🖹 01647 277223
Dir: Off A382 between Bovey Tracy and Moretonhampstead
Originally a Devon longhouse, this 15th-century thatched inn is set in a beautiful village on the flanks of Dartmoor, a perfect stop for walkers. There is a cosy lounge bar with granite walls and a vast inglenook fireplace, and a bigger Victorian bar with an impressive array of musical instruments. The home-made soups, pies and quiches are popular choices, along with imaginative salads.

OPEN: 11-3 6.30-11 (summer 11-11). Closed (Mon Nov-Feb).
BAR MEALS: L served all week. D served all week 12-2.30 6.30-9.
Av main course £6.95. **RESTAURANT:** L served All. D served All12-2 6.30. Av 3 course à la carte £16.
BREWERY/COMPANY: Heavitree.
PRINCIPAL BEERS: Flowers Original, Bass, Wadworth 6X.
FACILITIES: Children welcome Garden: beer garden, food served outdoors Dogs allowed. **NOTES:** Parking 10

England

Pick of the Pubs

Castle Inn ♀
EX20 4BH ☎ 01822 820242 820241   📄 01822 820454
e-mail: castle1lyd@aol.com
Dir: Off A386 S of Okehampton

Located beside the medieval castle and within walking distance of Lydford Gorge (NT), this pretty, wisteria-clad inn dates from the 16th-century. The interior oozes atmosphere and period charm, with its slate floors, low, lamp-lit beams, decorative plates and huge Norman fireplace.

Lengthy, all-embracing menu listing duck liver and bacon terrine with Cumberland sauce and Thai fishcakes with chilli dipping sauce for starters, followed by game casserole, steak and kidney pie, crispy confit of duck leg with celeriac and chive mash and port jus, and warm chicken tagliatelle with a spiced mango sauce. For pudding try the treacle tart with clotted cream or a selection of West Country cheeses.

Comfortable accommodation; shrub-filled garden for summer alfresco eating. Close to Dartmoor and miles of beautiful walks. Now owned by Heavitree Inns.
OPEN: 11.30-3 (Apr-Nov Open all day) 6-11 (Nov-Apr Fri, Sat& Sun Open all day). **BAR MEALS:** L served all week. D served all week 12-2.30 6.30-9.15. **RESTAURANT:** L served all week. D served all week 12-2.30 7-9.15. Av 3 course à la carte £17.
BREWERY/COMPANY: Free House.
PRINCIPAL BEERS: Fullers London Pride, Flowers IPA, Greene King Old Speckled Hen. **FACILITIES:** Children welcome Garden: patio, outdoor eating, BBQ Dogs allowed allowed in bar, patio & bedrooms. **NOTES:** Parking 10.
ROOMS: 9 bedrooms 9 en suite s£58 d£96

Pick of the Pubs

Dartmoor Inn ◉ ◉ 🐾 ♀
EX20 4AY ☎ 01822 820221   📄 01822 820494
Dir: On A386 S of Okehampton
Set within the beautiful and dramatic landscape of Dartmoor National Park and close to the National Trust's Lydford Gorge, this rather plain-looking 16th-century inn has been rejuvenated and neatly refurbished within, yet retains the character of contemporary co-ordinating styles through a succession of wooden and slate-floored dining-rooms.

Imaginative modern dishes have a down-to-earth feel, combining an honest farmhouse kitchen style with some sophisticated use of contrasting flavours. Set weekday lunch and dinners offer daily soups such as celeriac with thyme cream, perhaps grilled smoked salmon with a hot vinaigrette of leeks, followed by peppered fillet steak and crème brûlée or West Country farmhouse cheeses.

Light bites of the day might be char-grilled vegetables with pesto or baked goats' cheese salad, followed by smoked haddock risotto with chives or a small fillet steak and chips. Individually priced alternatives include pan-fried fishcakes with spiced saffron sauce, braised oxtail with creamed leeks and root vegetables and fillet of chicken with butternut squash, bacon and pesto. Don't miss the Devon clotted cream with black cap apples and vanilla sauce.
OPEN: 11.30-3 6.30-11 (6-11 in Summer). **BAR MEALS:** L served Tue-Sun. D served Tue-Sat 12-2.15 6.30-10. Av main course £9.50. **RESTAURANT:** L served Tue-Sun. D served Tue-Sat 12-2.15 6.30-10. Av 3 course à la carte £23.75. Av 3 course fixed price £19.75. **BREWERY/COMPANY:** Free House. **PRINCIPAL BEERS:** Bass, Greene King Old Speckled Hen, St Austell Hicks Special & Dartmoor Best.
FACILITIES: Children welcome Garden: Food served outside Dogs allowed. **NOTES:** Parking 35. **ROOMS:** 3 bedrooms 3 en suite s£50 d£60
See Pub Walk on page 137

The Globe Inn
The Strand EX8 5EY ☎ 01395 263166
Set in the harbour village of Lympstone, this traditional beamed inn has a good local reputation for seafood. The separate restaurant area serves as a coffee bar during the day.

BAR BILLIARDS

The ingenious blend of billiards and skittles is a relative newcomer to the pub scene. It was introduced here from Belgium in the 1930s, with support from billiard table manufacturers. The game caught on rapidly, especially in the South and Midlands, and leagues had been organised by the time the Second World War began. Its much more recent rival is pool, which came here from America in the 1960s in the wake of the Paul Newman film The Hustler.

LYNMOUTH
Map 03 SS74

Pick of the Pubs

Rising Sun Hotel ⊛ ⊛ ★ ★ 🐾 ♀
Harbourside EX35 6EG ☎ 01598 753223
📠 01598 753480
e-mail: risingsunlynmouth@easynet.co.uk
Dir: From M5 J25 to Minehead, A39 to Lynmouth

Hugo Jeune's part-thatched 14th-century hotel on
Lynmouth's waterside has been a trail-blazer for some two
decades. Backed by hog-back cliffs the inn is steeped in
Lorna Doone history and boasts a garden cottage where
Percy Bysshe Shelley once stayed: he wrote that the
climate is so mild that myrtles twine up the walls and
roses sway in the air in winter.
    Following a change of chef the food is as consistent as
ever, with jacket potatoes, sandwiches and ploughman's
through lunch supplemented by hot food selections of
market-fresh fish, such as cod cakes with sweet chilli and
smoked haddock with spinach and soft-poached egg.
Meatier alternatives include Toulouse sausage soubise
with black pudding and sirloin steak with fries and
béarnaise sauce.
    At night the oak-panelled, candlelit dining-room
exemplifies quintessentially romantic British inn-keeping at
its best. Bedrooms are individually designed and offer
good modern facilities and harbour views.
OPEN: 11-3 6.30-11. **BAR MEALS:** L served all week.
D served all week 12-2 7-9. Av main course £7.
RESTAURANT: L served all week. D served all week 12-2
7-9. Av 3 course à la carte £27.50. Av 3 course fixed price
£19.95. **BREWERY/COMPANY:** Free House.
PRINCIPAL BEERS: Exmoor - Gold, Fox and Exmoor Ale.
FACILITIES: Garden: outdoor eating, patio. **ROOMS:** 16
bedrooms 16 en suite s£60 d£94

MEAVY
Map 02 SX56

The Royal Oak Inn
PL20 6PJ ☎ 01822 852944
e-mail: royaloakinn.meavy@barbox.net
Dir: Off A386 between Tavistock & Plymouth
Standing on the edge of Dartmoor, between Tavistock and
Plymouth, this 12th-century brew house is a popular watering
hole for those touring and exploring the National Park. Good
quality fare is prepared from produce bought locally and
much of the meat is free-range. A local fishmonger delivers
fresh fish from Plymouth. Expect filled baguettes, local pasties
and salads at lunchtime, while the evening menu consists of
stuffed plaice, lemon butterfly chicken, gammon steak and
salsa sardines.
OPEN: 11.30-3 (Sun 12-3, 6.30-10.30 6.30-11. **BAR MEALS:** L
served all week. D served all week 11.30-2.00 6.30-9.00.
BREWERY/COMPANY: Free House. **PRINCIPAL BEERS:** Bass,
Courage Best, Princetown Jail Ale, IPA. **FACILITIES:** Dogs
allowed

NEWTON ABBOT
Map 03 SX87

The Court Farm Inn ♀
Wilton Way, Abbotskerswell TQ12 5NY ☎ 01626 361866
Grade II former Devon longhouse, rebuilt in 1721 and
converted to a pub in 1972. Prior to that it was a farmhouse.
Cosy, relaxed atmosphere, good home-cooked food and the
chance to enjoy a drink in the garden. Extensive menu offers
cottage pie, honey roast ham, Chinese beef stir-fry, fillet of
cod, lambs liver and bacon, and oven-baked breast of chicken.

OPEN: 11-11 (Sun 12-10.30). **BAR MEALS:** L served all week.
D served all week 11.30-2.30 5-10.
BREWERY/COMPANY: Heavitree. **PRINCIPAL BEERS:** Bass,
Flowers IPA, Fullers London Pride, Wadworth 6X.
FACILITIES: Children welcome Garden: outdoor eating, flower
beds, bird table Dogs allowed. **NOTES:** Parking 70

The Linny Inn & Hayloft Dining Area 🐾 ♀
Coffinswell TQ12 4SR ☎ 01803 873192
e-mail: andrew@linny.com
Dir: follow signs from A380
14th-century family-run inn situated in a picture-postcard
village outside Torquay. Beamed bar, snugs and hayloft
restaurant with two log fires blazing in winter and the popular
patio a delightful setting in summer. The name means barn or
outbuilding. Guest ales from local micro breweries change
daily and the same menu throughout offers stuffed chicken
breast with smoked cheese wrapped in bacon and wild
mushroom and asparagus lattice with spicy tomato sauce.
Good choice of fresh fish.
continued

England

OPEN: 11.30-3 6.30-11. **BAR MEALS:** L served all week.
D served all week 12-2 6.30-9.30. Av main course £7.
RESTAURANT: 12-2 6.30-9.30. Av 3 course à la carte £18.
BREWERY/COMPANY: Free House.
PRINCIPAL BEERS: Tetley, Bass, Sharps Cornish Ale.
FACILITIES: Children welcome Garden: patio/terrace, outdoor
eating Dogs allowed (in garden only). **NOTES:** Parking 30

The Wild Goose Inn 🍴 ♀

Combeinteignhead TQ12 4RA ☎ 01626 872241
*Dir: from A380 at the Newton Abbot rdbt, take the B3195 Shaldon rd,
signed Milber, for 2.5m into village then R at signpost*
Traditional 17th-century inn which has been licensed since
1840 and prides itself on being a true classic local. Secluded
beer garden overlooked by a 14th-century church tower and a
smallholding where sheep and cattle graze. Beyond the
garden, a stream winds its way through the valley.
  Real ales from West Country micro-breweries and a good
choice of chef's specials, including fresh fish dishes, grills,
game and whole rack of barbecued pork ribs. Other options
might feature BLT, Club sandwiches and chicken breast with
Stilton sauce.
OPEN: 11.30-2.30 6.30-11 Sun 12-2.30, 7-10.30). **BAR MEALS:** L
served all week. D served all week 12-2 7-10. Av main course
£7.50. **RESTAURANT:** L served all week. D served all week 12-2
7-10. Av 3 course à la carte £14. **BREWERY/COMPANY:** Free
House. **PRINCIPAL BEERS:** Teignworthy, Otter, Cotleigh,
Sharps. **FACILITIES:** Garden: outdoor eating, patio Dogs
allowed Water. **NOTES:** Parking 40

NEWTON ST CYRES   Map 03 SX89

The Beer Engine

EX5 5AX ☎ 01392 851282 ▤ 01392 851876
e-mail: enquiries@thebeerengine.co.uk
*Dir: from Exeter take A377 towards Crediton, pub is opp train station
in Newton St Cyres*
A former railway hotel, this straightforward white-painted local
has been brewing its own beer since 1983, mainly for the inn's
own consumption. Occasional live music in the cellar bar.
Expect a range of steaks and vegetarian dishes, as well as fish
and lamb chops.
OPEN: 11-11 (Sun 12-10.30). **BAR MEALS:** L served all week.
D served all week 12-2 6.30-9.30. Av main course £6.
BREWERY/COMPANY: Free House. **PRINCIPAL BEERS:** Beer
Engine: Piston Bitter, Rail Ale, Sleeper Heavy.
FACILITIES: Children welcome Garden: outdoor eating,
pario/terrace, BBQ Dogs allowed on lead only.
NOTES: Parking 30

Crown and Sceptre

EX5 5DA ☎ 01392 851278
Dir: 2m NW of Exeter on A377
The pub has burnt down twice and been rebuilt on the same
site. It has always had the same name, dating back to the
1800s. Under new management.

NOSS MAYO   Map 02 SX54

The Ship Inn ♀

PL8 1EW ☎ 01752 872387 ▤ 01752 873294
e-mail: ship@nossmayo.com
Dir: 3m S of Yealmpton, on the S side of the Yealm estuary
Traditional 16th-century waterside inn attracting yachtsmen
and tourists alike. It's fun to reach the pub at high tide and
relax at one of the terrace tables overlooking the scenic
estuary. The Ship underwent an extensive refit in 2000,
retaining its welcoming atmosphere and character. No music,
fruit machines or darts inside. Menu varies from day to day
and might include Devon lamb, fish and chips, local plaice, 8oz
steak burger, steak and kidney pie and wild mushroom risotto
served with Parmesan crostini.
OPEN: 11-11. **BAR MEALS:** L served all week. D served all week
12-9.30. Av main course £10. **BREWERY/COMPANY:** Free
House. **PRINCIPAL BEERS:** Tamar, Exmoor Gold, Wadworth 6X.
FACILITIES: Garden: Dogs allowed downstairs only

OTTERY ST MARY

The Talaton Inn

Talaton EX5 2RQ ☎ 01404 822214
Timber-framed, well-maintained 16th-century inn. Popular
with the locals. Themed food nights.

OTTER BREWERY

The founders of the Otter Brewery
both have hops and barley in their
blood. David McCaig was a brewer for
Whitbread for 17 years, and his wife Mary
Ann is the daughter of an erstwhile
Whitbread managing director. However, the
large brewery style has been tempered by
this couple who originally opted for a micro-
brewery approach but have ended up
running what has become the largest
brewery in Devon. Producing some 30,000
pints per week, and supplying more than
150 free houses, the Otter is as big as a
micro-brewery can get. Thankfully concerns
about quality control have led to a lid being
put on any further increase in quantity. Look
out for Otter Head (5.8%) and Otter
Bright (4.3%) in your local
quality supermarket.

England

PETER TAVY

Map 02 SX57

Pick of the Pubs

The Peter Tavy Inn ♀
PL19 9NN ☎ 01822 810348 📠 01822 810835
e-mail: Peter.tavy@virgin.net
Dir: Off A386 NE of Tavistock

Surrounded by moorland on the very edge of Dartmoor, this 15th-century inn is directly adjacent to the national cycle route, and also provides hitching posts for horses in the paddock. A true pub in the best English tradition, it retains all the character of slate floors, low beams and large fireplaces ablaze with logs in cold weather.

Pride is taken in the daily-changing blackboard menus, using fresh local ingredients wholly prepared on the premises, and carefully selected real ales that are a particular draw. Firm favourites include steak and kidney pie and boozy game casserole with a Stilton dumpling. Starters and snacks include wild boar and port and Stilton pâtés, spinach pancakes with savoury mushrooms, and a seafood gateau of layered salmon, cod and prawns.

Dinner choices broaden out to include duck breast with orange and Cointreau sauce, blackened tuna with Cajun spices and a game platter of ostrich, pheasant, wild boar, rabbit and venison, followed perhaps by banana toffee pudding, chocolate truffle torte or half a dozen local Devon cheeses.
OPEN: 12-2.30 (Wknd 12-3) 6.30-11 (Fri-Sat 6-11, Sun 7-10.30). Closed 25 Dec. **BAR MEALS:** L served all week. D served all week 12-2 7-9. **RESTAURANT:** L served all week. D served all week 12-2 7-9.
BREWERY/COMPANY: Free House.
PRINCIPAL BEERS: Princetown Jail Ale, Bass, Summerskills Tamar, Badger Dorset Best. **FACILITIES:** Children welcome Children's licence Garden: patio, outdoor eating Dogs allowed Water. **NOTES:** Parking 40

PLYMOUTH

Map 02 SX45

The China House ♀
Marrowbone Slip, Sutton Harbour PL4 0DW
☎ 01752 260932 📠 01752 268576
Dir: A38 to Plymouth centre, follow Exeter St to Sutton Rd, follow signs for Queen Anns Battery
Built as a warehouse in the mid-17th century, this waterfront pub has also been used as a gun wharf, a bakehouse, a wool warehouse and even a prison. The current name comes from the short-lived local manufacture of porcelain by William Cookworthy in the 1770s.
Expect dishes such as chargrilled tuna with warm potato
continued

salad, Cumberland sausage with cheese mash and onion gravy, or Bantry Bay mussels, on a typical menu. Fresh baguettes and doorstops served all day.
OPEN: 10-11.30. **BAR MEALS:** L served all week 12-3. Av main course £6. **RESTAURANT:** . D served all week 7-10.30. Av 3 course à la carte £15. **BREWERY/COMPANY:** Bass.
PRINCIPAL BEERS: Bass. **FACILITIES:** Children welcome Garden: Food served outisde Dogs allowed.
NOTES: Parking 120

Langdon Court Hotel ◉ ★ ★
Down Thomas PL9 0DY ☎ 01752 862358
📠 01752 863428
e-mail: langdon@eurobell.co.uk
Dir: On A379 from Elburton follow brown tourist signs, also HMS Cambridge signs
Once owned by Henry VIII, this historic, picturesque manor became the home of his last wife Catherine Parr. Close to outstanding coastal scenery. Primarily a hotel, Langdon Court offers a comfortable bar with freshly cooked meals and real ale.

POSTBRIDGE

Map 03 SX67

Warren House Inn
PL20 6TA ☎ 01822 880208
Dir: Take B3212 through Morehamptonstead on for 5m
High up on Dartmoor, this old tin miners' inn was cut off during the harsh winter of 1963 and supplies were delivered by helicopter. A peat fire has burned here continuously since 1845.
Home-made cauliflower cheese, seafood platter, mushroom Stroganoff, rabbit pie and venison steak in a port and cranberry sauce feature among the popular dishes. Good choice of snacks and sandwiches.
OPEN: 11-3 Open all day Easter - Oct 6-11 (Sun til 10:30).
BAR MEALS: L served all week. D served all week 12-2 6-9.30. Av main course £6. **BREWERY/COMPANY:** Free House.
PRINCIPAL BEERS: Sharps Special, Butcombe Bitter, Badger Tanglefoot. **FACILITIES:** Children welcome Garden: Food served outside Dogs allowed Water. **NOTES:** Parking 30

RATTERY

Map 03 SX76

Church House Inn
TQ10 9LD ☎ 01364 642220
One of Britain's oldest pubs, parts of which date from about 1028. Previously a rest home for monks, and lodgings for the craftsmen who built the Norman church. Large fireplaces, solid oak beams and an original spiral staircase.
Expect steak and kidney, chicken and cranberry curry, Moroccan lamb, rump steak and stilton pie.
OPEN: 11-3 6-11 (Winter 11-2.30, 6.30-10.30). **BAR MEALS:** L served all week. D served all week 12-2 7-9.00. Av main course £6.50. **RESTAURANT:** L served all week. D served all week 12 7-9. Av 3 course à la carte £12.50. **BREWERY/COMPANY:** Free House. **PRINCIPAL BEERS:** St Austell Dartmoor Best, Marstons Pedigree, Greene King Abbot Ale. **FACILITIES:** Children welcome Garden: Patio, Food served outside Dogs allowed Water. **NOTES:** Parking 30 No credit cards

 ♀ Pubs offering six or more wines by the glass

ROCKBEARE
Map 03 SY09

Pick of the Pubs

Jack in the Green Inn
London Rd EX5 2EE ☎ 01404 822240
📠 01404 823445
e-mail: info@jackinthegreen.uk.com
Dir: from M5 take A30 towards Honiton signed Rockbeare
A thoroughly pleasant destination pub, though not one of
the nation's loveliest, offering peace and tranquillity since
the recent opening of the A30 trunk road into Exeter.

The young staff show real confidence and a willingness
to please - now there's a novelty! Consistency, attention to
detail and use of fresh local produce are central to the
philosophy of a caring kitchen that allows the fruits of its
endeavour to speak for themselves.

Set-price dinner and Sunday lunch menus - duck liver
pate, loin of pork with green peppercorns and apple,
lemon parfait with lemon curd ice cream - offer fair value
for money. Bar snacks weigh in with warm Coronation
chicken salad, smoked haddock risotto, venison stew with
chestnut dumplings and seared salmon fillet with wasabi
dressing.

Of special note are the cheese selection that includes
Sharpham, Somerset Camembert and Cornish Yarg, real
ales from Cotleigh and Hardy Country, wines by the glass
from the Old and New Worlds and regular special events,
gourmet dinners and corporate events.
OPEN: 11-2.30 (Sun 12-10.30) 6-11 (Sun 12-10.30). Closed
Dec 25 - Jan 1 inclusive. **BAR MEALS:** L served all week.
D served all week 11-2 6-9.30. Av main course £8.
RESTAURANT: L served all week. D served all week 11-2
6-9.30. Av 3 course à la carte £19. Av 3 course fixed price £19.
BREWERY/COMPANY: Free House.
PRINCIPAL BEERS: Bass, Cotleigh Tawny, Hardy Country,
Otter Ale. **FACILITIES:** Children welcome Garden:
Courtyard, Food served outside Dogs allowed garden only.
NOTES: Parking 120

SHEEPWASH
Map 02 SS40

Half Moon Inn
EX21 5NE ☎ 01409 231376 📠 01409 231673
e-mail: lee@halfmoon.demon.co.uk
*Dir: from M5 take A30 to Okehampton then A386, at Hatherleigh, L
onto A3072, after 4m R for Sheepwash*

New owners Nathan and Lee Adey have taken over this white-
painted village inn. It overlooks the square in a remote Devon
village and has fishing rights for 10 miles of the River Torridge
(very popular with anglers). Inside there are slate floors and a
continued

huge inglenook fireplace. Bar snacks are available at
lunchtime, and at dinner there is a set menu of traditional fare.
OPEN: 11-2.30 6-11. Closed 25 Dec. **BAR MEALS:** L served all week
12-1.45. Av main course £3.50. **RESTAURANT:** D served all week 8.
Av 5 course fixed price £20.50. **BREWERY/COMPANY:** Free
House. **PRINCIPAL BEERS:** Courage Best, Marstons Pedigree,
Ruddles Best Bitter. **NOTES:** Parking 30. **ROOMS:** 14 bedrooms 12
en suite d£80

SIDMOUTH

The Blue Ball
Stevens Cross, Sidford EX10 9QL ☎ 01395 514062
e-mail: rogernewton@blueballinn.net
Popular and characterful thatched pub with beams and log
fires. Dating back to 1385, the Blue Ball has been run by the
same family since 1912. The current landlord has been there
for over 30 years. Terrace, gardens, BBQ pit and playhouse.
Simple but colourful bedrooms.

SLAPTON
Map 03 SX84

Pick of the Pubs

The Tower Inn
Church Rd TQ7 2PN ☎ 01548 580216
📠 01548 580140
e-mail: towerinn@slapton.org
Dir: Off A379 south of Dartmouth, turn L at Slapton Sands

Hidden away behind cottages and the church and
standing beside the ivy-covered ruins of a Chantry Tower,
the 14th-century Tower Inn, built to accommodate the
artisans working on the adjacent tower, is a classic and
very atmospheric village pub. Rambling series of
interconnecting rooms, featuring stone walls, low ceilings
and open fires, in which to sample some good and
improving pub food.

Typical dishes may include game pie with shortcrust
pastry, seared salmon with pink peppercorn vinaigrette,
duck confit on celeriac mash with black cherry and red
wine sauce, pan-fried monkfish with tomato and red onion
salsa, tangy lemon tart and Salcombe ice creams.
OPEN: 12-3 6-11 (Sun 7-10.30). **BAR MEALS:** L served all
week. D served all week 12-2.30 6-9.30. Av main course
£9.50. **RESTAURANT:** L served all week. D served all week
12-2.30 6-9.30. Av 3 course à la carte £15.
BREWERY/COMPANY: Free House.
PRINCIPAL BEERS: Adnams Southwold, Badger Tanglefoot,
St Austell Dartmoor Best, Exmoor Ale. **FACILITIES:** Children
welcome Garden: patio, food served outdoors Dogs
allowed Water. **NOTES:** Parking 6. **ROOMS:** 3 bedrooms
3 en suite s£30 d£50

SOURTON
Map 02 SX59

The Highwayman Inn
EX20 4HN ☎ 01837 861243
e-mail: info@thehighwaymaninn.net
Dir: Situated on the A386 Okehampton to Tavistock Rd. Come off main A30 following directions for Tavistock (4m from Okehampton and 12 from Tavistock)
Looking out on Dartmoor National Park, this highly unusual pub is the eccentric vision of one man, Buster Jones. Although he and his wife Rita, have handed over the pub to their daughter, the bizarre jigsaw puzzle that is the Highwayman remains. Parts of the bar are made from old sailing ships, gnarled wood dragged from Dartmoor bog, and gothic church arches. The place is packed with bric-a-brac, odd items, and peculiar antiques. Popular with tourists, this is a startling pub, well worth a visit.
OPEN: 11-2 (Sun 12-2, 7-10.30) 6-10.30. **BAR MEALS:** L served all week. D served all week 11-10.15 11-10.15. Av main course £2.
BREWERY/COMPANY: Free House.
PRINCIPAL BEERS: Whitbread Best, Flowers Best.
FACILITIES: Garden: outdoor eating Dogs allowed On lead only. **NOTES:** Parking 150. **ROOMS:** 3 bedrooms 2 en suite d£36 No credit cards

OPEN: 11-2.30 6-11. **BAR MEALS:** L served all week. D served all week 12-2 7-9.15. Av main course £6.25. **RESTAURANT:** L served all week. D served all week 12-2 7-9. Av 3 course à la carte £15. Av 2 course fixed price £12.50.
BREWERY/COMPANY: Free House.
PRINCIPAL BEERS: Princetown Dartmoor IPA, Sharps.
FACILITIES: Garden: food served outdoors Dogs allowed Water. **NOTES:** Parking 8. **ROOMS:** 8 bedrooms 7 en suite s£40 d£50 FR£65.50-£71.00

SOUTH POOL
Map 03 SX74

Millbrook Inn 🍴 ♀
TQ7 2RW ☎ 01548 531581 📠 01548 531868
Dir: Take A379 from Kingsbridge to Frogmore then E
Customers can arrive at this quaint 16th-century village pub close to Salcombe estuary by boat when the tide is high. Inside, it is small, cosy and unspoilt, with open fires, fresh flowers cushioned wheelback chairs, and original beams adorned with old banknotes and clay pipes. Good local reputation for simple, wholesome bar food, notably the selection of fresh crab dishes, especially the heavenly crab sandwiches, bouillabaisse, kiln-roasted salmon, roasted cod, halibut au poivre, and prime Scottish fillet steaks. Peaceful sunny rear terrace overlooking a stream with resident ducks.
OPEN: 11.30-2.30 5.15-11 (Sun 12-3, 7-10.30). **BAR MEALS:** L served all week. D served all week 12-2 7-9. Av main course £9.50.
BREWERY/COMPANY: Free House. **PRINCIPAL BEERS:** Bass, Wadworth 6X, Fullers London pride. **FACILITIES:** Children welcome Garden: outdoor eating, patio Dogs allowed garden only No credit cards

SOUTH ZEAL
Map 03 SX69

Oxenham Arms ★ ★
EX20 2JT ☎ 01837 840244 📠 01837 840791
e-mail: jhenry1928@aol.com
Dir: just off A30 4m E of Okehampton in the centre of the village
Historic inn believed to date from the 12th century and first licensed in 1477. Interesting features include the large granite fireplace in the lounge, and the granite pillar supporting the beam in the dining room. There is a daily set price dinner menu, and bar specials such as squab pie, curries, Devon porkers and seafood thermidor.

SPREYTON
Map 03 SX69

The Tom Cobley Tavern
EX17 5AL ☎ 01647 231314
e-mail: fjwfilor@tomcobley.fsnet.co.uk
Dir: From Merrymeet roundabout take A3124 north

According to legend, this is the pub that 'Uncle Tom Cobley and all' set off from en route to Widecombe Fair. Thomas Cobley was a wealthy man who owned eight properties in Spreyton and nearby parishes. Expect a welcoming atmosphere at this traditional village local.
Food is home-made and the menu ranges from rump steak and chicken and mushroom pancakes in a cheese sauce, to chicken lasagne and lamb and paprika pie with a selection of vegetables. Good choice of bar snacks and light meals.
OPEN: 12-2 (Sun 12-3, 7-10.30) 6-11 (closed Mon).
BAR MEALS: L served Tue-Sun. D served Tue-Sun 12-1.45 7-9.
RESTAURANT: L served Sun. D served Wed-Sat 1 7-9. Av course à la carte £17.50. **BREWERY/COMPANY:** Free House.
PRINCIPAL BEERS: Cotleigh Tawny. **FACILITIES:** Garden: outdoor eating, Dogs allowed. **NOTES:** Parking 8.
ROOMS: 4 bedrooms s£20 d£40 No credit cards

STAVERTON Map 03 SX76

Pick of the Pubs

The Sea Trout ◉ ◉ ★ ★ �‍
TQ9 6PA ☎ 01803 762274 🖺 01803 762506
Dir: M5/A38
Set in the heart of a quiet Devon village, this attractive 15th-century inn is a firm favourite with both locals and visitors. Inside the rambling, whitewashed building you'll find an easy combination of comfortable hotel, elegant restaurant, and village pub. Eleven comfortably furnished en suite bedrooms make this an ideal base for touring Dartmoor and the South Devon coast; Dartington Hall is on the doorstep, and Dart Valley steam trains cover the short journey to Buckfast Abbey. An interesting bar menu features steaks, plenty of fresh local fish, and daily specials like game pie or chargrilled venison. The attractive conservatory style restaurant overlooks pretty gardens; starters here include vegetable soup with home-made bread, or melon and citrus salad, with chargrilled venison medallions with game jus and cranberry compote, braised brill, chicken and leek pie or home-baked gammon to follow. Home-made desserts like apple and cinnamon strudel, crème brûlée or Salcombe Dairy ice creams round off the meal.

OPEN: 11-3 Sun 12-3, 7-10.30 6-11. **BAR MEALS:** L served all week. D served all week 12-2 7-9. **RESTAURANT:** L served Sun. D served Mon-Sat 12-2 7-9. Av 3 course fixed price £19.75. **BREWERY/COMPANY:** Palmers.
PRINCIPAL BEERS: Palmers IPA, Dorset Gold, Bridport Bitter. **FACILITIES:** Children welcome Garden: patio,outdoor eating, Dogs allowed. **NOTES:** Parking 80.
ROOMS: 11 bedrooms 11 en suite s£35 d£52 FR£62-£80

STOCKLAND Map 03 ST20

Kings Arms ◉ �‍
EX14 9BS ☎ 01404 881361 🖺 01404 881732
e-mail: info@kingsarms.net
By the Great West Way at the heart of the Blackdown Hills stands this pre-1700s thatched and whitewashed former coaching inn whose history is all around in the huge inglenook fireplace and bread oven, the mediaeval oak screen and many other original features. The atmospheric Farmers Bar is a popular and lively meeting place while the Cotley restaurant bar and non-smoking dining-room are the setting for vast choices of British and classic cooking, complemented by an interesting wine list, well-kept real ales and an outstanding collection of West Country cheeses. Blackboards list the dishes currently available at every session, with traditional roasts at

Sunday lunch. Portuguese sardines and Mediterranean fish soup rub shoulders with confit du canard and smoked ham and goats' cheese salad as a prelude to chicken in coriander, Cotley rack of lamb and Quantock calves' liver with Denhay bacon. Fish specials might be cod Grenobloise or monkfish Marseillaise while vegetarian options include banana Indienne and mushrooms thermidor. Lovely gardens and patio and three en suite bedrooms newly refurbished to a high standard.
OPEN: 12-3 6.30-11.30. Closed Dec 25. **BAR MEALS:** L served all week 12-3. Av main course £5.50. **RESTAURANT:** L served all week. D served all week 12-3 6.30-11. Av 3 course à la carte £17.
BREWERY/COMPANY: Free House.
PRINCIPAL BEERS: Otter Ale, Exmoor Ale, John Smiths, Courage Directors. **FACILITIES:** Children welcome Garden: patio, outdoor eating Dogs allowed. **NOTES:** Parking 45.
ROOMS: 3 bedrooms 3 en suite s£30 d£50
See Pub Walk on page 147

STOKENHAM Map 03 SX84

Pick of the Pubs

Trademan's Arms ◉
TQ7 2SZ ☎ 01548 580313
e-mail: elizabethsharman@hotmail.com
Dir: just off A379 between Kingsbridge & Dartmouth
This part-thatched free house dates from 1390 and forms the centre-piece of this picturesque old village close to Slapton Ley. Incorporating a former brewhouse and three cottages, it takes its name from the tradesmen who used to call at the brewhouse while working in the area. Unpretentious, simply furnished interior with stone fireplace and fine views of the parish church. Noted locally for innovative food cooked by the landlord who sources fresh local produce where possible, in particular fish, seafood and seasonal game. Short lunchtime blackboard may list venison stew, beef and stout casserole, fish pie, grilled sardines in garlic butter, and mixed bean casserole. Evening fare moves up a gear, the choice extending to pan-fried halibut with lime and ginger sauce, seared tuna with piquant tomato sauce, roast rack of lamb, sauté rabbit with fresh horseradish, and venison with wild mushroom sauce. Local farm cider and Adnams ales on tap.
OPEN: 12-2 (Closed Mon-Tue & Sat Lunch) 6.30-11 (Please ring for details times may vary). Closed 2wks Nove or Mar.
BAR MEALS: L served Wed-Fri & Sun. D served Tue-Sat 12-1.45 6.30-9. Av main course £9.50. **RESTAURANT:** L served Wed-Fri , Sun. D served Tue-Sat 12-1.45 6.30-9. Av 3 course à la carte £15. **BREWERY/COMPANY:** Free House.
PRINCIPAL BEERS: Adnams, Southwold, Adnams Broadside, Otter Ale. **FACILITIES:** Children welcome Garden: outdoor eating, patio Dogs allowed Water.
NOTES: Parking 14

TEDBURN ST MARY Map 03 SX89

Kings Arms Inn �‍ ◆◆◆
EX6 6EG ☎ 01647 61224 🖺 01647 61324
e-mail: reception@kingsarmsinn.co.uk
Dir: A30 W to Okehampton, 1st exit R signed Tedburn St Mary
Log fires and exposed beams characterise this charming village centre inn which is conveniently located for exploring the rugged beauty of nearby Dartmoor. Expect a good range of traditional bar meals, daily fish specials, perhaps monkfish
continued

in garlic, skate in Pernod sauce and freshly battered cod, and comfortable overnight accommodation in simply decorated bedrooms.

OPEN: 11-3 6-11 (Thu-Sat 11-11, Sun 12-10.30). **BAR MEALS:** L served all week. D served all week 11.30-2 6-9.30. Av main course £7.50. **RESTAURANT:** L served all week. D served all week 11.30-2 6-9.30. Av 3 course à la carte £15.
BREWERY/COMPANY: Free House. **PRINCIPAL BEERS:** Bass, Sharps Cornish, Whitbread Best, Worthingtons Best.
FACILITIES: Garden: outdoor eating, patio, Dogs allowed Guide dogs only in public bar. **NOTES:** Parking 40.
ROOMS: 8 bedrooms 1 en suite s£24 d£48

THURLESTONE   Map 03 SX64

The Village Inn 🏠 ♀
TQ7 3NN ☎ 01548 563525 ▤ 01548 561069
e-mail: enquires@thurlestone.co.uk
Dir: Take A379 from Plymouth towards Kingbridge at Bantham Rdbt go straight over on to the B3197, the right onto a lane Signed Thurlestone 21/2M

Just minutes from the south-west coast path and the stunning clifftop scenery of Bigbury Bay, this popular village haunt has been owned by the Grose family for over a century. Formerly run as a farmhouse B&B, the 16th-century free house now prides itself on good service, well-kept ales, and decent food. Expect smoked chicken with tagliatelle, bangers and mash with red wine gravy, scallops, and grilled whole plaice.
OPEN: 11.30-3 (July-Aug open all day) 6-11. **BAR MEALS:** L served all week. D served all week 12-2 6.30-9.30. Av main course £6. **BREWERY/COMPANY:** Free House.
PRINCIPAL BEERS: Palmers IPA, Bass, Courage Directors, Wadworth 6x. **FACILITIES:** Children welcome Garden: Terrace, Outdoor eating Dogs allowed On lead, Water.
NOTES: Parking 50

TOPSHAM   Map 03 SX98

The Lighter Inn 🏠 ♀
The Quay EX3 0HZ ☎ 01392 875439 ▤ 01392 876013
The imposing 17th-century customs house on Topsham Quay has been transformed into a popular waterside inn. A strong nautical atmosphere is reinforced with pictures, ship's instruments and oars beneath the pub's wooden ceilings, and the attractive quayside sitting area is popular in summer. Generous, well presented dishes include sandwiches, jacket potatoes, Thai chicken stir-fry, pan-fried sardines, and seasonal salads. There's a children's menu, too.
OPEN: 11-11 (Sun 12-10.30). **BAR MEALS:** L served all week. D served Mon-Sat 12-2.30 6-9. Av main course £6.
BREWERY/COMPANY: Woodhouse Inns.
PRINCIPAL BEERS: Badger Best, Badger Tanglefoot.
FACILITIES: Children welcome Children's licence.
NOTES: Parking 40

TORCROSS   Map 03 SX84

Pick of the Pubs

Start Bay Inn 🏠 ♀
TQ7 2TQ ☎ 01548 580553 ▤ 01548 580941
e-mail: cstubbs@freeuk.com
Dir: between Dartmouth & Kingsbridge on the A379
For the best 'fish and chips' in Devon head for the Start Bay Inn, a 14th-century thatched pub situated between Slapton Ley and the panoramic sweep of Start Bay in the beautiful South Hams. Fish is delivered from a local trawler and the landlord dives for plaice and scallops and catches sea bass by rod and line for the pub. The modest bar and dining areas are simply furnished with a mix of chairs and photographs of the storm-ravaged pub adorn the walls.
Served in small, medium and large portions, expect to find whole bass, skate, lemon sole, whole Dover sole, and the ever-popular cod, haddock and plaice deep-fried in a light and crispy batter - arrive soon after opening, especially in the summer. Crab and seafood platters are also available as are sandwiches, ploughman's lunches, Devon ham and chips, and sirloin steak with pepper sauce for carnivores.
OPEN: 11.30-2.30 6-11.30 (Summer 11.30-11.30).
BAR MEALS: L served all week. D served all week 11.30-2 6-10. Av main course £5.50.
BREWERY/COMPANY: Heavitree.
PRINCIPAL BEERS: Flowers Original, Bass.
FACILITIES: Children welcome Patio, food served outside Dogs allowed on leads, Water. **NOTES:** Parking 18 No credit cards

We endeavour to be as accurate as possible but changes in personnel and data can occur in establishments after the guide has gone to press

King's Arms, Stockland

KING'S ARMS, STOCKLAND
EX14 9BS. Tel: 01404 881361
Directions: signed off A30
between Chard and Honiton or
A35 W of Axminster
*Thatched former 17th-century
coaching inn retaining many
interesting interior features,
including a stone-flagged bar
and an elegant dining lounge
with a huge inglenook.
Interesting bar food and Devon
ales on tap. Accommodation.*
Open: 12-3, 6.30-11.30. Bar
Meals 12-3, 6.30-11. Children
and dogs welcome. Garden and
patio. Parking.
(see page 145 for full entry)

A scenic walk across rolling farmland and along country lanes through the heart of the Blackdown Hills, in a gloriously peaceful area of East Devon.

From the pub turn left along the road, then right by the telephone box to the church. Walk to the right of the church and exit the gate by the old thatched barn. Proceed straight on to a gate and follow the footpath marker right. Cross two fields to a footbridge and continue uphill across fields to a gate (in line with transmitter mast), then turn right along the lane.

Take the next turning left, pass Lower Seavington Farm and follow the waymarked path right before the stream. Keep the stream to your left and cross a footbridge to join the road in Millhayes. Turn left and head uphill to a bend, then take the footpath through a garden gate of a cottage on right. Proceed through two fields to a lane by a ford. Turn right and immediately take the arrowed path left. Cross the bridge over the weir and following the right-hand field edge to a stile to the right of a house to a road.

Take the road opposite, pass Hornshayes Farm, and take the footpath right. Cross stile, keep the hedge to your right and head for the break in the hedge, turn right, down to a gate and road. Cross straight over towards farm buildings, where you follow the yellow marker up the field to a stile and footbridge. Keep the hedge on your right and soon reach a farm track. Turn right, then right again at the road and soon climb the waymarked stile on left by Corrybrook Cottages. Head uphill and bear left across the field to a gate. Proceed up the field with the hedge on your right to a stile and road.

Turn right, pass Wytch Farm and take the next arrowed path right over a stile. Go through the gateway directly ahead of you, then walk to the small gate in the right-hand corner of the field. Head downhill and go through the gate at the bottom, then proceed diagonally left towards houses. Pass to the right-hand side of the houses to a gate and road. Turn right back to Stockland and the pub.

Distance: 5 miles (8km)
Map: OS Landranger 192
Terrain: farmland
Paths: field paths and farm tracks; can be very muddy in winter
Gradient: undulating but not strenuous

Walk submitted by:
Ken West

TOTNES   Map 03 SX86

Pick of the Pubs

Durant Arms 🏵 ♦♦♦♦ 🛏️ ☿

Ashprington TQ9 7UP ☎ 01803 732240
📠 01803 732471
Dir: Leave A38 at Totnes Jct, proceed to Dartington & Totnes, at 1st set of traffic lights R for Knightsbridge on A381, after 1m L for Ashprington

Situated close to the River Dart and just two miles from the Elizabethan town of Totnes, the 18th-century Durant Arms is ideally placed for exploring the local countryside. Bed and breakfast accommodation in the form of six en suite rooms make this is a popular choice for a short holiday or a weekend break. Taking its name from the owners of the original village estate, this award-winning inn prides itself on a good standard of cuisine, which is all freshly cooked to order and offers a wide variety of locally-sourced meat, fish and vegetables. Eat in one of three separate dining rooms and choose perhaps celery and coconut soup, followed by fillet of lamb with herb crust and a light mint sauce and finish with a delicious home-made treacle tart with shortcrust pastry.
OPEN: 11.30-2.30 (Sun 12-2.30, 7-10.30) 6.30-11.
BAR MEALS: L served all week. D served all week 12-2.30 7-9.15. Av main course £5.95. **RESTAURANT:** L served all week. D served all week 12-2.30 7-9.15. Av 3 course à la carte £18. **BREWERY/COMPANY:** Free House.
PRINCIPAL BEERS: Flowers Original, Wadworth 6X.
FACILITIES: Children welcome Garden: patio, outdoor eating Dogs allowed. **NOTES:** Parking 6.
ROOMS: 6 bedrooms 6 en suite s£30 d£50

The Steam Packet Inn ☿
St Peter's Quay TQ9 5EW ☎ 01803 863880
e-mail: Ezzythecastle@aol.com
The inn sign and logo at this stone-built West Country pub depicts the Amelia, one of three coastal steam packet ships that regularly called here before the introduction of the railways. A perfect venue for summertime relaxing and watching the bustling boating activity. Try rack of lamb, pork medallions, mixed grill platter or salmon fillet from the monthly-changing menu.
OPEN: 11.30-3 6-11. **BAR MEALS:** L served all week. D served all week 12-2.15 6.30-9.30. Av main course £5.50.
RESTAURANT: L served all week. D served all week 12-2.15 6.30-9.30. Av 3 course à la carte £15.
BREWERY/COMPANY: Free House.
PRINCIPAL BEERS: Courage Directors, Courage Best , Bass.
FACILITIES: Garden: Food served outside. **NOTES:** Parking 16.
ROOMS: 4 bedrooms 4 en suite s£35 d£45

Pick of the Pubs

The Watermans Arms 🛏️ ☿
Bow Bridge, Ashprington TQ9 7EG ☎ 01803 732214
📠 01803 732314
Dir: A38, follow signs for Kingsbridge out of Totnes, at top of hill turn L for Ashprington and Bow Bridge
This charming old free house is located in a wildlife paradise at the head of Bow Creek, close to the ancient Bow Bridge. Robert Ashwick used the building as a smithy in 1850, when he was also listed in the parish directory as a publican and brewer. At one time the inn was a favourite haunt of the hated press-gangs, who hauled their victims off for military service. Nothing could be further from the tranquil nature of the pub today, with its delightful riverside garden. The 15 en suite bedrooms are beautifully furnished, and guests qualify for a substantial discount at the nearby Dartmouth Golf and Country Club. Besides sandwiches and bar snacks, the full menu offers grills, pies, stuffed Gressingham duck, and oven baked sea bass.
OPEN: 11-11 (12-10.30). **BAR MEALS:** L served all week. D served all week 12-2.30 6.30-9.30. Av main course £9.
RESTAURANT: L served all week. D served all week 12-2.30 6.30-9.30. Av 3 course à la carte £15.
BREWERY/COMPANY: Eldridge Pope.
PRINCIPAL BEERS: Bass, Bow Bridge Bitter, Theakston XB.
FACILITIES: Children welcome Garden: patio, outdoor eating, Dogs allowed. **NOTES:** Parking 100. **ROOMS:** 15 bedrooms 15 en suite s£54 d£69 FR£79-£89

Pick of the Pubs

The White Hart Bar
Dartington Hall TQ9 6EL ☎ 01803 847111
e-mail: dhcc.reservations@btinternet.com
Dir: Totnes turning on A38 to Plymouth, approx 4m
Situated in the 14th-century courtyard on the Dartington Hall Estate, with its 30-acres of gardens and splendid riverside walks, this stylish bar and dining venue offers organic produce and west country ales. Menu choices range from lunctime baguettes (local ham and mustard), and short-crust pastry-topped pies, to crab fritters, and Cornish organic lamb steak with game chips and Madeira jus.
OPEN: 11-11 (Sun 12-10.30). Closed 24 Dec-6 Jan.
BAR MEALS: L served all week. D served all week 12-2.30 6-9. Av main course £7.95. **RESTAURANT:** L served all week. D served all week 12-2.30 6-9. Av 3 course à la carte £15. Av 4 course fixed price £15.95.
BREWERY/COMPANY: Free House.
PRINCIPAL BEERS: Princetown Jail Ale, Butcombe Bitter, Blackawton Bitter. **FACILITIES:** Children welcome Garden:.
NOTES: Parking 250. **ROOMS:** 55 bedrooms 14 en suite

 For pubs with AA rosette awards for food see page 10

PICK OF THE PUBS

OPEN: 11-3 6-11
(Sun 12-3 7-10.30).
BAR MEALS: L served all week.
D served all week 12-2 7-9.
Av main course £6.50
RESTAURANT: L served all week
D served all week 12-2 7-9.
Av 3 course a la carte £18.95.
Av 3 course fixed price £16.95.
BREWERY/COMPANY:
Free House.
PRINCIPAL BEERS: Jollyboat
Bitter, Bass, Clearwater Cavalier,
Barum BSE, Cotleight Tawny.
FACILITIES: Children welcome.
Garden: terrace, outdoor eating.
Dogs allowed.
NOTES: Parking 30.
ROOMS: 9 bedrooms 9 en suite
£36-£40 d£60-£77 FRE80-£92.

The Rising Sun Inn

★★ 🐘 ♀

EX37 9DU
☎ 01769 560447 📠 01769 564764
e-mail: risingsuninn@btinternet.com
Dir: At Umberleigh Bridge on A377,
Exeter/Barnstaple road, at junc of B3227.

Overlooking the River Taw with soothing rural views from its sunny raised front terrace, this 17th-century roadside inn is a haven for salmon and trout anglers and a popular base for visitors keen to explore this glorious, unspoilt part of North Devon. Comfortable accommodation and home-cooked food.

Fishing memorabilia is displayed throughout the traditional flagstoned bar, with its open fire, daily papers and magazines and fine mural depicting a scene along the Taw Valley. Adjoining 'River Room' lounge with sofas and easy chairs and a warming wood-burning fire. Popular with locals, the friendly bar offers Devon micro-brewery ales, perhaps Jolly Boat, Barum and Cotleigh brews, and is the ideal spot to relax after a riverside stroll or time spent fishing on one of the inn's exclusive beats. Charles and Heather Manktelow bought the inn two years ago and are gradually refurbishing and upgrading the nine comfortable en suite bedrooms.

The most significant impovement to date has been in raising the quality of the food served in both the bar and spacious dining room. Diners can now expect good home-cooked food prepared from fresh produce, including local game and fish. On the chalk board in the bar you may find Clovelly mussels cooked in cider, salmon and ginger fishcakes with Thai dressing, game casserole, fish pie, tagliatelle with pesto, whole Brixham plaice and freshly battered cod and chips, alongside lunchtime sandwiches and ploughman's. The short monthly-changing carte - also served in the bar - may list rabbit terrine with Cumberland sauce, roast Gressingham duck with orange and apricots and pan-fried rack of lamb with garlic and rosemary. Hearty nursery puds include apple crumble and sticky toffee pudding. Good Sunday roasts and 10 wines by the glass.

Cridford Inn 🌀
TQ13 0NR ☎ 01626 853694   📠 01626 853694
e-mail: cridford@eclipse.co.uk
Originally a Devon longhouse, this historic inn was also a farm at one time, owned by the same family for generations. The transept window in the bar is said to be the oldest domestic window in Britain. The present proprietor's wife is a Malaysian culinary expert from Kuala Lumpur, so Malaysian specialities are offered alongside traditional pub dishes like sausage and mash.
OPEN: 12-3 7-11. Closed 8 Jan- 31Mar,. **BAR MEALS:** L served all week. D served all week 12-3 7-10.30. Av main course £7.50.
RESTAURANT: D served all week 7-9.30. Av 3 course à la carte £18. **BREWERY/COMPANY:** Free House.
PRINCIPAL BEERS: Teign Valley Tipple, Greene King Ruddles County. **FACILITIES:** Children welcome Dogs allowed.
NOTES: Parking 35. **ROOMS:** 6 bedrooms 6 en suite s£40 d£50

Pick of the Pubs

The Maltsters Arms 🌀 ♀
TQ9 7EQ ☎ 01803 732350   📠 01803 732823
e-mail: pub@tuckenhay.demon.co.uk
In an idyllic location beside the wooded, tidal and beautiful Bow Creek, this splendid 18th-century pub has overcome many former dramas and re-invented itself as a residential inn and dining venue that exudes both class and enthusiasm.

Its many menus cater for all tastes - if not pockets - with imaginative "real food" for children and plenty of options from the bar and wine list to keep their elders occupied. From a plethora of menus, seafood soup with salmon, tuna, prawns and mussels (almost a meal in itself) and game pie of venison, wild boar, mallard, red wine and cranberries are well suited to a January lunch session.

Evening starters that might include Sevruga caviar for the super-rich and flash-fried squid in lime and saffron for the rest of us, are followed by Chinese-style braised chicken joints and massive rib-eye and T-bone steaks with peppercorn and red wine sauce. Of the puddings, blackcurrant and gooseberry crumble excels, as does a platter of West Country cheeses, offered with port as an optional extra: "OTT" perhaps, but great fun nonetheless.
OPEN: 11-11 (Sun 12-10.30). **BAR MEALS:** L served all week. D served all week 12-2.30 7-9.30. Av main course £8.
RESTAURANT: L served all week. D served all week 12 7. Av 3 course à la carte £15. **BREWERY/COMPANY:** Free House. **PRINCIPAL BEERS:** Princetown Dartmoor IPA, Youngs, Otter, Exe Valley Devon Glory. **FACILITIES:** Children welcome Garden: patio, outdoor eating Dogs allowed Dog Bowl, Biscuits, lots of pals. **NOTES:** Parking 50.
ROOMS: 7 bedrooms 5 en suite d£55

Room prices minimum single and minimum double rates are shown. FR indicates family room

---

Pick of the Pubs

The Rising Sun Inn ★ ★ 🌀 ♀
EX37 9DU ☎ 01769 560447   📠 01769 564764
e-mail: risingsuninn@btinternet.com
See Pick of the Pubs on page 149

Rugglestone Inn
TQ13 7TF ☎ 01364 621327   📠 01364 621224
Dir: *A38 Drumbridges exit towards Bovey Tracey, L at 2nd rdbt, L at sign Haytor 8 Widecombe, village is 5m*
Surrounded by peaceful moorland, this pretty Dartmoor inn was converted from a farm cottage in 1832. Open fires, stone floors, and a good local following gives the pub its unique atmosphere, and the attractive garden offers stunning views. Good home-cooked food includes soup with crusty bread, hot salt beef rolls, steak and kidney pie, and roast vegetable bake. Leave room for treacle tart with clotted cream. Just a short stroll for the village centre and well worth it for Bass and Butcombe ales drawn straight from the cask and local farm ciders.
OPEN: 11-2.30 (Sat-Sun 11-3) 6-11 (7-11 in winter).
BAR MEALS: L served all week. D served all week 12-2 7-9. Av main course £4. **BREWERY/COMPANY:** Free House.
PRINCIPAL BEERS: Butcombe Bitter, Bass.
FACILITIES: Garden: Beer garden, food served outside Dogs allowed Water and biscuits. **NOTES:** Parking 40

NATIONAL TRUST PUBS

The National Trust began in 1895 and secured its first property a year later, paying the princely sum of £10 for it. Today, it is the country's biggest landowner, with over 600,000 acres of countryside, 550 miles of coastline, over 300 historic houses and more than 150 gardens. As a rule, we don't associate the National Trust with Britain's pubs, but this long-established independent charity owns a number of notable hostelries around the country. Among the most famous are the ancient Fleece Inn - originally a medieval farmhouse - at Bretforton in the Cotswolds, the 18th-century Castle Inn in the picturesque Kent village of Chiddingstone, and the historic George at Lacock in Wiltshire. The National Trust's George in London's Borough High Street is the only surviving example of the capital's once numerous galleried coaching inns, while the Spread Eagle at Stourhead, close to the Somerset/Wiltshire border, was acquired by the Trust in 1947. A number of distinguished visitors have passed through its doors over the years, including Horace Walpole and David Niven.

WINKLEIGH | Map 03 SS60

Pick of the Pubs

The Duke of York 🐄 ♈
Iddesleigh EX19 8BG ☎ 01837 810253
📠 01837 810253
Thatched 15th-century inn set in a sleepy village in the heart of rural mid-Devon. Originally three cottages, built to house workers restoring the parish church, it has all the timeless features of a classic country pub - heavy old beams, a huge inglenook fireplace with winter log fires, old scrubbed tables and farmhouse chairs, and an unspoilt atmosphere free from electronic games. Popular with local farmers, business people and visitors alike, it offers great real ale and hearty home cooking, with all dishes displayed on the large blackboard menu being freshly prepared in the pub kitchen using local produce, including meat reared on nearby farms. From starters or light meals like port and Stilton pâté, smoked trout fillet with dill, and home-made soups, the menu choice extends to freshly battered cod and chips, beef and Guinness casserole, lamb and mint pie, Thai green chicken curry, and liver and bacon with mash and onion gravy. Delightful hosts and excellent value overnight accommodation.
OPEN: 11-11. Closed Dec 25. **BAR MEALS:** L served all week. D served all week. Av main course £7.
RESTAURANT: L served none. D served all week 7-10. Av 3 course à la carte £19. Av 3 course fixed price £19.
BREWERY/COMPANY: Free House.
PRINCIPAL BEERS: Adnams Broadside, Cotleigh Tawny, Sharps Doom Bar. **FACILITIES:** Children welcome Garden: patio/terrace, outdoor eating Dogs allowed water provided.
ROOMS: 7 bedrooms 7 en suite s£25 d£25

YARCOMBE | Map 03 ST20

The Yarcombe Inn 🐄
EX14 9BD ☎ 01404 861676
Dir: On A30 between Chard and Honiton, 1m from A303
Once owned by Sir Francis Drake, this historic pub offers a range of imaginatively devised chef's specials. Expect home-made steak and kidney pie, warm onion and potato tart, lobster and tiger prawn ravioli, stuffed guinea fowl with port jus, and farmhouse mixed grill on the interesting menu. Ploughman's and open sandwiches are always available.
OPEN: 12-3 (Closed Mon-Tue during Jan-Feb) 6-11 (Sun 12-10.30). **BAR MEALS:** L served all week. D served all week 12-2 7-9.30. Av main course £5.50. **RESTAURANT:** L served all week. D served all week 12-2 7-9.30. Av 3 course à la carte £25.
BREWERY/COMPANY: Free House.
PRINCIPAL BEERS: Cotleigh Tawny, St Austell Dartmoor Best.
FACILITIES: Children welcome Garden: Overlooks Yarty Valley, Dogs allowed. **NOTES:** Parking 20

YELVERTON | Map 02 SX50

The Skylark Inn
PL20 6JD ☎ 01822 853258
e-mail: skylarkinn@hotmail.com
Dir: 5 M North of Plymouth, just off the A386 to Tavistock Road
Set in the scenic Dartmoor National Park, this traditional village inn has a huge wood burning stove, a bread oven and plenty of atmosphere. Patio and garden. Wholesome pub food.

DORSET

ABBOTSBURY

Ilchester Arms
Market St DT3 4JR ☎ 01305 871243 📠 01305 871225
e-mail: enqs@ilchesterarms.co.uk
Rambling 16th-century coaching inn set in the heart of one of Dorset's most picturesque villages. Abbotsbury is home to many crafts including woodwork and pottery. A good area for walkers, and handy for the Tropical Gardens in Swannery. Comfortable en suite bedrooms. Under new management as we went to press.

ASKERSWELL

The Spyway Inn
DT2 9EP ☎ 01308 485250
Dir: On A35 between Dorchester & Bridport
There are outstanding views of the Dorset countryside from this quiet country pub, possibly an old smugglers look-out. Straightforward menu and interesting specialities.

BLANDFORD FORUM | Map 03 ST80

The Cricketers 🐄 ♈
Shroton, Iwerne Courtney DT11 8QD ☎ 01258 860421
📠 01258 861800
Dir: Off the A350 Shaftesbury to Blandford
Homely local nestling below Hambledon Hill and a popular watering hole with hikers on the nearby Wessex Way, as well as members of the local cricket team who gather in the homely bar and garden during the summer months. Food is freshly prepared and offers everything from bar snacks and blackboard specials to fresh fish bought from local markets. Try the steak and ale pie, smoked chicken breast salad or lamb hock cooked in rosemary, mint and garlic. Finish off with one of the inn's famous home-made puddings.
OPEN: 11.30-2.30 (Summer 11.30-3,6-11) 7-11 (Sun 12-3, 7-10.30). **BAR MEALS:** L served all week. D served all week 12-2 7-9.30. Av main course £5.95. **RESTAURANT:** L served all week. D served all week 12-2 7-9.30. Av 3 course à la carte £14.40.
BREWERY/COMPANY: Free House.
PRINCIPAL BEERS: Fullers London Pride, Greene King IPA.
FACILITIES: Children welcome Garden: patio, outdoor eating.
NOTES: Parking 19

The Crown Hotel ★ ★ ★
West St DT11 7AJ ☎ 01258 456626
Dir: M27 onto A31 to junction with A350 W to Blandford. 100 metres from town bridge
Classic Georgian coaching house with plenty of period atmosphere, overlooking Blandford's handsome red-brick-and-stone town centre. Bar fare includes grilled pork and leek sausages, hot baguettes, and popular daily specials, while lemon sole, fillet steak, chicken with stilton, and lamb cutlets feature on the restaurant menu.
OPEN: 10am-11pm. Closed 25-28 Dec. **BAR MEALS:** L served all week. D served all week 12-2 7-9. Av main course £6.
RESTAURANT: L served Sun-Fri. D served Mon-Sat 12.30-2 7.15-9.15. Av 3 course à la carte £15. Av 3 course fixed price £15.
BREWERY/COMPANY: Hall & Woodhouse.
PRINCIPAL BEERS: Badger Tanglefoot, Badger Best.
FACILITIES: Children welcome Garden: Dogs allowed.
NOTES: Parking 70. **ROOMS:** 32 bedrooms 32 en suite s£68 d£82

England

Map 03 ST73

The White Lion Inn
High St SP8 5AT ☎ 01747 840866 🗎 01747 840799
Dir: Off A303, opposite B3092 to Gillingham
The epitomy of an English pub, this stone-built village inn features old beams, flagstones, real fires and fishing mementoes. Good range of home-cooked food and traditional pub favourites. Bedrooms.

Map 03 SY49

Pick of the Pubs

The Anchor Inn 🐑
Seatown DT6 6JU ☎ 01297 489215
e-mail: david@theanchorinn.co.uk
Dir: On A35 turn S in Chideock opp church & follow single track rd for 0.75m to beach
Smack on the Dorset coast path west of Bridport - nestling beneath Golden Cap, at 190m the south coast's highest point - this is a spectacular location, with its large sun terrace and cliff-side beer garden overlooking the beach. Thronging with folk on fine summer days; blissfully peaceful on winter weekdays.
   Deservedly popular in season are the speciality dishes that offer Seatown lobster and crab, the latter in heavenly sandwiches and salads, whole local plaice and a celebrated seafood platter. Blackboard specials in the bar may include Boston seafood chowder, thick curried potato and parsnip soup, monkfish in Thai sauce, fish pie, rabbit casserole, beef in Guinness and 'The Memsahib's' authentic beef curry. Traditional printed menu fare offering burgers, ploughman's lunches and filled jacket potatoes. Perfect for pint of Palmers ale after a strenuous morning's walk along the 'rollercoaster' cliff path.
OPEN: 11-2.30 6-11 (Whitsun-end Aug 11-11. Food all day).
BAR MEALS: L served all week. D served all week 12-2 .30-9.30. Av main course £5.
BREWERY/COMPANY: Palmers.
PRINCIPAL BEERS: Palmers - Bridport, IPA & Tally Ho & Gold. **FACILITIES:** Children welcome Garden: patio, outdoor eating, Dogs allowed Water, Dog treats.
NOTES: Parking 20. **ROOMS:** 2 bedrooms s£25 d£45

The George Hotel 🐑 ☿
4 South St DT6 3NQ ☎ 01308 423187
Dir: Town centre
Handsome Georgian town house, with a Victorian-style bar and a mellow atmosphere, bustles all day, and offers a traditional English breakfast, decent morning coffee and a good menu featuring fish and crab from West Bay, home-made rabbit pie, Welsh rarebit, and lambs' kidneys in Madeira.
OPEN: 8.30-11 (Sun 9.30am-10.30pm). **BAR MEALS:** L served Mon-Sat. D served Mon-Sat (seasonal please ring)12-2.30 6.30-9. Av main course £7.50. **BREWERY/COMPANY:** Palmers.
PRINCIPAL BEERS: Palmers - IPA, Bridport Bitter & 200.
FACILITIES: Children welcome Dogs allowed

Pick of the Pubs

Shave Cross Inn 🐑 ☿
Shave Cross, Marshwood Vale DT6 6HW
☎ 01308 868358
Dir: From Bridport take B3162 2m turn L signed 'Broadoak/Shave Cross' then Marshwood
Thatched, 14th-century cob and flint inn tucked away down narrow lanes in the heart of the beautiful Marshwood Vale. Once a resting place for pilgrims and travelling monks, it is worth the short drive from the coast for its delightful sun-trap garden and the imaginative food prepared by chef patron Nic Tipping. Eat outside in summer and in the tastefully refurbished interior on cooler days; classic flagstone-floored bar with warming log fire in a huge inglenook.
   Lunchtime fare changes daily and the short blackboard list may highlight spicy seafood soup, corned beef hash, a delicious warm salad of chorizo, and salmon fishcakes. Civilised evening dining in warm yellow and terracotta-painted rooms may take in sautéed chicken liver and king prawns sautéed with sweet chilli and fresh ginger for starters.
   Main course options may include confit of fresh tuna with roasted garlic and red wine sauce or beef fillet with peppercorn and port jus. Excellent Otter Ale, a changing local guest ale and farmhouse cider on tap.
OPEN: 11-3 7-10. **BAR MEALS:** L served Tue-Sun. D served Tue-Sun 12-2 7-9. **RESTAURANT:** L served Tue-Sun. D served Tue-Sun 12-2 7-9.
BREWERY/COMPANY: Free House.
PRINCIPAL BEERS: Otter Ale, Local guest beer.
FACILITIES: Children welcome Garden: Dogs allowed.
NOTES: Parking 30 No credit cards

The White Lion
The Square DT8 3QD ☎ 01308 867070 🗎 01308 867740
e-mail: johnandsuebei@aol.com
17th-century village inn close to the Marshwood Vale and Dorset coast. Modernised interior with open fire, Palmers ales on tap, and a varied menu of home-cooked food.

Map 03 ST60

Gaggle of Geese ☿
DT2 7BS ☎ 01300 345249
e-mail: Gaggle@bucklandnewton.freeserve.co.uk
Dir: On B3143 N of Dorchester
Changing its name from the Royal Oak 20 years ago, when the previous landlord started breeding geese, this pub was built in 1834 as a village shop, and became a pub in 1846. Traditional pub dishes are served, including homemade casseroles, steak, plaice with prawns and mushrooms, or calamari.
OPEN: 12-2.30 6.30-11. **BAR MEALS:** L served all week. D served all week 12-2 7-10. Av main course £6. **RESTAURANT:** L served all week. D served all week 12-2 7-10. Av 3 course à la carte £12. **BREWERY/COMPANY:** Free House.
PRINCIPAL BEERS: Badger Dorset Best, Ringwood Best, Ringwood 49er. **FACILITIES:** Children welcome Garden: outdoor eating, patio/terrace, Dogs allowed. **NOTES:** Parking 30
See Pub Walk on page 153

The Gaggle of Geese, Buckland Newton

THE GAGGLE OF GEESE, BUCKLAND NEWTON

DT2 7BS. Tel: 01300 345249

Directions: B3143 N Dorchester

Built in 1834 as the village shop and The Royal Oak pub since 1846, this homely hostelry changed its name 20 years ago when a previous landlord started breeding geese. Attractive bar, traditional pub food and a streamside garden.

Open: Open: 12-2.30 6.30-11. Bar Meals: 12-2 7-10. Children and dogs welcome. Garden and patio. Parking.

(see page 152 for full entry)

This undulating ramble explores unspoilt farmland between Buckland Newton and Glanville Wootton. Fine views across the Blackmore Vale to Bulbarrow Hill, the second highest point in Dorset.

Turn right on leaving pub and walk up the lane, ignoring the right turn. Turn left at kissing-gate and walk down field to gate. Continue ahead through churchyard, turn right and soon turn left at road junction. Pass the farm and take arrowed path right through gate. Cross paddock into the yard and bear left along farm track to gate on right. Keep straight ahead across field to stile and continue to gate and road.

Turn left, then left again at the junction and take bridleway right. Proceed uphill (NE) across field keeping fence left. Crest the hill, continue through gate and head downhill towards gate. Bear left, keeping woodland left, to gate and follow path ahead over White Down. Go through gap in hedge and head downhill (NW) to gate. Follow waymarker diagonally across field to gate beside copse, then bear left along hedge to stile.

Head downhill (SW) to gate in far corner. Continue to gate and take path left. Pass beside pond, cross footbridges and walk towards the house. Go through gate, pass between farm buildings and follow the road, keeping Glanville Wootton church right, to reach village road. Turn left and soon take arrowed path right. Bear SW across field, go through gap in hedge ahead and proceed SSW towards the distant house to a gate and road.

Bear right, pass Lower Grange Farm and turn left along track leading to Grange Farm. Pass stables and cottage, then bear right towards house. At second conifer hedge follow path diversion signs and bear right into field. Turn left to gate and bear diagonally left to further gate. Bear diagonally left to stile in far corner and continue across next field to stile. Bear diagonally right to gate, then climb to gate and track on left-hand edge of field. Follow track and waymarkers to the farm and road. Turn left, then right at junction and continue to church. Pass through churchyard and turn right back to pub.

Distance: 6 miles (10km)

Map: OS Landranger 194

Terrain: farmland

Paths: well waymarked footpaths and bridleways

Gradient: undulating: two gentle climbs

Walk submitted by: The Gaggle of Geese

View from Bulbarrow Hill

153

England

BURTON BRADSTOCK — Map 03 SY48

The Anchor Inn 🐾 ♀ NEW
High St DT6 4QF ☎ 01308 897228 🖹 01308 897228
e-mail: aexo13@dialpipex.com
Dir: *2M SE of Bridport on B3157 in the centre of the village of Burton Bradstock*
A short walk from the beach, this cosy old village pub lives up to its name with a maritime theme. Carnivores and vegetarians won't go hungry; witness Barbary duck, mini-lamb leg, or cheese and lentil loaf. But speciality seafood is the main reason for booking a table at this popular inn. Green-lipped mussels, fresh local scallops, sea bass or tuna steaks, brill, monkfish, or lobster - the list just goes on!
OPEN: 11-3 6-11.30. **BAR MEALS:** L served all week. D served all week 12 6.30. Av main course £15. **RESTAURANT:** L served all week. D served all week 12 6.30. Av 3 course à la carte £24.
BREWERY/COMPANY: PRINCIPAL BEERS: Ushers Best, Bass, Wadsworth 6X, Flowers IPA. **FACILITIES:** Dogs allowed.
NOTES: Parking 24

CERNE ABBAS — Map 03 ST60

The Red Lion
24 Long St DT2 7JF ☎ 01300 341441
Following a fire in the 1890s, parts of this 16th-century cottagey pub have been rebuilt in the Victorian style. Note the impressive original fireplace and picturesque south-facing garden.

The Royal Oak ♀
23 Long St DT2 7JG ☎ 01300 341797 🖹 01300 341797
Dir: *On A352 N of Dorchester*
Thatched, creeper-clad, 16th-century inn, formerly a coaching inn and blacksmiths, situated in a picturesque village below the Dorset Downs. Home-cooked food is served in the cosy, traditional interior.
Expect pub favourites and specialities like game pie, lamb shank, venison casserole, Dublin Bay prawns, scallops and home-made puddings. Attractive courtyard garden.

OPEN: 11-3 6-11 (Sun 12-3, 7-10.30). **BAR MEALS:** L served all week. D served all week 12-2 7-9. Av main course £7.25.
BREWERY/COMPANY: Free House.
PRINCIPAL BEERS: Morland Old Speckled Hen, Butcombe, Royal Oak, Tisbury. **FACILITIES:** Children welcome Garden: Courtyard, outdoor eating Dogs allowed

---

CHIDEOCK — Map 03 SY49

The George Inn 🐾 ♀
Main St DT6 6JD ☎ 01297 489419 🖹 01297 489411
e-mail: george.inn@virgin.net
Dir: *On A35*
Traditional Dorset thatched inn situated close to the Golden Cap, the highest cliff in southern England. An impressive range of snacks, home-made pies and light lunches is available, plus various exotic specials. There are at least eight vegetarian dishes, and grilled cod on roasted vegetables, sea bass, Portuguese sardines and skate wings feature among the seafood attractions.
OPEN: 11-2.30 6-11. **BAR MEALS:** L served all week. D served all week 12-2 6-9. **RESTAURANT:** L served all week. D served all week 12-2 6-9. Av 3 course à la carte £12.
BREWERY/COMPANY: Palmers. **PRINCIPAL BEERS:** Palmers IPA & 200, Dorset Gold. **FACILITIES:** Children welcome Garden: Patio, Outdoor eating Dogs allowed. **NOTES:** Parking 40

CHRISTCHURCH — Map 03 SZ19

Fishermans Haunt Hotel ♀
Salisbury Rd, Winkton BH23 7AS ☎ 01202 477283 484071 🖹 01202 478883
Dir: *2.5m north on B3347(Christchurch/Ringwood rd)*
Overlooking the sparkling waters of the River Avon, this old-world inn, dating back to 1673, is a popular base for those who enjoy angling and walking. Winkton has its own fishery and many others are situated locally. There are also a number of golf courses in the area. Pub dishes include mixed grill, steak and kidney pie, battered cod, sandwiches and jacket potatoes.
OPEN: 10.30-2.30 5-11 (Sat-Sun open all day). **BAR MEALS:** L served all week. D served all week 12-2 7-9.30. Av main course £6.50. **RESTAURANT:** L served all week. D served all week 12-2 7-9.30. Av 3 course à la carte £14.50. Av 3 course fixed price £14.50. **BREWERY/COMPANY:** Gales.
PRINCIPAL BEERS: Gales GB, HSB. **FACILITIES:** Children welcome Children's licence Garden: outdoor eating Dogs allowed Water. **NOTES:** Parking 80. **ROOMS:** 17 bedrooms 17 en suite s£49.50 d£66 FR£77

The Ship In Distress 🐾
66 Stanpit BH23 3NA ☎ 01202 485123
e-mail: seafood@shipindistress.co.uk
Seafood predominates at this 300-year-old smugglers' pub, close to Mudeford quay. The unusual name derives from an incident when the regulars rescued a smuggling vessel that had run aground in a nearby creek; nowadays, the nautical theme continues with imaginative fresh fish dishes. Expect roast pollack with sun-dried tomatoes, pan-fried Cornish squid, baked haddock with crab and Parmesan crust, or stir-fried tiger prawns with ginger, chilli and mange-tout. Meat and vegetarian options are also available.
OPEN: 11-11 (Sun 12-3) BH Open till Midnight. Closed Dec 25 & Jan 1. **BAR MEALS:** L served all week. D served all week 12-2 7-9. Av main course £12. **RESTAURANT:** L served all week. D served all week 12-2 7-9. Av 3 course à la carte £22.
BREWERY/COMPANY: Inn Partnership.
PRINCIPAL BEERS: Ringwood Best & 49er, Bass.
FACILITIES: Garden: patio/terrace, outdoor eating Dogs allowed Water upon request. **NOTES:** Parking 40

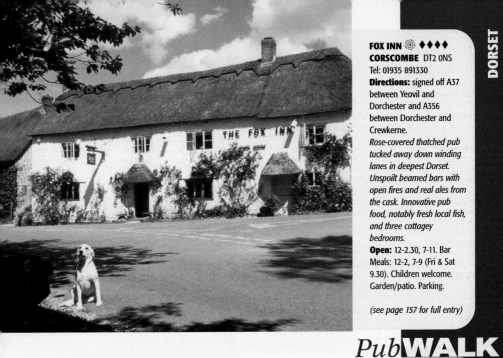

DORSET

FOX INN ✦✦✦✦
CORSCOMBE DT2 0NS
Tel: 01935 891330
Directions: signed off A37
between Yeovil and
Dorchester and A356
between Dorchester and
Crewkerne.
*Rose-covered thatched pub
tucked away down winding
lanes in deepest Dorset.
Unspoilt beamed bars with
open fires and real ales from
the cask. Innovative pub
food, notably fresh local fish,
and three cottage
bedrooms.*
Open: 12-2.30, 7-11. Bar
Meals: 12-2, 7-9 (Fri & Sat
9.30). Children welcome.
Garden/patio. Parking.

(see page 157 for full entry)

*Pub*WALK

Fox Inn, Corscombe

A peaceful walk along established paths around Corscombe affording spectacular views into Somerset towards the Mendip Hills. The route is hilly and often muddy.

Turn right on leaving the Fox. In 100 yards (91m), opposite a road on your right, turn left through a gateway and pass the staddlestones and the walled garden to Corscombe Court. Go through another gate, keep left of the lone tree ahead and cross the fence in the corner into the next field. Do not cross the stile to your left in the corner, instead go through the gate a few yards further on. Follow the left-hand hedge uphill towards houses to a gate and lane.

Turn left, then at a junction by 'The Pines', turn right towards the village centre. In 400 yards (365m), beyond the playground, turn left into Barrow Lane. Steeply ascend this lane

(often muddy) to a gate, signed permissive path. Go through another gate, then pass between a coppice and chalets, and a group of standing stones, to reach a gate and field.

The footpath continues along the valley and straight up the hill to a fence. Turn left alongside the fence and go through two gates to reach the road. Go through the gate opposite. Bear diagonally left and go through an opening to the left of a single tree into another field. Head diagonally left downhill to a gate, then skirt round the edge of the woodland on your right to reach a gate to the left of Ford Glen Cottage. Turn left along the lane, pass St Mary's Church (worth a visit), and Corscombe House, to a junction. Turn right, ignore the left turn for the village, and continue downhill (steep and often busy) back to the Fox.

Distance: 3 miles (4.8km)
Map: OS Landranger 194
Terrain: farmland and country lanes
Paths: footpaths (can be muddy); road walking
Gradient: two steep climbs and long descents

Walk submitted by:
Corscombe Parish Council

England

CHURCH KNOWLE Map 03 SY98

The New Inn 🛏 ♈
BH20 5NQ ☎ 01929 480357 📠 01929 480357
Overlooking the Purbeck Hills and just a gentle walk from historic Corfe Castle, this 16th-century stone and thatch inn is a popular destination among visitors exploring the beautiful surrounding area.

The attraction, apart from the ever-changing selection of real ales, is the impressive range of daily delivered fresh fish listed on huge blackboards. Typical choices include beer-battered haddock, whole Brixham plaice, roast cod with wild mushroom sauce, local mussels and sea bass, in addition to roast Dorset lamb, shepherds pie, lasagne and traditional snacks.

OPEN: 11-3 6.30-11 (closed Mon Jan-Mar). Closed Mon Jan-Mar. **BAR MEALS:** L served all week. D served all week 12-2.15 6-9.15. Av main course £10. **RESTAURANT:** L served all week. D served all week 12-2.15 6-9.15. **BREWERY/COMPANY:** Inn Partnership. **PRINCIPAL BEERS:** Wadworth 6X, Greene King Old Speckled Hen, Flowers Original. **FACILITIES:** Children welcome Garden: food served outdoors Dogs allowed only on lead. **NOTES:** Parking 100

CORFE CASTLE Map 03 SY98

The Greyhound Inn 🛏
The Square BH20 5EZ ☎ 01929 480205
Dir: W from Bournemouth, take A35, after 5m L onto A351, 10m to Corfe Castle
16th-century coaching house on National Trust land in the shadow of Corfe Castle: extensive grounds by the castle wall include a herb garden. The young chef puts these to good use in confit of lamb shank, chicken chausseur, crab gratin or local plaice. Food all day in high season; childrens' menu; Sunday lunch.

OPEN: 11-3 Summer open all day 6-11.30. **BAR MEALS:** L served all week. D served all week 12-2.30 6-9. Av main course £6.95. **RESTAURANT:** L served all week. D served all week 12-2.30 6-9. Av 3 course à la carte £9.95. **BREWERY/COMPANY:** Free House. **PRINCIPAL BEERS:** Flowers, Ringwood, Whitbread Best. **FACILITIES:** Children welcome Garden: outdoor eating, herb garden, patio, BBQ Dogs allowed Water. **NOTES:** Parking 10. **ROOMS:** 2 bedrooms s£40 d£50

Scott Arms
West St, Kingston BH20 5LH ☎ 01929 480270
Creeper-clad stone inn with excellent views of the Purbeck Hills and Corfe Castle from its attractive garden. Family rooms.

CORSCOMBE Map 03 ST50

Pick of the Pubs

The Fox Inn ⊛ ♦♦♦♦ 🛏 ♈
DT2 0NS ☎ 01935 891330 📠 01935 891330
e-mail: dine@fox-inn.co.uk

See Pub Walk on page 155
See Pick of the Pubs on page 157

EAST CHALDON Map 03 SY78

The Sailors Return 🛏
DT2 8DN ☎ 01305 853847 📠 01305 851677
Dir: 1m S of A352 between Dorchester & Wool
Tucked away in rolling downland, this splendid 17th-century thatched country inn is close to Lulworth Cove and miles of cliff walks. Comfortable beamed and flagstoned bar where a blackboard lists available dishes. Expect steak and kidney pie, half shoulder of lamb, fresh fish, and various steaks.
OPEN: 11-3 (all day open from Easter-end Sept) 6-11. **BAR MEALS:** L served all week. D served all week 12-2 6.30-9.30. Av main course £5.25. **RESTAURANT:** L served all week. D served all week 12-2 6.30-9.30. Av 3 course à la carte £11.50. **BREWERY/COMPANY:** Free House. **PRINCIPAL BEERS:** Flowers IPA, Wadworth 6X, Ringwood Best, Greene King Old Speckled Hen. **FACILITIES:** Children welcome Children's licence Garden: outdoor eating, patio, Dogs allowed. **NOTES:** Parking 100

Naval and Military

Britain's seafaring tradition has influenced inn signs on the coast and far inland. The ship is sometimes Noah's Ark, but more often the sign depicts a famous vessel such as the Victory or the Royal George. Names like the Anchor, the Channel Packet, the Jolly Tar and the Drum and Monkey (meaning a naval powder monkey) are in the same tradition and Lord Nelson leads the famous admirals loyally honoured on inn signs. Plenty of pubs celebrate British military history, too, with names like the Artilleryman, the Rifleman, the Volunteer, the Gurkha and the Bugle. Battles from the Alma to Waterloo are remembered, Wellington is pre-eminent among generals and the Marquis of Granby, an 18th-century war hero, still has many pubs to his name.

OPEN: 12-2.30 7-11 Closed 25 Dec.
BAR MEALS: L served all week.
D served all week 12-2 7-9 (9.30
Fri & Sat). Av main course £9.
RESTAURANT: L served all week.
D sercved all week 12-2 7-9 (9.30
Fri & Sat). Av 3 course a la carte
£18.95.
BREWERY/COMPANY:
Free House.
PRINCIPAL BEERS: Exmoor Ale &
Fox, Fullers London Pride.
FACILITIES: Children welcome.
Garden: patio, outdoor eating.
Dogs allowed - garden only.
NOTES: Parking 50.
ROOMS: 3 beroooms 2 en suite
s£55-£60 d£65-£80.

The Fox Inn

◉ ◆◆◆◆ 🫖 ♈

DT2 0NS
☎ 01935 891330 📠 01935 891330
e-mail: dine@fox-inn.co.uk
Dir: Signed from A37 Yeovil-Dorchester
road and the A356 S of Crewkerne

Idyllic, rose-adorned thatched pub tucked away down winding narrow lanes deep in unspoilt Dorset countryside. Renowned locally for its character bars, tip-top real ales, imaginative daily menus featuring excellent fresh fish dishes, and comfortable cottagey accommodation.

Built in 1620 as a cider house, The Fox stands on the old droving route to Yeovil, opposite the stream where the sheep used to be dipped. Hollyhocks and roses climb the cream-painted exterior walls and beyond the tiny entrance lobby lie two unspoilt beamed bars, one with old hunting prints, old pine furniture and chatty locals, the other prettily furnished with sturdy tables topped with blue gingham tablecloths and fronting a huge old stone fireplace with a warming winter log fire. The attractive, plant-festooned rear conservatory boasts a long wooden table; it seats 20 and is ideal for parties.

In addition to a cracking pint of Exmoor ale, local farm cider and home-made damson vodka and sloe gin, the attraction of Martyn and Susie Lee's gem of a country pub is the excellent food prepared from quality local produce, including fish from Bridport - 'No Chips or Microwaves' here! Begin with a chunky fish soup, quail stuffed with thyme risotto or a Szechuan peppered squid with roast red pepper relish, then move on to Moroccan lamb tagine, venison braised in red wine, a perfectly cooked rack of lamb with a rich rosemary gravy, or fishy options like whole Dover sole, pan-seared scallops with orange braised fennel, and halibut with lemon and dill sauce. Finish with vanilla cream terrine with redcurrant coulis.

Alfresco eating across the lane by the brook and thoughtfully furnished accommodation in three spacious en suite bedrooms; two delightful cottagey rooms tucked beneath the heavy thatch.

See Pub Walk on page 155

England

EAST KNIGHTON   Map 03 SY88

The Countryman Inn ⌐
Blacknoll Ln DT2 8LL ☎ 01305 852666   ▤ 01305 854125
Dir: On A352 between Warmwell Cross & Wool
There's a comfortable, farmhouse atmosphere at this attractive
whitewashed free house, tucked away just off the A352 in the
heart of Hardy country. There are open fires in the bars, plus a
family room, garden and play area.
   The menus cater for all tastes; everything from sandwiches,
ploughman's and jacket potatoes to pan-fried chicken, lemon
sole, or tomato and lentil lasagne. Daily carvery roasts and
specials include old-fashioned home-made puddings.
OPEN: 11-2.30 6-11. Closed 25 Dec. **BAR MEALS:** L served all
week. D served all week 12-2 6.30-9.30. **RESTAURANT:** L served
all week. D served all week 12-2 6.30-9.30.
BREWERY/COMPANY: Free House.
PRINCIPAL BEERS: Greene King Old Speckled Hen, Courage
Directors & Best, Ringwood Best & Old Thumper.
FACILITIES: Children welcome Garden: Food Served outside
Dogs allowed. **NOTES:** Parking 200. **ROOMS:** 6 bedrooms 6 en
suite s£48 d£58

EAST MORDEN   Map 03 SY99

Pick of the Pubs

The Cock & Bottle ⌐
BH20 7DL ☎ 01929 459238
Dir: From A35 W of Poole take B3075. Pub 2m on R
Rambling, cob-walled Dorset longhouse, dating in parts
back some 400 years, set hard beside the B3075 with
lovely pastoral views from the modern rear extension and
adjoining garden. Comfortably rustic inside with low-
beamed ceilings, attractive paintings and plentiful nooks
and crannies around its two log fires.
   Handily placed for Wareham, Poole and Blandford, the
Cock & Bottle is a popular dining destination for good
traditional pub food and more imaginative dishes, in
particular fresh and local game. Daily-changing
chalkboards may offer steak and kidney suet pudding,
partridge with port wine jus, and pork fillet with pepper
ragout and mustard sauce, alongside seafood ragout,
herb-crusted monkfish with white wine sauce, red Thai
chicken curry, and seared tuna with Mediterranean
tapenade.
   Those popping in for a snack will find a range of Club
sandwiches and filled baguettes. Classic pub puddings like
sticky toffee pudding or fine British cheeses to finish.
Expect a warm welcome and the full range of Hall &
Woodhouse ales.
OPEN: 11-3 (Sun 12-3, 7-10.30) 6-11. **BAR MEALS:** L
served all week. D served all week 12-2 6-9. Av main course
£8.95. **RESTAURANT:** L served all week. D served all week
12-2 6-9. Av 3 course à la carte £18.50.
BREWERY/COMPANY: Hall & Woodhouse.
PRINCIPAL BEERS: Badger Dorset Best & Tanglefoot, King &
Barns, Sussex,. **FACILITIES:** Children welcome Garden:
outdoor eating, patio Dogs allowed Water.
NOTES: Parking 40

EVERSHOT   Map 03 ST50

Pick of the Pubs

The Acorn Inn ⌐ ◆◆◆◆
DT2 0JW ☎ 01935 83228   ▤ 01935 83707
e-mail: stay@acorn-inn.co.uk
See Pick of the Pubs on page 159

FARNHAM   Map 03 ST91

Pick of the Pubs

The Museum Arms ⌐
DT11 8DE ☎ 01725 516261
e-mail: themuseuminn@supernet.co.uk
Dir: From Salisbury take the A354 to Blandford Forum. After
Approx 12 M , Farnham is Signposted to the R, the pub is in the
centre of the village
At the time of going to press, new owners Vicky Eliot and
Mark Stephenson were putting the last touches to their
year-long renovation of this fine village inn, which owes its
name and present existence to General Pitt Rivers who
took over a Gypsy School nearby and housed one of his
Museum's in it.
   Following re-thatching, total refurbishment of the bar,
and the addition of eight en suite bedrooms, this country
retreat should be well worth visiting, especially as Vicky
Eliot's background in the trade includes creating the
excellent Fox Inn at Oddington in Gloucestershire. Expect
modern pub food, a relaxing dining atmosphere, good
local ales and a decent list of wines. Watch this space!
OPEN: 12-3 6-11. Closed Dec 25. **BAR MEALS:** L served all
week. D served all week 12-2 7-9. Av main course £8.95.
RESTAURANT: L served all week. D served all week 12-2
7-9. Av 3 course à la carte £21. **BREWERY/COMPANY:** Free
House. **PRINCIPAL BEERS:** Ringwood Best Bitter, Hopback
Glory, Quay Best Bitter, Badger Tanglefoot.
FACILITIES: Garden: Food served outside Dogs allowed
Water. **NOTES:** Parking 12. **ROOMS:** 8 bedrooms
8 en suite s£50 d£65

PALMERS

Britain's only thatched brewery has
been in operation in the small town of
Bridport since 1794, and has been run by
the same family since two Palmer brothers
bought it in 1896. The current owners are
great grandsons of one of those brothers.
The current brews are Bridport Bitter
(3.2%), Dorset Gold (3.7%), IPA (4.2%)
and 200 (5%), which commemorates
the brewery's 200th anniversary.
Tours are available, but must be
booked in advance.

PICK OF THE PUBS

OPEN: 12-3 6-11.
BAR MEALS: L served all week.
D served all week 12-2 7-9.
Av main course £11.
RESTAURANT: L served all week.
D served all week 12-2 7-9.
Av 3 course a la carte £25.
BREWERY/COMPANY:
Free House.
PRINCIPAL BEERS: Butcombe
Bitter, Fullers London Pride,
Palmers IPA, guest ale.
FACILITIES: Children welcome.
Terrace, outdoor eating.
Dogs allowed.
NOTES: Parking 30.
ROOMS: 9 bedrooms 9 en suite
s£55-£65 d£75-£100 FR£100-£110

The Acorn Inn

♦♦♦♦ ⌂

DT2 0JW
☎ 01935 83228 🖷 01935 83707
e-mail: stay@acorn-inn.co.uk
Dir: A303 to Yeovil, then A37 towards
Dorchester, Evershot 1.5m off A37

Known as the 'Sow and Acorn' in Thomas Hardy's novel Tess of the d'Urbervilles, this 16th-century coaching inn enjoys a quaint historic setting in the heart of Dorset. Recently restored to its former glory, it now offers stylish accommodation and interesting food prepared from fresh local produce.

Acquired by the owners of the Fox Inn at nearby Corscombe three years ago, this fine stone building has been painstakingly restored and refurbished to create the perfect rural base from which to explore 'Hardy County' and the beautiful Dorset coastline. Oak panelled bars with flagstone floors and blazing log fires in carved Hamstone fireplaces and warmly decorated dining areas adorned with pictures by local artists offer a relaxing and civilised ambience in which to enjoy some good, freshly prepared bar food. Both menu style and quality of cooking continue to improve, with the sensibly short choice of dishes favouring fish from Bridport, estate game in season and organic produce from local suppliers.

From starters like wild mushroom risotto, terrine of duck confit with home-made chutney, warm monkfish salad with garlic and bacon, and grilled goats' cheese with pesto, oven-dried tomatoes and olives, the main course options may include grilled plaice with red onion and Dijon mustard butter, braised lamb shank with white wine and root vegetables, game casserole with port and junipers, and roast pork steak on Stilton and spring onion mash with red wine sauce. Good, hearty sandwiches and thick soups and home-made puddings - chocolate terrine with cappuccino sauce and traditional bread-and-butter pudding.

Comfortable, individually styled bedrooms, two with four-poster beds, vary in size and are thoughtfully equipped.

England

GILLINGHAM   Map 03 ST82

The Kings Arms Inn
East Stour Common SP8 5NB ☎ 01747 838325
e-mail: jenny@kings-arms.fsnet.co.uk
Dir: 4m W of Shaftesbury on A30
200-year-old coaching inn set in the beautiful Blackmore Vale,
opposite the conical Duncliffe Hill; a good base from which to
explore the heart of Dorset.
   Traditional pub food ranges from ploughman's lunches and
pizzas to orchard pork, beef in red wine sauce, a daily roast,
salmon and steaks. Live acoustic music once a month. Large
car park and beer garden.

OPEN: 12-2.30 5-11. **BAR MEALS:** L served All. D served All 12-2
6-9. Av main course £5.25. **RESTAURANT:** L served all week.
D served all week 12-2 6-9. Av 3 course à la carte £10.50. Av 3
course fixed price £7.75. **BREWERY/COMPANY:** Free House.
PRINCIPAL BEERS: Bass, Worthington Best.
FACILITIES: Children welcome Garden: outdoor eating,
patio/terrace. Dogs allowed Water provided. **NOTES:** Parking
40. **ROOMS:** 3 bedrooms 3 en suite s£25.50 d£45

GODMANSTONE

Smiths Arms
DT2 7AQ ☎ 01300 341236
With only around six tables, this is one of (if not the) smallest
pubs in Britain. 15th-century and thatched. Real ale from cask.
Riverside setting.

GUSSAGE ALL SAINTS   Map 03 SU01

The Drovers Inn
BH21 5ET ☎ 01258 840084
Dir: A31 Ashley Heath rdbt, R onto B3081
Re-opened under new ownership following total
refurbishment, this 16th-century pub with a fine terrace has
retained its traditional appeal with flagstone floors and oak
furniture.
   All the food is home-made including steak and kidney pie
and drover's lunches with a choice of five cheeses, pate and
beef.
OPEN: 11.45-2.30 6-11 (Sat 11-3, 6-11 Sun 12-3, 6-11).
BAR MEALS: L served all week. D served all week 12-1.45 7-8.45.
Av main course £6.95. **BREWERY/COMPANY:** Ringwood
PRINCIPAL BEERS: Ringwood Best, Old Thumper, Forty Niner.
FACILITIES: Children welcome Garden: Dogs allowed.
NOTES: Parking 35

LODERS   Map 03 SY49

Loders Arms
DT6 3SA ☎ 01308 422431
Dir: off the A3066, 2m NE of Bridport
Unassuming stone-built local tucked away in a pretty thatched
village close to the Dorset coast. Arrive early to bag a seat in
the bar or in the homely (and tiny) dining room. Interesting
blackboard menus may list fish soup, smoked haddock
fishcakes and filled baguettes for bar diners, with the likes of
scallops in Pernod, rack of lamb, and sea bass with salsa verde
available throughout. Lovely summer garden.
OPEN: 11.30-3 6-11 (Sun 11.30-11). **BAR MEALS:** L served all
week. D served all week 12.30-2 7.15-9. **RESTAURANT:** L served
all week. D served all week 12.30-2 7.15-9.
BREWERY/COMPANY: Palmers Brewery.
PRINCIPAL BEERS: Palmers Bridport Bitter, Palmers IPA,
Palmers 200. **FACILITIES:** Children welcome Garden: Dogs
allowed. **ROOMS:** 2 bedrooms 2 en suite d£40

LOWER ANSTY   Map 03 ST70

The Fox Inn ★ ★ ♀ NEW
DT2 7PN ☎ 01258 880328 📠 01258 881440
e-mail: hotel@fox-inn-ansty.co.uk
*Dir: A35 from Dorchester towards Poole, onto B3142, 1st R for
Cheselbourne, keep to road for 4 miles.*
This reassuringly civilised brick and flint dining pub with its
delightful en suite bedrooms makes a perfect base for touring
Hardy's Wessex. The Hall and Woodhouse brewing families
were both linked with The Fox, and old family photos decorate
the bar. Varied menus serve the bar and restaurants; choices
range from hot filled baguettes, or cod in beer batter, to lamb
shank on olive oil mash, aromatic duck leg, or mushroom and
red onion tart. Finish with meringue basket and fresh
strawberries, or tangy lemon tart.
BAR MEALS: L served all week. D served all week 12 6.30. Av
main course £9. **RESTAURANT:** L served all week. D served all
week 12 6.30. Av 3 course à la carte £17.50. Av 5 course fixed price
£29. **BREWERY/COMPANY:** Free House.
PRINCIPAL BEERS: Badger Tanglefoot, Badgers best.
FACILITIES: Garden: Food served outside. **NOTES:** Parking 40.
ROOMS: 14 bedrooms 14 en suite s£45 d£70

LYME REGIS   Map 03 SY39

Pilot Boat Inn ♀
Bridge St DT7 3QA ☎ 01297 443157
Busy town-centre pub close to the seafront with nautical
connections. This may also be the place where the legend of
Lassie, the canine hero of numerous Hollywood rescue
dramas was born. Food options include salads, sandwiches,
ploughmans', steaks and grills, and locally landed seafood.
Vegetarians may enjoy the avocado and sweetcorn bake.
OPEN: 11-11 (Sun 12-10.30). Closed Dec 25. **BAR MEALS:** L
served all week. D served all week 12-10. **RESTAURANT:** L
served all week. D served all week 12-10. Av 3 course à la carte
£11.50. **BREWERY/COMPANY:** Palmers.
PRINCIPAL BEERS: Palmers Dorset Gold, IPA, Palmers 200 &
Bridport Bitter. **FACILITIES:** Children welcome Children's licence
Garden: Patio, Outdoor eating Dogs allowed

MARSHWOOD   Map 03 SY39

Pick of the Pubs

The Bottle Inn
DT6 5QJ ☎ 01297 678254   📠 01297 678739
e-mail: info@thebottleinn.co.uk
Dir: *4m inland from the A35 on the B3165*
Standing beside the B3165 on the edge of the glorious
Marshwood Vale, the thatched Bottle Inn was mentioned
as an ale house back in the 1600s. It was the first pub in
the area during the 18th century to serve bottled beer
rather than beer from the jug - hence its name. Present-
day landlords, Shane Pym and Chloe Fox-Lambert, lead
the way locally in specialising (70%) in local organic food
and drink, the latter including organic Caledonian Golden
Promise on handpump.
    Rustic interior with simple wooden settles, scrubbed
tables and a blazing log fire. With a 'zero tolerance policy
to genetically modified foods', diners with find natural
breaded plaice, ploughman's lunches with organic
Cheddar and locally-baked organic bread, Dorset farm
pâté, moussaka, African vegetable curry, and various
salads and burgers on the menu. Blackboard specials may
feature Moroccan lamb and apricot tagine and pheasant
in red wine. Rear garden and campsite. Visit in mid-
summer for the annual nettle-eating competition.
OPEN: 12-3 6.30-11. **BAR MEALS:** L served all week.
D served all week 12-2 7.30-9. **RESTAURANT:** L served all
week. D served all week. Av 3 course à la carte £25.
BREWERY/COMPANY: Free House.
PRINCIPAL BEERS: Otter Ale, Marston Old Speckled Hen.
FACILITIES: Children welcome Garden: Food served
outside. **NOTES:** Parking 40

MILTON ABBAS   Map 03 ST80

The Hambro Arms 🍽 ♀
DT11 0BP ☎ 01258 880233
Traditional thatched pub located in a picturesque landscaped
village. The whitewashed exterior of this 18th-century
longhouse enhances the scene. Enjoy an appetising bar snack
or, perhaps, half shoulder of lamb with minted redcurrant
sauce, liver and bacon, duck with orange sauce or grilled sea
bass, in the comfortable lounge bar or on the popular patio.
OPEN: 11-3 6.30-11. **BAR MEALS:** L served all week. D served
all week 12-2 7-9. **RESTAURANT:** L served all week. D served all
week 12-2 7-9. **BREWERY/COMPANY:** Greenalls.
PRINCIPAL BEERS: Bass, Greene King Old Speckled Hen.
ROOMS: 2 bedrooms 2 en suite

MOTCOMBE   Map 03 ST82

The Coppleridge Inn 🍽 ♀
SP7 9HW ☎ 01747 851980   📠 01747 851858
e-mail: thecoppleridgeinn@btinternet.com
Set in 15 acres with beautiful views across the Blackmore Vale,
this tastefully converted farm complex offers spacious
bedrooms in refurbished barns and wide-ranging menus in
the old farmhouse, complete with flagstone floors, stripped
pine and country views. Choose, perhaps, a hearty
ploughman's lunch, home-made pizzas, steak and ale pie or
fresh fish - cod with herb and cheese crust - in the bar, or
roast partridge and rack of lamb in the light and airy
restaurant.   *continued*

OPEN: 11-3 5-11 All day Sat & Sun. **BAR MEALS:** L served all
week. D served all week 12-2.30 6-9.30. Av main course £6.75.
RESTAURANT: L served all week. D served all week 12-2.30
6-9.30. Av 3 course à la carte £17.50.
BREWERY/COMPANY: Free House.
PRINCIPAL BEERS: Butcombe Bitter, Adnams Southwold,
Wadworth 6X, Fullers London pride. **FACILITIES:** Children
welcome Garden: 3 gardens, outdoor eating, patio/terrace
Dogs allowed Garden:, Water. **NOTES:** Parking 60.
ROOMS: 10 bedrooms 10 en suite s£42.50 d£75 FR£95

NETTLECOMBE   Map 03 SY59

Marquis of Lorne ♦♦♦♦ 🍽
DT6 3SY ☎ 01308 485236   📠 01308 485666
e-mail: julie.woodruff@btinternet.com
Dir: *3m E of A3066 Bridport-Beaminster rd, after Mangerton Mill
& West Milton*
Tucked away along narrow country lanes, this friendly
16th-century inn, formerly a farmhouse, enjoys peaceful
rural views and offers good home-cooked food. Traditional
snacks are supplemented by daily specials such as steak,
ale and mushroom pie, fresh battered cod, and pan-fried
liver and bacon.
OPEN: 11-2.30 6.30-11 (Sun 12-2.30, 7-10.30).
BAR MEALS: L served all week. D served all week 12-2
6.30-9.30. Av main course £7.50.
BREWERY/COMPANY: Palmers.
PRINCIPAL BEERS: Palmers - Bridport, IPA & 200.
FACILITIES: Children welcome Garden: Dogs allowed.
NOTES: Parking 50. **ROOMS:** 6 bedrooms 6 en suite s£45
d£70

NORTH WOOTTON   Map 03 ST61

The Three Elms ♀
DT9 5JW ☎ 01935 812881   📠 01935 812881
e-mail: threeelms@talk21.com
Dir: *From Sherborne take A352 towards Dorchester then A3030.
Pub 1m on R*
An interesting choice of real ales and locally produced ciders
awaits you at this family run free house, overlooking
Blackmoor Vale. There are stunning views from the pub's
garden, and the landlord boasts a collection of around 1300
model cars.
    The wide-ranging menu includes steaks, home-made
snacks, and a good range of vegetarian fare. Try the all day
breakfast, Dorsetshire faggots, vegetable moussaka, or cheese,
nut and spinach strudel.
OPEN: 11-2.30 6.30-11 (Sun 12-3, 7-10.30). Closed 25-26 Dec.
BAR MEALS: L served all week. D served all week 12-2 6.30-10.
Av main course £6.50. **RESTAURANT:** L served all week. D
served all week 12-2 6.30-10. Av 3 course à la carte £12.50.
BREWERY/COMPANY: Free House.
PRINCIPAL BEERS: Fullers London Pride, Butcombe Bitter,
Shepherd Neame Spitfire, Otter Ale. **FACILITIES:** Children
welcome Garden: outdoor eating Dogs allowed.
NOTES: Parking 50. **ROOMS:** 1 bedrooms

England

OSMINGTON MILLS

The Smugglers
DT3 6HF ☎ 01305 833125 📱 832219
Enjoying a lovely location on the Dorset coastal path, with a stream running through the garden. Good views of Weymouth Bay and Portland. Once this was the HQ of French smuggler, Pierre Latour, hence the name. Good ale selection.

PIDDLEHINTON   Map 03 SY79

The Thimble Inn 🐷
DT2 7TD ☎ 01300 348270
Dir: A35 westbound, R onto B3143, Piddlehinton 4m
Thatched Grade II listed building, over 200 years old. The original well is now incorporated into the building and the River Piddle runs through the garden. The menu includes trio of lamb cutlets, game pie, fish crumble and a variety of steaks. Snacks such as jacket potato, ploughmans' and sandwiches are also available.
OPEN: 12-2.30 7-11 (Sun 12-2.30 7-10.30). Closed 25 Dec.
BAR MEALS: L served all week. D served all week 12-2 7-9.
BREWERY/COMPANY: Free House.
PRINCIPAL BEERS: Badger-Best & Tanglefoot, Hardy Country, Ringwood Old Thumper. **FACILITIES:** Children welcome Garden: outdoor eating, patio, Dogs allowed. **NOTES:** Parking 50

PIDDLETRENTHIDE   Map 03 SY79

The Piddle Inn 🐷
DT2 7QF ☎ 01300 348468 📱 01300 348102
This friendly village local stands in an unspoilt valley on the banks of the River Piddle. Good food, open fires and traditional pub games make this a favourite spot with visitors, and the riverside patio is popular in summer. Home-made soup or Cajun chicken baguettes will fill an odd corner, whilst heartier appetites might choose rack of lamb, rich game pie, baked red snapper, or mushroom and pinenut Stroganoff.
OPEN: 11-3 6-11. **BAR MEALS:** L served all week. D served all week 12-2 6.30-9.30. Av main course £4.50. **RESTAURANT:** L served all week. D served all week 12-2 6.30-9.30 9.30.
BREWERY/COMPANY: Free House.
PRINCIPAL BEERS: Courage Best & Directors, Ringwood 49er, Greene King Old Speckled Hen, Quay Bombshell.
FACILITIES: Children welcome Garden: patio, outdoor eating Dogs allowed. **NOTES:** Parking 20

The Poachers Inn ♦♦♦♦
DT2 7QX ☎ 01300 348358 📱 01300 348153
Dir: 8m from Dorchester on B3143
Friendly, family run inn located in the Piddle Valley. Lots of home cooked dishes are served in the bar, and during spring and summer guests can use the private pool at the rear. Accommodation is in a separate building, and comes with all expected facilities. The local church is well-known for its grotesque gargoyle carvings.

PLUSH   Map 03 ST70

The Brace of Pheasants 🐷 ♟
DT2 7RQ ☎ 01300 348357
e-mail: geoffreyknights@braceofpheasants.freeserve.co.uk
Dir: A35 onto B3143,5m to Piddletrenthide, then R to Mappowder & Plush
Tucked away in a fold of the hills east of Cerne Abbas, Plush is believed to have been Thomas Hardy's model for Flintcomb-
continued

Ash in Tess of the d'Urbevilles. This delightful 16th-century thatched inn was originally built as a row of cottages that included the village forge. The pub was restored after a devastating fire in 1979, and still retains its status as a listed building. Fresh flowers decorate the beamed bar with its solid tables and Windsor chairs; there's a heavily beamed inglenook, open log fires, and a big garden for the summer months, too.

This is good walking country, and the 'Brace' offers a welcome refreshment stop. You'll find a good selection of cask ales, and typical dishes include grilled tuna, calves' liver with bacon and mushrooms, or lamb and rosemary pie.

OPEN: 12-2.30 7-11 (Sun 12-3 7-10.30). Closed Dec 25.
BAR MEALS: L served all week. D served all week 12-1.45 7-9.30. Av main course £7. **RESTAURANT:** L served all week. D served all week 12-1.30 7-9.30. Av 3 course à la carte £18.50.
BREWERY/COMPANY: Free House.
PRINCIPAL BEERS: Fullers London Pride, Butcombe, Hop Back Summer Lightning. **FACILITIES:** Children welcome Garden: outdoor eating, patio Dogs allowed. **NOTES:** Parking 30

POWERSTOCK   Map 03 SY59

The Horseshoes
DT6 3TF ☎ 01308 485328 📱 01308 485328
Dir: E of A3066 (Bridport/Beaminster rd)
Well worth the tortuous drive down narrow country lanes, this stone and thatch village inn offers fine valley views from its sheltered rear terrace.

PUNCKNOWLE   Map 03 SY58

The Crown Inn
Church St DT2 9BN ☎ 01308 897711 📱 01308 898282
e-mail: thecrowninn@puncknowle48.fsnet.co.uk
Dir: From A35, into Bride Valley, thru Litton Cheney. From B3157, inland at Swyre.
Picturesque 16th-century thatched inn, once a popular haunt of smugglers en route from nearby Chesil Beach to visit prosperous customers in Bath. Traditional atmosphere within its rambling, low-beamed bars. Hearty pub fare and imaginative main courses range from mixed grill, jacket potatoes and sandwiches to home-made casserole, steak and kidney pie and whole trout.
OPEN: 11-3 (Sun 12-3, 7-10.30) 7-11 (Summer 6.30 opening). Closed 25 Dec. **BAR MEALS:** L served all week. D served all week 12-2 7-9. Av main course £12.
BREWERY/COMPANY: Palmers. **PRINCIPAL BEERS:** Palmers IPA, 200, Bridport & Tally Ho!. **FACILITIES:** Children welcome Garden: outdoor eating, patio Dogs allowed Water.
NOTES: Parking 12. **ROOMS:** 3 bedrooms 1 en suite s£23 d£42 No credit cards

SHERBORNE   Map 03 ST61

The Digby Tap
Cooks Land DT9 3NS ☎ 01935 813148
e-mail: p.lefevre@talk21.com
Old-fashioned town pub with stone-flagged floors, old beams and a wide-ranging choice of real ale. Simple pub food. Close to Sherborne Abbey.

Half Moon ♀
Half Moon St DT9 3LN ☎ 01935 812017 🖹 01935 815295
Half-timbered and Cotswold stone inn at the centre of town overlooking Sherborne Abbey: one of an expanding group of character accommodation inns. Make your choice from the tried and tested: home-made pies, cod in beer batter and grilled steaks. Sunday lunch. Bridal suite available.

OPEN: 11-11 (Sun 12-10.30). **BAR MEALS:** L served all week. D served all week 12-2 6-9.30. Av main course £5.25. **RESTAURANT:** L served all week. D served all week 12-2 6-9.30. Av 3 course à la carte £15. **BREWERY/COMPANY:** Eldridge Pope. **PRINCIPAL BEERS:** Bass. **FACILITIES:** Children welcome Garden: outdoor eating. **NOTES:** Parking 40. **ROOMS:** 16 bedrooms 16 en suite s£54 d£69 1 family room £79-£89

Queen's Head
High St, Milborne Port DT9 5DQ ☎ 01963 250314
🖹 01963 250339
A village pub for over 250 years, this listed building features a good range of real ale and is noted for its steak and curry evenings.

Skippers Inn 🕮 ♀
Horsecastles DT9 3HE ☎ 01935 812753
e-mail: chrisfrowde@lineone.net
Dir: From Yeovil A30 to Sherborne
End of terrace converted cider house which is much larger inside than it looks outside. Most of the food is cooked on the premises and the inn is known locally for its dozen or so varieties of fish, including tuna, hake, trout and scallops, listed on a blackboard. All produce is provided by a local source whenever possible and many of the dishes are suggested by the pub's own customers. Well kept Bass on tap.
OPEN: 11-2.30 5.30-11. **BAR MEALS:** L served all week. D served all week 11.15-2 6.30-9.30. Av main course £8.50. **RESTAURANT:** L served all week. D served all week 11.15-2 6.30-9.30. Av 3 course à la carte £12.50.
BREWERY/COMPANY: Wadworth.
PRINCIPAL BEERS: Wadworth 6X, Henrys IPA,.
FACILITIES: Garden: outdoor eating, Dogs allowed garden only, Water. **NOTES:** Parking 30

White Hart
Bishops Caundle DT9 5ND ☎ 01963 23301
Dir: On A3030 between Sherborne & Sturminster Newton
New owners at this historic inn, which boasts stone walls and beams. Once the site of a monks' brewhouse, notorious Judge Jeffries held court here.

STOKE ABBOTT   Map 03 ST40

The New Inn ♀
DT8 3JW ☎ 01308 868333
Expect a traditional welcome at this 17th-century thatched village inn. An attractive large garden is among the features, and inside is a cosy beamed bar with a roaring log fire. The Sunday roast is particularly memorable. Specials may include medallions of pork, stuffed pheasant breast, Cantonese prawn platter, and seared scallops in a cream and sherry sauce.
OPEN: 11.30-3 7-11 (Sun 12-3, 7-10.30). **BAR MEALS:** L served all week. D served all week 12-2 7-9.30. Av main course £7.95. **RESTAURANT:** L served all week. D served all week 12-2 7-9.30. Av 3 course à la carte £12.95. **BREWERY/COMPANY:** Palmers. **PRINCIPAL BEERS:** Palmers IPA, Gold, 200, & Tally Ho. **FACILITIES:** Children welcome Garden: outdoor eating, Dogs allowed. **NOTES:** Parking 25

STRATTON   Map 03 SY69

Saxon Arms 🕮 ♀ NEW
DT2 9WG ☎ 01305 260020 🖹 01305 264225
e-mail: saxonarms@btinternet.com
Dir: 3m NW of Dorchester on A37 Saxon arms is at the back of the village green between the church and new village hall
A unique new venture for hard working licensees Ian and Anne Barrett, formerly at the Marquis of Lorne in Nettlecombe where they won numerous awards. The pub, a brand new thatched, stone and flint building close to the village green and church opened in April 2000 and with the Barrett's come years of experience and a winning formula of good food, friendly, efficient service and general high standards. Expect changing menus featuring fresh local fish and seafood alongside home-cooked favourites like steak, ale and mushroom pie, lamb shank and ribeye steaks. Watch this space!
OPEN: 11-2.30 (All day Sat) 5.30-11. **BAR MEALS:** L served all week. D served all week 11.30 6.30. Av main course £6.50. **BREWERY/COMPANY:** Free House. **PRINCIPAL BEERS:** Fullers London Pride, Palmers IPA. **FACILITIES:** Garden: Food served outside, Patio. **NOTES:** Parking 35

STUDLAND   Map 03 SZ08

The Bankes Arms Hotel 🕮
Watery Ln BH19 3AU ☎ 01929 450225 📞 01929 450310
🖹 01929 450307
Dir: B3369 from Poole, across on Sandbanks chain ferry, or A35 from Poole, A351 then B3351
Just 500 yards from the beach and outstanding coastal walks, this creeper-clad old smugglers' inn overlooks Studland Bay. Popular in summer months and a peaceful retreat on winter weekdays, the inn offers eight changing real ales and a varied menu that specialises in fresh fish and seafood. Look for fresh cod, bream, sea bass, local pollack and fresh crab and lobster in season, in addition to a traditional pub ploughman's and

continued

chilli, and local estate venison. Handy overnight accommodation.

The Bankes Arms Hotel

OPEN: 11-11. Closed Dec 25. **BAR MEALS:** L served all week. D served all week 12-3.00 7-9.30. Av main course £7.50. **BREWERY/COMPANY:** Free House **FACILITIES:** Garden: patio, outdoor eating, Dogs allowed. **ROOMS:** 9 bedrooms 7 en suite d£50 1 family room £50-£74

SYDLING ST NICHOLAS   Map 03 SY69

The Greyhound Inn ♀ NEW
DT2 9PD ☎ 01300 341303 📠 01300 341303
Dir: Off A37 Yeovil to Dorchester Road, turn off at Cerne Abbas/Sydling St Nicholas
Located in one of Dorset's loveliest villages and surrounded by picturesque countryside, this traditional, brightly painted inn is characterised by its relaxed, welcoming atmosphere and delightful walled garden. Fresh home-cooked food served daily includes rib-eye steak, rack of lamb with a herb crust and port jus, pan-fried King scallops in a ginger butter, and goats' cheese topped with pesto and grilled on salad.
OPEN: 11-3.30 6-11. **BAR MEALS:** L served all week. D served all week 12 6. Av main course £10. **RESTAURANT:** L served all week. D served all week 12 6. Av 3 course à la carte £22.
BREWERY/COMPANY: Free House.
PRINCIPAL BEERS: Youngs Special, Greene King IPA,.
FACILITIES: Garden: Food served outside Dogs allowed.
NOTES: Parking 24. **ROOMS:** 6 bedrooms 6 en suite s£40 d£70

TARRANT MONKTON   Map 03 ST90

The Langton Arms ♀
DT11 8RX ☎ 01258 830225 📠 01258 830053
e-mail: info@thelangtonarms.co.uk
Dir: A31 from Ringwood, or A357 from Shaftesbury, or A35 from Bournemouth
This attractive 17th-century thatched free house serves a good choice of real ales in the rustic beamed bar. There's a skittle alley, and a separate bistro restaurant in an old converted stable. The bar menu features beef lasagne, braised wild rabbit, and four bean stew. In the restaurant, try red snapper with lime and ginger, chicken with pesto and smoked bacon, or spinach and ricotta tortellini.
OPEN: 11.30-11 (Sun 12-10.30). **BAR MEALS:** L served all week. D served all week 11.30-2.30 6-9.30. Av main course £7.
RESTAURANT: L served Sun. D served Wed-Sat 12-2 7-9. Av 3 course à la carte £24. Av 3 course fixed price £12.95.
BREWERY/COMPANY: Free House.
PRINCIPAL BEERS: Ringwood Best & 4 changing guest beers.
FACILITIES: Children welcome Garden: outdoor eating, Dogs allowed overnight only. **NOTES:** Parking 100.
ROOMS: 6 bedrooms 6 en suite s£45 d£70 family room £80

TOLPUDDLE   Map 03 SY79

The Martyrs Inn
DT2 7ES ☎ 01305 848249 📠 01305 848977
e-mail: jpa@highridge.demon.co.uk
Dir: Off A35 between Bere Regis (A31/A35 Junction)
Originally the Crown Inn, the pub was renamed in honour of the six local farm labourers deported for their union activities. Tolpuddle Martyrs' memorabilia is strongly featured.

TRENT   Map 03 ST51

Rose & Crown Inn 🍴 ♀
DT9 4SL ☎ 01935 850776
Dir: A30 W on A30 towards Yeovil. 3m from Sherborne R to Over Compton/Trent, 1.5m downhill, then R. Pub opp church
Stone-built thatched pub, with beams and flagstones, converted from two cottages in 1720. It reputedly hid the France-bound Charles II. Today's visitors come for the bistro-style food, in particular fresh fish and local game. Typical dishes are lemon peppered chicken, and Louisiana blackened swordfish.
OPEN: 12-2.30 7-11. Closed Dec 25. **BAR MEALS:** L served all week. D served Fri & Sat12-1.45 7-9.30. Av main course £7.50.
RESTAURANT: L served all week. D served Mon-Sat 12-1.45 7-9. Av 3 course à la carte £15. **BREWERY/COMPANY:** Free House.
PRINCIPAL BEERS: Shepherd Neame Spitfire, Butcombe Bitter, Wadworth 6X. **FACILITIES:** Children welcome Garden: outdoor eating, BBQ, play area Dogs allowed on lead only.
NOTES: Parking 30

WEST BEXINGTON   Map 03 SY58

The Manor Hotel ★ ★ 🍴
DT2 9DF ☎ 01308 897616 📠 01308 897035
e-mail: themanorhotel@btconnect.com

500 yards from Chesil Beach lies this 16th-century manor house, featuring Jacobean oak panelling and flagstone floors. Panoramic views and handy for exhilarating coast path walks. Imaginative cooking and freshly prepared specialities, with dishes such as cod in red wine, rabbit casserole, stir-fried pork, honey-glazed chicken, and mushroom crêpe with a beef, tomato and onion salad.
OPEN: 11-11. **BAR MEALS:** L served all week. D served all week 12-2 6.30-10. **RESTAURANT:** L served all week. D served all week 12-1.30 7-9.30. **BREWERY/COMPANY:** Free House.
PRINCIPAL BEERS: Hardy Royal Oak & County, Wadworth 6X.
FACILITIES: Children welcome Garden: outdoor eating.
NOTES: Parking 25. **ROOMS:** 13 bedrooms 13 en suite s£57 d£95

England

WEST KNIGHTON   Map 03 SY78

The New Inn
DT2 8PE ☎ 01305 852349
A 200-year-old pub with listed archway, formerly a row of
farm cottages. Good base for walks and exploring the
surrounding countryside.

WEST LULWORTH   Map 03 SY88

The Castle Inn
Main Rd BH20 5RN ☎ 01929 400311 ▤ 01929 400415
Dir: on the Wareham to Dorchester Rd, L approx 1m from Wareham
Beamed-and-thatched 17th-century inn with prize-winning
gardens close to Lulworth Cove. Extensive menus throughout
major in steaks from fillet stuffed with Stilton to
chateaubriand; fresh fish from tuna steak to scampi and
scallop provençale. Cold buffet available; good cheese
selection; a la carte dining Friday and Saturday.
OPEN: 11-2.30 6-11. **BAR MEALS:** L served all week. D served
all week 11-2.30 6-10.30. Av main course £5. **RESTAURANT:** D
served Fri & Sat 7-9.30. Av 3 course à la carte £15.
BREWERY/COMPANY: Free House. **PRINCIPAL BEERS:** Bass,
Caffreys, Ringwood, Gales. **FACILITIES:** Children welcome
Children's licence Garden: outdoor eating, patio, BBQ Dogs
allowed. **NOTES:** Parking 30. **ROOMS:** 15 bedrooms
12 en suite s£25 d£49 1 family room £65

WEST STAFFORD   Map 03 SY78

The Wise Man Inn
DT2 8AG ☎ 01305 263694
Dir: 2m from A35
Set in the heart of Thomas Hardy country, this thatched 16th-
century pub displays a large collection of brass, pipes and
Toby jugs.

WORTH MATRAVERS

The Square & Compass
BH19 3LF ☎ 01929 439229
Classic, unspoilt ale house run by the Newman family for the
last ninety years. Simple interior, ales from the cask, limited
food options, but lovely views and superb coastal walks along
Purbeck.

CO DURHAM

AYCLIFFE   Map 11 NZ22

The County ♀ NEW
☎ 01325 312273 ▤ 01325 308780
e-mail: enquiries@the-county.co.uk
Dir: Off the A167 into Aycliffe Village
Historic pub overlooking picturesque Aycliffe village green.
Sympathetically restored inside and with the emphasis on
interesting, well-presented modern pub food, this is where
Prime Minister Tony Blair entertained France's President
Jacques Chirac in the past year. Expect eggs Benedict and
home-cured salmon among the starters, while Cajun-spiced
chicken, herb-crusted roast cod with wilted spinach and lemon
butter sauce, and braised lamb shank on creamy mashed
potato with vegetables and rich gremolata jus are typical main
course dishes. *continued*

OPEN: 12-3 5.30-11. **BAR MEALS:** L served all week. D served
all week 12-2 6-7. Av main course £7. **RESTAURANT:** D served
all week 6-9.30. Av 3 course à la carte £20.
BREWERY/COMPANY: Scottish & Newcastle.
PRINCIPAL BEERS: Changing Ales. **FACILITIES:** Dogs allowed
Guide dogs only with notice. **NOTES:** Parking 30

BARNARD CASTLE   Map 11 NZ24

Pick of the Pubs

The Morritt Arms Hotel ★ ★ ★ ♀
Greta Bridge DL12 9SE ☎ 01833 627232
▤ 01833 627392
e-mail: relax@themorritt.co.uk
*Dir: At Scotch Corner take A66 towards Penrith, after 9m turn at
Greta Bridge. Hotel over bridge on L*
Standing in large mature gardens by the bridge over the
River Greta, this solid, 17th-century grey stone hotel
continues the tradition of coaching inn hospitality. Log
fires warm the building in winter, and there are pleasantly
landscaped gardens for alfresco summer dining.
Throughout the Dickensian era this was the second
overnight stop for the London to Carlisle mail coach, and
the novelist himself stayed at Greta Bridge whilst
researching Nicholas Nickleby. His visit is commemorated
by a fine set of Gilroy murals, running right around the
walls of the comfortable Dickens bar.
    Food is served here, as well as in Pallatt's Bistro and the
more formal Copperfield Restaurant. Expect deep-fried
avocado in poppy seed batter, fresh salmon with a basil
potato cake, marinated lamb with bubble and squeak, or
grilled veal cutlets. Seafood dishes include roast monkfish
in cracked black pepper, or grilled sea bass with roasted
fennel mash. Homely bedrooms come in all shapes and
sizes; some boast four-poster and brass beds, while all
have en suite bathrooms and modern facilities.
OPEN: 11.30-11 (Sun 11-10.45). **BAR MEALS:** L served all
week. D served all week 12-3 6-9.30. Av main course £6.95.
RESTAURANT: L served all week. D served all week 12-3
7-9.30. Av 3 course à la carte £18.95.
BREWERY/COMPANY: Free House.
PRINCIPAL BEERS: John Smiths, Theakston.
FACILITIES: Children welcome Children's licence Garden:
outdoor eating, Dogs allowed Water. **NOTES:** Parking 100.
ROOMS: 23 bedrooms 23 en suite s£59.50 d£83.50

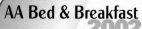

AA Bed & Breakfast 2002

Britain's best-selling B&B
guide featuring over 3500
great places to stay

www.theAA.com

AA Lifestyle Guides

England

BOLAM   Map 11 NZ12

Countryman Inn NEW
DL2 2UP ☎ 01388 834577 🖹 01388 834577
Fresh, wholesome ingredients are the foundation of The
Countryman's innovative home-cooked menu. Quietly situated
near the Roman Dere Street, this award winning village local is
handy for the surrounding urban centres. Starters like blue
cheese and smoked bacon soufflé or Tempura prawns
complement main courses such as braised lamb shank,
chorizo and chicken kebab, or baked trout with tomato
fondue.
OPEN: 12-3 6-12. **BAR MEALS:** L served all week. D served all
week 12-2 7-10. Av main course £11. **RESTAURANT:** L served all
week. D served all week 12-2 7-10. Av 3 course à la carte £20.
BREWERY/COMPANY: Free House.
PRINCIPAL BEERS: Black Sheep Bitter, Rudgate Battleaxe.
FACILITIES: Garden: Food served outside. **NOTES:** Parking 60

COTHERSTONE   Map 11 NZ01

The Fox and Hounds ◆◆◆
DL12 9PF ☎ 01833 650241 🖹 01833 650241
e-mail: mcarlisle@foxcotherstone.co.uk
Dir: 4m W of Barnard Castle, from A66 turn onto B6277, Cotherstone
signposted
Traditional coaching inn, with heavy beams and open fires,
situated in Upper Teesdale, an area of outstanding natural
beauty. The bar menu offers sandwiches and hot dishes with
home-made chips, typically Cumberland sausage in a giant
Yorkshire pudding. In the restaurant expect the likes of rack of
lamb, chargrilled sea bass, and chicken breast stuffed with
Cotherstone cheese.
OPEN: 11-3 6-11. Closed 25 Dec. **BAR MEALS:** L served all
week. D served all week 12-3 6-11. Av main course £6.
RESTAURANT: L served all week. D served all week 12-3 6-10.
Av 3 course à la carte £15. **BREWERY/COMPANY:** Free House.
PRINCIPAL BEERS: Black Sheep Best & Special.
FACILITIES: Children welcome Children's licence Garden: food
served outside Dogs allowed garden only, water.
NOTES: Parking 20. **ROOMS:** 5 bedrooms 3 en suite s£35 d£55

CROOK   Map 11 NZ13

Duke of York Country Inn
Fir Tree DL15 8DG ☎ 01388 762848 🖹 01388 767055
e-mail: suggett@firtree-crook.fsnet.co.uk
Dir: on A68 trunk road to Scotland, 12m W of Durham City
Former drovers' and coaching inn on the old York to
Edinburgh coach route, this 18th-century white-painted inn is
noted for its furniture which contains the famous carved
mouse trademark of Robert Thompson, a renowned Yorkshire
woodcarver. There is also a collection of flint arrowheads, axes
and Africana. Relax inside and choose from varied blackboard
menus characterised by fresh food, including chicken kiev,
lamb in hot pepper, sirloin in Stilton, and a range of
sandwiches. Large, landscaped beer garden.
OPEN: 11-2.30 6.30-10.30. **BAR MEALS:** L served all week.
D served all week 12-2 6.30-9. Av main course £7.50.
RESTAURANT: L served all week. D served all week 12-2 6.30-9.
Av 3 course à la carte £15. **BREWERY/COMPANY:** Free House.
PRINCIPAL BEERS: Black Sheep. **FACILITIES:** Children
welcome Children's licence Garden: outdoor eating,.
NOTES: Parking 65. **ROOMS:** 5 bedrooms 5 en suite s£52 d£69

DURHAM   Map 11 NZ24

Pick of the Pubs

Seven Stars Inn 🍽️
High St North, Shincliffe Village DH1 2NU
☎ 0191 3848454 🖹 0191 3860640
e-mail: sevenstarsinn.co.uk

A little gem tucked away on the edge of picturesque
Shincliffe, this quaint and cosy inn remains virtually
unaltered since 1724, although tasteful decoration and the
addition of antique furniture have improved levels of
comfort for discerning local diners.
   Pretty in summer with its tubs and window boxes and
cosily lit within in winter, it offers a fine setting for
imaginative British cuisine with exotic influences. Typically,
fresh local crab and avocado salad with gazpacho
dressing, and seared scallops with guacamole, coriander
and chilli; followed by Parma ham-wrapped salmon on
herb mash with tomato fondue, open ravioli of monkfish,
pan-fried calves' liver with bacon and red wine jus, and
Northumbrian aged beef steaks. Round off with lemon
and lime tart or banana and toffee pie. Individually
furnished bedrooms.
OPEN: 11.30-11. **BAR MEALS:** L served all week. D served
all week 12-2.30 6-9.30. **RESTAURANT:** L served all week.
D served all week 12-2.30 6-9.30.
BREWERY/COMPANY: Free House.
PRINCIPAL BEERS: Theaskstons, Marstons Pedigree,
Courage Directors. **FACILITIES:** Garden: Patio, Food served
outside. **NOTES:** Parking 20. **ROOMS:** 8 bedrooms
8 en suite s£40 d£50

MIDDLETON-IN-TEESDALE   Map 11 NY92

The Teesdale Hotel
Market Square DL12 0QG ☎ 01833 640264 & 640537
🖹 01833 640651
In the heart of the High Pennines this 17th-century coaching
inn has been tastefully modernised, yet retains much
traditional charm. Handy for Durham, the Metro Centre, the
Beamish Museum and the Lakes. Bedrooms.

 AA inspected guest accommodation

Rose & Crown, Romaldkirk

ROSE & CROWN ⊚ ⊚ ★ ★
ROMALDKIRK
Barnard Castle DL12 9EB.
Tel: 01833 650213
Directions: 6m NW of Barnard
Castle on B6277
*Splendid, stone-built Jacobean
coaching inn standing in the
middle of three greens by the
church in a pretty conservation
village. Retains much of its
original charm and offers
tasteful accommodation.
Innovative menus.*
Open: 11.30-3 5.30-11 (Sun 12-
3 7-10.30). Bar Meals: 12-1.30
6.30-9.30. Children welcome,
Garden/Patio. Parking.
(see page 169 for full entry)

A delightful ramble that takes in great views of Teesdale and finishes with a majestic walk beside the River Tees.

Turn left on leaving the inn and walk down to the bottom of the village. Take the waymarked footpath left down a track (Primrose Lane), crossing a beck and then a wall stile. Head diagonally across the field to a stile on the brow, then follow the right-hand field edge to a further stile. Proceed beside the concrete wall, soon to bear left to a gate and road by a stone barn, opposite Eggleston House.

Turn right, cross Eggleston Bridge and turn immediately right along a lane. In 1/2 mile (0.8km), cross the ladder stile on your left and ascend steep steps through Great Wood to enter a field. Cross the wall stile ahead, then bear left across the field to a stile. Head to the left of East Barnley Farm, aiming for the telegraph pole and the gate beyond. Head for the stile and gate beyond the beck and proceed across marshy ground to a stile in a wire fence. Bear left to a wall stile and join a track. Good views across Teesdale.

Walk along the track, passing through two field gates to enter a small wood. Continue past a waterfall and caravan site and head towards the River Tees, crossing the bridge ahead. Turn right and cross the stile at the top of the bank. Keep to the right-hand edge of the field to a stile, then head for stepping stones across a beck. Proceed to a gate in the top right-hand corner of the field and soon pass a large house (Woden Croft - one of the old Yorkshire schools which Charles Dickens researched for *Nicholas Nickleby*). Bear right past a farm cottage and barns to a gate, then follow the path immediately right down to the river.

At the river, bear left and follow it upstream through beautiful woodland to a wall stile. Climb towards abandoned farmhouse and pass through gate to its left. Follow drive through field, soon to bear off right to gate in hedge. Head for gate in top left-hand corner of field and follow footpath (Jennings Lane) back into Romaldkirk. Inn is across the green to your left.

Distance: 6 miles (10km)
Map: OS Landranger 92
Terrain: farmland and woodland
Paths: field and woodland paths
Gradient: gently undulating; one steep climb.

Walk submitted by:
The Rose & Crown

England

ROMALDKIRK   Map 11 NY92

Pick of the Pubs

Rose and Crown 🏨 🏨 ★ ★ 🛏 ⬚
DL12 9EB ☎ 01833 650213 📠 01833 650828
e-mail: hotel@rose-and-crown.co.uk
See Pub Walk on page 167
See Pick of the Pubs on page 169

ESSEX

ARKESDEN   Map 07 TL43

Pick of the Pubs

Axe & Compasses 🛏 ⬚
High St CB11 4EX ☎ 01799 550272 📠 01799 550906
See Pick of the Pubs on page 171

BLACKMORE END   Map 07 TL73

Pick of the Pubs

The Bull Inn
CM7 4DD ☎ 01371 851037 📠 851037
Off-the-beaten-track at the heart of tranquil north Essex
countryside, two 17th-century cottages and an adjoining
barn form this traditional village pub, full of original
beams and open hearths, that looks out over open
farmland little changed over 300 years. An attractive
garden also produces herbs for kitchen staff full of
enthusiasm and up-to-date ideas.

In the beginning are potted brown shrimps, chicken
and sun-dried tomato terrine and grilled goats' cheese
with raspberry vinaigrette. In the middle come beef
tournedos rossini with Marsala jus, monkfish in bacon
garnished with queen scallops and game and oyster suet
pudding in rich gravy with creamed mash. Vegetarians at
this point have their own menu - wild mushroom
Stroganoff or aubergine and Stilton polenta gateau
perhaps - before all join in at the end for apple and forest
fruits crumble, chocolate and hazelnut roulade and ice
cream sundae. Only on a Sunday is there a set-price lunch
with similar starters, traditional roasts and nursery
puddings.
OPEN: 12-3 6-11 (Summer open 12-3, 5-11).
BAR MEALS: L served all week. D served all week 12-3
6.30-9.45. Av main course £5.60. **RESTAURANT:** L served
all week. D served all week 12-3 6.30-9.30. Av 3 course à la
carte £22. **BREWERY/COMPANY:** Free House.
PRINCIPAL BEERS: Greene King IPA, Abbot Ale, Adnams
Best. **FACILITIES:** Children welcome Garden: outdoor
eating, BBQ Dogs allowed Guide dogs. **NOTES:** Parking 36

BRADWELL   Map 07 TL82

The Swan Inn
CM7 8ED ☎ 01376 562111
Dir: On A120 between Braintree & Coggeshall
Sympathically extended and refurbished old pub, with
exposed beams and brickwork, open fires, and cricketing
memorabilia in the character bars.

BRAINTREE   Map 07 TL73

Pick of the Pubs

The Green Dragon at Young's End ⬚
Upper London Rd, Young's End CM7 8QN
☎ 01245 361030 📠 01245 362575
e-mail: green.dragon@virgin.net
*Dir: M11 J8 take A120 towards Colchester. At Braintree b'pass
take A131 S towards Chelmsford*

A former private house and stables were the starting point
for this popular dining pub, which lies close to the Essex
County Showground. The cosy bars lead through to the
'Barn' and non-smoking first floor 'Hayloft' restaurants,
with their plain brick walls and wealth of old beams.
Outside, there's a large garden and children's play area,
with a slide, climbing frame and aviary. The extensive
menus range from starters like tiger prawns in filo pastry
and devilled whitebait, through kleftico, wild Black Forest
boar, and steak, kidney and mushroom pie. Seafood
lovers can enjoy skate wing with capers, supreme of
salmon, or cod in beer batter, whilst vegetarian options
include stuffed peppers, and leek, potato and mushroom
cakes. All this, plus a fixed-price menu, daily blackboard
specials and Sunday roasts. Lighter meals, ploughman's
lunches, baguettes and filled baked potatoes are also
served in the bars.
OPEN: 12-3 (Sat-Sun & BHs 12-11) 5.30-11. **BAR MEALS:** L
served all week. D served all week 12-2.30 6-9.30. Av main
course £9. **RESTAURANT:** L served all week. D served all
week 12-2.30 6-9.30. Av 3 course à la carte £15. Av 3 course
fixed price £14.50. **BREWERY/COMPANY:** Greene King.
PRINCIPAL BEERS: Greene King IPA & Abbot Ale.
FACILITIES: Garden: patio, outdoor eating,.
NOTES: Parking 40

PICK OF THE PUBS

OPEN: 11.30-3 5.30-11 (Sun 12-3 7-10.30). Closed 24-26 Dec.
BAR MEALS: L served all week. D served all week 12-1.30 6.30-9.30. Av main course £7.50.
RESTAURANT: L served Sun. D served Mon-Sat 12-1.30 7.30-9. Av 4 course fixed price £25.
BREWERY/COMPANY: Free House.
PRINCIPAL BEERS: Theakston Best, Black Sheep Bitter.
FACILITIES: Children welcome Garden: patio, outdoor eating. Dogs allowed.
NOTES: Parking 24.
ROOMS: 12 bedrooms 12 en suite s£62 d£86 FR£100

The Rose & Crown

◎ ◎ ★ ★ 🐾 ♀

DL12 9EB
☎ 01833 650213 🖨 01833 650828
e-mail: hotel@rose-and-crown.co.uk
Dir: 6m NW from Barnard Castle on B6277

Enjoying a picturesque village setting and exuding much of its original charm and character, this splendid 18th-century inn is one of the great all-rounders, boasting a cosy pub with excellent bar food, a smart restaurant and stylish bedrooms. Finalist in the AA Pub of the Year Award 2002.

The wood-panelled bar features original oak beams and a roaring log fire in a fine stone fireplace, and glass and copper, shuttered windows and early 1900s sepia prints complete its unique rustic charm; here is both a restaurant-with-rooms and a pub for casual visitors and fiercely loyal locals alike. Eat lunch in the intimate old bar and Crown Room where quality bar meals are popular with all-comers; Durham baps of smoked salmon and prawns or smoked Wensleydale with pickle, might suffice. More substantial combinations involve quail's egg and anchovy salad with black olive dressing, followed by wood pigeon breast with a fried potato cake and juniper berry sauce or creamy risotto with ratatouille, basil and pecorino.

More elaborate supper dishes run to corn-fed chicken with mushrooms, smoked bacon, cream and pasta, 'Whitby woof' with Welsh rarebit, roast tomatoes and fresh basil, and chargrilled beef fillet with green peppercorn sauce. Overnighters will more likely opt for a set-price four-course dinner offering leek, bacon and Shetland mussel chowder; roasted tomato soup; pan-fried guinea fowl breast with a casserole of leg meat; and dessert options of hot walnut tart with toffee ice cream or chocolate and praline ice cream.

Residents can relax in the cosy lounge, complete with stripped stone and beams, wing chairs and period furniture, while refurbished bedrooms offer luxurious bathrooms. The perfect base for exploring stunning Teesdale and enjoying country pursuits.

See Pub Walks on page 167

BURNHAM-ON-CROUCH
Map 05 TQ99

Ye Olde White Harte Hotel
The Quay CM0 8AS ☎ 01621 782106 🖹 01621 782106
Overlooking the River Crouch, the hotel dates from the 1600s and retains many original features. The food is mainly English-style with such dishes as gammon, lamb chops, sausage casserole, and steak and kidney pie. Fish is well represented on the menu and much of it is locally caught.
OPEN: 11-11. **BAR MEALS:** L served all week. D served all week 12-2 7-9. Av main course £5. **RESTAURANT:** L served all week. D served all week 12-2 7-9. Av 3 course à la carte £16. Av 3 course fixed price £12.80. **BREWERY/COMPANY:** Free House.
PRINCIPAL BEERS: Tolly Cobbold, Adnams, Crouch Vale.
FACILITIES: Children welcome Dogs allowed.
NOTES: Parking 15. **ROOMS:** 19 bedrooms 11 en suite s£19.80 d£37

CASTLE HEDINGHAM
Map 07 TL73

The Bell Inn
St James St CO9 3EJ ☎ 01787 460350
e-mail: bell-inn@ic24.net
Dir: On A1124(A604) N of Halstead, R to Castle Hedingham
Classic English pub which has been owned by the same brewery since 1897. Upstairs you will find a splendid barrel ceiling function room built during the 18th century and originally a theatre, a courthouse and an assembly room. Nowadays it is the venue for monthly live jazz. Downstairs, in the convivial beamed lounge, food includes daily specials and perennial favourites, all of which are home made using local produce. Expect steak and Guinness pie, Thai chicken curry, oak-smoked prawns and roast vegetable kebabs on the seasonally-changing menu.
OPEN: 11.30-3 (Sun, 12-3) 6-11 (Sun,7-10.30). Closed 25 Dec.
BAR MEALS: L served all week. D served Tue-Sat 12-2 7-9.30.
Av main course £6. **BREWERY/COMPANY:** Grays.
PRINCIPAL BEERS: Shepherd Neame Spitfire, Greene King IPA , Adnams. **FACILITIES:** Children welcome Garden: patio, food served outside Dogs allowed. **NOTES:** Parking 15

CHAPPEL
Map 07 TL82

The Swan Inn 🐑 NEW
CO6 2DD ☎ 01787 222353 🖹 01787 220012
Dir: Pub visible just off A1124 Colchester-Halstead road, from Colchester 1st L after viaduct

Set in the shadow of a magnificent Victorian viaduct, this rambling, low-beamed old free house boasts a charming riverside garden, cobbled courtyard and overflowing flower tubs. Fresh market meat and fish arrives daily; expect steaks, gammon and prime English lamb, as well as whole grilled sea bass, halibut with citrus sauce, or grilled smoked salmon salad.
OPEN: 11-3 Sat 11-11, Sun 12-10.30) 6-11. **BAR MEALS:** L served all week. D served all week 12-2.30 7-10.30. Av main course £8.95. **RESTAURANT:** L served all week. D served all week 12-2.15 7-10. Av 3 course à la carte £16.
BREWERY/COMPANY: Free House.
PRINCIPAL BEERS: Greene King IPA, Abbot Ale.
FACILITIES: Children welcome Garden: Food served outside Dogs allowed Water, on a lead please. **NOTES:** Parking 55

CHELMSFORD

Prince of Wales
Woodham Rd, Stow Maries CM3 6SA ☎ 01621 828971
Simple, friendly marshland pub specialising in real ale - six on handpump - and unusual continental beers. Barbeques every Sunday in summer. Pub incorporates old bakery with bread oven.

Curiouser and Curiouser

Some pub names are exceedingly old, and the suggested explanations often older still. The Goat and Compasses is most unlikely to be a corruption of a supposed Puritan slogan 'God encompasses us', the Bag o' Nails to come from Bacchanals of the Roman wine god or the Pig and Whistle from Old English words for 'pail' and 'health'. The Cat and Fiddle may come from the nursery rhyme, but then where did the nursery rhyme image itself come from? The device of the Elephant and Castle is known in heraldry and was the badge of the Cutlers Company, so there is no need to find an Infanta of Castile to derive it from.

Many strange names are the product of humour and sarcasm, such as the Quiet Woman (she has no head), the Honest Lawyer (also beheaded), the Drop Inn, Nog Inn and Never Inn. Others, like the Case is Altered, the Who'd Have Thought It, the Live and Let Live, the Labour in Vain and the World Turned Upside Down are creations of rich and philosophical whimsy.

OPEN:11.30-2.30 6-11
(Sun 12-3 7-10.30).
BAR MEALS: L served all week.
D served all week 12-2 6.45-9.30.
Av main course £8.95.
RESTAURANT: L served all week
D served Mon-Sat 12-2 6.45-9.30.
Av 3 course a la carte £22.
Av 3 course Sun lunch £13.
BREWERY/COMPANY:
Greene King.
PRINCIPAL BEERS: Greene King
IPA, Abbot Ale, & Old Speckled
Hen.
FACILITIES: Garden: patio,
outdoor eating. Dogs allowed.
NOTES: Parking 12.

The Axe & Compass

High Street CB11 4EX
☎ 01799 550272 📠 01799 550906
Dir: From Buntingford B1038 towards
Newport. Then L for Arkesden

'Relax at the Axe' says all you need to know about Themis and Diane Christou's unassuming pub, the centrepiece of a pretty village whose narrow main street runs alongside the village stream, spanned by a succession of footbridges that give access to white, cream and pink-washed cottages.

At its centre the Axe's thatched section dates from around 1650, with stabling to one side that was in constant use until the 1920s, and a 19th-century extension that today houses a convivial public bar and laid-back lounge, the latter featuring easy chairs, settees, antique furniture and brass, and a warming log fire. Floral tubs and hanging baskets adorn the frontage in summer, whither the crowds flock for a selection of sandwiches and bar food that includes home-made soup, grilled sardines, chicken, leek and bacon crumble, cod in batter, lemon sole, and sausage-and-mash with onion gravy.

Accent on the restaurant's à la carte menu draws a higher-spending crowd to indulge in scallops, mushrooms and shallots in wine and cream glazed with Parmesan shavings, strips of roasted duck with plum sauce on a bed of noodles, or focaccia with sun-dried tomatoes and Stilton; followed by halibut steak with prawns on tomato and basil sauce, monkfish with roasted pepper sauce, pigeon breasts cooked rare with mushrooms, onions and Madeira or a puff-pastry case of stir-fried vegetables with French mustard sauce. Finish with one of the tempting home-made puddings displayed on the laden trolley.

Greene King's ales predominate, alongside a handy wine selection (10 available by the glass), and a notable collection of up to two dozen malt whiskies.

CHIPPING ONGAR

The Black Bull
Dunmow Rd, Fyfield CM5 0NN ☎ 01277 899225
Vine-covered pub which offers a wide range of bar meals in its
15th-century black-beamed rooms. Aviary with budgies and
cockateels in car park.

CLAVERING
Map 07 TL43

Pick of the Pubs

The Cricketers 🐑 ♀
CB11 4QT ☎ 01799 550442 ▤ 01799 550882
e-mail: cricketers@lineone.net
*Dir: From M11 J10 take A505 E. Then A1301, B1383. At Newport
take B1038*

Fully a quarter century in the hands of the Oliver family,
this celebrated 16th-century inn stands at the heart of a
beautifully unspoilt Essex village, opposite the local cricket
pitch which is the inspiration for the ubiquitous
memorabilia that adorn its interior.

Forever moving with the times, there are daily
blackboards of choices that make use of the best available
fresh produce and a set-price Italian-inspired menu serves
the dining-room. Starters or light snacks ordered in the
bar might include Piadina with grilled peppers, olives, mint
and feta cheese; pink pigeon breasts on a bed of fine
beans and fried prosciutto and squid with crispy onions
and bacon on bitter leaves. Larger main dishes regularly
include grilled swordfish steak with red pepper, chilli and
saffron risotto, richly-sauced pork meatballs with fusilli,
and roast rack of lamb with parsley crust and a rosemary
and garlic jus.

True to the theme, stylish individually furnished en suite
bedrooms are housed in the adjacent Pavilion.
OPEN: 10.30-3 6-11. Closed 25-26 Dec. **BAR MEALS:** L
served all week. D served all week 12.00-2.00 7.00-10.00.
Av main course £9. **RESTAURANT:** L served Sun. D served
Mon-Sat 12-2 7-10. Av 3 course à la carte £23. Av 3 course
fixed price £23. **BREWERY/COMPANY:** Free House.
PRINCIPAL BEERS: Adnams, Tetleys. **FACILITIES:** Children
welcome Garden: patio, outdoor eating.
NOTES: Parking 100. **ROOMS:** 8 bedrooms 8 en suite s£65
d£90

COLCHESTER
Map 07 TL92

Rose & Crown Hotel 🛏
East St CO1 2TZ ☎ 01206 866677 ▤ 01206 866616
e-mail: 101711.2201@compuserve.com
Dir: From M25 J28 take A12 N & follow signs for Colchester
Situated in the heart of Britain's oldest town, this splendid
14th-century posting house retains much of its Tudor
character. With ancient timbers, smartly decorated bedrooms,
and wide-ranging meus, it is a popular destination. The focus
is on fresh seafood, with other options such as rack of lamb,
or seared venison fillet.
OPEN: 12-2 7-11. **BAR MEALS:** L served all week. D served
Mon-Sat 12-2 7-10. Av main course £7.50. **RESTAURANT:** L
served all week. D served Mon-Sat 12-2 7-11. Av 3 course à la
carte £25. Av 3 course fixed price £23.95.
BREWERY/COMPANY: Free House.
PRINCIPAL BEERS: Tetley, Rose & Crown Bitter.
FACILITIES: Children welcome Garden: Dogs allowed garden
only. **NOTES:** Parking 50. **ROOMS:** 29 bedrooms 29 en suite
s£65 d£49

The Rose & Crown ♀ NEW
Nayland Rd, Great Horkesley CO6 4AH ☎ 01206 271251
e-mail: petitpour@dingley.freeserve.co.uk

17th-century pub with a warm, homely atmosphere, a log fire
and a choice of popular, well kept real ales. The licensees have
a wealth of experience of almost 30 years between them, and
by cooking everything on the premises and using fresh local
produce, they are able to offer an imaginative, regularly
changing menu. Enjoy a drink in one of four bar areas or relax
over a meal in the timbered restaurant. Typical dishes include
beef cobbler and smoked haddock and salmon fishcakes with
horseradish cream. Try the warm almond tart or lemon and
ginger steamed pudding.
OPEN: 12-3 6-11. **BAR MEALS:** L served all week. D served all
week 12-2 6-9.30. Av main course £8. **RESTAURANT:** L served
Sun. D served Tue-Sat 12-2 7-9.30. Av 3 course à la carte £19.95.
BREWERY/COMPANY: Greene King.
PRINCIPAL BEERS: Greene King IPA, Abbot Ale.
FACILITIES: Children welcome Garden: Food served outside
Dogs allowed Water. **NOTES:** Parking 32

The Whalebone 🛏
Chapel Rd CO5 7BG ☎ 01206 729307 ▤ 01206 729307
In the shadow of the oldest tree in Essex, the 250-year-old
Whalebone is situated next to the village green and pond,
close to Colchester, the Fingrinhoe Nature Reserve, and the
foot ferry that crosses the River Colne from Wivenhoe. A good
choice of dishes is offered from the lunchtime snack menu,
daily specials and interesting evening carte - game in season,
confit of duck, and roast cod on herb potato with lime butter.

continued

OPEN: 10-3 5.30-11 (Sun 10-3, 7-10.30). **BAR MEALS:** L served all week. D served all week 12-2.30 6.30-9.30. Av main course £9. **RESTAURANT:** 12 6.30. Av 3 course à la carte £18. Av 3 course fixed price £9.95. **BREWERY/COMPANY:** Free House. **PRINCIPAL BEERS:** Greene King IPA, Old Speckled Hen & Abbot Ale, Mauldon Moletrap. **FACILITIES:** Garden: patio/terrace, outdoor eating Dogs allowed. **NOTES:** Parking 25

DEDHAM Map 07 TM03

Marlborough Head Hotel ♀
Mill Ln CO7 6DH ☎ 01206 323250 📧 01206 322331
Dir: E of A12, N of Colchester
Set in glorious Constable country, close to Flatford Mill and peaceful walks, this former wool merchants house dates from 1455. Became an inn in 1704, the year of the Duke of Marlborough's famous victory over the French at the Battle of Blenheim. Extensive menu might feature fisherman's pie, king cod, hot cross bunny, or duck delight.
OPEN: 11-3 6-11 (Sat 11-11, Sun 12-10.30). **BAR MEALS:** L served all week. D served all week 12-2.30 7-9.30. Av main course £8. **RESTAURANT:** L served all week. D served all week 12-3 7-9.30. Av 3 course à la carte £16. **PRINCIPAL BEERS:** Adnams Southwold, Greene King IPA, Adnams Broadside.
FACILITIES: Children welcome Children's licence Garden: beer garden outdoor eating, Dogs allowed garden only.
NOTES: Parking 28. **ROOMS:** 3 bedrooms 3 en suite s£45 d£55

ELSENHAM Map 07 TL52

The Crown 🛏️
The Cross, High St CM22 6DG ☎ 01279 812827
Dir: M11 J8 towards Takeley L at traffic lights
A pub for 300 years, with oak beams, open fireplaces and Essex pargeting at the front. The menu, which has a large selection of fresh fish, might offer seafood, mixed grill or pork fillet with Calvados.

OPEN: 11-3 (Sun 12-2.30, 7-10.30) 6-11. **BAR MEALS:** L served all week. D served Mon-Sat 12-2 7.30-9.00. Av main course £7.95. **RESTAURANT:** L served all week. D served Mon-Sat 12-2 7.30-9.00. Av 3 course à la carte £15.95.
BREWERY/COMPANY: Allied Domecq.
PRINCIPAL BEERS: Crouch Vale IPA, Youngs Special, Adnams Broadside. **FACILITIES:** Children welcome Garden: outdoor eating. **NOTES:** Parking 28

FEERING Map 07 TL82

The Sun Inn
Feering Hill CO5 9NH ☎ 01376 570442
Dir: On A12 between Colchester and Witham
Thought to date from 1525 and originally part of a gentleman's residence, this lively pub offers between 20 and 30 different
continued

beers a week and is home to the Feering Beer Festival. An ever-changing menu board of home-cooked dishes includes some Maltese specialities, courtesy of the landlord. Peppered wild boar, Maltese rabbit, and BOG pie (beef, oyster and Guinness) are fairly typical.
OPEN: 12-3 6-11 (Sun 12-3, 6-9.30). **BAR MEALS:** L served all week. D served all week 12-2 6-10. Av main course £4.
BREWERY/COMPANY: Free House **FACILITIES:** Children welcome Garden: Outdoor eating Dogs allowed Water.
NOTES: Parking 19 No credit cards

GOSFIELD Map 07 TL72

The Green Man ♀
The Street CO9 1TP ☎ 01787 472746
Dir: Braintree A131 then A1017
Smart yet traditional village dining pub with old beams, named after a pagan symbol of fertility. Popular for the relaxing atmosphere, Greene King ales and decent bar food. Blackboard menus may list steak and kidney pudding, pheasant in red wine, lamb chops in a port and cranberry sauce or chicken curry. Cold buffet table available at lunch time.
OPEN: 11-3 6.15-11 (Sun 12-3, 7-10.30). **BAR MEALS:** L served all week. D served Mon-Sat 12-2 6.45-9. Av main course £6.95. **RESTAURANT:** L served all week. D served Mon-Sat 12-2 6.45-9. Av 3 course à la carte £15. **BREWERY/COMPANY:** Greene King. **PRINCIPAL BEERS:** Greene King IPA & Abbot Ale. **FACILITIES:** Children welcome Garden: beer garden, patio, food served outdoors Dogs allowed. **NOTES:** Parking 25

GREAT BRAXTED Map 07 TL81

Du Cane Arms ♀
The Village CM8 3EJ ☎ 01621 891697
Dir: Great Braxted signed between Witham and Kelvedon on A12
Forming part of a village that was displaced by Lord Du Cane in the 19th century, this friendly pub was built in 1935 and welcomes walkers and cyclists. Fresh fish is served daily, and fresh herbs and local produce form the major part of the kitchen's output. Dishes include prawn fetuccinni, salmon linguine, deep fried cod or haddock, and oven baked trout.

OPEN: 11.30-3 6.30-11. **BAR MEALS:** L served all week. D served all week 12-2.30 7-9.30. Av main course £8.95. **RESTAURANT:** L served all week. D served all week 12-2.30 7-9.30. Av 3 course à la carte £16. **BREWERY/COMPANY:** Free House. **PRINCIPAL BEERS:** Adnams, Greene King IPA,. **FACILITIES:** Garden: food served outdoors. **NOTES:** Parking 25

England

GREAT YELDHAM   Map 07 TL73

Pick of the Pubs

The White Hart 🌸 👓 𝟵
Poole St CO9 4HJ ☎ 01787 237250 📠 01787 238044
e-mail: whitehartgreatyeldham@hotmail.com
Dir: On A1017 between Haverhill & Halstead

Set in four acres and dating from 1305, this elegantly restored, black and white timbered inn has offers some of the best pub food in the area. Recently take over by experienced restauranteurs, John and Maria Dicken, who also own Dicken's Restaurant in nearby Wethersfield, the food remains innovative with modern dishes having a distinct Mediterranean flavour. What has changed is that the pub now has a good pubby atmosphere, the spacious, wooden-floored bar offering a range of Belgian bottled beers, organic fruit juices, a first-rate list of wines (10 by the glass), and excellent Adnams bitter and micro-brewery guest ales that are not repeated over the year. Good bar menu listing sandwiches and ploughman's for those short of time, and a daily-changing main menu offering, perhaps seared scallops with wilted rocket and balsamic dressing, confit of duck leg with diced potatoes, spinach and jus, roasted cod on a spring onion and parsley mash, and, for pudding, lemon tart with crème anglaise. Expect, also, freshly-made breads, and home-made petit fours to accompany decent coffee.
OPEN: 11-3 6-11. (Sun & BHs 12-3 7-10.30). **BAR MEALS:** L served all week. D served all week 12-2 7-9.30. Av main course £10. **RESTAURANT:** L served all week. D served all week 12-2 7-9.30. Av 3 course à la carte £20.
BREWERY/COMPANY: Free House.
PRINCIPAL BEERS: Adnams, changing guest beers.
FACILITIES: Children welcome Garden: 4.5 acres, stream.
NOTES: Parking 40

HARLOW   Map 07 TL41

Rainbow & Dove
Hastingwood Rd CM17 9JX ☎ 01279 415419
📠 01279 415419
Dir: M11 J7 take A414 towards Chipping Ongar. Then L into Hastingwood Rd

Quaint listed inn with many charming features, originally a farmhouse and staging post. Became a pub when Oliver Cromwell stationed his new model army on the common here in 1645. Relaxed atmosphere inside and good quality bar food.

The Green Man
The most uncanny and enigmatic of inn signs represents a figure of folk custom from the distant past, the Jack in the Green who appeared at May Day revels. He was a man covered with green leaves and branches, who probably stood for the rebirth of plants, trees and greenery in the spring. Virile and wild, part human and part tree, he is often found carved eerily in churches. A connection grew up between him and Robin Hood, the forest outlaw, and this is perpetuated in some Green Man pub signs, which show an archer or a forester in Lincoln green.

HORNDON ON THE HILL   Map 05 TQ68

Pick of the Pubs

Bell Inn & Hill House 👓 𝟵
High Rd SS17 8LD ☎ 01375 642463 📠 01375 361611
e-mail: enquiries@bell-inn.co.uk
Dir: Off M25 J30/31 signed Thurrock. Lakeside A13 then B1007 to Horndon

Family-run and at the centre of village life for over 50 years, the Bell was purchased in 1938 without the benefits of running water or electricity. Over the years Hill House, almost next door, underwent conversion to stylish beamed bedrooms and function facilities that enhance this fine old inn's latter-day appeal. The two bars offer real ales and guest beers - that number close to three per week - and a daily-changing menu that features throughout and in the popular restaurant.

Commitment to quality dishes and fresh ingredients shines through in starters such as cauliflower couscous with spiced tomato salsa and chicken liver ravioli with beetroot purée and lemon coulis. Follow then with peppered beef rib-eye with foie gras and caramelised onions or roast cod with macaroni, cockles and smoked cheese: for imaginative accompaniments choose from honey-roast carrots with cranberry or leeks with chestnuts and, of course, crisp fat chips with mayonnaise. Round off perhaps with treacle tart and home-made ice cream.
OPEN: 11-2.30 (Sat 11-3, 6-11) 6-11 (Sun 12-3, 7-10.30). **BAR MEALS:** L served all week. D served all week 12-2 6.45-10.00. Av main course £10.95. **RESTAURANT:** L served all week. D served all week 12-2 6.45-10. Av 3 course à la carte £15.95. Av 3 course fixed price £15.95.
BREWERY/COMPANY: Free House.
PRINCIPAL BEERS: Greene King IPA, Bass, Youngs Special, Crouch Vale Ash Vine Hop & Glory. **FACILITIES:** Children welcome Garden: Courtyard Food served outside Dogs allowed manager's discretion. **NOTES:** Parking 50.
ROOMS: 16 bedrooms 16 en suite d£40 FR£60-£85

LANGHAM   Map 07 TM03

The Shepherd and Dog 👓
Moor Rd CO4 5NR ☎ 01206 272711 📠 01206 273136
Dir: A12 toward Ipswich, 1st turning L out of Colchester, marked Langham

Popular village pub in the Dedham Vale known for speciality food events - a fish supper, an Indian evening, French weeks and Italian weeks.

On a daily basis you can expect eight to ten varieties of baked, grilled, poached or fried fresh fish, three vegetarian dishes and home-made puddings like treacle tart and apple crumble. All ingredients are locally sourced where possible.
OPEN: 11-3 5.30-11. **BAR MEALS:** L served Mon-Sun. D served Mon-Sun 12-2.15 6-10. Av main course £7.50. **RESTAURANT:** L served Mon-Sun. D served Mon-Sun 12-2.15 6-10. Av 3 course à la carte £13.50. **BREWERY/COMPANY:** Free House.
PRINCIPAL BEERS: Greene King IPA, Abbot Ale & Triumph Ale, Black Pig Stout, Nethergate Suffolk Best. **FACILITIES:** Children welcome Garden: outdoor eating Dogs allowed.
NOTES: Parking 40

LEIGH-ON-SEA
Map 05 TQ88

Crooked Billet
51 High St, Old Town SS9 2EP ☎ 01702 714854
Dir: *A13 towards Southend, follow signs for Old Leigh*
Fine 16th-century timbered ale house, with open fires, original beams and local fishing pictures, set in the picturesque fishing village of Old Leigh. Enjoy views of cockle boats and the estuary from the terrace.

LITTLE CANFIELD
Map 07 TL52

The Lion & Lamb
CM6 1SR ☎ 01279 870257 ▤ 01279 870423
Dir: *M11 J8 A120 towards Braintree*
Comfortable bric-a-brac filled pub where the conservatory overlooks surrounding countryside. Coming under new management as guide went to press.

LITTLE DUNMOW
Map 07 TL62

Flitch of Bacon ♀
The Street CM6 3HT ☎ 01371 820323 ▤ 01371 820338
Dir: *A120 to Braintree for 10m, turn off at Little Dunmow, 1/2m pub on R*
The name of this 15th-century country inn refers to the ancient award of a flitch of bacon to a married couple that had achieved a harmonious first year of marriage. Expect liver and bacon, home-made lasagne, smoked salmon with scrambled eggs, and various steaks.
OPEN: 12-3 6-11. **BAR MEALS:** L served all week. D served Mon-Sat 12.30-2 7-9. **BREWERY/COMPANY:** Free House.
PRINCIPAL BEERS: Greene King IPA. **FACILITIES:** Children welcome Garden: BBQ, outdoor eating Dogs allowed.
NOTES: Parking 6. **ROOMS:** 3 bedrooms 3 en suite s£35 d£50 No credit cards

MANNINGTREE
Map 07 TM13

Thorn Hotel
High St, Mistley CO11 1HE ☎ 01206 392821
▤ 01206 392133
Historic pub in the centre of Mistley, which stands on the estuary of the River Stour near Colchester and is the only surviving Georgian port in England today. Wide choice of freshly cooked food is available, with dishes such as chicken curry, home-made cottage pie, beef and ale pie, seafood platter and mixed grill.
OPEN: 11-11. **BAR MEALS:** L served all week. D served Mon-Sat 12-2.30 7-9. Av main course £4. **RESTAURANT:** L served all week. D served Mon-Sat 12-2.30 7-9. Av 3 course fixed price £10.
BREWERY/COMPANY: Free House.
PRINCIPAL BEERS: Greene King IPA, Greene King Old Abbot, Adnams. **FACILITIES:** Children welcome Dogs allowed except in garden. **NOTES:** Parking 6. **ROOMS:** 4 bedrooms 4 en suite s£42.50 d£60 2 family rooms, £85

NORTH FAMBRIDGE
Map 05 TQ89

The Ferry Boat Inn
Ferry Ln CM3 6LR ☎ 01621 740208
e-mail: Sylviaferryboat@aol.com
Dir: *From Chelmsford take A130 S then A132 to South Woodham Ferrers, then B1012. R to village*
The 500-year-old inn is located by the Essex Wildlife Trust's 600-acre sanctuary. It is believed to have a poltergeist but, while they have seen some strange things, the proprietors are

keeping an open mind. Meanwhile the log fire keeps burning, the beams are still head-achingly low, the River Crouch just flows on by. Pub fare includes local fish, steaks, and comfort food puddings.
OPEN: 11.30-3 (Sun 12-4) 7-11 (Sun 7-10.30). **BAR MEALS:** L served all week. D served all week 12-2.00 7-9.30. Av main course £5.50. **RESTAURANT:** L served all week. D served all week 12-1.30 7-9.30. Av 3 course à la carte £15.
BREWERY/COMPANY: Free House.
PRINCIPAL BEERS: Shepherd Neame Bishops Finger, Spitfire, Best Bitter. **FACILITIES:** Children welcome Garden: Beer garden, food served outdoors Dogs allowed On leads.
NOTES: Parking 30. **ROOMS:** 6 bedrooms 6 en suite s£30 d£40 FR£40

PAGLESHAM
Map 05 TQ99

Plough & Sail 🍴 ♀
East End SS4 2EQ ☎ 01702 258242 ▤ 01702 258242
Charming weatherboarded 17th-century dining pub on the bracing Essex marshes, within easy reach of the rivers Crouch and Roach. Inside are pine tables, brasses and low beams, giving the place a quaint, traditional feel. The attractive, well-kept garden is a popular spot during the summer months. Renowned for its good quality food and fresh fish dishes, including sea bass, smoked haddock and chargrilled tuna steak with pepper and lime chilli salsa.
OPEN: 11.30-3 6.45-11. **BAR MEALS:** L served all week. D served all week 12-2.15 7-9.30. Av main course £7.
RESTAURANT: L served all week. D served all week 12-2.15 7-9.30. Av 3 course à la carte £14. **BREWERY/COMPANY:** Free House. **PRINCIPAL BEERS:** Greene King IPA, Ridley's.
FACILITIES: Children welcome Garden: outdoor garden, patio. **NOTES:** Parking 30

The Punchbowl
Church End SS4 2DP ☎ 01702 258376
Weatherboarded pub with rural views and a small garden. Bar food and dining room. Changing guest ale.

PATTISWICK
Map 07 TL82

The Compasses Inn 🍴 ♀
CM7 8BG ☎ 01376 561322 ▤ 01376 561780
e-mail: chris.heap@btconnect.com
Dir: *off A120 between Braintree & Coggeshall*

Set in idyllic Essex countryside surrounded by woodland and rolling fields and much extended from the original, this inn dates back to the 13th century. Lighter bar bites are supplemented on the bistro menu by local favourites such as Trucker's Platter, liver and bacon, toad-in-the-hole, braised Scottish steak and kidney pie, and spinach and goats cheese cannelloni. Multi-choice Sunday lunch. *continued*

England

OPEN: 11-3 6-11 (open all day wknds). **BAR MEALS:** L served all week. D served all week 12-2.30 7-9.30. Av main course £9. **RESTAURANT:** L served all week. D served all week 12-2.30 7-9.30. Av 3 course à la carte £20. **BREWERY/COMPANY:** Free House. **PRINCIPAL BEERS:** Greene King - IPA, Abbot Ale & Triumph. **FACILITIES:** Children welcome Garden: patio, outdoor eating Dogs allowed Water. **NOTES:** Parking 40

RADWINTER   Map 07 TL63

The Plough Inn  ♈
CB10 2TL ☎ 01799 599222 ▤ 01799 599161
Dir: 4m E of Saffron Walden, at Jct of B2153 & B2154

An Essex woodboard exterior, old beams and a thatched roof characterise this listed inn, once frequented by farm workers. The menu extends from lunchtime snacks to three course meals, with fresh fish from Lowestoft from Wednesday to Saturday, including cod in beer batter and seared fillet of red bream with honey and Grand Marnier. Home-made pies, steaks and grills are available daily.
OPEN: 11-3 6.30-11 (Sat-Sun 11-10.30). Closed Dec 25. **BAR MEALS:** L served all week. D served all week 12-2.15 7-9. Av main course £6.95. **RESTAURANT:** L served all week. D served all week 12-2.15 7-9. **BREWERY/COMPANY:** Free House. **PRINCIPAL BEERS:** Adnams Best, Youngs Best, Brakspear Special, Greene King IPA. **FACILITIES:** Children welcome Garden: patio/terrace, outdoor eating, Dogs allowed on a lead, Water provided. **NOTES:** Parking 28.
ROOMS: 3 bedrooms 3 en suite s£50 d£50 1 family room £65

SAFFRON WALDEN   Map 07 TL53

The Cricketers' Arms ♦♦♦  ♈
Rickling Green CB11 3YG ☎ 01799 543210
▤ 01799 543512
e-mail: reservations@cricketeers.demon.co.uk
Dir: exit B1383 at Quendon. Pub 300yds on L opp cricket ground
Historic inn originally built as a terrace of timber framed cottages, now offering accommodation in 10 en suite bedrooms. The cricketing connection began in the 1880's when Rickling Green became the venue for London society cricket matches. One menu serves all three dining areas with choices ranging from snacks to full meals, including speciality mussel dishes.
OPEN: 11-11 Sun 12-10.30. **BAR MEALS:** L served all week. D served all week 12-2.30 7-9.30. **RESTAURANT:** L served all week. D served all week 12-2 7-9.30. Av 3 course fixed price £10.50. **BREWERY/COMPANY:** Free House.
PRINCIPAL BEERS: Flowers IPA, Wadworth 6X, Fullers ESB,. **FACILITIES:** Children welcome Garden: outdoor eating, patio/terrace Dogs allowed On lead. **NOTES:** Parking 40.
ROOMS: 10 bedrooms 10 en suite s£55 d£70 FR£70-£95

Queen's Head ♈
Littlebury CB11 4TD ☎ 01799 522251
16th-century inn only a short drive from the Duxford Air Museum. Quarry tiled floors, rustic furniture and beams characterise the bar which is enhanced by an informal and relaxing atmosphere. Food is prepared on the premises and barbecues are a regular feature in the walled garden. Try smoked haddock baked with Welsh rarebit, salmon fillet on Parmesan mash or the pot-roast guinea fowl.
OPEN: 12-3 5.30-11. **BAR MEALS:** L served all week. D served all week 12-2.30 6.30-9.30. Av main course £7.25. **RESTAURANT:** L served all week. D served all week 12-2.30 6.30-9.30. Av 3 course à la carte £20.
PRINCIPAL BEERS: Greene King IPA, Ruddles Best, Batemans XXXB. **FACILITIES:** Children welcome Garden: Food served outside Dogs allowed. **NOTES:** Parking 25.
ROOMS: 6 bedrooms 6 en suite s£40 d£55

STOCK   Map 05 TQ69

The Hoop
21 High St CM4 9BD ☎ 01277 841137
Dir: On B1007 between Chelmsford & Billericay
Built as weavers' cottages in the 15th-century, The Hoop became an alehouse inthe 17th-century and has been serving good ale ever since. An annual beer festival is held at the end of May. The homely little bar offers a good selection of snacks and light meals. Expect sandwiches, steak and kidney pie, fish pie, and ploughmans', and don't forget to check the blackboards for today's specials.
OPEN: 11-11 (Sun 12-10.30). **BAR MEALS:** L served all week. D served all week 11-9. Av main course £5.
BREWERY/COMPANY: Free House.
PRINCIPAL BEERS: Fullers, Hop Back, Crouch Vale, Adnams. **FACILITIES:** Garden: Outside eating, covered seating area,

---

TILLINGHAM   Map 07 TL90

Cap & Feathers Inn  ♈
South St CM0 7TH ☎ 01621 779212 ▤ 01799599161
Dir: From Chelmsford take A414, follow signs for Burnham-on-Crouch, then for Tillingham
Delightfully unspoilt, classic, white-painted, weather-boarded Essex village inn, reputedly an ale house since 1427, that changed its name from the King's Head to the Cap and Feathers during the Civil War. Timeless, old-fashioned interior with traditional furnishings, time-honoured pub games, tip-top Crouch Vale ales and home-cooked blackboard specials. Choose from Tillingham pie, locally-smoked fish and meats and freshly caught haddock, sole and monkfish.
OPEN: 12-3 (Open all day Sat-Sun Summer) 5.30-11 (Sun 12-4, 7-10.30). **BAR MEALS:** L served all week. D served all week 12-2.30 7-9.30. Av main course £5.20. **RESTAURANT:** L served all week. D served all week 12-2.30 7-9.30. Av 3 course à la carte £12. **BREWERY/COMPANY:** Crouch Vale.
PRINCIPAL BEERS: Crouch Vale Best & Woodham IPA, Fullers London Pride. **FACILITIES:** Children welcome Garden: outdoor eating Dogs allowed. **NOTES:** Parking 30.
ROOMS: 3 bedrooms s£30 d£40

For pubs with AA rosette awards for food
see page 10

WENDENS AMBO — Map 07 TL53

The Bell
Royston Rd CB11 4JY ☎ 01799 540382
Dir: Near Audley End train station
Formerly a farm, this 16th-century timber-framed building nestles in a picturesque village close to Audley End House. Extensive and attractive gardens, and cottagey low-ceilinged rooms.

WICKHAM BISHOPS — Map 07 TL81

The Mitre
2 The Street CM8 3NN ☎ 01621 891378 ▤ 01621 891378
Dir: Off B1018 between Witham and Maldon
The Bishops of London used to stay at this 19th-century pub - hence the name. Noted for its friendly atmosphere and character.

WIVENHOE — Map 07 TM02

The Black Buoy Inn ▤
Black Buoy Hill CO7 9BS ☎ 01206 822425
▤ 01206 827834
e-mail: enquiries@blackbuoy.com
Dir: From Colchester take A133 towards Clacton, then B1027, B1028. In Wivenhoe turn L after church into East St

Wivenhoe's oldest inn has a smugglers' tunnel running from the quay - though we are reliably informed that it is no longer in use. The landlord has a passion for food, particularly Far Eastern and Asian cooking, examples of which can be found on the extensive menu. Produce is locally sourced, and the daily blackboard menu depends on the day's catch and the chef's mood.
OPEN: 11.30-2.30 6.30-11 (Sun 12-3.30 7-10.30).
BAR MEALS: L served all week 12-2. Av main course £4.50.
RESTAURANT: L served all week. D served Tue-Sat 12-2 7-9.30.
Av 3 course à la carte £15. **BREWERY/COMPANY:** Pubmaster.
PRINCIPAL BEERS: Greene King IPA & Old Speckled Hen, Adnams Bitter, Broadside, Marston's Pedigree.
FACILITIES: Children welcome Garden: small patio area, food served outdoors Dogs allowed On lead water and biscuits available. **NOTES:** Parking 12

Ⴑ Pubs offering six or more wines by the glass

The Birds of the Air

Pride of place among bird signs is taken by the Swan, often adopted by inns close to a river. The eccentric Swan with Two Necks probably began as a swan with two nicks in its beak. The Cock may be related to cock-fighting or to St Peter. Geese and chickens appear alone or keeping dangerous company with the Fox. The Bird in Hand comes from falconry and the Dog and Duck either from fowling or from the amusement of setting a dog on a pinioned duck. The Eagle is from Heraldry and the Magpie and Stump from the countryside, while rarities include the Parrot and the Peahen.

England

GLOUCESTERSHIRE

ALMONDSBURY — Map 03 ST68

The Bowl Ⴑ
Church Rd BS12 4DT ☎ 01454 612757 ▤ 01454 619910
e-mail: reception@theoldbowlinn.co.uk
Nestling on the edge of the Severn Vale, this character whitewashed pub originally housed monks building the adjoining church and gets its name from the surrounding bowl-shaped landscape. Handy for Bristol and the M4 and M5 motorways. Wide-ranging and well planned bar fare menu includes warm baguettes, ploughman's lunches, pasta and fish dishes, grills and various salads.

OPEN: 11-3 5-11 (Sun 7-10.30). **BAR MEALS:** L served all week. D served all week 12-2.30 6-10. Av main course £7.
RESTAURANT: L served all week. D served all week 12-2.30 7-10. Av 3 course à la carte £25. **BREWERY/COMPANY:** Free House.
PRINCIPAL BEERS: Courage Best, Smiles Best.
FACILITIES: Children welcome Garden: Food served outside Dogs allowed. **NOTES:** Parking 50. **ROOMS:** 13 bedrooms 13 en suite s£39.50 d£64

ANDOVERSFORD — Map 03 SP01

The Frogmill Inn
Shipton GL54 4HT ☎ 01242 820547 ▤ 820237
Just off the A40 this 14th-century inn is set on the banks of the River Coln, and a smaller river runs through the car park. The mill wheel still turns, and can be seen under the restaurant window. Traditional pub food. Bedrooms.

ANDOVERSFORD continued

Pick of the Pubs

The Kilkeney Inn 🐑
Kilkeney GL54 4LN ☎ 01242 820341
📄 01242 820133

      See Pick of the Pubs on page 181

The Royal Oak Inn 🐑 ♀
Old Gloucester Rd GL54 4HR ☎ 01242 820335
e-mail: bleninns@clara.net
Dir: 200metres from A40, 4m E of Cheltenham
The pub stands on the banks of the River Coln four miles east of Cheltenham and is a focus for village life. It is a former coaching inn on the Oxford and Cheltenham route, and the old stables have been converted into a galleried restaurant. The menu incorporates a fresh fish choice, grills and country dishes like venison casserole and braised rabbit.

OPEN: 11-2.30 5.30-11 (Sat 11-11, Sun 12-3, 7-10.30).
BAR MEALS: L served all week. D served all week 12-2.30 7-9.30.
Av main course £5.95. **RESTAURANT:** L served all week.
D served all week 12-2.30 7-9.30. Av 3 course à la carte £12.50.
BREWERY/COMPANY: Free House.
PRINCIPAL BEERS: Marstons Pedigree, Fullers London Pride,
Hook Norton Best. **FACILITIES:** Children welcome Garden:
patio, Outdoor eating, Dogs allowed. **NOTES:** Parking 44

THE SEVERN WAY – GLOUCESTERSHIRE SECTION

Beyond the riverside towns of Bewdley and Stourport and south of the historic city of Worcester, the Severn Way enters Gloucestershire. As you approach picturesque Tewkesbury, famous for its magnificent abbey, make a short detour to the riverside Fleet Inn at Twyning and then follow the Avon into the town to rejoin the trail. South of Gloucester, the way makes for Berkeley, where you can pause for refreshment at the Malthouse, and then follows the bank of the Severn Estuary to the village of Oldbury. Close to the river lies the welcoming, stone-built Anchor Inn. The way continues alongside the river, passing the original Severn Bridge, opened in 1966, and finishing by the new Severn crossing, completed in 1996.

ASHLEWORTH   Map 03 SO82

Boat Inn
The Quay GL19 4HZ ☎ 01452 700272 📄 01452 700272
Occupied by the same family for over three centuries and situated beside the River Severn, this traditional inn is a gem among country pubs. Inside, there is lots of character, with a small front parlour, flagstone floors and an old kitchen range. Filled baps available at lunchtime. Nearby are several medieval buildings including a church and tithe barn.
OPEN: 11-2.30 6-11 (Oct-Mar 11-2.30, 7-11). **BAR MEALS:** L served all week 12-2. **BREWERY/COMPANY:** Free House.
PRINCIPAL BEERS: Wye Valley, Churchend, Arkells.
FACILITIES: Children welcome Garden: patio, outdoor eating
Dogs allowed garden only. **NOTES:** Parking 10 No credit cards

Pick of the Pubs

The Queens Arms 🐑
The Village GL19 4HT ☎ 01452 700395
Brick-fronted Elizabethan inn with Victorian additions, patio and herb garden. Spick-and-span interior and careful home cooking of fresh local produce is a feature of the changing menus served throughout the bar and dining areas. King prawns in garlic butter and scallops wrapped in Parma ham may precede crispy duck with Grand Marnier sauce, Greek lamb shank, roast pheasant with smoked bacon and cabbage, or roast cod on tomatoes with Mozzarella and basil. Good desserts; good value Sunday lunch.
OPEN: 12-2.30 7-11. Closed Dec 25. **BAR MEALS:** L served all week. D served all week 12-2 7-9. Av main course £10.
RESTAURANT: L served all week. D served all week 12-2
7-9. Av 3 course à la carte £17. **BREWERY/COMPANY:** Free
House. **PRINCIPAL BEERS:** Shepherd Neame Spitfire,
Donningtons, Bass, Youngs Special. **FACILITIES:** Children
welcome Garden: outdoor eating. **NOTES:** Parking 80

AUST   Map 03 ST58

The Boar's Head
Main Rd BS35 4AX ☎ 01454 632278 📄 01454 632570
e-mail: boarshead.aust@eldridge-pope.co.uk
Dir: Off the M48 just before the first built Severn Bridge, A403 to Avonmouth about 60 yds from Rdbt L into Aust Village. 1/2 mile ion L the house
For the cognoscenti, this popular 16th-century pub close to the M48 Severn Road Bridge offers a fine alternative to the nearby motorway service area. Seasonal log fires and a large stone-walled garden still provide hospitality to travellers, as they did in the days of the old Aust ferry. Expect chicken Caesar salad, sausage and mash, chilli with garlic bread, fresh trout, or salmon and broccoli fishcakes.
OPEN: 11.30-3 6.30-11.30 (Sun 10.30 close). **BAR MEALS:** L served all week. D served all week 12-2.30 6.30-9.30. Av main course £8. **RESTAURANT:** L served all week. D served all week 12-2.30 6.30-9.30. Av 3 course fixed price £15.
BREWERY/COMPANY: Eldridge Pope.
PRINCIPAL BEERS: Courage Best, Directors, Thomas Hardy Country Bitter. **FACILITIES:** Children welcome Garden: Food served outside. **NOTES:** Parking 30

Rose & Crown, Redmarley D'Abitot

ROSE & CROWN, REDMARLEY D'ABITOT
Playley Green GL19 3NB.
Tel: 01531 650234
Directions: on the A417
Gloucester to Ledbury road, 6
miles east of Ledbury
*Friendly, family-run village pub
dating from 1770 and formerly
part of the Beauchamp Estate.
Traditional pub food and good
daily specials. Detailed leaflet
on walk available in the pub.*
Open: 11-2.30 6-11 (Sun 12-3
7-10.30). Bar Meals: 12-2 6.30-
9. Children and dogs welcome.
Garden. Parking.
(see page 197 for full entry)

A walk across fields and along quiet lanes with views towards the Malvern and Cotswold Hills.

From pub turn left along road and cross stile on left before layby. Go through gate and bear half-right to gate, then bear slightly left and pass right of trees to stile. Bear slightly right over rise, then aim towards right side of oak to stile. Walk through orchard, crossing two stiles, to stile and road.

Cross stile opposite and bear diagonally right across field towards pole on skyline. Go through gate and keep beside hedge to gate by bungalow. Join drive, reach lane and turn left, then left again at junction. In 100yds (91m) take the path opposite Lowbands Farm. Go through gate and follow track around the right-hand edge of field to gateway. Bear left, then sharp right in corner and soon go left through gate. Walk beside brook, turn right through gate and cross bridge over brook, soon to reach gate. Take left-hand path beside hedge and bear left through gate in corner. Walk through farmyard to gate and follow drive for 90yds (82m) as it bears left around Redmarley Park to gate.

Immediately turn left through gate into field and proceed down to a stile in corner. Maintain direction, cross bridge over brook and bear left up bank to stile. Continue uphill to gate and A417. Cross stile opposite and cross field to stile beside farm. Ignore drive right, turn left, then bear right to gate and stile leading to adjoining house. Keep right to another stile and bear right to left of oak and right of sheds to cross left-hand of two stiles. Continue along right-hand side of garden fence to gate in corner and Drury Lane.

Turn right and take arrowed path left up steps to stile. Walk beside right-hand hedge and through trees to stile. Cross stile ahead and walk along bottom of field below Drury Lane House to stile. Continue beside garden to cottage and lane. Turn left, then right in 100yds (91m) through gate into field. Continue to stile beside garden wall to Old Rectory, cross drive and continue to stile in corner of car park. Turn left along hedge and boundary of cricket field. Cross cattle grid and follow drive to road. Turn right, then where it curves left to A417, follow path back to pub.

Distance: 3 1/2 miles (5.6km)
Map: OS Landranger 150
Terrain: farmland, parkland, country lanes
Paths: field paths and tracks; some road walking
Gradient: gently undulating; few steep climbs

Walk submitted by:
John Beech

AWRE Map 03 SO70

The Red Hart Inn

GL14 1EW ☎ 01594 510220 📠 01594 517249
Dir: E of A48 between Gloucester & Chepstow, access is from Blakeney or Newnham villages
Charming, 15th-century pub in a sleepy hamlet close to the meandering estuary of the River Severn. Quite inaccessible by road but well worth the effort. Plenty of attractive features inside, including a glass-covered illuminated well. Food bought locally whenever possible, with lamb and beef provided by local farmers. Expect scallops and prawns in a crab and garlic sauce and roast venison filled with apple and Stilton and set on a port glaze. Good range of traditional bar meals, a popular choice of real ales and several malt whiskies.
OPEN: 12-3 6.30-11. Closed Jan 1-2. **BAR MEALS:** L served Tue-Sun. D served all week 12-2 7-9. Av main course £7.
RESTAURANT: L served Tue-Sun. D served all week 12-2 7-9. Av 3 course à la carte £20. **BREWERY/COMPANY:** Free House.
PRINCIPAL BEERS: Fullers London Pride, Bass, Freeminer Speculation. **FACILITIES:** Children welcome Garden: food served outside. **NOTES:** Parking 30. **ROOMS:** 2 bedrooms 2 en suite s£45 d£55

BARNSLEY Map 03 SP00

Pick of the Pubs

The Village Pub ◉ ◉ ♀

GL7 5EF ☎ 01285 740421 📠 01285 740142
e-mail: reservations@thevillagepub.co.uk
Dir: On B4425 3m NE of Cirencester
Finalist in the AA Pub of the Year Award 2002.
Unique in preserving its unusual name, this 'Village Pub' is not your average 'local'. Mellow-stoned and set hard by the B4425 in a charming Cotswold village, it has been transformed in just two years by Tim Haigh and Rupert Pendered and now ranks among the best of the new breed of successful pub-restaurants, where innovative, modern British food is served in a relaxed and informal pub atmosphere.
Warm terracotta walls, rug-strewn stone floors and an eclectic mix of furnishings throughout a warren of beautifully refurbished rooms set the style in which to enjoy ambitious dishes cooked with flair and imagination. Order a pint and a sandwich and sit at the bar or go the whole hog and linger over four courses by the open fire in the bar. Local, organic or traceable meats and fresh produce from quality suppliers are used in the preparation of pan-fried pork chop with confit potatoes and parsnips, navarin of lamb with braised beans and pasta, and grilled sea bass with sweet potato purée, clams and coriander.
Precede with onion and cider soup or salmon fishcake, mixed leaves and lemon butter; finish with chocolate and almond torte with clotted cream. Distinctly a dining destination but still very much the 'village pub', attracting both local drinkers and well heeled 'foodies'. Classy accommodation.
OPEN: 11-3.30 6-11. Closed 25 Dec. **BAR MEALS:** L served all week. D served all week 12-3 7-10. Av main course £12. **BREWERY/COMPANY:** Free House.
PRINCIPAL BEERS: Hook Norton Bitter, Wadworth 6X.
FACILITIES: Children welcome Garden: patio, Food served outside Dogs allowed. **NOTES:** Parking 35.
ROOMS: 6 bedrooms 6 en suite s£55 d£70

BERKELEY Map 03 ST69

The Malthouse NEW

Marybrook St GL13 9AB ☎ 01453 511177
📠 01453 810257
Dir: From A38 towards Bristol from exit 13 of M5, Aprox 8 M Berkeley is signposted, the Malthouse is situated on the main road heading towards Sharpness
Family-run pub located in the historic town of Berkeley. Close by is the Severn Way and only a stone's throw are the battlemented walls of a Norman castle and the Jenner Museum, dedicated to the life and work of Dr Edward Jenner, a local man who invented a vaccine for smallpox. Good choice of starters, followed by lamb shank with root vegetables and a herb mash, and prime ribeye steak with fondant potatoes and red onion marmalade. Wholesome bar meals and snacks.
OPEN: 12-3.30 6-11. **BAR MEALS:** L served all week. D served all week 12-2.30 6.30-10. Av main course £6. **RESTAURANT:** L served all week. D served all week 12-2.30 6.30-10. Av 3 course à la carte £20. **BREWERY/COMPANY:** Free House.
PRINCIPAL BEERS: Regular changing real ales.
FACILITIES: Children welcome Garden: Food served outside.
NOTES: Parking 40. **ROOMS:** 9 bedrooms 9 en suite s£40 d£60

BIBURY

Catherine Wheel

Arlington GL7 5ND ☎ 01285 740250 📠 01285 740779
e-mail: Catherinewheel.bibury@eldridge-pope.co.uk
Low-beamed 15th-century pub situated in a classic Cotswold village, close to Arlington Row (NT) and the River Coln. Traditional home-made pub food. Bedrooms.

BIRDLIP Map 03 SO91

The Golden Heart ♀

Nettleton Bottom GL4 8LA ☎ 01242 870261
📠 01242 870599
Dir: on the main road A417 Gloucester to Cirencester
Listed stone-built inn situated in glorious Cotswold countryside and close to the tourist attractions of Gloucester and Cheltenham. Formerly three cottages, the pub offers memorable views from its terraced gardens. The Golden Heart uses prize-winning stock from local markets and national shows and to complement the best quality English meat, exotic dishes are prepared, including crocodile, ostrich and kangaroo. Award-winning wines and real ales enhance the menu.
OPEN: 11-3 5-11 (Fri-Sat 11-11, Sun 12-10.30). **BAR MEALS:** L served all week. D served all week 12-3 6-10. Av main course £8.95. **RESTAURANT:** L served all week. D served all week 12-3 6-10. Av 3 course à la carte £14.95. **BREWERY/COMPANY:** Free House. **PRINCIPAL BEERS:** Bass, Timothy Taylor Landlord, Archers Bitter & Golden Best. **FACILITIES:** Children welcome Garden: outdoor eating, patio/terrace, Dogs allowed Kennel, water. **NOTES:** Parking 60. **ROOMS:** 3 bedrooms 3 en suite s£35 d£55 1 family room £60

All AA listed accommodation can also be found on the AA's internet site **www.theAA.com**

OPEN: 11.30-2.30 6.30-11 (Sun 12-2.30 7-10.30. Sat 11-11, Sun 12-10.30 Easter-Sep).
Closed 25-26 Dec.
BAR MEALS: L served Mon-Sat 12-2. Av main course £6.95
RESTAURANT: L served all week D served all week 12-2 7-9.
Av 3 course a la carte £18.50.
BREWERY/COMPANY: Free House.
PRINCIPAL BEERS: Bass, Hook Norton Best.
FACILITIES: Garden: patio, outdoor eating. Guide dogs only.
NOTES: Parking 50.

The Kilkeney Inn

Kilkeney GL54 4LN
☎ 01242 820341 📠 01242 820133
Dir: On A436 Gloucester to Cirencester road, 1m W of Andoversford

Formerly a terrace of six stone cottages (dating from 1856), this charming country pub-restaurant commands delightful views from mature gardens and a conservatory brasserie across a beautiful rolling Cotswold landscape.

Very much a dining venue, with its fine conservatory dining room and a spacious and airy open-plan bar sporting numerous watercolours, daily papers and an effective log fire and woodburner for those chilly winter nights. Certainly the 'place to eat' in the area, with the intimate dining atmosphere enhanced by candlelight in the evenings.

Light lunches run to smoked chicken and avocado salad, Spanish omelette with salad and a tomato and fresh herb jus, and local sausage and bacon in puff pastry parcels with onion gravy. Dedicated snackers will be satisfied with filled breads such as prawns Marie Rose in a crisp white baguette. Dinner is a tad more serious, offering such starters as warm smoked fish salad with virgin olive oil dressing and goats' cheese parcels with crushed black olives. Main dishes on the seasonal menu might include pork fillets stuffed with young spinach leaves and local venison and mushroom casserole with celeriac mash. Fishy daily specials may include mussel and coconut curry and John Dory with tagliatelle and lemon butter.

Fruity, often meringued, desserts include a platter to share: otherwise try the hand-made British cheeses with a small bottle of Port of Leith. Advertised special events include fresh fish evenings, authentic Viennese cuisine, Caribbean nights, and twice-monthly jazz supper evenings. Traditional Sunday lunches - booking advised.

BISLEY   Map 03 SO90

The Bear Inn
George St GL6 7BD ☎ 01452 770265
e-mail: thebear@cyberphile.co.uk
Dir: E of Stroud off B4070
A priest hole, a bread oven and a huge inglenook fireplace are among the fascinating features at this charming village inn, supposedly used by gunpowder conspirators. Extensive bar menu features Bear burgers, a selection of home-made pies and casseroles and a wide choice of filled baguettes.
OPEN: 11-3 6-11. **BAR MEALS:** L served all week. D served Mon-Sat 12-2.30 7-9. Av main course £7.50.
BREWERY/COMPANY: Pubmaster. **PRINCIPAL BEERS:** Bass, Tetley, Flowers IPA, Charles Wells Bombardier.
FACILITIES: Children welcome   Garden: Boule pitch   Dogs allowed. **NOTES:** Parking 20. **ROOMS:** 2 bedrooms d£18

Coaching Days
The traditional English inn reached its apogee in the coaching age in the 18th century. This was the period of the capacious Georgian inn of popular nostalgia, with its jovial, welcoming landlord and army of maids, tapsters, ostlers and pot-boys. Here the stagecoaches halted to change horses, while the passengers went inside to warm themselves by a roaring fire, eat and drink and clean up. The best inns were social centres for affluent locals, tastefully furnished and lavishly provided with clocks, mirrors and barometers. In the second half of the century the smartest ones began to call themselves 'hotels', French-style.
While drinking had fallen off by this time and the old-style tavern disappeared, the alehouses were growing far more comfortable. Some of them now called themselves taverns and from the late 17th century the term 'public house' came in. Some were now purpose-built, instead of being ordinary dwelling houses. The bigger ones had upstairs lodging rooms, decently furnished, and games rooms for shove halfpenny, billiards or bagatelle. They sold simple food - pies, bread and cheese, buns - eaten in a thick fug of tobacco smoke, and you could buy all sorts of things in the bar from small traders, from butter to gloves or pens.

BLEDINGTON   Map 06 SP22

Pick of the Pubs

Kings Head Inn & Restaurant ◆◆◆◆ ♀
The Green OX7 6XQ ☎ 01608 658365
▤ 01608 658902
e-mail: kingshead@orr-ewing.com
Dir: On B4450 4m from Stow-on-the-Wold

Enthusiastic young owners, Archie and Nicola Orr-Ewing, bought this well respected, quintessential Cotswold inn in June 2000 and have set about improving the menus and plan to revamp the bedrooms. Built of honey-coloured stone in the 15th century, it enjoys an idyllic setting on the Oxford/Gloucester county boundary and the village green with its brook and border-patrolling ducks. Parts of the original cider house have survived, adding character to an interior of low ceilings, exposed stone walls, open fires and sturdy wooden furnishings. Seasonal local game and fresh fish feature on the now manageable main menu, which may list warm tomato and Mozzarella tart with pesto sauce and lentil and ham broth among the starters, followed by Italian rabbit ragout, jugged hare, steak and Hook Norton pie, braised lamb shank with root vegetables, and baked cod with ratatouille, dill pesto and chard red pepper dressing. Good vegetarian options and nursery puddings to finish. Stylish en suite bedrooms are well equipped with thoughtful extras.
OPEN: 11-2.30 6-11. Closed 24-25 Dec. **BAR MEALS:** L served all week. D served all week 12-2 7-9.30. Av main course £7. **RESTAURANT:** L served Mon-Sat. D served all week 12-2 7-9.30. Av 3 course à la carte £15.50.
BREWERY/COMPANY: Free House.
PRINCIPAL BEERS: Hook Norton Bitter, Wadworth 6X, Shepherds Neam Spitfire, Timothy Taylor Landlord.
FACILITIES: Garden: patio, outdoor eating   Dogs allowed manager's discretion only. **NOTES:** Parking 60.
ROOMS: 12 bedrooms 12 en suite s£45 d£60 FR£90.00-£90.00

BLOCKLEY   Map 03 SP13

The Crown Inn & Hotel 🐑
High St GL56 9EX ☎ 01386 700245   ▤ 01386 700247
e-mail: info@thecrownatblockley.co.uk
Mellow, 16th-century coaching inn set in one of the most attractive of the Cotswold villages. Charming interior with old beams, log fires and exposed stonewalls. Good pub food includes fish cakes, fish and chips, Thai crab cakes and moules mariniere.   *continued*

OPEN: 11-11. **BAR MEALS:** L served all week. D served all week 12-2 7-9.30. Av main course £8.95. **RESTAURANT:** L served all week. D served all week 12-2 7-9.30. Av 3 course à la carte £25. **BREWERY/COMPANY:** Free House. **PRINCIPAL BEERS:** Hook Norton Bitter, Fullers London Pride, John Smiths. **FACILITIES:** Garden: Food served outside in summer. **NOTES:** Parking 40. **ROOMS:** 24 bedrooms 24 en suite s£55 d£99 FR£120

BOURTON-ON-THE-WATER
Map 03 SP12

The Duke of Wellington
Sherborne St GL54 2BY ☎ 01451 820539
🖹 01451 810919
e-mail: mail@dukeofwellingtonbourton.co.uk
Offering a wide range of celebratory themed evenings, including Chinese New Year, St David's Day and Aquitaine Evening, this 16th-century Cotswold-stone coaching inn is right by the River Windrush.

Kingsbridge Inn ♀
Riverside GL54 2BS ☎ 01451 820371 🖹 01451 810179
Village-centre inn with waterside bar, garden and patios by the Windrush, and a childrens' play area. Diverse menu choices include cod in home-made beer batter, guinea fowl with chicken and cranberry mousse, daily pies, curries and roast lunches: variously filled baguettes; childrens' menu: Sunday lunch.
OPEN: 11-11 (Sun 12-10.30). **BAR MEALS:** L served all week. D served all week 11-3 6-9. Av main course £4.50. **BREWERY/COMPANY:** Eldridge Pope. **PRINCIPAL BEERS:** Deuchars IPA, Bass, Courage Best. **FACILITIES:** Children welcome Garden: outdoor eating, patio Dogs allowed. **NOTES:** Parking 5. **ROOMS:** 3 bedrooms 3 en suite s£39 d£54

BROCKWEIR
Map 03 SO50

Brockweir Country Inn
NP16 7NG ☎ 01291 689548
A 400-year-old inn, with a small garden and covered courtyard, close to the River Wye in the old village of Brockweir. It is popular with locals and retains many characteristics of a traditional alehouse. Ideal for walkers enjoying the unspoilt Wye Valley.

CHALFORD
Map 03 SO80

The Crown Inn ♀
Frampton Mansell GL6 8JG ☎ 01285 760601
🖹 01285 760681
Gloriously situated in the heart of Stroud's Golden Valley, this 17th-century coaching inn lies close to the Royal residences at Highgrove and Gatcombe Park. The cosy beamed bar with its honey coloured stone walls and open fire offers a warm welcome; and, although the cellar is alleged to be haunted, new owners Gareth and Karal Rees comment that "we've enough spirits behind the bar, anyway!" With its 12 tastefully furnished en suite bedrooms, the Crown makes an excellent base for touring Cirencester and the Cotswolds. The pub garden enjoys superb views of the surrounding countryside, and you may be lucky enough to spot buzzards soaring overhead.

An imaginative selection of home-cooked fare is offered in the spacious panelled restaurant. Salmon and prawn paté, deep-fried British cheeses, or home-cured gravad lax, precede marinated lamb steak, pan-fried pork loin on herb mash, home-made fishcakes, or oriental vegetable stir-fry. Finish with chocolate box cake, or gin and lavender ice cream in a crispy brandy basket.
OPEN: 11-3 (Open all day summer months) 5.30-11 (Sat 11.30-11, Sun 12-3, 7-11). **BAR MEALS:** L served all week. D served all week 12-2.30 6.30-9.45. Av main course £6.95. **RESTAURANT:** L served all week. D served all week 12-2.30 6.30-9.45. Av 3 course à la carte £11.95. Av 2 course fixed price £7.95. **BREWERY/COMPANY:** Lionheart. **PRINCIPAL BEERS:** Bass, Courage Directors & Best, John Smiths. **FACILITIES:** Children welcome Garden: outdoor eating, patio Dogs allowed on leads. **NOTES:** Parking 100. **ROOMS:** 12 bedrooms 12 en suite s£52 d£69 FR£120

CHEDWORTH
Map 03 SP01

Hare & Hounds
Foss Cross GL54 4NN ☎ 01285 720288
Dir: On A429(Fosse Way), 6m from Cirencester
Situated on a remote stretch of the ancient Foss Way and surrounded by beautiful Cotswold countryside, this rustic stone pub features flagged floors, splendid open fires, low beams and various farm implements throughout its simply adorned interior. Well respected for innovative pub food but due to change hands as we went to press: reports please!

Seven Tuns ♀
Queen St GL54 4AE ☎ 01285 720242 🖹 01285 720242
e-mail: sevevtuns@smiles.co.uk
Dir: A40 then A429 towards Cirencester, after 5m R for Chedworth, 3m then 3rd turning on R
Traditional village inn dating back to 1610 and the ideal place to relax in after an exhilarating walk in the Cotswolds. Handy also for visiting nearby Chedworth Roman villa which can be reached on foot. Directly opposite the inn, which takes its name from seven chimney pots, is a waterwheel, a spring and a raised terrace for summer drinking. The freshly prepared daily-changing menu might feature braised rabbit, cheese and walnuts with a Stilton sauce, steak and kidney pie and ravioli. Well-kept real ales.
OPEN: 11-11 (Sun 12-10.30) (Winter 11-3, 6-11). **BAR MEALS:** L served all week. D served Mon-Sat 12-2.30 6.30-9.30. Av main

continued

course £6.95. **RESTAURANT:** L served all week. D served Mon-Sat 12-2.30 6.30-9. Av 3 course à la carte £18.
BREWERY/COMPANY: Free House.
PRINCIPAL BEERS: Youngs, Everards, Greene King Abbot Ale.
FACILITIES: Children welcome Garden: patio outside eating Dogs allowed Water,. **NOTES:** Parking 30.
ROOMS: 2 bedrooms 2 en suite s£50 d£60

CHELTENHAM
Map 03 SO92

The Little Owl ♀
Cirencester Rd, Charlton Kings GL53 8EB ☎ 01242 529404
🖹 01242 252523
e-mail: alan@littleowl.totalserve.co.uk
Dir: on A435 Cirencester Rd, 2.5m from Cheltenham Spa
Named after the famous 1981 Cheltenham Gold Cup winner, this double-fronted pub is situated near the popular Cotswold Way long-distance trail, Lilley Brook Golf Club and the Cheltenham Race Course. Menu includes wild boar sausages, beef and Guinness pie, grilled supreme of salmon, and green Thai chicken curry.
OPEN: 11.30-2.30 5.30-11.30. **BAR MEALS:** L served all week. D served all week 12-2 6.30-9.30. Av main course £8.95.
RESTAURANT: L served all week. D served all week 12-2 6.30-9.30. Av 3 course à la carte £15.95.
BREWERY/COMPANY: Whitbread.
PRINCIPAL BEERS: Wadworth 6X, Tetley, Fullers London Pride, Smiles Best Bitter. **FACILITIES:** Children welcome Garden: outdoor eating, plum and apple trees Dogs allowed Water.
NOTES: Parking 40

CHIPPING CAMPDEN
Map 03 SP13

The Bakers Arms
Broad Campden GL55 6UR ☎ 01386 840515

Small Cotswold inn with a great atmosphere - visitors are welcomed and regulars are involved with the quiz, darts and crib teams. The traditional look of the place is reflected in its time-honoured values, with good meals at reasonable prices and a choice of four to five real ales. Typical specials are marinated duck breast, trout and almonds, and paprika chicken.
OPEN: 11.30-2.30 6-11. Closed 25 Dec. **BAR MEALS:** L served all week. D served all week 12-2 6.30-9. Av main course £6.
RESTAURANT: 6-9. **BREWERY/COMPANY:** Free House.
PRINCIPAL BEERS: Timothy Taylor Landlord, Hook Norton.
FACILITIES: Children welcome Garden: outdoor eating Dogs allowed garden only, Water. **NOTES:** Parking 30 No credit cards

---

Pick of the Pubs

The Churchill Arms ◉ ◉ 🍴 ♀
Paxford GL55 6XH ☎ 01386 594000 🖹 01386 594005
e-mail: the-churchill-arms@hotmail.com
Dir: 2m E of Chipping Campden, 4m N of Moreton-in-Marsh
Respected restaurant chef Sonya Kidney from the well established Marsh Goose in nearby Moreton-in-Marsh ventured boldly into the pub market two years ago to find a more informal and flexible set-up where she would have the freedom to experiment with her cooking.
The Churchill Arms, a traditional Cotswold stone village local, continues to go from strength to strength, winning praises from far and wide for the innovative modern cooking using fresh seasonal produce. This is pub-restaurant food at its best!
Expect wooden floors, rustic stone walls, an eclectic mix of furnishings and a bustling dining atmosphere alongside an ever-changing blackboard menu that may list spiced tomato and herb soup and fresh squid with harrisa dressing and apricot couscous for starters; followed by loin of rabbit filled with spiced aubergine lentils and mustard dressing, herb-crusted lemon sole with sweet red pepper sauce or breast of guinea fowl with Madeira and mushroom cream sauce. Round off a memorable meal with a perfect chocolate torte or panacotta with orange and nutmeg parfait Hook Norton ales; 9 wines by the glass; comfortable en suite bedrooms.
OPEN: 11.30-3 6-11. **BAR MEALS:** L served all week. D served all week 12-2 7-9. Av main course £10.
RESTAURANT: L served all week. D served all week 12-2 7-9. Av 3 course à la carte £20.
BREWERY/COMPANY: Free House.
PRINCIPAL BEERS: Hook Norton Bitter, Arkells 3B.
FACILITIES: Children welcome Garden: outdoor eating, patio. **ROOMS:** 4 bedrooms 4 en suite s£40 d£70

Pick of the Pubs

Eight Bells Inn
Church St GL55 6JG ☎ 01386 840371
🖹 01386 841669
Built in the 14th-century to house the stone masons and store the bells during the construction of the fine church, the Eight Bells has a tiny, low Cotswold stone frontage hung with flowers baskets. Beyond the cobbled entranceway are two cosy bars with open fires, old beams and a warm, welcoming atmosphere, and beyond an enclosed courtyard for fine weather drinking.
Fresh local produce is utilised well here, daily-changing blackboard dishes may include chicken and mushroom shortcrust pie, braised ham hock with parsley sauce, and apple, cinnamon and sultana crumble. A converted barn houses the en suite bedrooms.
OPEN: 11-3 5.30-11 (all day Wed-Sun). Closed 25 Dec.
BAR MEALS: L served all week. D served all week 12-2 6.30-9. Av main course £10. **BREWERY/COMPANY:** Free House. **PRINCIPAL BEERS:** Marstons Pedigree,.
FACILITIES: Children welcome Garden: patio, outdoor eating Dogs allowed Water. **ROOMS:** 5 bedrooms 5 en suite s£35 d£60 FR£60-£90

England

Pick of the Pubs

The Noel Arms Hotel @ @ ★ ★ ★ ♀
High St GL55 6AT ☎ 01386 840317 ▤ 01386 841136
e-mail: bookings@cotswold-inns-hotels.co.uk
Originally a 14th-century coaching inn with a fine stone façade and Regency portico, standing on the main street of arguably the Cotswolds' prettiest town.

Light meals served in the historic beamed bar and modern conservatory might include chicken and mushroom pie, home-made pâté and toast, and tomato, mozarella and basil salad. Round off with rich chocolate cake or hot apple pie.

The restaurant is à la carte: rib-eye steak with pomme fondant served with haricot verte, sun-dried tomatoes, Worcester sauce and mushrooms, roasted Mediterranean vegetables in a filo basket with aubergine, caviar and red and yellow cherry tomatoes with a light basil sauce.
OPEN: 11-11 (Sun 12-10.30). **BAR MEALS:** L served all week. D served all week 12-2 7-9. Av main course £6.95.
RESTAURANT: L served Sun. D served all week 12-2 7-9.30. Av 3 course à la carte £24.95. **BREWERY/COMPANY:** Free House. **PRINCIPAL BEERS:** Hook Norton, Bass.
FACILITIES: Children welcome Dogs allowed.
NOTES: Parking 25. **ROOMS:** 26 bedrooms 26 en suite s£75 d£135 FR£135

The Volunteer NEW
Lower High St ☎ 01386 840688 ▤ 01386 840543
e-mail: saravol@aol.com
Family-run pub attracting locals and tourists alike - many ramblers start the Cotswold Way from here. There are log fires in winter and a large beer garden with a collection of mad pets in summer. A good choice of real ales is offered and home-made dishes cater for traditional and exotic tastes. Paella days, pig roasts and curry nights are held seasonally.
OPEN: 11.30-3 (Sun 12-3, 7-10.30) 5-11. **BAR MEALS:** L served all week. D served all week 12-2 7-9. Av main course £7.
BREWERY/COMPANY: Free House.
PRINCIPAL BEERS: Hook Norton Best, North Cotswold Genesis, Stanway bitter,. **FACILITIES:** Garden: Food served outside.
ROOMS: 5 bedrooms 5 en suite

CIRENCESTER   Map 03 SP00

Bathurst Arms ♀
North Cerney GL7 7BZ ☎ 01285 831281 ▤ 01285 831155
Dir: The Bathurst Arms is setback from the Cheltenham Rd (A435)
Former coaching inn with bags of period charm - antique settles on flagstone floors, stone fireplaces, beams and panelled walls. The pretty garden stretches down to the River Churn, and a large barbecue is in use most summer weekends. Local delicacies include grilled Cerney goats' cheese with mixed leaves and walnuts, and trio of organic sausages with garlic mash and red onion gravy.
OPEN: 11-3 (Sun 12-2.30, 7-10.30) 6-11. **BAR MEALS:** L served all week. D served all week 12-2 7-9. Av main course £9.50.
RESTAURANT: L served all week. D served all week 12-2 7-9. Av 3 course à la carte £15. **BREWERY/COMPANY:** Free House.
PRINCIPAL BEERS: Hook Norton, Wadworth 6X.
FACILITIES: Children welcome Garden: Food served outside.
NOTES: Parking 30. **ROOMS:** 5 bedrooms 5 en suite s£45 d£65

Pick of the Pubs

The Crown of Crucis @ ★ ★ ★ ♀
Ampney Crucis GL7 5RS ☎ 01285 851806
▤ 01285 851735
e-mail: info@thecrownofcrucis.co.uk
Dir: On A417 to Lechlade, 2m E of Cirencester

In a lovely Cotswold setting, the hotel takes its name from the unusual old cross that stands in the village churchyard. Built in two parts, the bar and dining areas are housed in the original 16th-century inn, while bedrooms are in a modern block that surrounds the courtyard. Swans wander by the riverside, where assorted tables and chairs look out over the local cricket pitch. The atmosphere is casual, busy and bubbling, attracting a broad cross-section of clientele.

Bar food ranges from nachos with dips and goats' cheese with roast Mediterranean vegetables to steak and kidney pie, cod in beer batter and grilled rump steak topped with cheese: a fish special might be pan-fried halibut with saffron and mussel cream sauce.

The restaurant features modern British cooking with traditional influences, as in shellfish terrine, roast duck breast and pear and almond crumble.
OPEN: 10.30am-11pm (Sun 12am-11pm). Closed Dec 25.
BAR MEALS: L served all week 12. Av main course £7.
RESTAURANT: L served all week. D served all week 12-2.30 7-10. Av 3 course à la carte £18.50.
BREWERY/COMPANY: Free House.
PRINCIPAL BEERS: Wadworth 6X, Archers Village, Theakston XB, Marstons Pedigree. **FACILITIES:** Children welcome Garden: outdoor eating, patio, riverside setting Dogs allowed. **NOTES:** Parking 70. **ROOMS:** 25 bedrooms 25 en suite s£44 d£62 FR£102.00

185

CLEARWELL   Map 03 SO50

Pick of the Pubs

Wyndham Arms ★ ★ ★ 🛏 ♀
GL16 8JT ☎ 01594 833666 📠 01594 836450
Dir: In centre of village on the B4231
Set in several acres of glorious sloping gardens, woods and lawns, this 600-year-old inn of long pedigree stands in the heart of this medieval village close to the towering castle.

The Stanford family, here since 1973, are splendid hosts and have created a civilised small hotel with a bustling bar offering traditional hand-pulled ales and a notable malt whisky collection, and a thriving bar and restaurant food trade. Bar snacks, grills and meals cover six dozen choices on a three-page menu, from cheese and herb pâté, ploughman's platter, gammon ham, egg and chips and smoked salmon sandwiches to kidneys' Stroganoff, mixed grills and daily specials like lamb cobbler and haddock and prawn pie.

Restaurant additions include beef en croûte, roast local lamb with redcurrant gravy, and seafood thermidor. Bedrooms are divided between the evocative main building and a modern extension.
OPEN: 11-11 (Sun 12-10.30). **BAR MEALS:** L served all week. D served all week 12-2 6.45-9. Av main course £10. **RESTAURANT:** L served all week. D served all week 12-2 6.45-9. Av 3 course à la carte £21.25. Av 3 course fixed price £21.25. **BREWERY/COMPANY:** Free House. **PRINCIPAL BEERS:** Bass. **FACILITIES:** Children welcome Garden: Food served outside. **NOTES:** Parking 50. **ROOMS:** 18 bedrooms 18 en suite s£55 d£65

COLD ASTON   Map 03 SP11

The Plough Inn
GL54 3BN ☎ 01451 821459 📠 01451 824000
Dir: village signed from A436 & A429 SW of Stow-on-the-Wold

A delightful 17th-century pub standing at the heart of this lovely Cotswold village close to Stow-on-the-Wold. Full of old beams, flagstone floors, cottagey windows and open log fires in winter, it offers local Donnington ales and daily-changing menus. Dishes are freshly prepared by the chef/landlord and may include soup with home-made bread, crispy chicken and watercress salad, shank of lamb with mint and redcurrant, steak, mushroom and ale pie, and mixed fish grill with olive oil and garlic. Patio and garden for summer alfresco drinking.
OPEN: 11.30-2.30 6.30-11 (Sun 12-3, 7-10.30). **BAR MEALS:** L served all week. D served all week 12-2 6.30-9. Av main course

continued

£7.95. **BREWERY/COMPANY:** Free House. **PRINCIPAL BEERS:** Hook Norton. **FACILITIES:** Children welcome Garden: Patio, food served outside Dogs allowed Garden: only. **NOTES:** Parking 12

COLESBOURNE   Map 03 SP01

The Colesbourne Inn
GL53 9NP ☎ 01242 870376 📠 01242 870397
e-mail: info@colesbourneinn.com
Dir: On A435 (Cirencester to Cheltenham road)
An 18th-century coaching inn with exposed beams and log fires, and a large garden overlooking wooded hills. Appetising main courses include collops of beef with a garlic and thyme sauce, and breast of chicken with smoked cheese wrapped in parma ham. Sweets include dark and white chocolate tart and banana and coffee brûlée.
OPEN: 11.30-3 6.30-11. **BAR MEALS:** L served all week. D served all week 12-2.30 7-10. Av main course £7.50. **RESTAURANT:** L served all week. D served all week 12-2.30 7-10. Av 3 course à la carte £20. **BREWERY/COMPANY:** Wadworth. **PRINCIPAL BEERS:** Wadworth 6X, Henrys IPA & Farmers Glory. **FACILITIES:** Garden: pond and water features Dogs allowed. **NOTES:** Parking 40. **ROOMS:** 9 bedrooms 9 en suite s£45 d£65

COLN ST-ALDWYNS   Map 03 SP10

Pick of the Pubs

The New Inn at Coln ⊛ ⊛ ★ ★ 🛏 ♀
GL7 5AN ☎ 01285 750651 📠 01285 750657
e-mail: stay@new-inn.co.uk
Dir: Between Bibury(B4425) & Fairford(A417), 8m E of Cirencester
Entering its tenth year since rescue from near-dereliction, this is a remarkable tale of an inn that was old when Christopher Wren was building St Paul's, for over the intervening centuries little of the inn's fabric has changed, but how times have. The bedrooms offer every modern comfort yet the bars with flagstone floors, exposed beams and open fires, as well as the flower-filled summer courtyard, show that the 16th century has ceded gracefully to the 21st.

Freshly prepared dishes such as gratin of whiting and macaroni, satay chicken with roasted peanuts and Caesar salad with poached egg may be taken in small or large portions, while ambitious choices from an ever-changing main menu may likely include traditional fish and chips with mushy peas alongside ribeye steak, field mushrooms and tomato. More adventurously, go for salmon omelette with crème fraiche, sweet and sour pork stir-fry with pineapple or daube of beef with smoked bacon and mushrooms; following with an envious choice between apple and cinnamon crumble and pannacotta with a thyme-roasted plum.

Real ales and quality wines are legion, appealing equally to partakers of the imaginative fixed-price menus offered in the restaurant. Remarkable indeed.
OPEN: 11-11 (Sun 12-10.30). **BAR MEALS:** L served all week. D served all week 12-2 7-9. Av main course £10. **RESTAURANT:** L served all week. D served all week 12-2 7-9. Av 3 course fixed price £22.50. **BREWERY/COMPANY:** Free House. **PRINCIPAL BEERS:** Hook Norton Best Bitter, Wadworth 6X, Butcombe Bitter. **FACILITIES:** Garden: Patio, food served outside Dogs allowed. **NOTES:** Parking 24. **ROOMS:** 14 bedrooms 14 en suite s£72 d£99

England

England

COWLEY   Map 03 SO91

Pick of the Pubs

The Green Dragon Inn NEW
Cockleford GL53 9NW ☎ 01242 870271
▣ 01242 870171
Attractive 17th-century character pub with a growing
reputation for attracting discerning diners in search of
modern pub food. Located in the Cotswolds, the inn is
also an ideal base for touring the region's many
attractions, as well as visiting historic Cirencester and the
elegant spa town of Cheltenham.

Inside crackling log fires, beamed ceilings and stone-
flagged floors give the Green Dragon a cosy individuality.
Even the furniture is distinctive, hand-crafted by Robert
Thompson, the famous Yorkshire woodcarver whose
renowned trademark signature was in the form of a
mouse.

Enjoy an appetising snack or meal in the delightfully
informal surroundings of the Mouse Bar where meals
range from avocado pear and smoked bacon salad to Thai
chicken curry with aromatic spices. Excellent choice of real
ales, decent wines and coffee, heated rear terrace for
summer dining, and comfortable courtyard bedrooms.
OPEN: 11-11. **BAR MEALS:** L served all week. D served all
week 12-2.30 6.30-10.30. Av main course £7.95.
BREWERY/COMPANY: Free House.
PRINCIPAL BEERS: Hook Norton, Wadsworth 6X, Courage
Best Bitter, Smiles Best Bitter. **FACILITIES:** Children welcome
Garden: Food served outside Dogs allowed Water.
NOTES: Parking 100. **ROOMS:** 9 bedrooms 9 en suite s£40
d£55

CRANHAM   Map 03 SO81

The Black Horse Inn
GL4 8HP ☎ 01452 812217
Dir: *A46 towards Stroud, follow signs for Cranham*
Situated in a small village surrounded by woodland and
commons, a mile from the Cotswold Way and Prinknash
Abbey, this is a traditional inn with two open fires, a stone-
tiled floor and two dining rooms upstairs.

On the menu you may find beef and Guinness pie, toad-in-
the-hole, chicken italienne or Mediterranean cod fishcakes. A
wide range of fresh fish is also served.
OPEN: 11.30-2.30 (Sun 12-3, 7-10.30) 6.30-11. Closed 25 Dec.
BAR MEALS: L served all week. D served Mon-Sat 12-2 6.45-9.
Av main course £7. **RESTAURANT:** L served all week. D served
Mon-Sat . **BREWERY/COMPANY:** Free House.
PRINCIPAL BEERS: Wickwar Brand Oak, Hook Norton, Marstons
Pedigree, Flowers Original. **FACILITIES:** Children welcome
Garden: outdoor eating, patio, BBQ Dogs allowed In public bar
or garden. **NOTES:** Parking 25

★   AA inspected hotel accommodation

DIDMARTON   Map 03 ST88

Pick of the Pubs

The Kings Arms ♦♦♦ 🐽 ♀
The Street GL9 1DT ☎ 01454 238245
▣ 01454 238249
e-mail: kingsarm@kingsarm.freeserve.co.uk
Dir: *M4 Junct 18 take A46 N signed Stroud, after 8m take A433
signed Didmarton 2m*

Just six miles west of Tetbury and a few minutes' drive
from Westonbirt Arboretum, the pub is situated at the
heart of the South Cotswolds on the fringe of the
Badminton Estate. An attractive 18th-century coaching inn,
standing within its own walled gardens, it offers
comfortable en suite bedrooms and three self-contained
holiday cottages in the former stable block.

The two beamed bars are a busy meeting point for
locals and tourists, with a selection of guest cask-
conditioned ales and prominent blackboards announcing
the outcome of daily local shopping.

On offer here are pork and hop sausages with red
pesto mash, salmon and dill fishcakes with citrus
mayonnaise and tortillas of stir-fried vegetables in
Szechuan sauce: desserts might be treacle tart with whisky
cream or nougat glace with raspberry coulis.

Further dining-room options include venison carpaccio
marinated in Madeira and warm spinach mousse with
tomato and garlic dressing, followed by thyme-scented
pollock with mussels, shallots and lemon butter sauce and
oven-roast Barnsley chop with redcurrant and mint jus.
OPEN: 12-3 6-11 (Sun 12-3, 7-10.30). **BAR MEALS:** L
served all week. D served all week 12-1.45 7-9.45. Av main
course £5.95. **RESTAURANT:** L served all week. D served
Mon-Sat 12-1.45 7-9.45. Av 3 course à la carte £21.25.
BREWERY/COMPANY: Free House.
PRINCIPAL BEERS: Uley Bitter, John Smiths, Smiles Best.
FACILITIES: Garden: outdoor eating, patio, Cotswold stone
walls Dogs allowed. **NOTES:** Parking 28.
ROOMS: 4 bedrooms 4 en suite s£45 d£70

DURSLEY

Pickwick Inn
Lower Wick GL11 6DD ☎ 01453 810259
18th-century pub serving local produce and populated by
locals. Large garden with play area.

EBRINGTON   Map 03 SP14

Ebrington Arms NEW
Ebrington ☎ 01386 593223

An ale house since 1764, the Ebrington Arms is a delightfully unpretentious village inn boasting a wealth of exposed low beams, two stone inglenook fireplaces and traditional furnishings in the music-free bar.

Popular with the walking fraternity for locally-brewed ales and home-cooked food, notably the speciality fresh cod and chips, steak, mushroom and Guinness pie, and the hearty ploughman's lunch. Handy for Kiftsgate and Hidcote Garden:s.

OPEN: 11-2.30 (Sun12-3, 7-10.30) 6-11 (Winter 12-2.30, 7-11 Sun 8-10.30). **BAR MEALS:** L served all week. D served Mon-Sat 12-2 7-9. Av main course £5. **RESTAURANT:** L served all week. D served Mon-Sat 12-2 7-9. Av 3 course à la carte £10.
BREWERY/COMPANY: Free House.
PRINCIPAL BEERS: Hook Norton BB. **FACILITIES:** Children welcome Garden: Food served outisde Dogs allowed Water.
NOTES: Parking 12. **ROOMS:** 3 bedrooms 1 en suite s£25 d£35 No credit cards

---

THE THAMES PATH

Historically the most important river in Britain, the Thames has been used as a highway since early times. The riverbank's user-friendly terrain and level, easy-going surface enables walkers to trace the Thames from its source in Gloucestershire to the heart of London, and the 180-mile Thames Path is really the only way to appreciate the river's gentle beauty and unique, ever-changing character. The route has certainly come a long way since the 1920s when the idea of providing public access along the length of the Thames was first mooted.

Much of the trail is set against an urban backdrop but even here there are many historic buildings and famous monuments to be seen, reflecting Britain's history and tradition. Along the way there are also numerous pubs where you can relax and enjoy the tranquil scene. Close to where the infant Thames begins its journey lies the Wild Duck at Ewen, a Cotswold stone inn peacefully located on the edge of the village. Further downstream, near Buscot Weir, is the 15th-century Trout Inn, while not far from the route of the trail are the Five Alls at Filkins and the Five Bells at neighbouring Broadwell.

EWEN   Map 03 SU09

Pick of the Pubs

The Wild Duck 🏵 ★ ★ 💤 ♀
Drakes Island GL7 6BY ☎ 01285 770310
📖 01285 770924
e-mail: wduckinn@aol.com
Dir: From Cirencester take A429, at Kemble take L turn to Ewen, pub in village centre

A long-standing favourite under its present ownership, this originally Elizabethan Cotswold stone inn is steeped in character, with a wealth of old beams, oak panelling and open fires. Well-equipped bedrooms, all en suite, feature several four-poster beds and fully up-to-date facilities.

Food served throughout remains traditionally British with an occasional nod to Europe and the Orient, with vegetarian options always available. A daily board highlights snacks served throughout the day to supplement light lunches such as penne with sun-dried tomatoes, feta and garlic or grilled tuna burger stacked with Mediterranean vegetables.

More home-grown options include venison and bacon terrine with port wine dressing, rare fillet of spring lamb with honey and lavender, crispy roast duck on spring onion mash and sticky toffee pudding with chocolate sauce.

Real ales here are the tops, while an eclectic wine list offers wide variety of choice. Lovely secluded garden, friendly owners and staff and a warm welcome to all-comers - most of the time.
OPEN: 11-11 (Sun 12-10.30). **BAR MEALS:** L served all week. D served all week 12-2 7-10. Av main course £6.95. **RESTAURANT:** L served all week. D served all week 12-2 7-10. Av 3 course à la carte £20.
BREWERY/COMPANY: Free House.
PRINCIPAL BEERS: Theakston Old Peculier, Wells Bombardier, Greene King Old Speckled Hen, Smiles.
FACILITIES: Children welcome Garden: Secluded, food served outside Dogs allowed none. **NOTES:** Parking 50.
ROOMS: 11 bedrooms 11 en suite s£55 d£75

Pubs offering a good choice of seafood on the menu.

FORD
Map 03 SP02

Plough Inn ♀
GL54 5RU ☎ 01386 584215 📠 01386 584215
e-mail: Plough.ford.glos@ukonline.co.uk
Dir: *4m from Stow-on-the-Wold on the Tewkesbury road*
Long a favourite of Cotswold ramblers and lovers of the traditional English pub everywhere, the interior of the idyllic little 13th-century Plough Inn, with its flagstone floors, warming open fires, sturdy pine furnishings and lively conversation, has all the atmosphere you could wish for. Blackboards list the day's menu, the interesting choice may list home-made soups and pâtés, steak and Guinness pie, home-baked gammon and eggs, beef and mushrooms in red wine, pork tenderloin in mustard sauce and fresh Donnington trout. A notable event is the traditional spring asparagus feasts (April-June). Excellent Donnington ales and accommodation in simple en suite bedrooms.
OPEN: 11-11 (Sun 12-10.30). Closed Dec 25. **BAR MEALS:** L served all week. D served all week 12-2 6.30-9. Av main course £8.95. **PRINCIPAL BEERS:** Donnington BB & SBA.
FACILITIES: Children welcome Garden: outdoor eating, patio,.
NOTES: Parking 50. **ROOMS:** 3 bedrooms 3 en suite d£50

PUBS AT WAR
With its reputation for long opening hours and drunken behaviour, the British pub was viewed as a serious threat to the war effort during the dark days of the First World War. The Prime Minister, David Lloyd George, who in 1915 commented 'we are fighting Germany, Austria and drink, and the greatest of these foes is drink,' drastically curtailed opening hours and even considered prohibition. It was only after the war that the situation gradually improved. The storm clouds had passed and people looked optimistically to the future. 20 years later, however, in September 1939, the British pub once again faced the uncertainty of war. But instead of locking its doors and turning away custom, the traditional local became a social focal point at the heart of the community, where service men and women, air raid wardens, fire-watchers, grocers and butchers could relax and forget, albeit briefly, the terrible effects of bombs and bullets. The writer AP Herbert described the British pub during the Second World War as 'the one place where, after dark, the collective heart of the race could be seen and felt, beating resolute and strong.' Many inns were frequented by British and American airmen based nearby, and if you happen to visit the splendid 17th-century Eagle pub in Cambridge, have a look at their signatures scrawled on the pub's high red ceiling.

FOSSEBRIDGE
Map 03 SP01

Pick of the Pubs

Fossebridge Inn 🏵 ★ ★ 🍴
GL54 3JS ☎ 01285 720721 📠 01285 720793
e-mail: fossebridgeinn@compuserve.com
Dir: *From M4 J15, take A419 towards Cirencester, then take A429 towards Stow, pub approx 7m on L*

A splendid spot in the heart of the Cotswolds with grounds that run alongside the River Coln at the spot where the Fosse Way once crossed it. Recently discovered Roman settlements suggest that its history as a hostelry is much longer than first imagined, though the beamed Bridge Bar with flagstone floors and open fires is Tudor and the main hotel building looking out on the gardens is certainly Regency. Still offering sustenance to travellers, today's family-run inn is informal and relaxed without ever overlooking standards of service. Lunch specials posted on blackboards include local game and fish catches-of-the-day such as grilled mackerel with ginger and spring onion salsa and chargrilled tuna with tomato chutney. Other typical choices include roast black pudding with quails eggs and béarnaise, beer-battered cod with mushy peas and slow-roast lamb shank with rose lentils - with plainer grills and vegetarian options listed. Two- or three-course lunches have a limited choice: dinner is à la carte.
BAR MEALS: L served all week D served all week 12-2.30 6.30-9.30. **BREWERY/COMPANY:** Free House.
PRINCIPAL BEERS: Hook Norton Bitter, Bass, Wadworth 6X, Fullers London Pride. **FACILITIES:** Children welcome Garden: outdoor eating, patio Dogs allowed.
NOTES: Parking 70. **ROOMS:** 10 bedrooms 10 en suite

GLOUCESTER
Map 03 SO81

Queens Head NEW
Tewkesbury Rd, Langford GL2 9EJ ☎ 01422 301882
📠 01422 524 368
e-mail: finefoodpub@aol.com
Dir: *On the A38 Tewkesbury to Gloucester road in the village of Longford*
Situated in a village within sight of Gloucester cathedral, this 250 year-old pub restaurant is festooned with hanging baskets during the summer months. There's a flagstoned floor in the lovely old locals bar, plus two popular dining areas where booking is essential at weekends. Expect tender Longford lamb, chargrilled steaks, chicken in broccoli and Stilton sauce, seafood bouillabaisse, and vegetable and blue cheese filo parcels.
OPEN: 11-3 5.30-11. **BAR MEALS:** L served all week 12-2. Av main course £8.95. **RESTAURANT:** D served all week 6.30-9.30.
continued

Av 3 course à la carte £14. **BREWERY/COMPANY:** Free House. **PRINCIPAL BEERS:** Bass, Greene King Morland Old Seckled Hen, Wadworth 6X. **FACILITIES:** Garden: Food served outside. **NOTES:** Parking 40

GREAT BARRINGTON	Map 06 SP21

The Fox ♀

OX18 4TB ☎ 01451 844385

Few pubs in this area offer a more picturesque setting than the Fox. On warm days the delightful patio and large beer garden overlooking the River Windrush attract drinkers and alfresco diners, making it a perfect summer watering hole.

Built of mellow Cotswold stone and characterised by low ceilings and log fires, the inn offers a range of well-kept Donnington beers and a choice of food which might include beef and ale pie, sea bass, Thai curry and various home-made chillies and casseroles. **OPEN:** 11-11. **BAR MEALS:** L served all week. D served all week 12-2.30 6.30-9.30. Av main course £7.95. **RESTAURANT:** L served all week. D served all week 12-2.30 6.30-9.30. Av 3 course à la carte £13.95. **PRINCIPAL BEERS:** Donnington BB, SBA. **FACILITIES:** Children welcome Garden: Food served outside Dogs allowed. **NOTES:** Parking 60. **ROOMS:** 4 bedrooms 3 en suite s£37.50 d£55

GREAT RISSINGTON	Map 03 SP11

The Lamb Inn

GL54 2LP ☎ 01451 820388 📠 01451 820724

Dir: Between Oxford & Cheltenham off A40

Make this delightful former farmhouse your base for exploring the picturesque Cotswold countryside on foot and touring the region's famous old towns by car. Many other popular attractions lie within easy reach of this busy inn, parts of which date back 300 years.

Among the more unusual features here is part of a Wellington bomber which crashed in the garden in 1943. Home-cooked pub food might include salmon fishcakes and steak and Guinness pie. **OPEN:** 11.30-2.30 6.30-11 (evening residents only). **BAR MEALS:** L served all week. D served all week 12-2 7-9. Av main course £5.95. **RESTAURANT:** L served all week. D served all week 12-2 7-9. Av 3 course à la carte £15. **BREWERY/COMPANY:** Free House. **PRINCIPAL BEERS:** Hook Norton, John Smiths, Wychwood. **FACILITIES:** Children welcome Children's licence Garden: outdoor eating, patio, Dogs allowed. **NOTES:** Parking 15. **ROOMS:** 14 bedrooms 14 en suite s£35 d£50

GREET	Map 03 SP03

The Harvest Home ♀

Evesham Rd GL54 5BH ☎ 01242 602430

e-mail: karlisa@compuserve.com

Dir: M5 J9 take A435 towards Evesham, then B4077 & B4078 towards Winchcombe

This popular country inn was built around the same time as the famous Great Western Railway, and is only 200 yards from Winchcombe station. It is also handy for Sudeley Castle and Cheltenham. Blackboard specials include fish and vegetarian dishes. A range of snacks are available, as well as a selection of home-made puddings. **OPEN:** 11-3 6-11. **BAR MEALS:** L served all week. D served all week 12-2.30 6-9.30. Av main course £7. **RESTAURANT:** L served all week. D served all week 12-2.30 6-9.30.

continued

BREWERY/COMPANY: Whitbread. **PRINCIPAL BEERS:** Fullers London Pride, Greene King IPA, & Guest. **FACILITIES:** Children welcome Children's licence Garden: patio/terrace, BBQ, children's area Dogs allowed. **NOTES:** Parking 30

GUITING POWER	Map 03 SP02

The Hollow Bottom ♦♦♦

GL54 5UX ☎ 01451 850392 📠 01451 850392

e-mail: hollow.bottom@virgin.net

Dir: From Stow-on-the-Wold take B4068 (approx 5m) past golf course, 2nd R signed Guitings, at T-junc, R again,next left signed Guiting Power

An 18th-century building constructed of Cotswold stone, the pub has a horse racing theme and is frequented by racing personalities. The same menu is available in the bar and restaurant, and offers filled baguettes, chicken and mushroom pie, steaks, fresh fish, pasta and Sunday roasts. **OPEN:** 11-11. **BAR MEALS:** L served all week. D served all week 12-2 7-9. Av main course £8.95. **RESTAURANT:** L served all week. D served all week 12-2 7-9. Av 3 course à la carte £20. **BREWERY/COMPANY:** Free House. **PRINCIPAL BEERS:** Hook Norton Bitter, Bass. **FACILITIES:** Children welcome Garden: outdoor eating. **NOTES:** Parking 10. **ROOMS:** 3 bedrooms 2 en suite s£25 d£50 1 family room

HINTON	Map 03 ST77

The Bull Inn

SN14 8HG ☎ 0117 9372332 📠 0117 937 2332

Dir: From M4 Junc 18, A46 to Bath for 1m then R, 1m down hill, Bull on R

15th-century farmhouse off the old London to Bath road and converted to an inn about 100 years ago. Traditional pub

continued

atmosphere and the bars and non smoking area are candlelit in the evening. Food is freshly prepared on the premises, and the varied menu is offered throughout. Expect beef, ale and mushroom pie, Thai green seafood curry and wild boar and apple sausages with mash.
OPEN: 11.30-3 6-11 (Sun 6.30-10.30). **BAR MEALS:** L served all week. D served all week 11.30-2 6-9.00. Av main course £7.25.
BREWERY/COMPANY: Wadworth.
PRINCIPAL BEERS: Wadworth 6X & Henrys IPA, Bass.
FACILITIES: Children welcome Garden: food served outdoors, Dogs allowed. **NOTES:** Parking 30

HYDE Map 03 SO80

Ragged Cot Inn ♀
Cirencester Rd GL6 8PE ☎ 01453 884643
☷ 01453 731166
e-mail: davidsauagk-@oasisholdings-.com
Dir: *From M5 take A429 for Cirencester, Hyde 2m after Stroud on R*
17th-century Cotswold free house high up on Minchinhampton Common. A perfect base for a weekend break and situated within easy reach of Stratford, Bath and Cheltenham. The bar is the focal point and is characterised by stripped stone, old beams and comfortable settles. Traditional games are played here and there is a reference library for crossword and quiz addicts. Home-cooked food using fresh produce from local suppliers and a bar menu offering a wide range of meals, from sandwiches to daily specials. Good vegetarian options.
OPEN: 11-3.00 5-11 (open all day Sat-Sun). **BAR MEALS:** L served all week. D served all week 12-2 6.30-9. Av main course £6. **RESTAURANT:** L served all week. D served all week 12 6.30. Av 3 course à la carte £12. **BREWERY/COMPANY:** Free House. **PRINCIPAL BEERS:** Bass, Theakston Best, Uley Old Spot, Badger Tanglefoot. **FACILITIES:** Children welcome Garden: Food served outside Dogs allowed manager's discretion. **NOTES:** Parking 55. **ROOMS:** 10 bedrooms 10 en suite s£40 d£60 FR£60-£75

LECHLADE Map 04 SU29

The Five Alls
Filkins GL7 3JQ ☎ 01367 860306 ☷ 01367 860776
Dir: *A40 exit Burford, Filkins 4m, A361 to Lechlade*

This 17th-century inn is set in a peaceful Cotswold village close to Lechlade and the River Thames. The daily-changing blackboard menu lists some innovative pub food. Typical choices include pan-fried scallops with tarragon risotto and roast pepper salsa, caramelised sea bass with wilted spinach, pancetta and chilli dressing, and duck with ginger and coriander sauce. Sunday lunch; gourmet evenings.
OPEN: 11-2.30 6-11.30. **BAR MEALS:** L served all week. D served all week 11.30-2 7-9.30. Av main course £5.95.

continued

BREWERY/COMPANY: Free House. **PRINCIPAL BEERS:** Bass, Hook Norton, Wadworth 6X. **FACILITIES:** Children welcome Garden: patio/ outdoor eating Dogs allowed.
NOTES: Parking 100. **ROOMS:** 6 bedrooms 6 en suite s£38.50 d£50

The Five Bells ♦♦♦
Broadwell GL7 3QS ☎ 01367 860076
Dir: *A351 from Lechlade to Burford, after 2m R to Kencot Broadwell, then R after 200m, then R at crossrds*

Attractive 16th-century Cotswold stone inn overlooking the manor and parish church. The bars are full of character with beams and flagstones, and the conservatory leads to a pretty garden. An extensive choice of dishes includes salmon and prawn gratin, pheasant in red wine, and steak and kidney pie. Accommodation comes in the shape of five luxury chalets.
OPEN: 11.30-2.30 (Sun 12-3, 7-10.30) 6.30-11 (Winter 7-11). Closed 25 & 26 Dec, closed Mon except BHs. **BAR MEALS:** L served Tue-Sun. D served Tue-Sat 12-1.45 7-9. **RESTAURANT:** L served Tue-Sun. D served Tue-Sat 12-1.45 7-9. Av 3 course à la carte £12. Av 4 course fixed price £12.95. **BREWERY/ COMPANY:** Free House. **PRINCIPAL BEERS:** Wadworth 6X, Archers Village. **FACILITIES:** Children welcome Garden: outdoor eating Dogs allowed In public bar. **NOTES:** Parking 30. **ROOMS:** 5 bedrooms 5 en suite s£50 d£50

The Trout Inn ♀
St Johns Bridge GL7 3HA ☎ 01367 252313
Dir: *From A40 take A361 then A417. From M4 to Lechlade then A417 to Trout*
Stone-built former almshouse, dating from around 1220, located by the weir pool at the first lock on the River Thames. The inn has ancient fishing rights and a slipway for small boats. Local trout appears on the extensive menus and among the daily specials. The latter offers dishes such as orange tilapia with grapes, pork cobbler, and mushrooms in Marsala. Live jazz twice a week.

LITTLE WASHBOURNE Map 03 S093

Hobnail's Inn ♀ NEW
GL20 8NQ ☎ 01242 620237 ☷ 01242 620458
e-mail: finefoodpub@aol.com
Dir: *From J9 of the M5 take A46 towards Evesham then B4077 to Stow on Wold. Hobnails is1 1/2 M on the L*
15th century exposed beams, a log fire and various other character features complement this charming old inn which, until recently, was owned by the same family for about 250 years. Well-known in the area, the pub is within easy reach of the region's many attractions, including the scenic Cotswolds, Beckford Silk Mill and Sudeley Castle. Food ranges from filled

continued

England

baps to marinated lamb, beef cooked in beer and herbs with creamed horseradish potato, and scampi.
OPEN: 11-3 6-11 (May-Sept 11-11). **BAR MEALS:** L served all week. D served all week 11-2. Av main course £6.25.
RESTAURANT: D served all week 6.30-9.30. Av 3 course à la carte £12. **BREWERY/COMPANY:** Free House.
PRINCIPAL BEERS: Wadworth 6X, Fullers London Pride.
FACILITIES: Garden: Food served outside. **NOTES:** Parking 80

LOWER APPERLEY   Map 03 S082

The Farmers Arms
Ledbury Rd GL19 4DR ☎ 01452 780307
Dir: On B4213 SE of Tewkesbury (off A38)
Traditional country pub in the heart of Gloucestershire, between the Cotswolds and the Malverns. Home-brewed ales.

LOWER ODDINGTON   Map 06 SP22

Pick of the Pubs

The Fox Inn ♀
GL56 0UR ☎ 01451 870555 ▤ 01451 870669
e-mail: info@foxinn.net
See Pick of the Pubs on page 193

LYDNEY   Map 03 SO60

The George Inn ♀
St Briavels GL15 6TA ☎ 01594 530228 ▤ 01594 530260
Overlooking the moody 12th-century castle ruin, once a hunting lodge used by King John, this inn stands in a quiet village above the Wye Valley close to the Forest of Dean. The 16th-century inn houses interlinked dining areas where local produce features on grills and specials menus: traditional Sunday lunch.

OPEN: 11-2.30 6.30-11. **BAR MEALS:** L served all week. D served all week 11-2.30 6.30-9.30. **RESTAURANT:** 6.30-9.30. **BREWERY/COMPANY:** Free House.
PRINCIPAL BEERS: Marston's Pedigree, Bass, RCH Pitchfork.
FACILITIES: Children welcome Garden: Food served outside Dogs allowed. **NOTES:** Parking 20. **ROOMS:** 4 bedrooms 4 en suite s£35 d£45

♀   Pubs offering six or more wines by the glass

The Wool Business

The trade in wool and cloth, which was the backbone of England's economy all through the Middle Ages and on into modern times, has left its mark behind it in such names as the Woolpack, the Ram, the Lamb (sometimes religious), the Shears, the Weavers Arms and the Fleece, often with sign of a dangling ram or sheep. The Golden Fleece is a neat reference to both the wealth derived from the wool business and the classical legend of Jason and the Argonauts.

MARSHFIELD   Map 03 ST77

The Catherine Wheel NEW
High St ☎ 01225 892220
Old-style country pub, with a friendly staff and broad spectrum clientele including plenty of locals. Home-cooked food features a fish of the day and vegetarian options like mushroom Stroganoff and vegetable and bean curry. Typical dishes are pork apricot tenderloin, Thai green curry, steaks, and chicken strips with mushrooms.
OPEN: 11-3 6-11. **BAR MEALS:** L served Tue-Sun. D served Mon-Sat 12-2 7-10. Av main course £9.95. **RESTAURANT:** L served Tue-Sun. D served Mon-Sat 12-2 7-10. Av 3 course à la carte £17. **BREWERY/COMPANY:** Free House.
PRINCIPAL BEERS: Wadworth 6X, Bass, Courage Best, John Smiths. **FACILITIES:** Children welcome Garden: Court Yard Dogs allowed. **NOTES:** Parking 10. **ROOMS:** 3 bedrooms 3 en suite s£33.50 d£55

MEYSEY HAMPTON   Map 03 SP10

The Masons Arms ♦♦♦
28 High St GL7 5JT ☎ 01285 850164 ▤ 01285 850164
e-mail: jane@themasonsarms.freeserve.co.uk
Dir: A417 from Cirencester toward Fairford, after 6m R into village, pub on R by village green
17th-century stone building situated on the southern edge of the Cotswolds. Ideal base for touring this beautiful area. Good, home-cooked food is served in the bar and separate restaurant. Varied menus and daily specials offer tomato and broccoli pasta bake, The Masons mixed grill, salmon steak with citrus fruits on a bed of spinach, jumbo fish and chips, and a variety of baguettes, salads, platters and jacket potatoes. Comfortable bedrooms.
OPEN: 11.30-2.45 6-11. **BAR MEALS:** L served all week. D served Mon-Sat 12-2 7-9.30. Av main course £6.90.
RESTAURANT: L served all week. D served Mon-Sat 12-2 7-9.30. **BREWERY/COMPANY:** Free House. **PRINCIPAL BEERS:** Bass, Hook Norton Best. **FACILITIES:** Garden: Food served outside Dogs allowed Water, £5 for over night. **ROOMS:** 9 bedrooms 9 en suite s£40 d£58 FR£68-£108

OPEN: 12-3 6.30-11 (Sun 12-3 7-10.30). Closed 25 Dec & 1 Jan.
BAR MEALS: L served all week. D served all week 12-2 7-10. Av main course £8.50
RESTAURANT: L served all week. D served all week 12-2 7-10. Av 3 course a la carte £16.50. .
BREWERY/COMPANY: Free House.
PRINCIPAL BEERS: Hook Norton Best, Shepherd Neame Spitfire, Badger Tanglefoot, Ash Vine Challenger.
FACILITIES: Children welcome. Garden: terrace outdoor eating.
NOTES: Parking 14.
ROOMS: 3 bedrooms 3 en suite d£58-£85.

The Fox Inn

GL56 0UR
☎ 01451 870555 📠 01451 870669
e-mail; info@foxinn.net
Dir: A436 from Stow-on-the-Wold then R to Lower Oddington

In a totally unspoilt Cotswold village - a rarity itself - the Fox displays a rare interest in all things good; food, wines, ales, décor and engaging company. Since Kirk and Sally Ritchie (ex Lygon Arms, Broadway), arrived in Spring 2000, subtle improvements have lifted this inn to an even higher plane.

Behind the creeper-clad, 16th-century, mellow Cotswold stone façade lies a first-class interior that has been fitted out with style and flair. Expect polished slate floors, rustic pine tables topped with candles and fresh flowers, rag-washed walls adorned with tasteful prints, classical music, daily papers and a blazing winter log fire in the convivial bar. A wine-related dining room is full of imbibers' curios. Well worth the short drive from nearby Stow-on-the-Wold or Chipping Campden.

Food asserts itself in imaginative and colourful dishes, the modern menu and daily specials offering the likes of goat's cheese, tomato and red pepper tart, shoulder of lamb with sage, garlic and cider sauce, pan-fried calves' liver with parsnip mash, port and peppercorns, and confit of duck with onion and date marmalade. Speciality fresh fish dishes may include roast sea bass with citrus fruits and olive oil. For pudding try the treacle and orange tart or mixed berry parfait. Hearty french bread sandwiches (smoked chicken, rocket and tomato) are available weekday lunchtimes. Traditional Sunday roast. Wash an enjoyable meal down with a pint of local Hook Norton ale or a decent wine from the excellent, well-chosen list.

The splendid, immaculately kept walled cottage garden, equipped with upmarket furnishings and heat lamps, is the perfect spot for civilised summer alfresco dining. A peaceful night's sleep is assured in one of the three en suite bedrooms, each kitted out with tasteful fabrics and antiques.

193

England

MINCHINHAMPTON
Map 03 SO80

The Old Lodge Inn
Minchinhampton Common GL6 9AQ ☎ 01453 832047
Former 16th-century hunting lodge set in the middle of a 600
acre common. Pleasing rural outlook from pine-furnished
rooms, good real ales and an imaginative choice of food. From
sandwiches and jacket potatoes, the menu may also feature
lamb and vegetable broth, stuffed saddle of lamb with port
and redcurrant gravy, and beef ragout.
OPEN: 12-3 6.30-11 (Closed Sun night). **BAR MEALS:** L served
Tue-Sun. D served Tue-Sun 12-2 7-9.30. Av main course £7.95.
BREWERY/COMPANY: Free House.
PRINCIPAL BEERS: Smiles, Youngs. **FACILITIES:** Children
welcome Garden: Dogs allowed

MISERDEN
Map 03 SO90

The Carpenters Arms ♀
GL6 7JA ☎ 01285 821283
e-mail: Bleninns@clara.net
*Dir: Leave A417 at Birdlip, take B4010 toward Stroud, after 3m
Miserden signed*

Historic inn on the Miserden Park Estate, retaining large
inglenook fireplaces and original stone floors, and taking its
name from the old carpenter's workshop at the rear. The
menu is displayed on daily changing chalkboards. Traditional
dishes include sirloin steak with seasonal vegetables, home-
made pies, and large Gloucester sausages with mash and
onion gravy.
OPEN: 11.30-2.30 (Sun 12-3, 7-10.30) 6.30-11. **BAR MEALS:** L
served all week. D served all week 12-2.30 7-9.30. Av main course
£7. **RESTAURANT:** L served all week. D served all week 12-2.30
7-9.30. Av 3 course à la carte £12.50.
BREWERY/COMPANY: Free House.
PRINCIPAL BEERS: Marston Pedigree, Fullers London Pride,
Goff's Jouster. **FACILITIES:** Children welcome Children's licence
Garden: outdoor eating, patio, Dogs allowed Water.
NOTES: Parking 22

NAILSWORTH
Map 03 ST89

The Britannia ⬡ ♀ NEW
Cossack Square GL6 0DG ☎ 01453 832501
▤ 01453 872228
Impressive17th-century former manor house occupying a
prominent position on the south side of Nailsworth's Cossack
Square. Refurbished several years ago, the interior is bright
and uncluttered with an open plan design and a blue slate
floor. Modern works of art separate the restaurant from the
bar which is heated by a large open fire. Spiral staircases and
glass-topped wells are also among the more interesting
continued

features inside. The Britannia's menu is a mix of modern
British and continental food with an extensive choice of dishes
for vegetarians.
OPEN: 11-11. Closed 25 Dec. **BAR MEALS:** L served all week.
D served all week 11-2.45 5.30-10. Av main course £10.
RESTAURANT: L served all week. D served all week 11-2.45
5.30-10. Av 3 course à la carte £18. **PRINCIPAL BEERS:** Greene
King Abbot Ale, Fullers London pride,. **FACILITIES:** Garden:
Food served outside Dogs allowed **NOTES:** Parking 100

Pick of the Pubs

Egypt Mill ⬡ ★ ★ 🛏
GL6 0AE ☎ 01453 833449 ▤ 01453 836098
This delightful hotel dates back to the 16th century, when
it started life as a corn and woollen mill. Many of the
original features are still in place, including two working
water wheels, original millstones and lifting equipment.
The name is thought to be corrupted from the gypsies
who settled beside the river in the 17th century.
A riverside patio and views over the water gardens
enhance the setting, and the hotel is ideally placed for
touring the Cotswolds, and eisiting Bath, or Cirencester
Polo Park. The bedrooms are well equipped and tastefully
furnished, and guests can relax in either the split-level
restaurant or the Mill Bistro.
The snack menu features sandwiches, baguettes, and
hot dishes like home-made meatballs, or fresh fish pasties.
Typical main courses include braised lamb shank, pancetta
wrapped chicken breast, grey mullet with tapenade sauce,
or tomato and Mozzerella tart. Finish with lemon sponge
pudding or peach crème brûlée.
OPEN: 10-3 6.30-11. **BAR MEALS:** L served all week.
D served all week 12-2 7-10. Av main course £9.
RESTAURANT: L served all week. D served all week. Av 3
course à la carte £20. **BREWERY/COMPANY:** Free House
FACILITIES: Children welcome Garden: outdoor eating,
patio. **NOTES:** Parking 100. **ROOMS:** 17 bedrooms
17 en suite s£49.50 d£75 FR£75-£95

NAUNTON

The Black Horse
GL54 3AD ☎ 01454 850565
Owned by Donnington Brewery serving a wide range of ales,
this friendly inn enjoys a typical Cotswold village setting, sunk
deep in beautiful countryside. Very popular with walkers.
Home cooked traditional meals. Bedrooms.

AA The Hotel Guide
2002

Britain's best-selling hotel
guide for all your business
and leisure needs

www.theAA.com

AA Lifestyle Guides

OPEN: 12-3 6-11. Closed Mon.
BAR MEALS: L served Tue-Sun.
D served Tue-Sun 12-3 6.30-10.30.
Av main course £9.50.
RESTAURANT: L served Tue-Sun.
D served Tue-Sun 12-3 6.30-10.30.
Av 3 course a la carte £24.50.
BREWERY/COMPANY:
Free House.
PRINCIPAL BEERS: Shepherd
Neame Spitfire, Wye Valley Butty
Bach, RCH Pitchfork.
FACILITIES: Children welcome.
Garden: patio, outdoor eating
dogs allowed.
NOTES: Parking 30.
ROOMS: 2 bedrooms 2 en suite
s£40 d£60

The Yew Tree

☼ ♀ NEW

GL18 1JS

☎ 01531 820719 ▤ 01531 820719

Dir: A40 to Ross-on-Wye, 2m past turn
for Huntley, turn R for Mayhill & Clifford
Mesne. Pass glasshouse, turn L for pub

Perched on the lip of Mayhill, some 900ft high with
magnificent views across the Malverns, Gloucester and out
towards the Brecon Beacons, this 18th-century former cider
press has been transformed in just two years from run-down
village pub to distinctive dining venue.

Under the direction of chef/patron Paul Hackett, the kitchen's entire
philosophy revolves around local produce, fresh fish from Brixham and
Plymouth and home-generated produce that includes herbs, fruit and free-range chicken and duck eggs. There are
five acres of grounds for the children to roam in and picnic tables on a patio whose hanging baskets and window
boxes are ablaze with summer colours. Both the open-plan L-shaped bar and separate dining area have been
refurbished, featuring plenty of plush banquette seating and a smart, 'yew tree' patterned carpet.

Two distinct menu types operate within, taking in traditional fish
and chips in the bar and Scottish lobster with tomato and saffron
cream in the dining-room. Simple blackboard options might include
risotto of wild forest mushrooms, leeks and white wine and a
toasted English muffin of spinach, smoked salmon and chive butter.
On the more complex fixed-price dinner menu choose from Asian
broth with noodles and coriander or chicken mousseline with sun-
dried tomato butter sauce, followed by roast turbot with port and
shallot sauce, roast venison saddle infused with bitter chocolate or
local pheasant sauced with red wine and blackcurrants. Round off
with apple crumble and lemon custard, rice pudding with kiwi plum
sauce or British farmhouse cheeses.

Real ale imbibers will find Wye Valley and Shepherd Neame
brews on handpump; wine lovers are treated to an extensive list.

195

NEWENT

Pick of the Pubs

The Yew Tree 🐑 ♟ NEW
Clifford Mesne GL18 1JS ☎ 01531 820719
See Pick of the Pubs on page 195

NEWLAND   Map 03 SO50

The Ostrich Inn ♟
GL16 8NP ☎ 01594 833260
Dir: *Follow Monmouth signs from Chepstow (A466)m Newland is signed from Redbrook*
A late 13th-century inn situated opposite the fine church known as the 'Cathedral of the Forest'. A good choice of food is offered, from griddled salmon in lime and dill sauce, or duck breast with blueberry and ginger, to goat's cheese with char-grilled aubergines, pementoes and basil and walnut dressing.
OPEN: 12-2.30 6.30-11. **BAR MEALS:** L served all week. D served all week 12-2.30 7-9.30. **RESTAURANT:** L served all week. D served all week 12-2.30 7-9.30.
BREWERY/COMPANY: Free House **FACILITIES:** Children welcome Garden: patio, outdoor eating Dogs allowed

---

NORTHLEACH   Map 03 SP11

Wheatsheaf Inn ♟ NEW
GL54 3EZ ☎ 01451 860244 📠 01451 861037
e-mail: wheatsheaf@establishment.ltd.uk
Newly refurbished period coaching inn quietly situated in the celebrated Wood Town. Eight en suite bedrooms are popular with walkers and Cotswold explorers, while good ales and wines and modern British food can be found in the civilised bar and dining areas. Typical dishes include duck and foie gras terrine with pear and apple compote, marinated venison with Savoy cabbage and pommes Anna, chicken breast stuffed with Mozzarella and pumpkin with herb risotto, and chocolate praline parfait with Bailey's sauce.
OPEN: 12-3 6-11. **BAR MEALS:** L served all week. D served all week 12-2.30 7-10. Av main course £9. **RESTAURANT:** L served all week. D served all week 12-2.30 7-10. Av 3 course à la carte £18. **BREWERY/COMPANY:** Free House.
PRINCIPAL BEERS: Wadsworth 6X, Fullers London Pride, Hook Norton. **FACILITIES:** Garden: Food served outside.
NOTES: Parking 15. **ROOMS:** 8 bedrooms 8 en suite s£45 d£45

OAKRIDGE   Map 03 SO90

The Butcher's Arms
GL6 7NZ ☎ 01285 760371
Dir: *From Stroud take A419 turn L for Eastcombe. Then follow signs for Bisley. Just before Bisley turn R to Oakridge*
Traditional Cotswold country pub with stone walls, beams and log fires in the renowned Golden Valley. Once a slaughterhouse and butchers shop. A full and varied restaurant menu offers steak, fish and chicken dishes, while the bar menu ranges from ploughman's lunches to home-cooked daily specials.
OPEN: 11-3 6-11. Closed 25-26 Dec, 1 Jan. **BAR MEALS:** L served all week. D served Mon-Sat 12-2 6.30-9.30. Av main course £5. **RESTAURANT:** L served Sun. D served Wed-Sat 12-3 7.30-9.30. Av 3 course à la carte £16.50. **BREWERY/COMPANY:** Free House. **PRINCIPAL BEERS:** Greene King Abbot Ale, Berkely Brewery Old Friend, Tetleys, Wickwar Bob. **FACILITIES:** Children welcome Garden: tubs and hanging baskets Dogs allowed.
NOTES: Parking 50

OLDBURY-ON-SEVERN   Map 03 ST69

The Anchor Inn ♟
Church Rd BS35 1QA ☎ 01454 413331
Dir: *From N A38 towards Bristol, 1.5m then R, village signed. From S A38 through Thornbury*
Traditional stone-built 17th-century pub on an old mill site near the River Severn. Renowned for its summer gardens and one of the largest boules areas in the region, with more than 100 players in league teams. Original paintings, window seats and open fires create a welcoming atmosphere inside. Food is traditional with a continental flavour, using fresh produce where possible. Typical dishes might include seafood pancake, pork and garlic sausages and lamb cooked in red wine with aubergine and onions. Only real ales are served and there is a choice of over 75 malt whiskies.
OPEN: 11.30-2.30 6.30-11 (Sat 11.30-11, Sun 12-10.30). Closed Dec 25. **BAR MEALS:** L served all week. D served all week 11.30-2.30 6.30-9.30. Av main course £6.45. **RESTAURANT:** L served all week. D served all week 11.30-2.30 6.30-9.30. Av 3 course à la carte £11. **BREWERY/COMPANY:** Free House.
PRINCIPAL BEERS: Bass, Theakston Best & Old Peculier, Butcombe Best. **FACILITIES:** Children welcome Garden: Beer garden, outdoor eating, patio Dogs allowed. **NOTES:** Parking 15

PAINSWICK   Map 03 SO80

The Falcon Inn 🐑 ♟
New St GL6 6UN ☎ 01452 814222 📠 01452 813377
e-mail: bleninns@clara.net
Dir: *On A46 in centre of Painswick*
Handsome coaching inn standing in a conservation village right on the Cotswold Way. Walkers are welcome, and a special drying room is provided. The inn has a colourful history and the world's oldest bowling green is to be found in the gardens. Interesting dishes include pork roulade with apricot stuffing, and chargrilled chicken supreme marinated in lime.

OPEN: 11-4 (Sun 12-4, 6-10.30) 5.30-11. **BAR MEALS:** L served all week. D served all week 12.30-2.30 7-9.30. Av main course £7.50. **RESTAURANT:** L served all week. D served all week 12-2.30 7-9.30. Av 3 course à la carte £15.50.
BREWERY/COMPANY: Free House.
PRINCIPAL BEERS: Hook Norton Best, Greene King Abbot Ale, Wadsworth 6X, Boddingtons. **FACILITIES:** Children welcome Children's licence Garden: Beer garden, outdoor eating, Dogs allowed manager's discretion only. **NOTES:** Parking 35.
ROOMS: 12 bedrooms 12 en suite s£39.50 d£59 FRE77.50

England

REDMARLEY D'ABITOT   Map 03 SO73

Rose & Crown 🍴
Playley Green GL19 3NB ☎ 01531 650234
Dir: on the A417 Gloucester to Ledbury, 1M from exit 2 of the M50
The pub, which dates from around 1770, was formerly part of
the Beauchamp Estate, and in the dining room tenants once
assembled to pay their annual rent. After WWI Lord
Beauchamp gave the pub to his best man and so it passed into
private hands. Seasonal menus offer well-sourced fresh fish
and prime Herefordshire beefsteaks.
OPEN: 11-2.30 6-11 (Sun 12-3, 7-10.30). Closed Dec 25.
BAR MEALS: L served all week. D served all week 12-2 6.30-9. Av
main course £6.95. **RESTAURANT:** L served All. D served All12-2
6.30-9. Av 3 course à la carte £15.
BREWERY/COMPANY: Pubmaster.
PRINCIPAL BEERS: Flowers Original, Youngs Special, Ruddles
County, Wadworth 6X. **FACILITIES:** Children welcome Garden:
outdoor eating, patio, Dogs allowed Water. **NOTES:** Parking 50
See Pub Walk on page 179

SHEEPSCOMBE   Map 03 SO81

The Butchers Arms 🍴 ♟
GL6 7RH ☎ 01452 812113 📠 01452 814358
e-mail: bleninns@clara.net
Dir: 1.5m south of A46 (Cheltenham to Stroud road), N of Painswick

The Butchers Arms, dating from about 1670, is in the Royal
Deer Park and offers marvellous views from its hillside location.
Deer were butchered and hung on the premises - hence the
name - and the famous carved sign depicts a butcher supping
ale with a pig tied to his leg. Favourite dishes include Katie's
salmon and haddock fishcakes, home-made steak and Stilton
pie, and venison medallions with chasseur sauce.
OPEN: 11.30-2.30 (Sun 12-3, 7-10.30) 6-11.30. **BAR MEALS:** L
served all week. D served all week 12-2.30 7-9.30. Av main course
£6.75. **RESTAURANT:** L served all week. D served all week
12-2.30 7-9.30. Av 3 course à la carte £13.50.
BREWERY/COMPANY: Free House.
PRINCIPAL BEERS: Hook Norton Best & Old Hooky, Timothy
Taylor Landlord, Wychwood Hobgoblin. **FACILITIES:** Children
welcome Children's licence Garden: outdoor eating, patio,
Dogs allowed in garden and on terrace only, Water.
NOTES: Parking 16

SIDDINGTON   Map 03 SU09

The Greyhound
Ashton Rd GL7 6HR ☎ 01285 653573 📠 01285 650054
*Dir: A419 from Swindon, turn at sign for industrial estate, L at main
rdbt, follow Siddington signs, pub at far end of village on R*
Village pub, formally a coach house, built of Cotswold stone
with flagstone floors inside. Friendly, relaxed atmosphere.

SOUTHROP   Map 03 SP10

The Swan 🍴
GL7 3NU ☎ 01367 850205 📠 01367 850555
Dir: Off A361 between Lechlade and Burford
Creeper-clad Cotswold pub, refurbished under new
ownership. Emphasis on good quality pub food and classic
country pub atmosphere.
Expect crab risotto with spring onions and chilli oil, and pan
fried calves' liver with mashed potato and red onion
marmalade.
OPEN: 12-3 7-11 Closed Mon. **BAR MEALS:** L served Tue-Sun.
D served Tue-Sun 12-2.30 7-9.30. Av main course £5.95.
RESTAURANT: L served Tue-Sun. D served Tue-Sun 12-2.30
7-9.30. Av 3 course à la carte £19. **BREWERY/COMPANY:** Free
House. **PRINCIPAL BEERS:** Hook Norton, Greene King IPA,
guest ale. **FACILITIES:** Children welcome Dogs allowed

STONEHOUSE

The George Inn ♦♦♦
Bath Rd, Frocester GL10 3TQ ☎ 01453 822302
📠 01453 791612
e-mail: enquiries@georgeinn.fsnet.co.uk
Since 1994 The George has been run by a group of
enterprising villagers, determined to keep local traditions alive.
It is a lively and welcoming inn with log fires, real ales and
home cooked food using local produce.
There is a popular choice of soups, steaks, curries, pies and
puddings, with specials such as beef, venison and pheasant
stew, stuffed mushrooms, and salmon steak in raspberry
sauce.
OPEN: 11.30-11 (Sun 12-10.30). **BAR MEALS:** L served all week.
D served Mon-Sat 12-2 6.30-9.30. Av main course £6.
RESTAURANT: L served all week. D served Mon-Sat 12-2
6.30-9.30. **BREWERY/COMPANY:** Enterprise Inns.
PRINCIPAL BEERS: Wadworth 6X, Ruddles County, John Smiths.
FACILITIES: Children welcome Garden: outdoor eating..
NOTES: Parking 25. **ROOMS:** 8 bedrooms 3 en suite

STOW-ON-THE-WOLD   Map 03 SP12

Coach and Horses
Ganborough GL56 0QZ ☎ 01451 830208
Dir: On A424 2.5m from Stow-on-the-Wold
Built of Cotswold stone and set beside an old coach road, this
250-year-old inn boasts a welcoming bar with beams,
flagstones and an open fire. Well-kept Donnington ales.

England

Pick of the Pubs

The Eagle and Child 🐾 ♀ NEW
The Royalist Hotel, Digbeth St GL54 1BW
☎ 01451 830670 ▤ 01451 870048
e-mail: info@theroyalisthotel.co.uk
Dir: *From the A40 take the A429 towards Stow on the Wood turn into town and we are situated by the green on the L handside*
In the Spring of 2000 Australian-born chef Alan Thompson sold his successful 3-rosette restaurant in London (755) and invested heavily in refurbishing the Grade II listed Royalist Hotel in the heart of historic Stow. Now this beautiful Cotswold stone hostelry, which dates back to 947AD, has12 bedrooms, a stylish restaurant and, next door, a cracking good pub - the Eagle and Child. With its stone walls, polished flagstone floor, rustic wooden furnishings and airy rear conservatory, it is a relaxing venue in which to sample the local Donnington Brewery ales and some 'jolly good pub food' that arrives from the hotel kitchen. So, expect a basket of home-made bread to precede crab, spring onion and salmon sausage with aïoli or warm chorizo and shallot tart with Parmesan shavings. Modern makeovers are given to traditional dishes - local sausages with sage, onion gravy and mash - with more adventurous options including seared scallops with saffron risotto and pesto dressing and Thai sea bass with spicy Puy lentils and bok choi. Good puddings.
OPEN: 11-11 (Winter open at 12). **BAR MEALS:** L served all week. D served all week 12 6.30. Av main course £7.95.
RESTAURANT: L served all week. D served all week 12 6.30. Av 3 course à la carte £14. **BREWERY/COMPANY:** Free House. **PRINCIPAL BEERS:** Hook Norton, Greene King Abbot Ale,. **FACILITIES:** Children welcome Garden: Food served outside Dogs allowed. **NOTES:** Parking 10.
ROOMS: 10 bedrooms 10 en suite s£60 d£130

Pick of the Pubs

Bear of Rodborough Hotel ★ ★ ★ ♀
Rodborough Common GL5 5DE ☎ 01453 878522
▤ 01453 872523
Dir: *From M5 J13 follow signs for Stonehouse then Rodborough*
300-year-old imposing former coaching inn situated high above Stroud in acres of National Trust parkland, with magnificent Cotswolds views. Minchinhampton and Rodborough Commons comprise open grassland and woodland which form a steep-sided plateau particularly important for wild flowers.
The hotel is worth seeking out for the comfortable accommodation, open log fires, stone walls and solid wooden floors. There is certainly plenty of character here and the elegant Mulberry restaurant epitomises the inherent charm of the building.
Appetising menu uses Cotswold produce where possible, including good local cheeses. Try the home-made chicken pie, Cotswold cheese platter, local hot buttered crumpets or the fish of the day.
OPEN: 10.30am-11pm. **BAR MEALS:** L served all week. D served all week. Av main course £7.95. **RESTAURANT:** L served Sun. D served Sun. Av 3 course à la carte £21.95. Av 3 course fixed price £24.95. **BREWERY/COMPANY:** Free House. **PRINCIPAL BEERS:** Bass, Uley Bitter.
FACILITIES: Children welcome Children's licence Garden: outdoor eating, patio, BBQ Dogs allowed. **NOTES:** Parking 175. **ROOMS:** 46 bedrooms 46 en suite s£75 d£120 FR£120

From Gin Shop to Gin Palace
As the alehouses moved further up in the world in the 18th century, new drinking-houses filled the vacant space at the foot of the social ladder. These were the gin shops (or dram shops, for brandy). Gin was cheap and strong, it was adulterated with anything from turpentine to sulphuric acid, and in the slums of London and other towns the poor could get 'drunk for a penny, dead drunk for twopence' as the slogan went, in squalid cellars, hovels and back alleys. The scenes of drunkenness and degradation - vividly depicted in Hogarth's 'Gin Lane' - were so appalling that Parliament moved decisively in the 1750s to make spirits more expensive.

Following the sharp rise in beer prices at the end of the century, gin made a comeback in the industrial slums and from the 1820s on the distillers made a bid for working-class custom by opening gin palaces of ostentatious grandeur. The brewers followed this lead, hence the creation of magnificent Victorian and Edwardian pubs opulently provided with mahogany panelling, tiles and gilt, engraved mirrors and decorated glass, ornate gas lamps and richly elaborate ceilings. A few of them survive as reminders of vanished splendour.

Pick of the Pubs

Halfway Inn ◉
Box GL6 9AE ☎ 01453 832631 🖹 01453 835275
Clean, bright and trendy following its latest make-over, the inn stands on the edge of Minchinhampton Common high in the Cotswold Hills. Decor features stripped wood floors and solid tables set around a central bar, while the dining area is rather more intimate and overlooks the common through swagged picture windows. Modern informal eating is qualified by a seasonal menu backed up by blackboard specials of the day that might include chicken liver and wild mushroom tartlet, cod fishcakes with chive and tomato hollandaise and leek and mushroom crumble. Typical lunch dishes include slow-roast duck leg with bacon and orange balsamic dressing and pan-fried scallop and avocado salad, while dinner favourites include chump of lamb with fondant potato, roast monkfish tail with prosciutto in red wine and truffle oil, and wild mushroom pithivier with mustard greens and Madeira sauce. Round off perhaps with apricot bread-and-butter pudding or orange posset. There are baguettes, burgers and things for children and a landscaped garden to relax in.

OPEN: 11-11. **BAR MEALS:** L served all week. D served all week 12 7. Av main course £8.50. **RESTAURANT:** L served all week. D served all week 12 7. Av 3 course à la carte £25. **BREWERY/COMPANY:** Free House. **PRINCIPAL BEERS:** Wickwar Oak Brand Bitter, Archers Village Bitter, Bass. **FACILITIES:** Garden: outdoor eating, patio. **NOTES:** Parking 60

The Ram Inn ♀
South Woodchester GL5 5EL ☎ 01453 873329
🖹 01453 872880
Dir: A46 from Stroud to Nailsworth, R after 2m into S.Woodchester (brown tourist signs)
Atmospheric inn built of Cotswold stone with beautiful valley views from its summer patio. In winter a big log fire and a Scandinavian-style burner make for a warm welcome. Food is cooked on the premises and there is a good range of real ales - around 400 over a year. Dishes vary continuously, but could include roast pheasant, smoked haddock au gratin, and chicken jalfrezi.
OPEN: 11-11 (Sun 12-10.30). **BAR MEALS:** L served all week. D served all week 12-2.30 6.00-9.30. Av main course £6.95. **RESTAURANT:** L served all week. D served all week 12-2.30 6-9.30. Av 3 course à la carte £12.85. **BREWERY/COMPANY:** Free House. **PRINCIPAL BEERS:** Archers Best, John Smiths, Theakston Old Peculiar, Wychwood Hobgoblin. **FACILITIES:** Children welcome Garden: Patio, Outdoor eating Dogs allowed. **NOTES:** Parking 60

Pick of the Pubs

Rose & Crown Inn ♦♦♦ ♀
The Cross, Nympsfield GL10 3TU ☎ 01453 860240
🖹 01453 860900
Dir: M5 J13 off B4066 SW of Stroud

Acquired and refurbished two years ago by Red Rose Taverns, who also own two other select Cotswold inns, this 16th-century coaching inn stands in the heart of the village close to the Cotswold Way, ideal for walkers seeking well earned refreshment. Expect neat, stone-walled bars with warming log fires, evening candlelight, an informal dining atmosphere and a good range of well cooked traditional pub food.
Menu choices range from chicken liver pâté, beef and ale pie, lasagne, fish pie, chilli and rump steak with chips and fresh salad. Bedrooms are spacious and comfortable with en suite bathrooms and a good range of amenities.
OPEN: 12-11. **BAR MEALS:** L served all week. D served all week 12-9. Av main course £8. **RESTAURANT:** L served all week. D served all week 12-9 9. Av 3 course à la carte £14. **BREWERY/COMPANY:** Free House. **PRINCIPAL BEERS:** Greene King IPA, Wickwar Brand Oak Bitter, Archers Best. **FACILITIES:** Children welcome Garden: outdoor eating, pati. Dogs allowed Water Provided. **NOTES:** Parking 20. **ROOMS:** 3 bedrooms 3 en suite s£42.50 d£70 FR£99

Horse-brasses
Delightful and attractive as they are, horse-brasses are nothing like as old as is generally believed. The working horse in a harness gleaming with ornamental hanging brasses is a creature of the period since 1850. The brasses were mass-produced folk art, following the earlier precedent of the heraldic badges worn by the carriage horses of aristocratic families. Favourite symbols include the sun, the moon, the stars and such heraldic creatures as the lion, the stag, the unicorn and the eagle, as well as railway locomotives and ships.

TETBURY   Map 03 ST89

Pick of the Pubs

Gumstool Inn 🐾 ♉
Calcot Manor GL8 8YJ ☎ 01666 890391
🖥 01666 890394
e-mail: reception@calcotmanor.co.uk
Dir: In Calcot (on jct of A4135 & A46, 4m W of Tetbury)

Right in the heart of the Cotswolds Calcot Manor is a charming English farmhouse set around a flower-filled courtyard of ancient barns and stables built in the 14th century by Cistercian monks. In this setting, the Gumstool is the Manor's own pub where the chefs can exhibit their skills in a rustic style that well matches the informal surroundings.

Local real ales and an impressive selection of wines by the glass are the added draw when contemplating a comprehensive list of eating options. In addition to baked Cheddar cheese soufflé and potted shrimps with granary toast are dishes offered in 'ample' or 'generous' portions - such as devilled lambs' kidneys in pastry and Thai-spiced crab cakes with cucumber and crème fraiche.

Substantial main dishes such as Gloucestershire Old Spot pork and beer sausages and Calcot shepherds pie are supplemented by daily specials embracing perhaps warm goats' cheese and avocado salad and chargrilled liver and bacon. Round off with Old English trifle or local cheeses with celery, grapes and pickle.
OPEN: 11.30-2.30 6-11 (Sat-Sun 11.30-11). **BAR MEALS:** L served all week. D served all week 12-2 7-9.30. Av main course £9. **RESTAURANT:** L served all week. D served all week 12-2 7-9.30. Av 3 course à la carte £25.
BREWERY/COMPANY: Free House.
PRINCIPAL BEERS: Courage Directors, Courage Best,.
FACILITIES: Children welcome Children's licence Garden: outdoor eating, patio, BBQ. **NOTES:** Parking 100.
ROOMS: 28 bedrooms 28 en suite s£120 d£135 FR£175-£185

Pick of the Pubs

Trouble House Inn 🏵 🏵
Cirencester Rd GL8 8SG ☎ 01666 502206
🖥 01666 502206
Dir: On A433 between Tetbury & Cirencester
This historic Cotswold inn, set beside the A433 between Tetbury and Cirencester, is now the unlikely workplace of former City Rhodes head chef, Michael Bedford. From heading a brigade of 15 he has turned his back on London and is now solo in the kitchen at this spruced-up Wadworth pub which he runs with his wife Sarah. Low-beamed rooms with three open fires, rustic wooden furnishings and a classic pub ambience, is now the setting for Bedford's quality cooking.

Gone are the scampi, steaks and hotpots; in comes a sensibly-short, twice daily-changing blackboard menu listing the innovative dishes that are attracting affluent diners from surrounding Cotswold towns and villages. Tip-top fresh ingredients and general attention to detail are evident in dishes like crispy duck confit with white beans and lentils, braised oxtails with roast parsnips, seared salmon with creamed Savoy cabbage, and roasted skate with garlic mash and parsley butter. Starters include mushroom risotto and curried parsnip soup; for pudding try the delicious vanilla cream parfait with marinated pineapple.
OPEN: 11-3 6.30-11 (Sun 12-3, 7-10.30). Closed Dec 25.
BAR MEALS: L served all week. D served all week 12-2 7-9.30. Av main course £9.50. **RESTAURANT:** L served all week. D served all week 12-2 7-9.30. Av 3 course à la carte £18. **BREWERY/COMPANY:** Wadworth.
PRINCIPAL BEERS: Wadworth 6X & Henrys IPA.
FACILITIES: Children welcome Garden: outdoor eating, patio Dogs allowed. **NOTES:** Parking 30

TEWKESBURY   Map 03 SO83

The Fleet Inn ♉
Twyning GL20 6DG ☎ 01684 274310   🖥 01684 291612
e-mail: fleetinn@hotmail.com
Dir: 1/2M Junction 1 -M50
On the banks of the River Avon, this 15th-century pub with restaurant has lawns and patios that can seat up to 350. Fishing, boules, play area, pet's corner, bird garden, craft shop, tea room and a Japanese water garden are all to hand. The olde worlde bars and themed areas provide a wide range of dishes including jumbo cod fillet, Cajun chicken, Norwegian prawn salad, vegetarian cannelloni, traditional Sunday lunch and Atlantic tuna pasta bake.
OPEN: 11-11. **BAR MEALS:** L served all week. D served all week 12-9.30 6-9.30. Av main course £6.50. **RESTAURANT:** L served all week. D served all week 12-2.30 6.00-9.30. Av 3 course à la carte £11.50. **BREWERY/COMPANY:** Whitbread.
PRINCIPAL BEERS: Boddingtons, Greene King Abbot Ale, Bass, Fullers London Pride. **FACILITIES:** Children welcome Garden: outdoor eating,. **NOTES:** Parking 50. **ROOMS:** 3 bedrooms 3 en suite d£55 FR£69

TORMARTON   Map 03 ST77

Compass Inn ★ ★
GL9 1JB ☎ 01454 218242   🗎 01454 218741
e-mail: info@compass-inn.co.uk
Dir: From M4 take A46 towards Stroud for 100yds then R
Busy country inn well placed on the village edge, convenient
for the M4 (J18). The 18th-century building has been extended
to offer accommodation, conference facilities and a choice of
restaurants. Bar fare includes Thai curry, lasagne and roasted
venison, while the restaurant might offer rainbow trout, and
stir fry beef fillet. Clay pigeon shooting, hot-air ballooning, or
riding activities can be arranged. Bedrooms come complete
with all modern facilities.
OPEN: 7-11. Closed 25-26 Dec. **BAR MEALS:** L served all week.
D served all week 11-10. Av main course £8. **RESTAURANT:** D
served Mon-Sat 7pm-10. Av 3 course à la carte £18.
BREWERY/COMPANY: Free House. **PRINCIPAL BEERS:** Bass,
Smiles, Worthington. **FACILITIES:** Children welcome Garden:
patio/terrace, outdoor eating, BBQ. **NOTES:** Parking 200.
ROOMS: 26 bedrooms 26 en suite s£55 d£65

WINCHCOMBE   Map 03 SP02

Royal Oak
Gretton GL54 5EP ☎ 01242 602477   🗎 01242 602387
Lovely views across the Malvern Hills can be enjoyed from the
extensive gardens and conservatory at this old Cotswold inn,
complete with beamed and flagstoned bars. An unusual
attraction is the steam train at the bottom of the garden. Plenty
of live music.

WITHINGTON   Map 03 SP01

The Mill Inn ♀
GL54 4BE ☎ 01242 890204   🗎 01242 890195
Dir: 3m from the A40 between Cheltenham & Oxford
The Mill has stood in this delightful situation on the River Coln
for over 400 years. With flagstone floors, oak beams and huge
open fireplaces, little has changed over the centuries, and the
letting rooms under the eaves could tell many a story. Chicken
in a basket started here in the 1950s, and other pub favourites
include lasagne and steak and ale pie.
OPEN: 11.30-3 6.30-11 (Sun 12-3, 6.30-10.30). **BAR MEALS:** L
served all week. D served all week 12-2 6.30-9. Av main course £6.
BREWERY/COMPANY: Samuel Smith.
PRINCIPAL BEERS: Samuel Smith. **FACILITIES:** Children
welcome Garden: outdoor eating, Dogs allowed Water,
biscuits,. **NOTES:** Parking 80. **ROOMS:** 4 bedrooms 4 en suite
s£45 d£55 FR£70

WOODCHESTER   Map 03 SO80

The Old Fleece ♀ NEW
Bath Rd, Rooksmoor GL5 5NB ☎ 01453 872582
🗎 01453 872228
Dir: 2M S of Stroud on the A46
Popular 17th-century coaching inn built of Cotswold stone with
a traditional stone roof. Cosy log fires bring a welcome glow to
the inn's timeless, open-plan interior, characterised by
wooden floors, wood panelling and exposed stone. Fine food
cooked daily by the proprietor, with an extensive menu
offering modern English and continental dishes. Sample
seared scallops wrapped in smoked bacon, tournedos Rossini
continued

or filo parcels with ricotta, basil and sun-dried tomatoes. Wide-
ranging choice of starters and light meals, fish dishes and
puddings.
OPEN: 11-11. Closed 25 Dec. **BAR MEALS:** L served all week. D
served all week 11-2.45 5.30-10. Av main course £10.
RESTAURANT: L served all week. D served all week 11-2.45
5.30-10. Av 3 course à la carte £18.
BREWERY/COMPANY: Pubmaster. **PRINCIPAL BEERS:** Bass,
Greene King Abbot Ale, Boddington. **FACILITIES:** Garden: Food
served outside Dogs allowed. **NOTES:** Parking 40

The Royal Oak
Church Rd GL5 5PQ ☎ 01453 872753   🗎 01453 873150
*Dir: Take A46 south from Stroud, R at N Woodchester sign onto
Selsley Road. Church Rd on L*
At the heart of the glorious Cotswolds and situated at the start
of the popular Five Valleys Walk, it's not surprising this
welcoming 17th-century inn attracts many walkers and
tourists. The rural views are stunning and the new owners
have recently carried out major improvements to the popular
beer garden.
   A good range of local real ales, including Uley Old Spot,
CAMRA's beer of the year for 2001, and traditional home
cooking using local produce. Bar food includes cottage pie,
lasagne, local sausages and ploughman's lunches while
venison, sirloin steak and salmon feature on the restaurant
menu.
OPEN: 11-3 (Sun 12-10.30) 5.30-11 (all day Sat). Closed 1 Jan.
BAR MEALS: L served all week. D served all week 12-2.30
6.30-9.30. Av main course £4. **RESTAURANT:** L served all week.
D served all week 12-2.30 6.30-9.30. Av 3 course à la carte £25.
BREWERY/COMPANY: Free House.
PRINCIPAL BEERS: Hook Norton Best, Uley Old Spot, Archers
Best, Berkeley Old Friend. **FACILITIES:** Garden: Food served
outside Dogs allowed. **NOTES:** Parking 15

GREATER LONDON

COULSDON   Map 07 TQ25

The Fox
Coulsdon Common CR3 5QS ☎ 01883 330401
Dir: Off B2030 between Caterham & Coulsdon
Standing above Happy Valley, - a site of special scientific
interest - yet convenient for major roads into London, this
Victorian pub is in a tranquil and secluded location. Traditional
pub menu.

KESTON   Map 07 TQ46

The Crown
Leaves Green BR2 6DQ ☎ 01959 572920
Dir: A21 onto A232, then L onto A233, pub 4m
An old pub, not far from Biggin Hill, where the food ranges
from sandwiches and ploughman's to a filo basket filled with
fresh mussels and white wine, garlic and bacon sauce, or fillet
of halibut with tarragon mash and fresh broccoli.
OPEN: 11-2.30 5-11 (Sat-Sun , all week in summer 11-11).
BAR MEALS: L served all week. D served Mon-Sat 12-2 6-9. Av
main course £5.95. **RESTAURANT:** L served all week. D served
Mon-Sat 12-2 6-9. Av 3 course à la carte £15.
BREWERY/COMPANY: Shepherd Neame.
PRINCIPAL BEERS: Shepherd Neame Master Brew, Spitfire &
Best. **FACILITIES:** Garden: BBQ. **NOTES:** Parking 30

England

UXBRIDGE Map 06 TQ08

The Turning Point
Canal Cottages, Packet Boat Ln, Cowley Peachey UB8 2JS
☎ 01895 440550 ▤ 01895 422144
Dir: From M4 J4 2m N on A408
This is the point on the Grand Union Canal where horsedrawn barges were able to be turned around, and the building housed employees who repaired the barges. The waterside bar and restaurant offer pleasant surroundings for a comprehensive selection of snacks and freshly cooked meals.
OPEN: 12-11. **BAR MEALS:** L served all week. D served all week 12-9.30. Av main course £5.95. **RESTAURANT:** L served all week. D served all week 12-2.30 6.30-9.30. Av 3 course à la carte £20. Av 3 course fixed price £19.95.
BREWERY/COMPANY: Free House **FACILITIES:** Children welcome Garden: Dogs allowed. **NOTES:** Parking 60

GREATER MANCHESTER

ALTRINCHAM Map 08 SJ78

The Old Packet House ◆◆◆◆
Navigation Rd, Broadheath WA14 1LW ☎ 0161 929 1331
▤ 0161 233 0048
Standing by the Bridgewater Canal, this charming black and white traditional inn takes its name from the horse-drawn post boat that once travelled the canal to Manchester. Colourful floral displays adorn the pub and garden in summer, and make outdoor dining a pleasure. Among the dishes on offer are lamb Henry, tuna steak in dill and lemon butter, fresh salmon, and Cumberland sausage. The comfortable bedrooms come with many extras.
OPEN: 11-11. **BAR MEALS:** L served all week. D served all week 12-2.30 7-9.30. Av main course £8. **FACILITIES:** Children welcome Garden: outdoor eating. **NOTES:** Parking 10.
ROOMS: 4 bedrooms 4 en suite

ASHTON-UNDER-LYNE Map 09 SJ99

The Station
2 Warrington St OL6 6XB ☎ 0161 3306776 & 3437778
Dir: A627
Built in 1845 to serve the railway, the Station has a collection of 'railwayana'.

BAMFORD Map 09 SD81

Egerton Arms ♀
Ashworth Rd, Ashworth Valley OL11 5UP ☎ 01706 646183
▤ 01706 715343
e-mail: barry@egertonarms.co.uk
Dir: Bamford on B6222
Old-world pub, next to the ancient chapel, haunted by the ghost of a tragic woman, killed with her lover while trying to defend her from crossbow attack. Bar favourites are the pies, daily roast and fish and chips, while the restaurant may offer chateaubriand and sole with asparagus mousse.
OPEN: 12-3 (Restaurant lunch on Sun only) 5.30-11.
BAR MEALS: L served all week. D served all week 12-2.30 5.30-9. Av main course £4. **RESTAURANT:** L served Sun. D served all week 12-2.30 5.30-10.30. Av 3 course à la carte £17.
BREWERY/COMPANY: Free House.
PRINCIPAL BEERS: Theakston Old Peculier, Greene King Old Speckled Hen, Ruddles County. **FACILITIES:** Children welcome Garden: BBQ, patio, outdoor eating Dogs allowed garden only. **NOTES:** Parking 100

DELPH Map 09 SD90

Green Ash Hotel 🛏
New Tame, Denshaw Rd OL3 5TS ☎ 01457 871035
▤ 01457 871414
Dir: Just off A670 NE of Oldham
Dating back to 1800 and originally a branch of the Co-op, this stone-built country pub stands in a third of an acre garden with magnificent views in all directions. Solid oak furniture and stone fireplaces are among the character features inside. Varied and well-designed menu might offer flash-fried beef with nuts and noodles, coconut-spiced King prawns, and sirloin steak with goats' cheese galette.

OPEN: 7am-midnight (Sun 8-11). **BAR MEALS:** L served all week. D served all week 12-2 6-10. Av main course £7.
RESTAURANT: L served all week. D served all week 12-2 7-10. Av 3 course à la carte £17.50. **BREWERY/COMPANY:** Free House. **PRINCIPAL BEERS:** Black Sheep. **FACILITIES:** Garden: Food served outside. **NOTES:** Parking 37.
ROOMS: 18 bedrooms 18 en suite s£30 d£60

DIDSBURY Map 08 SJ89

The Royal Oak
729 Wilmslow Rd M20 6WF ☎ 0161 434 4788
Character town pub gutted by fire in 1995 but now fully restored. Victorian fireplaces and old theatre memorabilia. Sources suggest the pub was once run by an ex-zookeeper who trained a monkey to clear glasses in the bar. Renowned for cheese and pâté lunches, with a daily choice of about 30 cheeses.
OPEN: 11-11 (Sun 12-10.30). **BAR MEALS:** L served Mon-Fri 12-2. Av main course £3.70.
BREWERY/COMPANY: W'hampton & Dudley.
PRINCIPAL BEERS: Marstons Pedigree, Banks Bitter, Banks Original, Marstons Bitter.

J.W. Lees & Co. of Manchester
In 1828 John Lees, a retired twill and linen manufacturer, bought the premises at Middleton Junction that are now the home of one of the North West's most respected breweries. The company is still run by a Lees, Richard Lees-Jones, who is the great great grandson of the founder. Lees doesn't just produce beer, but also includes a range of wines, spirits, ciders and soft drinks. The pride of the brewery however, remains its beers, and these include John Willie's (5.0%), Malted Mayhem (4.5%), Winter Storm (4.8%), Moonraker Strong Ale (7.5%) and Greengate Pale Ale (3.2%).

THE ROEBUCK, OLDHAM
Strinesdale OL4 3RB.
Tel: 0161 624 7819
Directions: A62 from
Oldham then A672 towards
Ripponden. 1m turn R into
Turf Pit Lane, Pub 1m
*Located on the edge of
Saddleworth Moor in the
Pennines, this unpretentious
18th-century inn offers an
extensive menu of good-
value food, Marston's ales,
great views over the town.*
Open: 12-2.30 5-12.
Bar Meals: 12-2.15 5-9.30.
Children and dogs welcome.
Garden. Parking.
(see page 204 for full entry)

GREATER MANCHESTER

*Pub*WALK

The Roebuck, Oldham

An interesting walk through Strinesdale Country Park and across moorland to the monument in Bishop Park, where you can savour views over four counties - Lancashire, Yorkshire, Cheshire and Derbyshire.

Turn left on leaving the pub, then left again to walk down Green Lane for about 1/2 mile (0.8km) to reach Strinesdale Country Park. Turn half-left and follow the rough track through a small copse and then between fences beside the River Medlock. You will soon cross the river where it begins to cascade down a series of stone steps. Follow the track beside the steps until you reach the Strinesdale Centre (information & toilets). Go through the car park and leave by the gate in the top left-hand corner.

Follow the path uphill, which soon bears left to reach the one-time Waterman's Cottage on Waterworks Road. Turn right and keep to the road

as it follows the western edge of both the lower & upper lakes to a stile by a bridge over the point where the river feeds the upper lake. Cross the stile and keep to the well waymarked path as it ascends uphill and away from the stream to reach a metalled road. Cross over and walk across what can be a boggy field to a footbridge. Begin climbing again, go round a fenced right bend, just below the monument, then, in 55 yards (50m), go through a gate on your right. Follow the path straight ahead to reach the monument and viewpoint. From the monument make for the car park.

Turn right along the road and in 500 yards (457m) turn right along High Lee Lane. This becomes Two Acre Lane and remain on this lane to the road junction opposite the inn.

Distance: 3.5 miles (5.6km)
Map: OS Landranger 109
Terrain: patches of woodland, open moorland dotted with lakes & streams
Paths: field paths, broad tracks through Bishop Park, country lanes
Gradient: one short, fairly steep climb

Walk submitted by:
Jack Robinson

England

MANCHESTER
Map 08 SJ89

Dukes 92
14 Castle St, Castlefield M3 4LZ ☎ 0161 8398646
🖥 0161 834 2851
Dir: Town centre
Trendy, bustling pub by the side of Dukes Lock. Originally a stable for working horses, Dukes 92 has two function rooms, one is a venue for concerts, wedding receptions and theatre productions. Look out for celebrities from nearby Granada Studios among the varied clientele. Visit the cheese and pâté bar, sample one of the themed buffets or try something from the regular specials selection which includes curry and pasta dishes.
OPEN: 11-11 (Fri-Sat 11-12, Sun12-10.30). Closed 25-26 Dec, 1 Jan. **BAR MEALS:** L served all week. D served Mon-Fri 12-3 5-8. Av main course £4.95. **RESTAURANT:** L served all week. D served Mon-Fri 12-3 5-8. Av 3 course à la carte £12.
BREWERY/COMPANY: Free House.
PRINCIPAL BEERS: Boddingtons. **FACILITIES:** Children welcome Garden: Food served outside. **NOTES:** Parking 30

Lass O'Gowrie 🍷
36 Charles St, Chorlton-cum-Medlock M1 7DB
☎ 0161 273 6932
Not far from the BBC complex, this is a traditional pub with wooden floors, 10 constantly changing cask beers, and its own brewery. The real gas lamps add to the atmosphere. Straightforward bar menu includes lasagne, baked potatoes, chicken and bacon, chilli and steak and ale pie.
OPEN: 11-11. **BAR MEALS:** L served all week. D served all week 11-6. Av main course £3.50. **BREWERY/COMPANY:** Whitbread.
PRINCIPAL BEERS: Marstons Pedigree, Hook Norton Old Hooky. **FACILITIES:** Dogs allowed

The White Lion
43 Liverpool Rd, Castlefield M3 4NQ ☎ 0161 8327373
🖥 0161 832 9008
One of the oldest licensed premises in Manchester, adjacent to Castlefields historic Roman fort and Granada Studios.

MELLOR
Map 08 sd63

The Oddfellows Arms 🍴 🍷
73 Moor End Rd SK6 5PT ☎ 0161 449 7826
Drinkers and diners will find an equal welcome in the stone-flagged bars of this 300-year-old free house, which prides itself on quality ales and freshly-cooked food. Dishes like pasta with pesto, smoked pork cassoulet and a range of authentic curries give the menu an international flavour, whilst fish dishes include roasted sea bass and Cajun swordfish.
OPEN: 12-3 5-11 (Sun 12-3, 7-10.30). **BAR MEALS:** L served all week. D served all week 12-2 6.30-9.30. Av main course £9.
RESTAURANT: L served Sun. D served Tue-Sun 12-2 7-9.30. Av 3 course à la carte £20. **BREWERY/COMPANY:** Free House.
PRINCIPAL BEERS: Adnams Southwold, Marstons Pedigree, Flowers IPA. **FACILITIES:** Patio, food served outside Dogs allowed. **NOTES:** Parking 21

OLDHAM
Map 09 SD90

The Rams Head Inn 🍷
Denshaw OL3 5UN ☎ 01457 874802 🖥 01457 820978
e-mail: ramsheaddenshaw@btconnect.com
Dir: From M62 towards Oldham, Denshaw 2m on R
Situated 1212 feet above sea level with panoramic views of Saddleworth Moor, this historic 400-year-old inn stands by the old pack horse route from Huddersfield to Rochdale. *continued*

A deceptively modest interior is packed with fascinating memorabilia, but the fresh, exciting food is its major draw. Ubiquitous blackboards proclaim enviable choices from smoked chicken sandwiches to lobster thermidor.
OPEN: Please ring for opening times -11. Closed 25 Dec.
BAR MEALS: L served Tue-Sun. D served all week 12-2.30 6-10.
Av main course £8.95. **RESTAURANT:** L served Tue-Sun. D served all week 12-2.30 6-10. Av 3 course à la carte £20.
BREWERY/COMPANY: Free House.
PRINCIPAL BEERS: Tetley, Timothy Taylor Landlord, Golden & Best. **FACILITIES:** Children welcome. **NOTES:** Parking 30

The Roebuck Inn
Strinesdale OL4 3RB ☎ 0161 6247819 🖥 0161 624 7819
Dir: From Oldham take A62 then A672 towards Ripponden. 1m turn R at Moorside Public Hose into Turf Pit Lane. Pub 1m.
An 18th-century inn located on the edge of Saddleworth Moor in the Pennines. An upstairs room was once used for the 'laying out' of bodies - often taken from the reservoirs at Strinesdale - and the last of these, a young woman, is believed to revisit on occasion. Favourite fare includes steak and kidney pudding, roast duck with orange stuffing and Grand Marnier sauce, and fresh seafood salad.
OPEN: 12-2.30 5-12. **BAR MEALS:** L served all week. D served all week 12-2.15 5-9.30. Av main course £6. **RESTAURANT:** L served all week. D served all week 12-2.15 5-9.30. Av 3 course à la carte £16. Av 3 course fixed price £7.25. **BREWERY/COMPANY:** Free House.
PRINCIPAL BEERS: Marstons Pedigree. **FACILITIES:** Children welcome Garden: outdoor eating Dogs allowed. **NOTES:** Parking 40

See Pub Walk on page 203

Pick of the Pubs

The White Hart Inn 🅰 🅰 🍷
Stockport Rd, Lydgate OL4 4JJ ☎ 01457 872566
🖥 01457 875190
e-mail: charles@thewhitehart.co.uk
Dir: From Manchester A62 to Oldham. R onto bypass, A669 through Lees. Inn 500yds past Grotton brow of hill turn R
A 200-year-old inn restored to traditional standards high up on the rugged moors above Oldham overlooking the Pennines; as it has expanded, so the food has simply become better and better. New bedrooms have been added and dining options varied, while sheer quality and attention to the use of best available local produce shines through on the various menus. The brasserie offers 'quick dishes' such as moules marinière, deep-fried cheese soufflé and wild mushroom spring roll with spinach and pine nuts. Those with more time can sample the Saddleworth Sausage Co's varied options with crushed new season's potato or pig out on slow-roast belly pork with pak choi and tagliatelle, or broccoli and Parmesan quiche with grilled vegetables. Baked apple tart and chocolate marquise with cherry compote are typical desserts: meanwhile the cheese selection of Smoked Lancashire, Sharpham Brie. Cropwell Bishop and Mrs Appleby's Cheshire is exemplary. A newly extended restaurant adds more of the same with a welcome touch of extra class.
OPEN: 12-11 (Sun 1-10.30). **BAR MEALS:** L served all week. D served all week 12-2.30 6-9.30. Av main course £12.
RESTAURANT: L served Sun. D served Tue-Sat 1-3.30 6.30-9.30. Av 3 course à la carte £24. Av 5 course fixed price £25. **BREWERY/COMPANY:** Free House.
PRINCIPAL BEERS: Boddingtons, Flowers IPA, Wadworth 6X. **FACILITIES:** Children welcome Garden: patio, outdoor eating. **NOTES:** Parking 60. **ROOMS:** 12 bedrooms 12 en suite s£62.50 d£90 FR£90+

England

SALFORD

Mark Addy
Stanley St M3 5EJ ☎ 0161 832 4080
On the banks of the River Irwell close to Salford Quays, a former river-ferry landing stage - where Mark Addy saved 50 passengers from drowning in Victorian times. Up to 50 cheeses from eight countries and eight Belgian pâtés are served with granary bread - and soup in winter. Wine tasting notes accompany: free doggy bags.
OPEN: 11.30-11. Closed 25/26 Dec, Jan1. **BAR MEALS:** L served all week. D served all week. Av main course £3.50.
RESTAURANT: L served all week. D served all week.
BREWERY/COMPANY: Free House.
PRINCIPAL BEERS: Boddingtons, Timothy Taylor Landlord, Greene King Triumph, Shepherd Neame Spitfire.
FACILITIES: Children welcome Children's licence Garden: Riverside patio

STALYBRIDGE   Map 09 SJ99

Stalybridge Station Buffet Bar ♀
The Railway Station SK15 1RF ☎ 0161 303 0007
e-mail: esk@buffetbar.com
Unique Victorian railway station refreshment rooms dating from 1885 and including original bar fittings, open fire and conservatory. Recently extended using the old living accommodation and first class ladies waiting room. The bar hosts regular beer festivals. Expect lamb hotpot, pasta bake and curry on the bar menu.
OPEN: 11-11. Closed Dec 25. **BAR MEALS:** L served all week. D served all week. Av main course £3.
BREWERY/COMPANY: Free House.
PRINCIPAL BEERS: Boddingtons, Flowers, Wadworth 6X.
FACILITIES: Children welcome Dogs allowed Water.
NOTES: Parking 60 No credit cards

SWINTON

The New Ellesmere
East Lancs Rd M27 3AA ☎ 0161 728 2791
▤ 0161 794 8222
Under new management. Family friendly. Bedrooms. Handy for M6 and M62.

AA Bed & Breakfast
2002
Bed & Breakfast Guide
Britain's best-selling B&B guide featuring over 3500 great places to stay
www.theAA.com
AA Lifestyle Guides

HAMPSHIRE

ALRESFORD   Map 04 SU53

The Fox Inn 🍴 ♀
Bramdean SO24 0LP ☎ 01962 771363
e-mail: thefoxinn@callnet.com
400-year-old village pub situated in the beautiful Meon Valley surrounded by copper beech trees. Produce is locally sourced and a good choice of fresh fish is featured on blackboard menus written up twice a day. Options might include pan-fried wing of skate, whole sea bass with a chilli salsa, roast rack of lamb, and fillet steak in a mushroom cream sauce.
OPEN: 11-3 6-11 (Winter open at 6.30). **BAR MEALS:** L served Tue-Sat. D served Tue-Sat 12-2 7-9. Av main course £9.95.
BREWERY/COMPANY: Greene King.
PRINCIPAL BEERS: Greene King Abbot Ale, Greene King IPA,.
FACILITIES: Garden: Food served outside. **NOTES:** Parking 25

Pick of the Pubs

Globe on the Lake ♀
The Soke, Broad St SO24 9DB ☎ 01962 732294
▤ 01962 736211
e-mail: duveen-conway@supernet.com
See Pick of the Pubs on page 207

BASINGSTOKE   Map 04 SU65

Hoddington Arms
Upton Grey RG25 2RL ☎ 01256 862371 ▤ 01256 862371
e-mail: justinhoddy@lineone.net
The bars are warm and inviting at this 18th-century pub in a charming village setting by the local duck pond. Peaceful rear terrace and garden for summer alfresco drinking.

BEAUWORTH   Map 04 SU52

The Milburys
SO24 0PB ☎ 01962 771248 ▤ 01962 7771910
Dir: A272 towards Petersfield, after 6m turn R for Beauworth
Rustic hill-top pub dating from the 17th century and named after the Bronze Age Mill-barrow nearby. Noted for its massive, 250-year-old treadmill that used to draw water from the 300ft well in the bar, and for the far-reaching views across Hampshire that can be savoured from the lofty garden. Traditional food ranges from filled baguettes and jacket potatoes to lasagne, chilli, beer-battered fish and beef steak pie with rich real ale gravy.
OPEN: 11-11 (Sun 12-10.30) 6-11 (Sun 6-10.30). **BAR MEALS:** L served all week. D served all week 12-2 6.30-9.30.
BREWERY/COMPANY: Free House.
PRINCIPAL BEERS: Hampshire King Alfred & Pride of Romsey.
FACILITIES: Children welcome Garden: beer garden with seating, Dogs allowed Water. **NOTES:** Parking 60.
ROOMS: 2 bedrooms s£28.50 d£40 FR£52.50

PICK OF THE PUBS

OPEN: 11-3 6-11. (all day summer weekends). Closed 25 Dec.
BAR MEALS: L served all week. D served all week 12-2 6.30-9.30. Av main course £7.95.
RESTAURANT: L served Sun D served all week 12-2 6.30-9.30. Av 3 course a la carte £17.95.
BREWERY/COMPANY: Unique Pub Company.
PRINCIPAL BEERS: Courage Best, Wadworth 6X, Marston's Pedigree, Brakspear Bitter.
FACILITIES: Children welcome. Garden: terrace, outdoor eating, 20 acre pond & wildlife reserve. Dogs allowed in garden.
NOTES: Park in Broad Street.

Globe on the Lake

20 The Soke, Broad Street SO24 9DB
☎ 01962 732294 ▤ 01962 736211
e-mail: duveen-conway@supanet.com
Dir: Alresford is situated off A31 6m E of Winchester. Pub at bottom of Broad St

Superbly sited on the banks of a reed-fringed lake at the bottom of Alresford's Georgian main street, the 17th-century Globe boasts a delightful waterside garden, in addition to convivial bars where visitors will find log fires, good wines and an interesting choice of freshly prepared food.

Tucked away from busy Broad Street beside Alresford Pond, this popular dining pub is the perfect summer lunch venue. Sit in the peaceful lakeside garden, complete with swans and dabbling ducks, sip a glass of Chablis and order a satisfying snack from the ever-changing blackboard menus in the bar. The pleasing view can be equally enjoyed on cooler days from the neatly appointed restaurant and the enclosed rear terrace which is warmed by efficient heaters in winter. Character, terracotta-painted beamed bar with a comfortable sofa fronting a blazing winter log fire; local photographs and prints decorate the walls and four handpumps dispense well kept real ale; 17 wines available by the glass.

For a light snack you may choose home-made watercress soup, Stilton and walnut pâté, spinach and goat's cheese lasagne, beer-battered cod with chunky chips, or a decent sandwich from the blackboard list above the bar. More substantial options range from sautéed tenderloin of pork with cheese and brandy sauce, braised lamb shank with mash and onion gravy, confit of duck with cranberry sauce, fillet steak au poivre and a fair range of fresh fish and seafood - scallops with buttered spinach and rich seafood sauce, Thai fishcakes with noodles and chilli sauce, and baked spiced salmon with strawberry salsa. Finish with vanilla terrine with raspberries and blackcurrant coulis.

Please park in Broad Street as there are few spaces at the pub.

BENTLEY   Map 04 SU74

The Bull Inn 🐑
GU10 5JH ☎ 01420 22156 & 23334   📠 01420 520772
Dir: 2m out of Farnham on the A31 towards Winchester

A welcome retreat for A31 travellers, the 15th-century Bull Inn offers an interesting selection of food, especially fish and seafood, in its civilised bar. Diners may well find smoked haddock risotto, confit of duck, braised shin of beef, liver and bacon, and chargrilled steak, alongside an extensive bar menu. **OPEN:** 11-11 (Sun 12-10.30). **BAR MEALS:** L served all week. D served all week. Av main course £9.95. **RESTAURANT:** L served all week. D served all week. Av 3 course à la carte £25.
BREWERY/COMPANY: Free House.
PRINCIPAL BEERS: Courage Best, Hogs Back TEA, Youngs, Marstons Pedigree. **FACILITIES:** Children welcome Garden: patio Dogs allowed. **NOTES:** Parking 40

BENTWORTH   Map 04 SU64

The Star Inn
GU34 5RD ☎ 01420 561224
Dir: N of Alton 3 M off A339
Opposite the village green in the charming village of Bentworth, this 19th-century pub is popular with those visiting the nearby Woodland Trust. Eye-catching floral displays, regular live entertainment and midweek darts matches.

Hampshire Brewery
After spending decades between them at various major breweries Steve Winduss and Dan Thomasson now run this small brewery which was founded in 1992 and relocated to Romsey in 1997. The beers convey a flavour of medieval history, with names like King Alfred's Hampshire Bitter (3.8%), Ironside Best (4.2%) (named for Edmund II), Arthur Pendragon Strong Ale (4.8%) and 1066 (6.0%). In 1999 Hampshire Brewery relaunched Strongs Best (3.8%), a Whitbread favourite, originally brewed in Romsey at Strong & Co.

Pick of the Pubs

The Sun Inn ♀
Sun Hill GU34 5JT ☎ 01420 562338
Located down a narrow lane on the village edge, this delightful, flower-adorned 17th-century pub, originally two cottages, has three interconnecting rooms, each with open log fires, brick or boarded floors, low-beamed ceilings, and lots of old pews, settles and scrubbed pine tables. A thriving free house it offers eight real ales, including local Hogs Back TEA and Cheriton Brewhouse Pots Ale, on handpump and a traditional pub atmosphere. It is particularly cosy and inviting in the evenings when candles top the tables. Food is equally traditional; expect filled giant Yorkshire puddings, bacon, mushroom and tomato pasta salad, cheesy haddock bake, liver and bacon with creamy mash and braised steak in red wine and mushroom sauce, alongside Mediterranean lamb and venison in Guinness and pickled walnuts.
OPEN: 12-3 6-11 (Sun 12-10.30). **BAR MEALS:** L served all week. D served all week 12-2 7-9.30.
BREWERY/COMPANY: Free House.
PRINCIPAL BEERS: Cheriton Brewhouse Pots Ale, Ringwood Best & Old Thumper, Brakspear Bitter, Fullers London Pride. **FACILITIES:** Children welcome Garden: patio, outdoor eating Dogs allowed

BISHOP'S WALTHAM   Map 04 SU51

The Priory Inn
Winchester Rd SO32 1BE ☎ 01489 891313
📠 01489 896370
Dir: from M3 take Marwell Zoo turn off thru Twyford, L at Queens Head pub, follow Winchester Rd into Bishops Waltham
Traditional, friendly inn, originally known as The Railway, located in one of Hampshire's most famous villages, renowned for its ruined palace, built around 1135. Handy for Winchester and the coast. Real log fire, garden and games bar are among the features.
OPEN: 11.30-11 (Sun 12-10.30). **BAR MEALS:** L served all week. D served all week 11.30-2 5-9.30. Av main course £5.50.
RESTAURANT: 11.30-2 5.00-9.30.
BREWERY/COMPANY: Whitbread.
PRINCIPAL BEERS: Wadworth 6X, Hampshire Pride of Romsey.
FACILITIES: Children welcome Garden: outdoor eating, patio, BBQ. **NOTES:** Parking 15. **ROOMS:** 2 bedrooms 2 en suite s£20 d£40 FR£45

BOLDRE   Map 04 SZ39

The Red Lion Inn 🐑 ♀
Rope Hill SO41 8NE ☎ 01590 673177   📠 01590 676403
Dir: 0.25m E off A337, 1m N of Lymington
Dating from around 1650 and mentioned as an alehouse in the Domesday Book, this most attractive New Forest pub stands in the village centre opposite the village green. An old cart stands outside and is strewn with flowers, and the hanging baskets and troughs are a riot of colour in summer. Collections of old bottles and chamber pots and various farm implements adorn the rambling series of interconnecting beamed rooms inside. Choose from ploughman's lunches, sandwiches, salmon and prawn tagliatelle and steak and kidney pie on the main menu, or the more inventive specials list, perhaps venison pie, duck confit and sea bass with stir-fried vegetables and a honey balsamic sauce.

continued on p210

HAMPSHIRE

FLOWER POTS INN, CHERITON

SQ24 0QQ. Tel: 01962 771318
Directions: in village
(B3046), off A272 E of
Winchester

*Award-winning ales brewed
on the premises, an unspoilt
village pub atmosphere, and
honest home cooking are
among the attractions at this
traditional rural inn, built as
a farmhouse in the 1820s. En
suite bedrooms in a well
converted outbuilding.*
Open: 12-2.30 6-11. Bar
Meals: 12-2 7-9. No food Sun
eve. Dogs welcome. Garden.
Parking
(see page 212 for full entry)

*Pub***WALK**

Flower Pots Inn, Cheriton

From a traditional village local, this short rural ramble passes the site of a Civil War battle and affords lovely views across the peaceful Itchen Valley.

Turn right out of the pub, then at the main village road, cross over to pass the green and shop. Shortly, bear right over the small brick bridge close to Freeman's Yard and bear right in front of the school. Just beyond a house called 'Martyrwell', turn left along a narrow fenced path and climb to a stile. Turn right around the field edge to a stile and crossing of paths.

Proceed straight ahead along the grassy track to a crossing of routes. The fields in the shallow valley away to your right are the site of the Battle of Cheriton in 1644. Turn left downhill and keep to the track to a lane by a barn. Cross the lane and walk along the farm track. A path merges from the left, beyond which you climb to a

junction of paths. With lovely views across the Itchen Valley, turn left downhill, following the track to the B3046.

Cross straight over into the lane for Tichborne. Cross the River Itchen and follow the Wayfarers Walk left beside Cheriton Mill to a gate. Walk in front of a cottage to a stile and continue ahead parallel with the river. Cross double stiles and maintain direction through pasture to a stile by a gate.

Continue to a further stile and lane. Cross the stile opposite and bear half-right to a stile by a children's play area. Turn left along the edge of the cricket field and join a concrete path leading to a cul-de-sac. Walk to the lane and the pub lies opposite.

Distance: 3 miles (4.8km)
Map: OS Landranger
Terrain: farmland and river valley
Paths: field paths, bridleways and tracks
Gradient: undulating

*Walk submitted by:
David Hancock*

The Wayfarers Walk at Cheriton

209

OPEN: 11-11. **BAR MEALS:** L served all week. D served all week 11.30-2.30 6.30-9.30. Av main course £6.50. **RESTAURANT:** L served all week. D served all week 11.30-2.30 6.30-9.30. **BREWERY/COMPANY:** Eldridge Pope. **PRINCIPAL BEERS:** Hardy Royal Oak, Bass, Thomas Hardy Best. **FACILITIES:** Garden: Food served outside. **NOTES:** Parking 50

BROCKENHURST   Map 04 SU30

The Filly Inn ♀
Lymington Rd, Setley SO42 7UF ☎ 01590 623449
🖷 01590 623449
e-mail: pub@fillyinn.co.uk
Situated close to Roydon Wood nature reserve in the heart of the New Forest, locals believe that this picturesque 16th-century free house is haunted by the ghost of a repentant highwayman.
Wholesome, home-cooked pub fare, with blackboard specials that might include chilli, barbecued ribs, ham, egg and chips, or plaice with prawn mousse. Curry evenings are held on the last Friday of every month.
OPEN: 10-3 6-11 (Summer Open all day). **BAR MEALS:** L served All. D served All10-2.15 6.30-10. Av main course £6. **RESTAURANT:** 10-2.15 6.30-10. **BREWERY/COMPANY:** Free House. **PRINCIPAL BEERS:** Ringwood Best, Old Thumper, Fortyniner & True Glory. **FACILITIES:** Children welcome Children's licence Garden: Outdoor eating, Dogs allowed Not in bar. **NOTES:** Parking 90. **ROOMS:** 3 bedrooms 1 en suite s£40 d£40

BROOK   Map 04 SU21

Pick of the Pubs

The Bell Inn ★ ★ ★ ◉ 🐾 ♀
SO43 7HE ☎ 023 80812214 🖷 023 80813958
e-mail: bell@bramshaw.co.uk
Dir: From M27 J1 (Cadnam) take B3078 signed Brook, 0.5m on R
This handsome listed inn is part of the Bramshaw Golf Club, but also makes an ideal base for touring the New Forest and the nearby south coast. There's a cosy, friendly atmosphere, and the 18th-century hotel retains many period features. The bar has an inglenook fireplace, and the en suite bedrooms are attractive and comfortably furnished.
Bar specials might include home-made cottage pie, or medallions of pork with brandy, whilst the daily-changing restaurant menu includes grilled sardines, beef Stroganoff, supreme of chicken, and peppered salmon fillet.
OPEN: 11-11 (Sun 12-10.30). **BAR MEALS:** L served all week. D served all week 12-2.30 6.30-9.30. Av main course £7.25. **RESTAURANT:** L served all week. D served all week 12-2.00 6.30-9.30. Av 3 course à la carte £26.50. Av 0 course fixed price £26.50. **BREWERY/COMPANY:** Free House. **PRINCIPAL BEERS:** Ringwood Best, Courage Directors. **FACILITIES:** Children welcome Children's licence Garden: outdoor eating, patio. BBQ Dogs allowed except in garden. **NOTES:** Parking 60. **ROOMS:** 25 bedrooms 25 en suite s£55 d£80

BROUGHTON   Map 04 SU33

The Tally Ho!
High St SO20 8AA ☎ 01794 301280
Dir: Winchester to Stockbridge rd then A30, 1st L to Broughton
Traditional, well restored pub nestling in a pretty village close to the Test Valley and a popular refreshment stop for walkers undertaking the Clarendon Way. New licensees.

BUCKLERS HARD   Map 04 SU40

Pick of the Pubs

The Master Builders House Hotel ◉ ◉ ★ ★ ★ ♀
SO42 7XB ☎ 01590 616253 🖷 01590 616297
e-mail: res@themasterbuilders.co.uk
On the banks of the Beaulieu River in the heart of the Beaulieu Manor Estate, this former house of the master shipbuilder Henry Adams has been carefully refurbished by Jeremy Willcock and John Illsley, who also own The George at Yarmouth and the nearby East End Arms. Grassy areas in front of this fine 18th-century building run right down to the river - a delightful spot. Heavy beams, rustic furnishings and a huge inglenook characterise the Yachtsman's Bar which is very popular in summer with people visiting this unique estate village.
Good light snacks with lunchtime filled ciabatta and home-made soup; short evening menu offering fish pie, lambs' liver on mash and beef bourguignonne. Imaginative restaurant menu, smart lounges and stylish bedrooms in more upmarket hotel side of the operation.
OPEN: 11-11 (Sun 12-10.30). **BAR MEALS:** L served all week. D served all week 12-2.30 6.30-9. **RESTAURANT:** L served all week. D served all week 12-2.30 6.30-9. Av 3 course à la carte £19.60. **BREWERY/COMPANY:** Free House. **PRINCIPAL BEERS:** Courage Directors, Samuel Smith, Ringwood Best. **FACILITIES:** Children welcome Garden: Dogs allowed Water. **NOTES:** Parking 50.
ROOMS: 25 bedrooms 25 en suite s£115 d£155

BURITON   Map 04 SU71

The Five Bells 🐾 ♀
High St GU31 5RX ☎ 01730 263584 🖷 01730 263584
Dir: village signposted off A3 S of Petersfield
The South Downs Way runs through Buriton on its way to Winchester and this character 17th century village inn makes a welcome refreshment stop. In addition to its quaint beams, cosy fires and solid stone walls, the Five Bells offers two self-catering cottages located within the pub's courtyard.
An extensive menu offers lunchtime snacks and pub favourites like steak and kidney pudding, duck breast with citrus sauce, Cajun rump steak and salmon fillet with orange and basil. Game in season; home-made puddings; excellent choice of real ale.
OPEN: 11-2.30 (11-3 Fri-Sat , 12-3Sun) 5.30-11 (7-10.30 Sun). **BAR MEALS:** L served Mon-Fri. D served Mon-Sat 12-2 6-10. Av main course £7.50. **RESTAURANT:** L served Sat-Sun. D served Sun12-2 7-9.30. Av 3 course à la carte £15. **BREWERY/COMPANY:** Hall & Woodhouse. **PRINCIPAL BEERS:** Badger Best, Tanglefoot, Champion, K&B Sussex. **FACILITIES:** Children welcome Garden: patio, outdoor eating, BBQ Dogs allowed Water, biscuits. **NOTES:** Parking 12. **ROOMS:** 2 bedrooms 2 en suite s£35 d£35

England

BURLEY   Map 04 SU20

The Burley Inn 🍴 ♉
BH24 4AB ☎ 01425 403448   🖹 01425 402058
Dir: between the A31 & A35
At the centre of Burley village in the New Forest, a brand-new
conversion of an Edwardian country house into a comfortable
country inn. Typical dishes on the menu include breast of duck
in orange and cranberry, and salmon fillet with citrus herb
butter.

OPEN: 11-11 (Sun 12-10.30). **BAR MEALS:** L served all week.
D served all week 12-2 6-9. Av main course £6.
BREWERY/COMPANY: Wadworth.
PRINCIPAL BEERS: Wadworth 6X & Summersault.
FACILITIES: Children welcome Dogs allowed.
ROOMS: 9 bedrooms 9 en suite s£45 d£60

CADNAM   Map 04 SU31

The White Hart 🍴 ♉
Old Romsey Rd SO40 2NP ☎ 023 80812277
Dir: M27 J1 Just off rdbt to Lyndhurst
Smartly refurbished old coaching inn located on the edge of
the New Forest and a very convenient refreshment for
M27/A31 travellers. Rambling series of interconnecting rooms
with open fires, a comfortable mix of old and new furniture,
tiled floors and traditional decor. Food is the attraction here,
the extensive blackboard menu listing home-cooked dishes
prepared from fresh local produce, including fish and game.
Typical dishes may include lamb noisettes on garlic mash with
red wine sauce, pan-fried monkfish with Thai curry sauce, and
game casserole; good snacks like open sandwiches and pasta
dishes. Large rear garden.
OPEN: 11-3 6-11. **BAR MEALS:** L served all week. D served all
week 12-2 6-9.30. Av main course £9.25. **RESTAURANT:** L
served all week. D served all week 12-2 6-9.30. Av 3 course à la
carte £16.95. **BREWERY/COMPANY:** Whitbread.
PRINCIPAL BEERS: Wadworth 6X, Ringwood Best, Greene King
Old Speckled Hen, Courage Best. **FACILITIES:** Children welcome
Garden: Food served outside. **NOTES:** Parking 60

CHALTON   Map 04 SU71

The Red Lion 🍴 ♉
PO8 0BG ☎ 023 92592246   🖹 023 92596915
e-mail: redlionchalton@aol.com
*Dir: Just off A3 between Horndean & Petersfield. Take exit near
Queens Elizabeth Country Park*
Hampshire's oldest pub, dating back to 1147, was originally a
workshop for craftsmen building the Norman church opposite.
In addition to real ales, there's a choice of over 20 malts and
imaginative dishes from the daily menu. Expect the likes of
continued

---

mahi-mahi fillets poached in coconut milk, guinea fowl in
Calvados, and fresh sea bass with roasted macadamia nuts
and honey dressing - as well as the usual pub snacks.

OPEN: 11-3 6-11. **BAR MEALS:** L served all week. D served
All12-2 6.30-9.30. Av main course £8.95. **RESTAURANT:** L
served all week. D served Mon-Sat 12-2 6.30-9.30. Av 3 course à la
carte £8.95. **BREWERY/COMPANY:** Gales.
PRINCIPAL BEERS: Gales Butser, Winter Brew, GB & HSB.
FACILITIES: Children welcome Garden: outdoor eating Dogs
allowed Dogs welcome in public bar. **NOTES:** Parking 80

CHARTER ALLEY   Map 04 SU55

The White Hart ♉
White Hart Ln RG26 5QA ☎ 01256 850048
🖹 01256 850524
e-mail: h4howard@aol.com
*Dir: From M3 J6 take A339 towards Newbury.Take turning to
Ramsdell. Turn R at church, then 1st L into White Hart Lane*
Dating from 1815, but considerably extended, this traditional
beamed pub is where the local farrier and blacksmith once
worked. Good local reputation for its range of well-kept real
ales, and list of English country wines. On the food side, you
may find a variety of pies, steaks from the grill, seafood bake,
wild boar sausages, or chicken madras curry.
OPEN: 12-2.30 7-11. Closed Dec 25-26. **BAR MEALS:** L served
all week. D served Tue-Sun 12-2 7-9. Av main course £7.50.
RESTAURANT: L served all week. D served Tue-Sun 12-2 7-9.
Av 3 course à la carte £16. **BREWERY/COMPANY:** Free House.
PRINCIPAL BEERS: Morrells Varsity , Ringwood Fortyniner,
Harveys, Fullers London Pride. **FACILITIES:** Garden: patio,
outdoor eating. **NOTES:** Parking 30

CHERITON BREWHOUSE

Purpose-built brewery set up in 1993 by Paul
Tickner beside his unspoilt village local in the the
heart of Hampshire, the Flower Pots Inn. Now
working close to capacity, it produces the pale
brown, hoppy and well balanced Pots Ale (3.8%),
the malty Cheriton Best (4.2%), the award-
winning Diggers Gold (4.6%) and popular
seasonal beers (Village Elder (3.8%), Beltane
(4.5%), Flower Power (5.2%), Turkeys Delight
(5.9%) for the pub and the local free trade. Tours
by arrangement.

England

CHERITON
Map 04 SU52

Pick of the Pubs

The Flower Pots Inn
SO24 0QQ ☎ 01962 771318 🖹 01962 771318
Dir: A272 toward Petersfield, L onto B3046, pub 0.75m on R
Originally built as a farmhouse in the 1840s by the head gardener of nearby Avington House, this unassuming and homely brick village pub has become a popular place in which to sample award-winning ales, brewed in the micro-brewery across the car park, and simple, honest bar food. Two traditional bars are delightfully music- and electronic game-free, the rustic public bar being furnished with pine tables and benches and the cosy saloon having a relaxing sofa among other chairs; both have warming winter log fires. A short value for money menu offers home-cooked meals, including jacket potatoes with decent filling, giant baps (try the home-baked ham), hearty soups and casseroles and a bowl of delicious chilli served with garlic bread or rice. Come on a Wednesday night for an authentic Punjabi curry and wash it down with a first-rate pint of Pots Ale or Diggers Gold. Neat, pine-furnished bedrooms are housed in a well-converted outbuilding. Beer Festival August Bank Holiday.
OPEN: 12-2.30 6-11 (Sun 12-3, 7-10.30). **BAR MEALS:** L served Mon-Sun. D served Mon-Sat 12-2 7-9. Av main course £5. **BREWERY/COMPANY:** Free House.
PRINCIPAL BEERS: Cheriton Pots Ale, Best Bitter, Diggers Gold. **FACILITIES:** Garden: Dogs allowed.
NOTES: Parking 30. **ROOMS:** 5 bedrooms 5 en suite s£35 d£58 No credit cards

See Pub Walk on page 209

DAMERHAM
Map 03 SU11

The Compasses Inn ◆◆◆ 🐾 ♀
SP6 3HQ ☎ 01725 518231 🖹 01725 518880
Dir: From Fordingbridge (A338) follow signs for Sandleheath/Damerham. Or signs from B3078

Attractive 400-year-old coaching inn in a splendid village centre location next to the cricket green, with a lovely flower-filled garden - ideal for watching an innings or two with a pint on sunny summer Sunday evenings. Plenty of character and atmosphere inside, with pine-furnished bars and cottagey bedrooms. Extensive menu includes plenty of fresh fish, light snacks and main meals like beef Stroganoff and steak and mushroom pie.
OPEN: 11-3 (all day Sat, Sun 12-4, 7-10.30) 6-11. **BAR MEALS:** L served all week. D served all week 12-2.30 7-9.30. Av main course £7. **RESTAURANT:** L served all week. D served all week 12-2.30 7-9.30. Av 3 course à la carte £15. **BREWERY/COMPANY:** Free
continued

House. **PRINCIPAL BEERS:** Compasses Ale, Ringwood Best, Hop Back Summer Lightning, Wadworth 6X.
FACILITIES: Children welcome Children's licence Garden: patio area, Outdoor eating Dogs allowed By arrangement.
NOTES: Parking 30. **ROOMS:** 6 bedrooms 6 en suite s£39.50 d£69 FR£69.00-£138.00

DUMMER
Map 04 SU54

The Queen Inn
Down St RG25 2AD ☎ 01256 397367 🖹 01256 397601
Dir: M3 J7, turn into Dummer
You can dine by candlelight at this 16th-century village pub, with its low beams and huge open log fire. Everything is home made, from the soup and light bites to the famous fish and chips with beer batter, fresh sea bass, and prime steaks.

OPEN: 11-3 (Sun 12-3) 6-11 (Sun 7-10.30). **BAR MEALS:** L served all week. D served all week 12-2 6-9.30. Av main course £7.95. **RESTAURANT:** L served all week. D served all week 12-2 6-9.30. Av 3 course à la carte £17.50.
BREWERY/COMPANY: Free House. **PRINCIPAL BEERS:** Courage Best, Greene King IPA, Fullers London Pride.
FACILITIES: Children welcome Garden. **NOTES:** Parking 20

EAST END
Map 04 SZ39

Pick of the Pubs

The East End Arms 🐾
Main Rd SO41 5SY ☎ 01590 626223
Dir: From Lymington follow signs for Isle of Wight ferry. Pass ferry terminal on R & continue for 3m
Traditional New Forest pub tucked away down quiet lanes, close to Beaulieu and historic Buckler's Hard. Worth the short diversion off The Solent Way for the short, interesting range of modern, brasserie-style dishes served in the comfortably refurbished lounge bar. Oven-baked ciabatta, filled baguettes, fish pie and liver and bacon appear on the light snack menu, while the main menu could list duck and apple terrine, slow-roasted lamb shank with forest mushrooms, and pan-fried ribeye steak with roast red pepper butter and fresh-cut chips. Fish specials may include roast haddock with mussels and chorizo. Rustic Foresters Bar with open fires.
OPEN: 11.30-3 6-11 (Sun 12-9). Closed 1 Jan.
BAR MEALS: L served Tue-Sun 12-2. Av main course £6.
RESTAURANT: L served Tue-Sun. D served Tue-Sat 12-2 7-9. Av 3 course à la carte £18. **BREWERY/COMPANY:** Free House. **PRINCIPAL BEERS:** Ringwood Best & Fortyniner.
FACILITIES: Children welcome Garden: Food served outside Dogs allowed Water. **NOTES:** Parking 10

EAST MEON   Map 04 SU62

Ye Olde George Inn
Church St GU32 1NH ☎ 01730 823481 📠 01730 823759
Dir: S of A272 (Winchester/Petersfield) turning 1.5m from Petersfield on L opp church
Rambling 17th-century pub, with open fires, heavy beams and rustic artefacts, nestling close to the magnificent Norman church in this peaceful downland village. Nearby is the vast Queen Elizabeth Country Park, ideal for walking and cycling. Rack of lamb, whole grilled sole and a variety of steaks feature on the popular menu. Real ale fans will find a good choice of beers, and during the summer months cream teas with home-made scones are served.

OPEN: 11-3 (Sun 12-3, 7-10.30) 6-11. **BAR MEALS:** L served all week. D served all week 12-2 7-9. Av main course £8.
RESTAURANT: L served all week. D served all week 12-2 7-9. Av 3 course à la carte £8. **BREWERY/COMPANY:** Hall & Woodhouse. **PRINCIPAL BEERS:** Badger Best, Tanglefoot, K & B Sussex. **FACILITIES:** Children welcome Garden: outdoor eating, patio Dogs allowed Water. **NOTES:** Parking 30. **ROOMS:** 5 bedrooms 5 en suite s£27.50 d£50

EASTON   Map 04 SU53

The Chestnut Horse 🍽 🍷
SO21 1EG ☎ 01962 779257 📠 01962 779014
Dir: From M3 J9 take A33 towards Basingstoke, then B3047. Take 2nd R

The Itchen Valley is great for walking, and the Three Castles Path passes this delightful old dining pub en route to Windsor. A magnificent open fire warms the cosy bar, where the hand pulled ales include Chestnut Horse Special from the nearby Itchen Valley Brewery. The low beamed ceilings are festooned with old beer mugs and potties, whilst the intimate candlelit dining areas are divided by standing timbers. Outside, you'll find flower tubs and a couple of picnic sets on the quiet

continued

forecourt, and a small decked patio at the back. Lunchtime snacks, grilled open ciabatta sandwiches, and blackboard specials stand beside more substantial dishes like calves liver and bacon, Loch Ness chicken, baked cod rarebit, and traditional Sunday roasts.
OPEN: 11-3 5.30-11. **BAR MEALS:** L served all week. D served all week 12-2.30 6.30-9.30. Av main course £10.
RESTAURANT: L served all week. D served all week 12-2.30 6.30-9.30. Av 3 course à la carte £18.
BREWERY/COMPANY: Free House. **PRINCIPAL BEERS:** Bass, Courage Best, Chestnut Horse Special, Fullers London Pride.
FACILITIES: Children welcome Garden: Beer garden, outdoor eating Dogs allowed Water. **NOTES:** Parking 40

EAST STRATTON   Map 04 SU54

The Northbrook Arms
SO21 3DU ☎ 01962 774150
Dir: just off A33, 9m S of Basingstoke, 7m N of Winchester, follow Kings Worthy signs from M3
Formally the Plough, this refurbished 18th-century pub, at the centre of a classic estate village, was once the village shop and bakery. Idyllic setting adjoining the green and an assortment of thatched cottages. The inn's bed and breakfast accommodation makes it a handy base for visiting Winchester, Alresford and Alton and enjoying some of mid-Hampshire's loveliest walks. The varied menu may offer home-made steak and kidney pie, rump steak, sausages and mash with onion gravy, and cod deep-fried in beer batter.

OPEN: 12-3 6-11 (Sun 12-3, 7-10.30). **BAR MEALS:** L served all week. D served All 12-2 7-9. Av main course £7.95.
RESTAURANT: L served Mon-Sun. D served Mon-Sat 12-2 7-9.30. Av 3 course à la carte £14.95. **BREWERY/COMPANY:** Free House. **PRINCIPAL BEERS:** Gales HSB, Gales GB, Otter, Ringwood Best. **FACILITIES:** Garden: patio/terrace, outdoor eating Dogs allowed Water. **NOTES:** Parking 30. **ROOMS:** 4 bedrooms s£35 d£45

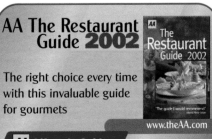

EAST TYTHERLEY   Map 04 SU22

Pick of the Pubs

Star Inn ⊛ ♦♦♦♦ 🛏 ♀
SO51 0LW ☎ 01794 340225 🖨 01794 340225
e-mail: info@starinn-uk.com
Dir: *5 M N of Romsey off A3057 take L Turn Dunbridge B3084 left turn for Awbridge & Lockerley follow Rd past Lockerly 1 M*

Brick-built former 16th-century coaching inn overlooking the village cricket ground on a quiet back lane between Salisbury and Romsey, close to the attractions of the Test Valley. Enthusiastic new owners have brought a contemporary slant to the interesting blackboard menu which hangs above the open fireplace in the modernised carpeted bar. Dine in the pine-furnished bar or at darkwood tables in the traditional restaurant. From rabbit and sage terrine with apple and prune compote, mussel soup and toasted foccacia with garlic field mushrooms and blue cheese salad for a snack or starter; the menu extends to lambs' liver, bacon and mash, tuna with smoked duck, aubergine caviar and sweet and sour vegetables, grilled sea bass on purple potato purée and citrus vinaigrette, and pan-fried beef fillet with mustard mousseline. Good puddings may include warm chocolate tart with white chocolate ice cream and British cheeses with walnut bread. Spacious bedrooms have high levels of quality and comfort.

OPEN: 11-2.30 6-11 Summer open all day. **BAR MEALS:** L served all week. D served all week 12-2.00 7-9. Av main course £6. **RESTAURANT:** L served all week. D served all week 12-2.00 7-9. Av 3 course à la carte £25. Av 3 course fixed price £15. **BREWERY/COMPANY:** Free House. **PRINCIPAL BEERS:** Gales HSB, Ringwood Best. **FACILITIES:** Children welcome Garden: Food served outside. **NOTES:** Parking 60. **ROOMS:** 3 bedrooms 3 en suite s£45 d£60

EMSWORTH   Map 04 SU70

The Sussex Brewery 🛏 ♀
36 Main Rd PO10 8AU ☎ 01243 371533 🖨 01243 379684
e-mail: sussexbrew@aol.com
Dir: *On A259 (coast road), between Havant & Chichester*
A traditional pub in every sense of the word, with Young's beers, sawdust on the floors and two open fires. It has an unassuming exterior and a warm welcome inside. The menu offers good food at realistic prices, including fresh fish and an amazing range of speciality sausages.   *continued*

OPEN: 11-11. **BAR MEALS:** L served all week. D served all week 12-2.30 7-10. Av main course £6. **RESTAURANT:** L served all week. D served all week 12-2.30 7-10. Av 3 course à la carte £12. **BREWERY/COMPANY:** Youngs. **PRINCIPAL BEERS:** Smiles Best Bitter, Youngs PA & Special, Timothy Taylor Landlord. **FACILITIES:** Children welcome Garden: Food served outside Dogs allowed Water. **NOTES:** Parking 30

EVERSLEY   Map 04 SU76

The Golden Pot ♀ NEW
Reading Rd RG27 0NB ☎ 0118 9732104
e-mail: justin.winstanley@excite.co.uk
Dir: *Between Reading and Camberley on the B3272 about 1/4m from the Eversley cricket ground*
Dating back to the 1700s and located in a famous village where 'The Water Babies' author Charles Kinglsey was once rector, this former standard local went more upmarket in the late 1990s when the pool bar was converted into a full à la carte restaurant. Strong emphasis on style, friendliness and good food cooked from fresh ingredients, as well as two bars with a connecting open fire which is always alight in winter. Live music once a week and an interesting bar and restaurant menu featuring sea bass with herbs, pork medallions with wild mushrooms, lamb shank braised in beer, and Cajun chicken salad.
OPEN: 11-3 6-11. **BAR MEALS:** L served all week. D served all week 12-2.15 6.30-9.15. Av main course £6. **RESTAURANT:** L served all week. D served all week 12-2 7-9.15. Av 3 course à la carte £20. **BREWERY/COMPANY:** Free House. **PRINCIPAL BEERS:** Ruddles Country, Wadworth 6X, Greene King Abbot Ale. **FACILITIES:** Garden: Food served outside Dogs allowed

FACCOMBE   Map 04 SU35

The Jack Russell Inn
SP11 0DS ☎ 01264 737315
Although the current building only dates back to 1982, there has been a pub on this site for more than a century, and the landlords still maintain a traditional Victorian pub atmosphere. Convenient for Pilot Hill, the highest point in Hampshire, and the towns of Hungerford and Newbury.

FORDINGBRIDGE   Map 03 SU11

The Augustus John ♀
116 Station Rd SP6 1DG ☎ 01425 652098
e-mail: peter@augustusjohn.com
Named after the renowned British painter who lived in the village (the pub was also his local), this unassuming brick building was transformed a few years into a smart dining pub with comfortable en suite accommodation - ideal base for exploring the New Forest. Of particular interest is the changing blackboard menu which may offer home-made soups, salmon and herb fishcakes, rack of lamb with redcurrant and mint, liver and bacon with mash and onion gravy and fresh Poole plaice. Good puddings and short list of good wines; 10 by the glass.
OPEN: 11.30-3.30 6-12. **BAR MEALS:** L served all week. D served all week 11.30-2 6.30-9. Av main course £7.95. **RESTAURANT:** L served all week. D served all week 11.30-2 6.30-9. Av 3 course à la carte £15. **BREWERY/COMPANY:** Eldridge Pope. **PRINCIPAL BEERS:** Hardy Country, Courage Best, John Smiths. **FACILITIES:** Children welcome Garden: outdoor eating, patio. **NOTES:** Parking 40. **ROOMS:** 8 bedrooms 8 en suite s£25 d£50 FR£75-£100

Pick of the Pubs

The Three Lions 🏵🏵🏵 ◆◆◆◆◆ ♟
Stuckton SP6 2HF ☎ 01425 652489 ▤ 01425 656144
Dir: .5m E of Fordingbridge from AA338 or B3078, signed from Q8 garage
Originally a farmhouse built in 1863 and converted into a pub in the early 1980s, the
Three Lions is an early example of the breed of fine dining pubs that are nowadays burgeoning in popularity. There is a small, intimate bar and an attractive terrace where all-comers are welcome to enjoy a bottle of wine or a pint of real ale; yet in the dining-room - warmed by a log fire on cooler days - the pub offers an internationally flavoured menu based on Mike Womersley's well-honed cooking techniques, enhancing the natural flavours and textures of finest quality ingredients grown locally by reputable suppliers.
Home-made farmhouse-style bread accompanies a crab and prawn bisque simply bursting with flavour, pink new season's lamb loin appears with rendered 'crispy bits', celeriac purée and dauphinoise potatoes, while tropical fruits and passion fruit sorbet garnish a smooth, tangy lime sorbet.
This is real food that is not sullied by over-complication - and is the better for it. Each day's menu, posted on large blackboards, is accompanied by an exemplary wine list. The three en suite bedrooms provide high levels of comfort and quality that one would expect from such a splendid and unpretentious inn.
OPEN: Closed: last 2wks Jan, 1st wk Feb. **RESTAURANT:** L served Tue-Sun. D served Tue-Sat 12-2 7-9. Av 3 course à la carte £27.50. Av 2 course fixed price £14.50.
BREWERY/COMPANY: Free House.
PRINCIPAL BEERS: Hampshire Lionheart.
FACILITIES: Children welcome Children's licence Garden: outdoor eating, patio/terrace, Dogs allowed.
NOTES: Parking 40. **ROOMS:** 3 bedrooms 3 en suite s£59 d£65

FROXFIELD GREEN Map 04 SU72

The Trooper Inn 🍴 ♟
Alton Rd GU32 1BD ☎ 01730 827293 ▤ 01730 827103
e-mail: bazziebaz@aol.com
Unpretentious roadside inn enjoying an isolated downland position west of Petersfield. A relaxing, laid-back atmosphere prevails throughout the rustic, pine-furnished interior; evening candlelight enhances the overall ambience. In addition to changing guest ales and decent wines by the glass, expect interesting home-cooked food. From lunchtime snacks like scrambled eggs and smoked salmon and fisherman's pie, freshly prepared evening dishes may include slow-roasted half-shoulder of lamb with honey and mint gravy, venison with Stilton sauce and cod with king prawns and lobster sauce. Visit on a Wednesday evening and experience excellent live jazz. Accommodation was due to come on line in June 2001.
OPEN: 12-3 6.30-12. Closed Dec 26, Jan 1. **BAR MEALS:** L served all week. D served all week 12-2 10.
BREWERY/COMPANY: Free House.
PRINCIPAL BEERS: Ringwood Best & Fortyniner, Bass, guest ales. **FACILITIES:** Children welcome Garden: Food served outside

---

HAVANT Map 04 SU70

The Royal Oak ♟
19 Langstone High St, Langstone PO9 1RY
☎ 023 92483125
Historic 16th-century pub, noted for its rustic, unspoilt interior with flagstone floors, exposed beams and open fires. Occupying an outstanding position on Langstone Harbour, there are benches at the front and a secluded rear garden for summer alfresco drinking. Bar food includes filled baguettes and jacket potatoes while the restaurant menu offers steak and ale pie and fresh fish dishes.
OPEN: 11-11 (Sun 12-10.30). **BAR MEALS:** L served all week. D served all week 12-9. Av main course £7.50. **RESTAURANT:** L served all week. D served all week 12-2.30 6-9. Av 3 course à la carte £17. **BREWERY/COMPANY:** Whitbread.
PRINCIPAL BEERS: Gales HSB, Flowers. **FACILITIES:** Children welcome Garden: patio, food served outdoors Dogs allowed Water

---

HAWKLEY

Hawkley Inn
Pococks Ln GU33 6NE ☎ 01730 827205
Unpretentious rural local tucked away down narrow lanes on the Hangers Way Path. Expect quality ale from micro-breweries, own cider and ambitious bar food.

HOLYBOURNE

White Hart ◆◆◆
GU34 4EY ☎ 01420 87654 ▤ 01420 543982
Dir: off A31 between Farnham & Winchester
Traditional village inn popular with locals and business guests. Comfortable bedrooms and good selection of bar food.

HOOK Map 04 SU75

Crooked Billet ♟
London Rd RG27 9EH ☎ 01256 762118 ▤ 01256 761011
e-mail: Richardbarwise@aol.com
Dir: From M3 J5 follow signs for A30/Hook.Pub 1m before Hook on A30, on L by river

Hook's only freehouse is a small pub with a large garden next to the River Whitewater. There's plenty to amuse the family, with a play area, ducks, fish, a barbecue, monthly quiz nights and regular meetings of the Morris Men. The straightforward bar menu is supplemented by daily specials, and options include snacks, curries, steaks, pies, smoked haddock, and lamb in rich mint gravy. *continued*

OPEN: 11.30-3 6-11. **BAR MEALS:** L served all week. D served all week 12.00-2.30 7-9.30. Av main course £6.50.
BREWERY/COMPANY: Free House.
PRINCIPAL BEERS: Courage Best & Directors, John Smith's.
FACILITIES: Children welcome Garden: Outdoor eating Dogs allowed Water. **NOTES:** Parking 60

IBSLEY   Map 03 SU10

Olde Beams Inn
Salisbury Rd BH24 3PP ☎ 01425 473387
Dir: On A338 between Ringwood & Salisbury
The cruck beam is clearly visible from the outside of this thatched, 14th-century building. In addition to the restaurant there is also a popular buffet counter. Located in the Avon Valley and handy for the New Forest.

LINWOOD   Map 03 SU10

Red Shoot Inn
Toms Ln BH24 3QT ☎ 01425 475792
Dir: From M27 take A338, take Salisbury turning and follow brown signs to the Red Shoot
Set in the heart of the New Forest, with its own micro-brewery, the bustling Red Shoot Inn offers real ale and real food in a real country pub.

LONGPARISH   Map 04 SU44

The Plough Inn
SP11 6PB ☎ 01264 720358 📠 01264 720377
Dir: Off A303 4m S of Andover
As it is only 100 yards away from the River Test this 400-year old pub is regularly visited by the local duck population. Typical menu includes scallops mornay, lobster thermidor, shoulder of lamb kleftico, wild boar sausage, and salmon hollandaise.
OPEN: 11-3.30 6-11 (11-3, 6-11 in winter). **BAR MEALS:** L served all week. D served all week 12-2.30 6.30-9.30. Av main course £5.95. **RESTAURANT:** L served all week. D served all week 12-2.30 6.30-9.30. Av 3 course à la carte £20. Av 3 course fixed price £20. **BREWERY/COMPANY:** Whitbread.
PRINCIPAL BEERS: Hampshire King Alfred, Greene King Old Speckled Hen, Wadworth 6X, Boddingtons. **FACILITIES:** Children welcome Garden: BBQ Dogs allowed. **NOTES:** Parking 60.
ROOMS: 2 bedrooms s£20 d£40

LYMINGTON   Map 04 SZ39

The Chequers Inn
Lower Woodside SO41 8AH ☎ 01590 673415
Dir: From Lymington take A337 towards New Milton. Turn L at White Hart PH

continued

Dating from about 1625, this was reputedly the salt exchange (or exchequer). A warm and friendly welcome awaits along with the open fire, antique furniture and old beams. The menu offers a good choice of traditional bar food: steaks, pork chops, burgers, and local fish straight from the boats.
OPEN: 11-3 6-11 (all day Sat-Sun). Closed 25 Dec.
BAR MEALS: L served all week. D served all week 12-2 7-10. Av main course £5. **RESTAURANT:** L served all week. D served all week 12-2 7-10. Av 3 course à la carte £12.50 10.
BREWERY/COMPANY: Enterprise Inns.
PRINCIPAL BEERS: Ringwood Best, Wadworth 6X, Bass.
FACILITIES: Children welcome Garden: Dogs allowed.
NOTES: Parking 16

The Kings Arms ◆◆◆ 🍷
St Thomas St SO41 9NB ☎ 01590 672594
Dir: Approaching Lymington from N on A337, head L onto St Thomas St. Kings Arms 50yds on R
Former coaching inn located in one of Hampshire's most attractive market towns. Charles II is reputed to have lodged here. Ideal base for visiting the New Forest and the Isle of Wight. Home made, appetising pub food offers the likes of liver and bacon, haddock and prawn pie, lasagne, creel prawns and curry among other dishes. Good choice of ploughman's lunches. Bedrooms are tastefully appointed and equipped with smart en suite facilities.
OPEN: 10.30-2.30 Sat 10.30-3 Sun 6-11 6-11. **BAR MEALS:** L served all week. D served all week 12-2 6.30-9.30. Av main course £5.95. **RESTAURANT:** L served all week. D served all week 12-2 6.30. Av 3 course à la carte £12.
BREWERY/COMPANY: Whitbread.
PRINCIPAL BEERS: Fullers London Pride, Greene King Abbot Ale, Gales HSB, Brakspear Special. **FACILITIES:** Garden: outdoor eating Dogs allowed Water. **NOTES:** Parking 8.
ROOMS: 2 bedrooms 2 en suite s£48 d£48 No credit cards

Mayflower Inn
Kings Saltern Rd SO41 3QD ☎ 01590 672160
e-mail: mayflower@fsbusiness.co.uk
Dir: A337 towards New Milton, L at rdbt by White Hart, L to Rookes Ln, R at mini-rdbt, pub 0.75m

Overlooking the Lymington River and the town's bustling yacht marina, this family-run inn is well placed for touring and exploring the Hampshire coast and the New Forest. Dine al fresco on the pub's flower-filled patio or relax over a drink by a warming log fire in winter. An ever-changing menu offers freshly cooked dishes, perhaps leek and mushroom risotto, chargrilled liver and bacon with onion gravy, smoked salmon with lemon and dill dressing, and lamb steak with mushroom and red wine sauce. *continued*

OPEN: 11-11 (Sun 12-10.30). **BAR MEALS:** L served all week. D served all week 12-2.30 6.30-9. Av main course £7.50. **BREWERY/COMPANY:** Whitbread. **PRINCIPAL BEERS:** Ringwood Best, Flowers Original. **FACILITIES:** Children welcome Garden: outdoor eating. **NOTES:** Parking 20. **ROOMS:** 6 bedrooms 6 en suite s£45 d£65 3 family rooms £75-£85

LYNDHURST   Map 04 SU30

New Forest Inn 🛏 ☍
Emery Down SO43 7DY ☎ 023 8028 2329
🖷 023 8028 3216
Delightfully situated in the scenic New Forest, this rambling inn lies on land claimed from the crown by use of squatters' rights in the early 18th-century. Ale was once sold from a caravan which now forms the front lounge porchway. Lovely summer garden and welcoming bars with open fires and an extensive menu listing local game in season and plenty of fresh fish - whole Dover sole, fresh tuna, monkfish thermidor - alongside traditional pub meals.

OPEN: 11-11. **BAR MEALS:** L served all week. D served all week 12-2.30 6-9. Av main course £8. **BREWERY/COMPANY:** Whitbread. **PRINCIPAL BEERS:** Flowers, Greene King Old Speckled Hen, Ringwood Best & True Glory. **FACILITIES:** Children welcome Children's licence Garden: outdoor eating Dogs allowed. **NOTES:** Parking 20. **ROOMS:** 4 bedrooms 3 en suite s£25 d£50

The Trusty Servant 🛏
Minstead SO43 7FY ☎ 02380 812137

Popular Victorian pub in the picturesque New Forest. An ideal watering hole for walkers and situated just a stone's throw from Sir Arthur Conan Doyle's grave at Minstead Church. The famous pub sign is a copy of a picture belonging to Winchester College. Huge selection of freshly prepared bar snacks and chef's specials includes pan roasted Barbary duck breast, lamb chump steak, fresh cut gammon with Stilton and *continued*

apricot sauce, steamed skate wing, mushroom and pimento stroganoff, and delice of farmed Scottish salmon.
OPEN: 11-11 (Sun 12-10.30). **BAR MEALS:** L served all week. D served all week 12-2.30 7-10. Av main course £7.95. **RESTAURANT:** L served all week. D served all week 12-2.30 7-10. Av 3 course à la carte £15. **BREWERY/COMPANY:** Whitbread. **PRINCIPAL BEERS:** Ringwood Best, Fullers London Pride, Wadworth 6X. **FACILITIES:** Children welcome Garden: outdoor eating, Dogs allowed Water. **NOTES:** Parking 16. **ROOMS:** 6 bedrooms 6 en suite s£27 d£55 2 family rooms £80

MATTINGLEY   Map 04 SU75

The Leather Bottle
Reading Rd RG27 8JU ☎ 01189 326371 🖷 01189 326547
Dir: *From M3 J5 follow signs for Hook then B3349*
Established in 1714, the Leather Bottle is a wisteria-clad pub with heavy beams, huge open winter fires and a new dining extension leading to a summer terrace. Standard extensive menu.

MEONSTOKE   Map 04 SU53

The Bucks Head
Bucks Head Hill SO32 3NA ☎ 01489 877313
Dir: *by the jct of A32 & B2150*
Nestling in a quaint village in the Meon valley, close to the Saxon church, and babbling chalk stream, this former coaching inn dates from the 16th century. Two welcoming bars with open fires, beams, and an enterprising eclectic menu that has an emphasis on English and continental dishes. Expect filled baguettes, platters, steak and kidney pudding, peppered steaks, pan-fried salmon, and game in season. Lovely riverside garden.
OPEN: 11-3 6-11. **BAR MEALS:** L served all week. D served all week 12-2.15 7-9.15. Av main course £7. **RESTAURANT:** L served all week. D served all week 12-2.15 7-9.15. Av 3 course à la carte £14. **BREWERY/COMPANY:** Greene King. **PRINCIPAL BEERS:** Greene King Old Speckled Hen & IPA, Ruddles County, Black Sheep. **FACILITIES:** Garden: Dogs allowed. **NOTES:** Parking 40. **ROOMS:** 5 bedrooms 5 en suite s£32.50 d£50

MICHELDEVER   Map 04 SU53

Half Moon & Spread Eagle
Winchester Rd SO21 3DG ☎ 01962 774339
🖷 01962 774834
Dir: *Take A30 from Winchester towards Basingstoke. After Kings Worthy turn L after petrol station. Pub 0.5m on L*
Conveniently located a mile off the A33 in the heart of a quintessential thatched and timbered Hampshire village, this well-maintained 16th-century pub has reverted back to its old name, having been called the Dever Arms for just eight years. The three neatly furnished and carpeted interconnecting rooms sport a village local atmosphere and an extensive menu offering a range of imaginative salads, half shoulder of lamb with mint gravy, pork escalope with fennel and a good range of fresh fish - mackerel fillets with mustard sauce and red mullet with Pernod.
OPEN: 12-3 6-11 (Sun 7-10.30). **BAR MEALS:** L served all week. D served all week 12-2 6-9. Av main course £9. **RESTAURANT:** L served all week. D served all week 12-2 6-9. Av 3 course à la carte £15. **BREWERY/COMPANY:** Greene King. **PRINCIPAL BEERS:** Greene King IPA Abbot Ale, Ruddles, XX Mild. **FACILITIES:** Children welcome Garden: Outdoor eating Dogs allowed Water. **NOTES:** Parking 20

NORTH WALTHAM   Map 04 SU54

The Fox
RG25 2BE ☎ 01256 397288 ☖ 01256 397288
Dir: From M3 J7 take A30 towards Winchester.
Village signposted on R
Built as three farm cottages in 1624, this peacefully situated
village pub enjoys splendid views across fields and farmland
and has its own award-winning garden.
   A varied bar menu features basket meals, baguettes and
jacket potatoes. In the restaurant, steaks, fish and game dishes
are offered, with vegetarian alternatives.
OPEN: 11-3 (all day w/end) 5.30-12. **BAR MEALS:** L served all
week. D served all week 12-2.30 6.30-10. Av main course £3.50.
RESTAURANT: L served all week. D served all week 12-2.30
6.30-10. **BREWERY/COMPANY:** Ushers.
PRINCIPAL BEERS: Ushers. **FACILITIES:** Children welcome
Children's licence Garden: BBQ, beer garden with seating, food
served outdoors Dogs allowed. **NOTES:** Parking 40

OLD BASING   Map 04 SU65

The Millstone
Bartons Mill Ln RG24 8AE ☎ 01256 331153
Dir: From M3 J6 follow brown signs to Basing House
Enjoying a rural location beside the River Loddon, close to a
country park and Old Basing House, this attractive old building
is a popular lunchtime spot for summer alfresco imbibing.

OVINGTON   Map 04 SU53

The Bush
SO24 0RE ☎ 01962 732764 ☖ 01962 735130
Dir: A31 from Winchester, E to Alton & Farnham, approx 6m turn L off
dual carriageway to Ovington. 0.5m to pub
Tucked away down a lane off the A31 is this delightful rose-
covered pub, situated by the gently flowing River Itchen. Take
a riverside stroll before relaxing over a meal in the character
bars, complete with roaring log fires in winter. Tuck into beef
and ale pie, venison casserole or spinach and wild mushroom
lasagne. Everything is fresh and home-cooked.
OPEN: 11-3 6-11 (Sun 12-2 7-10.30). Closed Dec 25.
BAR MEALS: L served all week. D served Mon-Sat 12-2 6.30-
9.30. Av main course £10. **BREWERY/COMPANY:** Wadworth.
PRINCIPAL BEERS: Wadworth 6X, IPA & Farmers Glory, Badger
Tanglefoot, Red Shoot Tom's Tipple. **FACILITIES:** Children
welcome Children's licence Garden: beer garden, outdoor
eating, Dogs allowed. **NOTES:** Parking 40

OWSLEBURY   Map 04 SU52

The Ship Inn
Whites Hill SO21 1LT ☎ 01962 777358 ☖ 01962 777458
e-mail: theshipinn@freeuk.com
Dir: M3 J11 take B3335 follow signs for Owslebury
Despite its name, this 17th-century inn is nowhere near the
sea, it's actually located on a chalk ridge offering wonderful
country views.
   There's plenty to keep the children occupied in the large
garden, with its play area, aviary and pet corner. Lunch,
evening and specials menus offer a good choice, from sea
bass with lime, ginger and coriander to a range of steaks*continued*

OPEN: 11-3 (Sun 12-10.30) 6-11 (Apr-Sep Open all day Sat).
BAR MEALS: L served all week. D served all week 12-2 6.30-9.30.
RESTAURANT: L served all week. D served all week 12 6.30.
BREWERY/COMPANY: Greene King.
PRINCIPAL BEERS: Greene King IPA & Triumph, Bateman XXXB,
Cheriton Pots Ale. **FACILITIES:** Children welcome Garden:
Food served outside. **NOTES:** Parking 50

PETERSFIELD   Map 04 SU72

The Good Intent ♉ NEW
40-46 College St GU31 4AF ☎ 01730 263838
☖ 01730 302239
Open fires, candlelit tables and well-kept ales characterise this
16th-century 'country pub in the town'. In summer, flower tubs
and hanging baskets festoon the front patio, and the pub is
well-known for live music on Sunday evenings. Expect home-
baked pies and baguettes, speciality sausages and mash,
seafood pasta, and fisherman's pie.
OPEN: 11-3 5.30-11. **BAR MEALS:** L served all week. D served
all week 12-2.30 6-9.30. Av main course £7.50. **RESTAURANT:** L
served all week. D served all week 12-2 6-9.30. Av 3 course à la
carte £16. **BREWERY/COMPANY:** Gales.
PRINCIPAL BEERS: Gale's HSB, GB, Buster.
FACILITIES: Children welcome Garden: Food served outside
Dogs allowed Water. **NOTES:** Parking 10

The White Horse Inn
Priors Dean GU32 1DA ☎ 01420 588387
☖ 01420 588387
Dir: A3/A272 to Winchester/Petersfield. In Petersfield L to Steep, 5m
then R at small X-rds to E Tisted, 2nd drive on R
Also known as the 'Pub With No Name' as it has no sign, this
splendid 17th-century farmhouse enjoys a remote downland
setting. Two classic unspoilt bars.

PILLEY   Map 04 SZ39

The Fleur de Lys 🐷
Pilley St SO41 5QG ☎ 01590 672158 ☖ 01590 672158
Originally a pair of foresters' cottages, this delightful thatched
property was established as an inn in 1096. It has a splendid
stone-flagged hall and cosy beamed bars. Bar food favourites
include British beef, fresh fish dishes, scampi and chips, and
venison and game dishes in season.
OPEN: 11.30-2.30 6-11 (11.30-3, 6-11 Sat-Sun). **BAR MEALS:** L
served all week. D served all week 12-2 6.30-9.30. Av main course
£8. **RESTAURANT:** L served all week. D served all week 12-2
6.30-9.30. Av 3 course à la carte £15. Av 2 course fixed price £8.99.
BREWERY/COMPANY: Whitbread.
PRINCIPAL BEERS: Ringwood Best, Gales HSB.
FACILITIES: Children welcome Garden: Dogs allowed.
NOTES: Parking 18

Rose & Thistle, Rockbourne

A gentle downland ramble linking two of Hampshire's most picturesque villages.

Turn right from pub and take drive left. Turn right, signed to church, and cross drive to stepped path to church. Continue along right-hand edge of churchyard to junction of paths. Keep straight on, ignoring two paths right, then cross stile and turn immediately right through gate. Follow field edge down to junction of paths. Keep left to gate and maintain direction across two stiles and along field edge to stile. Climb stile immediately right and bear left along meadow edge to stile. Pass in front of cottage to track.

Bear left, then right through gate and keep left to gate. Bear half-right to gate in corner and proceed along edge, eventually reaching stile and lane. Take track opposite. Enter copse, then at junction of tracks, take path left up steep bank into field. Keep to left-hand edge and head across field to track. Turn right, then left downhill through woodland edge to lane.

Turn right, then left and climb through wood. At fork, bear left and pass behind house to lane. Turn left, then right along track to lane. Turn right, then bear off right through woodland. At junction, bear left and walk beside paddocks to bungalow. Turn left along track towards church. Turn left at T-junction and shortly enter churchyard. Go through gate opposite church door and descend to lane. Turn right, then left along farm drive and keep ahead, bearing left, then right, uphill to gate. Turn left along field edge, then head across field to track. Turn right and follow track left to junction of tracks. Cross stile opposite to reach Rockbourne church. Retrace steps to pub.

Distance: 4.1/2 miles (7.2km)
Map: OS Landranger 184
Terrain: woodland, farmland
Paths: field paths, woodland bridleways and tracks
Gradient: gradual climbs

Walk submitted by:
David Hancock

Thatched cottages in picturesque Rockbourne

ROSE AND THISTLE, ROCKBOURNE
SP6 3NL. Tel: 01725 518236
Directions: village off B3078 1m W of Fordingbridge.
Set in one of Hampshire's most attractive downland villages and well placed for the New Forest, this delightful thatched 16th-century inn is the perfect retreat after a country stroll. Civilised beamed bar and restaurant country-style fabrics, oak tables and open log fires. Good light lunch menu and more elaborate evening fare.
Open: 11-3 6-11. Bar Meals: 12-2.30 6.30-9.30. Children welcome. Garden/patio. Parking.
(see page 221 for full entry)

England

PORTSMOUTH & SOUTHSEA   Map 04 SZ69

The Still & West
2 Bath Square, Old Portsmouth PO1 2JL ☎ 023 92821567
Nautically themed pub close to HMS Victory and enjoying
excellent views of Portsmouth Harbour and the Isle of Wight.
Gale's managed house with guest ales.

The Wine Vaults ♀
43-47 Albert Rd, Southsea PO5 2SF ☎ 023 92864712
📠 023 92865544
e-mail: Vinevalts@freeuk.com
Originally several Victorian shops converted into a Victorian-
style alehouse with wooden floors, panelled walls, and old
church pew seating. Partly due to the absence of a jukebox or
fruit machine, the atmosphere here is relaxed and there is a
good range of real ales and good-value food. A typical menu
includes simple dishes such as jacket potatoes, sandwiches,
ploughmans, and Mexican specials including nachos and
burritos.
OPEN: 12-9.30. Closed 1 Jan. **BAR MEALS:** L served all week.
D served all week 12-9.30pm. Av main course £5.60.
RESTAURANT: L served all week. D served all week .
BREWERY/COMPANY: Free House.
PRINCIPAL BEERS: Hopback GFB, Courage Best, Bass..
FACILITIES: Children welcome Children's licence Garden:
outdoor eating, patio Dogs allowed

PRESTON CANDOVER   Map 04 SU64

The Crown at Axford
near Preston Candover RG25 2DZ ☎ 01256 389492
📠 01256 389149
e-mail: crown@axfordc.fsnet.co.uk
This small country inn, set at the northern edge of Candover
Valley about five miles from Basingstoke, offers a good range
of beers, and a traditional pub menu.

RINGWOOD   Map 03 SU10

The Struan Country Inn
Horton Rd, Ashey Heath BH24 2EG ☎ 01425 473553
📠 01425 480529
Dir: M27 to A31, at rdbt take A338 Bournemouth, R for Ashey Heath
Built as a private house in the 1920s, this imposing inn is
handy for Bournemouth, the New Forest and the Avon Valley.
Interesting food and 10 en suite bedrooms.

ROCKBOURNE   Map 03 SU11

Pick of the Pubs

The Rose & Thistle 🐑 ♀
SP6 3NL ☎ 01725 518236
e-mail: enquiries@roseandthistle.co.uk
See Pub Walk on page 219
See Pick of the Pubs on page 221

ROMSEY   Map 04 SU32

The Dukes Head 🐑
Greatbridge Rd SO51 0HB ☎ 01794 514450
📠 01794 518102
This rambling 400-year-old pub, festooned with flowers in
summer, nestles in the Test Valley just a stone's throw from the
famous trout stream. An adventurous menu offers duck
sausages in hoi sin sauce, tian of crab, chicken breast stuffed
with pineapple, and fresh local trout delivered daily.

OPEN: 11-11. **BAR MEALS:** L served all week. D served all week
12-3 6-10.30. Av main course £9.95.
BREWERY/COMPANY: Free House.
PRINCIPAL BEERS: Theakston Old Peculier, Fullers London
Pride. **FACILITIES:** Garden: patio, outdoor eating.
NOTES: Parking 50

TRAILS AND ALES HAMPSHIRE

Tackle the 44-mile Test Way, which runs from Totton near Southampton to Inkpen Beacon in Berkshire, and you can
sample a pint at the listed George Inn at St Mary Bourne, renowned for its cricket memorabilia, enjoy lunch at the White
Lion in Wherwell - popular with Test Way ramblers - or relax in the riverside garden of the popular Mayfly near Stockbridge.
The 70-mile Wayfarers Walk starts at Emsworth on the edge of Chichester Harbour and runs north-west through Hampshire.
Like the Test Way, it finishes at Inkpen Beacon. Along the way the trail visits the much-photographed Royal Oak overlooking
Langstone Harbour before moving on to the White Horse at Droxford - a rambling old coaching inn in the picturesque Meon
Valley - and the Flower Pots at Cheriton, a classic village pub with its own brewery. Approaching Basingstoke, the way
reaches the 16th-century Queen Inn at Dummer before cutting across spectacular downland country to finish at Inkpen
Beacon on the Berkshire border. Running west to east is the spectacular 60-mile Solent Way, offering stunning coastal views,
bracing sea breezes and constant reminders of Britain's historic seafaring traditions. Starting at Milford near Lymington, the
walk heads for Bucklers Hard in the New Forest, setting for the Master Builders House Hotel where light snacks are
served in the Yachtsman's Bar. Beyond Southampton, the Solent Way makes for the picturesque waterside
village of Hamble, renowned for its many pubs, including the 12th century Bugle.

OPEN: 11-3 6-11
(Sun 12-3 7-10.30)
BAR MEALS: L served all week.
D served all week 12-2.30 6.30-
9.30. Av main course £10
RESTAURANT: L served all week
D served all week 12-2.30 6.30-
9.30. Av 3 course a la carte £16.
BREWERY/COMPANY:
Free House.
PRINCIPAL BEERS: Fullers
London Pride, Marston's Pedigree,
Adnams Broadside, Wadworth 6X.
FACILITIES: Children welcome.
Garden: patio, outdoor eating.
Dogs allowed.
NOTES: Parking 28.

The Rose & Thistle

SP6 3NL
☎ 01725 518236
e-mail: enquiries@roseandthistle.co.uk
Dir: village is signposted from B3078
NW of Fordingbridge & from A354 SW
of Salisbury

The idyllic appearance of this pretty downland village is maintained in the picture-postcard, thatched exterior of this 17th-century pub, which is located at the top of the fine village street lined with thatched cottages and period houses. Well placed for the New Forest, Salisbury and Breamore House.

Originally two 16th-century cottages, this delightful long and low whitewashed pub became an inn nearly 200 years ago and was recently owned by a consortium of locals until landlord Tim Norfolk bought the freehold. Country-house fabrics, floral arrangements and magazines are tasteful touches to the civilised and delightfully unspoilt low-beamed interior, the bar and dining area being furnished with polished oak tables and chairs, carved benches and cushioned settles. Relax inside in front of open fires in winter and soak up the sun in summer in the neat front garden, kitted out with upmarket benches and brollies, and a quaint dovecot.

Expect a relaxing atmosphere, good ale and wine and interesting pub food from well balanced lunch and dinner menus and daily dishes that favour fresh fish and local game in season. From light lunches like rare roast beef ploughman's, scrambled egg with smoked salmon and prawns and tagliatelle carbonara, main course choices extend to rack of lamb with redcurrant sauce, steak and kidney pudding and venison steak with spring onion and chestnut sauce. Fishy alternatives may include Cornish crab salad, grilled Portuguese sardines with salad and new potatoes, pan-fried John Dory stuffed with lime and coriander butter, and monkfish wrapped in bacon with creamy chive sauce. Round off with a good nursery pudding like sticky toffee pudding or home-made ice cream. Decent coffee and an imaginative Sunday lunch menu.

221

ROMSEY continued

The Mill Arms ♀
Barley Hill, Dunbridge SO51 0LF ☎ 01794 340401
▤ 01794 340401
e-mail: themillarms@zoom.co.uk
Former coaching inn with stables converted into a skittle alley,
function room and six bedrooms. Interior features fishing
memorabilia and old photographs of the area. Handy for
visiting the NT's Mottisfont Abbey and exploring the pretty Test
Valley. Expect lamb shank, cod in beer batter, local pheasant,
and 'tickled' sausage, mash and onion gravy.
OPEN: 12-3.00 6.00-11. **BAR MEALS:** L served all week. D
served all week 12-2.30 6.00-9.30. **RESTAURANT:** L served all
week. D served all week 12-2.30 6.00-9.30.
BREWERY/COMPANY: Free House.
PRINCIPAL BEERS: Dunbridge Test Tickler, Ringwood True
Glory, Hampshire Pride of Romsey, Taylor Landlord.
FACILITIES: Children welcome Garden: Outdoor eating.
NOTES: Parking 90. **ROOMS:** 6 bedrooms 6 en suite

ROWLANDS CASTLE   Map 04 SU71

Castle Inn ♦♦♦
1 Finchdean Rd PO9 6DA ☎ 023 92412494
Dir: N of Havant take B2149 to Rowlands Castle. Pass green, under
rail bridge, pub 1st on L opp Stansted Park
Victorian building directly opposite Stansted Park, part of the
Forest of Bere. Richard the Lionheart supposedly hunted here,
and the house and grounds are open to the public for part of
the year. Traditional atmosphere with wooden floors and fires
in both bars. Menu might list cod and chips, Angus rump
steak, casseroles, chicken curry and roasted vegetable platter.
OPEN: 12-3 (Sat all day, Sun 12-10.30). **BAR MEALS:** L served all week. D served Mon-Thu12-2. Av main
course £5. **RESTAURANT:** L served Sun. D served Mon-Sat 12-2
7-9. Av 3 course à la carte £15. **BREWERY/COMPANY:** Gales.
PRINCIPAL BEERS: Gales Butser, HSB & GB.
FACILITIES: Children's licence Garden: outdoor eating, BBQ
Dogs allowed Water, chews. **NOTES:** Parking 30.
ROOMS: 3 bedrooms s£20 d£30

The Fountain Inn
34 The Green PO9 6AB ☎ 023 9241 2291
Lovely Georgian building recently refurbished in a classical
English country style. Beside the village green. Bedrooms.
Children's play area.

ST MARY BOURNE   Map 04 SU45

The Bourne Valley Inn
SP11 6BT ☎ 01264 738361 ▤ 01264 738126
Situated in the picturesque rural community of St Mary
Bourne, this is the ideal location for conferences, exhibitions,
weddings or other celebrations. The riverside garden abounds
with wildlife, and the children can play safely in the special
play area. Traditional menu.

The George Inn
SP11 6BG ☎ 01264 738340 ▤ 01264 738877
Dir: M3 J8/A303, then A34 towards Newbury. Turn at Whitchurch &
follow signs for St Mary Bourne
Listed village inn in the picturesque Tarrant valley, with a bar
full of cricket memorabilia, one dining room decorated with
regimental battle scenes, and another one with a mural of the
River Test. Bedrooms.

Ringwood Brewery
The Wild Boar of Beers'

Founded in 1978, but continuing a
brewing tradition that goes back to
Tudor times, the Ringwood Brewery
now owns four local pubs, as well as a
vineyard in the Dordogne. Brewery
tours are available. The selection of
boar-bedecked beers includes Best
(3.8%), True Glory (4.3%), Fortyniner
(4.9%), Old Thumper (5.6%)
and Boondoggle (3.9%)

SHERFIELD ENGLISH   Map 04 SU22

The Hatchet Inn 🐑
SO51 6FP ☎ 01794 324033
Dir: A27 from Salisbury
Attractive 17th-century country inn ideally placed for exploring
the peaceful woodland and picturesque villages of the New
Forest. Delightful walks in the tranquil Test Valley close by.
Good emphasis on home-made food, with dishes such as
lamb chops, Cajun chicken strips with mixed vegetables, rump
steak, whole plaice, and duck with brandy, orange and green
peppercorn sauce.
OPEN: 12-3 (Sun 12-3, 7-10.30) 6-11. **BAR MEALS:** L served all
week. D served all week 12-2 7-9. Av main course £5.
RESTAURANT: L served all week. D served all week 12-2 7-9. Av
3 course à la carte £17.50. **BREWERY/COMPANY:** Inn Business.
PRINCIPAL BEERS: Bass, Worthington Best, Stonehenge.
FACILITIES: Children welcome Garden: outdoor eating, patio
Dogs allowed. **NOTES:** Parking 30

SOUTHAMPTON   Map 04 SU41

The Jolly Sailor ♀
Lands End Rd, Bursledon SO31 8DN ☎ 023 8040 5557
▤ 023 80402050
e-mail: jolly.sailor@ukonline.co.uk
Famous as the village local in the BBC's sailing soap Howards
Way, this charming character inn overlooks the yacht marina
and the River Hamble at Bursledon, occupying one of the
south coast's most picturesque settings. Access is quite novel
as you have to descend a steep path leading down from the
road. Fresh fish dishes, including red sea bream and moules
marinière, a good range of snacks and an impressive selection
of quality real ales.
OPEN: 11-11. Closed 25 Dec. **BAR MEALS:** L served all week.
D served all week 12-9.30. Av main course £9.50.
BREWERY/COMPANY: Woodhouse Inns.
PRINCIPAL BEERS: Badger Best, IPA & Tanglefoot, King &
Barnes Sussex. **FACILITIES:** Children welcome Garden: Food
served outside Dogs allowed Water

England

SPARSHOLT Map 04 SU43

Pick of the Pubs

The Plough Inn 🐑 ♀
Main Rd SO21 2NW ☎ 01962 776353
🖻 01962 776400
Dir: *From Winchester take B3049(A272) W, take L turn to village of Sparsholt. The Plough Inn is 1M down the lane*

Located on the village edge, just two miles from the cathedral city of Winchester, this extended, 200-year-old cottage overlooks open fields from its delightful flower- and shrub-filled garden - the perfect spot for a summer evening drink. Inside, you will find an often bustling bar, with pine tables, beams garlanded with hops, an open log fire, Wadworth ales on handpump and a decent selection of wines by the glass. The original cottage front rooms are particularly cosy and ideal for intimate dining. The draw here is the imaginative range of home-cooked food - best to book for evening dining. Extensive blackboard menus list above average pub meals. Expect lunchtime 'doorstep' sandwiches, pork and chive sausages with parsley mash and red wine jus, Thai seafood curry and more adventurous restaurant-style dishes like roast lamb rack with rosemary jus, pheasant breasts stuffed with chestnut farcie on a port and wild mushroom sauce, and monkfish with mussel cream sauce. The dessert board may list Eve's pudding or traditional fruit crumbles.
OPEN: 11-3 6-11 (12-3, 6-10.30). **BAR MEALS:** L served all week. D served all week 12-2 6-9. **RESTAURANT:** L served all week. D served all week 12-2 6-9. Av 3 course à la carte £16. **BREWERY/COMPANY:** Wadworth.
PRINCIPAL BEERS: Wadworth IPA, 6X, Farmers Glory & Old Timer. **FACILITIES:** Children welcome Garden: Food served outside Dogs allowed on leads. **NOTES:** Parking 90

STEEP Map 04 SU72

Pick of the Pubs

Harrow Inn
GU32 2DA ☎ 01730 262685
Dir: *Off A3 to A272, L through Sheet, take road opp church (school lane) then over A3 by-pass bridge*
Tucked away down a sleepy lane the Harrow is a gem of a rustic pub, still totally unspoilt and run by the McCutcheon family since 1929. Once a drovers' stop on the old Liss to Petersfield route, this 400 to 500 year old tile-hung building is now a popular watering hole with walkers hiking the Hanger's Way. There are two character bars, each with scrubbed wooden tables, boarded walls and seasonal flower and fruit decorations; one features a huge inglenook. Accompany a decent pint of local ale with a hearty bowl of ham and split pea soup, rare beef sandwiches, lasagne, ploughman's lunches and, for pudding damson and orange Bakewell tart. Delightful cottage garden.
OPEN: 12-2.30 6-11 (Sat 11-3, 6-11, Sun 12-3, 7-10.30).
BAR MEALS: L served all week. D served all week 12-2 7-9. Av main course £7. **BREWERY/COMPANY:** Free House.
PRINCIPAL BEERS: Ringwood Best, Cheriton Diggers Gold & Pots Ale, Ballards Trotton. **FACILITIES:** Garden: patio, outdoor eating Dogs allowed on a lead. **NOTES:** Parking 15

STOCKBRIDGE Map 04 SU33

Mayfly
Testcombe SO20 6AZ ☎ 01264 860283
Dir: *Between A303 & A30, on A3057*
A former farmhouse and now one of Hampshire's most famous riverside pubs, the Mayfly is the perfect watering hole for relaxing over a summertime drink and lunch in the delightful garden on the banks of the Test. Lots of local walks and the long-distance Test Way runs close by. Winchester, Stockbridge and Romsey are within easy reach. The pub operates a hot and cold buffet with a choice of up to 40 cheeses, as well as smoked chicken and a selection of cold meats and pies.
OPEN: 10-11. **BAR MEALS:** L served all week. D served all week 11.30-9. Av main course £6. **BREWERY/COMPANY:** Whitbread.
PRINCIPAL BEERS: Wadworth 6X, Flowers Original, Ringwood Old Thumper, Marstons Pedigree. **FACILITIES:** Children welcome Garden: Next to riverside Dogs allowed.
NOTES: Parking 48

Timeless Gems
At a time when the great institution of the British local is under threat, it's good to know that some classic country pubs continue to thrive. The Bell at Aldworth on the Berkshire Downs near Streatley, the isolated Pot Kiln at nearby Frilsham and the Harrow at Steep near Petersfield are classic examples of inns that have steadfastedly refused to pamper to modern trends. With no sign of juke boxes or fruit machines to spoil the cosy atmosphere, the intention is to try and promote the art of good conversation and preserve a disappearing way of life. If there were awards for timeless pubs that have hardly changed over the years, the picturesque Cricketers at Berwick in East Sussex, the Red Lion at Appledore in Kent and the Kings Head at Laxfield in Suffolk would surely be prime candidates. The historic Fleece at Bretforton in Worcestershire, the Drewe Arms at Drewsteignton in Devon, the 500-year-old Falkland Arms at Great Tew in Oxfordshire and the Flower Pots at Cheriton in Hampshire are also typical of pubs that have stood the test of time.

England

STOCKBRIDGE continued

Pick of the Pubs

The Peat Spade 🐾 ⏛
Longstock SO20 6DR ☎ 01264 810612
e-mail: peat.spade@virgin.net
Striking red-brick and gabled Victorian pub tucked away in a sleepy thatched village in the Test Valley, just 100 metres from Hampshire's finest chalk stream. Worth the short diversion off the A3057 north of Stockbridge for some good pub food, served throughout the uncluttered and tastefully furnished bar and adjacent eating areas. With its unusual paned windows, open fires, attractive prints and antique pine furniture, it offers a relaxed and informal atmosphere in which to enjoy a decent pint of Hampshire ale and a satisfying meal chosen from the short, daily-changing blackboard menu. Twice-baked goats' cheese soufflé or smoked mackerel pâté may precede ribeye steak with cracked pepper sauce, roast cod on coriander couscous with coconut sauce, or duck with roasted aubergine and hoi sin sauce. Lighter dishes may include beef casserole, warm salad of smoked duck and chorizo, fresh basil tagliatelle with blue cheese sauce, and sandwiches with imaginative fillings - Cornish Yarg and apple chutney. Finish, perhaps, with rhubarb crumble or treacle sponge. Small rear garden for summer sipping.
OPEN: 11.30-3 6.30-11. Closed Dec 25-26 & 31Dec-1 Jan.
BAR MEALS: L served Tue-Sun. D served Tue-Sat 12-2.30 7-9.30. Av main course £6.95. **RESTAURANT:** L served Tue-Sun. D served Tue-Sun 12-2 7-9.30. Av 3 course à la carte £21.50. **BREWERY/COMPANY:** Free House.
PRINCIPAL BEERS: Ringwood Best & 49er.
FACILITIES: Children welcome Garden: outdoor eating, patio, BBQ Dogs allowed on a lead. **NOTES:** Parking 22.
ROOMS: 4 bedrooms 4 en suite s£58.75 d£58.75 No credit cards

STRATFIELD TURGIS   Map 04 SU65

The Wellington Arms ★ ★ ★ ⏛
RG27 0AS ☎ 01256 882214 🖳 01256 882934
e-mail: wellington.arms@virgin.net
Dir: on A33 between Basingstoke & Reading
Former farmhouse, dating from the 17th century, situated at one of the entrances to the ancestral home of the Duke of Wellington. There is a monthly restaurant carte, and lounge bar favourites such as Wellington chicken liver pâté, home-made pie, and sirloin steak. Most of the bedrooms are located in the modern Garden Wing, though rooms in the original house with a more period feel are available.
OPEN: 11-11 (Sun 12-10.30). **BAR MEALS:** L served all week. D served all week 12-2.30 6-10. Av main course £8.95.
RESTAURANT: L served Sun-Fri. D served Mon-Sat 12-2 6.30-9.30. Av 3 course à la carte £25.
BREWERY/COMPANY: Woodhouse Inns.
PRINCIPAL BEERS: Badger Dorset Best, Tanglefoot.
FACILITIES: Children welcome Garden: Beer garden, food served outdoors Dogs allowed outside only. **NOTES:** Parking 60. **ROOMS:** 30 bedrooms 30 en suite s£65 d£75 FR£120-£145

TANGLEY   Map 04 SU35

The Fox Inn ⏛
SP11 0RU ☎ 01264 730276
Dir: 4m N of Andover
Well worth the detour off the A343, the 300-year-old Fox is a remote brick and flint cottage with a friendly atmosphere. In the bar, choose from steak and kidney pie, moussaka, or chicken tikka. The restaurant might offer fresh crab cakes, or tenderloin of pork in Calvados.

OPEN: 12-3 6-11. **BAR MEALS:** L served all week. D served all week 12-3 6-11. Av main course £5. **RESTAURANT:** L served all week. D served all week 12-3 6-11. Av 3 course à la carte £20.
BREWERY/COMPANY: PRINCIPAL BEERS: Flowers IPA, Wadworth 6X. **FACILITIES:** Children welcome Children's licence outdoor eating, patio Dogs allowed. **NOTES:** Parking 50.
ROOMS: 1 bedrooms 1 en suite s£50 d£55

TICHBORNE   Map 04 SU53

Pick of the Pubs

The Tichborne Arms ⏛
SO24 0NA ☎ 01962 733760 🖳 01962 733760
e-mail: kjjday@btinternet.com
Dir: off A31 towards Alresford, after 200yds R at sign for Tichborne
Real ales are served straight from cask at this heavily thatched red-brick pub set in an idyllic rural hamlet in the Itchen Valley. The village dates from 1100 and a pub has existed on the site since 1423; the present building was erected after a fire in 1939. Traditional home-cooked food ranges from toasted sandwiches and filled jacket potatoes to fillet steak in pepper sauce, dressed crab salad, whole lamb shank, and smoked salmon and scrambled eggs. Hearty nursery puddings. Two homely bars and a splendid rear garden for warm-weather imbibing.
OPEN: 11.30-2.30 6-11. **BAR MEALS:** L served all week. D served all week 12-1.45 6.30-9.45. Av main course £7.50.
BREWERY/COMPANY: Free House.
PRINCIPAL BEERS: Ringwood Best, Triple fff Moondance, Wadworth 6X, Otter Ale. **FACILITIES:** Garden: patio, outdoor eating, Dogs allowed Water. **NOTES:** Parking 30

UPPER FROYLE
Map 04 SU74

The Hen & Chicken Inn ♀
GU34 4JH ☎ 01420 22115 🖹 01420 23021
Dir: 6m from Farnham on A31 on R
Situated on the old Winchester to Canterbury road, this 16th-century inn was once the haunt of highwaymen. It retains its traditional atmosphere with large open fires, panelling and beams. Now owned by Hall & Woodhouse.

WARSASH

The Jolly Farmer Country Inn
29 Fleet End Rd SO31 9JH ☎ 01489 572500
🖹 01489 885847
Dir: Exit M27 Juct 9, head towards A27 Fareham, turn R onto Warsash Rd Follow for 2 M then L onto Fleet end Rd
Attractive white pub with an abundance of hanging baskets. Vintage car outside. Children's play area. Lots of farming equipment in bar. Look out for the 'talking' cat.

WELL
Map 04 SU74

The Chequers Inn
RG29 1TL ☎ 01256 862605 🖹 01256 862133
Dir: from Odiham High St turn R into Long Lane, follow for 3m, L at T jct, pub 0.25m on top of hill
A charming, old-world 17th-century pub with a rustic, low-beamed bar, replete with log fire, scrubbed tables and hand-pulled Badger ales, and vine-covered front terrace, set deep in the heart of the Hampshire countryside. Blackboard listed dishes range from sausages and mash, pasta meals and liver and bacon, to Cajun salmon fillet, tuna with Creole sauce, and rump steak with pepper sauce.
OPEN: 11-3 6-11. **BAR MEALS:** L served all week. D served all week 12-2.30 6-10. Av main course £9.50. **RESTAURANT:** L served all week. D served all week 12-2.30 6-10. Av 3 course à la carte £20. **BREWERY/COMPANY:** Hall & Woodhouse.
PRINCIPAL BEERS: Badger IPA, Tanglefoot & Best.
FACILITIES: Garden: Food served outside Dogs allowed.
NOTES: Parking 30

WHERWELL
Map 04 SU34

The White Lion
Fullerton Rd SP11 7JF ☎ 01264 860317 🖹 01264 860317
Dir: Off A303 onto B3048, pub on B3420
At the centre of one of Hampshire's loveliest villages, this former coaching inn is just a few minutes' walk from a picturesque reach of the River Test. A cannon ball is reputed to have come down the chimney, when fired by Oliver Cromwell during the Civil War. Expect lunchtime bar snacks and daily specials, and such dishes as rump steak, battered cod and local butcher's ham on the evening menu.
OPEN: 10-2.30 (Sat 10-3 Sun 12-3) 6-11 (Sun 7-10.30, Mon-Tue 7-11). **BAR MEALS:** L served all week. D served Mon-Sat 12-2 7-9.30. Av main course £6.25. **RESTAURANT:** L served all week. D served Mon-Sat 12-2 7-9.30. Av 3 course à la carte £14.50.
BREWERY/COMPANY: Inn Partnership.
PRINCIPAL BEERS: Flowers Original, Adnams Best Bitter, Ringwood Bitter. **FACILITIES:** Children welcome Garden: enclosed courtyard, food served outside Dogs allowed.
NOTES: Parking 40. **ROOMS:** 3 bedrooms s£32.50 d£42.50 FR£55

WHITCHURCH
Map 04 SU44

Pick of the Pubs

The Red House Inn 🕙 ♀
21 London St RG28 7LH ☎ 01256 895558
Dir: From M3 or M4 take A34 to Whitchurch
Busy 16th-century coaching inn with quaint flagstones and beams, only a few minutes' walk from southern England's only working silk mill. Nearby is the parish church which has some interesting features, and the late Lord Denning, former Master of the Rolls, was born over his parents draper's shop beside the Town Hall in 1899. Good modern cooking uses fresh local produce and imaginative, seasonally changing menus and daily specials may include seared scallops with mint pea purée, crispy sea bass with saffron mash and crayfish, lamb chump and honey roast sweet potato, and artichoke, chive and goats' cheese fritters with chilli and tomato dressing. Enterprising range of pasta dishes and baguettes. Impressive wine list.
OPEN: 11.30-3 6-11 (Sun 12-3, 7-10.30). **BAR MEALS:** L served all week. D served all week 12-2 6.30-9.30. Av main course £9. **RESTAURANT:** L served all week. D served all week 12-2 6.30-9.30. Av 3 course à la carte £18.
BREWERY/COMPANY: Free House.
PRINCIPAL BEERS: Cheriton Diggers Gold & Pots Ale, Itchen Valley Fagins. **FACILITIES:** Children welcome Garden: outdoor eating, patio, BBQ, Dogs allowed.
NOTES: Parking 20

Watership Down Inn
Freefolk Priors RG28 7NJ ☎ 01256 892254
e-mail: watershipdowninn@btinternet.com
Dir: On B3400 between Basingstoke & Andover
Enjoy an exhilarating walk on Watership Down before relaxing with a welcome pint at this homely 19th-century inn named after Richard Adams' classic tale of rabbits. A popular new conservatory and plenty of character are among the attractions, and the pub is renowned for its choice of beers. The same menu is offered throughout, including seafood platter, sausage and mash, ham, egg and chips and T-bone steak.
OPEN: 11.30-3.30 6-11. **BAR MEALS:** L served all week. D served all week 12-2.30 6-9.30. Av main course £5.50.
BREWERY/COMPANY: Free House.
PRINCIPAL BEERS: Archers Best, Brakspear Bitter, Ringwood, Bateman XB. **FACILITIES:** Children welcome Garden: beer garden, outdoor eating, Patio Dogs allowed garden only.
NOTES: Parking 18

WHITSBURY
Map 03 SU11

The Cartwheel Inn ♀
Whitsbury Rd SP6 3PZ ☎ 01725 518362 🖹 01725 518886
e-mail: thecartwheelinn@lineone.net
Dir: Off A338 between Salisbury & Fordingbridge
Handy for exploring the New Forest, visiting Breamore House and discovering the remote Mizmaze on the nearby downs, this extended, turn-of-the-century one-time wheelwright's and shop has been a pub since the 1920s. Venue for a beer festival held annually in August, with spit-roast pigs, barbecues, Morris dancing and a range of 30 real ales. Popular choice of well kept beers in the bar too. Home-made food on daily specials boards - steak and kidney pudding, fisherman's pie and chicken curry. *continued*

225

OPEN: 11-2.30 6-11. **BAR MEALS:** L served all week. D served all week 12-2 7-9.30. Av main course £6. **RESTAURANT:** L served all week. D served all week 12-2 7-9.30. Av 3 course à la carte £13.50. **BREWERY/COMPANY:** Free House. **PRINCIPAL BEERS:** Adnams Broadside, Ringwood Best, Smiles, Hop Back Summer Lightning. **FACILITIES:** Children welcome Garden: Food served outside Dogs allowed Water. **NOTES:** Parking 25

WINCHESTER   Map 04 SU52

Pick of the Pubs

Wykeham Arms 🏵 ♦♦♦♦ ♀
75 Kingsgate St SO23 9PE ☎ 01962 853834
▤ 01962 854411
Dir: Near Winchester College & Winchester Cathedral

Sandwiched between Winchester College and the famous Cathedral, the former Fleur de Lys of pre-Napoleonic times dates from 1755 and retains both its sense of history and its identity as a fine city local. Blazing log fires and ubiquitous pictures adorning the walls contribute to the great atmosphere in a pub that takes its food and wines seriously yet without pretension.

Sourced entirely from fresh local produce, menus are up-dated daily, while from an evolving list of some 40 wines, up to twenty are sold by the glass or carafe. Luncheon platters on the lines of chicken liver parfait, warm chicken salad and oak-smoked salmon are supplemented by daily offerings such as cottage pie, pasta carbonara and game casserole. More substantial options might be red sea bream with chilli, sun-dried tomato and coriander oil, pan-fried pheasant stuffed with mushroom mousseline and Aberdeen Angus fillet and sirloin steaks served peppered or plain.

Round off with kumquat and marscapone cheesecake or smoked Applewood cheese with a late bottled port, enjoying the bonus of an overnight stay in one of the first-class en suite bedrooms that are generously furnished with all modern comforts.
OPEN: 11-11 (Sun 12-10.30). Closed 25 Dec.
BAR MEALS: L served Mon-Sat. D served Mon-Sat 12-2.30 6.30-8.45. Av main course £6.25. **RESTAURANT:** D served Mon-Sat 6.30-8.45. Av 3 course à la carte £22.
BREWERY/COMPANY: Gales. **PRINCIPAL BEERS:** Bass, Gales Butser, Special & HSB. **FACILITIES:** Garden: patio, outdoor eating Dogs allowed. **NOTES:** Parking 12.
ROOMS: 13 bedrooms 13 en suite s£45 d£79.50

WOODLANDS   Map 04 SU31

The Game Keeper
268 Woodlands Rd SO40 7GH ☎ 023 80293093
Dir: M27 J2 follow signs for Beaulieu/Fawley(A326). At 1st rndbt after the Safeway rndbt turn R, then next L. 1m on L
Backing onto open fields on the very edge of the New Forest, this 150-year-old extended cottage is the perfect resting place after a long forest walk. Comfortable modernised interior and traditional pub food.

HEREFORDSHIRE

AYMESTREY   Map 03 SO46

Pick of the Pubs

Riverside Inn & Restaurant 🏡 ♀
HR6 9ST ☎ 01568 708440 ▤ 01568 709058
e-mail: riverside@aymestrey.fsnet.co.uk
Dir: Situated on A4110 between Hereford & Knighton

A handsome half-timbered 16th-century inn on the banks of the River Lugg with a mile of private trout fishing, accommodation in the main pub and a converted barn and a campsite in the grounds with views over the river and surrounding woods. Wherever possible, locally grown or farmed produce is used, including many vegetables, salads and herbs from their own gardens and Marches quality meats: a totally organic menu is now planned to complement the current one.

This serious approach to food is reflected in daily fresh fish and vegetarian dishes and a wide choice of imaginative alternatives. Tartelette of kedgeree with poached egg and vierge dressing and carpaccio of beef with fresh Parmesan might typically start the meal, followed by rack of Marches lamb with clapshot and sea bass fillets on cumin flavoured leeks, with vegetarian options typified by plum tomato tart tatin with herb Mascarpone. All the desserts and ice creams are home made and there is an impressive cheese selection including Long Clawson Stilton and Shropshire Blue.
OPEN: 11 Open All day. Closed Dec 25. **BAR MEALS:** L served all week. D served all week 12-2.30 7-10. Av main course £6. **RESTAURANT:** L served all week. D served all week 12-2.30 7-10. Av 3 course à la carte £23. Av 3 course fixed price £18.95. **BREWERY/COMPANY:** Free House. **PRINCIPAL BEERS:** Woodhampton. **FACILITIES:** Children welcome Garden: 3 acres/woodland, Food served outside Dogs allowed Water, Food Bowls. **NOTES:** Parking 40. **ROOMS:** 5 bedrooms 5 en suite s£25 d£45 FR£55-£75

STAGG INN, KINGTON
Titley HR5 3RL.
Tel: 01544 230221
Directions: on B4355 between Kington and Presteigne
Tiny Titley and the rejuvenated Stagg Inn stand by the Mortimer Trail and the Offa's Dyke Path in beautiful countryside close to the Welsh border. Expect award-winning food, from decent bar meals to imaginative dishes listed on innovative main menus. Accommodation.
Open: 12-3, 6.30-11. Closed Mon & 2 wks early Nov. Bar Meals: 12-2 6.30-10. Children welcome. Garden. Parking.
(see page 230 for full entry)

*Pub*WALK

Stagg Inn, Kington

This delightful short walk explores unspoilt, rolling countryside close to the Welsh Border, including a section of the Mortimer Trail. Visit Titley Church and look out for Titley Court, an impressive building dating from the mid 19th century.

Turn left on leaving the pub and walk down the main road and past the entrance to Titley church. Just beyond, and before two houses, turn left on to the waymarked Mortimer Trail. With the church to your left, the tracks bears slightly right to follow the hedge up the hillside. Go through a gate, keep ahead until the field dips right and continue to a stile. Bear slightly right in the next field to a gate and continue forward through Green Lane Farm, heading for a stile to the right of a gate. Proceed straight on to pass to the right of the farm and outbuildings.

Cross a stile, pass through the gate on your left and turn immediately right to leave the farm via a green lane. Go through a gate and continue along this secluded lane, heading gradually uphill to the ruins of Burnt House Farm. Bear left at the ruins and walk through a small wood to a stile. Follow the left-hand hedge to the field corner, bear left to the next corner, and then turn right down to a gate. Continue ahead to cross a stile and go through the right-hand gate in front of you. Proceed ahead to another gate and follow the track ahead to a gate, passing a farm on your right. The lane becomes metalled at Turning Ways. At the T-junction by the farm, bear right to descend a sunken road down to the village. Ignore the left turn and keep ahead back to the pub.

Distance: 3 miles (4.8km)
Map: OS Landranger 148
Terrain: farmland
Paths: well established Mortimer Trail, field paths, tracks and some road
Gradient: undulating; one long gradual climb

*Walk submitted by:
The Stagg Inn*

The River Wye at Symonds Yat

227

BRIMFIELD   Map 03 SO56

Pick of the Pubs

The Roebuck Inn ◎ ◎ ♦♦♦♦ 🛏 ♀

SY8 4NE ☎ 01584 711230 📠 01584 711654
e-mail: dave@roebuckinn.demon.co.uk
Dir: Just off the A49 between Ludlow & Leominster
In a sleepy Marches village nestling just off the A49 as it
by-passes Ludlow this relaxed country inn lays emphasis
on its variety of fine food. The three bedrooms are
cottagey and comfortable; the dining-room bright and airy
with terracotta walls and colourful table settings.
Altogether more traditional are three bars with inglenooks,
wood panelling and plenty of eating space.
  Everything from daily home-made breads to
sweetmeats with coffee is made on the premises from
first-class local ingredients and the variety of choice is
impressive. Large boards display fresh fish and special
dishes, one entirely devoted to a British cheese selection
among the best in the land. Small and large portions
according to appetite include wild mushroom risotto, crab
filo parcels, spring rolls of confit duck and Mediterranean
mixed salad with herbed olive oil. Heartier main dishes
include steak and mushroom suet pudding and famous
fish pie, pan-roast duck breast and prime fillet steaks;
followed by citrus meringue pie, steamed mincemeat
pudding and passion fruit tiramisu.
OPEN: 11.30-3 6.30-11 (Sun 12-3, 7-10.30). **BAR MEALS:** L
served all week. D served all week 12-2.30 7-9.30. Av main
course £11.50. **RESTAURANT:** L served all week. D served
all week 12-2.30 7-9.30. Av 3 course à la carte £22. Av 3
course fixed price £17.50. **BREWERY/COMPANY:** Free
House. **PRINCIPAL BEERS:** Tetley, Woods, Hook Norton
Old Hooky. **FACILITIES:** Children welcome Garden:
outdoor eating, patio. **NOTES:** Parking 24.
ROOMS: 3 bedrooms 3 en suite s£45 d£60

CANON PYON   Map 03 SO44

The Nags Head Inn 🛏

HR4 8NY ☎ 01432 830252
Listed building, dating back 400 years, with flagstone floors,
open fires and beams. The large garden features a children's
adventure playground. Pub food ranges from filled baguettes,
through grills and fish dishes, to specials such as pork
casserole or chicken and mushroom pie.
OPEN: 11-3 6-11. **BAR MEALS:** L served all week. D served all
week 12-2 6.30-9. Av main course £5.50. **RESTAURANT:** L
served all week. D served all week 12-2 6.30-9. Av 3 course à la
carte £15. **BREWERY/COMPANY:** Free House.
PRINCIPAL BEERS: Wadworth 6X, Flowers IPA, Fullers London
Pride. **FACILITIES:** Children welcome Garden: patio, outdoor
eating, BBQ. **NOTES:** Parking 50. **ROOMS:** 6 bedrooms
6 en suite s£30 d£40 FR£50.00

◆   AA inspected guest accommodation

CAREY   Map 03 SO53

Cottage of Content

HR2 6NG ☎ 01432 840242 📠 01432 840208
*Dir: From A40 W of Ross-on-Wye take A49 towards Hereford.Follow
signs for Hoarworthy,then Carey*
A 500-year-old building, formerly three cottages, situated
beside a stream. The specials board is likely to feature chargrilled chicken with apricot, mango and green pepper sauce,
salmon with saffron and herb butter sauce, fillet of beef with
wild mushrooms and port sauce, and vegetarian options.
OPEN: 12-2.30 7-11. Closed 25 Dec. **BAR MEALS:** L served all
week. D served all week 12-2 7-9.30. Av main course £7.95.
BREWERY/COMPANY: Free House.
PRINCIPAL BEERS: Hook Norton. **FACILITIES:** Children
welcome Garden: Dogs allowed. **NOTES:** Parking 30.
ROOMS: 4 bedrooms 3 en suite s£35 d£48

CRASWALL   Map 03 SO23

Bulls Head 🛏 NEW

HR2 0PN ☎ 01981 510616 📠 01981 510383
In the heart of some great walking country, this isolated 300
year-old drover's inn offers rough camping as well as bed and
breakfast. Recent refurbishments have retained the traditional
atmosphere, with flagstone floors, a farmhouse range and
butler sink. Local ingredients drive the menu; try the huge
home-baked wholemeal sandwiches, Crassie pie, or Ledbury
lamb chops. Lots of authentic curries, plus vegetarian options
and sticky puddings, too.
OPEN: 11-3 6-11. **BAR MEALS:** L served all week. D served all
week 12-3 6-9.30. Av main course £8. **RESTAURANT:** L served
all week. D served all week 12-3 6-9.30. Av 3 course à la carte £12.
BREWERY/COMPANY: Free House. **PRINCIPAL BEERS:** Wye
Valley Butty Bach. **FACILITIES:** Children welcome Garden:
Food served outside Dogs allowed. **NOTES:** Parking 6.
ROOMS: 3 bedrooms 1 en suite s£30 d£40

DORMINGTON   Map 03 SO54

Yew Tree Inn 🛏

Len Gee's Restaurant, Priors Frome HR1 4EH
☎ 01432 850467 📠 01432 850467
*Dir: A438 Hereford to Ledbury, turn at Dormington towards
Mordiford, 1/2 mile on L.*
Enjoy panoramic views of the Wye Valley across to the Brecon
Beacons and the Black Mountains while you relax in the
spacious gardens of this popular country pub. Inside are three
bars where you can sample a range of local ciders and real
ales, including the inn's own Yew Tree Bitter. The menu
features fresh local produce and quality ingredients, fish is a
speciality and the imaginative selection of desserts changes
daily.
OPEN: 12-2 7-11. **BAR MEALS:** L served all week. D served all
week 12-2 7-9. Av main course £5.50. **RESTAURANT:** L served
all week. D served all week 12-2 7-9. Av 3 course à la carte £12.
BREWERY/COMPANY: Free House.
PRINCIPAL BEERS: Tetley, Wye Valley, Red Kite.
FACILITIES: Children welcome Garden: outdoor eating, patio,
Dogs allowed Public bar only. **NOTES:** Parking 25

DORSTONE
Map 03 SO34

The Pandy Inn
HR3 6AN ☎ 01981 550273 🖻 01981 550277
Dir: Off B4348 W of Hereford
The oldest inn in Herefordshire, the Pandy was built in 1185, originally to house workers building Dorstone Church. Oliver Cromwell was a frequent visitor in the 17th-century. Alongside the usual pub favourites, the South African owners offer traditional dishes from back home, bobotie and tomato bredie, along with English dishes such as Herefordshire rump steak, grilled rainbow trout, or lamb shank with rosemary and red wine gravy.
OPEN: 12-3 (Mon 6-11 only) 7-11 (Sat 12-11, Sun 12-10.30).
BAR MEALS: L served all week. D served all week 12-2.30 7-9.30.
RESTAURANT: L served all week. D served all week 12-2.30 7-9.30. Av 3 course à la carte £15. **BREWERY/COMPANY:** Free House. **PRINCIPAL BEERS:** Wye Valley Butty Bach & Dorothy Goodbody. **FACILITIES:** Children welcome Children's licence Garden: patio, BBQ Dogs allowed garden only.
NOTES: Parking 30

FOWNHOPE
Map 03 SO53

The Green Man Inn ★ ★ ♀
HR1 4PE ☎ 01432 860243 🖻 01432 860207
Dir: From M50 take A449 then B4224 to Fownhope
15th-century black and white timbered former coaching inn situated in picturesque countryside amidst wooded hills and the valley scenery of the River Wye. Ideal base for walking, touring and local salmon fishing. Petty Sessions Court used to be held here and one of its original landlords was a bare fist prize fighter. Food includes seafood platter, home-made chilli con carne, liver and bacon casserole and lamb steak with orange and mint gravy.
OPEN: 11-11. **BAR MEALS:** L served all week. D served all week 12-2 6-10. Av main course £5.95. **RESTAURANT:** L served Sun. D served all week 12-2 7-9. Av 3 course à la carte £15.95.
BREWERY/COMPANY: Free House.
PRINCIPAL BEERS: Marstons Pedigree, Courage Directors, Hook Norton. **FACILITIES:** Children welcome Garden: Beer garden, patio, food served outdoors Dogs allowed By arrangement.
NOTES: Parking 80. **ROOMS:** 20 bedrooms 20 en suite s£37.50 d£62

GLADESTRY

Royal Oak
HR5 3NR ☎ 01544 370669 🖻 01544 370669
Dir: 2m off A44
On the route of the Offa's Dyke Path, one of Britain's most popular long-distance trails, this beamed character pub is under new ownership. A friendly, inviting atmosphere greets the customer, with cosy coal fires in winter and Welsh cream teas and home-made cakes available during the summer. Popular with walkers, village locals and hill farmers. Beef and ale pie, stuffed trout with almonds, lamb chops and home-made faggots feature on the traditional pub menu.
OPEN: 11.30-2 7-11. Closed Dec 25. **BAR MEALS:** L served all week. D served all week 12-2 7-9.30. Av main course £5.50.
RESTAURANT: L served all week. D served all week 12-2.00 7-9.30. Av 3 course à la carte £12. **BREWERY/COMPANY:** Free House. **PRINCIPAL BEERS:** Hancocks HB, Albright, Bass.
FACILITIES: Children welcome Children's licence Garden: outdoor eating Dogs allowed Water, food. **NOTES:** Parking 20.
ROOMS: 4 bedrooms s£20 d£40 No credit cards

HAMPTON BISHOP
Map 03 SO53

The Bunch of Carrots 🍴 ♀
HR1 4JR ☎ 01432 870237 🖻 01432 870237
Dir: From Hereford take A4103, A438, then B4224
Friendly pub with real fires, old beams and flagstones. Its name comes from a rock formation in the River Wye which runs alongside the pub. There is an extensive menu (steaks, salmon fillet and Cajun chicken) plus a daily specials board, a carvery, salad buffet and simple bar snacks.
OPEN: 11-3 6-11. **BAR MEALS:** L served all week. D served all week 12-2 6-10. Av main course £6.95. **RESTAURANT:** L served all week. D served all week 12-2 6-10.
BREWERY/COMPANY: Free House. **PRINCIPAL BEERS:** Bass, Hook Norton, Wye Valley. **FACILITIES:** Children welcome Garden: patio, outdoor eating, BBQ Dogs allowed.
NOTES: Parking 100

HEREFORD
Map 03 SO54

Pick of the Pubs

The Ancient Camp Inn ★ ★
Ruckhall HR2 9QX ☎ 01981 250449 🖻 01981 251581
e-mail: enquiries@theancientcamp.co.uk
Dir: Take A465 from Hereford, then B4349.Follow signs 'Belmont Abbey/Ruckhall'
From its elevated position some 70 feet above the winding River Wye the views across the river and Golden Valley from the terrace are stunning; an iron age fort nearby being the inspiration for the inn's unusual name. The low-beamed interior with its stone-flagged floors and simple furnishings sets the scene for some fine cooking that is similarly rustic in style. Commendable dishes include glazed goats' cheese salad and spiced fishcakes with tomato and ginger dressing, leading on to pan-fried sea bass with red mullet jus, pork loin with honey and sherry glaze and roasted vegetable terrine. Leave room for sticky lime pudding or bitter chocolate tart.
OPEN: 12-2 (Sun 12-2.30 only) 7-11. Closed 2 weeks Jan.
BAR MEALS: L served Mon-Sun 12-2. Av main course £7.
RESTAURANT: L served Tue-Sun. D served Tue-Sat 12-2 7-9. Av 3 course à la carte £25. **BREWERY/COMPANY:** Free House. **PRINCIPAL BEERS:** Hook Norton, Wye Valley.
FACILITIES: Garden: patio, outdoor eating Dogs allowed garden only. **NOTES:** Parking 30. **ROOMS:** 5 bedrooms 5 en suite s£45 d£55

The Crown & Anchor 🍴 ♀
Cotts Ln, Lugwardine HR1 4AB ☎ 01432 851303
🖻 01432 851637
e-mail: jscrownandanchor@care4free.net
Dir: 2 miles from Hereford city centre on A438, turn left into Lugwardine down Cotts Lane
Attractive old black-and-white pub on the Lugg flats, with quarry tile floors and a large log fire. An extensive list of sandwiches includes smoked trout, apple and horseradish, and cambazola, cucumber and kiwi. Interesting main courses offer an imaginative vegetarian choice, and the likes of baked whole bass with ginger and spring onions and medallions of venison with onions, mushrooms and red wine sauce.
OPEN: 12-11. **BAR MEALS:** L served all week. D served all week 12-2 7-10. Av main course £6.50. **BREWERY/COMPANY:** Free House. **PRINCIPAL BEERS:** Worthington Best, Hobsons Best, Theakstons XB. **FACILITIES:** Children welcome Garden: outdoor eating, patio Dogs allowed garden only. **NOTES:** Parking 30

The Mortimer Trail

Officially opened in 1996, the 30-mile Mortimer Trail takes you to the heart of the Welsh Marches, a once bitterly contested land of lush pastures, wooded valleys and rolling hills. Taking its name from the autocratic Mortimer family whose seat was at Wigmore, the route climbs a series of spectacular ridges, with magnificent views of the Black Mountains and the Clee Hills. From these breezy tops the trail runs down to the Rivers Lugg and Arrow and here you might spot a kingfisher or perhaps a heron. Starting at Ludlow in neighbouring Shropshire, where you can enjoy a pint or a leisurely lunch at the Unicorn Inn in Corve Street or the historic Church Inn in Buttercross, the walk makes for the delightfully situated Riverside Inn at Aymestrey. Ideally, you'll want to stop here for an overnight break before continuing to the Bateman Arms at Shobdon, just off the route, and the Stagg Inn at Titley, near the end of the walk. If time allows, you may like to extend the Mortimer Trail and follow a section of the Offa's Dyke long-distance trail to the Royal Oak at Gladestry.

HOWLE HILL   Map 04 SO62

The Crown

HR9 5SP ☎ 01989 764316

Dir: *End M50 thru Ross to B4234, 1st L after entering Walford, then 1st R signed Howle Hill*

Roses round the door greet visitors to this simple 19th-century country pub nestling in a sheltered spot of this scattered hamlet.

KIMBOLTON   Map 03 SO56

Pick of the Pubs

Stockton Cross Inn

HR6 0HD ☎ 01568 612509

Dir: *On the A4112 between Leominster and Ludlow*

Picturesque black and white drovers' inn dating back to the 16th century. The building and its pretty garden are endlessly photographed by tourists and the pub regularly appears on a variety of calendars and chocolate boxes. The food here is equally popular. Good home-cooked specials might include venison Cumberland sausage with red onion gravy, pork tenderloin filled with spinach and wrapped in smoked bacon, and lamb cutlets with redcurrant and port sauce. Hake, sea bass, turbot and smoked haddock among the fish options.

OPEN: 12-3 (Mon 12-3) 7-11. **BAR MEALS:** L served all week. D served Tues-Sun 12-2.15 7-9. Av main course £6.50. **RESTAURANT:** L served all week. D served Tues-Sun 12-2.15 7-9. Av 3 course à la carte £20.

BREWERY/COMPANY: Free House.
PRINCIPAL BEERS: Castle Eden Ale, Whitbread OB Mild, Wye Valley Butty Bach, Bass. **FACILITIES:** Garden: outdoor eating Dogs allowed garden only. **NOTES:** Parking 30

KINGTON   Map 03 SO25

Pick of the Pubs

The Stagg Inn

Titley HR5 3RL ☎ 01544 230221
e-mail: reservations@thestagg.co.uk

In beautiful rolling countryside close to the Welsh border, tiny Titley stands by the Mortimer Trail and the Offa's Dyke Path. Here the Marches are a treasure-trove of fine produce, put to best use by the Stagg's Roux-trained chef proprietor Steve Reynolds. Menus served throughout the homely, pine-furnished bar, complete with wood-burner and jolly, pint-drinking farmers, and the separate, informal dining-room, reflect his pedigree with bar meals of organic local pork sausages with mash and onion gravy, crispy duck leg with cider sauce, local cheese ploughman's, and steak sandwich with home-made chips.

Main seasonal menus start with seared scallops with creamed leeks and black pepper oil, through rack of lamb with fennel and garlic purée, brill with saffron and roast garlic, and Herefordshire beef with béarnaise sauce to end with apple crumble parfait or the splendid cheeseboard. Local Hobson Brewery ales, Dunkerton's organic cider and a well chosen list of wines; eight by the glass. A marvellous re-incarnation of traditional inn-keeping.

OPEN: 12-3 6.30-11 (Sun 12-3, 7-11). Closed 1st 2wks Nov. **BAR MEALS:** L served Tue-Sun. D served Tue-Sun 12-2 6.30-10.30. Av main course £6.50. **RESTAURANT:** L served Tue-Sun. D served Tue-Sun 12-2 6.30-10. Av 3 course à la carte £22. **BREWERY/COMPANY:** Free House.
PRINCIPAL BEERS: Hobsons Town Crier, Hobsons Old Henry, Hobsons Best Bitter. **FACILITIES:** Children welcome Garden: outdoor eating Dogs allowed. **NOTES:** Parking 40. **ROOMS:** 2 bedrooms 2 en suite s£30 d£50 FR£60-£80

See Pub Walk on page 227

LEDBURY   Map 03 SO73

The Farmers Arms

Horse Rd, Wellington Heath HR8 1LS ☎ 01531 632010

Two miles north of Ledbury in lush countryside with woodland views, the new venture of experienced licensees. Country cooking with style is the motto on menus that list starters such as Brie-filled mushrooms with redcurrant sauce followed by Farmer's hog roast, coriander chicken and fresh fish from the chalkboard.

OPEN: 12-3 6-11. **BAR MEALS:** L served all week. D served all week 12-2 7-10. Av main course £7.50. **RESTAURANT:** L served all week. D served all week 12-2 7-10. Av 3 course à la carte £20. **BREWERY/COMPANY:** Free House. **PRINCIPAL BEERS:** Fullers London Pride, Hancocks HB, **FACILITIES:** Children welcome Garden: outdoor eating, patio. **NOTES:** Parking 50

England

Pick of the Pubs

The Feathers Hotel ® ★ ★ ★ 🏠 ♈
High St HR8 1DS ☎ 01531 635266 📠 01531 638955
e-mail: mary@feathers-ledbury.co.uk
Dir: S from Worcester A449, E from Hereford A438, N from
Gloucester A417.
With its striking black-and-white timbered frontage that
dominates the High Street, this fine old coaching inn has
been a haven for travellers since Elizabethan times (the
first one!). Its character is enhanced by an interior full of
oak beams, panelled walls and open log fires. Fuggles
Brasserie is adorned with dried Herefordshire hops of the
same name, while local produce is a major feature of daily
menus posted on large blackboards.
Fresh pheasant breasts are served on wilted greens
with a mustard crust; Hereford beef tournedos come with
thyme, wild mushrooms and glazed shallots. Fresh
Cornish fish features strongly, as in hake fillet with garlic,
lemon and capers and crispy-skinned sea bass with
sesame, chilli and oyster glaze. An adjacent real ale bar
also offers world-famous Herefordshire ciders and a
selection of lunchtime sandwiches while across the foyer
the restaurant provides a more formal dining atmosphere.
Upstairs, and in modern extensions, bedrooms are
individually styled and well equipped.
OPEN: 11-11 (Sun 12-10.30). **BAR MEALS:** L served all
week 12-2. Av main course £11. **RESTAURANT:** L served all
week. D served all week 12-2 7-9.30. Av 3 course à la carte
£17.50. **BREWERY/COMPANY:** Free House.
PRINCIPAL BEERS: Worthington Best, Bass, Fullers London
Pride, Greene King Old Speckled Hen. **FACILITIES:** Children
welcome Garden: outdoor eating, patio.
NOTES: Parking 30. **ROOMS:** 19 bedrooms 19 en suite
s£72.50 d£89.50 FR£105-£150

The Talbot ♈
14 New St HR8 2DX ☎ 01531 632963
e-mail: talbot.ledbury@wadworth.co.uk
Dir: follow Ledbury signs, turn into Bye St, 2nd L into Woodley Rd,
over bridge to jct, L into New St. Talbot on R
Historic black and white coaching inn with a beautiful oak-
panelled dining room, once the scene of fighting between
Cavaliers and Roundheads. The carved overmantle is one of
the finest in the county. You can eat in here or in the cosy bar
from one menu offering Herefordshire steaks and dishes such
as grilled pork cutlet and roast shank of lamb.
OPEN: 11.30-3 5-11. **BAR MEALS:** L served all week. D served
all week 12-2.30 6.30-9.30. Av main course £7.50.
RESTAURANT: L served all week. D served all week 12-2.30
6.30-9.30. Av 3 course à la carte £16.50.
BREWERY/COMPANY: Free House.
PRINCIPAL BEERS: Wadworth 6X, Henrys IPA, Wye Valley Butty
Bach. **FACILITIES:** Dogs allowed. **NOTES:** Parking 10.
ROOMS: 7 bedrooms 6 en suite s£27.50 d£49.50

Map 03 SO45

The Royal Oak Hotel ★ ★
South St HR6 8JA ☎ 01568 612610 📠 01568 612710
Dir: Junc A44/A49
Coaching inn dating from before 1700, with log fires, antiques
and a minstrels' gallery in the original ball room.

Map 03 SO65

The Three Horseshoes Inn
HR7 4RQ ☎ 01885 400276 📠 01885 400276
Dir: Off A456 (Hereford/Bromyard).At Stokes Cross, take turning
signed Little Cowarne/Pencombe

Formerly a blacksmith's shop and alehouse, this country inn
offers home-made food using fresh local produce, and the
Garden Room conservatory is a pleasant place to eat at
lunchtime. The blackboard menu ranges from bar snacks to
prawn and haddock smokies, devilled kidneys, grilled sea bass
with lemon and lime dressing, and venison with blackcurrant
sauce.
OPEN: 11-3 6.30-11 Closed Sun eve Winter. Closed Dec 25.
BAR MEALS: L served all week. D served all week 12-2 6.30-10.
Av main course £9. **RESTAURANT:** L served all week. D served
all week 12-2 6.30-10. Av 3 course à la carte £15.
BREWERY/COMPANY: Free House. **PRINCIPAL BEERS:** Marstons Pedigree, Greene King Old Speckled Hen, Websters
Yorkshire Bitter, Wye Valley Bitter,. **FACILITIES:** Children
welcome Garden: outdoor eating, patio, BBQ. **NOTES:** Parking
50. **ROOMS:** 2 bedrooms 2 en suite s£27 d£46

Map 03 SO43

The Comet Inn
Stoney St HR2 9NJ ☎ 01981 250600 📠 01981 250643
Dir: approx 6m from Hereford on the B4352
Located in a prominent corner position and set in two and a
half acres, this black and white 19th-century inn has beamed
walls and ceilings, and a large open fire.

The Bridge Inn
HR2 0JW ☎ 01981 510646 📠 01981 510646
e-mail: lisabridge@tesco.net
Dir: from Hereford take A465 towards Abergavenny, then B4348
towards Peterchurch. Turn L at Vowchurch for village
By Escley Brook, at the foot of the Black Mountains and close
to Offa's Dyke, there are 14th-century parts to this oak-
beamed family pub: the dining-room overlooks the river and
garden, abundant in rose and begonias. The food-minded
landlady's home-produced dishes include steak and ale and
leek and parsnip pies and fine Herefordshire beef.
OPEN: 12-2.30 7-11 (Sun 12-10.30). Closed 25 Dec.
BAR MEALS: L served all week. D served all week 12-2 7-9.30. Av
main course £5. **RESTAURANT:** L served all week. D served all
week 12-2 7-9.30. Av 3 course à la carte £15.
BREWERY/COMPANY: Free House.
PRINCIPAL BEERS: Buckley's Best, Wye Valley IPA.
FACILITIES: Children welcome Garden: patio, outdoor eating,
BBQ Dogs allowed. **NOTES:** Parking 30

MUCH COWARNE
Map 03 SO64

Fir Tree Inn
HR7 4JN ☎ 01531 640619 📠 01531 640663
e-mail: richard@firtreeinn.co.uk
Dir: off the A4103 Hereford to Worcester
Set in three acres of grounds with fishing lake and small
caravan site, this this part 16th-century modernised inn is a
versatile establishment situated in unspoilt countryside. Dishes
may include home-made steak and ale pie, lamb, mint and
apricot bake, mixed grill, Dover sole, lasagne, and sirloin steak.

OPEN: 12-3 6-11. **BAR MEALS:** L served all week. D served Sun-
Thu12-2.30 6.30-10. Av main course £3.50. **RESTAURANT:** L
served all week. D served all week 12-2.30 6.30-10. Av 3 course à
la carte £12.50. Av 1 course fixed price £9.95.
BREWERY/COMPANY: Free House. **PRINCIPAL BEERS:** Bass.
FACILITIES: Children welcome Garden: Dogs allowed.
NOTES: Parking 80

MUCH MARCLE
Map 03 SO63

The Scrumpy House Bar & Restaurant 🐨
The Bounds HR8 2NQ ☎ 01531 660626 📠 01531 660626
e-mail: matt@scrumpyhouse.co.uk
*Dir: approx 5 miles from Ledbury & Ross-on-Wye on A449, follow
signs to Cidermill*
A renovated hay barn on the site of a family-run cider mill
with a bar and restaurant separated by a woodburner in the
fireplace. Over 20 different ciders are offered alongside local
bitters and a varied wine list. All food is prepared on the
premises, including 16 kinds of ice cream, and fresh fish on
Friday from Grimsby. Favourite dishes include award-winning
local bangers and oven-baked sea bass stuffed with home-
grown herbs.
OPEN: 12-2.30 7-12 (Fri-Sat 12-2.30, 6.30-12). Closed 25-26 Dec.
RESTAURANT: L served all week. D served all week 12-2.30 7-11.
Av 3 course à la carte £22. **BREWERY/COMPANY:** Free House
FACILITIES: Children welcome Children's licence Garden:
Patio, Food served outside. **NOTES:** Parking 30

The Slip Tavern ♀
Watery Ln HR8 2NG ☎ 01531 660246
Dir: Follow the signs off the A449 at the Much Marcle junction
This country pub, surrounded by cider apple orchards, is
named after the landslip of 1575. Sit in the cosy bar or the
attractive conservatory overlooking the award-winning garden.
A comprehensive menu ranges through steaks, salads, pork
and pears, crispy lemon chicken, and faggots with mushy peas
and chips.
OPEN: 11.30-2.30 6.30-11 (Sun 12-2.30, 6.30-10.30).
BAR MEALS: L served all week. D served all week 12-2 7-9.30. Av
main course £6.45. **RESTAURANT:** L served all week. D served
continued

all week 12-2 7. Av 3 course à la carte £12.
BREWERY/COMPANY: Free House.
PRINCIPAL BEERS: Hook Norton, Wadworth 6X, John Smiths
Bitter. **FACILITIES:** Children welcome Garden: patio, food
served outside Dogs allowed. **NOTES:** Parking 45

PEMBRIDGE
Map 03 SO35

The Cider House Restaurant
Dunkerton's Cider Mill, Luntley HR6 9ED ☎ 01544 388161
📠 01544 388654
*Dir: W on A44 from Leominster, L in Pembridge centre by New Inn,
1m on L*
Dunkertons own and run the 16th-century timber-framed
dining room that adjoins their orchards and cider mill. The
farm's own meat features on the menu and organic vegetables
and herbs are planned. Bread, cakes and pastries are all home
made too. The regularly changing menu might include
Hereford beef in cider with roast vegetables and herb
dumplings, and baked organic pork, as well as British
farmhouse cheeses - and cider.
OPEN: 10-5. Closed Jan, Feb, & Dec 25-26. **BAR MEALS:** L
served Mon-Sat 12-2.30. Av main course £10. **RESTAURANT:** L
served Mon-Sat 12-2.30. Av 3 course à la carte £17.
BREWERY/COMPANY: Free House.
PRINCIPAL BEERS: Dunkertons Ciders, Caledonian Golden
Promise. **FACILITIES:** Children welcome Terrace overlooking
fields. **NOTES:** Parking 30

New Inn ♀
Market Square HR6 9DZ ☎ 01544 388427
📠 01544 388427
*Dir: From M5 J7 take A44 W through Leominster towards Llandrindod
Wells*
At the centre of a picture-postcard village full of quaint
cottages, this black and white timbered inn dates from the
early 14th-century and is one of the oldest pubs in England. It
was once the local court house and the cellar used to be the
dungeon. Reputedly haunted by the ghosts of a young lady
and a red-coated soldier beating a drum. Full of old beams,
wonky walls and worn flagstones, it offers a traditional menu
which may list hearty, home-cooked dishes like pheasant in
elderberry wine, beef and vegetable stew and deep-fried cod,
alongside crab and avocado salad and crusty sandwiches.
OPEN: 11-3 Winter 11-2.30 6-11. **BAR MEALS:** L served all
week. D served Fri-Tue 12-2 7-9.30. Av main course £6.
RESTAURANT: L served all week. D served Fri-Tue 12-2 7-9.30.
Av 3 course à la carte £11.50. **BREWERY/COMPANY:** Free
House. **PRINCIPAL BEERS:** Fullers London Pride, Bass, Kington
Bitter. **FACILITIES:** Children welcome Garden: patio area,Food
served outside. **NOTES:** Parking 25. **ROOMS:** 6 bedrooms s£20
d£40 FR£40.00-£50.00

ROSS-ON-WYE

The Moody Cow ♀
Upton Bishop HR9 7TT ☎ 01989 780470
Older sister pub to the new 'Moody Cow' at the Wykeham
Arms at Sibford Gower, Oxfordshire. This old stone pub
incorporates a formerly derelict barn (now the restaurant), and
has been an established dining destination locally since
the early 1990s. Long menu of imaginative dishes that are
freshly prepared from local produce, including the famous
Moody Cow Pie - steak and kidney with potatoes under
shortcrust pastry - with 'fishy' special listed on the blackboard.

England

The Woodhampton Brewing Co.

What makes this Herefordshire micro-brewery unusual is the fact that it markets its beers using ornithological brands. These include Red Kite (3.6%), Jack Snipe (4.1%) and Kingfisher Ale (4.5%). Seasonal brews include Wagtail and Ravens Head. The brewery was founded in 1996, and uses a natural spring for its water.

ST OWEN'S CROSS   Map 03 SO52

The New Inn 🐾
HR2 8LQ ☎ 01989 730274 📠 01989 730547
Dir: Off A4137 W of Ross-on-Wye
Heavily beamed coaching inn on the Chepstow to Hereford route, with three Dobermans, several ghosts and many colourful hanging baskets in summer. It is probably the oldest site of refreshment in the county - as far back as the 6th century St Owen, a pilgrim saint, is known to have stopped here. Special dishes include rack of lamb, guinea fowl, pigeon, rabbit, venison, curries and chilli.

OPEN: 12-2.30 6-11. **BAR MEALS:** L served all week. D served all week 12-2.30 6.30-9.30. Av main course £6. **RESTAURANT:** L served all week. D served all week 12-2.30 6.30-9.30. Av 3 course à la carte £15. **BREWERY/COMPANY:** Free House.
PRINCIPAL BEERS: Wadworth 6X, Tetley, Bass, Fullers London Pride. **FACILITIES:** Children welcome Garden: Food served outside Dogs allowed Water, Food. **NOTES:** Parking 45.
ROOMS: 2 bedrooms 2 en suite s£35 d£35

SELLACK   Map 03 SO52

The Lough Pool Inn 🐾 ♀
HR9 6LX ☎ 01989 730236 📠 01989 730462
Dir: A49 from Ross-on-Wye toward Hereford, side rd signed Sellack/Hoarwithy, pub 2m from R-on-W

Half-timbered, 17th-century pub enjoying an off-the-beaten-track location amid rolling countryside close to the River Wye. Respected London chef/restaurateur, Stephen Bull, bought the pub towards the end of 2000. He has extended the kitchen and is gradually refurbishing the traditional flagstoned bar and the intimate beamed dining-room. As one would expect, food style and quality has improved but the Lough Pool will not become a country restaurant. Real ales and an improved wine list accompany good bar food prepared from tip-top ingredients sourced from local suppliers.

Typically, the daily menu may list chicken liver pâté with sweet grape relish, mussels with saffron, roast pepper and almond cream, steak and kidney pie, steak and Stilton baguette, a decent ploughman's with pear chutney, and the very popular roast duck (for two). Plans to introduce a separate, more adventurous restaurant menu were being finalised as we went to press. A truly peaceful spot; lovely front garden for summer alfresco imbibing.
OPEN: 11.30-2.30 (Sun 12-6) 6.30-11. Closed 25 Dec.
BAR MEALS: L served all week. D served all week 12-2 7-9.30. Av main course £10. **RESTAURANT:** L served all week. D served all week 12-2 7-9.30. Av 3 course à la carte £20. **BREWERY/COMPANY:** Free House.
PRINCIPAL BEERS: Wye Valley, John Smiths,.
FACILITIES: Children welcome Garden: Beer garden, outdoor eating. **NOTES:** Parking 40

SHOBDON   Map 03 SO46

The Bateman Arms
HR6 9LX ☎ 01568 708374
Dir: On B4362 off A4110 NW of Leominster
Black and white 18th-century coaching inn. Traditional interior with open fire, wooden settles and a welcoming atmosphere. Under new management. A great area for walking. The village also has an outstanding old church, an air field and a caravan park.

England

SYMONDS YAT (EAST)   Map 03 SO51

The Saracens Head Inn ★ ★ ♀
HR9 6JL ☎ 01600 890435 🖹 01600 890034
e-mail: email@saracensheadinn.co.uk
Riverside inn on the east bank of the glorious Wye, situated by
the ancient hand ferry which has been in use for 250 years.
Handy for exploring the Wye Valley and Forest of Dean. Wide
range of home-made bar food and restaurant dishes includes
lamb cutlets, fillet au poivre, red mullet and shepherds pie.
OPEN: 11-11 (Sun 12-10.30). **BAR MEALS:** L served all week. D
served all week 12-2.30 7-9.15. Av main course £6.50.
RESTAURANT: D served all week 7-9.15. Av 3 course à la carte
£20. **BREWERY/COMPANY:** Free House.
PRINCIPAL BEERS: Theakstons, Greene King Old Speckled Hen,
Wells Bombardier, Wye Valley HPA. **FACILITIES:** Children
welcome Garden: patio, outdoor eating Dogs allowed.
NOTES: Parking 38. **ROOMS:** 9 bedrooms 9 en suite s£35 d£60

ULLINGSWICK   Map 03 SO54

Pick of the Pubs

Three Crowns Inn 🍸 ♀
HR1 3JQ ☎ 01432 820279 🖹 01432 820279
e-mail: info@threecrownsinn.demon.co.uk
Dir: *From Burley Gate rdbt take A465 toward Bromyard, after 2m
L to Ullingswick, L after 0.5m, pub 0.5m on R*
As unspoilt as it gets deep in the countryside looking
across to the Welsh borders, the emphasis here is on
providing for lovers of good food and drink the best that
Herefordshire can provide. And they do it well with
organically grown produce, rare breed livestock and
artisans' cheeses to accompany beers from nearby
breweries and famous Hereford cider.

All food is made on the premises, much of it from
home-grown varieties of old herbs, fruit and vegetables
that are not commercially available. A distinctive,
individual style of cooking results, served in an informal
environment of simple sophistication.

Typical weekday lunches, at an affordable price, might
include grilled cod with curry butter, beef, stout and
mustard sausage and mash and ploughman's of
Monkland cheese with home-made pickles. The
sophistication is otherwise revealed in Cheddar and
spinach soufflé with Parmesan, crusted rack of Marches
lamb with a bacon and leek quiche and sticky toffee
pudding with malt whisky sauce. Flavours of Herefordshire
dinners are held quarterly.
OPEN: 12-2.30 7-11 (Sun 12-3, 7-10.30). Closed 2wks from
Dec 25. **BAR MEALS:** L served Wed-Mon. D served Wed-
Mon 12-3 7-10.30. Av main course £12.95.
BREWERY/COMPANY: Free House.
PRINCIPAL BEERS: Hobsons Best. **FACILITIES:** Garden:
outdoor eating, patio Dogs allowed except when food is
being served in bar. **NOTES:** Parking 20

For pubs with AA rosette awards for food
see page 10

Heraldic Devices

The animals on inn signs are
frequently drawn from heraldry.
The most common of all, the Red Lion,
was the badge of the kings of Scots from
time immemorial and had a prominent
place in the British royal arms after the
accession of James I in 1603. So did the
Unicorn, which is also a pub name, while the
Greyhound was a Tudor badge. The White Horse
was the Hanoverian emblem (and an ancient
badge of Kent). Other devices include the Eagle
and Child of the Stanleys, Earls of Derby, the Blue
Boar of the De Veres, Earls of Oxford, and the
Bear - with or without Ragged Staff - of the
Earls of Warwick. Other well-known heraldic
signs are the Chequers, the Spread Eagle
and the Stag's Head, and many pubs
display the coat of arms of the local
landowning family, which might
own the pub or with whom it
was desirable to be on
good terms.

WALTERSTONE   Map 03 SO32

Carpenters Arms ♀
HR2 0DX ☎ 01873 890353
Dir: *Off the A465 between Hereford & Abergavenny at Pandy*
Dating back over 300 years, this popular country pub is
located on the edge of the Black Mountains, and the owner
Mrs Watkins was born here. It has plenty of character, with
beams, antique settles and a leaded range where open fires
burn all winter. Options range from smoked salmon and
scrambled egg to 10oz sirloin steak, with home-made dishes
such as cod and prawn pie, lasagne and chicken curry.
OPEN: 11-3 7-11. **BAR MEALS:** L served all week. D served all
week 12-3 7-9.30. Av main course £6. **RESTAURANT:** L served
all week. D served all week 12-3 7-9.30. Av 3 course à la carte £20.
BREWERY/COMPANY: Free House.
PRINCIPAL BEERS: Wadworth 6X, Worthington Best.
FACILITIES: Children welcome Garden: patio, food served
outdoors Dogs allowed Only by arrangement.
NOTES: Parking 15 No credit cards

WEOBLEY   Map 03 SO45

Pick of the Pubs

Ye Olde Salutation Inn ◉ ◉ ♦♦♦♦ 🍸 ♀
Market Pitch HR4 8SJ ☎ 01544 318443
🖹 01544 318216
e-mail: info@salutationinn.com
See Pick of the Pubs on page 235

Open: 11-11 (Sun 12-10.30).
Bar Meals: L served all week.
D served all week 12-2 7-9.30. Av
main course £7.25.
RESTAURANT: L served all week
D served all week 12-2 7-9. Av 3
course a la carte £26.50.
BREWERY/COMPANY:
Free House.
PRINCIPLE BEERS: Hook Norton
Best, Fullers London Pride.
FACILITIES: Garden: patio,
outdoor eating.
NOTES: Parking 14.
ROOMS: 3 bedrooms 3 en suite
s£45-£50 d£69-£75

The Salutation Inn

◉ ◆◆◆◆ 🛏 ⚲
Market Pitch HR4 8SJ
☎ 01544 318443 📠 01544 318216
e-mail: info@salutationinn.com
Dir: In the village centre facing Broad
Street

This historic old inn, under new ownership this year, remains one of the area's favoured destinations for all the right reasons; peaceful accommodation overlooking the green, a comfortable blend of village pub, destination eating-house and food that has apparently lost none of its appeal.

A black-and-white timbered conversion of a former ale and cider house with adjoining cottages, the Salutation dates back 500 years and is full of old-world charm and character. There is a lounge bar and snack menu (at lunch only) that promises a choice of ploughman's lunches and baked baguettes, in addition to gratin of seafood, steak and stout pie and lamb and barley stew with freshly baked bread. Other specials posted on the boards might include whole grilled plaice, pheasant supreme with mushrooms, red onions and thyme and a bean and aubergine moussaka. For finishing touches turn to a further page listing Jamaican bananas in rum sauce, an 'orchard pancake' with orange sauce and Calvados ice cream and allegedly 'Mouse Trap' cheeses served with biscuits and celery. Sunday lunch, when the full alternatives might not be available, includes a selection of roasts preceded by baked goats' cheese or chicken and sweetcorn soup and apple crumble with vanilla ice cream or hazelnut parfait and chocolate sauce to round off a meal of undoubted quality served in convivial surroundings.

There remains another time to sample a classy restaurant menu that offers more of the same with a host of added extras. In the bars go for quality real ales or acceptable wines by the glass: again the Oak Room wine list journeys into another dimension.

Well equipped, traditionally furnished bedrooms include a family room, and a room with a four-poster bed.

England

Rhydspence Inn ★ ★ 🍴
HR3 6EU ☎ 01497 831262   🖹 01497 831751
Dir: *N side of A438 1m W of Whitney-on-Wye*
14th-century converted manor house on the English side of
the Welsh Borders, with a spacious dining room overlooking
the Wye valley. For many years it was a meeting point for
drovers on the Black Ox Trail, taking livestock as far as London.
It now offers an imaginative menu ranging from Cajun chicken
and roast half of Aylesbury duck, to baked supreme of salmon,
hand-made pork and leek sausage, and tagliatelli provençale.

OPEN: 11-2.30 7-11 (closed 2wks Jan). Closed 2 wks in Jan. **BAR
MEALS:** L served all week. D served all week 11-2.30 7-9.30. Av
main course £6.50. **RESTAURANT:** L served all week. D served
all week 11-2.30 7-9.30. Av 3 course à la carte £23. **BREWERY/
COMPANY:** Free House. **PRINCIPAL BEERS:** Robinsons Best,
Bass. **FACILITIES:** Children welcome Garden: Beer Garden:,
Food served outside. **NOTES:** Parking 30. **ROOMS:** 7
bedrooms 7 en suite s£27.50 d£55

Pick of the Pubs

The Sun Inn 🍴
HR3 6EA ☎ 01544 327677   🖹 01544 327677
The secret of the Sun's long-standing success lies in the
dedication of Welsh licensees Brian and Wendy Hibbards'
reliance on the best locally-bought ingredients, prepared
and cooked in a trendy mix of modern and traditional
guises. Results that score on the plate include grilled tuna
with lime, ginger and sesame dressing, pigeon pie
(secretly devised by Brian), so-called 'Grandma's' fish pie
and the pork-based 'Piggie-in-the-Orchard', flavoured with
Herefordshire cider apples - and an allegedly divine
Chocolate Heaven-on-a-plate. From the snacks board go
for the plate of pristine local cheeses served with Wendy's
home-made chutneys or vegetarian Welsh Dragon pie
with a generous dish of fresh vegetables. The recently
added en-suite bedrooms are cosily comfortable. In
summer relax in the orchard or tackle a novel golf
challenge that reflects these family proprietors' own
philosophy - original, imaginative and just slightly crazy.
OPEN: 11.30-3 6.15-11 (closed Tue). **BAR MEALS:** L served
Wed-Mon. D served Wed-Mon 12-2.00 6.45-9.30. Av main
course £8. **RESTAURANT:** L served Wed-Mon. D served
Wed Mon12-2 6.45-9.30. Av 3 course à la carte £17.
BREWERY/COMPANY: Free House. **PRINCIPAL BEERS:**
Jennings, Hook Norton, Woods. **FACILITIES:** Children welcome
Garden: patio, outdoor eating **NOTES:** Parking 40. **ROOMS:** 3
bedrooms 3 en suite s£32 d£50 FR£68 No credit cards

The Butchers Arms
HR1 4RF ☎ 01432 860281
e-mail: mark-vallely@lineone.net
Dir: *Off B4224 between Hereford & Ross-on-Wye*
Set in glorious walking country close to the Marcle Ridge, this
14th-century pub welcomes you with low beams, comfortable
old settles, and roaring log fires. Well-kept ales complement
substantial dishes like venison sausages and mash, mushroom
biryani or steak and kidney pie. There's plenty of seafood, too;
baked trout or ocean pie, as well as cod, plaice, scampi or
salmon.
OPEN: 11.30-2.30 6.30-11. **BAR MEALS:** L served all week.
D served all week 12-2 6.30-9.30. Av main course £7.
RESTAURANT: L served Sat-Sun. D served Sat-Sun 12-2.30 6.30-
9.30. Av 3 course à la carte £15. **BREWERY/COMPANY:** Free
House. **PRINCIPAL BEERS:** Hook Norton Best & Old Hooky.
Wye Valley, Shepherd Neame Spitfire. **FACILITIES:** Children
welcome Garden: patio, outdoor eating. **NOTES:** Parking 50.
ROOMS: 2 bedrooms 2 en suite s£30 d£39

The Crown Inn 🍺
HR1 4QP ☎ 01432 860468   🖹 01432 860633
Dir: *from Hereford take B4224 to Mordiford, L immediately after
Moon Inn. Crown Inn is in village centre*
Located in the centre of the village, next door to the church and
within a conservation area, this 18th-century stone-built pub,
adorned with colourful flowers in summer, offers a very
extensive menu. Starters range from garlic mushrooms on toast
to bacon and cheese crumpet, while bacon chop with plum
sauce, deep-fried plaice, rabbit pie and lamb, apricot and ginger
casserole might feature among the main courses. Good selection
of puddings. Beautifully kept lounge bar with open fires,
attractive wildlife pictures, and excellent Wye Valley ales on tap.
OPEN: 12-2.30 6.30-11 (Sun till 10.30, times vary in winter).
BAR MEALS: L served all week. D served all week 12-2 6.30/7-10.
Av main course £7.50. **RESTAURANT:** L served all week. D
served all week 12-2 6.30/7-10. Av 3 course à la carte £14.25.
BREWERY/COMPANY: Free House.
PRINCIPAL BEERS: Smiles Best, Wye Valley Best.
FACILITIES: Children welcome Garden: Beer garden, outdoor
eating, patio, Dogs allowed ex Guide dogs and in the garden.
NOTES: Parking 30

McMullen
since 1827
Peter McMullen, founder of this
Hertfordshire brewery, was a master cooper
who got fed up with making barrels of a higher
quality than the beers they contained. Before
long he was producing AK (3.7%) and buying up
pubs in the area. In 1891, his successor Osmond
Henry McMullen, built a new brewery at Hartham
Lane that has stood the test of time and still
produces McMullen brews today. Among
these are Gladstone (4.3%), Country Best
(4.3%), Strong Hart (7.0%) and
Special Reserve (5.0%).

HERTFORDSHIRE

ALDBURY
Map 06 SP91

The Greyhound Inn
19 Stocks Rd HP23 5RT ☎ 01442 851228 🖹 01442 851495
Situated in the valley between Ashridge Forest and The
Chilterns and surrounded by National Trust parkland, Aldbury
is an idyllic village: its historic coaching inn overlooks the old
stocks and duck pond. Bar snacks include fresh-cut bloomers
and home-made burgers alongside daily blackboard specials
such as steak and ale pie, wild boar, venison, sea bass and
vegetable and goats cheese lasagne.
OPEN: 7-11. Closed 25 Dec. **BAR MEALS:** L served all week. D
served all week 12-2.30 7-9.30. Av main course £6.95.
RESTAURANT: L served all week. D served all week 12-2.30
7-9.30. Av 3 course à la carte £18.50.
BREWERY/COMPANY: Hall & Woodhouse.
PRINCIPAL BEERS: Badger Best, Tanglefoot & Champion.
FACILITIES: Children welcome Garden: Food served outside
Dogs allowed Water. **NOTES:** Parking 9.
ROOMS: 11 bedrooms 11 en suite s£60 d£75

The Valiant Trooper ♀
Trooper Rd HP23 5RW ☎ 01442 851203 🖹 01442 851071
Dir: A41 Tring jct, follow signs for railway station, go past for about
1/2m, once at village green turn R then 200yds on L
Family-run free house in a pretty village surrounded by the
Chiltern Hills, where hikers, cyclists and dogs are all made
welcome. Local and guest beers feature, and interesting daily
specials from the blackboard are tarragon chicken on fennel
mash, and cod fillet with capers and prawns. The Duke of
Wellington is rumoured to have held a tactical conference at
the pub - hence the name.
OPEN: 11-11 (Sun 12-10.30). **BAR MEALS:** L served all week. D
served all week 12-2 6.30-9.15. Av main course £8.50.
RESTAURANT: L served all week. D served All12-2 6.30-9.15.
Av 3 course à la carte £15. **BREWERY/COMPANY:** Free House.
PRINCIPAL BEERS: Fullers London Pride, John Smiths, Marstons
Pedigree, Ruddles Best. **FACILITIES:** Children welcome Garden:
beer garden, food served in the garden Dogs allowed.
NOTES: Parking 36

ARDELEY
Map 06 TL32

The Jolly Waggoner
SG2 7AH ☎ 01438 861350
Dating back 500 years, this pink-washed village pub is
characterised by original beams and antique furniture. In
winter there are roaring log fires and in summer a beautiful
garden to enjoy. Favourite dishes range through omelette
Arnold Bennett, filled with smoked haddock and served with a
light béchamel sauce, home-made burgers topped with
cheddar and bacon, local sausages, and fillet of sea bass with
mash and fresh asparagus.
OPEN: 12-2.30 6.30-11 (open BH Mon, closed Tue after BH.
BAR MEALS: L served Tue-Sun. D served Tue-Sat 12-2 6.30-9.00.
Av main course £9. **RESTAURANT:** L served Sun. D served Tue-
Sat 12.30 6.30-9. Av 3 course à la carte £30.
BREWERY/COMPANY: Greene King.
PRINCIPAL BEERS: Greene King IPA & Abbot Ale.
FACILITIES: Children welcome Garden: Beer garden, Outdoor
eating,. **NOTES:** Parking 15

ASHWELL
Map 06 TL23

Bushel & Strike ♀
Mill St SG7 5LY ☎ 01462 742394 🖹 01462 742300
Popular inn located in a pretty village with ancient springs and
lovely local walks. The main bar has wooden floors, leather
chesterfields and open fires in winter, while the conservatory
restaurant is a conversion of the old school hall. Food based
on fresh, locally sourced ingredients is served in both areas,
with options such as cracker of pork fillet, knuckle of lamb,
and chicken balti.
OPEN: 11.30-3 6-11.20 (all day Sun). **BAR MEALS:** L served all
week. D served all week 12-2.30 7-9.30. Av main course £8.
RESTAURANT: L served all week. D served all week 12-2.30
7-9.30. Av 3 course à la carte £15. Av 3 course fixed price £8.
BREWERY/COMPANY: Charles Wells.
PRINCIPAL BEERS: Greene King Old Speckled Hen, Wells
Bombadier/Eagle, Adnams Broadside. **FACILITIES:** Children
welcome Garden: outdoor eating, Dogs allowed.
NOTES: Parking 40

The Three Tuns
High St SG7 5NL ☎ 01462 742107 🖹 01462 743662
e-mail: claire@tuns.co.uk
This 19th-century inn has a lot of original features, and is next
to an ancient natural spring. Parts of the building date back to
the 18th century. Old world atmosphere, and locally renowned
home-made food.

AYOT ST LAWRENCE
Map 06 TL11

Pick of the Pubs

The Brocket Arms ♦♦♦ ♀
AL6 9BT ☎ 01438 820250 🖹 01438 820068
Delightful 14th-century inn located in the village where
George Bernard Shaw lived for 40 years. Many charming
features inside, including oak-beamed, low-ceilinged bars
and restaurant. The extensive walled garden is a glorious
sun-trap in summer, while the inn's bedrooms vary in
shape and size, with the four-poster rooms being
especially popular. Traditional English dishes characterise
the menu, with medallions of local venison, steak and
kidney pie, and roast duck with orange and Grand Marnier
sauce among them.
OPEN: 11-11. **BAR MEALS:** L served all week. D served
Tue-Sat 12-2.30 7.30-10. Av main course £5.
RESTAURANT: L served all week. D served Tue-Sat 12-2.30
7.30-10. Av 3 course à la carte £18.
BREWERY/COMPANY: Free House.
PRINCIPAL BEERS: Greene King Abbot Ale & IPA, Adnams
Broadside, Fullers London Pride, Youngs IPA.
FACILITIES: Children welcome Garden: Food served
outside Dogs allowed garden only. **NOTES:** Parking 7.
ROOMS: 7 bedrooms 3 en suite s£60 d£70

Room prices minimum single and minimum double
rates are shown. FR indicates family room

England

BARLEY · Map 07 TL43

The Fox & Hounds
High St SG8 8HU ☎ 01763 848459 ▤ 01763 849274
Dir: A505 onto B1368 at Flint Cross, pub 4m
Enjoying a pretty thatched village setting, this former 17th-century hunting lodge is notable for its pub sign which extends across the lane. Real fires and a warm welcome. Watch the daily changing blackboard menus for today's specials. Under new management.

BERKHAMSTED · Map 06 SP90

Pick of the Pubs

Alford Arms ♀
Frithsden HP1 3DD ☎ 01442 864480
▤ 01422 876893
Surrounded as it is by beautiful National Trust woodland, follow the signs for Frithsden Vineyard - directly behind the pub - to find the former Tyrant Arms which was burned down in the 19th century. It is a pretty place, typically Victorian, full of traditional finishes, old furniture and pictures, quarry tiles and reclaimed wooden floors. The interior has a light modern touch in keeping with today's trends, blending well with a style of food that has become its great draw with walkers, cyclists and pub gourmands alike.

Small plates range from oak-smoked bacon, bubble-and-squeak, hollandaise and poached egg to Thai scented mussels with coconut offered in two sizes. Main meals mix rustic and eclectic styles as in salmon fishcakes with celeriac remoulade and roast monkfish on leek-and-bacon mash amongst the daily fish choices - and calves' liver on dauphinoise potatoes with blueberry and thyme jus, duck leg confit with bok choi, soy and garlic and penne with wild mushrooms and spicy chestnut pesto among popular alternatives. Best local free range and organic suppliers are used wherever possible; real ales and plenty of wines by the glass are chosen will equal care, and the service from David and Becky Salisbury's team is warm and friendly in the very best tradition.
OPEN: 11-11. **BAR MEALS:** L served all week. D served all week 12-2.30 7-10. Av main course £10. **RESTAURANT:** L served all week. D served all week 12-2.30 7-10. Av 3 course à la carte £20. **PRINCIPAL BEERS:** Marstons Pedigree, Wadworth 6X, Flowers. **FACILITIES:** Garden: Food served outside Dogs allowed Water. **NOTES:** Parking 25

The Boat
Gravel Path HP4 2EF ☎ 01422 877152
Very modern canalside pub that has a lot of character despite its relative youth. A summer terrace overlooks the canal. Fuller ales. Open all day.

BUNTINGFORD · Map 06 TL32

The Sword in Hand
Westmill SG9 9LQ ☎ 01763 271356
Dir: Off A10 1.5m S of Buntingford
Early 15th-century inn, once the home of the Scottish noble family, Gregs. Pubs name taken from a motif within their family crest. Regularly changing menu.

BURNHAM GREEN · Map 06 TL21

The White Horse
White Horse Ln AL6 0HA ☎ 01438 798416
▤ 01438 798002
Sympathetically restored and extended old pub situated on the village green. Civilised dining ambience within the neatly furnished beamed bar and galleried extension. Bar food ranges from traditional meals like fresh battered cod, lasagne, and home-cooked ham, to monthly specials such as beef Wellington and chargrilled calves' liver with red onion gravy.
OPEN: 11.30-3 6-11. **BAR MEALS:** L served all week. D served all week 12-2 6.30-9.30. Av main course £5. **RESTAURANT:** L served all week. D served all week 12-2 6.30-9. Av 3 course à la carte £14. **BREWERY/COMPANY:** Free House.
PRINCIPAL BEERS: Greene King IPA & Abbot Ale, Brakspear.
FACILITIES: Garden. **NOTES:** Parking 50

COTTERED · Map 06 TL32

The Bull at Cottered NEW
Cottered ☎ 01763 281243
Attractively situated in a pretty village, this traditional local boasts low-beamed ceilings, an open log fire and pub games like cribbage and dominoes. A good-sized garden, well kept ales and interesting, good quality meals makes this a pub worth visiting. Popular dishes include salads, chicken with Stilton and walnut sauce, rack of lamb, home-made burgers, and salmon fillet with prawns in a wine and parsley sauce.
OPEN: 12-2.30 6.30-11. **BAR MEALS:** L served all week. D served Wed-Mon 12-2 6.30-9. Av main course £10.
RESTAURANT: L served all week. D served all week 12-2 6.30-9. Av 3 course fixed price £19.50. **BREWERY/COMPANY:** Greene King. **PRINCIPAL BEERS:** Greene King IPA & Abbot Ale.
FACILITIES: Children welcome Garden: Food served outside.
NOTES: Parking 30

FLAUNDEN · Map 06 TL00

The Bricklayers Arms ♀
Hogpits Bottom HP3 0PH ☎ 01442 833322
e-mail: brickies-flaunden@talk21.com
Dir: M1 J8 through H Hempstead to Bovington then follow Flaunden sign. M25 J18 through Chorleywood to Chenies/Latimer then Flaunden

Traditional low-beamed freehouse and country pub characterised by a low-beamed bar, wooden wall seats and virginia creeper. Popular with locals and walkers who like to relax in the delightfully old-fashioned garden in the summer months. Once inside, the inn offers a friendly, informal ambience together with good quality, freshly prepared dishes.

continued

OPEN: 11.30-3 6-11 Summer Sat-Sun open all afternoon.
BAR MEALS: L served all week. D served all week 12-2.30 7-9.30.
Av main course £7. **RESTAURANT:** L served all week. D served
all week 12-2 7-9. Av 3 course à la carte £24.
BREWERY/COMPANY: Free House.
PRINCIPAL BEERS: Fullers London Pride, Brakspear Bitter,
Ringwood Old Thumper. **FACILITIES:** Children welcome
Garden: outdoor eating, patio, BBQ Dogs allowed Water.
NOTES: Parking 40

The Green Dragon
HP3 0PP ☎ 01442 832269
Dir: B4505 from Hemel Hempstead to Bovington then S to Flaunden
Walkers and cyclists visiting the Chilterns find this a welcome
watering hole, as did some other, rather more unlikely guests.
Both Hitler's ambassador Von Ribbentrop, and British spy Guy
Burgess, have visited this historic village inn. Food comes in
large portions, and children are very welcome.

HARPENDEN

Gibraltar Castle
70 Lower Luton Rd AL5 5AH ☎ 01582 460005
Bustling Fuller's pub located opposite a common in Batford.
Collection of militaria, comfortable carpeted bar and
traditional pub food; live Irish music on Tuesdays.
OPEN: 11-3 5-11 (Sun 12-4, 6-10.30). **BAR MEALS:** L served all
week. D served all week 12-2.30 6-9. Av main course £6.95.
BREWERY/COMPANY: Fullers. **PRINCIPAL BEERS:** Fullers
London Pride, ESB & Chiswick. **FACILITIES:** Children welcome
Small courtyard Dogs allowed Water. **NOTES:** Parking 25

HEXTON

The Raven ♀
SG5 3JB ☎ 01582 881209 📠 01582 881610
e-mail: ravenph@freenetname.co.uk
Named after Ravenborough Castle in the Chiltern Hills above
attractive Hexton, this neat 1920s pub has a large garden with
terrace and play area, comfortable bars, and an extensive
menu highlighting traditional pub food. Expect wild boar
sausages, scrumpy pork, Cajun chicken, gammon steak with
pineapple and egg, and plenty of steaks from the grill. Various
salads, ploughman's lunches and daily specials.

OPEN: 11-3 6-11 (Sun 12-10.30). **BAR MEALS:** L served all
week. D served Mon-Sat 12-2 6-10. Av main course £7.25.
RESTAURANT: L served all week. D served Mon-Sat 12-2 6-10.
BREWERY/COMPANY: Whitbread.
PRINCIPAL BEERS: Greene King Old Speckled Hen & IPA,
Fullers London Pride. **FACILITIES:** Children welcome Garden:
outdoor eating, patio, BBQ

HINXWORTH
Map 06 TL24

Three Horseshoes 🛏
High St SG7 5HQ ☎ 01462 742280
Dir: E of A1 between Biggleswade and Baldock
Thatched 18th-century country pub with a dining extension
into the garden. The same menu is served in the bar and
restaurant and has an emphasis on fresh fish and seafood.
Starters may include fresh dressed crabs and seared king
scallops when available. Main courses include Greenland
halibut, and char-grilled gigot of English spring lamb.
OPEN: 11.30-2.30 6-11. **BAR MEALS:** L served all week. D
served Mon-Sat 12-2 7-9. Av main course £10. **RESTAURANT:** L
served all week. D served Mon-Sat 12-2 7-9. Av 3 course à la carte
£19. **BREWERY/COMPANY:** Greene King.
PRINCIPAL BEERS: Greene King IPA & Abbot Ale.
FACILITIES: Garden:. **NOTES:** Parking 16

HITCHIN
Map 06 TL12

The Greyhound ♦♦♦ 🛏 ♀
London Rd, St Ippolyts SG4 7NL ☎ 01462 440989
Surrounded by farmland and convenient for the M1 and Luton
Airport, this family-run inn offers well appointed
accommodation and good bar food. In addition to steak and
ale pie, rabbit pie, faggots and steaks, the menu also offers a
wide choice of fresh fish, including seabass fillet, swordfish
steak, and smoked mackerel.
OPEN: 11.30-2.30 5-11. Closed Dec 25-26. **BAR MEALS:** L
served all week. D served all week 12-2 7-10. Av main course £7.
RESTAURANT: L served All. D served all week 12-2 7-10. Av 3
course à la carte £13.50. **BREWERY/COMPANY:** Free House.
PRINCIPAL BEERS: Adnams, Greene King IPA.
FACILITIES: Garden: patio, outdoor eating. **NOTES:** Parking 25.
ROOMS: 4 bedrooms 4 en suite

The Red Lion ♀ NEW
The Green SG4 7UD ☎ 01462 459585
e-mail: janebaerlein@hotmail.com
The first village-owned pub in Britain was bought in 1982 and
still has about 100 shareholders, most of whom live in or near
Preston. The driving force behind the venture was to ensure a
continuing social focal point for the village. The pub, a CAMRA
award-winner for the county, offers a regularly changing menu
board with options like home-made soup, fresh fillet of sole,
vegetarian lasagne, and venison casserole.
OPEN: 12-2.30 5.30-11. **BAR MEALS:** L served all week 12-2. Av
main course £5.95. **BREWERY/COMPANY:** Free House.
PRINCIPAL BEERS: Greene King IPA, Woodforde Wherry.
FACILITIES: Children welcome Garden: Food served outside
Dogs allowed. **NOTES:** Parking 60 No credit cards

KNEBWORTH
Map 06 TL22

The Lytton Arms ♀
Park Ln SG3 6QB ☎ 01438 812312 📠 01438 815289
e-mail: thelyttonarms@btinternet.com
*Dir: From A1(M)take A602.At Knebworth turn R at rail station.Follow
signs 'Codicote'.Pub 1.5m on R*
Inn designed by Sir Edwin Lutyens, brother-in-law to Lord
Lytton, dating from 1877. It adjoins Knebworth estate, the
Lytton family seat. Noted for a fine selection of real ales,
Belgian bottled beers, and whiskies, and popular pub food.
Typical dishes include salmon fishcakes, liver and bacon
casserole, and steak and kidney pie. *continued*

OPEN: 11-3 (Sun 12-10.30, Fri-Sat open all day) 5-11. **BAR MEALS:** L served all week. D served all week 12-2 6.30-9.30. Av main course £6.95. **BREWERY/COMPANY:** Free House. **PRINCIPAL BEERS:** Fullers London Pride, Adnams Best Bitter, Bass. **FACILITIES:** Children welcome Garden: Food served outside. **NOTES:** Parking 40

LITTLE HADHAM   Map 07 TL42

The Nags Head 🐭 ♀
The Ford SG11 2AX ☎ 01279 771555 📄 01279 771555
Dir: M11 J8 take A120 towards Puckeridge & A10. At lights in Little Hadham turn L. Pub 0.75m on R
Former coaching inn that has in its time been a brewery, a bakery and an arsenal for the home guard. It has an oak-beamed bar and a restaurant area with open brickwork and an old bakery oven (now seating two people). Popular features are the gravity pour IPA and Abbot ales, and the fresh fish specials, such as seafood platter, monkfish with Pernod sauce and cod in Abbot batter.
OPEN: 11-2.30 6-11 (Sun 12-3.30 7-10.30). **BAR MEALS:** L served all week. D served all week 12-2 6-9.00. Av main course £7.95. **RESTAURANT:** L served all week. D served all week 12-2 6-9.00. Av 3 course à la carte £14.50.
BREWERY/COMPANY: Greene King.
PRINCIPAL BEERS: Greene King Abbot Ale, IPA & Old Speckled Hen, Ruddles County, Marstons Pedigree. **FACILITIES:** Children welcome Garden: beer garden, Food served outside Dogs allowed garden only, Water

MUCH HADHAM   Map 07 TL41

Jolly Waggoners
Widford Rd SG10 6EZ ☎ 01279 842102
Dir: On B1004 between Bishops Stortford & Ware
The pub was built in 1840 and incorporates two older cottages. A menu of home-cooked fare is supported by daily specials.

POTTERS CROUCH

The Hollybush
AL2 3NN ☎ 01727 851792 📄 01727 851792
Dir: Ragged Ln off A405 or Bedmond Ln off A4147
Well kept and attractively furnished old pub close to St Albans, with a fine fireplace, splendid rear garden and Fuller's ales on draught. Simple food - ploughman's platters, salads, jacket potatoes and burgers.

ROYSTON

The Green Man
Lower St, Thriplow SG8 7RJ ☎ 01763 208855
📄 01763 208431
Dir: 1M W of junction 10 on M11
Refurbished early 19th-century pub in the heart of picturesque Thriplow. Good choice of changing guest ales; home-cooked food (wild mushroom and fennel timbale, game pie); landscaped garden with pond.
OPEN: 12-2.30 6-11. **BAR MEALS:** L served Wed-Mon. D served Wed-Mon 12-2 7-9.30. Av main course £8.
BREWERY/COMPANY: Free House.
PRINCIPAL BEERS: Timothy Taylor Landlord Bitter.
FACILITIES: Children welcome Garden: patio; guide dogs only.
NOTES: Parking 6

ST ALBANS   Map 06 TL10

Rose & Crown
10 St Michael St AL3 4SG ☎ 01727 851903
📄 01727 766450
Traditional 16th-century pub situated in a beautiful part of St Michael's 'village', opposite the entrance to Verulamium Park and Roman Museum. Classic beamed main bar with huge inglenook, and lovely flower-decked summer patio. Noted for excellent 'royalty' sandwiches served with potato salad, kettle crisps and pickled cucumber. Try the 'Clark Gable' - roast beef, American cheese, onions, cucumber, tomato and horseradish mustard!
OPEN: 11.30-3 5.30-11 (Sun 12-3, 7-10.30). **BAR MEALS:** L served Mon-Sat 12-2. Av main course £5.
BREWERY/COMPANY: Inn Partnership.
PRINCIPAL BEERS: Adnams, Tetley, Courage Directors, Marstons Pedigree. **FACILITIES:** Children welcome Garden: Dogs allowed. **NOTES:** Parking 6

SARRATT   Map 04 TQ09

The Cock Inn ♀
Church End, Church Ln WD3 6HH ☎ 01923 282908
📄 01923 286224
Dir: Between M25 J18 & A404 opposite St Clement Danes School
Cream-painted 17th-century pub opposite the 12th century church and overlooking open countryside at the rear. The pub takes its name from the cockhorse that pulled carts up the hill from the nearby mill. Character interior includes a cosy snug with a vaulted ceiling and original bread oven. The restaurant is a converted barn with exposed beams and high-pitched roof. Good quality menu and daily specials feature the likes of lamb shank, steak and ale pie, seafood pasta, wild boar sausages, red snapper and roasted vegetable kebabs.
OPEN: 11-3 (all day wknds) 5.30-11. **BAR MEALS:** L served all week. D served all week 12-2.30 6-9.30. Av main course £6.
RESTAURANT: L served all week. D served all week 12-2.30 6-9.30. Av 3 course à la carte £20. **BREWERY/COMPANY:** Hall & Woodhouse. **PRINCIPAL BEERS:** Badger Tanglefoot, Dorset Best & IPA, King and Barnes Sussex Bitter. **FACILITIES:** Children welcome Garden: outdoor eating Dogs allowed.
NOTES: Parking 40

STOTFOLD   Map 06 TL23

The Fox & Duck
149 Arlesey Raod SG5 4HE ☎ 01426 732434
📄 01426 835962
Set on a large site this picturesque family pub has a big garden, a children's playground, a caravan site, weekly football matches, and regular BBQs. Children's birthday parties catered for.

TEWIN

The Plume of Feathers
Upper Green Rd AL6 0LX ☎ 01438 717265
Dir: E from A1 J6 toward WGC, follow B1000 toward Hertford, Tewin signed on L
Built in 1596, this historic inn, a former hunting lodge of Elizabeth I and later the haunt of highwaymen, now boasts several ghosts including a 'lady in grey'. Interesting food.

WALKERN
Map 06 TL22

The White Lion
31 The High St SG2 7PA ☎ 01438 861251
🖥 01438 861160
Dir: B1037 from Stevenage
Late 16th-century timber-framed building, originally a coaching inn on the Nottingham to London route.

WARE
Map 06 TL31

The Sow & Pigs
Cambridge Rd, Thundridge SG12 0ST ☎ 01920 463281
Dir: On A10 just N of Ware turn off. Adj to entrance of Hanbury Manor
There is a predominantly porcine theme to this village pub, with piggy pictures and lots of little pigs in display cabinets (also pig roasts on Bank Holiday Mondays).

WESTON
Map 06 TL23

The Rising Sun
21 Halls Green SG4 7DR ☎ 01462 790487
Dir: A1(M)J9 take A6141(dual carriageway) towards Baldock (take outside lane) & turn R towards Graveley. 100yds take 1st L
Set in picturesque Hertfordshire countryside, The Rising Sun is especially welcoming to those with children. Play equipment, a children's menu, and tuck shop in summer are provided.

KENT

APPLEDORE
Map 05 TQ92

The Red Lion
Snargate TN25 6BD ☎ 01797 344648
Few pubs invite you to picnic in their garden but then, they don't serve food at this one. Doris Jemison's family has run this unspoilt free house since 1911, and little has changed here in fifty years. Well kept local ales and Double Vision cider are served over the original marble counter and, for entertainment, there's the piano, and traditional games like shove ha'penny or toad-in-the-hole.
OPEN: 12-3 7-11 Sun 12-3, 7-10.30).
BREWERY/COMPANY: Free House.
PRINCIPAL BEERS: Rother Valley Tailwagger, Hop Back Summer Lightning, Black Sheep Best,. **FACILITIES:** Children welcome Garden:. **NOTES:** Parking 15 No credit cards

BENENDEN
Map 05 TQ83

The Bull at Benenden NEW
The Street TN17 4DE ☎ 01580 240054
e-mail: thebullatbenenden@btinternet.com
Dir: Benenden is on the B2086 between Cranbrook and Tenterden
Adjoining the village green, this listed family-run pub is thought to date back to 1608. The subject of recent renovation work, it lies in a picturesque Kentish village and is also the headquarters of the local cricket club. Varied home-cooked fare might include poached salmon with a lemon and lime sauce, Italian pancakes and shoulder of lamb.
OPEN: 11.30-3 6-11. **BAR MEALS:** L served all week. D served all week 12-2.30 7-9.30. Av main course £6.90. **RESTAURANT:** L served all week. D served all week 12-2.30 7-9.30. Av 3 course à la carte £12.95. **BREWERY/COMPANY:** Free House
FACILITIES: Garden: Food served outside. **NOTES:** Parking 12

BIDDENDEN
Map 05 TQ83

Pick of the Pubs

The Three Chimneys
Biddenden Rd TN27 8LW ☎ 01580 291472
🖥 01233 820042
Dir: On A262 W of Biddenden
Unspoilt 15th-century country pub in the Kentish Weald, complete original, small room layout with old settles, low beams, wood-panelled walls, flagstone floors and warming fires. Evening candlelight enhances the atmosphere.
Everything is cooked to order here, the daily-changing menu may feature dishes such as chargrilled fish, rack of lamb, roast loin of venison, and tomato, red pepper and goats' cheese tartlet. Meat is supplied by a local farmer and the menu aims to reflect the changing seasons. A classic country pub.
OPEN: 11.30-2.30 (Sat 3) 6-11. Closed 25 Dec.
BAR MEALS: L served all week. D served all week 12-2 6-10. Av main course £8. **RESTAURANT:** L served all week. D served all week 12-2 6-10. Av 3 course fixed price £17.50.
BREWERY/COMPANY: Free House.
PRINCIPAL BEERS: Shepherd Neame Master Brew, Adnams.
FACILITIES: Children welcome Garden: Dogs allowed.
NOTES: Parking 70

BOYDEN GATE
Map 05 TR26

The Gate Inn ♀
CT3 4EB ☎ 01227 860498
Dir: From Canterbury on A28 turn L at Upstreet
Surrounded by farmland and marshes, 2 miles from the A28, this rustic and unpretentious rural retreat has a delightful summer garden with flowers, stream and duck pond with resident ducks and geese. Quarry-tiled floors, pine furnishings and lively conversation characterise the two welcoming interconnecting rooms.
Cooking is down to earth, with hearty soups, various hotpots and grills, home-made burgers, freshly-cut sandwiches, and pasta with pesto.
OPEN: 11-2.30 6-11 (Sun 12-4,7-10.30). **BAR MEALS:** L served all week. D served all week 12-2 6-9. Av main course £3.50.
BREWERY/COMPANY: Shepherd Neame.
PRINCIPAL BEERS: Shepherd Neame Master Brew, Spitfire & Bishops Finger. **FACILITIES:** Children welcome Garden: Beer garden, food served outside Dogs allowed, water & dog biscuits.
NOTES: Parking 14 No credit cards

BRABOURNE
Map 05 TR14

The Five Bells
The Street TN25 5LP ☎ 01303 813334 🖥 01303 814667
e-mail: five.bells@lineone.net
Dir: 5m E of Ashford
Retaining many original beams and a large inglenook fireplace, this 16th-century building enjoys a quiet village setting at the base of the North Downs.

BROOKLAND   Map 05 TQ92

Woolpack Inn
TN29 9TJ ☎ 01797 344321
Partly built from old ship timbers, this 15th-century cottage inn
is set in Kentish marshland, and has a large collection of
waterjugs. Homemade wholesome pub food.

BROUGHTON ALUPH

The Flying Horse Inn
TN25 4ET ☎ 01233 620914
15th-century inn with oak beams and open log fires.
Comfortable minstrel bar with sunken wells. Regular cricket
matches in summer on the spacious village green opposite.
Good selection of real ales and a varied menu which might
include roast rack of lamb, poached salmon, monkfish with
mushroom, lemon and butter sauce, baked avocado with
spinach, or braised lamb shank.
OPEN: 12-11. **BAR MEALS:** L served all week. D served all week
12-2 7-9. Av main course £8.50. **RESTAURANT:** L served all
week. D served all week 12-2 7-9. Av 3 course à la carte £25.
BREWERY/COMPANY: Unique Pub Co.
PRINCIPAL BEERS: Fullers London Pride, Courage Best, Youngs
Special, Greene King IPA. **FACILITIES:** Garden: outdoor eating,
patio/terrace, BBQ. **NOTES:** Parking 40. **ROOMS:** 3 bedrooms
s£25 d£40

BURHAM   Map 05 TQ76

The Golden Eagle
80 Church St ME1 3SD ☎ 01634 668975
🖹 01634 668975
Dir: South from M2 J3 or North M20 J6 on A229, signs to Burham

Situated on the North Downs with fine views of the Medway
Valley, this traditional free house has a friendly and informal
atmosphere. The kitchen specialises in oriental cooking, with
an extensive menu that includes a wide range of vegetarian
dishes. House specials include pork babibangang, sunset
chicken, crispy wor tip babycorn, and red hot chilli vegetables.
OPEN: 11.30-2.30 6.15-11. **BAR MEALS:** L served all week.
D served all week 12-2 7-10. Av main course £7.90.
RESTAURANT: L served all week. D served all week 12-2 7-10.
Av 3 course à la carte £17.50. **BREWERY/COMPANY:** Free
House. **PRINCIPAL BEERS:** Wadworth 6X, Marstons Pedigree.
FACILITIES: Terrace. **NOTES:** Parking 40.

CANTERBURY   Map 05 TR15

Pick of the Pubs

The Dove Inn 🏵 🏵 📷 ♀
Plum Pudding Ln, Dargate ME13 9HB ☎ 01227 751360
Tucked away in a sleepy hamlet on the delightfully named
Plum Pudding Lane, the Dove is the sort of pub you dream
of as your local. Roses round the door, a simple interior
with stripped wooden floors, plain tables, a hop-garlanded
bar, tip-top Shepherd Neame ales, a relaxing atmosphere,
and astonishingly good food sum up this charming rural
pub.
    Food is simply described on a series of blackboard
menus that feature fresh fish from Hythe and local game
and expertly prepared by talented chef/proprietor Nigel
Morris. For a lunchtime snack order a starter, perhaps
grilled local herrings flavoured with virgin olive oil and
garlic or pan-fried crevettes with fresh garden herbs and
pickled ginger.
    Main courses range from confit duck leg with braised
red cabbage and braised shank of lamb on chive potato
purée, to roast monkfish wrapped in Bayonne ham and
basil and wild sea bass on crushed new potatoes with
tapenade. Desserts such as lemon tart and classics. Good
Sunday lunch choices. Splendid sheltered garden for
summer meals.
OPEN: 11-3 6-11. **BAR MEALS:** L served Tue-Sun. D served
Tues-Sun 12-2. **RESTAURANT:** L served Tue-Sun. D served
Tue-Sat 12-2 7-9. Av 3 course à la carte £25.
BREWERY/COMPANY: Shepherd Neame.
PRINCIPAL BEERS: Shepherd Neame Master Brew.
FACILITIES: Children welcome Garden: herb garden, food
served outside. **NOTES:** Parking 14

The Duke William 📷 ♀
Ickham CT3 1QP
A family-run free house in a picturesque village between
Canterbury and Sandwich. There's an open fire in the
comfortable bar, with a summer garden and rural views. The
extensive menu in the conservatory-style restaurant features
home-cooked dishes like spatchcock poussin, pot-roasted pork
in cider, or chargrilled tuna. Vegetarian options include braised
leeks and wild mushrooms in puff pastry.
OPEN: 11-11. **BAR MEALS:** L served all week. D served all week
11 6. Av main course £3.50. **RESTAURANT:** L served all week.
D served all week 11 6. Av 3 course fixed price £14.95.
BREWERY/COMPANY: Free House.
PRINCIPAL BEERS: Shepherd Neame Master Brew, Youngs
Special, Adnams, Fullers London Pride,. **FACILITIES:** Children
welcome Garden: Food served outside Dogs allowed. Water

♀ Pubs offering six or more wines by the glass

CASTLE INN, CHIDDINGSTONE

TN8 7AH. Tel: 01892 870247

Directions: S of B2027 between Tonbridge and Edenbridge

Striking tile-hung building set in a timeless village owned by the National Trust.. The Castle dates from 1420, but became an inn in 1752. Classic, unspoilt bar with huge fireplace, beamed lounge bar, a secluded, garden and vine-hung courtyard.

Open: 11-11 (Sun 12-10.30). Bar Meals: all day. Children and dogs welcome, Garden and patio. Village car park.

(see page 245 for full entry)

KENT

Pub WALK

Castle Inn, Chiddingstone

A beautiful Wealden walk through peaceful meadows and woodland to picturesque Penshurst and the opportunity to visit Penshurst Place, a splendid 14th-century manor house.

Turn right on leaving the pub. Just east of the village, take the footpath on the right, signed 'Footpath to Chiddingstone Hoath', and head south on a well marked path, via stiles to a kissing-gate. Turn left along the old coach road that once linked Chiddingstone with Penshurst, then where the track divides, keep left to a road. Turn right, then cross the stile on the left and bear diagonally across the field to re-join the coach road.

Turn left to reach Watstock Farm and keep left through the farm buildings. Keep to the broad track, cross the River Eden and reach the main road, opposite Penshurst Place. Bear right for the village centre.

Return along the main road, pass your outward route, and continue to steps and a stile beyond house on your left.

Keep left-handed along the hedge, cross a track (Dutch barns left) and follow the path down to the river. Turn right, cross the footbridge over the River Eden, and bear half-right. Cross a ditch and a stile flanking a gate, then turn right along the field edge to a stile. Continue along the right-hand edge of the field to a gate and road by a group of houses called Wellers Town. Turn right, then in a few paces, go through the gate on the left and bear half-right across the field to a stile. Bear diagonally left across the next field to a stile and continue beside a wire fence to reach the path followed on your outward route. Turn right and retrace steps back to Chiddingstone.

Distance: 4 1/2 miles (7.2km)
Map: OS Landranger 188
Terrain: woodland and farmland, country lanes
Paths: tracks, field and woodland paths; some road walking
Gradient: gently rolling

Walk submitted by: The Castle Inn

Penshurst Place

243

CANTERBURY continued

The Old Coache House ⚲
A2 Barnham Downs CT4 6SA ☎ 01227 831218
🖃 01227 831932
Dir: 7M Sof Canterbury, on the A2 Turn at Jet Petrol Station.
A former stop on the original London-Dover coaching route,
and listed in the 1740 timetable, this inn stands some 300
metres from the Roman Way. Noteworthy gardens with home-
grown herbs and vegetables, weekend spit-roasts, and
unabashed continental cuisine mark it as an auberge in the
finest Gallic tradition. Food options include game in season,
venison, wild duck, lobster, sea bass and seafood.
OPEN: 11-11. **BAR MEALS:** L served all week. D served all week
12-2 6.30-9. **RESTAURANT:** D served all
week 6.30-9. Av 3 course à la carte £20.
BREWERY/COMPANY: Free House.
PRINCIPAL BEERS: Whitbread Best Bitter.
FACILITIES: Children welcome Garden: outdoor eating, Dogs
allowed. **NOTES:** Parking 60. **ROOMS:** 7 bedrooms 7 en suite
s£40 d£40 FR£55-£75

CHIDDINGSTONE   Map 05 TQ54

Pick of the Pubs

Castle Inn
TN8 7AH ☎ 01892 870247 🖃 01892 870808
e-mail: info@castleinn.co.uk
                See Pub Walk on page 243
                See Pick of the Pubs on page 245

CHILHAM   Map 05 TR05

The White Horse
The Square CT4 8BY ☎ 01227 730355
Dir: Take A28 from Canterbury then A252, 1m turn L
Built in 1422, the White Horse is located in the picturesque
Tudor square of Chilham, opposite the entrance to Chilham
Castle.

CHILLENDEN   Map 05 TR25

Griffins Head 🐾
CT3 1PS ☎ 01304 840325 🖃 01304 841290
Dir: A2 from Canterbury towards Dover,then B2046.Village on R
Wealden Hall House, dating from 1286, with a lovely garden.
Once occupied by monks who farmed the surrounding land, it
features inglenook fireplaces, beamed bars, fine Kentish ales
and home-made food. Typical dishes include warm salads,
fresh pasta, various pies and stews, good steaks and fresh fish.
OPEN: 10.30am-11pm. **BAR MEALS:** L served all week.
D served Mon-Sat 12-2 7-9.30. Av main course £8.50.
RESTAURANT: L served all week. D served Mon-Sat 12-2 7-9.30.
Av 3 course à la carte £17.50. **BREWERY/COMPANY:** Shepherd
Neame. **PRINCIPAL BEERS:** Shepherd Neame.
FACILITIES: Garden: BBQ at weekends. **NOTES:** Parking 25

CLIFFE   Map 05 TQ77

The Black Bull
186 Church St ME3 7QD ☎ 01634 220893
🖃 01634 221382
e-mail: the_black_bull@msn.com
Dir: On B2000 N of Rochester
Pip's meeting place with Magwitch in Dickens's Great
Expectations is within easy reach of this distinctive free house
situated near the Thames estuary. The Tapestries restaurant
has a 50ft ancient well. Authentic Malaysian, Thai and Chinese
cuisine includes mixed seafood, sweet and sour pork and
orange chicken.
OPEN: 12-2.30 7-11 (Mon 12-2.30 only). **BAR MEALS:** L served
all week. D served Tue-Sun 12-2.30 7-11. **RESTAURANT:** L
served all week. D served Tue-Sat 7-12. Av 3 course à la carte
£13.85. Av 0 course fixed price £18.50.
BREWERY/COMPANY: Free House.
PRINCIPAL BEERS: Flagship Destroyer, Shepherd Neame,
Courage Directors, Black Bull. **FACILITIES:** Children welcome
Garden: patio, outdoor eating, BBQ, Dogs allowed Water.
NOTES: Parking 16

The North Downs Way, (Kent section)
Crossing the Surrey border into Kent, the North Downs Way crosses fertile
farmland and gently rolling hills studded with picturesque villages and criss-crosssed by
narrow winding lanes. This picturesque region of the country is aptly known as the Garden
of England. The trail makes for the unspoilt Fox & Hounds at Westerham before continuing
to Wrotham. At this point you might also like to visit the 18th-century Green Man at nearby
Ash-cum-Ridley. Resuming the walk, the North Downs Way now zigzags across country to
reach the 15th-century White Horse at Chilham, one of Kent's loveliest villages. A little way
off the route, between Canterbury and Whitstable, lies the Dove Inn at Dargate -
ideal for rest and relaxtion before beginning the final leg of the walk to Dover.

PICK OF THE PUBS

OPEN: 11-11 (Sun 12-10.30).
BAR MEALS: L served all week.
D served all week 11-10.45
(Sun 12-10.15).
RESTAURANT: L served all week
D served all week 12-2 7.30-9.30.
Av 3 course a la carte £28. Av 3
course lunch £13/dinner £22.50.
BREWERY/COMPANY:
Free House.
PRINCIPAL BEERS: Larkins
Traditional & Porter, Youngs Bitter,
Harveys Sussex.
FACILITIES: Children welcome
Children's licence. Garden: patio,
outdoor eating. Dogs allowed.
NOTES: Parking - use village car
park.

The Castle Inn

TN8 7AH
☎ 01892 870247 🖷 01892 870808
e-mail: info@castleinn.co.uk
Dir: S of B2027 between Tonbridge and
Edenbridge

At the heart of Kent's famous National Trust village, the Castle - so named, 'tis said, in memory of Anne Boleyn who resided at nearby Hever Castle - is a mellow brick inn dating from the 1730s that is a picturesque and much-used film-set. The Wicked Lady and Room with a View were shot in the village.

Within its rambling interior the beamed bar, studiously remodelled so as not to destroy its unique character, is full of nooks and crannies, period furniture and evocative curios. In the same hands for nearly 40 years, it dispenses traditional ales such as Larkins Traditional and Porter ales, brewed just down the road at Larkins Farm, for the thirsty or simply curious, and similarly run-of-the-mill bar food throughout the inn and in the secluded, vine-hung courtyard garden on warm summer days.

'Of the moment' fresh soup and salad Niçoise indicate an awareness of seasonal ingredients, echoed by rolled and stuffed flounder with lobster and prawn mousse and braised English lamb in garlic with market-fresh vegetables. Followed by bread-and-butter pudding or warm spiced apple slice these feature on a fixed-price Fireside menu. 'Not too heavy' bar dishes offer Stilton ploughman's, filled whole wheat baguettes, tomato and anchovy or tuna and mixed bean salads; more substantially beef and vegetable curry and local pork sausages with jacket potato and cheese.

The à la carte restaurant menu passes into a different league with 30 grams of Sevruga caviar, beef fillet with green peppercorn and cream sauce, lobster Thermidor (for two) and rich cheeseboard selections - not for the faint-hearted, with serious wines to match. Fine clarets feature on the Castle Inn Cellars wholesale list of wines.

DARTFORD

Map 05 TQ57

The Rising Sun Inn ◆◆◆
Fawkham Green, Fawkham DA3 8NL ☎ 01474 872291
🖹 01474 872291

16th-century inn set in a peaceful picturesque village not far from the Thames and Medway estuaries. The Rising Sun has been a pub since 1702. Friendly atmosphere inside, inglenook log fire and cosy restaurant. Convenient for Brands Hatch racing circuit. Traditional fish 'n' chips, t-bone steak, steak and kidney pudding, oven baked trout, and tournedos royale are among the popular dishes. Barbecues, special events and jazz on the first Wednesday of each month.
OPEN: 12-3 6-11. Closed 1 Jan. **BAR MEALS:** L served all week. D served all week 12-2 6.30-9.30. Av main course £9. **RESTAURANT:** L served all week. D served all week 12-2 6.30-9.30. Av 3 course à la carte £16. **BREWERY/COMPANY:** Free House. **PRINCIPAL BEERS:** Courage Best, Courage Directors. **FACILITIES:** Garden: outdoor eating, BBQ Dogs allowed except in garden. **NOTES:** Parking 30. **ROOMS:** 5 bedrooms 5 en suite s£40 d£80 FR£100

DEAL

The King's Head
9 Beach St CT14 7AH ☎ 01304 368194 🖹 01304 364182
Traditional 18th-century seaside pub overlooking the seafront and situated in one of the south-east's most picturesque coastal towns. Deal's famous Timeball Tower is a few yards away and the pub is within easy reach of Canterbury, Walmer Castle and the Channel Tunnel. Bar meals and daily-changing specials board.
OPEN: 10-close. **BAR MEALS:** L served all week. D served all week 11-2.30 6-9. Av main course £5.95.
BREWERY/COMPANY: Free House.
PRINCIPAL BEERS: Shephard Neame Master Brew, Courage Best. **FACILITIES:** Children welcome Garden: outdoor eating, patio. **ROOMS:** 14 bedrooms 13 en suite s£38 d£56 FR£80-£100

DOVER

Map 05 TR34

The Cliffe Tavern ♖
High St, St Margaret's at Cliffe CT15 6AT ☎ 01304 852400
🖹 01304 851880
Dir: 3m NE of Dover
Located opposite the parish church and just half a mile from the white cliffs north of Dover, this 16th-century Kentish clapboard building, formerly an 'academy for young gentlemen', has undergone major refurbishment since new owners took over in February 2000. Convivial main bar and neatly furnished lounge leading out to the delightful walled
continued

rose garden. Food now includes fresh local fish, traditional dishes like toad-in-the-hole, steak and pie and calves' liver and bacon, and mushroom and herb tagliatelle, Thai curries, and home-made ice creams among the puddings.
OPEN: 11-3 (Sun 12-10.30) 5-11. **BAR MEALS:** L served all week. D served all week 11.30-2.30 6.30-9.30. Av main course £8. **RESTAURANT:** L served all week. D served all week 12-2.30 7-9.30. Av 3 course à la carte £25. **BREWERY/COMPANY:** Free House. **PRINCIPAL BEERS:** Shepherd Neame Spitfire, Masterbrew, Pickled Porter, Indian Summer ESB.
FACILITIES: Children welcome Garden: Food served outside Dogs allowed. **NOTES:** Parking 35. **ROOMS:** 15 bedrooms 15 en suite s£35 d£50

EASTLING

Map 05 TQ95

Carpenters Arms
The Street ME13 0AZ ☎ 01795 890234 🖹 01795 890654
e-mail: carpenters-arms@lineone.net
Dir: A251 towards Faversham, then A2, 1st L Brogdale Rd, 4m to Eastling
An early Kentish hall house, built in 1380, this listed building soon became an ale house serving carpenters working in the nearby sawmill. It features oak beams, an inglenook fireplace and a brick tiled floor. The bar offers home-cooked pub fare, snacks and daily specials, while restaurant dishes include steaks, local pheasant, and slow cooked lamb shank.
OPEN: 11-4 (Sun 12-6) 6-11. **BAR MEALS:** L served all week. D served Mon-Sat 12-2.30 7-10. Av main course £6.95.
RESTAURANT: L served all week. D served Mon-Sat 12-2.30 7-10. Av 3 course à la carte £20.
BREWERY/COMPANY: Shepherd Neame.
PRINCIPAL BEERS: Shepherd Neame Master Brew, Bishops Finger & Spitfire. **FACILITIES:** Children welcome Garden: outdoor eating Dogs allowed on lead only, Water.
NOTES: Parking 20. **ROOMS:** 3 bedrooms 3 en suite s£41.50 d£49.50

EDENBRIDGE

Map 05 TQ44

The Kentish Horse
Cow Ln, Markbeech TN8 5NT ☎ 01342 850493
Weatherboarded rural pub with a growing reputation for good pub food. Terrace and garden. Reports please!

Ye Old Crown ◆◆◆◆
74-76 High St TN8 5AR ☎ 01732 867896 🖹 01732 868316

An unmissable landmark on account of its unique street-bridging Kentish inn sign, this has been an inn since 1340: a concealed passage from the 1630s confirms its history as a smugglers' den. Today it dispenses local Larkins' ale, traditional English bar and restaurant food, and offers comfortable tourist accommodation. *continued*

OPEN: 11-11 (Sun 12-10.30). **BAR MEALS:** L served all week. D served all week 12-3 6-10. Av main course £4.95. **RESTAURANT:** L served all week. D served all week 12-3 6-10. Av 3 course à la carte £15. **BREWERY/COMPANY: PRINCIPAL BEERS:** Courage Directors & Best, Shepherd Neame, Larkins. **FACILITIES:** Children welcome Garden: outdoor eating, patio, BBQ Dogs allowed. **NOTES:** Parking 20. **ROOMS:** 6 bedrooms 6 en suite s£59 d£74 FR£85-£95

The Wheatsheaf

Hever Rd, Bough Beech TN8 7NU ☎ 01732 700254
🖹 01732 700141
Merrie England comes to life beneath the lofty timbered ceilings of this splendid medieval pub, originally built as a hunting lodge for Henry V. You'll find massive stone fireplaces, roasting chestnuts and mulled wine in winter, plus lovely summer gardens with swings for the children. The Wheatsheaf also has a well-deserved reputation for good food; expect ciabatta open sandwiches, liver and bacon, Welsh fillet steaks and home-made curries.

OPEN: 11-11. **BAR MEALS:** L served all week. D served all week 12-10. Av main course £5.95. **RESTAURANT:** L served all week. D served all week 12-10. Av 3 course à la carte £15. **BREWERY/COMPANY:** Free House. **PRINCIPAL BEERS:** Harveys Sussex Bitter, Shepherds Neame, Fullers London Pride, Greene King Old Speckled Hen. **FACILITIES:** Garden: Food served outside Dogs allowed Water. **NOTES:** Parking 30

AA Bed & Breakfast

2002

Britain's best-selling B&B guide featuring over 3500 great places to stay

AA Bed Breakfast Guide

www.theAA.com

AA Lifestyle Guides

EYNSFORD   Map 05 TQ56

Swallows' Malt Shovel Inn 🐑 Ⓨ

Station Rd DA4 0ER ☎ 01322 862164   🖹 01322 864132
Dir: A20 to Brands Hatch, then A225, 1m to pub
Close to the Darenth river, this charming village pub is very popular with walkers and those visiting the Roman villa in Eynsford, or Lullingstone Castle.
Fish is very well represented on the menu, and dishes may include grilled monkfish, best smoked Scotch salmon, whole lobster, sea bass, tiger prawns, tuna, plaice, trout, skate or dressed baby crab. Rack of ribs, venison pie, leek and lentil lasagne and vegetable curry also turn up on a typical menu.
OPEN: 11-3 7-11. Closed 25-26 Dec. **BAR MEALS:** L served all week. D served all week 12-2.30 7-10. Av main course £6.50. **RESTAURANT:** L served all week. D served all week 12-2.30 7-10. Av 3 course à la carte £12. **BREWERY/COMPANY:** Free House. **PRINCIPAL BEERS:** Greene King Old Speckled Hen, Harveys Armarda, Fullers London Pride, Taylor Landlord. **FACILITIES:** Children welcome patio. **NOTES:** Parking 26

FAVERSHAM   Map 05 TR06

Pick of the Pubs

The Albion Tavern 🐑

Front Brents, Faversham Creek ME13 7DH
☎ 01795 591411   🖹 591587
e-mail: patrickcoevdet@freeuk.com
Dir: From Faversham take A2 W. In Ospringe turn R just before Ship Inn, at Shepherd Neame Brewery 1m turn L over creek bridge
Popular white weatherboarded pub overlooking Faversham Creek and just a stone's throw from the owning brewery - Shepherd Neame. As one would expect, tip-top Masterbrew, Spitfire, Bishop's Finger and Porter ales are available on draught in the open-plan bar which is adorned with nautical artefacts, including oars, a hammock and photographs of old boats.
Picture windows looking out across the creek add to the charm, and the tiny, vine-festooned rear conservatory leads out to a pretty garden. Old pine tables are topped with candles and are generally reserved for diners (essential to book) as the food here, freshly prepared by French chef/patron Patrick Coevoet, draws a discerning local clientele.
Starters or light snacks range include New Zealand mussels grilled with garlic, tomato and herbs and scallop, prawn, crab and mushroom cassoulette. Main dishes range from local sausages with melted onions and mash, pan-fried calves' liver with lime and sage butter, and grilled marlin steak with red chilli and lime salsa. Filled baguettes served lunchtimes only.
OPEN: 11.30-3 6.30-11. **BAR MEALS:** L served all week. D served all week 12-2 6.30-9.30. Av main course £9.95. **RESTAURANT:** L served all week. D served all week 12-2 6.30-9.30. Av 3 course à la carte £17.95. **BREWERY/COMPANY:** Shepherd Neame. **PRINCIPAL BEERS:** Shepherd Neame Spitfire, Master Brew, Bishops Finger & Porter. **FACILITIES:** Children welcome Garden: patio, outdoor eating, BBQ. **NOTES:** Parking 50

Shipwrights Arms
Hollowshore ME13 7TU ☎ 01795 590088
Dir: A2 through Osprince then R at rdbt. Turn R at T-junct then L opp Davington School & follow signs
Find this classic pub on the Kent marshes on foot and savour its wonderful atmosphere. Once a haunt of pirates and smugglers, there are numerous nooks and crannies inside and beer is served traditionally by gravity straight from the cask. Frequently changing range of Kent-brewed real ales. Self-sufficient landlord generates his own electricity and draws water from a well. Home-cooked food might include mushroom Stroganoff and sausage and mash. Emphasis on English pies and puddings during the winter.
OPEN: 12-3 Summer Open all day 7-11 (Sun 12-3,6-10.30).
BAR MEALS: L served Tue-Sun. D served Tue-Sat 12-3 7-9.
Av main course £5.50. **BREWERY/COMPANY:** Free House
FACILITIES: Children welcome Garden: food served outdoors
Dogs allowed. **NOTES:** Parking 30 No credit cards

FORDCOMBE   Map 05 TQ54

Chafford Arms
TN3 0SA ☎ 01892 740267
e-mail: bazzer@chafford-armsfsnet.co.uk
Dir: On B2188 (off A264) between Tunbridge Wells & E Grinstead
Creeper-clad village pub with an award-winning garden, situated between Penshurst Place and Groombridge Place. One menu serves all in the homely bars and dining room. The main emphasis is on fish with the likes of fresh Dover sole from Hastings grilled with butter, prawn provençale or local Weald smoked trout served cold with horseradish sauce. There is also a good range of snacks, salads, vegetarian and meat dishes.
OPEN: 11.45-3 6.30-11. **BAR MEALS:** L served all week.
D served Tue-Sat 12.30-2 7.30-9.30. Av main course £5.95.
RESTAURANT: L served all week. D served Tue-Sat 12.30-2 7.30-9.30. Av 3 course à la carte £15.
BREWERY/COMPANY: Whitbread.
PRINCIPAL BEERS: Larkins Bitter, Wadworth 6X.
FACILITIES: Children welcome Garden: outdoor eating, 100 yr old cider press, Dogs allowed. **NOTES:** Parking 16
See Pub Walk on page 249

FORDWICH   Map 05 TR15

Fordwich Arms ♀
King St CT2 0DB ☎ 01227 710444 📠 01227 712811
Dir: From A2 take A28, on approaching Sturry turn R at 'Welsh Harp' pub into Fordwich Rd
Solid Tudor-style village pub situated opposite the tiny, half-timbered 16th-century town hall, a reminder of the days when Fordwich was a Borough. Large bar with log-burning fires, an oak-panelled dining room and delightful riverside patio and garden for summer sipping. Modern, daily-changing menus encompass grilled goats' cheese with Parma ham, roasted cod with hazelnut butter, apricot stuffed saddle of lamb, and honey-roasted duck with orange and walnut sauce. Good Sunday lunch menu.
OPEN: 11-11 (Sun 12-3, 7-10.30). **BAR MEALS:** L served all week. D served Mon-Sat 12-2.30 6.30-9.30. Av main course £8.95.
RESTAURANT: L served all week. D served Mon-Sat 12-2.30 6.30-9.30. Av 3 course à la carte £20.
BREWERY/COMPANY: Whitbread.
PRINCIPAL BEERS: Flowers Original, Shepherd Neame Masterbrew, Wadworth 6X, Boddingtons. **FACILITIES:** Garden: patio, outdoor eating Dogs allowed **NOTES:** Parking 12

GOUDHURST   Map 05 TQ73

Pick of the Pubs

Green Cross Inn 🍴 NEW
TN17 1HA ☎ 01580 211200 📠 01580 212905
Dir: Tonbridge A21 toward Hastings turn L A262 leading to Ashford 2 M from the turning on the A262 Station road Goudhurst on the R hand side
Food-orientated pub in a delightful unspoiled corner of Kent, ideally placed for visiting Tunbridge Wells, the Ashdown Forest and the remote fenland country of Pevensey Levels. The dining-room is prettily decorated with fresh flowers and white linen table cloths and, with a new chef/proprietor at the helm, the whole pub is undergoing a gradual but extensive makeover.
Fresh seafood is the house speciality here, with all dishes cooked to order and incorporating the freshest ingredients. Main courses in the bar range from home-made steak, kidney and mushroom pie with shortcrust pastry, to calves' liver and bacon Lyonnaise. Restaurant fish dishes might include fillet of turbot with spinach and a creamy cheese sauce, grilled lemon sole with home-made tartare sauce, and Cornish cock crab with fresh dressed leaves.
OPEN: 11-3 6-11. **BAR MEALS:** L served all week. D served Mon-Sat 12-2.30 7-9.45. Av main course £7.25.
RESTAURANT: L served all week. D served Mon-Sat 12-2.30 7-9.45. Av 3 course à la carte £27.
BREWERY/COMPANY: Free House.
PRINCIPAL BEERS: Harveys Best, Shepherd Neame Master Brew, Larkins. **FACILITIES:** Garden: Food served outside Dogs allowed. **NOTES:** Parking 26

The Star & Eagle ♀
High St TN17 1AL ☎ 01580 211512 📠 01580 212589
Dir: On A262 E of Tunbridge Wells
Fine 14th-century timbered and gabled hostelry which is reputed to have been an ancient monastery. Located in the heart of the beautiful Kentish Weald, with lovely views across orchards and hop gardens, the 18th-century Hawkhurst Gang of smugglers used it as their headquarters.
A typical menu includes lamb jalfrezie, salmon fillet with lobster sauce, beef stroganoff, baked oysters, moules et frites, and roasted aubergines stuffed with Stilton and roast peppers.
OPEN: 11-11 (Sun 12-10.30). **BAR MEALS:** L served all week. D served all week 12-2.30 7-9.30. Av main course £8.
RESTAURANT: L served all week. D served all week 12-2.30 7-9.30. Av 3 course à la carte £18.
BREWERY/COMPANY: Whitbread.
PRINCIPAL BEERS: Flowers Original, King & Barnes Sussex.
FACILITIES: Garden: outdoor eating, patio. **NOTES:** Parking 25.
ROOMS: 10 bedrooms 8 en suite d£55

Chafford Arms, Fordcombe

CHAFFORD ARMS, FORDCOMBE

TN3 0SA. Tel: 01892 740267

Directions: on B2188 between Tunbridge Wells & E Grinstead

Creeper-clad village pub with an award-winning garden, situated within easy reach of Hever Castle and Penshurst Place. Homely and relaxing bars, a good range of snacks and home-cooked main meals, and local Larkins ale on tap.
Open: 11.45-3 6.30-11. Bar Meals: 12.30-2 7.30-9.30 (no food Mon eve). Children welcome. Garden. Parking.
(see page 248 for full entry)

An easy walk along the Kent and Sussex border providing fine views across the Weald, the Ashdown Forest and the headwaters of the River Medway.

Walk uphill away from pub, passing village green, to reach cricket pitch. Follow left side of the pitch to top of field and turn right along hedge (Weald Way). Maintain direction across several fields and stiles for 3/4 mile (1.2km), with fine views over the Medway Valley. Join narrow lane by two houses and soon reach A264 at Stone Cross. Cross the road, turn left, then follow the Weald Way marker right across a stile. Follow the narrow path to open fields (woods to your right), and follow the contour to a stile by a gate.

Continue to gates on the brow of the hill. Go through the left-hand gate (good views) and head downhill beside the right-hand hedge. Halfway down, cross the stile in the hedge and head downhill with hedge to your left. Cross two stiles and turn right into a small field, the Weald Way leading to a tunnel under the railway. Ignore the Weald Way. Instead, follow the path

that leads out to the top right side of the field and soon pass a derelict barn. Go through a gate and follow a track for 1/4 mile (0.4km) Just before the top of the hill, turn left downhill along a track. Turn right in 100yds (91m) beside houses and follow the track to the A264.

Cross the road, turn left under the railway bridge and in 150yds (136m), take the waymarked footpath right into field. Turn left alongside hedge, ignoring gate, then track to farm buildings, then at top of field follow track to the main road. Turn right along the footpath, then right again in 50 yards (46m). Take footpath right to reach a short road and turn left, then immediately right at its end to follow tarmac track to Willetts Farm. Go through the farm and take the path, which veers slightly right, down a shallow incline to a footbridge across Kent Water. Proceed straight ahead to the top of the field (overhead cables) to a lane. Turn right, then right again at its T-junction. Follow the road back over the river and on up to Fordcombe and the pub.

Distance: 5 miles (8km)
Map: OS Landranger 188
Terrain: farmland and patches of woodland
Paths: broad tracks, field and woodland paths, country lane
Gradient: undulating

Walk submitted by:
David Leppard

The River Medway from the Weald Way

GRAVESEND

The Cock Inn
Henley St, Luddesdowne DA13 0XB ☎ 01474 814208
▤ 01474 812850
e-mail: cockinn@amserve.net
No jukebox and no children are permitted at this traditional
English alehouse. It is set in the beautiful Luddesdowne Valley,
and is an ideal watering hole for walkers, with its constantly
changing range of ales and good bar food. Typical dishes
include Mediterranean lamb and Thai green curry alongside
specials of liver and bacon, or steak and ale pie.
OPEN: 12-11 (Sun 12-10.30). **BAR MEALS:** L served Mon-Sat.
D served Mon-Sat 12-2.30 6-9. Av main course £6.
BREWERY/COMPANY: Free House.
PRINCIPAL BEERS: Adnams Southwold, Adnams Broadside
Shepherd Neame Masterbrew, Harveys Best.
FACILITIES: Garden: outdoor eating, patio/terrace Dogs
allowed. **NOTES:** Parking 60

HADLOW
Map 05 TQ65

The Artichoke Inn
Park Rd, Hamptons TN11 9SR ☎ 01732 810763
Dir: From Tonbridge take A26. In Hadlow turn L into Carpenters Lane.
L at junction, 2nd on R
Timber framed, tile hung pub built in 1483 as a farm worker's
cottage and licensed in 1585. Log fires burn in the large
inglenook fireplace in winter and in summer there is a covered
terrace. The Artichoke is a regular holder of the local council's
Clean Food Award. Bar food ranges through pasta dishes, pies,
stuffed plaice, mixed grill, and steak and kidney pudding.
OPEN: 12-3 7-11. **BAR MEALS:** L served all week. D served all
week 12-2 7-9. Av main course £7.25.
BREWERY/COMPANY: Free House.
PRINCIPAL BEERS: Youngs PA, Fullers London Pride,.
FACILITIES: terrace. **NOTES:** Parking 30

HARRIETSHAM
Map 05 TQ85

The Pepper Box Inn NEW
ME17 1LP ☎ 01622 842558 ▤ 01622 844218
e-mail: pbox@nascr.net
Dir: Take the Fairbourne Heath turning from A20 in Harrietsham and
follow for 2M to crossroads straight over follow for 200 yds pub is on
the L
Delightful 15th-century country pub situated on the Greensand
Ridge overlooking the Weald of Kent. The pub takes its name
from an early type of pistol with many barrels, a replica of
which hangs behind the bar. Cosy inglenook fireplaces,
comfortable furnishings, a separate non-smoking dining area
and a patio with spectacular views attract a good mix of
customers. Typical dishes include rack of lamb with redcurrant
and rosemary, spinach and Stilton crumble, pan-fried lambs'
liver and bacon with garlic mash, and fresh scampi and
prawns in basil and brandy.
OPEN: 11-3 6.30-11. **BAR MEALS:** L served all week. D served
all week 12-2.15 7-9.45. Av main course £9.50. **RESTAURANT:** L
served all week. D served all week 12-2 7-9.45. Av 3 course à la
carte £18. **BREWERY/COMPANY:** Shepherd Neame.
PRINCIPAL BEERS: Shepherd Neame Master Brew, Bishops
Finger, Spitfire. **FACILITIES:** Garden: Food served outside Dogs
allowed. **NOTES:** Parking 30

HERNHILL
Map 05 TR06

Pick of the Pubs

Red Lion ♈
The Green ME13 9JR ☎ 01227 751207
▤ 01227 752990
e-mail: theredlion@lineone.net
Dir: S of A299 between Faversham & Whitstable

Beams and flagstones, rustic pine tables and roaring
winter log fires are all part of the charm at this handsome,
half-timbered 14th-century hall house, which overlooks
the village green to the historic church. Now privately
ownwd, visitors will find local Shepherd Neame ales on
tap, a monthly-changing carte and a blackboard listing a
good range of daily specials. Begin with smoked salmon
tart, warm goats' cheese salad or moules marinière, then
move on to steak and kidney pudding, lamb en croûte,
home-baked ham, egg and chips, fresh beer-battered cod
or the Red Lion mixed grill. Traditional puddings include
chocolate fudge cake, fruit crumble and apple pie. Fully-
equipped two bedroom cottage with garden and patio to
rent.
OPEN: 11-.30 6-11. **BAR MEALS:** L served all week.
D served all week 12-3 6-9.30. Av main course £7.95.
RESTAURANT: D served all week 6-9.30.
BREWERY/COMPANY: Free House.
PRINCIPAL BEERS: Shepherd Neame Master Brew, Spitfire,
Wadworth 6X. **FACILITIES:** Children welcome Garden:
patio, outdoor eating. **NOTES:** Parking 40

HOLLINGBOURNE

The Dirty Habit
Upper St ME17 1UW ☎ 01622 880880 ▤ 01622 880773
The pub's name reflects its position on the Pilgrim's Way as a
haven for weary travellers. The original building was destroyed
(apparently by earthquake) in 1382. It was replaced by a
house occupied by monks, who introduced wine and ale to
serve to the pilgrims who stopped here to rest. Specialities
these days are sizzle dishes (perhaps monkfish, prawns and
potatoes), Thai curries, home-made pies and stir-fries.
OPEN: 11.30-3 6.30-11 (Sun 12-4, 7-10.30). **BAR MEALS:** L
served all week. D served all week 12-2.45 7-10.30. Av main
course £12. **RESTAURANT:** L served all week. D served all week
12-2.45 7-10.30. Av 3 course à la carte £22.
BREWERY/COMPANY: Free House.
PRINCIPAL BEERS: Fullers London Pride, Flowers IPA, Shepherd
Neame Spitfire, Bass. **FACILITIES:** Children welcome Garden:
2 level patio terrace, outdoor eating Dogs allowed Water.
NOTES: Parking 30

England

IDEN GREEN
Map 05 TQ73

The Peacock
Goudhurst Rd TN17 2PB ☎ 01580 211233
Dir: A21 from Tunbridge Wells to Hastings, onto A262, pub 1.5m past Goudhurst
Grade II listed building dating from the 12th century with low beams, an inglenook fireplace, Shepherd Neame ales on tap, and a wide range of traditional pub food.

IGHTHAM
Map 05 TQ55

George & Dragon
The Street TN15 9HH ☎ 01732 882440 ▤ 883209
Dir: From M20, A20 then A227 towards Tonbridge
Local legend has it that the Duke of Northumberland was imprisoned here after the discovery of the Gunpowder Plot. It is also believed that Guy Fawkes stayed here the night before the attempted plot was carried out. It is a fine example of Tudor architecture in a historic village setting, not far from Ightham Mote, one of the oldest continuously inhabited dwellings in England.

Pick of the Pubs

The Harrow Inn 🍴
Common Rd TN15 9EB ☎ 01732 885912
Dir: Off A25 between Sevenoaks & Borough Green. Signposted to Ightham Common
Within easy reach of both M20 and M26 motorways, yet tucked away down country lanes close to the National Trust's Knole Park and Igtham Mote, this Virginia creeper-hung stone inn clearly dates back to the 17th century and beyond.

The bar area comprises two rooms with a great brick fireplace, open to both sides, piled high with blazing logs: meanwhile the restaurant boasts a vine-clad conservatory that opens to a terrace that is ideal for summer dining.

Food options display imaginative use of fresh produce, with warm leek tart with garlic mayonnaise and beef stew with dumplings catching the eye in the bar; while tomato and anchovy salad before pan-fried duck breast with sweet-and-sour orange sauce are particularly tempting à la carte. Amongst popular house specialities, expect to find hot Kent smoked haddock pie, smoked salmon and halibut with creamed horseradish, wild mushroom and saffron risotto and Beef Wellington with Marsala sauce, followed by home-made apple tart or crispy roulade flavoured with lemon and lime.

OPEN: 12-3 6-11 (Sun 12-3 only). Closed Dec 26 Jan 1.
BAR MEALS: L served all week. D served Mon-Sat 12-2.30 6-9.30. Av main course £8. **RESTAURANT:** L served Tue-Sat. D served Tue-Sat 12-2.30 6-9.30. Av 3 course à la carte £22.
BREWERY/COMPANY: Free House.
PRINCIPAL BEERS: Greene King Abbot Ale & IPA,.
FACILITIES: Garden: outdoor eating, patio Dogs allowed guide dogs only. **NOTES:** Parking 20

IVY HATCH
Map 05 TQ55

Pick of the Pubs

The Plough 🍴 ♟
High Cross Rd TN15 0NL ☎ 01732 810268
▤ 01732 810451
Dir: M25 J5 take A25 towards Borough Green follow signs for Ivy Hatch

Long-established owners here have little to say except that they perennially produce more of the same - and if it ain't broke they don't fix it! Deep in Kent countryside and close to the National Trust's 14th-century Igham Mote, this a decidedly food-faceted dining pub whose special draw remains the variety of fish and sea-foods dished up daily according to market availability. Warm home-potted shrimps, fresh Irish oysters and sweet marinated anchovies with lemon dressing are precursors to steamed skate, grilled fillets of haddock and grilled or cold-dressed lobster as available.

At lunch only there may be wild boar sausages with herb mash and warm mushroom-and-bacon tart as alternatives to spicy fishcakes laid on a calypso sauce. Salads of smoked chicken and Stilton, or beef tomato with mozzarella, followed by honey-roast poussin and braised game casserole en croute extend choices for the less fishy-minded.

More than a dozen wines by the glass and some perfectly acceptable Larkin's ales ensure none shall go thirsty, even if not eating.
OPEN: 12-3 6-11. **RESTAURANT:** L served all week. D served all week 12-2 7-9.30. Av 3 course à la carte £19. Av 3 course fixed price £14.95. **BREWERY/COMPANY:** Free House. **PRINCIPAL BEERS:** Larkins. **FACILITIES:** Children welcome Garden: patio, outdoor eating.
NOTES: Parking 30

All AA listed accommodation can also be found on the AA's internet site **www.theAA.com**

LINTON
Map 05 TQ75

The Bull Inn
Linton Hill ME17 4AW ☎ 01622 743612
Dir: A229 through Maidstone to Linton
Traditional 17th-century coaching inn in the heart of the Weald with stunning views from the glorious garden. Popular with walkers and very handy for the Greensand Way. Large inglenook fireplace and a wealth of beams inside. Bar snacks and freshly prepared restaurant meals are available, ranging from Barnsley lamb chops with mint gravy and grilled salmon fillet to home-made lamb and apricot pie with Mediterranean vegetables and roast duck with Cumberland sauce.
OPEN: 12-3 6-11 (In summer-open all day). **BAR MEALS:** L served Tues-Sat. D served Tues-Sat 12-2.30 6.30-9. Av main course £6.95. **RESTAURANT:** L served all week. D served Mon-Sat 12-2.30 6.30-9. Av 3 course à la carte £16.
BREWERY/COMPANY: Shepherd Neame.
PRINCIPAL BEERS: Shepherd Neame Master Brew, Spitfire & Bishop's Finger. **FACILITIES:** Children welcome Garden: outdoor eating, patio Dogs allowed. **NOTES:** Parking 50

LITTLEBOURNE
Map 05 TR25

Pick of the Pubs

King William IV
4 High St CT3 1UN ☎ 01227 721244 📠 01227 721244
Dir: From A2 follow signs to Howletts Zoo. After zoo & at end of road, pub is straight ahead
Comfortable country inn located in the rural heartland of Kent, close to Canterbury and roughly mid-way between historic Sandwich and the coastal resort of Herne Bay. Exposed oak beams and open log fires help to generate a friendly, welcoming atmosphere and the pub's new owners offer a daily specials board featuring fish dishes and interesting vegetarian options, while the likes of ham and chips, jacket potatoes and a range of sandwiches are always available in the bar. The monthly-changing carte may offer Thai crab cakes with mango and red onion salsa, and fried chicken and turkey dumplings with a spicy plum sauce, followed by roasted pork fillet with apple and walnut stuffing to venison sausages with light horseradish mash, garlic and onion jus.
OPEN: 11-11. **BAR MEALS:** L served all week. D served all week 12-3 7-10. Av main course £5. **RESTAURANT:** L served all week. D served all week 12-2.30 7-10. Av 3 course à la carte £20. Av 2 course fixed price £11.95.
BREWERY/COMPANY: Free House.
PRINCIPAL BEERS: Shepherd Neame Master Brew, John Smiths. **FACILITIES:** Children welcome Garden: terrace, Food served outside. **NOTES:** Parking 15.
ROOMS: 7 bedrooms 7 en suite s£30 d£45

MAIDSTONE
Map 05 TQ75

Pick of the Pubs

The Ringlestone Inn ◆◆◆◆◆ ♀
Ringlestone Hamlet, Nr Harrietsham ME17 1NX
☎ 01622 859900 📠 01622 859966
e-mail: michelle@ringlestone.com
See Pick of the Pubs on page 253

NEWNHAM
Map 05 TQ95

Pick of the Pubs

The George Inn ♀
44 The Street ME9 0LL ☎ 01795 890237
📠 01795 890587
Dir: 5m SW of Faversham
Rugs on polished wooden floors, candlelit tables, exposed beams festooned with hopbines, open fires and splendid flower arrangements characterise the civilised interior at this attractive, tile-hung 16th-century village pub. Although under new management since December 2000, menus continue to show interest. For a hearty bar snack choose, perhaps, fisherman's pie, home-cooked ham, egg and chips, Caesar salad with pan-fried chicken, or a bacon and Brie baguette. Evening choices may include chicken liver and brandy pâté, followed by half shoulder of lamb with rosemary, garlic and red wine sauce or sirloin steak with peppercorn and cream sauce.
OPEN: 11-3 6.30-11. **BAR MEALS:** L served all week. D served all week 12-2..30 7-9.45. Av main course £8. **RESTAURANT:** L served all week. D served all week 12-2.30 7-9.45. Av 3 course à la carte £15. Av 0 course fixed price £12.50. **BREWERY/COMPANY:** Shepherd Neame.
PRINCIPAL BEERS: Shepherd Neame Master Brew, Spitfire, Bishops Finger. **FACILITIES:** Children welcome Garden: outdoor eating, BBQ Dogs allowed. **NOTES:** Parking 25

PLUCKLEY
Map 05 TQ94

Pick of the Pubs

The Dering Arms 🍴 ♀
Station Rd TN27 0RR ☎ 01233 840371
📠 01233 840498
Dir: M20 J8 take A20 to Ashford.Then R, B2077 at Charing
AA/Sea Fish Industry Authority
Seafood Pub of the Year for South & South East 2002
Located a mile from the village beside Pluckley Station, this impressive building with curved Dutch gables and uniquely arched windows was formerly a family hunting lodge for the Dering Estate. Splendid interior to match, with high ceilings, wood or stone floors, simple antique furniture and winter log fires. Expect a relaxing atmosphere, ale from Goacher's micro-brewery in Maidstone and good food using fresh vegetables from the family farm and herbs from the pub garden. Chef/patron James Buss has a real passion for fresh fish and seafood as is evident across the interesting menu, with starters like fish soup, Irish oysters with shallot and red wine vinegar, and herring roes pan-fried with smoked bacon. Follow with pan-fried scallops with basil spaghetti and saffron sauce, monkfish with bacon, orange and cream sauce, salmon fishcakes with sorrel sauce, or - given notice - Jim's massive seafood special. Pies of the day, sirloin steaks and confit of duck redress the balance.
OPEN: 11-3 6-11. Closed 26-29 Dec. **BAR MEALS:** L served Tues-Sun. D served Tue-Sat 12-2 7-9.30. Av main course £7.95. **RESTAURANT:** L served Tue-Sun. D served Tue-Sat 12-2 7-9.30. Av 3 course à la carte £22. **BREWERY/COMPANY:** Free House. **PRINCIPAL BEERS:** Goacher's Ales, Dering Ale, Maidstone Dark, Gold Star. **FACILITIES:** Children welcome Garden outdoor eating Dogs allowed Water. **NOTES:** Parking 20. **ROOMS:** 3 bedrooms s£30 d£40

OPEN: 12-3 6-11 (Sat-Sun 12-11). Closed 25 Dec.
BAR MEALS: L served all week. D served all week 12-2 7-9.30. Av main course £7.50
RESTAURANT: L served all week. D served all week 12-2 7-9.30. Av 3 course a la carte £17.
BREWERY/COMPANY: Free House.
PRINCIPAL BEERS: Shepherd Neame Bishops Finger & Spitfire, Greene King Abbot Ale, Theakston Old Peculier.
FACILITIES: Children welcome. Garden: landscaped, patio outdoor eating. Dogs allowed.
NOTES: Parking 50.
ROOMS: 20 bedrooms 20 en suite s£79-£96 d£89-£86 FR£99-£106.

The Ringlestone Inn

♦♦♦♦♦ ♀

Ringlestone, Harrietsham ME17 1NX
☎ 01622 859900 ▤ 01622 859966
e-mail: michelle@ringlestone.com
Dir: A20 E Maidstone. At rnbbt opp Great Danes Hotel turn L through Hollingbourne, R at crossroad top hill

As listed in Domesday, the 'ring stone' survives to this day with hooks for the tethering of one's mount still evident in the brickwork of this lamplit tavern and farmhouse hotel off the beaten track way up in the North Downs. Noted locally for its atmospheric bars, hearty country cooking and real ale.

A 'ryghte joyouse greetynge' emphasises the heritage of an historic hostelry that dates in all probability back to 1533, when it was used as a monks' hospice on the ancient Pilgrim's Way to Canterbury. Brick-and-flint walls, oak beams, inglenooks and antique furniture abound, and the well-stocked bar dispenses a mind-boggling range of country fruit wines alongside local cider and four real ales. Kentish fare with flair is today's thoroughly deserved slogan for home-created dishes produced wherever possible from local produce, enhanced by imaginative and exciting flavours.

Every lunchtime features a veritable feast of hot-and-cold buffet delights from traditional country recipes; coarse liver and apple pâté followed by turkey, bacon and walnut, lamb with apricot, or duck and damson wine pies with generous side dishes of the day's potato and vegetables, or a mixed salad. Of an evening, alternative main dishes 'from the stove' - how traditional - might well include fresh pink trout baked with lemon, almonds and oatmeal; lamb, coconut and almond curry; and spinach, cheese and herb pancakes with a touch of cayenne pepper. Follow with sweets that will likely include brandy bread pudding and treacle, orange and nut tart; or opt instead for a plate of decent cheese with crackers and celery.

Its smart modern bedrooms, housed in a nearby converted farmhouse, are furnished with plenty of individual touches such as CD players and fresh milk provided in the fridge.

PLUCKLEY continued

The Rose and Crown
Munday Bois TN27 0ST ☎ 01233 840393
📠 01233 756530
An ale house since 1780, the Rose and Crown is set in a remote hamlet - allegedly part of England's most haunted parish. The bar menu offers local sausages, steak and kidney pie and hearty brunches. Specials might include chilli and garlic tiger prawns, lamb fillets 'Shrewsbury' and spinach and mushroom pancakes. Childrens' and Sunday lunch menus.
OPEN: 11.30-3 6-11 (Sun 12-3, 7-11). **BAR MEALS:** L served all week. D served all week 12-2 6.30-9.30. Av main course £7.95. :**RESTAURANT:** L served all week. D served all week 12-2 6.30-9.30. Av 3 course à la carte £15. **BREWERY/COMPANY:** Free House. **PRINCIPAL BEERS:** Master Brew, Hook Norton, Shepherd Neame Bishops Finger. **FACILITIES:** Children welcome Garden: outdoor eating, Dogs allowed Garden only Water.
NOTES: Parking 30

SANDWICH

St Crispin Inn
The Street, Worth CT14 0DF ☎ 01304 612081
Set at the end of a dead-end village lane, this delightful inn has a carvery and char-grill, as well as summer barbeques. Close to Royal links courses. En suite bedrooms.

SELLING   Map 05 TR05

The Rose and Crown
Perry Wood ME13 9RY ☎ 01227 752214
Dir: A28 to Chilham R at Shottenden turning. R at Old Plough x roads, next R signed Perry Wood.Pub at top of hill
Set against 150 acres of natural woodland, this traditional 16th-century pub is decorated with local hop garlands and a unique corn dolly collection. Log fires in winter and a very attractive pub garden. Wide-ranging menu offers homemade steak and kidney pie, steak and mushroom suet pudding, curry, cod and smoked haddock mornay, and a variety of Chinese and Mexican specials.
OPEN: 11-3 6.30-11. **BAR MEALS:** L served all week. D served Tue-Sat 12-2 7-9.30. Av main course £6. **RESTAURANT:** L served Sun. D served Tue-Sat 12-2 7-9.30. Av 3 course à la carte £13.
BREWERY/COMPANY: Free House.
PRINCIPAL BEERS: Adnams Southwold, Harvey's Best.
FACILITIES: Children welcome Garden: Food served outside Dogs allowed Water, biscuit on welcome

---

SMARDEN   Map 05 TQ84

The Bell
Bell Ln TN27 8PW ☎ 01233 770283
Tiled and rose-covered Kentish inn in peaceful countryside. Rustic interior. Impressive choice of real ales. Pleasant garden. Bedrooms

---

Pick of the Pubs

The Chequers Inn 🐑 ♉
The Street TN27 8QA ☎ 01233 770217
📠 01233 770623
Dir: Through Leeds village, L to Sutton Valence/Headcorn then L for Smarden. Pub in village centre

Smart 14th-century inn with unique rounded weatherboarding located close to the church in the heart of this most attractive Wealden village. Newish owners have refurbished the rustic interior, the two character bars sporting a wealth of old beams, wood and flagstone floors, open fires and sturdy furnishings.

In addition to Harveys Sussex Bitter, Bass, changing guest beers and a dozen wines by the glass, visitors will find blackboard menus offering traditional bar snacks and more imaginative specials, including fresh fish, for example fish soup with rouille, queen scallops, smoked bacon and rocket salad, fresh cod in home-made batter and sea bass with tomato and chilli dressing. Meat alternatives may include honey-roast duck with cassis sauce and fillet steak with béarnaise. Four cottagey upstairs bedrooms featuring exposed beams, wall timbers and en suite facilities.
OPEN: 11-3 6-11 (Sat + Sun all day). **BAR MEALS:** L served all week. D served all week 12-2.30 6-9. Av main course £7. **RESTAURANT:** L served all week. D served all week 12-2.30 6-9. Av 3 course à la carte £20.
BREWERY/COMPANY: Free House.
PRINCIPAL BEERS: Harveys, Bass, Fullers London Pride.
FACILITIES: Children welcome Garden: Beer garden, patio, food served outdoors Dogs allowed. **NOTES:** Parking 15.
ROOMS: 4 bedrooms 4 en suite s£35 d£50

Pubs offering a good choice of seafood on the menu.

SMARTS HILL
Map 05 TQ54

Pick of the Pubs

The Bottle House Inn ♀
Coldharbour Rd TN11 8ET ☎ 01892 870306
📠 01892 871094
Dir: From Tunbridge Wells take A264 W then B2188 N

Formerly a barn belonging to a local estate, this solid, character dining pub was first licensed around the end of the 19th century when cider was produced here. Quaint beams, low ceilings and open fires characterise the cosy interior; splendid front terrace for summer alfresco imbibing. Diners can expect to find game terrine with fruit chutney, steak and kidney pudding, Thai prawn red curry, pan-fried calves liver, beef Stroganoff and chargrilled tuna on the extensive daily menu, and local Larkins bitter on tap. **OPEN:** 11-3 6-11. Closed Dec 25. **BAR MEALS:** L served all week. D served all week 12-2 6-10. Av main course £10. **RESTAURANT:** L served all week. D served all week 12-2 6-10. Av 3 course à la carte £18. **BREWERY/COMPANY:** Free House. **PRINCIPAL BEERS:** Larkins Ale, Harveys Best,. **FACILITIES:** Children welcome Children's licence Garden: patio, outdoor eating Dogs allowed. **NOTES:** Parking 36

Pick of the Pubs

The Spotted Dog ♀
TN11 8Ee ☎ 01892 870253
Relax and enjoy far-reaching views over the Weald from the terraced gardens of this 15th-century weatherboarded pub, situated within easy reach of Penshurst Place and Hever Castle. Rambling interior with a wealth of beams, open log fires, tiled and oak floors and intimate nooks and crannies. Blackboards list the day's interesting choice of food, perhaps including Indian ocean butter fish, Dublin Bay crayfish, chicken tagine, crispy aromatic duck, or spinach and ricotta filo parcels. Wide range of salads and light bites available. **OPEN:** 12-3 6-11 (Seasonal times vary, ring for details). Closed 25 & 26 Dec. **BAR MEALS:** L served all week. D served all week 12-2.30 6-9.30. Av main course £10. **RESTAURANT:** L served all week. D served Tue-Sun 12-2 7-9. Av 3 course à la carte £20. **BREWERY/COMPANY:** Carlsberg Tetley. **PRINCIPAL BEERS:** Greene King Abbot Ale, Adnams, Kentish Admiral, Old Spotty. **FACILITIES:** Children welcome Garden: beer garden with seating, patio. **NOTES:** Parking 60

SPELDHURST
Map 05 TQ54

The George and Dragon
Speldhurst Hill TN3 0NN ☎ 01892 863125
Dating from 1213, this is one of the oldest three pubs in England. It was used as a stopping off point by knights going to the Crusades.

STALISFIELD GREEN
Map 05 TQ95

The Plough
ME13 0HY ☎ 01795 890256
Dir: A20 to Charing, on dual carriageway turn L for Stalisfield
Splendid 15th-century hall house nestling beside the village green on top of the North Downs. Choose from a comprehensive snack menu or from the varied carte, the latter featuring Italian specialities.

TENTERDEN
Map 05 TQ83

White Lion Inn ◆◆◆◆ ♀
57 High St TN30 6BD ☎ 01580 765077 📠 01580 764157
e-mail: whitelion@lionheartinns.co.uk
Dir: on the A28 Ashford/Hastings road
On the tree-lined high street of this old cinque port, the White Lion is a 16th-century coaching inn that retains many original features. The area is known for cricket connections, and saw the first recorded county match between Kent and London in 1719. The chef's signature dishes include beer battered cod, brewer's pie, and salt and pepper king prawns. Menu regularly changes. Bedroom tariff includes use of local leisure facilities. **OPEN:** 11-11 (Sun 12-10.30). **BAR MEALS:** L served all week. D served all week 12-2.30 6-10. Av main course £7.50. **RESTAURANT:** L served all week. D served all week 12-2.30 6-10. Av 3 course à la carte £18. **BREWERY/COMPANY:** Lionheart. **PRINCIPAL BEERS:** Shepherd Neame, Bass, Worthington, Flowers IPA. **FACILITIES:** Children welcome Garden: Patio, Food served outside Dogs allowed. **NOTES:** Parking 30. **ROOMS:** 15 bedrooms 15 en suite s£40 d£55 2 family rooms £65-£89

TUNBRIDGE WELLS (ROYAL)
Map 05 TQ53

The Beacon ♀
Tea Garden Ln, Rusthall TN3 9JH ☎ 01892 524252
📠 01892 524252
Dir: From Tunbridge Wells take A264 towards East Grinstead. Pub 1m on L

The Beacon was built in 1895 as the elegant country home of a former Lieutenant of the City of London. Set in sixteen acres of grounds with lakes, woodland, and its own chalybeate spring, there's also a dining terrace with lovely rural views. Fresh local
continued

ingredients drive interesting menus, ranging from moules and chips or game casserole topped with flaky pastry, to Scotch beef on horseradish crushed new potatoes, baked Gressingham duck, or grilled swordfish with crab salsa. **OPEN:** 11-11 (Sun 12-10.30). **BAR MEALS:** L served all week. D served all week 12-2.30 6.30-9.30. Av main course £6.25. **RESTAURANT:** L served all week. D served all week 12-2.30 6-9.30. Av 3 course à la carte £23. **BREWERY/COMPANY:** Free House. **PRINCIPAL BEERS:** Harveys Best, Timothy Taylor Landlord, Fullers London Pride. **FACILITIES:** Children welcome Children's licence Garden: outdoor eating, patio, BBQ Dogs allowed. **NOTES:** Parking 40

The Crown Inn ♀
The Green, Groombridge TN3 9QH ☎ 01892 864742
Dir: Take A264 W of Tunbridge Wells, then B2110 S
Close to Groombridge Place (a fine moated manor with lovely gardens), this beamed 16th-century inn overlooks the village green and is popular with Weald Way walkers. The proprietors aim to please all tastes and meet all dietary requirements. The range of dishes includes skate wing with capers and black butter, braised pheasant in port, and vegetable goulash. **OPEN:** 11-3 6-11 (Sun 12-10.30, Sat in summer 11-11). **BAR MEALS:** L served all week. D served Mon-Sat 12-2 7-9.30. Av main course £7. **RESTAURANT:** L served all week. D served Mon-Sat 12-2 7-9.30. Av 3 course à la carte £16. **BREWERY/COMPANY:** Free House. **PRINCIPAL BEERS:** Harveys IPA, Courage Directors. **FACILITIES:** Children welcome Garden: patio, outdoor eating. **NOTES:** Parking 12. **ROOMS:** 4 bedrooms s£30 d£40

The Hare on Langton Green 🐇 ♀
Langton Rd TN3 0JA ☎ 01892 862419 📠 01892 861275
Dir: On A264 W of Tunbridge Wells
Rebuilt in 1901, with high ceilings, big windows and wooden floors, the pub has plenty of space and lots of old books and bric-a-brac to keep customers entertained. In addition to real ales, there is an impressive range of malt whiskies and wines by the glass. The imaginative menu takes in sandwiches and light bites like pasta with crab and ginger served with warm olive bread, to mains of Swedish meatballs, 10oz rump steak, and leek and cheddar soufflé. **OPEN:** 12-11 (Sun 12-10.30). **BAR MEALS:** L served all week. D served all week 12-9.30. Av main course £9.95. **RESTAURANT:** L served all week. D served all week 12-9.30. Av 3 course à la carte £17. **BREWERY/COMPANY: PRINCIPAL BEERS:** Greene King IPA & Abbot Ale. **FACILITIES:** Children's licence Garden: food served outdoors Dogs allowed. **NOTES:** Parking 15

Pick of the Pubs

Royal Wells Inn 🏵 🏵 ★ ★ ★ 💤 ♀
Mount Ephraim TN4 8BE ☎ 01892 511188
📠 01892 511908
e-mail: info@royalwells.co.uk
Dir: 75 yds from junction of A26 & A264

Family owned for nigh on 35 years, this handsome, white-painted small hotel is a significant landmark overlooking the common, its first-floor conservatory restaurant dominating the fine frontage. The informal Wells Brasserie and Bar is equally striking in its own right, with a classic and vintage car theme dominating its bright modern lines. Similarly up-to-date food of high quality is well in keeping, following the seasons with flair and imagination. As starters or main courses come Carlingford Lough oysters, warm crispy duck salad with aromatic dressing and smoked haddock and salmon fishcakes with parsley sauce. Poached skate and mussels in white wine, flash-fried calves' liver with balsamic and bacon and turkey and leek pie are among substantial alternatives. A fixed-price express lunch of one to three courses might well add smoked trout mousse with smoked salmon, roast stuffed loin of local lamb and apple and rhubarb crumble or chocolate tart with mango sorbet. Fine Kentish real ales and interesting wines by glass from France and the Antipodes. **OPEN:** 11-11 (Sun 12-10.30). **RESTAURANT:** L served all week. D served all week 12.15-2.15 6.30-10.15. Av 3 course à la carte £9.50. **BREWERY/COMPANY:** Free House. **PRINCIPAL BEERS:** Harveys Best, Shepherd Neame Master Brew, Bishop's Finger & Spitfire. **FACILITIES:** Children welcome Garden: outdoor eating, patio Dogs allowed. **NOTES:** Parking 28. **ROOMS:** 18 bedrooms 18 en suite s£65 d£85 FR£95-£135

Top of the Tree

Pubs called the Royal Oak were originally named in loyal remembrance of the day in 1651 when the youthful King Charles II hid in an oak tree at Boscobel in Shropshire, while Roundhead soldiers unsuccessfully searched the woods for him. The Royal Oak sign often shows simply the oak tree, or the king is shown perched among the branches - in plain view from all directions, but conventionally accepted as invisible to the purblind Parliamentarian troops. Sometimes, more subtly, the tree has a large crown among the foliage. Rarer variants include the king holding an oak spray with acorns, or acorns below a crown.

Pick of the Pubs

Sankey's Cellar Wine Bar 🍴 ♟
39 Mount Ephraim TN4 8AA ☎ 01892 511422
📠 01892 536097
e-mail: seafood@sankeys.co.uk
Dir: on A26
Seafood restaurant, oyster bar, cellar wine bar and pub supporting small local and international brewers, Sankeys has been a Tunbridge institution for over 15 years. The atmosphere is uniquely bustling and cluttered, with steps leading from the street down to the old cellars that open onto a sheltered garden protected from the weather by huge umbrellas and patio heaters. One menu at sensible prices applies throughout, with Cuan Bay Irish rock oysters and Scottish rope cultured mussels to the fore and specialities that include hand-dressed Cornish cock crab from Newlyn, 'mother's recipe' fishcakes and shellfish paella of faultless provenance. For further selections visit the blackboards promoting skate wings with caper butter, game casserole and steak and kidney pudding with side orders ranging from dauphinoise potatoes to mushy peas. Equal diligence in the provision of Caerphilly cheese from Wynford Evans of St Bride's Bay and wine selections from a master sommelier, Guy Sankey himself, all contribute to the uniqueness of this outstanding enterprise.
OPEN: 11-3.30 6-12 all day in summer. Closed 25-26 Dec, BHs. **BAR MEALS:** L served Mon-Sat. D served Mon-Sat 12-2.30 7-10. Av main course £8.50. **RESTAURANT:** L served Mon-Sat. D served Mon-Sat 12-2.30 7-10.00. Av 3 course à la carte £20. **BREWERY/COMPANY:** Free House. **PRINCIPAL BEERS:** Timothy Taylor Landlord, Larkins Traditional Bitter,. **FACILITIES:** Garden: sheltered, food served outside

WARREN STREET — Map 05 TQ95

The Harrow Inn ◆◆◆
Hubbards Hill ME17 2ED ☎ 01622 858727
📠 01622 850026
Dir: A20 to Lenham, follow sign for Warren St on L, pub on R
Once the forge and rest house for travellers heading for Canterbury on the Pilgrim's Way, this country inn is situated high up on the North Downs. The same menu is served in the bar and restaurant, with options such as paupiette of lemon sole filled with prawns and served with a white wine sauce, or fillet of lamb layered with wok-fried vegetables. Comfortable B&B.
OPEN: 12-3 7-11 (Sun 7-10.30). Closed 25-26 Dec. **BAR MEALS:** L served all week. D served all week 12-2 7-10. **RESTAURANT:** L served all week. D served Mon-Sat 12-1.30 7-9.30. Av 3 course à la carte £25. **BREWERY/COMPANY:** Free House. **PRINCIPAL BEERS:** Greene King Abbot, Adnams, Fullers London Pride. **FACILITIES:** Children welcome Garden: patio, outdoor eating, Dogs allowed only in garden. **NOTES:** Parking 80. **ROOMS:** 14 bedrooms 14 en suite s£39 d£49 5 family rooms, £59-£69

WESTERHAM — Map 05 TQ45

The Fox & Hounds
Toys Hill TN16 1QG ☎ 01732 750328
Unspoilt, traditional country pub with genuine atmosphere and no music or fruit machines. Furnished with old settees and armchairs. Open fires also add to the character. Ideally placed for good local country walks and National Trust land. Simple pub fare consists of filled rolls and hot snacks.
OPEN: 11.30-2.30 (Winter 12-2.30) 6-11 (Sun 12-3, 7-11). Closed Dec 25. **BAR MEALS:** . D served Snacks12-2. Av main course £4.
BREWERY/COMPANY: Greene King.
PRINCIPAL BEERS: Greene King IPA & Abbot Ale.
FACILITIES: Children welcome Garden: Dogs allowed at discretion of innkeeper. **NOTES:** Parking 15 No credit cards

WHITSTABLE — Map 05 TR16

Pick of the Pubs

The Sportsman 🍴 NEW
Faversham Rd CT5 4BP ☎ 01227 273370
Reached via a winding lane across open marshland from Whitstable and tucked beneath the sea wall, the Sportsman is the most unlikely place to find astonishingly good food, in particular fresh fish, listed on a sensibly-short blackboard menu. Most would drive past due to its unprepossessing appearance, but persevere and you will find a rustic, yet comfortable, interior decked out in modern style with sturdy open tables on wooden floors and interesting prints on the walls.
  Accompany a first-rate pint of Shepherd Neame Master Brew or a decent glass of wine with a pear and Roquefort or oyster with hot chorizo starter, moving on to whole roast sea bass, crispy duck with smoked chilli salsa and sour cream or roast ribeye of beef. Lunchtime bar food includes home-baked pizzas and salads.
OPEN: 12-3 6-11. Closed 25 Dec. **BAR MEALS:** L served all week 12-2.30. Av main course £4.95. **RESTAURANT:** L served all week. D served all week 12-2 7-9. Av 3 course à la carte £10.50. **BREWERY/COMPANY:** Shepherd Neame. **PRINCIPAL BEERS:** Shepherd Neame Bishops Finger & Master Brew. **FACILITIES:** Garden: Food served outside Dogs allowed, on leads please. **NOTES:** Parking 25

WROTHAM — Map 05 TQ65

The Green Man
Hodsoll St, Ash-cum-Ridley TN15 7LE ☎ 01732 823575
Dir: Off A227 between Wrotham & Meopham
An 18th-century brick and timber building with impressive floral displays in summer. The interior is warmly decorated with hops, horse brasses and local pictures.

WYE — Map 05 TR04

The New Flying Horse
Upper Bridge St TN25 5AN ☎ 01233 812297
400-year-old Shepherd Neame inn, characterised by low ceilings, black beams and open fire. Tucked away in pretty village beneath the North Downs. Bedrooms.

LANCASHIRE

BELMONT
Map 08 SD61

Black Dog
2/4 Church St BL7 8AB ☎ 01204 811218
Dir: M65 J3 onto A675
Traditional moorland pub adorned with antiques and bric-a-brac and noted for classical music with occasional live orchestras. Good value bar food includes everything from toasted sandwiches, ploughmans' and barm cakes, to lamb cutlets, grilled gammon, tandoori vegetable masala, and jumbo sausage.
OPEN: 12-4 7-11. **BAR MEALS:** L served all week. D served Wed-Sun (Mon-Tue residents only) 12-2 7-9. Av main course £5. **BREWERY/COMPANY:** Holts. **PRINCIPAL BEERS:** Holt-Bitter, DBA, Mild. **FACILITIES:** Children welcome Garden: small courtyard garden for residents only Guide dogs only.
NOTES: Parking 28. **ROOMS:** 3 bedrooms 3 en suite s£32 d£42 FR£42-£54 No credit cards

BILSBORROW
Map 08 SD52

Owd Nell's Tavern ♀
Guy's Thatched Hamlet, Canal Side PR3 0RS
☎ 01995 640010 📠 01995 640141
e-mail: guyshamlet@aol.com
Busy thatched pub tucked away in an expanding thatched tourist hamlet beside the Lancaster Canal. Always a wide selection of guest ales from all over the country. Great for families, specials include salmon hotpot, stuffed peppers, Cajun chicken wings, cottage pie, and bacon chop with champ.

OPEN: 11-11. Closed 25 Dec. **BAR MEALS:** L served all week. D served all week 11-9.30. Av main course £4.75. **RESTAURANT:** L served all week. D served all week 12-2.30 5.30-10.30. Av 3 course à la carte £8. **BREWERY/COMPANY:** Free House. **PRINCIPAL BEERS:** Boddingtons, Jennings, Flowers, Castle Eden. **FACILITIES:** Children welcome Garden: patio, BBQ, outdoor eating Dogs allowed. **NOTES:** Parking 300. **ROOMS:** 53 bedrooms 53 en suite s£42 d£42

We endeavour to be as accurate as possible but changes in personnel and data can occur in establishments after the guide has gone to press

BLACKBURN
Map 08 SD62

Pick of the Pubs

Millstone Hotel ⊛ ★ ★ ♀
Church Ln, Mellor BB2 7JR ☎ 01254 813333
📠 01254 812628
e-mail: millstone@shireinns.co.uk
Dir: From M6 J31 take A59 towards Clitheroe, past British Aerospace. R at rndbt signed Blackburn/Mellor. Next rndbt 2nd L. Hotel- top of hill on R
This fine inn, the original flagship of Daniel Thwaites' Brewery, was developed from a 17th-century tithe barn, retaining many of its original features such as oak beams, linen-fold panelling and the circular grinding-stone, incorporated in the facade, from which the hotel derives its name. Equally well preserved is the ambience of a traditional country inn with the options of bar food and restaurant dining. Bistro-style food, with its awareness of fresh produce, offers good value in the likes of casserole of beef in stout, pan-fried supreme of chicken and Loch Fyne scallops baked with garlic and gruyere. A la carte dinners and Sunday lunch.
OPEN: 11-11 (Sun 12-10.30). **BAR MEALS:** L served all week. D served all week 12-2 6.30-9.15. Av main course £7.25. **RESTAURANT:** L served all week. D served all week 12-2 6.30-9.15. Av 3 course à la carte £20. **BREWERY/COMPANY:** Shire Inns. **PRINCIPAL BEERS:** Thwaites. **FACILITIES:** Children welcome outdoor eating, patio Dogs allowed. **NOTES:** Parking 45. **ROOMS:** 23 bedrooms 23 en suite s£45 d£93 FR£78-£125

BLACKO
Map 08 SD84

Moorcock Inn
Gisburn Rd BB9 6NG ☎ 01282 614186
Dir: M65 J13, A682 for Kendal
Moorland inn, close to the Pendle Way, with good views and a traditional bar warmed by log fires in winter. Home-made Lancashire dishes are served, including daily specials, and there is a carvery at weekends in the dining room, with three joints and market vegetables. Daily specials are written up on blackboards.
OPEN: 12-2.30 6.30-9.30 (open all day wknd). **BAR MEALS:** L served all week. D served all week 12-2 6.30-9. Av main course £5.50. **RESTAURANT:** D served Sat-Sun 12-2 6.30-9. Av 3 course à la carte £10. **BREWERY/COMPANY:** Thwaites. **PRINCIPAL BEERS:** Thwaites Best Bitter. **FACILITIES:** Children welcome Garden: outdoor eating, patio Dogs allowed Water and Food. **NOTES:** Parking 80. **ROOMS:** 3 bedrooms 1 en suite s£20 d£35

BROOKHOUSE
Map 08 SD56

Black Bull Inn
LA2 9JP ☎ 01524 770329
Dir: Leave M6 at Juct 34, take A683 to Kirby Lonsdale for 2.5 M, at mini Rdbt turn R for .75 M pub is located on R
16th-century coaching inn situated in a picture postcard village. Originally made up of three cottages, the inn was also used as a local courthouse in the 1820s. Lots of old beams and local atmosphere.

England

CARNFORTH
Map 08 SD47

Dutton Arms
Station Ln, Burton LA6 1HR ☎ 01524 781225
📠 01524 782662
Dir: *from M6 take A6 signed Milnthorpe (Kendal), 3m before Milnthorpe turn R signed Burton/Holme*
Close to a host of tourist attractions, including Morecambe Bay, the Lancaster Canal and the northern Yorkshire Dales, the Dutton Arms boasts a new conservatory area which provides access to the pub's colourful gardens. Food is prepared from fresh ingredients and the landlord expertly demonstrates his cooking expertise here. Sample from a menu that may include pork and duck meatloaf, beef in beer, and spicy lamb and haggis pot with bacon, tomato and onion.
OPEN: 10-3.30 6-11 (11.30-11 winter wknd & summer evday).
BAR MEALS: L served all week. D served all week 11-2.30 6-9.30. Av main course £7. **RESTAURANT:** L served all week. D served all week 11-2.30 6-9.30. Av 3 course à la carte £12. Av 3 course fixed price £11. **BREWERY/COMPANY:** Free House.
PRINCIPAL BEERS: Boddingtons, Greene King Old Speckled Hen, Dent. **FACILITIES:** Children welcome Garden: outdoor eating Dogs allowed Water Provided. **NOTES:** Parking 30.
ROOMS: 4 bedrooms 4 en suite s£29.50 d£39.50 FR£39.50

CHIPPING
Map 08 SD64

Dog & Partridge
Hesketh Ln PR3 2TH ☎ 01995 61201 📠 01995 61446
Dating back to 1515 and originally known as the Cliviger Arms and then the Green Man, this comfortably modernised rural inn in the Ribble Valley enjoys wonderful views of the surrounding fells. The next door barn has been converted into an additional dining area and the emphasis is on home-made food using local produce. The menu is traditional English and roast duckling is the house speciality. Good range of local game in season, and a choice of fresh fish and steak.
OPEN: 11.45-3 6.45-11. **BAR MEALS:** L served Mon-Sat 12-1.45. Av main course £9. **RESTAURANT:** L served all week. D served all week 12-1.30 7-9. Av 3 course à la carte £16. Av 4 course fixed price £12.50. **BREWERY/COMPANY:** Free House.
PRINCIPAL BEERS: Tetleys. **FACILITIES:** Children welcome.
NOTES: Parking 30

Shove Halfpenny
The game is still played with pre-decimal halfpennies, lovingly preserved, but is not as popular and widespread in pubs as it used to be. It is a scaled-down version of shuffleboard, which involved propelling flat metal discs along a smooth wooden table up to 30ft long. Down to the First World War a playing area was often drawn in chalk on the bar or a tabletop, but today a special wooden or slate board is used, 24 inches long by 15 inches wide. As usual, the house rules vary in detail from one pub to another.

CLITHEROE
Map 08 SO74

Pick of the Pubs

Assheton Arms
Downham BB7 4BJ ☎ 01200 441227
e-mail: asshetonarms@aol.com
Dir: *From A59 take Chatburn turn. In Chatburn follow signs for Downham*
Standing at the head of the village by the Norman church and surrounded by picturesque cottages, the Assheton Arms retains a cheerfully warm traditional air. It is named after Lord Clitheroe's family who own the whole village. A single bar and sectioned rooms house an array of solid oak tables, wing-back settees, window seats, a large original stone fireplace, and a large blackboard listing interesting range of daily dishes available.
   Typical choices may include Loch Fyne oysters, pan-fried monkfish, sea bream with caper sauce, venison, bacon and cranberry casserole, beef Oriental, and home-made soups (cream of mushroom). A long menu of traditional pub favourites includes grills, chicken and mushroom pie, home-made ham and vegetable broth and toasted baguettes. Well-placed for a wild moorland walk up Pendle Hill which looms high above the village.
OPEN: 12-3 7-11 (closed 2nd week Jan). **BAR MEALS:** L served all week. D served all week 12-2 7-10. Av main course £8.50. **BREWERY/COMPANY:** Whitbread.
PRINCIPAL BEERS: Castle Eden Ale. **FACILITIES:** Children welcome patio, food served outside Dogs allowed.
NOTES: Parking 12

DARWEN
Map 08 SD62

Old Rosins Inn ★ ★
Treacle Row, Pickup Bank, Hoddlesden BB3 3QD
☎ 01254 771264
Dir: *M65 J5, follow signs for Haslingdon then R after 2m signed Egworth. 0.5m R & continue for 0.5m*
The original inn, set in the heart of the Lancashire Moors, has been extended to provide a variety of facilities. Bar food includes a variety of pies, including steak and ale, mixed grill, and a seafood platter, while the restaurant might offer local duck and a daily choice of fresh fish.
OPEN: 11-11 (Sun 12-10.30). **BAR MEALS:** L served all week. D served all week 11.30-10. Av main course £5.95.
RESTAURANT: D served all week 7-10. Av 3 course à la carte £14.95. Av 4 course fixed price £15.
BREWERY/COMPANY: Jennings.
PRINCIPAL BEERS: Jennings Bitter, Cumberland, Sneck Lifter & Fell Runner. **FACILITIES:** Children welcome Garden: Lawns and shrubbery Dogs allowed manager's discretion only.
NOTES: Parking 200. **ROOMS:** 15 bedrooms 15 en suite s£52 d£65

FENCE
Map 08 SD83

Fence Gate Inn
Wheatley Lane Rd BB12 9EE ☎ 01282 618101
📠 01282 615432
Dir: *From M65 L 1.5m, set back on R opposite T-junction for Burnley*
This substantial inn was originally a collection point for cotton delivered by barge and distributed to surrounding cottages to be spun into cloth. Wide-ranging menus are offered in the Topiary Brasserie.

England

FORTON   Map 08 SD45

Pick of the Pubs

The Bay Horse Inn ♀ NEW
LA2 0HR ☎ 01524 791204 📠 01524 791204
e-mail: cwilki5769@aol.com
Dir: 1 M S off Junct 33 of M6
Bay Horse is a name lent to this picturesque area to the
south of Lancaster that stretches to Cockerham Sands and
the Lune estuary. A stylish yet informal, traditional
coaching inn tucked just off the A6, Forton's eponymous
inn specialises in a combination of simple, fresh and
imaginative food from a chef who is wholly self-taught and
whose shopping policy reveals his total commitment. This
is a no-frills local with roughcast walls, bay windows and
window boxes and a small dining-room in which to
indulge the imagination.
   A platter of local seafood makes an ideal starter for
two, with bang-bang chicken with spicy peanut butter and
baked goats' cheese salad with Italian ham and marinated
olives typical of other choices. Thoughtful attention to
inherent flavours produces main dishes such as peppered
beef fillet with Stilton potatoes, ceps and Madeira cream,
seared salmon with buttered spinach and sweet chilli
sauce and a thick roast pork chop with black pudding
mash, roast apple and cider mustard sauce. Alternative to
desserts such as vanilla yoghurt pannacotta and pears
poached in red wine is a plate of British cheeses and
home-made chutney.
OPEN: 12-3 (Sun 12-5, 8-10.30) 6.30-11. **BAR MEALS:** L
served Tues-Sun. D served Tues-Sat 12-2 7-9.30. Av main
course £11. **RESTAURANT:** L served Tues-Sun. D served
Tues-Sat 12-2 7-9.30. Av 3 course fixed price £25.
PRINCIPAL BEERS: Wadworth 6X. **FACILITIES:** Children
welcome Garden: food served outside. **NOTES:** Parking 30

GALGATE   Map 08 SD45

The Stork Hotel
Conder Green LA2 0AN ☎ 01524 751234
📠 01524 752660
Dir: M6 J33 take A6 north. At Galgate turn L & next L to Conder
Green
Situated on the River Conder, the Stork has been a public
house, under various names, since the mid-17th century.
Handy for the Lake District and the Forest of Bowland.
Bedrooms.

GARSTANG

Th'Owd Tithebarn
Church St PR3 1PA ☎ 01995 604486
Set on the canal bank and adorned inside with antique
farming memorabilia. Open all day.

GOOSNARGH   Map 08 SD53

The Bushell's Arms
Church Ln PR3 2BH ☎ 01772 865235 📠 01772 865235
Georgian village pub named after the benefactors of a former
private hospital nearby. Cosy interconnecting beamed dining
area. Known locally for good, old-fashioned hospitality and
imaginatively cooked food, but long-serving landlord due to
leave Summer 2001. Reports on new regime please.

Ye Horns Inn
Horns Ln PR3 2FJ ☎ 01772 865230 📠 01772 864299
e-mail: yehornsinn@msn.co.uk
Dir: From M6 J32 take A6 N. At traffic lights turn R onto B5269.
In Goosnargh follow Inn signs
An 18th-century, black and white coaching inn with a new
patio and outdoor seating area. It has a peaceful country
setting and retains its original character. The food on offer
includes home-made pâté, steak and kidney pie, battered cod
and hot sticky toffee pudding.
OPEN: 11.30-3 (ex Mon) 6-11 (no bar food Sun lunch, Sat eve).
BAR MEALS: L served Tue-Sun. D served Sun-Fri 12-2 7-9.15.
RESTAURANT: L served Tue-Sun. D served all week 12-2 7-9.15.
BREWERY/COMPANY: Free House. **PRINCIPAL BEERS:** No
real ale. **FACILITIES:** Children welcome Garden: outdoor
eating, patio, BBQ, pond. **NOTES:** Parking 70.
ROOMS: 6 bedrooms 6 en suite s£55 d£75

HASLINGDEN   Map 08 SD72

Farmers Glory NEW
Roundhill Rd BB4 5TU ☎ 01706 215748 📠 01706 215748
Dir: 7 miles equidistant from Blackburn, Burnley and Bury, 1/2m from
M66
Stone-built 350-year-old pub situated high above Haslingden
of the edge of the Pennines. Formerly a coaching inn on the
ancient route to Whalley Abbey, it now offers locals and
modern A667 travellers a wide-ranging traditional pub menu
of steaks, seafood, pizzas and pasta meals.
OPEN: 12-3 7-11.30. **BAR MEALS:** L served all week. D served
all week 12-2.30 7-9.30. Av main course £5. **RESTAURANT:** L
served all week. D served all week 12-2.30 7-9.30. Av 3 course à la
carte £12.50. **BREWERY/COMPANY:** Pubmaster.
PRINCIPAL BEERS: Tetley Bitter, Marstons Pedigree, Greene
King IPA. **FACILITIES:** Children welcome Garden.
NOTES: Parking 60

HESKIN GREEN   Map 08 SD51

Farmers Arms
85 Wood Ln PR7 5NP ☎ 01257 451276 📠 01257 453958
e-mail: andy@farmersarms.co.uk
Dir: On B5250 between M6 & Eccleston
Long, creeper-covered country inn with two cosy bars decorated
in old pictures and farming memorabilia. Once known as the
Pleasant Retreat, this is a family-run pub proud to offer a warm
welcome. Typical dishes include steak pie, fresh salmon with
prawns and mushroom, rack of lamb, and chicken curry.
OPEN: 12-11. **BAR MEALS:** L served all week. D served all week
12-9.30. Av main course £6. **RESTAURANT:** L served all week.
D served all week 12-9.30. Av 3 course à la carte £12.
BREWERY/COMPANY: Whitbread. **PRINCIPAL BEERS:** Taylor
Landlord, Castle Eden, Flowers IPA, Boddingtons.
FACILITIES: Children welcome Garden: Dogs allowed.
NOTES: Parking 50. **ROOMS:** 5 bedrooms 5 en suite s£30 d£40

HEST BANK   Map 08 SD46

Hest Bank Hotel 🛏
2 Hest Bank Ln LA2 6DN ☎ 01524 824339
📠 01524 824948
e-mail: hestbankhotel@hotmail.com
Dir: From Lancaster take A6 N, after 2m L to Hest Bank
Formerly a staging post for coaches crossing Morecambe Bay,
this 16th-century inn is situated beside the Lancaster Canal.
Local produce is a feature of the extensive menu, which

continued

includes a selection from the chargrill and favourites such as Morecambe Bay potted shrimps and Hest Bank lamb hot pot. In addition, daily specials might offer fresh crab salad or salmon fillet with herb crust. **OPEN:** 11.30-11 (Sun 12-10.30). **BAR MEALS:** L served all week. D served all week 12-9. Av main course £5.
BREWERY/COMPANY: Inn Partnership.
PRINCIPAL BEERS: Boddingtons, Marstons Pedigree, Timothy Taylor Landlord. **FACILITIES:** Garden: outdoor eating, patio,.
NOTES: Parking 20

MERECLOUGH   Map 09 SD83

Kettledrum Inn
302 Red Lees Rd BB10 4RG ☎ 01282 424591
📧 01282 424591
Dir: from Burnley town centre, past Burnley FC, 2 1/2m, 1st pub on L
Inviting well-kept country inn with superb views of the famous Pendle Hills. Good range of traditional pub food.

PARBOLD   Map 08 SD41

Pick of the Pubs

The Eagle & Child 🛏 ♀
Maltkiln Ln L40 3SG ☎ 01257 462297
📧 01257 464718
Dir: From M6 J27 to Parbold. At bottom of Parbold Hill turn R on B5246 to Hilldale. Then 1st L to Bispham Green
  In an area not blessed with the best dining pubs, this one shines out for its lack of juke box, fruit machines and loud music, preferring instead to concentrate on good ales and cider, a daily-changing menu of fresh food and perennially popular special events and theme nights. An interior of flagged floors, coir matting, oak settles and antique furniture, with old paintings and prints adorning the walls, is conducive to the enjoyment of regularly changing guest ales, varied and interesting house wines and good fresh food at generally kind prices. From the specials menu try carrot and orange soup or home-made chicken liver parfait before chargrilled swordfish with a warm salad of green beans and wild mushrooms or pan-fried pork fillet with black pudding timbale, apple and tarragon beurre blanc. Lighter meals and salads include crispy duck with chorizo and lardons and roast Mediterranean vegetables on toasted ciabatta with balsamic and olive oil. Battered cod, steak in real ale pie and liver-and-onions redress the balance at what remains a fiercely traditional country pub.
OPEN: 12-3 (Sun open all day) 5.30-11. **BAR MEALS:** L served all week. D served all week 12-2 6-8.30. Av main course £9.50. **RESTAURANT:** L served all week. D served all week 12-2 6-8.30. Av 3 course à la carte £15.
BREWERY/COMPANY: Free House.
PRINCIPAL BEERS: 5 Changing guest beers.
FACILITIES: Children welcome Garden: food served outside. **NOTES:** Parking 50

PRESTON   Map 08 SD52

Cartford Country Inn
Little Eccleston PR3 0YP ☎ 01995 670166 📧 01995 671785
Located by a toll bridge over the River Wyre, this welcoming inn is home to the Hart Brewery, a small operation that enjoys a strong local reputation. Bar menu includes traditionally home made and 'spicy' dishes.

RIBCHESTER   Map 08 SD63

The White Bull
Church St PR3 3XP ☎ 01254 878303
Grade II listed former courthouse dating back to the 17th century and boasting four complete Tuscan pillars which are thought to have once been part of a Roman town here. Impressive view of the Bathhouse from the rear of the beer garden. Three well-equipped bedrooms have been converted from an old stable loft and traditional and imaginatively-planned pub food is served in pleasantly furnished bars, including sea bass, stuffed aubergine and chicken pizziola topped with a tomato, basil and fresh pepper sauce.
OPEN: 11.30-3 6.30-11 (Sun 12-10.30; food 12-8).
BAR MEALS: L served all week. D served Tue-Sun 11.30-2 6.30-9.30. Av main course £5.50. **RESTAURANT:** L served all week. D served Tue-Sun 11.30-2 6.30-9.30. Av 3 course à la carte £10.50.
PRINCIPAL BEERS: Flowers IPA, Planets Bobbins Bitter Wadworths 6X , Boddingtons. **FACILITIES:** Children welcome Garden: food served outdoors. **NOTES:** Parking 14.
ROOMS: 3 bedrooms 3 en suite s£25 d£30

SAWLEY   Map 08 SD74

Pick of the Pubs

The Spread Eagle 🛏 ♀
BB7 4NH ☎ 01200 441202 📧 01200 441973
See Pick of the Pubs on page 263

On the Inside

The earliest pubs were people's homes and were furnished and decorated accordingly. It was not until the 1820s that the bar-counter made its appearance, but already a distinction had grown up between the taproom for labourers and poorer customers, and the parlour began to sport carpets, pictures of the royal family and cases of butterflies or stuffed birds. The Victorian gin palaces introduced an altogether plushier style.

The big brewing chains have intruded a fake and regimental note into pub decor, but many pubs still nostalgically display Toby jugs or horse-brasses, agricultural bygones, ornamental brass plates or gleaming copper pans.

Some maintain their individuality with collections of oddities that have taken the landlord's fancy - police equipment or cigarette cards, neckties or man traps, or even fossilised hot cross buns.

England

Dominoes

Dominoes came to Britain from the Continent at the end of the 18th century, perhaps brought back by British soldiers serving in the Napoleonic Wars. French prisoners-of-war made sets of dominoes, not only for their own amusement but to sell to the British. Many different varieties are played in pubs besides the standard block game, and some pubs belong to dominoe leagues.

WHITEWELL   Map 08 SD64

Pick of the Pubs

The Inn At Whitewell ◆◆◆◆ 🛏 ♀
Forest of Bowland BB7 3AT ☎ 01200 448222
📠 01200 448298
Dir: Take B6243 and follow signs for Whitewell
Perched on the east bank of the River Hodder, in the Forest of Bowland, the earliest parts of the building date back to the 1300s, when it would have been the forest keeper's house. The interior is slightly eccentric, with its haphazard arrangement of bric-a-brac, rugs and furnishings. Comprehensive bar lunch and supper menus from a talented kitchen are supplemented by blackboard specials. Typical options include hot salmon mousse, lamb casserole and roast duck marinated in soy, ginger and garlic, home-made pasta with mushrooms and bacon, seafood chowder, and a selection of sandwiches.

OPEN: 11-3 6-11. **BAR MEALS:** L served all week. D served all week 12-2 7.30-9.30. Av main course £9.
RESTAURANT: D served all week 7.30-9.30. Av 3 course à la carte £29. **BREWERY/COMPANY:** Free House.
PRINCIPAL BEERS: Marstons Pedigree, Boddingtons.
FACILITIES: Children welcome Garden: patio, outdoor eating Dogs allowed. **NOTES:** Parking 50.
ROOMS: 17 bedrooms 17 en suite s£65 d£99

SLAIDBURN   Map 08 SD75

Hark to Bounty Inn
Townend BB7 3EP ☎ 01200 446246 📠 01200 446361
e-mail: manager@hark-to-bounty.co.uk
Dir: From M6 J31 take A59 to Clitheroe then B6478, through Waddington and Newton and on to Slaidburn
Situated in the renowned Trough of Bowland, this 13th-century stone-built inn takes its name from a hunting dog whose loud barking could be heard above the baying of the pack. His master, the village squire, called out 'Hark to Bounty.' Expect home-made fish pie, pan-fried scallops on tagliatelle, or Cumberland sausage with apple sauce.
OPEN: 11-11. **BAR MEALS:** L served all week. D served all week 12-2 6-9. Av main course £6.95. **RESTAURANT:** L served all week. D served all week 12-2 6-9. Av 3 course à la carte £12.
BREWERY/COMPANY: Scottish Courage.
PRINCIPAL BEERS: Theakston - Old Peculier, Mild & Bitter, Courage Directors. **FACILITIES:** Children welcome Children's licence Garden: outdoor eating Dogs allowed garden and rooms only. **NOTES:** Parking 25. **ROOMS:** 9 bedrooms 9 en suite s£25 d£50 FR£70

WHALLEY   Map 08 SD73

Freemasons Arms ♀
8 Vicarage Fold, Wiswell BB7 9DF ☎ 01254 822218
e-mail: freemasons@wiswell.co.uk
The menu has improved and expanded since food was first introduced here in the 1960s and today the inn offers a wide-ranging choice of home-cooked food. Relax in the bar area, old tap room or more formal upstairs dining room and enjoy black pudding with a mustard sauce, tiger prawns in Filo pastry and stuffed tomatoes with cheese from the appetising menu. House specialities include rack of lamb and spicy chicken ginger. Impressive selection of malt whiskies.
OPEN: 12-3 6.30-12 (closed Mon-Tue). Closed 25-26 Dec, 1-2 Jan. **BAR MEALS:** L served Wed-Sun. D served Wed-Sun 12-2 6.30-9.30. Av main course £8.95. **RESTAURANT:** L served Wed-Sun. D served Wed-Sun 12-2 6.30-9.30. Av 3 course à la carte £16.
BREWERY/COMPANY: Free House.
PRINCIPAL BEERS: Jennings Bitter, Jennings Cumberland Ale, Black Sheep Best.

WREA GREEN   Map 08 SD33

The Grapes Hotel
Station Rd PR4 2PH ☎ 01772 682927 📠 01772 687304
Dir: From M55 J3 follow signs for Kirkham then Wrea Green
Situated in the centre of the village opposite the green and duck pond. One menu caters for everybody, offering a selection of snacks and traditional pub meals.

Open: 11-11 (Sun 12-3 only). Closed Sun eve & all Mon.
Bar Meals: L served Tue-Sun. D served Tue-Sat 12-2 6-9.
RESTAURANT: L served Tue-Sun D Tue-Sat 12-2 6-9. Av 3 course a la carte £15. Av 3 course fixed price £10.25.
BREWERY/COMPANY: Free House.
PRINCIPLE BEERS: Black Sheep Bitter, Shepherd Neame Spitfire, Wells Bombardier.
FACILITIES: Children welcome. Garden: patio, outdoor eating
NOTES: Parking 50.

The Spread Eagle

BB7 4NH
☎ 01200 441202 📠 01200 441973
Dir: N on A59 to Skipton, 3m N of Clitheroe

Charting its history back to a mention in records of the 16th century, this renowned inn at the heart of the Forest of Bowland has a long and proud history of high quality. Its reputation for good food and accomplished cuisine appears undimmed under new ownership.

Large picture windows in the smart, split-level riverside restaurant facilitate sweeping views over the River Ribble and the Ribble Valley and the décor is light and modern, bringing a touch of the metropolitan brasserie to the hillside.

Mid-week lunches, following a familiar pattern, offer remarkable value for money when you might have smoked fish salad with dill and horseradish cream, baked ham with butter-bean broth and herb dumplings, farmhouse Lancashire cheese from Goosnargh and a decent pint of real ale or a glass of house red without breaking the bank (not the river's!). Expect rather more in terms of elaboration and quality from the dinner menu, though mid-week offers before 8.00pm still slant somewhat in the customer's favour. Starters might include potted rillettes of chicken and pork or poached salmon ballantine with a dill and horseradish cream, followed by braised local pheasant on red cabbage with red wine and prune jus, shoulder of Cumbrian lamb with roasted baby onions and minted braising sauce, or salmon fillet with grain mustard cream sauce. For pudding try the rich chocolate terrine with vanilla anglaise or the iced apricot and almond parfait. Expect carefully balanced flavours and studied presentation: decidedly one to watch.

Special events include dinner dances and regular wine tastings enlivened by the presence of their local wine merchant.

263

England

WRIGHTINGTON Map 08 SD51

Pick of the Pubs

The Mulberry Tree 🏵 🍴 ♀ NEW
WN6 9SE ☎ 01257 451400 📠 01257 451400
Dir: Juct 27 off M6 turn into Mossy Lea Road 2 M on the right
Former Roux brothers' head chef Mark Prescott has returned to the village of his birth to set up in partnership at this free house, formerly known as The Scarisbrick Arms. Locals and regular diners, since its recent refurbishment in clean airy style, can relax and feast from the hand of the master - a growing phenomenon since the turn of this century! At its simplest are chargrilled smoked salmon on Caesar salad and twice-baked Lancashire cheese soufflé, followed by roast beef sirloin with Yorkshire and penne pasta with asparagus, tomato, pesto and Parmesan. Dining-room starters run from white onion soup with tarragon cream to Sevruga caviar (at a price), while speciality main dishes always include fresh lobster - with champagne and herb sauce perhaps. Other regular choices are chargrilled tuna loin with Nicoise salad, slow-roast belly pork with apples and sage and Goosnargh duck breast with blood oranges. To start, maybe Lancashire pork terrine or black pudding with pancetta, poached egg and hollandaise, and to finish red fruits in mulled wine jelly or bread-and-butter pudding with apricot sauce. Extensive fixed-price Sunday lunches and wine choices.
OPEN: 12-3 6-11. Closed 26 Dec, 1 Jan. **BAR MEALS:** L served Tue-Sun. D served Tue-Sat 12-2 6-9. Av main course £8.95. **RESTAURANT:** L served all week. D served all week 12-2 6-10. Av 3 course à la carte £20.
BREWERY/COMPANY: Free House.
PRINCIPAL BEERS: Flowers IPA,. **FACILITIES:** Children welcome Tables outside. **NOTES:** Parking 100

YEALAND CONYERS

The New Inn
40 Yealand Rd LA5 9SJ ☎ 01524 732938 📠 01524 734502
e-mail: newinn.yealand@virgin.net
Dir: Join A6 between Carnforth & Milnthorpe, 3m then L after Yealand Conyers sign, .25m to pub

Quaint, ivy-clad, 400-year-old village pub located close to Leighton Hall, Leighton Moss Nature Reserve (RSPB) and the Cumbrian border. Locals, walkers and A6 travellers can expect a warm welcome, winter log fires and tip-top Robinsons ales in the cosy, simply furnished bar. Comfortable adjoining dining areas. Good snack menu listing warm filled baguettes and hearty jacket potatoes. From the main menu choose, beef in beer, Cumberland sausage casserole, salmon Wellington,

continued

prime steaks or look to the chalkboard for daily dishes like spicy Mexican bean pot and desserts like tangy lemon posset.
OPEN: 11-11 (Sun 12-10.30). **BAR MEALS:** L served all week. D served all week 12-9.30. Av main course £7. **RESTAURANT:** L served all week. D served all week 12-9.30. Av 3 course à la carte £13. **BREWERY/COMPANY:** Frederic Robinson.
PRINCIPAL BEERS: Hartleys XB,. **FACILITIES:** Children welcome Garden: food served outside Dogs allowed Water. **NOTES:** Parking 50

LEICESTERSHIRE

CASTLE DONINGTON Map 09 SK42

Pick of the Pubs

The Nag's Head 🍴 ♀
Hilltop DE74 2PR ☎ 01332 850652
Thought to have started life as an old barn, the Nags Head has been trading for over a hundred years. It's now a comfortable little country pub on the edge of the village, very handy for the nearby airport and motor racing circuit. Inside the plain, whitewashed building, you'll find low beamed ceilings and open coal fires.
There's a bistro atmosphere in the large, well decorated dining room, with its colour-washed walls and plain scrubbed tables. This bustling venue appeals to the airport and motor racing fraternity, as well as to a more traditional local clientele. The extensive menu features an upmarket range of starters and snacks, including hearty soups, warm tomato and Mozzarella salad, and generously filled ciabatta sandwiches. Unusual and inventive dishes like venison with parsnip mash, Cajun beef with tsatsiki dressing, John Dory with leek and watercress sauce or sea bass with sweet potato casserole precede good, traditional home-made puddings.

OPEN: 11.30-2.30 5.30-11. **BAR MEALS:** L served Mon-Sat. D served Mon-Sat 12-2 5.30-9.30. Av main course £4.95. **RESTAURANT:** L served all week. D served all week 12-2 5.30-9.30. Av 3 course à la carte £20.
BREWERY/COMPANY: PRINCIPAL BEERS: Banks, Marstons Pedigree. **FACILITIES:** Garden: outdoor eating, patio Dogs allowed. **NOTES:** Parking 20

 For pubs with AA rosette awards for food see page 10

**BELL INN,
EAST LANGTON**
Main Street LE16 7TW.
Tel: 01858 545278
Directions: follow sign for
Langtons off A6 N of Market
Harborough
*Creeper-clad 16th-century
village pub with a long, pine-
furnished bar, open fire and
head-cracklingly low beams.
Home-brewed ales,
enjoyable food, including
decent lunchtime sandwiches
and more imaginative
evening menu. Bedrooms.*
Open: 11.30-2.30 7-11 (Fri &
Sat from 6). Bar Meals: 12-2
7-10. Children and dogs
welcome. Garden. Parking.
(see page 266 for full entry)

Bell Inn, East Langton

This enjoyable rural ramble explores the peaceful, gently rolling countryside that surrounds the attractive Langton villages.

From the car park, cross the road to the cricket pitch and walk along the edge of the pitch to the far side. Follow footpath markers into the next field, turn right and proceed to the gate and road. Head straight up the road opposite into Church Langton. At the T-junction opposite the church, turn right and keep to the road out of the village and down the hill.

Just before the corner, take the footpath arrowed right. Head diagonally towards the farmhouse in the distance to reach the road. Turn right, pass Mill Farm (left), then in 100yds (91m), at a small crossroads, take the track on the right. Either follow the track (less muddy in wet weather) all the way to Thorpe Langton or, for a more scenic route, take the signed footpath on your left after the first field and head diagonally across the field to the top of the hill. Follow waymarkers right over the Caundle Hills until you reach a small spinney. Cross the bridge over the stream and soon join the track for Thorpe Langton.

Turn right along the village road, then left towards the church. Turn right in front of the church and follow the path straight across a paddock to reach a lane. Turn left, then at the end of the lane, cross the stile ahead into the field. Turn immediately right and follow the marker posts across several meadows back towards East Langton. In the last meadow before the village, walk to the bottom left-hand corner and cross stiles into Back Lane. Bear right, then right at the end and head up Main Street back to the pub.

Distance: 5 1/2 miles (8.8km)
Map: OS Landranger 141
Terrain: farmland and village streets
Paths: field paths, tracks and country lanes
Gradient: undulating; ascents in the Caundle Hills.

*Walk submitted by:
The Bell Inn*

CROXTON KERRIAL
Map 09 SK82

Peacock Inn
1 School Ln NG32 1QR ☎ 01476 870324 ▯ 01476 870171
e-mail: boblord@currentbun.com
Dir: Situated on A607, 3M from Junct with A1

300-year-old coaching inn situated in the renowned Vale of Belvoir. Nearby is Belvoir Castle and among the many popular outdoor pursuits in the area are walking, angling and hunting. All the dishes are freshly prepared on the premises and the award-winning chef is acknowledged for her quality food and home-made puddings. Lincolnshire sausages, chicken curry and fish and chips are among the favourites in the bar, while the restaurant menu might offer fillet steak, baked turbot fillet and English duckling.
OPEN: 12-3.30 6-11 (Summer open all day). **BAR MEALS:** L served all week. D served all week 12-3.30 6.30-10. Av main course £6. **RESTAURANT:** L served all week. D served all week 12-3.30 6.30-10. Av 3 course à la carte £25. Av 3 course fixed price £16.95. **BREWERY/COMPANY:** Free House.
PRINCIPAL BEERS: John Smiths, Timothy Taylor.
FACILITIES: Children welcome Garden: beautiful views, food served outside Dogs allowed Water. **NOTES:** Parking 40.
ROOMS: 8 bedrooms d£60

Langton Brewery

Reflecting the tastes of a local community that expects a lot from its beer, the Langton Brewery was founded by the landlord of the Bell Inn and a retired banker. Their concern over the potential loss of the local brewing heritage led to the creation of a micro-brewery that now produces two regular brews: Caudle Bitter, (3.9%) and Bowler (4.8%) which celebrates the association between the Bell Inn and the Langtons Cricket Club opposite.

EAST LANGTON
Map 06 SP79

Pick of the Pubs

The Bell Inn ♀
Main St LE16 7TW ☎ 01858 545278 ▯ 01858 545748
e-mail: achapman@thebellinn.co.uk

Attractive, creeper-clad 16th-century inn set back from the pretty street in the most upmarket of the Langton villages. Comfortably refurbished by enthusiastic landlord Alistair Chapman, who has recently installed a micro-brewery in the outbuildings, the inn boasts a long, pine-furnished bar, an open log fire, head-crackingly low beams and a neat, green-painted dining-room. In addition to Langton Brewery Caudle and Bowler brews, served straight from the barrel, you can tuck into some hearty, traditional pub food, all freshly cooked on the premises. There's a fresh fish board at weekends, while normal options include filled baguettes and bagels, smoked chicken salad, liver and bacon casserole, vegetable and Stilton cobbler, fish and leek pie, and fillet steak with home-made chips and fresh vegetables. Sunday carvery lunches and interesting changing specials.
OPEN: 11.30-2.30 7-11. Closed Dec 25. **BAR MEALS:** L served all week. D served all week 12-2 7-10. Av main course £10. **BREWERY/COMPANY:** Free House.
PRINCIPAL BEERS: Greene King IPA & Abbot Ale.
FACILITIES: Children welcome Garden: outdoor eating Dogs allowed. **NOTES:** Parking 20. **ROOMS:** 2 bedrooms 2 en suite s£39.50 d£55 FR£80

See Pub Walk on page 265

FLECKNEY
Map 06 SP69

The Old Crown ♀
High St LE8 8AJ ☎ 0116 2402223
e-mail: old-crown-inn@fleckney7.freeserve.co.uk
A traditional village pub that is especially welcoming to walking and hiking groups, the Old Crown is close to the Grand Union Canal and Saddington Tunnel. Families are well catered for, with plenty of entertainment and children's facilities. Food options include jacket potatoes, burgers, baguettes and grills. Special curry nights.
OPEN: 11-11 (Sun 12-10.30). **BAR MEALS:** L served all week. D served all week 12-2 5-9. Av main course £5.
BREWERY/COMPANY: Everards Brewery.
PRINCIPAL BEERS: Everards Tiger, Everards Beacon, Courage Directors, Adnams. **FACILITIES:** Children welcome Garden: outdoor eating, Dogs allowed. **NOTES:** Parking 60 No credit cards

PICK OF THE PUBS

OPEN: 12-3 6.30-11 (Sun from 7).
BAR MEALS: L served all week.
D served all week 12-2.30 7-9.30.
Av main course £11
RESTAURANT: L served all week
D served all week 12-2.30 7-9.
Av 3 course a la carte £20.
BREWERY/COMPANY:
Free House.
PRINCIPAL BEERS: Fullers
London Pride, Jennings Bitter,
Shepherd Neame Spitfire.
FACILITIES: Garden: patio,
outdoor eating. Dogs allowed
(not in bar).
NOTES: Parking 8.
ROOMS: 2 bedrooms 2 en suite
£55 per room.

The Old Barn Inn

Andrews Lane LE16 7ST
☎ 01858 545215 🖶 01858 545215
Dir: A6 from Market Harborough. At
Kibworth follow signs to Langtons &
Hallaton. Glooston signposted.

Sixteenth-century former coaching inn situated well-off-the-beaten track in a tiny rural hamlet at the dead-end of an old Roman Road, yet within easy reach of Rutland Water and Rockingham Castle. Worth finding for interesting pub food and peaceful accommodation in two cottagey bedrooms.

New owners have taken over the helm of this tucked away dining pub, set opposite a charming row of stone cottages, with chef/patron Phillip Buswell offering a good range of freshly prepared dishes, in particular seafood, on his regularly-changing menus. Dine at stripped pine tables in front of the log fire in the cellar bar to the rear of the building, or in one of the cosy alcoves in the beamed and more intimate upper dining area; both free from intrusive music or electronic games. Traditional pub meals are available at lunchtime, including sandwiches, filled baguettes, omelettes and freshly battered cod, while evening diners will find a varied carte and imaginative daily dishes chalked up on the blackboard.

Typical choices range from steamed mussels and freshly-made soups to home-made steamed steak and kidney suet pudding, roast rack of lamb with redcurrant and red wine jus, venison and cranberry pie, farmhouse mixed grill, beef medallions with a wild mushroom ragout and port jus, and seafod specialities - seafood lasagne and monkfish in grain mustard and Parmesan batter with chargrilled Mediterranean vegetables. Book early to sample whole Cromer crab, fresh seafood platters and stews and 16oz Dover soles at the popular Gourmet Seafood Evenings held every six weeks. Beer drinkers will find a choice of four real ales on tap.

With no passing traffic or noise, overnight guests should enjoy a peaceful night in one of the two homely en suite bedrooms.

GLOOSTON　　　　　　　Map 06 SP79

Pick of the Pubs

The Old Barn Inn & Restaurant 👁
Andrew's Ln LE16 7ST ☎ 01858 545215
▤ 01858 545215
See Pick of the Pubs on page 267

GRIMSTON　　　　　　　Map 09 SK62

The Black Horse
3 Main St LE14 3BZ ☎ 01664 812358　▤ 01664 813138
e-mail: joeblackhorsepub@virgin.net
Over 400 years old, the Black Horse is situated next to a
Roman road and was once the local blacksmith's premises.
Remains of the old stables can still be seen. Butterflies of pork,
T-bone steak, shank of lamb, steak and Belvoir ale pie, lasagne
and chicken fillets in a cream sauce are part of the weekly
changing menu.
OPEN: 12-3 6-11. **BAR MEALS:** L served all week. D served
Mon-Sat 12-2 6.30-9. Av main course £6.25. **RESTAURANT:** L
served all week. D served Mon-Sat 12-2 6.30-9. Av 3 course à la
carte £12.55. **BREWERY/COMPANY:** Free House.
PRINCIPAL BEERS: Belvoir, Bass, Marstons Pedigree.
FACILITIES: Children welcome Children's licence Garden:
patio, outdoor eating, patio Dogs allowed. **NOTES:** Parking 30

HALLATON　　　　　　　Map 06 SP49

Pick of the Pubs

The Bewicke Arms 👁
1 Eastgate LE16 8UB ☎ 01858 555217
▤ 01858 555598
Dir: *S of A47 between Leicester & junction of A47/A6003*
New owners have taken over this famous 400-year-old
thatched inn by the village green and buttercross and have
stylishly transformed the pub's interior and revamped the
menus. Modern design and colours blend well with the
traditional features of this historic inn, while on the
imaginative menus, pub favourites are given a modern
twist and innovative evening dishes, prepared from fresh
ingredients, are proving very popular with local discerning
diners. Lunchtime options range from speciality
sandwiches (glazed tuna with Cheddar cheese and spring
onion), warm salads, and lighter dishes like salmon and
prawn fishcakes with béarnaise and chicken and pork
terrine with red onion and sun-dried tomato dressing. In
the evening, try the salmon supreme with garlic mash and
spinach, seared scallops with ratatouille vegetables and
pancetta, Thai-style sea bass poached in coconut milk, and
beef medallions on mushroom mash with Stilton glaze.
Good global list of wines; 6 by the glass. Play area and
miniature farm with animals to keep children amused.
OPEN: 12-3 6-11 (Sun 12-3 7-10.30). **BAR MEALS:** L served
all week. D served all week 12-2 7-9.30. **RESTAURANT:** L
served all week. D served all week 12-2 7-9.30. Av 3 course à
la carte £20. **BREWERY/COMPANY:** Free House.
PRINCIPAL BEERS: Ruddles County, Bass, Greene King
Old Speckled Hen. **FACILITIES:** Garden: outdoor eating,
patio. **NOTES:** Parking 20

HALSTEAD　　　　　　　Map 06 SK70

Pick of the Pubs

The Salisbury Arms ♀ NEW
Oakham Rd LE7 9DJ ☎ 0116 2597333
▤ 0116 2597377
e-mail: info@thesalisburyarms.co.uk
In two acres of grounds that offer outstanding scenic
views, this classic inn, refurbished throughout in a
contemporary style using warm Mediterranean colours,
carefully balances the informality of traditional bar with an
open log fire with a dining conservatory that sparkles at
night with warm candlelight.
　Standard lunch and dinner menus are supplemented by
specials based on local market shopping: Friday is saved
for numerous fishy offerings from green-lip mussels with
Thai butter and monkfish wrapped in Parma ham to
lobster thermidor. Speciality lunch sandwiches include
minute steak on ciabatta with tomato chutney; main
courses encompass local sausages with apple and sage
mash, home-made chicken, mushroom and leek pie and
salmon supreme with dill and cucumber sauce.
　Up a step in accomplishment and price at night, look
for roast lamb loin with crab flan and curried apricot sauce
and chargrilled Cajun chicken with Caesar salad, followed
by warm glazed blackcurrant bread-and-butter pudding,
cool summer pudding with chantilly cream or a plate of
British farmhouse cheeses with celery and 'biccies'.
OPEN: 12-3 6-11 (Sun till 10.30). **BAR MEALS:** L served all
week. D served all week 12-2.30 6-9.30. Av main course £9.
RESTAURANT: L served all week. D served all week 12-2.30
6-9.30. Av 3 course à la carte £20.
BREWERY/COMPANY: Free House.
PRINCIPAL BEERS: Bass. **FACILITIES:** Garden: food
served outside. **NOTES:** Parking 45

HOSE　　　　　　　Map 09 SK72

Rose & Crown
43 Bolton Ln LE14 4JE ☎ 01949 860424
e-mail: brian@rosehose.freeserve.co.uk
Dir: *Off A606 N of Melton Mowbray*
200-year-old village pub in the picturesque Vale of Belvoir.
Known for its real ales and good food, the Rose & Crown has a
large lounge bar with open fires and a heavily beamed
restaurant.
　Dishes range from sausages and fried egg or battered cod
with chips and peas, to Mediterranean vegetable bake or
chicken breast with white wine sauce. Light bites include
baguettes and jacket potatoes.
OPEN: 12-2.30 7-11 (Sun 12-3, 7.30-10.30). **BAR MEALS:** L
served Thur-Sun. D served Thur-Sat 12-2.30 7-8.30. Av main
course £5. **RESTAURANT:** L served Thu-Sun. D served Thu-Sat
12-2.30 7-8.30. Av 3 course à la carte £11.
BREWERY/COMPANY: Free House.
PRINCIPAL BEERS: Greene King IPA/Abbot, Brains Mild.
FACILITIES: Garden: outdoor eating, patio,. **NOTES:** Parking 30

Pub WALK

Cap & Stocking, Kegworth

LEICESTERSHIRE

A fairly level walk that follows a peaceful stretch of the River Soar, returning to Kegworth across unspoilt meadowland.

Turn right out of the pub, cross straight over at the road junction and follow the metalled path past the village hall to a road. Cross over and follow the metalled path half-left, signed 'Bridge Fields'. Opposite the Anchor Inn, turn right along the pavement and cross the river bridge into Nottinghamshire. Once over the canal section, take the arrowed path right and follow the river/canal upstream, bearing right to Kegworth Deep Lock. Keep to the tow path, passing a weir and a large house (The Hermitage) on the opposite bank, then just before The Otter pub (inaccessible), take the path left across a footbridge, signed Sutton Bonington.

Proceed across a series of stiles,

pass a pond and keep the church spire to your right. Reach a stile beside a prominent ash tree, then bear diagonally left to reach a lane. Turn right, then in 100yds (91m), take the narrow fenced path between cottages on left, signed Kegworth. Pass through two kissing-gates and proceed between ponds and the boundary to a large house to a further kissing-gate. Keep to the right-hand edge of the field to a stile and bear half-left to a double stile and footbridge by bushes.

Bear right to a stile flanking a gate, then keep ahead to a stile in the hedge (Kegworth river bridge visible in distance). Continue through the next field to join the river bank. Retrace your outward route back over the bridge and left opposite the Anchor Inn back into Kegworth and the pub.

Distance: 4 1/2 miles (7.2km)
Map: OS Landranger 129
Terrain: riverbank and farmland
Paths: field paths, tow path, metalled paths
Gradient: mainly level

Walk submitted by:
David Buxton

St Andrew's Church, Kegworth

CAP & STOCKING, KEGWORTH
20 Borough Street DE74 2FF.
Tel: 01509 674814
Directions: M1 J24 follow A6 towards Loughborough. Pub in village centre
Traditional and genuinely unspoilt Victorian brick pub, affectionately known as the 'Cap', where Bass is served straight from the jug and home-cooked meals are provided in comfortable old-fashioned rooms.
Open: 11.30-2.30 (Sat & Sun till 3) 6.30-11 (Sun 7-10.30). Bar Meals: 11.30-2.15 6.30-8.45. Children and dogs welcome. Walled garden and patio. Limited parking.

(see page 270 for full entry)

England

KEGWORTH — Map 09 SK42

Cap & Stocking
20 Borough St DE74 2FF ☎ 01509 674814
Dir: *Village centre (chemist on LHS. Turn L, left & left again to Borough St)*
Traditional and genuinely unspoilt pub, affectionately known as the 'Cap', where Bass is served straight from the jug and home-cooked meals are provided in the comfortable old-fashioned rooms. Food options range from sandwiches and snacks, like ploughman's, or Welsh rarebit, to goulash, beef Stroganoff, and vegetarian green curry.
OPEN: 11.30-2.30 (Sat-Sun 11.30-3) 6.30-11 (Sun 7-10.30).
BAR MEALS: L served all week. D served all week 11.30-2.15 6.30-8.45. Av main course £6. **BREWERY/COMPANY:** Punch Taverns. **PRINCIPAL BEERS:** Hancocks HB, Draught Bass,. **FACILITIES:** Children welcome Garden: Food served outside Dogs allowed. **NOTES:** Parking 4 No credit cards
See Pub Walk on page 269

LOUGHBOROUGH — Map 09 SK51

The Swan in the Rushes
21 The Rushes LE11 5BE ☎ 01509 217014
Dir: *On A6 (Derby road)*
A 30s tile-fronted real ale pub with two drinking rooms, a cosmopolitan atmosphere and no frills. Ten ales always available, including six guests. Two annual beer festivals.

MARKET HARBOROUGH — Map 06 SP78

The Queens Head Inn ♀
Main St, Sutton Bassett LE16 8HP ☎ 01858 463530
Traditional English pub with real ale, bar meals and an upstairs restaurant specialising in regional Italian cuisine. Full range of pasta, pizza, fish, steak and chicken dishes, while the bar menu features chef's special grills, fresh Whitby scampi, beef Stroganoff, Harborough gammon and potato skins supreme. Well-kept real ales.
OPEN: 11-3 6.30-11. Closed 25 Dec. **BAR MEALS:** L served all week. D served Mon-Sat 12-2 7-9.30. Av main course £6.
RESTAURANT: D served Tue-Sat 7-11. Av 3 course à la carte £17.
BREWERY/COMPANY: Free House.
PRINCIPAL BEERS: Adnams, Taylor Landlord, Marstons Pedigree, Fullers London Pride. **FACILITIES:** Children welcome Garden: patio, BBQ, food served outside Dogs allowed garden only. **NOTES:** Parking 15

AA Bed & Breakfast
2002
Britain's best-selling B&B guide featuring over 3500 great places to stay

AA Bed & Breakfast Guide

AA Lifestyle Guides
www.theAA.com

Pick of the Pubs

The Sun Inn ⊛ ★ ★ ⌂ ♀
Main St, Marston Trussel LE16 9TY ☎ 01858 465531
🖥 01858 433155
e-mail: Manager@suninn.com
Dir: *S of A4304 between Market Harborough & Lutterworth*
Head for Marston Trussell, in the heart of the Leicester countryside some three miles south west of Market Harborough, to find this late 17th-century coaching inn that offers cosy, up-to-date accommodation and modern amenities subtly combined with its historic charm. Three separate dining areas include a popular locals' bar and an informal restaurant with roaring fires on cooler days offering a friendly welcome, well-kept real ales and a fair selection of wines by the glass.

Fresh local produce plays a major part on regularly up-dated menus that feature grilled Dover sole, Lobster thermidor and baked halibut, supplemented by the likes of pheasant and grouse in season. A typical dinner might consist of Thai fishcakes with fierce chilli dressing, robust venison and sliced pears in a mead sauce and heavily caramelised tarte tatin of apples on a sound vanilla crème anglaise. Charming waitress service. Quality breakfasts and food available all day.
OPEN: 12-6 6-11. Closed Dec 25, Jan 1. **BAR MEALS:** L served all week. D served all week 12-6 6-10. Av main course £5.95. **RESTAURANT:** L served all week. D served all week 12-6 6-10. Av 3 course à la carte £17. Av 3 course fixed price £13.95. **BREWERY/COMPANY:** Free House.
PRINCIPAL BEERS: Bass, Hook Norton Best, Marstons Pedigree, Charles Wells Bombardier. **FACILITIES:** Children welcome Garden: patio, BBQ, food served outdoors. **NOTES:** Parking 60. **ROOMS:** 20 bedrooms 20 en suite s£69 d£69

MEDBOURNE — Map 06 SP89

The Nevill Arms
12 Waterfall Way LE16 8EE ☎ 01858 565288
🖥 01858 565509
e-mail: nevillarms@hotmail.com
Dir: *From Northampton take A508 to Market Harborough then B664 for 5m.L for Medbourne*
Traditional village pub with mullion windows situated on the River Welland and by the village green. Eat outside in summer and enjoy the garden with its own dovecote. The inn is also very popular with children who like to feed the ducks. Two friendly Great Danes also provide plenty of amusement. Smoked haddock and spinach bake, beef in garlic and mushrooms, avocado and bacon salad and spicy lamb with apricots are typical examples of the menu.
OPEN: 12-2.30 (Sun 12-3) 6-11 (Sun 7-10.30). **BAR MEALS:** L served all week. D served all week 12-2 7-9. Av main course £5.75. **BREWERY/COMPANY:** Free House.
PRINCIPAL BEERS: Fullers London Pride, Adnams, Greene King Abbot Ale. **FACILITIES:** Children welcome Garden: Terrace, outdoor eating. **NOTES:** Parking 30. **ROOMS:** 8 bedrooms 8 en suite s£45 d£55 1 family room

MELTON MOWBRAY — Map 09 SK71

Anne of Cleves House
12 Burton St LE13 1AE ☎ 01664 481336
Fine old 14th-century building which was given to Anne of
Cleves as part of her divorce settlement. Log fires in winter
and a picturesque garden for summer enjoyment.

MOUNTSORREL — Map 09 SK51

The Swan Inn
10 Loughborough Rd LE12 7AT ☎ 0116 2302340
☷ 0116 2376115
e-mail: dmw@jvf.co.uk
Dir: On main road between Leicester & Loughborough
Privately-owned former coaching inn between Loughborough
and Leicester. Among the attractive interior features are
various exposed beams, open fires, flagstone floors and
comfortable seating. Food is freshly cooked on the premises
and the varied menu includes game and vegetarian dishes.
Expect rabbit and sausage hot pot, oven-baked red snapper,
fillet steak and lamb casseroled with tomato, garlic, onion and
carrots. Good quality cask conditioned ales and an extensive
wine list.
OPEN: 12-2 (all day Sat) 5.30-11 (Sun 12-3, 7-10.30).
BAR MEALS: L served all week. D served Mon-Sat 12-2 7-9.30.
Av main course £8. **RESTAURANT:** L served all week. D served
Mon-Sat 12-2 7-9.30. Av 3 course à la carte £14.
BREWERY/COMPANY: Free House.
PRINCIPAL BEERS: Theakston Best, XB & Old Peculier, Ruddles
County. **FACILITIES:** Children welcome Garden: Dogs allowed
manger's discretion. **NOTES:** Parking 12. **ROOMS:** 3 bedrooms
s£20 d£32

OLD DALBY — Map 09 SK62

Pick of the Pubs

The Crown Inn 🍷
Debdale Hill LE14 3LF ☎ 01664 823134
☷ 01664 822638
e-mail: lynn@phoenixcons.demon.co.uk
Dir: Newark A46 R at Upper Broughton, from A46 towards
Leicester take turn to Broughton 100mtrs turn L, 0.3miles L again.
1 mile take rd to Old Dalby
Here's a pub with a strong, traditional flavour. The
building dates back to 1590, and the interior layout hasn't
changed in many hundreds of years. A number of small,
cosy rooms are warmed by open fires, and you can enjoy
a quiet game of dominoes or solitaire without the
distraction of piped music or gaming machines. There's a
large garden, too, with rustic tables and chairs, lawns and
fruit trees. 'The Crown' is proud of its real ales, which
include local brews like Beaver Bitter and Peacock's Glory
served straight from the cask. Local ingredients feature
extensively on the menu, and all meals are freshly cooked
to order. Bar meals range from wholemeal sandwiches or
smoked salmon bagels to chicken and garlic pasta or steak
and ale pie. In the restaurant, try beef Wellington, Barbary
duck or poached salmon, followed by summer pudding,
crème brûlée or hot fruit crêpes.
OPEN: 12-3 (Sun 12-3, 7-10.30) 6-11 (Winter 12-2.30,
6.30-11). **BAR MEALS:** L served Tues-Sun. D served Mon-Sat
12-2.30 7-9.30. Av main course £7. **RESTAURANT:** L served
Wed-Sun. D served Tue-Sat 12-2.30 7-9.30. Av 3 course à la
carte £22. Av 3 course fixed price £11.50.
BREWERY/COMPANY: Free House.
PRINCIPAL BEERS: Marstons Pedigree, Wells Bombardier,
Ruddles County, Wadworth 6X. **FACILITIES:** Garden: patio,
outdoor eating Dogs allowed Water. **NOTES:** Parking 32

Tudor & Stuart Hostelries

After the closing down of the monasteries, prosperity and increasing travel brought a rise in
the number and standards of inns. By Elizabeth's I's time there were hostelries big enough to
lodge 300 people and their horses. Inns were commercial centres for local merchants and traders,
some were 'posthouses' for the developing mail service and in the 17th century smart shops
appeared in the largest inns.
The introduction of hops was stoutly resisted. Henry VIII would drink only hopless ale and the
brewers were castigated for ruining the traditional drink. Beer brewed with hops kept better for
longer, however, which stimulated the development of large-scale breweries and both inns and
alehouses gradually gave up brewing their own.
Alehouses were growing steadily less primitive. The main drinking room might still be the kitchen,
for warmth. Furniture would be simple - a few trestle tables, benches and stools. As the number
of people on the roads grew, alehouses began to offer a night's lodging, though in the poorer
ones the traveller might sleep on the kitchen table or in bed with the landlord and his wife.
Games were played just outside the house - quoits, skittles, bowls - and customers
relieved themselves there too.

England

REDMILE   Map 09 SK73

Pick of the Pubs

Peacock Inn 🐦 ☿
Church Corner NG13 0GB ☎ 01949 842554
🖥 01949 843746
e-mail: peacock@redmile.fsbusiness.co.uk
Dir: From A1 take A52 towards Nottingham
Is drinking at the Peacock a prescription for long life? At
the age of 85, one local claims not to have missed a day in
72 years - so perhaps it's simply important to start young!
This traditional 16th-century country inn stands in a pretty
village beside the Grantham Canal, and offers a relaxed,
informal setting for wining, dining, and socialising. Against
a background of beamed ceilings and roaring log fires,
murder mystery nights and Broadway evenings liven up
the tranquil setting, just a stone's throw from Belvoir
Castle. The new owners and their chef have put together
an imaginative menu with a continental flavour. Starters
like confit of duck leg with ginger purée, or seared king
scallops precede guinea fowl on tomato risotto, pan-fried
red snapper, or spinach and ricotta tortellini. Finish with
vanilla parfait, blackberry delice, or a selection of home-
made desserts to share.
OPEN: 11-11. **BAR MEALS:** L served all week. D served
all week 12-2.30 7-9.30. Av main course £10.95.
RESTAURANT: L served all week. D served all week 12-2.30
7-9.30. Av 3 course à la carte £35. Av 3 course fixed price
£13.95. **BREWERY/COMPANY:** Free House.
PRINCIPAL BEERS: Marstons Pedigree, Timothy Taylor
Landlord, Whitbread IPA. **FACILITIES:** Children welcome
Garden: patio, outdoor eating. **NOTES:** Parking 50.
ROOMS: 10 bedrooms 10 en suite s£55 d£65
FR£110-£130

SADDINGTON   Map 06 SP69

The Queens Head
Main St LE8 0QH ☎ 0116 2402536 🖥 0116 240 4467
Dir: Between A50 & A6 S of Leicester, NW of Market Harborough
Traditional English pub with real ale and bar meals ranging
from sandwiches to steaks, Harborough gammon, and fresh
Whitby scampi. Vegetarian and pasta dishes are also available
in the bar, while the adjacent restaurant offers such dishes as
Dover sole and steak and ale pie.
OPEN: 11-3 5.30-11. **BAR MEALS:** L served all week. D served
Mon-Sat 12-2.30 6.30-10. Av main course £5. **RESTAURANT:** L
served all week. D served Mon-Sat 12-2 6.30-10. Av 3 course à la
carte £15. **BREWERY/COMPANY:** Everards Brewery.
PRINCIPAL BEERS: Everards Tiger & Beacon, Adnams.
FACILITIES: Garden. **NOTES:** Parking 50

  AA inspected guest accommodation

SIBSON   Map 09 SK30

Pick of the Pubs

The Cock Inn ☿
Twycross Rd CV13 6LB ☎ 01827 880357
🖥 01827 880976
e-mail: cockinnsibson@aol.com
Dir: On A444 between Nuneaton & M42 J11
One of the oldest inns in the country, dating back to about
1250, this is reputedly where the notorious highwayman
Dick Turpin sought refuge, hiding in the bar chimney and
stabling his horse in the cellar. The lawn at the rear was
used for cock fighting until about 1870 - hence the name.
It was also a witness to the Battle of Bosworth in 1485.
Inside, low beams and ancient timbers add to the charm.
Expect a very varied and wide-ranging choice of restaurant
dishes and specials. Traditional steak and kidney pie,
haggis, neeps and tatties, lamb jalfrezi, turkey tikka, and
breast of Barbary duck are among the popular favourites.
Good choice of sandwiches, salads, children's dishes and
Sunday roasts.
OPEN: 11.30-2.30 6.30-11 (Sun 12-3, 7-10.30).
BAR MEALS: L served Mon-Sat. D served all week 11.30-2
6.30-9.45. Av main course £7.95. **RESTAURANT:** L served all
week. D served Mon-Sat 11.30-2 6.30-9.45. Av 3 course à la
carte £18.50. Av 4 course fixed price £15.75.
BREWERY/COMPANY: Punch Taverns.
PRINCIPAL BEERS: Bass, M&B Brew XI.
FACILITIES: Children welcome Garden: patio, outdoor
eating **NOTES:** Parking 60

SILEBY   Map 09 SK61

The White Swan 🐦
Swan St LE12 7NW ☎ 01509 814832 🖥 01509 815995
Beyond the unassuming exterior of this 1930s pub lies a
homely bar, an open fire and a book-lined restaurant. Twice-
weekly-changing menu and specials might include beef
cobbler, salmon and prawn pasta, Thai-style chicken, sirloin
steak, leg of lamb with a mint and vegetable stuffing and
baked fillets of sea bream. Good range of starters.
OPEN: 11.45-3 (Mon 7.30-11 only) 7-11. Closed 1-7 Jan.
BAR MEALS: L served Tue-Sun. D served Tue-Sat 12-2 7-10. Av
main course £8.75. **RESTAURANT:** L served Tue-Sun.
D served Tue-Sat 12-2 7-10. Av 3 course à la carte £17.
BREWERY/COMPANY: Free House.
PRINCIPAL BEERS: Marstons Pedigree, Shipstones, Ansells.
FACILITIES: Children welcome Garden. **NOTES:** Parking 10

SOMERBY   Map 06 SK71

The Old Brewery
High St LE14 2PZ ☎ 01664 454777 🖥 01664 454777
Dir: Between Melton Mowbray & Oakham off the A606 at Leesthorpe
Holder of the record for brewing the strongest beer in the
world, this 15th-century coaching inn offers eight traditional
cask ales. In addition to fine ale, the pub is also known for its
food. Open all day. Lots of good walking country around. Live
music every Saturday night.

England

Stilton Cheese Inn
High St LE14 2QB ☎ 01664 454394
At the heart of a working village in beautiful countryside, this sandstone building dates from the 16th century. The same menus service both bar and restaurant areas, with good selections to be found on the Specials boards. Try Somerby sausages and mash in onion gravy, spaghetti with home-made meatballs, rack of lamb, sliced duck breast in ginger and orange sauce, or maybe whole lemon sole or tuna steak with lemon and herb crust.

OPEN: 12-3 6-11. **BAR MEALS:** L served all week. D served all week 12-2 6-9. Av main course £5.50. **RESTAURANT:** L served all week. D served all week 12-2 6-9. Av 3 course à la carte £11.50. **BREWERY/COMPANY:** Free House. **PRINCIPAL BEERS:** Marstons Pedigree, Black Sheep,. **FACILITIES:** Children welcome Garden: patio, outdoor eating. **NOTES:** Parking 14

THORPE LANGTON   Map 06 SP79

Pick of the Pubs

The Bakers Arms
Main St LE16 7TS ☎ 01858 545201
Dir: Take A6 S from Leicester then L signed 'The Langtons'
First-class modern pub food and period charm attract diners from miles around to this charming thatched pub set in a pretty village. Despite the emphasis on good, well presented food prepared from fresh ingredients, an informal pub, rather than staid restaurant, atmosphere prevails throughout.

Low beams, rug-strewn quarry-tiled floors, open fires, large pine tables, antique pews and terracotta-painted walls set the relaxing scene in which to sample, perhaps, pan-fried scallops with black pudding, orange and cardamom sauce, lamb shank with roast parsnips, whole baked sea bass with spinach and mushrooms, brill fillet with creamed leeks, or cod wrapped in Parma ham from the daily-changing blackboard menu. For pudding try the hot chocolate fudge cake with vanilla ice cream. Quick and efficient service from friendly staff. Extensive list of wines, including six by the glass, and Tetley Bitter on handpump.
OPEN: 12-3 6.30-11 (closed all Mon, Tue-Fri lunch, Sun eve). **BAR MEALS:** L served Sat-Sun. D served Tue-Sat 12-2 6.30-9.30. Av main course £12. **RESTAURANT:** L served Sat-Sun. D served all week 12-2 6.30-9.30. Av 3 course à la carte £24.50. **BREWERY/COMPANY:** Free House. **PRINCIPAL BEERS:** Tetley. **FACILITIES:** Garden: outdoor eating. **NOTES:** Parking 12

TUR LANGTON   Map 06 SP72

The Bulls Head
Tur Langton LE8 0PN ☎ 01858 545373 ▨ 01858 545144
Set in the heart of the Leicestershire countryside, about 5 miles from Market Harborough, this free house serves home-made food and traditional ales.

WOODHOUSE EAVES   Map 09 SK51

The Pear Tree Inn
Church Hill LE12 8RT ☎ 01509 890243 ▨ 01509 891362
Dir: Village centre
Well refurbished, family-run inn at the centre of a lovely village in the beauty spot known as Charnwood Forest. Noted for freshly cooked food. Excellent local walks.

The Wheatsheaf Inn ⚲ NEW
Brand Hill LE12 855 ☎ 01509 890320 ▨ 01509 890891
Dir: M1 Juct 22 follow directions for Quorn
Richard and Bridget Dimblebee have just bought this charming 18th-century pub for the third time, so it must have a certain appeal! Now completely refurbished, the inn retains the solid character imposed by the local slate quarrymen who built it. The competent menu has something for everyone; daily sandwiches and ciabattas, nice salads, steaks, burgers and curries, plus beef bourguignon, vegetable chilli, and lots of fresh fish.
OPEN: 12-2.30 6-11. **BAR MEALS:** L served all week. D served Tue-Sat 12-2 7-9.30. Av main course £7. **RESTAURANT:** L served all week. D served Tues-Sat 12-2 7-9.30. Av 3 course à la carte £7. **BREWERY/COMPANY:** Free House. **PRINCIPAL BEERS:** Greene King Abbot Ale, Bass, Timothy Taylor Landlord, Marston's Pedigree. **FACILITIES:** Children welcome Garden: Food served outside Dogs allowed Water. **NOTES:** Parking 70

Belvoir Brewery
Mostly constructed from original equipment recovered from breweries all over the country, the Belvoir Brewery opened in 1995, and has revived a long-standing brewing tradition in the area. Beers include Whippling Golden Bitter (3.6%), Star Bitter (3.9%), Peacock's Glory (4.7%) and Melton Red, a bottled beer inspired by the story behind the phrase 'painting the town red', which has local significance.

England

WYMONDHAM
Map 09 SK81

Pick of the Pubs

The Berkeley Arms NEW
59 Main St LE14 2AG ☎ 01572 787587
Equi-distant from Oakham and Melton Mowbray in the heart of the county's largely unsung countryside, this chef-managed country inn has become a favoured dining destination since refurbishment some three years ago. Its interior comprises a village bar of exposed stonework and original beams hung with dried hops, a carpeted, non-smoking dining-room with well-spaced pine tables and a garden that is popular with families and walkers in summer. The landlord prides himself on utilising the best available locally produced meats, poultry and fresh herbs on monthly menus that are a modern mix of traditional and trendy. Typically, bar lunches might include slow-roast belly pork with a Thai curry risotto and seared lambs' liver with bubble-and-squeak cake and confit of carrots and celery. At night, begin perhaps with pan-fried foie gras and black pudding or Arbroath smokie with avocado and mango salsa before hoi-sin roast duck breast with stir-fried ginger vegetables or steamed plaice fillets in a minestrone-style sauce and followed by glazed lemon tart or strawberry cheesecake.
OPEN: 12-3 6-11. **BAR MEALS:** L served Tues-Sun. D served Tues-Sat 12-2 6-7.30. Av main course £4.50. **RESTAURANT:** L served Tues-Sun. D served Tues-Sat 12-2 7-9. Av 3 course à la carte £21. **BREWERY/COMPANY:** Pubmaster. **PRINCIPAL BEERS:** Marstons Pedigree,. **FACILITIES:** Children welcome Garden: Food served outside Dogs allowed Garden only

LINCOLNSHIRE

ALLINGTON
Map 09 SK84

The Welby Arms ☿
The Green NG32 2EA ☎ 01400 281361 📠 01400 281361
Dir: From Grantham take either A1 north, or A52 west. Allington is 1.5m
Village pub in the time-honoured style with no loud music or pinball machines, providing a welcoming retreat for travellers on the A1. Dishes are prepared from fresh ingredients and include a daily home-made soup and comforting puddings like treacle sponge. Sunday lunch is a traditional meal with freshly cooked joints of locally produced meat.
OPEN: 12-2.30 6-11 (Sun 12-2.30 6-10.30). **BAR MEALS:** L served all week. D served all week 12-2 6.30-9.30. **RESTAURANT:** L served all week. D served all week 12-2 6.30-9.30. **BREWERY/COMPANY:** Free House. **PRINCIPAL BEERS:** John Smiths, Bass, Taylor Landlord. **FACILITIES:** Children welcome Garden: Outdoor eating Dogs allowed garden only. **NOTES:** Parking 35. **ROOMS:** 3 bedrooms 3 en suite s£48 d£60

ASWARBY
Map 09 TF03

The Tally Ho Inn ◆◆◆
NG34 8SA ☎ 01529 455205 📠 01529 455205
Dir: From A1 take Grantham exit onto A52 towards Boston. Take A15 towards Sleaford.
Part of the Aswarby Estate in deepest rural Lincolnshire, this 17th-century coaching inn has exposed stone walls, oak beams
continued

and open log fires: tables outside, under the fruit trees, overlook sheep-grazing meadows. A selection of representative dishes includes salmon and spinach fishcakes, beef and ale pie, sausage with cheese and onion mash, and halibut with spicy salsa.

OPEN: 12-3 6-11. Closed Dec 26. **BAR MEALS:** L served all week. D served all week 12-2.30 6.30-10. Av main course £6.95. **RESTAURANT:** L served Sun. D served Mon-Sat 7-10. Av 3 course à la carte £20. **BREWERY/COMPANY:** Free House. **PRINCIPAL BEERS:** Batemans, Bass. **FACILITIES:** Garden: Food served outside Dogs allowed. **NOTES:** Parking 40. **ROOMS:** 6 bedrooms 6 en suite s£35 d£50

BARNOLDBY LE BECK
Map 09 TA20

The Ship Inn
Main Rd DN37 0BG ☎ 01472 822308
Dir: Off A46/A18 SW of Grimsby
Situated on the edge of the Lincolnshire Wolds, this 200-year-old inn is filled with interesting bric-a-brac, and has a beautiful garden. Award-winning cooking includes specials such as lobster thermidor, pan-fried lamb steak and parfait of duckling with smoked bacon in a cherry brandy sauce.
OPEN: 11-3 6.30-11. **BAR MEALS:** L served all week. D served all week 12-2 6.30-9.30. Av main course £3.95. **RESTAURANT:** L served all week. D served all week 12-2 6.30-9.30. Av 3 course à la carte £17.50. **BREWERY/COMPANY:** Free House. **PRINCIPAL BEERS:** Marstons Pedigree, Whitbread Castle Eden Ale. **FACILITIES:** Children welcome Garden: Dogs allowed in garden. **NOTES:** Parking 75

EVERARD'S OF LEICESTER

Most of the Everard's pubs are in the Leicester area. The company has been run by successive generations of the family since two brothers, William and Thomas Everard of Narborough, acquired a brewery in Leicester in 1849. The firm brewed its Tiger Bitter in Burton upon Trent, at the Tiger Brewery (now home to the Heritage Brewery Museum) for close on 100 years, until in 1979 it returned to the Everard's original home town and built a new brewery in Narborough, which opened in 1985.

Masons Arms, Louth

**MASONS ARMS, ◆◆◆
LOUTH**
Cornmarket LN11 9PY.
Tel: 01507 609525
Directions: off A16 between
Skegness and Grimsby
*18th-century former posting inn
located right in the centre of
the Cornmarket in this historic
market town. Friendly
welcome, imaginative menu,
good range of ales and
bedrooms - ideal base for
exploring the Lincolnshire
Wolds.*
Open: 10am-11pm (Sun 12-
10.30). Bar Meals: 12-2 6-9.
Children welcome. Parking.
(see page 280 for full entry)

A pleasant rural walk from an historic market town. Some determined hill climbing is rewarded by excellent views east to the sea and west across the gently rolling Wolds.

From the inn, turn right along Rosemary Lane, then turn left to the church and head north along Bridge Street, crossing the River Lud. Turn left into Fanthorpe Lane, cross the A16 (great care) and continue along the lane to Northfield Farm, where it becomes a green lane, then a footpath. Pass through the edge of a clump of trees, cross a footbridge in the field corner and proceed along the hedge to a lane.

Turn left and walk uphill, passing through Acthorpe Farm, to reach 104m (343ft), and enjoy good views before descending to South Elkington. Cross the A631 and walk along Church Lane. Pass the church and footpaths left, go round the right-hand bend and take the signed bridleway left through a gate. The track becomes a path after exiting trees at Kirk Vale and continues along the left-hand hedge to a gate. Descend to a gate and turn left downhill along a track.

Where it veers sharp left, keep ahead into the wood and turn left along the bridleway through Sand Pit Plantation. Ignore paths left and right, go through a gate and continue along-side woodland. Eventually go through a gate to join a track, following it left around the end of a lake. Follow the waymarked footpath across a track, then over a stile and along the left-hand edge of fields to a footbridge on the left. Ascend the field towards a hedge gap and cross a stile and the A631. Continue uphill to a gate into woodland and follow the main track, which soon swings right to a stile and field. Continue with the trees to your left, downhill past Pasture Farm and uphill along the field edge to cross the Louth by-pass.

Follow arrows past houses and along the lane to cross the A157. Turn left, head downhill and cross the river. Continue into Louth, bearing left at the junction to St James' Church, then follow Rosemary Lane back to the pub.

Distance: 6 miles (10km)
Map: OS Landranger 122
Terrain: town streets, farmland and woodland
Paths: field and woodland path and track; metalled lanes
Gradient: undulating; some steady climbs.

Walk submitted by:
The Masons Arms

Cornmarket - Market Day

Water and Steam

Many attractive pubs today stand on the banks of rivers and canals. The riverside ones reflect the fact that for centuries the quickest, safest and cheapest way to move people and goods about was by river, not by road. The 18th century saw the construction of artificial rivers, the canals, and hostelries quickly sprang up for boatmen and travellers on them too. Again, when the railways spread across the country from the 1840s om, pubs near stations proudly called themselves the Railway or the Railway Arms to cater for the new system.

BOURNE   Map 09 TF02

Pick of the Pubs

The Black Horse Inn ⊛ ⊛ ☜ ♈
Grimsthorpe PE10 0LY ☎ 01778 591247
🖥 01778 591373
e-mail: dine@blackhorseinn.co.uk
See Pick of the Pubs on page 277

The Wishing Well Inn
Main St, Dyke PE10 0AF ☎ 01778 422970
🖥 01778 394508
Dir: 1.5m from the A15, 12m from A1 Colsterworth rdbt
Modernised country inn with old oak beams and an inglenook fireplace with roaring open fires in winter, and named after the wishing well in the restaurant. Standard pub food.

BRIGG   Map 09 TA00

The Jolly Miller ♦♦♦
Brigg Rd, Wrawby DN20 8RH ☎ 01652 655658
🖥 01652 652048
e-mail: john@jollymiller.co.uk
Dir: 1.5m E of Brigg on the A18, on L
Popular country inn situated a few miles south of the Humber estuary. Pleasant bar and dining area fitted out in traditional pub style. Saturday night entertainment and facilities for christenings, weddings and other functions. As well as comfortable B&B accommodation, a five van caravan site is also available. Straightforward menu offers the likes of haddock, gammon, shepherd's pie and curry.
OPEN: 12-2 5-11. **BAR MEALS:** L served all week. D served Mon-Fri 12-2 5-7. Av main course £3.95.
BREWERY/COMPANY: Free House.
PRINCIPAL BEERS: Highwood Tom Wood Harvest Bitter, Timothy Taylor Landlord. **FACILITIES:** Children welcome Garden: outdoor eating, patio Dogs allowed By arrangement.
NOTES: Parking 40. **ROOMS:** 3 bedrooms 3 en suite s£30 d£37.50 1 family room £42.50

COLEBY

The Bell Inn
3 Far Ln LN5 0AH ☎ 01522 810240
Dir: 8m S of Lincoln on A607. In Coleby village turn right at church.
There is a cosy atmosphere at this 18th-century inn, with its low beamed ceilings, log fires and a barrel-shaped bar with lots of international number plates. Bedrooms.

CONINGSBY   Map 09 TF25

The Old Lea Gate Inn
Leagate Rd LN4 4RS ☎ 01526 342370
Dir: Off B1192 just outside Coningsby
Last of the Fen Guide Houses, places of safety in the days before the treacherous eastern marshes were drained. A small iron gantry outside once held a lamp to guide travellers safely on their way. These are also the oldest licensed premises in Lincolnshire, established in 1542. Also convenient for RAF Coningsby's Battle of Britain Memorial Flight. Heavy beams, high-backed settles and roaring fires enhance the cosy atmosphere. Typical menu includes chicken stuffed with Mozzarella, steak and kidney pie, fresh haddock, and Coquilles St Jacques.
OPEN: 11.30-2.30 6.30-11 (Sun 12-2.30, 6.30-10.30). Closed Oct 19-Oct 26. **BAR MEALS:** L served all week. D served all week 12-2 6.30-9.30. **RESTAURANT:** L served all week. D served all week 6.30. Av 3 course à la carte £14.
BREWERY/COMPANY: Free House.
PRINCIPAL BEERS: Theakstons XB, Marstons Pedigree.
FACILITIES: Children welcome Garden: seated area, patio, BBQ, food served outside. **NOTES:** Parking 60.
ROOMS: 8 bedrooms 8 en suite s£47.50 d£55 FR£60-£70

CORBY GLEN   Map 09 TF02

The Woodhouse Inn
NG33 4NS ☎ 01476 550316
e-mail: mikep-j@btconnect.com
Dir: 4m E of A1 Colsterworth roundabout on the A151
Late Georgian country inn with an imaginative range of freshly prepared dishes and a daily-changing menu. Halibut, trout fillets and salmon are among the fish favourites on the otherwise varied menu. The inn also has a Sardinian brick-built oven in the garden, and hosts regular authentic Sardinian banquets.
OPEN: 12-2.30 7-11 (Sun 12-3.30, 7-10.30). **BAR MEALS:** L served all week. D served all week 12-2 7-9.30. Av main course £7.95. **RESTAURANT:** L served all week. D served all week 12-2 7-9.30. Av 3 course à la carte £16. **BREWERY/COMPANY:** Free House. **PRINCIPAL BEERS:** Theakston - Best, XB.
FACILITIES: Children welcome Garden: Dogs allowed.
NOTES: Parking 30. **ROOMS:** s£37.50 d£45

OPEN: 11.30-2.30 6.30-11
BAR MEALS: L served all week.
D served all week 12-2 7-9.30.
Av main course £9.50
RESTAURANT: L served all week.
D served all week 12-2 7-9.
Av 3 course a la carte £23.
BREWERY/COMPANY:
Free House.
PRINCIPAL BEERS: Grimsthorpe
Castle, Black Horse Bitter.
FACILITIES: Garden: terrace
outdoor eating.
NOTES: Parking 30.
ROOMS: 6 bedrooms 5 en suite
s£45-£55 d£60-£95.

The Black Horse

Grimsthorpe PE10 0LY
☎ 01778 591247 📠 01778 591373
e-mail: dine@blackhorseinn.co.uk
Dir: turn off A1 onto A151, inn 9m on L,
0.5m after Grimsthorpe Castle

Nestling in the shadows of Grimsthorpe Castle in idyllic countryside on the Lincolnshire/Rutland border, The Black Horse was built in the early 18th century as a coaching inn. Renovated and modernised, today it houses stylish bedrooms and offers quality food that attracts a discerning clientele.

Very much a dining pub, with a small bar for pre-prandial drinks, a cosy lounge and a buttery restaurant with exposed stone walls housed in a more recent extension. Bar meals and light snacks mirror the style and presentation of the larger menu with interesting daily additions. Options include honey-roast duck breast salad, tagliatelle with plum tomato sauce and olives, smoked haddock with bubble-and-squeak and calves' liver and bacon with good rich gravy. In the restaurant add red pepper tart with crème fraiche and sultana relish, seared sea bream with bok choy and provençale vegetables and roast chicken breast with peas, smoked bacon and wild mushrooms.

'Today's additions' might weigh in with deep-fried haloumi cheese with sweet and sour sauce and pan-fried lamb steak with baby carrots and meaux mustard sauce. The pudding menu is exemplary, with choices such as baked white chocolate cheesecake with forest fruits, vacherin with passion fruit cream or a plate of cheeses with celery, apple and grapes. Speciality teas and coffees join good real ales - specially supplied Black Horse and Grimsthorpe Castle - and a well chosen wine list as worthy of special mention as the dedication and warm, personal welcome extended by chef/patron Brian Wey and his wife Elaine.

Attractively furnished bedrooms include one with a four-poster bed and a suite is also available.

England

DONINGTON ON BAIN   Map 09 TF28

The Black Horse
Main Rd LN11 9TJ ☎ 01507 343640 📄 01507 343640
Ideal for walkers, this old-fashioned country pub is set in the
heart of the Lincolnshire Wolds on the Viking Way. Bedrooms.

EAST BARKWITH   Map 09 TF18

The Crossroads Inn
Lincoln Rd LN8 5RW ☎ 01673 858363
Homely village pub with a pleasant atmosphere and a menu
offering fresh fish and chips, and wide range of English and
Mexican dishes.

EWERBY   Map 09 TF14

Finch Hatton Arms
43 Main St NG34 9PH ☎ 01529 460363 📄 01529 461703
e-mail: bookings@finchhatton.fsnet.co.uk
*Dir: from A17 to Kirkby-la-Thorne, then 2m NE. Also 2m E of A153
between Sleaford & Anwick*
Originally known as the Angel Inn, this 19th-century pub was
given the family name of Lord Winchelsea who bought it in
1875. After a short period of closure, it reopened as a new-
style pub/restaurant in the 1980s. Extensive, varied menu
includes lamb noisettes, sea bass, scrumpy pork chop and
Finch Hatton steak pie.
OPEN: 11.30-2.30 6.30-11. Closed 25/26 Dec. **BAR MEALS:** L
served all week. D served all week 11.30-2.30 6.30-11. Av main
course £7. **RESTAURANT:** L served all week. D served all week
11.30-2.30 6.30-11. Av 3 course à la carte £13.50.
BREWERY/COMPANY: Free House.
PRINCIPAL BEERS: Everards Tiger, Greene King Abbot Ale,
Courage Directors. **FACILITIES:** Children welcome Garden:
patio, outdoor eating. **NOTES:** Parking 60.
ROOMS: 8 bedrooms 8 en suite s£40 d£60

FREISTON   Map 09 TF34

Kings Head
Church Rd PE22 0NT ☎ 01205 760368
*Dir: from Boston take A52 towards Skegness. 3m turn R at Haltoft
End to Freiston*
Originally two cottages, this village pub is renowned for its
prize-winning hanging baskets and colourful window boxes.
Inside, you can relax by an open fire and enjoy
straightforward wholesome bar food. Home-made pies are a
speciality and include steak and kidney, chicken and
mushroom, sausage, and apple. The blackboard specials
change on a weekly basis.
OPEN: 11-2.30 (Sun 12-3) 7-11 (Sun 7.30-10.30).
BAR MEALS: D served Wed-Sat 12-2 7-9. Av main course £4.95.
RESTAURANT: L served Fri-Sun. D served Fri-Sat 12-2
7-9. Av 3 course à la carte £14.
BREWERY/COMPANY: Batemans.
PRINCIPAL BEERS: Batemans XB & Dark Mild.
FACILITIES: Children welcome. **NOTES:** Parking 30 No credit
cards

 ★ AA inspected hotel accommodation

FROGNALL   Map 09 TF11

The Goat
155 Spalding Rd PE6 8SA ☎ 01778 347629
e-mail: goat.frognall@virgin.net
*Dir: A1 to Peterborough, A15 to Market Deeping, old A16 to Spalding,
pub about 1.5m from jct of A15 & A16*

Welcoming country pub dating back to the 17th century, with a
large beer garden and plenty to amuse the kids. A
straightforward but comprehensive menu ranges through fish,
grills and chicken dishes, while the chef's home-made
selection includes battered sweet and sour chicken balls,
grilled rainbow trout, spaghetti bolognaise, and leek and
mushroom crumble.
OPEN: 11-2.30 6-11 (Sun 12-3, 7-10.30). Closed 25 Dec.
BAR MEALS: L served all week. D served all week 12-2 6.30-9.30.
Av main course £7. **RESTAURANT:** L served all week. D served
all week 12-2 6.30-9.30. Av 3 course fixed price £9.50.
BREWERY/COMPANY: Free House.
PRINCIPAL BEERS: Adnams. **FACILITIES:** Children welcome
Garden: Outdoor eating. **NOTES:** Parking 50

FULBECK

Hare & Hounds Country Inn ◆◆◆
The Green NG32 3JJ ☎ 01400 272090 📄 01400 273663

Family-owned inn dating from 1648, facing the church,
vicarage and green of one of Lincolnshire's prettiest villages.
The emphasis is on top quality, hand prepared food in both
the bar and restaurant. Steak and Stilton pie is a speciality,
alongside dishes of sea bass on bubble and squeak, and
poached chicken breast stuffed with smoked salmon and
topped with whisky cream.
OPEN: 12-2 6-11 (Sun 7-10.30). **BAR MEALS:** L served all week.
D served all week 12-2 6.30-9.30. Av main course £6.50.
RESTAURANT: L served all week. D served all week 12-2
7-9.30. Av 3 course à la carte £17. Av 3 course fixed price £10.95.

continued

BREWERY/COMPANY: Free House.
PRINCIPAL BEERS: Batemans XB, Fullers London Pride, Hook Norton, Ruddles County. **FACILITIES:** Children welcome Garden: outdoor eating, patio. **NOTES:** Parking 32. **ROOMS:** 8 bedrooms 8 en suite s£30 d£40 FR£60

GEDNEY DYKE · Map 09 TF42

The Chequers 🐾 ♀
PE12 0AJ ☎ 01406 362666 ▤ 01406 362666
e-mail: chequerspub@bllmember.net
Dir: From King's Lynn take A17, 1st roundabout after Long Sutton take B1359
An 18th-century country inn located in a remote Fenland village close to The Wash wildlife sanctuaries. Local venison, Gressingham duck breast and fillet of Lincoln red beef steaks are regulars on the menu, along with fishy options like sea bass with limes and ginger, lobster thermidor or salmon en croute. **OPEN:** 12-2 7-11 (Sun 12-2 7-10.30). Closed 26 Dec. **BAR MEALS:** L served all week. D served all week 12-2 7-9. Av main course £8.95. **RESTAURANT:** L served all week. D served all week 12-2 7-9. Av 3 course à la carte £17.50.
BREWERY/COMPANY: Free House.
PRINCIPAL BEERS: Adnams, Greene King Abbot Ale.
FACILITIES: Garden: patio, outdoor eating

GRANTHAM · Map 09 SK93

The Beehive Inn
10/11 Castlegate NG31 6SE ☎ 01476 404554
▤ 01476 405339
Dir: A52 to town centre, L at Finkin St, pub at end
Grantham's oldest inn (1550) is notable for having England's only living pub sign - a working beehive high up in a lime tree. Otherwise, this simple town hostelry offers a good pint of Batemans XB and good-value, yet basic bar food.

HECKINGTON

The Nags Head
34 High St NG34 9QZ ☎ 01529 460218
Dir: 5m E of Sleaford on A17
Overlooking the green of a village boasting the only 8 sailed windmill in the country, this white painted 17th-century coaching inn reputedly once played host to Dick Turpin. Garden and play area. Bedrooms.

HOLDINGHAM · Map 09 TF04

Jolly Scotchman
NG34 8NP ☎ 01529 304864
Dir: 200yds S of A15/A17 rdbt, 1m from Sleaford
With an indoor play room and a garden featuring an adventure playground, aviary and pets' corner, this friendly old pub is the perfect family destination. Victorian-style conservatory restaurant and homely bars where traditional pub food is served.

HOUGH-ON-THE-HILL

The Brownlow Arms ◆◆◆◆ 🐾 ♀
Grantham Rd NG32 2AZ ☎ 01400 250234
▤ 01400 250772
Dir: Take A607 Grantham to Sleaford Rd, Hough on the Hill is signposted from Barkston
Quaint 16th-century country inn, originally the game keepers house for

the Brownlow Estate of Belton House, situated in a tranquil village. Features include stone mullioned windows, open fires and tastefully decorated bedrooms. Daily-changing menus highlight freshly prepared dishes. The restaurant carte changes weekly and includes plenty of fresh fish.
OPEN: Sat 12-3, Sun 12-4, 7-11. Closed Mon-Fri lunch & Sun eve. **BAR MEALS:** L served Mon-Sat. D served Mon-Sat 12-2 7-9.30. Av main course £6.50. **RESTAURANT:** L served Mon-Sat. D served Mon-Sat 12-2 7-9.30. Av 3 course à la carte £14.95. Av 3 course fixed price £9.99. **BREWERY/COMPANY:** Free House. **PRINCIPAL BEERS:** Timothy Taylor Landlord, Marstons Pedigree, Greene King Old Speckled Hen, Fullers London Pride. **FACILITIES:** Children welcome Garden: patio, outdoor eating. **NOTES:** Parking 45. **ROOMS:** 7 bedrooms 7 en suite s£40 d£52 FR£60

LINCOLN · Map 09 SK97

Pyewipe Inn
Fossebank, Saxilby Rd LN1 2BG ☎ 01522 528708
▤ 01522 525009
e-mail: robert@pyewipeinn.co.uk
Dir: Out of Lincoln on A57 past Lincoln A46 Bypass, pub signed after 0.5m

The Pyewipe is an 18th-century alehouse on the Roman Fossedyke Canal, set in four acres with great views of the city and the cathedral - a 25-minute walk along the Fossedyke. A two-storey lodge housing 21 en suite bedrooms is a new addition to the grounds. All food from pâté to ice cream is freshly prepared and offered from a daily board in the bar or seasonal carte in the restaurant.
OPEN: 11-11 (Sun 12-10.30). **BAR MEALS:** L served all week. D served all week. Av main course £7. **RESTAURANT:** L served all week. D served all week 12-3 7-9.30. Av 3 course à la carte £17. **BREWERY/COMPANY:** Free House. **PRINCIPAL BEERS:** Taylor Landlord, Greene King Abbot Ale, Bass, Tetley. **FACILITIES:** Garden: outdoor eating, patio/terrace,. **NOTES:** Parking 100. **ROOMS:** 20 bedrooms 20 en suite d£50

The Victoria
6 Union Rd LN1 3BJ ☎ 01522 536048 ▤ 01522 536048
Traditional drinkers pub located in the historic heart of the city close to the Castle. Terraced wide range of ales, usual bar food, occasional jazz or blues.
OPEN: 11-11 (Sun 12-10.30). **BAR MEALS:** L served all week. D served all week 12-2.30. Av main course £3.75. **RESTAURANT:** L served Sun12-2. Av 3 course à la carte £7.50.
BREWERY/COMPANY: Tynemill Ltd.
PRINCIPAL BEERS: Taylor Landlord, Batemans XB, Everards Original. **FACILITIES:** Garden: patio, outdoor eating Dogs allowed not during food times

continued

LINCOLN continued

Pick of the Pubs

Wig & Mitre ◉ ♀
30/32 Steep Hill LN2 1TL ☎ 01522 535190
▤ 01522 532402
See Pick of the Pubs on page 281

LONG BENNINGTON   Map 09 SK84

The Reindeer
Main Rd NG23 5EH ☎ 01400 281382
e-mail: terry@reindeerinn.co.uk
Dir: *7m North of Grantham on the A1*
Welcoming pub, with exposed beams and open fireplaces, in a
pretty village setting. A varied menu may include mushroom
and celery Stroganoff, chicken with sherry cream and
mushroom, steak and kidney pie, or salmon on mixed leaves
with lemon mayonnaise.
OPEN: 12-3 7-11 (Sat/Sun 12-4, Sun 7-10.30). **BAR MEALS:** L
served all week. D served Mon-Sat 12-2 7-10. Av main course
£8.95. **RESTAURANT:** L served Mon-Sat. D served Mon-Sat 12-2
7-10. Av 3 course à la carte £20. **BREWERY/COMPANY:** Free
House. **PRINCIPAL BEERS:** John Smiths, Greene King Old
Speckled Hen, Ruddles County, Wells Bombadier.
FACILITIES: Children's licence Garden: Dogs allowed garden
only

LOUTH   Map 09 TF38

Masons Arms ◆◆◆ ♀
Cornmarket LN11 9PY ☎ 01507 609525
e-mail: justin@themasons.co.uk

18th-century former posting inn in the centre of Louth's
Cornmarket. Comfortable, well equipped bedrooms make this
an ideal base for exploring the historic market town and
touring the gently rolling Lincolnshire Wolds. Imaginative menu
ranges from loin of local pork and fillet of salmon to char-
grilled chicken breast and pan-fried pigeon. Tempting selection
of sweets might include lemon posset and mango tart.
OPEN: 10-11 (Sun 12-10.30). **BAR MEALS:** L served all week.
D served all week 12-2 6-9. Av main course £6.95.
RESTAURANT: L served all week. D served all week 12-2 7-9.30.
Av 3 course à la carte £16 9.30. **BREWERY/COMPANY:** Free
House. **PRINCIPAL BEERS:** Batemans XB, Taylor Landlord,
Marstons Pedigree, Tom Wood. **FACILITIES:** Children welcome
Children's licence Dogs allowed only in guests rooms.
NOTES: Parking 20. **ROOMS:** 10 bedrooms 5 en suite s£21
d£36 1 family
room £52-£65   *See Pub Walk on page 275*

MARSTON   Map 09 SK84

Thorold Arms
Main St NG32 2HH ☎ 01400 250899 ▤ 01400 251030
Dir: *Off A1 N of Grantham*
A typical country pub, this large Victorian building is situated
in the centre of the village on the Viking Way. Good range of
regularly changing real ales. Bar snacks and restaurant meals
are available.

NEWTON   Map 09 TF03

The Red Lion
NG34 0EE ☎ 01529 497256
Dir: *10m E of Grantham on A52*
A 17th-century pub set in a hamlet of around 20 houses, with
some lovely circular walks in the surrounding countryside and
cycle routes on local lanes and bridleways. A cold buffet is
prepared daily with roasted meats, fish, quiches and salads.
Hot dishes include Aberdeen Angus steaks, pies, gammon,
curries and chilli.
OPEN: 12-2.30 (Sun 12-4, 7-10.30) 6-11. **BAR MEALS:** L served
all week. D served all week 12-2 7-9. Av main course £6.95.
RESTAURANT: L served all week. D served all week 12-2 7-9. Av
3 course à la carte £12.20. Av 2 course fixed price £8.95.
BREWERY/COMPANY: Free House.
PRINCIPAL BEERS: Bateman XB. **FACILITIES:** Children
welcome Garden: outdoor eating, patio, Dogs allowed Water.
NOTES: Parking 40

OLD SOMERBY   Map 09 SK93

Fox & Hounds
NG33 4AB ☎ 01476 564121
Dir: *From A1 take A52 E, after 3m take B1176, then 1m to Old
Somerby*
Nestling in a rural village in the Lincolnshire Wolds, this
rambling, traditional country pub offers a wide ranges of
snacks and meals to suit all palates.

PARTNEY   Map 09 TF46

Red Lion Inn
PE23 4PG ☎ 01790 752271 ▤ 01790 753360
Dir: *On A16 from Boston, or A158 from Horncastle*
Parts of this Lincolnshire inn may date back 400 years, but
reports of a ghost seem to be unsubstantiated. Home-made
special dishes include lamb chops with mint gravy, sweet and
sour chicken and rice, cod and prawns in cheese sauce, and
spinach and mushroom lasagne.
OPEN: 11-2.30 7-11 (Sun 12-2.30, 7-10.30, closed Mon-Tue).
Closed 25-26 Dec, 1 Jan. **BAR MEALS:** L served Wed-Sun.
D served Wed-Sun 12-2 7-9.30. Av main course £7.
BREWERY/COMPANY: Free House.
PRINCIPAL BEERS: Marstons Pedigree, Bateman.
FACILITIES: Garden: food served in garden. **NOTES:** Parking
40. **ROOMS:** 3 bedrooms 3 en suite s£30 d£40

We endeavour to be as accurate as possible but changes
in personnel and data can occur in establishments after
the guide has gone to press

PICK OF THE PUBS

OPEN: 8am-midnight.
BAR MEALS: L served all week.
D served all week 8am-midnight.
Av main course £7.50
RESTAURANT: L served all week
D served all week 8am-midnight.
Av 3 course a la carte £22. Av 3
course fixed price £12.
BREWERY/COMPANY:
Free House.
PRINCIPAL BEERS: Timothy
Taylor Landlord, Marston's
Pedigre.
FACILITIES: Children welcome.
Dogs allowed.

The Wig & Mitre

30-32 Steep Hill LN2 1TL
☎ 01522 535190 ▤ 01522 532402
e-mail: reservations@wigandmitre.co.uk
Dir: adjacent to Lincoln cathedral and
castle car park at top of Steep Hill.

In the same hands since 1977 (though re-located from next door only two years ago) this is a reassuringly civilised place located towards the top of historic Steep Hill 'twixt castle and cathedral'. The perfect refreshment stop, open 8am till late, for those walking Lincoln's fascinating city trail.

Wonderfully evocative interiors in both the ground floor bar and upper restaurant have retained 14th-century timbers amongst other evidence of the building's long and colourful history. With continuous service from 8am until midnight, in an ambience free of piped music and amusement machines, it is justifiably popular for its food, served every day of each week, all year round. Typically, the multi-choice English breakfast, including Lincolnshire sausages, black pudding and eggs in many guises, can be ordered equally at 6pm as first thing in the morning. Sandwiches and light meals encompass toasted bacon and Brie sandwiches and bowls of chilli, while a fixed-price lunch menu might feature stir-fried chicken with chilli and noodles, gurnard fillets on crispy fried cabbage and steamed jam sponge - an eclectic mix indeed.

From the main menu, served throughout, specialities include baked cheese soufflé, bangers-and-mash with onion and red wine gravy, a full flavoured confit of duck served with a bold red wine sauce, and fillet steak with cracked black pepper sauce. Expect fresh and well cooked accompanying vegetables. Fish selections include Thai-spiced crab cakes and steamed salmon, seabass and brill with saffron velouté, while afters include a creamy rice pudding with stewed apricots, banoffi pie and a selection of farmhouse cheeses.

Fine real ales, such as Timothy Taylor Landlord, and many decent wines by the glass.

RAITHBY   Map 09 TF36

Red Lion Inn ♀
PE23 4DS ☎ 01790 753727
Dir: Take A158 from Horncastle, R at Sausthorpe, keep L into Raithby
Traditional beamed black-and-white village pub, parts of which date back 300 years. Log fires provide a warm welcome in winter. A varied menu of home-made dishes includes pizzas in the bar, and steaks, curries and fish in the restaurant - perhaps grilled haddock or Dover sole.

OPEN: 12-3 (Sat-Sun only) 7-11 Closed Mon-Fri lunch.
BAR MEALS: L served Sat-Sun. D served all week 12-2.30 7-10.
Av main course £7. **RESTAURANT:** L served Sat-Sun. D served all week 12-2.30 7-10. Av 3 course à la carte £12.
BREWERY/COMPANY: Free House.
PRINCIPAL BEERS: Raithby, Marstons Pedigree, Mansfield IPA.
FACILITIES: Children welcome Children's licence food served outdoors Dogs allowed. **NOTES:** Parking 20.
ROOMS: 3 bedrooms 3 en suite s£28 d£38

SAXILBY   Map 09 SK87

The Bridge Inn
Gainsborough Rd LN1 2LX ☎ 01522 702266
Dir: On A57 W of Lincoln
Traditional Sunday lunch goes down well at this canalside pub near Lincoln. Day to day food ranges from bar snacks to specials.

SKEGNESS

The Vine ★ ★ ★
Vine Rd, Seacroft PE25 3DB ☎ 01754 763018
🖷 01754 769845
e-mail: vinehotel@bateman.co.uk
Ivy-covered Victorian hotel, converted from a farmhouse and bought by Harry Bateman in 1928. Now this Bateman flagship offers a fine selection of ales, silver service in the restaurant and charming accommodation. Weddings a speciality. Once a haunt of poet Alfred Lord Tennyson, who has given his name to The Tennyson Lounge.

SOUTH WITHAM   Map 09 SK91

Blue Cow Inn & Brewery
High St NG33 5QB ☎ 01572 768432 🖷 01572 768432
e-mail: Bluecow@btclick.com
Dir: between Stamford & Grantham on the A1
Refurbished village pub brewing its own ale - Thirwell's Cuddy & Best. Flagstoned bar with low beams; wide-ranging menu of home-cooked dishes.   *continued*

OPEN: 12-11. **BAR MEALS:** L served all week. D served all week 12-2.30 6-9.30. Av main course £6.50. **RESTAURANT:** L served all week. D served all week 12-2.30 6-9.30. Av 3 course à la carte £13.50. **BREWERY/COMPANY:** Free House.
PRINCIPAL BEERS: Own beers. **FACILITIES:** Children welcome Garden: outdoor eating, Dogs allowed Water.
NOTES: Parking 45. **ROOMS:** 6 bedrooms 6 en suite s£40 d£45
1 family room £65

SPALDING   Map 09 TF22

The Ship Inn 🛏
154 Reservoir Rd, Surfleet-Seas-End PE11 4DH
☎ 01775 680384 🖷 01775 680384
Dir: Off A16 (Spalding to Boston) Follow tourist signs towards Surfleet reservoir then the ship inn.signs to the pub
A 17th-century village pub on the banks of the River Glen with free fishing nearby. Spalding is four miles away and the flat open country is ideal for cycling and walking. A good choice of seafood ranges from fish and chips with mushy peas to lobster thermidor. Alternatives include coq au vin or rabbit and prune casserole.
OPEN: 12-2.30 7-11. **BAR MEALS:** L served all week 12-3. Av main course £6.50. **RESTAURANT:** L served all week.
D served all week 12-3 7-11. Av 3 course à la carte £12.50.
BREWERY/COMPANY: Free House.
PRINCIPAL BEERS: Everards Tiger/Beacon, Tom Wood Best.
NOTES: Parking 30. **ROOMS:** 2 bedrooms s£19 d£38 No credit cards

SPILSBY

Blacksmiths Arms
Skendelby PE23 4QE ☎ 01754 890662 🖷 01754 890030
Old fashioned bar with 17th-century cellar and indoor wishing well. Open fire. Batemans beers. Standard pub food.

STAMFORD   Map 06 TF00

The Blue Bell Inn 🛏 ♀ NEW
Shepherds Walk, Belmesthorpe PE9 4JG ☎ 01780 763859
Dir: 2 m N of Stamford on the A6121 Bourn Road, turn R for Belmesthorpe and pub is on the L
After three years at the Blue Bell, a 350-year-old, partly thatched village pub, enthusiastic owners, Andrew Cunningham and Susan Bailey, are undertaking a major refurbishment programme. In addition to four en suite bedrooms, improved kitchen facilities will result in more innovative pub food using fresh local produce. Served throughout the homely, cottagey bars, both featuring impressive inglenook fireplaces, are a reliable range of traditional pub meals and interesting daily specials. The latter may list seafood risotto with saffron and sweet tomatoes, roasted scallops with Parmesan and rocket salad, and roast partridge with Madeira sauce.
OPEN: 12-2.30 6-11. **BAR MEALS:** L served all week. D served all week 12-2 7-9.30. Av main course £5.50. **RESTAURANT:** L served all week. D served all week 12-2 7-9.30. Av 3 course à la carte £17. **BREWERY/COMPANY:** Free House.
PRINCIPAL BEERS: Bass, Ruddles County, Badger Best.
FACILITIES: Children welcome Garden: Food served outside.
NOTES: Parking 30. **ROOMS:** 4 bedrooms 4 en suite

England

Pick of the Pubs

The George at Stamford ⊛ ★ ★ ★ 🐾 🍷
71 St Martins PE9 2LB ☎ 01780 750750
📠 01780 750701
e-mail: reservations@georgehotelofstamford.com
Dir: take A1 N from Peterborough. From A1 roundabout signposted B1081 Stamford, down hill to lights. Hotel on L

Arguably middle England's most celebrated coaching inn, dating back to the 16th century, this is a place full of history. Two panelled rooms by the main entrance are marked York and London, the original waiting rooms for passengers while their coaches changed horses in the hotel courtyard, whilst the walled monastery garden was the burial ground of a church built on the site some 800 years ago.
Do not expect accommodation at this highly commended hotel to come cheap, yet for pub-goers of all generations dining options offer something for everyone. At its simplest, the York Bar dispenses real ale and snacks with an Italian slant; Cheddar and Stilton, beef, ham and smoked salmon served on ciabatta and Daniel Lambert's open sandwich of sirloin steak, fried onions, tomato and mushrooms. In the oak-panelled restaurant dressed Scottish crab at lunch rubs shoulders with breaded lamb cutlets and half-lobster tagliatelle, while in the Garden Lounge lasagne al forno and chargrilled chicken with Caesar salad are alternatives to the impressive cold buffet.
OPEN: 11-2.30 6-11. (Sat-Sun open all day from 11)
BAR MEALS: L served all week. D served all week 12-2.30 7-11. Av main course £8.95. **RESTAURANT:** L served all week. D served all week 12-2.30 7-10. Av 3 course à la carte £34. Av 2 course fixed price £16.50.
PRINCIPAL BEERS: Adnams Broadside, Fullers London Pride. **FACILITIES:** Children welcome Garden: patio, outdoor eating, Dogs allowed Dog Pack, Towel, Blanket, feeding mat. **NOTES:** Parking 140. **ROOMS:** 47 bedrooms 47 en suite s£78 d£105 £20 for extra bed

St Peter's Inn and The Bistro
11 St Peter's St PE9 2PQ ☎ 01780 763298
Dir: From A1 take A6121 to Stamford. Pub 1m on R
Thai style dishes are among the specialities at this 18th-century pub and bistro in the conservation area of Stamford, where the television adaption of Middlemarch was filmed.

WOOLSTHORPE   Map 09 SK83

Rutland Arms
NG32 1NY ☎ 01476 870111
Better known to locals as the 'Dirty Duck', this family pub sits at the side of the Grantham canal, in the shadow of Belvoir Castle.

LONDON

E1 London

Prospect of Whitby
57 Wapping Wall E1W 3SH ☎ 020 7481 1095
📠 020 7481 9537
Pepys, Dickens, Whistler, Hanging Judge Jeffreys and Paul Newman have been among the clientele at this 16th-century riverside inn, once known as The Devil's Tavern. Pirate Captain Kidd was hung here in 1701. Flagstone bar, pewter counter and straightforward pub food.

Town of Ramsgate
62 Wapping High St E1W 2NP ☎ 020 7264 0001
Old pub close to The City. Plenty of bric-a-brac and old prints. Value for money bar food.

E3 London

Pick of the Pubs

The Crown 🍷 NEW
223 Grove Rd E3 5SW ☎ 020 8981 9998
📠 020 8980 2336
e-mail: crown@singhboulton.co.uk
Dir: Nearest tube: Mile End Central Line & District line. Bus 277 to Victoria Bank

Now here's something different - a pub with attitude, where the environmental ethic permeates everything from the secondhand furniture to the organic menu and wine list. Look elsewhere for juke boxes, muzak or pinball machines; here you'll find buzzing conversation or the rustle of the papers on a peaceful afternoon. Building on the success of their first pub, the Duke of Cambridge in Islington (qv), Geetie Singh and Esther Boulton have carefully restored this Grade II listed building to create a comfortable, open plan bar and a labyrinth of intimate first-floor dining-rooms and balconies overlooking Victoria Park. Seasonal by nature and European in style, the blackboard menus are changed twice daily. Come in for breakfast of kippers and poached egg on toast, or a £6 special weekday lunch and drink. Other choices include spicy black bean soup, pumpkin and roast pepper risotto, or ribeye steak with chips and Caesar salad.
OPEN: 10.30-11. (Sun 10.30-10.30). Closed 25-26 Dec, 1 Jan.
BAR MEALS: L served all week. D served all week 10.30-3.30 6.30-10.30. **RESTAURANT:** L served all week. D served all week 10.30-3.30 6.30-10.30. Av 3 course à la carte £20.
BREWERY/COMPANY: Free House. **PRINCIPAL BEERS:** St Peter's Organic Ale & Best Bitter, Caledonian Golden Promise, Pitfield Eco Warrior. **FACILITIES:** Children welcome Garden: Food served outside Dogs allowed

England

E14 London

Pick of the Pubs

The Grapes 🍴 ♀
76 Narrow St, Limehouse E14 8BP ☎ 020 7987 4396
🖷 020 7987 3137
Dir: *Docklands Light Railway stations: Limehouse or West Ferry*
Used by Charles Dickens as the model for The Six Jolly
Fellowship Porters in his novel Our Mutual Friend, the pub
has been standing on its narrow riverside site since 1720.
'The Grapes' has been carefully renovated since Dickens'
day, and the novelist might still recognise many of its
features though quite what he would have made of the
nearby Canary Wharf or the convenient Docklands Light
Railway is a matter of conjecture! A small wooden
verandah overlooks the river, and there are more
spectacular views of the Thames from the tiny upstairs
restaurant. Cask conditioned real ales accompany bar
meals such as club sandwiches, ploughman's lunches, or
crispy potato skins, whilst the restaurant menu offers a
wide selection of seafood. Starters include whitebait,
pickled herrings, or a smoked fish platter, whilst sea bass,
supreme of salmon, or deep-fried jumbo scampi are just
some of the main course options.
OPEN: 12-3 5.30-11 Sat 7-11, Sun 7-10.30. Closed BHs.
BAR MEALS: L served Sun-Fri. D served Mon-Sat 12-2 7-9.
Av main course £5.75. **RESTAURANT:** L served Mon-Fri.
D served Mon-Sat 12-2.15 7.30-9.15. Av 3 course à la carte
£30. **BREWERY/COMPANY:** Allied Domecq.
PRINCIPAL BEERS: Adnams, Burton Ale, Tetley, Marstons
Pedigree. **FACILITIES:** Dogs allowed Water

EC1 London

Bishop's Finger
9-10 West Smithfield EC1A 9JR ☎ 020 7248 2341
Close to Smithfield Market, this relaxed bar offers interesting
food from an open kitchen. Plenty of real ales on tap.

Pick of the Pubs

The Bleeding Heart Tavern ♀ **NEW**   Map E4
19 Greville St EC1N 8SQ ☎ 0207 4040333
🖷 0207 4040333
First recorded as a licensed premises in 1746 and recently
restored to its former glory, this bustling inn stands at the
entrance to Bleeding Heart Yard, so named following the
brutal murder of Lady Elizabeth Hatton in the 17th
century, in the heart of Hatton Garden. Plenty of glass
and stone and rustic scrubbed tables on wooden floors
give the place an authentic yet contemporary atmosphere,
which is enhanced by an interesting menu listing
traditional pub food with a modern twist. It is 'the' place to
find the full complement of tip-top ales from Adnams
Brewery and a range of their equally impressive wines, in
addition to ribeye steak sandwich and pork sausages on
bubble-and-squeak with onion gravy in the bar. In the
restaurant, sample spit-roasted Suffolk ale pork, roast leg
of Norfolk lamb, ale-battered haddock with fat chips and
mushy pea purée, and great nursery puddings.
OPEN: 11-11. Closed Sat, Sun, BHs, 10 days at Christmas.
BAR MEALS: L served Mon-Fri 11-10.30. Av main course
£5.95. **RESTAURANT:** L served Mon-Fri. D served Mon-Fri
12-3 6-10.30. Av 3 course à la carte £17.50. **BREWERY/
COMPANY:** Free House. **PRINCIPAL BEERS:** Adnams
Southwold Bitter, Broadside & Fisherman. **NOTES:** Parking 20

Pick of the Pubs

The Eagle ♀   Map E4
159 Farringdon Rd EC1R 3AL ☎ 020 7837 1353
🖷 020 7689 5882
Dir: *Angel/Farringdon Stn. North end Farringdon Road*
Never forgetting its role as a pub is the secret of the Eagle,
now celebrating its tenth anniversary at the hub of its local
community. Simple, random furniture from school chairs
to bare tables fill the single dining area, serviced from an
open kitchen that is an extension of the bar. The food is
randomly Mediterranean yet carefully constructed: grilled
plaice with roast winter vegetables, linguine with crab, Bife
Ana marinated rumpsteak sandwich, poached ham hock
with chickpeas, spinach and chives, and Sardinian ewe's
milk cheese with flatbread and marmalade.
OPEN: 12-11 (Sun 12-5 only). Closed Easter + 2Wks Xmas.
BAR MEALS: L served all week. D served Mon-Sat
12.30-2.30 6.30-10.30. Av main course £8.50.
BREWERY/COMPANY: Free House.
PRINCIPAL BEERS: Wells Eagle IPA, Bombardier.
FACILITIES: Children welcome Dogs allowed

Pick of the Pubs

The Jerusalem Tavern   Map F4
55 Britton St, Clerkenwell EC1M 5UQ
☎ 020 7490 4281   🖷 0207 490 4281
e-mail: beers@stpetersbrewery.co.uk
Dir: *100m NE of Farringdon tube, 300m N of Smithfield*

Named after the Priory of St John of Jerusalem, this
historic tavern has occupied several sites in the area since
the 14th century. The current building dates from 1720
when it was a merchant's house, and lies in a fascinating
and wonderfully atmospheric corner of London. The likes
of Samuel Johnson, David Garrick and the young Handel
were visitors and the inn has been used as a film set on
many occasions. Owned by St Peter's Brewery, it features
a dimly-lit bar with bare boards, rustic wooden tables, old
tiles magazines and daily papers, and candles, open fires
and cosy corners add to the unspoilt charm of the place.
Renowned as one of the finest pubs in the capital, it is
open every weekday and offers the full range of St Peter's
ales, as well as simple bar fare, including speciality
sandwiches, sausage baguettes, soup and roll and beef
casserole.
OPEN: 11-11. Closed Sat, Sun, 25 Dec, Etr, BH Mon's.
BAR MEALS: L served Mon-Fri. D served Mon-Fri 12-7. Av
main course £6. **BREWERY/COMPANY:** St Peters Brewery.
PRINCIPAL BEERS: St Peters (complete range).
FACILITIES: Dogs allowed

Pick of the Pubs

The Leopard Map F5
33 Seward St EC1V 3PA ☎ 020 7253 3587
▤ 020 7253 3587
The unassuming exterior belies the civilised interior of this
friendly pub near The Barbican. Splendid rear
conservatory, rug-strewn, wooden-floored bar and
meeting room upstairs.
   Expect a good range of beers and an open kitchen
serving such delights as Thai green chicken curry, Caesar
chicken salad, salmon fishcakes with steamed spinach, hot
steak baguette with caramelised onions and fries, and
sausage and mash with onion gravy. **OPEN:** 12-11 (wknds - private parties). **BAR MEALS:** L
served Mon-Fri. D served Mon-Fri 12-9.30. **RESTAURANT:** L
served Mon-Fri. D served Mon-Fri 12-9.30.
BREWERY/COMPANY: Free House.
PRINCIPAL BEERS: Ushers Salisbury Best & Founders Ale,
Greene King Abbot Ale, Batemans. **FACILITIES:** Children
welcome Garden

Pick of the Pubs

The Peasant ♉ Map D3
240 St John St EC1V 4PH ☎ 020 7336 7736
▤ 020 7251 8525
Dir: Angel & Faringdon Rd Tube Station
Standing on a handsome Victorian corner site close to
Sadler's Wells and the Barbican, the Peasant - with its
striking architectural features and inlaid mosaic floor - has
long enjoyed a reputation for Mediterranean, peasant-
style food.
   Recent changes of ownership and chef suggest
that this remains its chosen path with polenta and porcini,
Mozzarella and marscapone dotted throughout an
inventive modern menu. Required now is further cohesion
in production and service that previously appeared to
have faltered. Promising dishes include Jerusalem
artichoke soup with truffle oil and polenta with roast
tomatoes, red onions and basil amongst featured starters,
with porcini and smoked pancetta risotto and penne with
marscapone, spinach and leeks available in small and
large portions. Sea bass with roast fennel and salsa verde
and roast guinea fowl, cavalo nero, marsala and crème
fraiche show much promise and attention to detail. To
follow, passion fruit tiramisu and a plate of gorgonzola
with apple and ginger chutney are pleasing, if not wholly
peasant, improvements.
OPEN: 12.30-12.30. **BAR MEALS:** L served Mon-Fri.
D served Mon-Sat 12.30-11. Av main course £10.
RESTAURANT: L served Mon-Fri. D served Mon-Sat 12-3.30
6.30-12.30. Av 3 course à la carte £25.
BREWERY/COMPANY: Free House
FACILITIES: Patio/Balcony Dogs allowed

Ye Olde Mitre
13 Ely Place, Hatton Garden EC1N 6SJ ☎ 020 7405 4751
Located at the edge of The City, this has been the site of a pub
since 1546. In the bar is part of a cherry tree that Elizabeth I is
thought to have danced around. Gets very busy at lunchtimes.
Real ales from the handpump. Bar snacks.

EC2 London

Old Dr Butler's Head
Mason's Av, Coleman St, Moorgate EC2V 5BY
☎ 020 76063504 ▤ 020 7600 0417
Traditional, gas-lit pub that dates back to the 17th century. Split
over three floors, the bars offer up to six cask ales at any one
time. Straightforward pub food.

EC4 London

The Black Friar
174 Queen Victoria St EC4V 4EG ☎ 020 7236 5650
Boasting a fine collection of Edwardian art nouveau
decorations, this deceptively large pub is very busy with after-
work drinkers. Close to Blackfriars Bridge.

The Centre Page ♉ Map F3
29 Knightrider St EC4V 5BH ☎ 020 7236 3614
Situated in the shadow of St Paul's Cathedral, this historic pub
used to be known as the Horn Tavern and was mentioned by
Charles Dickens in The Pickwick Papers, and in Samuel Pepys'
diary.
   Varied menu offers the likes of baby spinach salad with
grilled goats' cheese, pan-fried tuna on a Niçoise salad, and
Cumberland sausages with colcannon and onion gravy.
OPEN: 11-11 (for hire at weekends). Closed all BHs.
BAR MEALS: L served all week 12-3. **BREWERY/
COMPANY:** Front Page Pubs Ltd. **PRINCIPAL BEERS:** Wells
Bombardier, Brakspear, Shepherd Neame Spitfire.
FACILITIES: Children welcome

The Old Bank of England ♉ Map E4
194 Fleet St EC4A 2LT ☎ 020 7430 2255
▤ 020 7242 3092
e-mail: oldbankofengland@fullers.co.uk
One of London's most historic pubs is squeezed between the
site of Sweeney Todd's barber shop and the pie shop owned
by his mistress. Despite its rather dubious associations, this
former bank is a gem of a place, with a wonderful atmosphere
and some stunning features inside.
   Gleaming chandeliers, prints and framed bank notes hang
from the walls and ceilings and outside blazing Olympic-style
torches make the building easily recognisable. Generous
portions of traditional bar food.
OPEN: 11-11. Closed Weekends & BHs. **BAR MEALS:** L served
Mon-Fri. D served Mon-Fri 12-8. Av main course £6.
BREWERY/COMPANY: Fullers. **PRINCIPAL BEERS:** Fullers
London Pride, ESB.

Ye Olde Cheshire Cheese
Wine Office Court, 145 Fleet St EC4A 2BU
☎ 020 7353 6170 ▤ 020 7353 0845
e-mail: cheshirecheese@compuserve.com
17th-century pub with a long history of entertaining literary
greats such as Arthur Conan Doyle, Yeats and Dickens. One of
the few remaining Chop houses rebuilt after the Great Fire of
London in 1666. Plenty of nooks and crannies, traditional pub
meals and quiet at weekends.

The Thames through London

On its approach to London, the Thames passes a variety of picturesque cottages and period houses - some of them once occupied by fishermen. At Wandsworth you can take a break from the riverside trail and relax in the comfortable surroundings of the brightly coloured Ship Inn, with its modern saloon and 1930s-style public bar. Resume the walk and continue downstream to the historic Anchor next door to Tate Modern and the Globe. Samuel Pepys witnessed the Great Fire of London from here in 1666. Follow the Thames Path through the capital and you'll find a wide-ranging choice of riverside pubs to tempt you off the trail. The Mayflower at Rotherhithe and the Cutty Sark at Greenwich are worth a visit; alternatively, you could cross to the north bank of the river and try two classic pubs in Wapping, the Prospect of Whitby and the Town of Ramsgate.

N1 London

The Albion
10 Thornhill Rd, Barnsbury N1 1HW ☎ 020 7607 7450
🖹 020 7607 8969
e-mail: keithinwood@aol.com
Often playing host to local TV celebrities, this ivy-clad pub is a warren of homely rooms decorated in country hotel style. Outdoor eating available. Traditional pub grub.

The Compton Arms
4 Compton Av, Off Canonbury Rd N1 2XD
☎ 020 7359 6883
Small peaceful pub in a mews. Low ceilinged, rural feel. Real ales from the handpump. Good value bar food.

The Crown ♀
116 Cloudsley Rd, Islington N1 0EB ☎ 020 7837 7107
🖹 020 7833 1084
Bustling, Grade II listed pleasantly situated in an upmarket and peaceful residential area in the heart of Islington. Wealth of period features, including Victorian etched glass, stylish furnishings, tip-top Fuller's ales, and a modern pub menu. Alongside traditional sausage and mash lookout for caramelised salmon steak, chargrilled lamb, Mediterranean vegetables with goats' cheese, and various casseroles.
OPEN: 12-11. Closed 25/26 Dec. **BAR MEALS:** L served all week. D served Mon-Sat 12-3 6-10. Av main course £8.
RESTAURANT: L served all week. D served all week 12-3 6.30-10. Av 3 course à la carte £15. **BREWERY/COMPANY:** Fullers.
PRINCIPAL BEERS: Fullers London Pride.
FACILITIES: Children welcome Garden: outdoor eating Dogs allowed

Pick of the Pubs

The Duke of Cambridge ♀
30 St Peter's St N1 8JT ☎ 020 7359 3066
🖹 020 7359 1877
e-mail: duke@singhboulton.co.uk

Arguably London's first gastro-pub that specialises in organic food, wines and beers, 'The Duke' - certified by the Soil Association - has established an impressive pedigree since its opening in 1998. Stylishly modernised, it can be found in a residential street close to the centre of Islington.

Blackboard menus change twice daily with uncomplicated seasonal menus in a modern European style. Its owners, Geetie and Esther combine their disparate skills with their passion for good food and a sound business ethic: there is no music nor TV, juke boxes or pin-ball machines. Genuine care goes into a weekday special of goats' cheese, tomato and olive tart with salad leaves and a choice of beverage: alternatives are likely to include white bean and chilli soup, roast pheasant with olive oil mash, prunes and red wine, and Roquefort served with fresh pear and oat-cakes. Fish dishes follow market prices and children's portions are always available by arrangement.
OPEN: 12-11 (Mon 5-11). Closed Dec 25-26, Jan 1.
BAR MEALS: L served Tue-Sun. D served all week 12.30-3 6.30-10.30. Av main course £11. **RESTAURANT:** L served Tues-Sun. D served all week 12.30-3 6.30-10.30. Av 3 course à la carte £15. **BREWERY/COMPANY:** Free House.
PRINCIPAL BEERS: Caledonian Golden Promise, Pitfield Singhboulton,. **FACILITIES:** Children welcome Children's licence Garden: patio, food served outside Dogs allowed

N16 London

The Fox Reformed
176 Stoke Newington Church Street N16 0JL
☎ 020 7254 5975 🖹 020 7254 5975
Wine bar at the heart of community life, with its own reading circle, backgammon club and wine tastings. Good food comes from regular and specials menus.

OPEN: 11-11 (Sun 12-10.30). Closed Mon lunch, 25-26 Dec & 1 Jan
BAR MEALS: L served Tue-Sun. D served all week 12-3 6.30-11. Av main course £10.
RESTAURANT: L served Tue-Sun D served all week 12-3 6.30-11. Av 3 course a la carte £25.
BREWERY/COMPANY: Free House.
PRINCIPLE BEERS: Marstons Pedigree, guest ales.
FACILITIES: Children welcome. Patio. Dogs allowed.
NOTES: Parking 56.

Seafood Pub of the Year for London 2002

♥ NEW

91 Junction Road, Archway N19 5QU
☎ 020 7272 1587 ▤ 020 7272 8023
e-mail: st.johnsarchwat@virgin.net
Dir: Archway or Tufnell Park tube

St John's

The ordinary exterior of this Victorian street corner drinking den is pure Albert Square. Yet, inside, the airy bar and spectacular dining room attract trendy North London thirty-somethings. Cross the threshold of this 19th-century pub and, like Dr Who's Tardis, the interior is unexpectedly spacious.

Beyond the long, attractively converted bar, owner Nic Sharpe has transformed the adjoining snooker hall into a vast, comfortable restaurant. Come to think of it, the tousle-haired Doctor with his multi-coloured scarf and young companions might not seem out of place amidst the idiosyncratic decor, solid oak and pine tables, deep red walls hung with a variety of modern works of art, and comfy settees around the fire.

Unless you're on first name terms with a couple of Time Lords, you'll need to book – and, in any case, be sure to come hungry. St John's portions are lavish, the food's very good, and the happy staff help generate a relaxed atmosphere that encourages diners to linger. Starters like celeriac and apple soup, ternine of rabbit, pork and black pudding with apricot chutney, spinach, red onion and blue cheese tart, or chargrilled sardines are chalked up on huge, daily-changing blackboards.

An interesting wine list accompanies the imaginative selection of modern British and global main courses. Ribeye steak with red onion potato cake and roast tomatoes, caramelised duck breast with celeriac rösti, apples and prunes, or pan-fried monkfish with saffron potato gratin, and lemon sole with pea and mint purée are typical. If you've space, dark chocolate and Amaretto tart, or strawberry and clotted cream fool with shortbread will round things off nicely.

England

Pick of the Pubs

St Johns 🍴 ♀ **NEW**
91 Junction Rd, Archway N19 5QU ☎ 020 7272 1587
📠 020 7272 8023
e-mail: st.johnarchway@virgin.net
AA/Fish Industry Seafood Pub of the Year for London 2002
See Pick of the Pubs on page 287

Pick of the Pubs

The Chapel ♀   Map B4
48 Chapel St NW1 5DP ☎ 020 7402 9220
📠 020 7723 2337
*Dir: By A40 Marylebone Rd & Old Marylebone Rd junc.
Off Edgware Rd by tube station*
A modern, open-plan gastro-pub, the Chapel derives its
name from nothing more than its location: bright and airy
within, its stripped floors and pine furniture create a
relaxed, informal atmosphere. Menus posted daily on the
chalk-boards have a trendy Anglo-Mediterranean feel.
On any given day expect starters such as chilled
watercress soup, fish croquette salad with roast vegetables,
and goats' cheese terrine with braised chicory. Follow with
wild mushroom tart, marlin steak with anchovy dressing,
and pan-fried bison with roast parsnips (for the less
adventurous, Brie-stuffed chicken breast), rounding off with
tarte tatin or banoffee pie.
OPEN: 12-11 (Sun 12-10.30). Closed Dec 24-Jan 4.
BAR MEALS: L served all week. D served all week 12-2.30
7-10. Av main course £10.
BREWERY/COMPANY: Punch Taverns.
PRINCIPAL BEERS: Fullers London Pride, Greene King IPA.
FACILITIES: Children welcome Garden: Dogs allowed in
garden only

Crown & Goose
100 Arlington Rd NW1 7HP ☎ 020 7485 2342
📠 020 7485 2342
Dir: nearest tube: Camden Town
One of the original gastro-pubs with a relaxed atmosphere
attracting a fashionable media crowd. The food has an Anglo-
Mediterranean flavour with bar snacks like potato skins and
ciabatta rolls, and daily specials often feature fish. Under new
management.
OPEN: 11-11 (Sun 12-10.30). Closed 25 Dec. **BAR MEALS:** L
served all week. D served all week 12-3 6-10. Av main course
£7.50. **RESTAURANT:** L served all week. D served all week 12-3
6-10. **BREWERY/COMPANY:** Scottish Courage.
PRINCIPAL BEERS: Fullers London Pride, Courage Directors.
FACILITIES: Children welcome patio

Pubs offering a good choice of
seafood on the menu.

Pick of the Pubs

The Engineer 🍴 ♀
65 Gloucester Av, Primrose Hill NW1 8JH
☎ 020 7722 0950   📠 020 7483 0592
e-mail: info@the-engineer.com
*Dir: Nearest tube: Camden Town/Chalk Farm, on the corner of
Princess Rd and Gloucester Ave*
Situated in a very residential part of Primrose Hill close to
Camden Market this unassuming corner street pub,
surprisingly built by Isambard Kingdom Brunel in 1841,
attracts a discerning dining crowd for imaginative and well
prepared food and its friendly, laid-back atmosphere.
Fashionably rustic interior with a spacious bar area, sturdy
wooden tables with candles, simple decor and changing
art exhibitions in the restaurant area. A walled, paved and
heated garden to the rear is extremely popular in fine
weather. A first-class, fortnightly-changing menu features
an eclectic mix of home-made, Mediterranean inspired
dishes and uses organic or free-range meats. Start,
perhaps, with split pea and ham soup with truffle oil and
home-made bread or Mozzarella with figs and Parma ham
with honey and grain mustard dressing, following on with
salmon fishcakes with coriander, chilli and ginger served
with roast garlic aïoli, whole roasted sea bass with coarse
chopped tapenade, or chargrilled organic sirloin steak
with herb butter. Excellent Sunday brunch.
OPEN: 9am-11pm. Closed 25-26 Dec, 1 Jan. **BAR MEALS:**
served all week. D served all week 12.30-3 7-10.30. Av main
course £7.50. **RESTAURANT:** L served all week. D served all
week 12.30-3 7-10.30. **BREWERY/COMPANY:** Bass.
PRINCIPAL BEERS: Fullers London Pride, Greene King Old
Speckled Hen. **FACILITIES:** Children welcome Garden: Food
served outside

The Globe
43-47 Marylebone Rd NW1 5JY ☎ 020 7935 6368
📠 020 7224 0154
Dir: Nr Baker St tube
Consisting of wine bar, main bar and restaurant, this 18th-
century, three storey pub, opposite Baker Street tube station,
was once frequented by such luminaries as Charles Dickens
and Alfred Lord Tennyson. Convenient for the Planetarium and
Madame Tussaud's.

Pick of the Pubs

The Lansdowne ♀
90 Gloucester Av, Primrose Hill NW1 8HX
☎ 020 7483 0409   📠 020 7586 1723
One of the earlier dining pubs in Primrose Hill, the
Lansdowne consists of a light, spacious bar area with
outdoor seating and a slightly more formal upper dining-
room with waiter service where tables can be reserved.
Decor remains simple without being minimal and unfussy,
modern food is the order of the day. The seasonal menu
offers such dishes as cod baked with clams, roast rack of
lamb with flageolet beans and mint, rigatoni with fennel,
garlic and Parmesan, and caldo verde (Portuguese potato,
cabbage and sausage soup). Desserts include pear and
almond tart, blackberry ice cream and apple crumble.
OPEN: 12-11 (Mon 6-11/Sun 12-4, 7-10.30). Closed Dec
25-26. **BAR MEALS:** L served Sun, Tue-Sat. D served all week
12.30-2.30 7-10. Av main course £8. **RESTAURANT:** D
served all week 7-10. Av 3 course à la carte £17. **BREWERY/
COMPANY:** Bass. **PRINCIPAL BEERS:** Woodfordes
Wherry, Bass. **FACILITIES:** Children welcome patio

The Lord Stanley
51 Camden Park Rd NW1 9BH ☎ 020 7428 9488
▤ 020 7209 1347
e-mail: winras@aol.com
In the mid-1990s, Lord Stanley was stripped and re-kitted in a gastro-pub garb that has served the pub well. At an open grill, food is produced in full view - a typically modern idiom producing, perhaps, chicken with mango salsa. Other dishes include seasonal soups, steaks, pasta or sausages with various accompaniments. Monday night jazz.
OPEN: 12-11. Closed 1 Jan. **BAR MEALS:** L served Tue-Sun. D served all week 12-3 7-10. Av main course £8. **RESTAURANT:** L served Tue-Sun. D served all week 12-3 7-10. **BREWERY/COMPANY:** Free House. **PRINCIPAL BEERS:** Greene King IPA, Brains, Youngs Special. **FACILITIES:** Children welcome Garden: outdoor eating Dogs allowed

The Queens
49 Regents Park Rd, Primrose Hill NW1 8XD
☎ 020 7586 0408 ▤ 020 7586 5677
Dir: Nearest tube station - Chalk Farm
With a balcony overlooking Primrose Hill, this Victorian pub is five minutes from Regents Park and the zoo. Specials may feature a tomato, garlic and okra pasta, and rainbow trout with almonds, while other main courses often include fried skate with tarragon butter, chargrilled steaks, and a zucchini and saffron risotto.
OPEN: 11-11. **BAR MEALS:** L served all week. D served all week 12-2.30 7-9.45. Av main course £8.95. **RESTAURANT:** L served all week. D served all week 12-2.30 7-9.45. Av 3 course à la carte £25. **PRINCIPAL BEERS:** Youngs. **FACILITIES:** Balcony, tables Dogs allowed

NW3 London

The Flask ♈
14 Flask Walk, Hampstead NW3 1HE ☎ 020 7435 4580
Dir: Nearest tube: Hampstead
Friendly local with a new landlord and a fascinating clientele - writers, poets, actors, tourists, locals, workmen, shopkeepers, office-workers, professors and medics. The name reflects the time when flasks were made on site for the healing waters of the Hampstead spa. Dishes range through home-made soup, pies and burgers, fish and chips, sausage and mash and various pastas.
OPEN: 11-11 (Sun 12-11). **BAR MEALS:** L served all week. D served Tue-Sat 12-3 6-8.30. Av main course £5.
continued

BREWERY/COMPANY: Young's. **PRINCIPAL BEERS:** Young's: Special, Winter Warmer. **FACILITIES:** Children welcome Dogs allowed on lead

The Holly Bush
Holly Mount, Hampstead NW3 6SG ☎ 020 7435 2892
Old-fashioned pub with lots of Edwardian fixtures and fittings. Set in the heart of Hampstead village. Guest ales.

Spaniards Inn ♈
Spaniards Rd, Hampstead NW3 7JJ ☎ 020 8731 6571
▤ 020 8731 6572
Formerly a toll house and the residence of the Spanish ambassador, this 16th-century pub is reputed to have been visited by Dick Turpin, Charles Dickens, Keats and Byron. Traditional pub fare is on offer, from filled baguettes and fish and chips to chargrilled tuna steak and rosemary lamb shanks.
OPEN: 11-11 (Sun 12-10.30). **BAR MEALS:** L served all week. D served Mon-Sat 12-10. Av main course £7.50. **RESTAURANT:** D served Mon-Sat 5-9. Av 3 course à la carte £15. **BREWERY/COMPANY:** Bass. Adnams Broadside, Coachhouse Dick Turpin. **FACILITIES:** Children welcome Children's licence Garden: outdoor eating, patio Dogs allowed. **NOTES:** Parking 50

Ye Olde White Bear
Well Rd, Hampstead NW3 1LJ ☎ 0207 4353758
Victorian pub with a Hampstead village feel and varied clientele. Friendly and traditional. "A country pub in the heart of London." Lots of theatrical memorabilia. All day bar food.

NW6 London

The Flask ♈
Highgate West Hill N6 6BU ☎ 020 8348 7346
▤ 020 8348 7506
17th-century former school in one of London's loveliest villages. Dick Turpin hid from his pursuers in the cellars, and TS Elliot and Sir John Betjeman enjoyed a glass or two of ale here. The interior is listed and includes the original bar with sash windows which lift up come opening time. Enjoy a glass of mulled wine or a malt whisky while you peruse the menu. Beer-battered cod, beef and horseradish burger, spaghetti and hand-made speciality sausages and mash are among the favourites.
OPEN: 11-11. Closed Dec 25. **BAR MEALS:** L served all week. D served all week 12-3 6-10. Av main course £5.50. **PRINCIPAL BEERS:** Bass, Rooster's Rooster, Adnams. **FACILITIES:** Children welcome Garden: Food served outside Dogs allowed Water, Doggie Snacks

---

THE MAKING OF BEER

The traditional ingredients of beer are water, barley malt, hops, yeast and ripe judgement. One traditional brewery's product will taste different from another's due to variations in the blending of ingredients and the timing of processes. It all starts with barley, malted in a kiln at the maltings: the higher the temperature, the darker the beer. The powdered malt is mixed with hot water to make a mash. How hot the mash is and how long it is allowed to stand will affect the taste and in the old days local spring water gave beer a distinctive local flavour. Burton upon Trent's reputation rested on the gypsum in the town's water. The liquid from the mash is boiled up with the hops - the more hops, the bitterer - and sugar is often added. Next the liquid is cooled and yeast is added to make it ferment. The 'green beer' was eventually run into casks to mature, but nowadays most beer is filtered, sterilised and carbonated. This is keg beer, stored in sealed containers and tasting more like bottled beers, which are put through the same processes.

NW8 London

Crocker's Folly
Map A4
24 Aberdeen Place, Maida Vale NW8 8JR ☎ 020 7286 6608
📠 020 7266 1543
Dir: Nearest tube station - Warwick Avenue
Named after its original owner, Mr Frank Crocker, who sadly jumped to his death on hearing that Marylebone Station (which he thought was going to be built opposite) was actually to be built in Marylebone, this is a remarkable pub. You can enjoy home-made pies, generous portions of hot roast joints, speciality sausages, and a fine selection of British cheeses.

OPEN: 11-11 (Sun 12-10.30). **BAR MEALS:** L served all week. D served all week 12-9. Av main course £6.50. **RESTAURANT:** L served all week. D served all week 12-2 6-8.
BREWERY/COMPANY: Regent Inns.
PRINCIPAL BEERS: Brakspear, Gales, Adnams.
FACILITIES: Children welcome Garden: Dogs allowed

Pick of the Pubs

The Salt House 🏵 🍷
63 Abbey Rd NW8 0AE ☎ 020 7328 6626
📠 020 7625 9168
Situated in a leafy area of St Johns Wood a compact and informal dining pub with a tiny open-plan kitchen that takes its food, though not itself, seriously. Expect nothing short of well prepared fresh ingredients along with decent pints of real ale and numerous house wines served by the glass with an occasional smile. Changed at every session there are set lunch options - split pea and bacon soup, black pudding, bacon and soft egg salad and lemon curd ice cream. Opt more ambitiously for provençale fish soup, roast pheasant with celeriac and quince and for afters chocolate pithivier.
Rather more choice in the evening produces terrine of skate with rivogote sauce and pan-fried duck livers with polenta before pan-fried brill with fennel purée, tagliatelle with ceps and gremolata and lamb rack with confit turnips and garlic. Rhubarb fool with shortbread, epoisses and cappuccino for those who wish to tarry a while longer.
OPEN: 12-11. Closed Dec 25-26 & Jan 1. **BAR MEALS:** L served all week. D served all week 12.30-3 6.30-10.30. Av main course £9. **RESTAURANT:** L served all week. D served all week 12-3 6.30-10.30. Av 3 course à la carte £18. Av 3 course fixed price £11.75. **BREWERY/COMPANY:** Greene King. **PRINCIPAL BEERS:** Greene King IPA, Abbot Ale,. **FACILITIES:** Children welcome Garden: outdoor eating, floral display

NW10 London

William IV Bar & Restaurant 🍷
786 Harrow Rd NW10 5JX ☎ 020 8969 5944
📠 020 8964 9218
Dir: Nearest tube: Ladbroke Grove or Kensal Green
Situated in a bustling, lively district of London, this popular and tastefully refurbished bar and restaurant is also a renowned venue for live music performances, art exhibitions and local theatre productions. An innovative menu offers a good range of bar food, including Greek salad tapenade and hoummus with grilled flatbread and Merguez sausage, chick pea and butter bean stew. Alternatively, try one of the quality main courses, perhaps sirloin steak with chips and vine tomatoes or gratinated leek and blue cheese cannelloni.
OPEN: 12-11 (Thu-Sat 12-12, Sun 12-10.30). Closed Dec 25.
BAR MEALS: L served all week. D served all week 12-4 7-8.30. Av main course £7. **RESTAURANT:** L served all week. D served all week 12-3 6-10.30. Av 3 course à la carte £18.
BREWERY/COMPANY: Free House.
PRINCIPAL BEERS: Fullers London Pride, Everards Equinox, Adnams. **FACILITIES:** Children welcome Garden: Food served outside Dogs allowed

SE1 London

The Anchor
Map C3
Bankside, 34 Park St SE1 9EF ☎ 020 7407 1577 & 7407 3003 📠 020 7407 0741
Standing on an old brewery site in the shadow of the Globe Theatre, this historic pub lies on one of London's most famous tourist trails. Samuel Pepys supposedly watched the Great Fire of London from this tavern in 1666 and Dr Johnson was a regular here, drinking with such acquaintances as Oliver Goldsmith and David Garrick. The river views are breathtaking and inside there is fading plasterwork, black beams and a maze of tiny rooms. Food is varied and appetising and the barbecue menu is especially popular.
OPEN: 11-11 (Sun 12-10.30). Closed Dec 24. **BAR MEALS:** L served all week 12-3. Av main course £5.95. **RESTAURANT:** L served all week. D served all week 12-2.30 6-9.30. Av 3 course à la carte £22. **PRINCIPAL BEERS:** Wadworth 6X, Courage Directors, Greene King IPA. **FACILITIES:** Children welcome Garden: riverside. **NOTES:** Parking 35

Young's & The Ram
The Ram Brewery has been producing Ale since 1581, which makes it the oldest site in Britain where beer has been brewed continuously. The Young connection began in 1831 when Charles Allen Young and his partner Bainbridge, bought the Ram. A Young has been in charge since then, and the current chairman is the great-great-grandson of C A Young. Some beer is still delivered locally by heavy horses. Brews include Triple 'A' (4.0%), Special London Ale (6.5%) and Waggle Dance (5.0%), which is brewed with honey. Double Chocolate Stout (5.0%) uses chocolate malt and real dark chocolate.

Pick of the Pubs

The Fire Station ◎ ♀   Map D2
150 Waterloo Rd SE1 8SB ☎ 020 7620 2226
📠 020 7633 9161
e-mail: firestation@regent-inn.plc.uk
Close to Waterloo Station, and handy for the Old Vic and
Imperial War Museum, this remarkable conversion of a
genuine early-Edwardian fire station has kept many of its
former trappings intact - possibly the high point being a
rear dining room facing the open kitchen. Simple, typically
trendy bar food offers ciabattas and sandwiches such as
soft Brie with smoked garlic chutney and blackened
chicken and tomato with sweet chilli salsa, as well as
salads and pasta. A full meal might start with foie gras
terrine or avocado Caesar salad, followed by tandoori
seared tuna loin or calves' liver with braised Puy lentils.
Imaginative midweek and Sunday set-price lunches.
OPEN: 11-11 (Sun 12-10.30). **BAR MEALS:** L served all
week. D served all week 12-5.30. Av main course £6.
RESTAURANT: L served all week. D served all week 12-2.45
5-11. Av 3 course à la carte £18.50. Av 2 course fixed price
£16.95. **BREWERY/COMPANY:** Regent Inns.
PRINCIPAL BEERS: Adnams Best, Brakspear, Youngs.
FACILITIES: Children welcome Patio

The George
77 Borough High St SE1 1NH ☎ 020 7407 2056
Impressive 17th-century coaching inn once owned by the
Great Northern Railway, but now preserved by the National
Trust. The single surviving wing recalls the days when galleried
coaching inns were a familiar sight in London. Brimming with
atmosphere, the place is a maze of bars full of dark oak,
benches and settles. Wholesome specials might include steak
and mushroom pie and traditional fish and chips.

The Market Porter   Map F3
9 Stoney St, Borough Market, London Bridge SE1 9AA
☎ 020 7407 2495 📠 020 7403 7697
Dir: Close to London Bridge Station
Traditional tavern serving a market community that has been
flourishing for about 1,000 years. Excellent choice of real ales.
Worth noting is an internal leaded bay window unique in
London. Menu includes beer battered fish and chips, sirloin
steak and Thai and Indian dishes.
OPEN: 6.30-8.30am & 11-11 (Sun 12-10.30). **BAR MEALS:** L
served all week. D served all week 12-2.30 5-8.30. Av main course
£4.95. **RESTAURANT:** L served Sun-Fri 12-2.30. Av 3 course à la
carte £13. **BREWERY/COMPANY:** Free House.
PRINCIPAL BEERS: Harveys Best, Courage Best, Youngs,
Brakspears.

The Old Thameside
St Mary Overy Wharf, Clink St SE1 9DG ☎ 020 7403 4243
Situated on Clink Street, site of the first prison in England, this
former spice warehouse is near to the Golden Hind,
Southwark Market and other attractions.

Room prices minimum single and minimum double
rates are shown. FR indicates family room

SE10 London

The Cutty Sark
4-7 Ballast Quay, Lassell St SE10 9PD
With commanding views of the Thames and the Millennium
Dome, this waterside pub has plenty of atmosphere, well kept
beers, wines by the glass and a wide selection of malt
whiskies. Busy at weekends.

Pick of the Pubs

North Pole Bar & Restaurant ♀
131 Greenwich High Rd, Greenwich SE10 8JA
☎ 020 8853 3020 📠 020 8853 3501
Located in a prime Greenwich location with views of the
Thames and the Millennium Dome, this fashionable bar
and restaurant, contrary to what the name suggests,
claims to be the hottest place in town. The kitchen exhibits
plenty of style and the menu transcends the overworked
gastropub image. From the top down, the North Pole has
a restaurant, a busy lounge bar, and a champagne and
cocktail bar in the basement. DJs at the weekends and live
jazz on a Thursday. Main courses include spatchcock
chicken with lentil and sweet potato mash, seafood
casserole with white beans and chilli, spinach and goats'
cheese pizzeta, and baked cod with basil and caper
fondant potatoes.
OPEN: 12-12. **BAR MEALS:** L served Mon-Sat 12-3. Av main
course £5. **RESTAURANT:** D served all week 6-11. Av 3
course à la carte £30. Av 3 course fixed price £17.
BREWERY/COMPANY: Free House **FACILITIES:** Patio

The Observatory Bar
56 Royal Hill, West Greenwich SE10 8RT
☎ 020 8692 6258
A bright modern bar serving traditional real ales and home-
cooked food - liver and bacon, steak and ale pie, pork goulash.

SE16 London

Mayflower Inn ♀
117 Rotherhithe St, Rotherhithe SE16 4NF
☎ 020 7237 4088 📠 020 7237 0548
Dir: Exit A2 at Surrey Keys roundabout onto Brunel Rd, 3rd L onto
Swan Rd, at T jct L, 200m to pub on R
Before embarking on her historic voyage to the New World, The
Mayflower was moored at the jetty you can still see today from
the patio of the Mayflower Inn - then known as The Spread
Eagle. Links with the voyage have been maintained through the
memorabilia now on display. Pub fare includes sausage and
mash, liver and bacon, and steak and Abbot Ale pie.
OPEN: Please Phone. **BAR MEALS:** L served Tue-Sat 12-3. Av
main course £7.50. **RESTAURANT:** L served Sun. D served Tue-
Sat 12-4 6.30-9. **BREWERY/COMPANY:** Greene King.
PRINCIPAL BEERS: Greene King Abbot Ale, IPA & Old Speckled
Hen. **FACILITIES:** Jetty over river, Food served outside

SE21 London

The Crown & Greyhound
73 Dulwich Village SE21 7BJ ☎ 020 8299 4976
📠 020 8693 8959
Turn of the century pub with spacious interior and family-
friendly policy. Daily changing menu. Previous guests have
included Dickens and Ruskin. Handy for walks through
Dulwich Park, or a visit to Dulwich Picture Gallery.

England

SW1 London

The Albert
Map D2
52 Victoria St SW1H 0NP ☎ 020 7222 5577 & 7222 7606
📠 020 7222 1044
Dir: Nearest tube - St James Park
Classic Grade II listed pub featuring original heavily etched windows, a division bell from the House of Commons and a staircase with prime ministers' portraits. Named after Queen Victoria's consort, Prince Albert, this is a truly Victorian pub with traditional dishes cooked on the premises. Wholesome menu offers roast turkey with cranberry and stuffing, roast leg of English pork, chicken Kiev, and prime roast rib of beef with Yorkshire pudding - among other popular dishes.
OPEN: 11-11 (Sun 12-10.30). Closed 25-26 Dec. **BAR MEALS:** L served all week. D served all week 11-10.30. Av main course £4.75.
RESTAURANT: L served all week. D served all week 12-9.30. Av 3 course à la carte £14.95. Av 3 course fixed price £14.95.
PRINCIPAL BEERS: Courage Directors & Best, Theakston Best.

The Buckingham Arms ♀
Map D2
62 Petty France SW1H 9EU ☎ 020 7222 3386
Dir: St James's Park tube
Known as the Black Horse until 1903, this elegant, busy Young's pub is situated close to Buckingham Palace. Popular with tourists, business people and real ale fans alike, it offers a good range of simple pub food, including the 'mighty' Buckingham burger, nachos with chilli, chicken ciabatta and old favourites like ham, egg and chips in its long bar with etched mirrors.
OPEN: 11-11 (Sat 12-5.30, Sun 12-5.30). **BAR MEALS:** L served all week. D served Mon-Sat 12-2.30 6-9. Av main course £3.95.
BREWERY/COMPANY: Young's. **PRINCIPAL BEERS:** Youngs Bitter, Special & Winter Warmer.

The Clarence
55 Whitehall SW1A 2HP ☎ 020 7930 4808
📠 020 7321 0859
e-mail: theclarence@hotmail.com
Dir: Between Big Ben & Trafalgar Sq
Haunted pub, situated five minutes' walk from Big Ben, the Houses of Parliament, Trafalgar Square and Buckingham Palace, with leaded windows and ancient ceiling beams from a Thames pier.

The Grenadier
Map B2
18 Wilton Row, Belgravia SW1X 7NR ☎ 020 7235 3074
📠 020 7235 3400
Regularly used for films and television series, once the Duke of Wellington's officers' mess and much frequented by King George IV, the ivy-clad Grenadier stands in a cobbled mews behind Hyde Park Corner, largely undiscovered by tourists. Outside is the remaining stone of the Duke's mounting block. Food ranges from traditional fish and chips and beef Wellington to steak and ale pie and queen scallops.
OPEN: 11-11 (Sun 12-10.30). **BAR MEALS:** L served all week. D served all week 12-3 6-9. Av main course £14. **RESTAURANT:** L served all week. D served all week 12-1.30 6-9.30. Av 3 course à la carte £20. **PRINCIPAL BEERS:** Courage Best & Directors, Marstons Pedigree, Greene King Old Speckled Hen. **FACILITIES:** Children welcome

Nags Head
Map B2
53 Kinnerton St SW1X 8ED ☎ 020 7235 1135
e-mail: bugsmoran@hotmail.com
Hidden away in a quiet mews near Harrods, this classic pub claims to be London's smallest, and has the feel of an old fashioned village local. Homely and welcoming with panelled front area and a narrow passage leading to an even smaller back bar. Look out for the old slot machines, including a 'What The Butler Saw' kinoscope, fed by old pennies from behind the bar. Decent food includes real sausages, chilli, mash and beans, and specials such as roasts and steak and mushroom pie.
OPEN: 11-11 (Sun 12-11). **BAR MEALS:** L served all week. D served all week 11-2.30. Av main course £5.
BREWERY/COMPANY: Free House No credit cards

The Orange Brewery ♀
Map C1
37-39 Pimlico Rd SW1 W8NE ☎ 020 7730 5984
Dir: Nr Sloane Sq or Victoria tube stations
The name comes from local associations with Nell Gwynne, a purveyor of oranges in her time. The building dates from 1790, and fronts onto an appealing square. Beers are produced in the cellar and, from the kitchen, traditional pub food like sausage and mash and fish and chips.
OPEN: 11-11 (Sun 12-10.30, bar food all day). **BAR MEALS:** L served all week. D served all week. Av main course £5.50.
PRINCIPAL BEERS: Orange SW1, Pimlico Passport, Pimlico Porter & Spiritual Reunion.

Westminster Arms
Storey's Gate SW1P 3AT ☎ 020 7222 8520
Busy Westminster pub crowded after work with staff from the Houses of Parliament which is just across the square. Wide choice of real ales. Traditional pub food.

Classic London Pubs
London prides itself on its pubs. They are an integral part of its history and heritage, and if you go for a leisurely stroll through the streets of the capital, you are never far from a classic boozer. Among London's gems are the Ye Olde Cheshire Cheese just off Fleet Street, the fascinating Jerusalem Tavern in a delightfully atmospheric corner of Clerkenwell, the Grenadier, which lies buried in a quiet cobbled mews near Hyde Park, and the Market Porter in Borough Market, a typical example of a traditional, unspoilt London pub. Further afield at Maida Vale lies Crocker's Folly, a wonderfully eccentric building distinguished by its exuberant architecture, while down the Thames at Wapping you'll find the historic Prospect of Whitby and the Town of Ramsgate.

SW3 London

Pick of the Pubs

The Coopers of Flood Street ♀   Map B1
87 Flood St, Chelsea SW3 5TB ☎ 020 7376 3120
🖹 020 7352 9187

Situated close to the Registry Office in Chelsea's quietly affluent back streets, this popular neighbourhood local is a regular venue for celebrations and celebrities. 'The Coopers' boasts a bright, vibrant atmosphere, and the stuffed birds and animals which decorate the bar give the place a character all of its own. A regularly-changing menu is served in the bar, as well as in the quieter upstairs dining area; choose from a selection of wholesome, freshly prepared dishes, with meat supplied from the pub's own organic farm. A typical day might bring spicy pumpkin soup, followed by chargrilled kangaroo rump with parsnip purée, home-reared bangers and mash with onion gravy, or asparagus tortellini in garlic and rocket sauce. Seafood options include garlic tiger prawns, chargrilled tuna steak with Oriental vegetables, or seared king scallops with endive salad. Leave room for a rich chocolate torte, or spotted Dick and custard.
OPEN: 11-11. **BAR MEALS:** L served all week. D served all week 12.30-3 6-10. Av main course £8.50.
BREWERY/COMPANY: Young's.
PRINCIPAL BEERS: Youngs Special, Smiles Bitter.

Pick of the Pubs

The Cross Keys 🐷 ♀
1 Lawrence St, Chelsea SW3 5NB ☎ 020 7349 9111
🖹 020 7349 9333
Now with new landlords, this fine Chelsea pub dates from 1765 and has a stylish interior including a Bohemian-style banqueting room and open-plan conservatory, restaurant and first-floor gallery. It has been a bolthole for the rich and famous since the 60s and is adorned with modern works of art. The food has a modern European flavour - chargrilled sirloin steak, pan-fried chicken breast with chorizo and crispy pancetta - but stays traditional on Sundays.
OPEN: 12-11 (Sun 12-10.30). Closed Dec 25-26, Jan1, Easter Mon. **BAR MEALS:** L served all week. D served all week 12-3 6-8. Av main course £8. **RESTAURANT:** L served Mon-Sat. D served Mon-Sat 12-3 6-8. Av 3 course à la carte £20. **PRINCIPAL BEERS:** Theakston Best, Courage Directors. **FACILITIES:** Children welcome

The Front Page
35 Old Church St, Chelsea SW3 5BS
☎ 020 7352 2908   🖹 020 7352 2908
Dir: Nearest tube-Sloane Square & Sth Kensington. (halfway between Albert Bridge & Battersea Bridge)
Backstreet pub nestled between the Thames and Kings Road in Chelsea. Offers a good meal, a chance to catch up on the big screen sporting action, or a quiet pint in front of the fire.

The Phene Arms
Phene St, Chelsea SW3 5NY ☎ 020 7352 3294
🖹 020 7352 7026
Dir: Nearest tubes: Sloane Square & South Kensington
Hidden away down a quiet Chelsea cul-de-sac, a short stroll from The Embankment, this welcoming neighbourhood pub has a charming roof terrace and large garden for summer alfresco eating. Food options range from Jerusalem salad, burgers and Cumberland sausage through to oven-baked cod and fillet steak.
OPEN: 11-11 (Sun 12-10.30). **BAR MEALS:** L served all week. D served all week 12-3 6-10. Av main course £6.95.
RESTAURANT: L served all week. D served all week 12-3 6-10.
BREWERY/COMPANY: Free House.
PRINCIPAL BEERS: Adnams Bitter & Broadside, Courage Best & Directors, Greene King Old Speckled Hen. **FACILITIES:** Garden

SW4 London   Map C2

The Belle Vue NEW
1 Clapham Common Southside SW4 7AA
☎ 020 7498 9473   🖹 020 7627 0716
Bistro-style food and a relaxing atmosphere are among the attractions of this popular dining pub overlooking Clapham Common. Expect scrubbed wooden panelling, comfortable sofas, modern art around the walls and a short blackboard menu listing home-made fish soup, roast cod and scallop gratin, slow-roasted lamb shank with winter vegetables and mash, and bruschetta with grilled vegetables, goats' cheese and pesto.
OPEN: Mon-Fri 5-11, Sat 12.30-1, Sun 12.30-10.30. Closed 4-5 days at Christmas. **BAR MEALS:** L served Sat & Sun. D served all week 12.30-4 6.30-10.30. Av main course £8.
BREWERY/COMPANY: Free House

The Windmill on the Common ★ ★ ★ ♀
Clapham Common South Side SW4 9DE ☎ 020 8673 4578
🖹 020 8675 1486
Dir: Nearest tube: Clapham Common
There was a windmill on this site in 1655 but it has long gone. In later years the building became a popular watering hole for crowds returning to London from the Epsom Derby and it even appears in the background of a famous painting, now in the Tate Gallery. Inside are two spacious bars, a conservatory and a back room with a roof in the shape of a flattened Byzantine dome. Dishes range from steak and ale pie and sausage and mash, to pasta carbonara and chicken satay with peanut sauce. Separate oak-panelled restaurant and hotel accommodation.
OPEN: 11-11 (Sun 12-10.30). **BAR MEALS:** L served all week. D served all week 12-2.30 7-10. Av main course £5.25.
RESTAURANT: D served Mon-Sat 7-10. Av 3 course à la carte £16. **BREWERY/COMPANY:** Young's.
PRINCIPAL BEERS: Youngs Bitter, Special & Winter Warmer, Youngs Triple A. **FACILITIES:** Children welcome Children's licence Garden: food served outdoors Dogs allowed Water bowls. **NOTES:** Parking 16. **ROOMS:** 29 bedrooms 29 en suite s£80 d£90

England

SW6 London

Pick of the Pubs

The Atlas  ♀
16 Seagrave Rd, Fulham SW6 1RX ☎ 020 7385 9129
▤ 020 7386 9113
e-mail: richardmanners@msn.com
Dir: *2mins walk from West Brompton underground*
Mediterranean-inspired cooking has proven a big success
at the Manners brothers' busy pub just a tack or two from
Earl's Court's Boat Show: just breeze in for anything you
like from tapas, crostini and risotto to roast meats,
casseroles and fresh fish. To go with this are famously
traditional ales and up to two dozen wines from old and
new worlds alike in a laid back atmosphere that has
caught the eye with customers from near and far.

This is not to decry food that takes itself seriously in
representative main dishes such as Fabada Asturiana -
pork and bean stew with chorizo and butter beans - and
provincial French beef daube with brandy, thyme and
button mushrooms. Fish arrives market-fresh: roast whole
sea bass is served with couscous, butternut squash,
almonds, dates and coriander, and rounded off with
cucumber, yoghurt and mint salsa.

Chef George Manners came to prominence in the early
days of London 'gastro-pubs' and remains currently
abreast - or even ahead - of a trend that is thankfully
dropping its unappealing label.

OPEN: 12-11 (Sun 12-10). Closed Dec 24-Jan 1, Easter.
BAR MEALS: L served all week. D served all week 12.30-3
7-10.30. Av main course £8.50.
BREWERY/COMPANY: Free House.
PRINCIPAL BEERS: Theakstons Best, Greene King, Charles
Wells Bombardier, Wadworth 6X. **FACILITIES:** Children
welcome Garden: patio, outdoor eating , heated

The Imperial Arms
577 Kings Rd SW6 2EH ☎ 020 7736 8549
▤ 020 7731 3780
e-mail: imperial@fulham.co.uk
Mid 19th-century food pub in one of London's most famous
and fashionable streets. Vibrant and spacious inside, with
wooden floors, striking features, and a lively and varied
clientele. Paved terrace at the back. Wild boar sausages with
bubble and squeak and onion gravy, grilled goats', cheese
salad, spinach and cheese in puff pastry, various burgers and a
selection of snacks feature on the popular menu.

OPEN: 11-11. Closed BHs. **BAR MEALS:** L served all week.
D served all week 12-2.30 7-9.30. Av main course £6.50.
BREWERY/COMPANY: Free House.
PRINCIPAL BEERS: Wells Bombardier, Hogs Back TEA.
FACILITIES: Garden: outdoor eating, patio Dogs allowed
garden only

Pick of the Pubs

The White Horse ♀
1-3 Parson's Green, Fulham SW6 4UL
☎ 020 7736 2115 ▤ 020 7610 6091
Dir: *140 mtrs from Parson's Green tube*
A coaching inn has existed here since at least 1688 and its
ribald history since has been well documented. Today's
product has advanced a little: in fact it's unique. The White
Horse cellarman is a City analyst by day and his ales have
received the highest accolades. In the menu's margin,
drink suggestions accompany most dishes: pinot blanc
with rocket, roast tomato and Parmesan salad; Harvey's
Sussex with pork sausages, mash and pickled red
cabbage; Big House Red with duck, Seville orange,
beetroot and spinach. Good value evening meals are
served in the new Coach House restaurant. Dubbed the
"Sloaney Pony" it's good for Sunday brunch, summer
barbeques and beer festivals.
OPEN: 11-11 (Sun 12-10.30). **BAR MEALS:** L served all
week. D served all week 12-3.30 6-10. Av main course
£8.75. **RESTAURANT:** L served all week. D served all week
12-3.30 6-11. Av 3 course à la carte £20.
BREWERY/COMPANY: Bass.
PRINCIPAL BEERS: Adnams Extra, Bass, Harveys Sussex
Best, Highgate Mild. **FACILITIES:** Children welcome
Garden: patio, outdoor eating,

SW7 London

The Anglesea Arms ♀
15 Selwood Ter, South Kensington SW7 3QG
☎ 020 7737 7960
The Anglesea Arms, dating from 1827, is one of the few
privately owned pubs in West London, serving real ales and
real foods every lunchtime and evening in the bar. Traditional
English fare is also available in the clubby dining room, with its
mahogany-panelled walls and leather chairs. Thai specialities
are featured Tuesdays and Wednesdays, and in summer
customers can eat out on the terrace.
OPEN: 11-11 (Sun 12-10.30). **BAR MEALS:** L served all week
12-3 6.30-9.30. Av main course £7.50. **RESTAURANT:** L served
all week. D served all week 12-3 6.30-9.30. Av 3 course à la carte
£7.50. **BREWERY/COMPANY:** Free House.
PRINCIPAL BEERS: Fullers London Pride, Brakspear, Adnams,
Wadworth 6X. **FACILITIES:** Children welcome Garden: patio,
food served outside Dogs allowed

Room prices minimum single and minimum double
rates are shown. FR indicates family room

OPEN: 11-11. Closed Sat, Sun & BH
BAR MEALS: L served Mon-Fri.
D served Mon-Fri 12-3 6-10.
Av main course £10.70.
RESTAURANT: L served Mon-Fri.
D served Mon-Fri 12-3 6-10.
Av 3 course a la carte £21.50.
BREWERY/COMPANY:
Free House.
PRINCIPAL BEERS: Marston's
Pedigree, Wells Bombardier.
FACILITIES: Children welcome.
Dogs allowed - bar only.

The Swag and Tails

10/11 Fairholt Street SW7 1EG
☎ 020 7584 6926 📠 020 7581 9935
e-mail: swag&tails@mway.com
Dir: In a residential mews off Brompton
Road. Nearest tube: Knightsbridge

Pretty, flower-adorned Victorian building tucked away in a quiet residential mews in Knightsbridge village, just two minute's stroll from Harrods. A civilised and peaceful retreat away from the hustle and bustle for modern pub food cooked with flair and imagination.

Licensee Annamaria Boomer-Davies has successfully created an informal, neighbourhood pub-restaurant over the past eleven years, attracting shoppers, business people and well-heeled local residents for quality pub food served in a warm, relaxing and decidedly civilised atmosphere. Pop in for a pint of Wells Bombardier and peruse the daily papers with a decent Club sandwich at the bar or look to the interesting, constantly-changing blackboard menu for something more substantial. Open fires original panelling, pine tables on a stripped wooden floor and full-length windows with attractive 'swag and tailed' curtains set the scene in which to savour Mediterranean-inspired dishes prepared from seasonal produce.

From appetisers like Cajun-crumbed squid with lemon aïoli, rocket salad with chargrilled haloumi and glazed figs, and tomato, pepper and goat's cheese soup, the menu may also feature chargrilled calves' liver with crispy pancetta mash and sage jus, braised lamb shank with spiced couscous, pecorino and parsley risotto roast and fresh Billingsgate fish - monkfish with creamed mussels and spaghetti, herb-crusted haddock with lemon, bacon and white bean cassoulet. Lighter bites include blinis with smoked salmon, sour cream and chives and a classic burger with fries. For pudding try the pear tart with cinnamon mascarpone.

Good list of wines arranged by grape variety with good tasting notes; 12 by the glass including champagne.

SW7 London continued

Pick of the Pubs

Swag and Tails ◉ 🍸   Map B2
10/11 Fairholt St SW7 1EG ☎ 020 7584 6926
📠 020 7581 9935
e-mail: swag&tails@mway.com
See Pick of the Pubs on page 295

SW8 London

Pick of the Pubs

The Artesian Well 🐾 🍸 NEW
SW8 3JF ☎ 020 7627 3353 📠 020 7627 2850
Blue-painted building on the corner of St John and
Compton streets that has seen a recent makeover by the
owners of the Cross Keys in Chelsea (qv). Floorboards, old
scrubbed wooden furniture and light painted wall and
brickwork characterise the unpretentious informality of
this small local bar-cum-restaurant. Downstairs the
Aquarium Bar, kitted-out with fish tanks, dark grey
banquettes and subdued lighting, offers a contrasting
contemporary tone. The eclectic, bistro-style menu has
distinct Mediterranean influences; try roasted cod with
pea and mint risotto with crispy chorizo or corn-fed
chicken wrapped in Parma ham with blue cheese and
balsamic grilled vegetables. Alternatives include lamb,
tomato and basil sausages with herb mash and gravy and
ribeye steak with green peppercorn sauce, with chocolate
tart and cardomom kumquat for pudding. In short, a
buzzy, trendy and informal dining venue.
OPEN: 12-3 6-11. **BAR MEALS:** L served all week. D served
all week 12-3 6-8

London Pride
London ranked second only to Burton-
upon-Trent as an early brewing centre and its
famous names have included Watney, Meux,
Charrington and Truman, but the most durable is
Whitbread. The company was founded by a
Bedfordshire man named Samuel Whitbread in 1742.
He used to sit up four nights a week at his brewing,
reading the Bible at intervals, and he ended up a rich
landowner, MP for Bedford and a generous
philanthropist who had his portrait painted by Sir
Joshua Reynolds before dying in 1796. His only son,
another Samuel, who had no head for business, was a
radical MP and close ally of Charles James Fox, who
committed suicide in 1815. The family has
continued in the trade, and the founder's
great-great-great-great-grandson
became Chairman in 1984.

The Masons Arms 🍸
169 Battersea Park Rd SW8 4BT ☎ 020 7622 2007
📠 020 7622 4662
Dir: Opposite Battersea Park BR Station
Opposite Battersea Park Station, more neighbourhood local
with tempting food than gastro-pub. Devoid of games
machines and juke-box, it also has open fires in winter and a
summer dining terrace. Things heat up on Friday and Saturday
nights, when DJ's play. Try blackeye bean, salt cod and prawn
fritters; Caesar salad with anchovy and parmesan; mint and
olive lamb burger open sandwich.
OPEN: 12-11. **BAR MEALS:** L served all week. D served all week
12-4 6-10. Av main course £8. **BREWERY/COMPANY:** Free
House. **PRINCIPAL BEERS:** Brakspear, Wadworth 6X.
FACILITIES: Children welcome Children's licence Garden:
outdoor eating, patio/terrace Dogs allowed

SW10 London

Pick of the Pubs

The Chelsea Ram 🐾 🍸
32 Burnaby St SW10 0PL ☎ 020 7351 4008
📠 020 73490885
e-mail: pint@chelsearam.com
Dir: Nearest tube - Earls Court
A busy neighbourhood gastro-pub just off the beaten
track, close to Lots Road and Chelsea Harbour, whose
distinct emphasis is on fresh produce including fresh
market fish and meat from Smithfield. Modern dishes are
interesting and eclectic, exemplified by starters of tomato
and green herb risotto with parmesan shavings, goats'
cheese and asparagus tartlet and smoked salmon
'properly garnished'. Blackboards will display the best
from the markets, alongside poached salmon with
vegetable nage, corn-fed chicken breast with woodland
mushrooms and tarragon jus, and Aberdeen Angus ribeye
steaks with proper chips. Roast Sunday lunch.
OPEN: 11-11 (Sun 12-10.30). Closed 25-26 Dec, 1 Jan.
BAR MEALS: L served all week. D served all week 12.30-3
7-10. Av main course £9. **RESTAURANT:** L served all week.
D served all week 12.30-3 7-10. Av 3 course à la carte £18.
BREWERY/COMPANY: Youngs.
PRINCIPAL BEERS: Youngs Bitter, Special & Winter Warmer,
Smiles Best Bitter.

The Sporting Page 🍸   Map A1
6 Camera Place SW10 0BH ☎ 020 7349 0455
📠 020 7352 8162
Smart Chelsea pub offering good quality food - modern British
and European - with friendly service. It's the largest retail
outlet in London for Bollinger Champagne, with all bottle sizes
up to jeroboam. Popular features are the terrace in summer
and large screen TV for major sporting events.
OPEN: 11-11 (Sun 12-10.30). **BAR MEALS:** L served all week.
D served all week 12-2.30 7-10. Av main course £7.50.
BREWERY/COMPANY: Front Page Pubs Ltd.
PRINCIPAL BEERS: Shepherd Neame Spitfire.
FACILITIES: Children welcome terrace Dogs allowed

England

Pick of the Pubs

The Battersea Boathouse ♀ NEW
2 Lombard Rd SW11 3RQ ☎ 020 7924 6090
Following a successful few years at the Perch & Pike at
South Stoke in Oxfordshire, the Gully's have, surprisingly,
moved into London for their new pub venture. But what a
site they chose! The Boathouse enjoys a superb Thames-
side position overlooking Chelsea Harbour and the sun-
trap riverside patio, replete with cotton parasols and
heaters, makes the most of the view. Inside, the newly
refurbished bar and dining areas are light and airy with a
Mediterranean feel.
   Other than its fantastic location, the appeal is the range
of modern, brasserie-style food listed on the main menu
and daily-changing blackboards. For a light snack, try the
salmon fishcake with rocket salad, pasta carbonara,
chargrilled chicken sandwich or sugar-cured beef fillet
with Parmesan onions, or for something more substantial
look to the board for roast cod fillet with garlic mash and
wild mushroom sauce, chargrilled sea bass with chilli
vinaigrette on wilted green, red Thai duck and pumpkin
curry with jasmine rice. Adnams ale on tap, interesting list
of wines.
OPEN: 12-3 (Open all day Sat-Sun) 5.30-11.
BAR MEALS: L served all week. D served all week 12-2
6.30-9.30. Av main course £8. **RESTAURANT:** L served all
week. D served all week 12-2 6.30-9.30. Av 3 course à la carte
£20. **BREWERY/COMPANY:** Free House.
PRINCIPAL BEERS: Adnams. **FACILITIES:** Children
welcome Garden: food served outside

The Castle
115 Battersea High St SW11 3HS ☎ 020 7228 8181
Dir: *Nearest tube - Clapham Junction*
Ivy-covered pub tucked away in 'Battersea Village', with rugs
and rustic furnishings on bare boards inside, and an outside
enclosed patio garden. From home-made soup and cod in
beer batter, the menu extends to beef stew, salmon fishcakes,
Creole fish stew, and organically-reared roast lamb.
OPEN: 12-11 (Sun 12-10.30). Closed 25-26 Dec. **BAR MEALS:** L
served all week. D served Mon-Sat 12-3 7-9.45. Av main course
£7.95. **BREWERY/COMPANY:** Youngs.
PRINCIPAL BEERS: Youngs Bitter, Special & Smiles.
FACILITIES: Garden: Dogs allowed

Duke of Cambridge ♀
228 Battersea Bridge Rd SW11 3AA ☎ 020 7223 5662
▤ 020 7801 9684
This modernised village-style pub makes a comfortable and
relaxing midweek meeting place for an eclectic mix of locals.
Things liven up a bit at weekends, with a Saturday brunch
menu and traditional Sunday roasts. The interesting range of
dishes includes chunky Irish stew, crisp belly of pork, charred
lemon and thyme chicken, sea bass with roast vegetables, and
the hearty Duke's Brunch.
OPEN: 11-11. **BAR MEALS:** 12-2.30 7-9.30. Av main course £9.
RESTAURANT: L served all week. D served all week 12-2.30
7-9.30. Av 3 course à la carte £20.
BREWERY/COMPANY: Youngs. **PRINCIPAL BEERS:** Youngs
Bitter & Special. **FACILITIES:** Children welcome Garden: patio,
outdoor eating, BBQ Dogs allowed

The Bull's Head ♀
373 Lonsdale Rd, Barnes SW13 9PY ☎ 020 8876 5241
e-mail: jazz@thebullshead.com
Internationally famous modern jazz and blues pub situated
beside the Thames in Barnes. Music has been performed
nightly here for over 40 years and continues to draw jazz
lovers from miles around. Light and airy main bar offering
Young's ales on tap and decent selection of wines; 34 by the
glass.
OPEN: 11-11. **BAR MEALS:** L served all week. D served all week
12-3 6-11. Av main course £4.50. **RESTAURANT:** D served all
week 6-11. Av 3 course à la carte £10.
BREWERY/COMPANY: Youngs. **PRINCIPAL BEERS:** Youngs
Special, Bitter, Tripple AAA. **FACILITIES:** Children welcome
Garden: Patio, food served outside Dogs allowed

Pick of the Pubs

The Alma Tavern 🛏 ♀
499 Old York Rd, Wandsworth SW18 1TF
☎ 020 8870 2537 ▤ 020 8488 6603
e-mail: drinks@thealma.co.uk
Dir: *Wandsworth town station opposite pub*
Conveniently located across from Wandsworth Station and
close to Young's brewery, the Alma is a classic Victorian
tavern with a very distinctive green-tiled façade and fine
etched-glass windows. The bar's high ceiling, decorative
hand-painted mirrors open fires, simple furnishings, daily
papers and lively conversation are all very traditional, but
there's a decidedly continental atmosphere to the airy
central room and rag-washed rear dining-room. This extends
to the imaginative food on offer, which includes organic
meats from their own livestock farm in Surrey and home-
made breads and pasta. Besides good value sandwiches,
moules marinière and chips, warm goats' cheese salad and
smoked haddock crostini, the daily-changing menu may list
tagliatelle with scallops in a lemon and thyme butter sauce,
Moroccan beef with steamed couscous, smoked haddock
fishcake with bok choy and poached egg and traditional
sausages and mash. Tip-top Young's ales, good house wines
(20 by the glass) and excellent coffee.
OPEN: 11-11. Closed 25-26 Dec. **BAR MEALS:** L served all
week. D served Mon-Sat 12-10.30. Av main course £8.50.
RESTAURANT: L served all week. D served Mon-Sat
12-10.30. Av 3 course à la carte £15.
BREWERY/COMPANY: Youngs.
PRINCIPAL BEERS: Youngs PA, SPA, Triple A, March Hare.
FACILITIES: Children welcome Dogs allowed Water

The Ship Inn 🛏 ♀
Jew's Row SW18 1TB ☎ 020 8870 9667 ▤ 020 8874 9055
e-mail: drinks@theship.co.uk
Dir: *Wandsworth Town BR station nearby*
Situated next to Wandsworth Bridge on the Thames, the Ship
has been extended and modernised over the years and now
exudes a lively, bustling atmosphere. Saloon bar and extended
conservatory area lead out to a large beer garden and in the
summer months the outside bar is open for business. There is
a popular restaurant and all-day food is chosen from a single
menu, with the emphasis on free-range produce from the
landlord's organic farm. Swordfish steak, cod and sea bass are
typical fish dishes. *continued*

OPEN: 11-11 (Sun 12-10.30). **BAR MEALS:** L served all week. D served all week 12-10.30. Av main course £7. **RESTAURANT:** L served all week. D served all week 12-10.30. Av 3 course à la carte £15. **BREWERY/COMPANY:** Young's. **PRINCIPAL BEERS:** Youngs: PA, SPA, Triple A, Winter Warmer. **FACILITIES:** Children welcome Garden: patio, outdoor eating, Dogs allowed Water

W1 London

The Argyll Arms   Map C4
18 Argyll St, Oxford Circus W1V 1AA ☎ 020 7734 6117
Dir: Nearest tube - Oxford Circus
A tavern has stood on this site since 1740, but the present building is mid-Victorian and is notable for its stunning floral displays. There's a popular range of sandwiches and the hot food menu might offer vegetarian moussaka, beef and Guinness pie, chicken and leek pie, haddock and lasagne. **OPEN:** 11-11. Closed 25 Dec. **BAR MEALS:** L served all week. D served Mon-Sat 11-7. Av main course £5.95.
BREWERY/COMPANY: Bass. **PRINCIPAL BEERS:** Tetley, Bass, Adnams, Fullers London Pride. **FACILITIES:** Children welcome

Freedom Brewing Co NEW   Map C3
WC2H 9LD ☎ 020 7287 5267 🖥 020 7287 2729
e-mail: info@freedombrew.com
Dir: 5 min walk from Oxford Circus Tube, the micro brew bar is half way down Carnaby street
The second of the Fulham-based Freedom Brewing Company's new micro-brew bars, this popular watering hole opened in 1999, taking advantage of the growing demand for fresh, hand-crafted beer. The bar sells a range of six ales made on the premises, as well as offering a varied choice of freshly prepared salads, sandwiches, tortilla wraps and main dishes. Expect fish and chips, baked chicken with steamed greens, Thai spiced mussels, and lamb steak with grilled vegetables. **OPEN:** 11-11. Closed 25-26 Dec, 1 Jan. **BAR MEALS:** L served Mon-Sat. D served Mon-Sat 12-5 6-10. Av main course £7.25.
PRINCIPAL BEERS: Freedom Beers. **FACILITIES:** Children welcome

French House
49 Dean St, Soho W1D 5BG ☎ 020 7437 2799
🖥 020 7287 9109
Self-proclaimed bohemian bar populated by actors, writers and artists. Turn off your mobile phone, browse the works of local artists, and enjoy a wide range of beers, spirits and wines.

The Glassblower
42 Glasshouse St W1R 5RH ☎ 020 7734 8547
🖥 020 7494 1049
Ideally placed for visiting the shops and theatres, this traditional pub is in the heart of the West End. Under new management.

Red Lion
No 1 Waverton St, Mayfair W1X 7FJ ☎ 020 7499 1307
🖥 020 7409 7752
e-mail: gregpeck@redlionmayfair.co.uk
Dir: Nearest tube - Green Park
Built in 1752, The Red Lion is one of Mayfair's most historic pubs. Originally used mainly by 18th-century builders, the clientele is now more likely to be the rich and famous of Mayfair, yet the friendly welcome remains.

W2 London

Pick of the Pubs

The Cow Saloon Bar & Dining Rooms 🐄 Ⴤ
89 Westbourne Park Rd W2 5QH ☎ 020 7221 5400
☎ 020 7727 8687
e-mail: thecow@thecow.freeserve.co.uk
Dir: Nearest tubes - Royal Oak & Westbourne Park
Close to the 500-year-old drovers' route to Smithfield Market - from which its unusual name is derived - it is hard to determine how seriously The Cow takes itself. It offers "fine dining, oysters, Guinness and cigars" on a menu that promises to give the house a good name. Eating, in fact, cheek-by-jowl with noisy neighbours with service from seemingly hard-pressed waiting staff rather gives the lie to its aspirations. Native and Rock oysters, moules marinières, fish soup with rouille and Gruyère and pints of prawns with mayonnaise are scarcely of a bovine persuasion: look instead for sausage, mash and onion gravy or rare bavette steak with first-class fat chips and anchovy butter to redress the balance somewhat. Guinness and beef stew, sea bass with lentils and salsa verde, and a giant seafood platter (a "Cow" special!) are about as imaginative as it gets. Wash down with good London beers or fairly priced house wines if the Guinness is not your bag; - and come early to bag a decent table of your choosing, where a better bet is to make a bee-line for the upper dining-room. **OPEN:** 12-11. Closed 25 Dec. **BAR MEALS:** L served all week. D served all week 12.30-3.30 6.30-10.30. Av main course £8. **RESTAURANT:** L served all week. D served all week 12.30-3.30 6.30-10.30. Av 3 course à la carte £35. **BREWERY/COMPANY:** Free House.
PRINCIPAL BEERS: Fullers ESB, Fullers London Pride.

The Prince Bonaparte Ⴤ
80 Chepstow Rd W2 5BE ☎ 020 7313 9491
🖥 020 7792 0911
A large Victorian pub, airy and open plan, offering modern British cooking with Eastern, African and Mediterranean influences. Typical dishes are grilled breast of chicken with olive mash and mushroom sauce, Cumberland sausages with onions, mash and gravy, lamb curry with basmati rice, and grilled ribeye steak with green peppercorn sauce and pommes anna. **OPEN:** 12-11 (Tue 5.30-11, Sun 12-10.30). Closed 25-26 Dec, 1 Jan. **RESTAURANT:** L served Wed-Mon. D served all week 12-3.30 6.30-10.30. Av 3 course à la carte £15. **BREWERY/COMPANY:** Bass. **PRINCIPAL BEERS:** Fullers London Pride. **FACILITIES:** Children welcome Dogs allowed on a leash only

The Westbourne Ⴤ
101 Westbourne Park Villas W2 5ED ☎ 020 7221 1332
🖥 020 7243 8081
e-mail: ollydna@aol.com
Classic Notting Hill new-wave pub/restaurant favoured by bohemian clientele, including a sprinkling of celebrities. Sunny terrace is very popular in summer. Tempting, twice-daily-changing menu is listed on a board behind the bar and might include skate with capers, Morrocan stew, duck breast salad and rabbit with mustard. **OPEN:** 11-11 (Mon 5.30-11 only) (Sun 12-10.30). Closed 24 Dec-5 Jan. **BAR MEALS:** L served Tue-Sun. D served all week 12.30-3.30 7-9.30. Av main course £8. **RESTAURANT:** L served all week. D served all week 12.30-3.30 7-9.30. Av 3 course à la carte

continued

£20. Av 3 course fixed price £10. **BREWERY/COMPANY:** Free House. **PRINCIPAL BEERS:** Boddingtons, Greene King Old Speckled Hen. **FACILITIES:** Children's licence Dogs allowed

W5 London

The Wheatsheaf
41 Haven Ln, Ealing W5 2HZ ☎ 020 8997 5240
Dir: 1m from A40 junction with North Circular
Large Victorian pub with rustic appearance inside. Wooden floors, panelled walls, beams from an old barn, and real fires in winter. Various Mexican and Thai specialities, plus traditional English dishes.

W6 London

Pick of the Pubs

Anglesea Arms 🏵 🐾 ♀
35 Wingate Rd W6 0UR ☎ 020 8749 1291
🖷 020 8749 1254
e-mail: Fievans@aol.com
Traditional corner pub, with a Georgian facade, basic decor, real fires and a relaxed, smoky atmosphere, that positvely bustles with eager diners. The attraction is the the range of simple, robust dishes, including, perhaps, shellfish minestrone with tarragon pesto, oysters with shallot relish, John Dory with spinach and cep butter sauce, and stuffed saddle of rabbit.
OPEN: 11-11 (Sun 12-10.30). Closed 24-31 Dec.
BAR MEALS: L served all week. D served all week 12.30-2.45 7.30-10.45. Av main course £8. **RESTAURANT:** L served all week. D served all week 12.30-2.45 7.30-10.45.
BREWERY/COMPANY: Free House.
PRINCIPAL BEERS: Courage Best & Directors, Marstons Pedigree, Greene King Old Speckled Hen, Fullers London Pride. **FACILITIES:** Children welcome

The Thatched House ♀ NEW
115 Dalling Rd W6 0ET ☎ 0208 7486174
e-mail: thatchedhouse@establishment.ltd.uk
Sister pub to the Chelsea Ram (qv), the Thatched House, in a leafy Hammersmith backwater, is not thatched at all - nor do the Mediterranean-style features of a 'modern British' menu evoke the English countryside. Cosmopolitan gastro-pub fare delivers instead all one expects of roasted red pepper soup, seared scallops with ginger and stir-fried vegetables and American-style doughnuts with coffee cream and chocolate sauce. English breakfast salad is borrowed from Rhodes, the man: grilled black pudding and sausage with bacon and poached egg on crisp salad leaves. Youngs' beers on tap; some 20 wines-by-glass on the list; art for sale on the walls: trendy.
OPEN: 11-3 5.30-11. **BAR MEALS:** L served all week. D served all week 12-2.30 7-10. Av main course £9.50.
BREWERY/COMPANY: Youngs. **PRINCIPAL BEERS:** Youngs Bitter, Special, AAA. **FACILITIES:** Garden: Food served outside Dogs allowed

W8 London

The Churchill Arms
119 Kensington Church St W8 7LN ☎ 020 7727 4242
Dir: Off A40 (Westway). Nearest tube-Notting Hill Gate
Thai food is the speciality at this traditional 200-year-old pub with strong emphasis on exotic chicken, beef and pork dishes. Try Thai rice noodles with ground peanuts, spicy sauce and a

choice of pork, chicken or prawns (Kwaitiew Pad Thai), or special Thai roast duck curry served with rice (Kaeng Ped Phed Yang). This Oriental feast notwithstanding the Churchill Arms has many traditional British aspects including oak beams, log fires and an annual celebration of Winston Churchill's birthday.
OPEN: 11-11 (Sun 12-10.30). **RESTAURANT:** L served all week. D served Mon-Sat 12-2.30 6-9.30.
BREWERY/COMPANY: Fullers. **PRINCIPAL BEERS:** Fullers London Pride, ESB & Chiswick Bitter. **FACILITIES:** Children welcome Garden: Conservatory with exotic butterflies and plants Dogs allowed

W10 London

The North Pole ♀
13-15 North Pole Rd W10 6QH ☎ 020 8964 9384
🖷 020 8960 3774
A former run-down local transformed by large new windows and bright decor into a modern 'gastro-pub' - now under new ownership. Expect leather sofas, armchairs, daily papers, a good range of wines by the glass and a lively atmosphere in the bar. Separate bar and restaurant menus continue to show real interest, dishes are modern in style and simply described. 'Small Plates' may include seared scallops with pineapple salsa, chicken Caesar salad and rocket and Parmesan salad. 'Main Flavours' include ribeye steak with roasted potatoes and asparagus risotto - reports on the new regime please.
OPEN: 12-11 (Sun 12-10.30). **BAR MEALS:** L served all week. D served all week 12-10. Av main course £7.50. **RESTAURANT:** L served all week. D served all week 12-10. Av 3 course à la carte £20. **BREWERY/COMPANY:** Free House.
PRINCIPAL BEERS: Fullers London Pride. **FACILITIES:** Patio, food served outside Dogs allowed

Pick of the Pubs

Paradise by Way of Kensal Green
19 Kilburn Ln, Kensal Rise W10 4AE ☎ 020 8969 0098
🖷 020 8960 9968
e-mail: seeyou@theparadise.co.uk
There's been a pub on this site since the 17th century, though the farming community that supported the former 'Plough' has long since vanished. The present building dates from 1895, and the unusual name derives from the last line of G K Chesterton's poem 'The Rolling English Road'. Bare boards, bric-a-brac and wrought iron chandeliers now provide a Bohemian setting for artists, musicians and actors; but don't drop in for a bar snack as the mainly fixed-priced menus at this self-styled gastropub don't encourage spontaneity. With weekly live jazz, special events and even weddings, the food at this lively venue measures up manfully. Expect smoked chicken and pink grapefruit salad, Italian-style sausages with red cabbage and Parmesan mash, Scotch beef fillet and garlic roast potatoes, sea bass with saffron rice, or tuna steak with spinach mash and green salsa. There are daily blackboard specials and desserts, too.
OPEN: 12-11 (Sun 12-10.30). Closed 25 Dec & Jan 1.
BAR MEALS: L served all week. D served all week 12-4 7.30-11. Av main course £12.50. **RESTAURANT:** L served all week. D served all week 12.30-4 7.30-11. Av 3 course à la carte £18.50. Av 2 course fixed price £15.
BREWERY/COMPANY: Free House.
PRINCIPAL BEERS: Shepherd Neame Spitfire.
FACILITIES: Children welcome Children's licence Garden: outdoor eating, patio Dogs allowed Water.

England

Pick of the Pubs

The Ladbroke Arms ♀
54 Ladbroke Rd W11 3NW ☎ 020 7727 6648
▤ 020 7727 2127
Situated in one of London's trendier districts, close to Holland Park and fashionable Notting Hill, renowned for its street market, swanky restaurants and film location image. A relaxed chatty atmosphere inside attracts a broad spectrum of regular custom, including the well-heeled young. Sitting areas include a popular front courtyard and a split-level dining area to the rear. Meals are not outlandishly gastro and the menu changes daily with highlighted specials. Try an appetising starter, perhaps six rock oysters or steak tartare, followed by one of the imaginatively prepared main courses which might include lamb with lentils and garlic purée, pan-fried sea bass with artichoke and sage risotto, and ribeye steak with chorizo, pimento, olive and basil butter. Leave room for chocolate fondant with vanilla ice cream and blood orange and champagne jelly with honey madelines.
OPEN: 11-3 5.30-11 (Sat-Sun & Summer months11-11). Closed Dec 25. **BAR MEALS:** L served all week. D served all week 12-7. Av main course £11. **RESTAURANT:** D served Same as bar. **BREWERY/COMPANY:** Free House. **PRINCIPAL BEERS:** Wadworth 6X, Everards Tiger, Greene King Abbot Ale, Courage Directors.

Pick of the Pubs

The Havelock Tavern ♀
57 Masbro Rd, Brook Green W14 0LS ☎ 020 7603 5374
▤ 020 7602 1163
Dir: Nearest tubes: Shepherd's Bush & Olympia
Located between Shepherds Bush and Olympia and renowned as one of the first gastro-pubs, the popular Havelock Tavern occupies a spacious, sunny corner site with the emphasis very much on an eclectic, ever-changing menu presented in comfortable, informal surroundings. Large wooden tables, dark floorboards and a broadly-based clientele help give the place atmosphere and a distinctive character. Food is reasonably priced and the menu changes twice daily. It's often busy at lunchtime with working diners having much time to relax and savour their meal, and though it's equally crowded in the evening, most regulars are far more relaxed and stress-free. Try the yellow chicken curry with basmati rice, chargrilled veal escalope with Parmesan mash, green beans and salsa verde, or seared scallops with shaved fennel salad, rocket and lemon.
OPEN: 11-11 (Sun 12-10.30). Closed Xmas 5 days. **BAR MEALS:** L served all week. D served all week 12.30-2.30 7-10. Av main course £9.50. **BREWERY/COMPANY:** Free House. **PRINCIPAL BEERS:** Brakspear, Marston's Pedigree, Wadworth 6X. **FACILITIES:** Garden: Food served outside No credit cards

Cittie of Yorke ♀   Map E4
22 High Holborn WC1V 6BS ☎ 020 7242 7670
▤ 020 7405 6371
A pub with a history, dating from 1695 and located next to the gatehouse to Gray's Inn. There is a large cellar bar and the panelled front bar featuring an original chandelier and portraits of illustrious locals, including Dickens and Sir Thomas More. A variety of sandwiches and six hot dishes are prepared each day, such as sausage hotpot, and pork chop in apple and cider sauce.
OPEN: 11.30-11 (closed Sun). **BAR MEALS:** L served Mon-Sat. D served Mon-Sat 12-9. Av main course £4.50.
BREWERY/COMPANY: Samuel Smith.
PRINCIPAL BEERS: Samuel Smith Old Brewery.
FACILITIES: Children welcome

The Lamb ♀   Map E4
94 Lamb's Conduit St WC1N 3LZ ☎ 020 7405 0713
▤ 020 7405 0713
Dir: Nearest tube: Holborn or Russell Square
Built in 1729, this traditional pub is where Dickens supposedly enjoyed a drink. Unspoilt Victorian gem of a pub, with very rare etched glass snob screens, dark polished wood, and original sepia photographs of music-hall stars who performed at the old Holborn Empire. Home-cooked bar food may include steak and ale pie, lambs liver and bacon, fish and chips, sausage and mash, or ham baguettes.
OPEN: 11-11 (Sun 12-4, 7-10.30). **BAR MEALS:** L served all week. D served Mon-Sat 12-2.30 6-9. Av main course £5.25.
BREWERY/COMPANY: Young's. **PRINCIPAL BEERS:** Youngs (full range). **FACILITIES:** patio, outdoor eating

The Museum Tavern
Museum St WC1B 3BA ☎ 020 7242 8987
Built long before the British Museum, which is just across the road, this historic inn first opened its doors in 1723. Real ales from the pump and wines by the glass. Food available all day.

Map D4

Freedom Brewing Company NEW
41 Earlham St WC2H 9LD ☎ 020 7240 0606
▤ 020 7240 4422
e-mail: info@freedombrew.com
Dir: 5 min walk from Leicester Square or Covent Garden tube station
Launched in 1995, the Freedom Brewing Company is Britain's first dedicated lager micro-brewery, establishing a reputation for quality beer and lager among London's more discerning drinkers. The Earlham Street bar in Covent Garden was originally part of the Soho Brewing Company and when it opened, it was the new company's first branded micro-brew bar. Interesting restaurant and bar menus offering grilled chicken, rocket salad and bacon, seafood hotpot, calves' liver with bacon and mash, steak sandwich, fish and chips, and a daily-changing risotto.
OPEN: 11-11. Closed 25-26 Dec, 1 Jan. **BAR MEALS:** L served Mon-Sat. D served Mon-Sat 12-2 6-10. Av main course £7.25.
PRINCIPAL BEERS: Freedom Beers. **FACILITIES:** Children welcome

The Lamb and Flag
33 Rose St, Covent Garden WC2E 9EB ☎ 020 7497 9504
Covent Garden: pub well loved by Londoners meeting after work. Low-ceiling back bar with an open fire. Plenty of ales and whiskies.

Prince of Wales
150-151 Drury Ln, Covent Garden WC2B 5TB
☎ 020 7836 5183 & 7240 9935 ▤ 020 7240 6900
Opened in 1852, this pub is a useful venue for those visiting the many theatres in London's West End. Covent Garden is close by for shopping and an abundance of street entertainment.

The Seven Stars
53 Carey St WC2A 2JF ☎ 020 7242 8521
▤ 020 7404 3403
Shakespeare was living in London when The Seven Stars was constructed in 1602. First frequented by Dutch sailors, the pub's clientele is now drawn from the nearby Law Courts, and 'Spy' cartoons of eminent lawyers decorate the walls. Owned by the author/publican Roxy Beaujolais, this highly individual free house serves Adnams ales, and home-made dishes cooked by Roxy himself. Expect hot pastrami sandwiches, corned beef hash, omelettes, and kedgeree.
OPEN: 11-11 (Winter Mon-Tue 9pm close). Closed 25 Dec.
BAR MEALS: L served all week. D served all week. Av main course £5. **BREWERY/COMPANY:** Free House

MERSEYSIDE

BARNSTON   Map 08 SJ28

Fox and Hounds
Barnston Rd CH61 1BW ☎ 0151 6487685
Dir: From M53 J4 take A5137 to Heswell. R to Barnston on B5138
Situated in the conservation area of Barnston, this pub displays an assortment of 1920s/30s memorabilia, featuring a collection of policemen's helmets. Traditional pub fare is on offer, including a range of platters, sausage and mash, hot pot, lasagne, and chilli, along with daily specials - notably fish dishes.
OPEN: 11-11 (Sun 12-10.30). **BAR MEALS:** L served all week 12-2. Av main course £4.95. **BREWERY/COMPANY:** Free House. **PRINCIPAL BEERS:** Websters Yorkshire Bitter, Ruddles County, Theakston XB & Best. **FACILITIES:** Children welcome Garden: patio, outdoor eating Dogs allowed on leads at all times. **NOTES:** Parking 60 No credit cards

LIVERPOOL   Map 08 SJ39

Everyman Bistro ♀
9-11 Hope St L1 9BH ☎ 0151 708 9545 ▤ 0151 708 9545
e-mail: info@everyman.co.uk
Dir: Town centre. Bistro in basement of Everyman Theatre, between the two cathedrals
The bistro under the Everyman Theatre (which it now owns), popular with the theatrical and artist communities. Dishes are made from scratch using prime ingredients; there's a good vegetarian choice and the sweets are legendary. The menu changes twice a day, and after 8pm there are 'Small Eats', the place becomes more of a candlelit pub, with cask beers and wines by the bottle or glass.
OPEN: 12-12 (Thur 1am Fri-Sat 2am). Closed BHs.
BAR MEALS: L served Mon-Fri 10-2. Av main course £6.
RESTAURANT: L served Mon-Sat. D served Mon-Sat 12-8 4.30-8.

Av 3 course à la carte £11. **BREWERY/COMPANY:** Free House. **PRINCIPAL BEERS:** Cains, Timothy Taylor, Castle Eden, Wadworth 6X. **FACILITIES:** Children welcome Children's licence

Ship & Mitre
133 Dale St L2 2JH ☎ 0151 236 0859 ▤ 0151 236 0855
e-mail: shipandmitre.co.uk
Dir: 5mins from Moorfields underground, 5mins from Lime St Station
Award-winning pub in the heart of bustling Liverpool. Built in the art deco style of the 1930s and boasting the city's largest and most varied range of independent or micro-brewery ales; regular beer festivals. Choose something from the frequently-changing menu, perhaps chicken and mushroom pie or stuffed aubergine. There is always a selection of sausages, provided by a local butcher.
OPEN: 11.30-11 (Sat 12.30-11, Sun 12.30-10.30). Closed Dec 25-26, Jan 1. **BAR MEALS:** L served Mon-Fri 11.30-2.30. Av main course £2.75. **BREWERY/COMPANY:** Free House. **PRINCIPAL BEERS:** Chadwicks Finest, Hydes Bitter, Roosters. **FACILITIES:** Dogs allowed No credit cards

NORFOLK

ATTLEBOROUGH

Griffin Hotel
Church St NR17 2AH ☎ 01953 452149
Town centre inn dating back to the 16th century. Bedrooms.

BAWBURGH   Map 07 TG10

Kings Head ☜ ♀
Harts Ln NR9 3LS ☎ 01603 744977 ▤ 01603 744990
Dir: From A47 W of Norwich take B1108 W
There are beautiful views of the River Yare and the old mill from this village pub, which dates from 1602. Log fires make for a warm welcome in winter and in summer customers enjoy the pretty garden. A good range of real beer is offered and a varied menu featuring fresh fish dishes (crayfish cocktail, pan-fried cod, roasted halibut), steaks and Thai chicken curry.
OPEN: 11.30-11 (Sun 12-10.30). **BAR MEALS:** L served all week. D served all week 12-2.30 7-9.45. **RESTAURANT:** L served all week. D served all week 12-2 7-9.45.
BREWERY/COMPANY: Free House.
PRINCIPAL BEERS: Adnams, Woodforde's Wherry, Green King IPA, Courage Directors. **FACILITIES:** Children welcome Garden: Beer Garden:, Outdoor eating Dogs allowed Water provided.
NOTES: Parking 100

BINHAM   Map 07 TF93

Chequers Inn ♦♦♦
Front St NR21 0AL ☎ 01328 830297
Dir: On B1388 between Wells next the Sea & Walsingham
Located between the picturesque yachting harbour at Blakeney and the village of Walsingham, famous for its shrine, the 17th-century Chequers is ideally placed for exploring North Norfolk's scenic coastline and the famous Stiffkey salt marshes. Popular for good food and real ales, served throughout the beamed bars which feature open fires. Extensive menu highlighting local game, including venison casserole and game pie. A variety of curry dishes, local meats, steaks and grills are also available. Pine-furnished bedrooms are equipped with many useful extras.   *continued*

OPEN: 11.30-3 (Sun 12-3, 7-10.30) 5.30-11. Closed 25 Dec.
BAR MEALS: L served all week. D served all week 12-2 6-9. Av main course £6. **RESTAURANT:** L served all week. D served all week 12-2 6-9. Av 3 course à la carte £15.
BREWERY/COMPANY: Free House.
PRINCIPAL BEERS: Greene King Abbot Ale, & IPA, Woodforde's Wherry, Adnams. **FACILITIES:** Garden: outdoor eating.
NOTES: Parking 20. **ROOMS:** 2 bedrooms 2 en suite s£30 d£50

BLAKENEY   Map 07 TG04

The Kings Arms 🕭 ♀
Westgate St NR25 7NQ ☎ 01263 740341   📄 01328 711733
Grade II listed building on the wonderfully atmospheric North Norfolk coast. An ideal spot for walking and birdwatching. Regular ferry trips to unique seal colony and world-famous bird sanctuaries. Large beer garden with swings for children. Menu offers locally caught fish including cod, haddock, plaice and trout. Other food options include jacket potatoes, sandwiches, steaks and a vegetarian selection.
OPEN: 11-11. **BAR MEALS:** D served 12-9.30pm. Av main course £6. **BREWERY/COMPANY:** Free House.
PRINCIPAL BEERS: Greene King Old Speckled Hen, Woodfordes Wherry, Marstons Pedigree, Adnams Best Bitter.
FACILITIES: Children welcome Garden: outdoor eating Dogs allowed Water. **NOTES:** Parking 10. **ROOMS:** 7 bedrooms 7 en suite s£30 d£50

Pick of the Pubs

White Horse Hotel 🕭 ♀
4 High St NR25 7AL ☎ 01263 740574
📄 01263 741303
e-mail: whitehorse4@lineone.net
Dir: From A148 (Cromer to King's Lynn rd) turn onto A149 signed to Blakeney.
Set in the National Trust marshes with fine views across the harbour, this 17th-century coaching inn, built of traditional brick-and-flint and set around the old courtyard and stables, has a deserved reputation for both its accommodation and its food. Comprehensive bar menus have an unsurprisingly strong aquatic bias - herring roes on toast, plaice or cod in beer batter with home-cut chips and home-made fisherman's pie - supplemented by a blackboard of daily specials that embraces salmon fillet with mussel and thyme sauce and sea bass grilled with caramelised onions. Salads, sandwiches and children's items all play their part here.
   Dinner in the restaurant overlooking a walled garden, by comparison, takes a more serious if well-tried route that offers poached chicken and crayfish salad with sweet pepper mayonnaise and fricassee of monkfish, leeks and wild mushrooms followed by traditional treacle tart. Alternatives include tomato, spinach and Brie flan, roast partridge with bread sauce and bacon and fillet of beef with roasted butternut squash.
OPEN: 11-3 (Sun 12-3, 7-10.30) 6-11. Closed 4-19 Jan.
BAR MEALS: L served all week. D served all week 12-2 6-9. Av main course £6.50. **BREWERY/COMPANY:** Free House. **PRINCIPAL BEERS:** Adnams, Bass.
FACILITIES: Children welcome Garden: courtyard, patio, outdoor eating Dogs allowed garden only, Water.
NOTES: Parking 14. **ROOMS:** 10 bedrooms 10 en suite s£30 d£60

BLICKLING   Map 07 TG12

Pick of the Pubs

The Buckinghamshire Arms
Blickling Rd NR11 6NF ☎ 01263 732133
📄 01263 732133
Dir: From Cromer (A140) take exit at Aylsham onto B1354
There's a strongly traditional feel at this late 17th-century coaching inn, right by the gates of the National Trust's spectacular Blickling Hall. The inn was originally built for house guests and their servants, and Anne Boleyn is said to wander in the adjacent courtyard and charming garden. But there's nothing ethereal about the night's strong local following, or the solid furniture and wood-burning stoves in the lounge bar and restaurant. House guests are still welcome in three charming four-poster bedrooms, two of which enjoy majestic views of Blickling Hall. The same menu is served throughout and makes good use of fresh local ingredients. Start with soup, or deep-fried whitebait, before moving on to rabbit pie, baked chicken breast, beef and beer casserole, or poached salmon. Favourite puddings include treacle tart and banoffee pie.
OPEN: 11-3.30 6-11. Closed 25 Dec. **BAR MEALS:** L served all week. D served all week 12.30-2 7.30-9. Av main course £7.
RESTAURANT: L served all week. D served all week 12.30-2 7.30-9. Av 3 course à la carte £14.
BREWERY/COMPANY: Free House.
PRINCIPAL BEERS: Reepham, Adnams, Woodforde's Blickling.
FACILITIES: Garden: outdoor eating. **NOTES:** Parking 60.
ROOMS: 3 bedrooms 1 en suite s£25 d£40

BRANCASTER   Map 07 TF74

Pick of the Pubs

The White Horse ⊛ ★ ★ 🕭 ♀
Main Rd, Brancaster Staithe PE31 8BY
☎ 01485 210262   📄 01485 210930
e-mail: whitehorse.brancaster@virgin.net
AA/Sea Fish Industry Authority Seafood Pub of the Year for Central & East Anglia 2002.
See Pick of the Pubs on page 305

BRISTON   Map 07 TG03

The John H Stracey ♦♦♦ ♀
West End NR24 2JA ☎ 01263 860891   📄 01263 862984
e-mail: Johnhstracey@btinternet.com
15th-century inn originally known as the Three Horseshoes. Renamed after the boxer. Plenty of character inside, with log fire and copper features. Norfolk's spectacular coast is close by. Wide choice of good food includes home-cooked ham, steak and ale pie, chicken and prawn curries, and lemon sole.
OPEN: 11-2.30 6.30-11. **BAR MEALS:** L served all week. D served all week 12-2.30 6.30-10. Av main course £6.50.
RESTAURANT: L served all week. D served all week 12-2.30 6.30-10. Av 3 course à la carte £11.50. **BREWERY/COMPANY:** Free House. **PRINCIPAL BEERS:** Greene King Old Speckled Hen. **FACILITIES:** Children welcome Garden: outdoor eating. **NOTES:** Parking 30. **ROOMS:** 3 bedrooms 1 en suite s£19.50 d£39

The Hoste Arms, Burnham Market

THE HOSTE ARMS, ◎ ◎
★ ★ BURNHAM MARKET
The Green PE31 8HD.
Tel: 01328 738777
Directions: off B1155, 5m W of
Wells-next-the-Sea
*Handsome 17th-century
coaching inn overlooking the
green and church in a
delightful village close to
coastal bird reserves and
Holkham Hall. Noted for
innovative food, tip-top East
Anglian ales and first-class
accommodation.*
Open: 11-11. Bar Meals: 12-2
7-9. Children welcome in
conservatory. Garden & patio.
Parking.
(see page 304 for full entry)

A delightful short stroll from charming small market town of Burnham Market. Varied and interesting, it explores the breezy salt marsh and its rich birdlife, and visits the hamlets of Burnham Norton and Burnham Overy Staithe.

Turn left out of the inn, then left again along Herring Lane. Gently climb, passing a byway on the left and descend, soon to take the footpath left, signed to Burnham Norton. Follow the defined path along the left-hand field edge, with salt marsh and sea views, and bear right along a track to the main road.

Cross straight over and follow the lane through Burnham Norton. Where the lane veers sharp left, turn right along a waymarked track passing a cottage. At a junction of paths, bear right signed Burnham Overy Staithe and head towards the windmill along a raised path, affording views over open grassland and salt marsh. In 1/4 mile (0.4km) join with the Peddars Way

(coast path) converging from the left. Turn left here and follow the embankment if you wish to explore the marshes in search of the birdlife, and return to this point.

Keep right, cross a stream and waymarked stile, then keep to the worn path across the field (windmill right) to the road. Follow the field edge left and soon cross the road (fingerpost) to join a wide track heading inland. At a lane, turn right, then in 1/4 mile (0.4km), where it turns sharp right in Burnham Overy Town, keep ahead along the grassy path and enter the churchyard.

Exit by the main gate, turn right along the B-road and soon pick up the pavement. Pass a converted mill, then just beyond the Burnham Market sign, turn right into Friars Lane. Turn left before the school, signed to Norton Church, then at the next road turn left to pass the splendid round-towered church. Gently climb to Herring Lane, turn left and retrace steps back to the inn.

Distance: 4 miles (6.4km)
Map: OS Landranger 132
Paths: field and coastal paths, tracks, metalled lanes
Terrain: farmland, coast, village streets
Gradient: gently undulating

Walk submitted by:
David Hancock

Burnham Overy Staithe

Pick of the Pubs

The Hoste Arms ⊛ ⊛ ★ ★ 🍴 ⍙
The Green PE31 8HD ☎ 01328 738777
🖨 01328 730103
e-mail: thehostearms@compuserve.com
Dir: Signposted off B1155, 5m w of Wells-next-the-Sea

One of the truly great inns of Britain, the 17th-century Hoste Arms has over the last 12 years expanded from a rather seedy village pub, in danger of ruination by unsympathetic brewers, to today's classy small hotel with a classically egalitarian atmosphere, thanks to the enthusiasm of dedicated owners, Paul and Jeanne Whittome. Restored are the non-food village bar where local fishermen may literally drop in with their catch and added are several interlinked and air-conditioned dining areas serviced by a kitchen of prodigious output. Beers, wines, digestifs and malt whiskies are legion and meticulously chosen to accompany all manner of good food. Starters and light lunches list salmon and chilli fishcakes with sweet and salt spinach, crisp duck confit with honey-glazed parsnips, and Hoste Caesar salad in a choice of sizes. Main courses may add pan-fried monkfish with mild ginger sauce and Szechuan chilli beef with stir-fried Oriental vegetables, rounding off perhaps with lemon sponge and crème anglaise. In the tranquil restaurant dinner runs the gamut of fresh fish, seasonal game and high quality butchers' meats of sufficient variety to assuage the most demanding appetite. Comfortable, individually designed bedrooms.
OPEN: 11-11. **RESTAURANT:** L served all week. D served all week 12-2 7-9. **BREWERY/COMPANY:** Free House.
PRINCIPAL BEERS: Woodforde's Wherry, Greene King Abbot Ale, & IPA, Adnams Broadside. **FACILITIES:** Garden: patio, outdoor eating Dogs allowed Dog bowls, Blanket if requested. **NOTES:** Parking 30. **ROOMS:** 28 bedrooms 28 en suite s£64 d£86

See Pub Walk on page 303

Pick of the Pubs

The Lord Nelson
Walsingham Rd PE31 8HN ☎ 01328 738241
e-mail: lucy@nelsonslocal.co.uk
An unspoilt gem tucked away in a sleepy village and named after England's most famous seafarer, who was born in the rectory in 1758. Step inside this 350-year-old cottage, with its huge high-backed settles, old brick floors, traditional atmosphere and Nelson memorabilia, and sample Greene King and Woodforde ales tapped from the cask in the cellar room, or a dram of the popular rum concoction called 'Nelson's Blood', which is made to a secret recipe. Enjoyable bar food ranges from good pub favourites - baguettes, ploughman's lunches, breaded plaice - to Brancaster mussels in white wine and cream, lambs' liver and mash, home-made steak and ale pie, mixed grill and fresh local crab (in season) listed on a blackboard. Warm welcome to families - good-sized garden with climbing frame, wooden play area and basketball net for youngsters to let off steam. Monthly live jazz and blues in winter.
OPEN: 11-3 6-11 (Sun 12-3,7-10.30). **BAR MEALS:** L served all week. D served all week 12-2 7-9. Av main course £10.50.
BREWERY/COMPANY: Greene King.
PRINCIPAL BEERS: Greene King Abbot Ale, & IPA, Woodforde's Nelsons Revenge. **FACILITIES:** Children welcome Garden: outdoor eating Dogs allowed on lead, water. **NOTES:** Parking 25

George & Dragon Hotel 🍴 ⍙
High St NR25 7RN ☎ 01263 740652 🖨 01263 741275
Dir: On coast road (A149). Centre of village
Classic Edwardian inn, with high ceilings and terracotta features, overlooking the marshes to the sea. The first naturalist trust was formed here in 1926, and the inn still has strong links with the bird reserve. A local smokehouse supplies delicacies in addition to those cooked on the premises, including local seafood, samphire in season, and trio of Norfolk lamb cutlets in port and redcurrant gravy.
OPEN: 11-3 (Winter 11.30-2.30 6.30-11) 6-11. **BAR MEALS:** L served all week. D served all week 12-2 7-8.45. Av main course £6. **RESTAURANT:** L served all week. D served all week 12-2 7-8.45. Av 3 course à la carte £13. **BREWERY/COMPANY:** Free House.
PRINCIPAL BEERS: Greene King-IPA, Abbot Ale, Old Speckled Hen. **FACILITIES:** Children welcome Garden: Beer garden, outdoor eating Dogs allowed Not bar during meals.
NOTES: Parking 30. **ROOMS:** 9 bedrooms 6 en suite s£40 d£44 FR£72.50-£90

Woodforde's Norfolk Ales

Woodforde's Norfolk Ales has a fascinating history. The brewery takes its name from James Woodforde, a renowned bon viveur and clergyman whose revealing diary of life between 1758 and 1802 is seen as a unique record of rural England at that time. Woodforde acquired something of a reputation for good food and good ale - which he often brewed himself. The brewing company was established in 1981 and soon afterwards moved to a converted stable complex at Erpingham. By 1988 the demand for Woodforde's expanding range of ales had outgrown their second premises and a group of farm buildings at Woodbastwick eventually became the brewery's new home. With its own visitor centre, Woodforde's is one of Norfolk's largest and most successful breweries. Among the more popular beers are Nelson's Revenge (4.5%), named after Britain's most famous seafaring hero who was born at Burnham Thorpe in 1758, and the award-winning Wherry Bitter (3.8%), which takes its name from the unique shallow-draught sailing craft built for trading on the waterways of Norfolk in the early part of the 20th century. Tours are available.

OPEN: 11.30-11 (Sun 12-10.30)
Closed 25 Dec eve.
BAR MEALS: L served all week.
12-2. Av main course £8
RESTAURANT: L served all week.
D served all week 12-2 7-9.
Av 3 course a la carte £17.
BREWERY/COMPANY:
Free House.
PRINCIPAL BEERS: Adnams
Southwold, Greene King IPA &
Abbot Ale, guest ale (summer).
FACILITIES: Children welcome.
Garden: terrace, outdoor eating.
Dogs allowed.
NOTES: Parking 45.
ROOMS: 8 bedrooms 8 en suite
s£50-£65 d£60-£90 FR£75-£105.

The White Horse

Main Rd, Brancaster Staithe PE31 8BW
☎ 01485 210262 📄 01485 210930
e-mail: whitehorse.brancaster@virgin.net
Dir: mid-way between Hunstanton &
Wells-next-the-Sea on A419

Stunning views across glorious, wildlife-rich coastal marshland can be savoured from the airy conservatory restaurant, summer sun deck and the elegant bedrooms at this stylish dining pub, situated on the Norfolk Coastal Path.
Seafood Pub of the Year for Central & East Anglia 2002

Scrubbed pine tables, high-backed settles and cream painted walls all combine to create a bright, welcoming atmosphere. From the conservatory restaurant with its adjoining sun deck, diners can watch the sea retreating from the salt marsh, leaving a jumble of little boats stranded high and dry with their masts pointing crazily at the wide East Anglian sky. And, if you just can't tear yourself away from the view, eight tastefully furnished bedrooms, each with their own terrace (perfect for that summer alfresco breakfast!), look out over the water towards Scolt Head Island.

The pub's reputation for food rests on its four local chefs, all of whom have wide experience outside Norfolk. Local seafood is a particular speciality, and freshly harvested local mussels, oysters and samphire often appear on the menu. Typical starters include tempura of red mullet with sweet pepper and vanilla salsa, chargrilled langoustines with Asian dressed rocket and guacamole, and grilled belly pork with noodles and oyster sauce.

Moving on, an extensive wine list accompanies main courses like seared mahi-mahi with chargrilled vegetables and sun-dried tomato tapenade, and baked cod with white bean risotto and chilli sauce. Pan-roasted duck with red wine jus, and chargrilled T-bone steak with salad and fries add to the variety, whilst vegetarians can choose imaginative options like roasted tomato and wild mushroom tart, or pumpkin tortelli with mange-tout cream.

England

COLKIRK　　　　　　　　　　Map 07 TF92

The Crown 🛏 ♀
Crown Rd NR21 7AA ☎ 01328 862172 🖹 01328 863916
Dir: *2m from B1146 Fakenham-Dereham rd*
Comfortable country pub with open fires, a sunny terrace,
comfortable country furnishings, and a lively atmosphere.
There's an emphasis on good food, from filled baguettes to
steaks or roast duck with Cumberland sauce. Fresh seafood
from the specials board includes deep-fried wholetail scampi,
battered cod, chips and peas, grilled plaice and herb butter,
and fresh crab with salad.
OPEN: 11-2.30 6-11 (Sun 12-2.30, 7-10.30). **BAR MEALS:** L
served all week. D served all week 12-1.45 7-9.30. Av main course
£7. **RESTAURANT:** L served all week. D served all week 12-1.45
7-9.30. Av 3 course à la carte £14.
BREWERY/COMPANY: Greene King.
PRINCIPAL BEERS: Greene King - IPA, Abbot Ale, Mild, Ruddles
County. **FACILITIES:** Children welcome Garden: outdoor eating
Dogs allowed. **NOTES:** Parking 30

COLTISHALL　　　　　　　　Map 07 TG21

Pick of the Pubs

Kings Head 🏨 ♦♦♦ 🛏
26 Wroxham Rd NR12 7EA
☎ 01603 737426 🖹 01603 736542
Dir: *A47 Norwich ring road onto B1150 to North Walsham at
Coltishall. R at petrol station, follow rd to R past church, on R next
to car park*

Homely 17th-century beamed inn, located on the banks of
the River Bure, at the heart of the Norfolk Broads. Fish
figures highly on a menu that includes pan-fried wing of
skate, lemon sole fillets with a parsley crust, roast fillet of
cod, grilled salmon steak and sea bass fillet. Other dishes
include chicken filled with mushrooms and bacon, crispy
aromatic duck and roast Norfolk partridge.
OPEN: 11-3 6-11 (Sun all day). **BAR MEALS:** L served
all week. D served all week 12-2 7-9. Av main course £5.95.
RESTAURANT: L served all week. D served all week 12-2
7-9. Av 3 course à la carte £9.75.
BREWERY/COMPANY: Free House.
PRINCIPAL BEERS: Adnams, Courage Best, Marstons
Pedigree. **FACILITIES:** Children welcome outdoor eating.
NOTES: Parking 20. **ROOMS:** 4 bedrooms 2 en suite s£25
d£50 FR£75

DITCHINGHAM　　　　　　　Map 07 TM39

Duke of York 🛏
8 Norwich Rd NR35 2JL ☎ 01986 895558
Dir: *L off A143 at Bungay/Ditchingham rdbt 200yrds on R*
Cosy traditional pub fronted by two large bay windows. The
menu offers home cooking featuring grills, steaks and fish.
OPEN: 11-3.30 6-11. **BAR MEALS:** L served all week. D served
all week 12-2 7-9. Av main course £6.50.
BREWERY/COMPANY: Free House.
PRINCIPAL BEERS: Adnams, Greene King, Tindalls.
FACILITIES: Children welcome Garden: BBQ Dogs allowed No
credit cards

DOCKING　　　　　　　　　Map 07 TF73

Pilgrims Reach 🛏 ♀
High St PE31 8NH ☎ 01485 518383
Dir: *From Hunstanton take A1495 then B1454 or A149 E then B1153*
Once a resting place for pilgrims journeying to the shrine at
Walsingham, parts of this traditional flint and chalk building
date from 1580. Now a warm and friendly village inn, the pub
is deservedly popular for its excellent food. There's an
extensive range of fish, from Blakeney whitebait to salmon,
halibut and monkfish, with special seasonal menus, too. Other
dishes include pies, steaks and pasta.
OPEN: 12-2.30 6-11 (closed Tue). Closed 1st Week in Feb.
BAR MEALS: L served Sun-Mon, Wed-Sat. D served Sun-Mon ,
Wed-Sat 12-2 6-9. Av main course £7. **RESTAURANT:** L served
Sun-Mon, Wed-Sat. D served Sun-Mon, Wed-Sat 12-2 6-9. Av 3
course à la carte £19. **BREWERY/COMPANY:** Free House.
PRINCIPAL BEERS: Shepherd Neame Spitfire & Bishops Finger,
FACILITIES: Children welcome Garden: Food served outside
Dogs allowed. Water. **NOTES:** Parking 50

The Peddars Way and
North Norfolk Coast Path
Best-selling author Jack Higgins perfectly summed up
North Norfolk as 'a strange mysterious sort of place, the
kind that made the hair lift on the back of your head.
Sea creeks and mud flats, the great pale reeds merging
with the mist and somewhere out there, the occasional
cry of a bird, the invisible beat of wings.' Following the
93-mile Peddars Way and North Norfolk Coast Path is
the best way to capture the unique flavour and
atmosphere of this wonderfully preserved corner of the
country. Consisting of two paths joined together and
officially opened by the Prince of Wales in 1986, the trail
begins near Telford and follows ancient tracks and
Roman roads north to meet the sea near Hunstanton.
The coastal stretch of the trail is dotted with quiet towns,
old ports and sleepy villages, and plenty of character
pubs and inns offer a warm welcome and much-needed
sustenance en route to Cromer, the walks final
destination. Among them are the 16th-century Lifeboat
Inn at Thornham, the Titchwell Manor Hotel, the
superbly located White Horse at Brancaster and the
striking 17th-century Hoste Arms at Burnham Market.
The Crown coaching inn at Wells-next-the-Sea and the
Grade II listed Kings Arms at Blakeney are perfectly
situated for rest and refreshment on the final leg of the
trail.

EASTGATE Map 07 TG12

Pick of the Pubs

Ratcatchers Inn
Easton Way NR10 4HA ☎ 01603 871430
🖷 01603 873343
Dir: Off A140, past Norwich Airport take B1149 to Holt, thru Horsford, 6m then pub signed

A white pan-tiled Norfolk country inn that, 'tis said, derives its unusual name from the 'one-penny-per-tail' bounty paid to local rat catchers in the 19th century. Today's home-made, home-cooked policy includes no such delicacy but promises their own bread baked on the premises, herb oils, chutneys, purées and stocks.

All menu items are cooked to order, with vegetarians especially spoiled for choice, so do not expect to cut and run. Enjoy instead a choice of real ales and a sensible selection of wines by glass or bottle whilst awaiting Cley smoked mackerel, locally-smoked sausage with Norfolk mustard and parcels of deep-fried Camembert and Stilton.

Move on to steak and kidney pie, Coxwain's fish pie or vegetable Stroganoff, and for massive appetites steaks with speciality sauces, Continental and Eastern dishes and the best available local or Billingsgate fish listed daily on blackboards. Various choices for youngsters and loads of home-made desserts reward the adventurous.
OPEN: 11.45-3 6-11. Closed 26 Dec. **BAR MEALS:** L served all week. D served all week 11.45-2 6-10. Av main course £9.50. **RESTAURANT:** L served all week. D served all week 11.45-2 6-10. Av 3 course à la carte £17.
BREWERY/COMPANY: Free House.
PRINCIPAL BEERS: Adnams, Hancocks, Greene King IPA.
FACILITIES: Children welcome Garden: patio, outdoor eating, Dogs allowed garden only. **NOTES:** Parking 30

EATON Map 07 TG20

Red Lion
50 Eaton St NR4 7LD ☎ 01603 454787
Dir: off the A11
17th-century coaching inn retaining original features such as Dutch gables, beams, panelled walls and inglenook fireplaces. Bar food includes home-made soups, freshly-cut sandwiches, and sausages and mash. The restaurant offers a selection of fresh Lowestoft fish, carvery joints, prime steaks and game in season.

Red Lion Eaton 17th Century Inn,

OPEN: 11-3 6-11 (Sun 12-3, 7-10.30). **BAR MEALS:** L served all week. D served all week 12-2.15 7-9. **RESTAURANT:** L served all week. D served all week 12-2 7-9. Av 3 course à la carte £16.50.
BREWERY/COMPANY: Free House.
PRINCIPAL BEERS: Theakston, Courage Best/Directors, Greene King IPA. **FACILITIES:** Garden: food served outdoors.
NOTES: Parking 40. **ROOMS:** 7 bedrooms 7 en suite s£29 d£38

ERPINGHAM Map 07 TG13

Pick of the Pubs

Saracen's Head
Wolterton NR11 7LZ ☎ 01263 768909
🖷 01263 768993
Dir: A140 2.5m N of Aylsham, L through Erpingham, signs 'Calthorpe'. Through Calthorpe 1m on R (in field)

This eccentric old inn, modelled on a Tuscan farmhouse at the heart of the famed Wolterton Estate, is lent a continental feel by its walled garden and dining courtyard. A true sense of fun is engendered by its self-effacing accent on humble pleasures that belie a cultured attitude to both food and hospitality.

Seasonally inspired blackboard menus produce the goods: parsnip and spring onion soup or seafood bisque, followed perhaps by pan-fried monkfish with orange and ginger and seared duck breast with "drunken" pears. Bold, imaginative seasoning lifts fricassée of "wild and tame" mushrooms and saddle of hare with sherry and cream to an exalted plane, to which old-style treacle tart and mulled wine and red fruit pudding live up just as manfully. Look out for the monthly feasts that might celebrate Empire Day, U.S. Independence or the start of the venison season:- an ideal opportunity to book in early for an overnight touch of Saracen civilisation truly away from it all.
OPEN: 11.30-3 6-11.30. Closed 25 Dec. **BAR MEALS:** L served all week. D served all week 12.30-2.15 7.30-9.15.
RESTAURANT: L served same as bar.
BREWERY/COMPANY: Free House.
PRINCIPAL BEERS: Woodforde's, Greene King Abbot Ale.
FACILITIES: Children welcome Garden: outdoor eating.
NOTES: Parking 50. **ROOMS:** 4 bedrooms 4 en suite s£30 d£40

FAKENHAM Map 07 TF92

The Wensum Lodge Hotel
Bridge St NR21 9AY ☎ 01328 862100 🖷 01328 863365
Originally built around 1750 as the grain store to Fakenham Mill, this privately-owned family establishment opened as a restaurant in 1983. It later became the Wensum Lodge Hotel, taking its name from the river it overlooks. The emphasis is on friendly service and quality home-cooked food. Expect mixed seafood, giant filled Yorkshire pudding, chicken and asparagus pie, half spring Norfolk chicken, or roast Gressingham duck breast.
OPEN: 11-11. **BAR MEALS:** L served all week. D served all week 11.30-3 6.30-10. Av main course £12. **RESTAURANT:** L served all week. D served all week 11.30-3 6.30-10. Av 3 course à la carte £20. Av 3 course fixed price £15.50.
BREWERY/COMPANY: Free House.
PRINCIPAL BEERS: Greene King IPA,. **FACILITIES:** Children welcome Garden: outdoor eating, patio. **NOTES:** Parking 20.
ROOMS: 17 bedrooms 17 en suite s£50 d£65

FAKENHAM continued

The White Horse Inn ♦♦♦
Fakenham Rd, East Barsham NR21 0LH
☎ 01328 820645 📠 01328 820645
Near 10th-century East Barsham Manor, this refurbished 17th-century inn with its log-burning inglenook has lost none of its character. Freshest ingredients are assured in daily specials that may include skate with black butter, chicken with tomato and olives, pan-fried Mediterranean lamb, parcels of beef with red wine and mushroom sauce, or lamb shank korma.
OPEN: 11-3 6-11. **BAR MEALS:** L served all week. D served all week 12-2 7-9.30. Av main course £7.50. **RESTAURANT:** L served all week. D served all week 12-2 7-9.30. Av 3 course à la carte £13.50. **BREWERY/COMPANY:** L & J Leisure.
PRINCIPAL BEERS: Adnams, Greene King, Woodforde's,.
FACILITIES: Children welcome Garden: outdoor eating, patio.
NOTES: Parking 50. **ROOMS:** 3 bedrooms 3 en suite s£25 d£50

GREAT BIRCHAM Map 07 TF73

King's Head Hotel
PE31 6RJ ☎ 01485 578265

Attractive 17th-century inn with a beamed snug, comfortable lounge and a wood-burning stove in the inglenook fireplace. The village has an impressive restored windmill, and is close to Houghton Hall.
OPEN: 11-2.30 7-11. **BAR MEALS:** L served all week. D served all week 12-2 7-9.30. **RESTAURANT:** L served Sun-Mon, Wed-Sat. D served Mon, Wed-Sat 12-2 7-9.30.
BREWERY/COMPANY: Free House. **PRINCIPAL BEERS:** Bass, Adnams. **FACILITIES:** Children welcome Garden.
NOTES: Parking 100. **ROOMS:** 6 bedrooms 6 en suite

GREAT RYBURGH Map 07 TF92

The Boar Inn
NR21 0DX ☎ 01328 829212
e-mail: boarinn@aol.com
Dir: Off A1067 4m S of Fakenham
Nestling deep in rural Norfolk in the Wensum Valley, this 300-year-old inn sits opposite Great Ryburgh's round-towered Saxon church. Expect chicken cordon bleu, courgette and pasta bake, madras beef curry and veal cuisinière. A good range of sandwiches, cheesy melts, jacket potatoes, and prime Norfolk steaks are also available. *continued*

OPEN: 11-2.30 6.30-11. **BAR MEALS:** L served all week. D served all week 12-2 7-9.30. Av main course £6.50. **RESTAURANT:** L served all week. D served all week 12-2 7-9.30. Av 3 course à la carte £12. **BREWERY/COMPANY:** Free House. **PRINCIPAL BEERS:** Adnams, Wensum Bitter.
FACILITIES: Children welcome Children's licence Garden: outdoor eating Dogs allowed. **NOTES:** Parking 30.
ROOMS: 5 bedrooms 5 en suite s£20 d£35 FR£39-£60

HAPPISBURGH Map 09 TG33

The Hill House
NR12 0PW ☎ 01692 650004 📠 01692 650004
Dir: 5m from Stalham, 8m from North Walsham
16th-century coaching inn with original timbers situated in an attractive coastal village. Sir Arthur Conan Doyle stayed here and was inspired to write a Sherlock Holmes story called The Dancing Men. One of the bedrooms is in a converted railway signal box. Changing guest ales; good value bar food; large summer garden.

HETHERSETT Map 07 TG10

Kings Head
36 Norwich Rd NR9 3DD ☎ 01603 810206
Dir: Old Norwich Road just off B1172 Cringleford to Wymondham road. 5m SW of Norwich
Attractive 17th-century roadside inn with a beamed snug and comfortable lounge. Pleasant, enclosed rear garden with trees and shrubs.

HEVINGHAM Map 07 TG12

Marsham Arms ⬚
Holt Rd NR10 5NP ☎ 01603 754268 📠 01603 754839
e-mail: m.arms@paston.co.uk
Dir: 4M Nof Norwich Airport on B1149 through Horsford

Built by local Victorian landowner and philanthropist Robert Marsham as a hostel for farm labourers, this beamed inn has
continued

brick interiors and a large open fire. Traditional English fare is the order of the day, and main dishes include steak and kidney pie, peppered steak, salmon fillet, seafood mornay, cashew nut roast, and a variety of grills.
OPEN: 10-3 6-11 (all day Summer). Closed 25 Dec.
BAR MEALS: L served all week. D served all week 11-3 6-9.30. Av main course £9.95. **RESTAURANT:** L served all week. D served all week 12-3 6-9.30. Av 3 course à la carte £13.
BREWERY/COMPANY: Free House.
PRINCIPAL BEERS: Adnams, Woodforde's, Greene King IPA, Mauldons. **FACILITIES:** Children welcome Garden: outdoor eating. **NOTES:** Parking 100. **ROOMS:** 8 bedrooms 8 en suite s£40 d£60 FR£60-£70

| HEYDON | Map 07 tg12 |

Earle Arms
The Street NR11 6AD ☎ 01263 587376
Dir: signed off the main Holt to Norwich rd, between Cawston & Corpusty
17th-century pub situated opposite the village green in a classic, unspoilt estate village. Aylsham is often used as a film and television location - The Go-Between and Uprising among other productions. Ideal base for touring and exploring the North Norfolk Coast. Expect a good range of interesting main courses, including home-made game pie, local mussels, duck breast and Thai green chicken curry, in the two homely bars.
OPEN: 12-3 6-11 (Sun 12-3, 7-10.30). **BAR MEALS:** L served all week. D served Tue-Sat 12-2 7-9. Av main course £5.
BREWERY/COMPANY: Free House. **PRINCIPAL BEERS:** Adnams, Woodfordes Wherry, Adnams Broadside, Bass. **FACILITIES:** Children welcome Garden: patio/terrace, outdoor eating Dogs allowed. **NOTES:** Parking 6 No credit cards

| HORSEY | Map 07 TG42 |

Nelson Head
The Street NR29 4AD ☎ 01493 393378
Dir: On coast rd (B1159) between West Somerton & Sea Palling
Convenient for the coast path and local bird reserves, this homely 16th-century pub offers hot home-made dishes. Now under new management.

| HORSTEAD | Map 07 TG21 |

Recruiting Sergeant
Norwich Rd NR12 7EE ☎ 01603 737077 ▤ 01603 736905
Dir: on the B1150 between Norwich & North Walsham
Dating from the Domesday, this inviting country pub has a large inglenook fireplace and offers a good menu featuring fresh local fish and seafood. Reports please.

| ITTERINGHAM | |

Walpole Arms
NR11 7AR ☎ 01263 587258
Dining pub with open-plan timbered bar set on the edge of the village. Wines by glass, real ales and good home-cooked food. Reports please.

| KING'S LYNN | Map 07 TF62 |

The Tudor Rose Hotel ★ ★
St Nicholas St PE30 1LY ☎ 01553 762824 ▤ 01553 764894
e-mail: diane@tudorrosehotel.com
Dir: Hotel is off Tuesday Market Place in the centre of Kings Lynn
Built by a local wool merchant and situated in the heart of King's Lynn, the oldest part of this historic inn dates back to

1187 and was originally part of the winter palace of a Norfolk bishop. The Dutch gable extension of 1645 remains one of the best examples of its kind in the town. Cosy snug and medieval-style tapestries inside. Dishes range from steak and kidney pie and ham, egg and chips to Mexican chilli and prawn salad. Various light bites and starters and a good choice of well-kept beers, whiskies and popular wines.
OPEN: 11-11 (Sun 7-10.30). **BAR MEALS:** L served Mon-Sat. D served Mon-Sat 12-2 7-9. Av main course £5.50.
RESTAURANT: D served Mon-Sat 7-9. Av 3 course à la carte £16 9. **BREWERY/COMPANY:** Free House.
PRINCIPAL BEERS: Batemans XB, Timothy Taylor Landlord, Bass. **FACILITIES:** Garden: outdoor eating, patio.
ROOMS: 13 bedrooms 11 en suite s£30 d£50

| LARLING | Map 07 TL98 |

Angel Inn ♀
NR16 2QU ☎ 01953 717963 ▤ 01953718561
In 1983, after a forty year gap, the current landlord resumed the family residency at this traditional and charming roadside pub that was once managed by his great-grandfather. There is a big collection of jugs in the bar, which also houses a big woodburner in its brick fireplace. Over a hundred malt whiskies are available. The menu includes steaks, grills, seafood, Indian dishes, a vegetarian selection, burgers, sandwiches and salads.
OPEN: 10-11. **BAR MEALS:** L served all week. D served all week 12-2 6.30-9.30. Av main course £6.95. **RESTAURANT:** L served all week. D served all week 12-2 6.30-9.30. Av 3 course à la carte £12.95. **BREWERY/COMPANY:** Free House.
PRINCIPAL BEERS: Adnams,. **FACILITIES:** Children welcome Garden: outdoor eating,. **NOTES:** Parking 100.
ROOMS: 5 bedrooms 5 en suite s£30 d£50

| LITTLE FRANSHAM | Map 07 TF91 |

The Canary and Linnet NEW
Main Rd NR19 2JW ☎ 01362 687027 ▤ 01362 687021
e-mail: canaryandlinnet@btinternet.co.uk
Pretty former blacksmith's cottage with exposed beams, low ceilings, inglenook fireplace and a conservatory dining area overlooking the rear garden. Food is offered from a bar blackboard or evening carte and there's a choice of three real ales and 20 malt whiskies in addition to the wine list. Favourite dishes are aromatic duck, steak and kidney pudding, and medley of seafood.
OPEN: 12-3 6-11 (Sun 12-3 7-10). **BAR MEALS:** L served all week. D served all week 12-2 7-9.30. Av main course £6.50.
RESTAURANT: D served all week 7-9.30. Av 3 course à la carte £13. **BREWERY/COMPANY:** Free House.
PRINCIPAL BEERS: Greene King IPA & Old Speckled Hen, Woodfordes Wherry, Adnams Bitter. **FACILITIES:** Children welcome Garden: Food served outside Dogs allowed.
NOTES: Parking 70

| MARSHAM | Map 07 TG12 |

The Plough Inn
Old Norwich Rd NR10 5PS ☎ 01263 735000
Smart, traditional style country pub and restaurant close to the historic town of Aylsham and ideally placed for the Norfolk Broads. Good base for fishing and walking; 10 en suite bedrooms. Traditional bar food and daily specials.

continued

MUNDFORD   Map 07 TL89

Crown Hotel
Crown Rd IP26 5HQ ☎ 01842 878233 ▤ 01842 878982
*Dir: Take A11 until Barton Mills interception, then A1065 to Brandon &
thru to Mundford*
Ideal for those who enjoy walking, the Crown is surrounded
by the Thetford Forest and was once a hunting inn. Unusually
for Norfolk, the property is built on a hill so the garden is on
the first floor. The Court Restaurant was once used as a
magistrate's court. Today's menu may offer monkfish and
lobster tails with savoury citrus butter, or beef roulade with
pork forcemeat.
OPEN: 11-11. **BAR MEALS:** L served all week. D served all week
12-3 7-10. **RESTAURANT:** L served all week. D served all week
12-3 7-10. **BREWERY/COMPANY:** Free House.
PRINCIPAL BEERS: Woodforde's Wherry, Courage Directors,
Marstons Pedigree, Theakston Best. **FACILITIES:** Children
welcome Garden: beer garden patio, food served outside Dogs
allowed. **ROOMS:** 16 bedrooms 16 en suite

NORWICH   Map 05 TG20

Adam & Eve ♉
Bishopsgate NR3 1RZ ☎ 01603 667423
e-mail: theadamandeve@hotmail.com
The oldest pub in Norwich, built around a Saxon well which
still exists beneath the Lower Bar floor, originally a brewhouse
for the workmen constructing the nearby Cathedral. The living
accommodation and the Flemish gables were added in the
14th and 15th centuries. Recently refurbished and under new
management, with bar food now offering home-made beef
and ale pie, sausage and mash, smoked haddock, cod and
prawns topped with potato and cheese, and breaded French
Brie with gooseberry sauce. Crab salad and Irish stew are
seasonal specials.
OPEN: 11-11 (Sun 12-10.30, food 12-2.30). Closed 25/26 Dec, Jan
1st. **BAR MEALS:** L served all week 12-7. Av main course £5.
BREWERY/COMPANY: Free House.
PRINCIPAL BEERS: Adnams Best, Old Peculier, Greene King
IPA, Wells Bombardier. **FACILITIES:** patio. **NOTES:** Parking 10

The Fat Cat
49 West End St NR2 4NA ☎ 01603 624364
Back street pub with a wide choice of up to 26 real ales and
four Belgian draught beers. Food is limited to filled rolls, and
there are tables outside in summer.

Ribs of Beef
24 Wensum St NR3 1HY ☎ 01603 619517
▤ 01603 625446
e-mail: roger@cawdron.co.uk
Welcoming riverside pub incorporating remnants of the
original 14th-century building destroyed in the Great Fire in
1507. Once used by the Norfolk wherry skippers, it is still
popular among boat owners cruising the Broads. The pub is
named after one of Henry VIII's favourite dishes. Wide range
of real ales.

REEDHAM   Map 05 TG40

Railway Tavern
17 The Havaker NR13 3HG ☎ 01493 700340
Serving its own brew of Humpty Dumpty beers, the Railway
Tavern is a classic Victorian inn that plays host to beer festivals
and has regular jazz nights. Talented chef Simon Leese has
continued

recently forsaken the London restaurant scene and has taken
control of the kitchen here. Expect innovative menus using
fresh local produce. En suite bedrooms. Reports welcome.

The Reedham Ferry Inn 🍴
Ferry Rd NR13 3HA ☎ 01493 700429 ▤ 01493 700999
Dir: 6m S of Acle on B1140 (Acle to Beccles rd)
Quaint 17th-century inn, situated in lovely Norfolk Broads
country and associated with the last working chain ferry in
East Anglia. With the same name over the door for more than
fifty years, this is one of the longest running family inns in East
Anglia. Typical bar food includes ploughman's lunches, prawn
submarine and home-made curry, while the restaurant offers
market fresh fish, roast duckling and home-made pies.

OPEN: 11-3 (Sun all day in summer) 6.30-11 (Sun 12-4, 7-10.30).
BAR MEALS: L served all week. D served all week 12-2 7-9. Av
main course £5.85. **RESTAURANT:** L served all week. D served
all week 12-2 7-9. Av 3 course à la carte £11.95.
BREWERY/COMPANY: Free House.
PRINCIPAL BEERS: Woodforde's Wherry, Adnams - Best &
Broadside, Greene King Abbot Ale. **FACILITIES:** Children
welcome Garden: Riverside terrace, food served outside Dogs
allowed Water. **NOTES:** Parking 50

REEPHAM   Map 07 TG12

The Old Brewery House Hotel ★ ★
Mallet Place NR10 4JJ ☎ 01603 870881 ▤ 01603 870969
e-mail: enquiries@oldbrewery.fsbusiness.co.uk
Dir: off the A1067 Norwich to Fakenham rd, B1145 signed Aylsham

Built in 1729 and originally a private house with a grand
staircase, highly polished floors and wood panelling, the Old
Brewery House became a commercial hotel in 1972. Many
original Georgian features have been retained. Choose from
the extensive, constantly-changing bar menu or specials
board, complemented by real ales and fine wines.
continued

OPEN: 11-11 (Sun 12-10.30). **BAR MEALS:** L served all week.
D served all week 12-2 6.30-9.30. Av main course £5.
RESTAURANT: L served all week. D served all week 12-2
6.30-9.30. Av 3 course à la carte £18. Av 3 course fixed price
£16.95. **BREWERY/COMPANY:** Free House.
PRINCIPAL BEERS: Adnams, Reepham, Greene King Abbot Ale
& Old Speckled Hen. **FACILITIES:** Children welcome Children's
licence Garden: outdoor eating, patio/terrace, BBQ Dogs
allowed Not in bar. **NOTES:** Parking 80. **ROOMS:** 23
bedrooms 23 en suite s£42 d£68

RINGSTEAD

Gin Trap Inn
High St PE36 5JU ☎ 01485 525264
e-mail: margaret@gintrap.co.uk
Dir: take A149 from Kings Lynn to Hunstanton, after 15m R at
Heacham
Gin traps adorn the beamed interior of this 17th-century
former coaching inn set in a peaceful village on the Peddars
Way, a short drive from the North Norfolk coast.
  Good range of traditional pub food on varied menus,
including steak and kidney pie, fresh cod and chips, shepherd
pie, lasagne and home-made soups, are served in the split-
level bar. Excellent East Anglian ales and peaceful garden for
summer sipping.
BAR MEALS: L served all week. D served all week 12-2 7-9.
Av main course £6. **BREWERY/COMPANY:** Free House.
PRINCIPAL BEERS: Gin Trap, Adnams Best, Greene King Abbot
Ale, Woodfordes Norfolk Nog. **FACILITIES:** Children welcome
Garden: outdoor eating, patio. **NOTES:** Parking 50 No credit
cards

SALTHOUSE   Map 07 TG04

The Dun Cow NEW
NL25 7XG ☎ 01263 740467
Dir: Situated on A149 main coast road, 3 miles E from Blakeney, 6
miles West from Sheringham
The front garden of this attractive pub overlooks a large
swathe of freshwater marsh. The bar area was formerly a
blacksmith's forge, and many of the original 17th-century
beams have been retained. Children are welcome, but there's
also a tranquil rear garden reserved for adults.
  The bar menu includes snacks, pub favourites like burgers
and jacket potatoes, as well as home-made daily specials,
seasonal seafood, and vegetarian dishes.
OPEN: 11-11 (Sun 12-10.30). Closed 25 Dec. **BAR MEALS:** L
served all week. D served all week 12-9. Av main course £6.50.
BREWERY/COMPANY: Pubmaster.
PRINCIPAL BEERS: Greene King IPA & Abbot Ale, Adnams
Broadside. **FACILITIES:** Children welcome Garden: Food
served outside Dogs allowed. **NOTES:** Parking 12.
ROOMS: 2 bedrooms 2 en suite s£50 d£50

SCOLE

Scole Inn ⌾
Norwich Rd IP21 4DR ☎ 01379 740481 ▤ 01379 740762
Built in 1655 as a coaching inn, this lovely pub has a striking
Dutch facade and is full of original authentic features. The inn
was once the headquarters of notorious highwayman John
Belcher, who regularly rode his horse up the great oak
staircase. Reliable pub food and comfortable accommodation.

SCULTHORPE

Sculthorpe Mill ★ ★
Lynn Rd NR21 9QG ☎ 01328 856161 ▤ 01328 856651
Dir: 0.25m off A148, 2m from Fakenham
Splendid 18th-century listed watermill straddling the River
Wensum, with extensive riverside gardens for summer alfresco
drinking. Character oak-beamed bar and upstairs restaurant
serving reliable food.

SNETTISHAM   Map 07 TF63

Pick of the Pubs

The Rose & Crown ♦♦♦♦ ⌾
Old Church Rd PE31 7LX ☎ 01485 541382
▤ 01485 543172
e-mail: roseandcrown@btclick.com
Dir: Head N from Kings Lynn on A149 signed to Hunstanton. Inn
in centre of Snettisham between market square and the church

History records that this inn of many parts was built in
1397 to house workmen building the nearby Snettisham
Church: its location opposite the village cricket pitch with
views of the coast and sprawling sandy beaches is
quintessentially English. Recent years has seen the addition
of further bedrooms and the incorporation of a cellar
dining bar that is true to its 14th-century origins. With their
open fires the main bars, set around a central servery, add
to the informality of an exciting country product. Attention
to the freshness of supplies complements food which goes
from strength to strength, well balanced by four real ales
and six or more wines by the glass. Daily specials feature
plenty of local produce, perhaps calves' liver with mustard
mash and crispy Parma ham and wild mushroom and red
onion tart with mustard seed dressing. Casserole of local
game, green Thai chicken curry and roast monkfish with
kumquat and onion marmalade are innovative additions
to the main menu. Brancaster mussels, Caesar salad with
croutons and smoked haddock kedgeree, all in small or
large portions, supplement steak and kidney casserole, the
Stockbroker warm ciabatta of grilled steak and onions and
smoked salmon sandwiches with cream cheese for a
whistle-stop lunch.
OPEN: 11-11 (Sun 12-10.30). **BAR MEALS:** L served all
week. D served all week 12-2 6.30-9. Av main course £8.50.
RESTAURANT: L served all week. D served all week 12-2
6-9. Av 3 course à la carte £15.
BREWERY/COMPANY: Free House.
PRINCIPAL BEERS: Adnams, Broadside, Bass, Fullers
London Pride. **FACILITIES:** Children welcome Garden:
outdoor eating, patio, Dogs allowed Water.
NOTES: Parking 70. **ROOMS:** 11 bedrooms 11 en suite s£50
d£80

STIFFKEY Map 07 TF94

Pick of the Pubs

Stiffkey Red Lion 🍺 ⅃
44 Wells Rd NR23 1AJ
☎ 01328 830552 📠 01328 830882
e-mail: matthewredlion@aol.com
Dir: Take A149 from Wells toward Sheringham, 4m on L
Rustic, 16th-century brick-and-flint cottage nestling in the Stiffkey Valley amid rolling Norfolk countryside. Fresh fish from King's Lynn, crab from Cromer, mussels from local beds, and first-rate ales from East Anglian brewers like Woodfordes, Elgoods, Adnams and Greene King, draw coast path walkers, birdwatchers, holidaymakers and devoted fish fanciers to this welcoming watering-hole. Charming interior comprising three bare board or quarry-tiled floored rooms with open fires and a simple mix of wooden settles, pews and scrubbed tables. Ever-changing blackboard menus may list deep-fried Blakeney whitebait, fish pie, local cod, sole, plaice and lobster, alongside Norfolk game casserole, lambs' liver and bacon in onion gravy and prime beef steaks from local farms. Lighter bites include filled baguettes and ploughman's lunches. After a day on the beach or strolling the Peddars Way this is a good stop for families, who have use of a large and airy rear conservatory with access to the terraced garden.
OPEN: 11-3 6-11. **BAR MEALS:** L served all week. D served all week 12-2 6-9. Av main course £6.95.
BREWERY/COMPANY: Free House.
PRINCIPAL BEERS: Woodforde's Wherry, Adnams, Greene King Abbot Ale. **FACILITIES:** Children welcome Garden: patio, outdoor eating Dogs allowed Water.
NOTES: Parking 40

STOKE HOLY CROSS Map 07 TG20

Pick of the Pubs

The Wildebeest Arms 🍺 ⅃
82-86 Norwich Rd NR14 8QJ
☎ 01508 492497 📠 01508 494353
A passion for fine cuisine runs through the entire ethos of this unusually named dining pub situated just three miles south-east of Norwich. Its former striking and unusual interior has had a fairly sophisticated face-lift, yet its casual, efficient service remains the result of years of practice. Menus are simply divided; a set menu offering perhaps goats' cheese salad with confit onion and chargrilled smoked salmon with guacamole followed by grilled sea bream on crushed new potatoes and pot-roast pork with lardon cabbage and cocotte potatoes. On a larger carte are daily-changing speciality soups and fresh fish direct from the market alongside perhaps a salad of Parmesan, orange and baby spinach, corn-fed chicken breast with wild mushrooms, roast chump of lamb with rustic ratatouille and chocolate and hazelnut torte. Side orders are generous and the two-course traditional Sunday lunch is a give-away.
OPEN: 12-3 6-11 (Sun 12-3 7-10.30). Closed Dec 25-26.
RESTAURANT: L served all week. D served all week 12-2 7-10. Av 3 course à la carte £17. Av 3 course fixed price £15.
BREWERY/COMPANY: Free House.
PRINCIPAL BEERS: Adnams. **FACILITIES:** Children welcome Garden: outdoor eating. **NOTES:** Parking 30

STOW BARDOLPH Map 07 TF60

Pick of the Pubs

The Hare Arms 🍺
PE34 3HT ☎ 01366 382229 📠 01366 385522
e-mail: info@harearms.freeserve.co.uk
Dir: From King's Lynn take A10 to Downham Market. After 9m village signed on L
At the heart of a quiet Norfolk village, mostly surrounded by the Hare Estate from which the pub derived its name over 200 years ago, the ivy-covered exterior, conservatory and garden look particularly appealing, with peacocks wandering freely in the grounds. The warm and friendly atmosphere within appeals to a real mix of clientele and ages, attracted by its excellent food for fully a quarter century.
Using only fresh ingredients, seasonal game, fish and shellfish from the coast, local lamb, beef and vegetables, the team of chefs produces fine bar food and a range of dining options in the restaurant. Daily specials in abundance are noted for Stilton and broccoli soup, home-made steak and mushroom pie, pork steak with peppercorn sauce and chicken breast in oak-smoked ham with wild mushrooms. Generous salads accompany lemon sole with basil and lemon butter, luxury fish pie, wild mushroom lasagne and nut cutlets with chilli dip. Sandwiches, ploughman's and Sunday roasts, set-price and à la carte dining menus extend its egalitarian allure.
OPEN: 11-2.30 6-11. Closed 25-26 Dec. **BAR MEALS:** L served all week. D served all week 12-2 7-10. Av main course £8. **RESTAURANT:** L served Sun. D served Mon-Sat 12-2 7-9.30. Av 3 course à la carte £22. Av 3 course fixed price £18.50. **BREWERY/COMPANY:** Greene King.
PRINCIPAL BEERS: Greene King - Abbot Ale, IPA,.
FACILITIES: Garden: patio, outdoor eating.
NOTES: Parking 50

SWANTON MORLEY Map 07 TG01

Darbys Freehouse
1&2 Elsing Rd NR20 4NY ☎ 01362 637647
📠 01362-637987
Dir: From A47 (Norwich/King's Lynn) take B1147 to Dereham
Converted from two cottages in 1988 and originally built as a large country house in the 1700s, this popular freehouse opened when the village's last traditional pub closed. Named after the woman who lived here in the 1890s and farmed the adjacent land.
Stripped pine tables, exposed beams and inglenook fireplaces enhance the authentic country pub atmosphere. Up to eight real ales are available and home-cooked food includes pigeon breast, steak and mushroom pudding, pesto pasta and salmon fillet. Farmhouse bed and breakfast accommodation at the landlord's farm 2 miles away.
OPEN: 11.30-3 6-11 (Sat 11.30-11, Sun 12-10.30). **BAR MEALS:** L served all week. D served all week 12-2 6.30-9.15. Av main course £6.95. **RESTAURANT:** L served all week. D served all week 12-2 7-9.15. Av 3 course à la carte £6.95.
BREWERY/COMPANY: Free House.
PRINCIPAL BEERS: Woodforde's Wherry, Badger Tanglefoot, Greene King IPA, Adnams Broadside. **FACILITIES:** Children welcome Garden: outdoor eating, Dogs allowed.
NOTES: Parking 75. **ROOMS:** 5 bedrooms 5 en suite s£15 d£48

England

THOMPSON   Map 07 TL99

Pick of the Pubs

Chequers Inn ⓘ
Griston Rd IP24 1PX
☎ 01953 483360   ▤ 01953 488092
Dir: From A11 at Thetford, L to Watton at main rdbt,
after 10m 2nd L to Thompson, pub 1m on R

In a quiet village close to Thompson Water and the
Peddars Way, the 14th-century Chequers is full of wonky
timbers, exposed beams and low ceilings with its Norfolk
reed thatch swooping almost to the ground, and stands in
a secluded country garden surrounded by open fields.
Adjacent purpose-built guest accommodation offers all the
comforts appreciated by today's discerning traveller and
makes an ideal base for touring this lesser-known heart of
Norfolk.
   Freshly prepared food, made largely on the premises,
incorporates local seasonal produce wherever possible
and continues to attract a wide-ranging clientele of old-
and new-comers. Steak, gammon and mixed grills occupy
a lion's share of the main menu with a varied choice of
sauces; pork, chicken and duck dishes making up the
numbers. Daily specials address the balance, offering
perhaps parsnip and apple soup, tiger prawns in filo
pastry, chargrilled skate wings with prawns and capers
and medallions of ostrich with wild mushroom sauce.
OPEN: 11.30-2.30 6.30-11. **BAR MEALS:** L served all week.
D served all week 12-2 6.30-9.30. Av main course £6.50.
RESTAURANT: L served all week. D served all week 12-2
6.30-9.30. Av 3 course à la carte £15.
BREWERY/COMPANY: Free House.
PRINCIPAL BEERS: Fullers London Pride, Adnams Best,
Wolf Best, Greene King IPA. **FACILITIES:** Children welcome
Garden: patio, outdoor eating Dogs allowed Water,
Sweeties. **NOTES:** Parking 35. **ROOMS:** 3 bedrooms
3 en suite

AA Hotel Booking Service on 0870 5050505 to book
at AA recognised hotels and B & Bs in the
UK and Ireland, or through our Internet site:
www.theAA.com

THORNHAM   Map 07 TF74

Pick of the Pubs

Lifeboat Inn ⊚ ★ ★ ⓘ
Ship Ln PE36 6LT ☎ 01485 512236   ▤ 01485 512323
e-mail: reception@lifeboatinn.co.uk
Dir: A149 to Hunstanton, follow coast rd to Thornham, pub 1st L
A much-extended 16th-century inn overlooking the salt
marshes and Thornham Harbour that has a long and
colourful history. Much original character has been
retained; there are roaring log fires in winter and fine
summer views across open meadows to a sandy beach.
Central is the centuries-old Smugglers' Bar with its
hanging paraffin lamps and creaking oak door. Beyond,
the conservatory is renowned for its ancient vine and
attendant walled patio garden.
   Traditional country fare is the main theme of daily
shopping for the best available fish and game. Poached
mussels in white wine, garlic and cream and spiced crab
and ginger fishcakes; pan-fried liver with smoked bacon
and chargrilled steaks with spicy herb butter ensure
masses of choice. Also getting a look in are baguette-
lovers, vegetarians and small people who all have their
own menu selection. Most bedrooms share a view of the
sea, and provision is made for children and well-behaved
dogs.

OPEN: 11-11. **BAR MEALS:** L served all week. D served all
week 12-2.30 6.30-9.30. Av main course £8.
RESTAURANT: L served Sun. D served all week 7-9.30. Av 3
course fixed price £22. **BREWERY/COMPANY:** Free House.
PRINCIPAL BEERS: Adnams, Woodforde's Wherry, Greene
King Abbot Ale. **FACILITIES:** Children welcome Children's
licence Garden: patio, outdoor eating Dogs allowed Water.
NOTES: Parking 100. **ROOMS:** 22 bedrooms 22 en suite
s£40 d£68 FR£83-£103

THORPE MARKET   Map 07 TG23

Green Farm Restaurant & Hotel ♦♦♦
North Walsham Rd NR11 8TH
☎ 01263 833602   ▤ 01263 833163
e-mail: grfarmh@aol.com
Dir: Situated on A149
Conveniently situated for exploring the Norfolk Broads, or the
historic houses at Blickling, Felbrigg and Sandringham, this
16th-century former farmhouse features a pubby bar and an
interesting menu. Typical dishes may include ribeye of beef,
crispy duck leg salad, Cromer crab salad, and lobster in
season. Bedrooms are attractively furnished in pine.

continued

OPEN: 11-2.30 6.30-11. **BAR MEALS:** L served all week. D served all week 12-2 7-8.30. Av main course £7.95. **RESTAURANT:** L served Sun. D served all week 12-2.30 7-8.30. Av 3 course à la carte £21.50. **BREWERY/COMPANY:** Free House. **PRINCIPAL BEERS:** Greene King IPA, Wolf - Best, Granny Wouldn't Like It. **FACILITIES:** Children welcome Garden: Food served outside Dogs allowed manager's discretion. **NOTES:** Parking 75. **ROOMS:** 14 bedrooms 14 en suite s£55 d£70

TITCHWELL — Map 07 TF74

Pick of the Pubs

Titchwell Manor Hotel ⬦ ★ ★ 🔟
PE31 8BB ☎ 01485 210221 📠 01485 210104
e-mail: margaret@titchwellmanor.co.uk
Dir: A149 (coast rd) between Brancaster & Thornham
A charming hotel in an unspoilt country location near to the RSPB nature reserve and handy for golden sands, historic houses and all manner of outdoor pursuits. Several bedrooms, courtyard-style with private terrace doors, are separate from the main building: all are spacious and stylishly furnished.
Fish clearly takes precedence on the Seafood Bar menu, an encyclopaedic listing of Brancaster mussels, crab and oysters and main dishes such as plaice fillets glazed with cheese and prawns and smoked haddock on an oyster and saffron chowder. Neither carnivores nor vegetarians need feel left out, with alternatives that seasonally include pot-roast local pheasant with apricots, sage and garlic and Thai Green curry of roast vegetables with steamed rice. Ingredients throughout take great care in provision of the best available market produce: this is the mainstay of the hotel's more formal Garden Restaurant. Family-run for many years, children are welcomed with affection - and early teas always provided by arrangement.
OPEN: 11-11. **BAR MEALS:** L served all week. D served all week 12-2 6.30-9.30. Av main course £11. **RESTAURANT:** L served all week. D served all week 12-2 6.30-9.30. Av 3 course à la carte £15. **BREWERY/COMPANY:** Free House. **PRINCIPAL BEERS:** Greene King IPA & Abbot Ale. **FACILITIES:** Children welcome Garden: patio, outdoor eating Dogs allowed not in bar, Water bowls, kennel. **NOTES:** Parking 50. **ROOMS:** 16 bedrooms 16 en suite

TIVETSHALL ST MARY — Map 07 TM18

The Old Ram Coaching Inn ★ ★ 🔟 ♀
Ipswich Rd NR15 2DE ☎ 01379 676794 📠 01379 608399
e-mail: theoldram@btinternet.com
Dir: On A140 approx 15m S of Norwich
Grade II listed property dating from the 17th century. Sympathetically refurbished with exposed brickwork and original beams throughout, the inn features comfortably furnished bedrooms, including one with a four poster bed. Generously served food includes an excellent choice at breakfast (served from 7.30am), good snacks (filled baguettes, chicken goujons) and daily specials such as swordfish with coriander and lemon, teriyaki sirloin steak marinated in sherry and paprika, or honey roast duck breast.
OPEN: 7.30-11. Closed Dec 25-26. **BAR MEALS:** L served all week. D served all week 7.30am-10pm. Av main course £9.95. **RESTAURANT:** L served all week. D served all week 11.30-10. Av 3 course à la carte £17.50. **BREWERY/COMPANY:** Free House. **PRINCIPAL BEERS:** Adnams, Woodforde's, Bass. **FACILITIES:** Children welcome Garden: outdoor eating, patio Dogs allowed ex guide dogs. **NOTES:** Parking 150. **ROOMS:** 11 bedrooms 11 en suite s£45 d£57 FR£67-£77

UPPER SHERINGHAM — Map 07 TG14

The Red Lion Inn 🔟
The Street NR26 8AD ☎ 01263 825408
Dir: A140 (Norwich to Cromer) then A148 to Sheringham/Upper Sheringham
17th-century cottage inn situated in small village close to a steam railway and North Norfolk's splendidly isolated coast. A lack of music and fruit machines ensures a peaceful atmosphere, and an imaginative menu ensures good eating. Dishes include steak and ale pie, stir-fry duck in Hoi Sin, lobster, halibut, and 'Drunken Thumper'.
OPEN: 11.30-11 (Winter 11.30-3, 6.30-11).
BAR MEALS: L served all week. D served all week 12-2 6.30-8. Av main course £7. **RESTAURANT:** L served all week. D served all week 12-2 6.30-8. **BREWERY/COMPANY:** Free House. **PRINCIPAL BEERS:** Woodfordes Wherry, Greene King IPA. **FACILITIES:** Garden: outdoor eating, Dogs allowed Water. **NOTES:** Parking 10. **ROOMS:** 3 bedrooms s£25 d£40 No credit cards

WARHAM ALL SAINTS   Map 07 TF94

Pick of the Pubs

Three Horseshoes 🍴
NR23 1NL ☎ 01328 710547
Dir: *From Wells A149 to Cromer, then R onto B1105 to Warham*
Wellingtons are welcome on the stone floors of this timeless 18th-century brick and flint alehouse, tucked away in a sleepy village just a mile from the North Norfolk coast. The interior of the building is little changed since the 1930s, and the three unspoilt bars still feature scrubbed deal tables, gas lighting, and Victorian fireplaces. There's a rare example of Norfolk 'twister' set into the pub ceiling; a curious red and green dial for playing village roulette. Other entertainments include vintage one-arm bandits, now converted to take modern coins.

Expect East Anglian ales from the cask, and hearty Norfolk cooking using fresh local ingredients. The pub doesn't take bookings, so arrive early to sample snacks like filled jacket potatoes, sandwiches, and farmer's lunch with local smoked ham. Starters include shellfish cheese bake or farmhouse terrine, followed by pheasant, steak and kidney pudding, plaice in watercress sauce, or cottage garden bake.
OPEN: 11.30-2.30 (Sun 12-3) 6-11 (Sun 6-10.30).
BAR MEALS: L served all week. D served all week 12-2 6.30-8.30. Av main course £6.20.
BREWERY/COMPANY: Free House.
PRINCIPAL BEERS: Greene King IPA, Woodforde's Wherry.
FACILITIES: Children welcome Garden: food served outside Dogs allowed. **ROOMS:** 4 bedrooms 1 en suite s£22 d£48 No credit cards

---

WELLS-NEXT-THE-SEA   Map 07 TF94

Crown Hotel
The Buttlands NR23 1EX
☎ 01328 710209   📠 01328 711432
Dir: *10m from Fakenham on B1105*
Locally-born Horatio Nelson brought his wife home from the West Indies to live in the picturesque old fishing port of Wells and may even have called at this charming 16th-century coaching inn. The Crown's interior has some delightful features, including bowed beams, old maps of the town and a roaring log fire. The menu bears the hallmark of fresh local produce and dishes include venison casserole, steak in ale cobbler, corn-fed chicken supreme and lamb with ginger and almonds.

OPEN: 11-2.30 (Sun 12-3, 7-10.30) 6-11. **BAR MEALS:** L served all week. D served all week 12-2 6.30-9. Av main course £6.
RESTAURANT: L served all week. D served all week 12-2 7-9. Av 3 course à la carte £21.50. Av 2 course fixed price £18.50.
BREWERY/COMPANY: Free House. **PRINCIPAL BEERS:** Bass, Adnams. **FACILITIES:** Children welcome Garden: Patio, Outdoor eating Dogs allowed on leads. **NOTES:** Parking 8.
ROOMS: 15 bedrooms 10 en suite s£40 d£69 FR£79-£100

WEST BECKHAM   Map 07 TG13

The Wheatsheaf 🍷
Manor Farm, Church Rd NR25 6NX
☎ 01263 822110   📠 01263 822110
Dir: *off the A148 (between Holt & Cromer) opp Sheringham Park, signed Baconsthorpe Castle, L at village triangle after 1m*
Former manor house converted to a pub in 1984 and retaining many original features. Sample one of the real ales from Woodfordes Brewery and relax in the large garden where a fully restored gypsy caravan is on display. On summer evenings you can even enjoy a game of floodlit petanque. Great pub atmosphere inside and a mix of traditional pub food and more adventurous specials. Expect smoked haddock topped with a Brie sauce, steak and kidney pie, roast duck breast, and lamb chump chop with caramelised onions and a tarragon gravy.
OPEN: 11.30-3 (Sun 12-3, 7-10.30) 6.30-11. **BAR MEALS:** L served all week. D served Mon-Sat 12-2 7-9. Av main course £6.50. **RESTAURANT:** L served all week. D served Mon-Sat 12-2 7-9. Av 3 course à la carte £12.50.
BREWERY/COMPANY: Free House.
PRINCIPAL BEERS: Woodforde's: Wherry, Nelsons Revenge, Norfolk Nog, Headcracker. **FACILITIES:** Children welcome Garden: outdoor eating, Dogs allowed Water.
NOTES: Parking 50

WEST RUDHAM   Map 07 TF82

The Dukes Head 🍴
Lynn Rd PE31 8RW ☎ 01485 528540
Dir: *from King's Lynn follow A148 towards Cromer, after 8.5m enter village of W Rudham*
Beamed country inn, once used as the local court and handy for exploring the Norfolk countryside, Houghton Hall, Royal Sandringham, Holkham Hall and Little Walsingham. It's known not only for its good beers but also for Norfolk Nudge Pudding, developed by owners David and John. Other house specialities are gourmet sausages, stuffed duck's leg, and sea bass with ginger and spring onions.
OPEN: 11.30-2 6.30-11 (May vary if quiet). **BAR MEALS:** L served all week. D served all week 12-2 6.30-9.30. Av main course £7.50. **RESTAURANT:** L served all week. D served all week 12-2 6.30-9.30. Av 3 course à la carte £15.
BREWERY/COMPANY: Free House.
PRINCIPAL BEERS: Woodfordes Wherry, Ketts, Great Eastern & Nelsons Revenge. **FACILITIES:** Children welcome Garden: Food served outside Dogs allowed Water. **NOTES:** Parking 14.
ROOMS: 2 bedrooms 2 en suite s£30 d£45

For pubs with AA rosette awards for food
see page 10

continued

?turn

The ... .9 4BN ☎ 01493 393305 📄 01493 393951
Dir: N of Gt ␣u,mouth on B1159
Brick and flint pub dating back over 300 years in a village location just a short stroll from the beach and nature reserves. The two simply furnished bars are popular with locals and holidaymakers too in summer. There's a straightforward bar menu, but look to the blackboard for regional and seasonal specialities including fish and game.
OPEN: 11-2.30 6.30-11 (Sat 11-11, Sun 12-10.30).
BAR MEALS: L served all week. D served all week 11.30-2 6.30-9. Av main course £7.50. **BREWERY/COMPANY:** Free House.
PRINCIPAL BEERS: Woodforde's Wherry & Norfolk Nog, Adnams Fisherman & Broadside. **FACILITIES:** Children welcome Garden: patio, outdoor eating, Dogs allowed Water.
NOTES: Parking 50. **ROOMS:** 3 bedrooms s£30 d£60 FR£60 (+ £5 Per Child)

WIVETON   Map 07 TG04

Wiveton Bell
Blakeney Rd NR25 7TL ☎ 01263 740101
Close to the green and church, this heavily-beamed village pub uses mainly fresh produce. The owner is Danish so expect some native influence here. Dishes might include venison steak with a cranberry and ginger sauce, chicken stir-fry in noodles, cod fillet in home-made batter and mussels and crab in season.
OPEN: 11-2.30 (Summer 12-3, 6-11) 6.30-11. **BAR MEALS:** L served all week. D served all week 12-2 7-9. Av main course £7.50.
RESTAURANT: L served all week. D served all week 12-2 7-9. Av 3 course à la carte £15. **BREWERY/COMPANY:** Free House.
PRINCIPAL BEERS: Bass, Adnams. **FACILITIES:** Garden: patio, outdoor eating

WOODBASTWICK   Map 07 TG31

The Fur & Feather
Slad Ln NR13 6HQ ☎ 01603 720003 📄 01603 722266
Dir: 1.5m N of B1140, 8m NE of Norwich
Converted in 1992 from a pair of farm cottages, this splendid old thatched inn is within easy reach of Norwich, the Norfolk Broads and the coast. Expect a wide range of pub food, including pork and leek sausages, home-made meat loaf, Madras chicken curry and salmon and prawn tagliatelle. Woodfordes brewery and its shop are adjacent so after sampling a pint of gravity-fed real ale at the bar, pop next door and purchase some beer to take home.
OPEN: 12-3 6-11. **BAR MEALS:** L served all week. D served all week 12-2 6.30-9.30. Av main course £7.95. **RESTAURANT:** L served all week. D served all week 12-2 7-9. Av 3 course à la carte £15.95. **BREWERY/COMPANY:** Woodforde's.
PRINCIPAL BEERS: Woodforde's Broadsman, Wherry, Great Eastern, Norfolk Nog. **FACILITIES:** Garden: pond, outdoor eating Dogs allowed garden only, Water. **NOTES:** Parking 100

AA inspected guest accommodation

WRENINGHAM   Map 07 TM19

Pick of the Pubs

Bird in Hand  🍺 ♀
Church Rd NR16 1BH ☎ 01508 489438
📄 01508 488004
Dir: 6m S of Norwich on the B1113

An eclectic mixture of styles characterises this interesting pub-restaurant in the heart of the Norfolk countryside. The quarry tiled bar features an attractive, open beamed roof, whilst diners can choose between the elegant Victorian-style dining room and the more traditional farmhouse restaurant. The pub's reputation for an extensive range of freshly cooked food is more consistent.

The bar menu combines traditional pub favourites like chargrilled burgers and filled jacket potatoes with more adventurous offerings which include grilled duck with red cabbage, or vegetarian roulade. In the restaurant, you'll be spoilt for choice; pan-fried venison, marinated chicken supreme, seared red mullet, or tortellini with Gorgonzola and walnuts are typical choices. Award-winning desserts like mulled wine pudding, raspberry pavlova, or white chocolate and Malibu cheesecake round off your visit.
OPEN: 11.30-3 6-11. **BAR MEALS:** L served all week. D served all week 12-2 6-9.30. Av main course £6.95.
RESTAURANT: L served all week. D served all week 12-2 6-9.30. Av 3 course à la carte £18.
BREWERY/COMPANY: Free House.
PRINCIPAL BEERS: Adnams, Woodforde's Wherry, Fullers London Pride, Greene King IPA. **FACILITIES:** Children welcome Garden: Food served outside. **NOTES:** Parking 55

NORTHAMPTONSHIRE

ASHBY ST LEDGERS   Map 06 SP56

The Olde Coach House Inn 🍺 ♀
CV23 8UN ☎ 01788 890349 📄 01788 891922
Dir: M1 J18 follow signs A361/Daventry.Village on L
One of the gunpowder conspirators lived near where this 19th-century pub is situated. Originally a farm, the dining area and meeting rooms were once the farmhouse and cattle sheds. Popular menu offers an extensive choice of pub favourites and house specialities. Imaginatively designed main courses at lunchtime range from battered Thai pearl snapper and burger with bacon and cheese between a floured bap to chilli con carne and chunky venison sausages on garlic and leek mash with mushroom and onion gravy. *continued*

OPEN: 12-2.30 6-11. Closed 25 Dec. **BAR MEALS:** L served all week. D served all week 12-2 6-9.30. **RESTAURANT:** L served all week. D served all week 12-2 6-9.30.
BREWERY/COMPANY: Free House.
PRINCIPAL BEERS: Everards Old Original, Flowers Original, Fullers London Pride, Hook Norton. **FACILITIES:** Children welcome Garden: food served outside Dogs allowed By arrangement only. **NOTES:** Parking 50. **ROOMS:** 6 bedrooms 6 en suite s£51 d£65 FR£65+ £18 per child over 5

BADBY   Map 06 SP55

The Windmill Inn ♀

Main St NN11 3AN ☎ 01327 702363 📠 01327 311521
Dir: M1 J16 take A45 to Daventry then A361 S. Village 2m
A relaxing air pervades this traditional 17th-century thatched inn at the centre of a picturesque village. Blenheim Palace, Stratford and Silverstone are nearby. Inside are friendly beamed and flagstoned bars decorated with cricketing, rugby and racing pictures. There are also good hotel facilities with a modern extension discreetly sited at the rear. Varied menu and daily specials might include leg of lamb, vegetarian nut roast, venison burgers, and Whitby battered scampi. Good choice of sandwiches and snacks.
OPEN: 11.30-3.30 5.30-11. **BAR MEALS:** L served all week. D served all week 12-3 7-10.30. Av main course £9.
RESTAURANT: L served all week. D served all week 12-3 7-10.30. Av 3 course à la carte £16. **BREWERY/COMPANY:** Free House.
PRINCIPAL BEERS: Bass , Flowers, Boddingtons, Wadworth 6X.
FACILITIES: Children welcome Garden: patio, outdoor eating Dogs allowed. **NOTES:** Parking 25. **ROOMS:** 8 bedrooms 8 en suite s£52.50 d£65 FR£69-£89

BULWICK   Map 06 SP99

Pick of the Pubs

The Queen's Head ♀

High St NN17 3DY ☎ 01780 450272
Dir: Just off the A43 nr Corby, 12m from Peterborough, 2m from Dene Park
Restored some three years ago, this meandering 17th-century inn opposite the village church boasts a host of small connecting rooms replete with stone floors and open log fires. It has remained essentially a pub, with no separate restaurant, serving real food, up to five guest beers and over 30 wines, of which a dozen come by the glass. Weekly-changing blackboard menus offer dishes of starter or main course size that include crab, prawn and avocado on citrus couscous and warm salad of bacon and black pudding. Substantial main dishes include grilled sea bream with caper butter, roast lamb joint with port, rosemary and redcurrants and pan-fried venison with wild mushrooms and smoked bacon. Seasonal puddings include the exotic - say poached pear in a brandy snap basket - and the traditional, such as treacle-and-walnut tart or caramelised rice pudding.
OPEN: 12-2 6-11. **BAR MEALS:** L served all week. Av main course £10.25. **RESTAURANT:** D served Tue-Sat 6-10. Av 3 course à la carte £18.
BREWERY/COMPANY: Free House.
PRINCIPAL BEERS: Timothy Taylor Landlord, Greene King Old Speckled Hen, Fullers London Pride, Jennings SneckLifter. **FACILITIES:** Garden: food served outside.
NOTES: Parking 40

CASTLE ASHBY   Map 06 SP85

Falcon Hotel ★ ★

NN7 1LF ☎ 01604 696200 📠 01604 696673
e-mail: falcon@castleashby.co.uk
Dir: A428 between Bedford & Northampton, Opposite War Memorial
Claimed to be the prettiest hotel in the county, the 400-year-old Falcon stands in the centre of a privately-owned village. Visitors will find a choice of bars, a first-floor lounge, individually decorated bedrooms and a range of menus.

CHACOMBE   Map 06 SP44

Pick of the Pubs

George and Dragon 🍴

Silver St OX17 2JR ☎ 01295 711500
Dir: From M40 take A361 to Daventry, 1st R to Chacombe, 2nd L in village
Well placed for M40 travellers (J11/2 miles) and popular with business folk from nearby Banbury, the George & Dragon is an attractive, honey-stoned, 16th-century pub tucked away by the church in a pretty conservation village. Expect a welcoming atmosphere within the three comfortable bars, with low beams, log fires, simple wooden chairs and settles, and a warm terracotta decor enhancing the overall charm of the inn. Blackboards list the interesting choice of food, from sandwiches, filled jacket potatoes and unusual pasta dishes to crispy duck breast with chilli and cranberry sauce, collops of pork with creamy leek and sage sauce, and decent fish specials - roasted monkfish with spring onion and mushroom sauce. Comfortable accommodation in three en suite upstairs bedrooms.
OPEN: 12-11. **BAR MEALS:** L served all week. D served all week 12-2 6-9.30. Av main course £9.95. **RESTAURANT:** L served all week. D served all week 12-2 6-9.30. Av 3 course à la carte £16. **BREWERY/COMPANY:** Free House.
PRINCIPAL BEERS: Theakston-Best,XB, Courage Directors.
FACILITIES: Children welcome Dogs allowed.
NOTES: Parking 40. **ROOMS:** 3 bedrooms 3 en suite s£41 d£58.50 FR£68.50

CLIPSTON   Map 06 SP78

The Bulls Head ♀

Harborough Rd LE16 9RT ☎ 01858 525268
📠 01858 525266
Dir: On B4036 S of Market Harborough
Have a look at the walls at this character village pub and you'll see they are studded with coins dating back to the Second World War. This tradition originated when locally-based US airmen wedged them in as a good luck gesture while waiting for their next pint. As well as its choice of real ales, the inn is noted for stocking over 500 different brands of whisky. Straightforward but wholesome menu offers steak and kidney pie, scampi and chips, T-bone steak and mixed grill among other dishes.
OPEN: 11.30-2.30 6.30-11. **BAR MEALS:** L served Tue-Sun. D served Tue-Sat 11.30-2.30 6.30-11. Av main course £7.95.
RESTAURANT: L served Tue-Sun. D served Tue-Sat 11.30-2.30 6.30-11. Av 3 course à la carte £15. **BREWERY/COMPANY:** Free House. **PRINCIPAL BEERS:** Bateman's, Timothy Taylor Landlord, Flowers, Black Sheep. **FACILITIES:** Children welcome Children's licence Garden: patio, outdoor eating, BBQ Dogs allowed. **NOTES:** Parking 40. **ROOMS:** 3 bedrooms 3 en suite s£29.50 d£45

COSGROVE

Map 06 SP74

The Navigation Inn
Thrupp Wharf, Castlethorpe Rd MK19 7BE
☎ 01908 543156
Dir: From A5 W of Milton Keynes take A508 N. Take 2nd R, 1st L. Inn 0.5m
Built 200 years ago at the same time as the Grand Union Canal beside which it stands. Home-made specials are available.

CRICK

Map 09 SP57

The Red Lion Inn
52 Main Rd NN6 7TX ☎ 01788 822342 ▤ 01788 822342
Dir: M1 J18 0.75m E on A428
A thatched, stone-built former coaching inn dating from the 1600s, with open fires, beams and horse brasses. It is a friendly, family-run establishment with a good name for its real beers and good pub food. Steaks are a speciality of the evening menu, along with trout or duckling, while at lunchtime there is a daily roast, home-made pies, and lasagne.
OPEN: 11-2.30 (Sun 12-3) 6.15-11 (Sun 7-10.30).
BAR MEALS: L served all week. D served Mon-Sat 12-2 7-9. Av main course £3.95. **BREWERY/COMPANY:** Wellington Pub Co.
PRINCIPAL BEERS: Websters, Marstons Pedigree, Theakston Best, Greene King Old Speckled Hen. **FACILITIES:** Garden: patio, outdoor eating Dogs allowed Water. **NOTES:** Parking 40

EASTCOTE

Map 06 SP65

Eastcote Arms
6 Gayton Rd NN12 8NG ☎ 01327 830731
Brick and stone village inn dating from 1670 with inglenook fireplaces, original beams, a welcoming atmosphere, and a splendid south-facing garden. Under new management that intends to retain the pub's traditional style. Good value lunchtime snacks include filled baguettes, old favourites like ham, egg and chips, and fish and chips, while evening fare features steak with pepper sauce and steak and ale pie.
OPEN: 12-3 6-11 (Sun 12-4, 7-10.30, Mon closed lunch).
BAR MEALS: L served Tue-Sun 12-2. Av main course £4.
RESTAURANT: L served Sun. D served Thu-Sat 12-3 6.30-9.30.
Av 3 course à la carte £20. **BREWERY/COMPANY:** Free House.
PRINCIPAL BEERS: Adnams, Greene King IPA, Fullers London Pride, Youngs. **FACILITIES:** Children welcome Garden.
NOTES: Parking 20 No credit cards

EAST HADDON

Map 06 SP66

Red Lion Hotel ♀
NN6 8BU ☎ 01604 770223 ▤ 01604 770767
e-mail: red_lion_hotel@yahoo.co.uk
Dir: 7m NW of Northampton on A428, 8m from J18 of M1. Midway between Northampton & Rugby.
Handy for visiting nearby Althorp Park, the final resting place of Diana, Princess of Wales, this smart 17th-century inn is built of eye-catching golden stone and thatch with a popular walled side garden where you can relax over coffee or a drink amid lilac, roses and fruit trees. Oak panelled settles, cast-iron framed tables and recessed china cabinets characterise the interior. Wide-ranging menu features the likes of pheasant casserole, beef Wellington and grilled Scottish salmon. Extensive wine list and a good selection of real ales.

OPEN: 11-2.30 6-11 (Sun 12.15-2 only). Closed Dec 25-26.
BAR MEALS: L served all week. D served Mon-Sat 12.15-2 7-9.30.
Av main course £12. **RESTAURANT:** L served all week. D served Mon-Sat 12.15-2 7-9.30. **BREWERY/COMPANY:** Charles Wells.
PRINCIPAL BEERS: Greene King Old Speckled Hen, Wells Eagle IPA, & Bombardier, Adnams Broadside. **FACILITIES:** Children welcome Garden: outdoor eating, patio,. **NOTES:** Parking 40.
ROOMS: 5 bedrooms 5 en suite s£60 d£75

EASTON-ON-THE-HILL

Map 06 TF00

The Exeter Arms ⌷ ♀
Stamford Rd PE9 3NS ☎ 01780 757503 ▤ 01780 757503
e-mail: crook@exeter13.fsnet.co.uk
Dir: A43 & A1 junct
An old, white-painted stone building - dating from 1765 - the inn gets its name from the estates of the Marquis of Exeter on which it once stood. The garden and patio enjoy views of the superb Welland Valley. Favourite dishes include grilled duck breast with an orange and Grand Marnier sauce, beef Wellington with shallots, salmon en croute with spinach, and monkfish medallions.
OPEN: 12-3 7-11 (closed Mon). **BAR MEALS:** L served Tue-Sun.
D served Tue-Sat 12-2.30 7-9.30. Av main course £12.50.
RESTAURANT: L served Tue-Sun. D served Tue-Sat 12-2.30 7-9.30. Av 3 course à la carte £12.50. Av 3 course fixed price £16.75. **BREWERY/COMPANY:** Free House.
PRINCIPAL BEERS: Theakstons. **FACILITIES:** Garden: patio, outdoor eating, BBQ. **NOTES:** Parking 100

FARTHINGSTONE

Map 06 SP65

The Kings Arms ⌷
Main St NN12 8EZ ☎ 01327 361604 ▤ 01327 361604
e-mail: paul@kingsarms.fsbusiness.co.uk
Dir: from M1 take A45 W, at Weedon join A5 then R on road signed Farthingstone
Tucked away in unspoilt countryside near Canons Ashby (NT), this cosy, 18th-century Grade II listed inn is adorned by a collection of stone gargoyles. Interesting weekend menus feature home-made dishes, including spiced lamb tagine, game casserole, mustard and bacon pork steak, and vegetable and bean pie. Excellent real ales.
OPEN: 12-3 (wknds only) 7-11. **BAR MEALS:** L served Sat-Sun 12-2. Av main course £6.50. **BREWERY/COMPANY:** Free House. **PRINCIPAL BEERS:** Hook Norton, Timothy Taylor Landlord, Shepherd Neame Spitfire, Jennings Best.
FACILITIES: Children welcome Garden: Herb Garden With Scarecrows And A Pond Dogs allowed. **NOTES:** Parking 20 No credit cards

---

Dominoes

Dominoes came to Britain from the Continent at the end of the 18th century, perhaps brought back by British soldiers serving in the Napoleonic Wars. French prisoners-of-war made sets of dominoes, not only for their own amusement but to sell to the British. Many different varieties are played in pubs besides the standard block game, and some pubs belong to dominoe leagues.

STAR INN, SULGRAVE
Manor Road OX17 2SA.
Tel: 01295 760389
Directions: village signed off B4525 E of Banbury
Immaculate 300-year-old former farmhouse situated close to Sulgrave Manor (open). Cosy interior with civilised flagstoned bar and a comfortable dining room. Good Hook Norton ales and an interesting changing blackboard menu. Bedrooms.
Open: 11-2.30 6-11 (Sun 12-5 only). Bar Meals: 12-2 6.30-9.30 (Sun 12-4 only). No children or dogs inside. Garden/patio. Parking.
(see page 323 for full entry)

*Pub*WALK

Star Inn, Sulgrave

A gentle ramble along well waymarked footpaths and quiet country lanes, linking the attractive villages of Sulgrave and Culworth. Make time to visit 16th-century Sulgrave Manor, George Washington's ancestral home.

With your back to the inn, turn right and proceed to Stockwell Lane, a gravel track on the right which leads to a pond and watermill. Before reaching the mill, go through a gate on your left and take the path diagonally across to the field corner. In the next field, keep the hedge on your left and head towards a converted windmill. Go through a gate on the left on to a gravel path. Follow the path as it bends right, then where it bends left, go through a gate and head diagonally across a field to cross a stile to the right of a group of trees.

Cross the road and the stile opposite, then keep the hedge on your left and soon maintain direction across an open field to a fence to the far corner. Cross the fence and small field to another fence and lane. Turn right and walk through Culworth village to the church, then turn left (Post Office on your left) and leave the village on the road leading to Lower Thorpe.

In a mile (1.6km), go through a gate on your left and ascend the field to the skyline, with farm buildings to your left. Go through the gate in the far corner and follow the well marked path along the left-hand hedge to Magpie Farm (on left). Cross a busy road junction, with Sulgrave waymarked opposite, and take the arrowed footpath into a field and walk parallel with the road through a further field. Exit at the first of the village buildings and turn right, heading downhill to the pub.

Distance: 4 miles (6.4km)
Map: OS Landranger 152
Terrain: farmland and village streets
Paths: tracks, field paths and some road walking
Gradient: undulating

*Walk submitted by:
The Star Inn*

16th-century Sulgrave Manor

FOTHERINGHAY   Map 06 TL09

Pick of the Pubs

The Falcon Inn ⑯ ⑯ ♀
PE8 5HZ ☎ 01832 226254
Dir: N of A605 between Peterborough & Oundle
Attractive 18th-century stone pub set in an historic village close to the site of Fotheringhay Castle where Mary Queen of Scots was beheaded. The Falcon and chef/patron Ray Smikle are the latest additions to the select Huntsbridge Inns group of pubs that offer innovative food in a relaxing pub environment.

Eat what you like, where you like and accompany your meal with excellent wines or a pint of ale. Sit in the unpretentious bar or head for the smart rear dining room or conservatory extension and order from the short, imaginative seasonally-changing menu. Dishes are robust and gutsy and the choice cosmopolitan with sound Mediterranean influences. Follow decent breads and quality olives with potted salmon with roast peppers and green bean salad, or terrine of pork, bacon and roast red onions with salsa verde. For main course choose, perhaps, chicken breast stuffed with chorizo sausage, ricotta and basil with couscous salad and pesto, or daube of beef with bubble-and-squeak and fried carrots. Finish with steamed orange and marmalade sponge pudding or a plate of unpasteurised cheeses.

OPEN: 11.30-3 6-11 (Sun 12-3,7-10.30). **BAR MEALS:** L served Sun, Tue-Sat. D served all week 12-2.15 7-9.30. Av main course £10. **RESTAURANT:** L served all week. D served Sun, Tue-Sat 12-2.15 7-9.30. Av 3 course à la carte £22. Av 2 course fixed price £9.75. **BREWERY/COMPANY:** Free House. **PRINCIPAL BEERS:** Fullers London Pride, Adnams Best, Greene King IPA, John Smiths Best. **FACILITIES:** Children welcome Children's licence Garden: patio, outdoor eating. **NOTES:** Parking 30

GRAFTON REGIS   Map 06 SP74

The White Hart ♀
Northampton Rd NN12 7SR ☎ 01908 542123
Dir: M1 J15 on A508 between Northampton & Milton Keynes
Small, stone-built thatched pub, licensed since 1750. The historic village of Grafton Regis is where Edward IV married Elizabeth Woodville, a locally-born widow, in 1464. Expect smoked salmon, prawn and fresh fruit melange, home-cooked pies and various home-made soups on the varied menu.

OPEN: 12-2.30 6-11 (Sun 12-2.30, 7-10.30). **BAR MEALS:** L served Tue-Sun. D served Tue-Sat 12-2 6-9.30. Av main course £7.50. **RESTAURANT:** L served Tue-Sun. D served Tue-Sat 12-1.30 6.30-9. Av 3 course à la carte £17.50. **BREWERY/COMPANY:** Free House. **PRINCIPAL BEERS:** Greene King Abbot Ale & IPA. **FACILITIES:** Garden: flowers, herbs etc Dogs allowed. **NOTES:** Parking 40

GREAT OXENDON   Map 06 SE48

The George Inn ♀ NEW
LE16 8NA ☎ 01858 465205   🖳 01858 465205
Country inn where you can enjoy a pint, a snack or a full-scale meal, including a traditional Sunday lunch. Full service is provided in the restaurant, but food is also available in the bar or the attractive conservatory overlooking the flower garden. Dishes based on fresh local produce are cooked to order - typically grilled haddock, baked sea bass, confit of duck, and beef and Guinness pie. **OPEN:** 11.30-3 6-11. **BAR MEALS:** L served all week. D served all week 12-2.30 7-10. Av main course £8. **RESTAURANT:** L served all week. D served all week 12-2.30 7-10. Av 3 course à la carte £20.50. **BREWERY/COMPANY:** Free House. **PRINCIPAL BEERS:** Bass, Adnams,. **FACILITIES:** Children welcome Garden: food served outside Dogs allowed garden only, water. **NOTES:** Parking 34. **ROOMS:** 3 bedrooms 3 en suite d£52.50

HARRINGTON   Map 06 SP78

The Tollemache Arms 🐱
High St NN6 9NU ☎ 01536 710469
Dir: 6M from Kettering directly off the A14 both E & W bound signposted as Harrington
New licensees have recently taken over this pretty, thatched 16th-century village inn, situated near to Harrington Airfield and Museums. In addition to ales from Wells and Greene Kings breweries, freshly prepared food from local produce is served throughout the character bars and restaurant. Typical dishes include smoked haddock and horseradish parfait, roast rack of lamb with red wine jus and good fish options like whole sea bass with sweet and sour sauce. Popular Sunday lunch menu. **OPEN:** 12-3 6-11. **BAR MEALS:** L served all week. D served all week 12-2.30 6.30-9. Av main course £7.50. **RESTAURANT:** L served all week. D served all week 12-2.30 6.30-9. Av 3 course à la carte £20. **BREWERY/COMPANY:** Charles Wells. **PRINCIPAL BEERS:** Wells Eagle IPA & Bombardier, Adnams Broadside, Greene King Triumph & Old Speckled Hen. **FACILITIES:** Garden: Food served outisde Dogs allowed. **NOTES:** Parking 60

England

HARRINGWORTH
Map 06 SP99

Exeter Arms
Main Rd, Wakerley LE15 8PA ☎ 01572 747817
Set in a lovely walking area, close to Wakerley Woods and the
Welland Valley, this 17th-century stone pub has a garden with
fish pond. Bedrooms are in a converted stable block. Adnams
and more.

The White Swan
Seaton Rd NN17 3AF ☎ 01572 747543 ▤ 01572 747323
e-mail: white.swan1@virgin.net
Dir: Off B672 NE of Corby
Photographs recalling the nearby World War II airbase
decorate the bar of this stone-built 15th century coaching inn.
The prettily-situated free house also displays an old collection
of craftsman's tools and memorabilia. There's a nice selection
of well-kept real ales, and the constantly changing blackboard
menu offers dishes like braised lamb knuckle, beef Wellington,
duck with plum sauce, grilled salmon, or parsnip, ginger and
mushroom bake.

OPEN: 11.30-2.30 6.30-11 (Sun 12-3.30, 7-10.30).
BAR MEALS: L served all week. D served all week 12-2 7-10.
Av main course £7.25. **RESTAURANT:** L served all week.
D served all week 12-2 7-10. Av 3 course à la carte £14.50.
BREWERY/COMPANY: Free House.
PRINCIPAL BEERS: Greene King IPA, Abbot Ale & Old Speckled
Hen, Marstons Pedigree. **FACILITIES:** Children welcome Garden:
outdoor eating, patio Dogs allowed (except in garden).
NOTES: Parking 10. **ROOMS:** 6 bedrooms
6 en suite s£30 d£42

KETTERING
Map 06 SP87

The Overstone Arms
Stringers Hill, Pytchley NN14 1EN ☎ 01536 790215
▤ 01536 791098
Dir: village situated 1m from Kettering, 5m from Wellingborough
An 18th-century coaching inn, with its own orchard and
country garden, in the village of Pytchley. A varied menu is
supported by a list of daily specials.

Vane Arms
Main St, Sudborough NN14 3BX ☎ 01832 733223
Serving nine real ales that change regularly, this thatched pub
is in a beautiful conservation village. Close to new Indy
racetrack. Mexican menu.

LITTLE ADDINGTON
Map 06 SP97

The Bell Inn
High St NN14 4BD ☎ 01933 651700
Dir: From A14, S of Kettering, follow signs for The Addingtons
Tastefully modernised country pub with open fires, oak beams
and interesting blackboard menus. The kitchen makes good
use of fresh produce, creating such dishes as supreme of
chicken Italienne, pork chops Somerset, pie of the day,
mushroom, pepper and onion medley, pasta and pesto with
olives, and salmon in watercress sauce.
Lighter meals include salads, ploughmans', omelettes,
sandwiches and baked potatoes. Also look out for the specials
board.
OPEN: 12-2 6.30-11. Closed 1-8 Jan. **BAR MEALS:** L served all
week. D served all week 12-2 7-10. Av main course £8.
RESTAURANT: L served all week. D served all week 12-2 7-10. Av
3 course à la carte £14.50. **BREWERY/COMPANY:** Free House.
PRINCIPAL BEERS: Greene King IPA, Bass.
FACILITIES: Terrace, food served outside. **NOTES:** Parking 40

LITTLE HARROWDEN
Map 06 SP87

The Lamb
Orlingbury Rd NN9 5BH ☎ 01933 673300
▤ 01933 403131
Tucked away in a delightful village, this neatly refurbished
17th-century pub offers a friendly welcome in its comfortable
lounge bar and adjoining public bar with games area.
Home-cooked food is served in the restaurant, while cold
snacks are available in the bar during the afternoon. Steaks,
lasagne, jacket potatoes, omlettes and baguettes are readily
available. Under new management, and unusual in a way, as it
is run entirely by women.
OPEN: 12-11. **BAR MEALS:** L served all week. D served Mon-Sat
12-2.30 7-9. Av main course £4.95. **RESTAURANT:** L served all
week. D served all week 12-2.30 7-9. Av 3 course à la carte £12.
BREWERY/COMPANY: Charles Wells.
PRINCIPAL BEERS: Wells-Eagle & Bombardier, Marstons
Pedigree. **FACILITIES:** Children welcome Garden: barbecue,
patio, food served outside. **NOTES:** Parking 14

LOWICK
Map 06 SP98

The Snooty Fox
NN14 3BS ☎ 01832 733434
*Dir: off the A14 5 m E of Kettering on A6116. Straight over at 1st
roundabout and L into Lowick*
Exquisite carved beams are among the more unusual features
at this 16th-century pub. Originally the manor house, it is
supposedly haunted by a horse and its rider killed at the Battle
of Naseby. Varied bar food includes steaks, chicken and pork;
a good vegetarian selection, and fresh fish delivered daily.
OPEN: 12-3 6.30-11. **BAR MEALS:** L served all week. D served
all week 12-2 7-10. Av main course £5.95. **RESTAURANT:** L
served all week. D served all week 12-2 7-10. Av 3 course à la
carte £13. **PRINCIPAL BEERS:** Banks, Morrells, Adnams,
Marstons. **FACILITIES:** Children welcome Garden: BBQ in
summer Dogs allowed. **NOTES:** Parking 100

MARSTON ST LAWRENCE   Map 06 SP54

The Marston Inn
OX17 2DB ☎ 01295 711906
e-mail: marstonpub@easynet.co.uk
Dir: 5m from M40 J11
Originally three cottages, this 15th-century inn was seized by
Cromwell prior to the Battle of Edgehill and sold to raise
money for his army. Used to be known as 'The Case is
Altered'. Caravans and tents are welcome in the grounds, but
be sure to book in advance. One of the two dining rooms is
non-smoking. A typical menu offers tuna steak with salsa
glaze, lamb, apricot and coriander casserole, and salmon and
broccoli mornay. A large vegetarian menu is also available.
OPEN: 12-2.30 7-11 (closed Sun eve winter). **RESTAURANT:** L
served Tue-Sun. D served Tue-Sat 12-2 7-9.30. Av 3 course à la
carte £15. **BREWERY/COMPANY:** Hook Norton.
PRINCIPAL BEERS: Hook Norton Best, Old Hooky &
Generation. **FACILITIES:** Garden: outdoor eating, patio.
NOTES: Parking 12 No credit cards

NORTHAMPTON

The Fox & Hounds
Main St, Great Brington NN7 4JA ☎ 01604 770451
Restored stone thatched inn close to Althorp Hall. Plenty of
real ale choice. Courtyard, garden, play area.

OUNDLE   Map 06 TL08

The Mill at Oundle ♀
Barnwell Mill PE8 5PB ☎ 01832 272621   📠 01832 272221
e-mail: reservations@millatoundle.com
Dir: A14 Thrapston exit, A605 toward Peterborough, 8m Oundle
turning, 1m to pub
Set on the banks of the River Nene, this converted watermill
has a bar at the waterside, a Trattoria that serves lunch and
dinner, and the Granary Restaurant on the roof which can be
used for conferences. The mill itself has a history that dates
back to the Domesday Book, and was in use until 1947. A
typical menu includes steak, ale and mushroom pie, grills and
Tex-Mex dishes.
OPEN: 11-3 6.30-11 (Summer Sat 11-11, Sun12-10.30). Closed
Dec 26. **BAR MEALS:** L served all week. D served all week 12-2
6.30-9. Av main course £7.95. **RESTAURANT:** L served all week.
D served all week 12-2 6.30-9. Av 3 course à la carte £20.
BREWERY/COMPANY: Free House. **PRINCIPAL BEERS:** 3-6
regularly changing guest ales. **FACILITIES:** Children welcome
Garden: food served outside Dogs allowed Garden only.
NOTES: Parking 80

The Montagu Arms
Barnwell PE8 5PH ☎ 01832 273726   📠 01832 275555
Dir: off A605 opposite Oundle slip Rd, access to A605 via A14 or A1
One of Northamptonshire's oldest inns, the Montagu Arms
was originally three cottages built for workmen constructing
the manor house, and is set on the banks of a babbling brook.
Named after Edward Montagu, one-time lord of the manor
and chief justice to the court of the King's bench during the
reign of Henry VIII. Baguettes, sandwiches, burgers, steaks,
grills and pasta are available from a brightly coloured menu.
OPEN: 12-3 6-11 (Sat-Sun all day). **BAR MEALS:** L served all
week. D served all week 12-2.30 7-10. Av main course £6.50.
RESTAURANT: L served all week. D served all week 12-2.30 7-10.
Av 3 course à la carte £12. **BREWERY/COMPANY:** Free House.
PRINCIPAL BEERS: Adnams Broadside, Southwold Bitter,

continued

Flowers IPA. **FACILITIES:** Children welcome Garden: outdoor
eating Dogs allowed garden only, Water. **NOTES:** Parking 25.
ROOMS: 5 bedrooms 5 en suite s£27.50 d£45

SIBBERTOFT   Map 06 SP68

The Red Lion ♀
43 Welland Rise LE16 9UD ☎ 01858 880011
📠 01858 880011
e-mail: redlion@sibbertoft.demon.co.uk
Dir: From Market Harborough take A4304, then A50. After 1m turn L
Friendly and civilised village pub, believed to be 300 years old,
with a cottage-like frontage. The same menu is offered in both
the beamed restaurant and comfortably furnished bar, the
chalkboard listing specials such as steak and Stilton pie,
chicken Mississippi, haddock and poached egg, game pie,
and liver and onions.
OPEN: 12-2 6.30-11. **BAR MEALS:** L served Wed-Sun. D served
all week 12-2 7-9.45. Av main course £8.
BREWERY/COMPANY: Free House.
PRINCIPAL BEERS: Everards Tiger, Adnams Bitter, Bass.
NOTES: Parking 15. **ROOMS:** 2 bedrooms 2 en suite s£30 d£50

STOKE BRUERNE   Map 06 SP74

The Boat Inn
NN12 7SB ☎ 01604 862428   📠 01604 864314
e-mail: info@boatinn.co.uk
Dir: just off A508
Thatched canalside inn by working locks and opposite the
canal museum, where narrowboat trips on the 40-seater
Indian Chief are a feature. The bar menu offers the likes of
battered cod, steaks and jacket potatoes, while restaurant
dishes might include baked stuffed sea bass, and venison
chasseur.

OPEN: 11-11 (closed 3-6 Mon-Thu in winter). **BAR MEALS:** L
served all week. D served all week 9.30-9. **RESTAURANT:** L
served Tue-Sun. D served all week 12-2 7-9.
BREWERY/COMPANY: Free House.
PRINCIPAL BEERS: Banks Bitter, Marstons Pedigree, Adnams
Southwold, Thwaites. **FACILITIES:** Children welcome Children's
licence Garden: **NOTES:** Parking 50

We endeavour to be as accurate as possible but changes
in personnel and data can occur in establishments after
the guide has gone to press

SULGRAVE
Map 06 SP54

Pick of the Pubs

The Star Inn ♉
Manor Rd OX17 2SA
☎ 01295 760389 📠 01295 760991
e-mail: repose@starinnsulgrave.co.uk
Dir: M1 J15A follow signs for Silverstone race circuit then M40 J11
follow brown signs for golf course, then for Sulgrave Manor
Situated on the Oxfordshire/Northamptonshire border,
this delightful, 300-year-old creeper-clad inn is spotlessly
maintained and full of character. Handy for visiting
Silverstone and historic Sulgrave Manor, ancestral home
of George Washington. The pub describes itself as an adult
sanctuary offering fine ales and authentic, home-cooked
food. Shank of lamb with rosemary and garlic, beef stew
and dumplings, home-made corned beef with bubble-and-
squeak, and Vietnamese-style chicken curry are typical
examples of the interesting, frequently-changing menu.
OPEN: 11-2.30 6-11 (Sun 12-5 only). Closed 25 Dec.
BAR MEALS: L served all week. D served all week 12-2
6.30-9.30. Av main course £10. **RESTAURANT:** L served all
week. D served all week 12-2 6.30-9.30. Av 3 course à la carte
£17.50. **BREWERY/COMPANY:** Hook Norton.
PRINCIPAL BEERS: Hook Norton Best, Old Hooky,
Generation, & Haymaker. **FACILITIES:** Garden: Food served
outside Dogs allowed only in garden,Water.
NOTES: Parking 20. **ROOMS:** 4 bedrooms 4 en suite s£35
d£60

See Pub Walk on page 319

THORPE MANDEVILLE
Map 06 SP54

The Three Conies 🐾 ♉
Banbury Ln OX17 2EX ☎ 01295 711025
A uniquely named drovers' inn dating from 1622, with
inglenook fireplaces and herb terracing leading from the
dining room. Renowned for its speciality fish menu. Under
new management who aim to maintain the Three Conies good
local reputation.
OPEN: 12-3 6-11. **BAR MEALS:** L served all week. D served all
week 12-3 6-11. Av main course £5. **RESTAURANT:** L served all
week. D served all week 12-3 6-11. Av 4 course fixed price £15.
BREWERY/COMPANY: Hook Norton.
PRINCIPAL BEERS: Hook Norton BB, Hook Norton Hooky.
FACILITIES: Children welcome Garden: outdoor eating, patio,
BBQ, fountain & fish Dogs allowed. **NOTES:** Parking 30

AA Bed & Breakfast
2002

Britain's best-selling B&B
guide featuring over 3500
great places to stay

www.theAA.com

AA Lifestyle Guides

WADENHOE
Map 06 TL08

Pick of the Pubs

The King's Head ♉
Church St PE8 5ST ☎ 01832 720024 📠 01832 720024
e-mail: thekingshead@wadenhoe.freeserve.co.uk
Peacefully situated beside the River Nene down a dead-end
lane lined with honey-coloured stone cottages, this part-
thatched, 17th-century stone inn has seen new owners take
over in early 2001. Early indications are that they intend to
maintain the two en suite bedrooms and continue to offer an
interesting range of home-cooked food. Oak beams, quarry-
tiled floors and open fires characterise the welcoming and
neatly refurbished interior. From lunchtime soups,
sandwiches, pâtés and home-made burgers, the evening
menu may list venison casserole in sherry and Guinness,
queen scallops in garlic and cream, sirloin steak with
Madagascan green peppercorn sauce, fresh cod and chips,
and other fish specials featuring sea bass and skate among
others. Dine alfresco in the summer by the river.
OPEN: 12-3 7-11 (Sun 7-10.30, Summer all day Sat-Sun).
BAR MEALS: L served all week. D served all week 12-2.
Av main course £5. **RESTAURANT:** D served all week 7-9.
Av 3 course à la carte £12. **BREWERY/COMPANY:** Free
House. **PRINCIPAL BEERS:** Adnams Broadside.
FACILITIES: Children welcome Garden: patio
Dogs allowed. **NOTES:** Parking 20. **ROOMS:** 2 bedrooms
2 en suite s£35 d£55

WELFORD

Shoulder of Mutton Inn
12 High St NN6 6HT ☎ 01858 575375
e-mail: shoulderofmutton@hotmail.com
Dir: 2m N of A14 J1
17th-century low-beamed village inn close to Foxton Locks and
Naseby Battlefield. Open-plan bar, real ales and a varied menu
of traditional pub food.

WESTON

The Crown
Helmdon Rd NN12 8PX ☎ 01295 760310
This 16th-century listed building has exposed beams and an
inglenook fireplace, and is very good for local walks.
Reputedly this was the last place that Lord Lucan was seen
before his mysterious disappearance. Llama trekking available.

WOODNEWTON
Map 06 TL09

The White Swan
22 Main St PE8 5EB ☎ 01780 470381
Welcoming village local with a simple, single oblong room,
one end focusing on the bar and wood-burning stove, the
other set up as a dining area. The regularly-changing
blackboard may list fillet of beef Wellington, rack of lamb with
rosemary, redcurrant and port, and daily fresh fish specials.
OPEN: 12-2.30 7-11 (6-11 Fri, 7-10.30 Sun). **BAR MEALS:** L
served Tue-Sun. D served Tue-Sun 12-1.45 7-9. Av main course
£7.95. **RESTAURANT:** L served Tue-Sun. D served Tue-Sun
12-1.45 7-9. Av 3 course à la carte £16.50.
BREWERY/COMPANY: Free House.
PRINCIPAL BEERS: Fullers London Pride.
FACILITIES: Children welcome Garden: Petanque pitch Dogs
allowed garden only. **NOTES:** Parking 20

NORTHUMBERLAND

ALLENDALE
Map 11 NY85

Kings Head Hotel
Market Place NE47 9BD ☎ 01434 683681
Dir: From Hexham take B6305/B6304/B6295
Dating from 1754, the Kings Head is the oldest inn in Allendale, situated in the centre of the North Dales village. Traditional food. Bedrooms.

ALLENHEADS
Map 11 NY84

The Allenheads Inn
NE47 9HJ ☎ 01434 685200 ▤ 01434 685200
Dir: From Hexham take B6305, then B6295 to Allenheads
Unique 18th-century pub situated in a remote village high in the Pennines. Under new management since Easter 2001, the extraordinary bar is festooned with curios, antiques and assorted bric-a-brac. The straightforward bar menu steak pie, sweet and sour chicken, and lamb and vegetarian specials.
OPEN: 11-2.30 7-11 (wknd 12-4, 7-11, closed lunch winter).
BAR MEALS: L served Fri-Sun. D served all week 7-7.10. Av main course £5. **BREWERY/COMPANY:** Free House.
PRINCIPAL BEERS: Tetley. **FACILITIES:** Garden:
ROOMS: 8 bedrooms 8 en suite s£25 d£43 No credit cards

ALNWICK
Map 11 NU11

Masons Arms
Stamford, Nr Rennington NE66 3RX ☎ 01665 577275
▤ 01665 577894
e-mail: masonarms@lineone.net
Dir: 3.5m from A1 on B1340
Former coaching inn built about 200 years ago and an ideal base for discovering the wide open spaces of Northumberland and its majestic coastline. Within easy reach are Hadrian's Wall and the magnificent Cheviot Hills. The same menu is offered throughout and includes such dishes as gammon steak, fresh haddock and lamb cutlets. Game casserole, chicken and asparagus bake and seafood gratin feature may be found on the specials board.
OPEN: 12-2 6.30-11 (Sun 12-2 7-10.30). **BAR MEALS:** L served all week. D served all week 12-2 7-9. Av main course £6.45.
RESTAURANT: L served all week. D served all week 12-2 7-9. Av 3 course à la carte £12. **BREWERY/COMPANY:** Free House.
PRINCIPAL BEERS: Courage Directors. **FACILITIES:** Children welcome Garden: patio, food served outside.
NOTES: Parking 25. **ROOMS:** 6 bedrooms 6 en suite s£19.50 d£39

BAMBURGH
Map 11 NU13

Lord Crewe Arms Hotel ★ ★
Front St NE69 7BL ☎ 01668 214243 ▤ 01668 214273
e-mail: lca@tinyonline.co.uk
Historic coaching inn named after Lord Crewe who was one of the Prince Bishops of Durham. Perfect base for touring Northumberland, exploring the Cheviot Hills and visiting nearby Holy Island. Good, wholesome pub food ranges from local kippers and pan-fried supreme of garlic chicken, to steak pie in a Guinness and Bass Ale gravy or lamb and cider casserole.
continued

OPEN: 12-3 6-11. **BAR MEALS:** L served all week. D served all week 12-2.30 6-9. Av main course £6. **RESTAURANT:** L served all week. D served all week 12-2.30 6.30-9. Av 3 course à la carte £15. **BREWERY/COMPANY:** Free House.
PRINCIPAL BEERS: Bass. **FACILITIES:** Children welcome Children's licence Garden: patio, outdoor eating.
NOTES: Parking 20.
ROOMS: 18 bedrooms 17 en suite s£25 d£40

Pick of the Pubs

Victoria Hotel 🏵 ★ ★ 🐑 ♀
Front St NE69 7BP ☎ 01668 214431 ▤ 01668 214404
e-mail: enquiries@victoriahotel.net
Dir: In centre of Bamburgh village green

Friendly and attentive service is just one feature of this stylishly refurbished hotel, overlooking Bamburgh's historic village green.

The exuberant stone building dates from the late nineteenth century, but the welcome is uncompromisingly modern; there's an airy candlelit brasserie, a specially designed children's playden and 29 cheerful, well-equipped en suite bedrooms.

Two real ales are always available in the popular bar, plus seasonal mulled wine or sangria.

Meanwhile, carefully prepared fresh produce underpins the menus; lunchtime bar fare includes fresh soup, pasta, burgers, and smoked salmon salad, followed by appetising sweets or Northumbrian cheeses. In the brasserie, kick off with goats' cheese and tomato tart, posh prawn cocktail, or filled ogen melon. Main courses like roast Gressingham duck, beef with thyme roasted shallots, seared salmon steak or wild mushroom risotto precede Border fruit tart, white chocolate cheesecake, or strawberries with crème Chantilly.
OPEN: 11-11. **BAR MEALS:** L served all week. D served all week 12-3 6-9. Av main course £6. **RESTAURANT:** L served Sun. D served all week 12-3 7-9. Av 3 course à la carte £20.
BREWERY/COMPANY: Free House.
PRINCIPAL BEERS: Northumberland Secret Kingdom, Courage Directors, John Smiths. **FACILITIES:** Children welcome Patio, food served outside Dogs allowed Water.
NOTES: Parking 6. **ROOMS:** 29 bedrooms 29 en suite s£45 d£80

NORTHUMBERLAND

Dipton Mill Inn, Hexham

A pleasant, undulating ramble that meanders through woodland beside Dipton Burn before climbing to Hexham Racecourse and fine views across rolling Northumberland countryside.

Turn left from the inn, cross the bridge over Dipton Burn and turn immediately left into woodland, waymarked West Dipton Wood. Cross a stile and proceed through the wood with stream on your left. Where the trees thin on your right, with meadow beyond, follow the path alongside the fence. In the corner, pass beneath beech trees and then follow rocky path beside the stream again.

Pass a footbridge, then soon veer half-right to follow a zig-zag path up the bank, then along a sunken path to a gate on the woodland fringe. Walk straight across the field, with Hexham Racecourse soon coming into view. Go through several gates, draw level with

the grandstand and pass through a further gate, heading towards woodland.

Join a drive leading to house called Black Hill and pass beneath trees to a junction. Turn right along the lane, pass racecourse entrance and footpath to Dipton Burn, then at main junction, cross over and follow road uphill. Take the path right, signed to Hole House, and cross stile in the field corner. Turn right, then immediately left by old building and follow left-hand field edge towards Hole House.

Cross several stiles towards woodland and cross a stile into the wood. Pass Hole House, climb a stile on the right and follow the grassy swathe beside paddocks to a stile. Go through the gate ahead and follow the track beside Dipton Burn to the road. Turn left for the pub.

Distance: 4 miles (6.4km)
Map: OS Landranger 87
Terrain: woodland, farmland, country lanes
Paths: riverside, woodland and field paths; lanes
Gradient: undulating; steady climb to racecourse

Walk submitted by:
Nick Channer

The rolling hills beyond Hexham

DIPTON MILL INN, HEXHAM
Dipton Mill Road NE46 1YA.
Tel: 01434 606577
Directions: 2m S of Hexham on B6306 to Blanchland
Former mill house with beamed and panelled bars, built around 1750 and tucked away in a quiet wooded valley south of Hexham. Offers beers from the family-owned Hexhamshire Brewery and home-cooked food.
Open: 12-2.30 6-11 (Sun 12-4.30 7-10.30). Bar Meals: 12-2.30 6.30-8.30. Children welcome. Streamside garden and patio. Parking.
(see page 329 for full entry)

BELFORD

Pick of the Pubs

Blue Bell Inn ★★★
Market Place NE70 7NE ☎ 01668 213543
01668 213787
Long-established and popular creeper-clad coaching inn located in the centre of Belford just off the A1. Convenient base for exploring Northumberland's magnificent coastline and the Cheviot Hills, offering a friendly, relaxed atmosphere, a good range of real ales and an extensive choice of food, including a good choice of seasonal fish dishes, in the bar, bistro and elegant restaurant. Individually decorated bedrooms.
OPEN: 11-2.30 (Sat 3) 6.30-11 **BAR MEALS:** L served all week. D served all week 12 6.30. Av main course £6.95.
RESTAURANT: L served all week. D served all week 12 7.00. Av 3 course à la carte £23. Av 5 course fixed price £23.
BREWERY/COMPANY: Free House.
PRINCIPAL BEERS: Boddingtons Bitter.
FACILITIES: Children welcome Garden: Food served outside. **NOTES:** Parking 17. **ROOMS:** 17 bedrooms 17 en suite s£30 d£75

BELSAY Map 11 NZ09

The Highlander
NE20 0DN ☎ 01661 881220
Dir: *On A696, 2m S of Belsay*
Traditional pub meals, interesting home-cooked specials and all-day food are available at this popular, flower-adorned roadside hostelry. Choose from salads, casseroles, pasta meals, and substantial dishes like rack of lamb with minted jus, and pork with apple and cider sauce.

OPEN: 9.30-11 (Sun 12-10.30). **BAR MEALS:** L served all week. D served all week 12-9.30. Av main course £7.
PRINCIPAL BEERS: John Smiths, Theakston Best.
FACILITIES: Children welcome Garden: Heated

BERWICK-UPON-TWEED Map 11 NT95

The Rob Roy
Dock Rd, Tweedmouth TD15 2BE ☎ 01289 306428
01289 303629
e-mail: therobroy@btinternet.com
Dir: *Exit A1 2m S of Berwick at A1167 signed Scremerston, to rdbt signed Spittal, then R. 1m to Albion PH, L, 1m to pub*
Situated on the south bank of the Tweed, one of the world's most famous salmon rivers, the Rob Roy has been capably run by Keith and Julie Wilson for 20 years. In the time they have been here, they have transformed it from a small steak house into a cosy pub with a strong fishing theme and the accent very much on seafood. Expect lobster, crab and fresh white fish, with salmon and sea trout in season from the Tweed itself.

OPEN: 12-2.30 7-11. Closed 3wks Feb or Mar. **BAR MEALS:** L served all week. D served all week 12-2 7-9. Av main course £7.50.
RESTAURANT: L served all week. D served all week 12-1.45 7-9.30. Av 3 course à la carte £25. **ROOMS:** 2 bedrooms 2 en suite s£30 d£48

BLANCHLAND Map 11 NY95

Lord Crewe Arms ★★
DH8 9SP ☎ 01434 675251 01434 675337
e-mail: lordcrewearms@freeserve.co.uk
Dir: *10m S of Hexham via B6306*
Once the abbot's house of Blanchland Abbey, this is one of England's oldest inns. Antique furniture, blazing log fires and flagstone floors make for an atmospheric setting. Wide-ranging bar and restaurant menus, and well equipped period bedrooms split between the main hotel and a former estate building.
OPEN: 11am-11pm. **BAR MEALS:** L served Mon-Sat. D served all week 12-2 7-9. Av main course £6. **RESTAURANT:** L served Sun only. D served all week 12-2 7-9.15. Av 3 course à la carte £28. Av 4 course fixed price £28. **BREWERY/COMPANY:** Free House. **PRINCIPAL BEERS:** Castle Eden Ale.
FACILITIES: Children welcome Garden: Dogs allowed.
ROOMS: 19 bedrooms
19 en suite s£80 d£110

Quoits

Throwing a ring over a low post in the ground is the basis of a pastime which was repeatedly forbidden by law from the 14th century on and at some unknown date became a popular pub game. Clubs were competing in Scotland and the North of England before 1850. The game has always been especially strong in the North East, where a standard throwing distance of 11 yards emerged, but 18 yards is the pitch length in East Anglia. The game is subtler and more elaborate than might be supposed, as is the allied pastime of throwing horseshoes.

CARTERWAY HEADS
Map 11 NZ05

Pick of the Pubs

The Manor House Inn 🅰 ♇
DH8 9LX ☎ 01207 255268
Dir: *A69 W from Newcastle, L onto A68 then S for 8m. Inn on R*
From its lonely position high on the A68, this small, family-run free house enjoys spectacular views across open moorland and the Derwent Reservoir. A good range of well kept real ales is available in the stone-walled bar, with its log fires, low-beamed ceiling, and massive timber support. Built around 1760, the building houses a succession of dining areas, and a huge collection of mugs and jugs hangs from the beams in the informal, candlelit restaurant. The unpretentious menus have a cosmopolitan feel: witness smoked trout or local kippers, alongside green-lipped mussels in Thai curry sauce. Again, liver and bacon, or pigeon and lamb casserole with black pudding, stands beside stir-fried Szechuan vegetables in a filo pastry basket. And, if you can't face driving home after dinner, four recently refurbished bedrooms offer a comfortable night's rest.
OPEN: 11-3 5.30-11. **BAR MEALS:** L served all week. D served all week 12-2.30 6.30-9.30. Av main course £10. **RESTAURANT:** L served all week. D served all week 12-2.30 7-9.30. Av 3 course à la carte £18. **BREWERY/ COMPANY:** Free House. **PRINCIPAL BEERS:** Theakstons Best, Mordue Workie Ticket, Morland Ruddles County, Courage Directors. **FACILITIES:** Children welcome Children's licence Garden: patio, outdoor eating Dogs allowed. **NOTES:** Parking 60. **ROOMS:** 4 bedrooms 4 en suite s£33 d£55

CHATTON
Map 11 NU02

The Percy Arms Hotel
Main Rd NE66 5PS ☎ 01668 215244
Dir: *From Alnwick take A1 N, then B6348 to Chatton*
Built in the early 19th-century as a hunting lodge by the Duke of Northumberland, this ivy-covered pub enjoys a peaceful village setting in the unspoilt Till Valley. Bar food includes game and vegetable pie, grilled lamb chops with rosemary and garlic butter, Aberdeen Angus fillet and fresh Lindisfarne crab salad.
OPEN: 11-3 6-11 (Sun 12-3, 7-10.30). **BAR MEALS:** L served all week. D served all week 12-2.30 6.30-9.30. Av main course £6.95. **RESTAURANT:** L served all week. D served all week 12-2.30 6.30-9.30. **BREWERY/COMPANY:** Free House. **PRINCIPAL BEERS:** Northumbrian Ales. **FACILITIES:** Children welcome Children's licence Garden: patio/terrace, outdoor eating Dogs allowed garden only. **NOTES:** Parking 30. **ROOMS:** 7 bedrooms 5 en suite s£25 d£50 2 family rooms £65-£85

CORBRIDGE
Map 11 NY96

The Angel Inn ★ ★ 🅰 ♇
Main St NE45 5LA ☎ 01434 632119 📠 01434 632119
e-mail: 2027unit@snr.co.uk
Dir: *0.5m off A69, signed Corbridge*
Stylish 17th-century coaching inn overlooking the River Tyne. Relax with the daily papers in the panelled lounge or attractive bars, or enjoy a made mode dish or two from the extensive menu choice. Options range from freshly battered cod and chips, and deluxe sandwiches, to lamb hotpot, rabbit in

continued

mustard cream, and cheese and vegetable bake.
OPEN: 11-11 (Sun 12-10.30). **BAR MEALS:** L served all week. D served all week 12-2.30 6-9.30. Av main course £6.95. **RESTAURANT:** L served Thu-Tue. D served all week 12-2 6-9.15. Av 3 course à la carte £13. Av 4 course fixed price £16.95. **PRINCIPAL BEERS:** Theakston Best, Courage Directors. **FACILITIES:** Children welcome Children's licence Garden: patio/terrace. **NOTES:** Parking 25. **ROOMS:** 5 bedrooms 5 en suite s£49.50 d£74

CRASTER
Map 11 NU22

Cottage Inn ♦♦♦ ♇
Dunstan Village NE66 3SZ ☎ 01665 576658
📠 01665 576788
Dir: *NW of Howick to Embleton road*
An 18th-century building with a walled garden situated just a few minutes from the sea in beautiful countryside. English and local dishes feature on the menus, with plenty of fresh fish and vegetarian options. Favourites are Craster fish stew, whole joint of lamb, and rabbit and ale pie.
OPEN: 11-3 6-11 (Sun 12-3, 7-10.30). **BAR MEALS:** L served all week. D served all week 12-2.30 6-9.30. Av main course £6. **RESTAURANT:** L served Sun. D served all week 12-2.30 6-9.30. Av 3 course à la carte £15. **BREWERY/COMPANY:** Free House. **PRINCIPAL BEERS:** McEwans 80/-, Wells Bombardier. **FACILITIES:** Children welcome Garden: outdoor eating, patio. **NOTES:** Parking 60. **ROOMS:** 10 bedrooms 10 en suite s£35 d£63

Jolly Fisherman Inn
Haven Hill NE66 3TR ☎ 01665 576461
e-mail: muriel@silk.fsnet.co.uk
Authentic, unpretentious pub situated in a tiny fishing village famous for its kipper sheds. Handy for local walks, visiting Dunstanburgh Castle and exploring the scenic delights of Northumberland and the beautiful Scottish Borders. Delicious home-made Craster kipper pâté, crab soup with fresh cream and whisky, and fresh salmon sandwiches feature on the menu.
OPEN: 11-3 6-11 (all day from Jun-Aug). **BAR MEALS:** L served all week. D served all week 11-2.30 6-8. Av main course £2.50. **BREWERY/COMPANY:** Pubmaster. **PRINCIPAL BEERS:** Tetley, John Smiths. **FACILITIES:** Children welcome Garden: outdoor eating Dogs allowed. **NOTES:** Parking 10 No credit cards

EGLINGHAM
Map 11 NU21

Tankerville Arms 🅰 ♇
NE66 2TX ☎ 01665 578444 📠 01665 578444
Dir: *B6346 from Alnwick*
Traditional stone village pub serving real ales and food prepared with local produce. Lots of walkers call here, savouring the beamed bar and bustling atmosphere inside or enjoying the spectacular views from the popular beer garden. Expect a varied, well balanced range of English and European dishes, perhaps including roast cod on baked vegetables with a smoked bacon parsley sauce, steak and ale pie, and baked gammon with a cheese and tomato crust. Specials might feature sea bream with sautéed vegetables and Thai sauce, and supreme of corn-fed chicken on a smoked bacon mash with rosemary sauce.
OPEN: 12-3 6-11 (Sun 6-10.30) (winter 6:30-11). Closed 25 Dec. **BAR MEALS:** L served all week. D served all week 12-2 6-9. Av main course £6.50. **RESTAURANT:** L served all week. D served all week 12-2 6-9. Av 3 course à la carte £15. *continued*

BREWERY/COMPANY: Free House.
PRINCIPAL BEERS: Ruddles Best, Courage Directors, Northumberland Secret Kingdom. **FACILITIES:** Children welcome Garden: food served outside Dogs allowed garden only. **NOTES:** Parking 15

ETAL   Map 11 NT93

Black Bull
TD12 4TL ☎ 01890 820200
Dir: 10m N of Wooler R off A697, L at Jct for 1m then L into Etal.
This 300-year-old hostelry is the only thatched pub in Northumberland, located by the ruins of Etal Castle. Close to the River Till and a short distance to the grand walking country of the Cheviots. Typical dishes include steak and kidney pie, liver and onions, cottage pie with cheese topping and giant Yorkshire puddings. **OPEN:** 12-3 6.30-11 (11-11 summer). **BAR MEALS:** L served all week. D served all week 12-3 7-9. Av main course £5.95. **RESTAURANT:** 6.30-9.30. **BREWERY/COMPANY:** Pubmaster. **PRINCIPAL BEERS:** Stones, Tetley, John Smiths. **FACILITIES:** Children welcome. **NOTES:** Parking 6 No credit cards

FALSTONE   Map 11 NY78

The Blackcock Inn ◆◆◆ ⁊
NE48 1AA ☎ 01434 240200 ▤ 01434 240200
e-mail: Blackcock@falstone.fsbusiness.co.uk
Dir: off unclassified rd from Bellingham (accessed from A68 or B6320)
Traditional 18th-century stone-built inn, close to Kielder Reservoir and Forest, with comfortable, well equipped bedrooms. Old beams and open log fires make for a welcoming atmosphere. Typical bar fare includes filled Yorkshire puddings and cod and chips, while the restaurant offers various steaks and dishes such as game pie, smoked duck breast and salmon and asparagus.
OPEN: 11-3 6-11 (Sun 12-3, 6-10.30) (Closed Mon-Tues lunch in winter). **BAR MEALS:** L served all week. D served all week 11-2 7-9. Av main course £6. **RESTAURANT:** D served all week 7-9. Av 3 course à la carte £15. **BREWERY/COMPANY:** Free House. **PRINCIPAL BEERS:** Blackcock Ale, Ruddles County, John Smiths Magnet, Marston Pedigree. **FACILITIES:** Children welcome Garden: outdoor eating Dogs allowed. **NOTES:** Parking 20. **ROOMS:** 5 bedrooms 5 en suite s£28 d£50 FR£60-£80

The Pheasant ◆◆◆◆
Stannersburn NE48 1DD ☎ 01434 240382
▤ 01434 240382
e-mail: enquiries@thepheasantinn.com
Dir: From A68 onto B6320, or from A69, B6079, B6320, follow signs 'Kielder Water'
Close to Kielder Water, this was originally a farmstead, and dates back to the 1600s, with a wealth of beams, exposed stone walls and open fires. Simple menus of carefully prepared dishes are offered, using fresh local produce wherever possible. Expect home-made pies, roast Northumbrian lamb, cider baked gammon, or seafood tagliatelle, with sticky toffee pudding or crème brûlée to follow. The comfortable modern bedrooms open onto an adjoining courtyard.

OPEN: 11-3 6-11 (opening times vary, ring for details). Closed Dec 25-26. **BAR MEALS:** L served all week. D served all week 12-2 7-9. Av main course £6.25. **RESTAURANT:** L served Sun. D served all week 12-2 7-9. Av 3 course à la carte £17. **BREWERY/COMPANY:** Free House. **PRINCIPAL BEERS:** Theakston Best, Marstons Pedigree, Timothy Taylor Landlord, Greene King Old Speckled Hen. **FACILITIES:** Children welcome Garden: outdoor eating Dogs allowed by arrangement only. **NOTES:** Parking 30. **ROOMS:** 8 bedrooms 8 en suite s£35 d£55 FR£68-£80

GREAT WHITTINGTON   Map 11 NZ07

Pick of the Pubs

Queens Head Inn & Restaurant 🖢
NE19 2HP ☎ 01434 672267
Dir: Off A68 & B6318 W of Newcastle upon Tyne
At the heart of Hadrian's Wall country this old pub/restaurant, once a coaching inn, radiates a welcoming atmosphere in comfortable surroundings of beamed rooms, oak settles and open fires. In addition to Black Sheep beers there can be found some three dozen wines of choice and nearly as many malt whiskies.

Menus combine the best of local and international cuisine, taking in avocado, prawn and apple tian, vegetable tempura with sweet and sour sauce and venison medallions with celery and chestnut confit. Speciality dishes include baked cod fillet with herb and cheese crust, prime sirloin and pork tenderloin steaks and home-made desserts such as chocolate mousse with coffee custard. Sunday lunch can start with home-made soup or chef's game pâté before traditional butchers' meats or pot-roasted pheasant with mushroom, bacon and baby onion jus.
OPEN: 12-3 6-11. **BAR MEALS:** L served Tues-Sun. D served Tues-Sun 12-2 6.30-9. Av main course £8.95. **RESTAURANT:** L served Tues-Sun. D served Tues-Sun 12-2 6.30-9. Av 3 course à la carte £18.95. **BREWERY/COMPANY:** Free House. **PRINCIPAL BEERS:** Black Sheep, Queens Head, Hambleton. **FACILITIES:** Children welcome Garden. **NOTES:** Parking 20

HALTWHISTLE
Map 11 NY76

Milecastle Inn
Military Rd, Cawfields NE49 9NN
☎ 01434 321372 & 320682 📄 01434 321671
e-mail: milecastleinn@fsbdial.co.uk
Dir: Leave A69 at Haltwhistle, pub about 2 miles from Haltwhistle at junction with B6318
Small stone-built rural inn overlooking Hadrian's Wall, popular with locals as well as tourists from all over the world. The bar and restaurant both have beamed ceilings, lots of old brasses and open fires. There is a large car park and a walled garden with spectacular views. Home-made pies are a feature - maybe rabbit and musheoom or wild boar and duckling - washed down with a good choice of ales.

OPEN: 12-2.30 6.30-11. **BAR MEALS:** L served all week. D served all week 12-2 6.30-9. **RESTAURANT:** L served Sun. D served Wed-Sat 12-2 7-8.30. Av 3 course à la carte £18. **BREWERY/COMPANY:** Free House. **PRINCIPAL BEERS:** Northumberland Castle, Tetley, Jennings Cumberland Ale, Thwaites Bitter. **FACILITIES:** Garden: outdoor eating, patio, small dovecote. **NOTES:** Parking 30

HAYDON BRIDGE
Map 11 NY86

The General Havelock Inn
Ratcliffe Rd NE47 6ER ☎ 01434 684376
e-mail: GeneralHavelock@aol.com
Dir: On A69, 7m west of Hexham
Built as a private house in 1840, but licensed since 1890, this pub occupies a pleasant riverside setting. Its name comes from a British Army officer who fought in India in the 19th century. The food is all home-made and the wide-ranging menu offers cullen skink, poached fillet of cod with mussels and parsley liquor, seafood crumble, smoked haddock, and beef and Guinness stew with wild mushrooms.
OPEN: 12-2.30 7-11 (closed Mon). **BAR MEALS:** L served Tue-Sat. D served Tues-Sat 12-2 7-9. Av main course £6. **RESTAURANT:** L served Tue-Sun. D served Tue-Sat 12-2 7-9. Av 3 course à la carte £16.75. **BREWERY/COMPANY:** Free House. **PRINCIPAL BEERS:** Greene King Old Speckled Hen, Exmoor Gold, Cumberland Ale, Taylor Landlord, Courage Directors. **FACILITIES:** Children welcome Garden: garden, patio, food served outside Dogs allowed

HEDLEY ON THE HILL
Map 11 NZ05

Pick of the Pubs

The Feathers Inn
NE43 7SW ☎ 01661 843607 📄 01661 843607
From its hill-top position, this small stone-built free house overlooks the classic walking country of the Cheviots. The three-roomed pub is well used by the local community, but strangers are frequently charmed by its friendly and relaxed atmosphere. Families are welcome, and a small side room can be booked in advance if required. Old oak beams, open coal fires and rustic settles set the scene; there's a good selection of traditional games like shove ha'penny and bar skittles, and the stone walls are decorated with old local photographs of rural life. Although the pub has no garden, food and drinks can be served at tables on the green in fine weather. The menus change regularly, and the imaginative home cooking includes lots of vegetarian choices. Expect beef in red wine, honey seared soy salmon steak, sweet potato and goats' cheese casserole, or spring vegetable tart, plus an appetising range of home-made puddings.
OPEN: 12-3 (Sat & Sun only) 6-11 (Sun 7-10.30 only). Closed Dec 25. **BAR MEALS:** L served Sat-Sun. D served Tue-Sun 12-2.30 7-9. **BREWERY/COMPANY:** Free House. **PRINCIPAL BEERS:** Mordue Workie Ticket, Big Lamp Bitter, Fullers London Pride, Yates Bitter. **FACILITIES:** Children welcome Children's licence Dogs allowed. **NOTES:** Parking 12

HEXHAM
Map 11 NY96

Pick of the Pubs

Dipton Mill Inn
Dipton Mill Rd NE46 1YA ☎ 01434 606577
Dir: 2m S of Hexham on HGV route to Blanchland (B6306)
Originally part of a farmhouse, the inn has been here since the 1800s. Enjoy a delightful walk through the woods to Hexham racecourse and back before relaxing with a pint of home-brewed Hexhamshire ale in the low-ceilinged bar. Freshly prepared food utilises ingredients from local suppliers; rolls are made by a local baker and the inn offers a good selection of local cheeses. Sample steak and kidney pie, mince and dumplings, dressed crab salad or tomato, bean and vegetable casserole from the enterprising menu.
OPEN: 12-2.30 6-11 (Sun 12-4.30, 7-10.30). Closed 25 Dec. **BAR MEALS:** L served all week. D served all week 12-2.30 6.30-8.30. Av main course £5.15. **BREWERY/COMPANY:** Free House. **PRINCIPAL BEERS:** Tetley, Hexhamshire Shire Bitter, Devil's Water & Whapweasel. **FACILITIES:** Children welcome Children's licence Garden: stream, outdoor eating, patio. No credit cards

See Pub Walk on page 325

Miners Arms Inn
Main St, Acomb NE46 4PW ☎ 01434 603909
Close to Hadrian's Wall in a peaceful village, this charming 18th-century pub offers real ales and traditional pub food. No music, no juke box.

HEXHAM continued

The Rose & Crown Inn ♦♦♦ ♀
Main St, Slaley NE47 0AA ☎ 01434 673263
🖷 01434 673305
e-mail: rosecrowninn@supanet.com
Ideally placed for visiting Hadrian's Wall and exploring the
spectacular scenery of Northumberland, this 200-year-old
family-run inn combines traditional features with modern
service and comfort. Good wholesome cooking is the hallmark
here and among the dishes on the blackboard menu you
might find chicken breast in a wild mushroom cream sauce,
turkey and ham pie, breaded scampi and locally-made
Cumberland sausage with mash and onion gravy. Pine-
furnished bedrooms are attractively decorated and
thoughtfully equipped.
OPEN: 11.30-3 6-11. **BAR MEALS:** L served all week. D served
all week 12-2.15 6.30-9.30. Av main course £5.50.
RESTAURANT: L served all week. D served all week 12-2.15 6.30-
9.30. Av 3 course à la carte £16. **BREWERY/COMPANY:** Free
House. **PRINCIPAL BEERS:** Black Sheep Special, Theakstons,
Timothy Taylor Landlord, Ruddles County. **FACILITIES:** Children
welcome Garden: outdoor eating, BBQ. **NOTES:** Parking 36.
ROOMS: 3 bedrooms 3 en suite s£27.50 d£45

LONGFRAMLINGTON Map 11 NU10

Granby Inn ♀
Front St NE65 8DP ☎ 01665 570228 🖷 01665 570736
Dir: On A697, 11m N of Morpeth

Situated at the heart of Northumberland, between the
Cheviots and the coast, this 200-year-old coaching inn is a
family-run business which retains much of its original
character. Expect poached salmon, steak pie, grilled trout, or
roast duckling. Good range of traditional desserts.
OPEN: 11-3 6-11. Closed 25-26 Dec. **BAR MEALS:** L served all
week. D served all week 11-2 6-9.30. Av main course £6.50.
RESTAURANT: L served all week. D served all week 11-2 6-9.30.
Av 3 course fixed price £11. **BREWERY/COMPANY:** Free House.
NOTES: Parking 20. **ROOMS:** 5 bedrooms 5 en suite s£32 d£56

LONGHORSLEY Map 11 NZ19

Linden Tree Bar & Grill ★ ★ ★
Linden Hall NE65 8XF ☎ 01670 500033 🖷 01670 500001
e-mail: stay@lindenhall.co.uk
Dir: Off the A1 on the A697 1m N of Longhorsley

Originally two large cattle byres, this popular bar takes its
name from the linden trees in the grounds of Linden Hall
Hotel, an impressive Georgian mansion offering smartly
furnished bedrooms. Straightforward meals range from
aubergine and broccoli bake, braised lamb shank, or
medallions of pork, to grilled salmon, or poached smoked cod
fillets.
OPEN: 11-11 (Sun 12-10.30). Closed 1 Jan. **BAR MEALS:** L
served all week. D served all week 12-2 6-9.30. Av main course
£7.95. **RESTAURANT:** L served all week. D served all week 12-2
6-9.30. Av 3 course à la carte £13.95.
BREWERY/COMPANY: Free House.
PRINCIPAL BEERS: Black Bull, Ruddles Best.
FACILITIES: Children welcome Garden: outdoor eating.
NOTES: Parking 200. **ROOMS:** 50 bedrooms 50 en suite
s£73 d£52

LOW NEWTON BY THE SEA Map 1112 NU22

The Ship
The Square NE66 3EL ☎ 01665 576262
Dir: NW from A1 at Alnwick
The village of Low Newton was purpose-built as a fishing
village in the 18th century and is in the shape of an open-sided
square. The unspoilt Ship overlooks the green and is just a
stroll away from the beach. Bustling in summer and a peaceful
retreat in winter, it offers a simple bar menu that includes
fresh fish, vegetable broth, and a variety of sandwiches and
toasties.
OPEN: 11-4 6.30-11 (Nov-Easter 12-3, 8-11). **BAR MEALS:** L
served all week. D served all week .
BREWERY/COMPANY: Free House.
PRINCIPAL BEERS: Northumberland Castles.
FACILITIES: Children welcome Dogs allowed No credit cards

MATFEN Map 1112 NZ07

The Black Bull
NE20 0RP ☎ 01661 886330
Dir: Leave A69 at Corbridge, join B6318. 2m N sign to Matfen
A 200-year-old, creeper-covered inn fronting the village green,
which has a river running through it. The comfortable
restaurant and carpeted bar have low beams and open fires.

NEWTON ON THE MOOR   Map 11 NU10

Pick of the Pubs

Cook and Barker Inn 🛏 ♀
NE65 9JY ☎ 01665 575234   📠 01665 575234
Dir: 0.5m from A1 S of Alnwick
This very traditional English pub, warm and friendly, is
easily located just off the A1 just north of Morpeth.
Extensive bar menus are engagingly diverse to suit a wide
range of tastes and pockets, with a long list of real ales
and extensive wines to accompany. East Coast seafood
selections include fresh sardines in large or small portions,
pan-fried lemon sole with garlic king prawns and sea bass
fillets on roast vegetables. From 'forest and fields' come
roast venison fillet with black pudding, corn-fed chicken
supreme - perhaps with a lobster tail and shrimp sauce -
and beef fillet with mushroom duxelle or T-bone steak
with cracked peppercorn crust. Lunch and dinner
alternatives are legion with consistently pleasing results.
Special offers include mid-week dinner for two at a set
price: those fortunate to turn this into an overnight stay
are rewarded in the morning with fine Northumbrian
coastal views from its elevated position.
OPEN: 12-3 6-11. **BAR MEALS:** L served all week. D served
all week 12-2 6-9. **RESTAURANT:** L served all week.
D served all week 12-2 7-9. **BREWERY:** Free
House. **PRINCIPAL BEERS:** Timothy Taylor Landlord,
Theakstons, Fullers London Pride, Batemans XXXB.
FACILITIES: Children welcome Garden: outdoor eating
Dogs allowed garden only. **NOTES:** Parking 60.
ROOMS: 4 bedrooms 4 en suite

ROWFOOT   Map 11 NY66

The Wallace Arms
NE49 0JF ☎ 01434 321872   📠 01434 321872
The pub was originally the Railway Inn at Featherstone Halt,
on the Haltwhistle-Alston line (now the South Tyne Trail) and is
set in beautiful parkland half a mile south of Featherstone
Castle. Excellent local ales; great walking country.

SEAHOUSES   Map 11 NU23

The Olde Ship Hotel ★ ★ 🛏 ♀
9 Main St NE68 7RD ☎ 01665 720200   📠 01665 721383
Dir: lower end of main street above harbour
Originally a farmhouse and first licensed in 1812, this historic
hotel has been managed by the present owner's family for
more than 80 years. There is a strong nautical theme to the
cosy, comfortable surroundings and the well-equipped
bedrooms have been stylishly upgraded. An ideal base for a
weekend break visiting the Farne Islands or enjoying a bracing
coastal walk. Expect tip-top ales and home-cooked food,
perhaps including crab soup, freshly-cut sandwiches, liver
casserole, poached salmon with parsley sauce, cheese and
haddock hotpot and roast rib of beef.
OPEN: 11-3 6-11. **BAR MEALS:** L served all week. D served all
week 12-2 7-8.30. Av main course £5.50. **RESTAURANT:** L
served all week. D served all week 12-2 7-8.30. Av 3 course fixed
price £15. **BREWERY/COMPANY:** Free House.
PRINCIPAL BEERS: John Smiths, Theakston, Bass, McEwans.
FACILITIES: Children welcome Garden: Putting Green available.
NOTES: Parking 18. **ROOMS:** 18 bedrooms 18 en suite s£35
d£70

WARDEN   Map 11 NY96

The Boatside Inn
NE46 4SQ ☎ 01434 602233
Dir: Just off A69 west of Hexham, follow signs to Warden
Newborough & Fourstones
The pub, situated below Warden Hill and the Iron Age fort,
gets its name from the rowing boat that ferried people across
the Tyne before the bridge was built. The Iron Age hillfort that
stands behind the pub is a popular destination for walkers.
Home cooked food, locally sourced.

WARENFORD   Map 11 NU12

Pick of the Pubs

Warenford Lodge 🛏
NE70 7HY ☎ 01668 213453   📠 01668 213453
e-mail: warenfordlodge@aol.com
Dir: 100yds E of A1,10M N of Alnwick
Near the old toll bridge over Warren Burn, at the heart of
some fine walking country, this 200-year-old coaching inn
is just a stone's throw from the A1. Within it boasts
exposed thickset stone walls and fireplaces with a
welcoming open fire on colder days.
    Certainly a mainly dining venue, lunches are served on
weekends only from a menu that shows considerable
reliance on local produce - Bamburgh sausages and
Berwick Edge Pie for instance. Starters include traditionally
prepared soup with Turkestan brown bread and a mixed
platter of charcuterie. To follow, plaice fillets are stuffed
with prawns, mushrooms and chardonnay sauce and in
season expect to encounter a pork and pigeon pie served
with herb dumplings and a platter of fresh vegetables.
    In addition to special baked lemon pudding and spiced
pears in red wine, special mention should be made of the
selection of Northumberland cheeses such as
unpasteurised Doddington and Cuddy's Cave.
OPEN: Sat & Sun 12-2, Tue-Sat 7-11 (Sun 7-10.30). Closed all
Mon & Tue-Fri lunch. Seasonal variations Please phone.
Closed 25/26 Dec, 1 Jan. **BAR MEALS:** L served Sat-Sun.
D served Wed-Sun 12-1.30 7-9.30. Av main course £8.50.
RESTAURANT: L served Sun. D served Tues-Sun 12-1.30
7-9.30. Av 3 course fixed price £14.95.
BREWERY/COMPANY: Free House **FACILITIES:** Children
welcome Garden: Dogs allowed garden only, Water.
NOTES: Parking 60

WOOLER

Tankerville Arms ★ ★
Cottage Rd NE71 6AD ☎ 01668 281581
17th-century coaching inn. Bar popular for lunch. Well
equipped bedrooms. Characterful bar.

> **Room prices** minimum single and minimum double
> rates are shown. FR indicates family room

England

NOTTINGHAMSHIRE

BEESTON   Map 09 SK53

Pick of the Pubs

Victoria Hotel ♀
Dovecote Ln NG9 1JG ☎ 0115 9254049
▤ 0115 922 3537
*Dir: M1 J25 take A52 E. R at Nursuryman PH & R opp Rockaway
Hotel into Barton St 1st L*
The original 100-year-old hotel came to life in the hey-day
of the railways and the large patio garden remains handy
for a touch of trainspotting. Almost derelict with trees
growing out of the roof in 1994, this unpretentious brick
building has been restored and transformed into a great
pub, popular with ale drinkers, lovers of fresh food and
pub-goers seeking a traditional, music and electronic
game-free atmosphere. In addition to 12 tip-top real ales,
farm ciders and 150 malt whiskies, the attraction is the
single, daily-changing menu: there's always roast beef on
Sundays and fresh fish on Fridays - Dartmouth smoked
salmon, pan-fried whiting popular as ever. Sausage and
mash and steak and Hemlock pie are perennial favourites:
more up-to-date alternatives include sautéed corn-fed
chicken with chorizo and pancetta and Mediterranean
mezes platter. Good vegetarian choice; regular themed
evenings.
OPEN: 11-11. **BAR MEALS:** L served all week. D served all
week 12-9. Av main course £5.95. **RESTAURANT:** L served
all week. D served all week 12-9.
BREWERY/COMPANY: Tynemill Ltd.
PRINCIPAL BEERS: Batemans XB, Marstons Pedigree,
Caledonian IPA, Castle Rock Hemlock. **FACILITIES:** Garden:
patio, outdoor eating, Dogs allowed Public bar.
NOTES: Parking 10

CAUNTON   Map 09 SK76

Caunton Beck 🐑 ♀
NG23 6AB ☎ 01636 636793 ▤ 01636 636828
Dir: 5m NW of Newark on A616

Set amid herb gardens and a dazzling rose arbour, this
civilised pub-restaurant has been lovingly reconstructed
around a single 16th-century cottage. Original Elizabethan oak
trusses and reclaimed pitch pine create a relaxed, informal
environment, with no music or electronic games. Although
there's an emphasis on food 'in perpetual motion' throughout
the day, customers are encouraged to meet, eat and drink, or
simply unwind with a good book or the daily papers. Indoors
continued

you'll find low beams, rag-rolled paintwork and scrubbed pine
tables, with the option of al fresco meals on the flower-filled
open air terraces in summer.
Look in for breakfast at weekends (and weekdays by
arrangement) or come later for sandwiches, a varied menu
and a decent wine list. Expect bacon-wrapped pheasant with
parsnip mash, spiced lamb and rice, cheese soufflé with leeks,
salmon and crab fishcakes, or tuna steak with coriander and
lime couscous.
OPEN: 8am-midnight. **BAR MEALS:** L served all week. D served
all week 8am-midnight. Av main course £5.75. **RESTAURANT:** L
served all week. D served all week. Av 3 course à la carte £20. Av
3 course fixed price £12. **BREWERY/COMPANY:** Free House.
PRINCIPAL BEERS: Timothy Taylor Landlord.
FACILITIES: Children welcome Garden: Food served outside
Dogs allowed. **NOTES:** Parking 40

CAYTHORPE   Map 09 SK64

Black Horse Inn
NG14 7ED ☎ 0115 966 3520
This small, old-fashioned village pub has its own micro-
brewery and is very popular with locals, cyclists and walkers.
No hot food on a Sunday.

COLSTON BASSETT   Map 09 SK73

Pick of the Pubs

The Martins Arms Inn 🐑 ♀
School Ln NG12 3FD ☎ 01949 81361 ▤ 01949 81039
*Dir: M1 J22, Take A50 then A46 North towards Newark. Colston
Bassett is situated East of Cotgrave.*
During the middle years of the nineteenth century, Squire
Martin created this village inn from a 300-year-old estate
farmhouse. Nowadays the Grade II listed building has
something of a country house feel; there are seasonal fires
in the Jacobean fireplace, and the period furnishings and
ubiquitous hunting prints are redolent of a bygone age.
The acre of landscaped grounds includes a herb garden,
as well as established lawns for al fresco dining during the
summer months.
All meals are freshly cooked to order, and local
ingredients like Colston Bassett Stilton and Melton
Mowbray pork pies rub shoulders with more adventurous
dishes. Snacks such as toasted brioche with smoked
salmon and scrambled egg share the menu with daube of
beef with celeriac, fillets of sea bream on sea asparagus,
or roasted vegetable gateau layered with Brie and potato
rösti on a tomato fondue. Naturally, there's also an
extensive wine list.
OPEN: 12-3 6-11. Closed 25 Dec. **BAR MEALS:** L served all
week. D served Mon-Sat 12-2 6-10. Av main course £12.95.
RESTAURANT: L served all week. D served Mon-Sat 12-2
6-9.30. Av 3 course à la carte £25.
BREWERY/COMPANY: Free House.
PRINCIPAL BEERS: Marstons Pedigree, Bass, Greene King
Abbot Ale, Timothy Taylor Landlord. **FACILITIES:** Children
welcome Garden: Marquee for Weddings. Food served
outside Dogs allowed outside only, water.
NOTES: Parking 35. **ROOMS:** 2 bedrooms 1 en suite
s£35 d£65

EASTWOOD
Map 09 SK44

The Nelson & Railway Inn
12 Station Rd, Kimberley NG16 2NR ☎ 0115 9382177
Dir: *One mile north of junction 26 M1*
Originally 17th-century, this village pub includes various
Victorian additions and was previously known as The Pelican.
Renamed the Lord Nelson in 1804 before becoming the Lord
Nelson Railway Hotel during the railway era. Nearby station
buildings are now derelict. Next door is the Hardy & Hanson
brewery, which supplies many of the ales found behind the
bar. Freshly cooked dishes and daily specials might include
steak and kidney pie, grilled gammon, stir-fry duck with crispy
vegetables, mushroom Stroganoff, cod in batter or chicken
tikka masala.
OPEN: 10.30-3 5-11 (Thu-Sat 10.30-11, Sun 12-10.30).
BAR MEALS: L served all week. D served all week 12-2.30 5.30-9.
Av main course £5. **RESTAURANT:** L served all week. D served
all week 12-2.30 5.30-9. Av 3 course à la carte £10.
BREWERY/COMPANY: Hardy & Hansons.
PRINCIPAL BEERS: Hardys, Hansons Best.
FACILITIES: Children welcome Garden: outdoor eating,
patio/terrace Dogs allowed water provided. **NOTES:** Parking 50.
ROOMS: 3 bedrooms s£22 d£37 1 family room £49

ELKESLEY
Map 09 SK67

Pick of the Pubs

Robin Hood Inn ⌖ ♀
High St DN22 8AJ ☎ 01777 838259
Unassuming Whitbread pub located just off the A1 4 miles
south of Retford. Run by an enthusiastic landlord/chef,
Alan Draper, the modestly comfortable lounge and tiny
dining-room are the unlikely setting in which to enjoy
some good bar food - well worth passing every Little Chef
on the A1 for!
    Regular printed menu favourites like decent filled
baguettes and ploughman's lunches are supplemented by
an imaginative choice of daily blackboard dishes. Follow a
bowl of moules or chicken liver pâté with plum and apple
chutney with seared sea bass with mussel broth, roast
rump of lamb with ratatouille, confit of duck with port
wine and redcurrant, and casserole of plaice and mussels
in cream and garlic. Finish with baked bananas with
caramel sauce or tiramisu.
OPEN: 11.30-3 6.30-11. **BAR MEALS:** L served all week.
D served Mon-Sat 12-2 7-9.30. Av main course £7.
BREWERY/COMPANY: Whitbread.
PRINCIPAL BEERS: Flowers Original IPA, Boddingtons
Bitter. **FACILITIES:** Garden: outdoor eating.
NOTES: Parking 40

LAXTON
Map 09 SK76

The Dovecote Inn
Moorhouse Rd NG22 0NU ☎ 01777 871586
📠 01777 871586
e-mail: dovecoteinn@yahoo.co.uk
Set in the only village that still uses the '3 field system' (pop
into the local Visitor Centre to find out what that is), this pub is
an ideal stopping point for walkers.

MAPLEBECK

The Beehive
NG22 0BS ☎ 01636 636306
Nestling down a country lane, this popular family pub is by a
stream and has a play area in the garden. Mansfield beers.

NORMANTON ON TRENT
Map 09 SK75

The Square & Compass
Eastgate NG23 6RN ☎ 01636 821439
Dir: *Off A1 & B1164 N of Newark-on-Trent*
Refurbished and open-up pub, originally three cottages and
dating back some 400 years, with low-beamed ceilings and
open fires.

NOTTINGHAM
Map 09 SK54

Fellows Morton & Clayton ♀
54 Canal St NG1 7EH ☎ 0115 950 6795 📠 0115 953 9838
Originally a warehouse belonging to the brewers Samuel
Fellows and Matthew Claytons, this is an unusual and
atmospheric city centre pub with a cobbled courtyard
overlooking the canal. Apart from an award-winning flower
display, it offers a range of snacks, including red snapper,
steak and kidney pie and Moby Dick haddock.
OPEN: 11-11 (Sun 12-10.30). **BAR MEALS:** L served all week.
D served all week 11.30-10 (6pm wkends). Av main course £7.
RESTAURANT: L served all week. D served all week 11.30-2.30
5.30-9.30. Av 3 course à la carte £12. Av 2 course fixed price £4.99.
BREWERY/COMPANY: Free House.
PRINCIPAL BEERS: Taylor Landlord, Fellows Bitter, Fullers
London Pride. **FACILITIES:** Garden. **NOTES:** Parking 4

Lincolnshire Poacher
161-163 Mansfield Rd NG1 3FR ☎ 0115 9411584
Dir: *M1 J26. Town centre*
Traditional wooden-floored town pub with settles and sturdy
wooden tables. Bustles with real ale fans in search of the 12
real ales on tap - regular brewery evenings and wine tastings.
Also, good cider and 70 malt whiskies - a great drinkers pub.
Large summer terrace.

Ye Olde Trip to Jerusalem
1 Brewhouse Yard, Castle Rd NG1 6AD ☎ 0115 947 3171
📠 0115 950 1185
e-mail: cunderdown1@excite.co.uk
Thought to be the oldest inn in England, dating from 1070 and
associated with Richard the Lionheart's crusaders. In addition
to its range of sandwiches and snacks, the pub is known for its
giant filled Yorkshire puddings. Also on offer are bangers and
mash, Kimberley pie, or cheesy leek and potato bake.
OPEN: 11-11 (Sun 12-10.30). **BAR MEALS:** L served all week
11-6. Av main course £4.99. **PRINCIPAL BEERS:** Marstons
Pedigree. **FACILITIES:** Children welcome

SOUTHWELL

French Horn
Main St, Upton NG23 5SY ☎ 01636 812394
This 18th-century former farmhouse is handy for those visiting
the racecourse and nearby Southwell Minster. Real ales and
wines. Children welcome. Snacks all day & dining menus.

THURGARTON Map 09 SK64

The Red Lion
Southwell Rd NG14 7GP ☎ 01636 830351
Dir: *On A612 between Nottingham & Southwell*
16th-century inn that was once a monk's ale house. Try not to be put off your meal by the 1936 Nottingham Guardian cutting on the wall which tells of the murder of Sarah Ellen Clarke. Not far from Thurgarton Priory. The kitchen has a fine local reputation.

TUXFORD Map 09 SK77

The Mussel & Crab NEW
NG22 0PJ ☎ 01777 870491 01777 871096
Dir: *From the Ollerton/Tuxford Junction of the A1 & the A57 go N on the B1164 to Sibthorpe Hill and the pub is 800 yds on the R*
The daily catch is transformed into a comprehensive choice of seafood dishes at this quirky fish restaurant. Notable features of the establishment are the cupped hand carved seats in the bar, the aquarium in the gents' cistern, and the famous 'lifeboat', a sample of five wines from the restaurant's cellar presented in a model lifeboat to the sound of the captain's horn.
OPEN: 11.30-2.30 6.30-11. **BAR MEALS:** L served all week. D served all week 11.30-2 6.30-9. Av main course £10. **RESTAURANT:** L served all week. D served all week 12-2 6.30-9. Av 3 course à la carte £16.50. **BREWERY/COMPANY:** Free House **FACILITIES:** Garden: Food served outside Dogs allowed. **NOTES:** Parking 74

WALKERINGHAM Map 09 SK78

The Three Horse Shoes
High St DN10 4HR ☎ 01427 890959 01427 890437
e-mail: turnershoe@aol.com

A quiet village pub festooned with hanging baskets and some 10,000 bedding plants, all grown and tended by the owner. There's also an aviary, and a Japanese water garden. Medallions of pork in a white wine herb mustard and cream sauce, roast stuffed breast of lamb, spinach and courgette lasagne, or home-made steak and kidney pie may be on today's menu.
OPEN: 11.30-3 7-11 (from June 5-11). **BAR MEALS:** L served Tues-Sun. D served Tues-Sat 12-2 7-9.30. Av main course £7.50. **RESTAURANT:** L served Sun. D served Tues-Sat 12-2 7-9.30. Av 3 course à la carte £13. **BREWERY/COMPANY:** Free House. **PRINCIPAL BEERS:** Stones, Bass, Worthington. **FACILITIES:** Children welcome Garden: Dogs allowed garden only. **NOTES:** Parking 40

WELLOW

Olde Red Lion
Eakring Rd NG22 0EG ☎ 01623 861000
Dir: *From Ollerton on the A616 to Newark after 2 miles, Wellow village turn L.*
400-year-old pub opposite the maypole in a quiet Nottinghamshire village; popular with walkers. Unspoilt atmosphere; traditional pub food.

WEST LEAKE Map 09 SK52

Star Inn
Melton Ln LE12 5RQ ☎ 01509 852233
e-mail: lcollins1@ntlworld.com
Dir: *A6 toward Loughborough, 0.33m L to Kingston, over canal, R to Sutt Bonn, over crossroad, 1m Star on L*
Whitewashed walls and flowering window boxes and tubs add a touch of colour to this picturesque inn known to locals as the Pit House. Look out for the cock-fighting prints and foxes' masks on the ochre-painted walls in the public bar. Straightforward yet appetising pub food might include mixed grill, vegetable chilli, savoury lamb meat balls, gammon steak and scampi, as well as a choice of pies, casseroles and quiches.
OPEN: 11-2.30 6-11 (Sun 12-4, 7-10.30). **BAR MEALS:** L served all week. D served Tue-Sat 12.15-2 6.30-8.30. Av main course £6. **RESTAURANT:** L served all week. D served Tue-Sat 12.15-2 6.30-8.30. Av 3 course à la carte £11. **BREWERY/COMPANY:** Enterprise Inns. **PRINCIPAL BEERS:** Bass, Adnams Broadside, Greene King IPA, Fullers London Pride. **FACILITIES:** Children welcome Garden: patio, Food served outside Dogs allowed. **NOTES:** Parking 40

OXFORDSHIRE

ABINGDON Map 04 SU49

The Merry Miller
Cothill OX13 6JW ☎ 01865 390390 01865 390040
e-mail: rob@merrymiller.fsbusiness.co.uk
Dir: *1m from the Marcham interchange on the A34*
Former 17th-century granary situated in a quiet village close to Oxford. Beams, flagstones, log fires and pine furnishings characterise the tastefully refurbished bar and restaurant. Snack or main meals may be taken in either bar or restaurant, and include a range of fresh-filled baguettes as well as fish and chips, half shoulder of lamb, or fish risotto.
OPEN: 11-11 (Sun 12-10.30). **BAR MEALS:** L served all week. D served all week 12-2.45 6.30-9.45. **RESTAURANT:** L served all week. D served all week 12-2.45 6.30-9.45. Av 3 course à la carte £17. **BREWERY/COMPANY:** Greene King. **PRINCIPAL BEERS:** Greene King IPA & Old Speckled Hen. **FACILITIES:** Children welcome Dogs allowed. **NOTES:** Parking 60

ADDERBURY

The Red Lion
The Green OX17 3LU ☎ 01295 810269 01295 811906
Civilised old stone coaching inn on the Banbury to Oxford road. Once known as the King's Arms it had a tunnel in the cellar used by Royalists in hiding during the Civil War. Expect a rambling, beamed interior, daily papers, good wines and a varied menu. Comfortable bedrooms.

**THE LORD NELSON,
BRIGHTWELL BALDWIN**
OX9 5NP. Tel: 01491 612330
Directions: off B4009
between Watlington and
Benson
*An elegant, stone-built 18th-
century pub located opposite
the parish church. Attractively
modernised with a mix of
furnishings, open log fires
and lots of Nelson
memorabilia. Interesting
daily-changing menus using
fresh local produce.*
Open: 12-3 (Sat from 10, Sun
till 4) 6.30-11. Closed Sun eve
& all Mon. Bar Meals: 12-3
6.30-10. Children welcome.
Garden/patio. Parking.
(see page 338 for full entry)

*Pub*WALK

The Lord Nelson, Brightwell Baldwin

With lovely views of the
Chiltern Hills, this short
country ramble explores Brightwell
Park, an 18th-century parkland
landscaped by Repton, and nearby
farmland. Take your binoculars and
look out for red kites.

On leaving the pub and facing the
mainly 14th-century parish church,
turn left up the village street. In 50
yards (46m), at the entrance to
Brightwell Park, turn right by the
Lodge House into Cadwell Lane. Walk
along the lane, which becomes a track
between woods, and ignore the
turning left for Whitehouse Farm.
Continue ahead, the lane opening out
with good views across fields and look
out for red kites which are often seen
here.

Short walk - turn right on reaching
a junction with a track and head
downhill until you come to a stile on
your right, next to a horse jump. Cross
the stile and continue along the grassy
path to a gate into Brightwell Park (see
* below)

Longer walk - at the junction with
the track, enter the large field ahead
and walk along the field edge for 1/2
mile (0.8km) as it bends right towards
Cadwell Farm. Just beyond the farm,
take the waymarked footpath right,
crossing the large field in the direction
of Brightwell Park. Pass the horse jump
and stile and follow the grassy path to
a gate and enter Brightwell Park.
*Follow the footpath through another
gate and diagonally cross the park,
heading for the very large cedar tree.
Eventually, cross a stile and turn right
along the village street back to the
pub.

Distance: 4 miles (6.4km)
Map: OS Landranger 164
Terrain: parkland and
farmland
Paths: tracks, field and
parkland paths
Gradient: gentle climbs

*Walk submitted by:
The Lord Nelson*

ARDINGTON — Map 04 SU48

Pick of the Pubs

The Boars Head 🔊 ♀
Church St OX12 8QA ☎ 01235 833254
📠 01235 833254
e-mail: bruce-buchan@talk21.com
Dir: Off A417 W of Wantage
Chef/patron Bruce Buchan arrived here in January 2001
having established a fine reputation at several Oxfordshire
dining pubs in recent years. His plans look very promising
for this attractive, 400-year-old timbered pub set beside
the church in a timeless estate village. The tastefully
furnished series of rooms are mainly given over to dining
but the intention is to reinstate a locals' bar and build a
new conservatory dining area to the rear, and add four en
suite bedrooms. Logs fires, evening candlelight and fresh
flowers enhance to ambience in which to savour some
innovative pub food. A short menu lists simply described
dishes which utilise fresh local produce. From chicken and
foie gras terrine and grape chutney and crispy duck confit
with five spices to start, main course options may include
grilled Cornish cod with toasted ratatouille, seared
scallops with lentils and chardonnay, and herb-crusted
rump of English lamb. Puddings range from chocolate
truffle cake with cherry compote to an assiette of lemon
desserts.
OPEN: 12-3 6.30-11. **BAR MEALS:** L served all week.
D served all week 12-2.30 7-10. Av main course £12.
RESTAURANT: L served all week. D served all week 12-2.30
7-10. Av 3 course à la carte £25.
BREWERY/COMPANY: Free House.
PRINCIPAL BEERS: Brakspear Bitter, Hook Norton Old
Hooky,. **FACILITIES:** Children welcome Dogs allowed.
NOTES: Parking 10

ASTHALL — Map 06 SP21

The Maytime Inn ♦♦♦ 🔊 ♀
OX18 4HW ☎ 01993 822068 📠 01993 822635
Dir: A361 from Swindon, R onto A40 then onto B4047 to Asthall

Traditional Cotswold pub in the Windrush valley. Close by is
the former home of the famous Mitford sisters, one of whom,
Nancy, wrote Love in a Cold Climate. The present owners
acquired the then derelict local in 1975 and set about
transforming it into the character inn it is today. Daily menus
are listed on a blackboard and dishes might include Barbary
duck on potato cake, sirloin steak, bangers and mash with
onion gravy and pie of the day. Comfortable, well equipped
bedrooms, all with modern en suite facilities.

OPEN: 11-3 6-11. **BAR MEALS:** L served all week. D served all
week 12.30-2.15 7-9.30. Av main course £7.50. **RESTAURANT:** L
served all week. D served all week 12.30-2.15 7-9.30. Av 3 course à
la carte £14.95. **BREWERY/COMPANY:** Free House.
PRINCIPAL BEERS: Bass, Fullers London Pride, Greene King Old
Speckled hen. **FACILITIES:** Children welcome Garden:
patio/terrace, pond, outdoor eating Dogs allowed.
NOTES: Parking 100. **ROOMS:** 6 bedrooms 6 en suite s£49.50
d£67.50

BAMPTON — Map 06 SP30

The Romany ♦♦♦
Bridge St OX18 2HA ☎ 01993 850237 📠 01993 852133
e-mail: romany@barbox.net
A shop until 20 years ago, The Romany is housed in an 18th-
century building of Cotswold stone with a beamed bar, log
fires and intimate dining room. Food ranges from
ploughmans' to steaks, with home-made specials like hot pot
or steak and ale pie. Regional singers provide live
entertainment a couple of times a month.
OPEN: 11-11 (Sun 12-10.30). **BAR MEALS:** L served all week.
D served all week 11 5. Av main course £4.
RESTAURANT: L served all week. D served all week 11 5.
Av 3 course à la carte £10. **BREWERY/COMPANY:** Free
House. **PRINCIPAL BEERS:** Archers Village, Bass,.
FACILITIES: Children welcome Garden: Food served
outside Dogs allowed Water. **NOTES:** Parking 8.
ROOMS: 11 bedrooms 11 en suite s£22.50 d£35

The Vines ♀
Burford Rd, Black Bourton OX18 2PF
☎ 01993 843559 📠 01993 843559
*Dir: From A40 Witney, take A4095 to Faringdon, then 1st R after
Bampton to Black Bourton*
Mediterranean-style restaurant in a tiny village pub designed
by BBC Real Rooms personality John Cregg, with hand-painted
murals themed on Bacchus.
The menu offers a choice of light bites, salads and pasta in
addition to main meals. Favourite dishes are cheese soufflé
made with locally smoked mature cheddar, steamed Bantry
Bay mussels, baked calves' liver in a filo case, and fillet steak
Diane.

OPEN: 11-2.30 6-11 (Sun 12-10.30). **BAR MEALS:** L served all
week. D served all week 12-2 6.30-9.30. Av main course £5.
RESTAURANT: L served all week. D served all week 12-2 6.30-
9.30. Av 3 course à la carte £19.50. **BREWERY/COMPANY:** Free
House. **PRINCIPAL BEERS:** Greene King IPA, Marston's
Pedigree. **FACILITIES:** Children welcome Garden: outdoor
eating Dogs allowed except in garden. **NOTES:** Parking 70

continued

England

BANBURY   Map 06 SP44

The George Inn ♀
Lower St, Barford St Michael OX15 0RH
☎ 01869 338226   📠 01869 337804
300-year-old thatched building featuring old beams, exposed
stone walls and open fireplaces. Handy for visiting Banbury
and Oxford. Extensive clientele and a very large pub garden
overlooking unspoilt countryside. One menu throughout offers
dishes such as lamb stew and mint mash, hot chilli,
Cumberland sausage and fish and chips with mushy peas.
OPEN: 12-3 7-11 (Fri 12-3, 5-11, Sun 12-3, 7-10.30).
BAR MEALS: L served all week. D served all week 12-2 7-9.
Av main course £6.   **BREWERY/COMPANY:** Free House.
PRINCIPAL BEERS: Hook Norton, Wadworth 6X, Greene King
Abbot Ale, Shepherd Neame Spitfire.   **FACILITIES:** Children
welcome Garden: outdoor eating, patio/terrace Dogs allowed.
NOTES: Parking 20

Ye Olde Reine Deer Inn
47 Parsons St OX16 5NA ☎ 01295 264031
📠 01295 264018
Dir: One mile from M40 J11, in town centre just off market square
Historic town centre pub dating from 1570, where Oliver
Cromwell once held court in the oak-panelled Globe Room.
Noted for its atmosphere, tip-top Hook Norton ales, Irish
whiskey, and popular lunchtime bar food. Look to the menu
for Cromwell Pie, bubble and squeak, shepherd's pie, cod and
prawn pie, or mushroom florentine.   **OPEN:** 11-11 (closed Sun & BHs).   **BAR MEALS:** L served Mon-
Sat 11-2.   **BREWERY/COMPANY:** Hook Norton.
PRINCIPAL BEERS: Hook Norton, Best, Mild, Old.
FACILITIES: Children welcome Garden: Outdoor eating Dogs
allowed water provided.   **NOTES:** Parking 14

Pick of the Pubs

Moody Cow @ The Wykham Arms 🔖
Sibford Gower OX15 5RX ☎ 01295 788808
📠 01295 788013
e-mail: james@moodycow.co.uk
Picture-postcard 17th-century village pub, built of mellow
Hornton stone with a thatched roof and overlooking rolling
Oxfordshire countryside. Beautifully refurbished by new
owners (who also own The Moody Cow, Upton Bishop,
Herefordshire - see entry) during 2000, who have exposed
original features and created a smart, modern feel
throughout the rambling series of five rooms. Expect slate
floors, exposed stone, sturdy pine furnishings, tasteful
prints and open fires. Interesting, well presented home-
made food, freshly prepared from local produce, matches
the style of the place. From starters like bouillabaisse,
chicken Caesar salad and smoked salmon fishcakes with
horseradish crème fraiche, the choice extends to freshly
battered cod and chips, bangers and mash with onion
gravy, guinea fowl casserole, canon of lamb with chicken
and herb mousse and orange jus, and daily fish specials
(grey mullet with herb dressing). Puddings include gooey
chocolate pudding. South-facing terrace.
OPEN: 12-2.30 6.30-11.   **BAR MEALS:** L served Tue-Sun.
D served Tue-Sat 12 6.30. Av main course £11.
RESTAURANT: L served Tue-Sun. D served Tue-Sat 12 6.30.
Av 3 course à la carte £20.   **BREWERY/COMPANY:** Free
House.   **PRINCIPAL BEERS:** Hook Norton Best, Flowers IPA,
Wadsworth 6X.   **FACILITIES:** Garden: Food served outside
Dogs allowed.   **NOTES:** Parking 30

BARNARD GATE   Map 06 SP41

Pick of the Pubs

The Boot Inn ♀
OX29 6XE ☎ 01865 881231   📠 01865 882119
Dir: off the A40 between Witney & Eynsham
For reasons unexplained, the good-and-famous who have
donated footwear to this extraordinary Cotswold stone
pub include Ian Botham, George Best, Eddie Irvine, The
Bee Gees and Sir Ranulph Fiennes: new licensees pledge
to continue the tradition, adding recently the coveted
boots that once belonged to Sir Stanley Matthews. Set
back from the hum-drum of the busy A40 and surrounded
by open fields and hedgerows, the accent here is on
brasserie-style pub food in a modern idiom. Smart and
civilised interior with a spacious quarry-tiled bar and
attractively decorated dining areas either side. A typical
meal may begin with Thai-style mussels, salmon and crab
fishcakes with spicy noodles and mango salsa, or Caesar
salad, followed by seared salmon with pancetta, ratatouille
and foie gras, seafood linguine with scallops, king prawns,
shallots, cream and basil, or 'Lamboot' - slow-roasted
lamb shank with mashed roots, with beetroot and mint
jus. Interesting list of wines; 12 by the glass.
OPEN: 11-3 6-11.   **BAR MEALS:** L served all week 12-2.30.
Av main course £7.   **RESTAURANT:** L served all week.
D served all week 12-2.30 7-9.30. Av 3 course à la carte £20.
BREWERY/COMPANY: Free House.
PRINCIPAL BEERS: Hook Norton.   **FACILITIES:** Children
welcome Courtyard.   **NOTES:** Parking 30

BINFIELD HEATH   Map 04 SU77

Bottle & Glass ♀
RG9 4JT ☎ 01491 575755
Dir: N of B4155 between Reading & Henley

Located near the glorious Chilterns, this 15th-century thatched
and timbered inn is reputedly where sheep and cattle drovers
stopped for a 'bottle and glass' en route to market. Cosy
beamed bar with roaring open fire and scrubbed tables to
retreat to after enjoying one of the spectacular walks nearby.
Virtually everything on the menu is prepared from fresh
produce and cooked to order. Straightforward pub snacks
include ham, egg and chips and vegetarian quiche, while on
the blackboard the range of specials might feature beef
Stroganoff, country lamb casserole and Cornish fish pie with
leeks and smoked bacon.
OPEN: 11-3.30 6-11. Closed Dec 25.   **BAR MEALS:** L served all
week. D served Mon-Sat 12-1.45 7-9.30. Av main course £7.95.

continued

BREWERY/COMPANY: Brakspear.
PRINCIPAL BEERS: Brakspear. **FACILITIES:** Garden: outdoor eating Dogs allowed garden only,Water. **NOTES:** Parking 30

BLEWBURY   Map 04 SU58

Pick of the Pubs

Blewbury Inn ◉ ◉
London Rd OX11 9PD ☎ 01235 850496
▤ 01235 850496

See Pick of the Pubs on page 339

BLOXHAM   Map 06 SP43

The Elephant & Castle
OX15 4LZ ☎ 01295 720383
Dir: Just off A361
Pleasant Cotswold stone pub in hilltop village with a striking church and spire. Attractive features inside, including inglenook fireplace and strip wood floor. Well-planned lunchtime menu offers such dishes as minty lamb pie, roast chicken breast, beer battered cod and sausage, egg and beans. Baguettes, ploughmans lunches and toasted sandwiches.
OPEN: 10-3 5-11 (Sat-Sun all day). **BAR MEALS:** L served Mon-Sat 12-2. Av main course £3.50. **RESTAURANT:** L served all week. D served all week 12-2. Av 3 course à la carte £6.50.
BREWERY/COMPANY: Hook Norton.
PRINCIPAL BEERS: Hook Norton. **FACILITIES:** Children welcome Garden: outdoor eating, patio. **NOTES:** Parking 20

BRIGHTWELL BALDWIN   Map 04 SU69

Pick of the Pubs

The Lord Nelson Inn ♀
OX9 5NP ☎ 01491 612330 612497   ▤ 01491 612118
e-mail: diane@lordnelsoninn.fsnet.co.uk
Dir: Off the B4009 between Watlington & Benson
Having been closed for 66 years, this impressive 300-year-old inn was re-opened on 21st October 1971 - Trafalgar Day. Originally a thatched cottage and extended in the late-18th century, the Lord Nelson boasts a splendid inglenook fireplace - the perfect antidote after an invigorating country walk in the fresh air. During summer, the pretty garden with its weeping willow and rear terrace prove to be a popular attraction. Brakspears real ale is served in the attractive beamed bar, there is a comprehensive wine list and all food is freshly cooked to order by the inn's experienced chefs. Interesting, well designed specials include the likes of wild rabbit casserole with parsnip and potato mash and pan-fried foie gras, baked brill with grilled whole artichoke and pea sauce and salmon and herb fishcakes. Imaginative Sunday lunch menu.
OPEN: 12-4 6-11. **BAR MEALS:** L served all week. D served all week 12-3 6-10. Av main course £8. **RESTAURANT:** L served all week. D served all week 12-3 6-10. Av 3 course à la carte £20. Av 3 course fixed price £10.
BREWERY/COMPANY: Old English Inns.
PRINCIPAL BEERS: Brakspears. **FACILITIES:** Children welcome Garden: patio, outdoor eating.
NOTES: Parking 20

See Pub Walk on page 335

The Thames Path

The Oxfordshire stretch of the Thames Path boasts many pubs and inns. The Plough at Kelmscott, a short walk from the riverbank, is a popular watering hole; alternatively, you could continue downstream to the Trout at Tadpole Bridge or the White Hart at nearby Fyfield, south of the river. Another Trout, this time at Lower Wolvercote, offers the chance to sit outside and enjoy the tranquility of the timeless river, while historic Oxford has scores of character inns, including the charming Turf Tavern, splendidly hidden down a winding alleyway in the heart of the city. Beyond Abingdon, the trail's next stop is Dorchester, home to the 15th-century George and the White Hart. Suitably refreshed, continue downstream to the Perch and Pike at South Stoke and the ivy-clad Miller of Mansfield at Goring.

BRITWELL SALOME   Map 04 SU69

Pick of the Pubs

The Goose ◉ ♀
OX9 5LG ☎ 01491 612304   ▤ 01491 614822
e-mail: barber@thegoose.freeserve.co.uk
Dir: 1.5 from Watlington on B4009 towards Benson & Wallingford
Unassuming brick-and-flint village pub dating back to the 17th century, with a simple bar adorned with local works of art and an intimate, bottle-green painted dining room. Chef/proprietor Chris Barber makes the best use of fresh, local and largely organic ingredients on its sensibly short daily-changing menus, charged according to the number of courses chosen. At lunch, for instance, choose starter or main course portions of foie gras and duck liver parfait or grilled scallops on a salad of tomato and dressed leaves, or indulge in generous portions of sea bass with ratatouille and Orkney beef with root vegetable purée and shallots. Dinner, served only in the dining room, might add cauliflower soup with white truffle oil and crab salad with saffron mayonnaise, followed by free-range English veal with duchesse potatoes and turbot fillet with fondant potato and a gratin of spinach. Puddings range from traditional spotted dick and custard to crème brûlée and dark chocolate mousse, with an imaginative platter of British farmhouse cheeses also on offer. Good list of wines and Brakspears Bitter on tap.
OPEN: 12-3 6-11 (closed Sun eve & all Mon).
BAR MEALS: L served Tue-Sat. D served Tues-Sat 12-2 7-9. Av main course £15. **RESTAURANT:** L served Tue-Sun. D served Tue-Sat 12-2 7-9. Av 3 course à la carte £27.50.
BREWERY/COMPANY: Free House.
PRINCIPAL BEERS: Brakspears. **FACILITIES:** Children welcome Garden: patio, outdoor eating Dogs allowed Water. **NOTES:** Parking 20

OPEN: 12-3 6-11. Closed Sun eve, Mon lunch & 25 Dec.
BAR MEALS: L served Tue-Sun 12-2. Av main course £7.50.
RESTAURANT: L served Tue-Sun. D served Mon-Sat 12-2 6-11. Av 3 course a la carte £25. Av 3 course fixed price £23.50.
BREWERY/COMPANY: Free House.
PRINCIPAL BEERS: Hook Norton Best, Wadworth 6X, Timothy Taylor Landlord.
FACILITIES: Children welcome. Garden: patio, outdoor eating. Dogs allowed.
NOTES: Parking 20.
ROOMS: 2 bedrooms 2 en suite d£40-£50.

The Blewbury Inn

London Road OX11 9PD
☎ 01235 850496 📠 01235 850496
Dir: At the junction of the A417 & B4016 between Wantage and Reading, south of Didcot

Modest but appealing, white-painted 200-year-old pub set beside the A417 on the edge of Blewbury, a rambling village nestling beneath the Oxfordshire Downs. Justifiably popular among local diners for Franck Péigne's inventive menus which have a distinct Gallic flavour reflecting his Brittany origins.

The once very homely interior has recently been given a 'modern' makeover, the decor in the single bar and intimate restaurant now featuring a light seafaring theme. Although locals and passers-by are welcome to pop in for a pint at the bar, the real emphasis here is on dining, with the bar serving as an area for pre-prandial drinks prior to diners heading next door into the restaurant. At lunchtimes though the atmosphere is more relaxed and the menu lighterand simpler, perhaps including ham, Brie and tomato bagel and penne pasta with smoked salmon. The draw in the evening - booking advisable - is Franck Péigne's interesting, often adventurous dishes which make good use of quality local ingredients.

Follow terrine of lobster and seafood with mussels and artichokes tossed in basil oil, onion and organic cider soup with a Cheddar crust, or goat's cheese and chorizo tart, with medallions of beef with truffle mash, red onion marmalade and port jus, roast cod served with provençale vegetables, anglaise potato and basil and tomato Brittany butter, or sea bass with spinach fondue and a cider and coriander butter. Round off with traditional raspberry crème brûlée with blackcurrant sorbet, caramel mousse with passion fruit coulis and baby pears, or a plate of cheese with grapes and bread.

Book early for the popular theme nights - Brasserie, Irish, Game - or join the Gourmet Club for monthly set 4-course dinners with wine or whisky tastings. Accommodation in two en suite bedrooms.

BURCOT Map 04 SU59

The Chequers
OX14 3DP ☎ 01865 407771 ▤ 01865 407945
Dir: *On A415 (Dorchester/Abingdon rd)*
Partly dating back to the 16th century and originally a staging
post for barges on the Thames. Expect big changes under the
new management.
OPEN: 11-2.30 6-11 (Sun 7-10.30). **BAR MEALS:** L served all
week. D served Mon-Sat 12-2 6.30-9.30. Av main course £6.50.
RESTAURANT: L served all week. D served Mon-Sat 12-2 6.30-
9.30. **BREWERY/COMPANY:** Free House.
PRINCIPAL BEERS: Wadworth 6X, Brakspear.
FACILITIES: Children welcome Garden. **NOTES:** Parking 40

BURFORD Map 06 SP21

Golden Pheasant ★ ★
91 High St OX18 4QA ☎ 01993 823223 ▤ 01993 822621
Dir: *Leave M40 at junction 8 and follow signs A40 Cheltenham into
Burford*
Attractive, honey-coloured, 15th-century stone inn situated in
the centre of Burford. Expect an informal atmosphere,
comfortable bedrooms and a wide range of food. Old English
Inns.

Pick of the Pubs

The Inn for All Seasons ⓦ ★ ★ ★ 🛏 ♀
The Barringtons OX18 4TN ☎ 01451 844324
▤ 01451 844375
e-mail: sharp@innforallseasons.com
See Pick of the Pubs on page 341

Hook Norton

The Hook Norton Brewery Visitors' Centre
is the ideal place to brush up on your
knowledge of slightly obscure traditional
brewing equipment. Find out what a
Hummeller is good for, why a malt shovel
is wooden, and discover the startling
secret of how the Chrondometer can
detect the difference between a bushel of
malt and a bushel of barley. The
Saccharometer, the Wort Cooler and a
range of Hook Norton memorabilia are
also on show. Hook Norton's brews
include Old Hooky (4.6%), Generation
(4%) and Double Stout (4.8%).

Pick of the Pubs

The Lamb Inn ⓦ ⓦ ★ ★ ★ 🛏 ♀
Sheep St OX18 4LR ☎ 01993 823155 ▤ 01993 822228
Dir: *from M40 J8 follow signs for A40 & Burford, off High Street*
Four log fires burn constantly in winter (and most of
autumn and the spring!) at this archetypal English
coaching inn with roots back in the 15th century. Known
as the Gateway to the Cotswolds, Burford nestles on a
hillside above the Windrush Valley and The Lamb, with its
individually decorated bedrooms and pretty cottage
garden, makes an ideal base for exploring the area. In the
lounge and bar stone flagstones reflect the passing of the
centuries, enhanced by antique furniture, copper and
brass.
  Daily bar lunches offer an exhaustive choice from
smoked salmon fritters with pink peppercorn cream,
through guinea fowl breast with bay leaf jus and wild boar
and apple sausages to sauté of lambs' kidneys and salmon
fillets with lemon sauce. Traditional desserts such as crème
caramel and lemon meringue parfait further illustrate the
kitchen's pedigree. Candle-lit dinner in the pretty, pillared
restaurant offers two- or three-course menus at fixed
prices, as does Sunday lunch that begins with a glass of
Buck's Fizz.
OPEN: 11-2.30 (Sun 12-2.30) 6-11 (Sun 7-10.30). Closed
25-26 Dec. **BAR MEALS:** L served Mon-Sat 12-2. Av main
course £8.50. **RESTAURANT:** L served Sun. D served all
week 12.30-1.45 7-9. Av 3 course à la carte £27.
BREWERY/COMPANY: Free House.
PRINCIPAL BEERS: Wadworth 6X, Hook Norton Best,
Badger Dorset Bitter. **FACILITIES:** Children welcome
Garden: walled cottage garden, outdoor eating Dogs
allowed Water. **NOTES:** Parking 5. **ROOMS:** 15 bedrooms
15 en suite s£70 d£105

CHADLINGTON Map 06 SP32

The Tite Inn ♀
Mill End OX7 3NY ☎ 01608 676475
e-mail: willis@titeinn.co.uk
Dir: *3m S of Chipping Norton*
Delightful Cotswold inn which takes its name from the
constantly running stream, or tite, beneath it. Roses
clambering up the stone walls attract customers in summer,
while log fires and mulled wine help create a cosy atmosphere
in winter. Troops stopped here en route to the Battle of Edge
Hill. Varied choice of locally brewed ales and a bar menu
offering light meals, fresh salads and home-made soup.
Among the popular dishes are chicken Jalfrezi, salmon en
croûte, chilli con carne and lamb kidneys braised in red wine.
OPEN: 12-2.30 (Sun 12-3, 7-10.30) 6.30-11 (Closed Mon &
Dec 25-26. **BAR MEALS:** L served Tue-Sun. D served Tue-Sun
12-2 7-9. Av main course £6.95. **RESTAURANT:** L served Sun.
D served Tue-Sat 12-2 6.30-11. Av 3 course à la carte £15.85.
BREWERY/COMPANY: Free House.
PRINCIPAL BEERS: Archers, Fullers, Youngs, Guest Beers.
FACILITIES: Children welcome Garden: views , patio, beer
garden. **NOTES:** Parking 30

See Pub Walk on page 343

OPEN: 11-2.30 6-11
(Sun 12-3 7-10.30).
BAR MEALS: L served all week.
D served all week 11.30-2 6.30-
9.30. Av main course £8.50.
RESTAURANT: L served all week
D served all week 11.30-2 6.30-
9.30. Av 3 course a la carte £21.
BREWERY/COMPANY:
Free House.
PRINCIPAL BEERS: Wadworth 6X,
Bass, Wychwood.
FACILITIES: Children welcome.
Garden: outdoor eating.
Dogs allowed.
NOTES: Parking 80.
ROOMS: 10 bedrooms 10 en suite
s£35-£49.50 d£75-£85 FR£100-
£118

Inn For All Seasons

◎ ★★★ 🐑 ⚗

The Barringtons OX18 4TN
☎ 01451 844324 📠 01451 844375
e-mail: sharp@innforallseasons.com
Dir: 3 miles W of Burford on the A40

Head for The Barringtons, 3 miles west of Burford on the A40, to discover an engaging 16th-century English Grade II listed mansion, that has lost nothing of its charm in its conversion to a 10-bedroom country inn. Expect to find the original fireplaces, ancient oak beams and period furniture.

Close by are several walks around the National Trust's Sherborne Park estate with its remarkable collection of early spring flowers - snowdrops, winter aconites and wild daffodils. Menus are naturally seasonal, whether it be for informal bar snacks or dinner in a rather more staid restaurant.

Pride of place goes to the fish boards from which to choose County Louth rock oysters, flash-fried squid with lime and baby spinach leaf salad, grilled lobster with sweet mustard and brandy sauce or the classic fillet of deep-fried fresh cod with chunky hand-cut chips. Simpler starters can include cauliflower, broccoli and Stilton soup or Irish mussel tart with avocado in a basil cream sauce, followed by Herefordshire rib-eye peppered steak or roast partridge filled with leek farce on a game and rosemary sauce, and warm treacle tart with ice cream. In a higher gear à la carte choices range from pork and leek pâté with red onion and raisin chutney and River Dart gravad lax, to shank of Cotswold lamb with vegetable ragout and Thai and French bean curry flavoured with lemongrass and lime leaves.

Round off with hot chocolate brownie in a rich chocolate sauce or regional farmhouse cheeses; to accompany, some average house wines - or a cracking pint of Wychwood Ale.

Guests are assured of a warm and friendly welcome, while en suite bedrooms are spacious and comfortably furnished.

England

Pick of the Pubs

The Red Lion Inn
The High St OX44 7SS ☎ 01865 890625
📠 01865 890795
Dir: *B480 from Oxford Ring rd, thru Stadhampton, L then R at mini-rdbt, at Chalgrove Airfield R fork into village*

Set back from the road beside a babbling brook in a delightful village, this lovely cream-painted pub dates back to the 11th century and has been owned by Chalgrove Parish Church since 1637. It enjoys a good local following for the imaginative food served throughout the beamed and tastefully refurbished bar and dining areas.

Expect a civilised atmosphere, an upmarket clientele and well presented dishes, with perennial pub favourites given a welcome modern twist. From warm open baguettes (bacon, sausage and melted cheese), leek and potato soup, moules et frites, pasta with anchovies, thyme, tomatoes and garlic, and beer-battered cod on the lunchtime menu, the evening choice may feature seared lamb loin with rosemary crust, roasted spiced aubergine and port jus, Oxford sausages with spicy red cabbage and mash, beef Stroganoff, and dark chocolate cold soufflé with home-made shortbread. Lovely rear garden for summer imbibing; 6 wines by the glass.
OPEN: 12-3 6-11 (Sun 7-10.30). **BAR MEALS:** L served all week. D served Mon-Sat 12-2 7-9. Av main course £8.50.
RESTAURANT: L served all week. D served Mon-Sat 12-2 7-9. Av 3 course à la carte £18.
BREWERY/COMPANY: Free House.
PRINCIPAL BEERS: Brakspear, Fullers London Pride.
FACILITIES: Garden: patio, outdoor eating Dogs allowed.
NOTES: Parking 20

Drays and Horses

A few breweries still engagingly use Shire horses and old-style drays to deliver their as in days of yore. The older 18th-century drays were two-wheeled wagons drawn by a pair of horses in tandem, with the driver sitting on one of the barrels. From this developed the more familiar four-wheeled dray, drawn by two horses abreast, with the driver perched up on a high seat. Some of them had open sides, other rails or low boards, while some had iron stanchions supporting chains. Strong, hardy and weighing in at about a ton, Shire horses trace their ancestry from the vast, tank-like warhorses of the Middle Ages, which rumbled into battle at a ground-shaking trot. Their descendants today rumble through the streets on more peaceful and merciful errands.

Pick of the Pubs

The Bull Inn 🛏
Sheep St OX7 3RR ☎ 01608 810689
Dir: *On A40 at Oxford R to Woodstock, thru Woodstock & after 1.5m L to Charlbury*
Overlooking the main street of this handsome, small Cotswold town, the civilised Bull Inn dates from the 16th century and offers good old-fashioned hospitality and imaginative, freshly prepared food. Highly personable owners, Roy and Suzanne Flynn, have created a most appealing inn, attracting discerning diners from Oxford and across the Cotswolds. The smart stone exterior is matched by inside with a most relaxing and tastefully furnished lounge and dining-room. Friendly, unspoilt bar that is devoid of music and features wooden floors, lively conversation and Greene King ales.

Visitors popping in for just a snack in the bar will find hot jumbo baguettes (lunchtimes only) and daily specials on the blackboard. More adventurous dishes, best enjoyed in the dining room, may include smoked haddock, mussel and prawn chowder, salmon and chive fishcakes with tarragon hollandaise, and roast cod with herb and garlic crust with a spicy tomato and red pepper sauce. Round off warm pineapple upside down cake with rum sauce and coconut ice cream. Attractive vine-covered side terrace and overnight accommodation in three en suite bedrooms.
OPEN: 12-2.30 7-11 (Sun 12-3 only). Closed Sun eve, Dec 25-26 & Jan 1. **BAR MEALS:** L served Tues-Sat. D served Tues-Sat 12-2 7-9. (9.30 Fri & Sat). Av main course £9.
RESTAURANT: L served Tues-Sat. D served Tues-Sat 12-1.30 7-9. (9.30 Fri & Sat). Av 3 course à la carte £20.
BREWERY/COMPANY: Free House.
PRINCIPAL BEERS: Greene King-IPA, Abbot Ale & Triumph.
FACILITIES: Garden: terrace, BBQ, Food served outside
NOTES: Parking 14. **ROOMS:** 3 bedrooms 3 en suite s£50 d£60

Tite Inn, Chadlington

An easy walk across gently rolling farmland through the picturesque Evenlode Valley.

Turn left on leaving the inn, then right at the path, signed Brookend. Cross the second bridge on your right, turn left and follow the stream down valley. Shortly, go through a gate and turn left along the lane. Turn right at the crossroads, then left by the Brookend Street sign, following track between houses. Just beyond Boot Cottage, cross iron railings and continue with the stream to your left to cross a bridge in the field corner. Turn right over stile and proceed to next stile. Bear diagonally left under power lines to a stile and turn left along the Oxfordshire Way. Cross a road and keep ahead, gently climbing to a wood on your right.

Short walk - At the top of the rise, turn left through the gap in the hedge and follow track towards Chadlington church. Take path to left of 'no footpath' sign in the field corner and bear diagonally left to the field corner. Cross a stream and follow the left-hand fence to a stile. Turn right along the hedge to a track. Keep the wall on your right and

proceed ahead past a house to the road. Turn right, then left through gate into recreation field, signed Mill End (long walk joins here). * Walk parallel with road, turn right at hedge and go past pavilion to a gate in corner. In a few paces, go through gap on left and bear diagonally across field to houses and road. Turn right, then left back to the inn.

Long walk - Proceed beside woodland to a gate and continue ahead across Dean Common. Cross a track and continue towards Spelsbury church, then at top of field, turn left and follow right-hand boundary to a road. Turn right, then take the bridleway, signed to Dean, at the sharp right bend. Keep ahead at the fork down to a stream and road. Turn right through Dean, then at end of high wall, take footpath left to reach a road. Turn left past Dean Manor, then take the bridleway right for Chadlington. Cross a stream and gently climb to the road. Turn right, pass the church and hotel, then turn right into the recreation field (see directions above *)

Distance: 3 miles (4.8km) or 5 miles (8km)
Map: OS Landranger 164
Paths: field paths and tracks; some road walking
Terrain: farmland and village streets
Gradient: gently undulating

Walk submitted by:
The Tite Inn

St Philip's Church, Little Rollright

TITE INN, CHADLINGTON
Mill End OX7 3NY.
Tel: 01608 676475
Directions: S of Chipping Norton
Warm 16th-century Cotswold stone pub named after the constantly flowing (tite) stream beneath it. Pretty as a picture in summer with roses clambering up the walls, it offers home-cooked food and a good choice of real ale in its stone-walled bars.
Open: 12-2.30 6.30-11 (Closed Mon ex BH). Bar Meals: 12-2 6.30-9. Children welcome. Garden/patio. Parking.
(see page 340 for full entry)

Country Matters

Country occupations and pursuits provide many inns with their names. The Wheatsheaf, the Barley Mow, the Haywain, the Dun Cow, the Heifer. the Plough (sometimes the constellation) and the Harrow recall the farming year's immemorial round. Horses, long essential to agriculture, communications and sport, figure frequently - the Black Horse, the Nag's Head, the Grey Mare and many more. The Bull and the Bear are often related to the once popular sport of baiting the animals with dogs. The dog is usually a sporting dog and hunting has supplied many names, from the Fox and Hounds and the Hare and Hounds to numerous deer (also from heraldry), including the Stag and Hounds, the White Hart and the Roebuck. There are signs related to angling, too, such as the Angler and the Trout, and there are Jolly Cricketers and even Jolly Farmers.

CHECKENDON   Map 04 SU68

Pick of the Pubs

The Highwayman ♀
Exlade St RG8 0UA ☎ 01491 682020
📠 01491 682229
e-mail: info@thehighwaymancheckendon.co.uk
Dir: On A4074 Reading to Wallingford Rd

Overlooking open fields on the edge of the wooded Chiltern Hills, the 300-year-old Highwayman exudes a wonderfully warm atmosphere; its rambling interior is packed with curios and old artefacts, and dining at sunken tables in glimmering candlelight. The character bar is just the place to relax with a pint of Black Sheep, with the tastefully furnished interconnecting dining-rooms and adjoining conservatory the place to enjoy imaginative pub food.

New owners have maintained food standards here, offering ploughman's lunches, sandwiches and home-made soups on the bar menu, and the likes of honeyed ham hock terrine with red onion marmalade, smoked haddock and crab fishcake with basil pesto, calves' liver with rocket mash, spiced onion and lemon potatoes, and roast chump of lamb on braised red cabbage with rosemary and port glaze on the dining-room menu. Fishy dishes may include red mullet on ratatouille with olive oil mash. Attractive rear garden for summer imbibing; Peaceful overnight accommodation in four comfortable en suite bedrooms.
OPEN: 11-11 (Sun 12-11). **BAR MEALS:** L served all week. D served all week 12-2.30 7-9.30. Av main course £14.50. **RESTAURANT:** L served all week. D served all week 12-2.30 7-9.30. Av 3 course à la carte £27. **BREWERY/COMPANY:** Free House. **PRINCIPAL BEERS:** Gales HSB, Fullers London Pride, Black Sheep, Youngs Special. **FACILITIES:** Garden: food served outdoors, patio Dogs allowed. **NOTES:** Parking 30. **ROOMS:** 4 bedrooms 4 en suite s£55 d£70

CHINNOR   Map 06 SP70

Pick of the Pubs

Sir Charles Napier ◉ ◉ 🛏 ♀
Spriggs Alley OX9 4BX ☎ 01494 483011
📠 01494 485311
Dir: M40 J6 to Chinnor. Turn R at rdbt carry on straight up hill to Spriggs Alley

Situated in the Chiltern Hills and surrounded by beech woods and fields - boasting nonetheless a helicopter pad! - a classic old inn noted for consistently good food in an eclectic atmosphere of unmatching old chairs and tables. Surrounded indoors by sculptures and paintings by local artists, there is an air of suggestion that the fungi, game and local berries are part of a long-standing heritage.

In summer, lunches can also be served on a terrace shaded by vines and wisteria. Wild mushroom soup and brandade of cod with poached egg and hollandaise are indicative of the style, followed perhaps by beef bourguignon, lamb fillet with cumin and rosemary jus and pan-fried asparagus with guacamole. A higher premium at dinner will likely embrace foie gras terrine with brioche, calves' liver, braised cabbage and balsamic sauce and vanilla crème brûlée. Yet this remains truly a peoples' pub with good real ale and highly recommended wines from an exhaustive list.
OPEN: 12-2.30 6.30-10. Closed Mon & 25/26 Dec.
BAR MEALS: L served Tue-Fri 12-2.30. **RESTAURANT:** L served Tue-Sun. D served Tue-Sat 12-2.30 7-10. Av 3 course à la carte £26.50. **BREWERY/COMPANY:** Free House.
PRINCIPAL BEERS: Wadworth 6X. **FACILITIES:** Children welcome Garden: vine covered terrace, outdoor eating.
NOTES: Parking 50

CHIPPING NORTON   Map 06 SP32

Chequers ♀
Goddards Ln OX7 5NP ☎ 01608 644717   📠 01608 646237
e-mail: enquiries@chequers-pub.co.uk
Dir: Town centre, next to theatre

Located at the heart of an old Cotswold market town, this straightforward local dates back to the 16th century when it was known to be an ale house. Stonemasons working on the local church in the 1500s also lodged here. A warm welcome awaits inside and the inn offers a good choice of real ales and good quality specials. Expect pork and leek sausages, half-shoulder of lamb, Thai fishcakes, home-cooked honey and cider roast ham and vegetable lasagne among other imaginative dishes. *continued*

OPEN: 11-11 (Sun 11-10.30). Closed 25 Dec. **BAR MEALS:** L served all week. D served all week 12-2.30 6-9. Av main course £6.50. **RESTAURANT:** D served all week 12-2.30 6-9. Av 3 course à la carte £15. **BREWERY/COMPANY:** Fullers. **PRINCIPAL BEERS:** Fullers - Chiswick Bitter, London Pride, ESB.

Pick of the Pubs

The Falkland Arms ♀
Great Tew OX7 4DB ☎ 01608 683653
🖩 01608 683656
e-mail: sjcourage@btconnect.com
Dir: Off A361 1.25m, signposted Great Tew

An unspoilt and historic village is the tranquil setting for this 500-year-old, creeper-clad, Cotswold stone inn. Nestling at the end of a row of charming thatched cottages - the quintessential English village scene - the Falkland Arms is a real classic gem.

Flagstone floors, shuttered windows, heavy oak beams, an inglenook fireplace and high-backed settles characterise the intimate bar, where a huge collection of beer and cider mugs hangs from the ceiling. In addition to Wadworth ales, there is fine range of guest beers, country wines and malt whiskies.

Enthusiastic new licensees offer filled baguettes and ploughman's at lunchtime, in addition to home-cooked specials - pork and leek sausages with mash and onion gravy and beef and ale pie - and more inventive evening dishes, all cooked by the landlord. Expect sweet tomato and basil soup, followed by slow-cooked lamb shank with mash and rosemary and garlic gravy, baked herb-crusted cod with tomato coulis, or sweet pepper pot beef and tomatoes with sour cream. Finish with warm sticky toffee pudding. Cottagey, antique-furnished bedrooms.
OPEN: 11.30-2.30 6-11 (Summer Sat 11-11, Sun 12-10.30). **BAR MEALS:** L served all week 12-2. Av main course £6.50. **RESTAURANT:** L served all week. D served Mon-Sat 12-2 7-8. Av 3 course à la carte £18.
BREWERY/COMPANY: Wadworth.
PRINCIPAL BEERS: Wadworth 6X, Badger Tanglefoot, Wadworth Henry's IPA. **FACILITIES:** Garden: Food served outside Dogs allowed on lead, water.
ROOMS: 6 bedrooms 6 en suite s£40 d£65

The Plough
High St, Finstock OX7 3BY ☎ 01993 868333
Great pub for walkers and those with dogs. Some ales served from cask. Children not allowed in bar. Bedrooms.

Coach And Horses Inn ♦♦♦ 🖼 ♀
Watlington Rd OX44 7UX ☎ 01865 890255
🖩 01865 891995
e-mail: david-mcphillips@lineone.net

A 16th-century coaching inn retaining plenty of character with its beams, large fireplaces, old bread oven and well. Only 200 yards from the River Thame. There's a selection of grills, vegetarian dishes, and house favourites such as chicken curry madras, medallions of pork fillet Dijon, and venison steak. Seafood specials include grilled fresh Scottish salmon, Dover sole, red snapper fillet, and deep-fried scampi.
OPEN: 11.30-3 6-11 (Sun 11.30-3 only). **BAR MEALS:** L served all week. D served Mon-Sat 12-2 7-10. Av main course £10.
RESTAURANT: L served all week. D served Mon-Sat 12-2 7-10. Av 3 course à la carte £15. Av 2 course fixed price £13.
BREWERY/COMPANY: Free House.
PRINCIPAL BEERS: Hook Norton, Flowers Original.
FACILITIES: Children welcome Garden: outdoor eating, patio, well Dogs allowed garden only. **NOTES:** Parking 40.
ROOMS: 9 bedrooms 9 en suite s£48 d£60

Pick of the Pubs

The Hand & Shears 🖼 ♀ NEW
OX8 8AB ☎ 01993 88337 🖩 01993 883575
Stylishly refurbished pub-restaurant drawing discerning diners from far and wide for innovative brasserie-style food served in an informal pub atmosphere. Pop in for a pint of Hook Norton or a decent glass of wine and tuck into a roasted vegetable and goats' cheese ciabatta sandwich or Caesar salad. Alternatively, relax over three courses, beginning, perhaps, with chicken liver and foie gras parfait with Sauternes jelly or roasted monkfish with avocado, then move on to sea bass with roast vine tomatoes and hollandaise, roast rump of lamb with leek and basil purée and redcurrant jus, or lambs' liver with olive mash and red wine jus. Home-made puddings. Regular theme evenings.
OPEN: 11-3 6-11. **BAR MEALS:** L served all week. D served all week 12-2.30 7-9.30. Av main course £9.95.
RESTAURANT: L served all week. D served all week 12-2.30 7-9.30. Av 3 course à la carte £20.
PRINCIPAL BEERS: Hook Norton, Flowers IPA, Greene King Old Speckled Hen. **NOTES:** Parking 30

England

CHURCH ENSTONE
Map 06 SP32

Crown Inn
Mill Ln OX7 4NN ☎ 01608 677262
A 17th-century free house in a village setting on the edge of the Cotswolds. All dishes are home cooked, and may include Gressingham duck breast with plum sauce, liver and bacon, or fresh halibut. The Crown has recently come under new management. Reports welcome.
OPEN: 12-3 6-11 (Sun 7-10.30). **BAR MEALS:** L served Tue-Sun. D served Tue-Sat 12-2 7-9. Av main course £8.
RESTAURANT: D served Mon-Sat 7-9.
BREWERY/COMPANY: Free House.
PRINCIPAL BEERS: Everards. **FACILITIES:** Children welcome Garden: Dogs allowed. **NOTES:** Parking 10.
ROOMS: 4 bedrooms 3 en suite s£35 d£45

CLIFTON
Map 06 SP43

Duke of Cumberland's Head 🐑
OX15 0PE ☎ 01869 338534   📠 01869 338643
Dir: A4260 from Banbury, then B4031 from Deddington
Stone and thatch pub situated in the hamlet of Clifton, between the historic villages of Deddington and Aynho. It was built in 1645, originally as cottages, and is named after Prince Rupert who led the king's troops at the battle of Edge Hill.
 A good range of food is offered from sandwiches and deep-fried haddock to substantial dishes of rabbit in cream and bacon sauce, and boeuf bourguignon.

OPEN: 12-2.30 (w/end 12-3) 6.30-11. Closed Nov 1-Easter.
BAR MEALS: L served all week. D served all week 12-2 6-9. Av main course £8.50. **RESTAURANT:** L served Wed-Sun. D served Wed-Sat 12-2 7-9.30. Av 3 course à la carte £18. Av 2 course fixed price £15. **PRINCIPAL BEERS:** Hook Norton, Adnams, Wadworth 6X, Jennings.. **FACILITIES:** Children welcome Children's licence Garden: outdoor eating, BBQ Dogs allowed. **NOTES:** Parking 20. **ROOMS:** 7 bedrooms 5 en suite s£35 d£60

CLIFTON HAMPDEN
Map 04 SU59

Pick of the Pubs

The Plough Hotel ♀
Abingdon Rd OX14 3EG ☎ 01865 407811
📠 01865 407136
e-mail: reservation@the-ploughinn.co.uk

Picture-postcard, thatched and timber-framed 16th-century building set beside the A415 yet only a short walk from the River Thames and peaceful riverside walks. Tirelessly run by enthusiastic Turkish-born landlord Yuksel Bektas, always immaculately dressed in a morning suit, and his family, who have created a delightful country pub that not only oozes charm and character but offers tasteful overnight accommodation in en suite bedrooms. The cosy main bar and adjoining dining room feature low beams, deep red-painted walls and warming open fires. Visitors are guaranteed a warm welcome, impeccable service and good food, the interesting menus listing, perhaps, generous sandwiches served with dressed salad, goat's cheese soufflé, crispy duck salad, and home-made puddings like treacle tart. In addition, the restaurant carte may offer salmon with lemon butter sauce, rack of lamb with creamy mint sauce. Excellent Turkish coffee and a lovely rear summer garden in which to enjoy it in. Nothing is too much trouble here!
OPEN: Open all day. **BAR MEALS:** L served all week. D served all week. Av main course £12.95. **RESTAURANT:** L served all week. D served all week .
BREWERY/COMPANY: Free House.
PRINCIPAL BEERS: John Smiths, Courage Best, Directors.
FACILITIES: Children welcome Children's licence Garden: patio, outdoor eating. **NOTES:** Parking 35.
ROOMS: 11 bedrooms 11 en suite s£67.50 d£82.50

CUMNOR
Map 06 SP40

Bear & Ragged Staff
28 Appleton Rd OX2 9QH ☎ 01865 862329
📠 01865 865947
e-mail: gavinmansfield@hotmail.com
Dir: A420 from Oxford, R to Cumnor on B4017
Haunted by the Earl of Warwick's mistress, this 13th-century inn has two massive fireplaces and original beams and floors. The royal emblem above one fireplace was apparently chiselled out by Cromwell's brother. New landlord, new menus and a serious approach to modern pub dining. Reports please.

Claims to Fame

Candidates for the appealing title of the country's tiniest pub include the diminutive Smiths Arms - originally the village smithy - at Godmanstone, Dorset, and the miniature Nutshell in Bury St Edmunds, Suffolk, while the Two Brewers in Rochester, Kent, is not big enough for three brewers. The highest pub in Britain is generally agreed to be the remote Tan Hill Inn in North Yorkshire, 1732ft (528m) up on the Pennine Way, built for local miners in the 18th century, Other elevated pubs include the Cat and Fiddle on the moors outside Buxton in Derbyshire and the Sportsman's Arms at Bylchau in Conwy.

The Vine Inn
11 Abingdon Rd OX2 9QN ☎ 01865 862567
▤ 01865 863302
Dir: A420 from Oxford, R onto B4017
Country village pub-restaurant dating from 1743 and situated just off the A420 south-west of Oxford. Vine-covered stone façade, homely main bar with a relaxing atmosphere and a modern rear dining room. New licensees but still emphasis on modern pub food, with pan-fried calves' liver with onion and bacon jus and grilled tuna on king prawns, black olives, Parma ham with lemon beurre blanc setting the style - reports please!
OPEN: 11-2.30 (Sun 12-4, 7-10.30) 6-11. **BAR MEALS:** L served all week. D served all week 12.30-2.15 6.30-9.15. Av main course £8.50. **RESTAURANT:** L served all week. D served all week 12.30-2.15 6.30-9.15. Av 3 course à la carte £18.
BREWERY/COMPANY: Punch Taverns.
PRINCIPAL BEERS: Wadworth 6X, Adnams, Greene King Old Speckled Hen. **FACILITIES:** Children welcome Garden: food served outside Dogs allowed Water. **NOTES:** Parking 45

CUXHAM   Map 04 SU69

The Half Moon
OX49 5NF ☎ 01491 614110
Judith Bishop presides over this 17th-century thatched pub, tucked away beside a stream in a quiet village 4 miles from the M40 (J6). She ventures daily into the pretty rear garden to pick fresh herbs for her country dishes that appear on the regularly-changing menu in the low-beamed, cottagey interior. Relax by the open log fire with a pint of Brakspears and order a satisfying venison, blackcurrant and liquorice casserole, partridge and prune pie, 'posh' bangers and mash, or perhaps pan-fried duck with wild berry gravy. Snackier items include fresh baked filled baguettes.
OPEN: 12-2.30 6-11 (Sun 12-10.30). **BAR MEALS:** L served all week. D served all week 12-2 7-9. Av main course £6.95.
RESTAURANT: L served all week. D served all week 12-2 7-9.30. Av 3 course à la carte £15. **PRINCIPAL BEERS:** Brakspear Ordinary , 4 Seasons. **FACILITIES:** Garden: food served outside. **NOTES:** Parking 20

DEDDINGTON   Map 06 SP43

Pick of the Pubs

Deddington Arms ★ ★ ★ ▨ ♀
Horsefair OX15 0SH ☎ 01869 338364
▤ 01869 337010
e-mail: deddarms@aol.com
Dir: A43 to Northampton, B4100 to Aynho, B4031 to Deddington

Customers have been offered hospitality at this traditional village inn for the last 400 years. Character bar with timbers, open log fires, and village views. Fresh ingredients are used and the innovative menu may offer dressed crab, fillet steak Diane, pot-roasted duck, monkfish with tomato, basil and cream, and good home-made puddings. Good modern facilities in upgraded, smart bedrooms, split between character main building and rear extension.
OPEN: 11-11. **BAR MEALS:** L served all week. D served all week 12-3 6.30-9.30. Av main course £6. **RESTAURANT:** L served all week. D served all week 12-3 6.30-10.00. Av 3 course à la carte £20. **BREWERY/COMPANY:** Free House.
PRINCIPAL BEERS: Tetleys, Greene King, Marston Pedigree.
FACILITIES: Children welcome. **NOTES:** Parking 36.
ROOMS: 27 bedrooms 27 en suite s£60 d£65

DORCHESTER-ON-THAMES   Map 04 SU59

Pick of the Pubs

The George ◉ ★ ★ ★ 🐦 ♀
25 High St OX10 7HH ☎ 01865 340404
▤ 01865 341620

Dir: *From M40 J7 take A329 S to A4074 at Shillingford. Follow signs to Dorchester. From M4 J13 take A34 to Abingdon then A415 E to Dorchester*

Historic features throughout this 15th-century hostelry, the centrepiece of the village, include the inglenook fireplaces of Potboys Bar and a fine vaulted ceiling in the hotel restaurant. Bar menus change daily with a weather eye to high quality fresh produce from near and far.

Starters might include roast plum tomato soup and rabbit confit with mustard sauce, followed by boar and apple sausages with chive mash, wild mushroom and basil tagliatelle, and grilled salmon fillet with sauce vierge. Dinner menus offer chargrilled scallops with pancetta, roast peppered saddle of lamb, home-made blueberry ice cream and commendable British farmhouse cheeses.

OPEN: 11.30-11 (Sun 12-10.30). **BAR MEALS:** L served all week. D served all week 12-2.15 7-9.45. Av main course £13. **RESTAURANT:** L served all week. D served all week 12-2.15 7-9.45. Av 3 course à la carte £22.

BREWERY/COMPANY: Free House.
PRINCIPAL BEERS: Brakspear. **FACILITIES:** Children welcome Children's licence Garden: Dogs allowed.
NOTES: Parking 150. **ROOMS:** 18 bedrooms 18 en suite s£65 d£85 FR£100

Pick of the Pubs

The White Hart ◉ ★ ★ ★ ♀ NEW
High St OX10 7HN ☎ 01865 340074   ▤ 01865 341082
e-mail: whitehartdorches@aol.com
Dir: *A4074 Oxford to Reading, 5M J7 M40 A329 to Wallingford*

Privately-owned hotel situated in one of Oxfordshire's most famous villages. The Romans built a town here, though its ramparts are now only faintly recognisable. The abbey, at the heart of Dorchester, dates back to the 12th century and the adjoining gatehouse is now a museum.

A perfect base for exploring the Cotswolds and the Chilterns, taking a cruise on the Thames or visiting Oxford, the historic White Hart offers the chance to relax and dine in comfortably furnished surroundings. Food ranges from sandwiches and hot bar meals, to imaginative dishes and a weekly-changing menu.

Expect venison steak with sweet potato farls and roasted vegetable ratatouille, braised lamb shank with rosemary and port wine sauce, and pan-fried calves' liver on horseradish mash with cassis sauce.

OPEN: 11-11. **BAR MEALS:** L served all week. D served all week 12-2.30 6.30-9.30. Av main course £7.50.
RESTAURANT: L served all week. D served all week 12-2.30 6.30-9.30. Av 3 course à la carte £22.50.
BREWERY/COMPANY: Free House.
PRINCIPAL BEERS: Greene King, Marstons Pedigree,.
FACILITIES: Children welcome. **NOTES:** Parking 28.
ROOMS: 24 bedrooms 24 en suite s£69 d£79

Pubs in Unusual Buildings

The classic image of a traditional country pub is surely a charming thatched building overlooking a picturesque village green and boasting cosy log fires and quaint beams adorned with horse brasses. In reality, many inns are like that, but throughout the country there are also many pubs that began life as something entirely different. For example, the Castle Inn at Edgehill in Warwickshire was originally built as a battlemented folly, while the Old Bank in England in London's Fleet Street was once, as the name suggests, a branch of the Bank of England. Opened to service the nearby Law Courts, it became a pub in 1995. The unspoilt Ring O'Bells at Thornton in West Yorkshire began as a Wesleyan chapel, the Cholmondeley Arms in Cheshire was a village school before being converted to a pub in the late 1980s, and the West Riding Licensed Refreshment Rooms at Dewsbury near Wakefield is a converted 19th-century railway station building on the Trans-Pennine route. Right down at the other end of the country, the Chequers at Rookley on the Isle of Wight used to be a customs and excise house.

DUNS TEW
Map 06 SP42

The White Horse Inn
OX6 4JS ☎ 01869 340272 🖹 01869 347732
Dir: M40 J11, A4260, follow signs to Deddington and then onto Duns Tew
Dating back to the 17th century, this Cotswold coaching inn has a wealth of charming features, including log fires, oak panelling and flagstone floors.

EAST HANNEY
Map 04 SU49

The Black Horse ♀
Main St OX12 0JE ☎ 01235 868212 🖹 01235 868989
e-mail: black-horse-at-hanney@cwcom.net
Bavarian home-cooked specialities reflect the origin of this traditional pub's chef/proprietor, whose schnitzels come in various guises. Lighter eclectic selections include garlic chilli chicken, fish 'n' chips, lamb pasanda, as well as baguettes, ploughmans' and salads.

Main courses include peppered pork steak, knuckle of lamb, spinach ricotta cannelloni and mushroom Stroganoff. German apfelkuchen to finish.

OPEN: 12-3, 6-11. Closed Mon. **BAR MEALS:** L served Tue-Sun. D served Tue-Sun 12-2.30 6.30-9.30. **RESTAURANT:** L served Tue-Sun. D served Tue-Sun 12-2.30 6.30-9.30.
BREWERY/COMPANY: Free House.
PRINCIPAL BEERS: Hook Norton, Brakspear, Greene King Abbot Ale. **FACILITIES:** Children welcome Garden: patio/terrace, outdoor eating. **NOTES:** Parking 10

EAST HENDRED
Map 04 SU48

The Wheatsheaf ♀
Chapel Square OX12 8JN ☎ 01235 833229
Dir: 2m from the A34 Milton interchange
Two miles from the Ridgeway path in a pretty village of thatched properties, this 16th-century beamed pub was formerly the magistrates' court. Freshly prepared food includes steak-and-kidney pie and home-made puds. Specials such as home-smoked local trout and English beef steaks. Sunday lunch.
OPEN: 12-3 6-11 (Sun 7-10.30). **BAR MEALS:** L served all week. D served Mon-Sat 12-2 7-9.30. Av main course £6.75.
BREWERY/COMPANY: Greene King.
PRINCIPAL BEERS: Morland Original, Greene King Abbot Ale.
FACILITIES: Children welcome Garden: patio/terrace, outdoor eating, aviary Dogs allowed. **NOTES:** Parking 10

Jugs
Toby jugs grin cheerfully from their vantage points in many a pub interior. They were first made in the Staffordshire Potteries in the 18th century and the standard figure wears a black tricorn hat, holds a foaming jug of beer and sits in a chair whose sides are covered by the skirts of his ample topcoat. This is the Ordinary Toby, but connoisseurs distinguish between the Long Face, the Sharp Face and the Roman Nose variations. Numerous variants include the Sailor, the Squire, the Tipsy Man and the Drunken Parson. Other jugs represent famous figures of history or literature, from Nelson and Mr Gladstone to Falstaff and John Bull, while modern examples include Winston Churchill and Clark Gable. There are a few female Tobies, but essentially the jugs depict the jovial male toper, benevolent and beery.

FARINGDON
Map 04 SU29

Pick of the Pubs

The Lamb at Buckland ◉ 🐾 ♀
Lamb Ln, Buckland SN7 8QN ☎ 01367 870484
🖹 01367 870675
Dir: Just off A420 3m E of Faringdon
Quietly situated just off the Oxford to Swindon road, this civilised little 18th-century inn stands on the very edge of the Cotswolds, with spectacular views across the Thames flood plain. Inside the charming stone building, the tastefully furnished bar and restaurant subtly reinforce the brand image with sheep prints and models, and even the carpet has a specially woven Lamb motif!

Peta and Paul Barnard have earned an enviable reputation for their real ales, restaurant quality food and decent wine list. The varied and imaginative menu makes good use of the finest quality local ingredients, and food can be served in either the bar or restaurant areas. There's a garden, too, for alfresco dining and family barbecues on summer Sunday evenings. Lighter meals include dependable ploughman's lunches and baked seafood pancakes, whilst boiled beef and carrots, roast grouse, and grilled fresh tuna satisfy heartier appetites. Finish with summer pudding, hot poached dates, or the intriguing dieters' despair. Useful overnight accommodation in four en suite upstairs bedrooms.
OPEN: 10.30-3pm 5.30-11pm. Closed 25/26 Dec.
BAR MEALS: L served all week. D served all week 12-2 6.30-9.30. Av main course £10.95. **RESTAURANT:** L served all week. D served all week 12-2 6.30-9.30. Av 3 course à la carte £20. **BREWERY/COMPANY:** Free House.
PRINCIPAL BEERS: Hook Norton, Wadworth 6X, Adnams Broadside. **FACILITIES:** Children welcome Children's licence Garden: patio, outdoor eating. **NOTES:** Parking 50.
ROOMS: 4 bedrooms 4 en suite s£39 d£39 FR£58

FARINGDON continued

Pick of the Pubs

The Trout at Tadpole Bridge ♀
Buckland Marsh SN7 8RF ☎ 01367 870382
e-mail: info@troutinn.co.uk
Dir: Halfway between Oxford & Swindon on the A420, take rd signed Bampton, pub is approx 2m down it.
Originally a coal storage house, this 17th-century building was converted into cottages and then to an inn towards the late 19th century. Situated on the banks of the River Thames with a pretty riverside garden for summer alfresco drinking, it has a modern, light and airy feel to the refurbished interior, with polished wooden tables, oak beams and a roaring winter log fire.
Above average pub food cooked with style and flair using fresh local produce is the key to the success of the Trout. Diners beat a path to the door to sample such dishes as deep-fried crispy scallops with Parma ham and chilli tartare sauce, crab and pepper cakes with spicy tomato salsa, chargrilled venison on herb couscous with blackcurrant dressing, local game casserole with coriander mash, Thai-style red snapper, and Aberdeen Angus steaks with game chips and herb butter. Hearty bar snacks include filled baguettes. Lovely walks along the Thames Path. New en suite bedrooms.
OPEN: 11.30-3 6-11. Closed 25 Dec-1 Jan. **BAR MEALS:** L served all week. D served all week 12-2 7-9. Av main course £11. **RESTAURANT:** L served all week. D served all week 12-2 7-9. Av 3 course à la carte £20.
BREWERY/COMPANY: Free House.
PRINCIPAL BEERS: Archers Village & Golden, Fullers London Pride, Hook Norton Old Hooky, Wychwood Special.
FACILITIES: Children welcome Garden: food served outside Dogs allowed Water. **NOTES:** Parking 70
ROOMS: 3 bedrooms 3 en suite s£55 d£80

FERNHAM   Map 04 SU29

Woodman Inn
SN7 7NX ☎ 01367 820643 ▤ 01367 820643
Stone walls, heavy beams and real ale straight from the barrel are features of this traditional 17th-century village local in the Vale of the White Horse. Expect a good range of bar food, from filled baguettes to specialities like herb-crusted rack of lamb with mint jus, Woodman pie and steak au poivre.
OPEN: 12-3 7-11. Closed Dec 25. **BAR MEALS:** L served Wed-Sun. D served Tue-Sun 7-9.30. Av main course £7. **RESTAURANT:** L served Wed-Sun. D served Tue-Sun 12-2.30 7-9.30. Av 3 course à la carte £14. **BREWERY/COMPANY:** Free House. **PRINCIPAL BEERS:** Greene King Abbot Ale, Tanners Jack, Old Speckled Hen, & Ruddles County. **FACILITIES:** Children welcome Garden: Dogs allowed. **NOTES:** Parking 25

FRINGFORD   Map 06 SP62

The Butchers Arms
OX27 8EB ☎ 01869 277363
Boasting a mention in Flora Thompson's novel 'Lark Rise to Candleford', this traditional village pub has a wide range of ales on offer. From the patio you can watch cricket matches in progress during the summer.

FYFIELD   Map 04 SU49

The White Hart ♀
Main Rd OX13 5LW ☎ 01865 390585 ▤ 01865 390671
Dir: Just off A420, 8m SW of Oxford
The White Hart was originally built as a chantry house for five people engaged solely to pray for the soul of the Lord of Fyfield Manor. Today it comprises three separate restaurants and a main bar with original beams, a 30-foot ceiling and a large inglenook fireplace.
Snacks and full meals are served, with specials such as roast rack of lamb or chicken marinated in tandoori spices. Extensive gardens include a children's play area.
OPEN: 11-3 6-11 (Sun 12-3, 6.30-10.30). Closed Dec 25.
BAR MEALS: L served all week. D served all week 12-2 7-10. Av main course £7.50. **RESTAURANT:** L served all week. D served all week 12-2 7-10. Av 3 course à la carte £14. Av 3 course fixed price £17.50. **BREWERY/COMPANY:** Free House.
PRINCIPAL BEERS: Hook Norton, Wadworth 6X, Theakstons Old Peculier,. **FACILITIES:** Children welcome Garden: patio, food served outside Dogs allowed. **NOTES:** Parking 40

GORING   Map 04 SU68

Miller of Mansfield ♀
High St RG8 9AW ☎ 01491 872829 ▤ 01491 874200
Dir: From Pangbourne A329 to Streatley, then R on B4009, 0.5m to Goring

Historic ivy-clad pub in a sprawling riverside village between the Chilterns and the Berkshire Downs. Close to the River Thames and very handy for the Ridgeway national trail and the Thames Path. Menu features various steaks and such dishes as Thai chicken, shoulder of lamb and salmon fishcakes.
OPEN: 11-11 (Sun 12-10.30). **BAR MEALS:** L served all week. D served all week 12-2 6.30-10 (all day weekends).
RESTAURANT: L served all week. D served all week 12-2 7-10.
BREWERY/COMPANY: Free House.
PRINCIPAL BEERS: Courage Best, Marstons Pedigree, Greene King Old Speckled hen. **FACILITIES:** Children welcome.
NOTES: Parking 8. **ROOMS:** 10 bedrooms 10 en suite s£54.50 d£70

 Pubs offering six or more wines by the glass

HAILEY   Map 06 SP31

Pick of the Pubs

Bird in Hand 🕯 ♀
Whiteoak Green OX29 9XP ☎ 01993 868321
📧 01993 868702
Dir: Leave A40 for Witney town centre, onto B4022, through Hailey, inn 1m N
The origins of an old 17th-century inn, nestling in the Windrush Valley, are evident in the natural Cotswold stone, heavily beamed bars and inglenook fireplace that give the Bird in Hand its special charm. Its gallery of historical prints and the informal, friendly atmosphere add a sophisticated air. Light meals offer Arbroath smokies, chicken Caesar salad and Thai green curry, while a daily specials board exhibit similar Mediterranean and exotic influences. Red mullet bouillabaisse or tiger prawns with mango salsa; venison casserole with apricot dumplings and pork dolcellate with cheese scones are typical options.
OPEN: 11-11 (Sun 12-10.30). **BAR MEALS:** L served all week. D served all week 12-2.30 7-9.30. Av main course £6.95. **RESTAURANT:** L served all week. D served all week 12-2.30 7-9.30. Av 3 course à la carte £20.
BREWERY/COMPANY: Heavitree.
PRINCIPAL BEERS: Wadworth 6X, Boddingtons.
FACILITIES: Children welcome Garden: outdoor eating, patio Dogs allowed. **NOTES:** Parking 100.
ROOMS: 16 bedrooms 16 en suite s£49.50 d£58 FR£88

Pilgrims, Shrines and Inns

All through the Middle Ages hospitality to strangers was considered a fundamental Christian duty and travellers could stay overnight free at monasteries or bed down with the servants in a nobleman's hall. Gradually, however, with growing prosperity and burgeoning trade, more people began to travel. Among them were pilgrims making their way to the shrines of saints, to acquire religious merit or be cured of sickness. The two most popular pilgrimage centres were the tomb of St Thomas ‡ Becket at Canterbury and the Virgin Mary's shrine at Walsingham in Norfolk, but many other churches possessed wonder-working relics of great sanctity.
Monasteries put poor pilgrims up free in wooden sheds with rush-strewn floors, a brazier for warmth and a few benches, but with mounting affluence better-off pilgrims were ready to pay for greater comfort, a decent meal and congenial company. Scenting a profit, monasteries built inns to meet the demand and others were opened by local landowners and town merchants. Most of Britain's oldest inns go back to these beginnings.

HENLEY-ON-THAMES   Map 04 SU78

Pick of the Pubs

The Five Horseshoes 🕯 ♀
Maidensgrove RG9 6EX ☎ 01491 641282
📧 01491 641086
e-mail: info@totalevents.co.uk
Dir: A4130 from Henley, onto B480
Just 10 minutes' drive from Henley and set beside a single-track lane high in the Chilterns, this 17th-century, vine-covered inn enjoys spectacular views from its dining conservatory and sheltered garden. Lookout for red kites soaring above the beech trees as you sip your pint of Brakspear Special or one of the seven dozen wines available by the glass; try the champagne! Attractive features include a low-beamed bar with wood-burning stove, rustic stripped tables and collections of banknotes and old tools, and these are matched with imaginative food that scores high on quality and freshness. Typical offerings include braised shank of lamb with minted mash, grilled calves' liver, chicken breast with lobster mousseline, Scottish grass-fed beef steaks, and interesting fishy alternatives like herb-crusted cod and baked halibut on creamed spinach. Good snacks include hearty soups, sandwiches, ploughman's lunches and filled baked potatoes.

OPEN: 11.30-3 6-11. **BAR MEALS:** L served all week. D served all week 12-2 7-10. Av main course £11.50.
RESTAURANT: L served all week. D served Mon-Sat 12-2 7-10. Av 3 course à la carte £20. Av 3 course fixed price £12.50. **BREWERY/COMPANY:** Brakspear.
PRINCIPAL BEERS: Brakspear - Ordinary, Special.
FACILITIES: Children welcome Garden: Patio, outdoor eating Dogs allowed Water. **NOTES:** Parking 85

The Golden Ball ♀
Lower Assendon RG9 6AH ☎ 01491 574157
📧 01491 576653
e-mail: Golden.Ball@theseed.net
Dir: A4130, R onto B480, pub 300yrds on L
Dick Turpin hid in the priest hole at this 400-year-old building tucked away in the Stonor Valley close to Henley. Traditional pub food includes soup, pâté and toast, Cumberland sausages, chicken breast wrapped in Parma ham, enchiladas filled with chicken or chilli, and pancakes with cheese, leeks and wine.
OPEN: 11-3 6-11. **BAR MEALS:** L served all week. D served all week 12-2.15 7-9.30. Av main course £6.50.
BREWERY/COMPANY: Brakspear.
PRINCIPAL BEERS: Brakspear-Bitter, Special.
FACILITIES: Children welcome Garden: outdoor eating Dogs allowed on lead only. **NOTES:** Parking 50

HENLEY-ON-THAMES continued

The Little Angel 🍸
Remenham Ln RG9 2LS ☎ 01491 574165   📠 01491 411879
e-mail: info@thelittleangel.com
Dir: from M4, pub is on the R at bottom of hill as you arrive in Henley
Grade II listed building reputedly haunted by Mary Blandy
who poisoned her father in 1751. The pub overlooks Henley
Cricket Club and is the place to go for the Regatta and the
Henley Festival. The Spanish proprietor has introduced a warm
Mediterranean feel to the décor and a tapas menu to run
alongside the bar snacks and brasserie restaurant carte. Dishes
encompass dim sum, nachos, moules marinière and steak pie.
OPEN: 11-3 (Sun 12-3) 6-11 (Sun 7-10.30). **BAR MEALS:** L
served all week. D served all week 12-2.30 7-10. Av main course
£7.95. **RESTAURANT:** L served all week. D served all week
12.30-2.30 7-10. Av 3 course à la carte £25.
BREWERY/COMPANY: Brakspear.
PRINCIPAL BEERS: Brakspear Ordinary Bitter, Special Bitter &
Seasonal Ales. **FACILITIES:** Garden. **NOTES:** Parking 40

HENTON

Peacock Inn
OX9 4AH ☎ 01844 353519
Black and white timbered inn in quiet village setting. Patio with
outdoor eating facilities. Children welcome. Bedrooms. Look
out for the peacocks!

HOOK NORTON   Map 06 SP33

The Gate Hangs High 🍸
Whichford Rd OX15 5DF ☎ 01608 737387
Dir: Off A361 SW of Banbury
Originally a toll house on the road to Banbury market, this
charming country pub in picturesque ironstone country is well
worth finding. 'The gate hangs high and hinders none, Refresh
and pay, and travel on,' reads the sign outside. Handy for
exploring the Cotswolds and visiting Broughton Castle or
nearby Upton House. Just down the lane is the famous Hook
Norton Brewery from where the pub sources its tip-top ales.
Imaginative and traditional home cooking ranges from duck
with a cider apple and sage sauce to chargrilled noisettes of
lamb and oven-baked salmon supreme. Good wine list and a
range of malt whiskies.
OPEN: 11.30-3 6.30-11. Closed 25 & 26 Dec. **BAR MEALS:** L
served all week. D served Mon-Sat 12-2 7-9.30. **RESTAURANT:** L
served all week. D served Mon-Sat 12-2 7-9.30.
BREWERY/COMPANY: Hook Norton.
PRINCIPAL BEERS: Hook Norton - Best, Old Hooky, Haymaker
& Generation. **FACILITIES:** Children welcome Garden: outdoor
eating, patio, Dogs allowed in garden. **NOTES:** Parking 20

Sun Inn 🍸
High St OX15 5NH ☎ 01608 737570   📠 01608 730770
e-mail: enquiries@the-sun-inn.com
Traditional, extended pub in good walking country close to the
Oxfordshire/Warwickshire border. Hook Norton is a sizeable
village and close by is the famous, old-established Hook
Norton Brewery. Festooned with hops, the candlelit bar has a
cosy log fire and relaxed atmosphere. Fresh food is cooked to
order and among the imaginative specials you may find loin of
venison, chilli- and herb-crusted monkfish with roasted
shallots and a thyme sauce, and saddle of venison with
redcurrant and red wine sauce. Appetising bar menu for those
popping in for a pint and a light snack. Combine a visit with a
tour of the brewery. *continued*

OPEN: 11.30-3 6-11.30. **BAR MEALS:** L served all week. D
served all week 12-2 7-9.30. Av main course £12.50.
RESTAURANT: L served all week. D served all week 12-2 7-9.30.
Av 3 course à la carte £19.50. **BREWERY/COMPANY:** Hook
Norton. **PRINCIPAL BEERS:** Hook Norton Best Bitter, Old
Generation, Mild & Double Stout. **FACILITIES:** Garden: food
served outside. **NOTES:** Parking 20. **ROOMS:** 6 bedrooms
6 en suite s£30 d£50

KELMSCOT   Map 04 SU29

The Plough Inn
GL7 3HG ☎ 01367 253543   📠 01367 252514
Dir: From M4 onto A419 then A361 to Lechlade & A416 to Faringdon,
pick up signs to Kelmscot
Peacefully situated in an unspoilt village close to Kelmscot
Manor and the Thames, the 17th-century Plough is a favoured
refreshment stop among the walking and boating fraternity.
Good home-made food includes traditional snacks and decent
specials like venison casserole, beef stew and dumplings,
grilled sea bass, bouillabaisse, and game pie.

OPEN: 12-2.30 7-10.30. **BAR MEALS:** L served all week. D
served all week 12-2 7-9. Av main course £8.
BREWERY/COMPANY: Free House.
PRINCIPAL BEERS: Wadworth 6X, Flowers Original,
Boddingtons, Morland Original. **FACILITIES:** Children welcome
Children's licence Garden: outdoor eating, BBQ, English flowers
Dogs allowed. **NOTES:** Parking 10. **ROOMS:** 8 bedrooms
8 en suite s£30 d£55 FR£60-£70

KINGSTON LISLE   Map 04 SU38

The Blowing Stone Inn 🍸
OX12 9QL ☎ 01367 820288   📠 01367 820288
Dir: B4507 from Wantage toward Ashbury/Swindon, after 6m R to
Kingston Lisle
Situated in a pretty village in the Vale of the White Horse. The
name of the inn comes from a local legend that King Alfred
used a local sarsen stone pierced with holes to summon his
troops. Open fires and warm hospitality. Specialities include
seafood and local game in season.
OPEN: 11-2.30 6-11. **BAR MEALS:** L served Tues-Sun. D served
Mon-Sat 11-2.30 6.30-9.30. Av main course £6.50.
RESTAURANT: L served Tues-Sun. D served Mon-Sat 12-2 7-9.
Av 3 course à la carte £20. **BREWERY/COMPANY:** Free House.
PRINCIPAL BEERS: Wadworth 6X, Courage Best, Fullers London
Pride. **FACILITIES:** Children welcome Garden Dogs allowed.
NOTES: Parking 30. **ROOMS:** 3 bedrooms 3 en suite d£40

England

LEWKNOR

The Leathern Bottel
1 High St OX9 5TW ☎ 01844 351482
450-year old oak-beamed pub in a pretty village built in the Chiltern style. Low ceilings and open fires help to create an inviting atmosphere. The view of Lewknor from nearby Beacon Hill is breathtaking, and the pub is also handy for exploring the Thames Valley. Wholesome, appetising pub fare may include Scottish Angus steak, curries, salmon supreme, whole rainbow trout, Irish wholetail scampi and haddock with prawns and mushrooms.
OPEN: 10.30-3 6-11. **BAR MEALS:** L served all week. D served all week 12-2 7-9.30. Av main course £6.95.
BREWERY/COMPANY: Brakspear.
PRINCIPAL BEERS: Brakspear Ordinary/Special/Old.
FACILITIES: Children welcome Children's licence Garden: outdoor eating Dogs allowed Water. **NOTES:** Parking 35

LOWER WOLVERCOTE   Map 06 SP41

The Trout Inn ⚏
195 Godstow Rd OX2 8PN ☎ 01865 302071
Dir: From A40 at Wolvercote rdbt (N of Oxford) follow signs for Wolvercote

A riverside inn which has associations with Matthew Arnold, Lewis Carroll and Colin Dexter's Inspector Morse. Constructed in the 17th century from the ruins of Godstow Abbey, its rich history includes being torched by Parliamentarian troops. A good choice of food offers baked whole trout with garlic mushrooms and cheddar mash, lemon chicken, beef, mushroom and Bass pie, or Cumberland sausage wrapped in Yorkshire pudding, with liver and bacon.
OPEN: 11-11 (Sun 12-10.30). **BAR MEALS:** L served all week. D served all week . **BREWERY/COMPANY:** Vintage Inns.
PRINCIPAL BEERS: Bass, Worthington. **FACILITIES:** Garden: patio, outdoor eating. **NOTES:** Parking 100

MARSTON   Map 06 SP50

Victoria Arms
Mill Ln OX3 0PZ ☎ 01865 241382
Dir: From A40 follow signs to Old Marston, sharp R into Mill Lane, pub lane 500yrds on L
Friendly country pub situated on the banks of the River Cherwell, only 10 minutes from the centre of Oxford, and accessible by punt. Wadworth ales.

MIDDLETON STONEY   Map 06 SP52

Pick of the Pubs

The Jersey Arms ◉ ★ ★ ⚏
OX6 8SE ☎ 01869 343234 📠 01869 343565
e-mail: jerseyarms@bestwestern.co.uk
Charming family-run hotel, formerly a coaching inn with the original courtyard housing spacious and comfortable bedrooms which are quieter than main building rooms. Cosy bar offering good range of popular bar food with the extensive menu supplemented by daily blackboard specials, including soups, pâtés, pasta dishes and traditional main courses like steak and kidney pie. Beamed and panelled restaurant with Mediterranean terracotta decor and cosmopolitan brasserie-style menu.
OPEN: 12-3 7-11. **BAR MEALS:** L served all week. D served all week 12-2.15 6.30-9.30. Av main course £7.95.
RESTAURANT: L served all week. D served all week 12-2.15 6.30-9.30. Av 3 course à la carte £21.
BREWERY/COMPANY: Free House.
PRINCIPAL BEERS: Courage, John Smiths.
FACILITIES: Children welcome Garden: food served outside. **NOTES:** Parking 50. **ROOMS:** 20 bedrooms 20 en suite s£79 d£92

MINSTER LOVELL   Map 06 SP31

The Mill & Old Swan ⚏
OX8 5RN ☎ 01993 774441 📠 01993 702002
e-mail: themill@initialstyle.co.uk
Dir: On A4095 W of Witney

Historic, 650-year-old riverside inn within easy reach of Oxford, Stratford and Blenheim Palace. The original weir, from which the mill was powered, can still be seen today. Inside you'll find a fine mix of oak beams, original flagstone floors and winding staircases. Individually furnished bedrooms with views over the river enhance the style and charm of this civilised hotel-cum-inn. Good choice of bar and restaurant menus. Cream teas are a speciality and the Sunday buffet lunch is particularly popular - booking advisable.
OPEN: 11-5 6-11. **BAR MEALS:** L served all week. D served all week 12.30-2.30 7-9.30. Av main course £6.50. **RESTAURANT:** L served Sat-Sun. D served all week 12.30-2.30 7-9.30. Av 3 course à la carte £20. Av 4 course fixed price £40.
BREWERY/COMPANY: Free House.
PRINCIPAL BEERS: Hook Norton,. **FACILITIES:** Children welcome Children's licence Garden: outdoor eating, BBQ Dogs allowed Water. **NOTES:** Parking 120. **ROOMS:** 63 bedrooms 63 en suite s£30 d£40

MURCOTT　　　　　　　　　　　Map 06 SP51

The Nut Tree ♀
Main St OX5 2RE ☎ 01865 331253 ▤ 331957
e-mail: jameswood100@hotmail.com
Dir: *off B4027 NE of Oxford via Islip and Charlton-on-Moor*
15th-century thatched pub set in five acres of gardens,
including a duck pond. There are donkeys, geese, peacocks
and chickens, which supply the pub with eggs. Beamed
interior with brasses, paintings and antiques. Conservatory
serves as a non-smoking restaurant. Comprehensive menu
specialises in fish and contemporary traditional dishes.

NORTH MORETON　　　　　　　　　Map 04 SU58

The Bear
High St OX11 9AT ☎ 01235 813236
Dir: *Off A4130 between Didcot & Wallingford*
15th-century inn on the village green, with exposed beams,
open fireplaces and a cosy, relaxed atmosphere. Hook Norton
ales.

NUFFIELD　　　　　　　　　　　Map 04 SU68

The Crown ♀
RG9 5SJ ☎ 01491 641335 ▤ 01491 641335
Dir: *Follow Henley signs, then Wallingford rd on L past turning for village*
Heavily beamed 17th-century pub, originally a waggoners' inn.
Located in the wooded country of the Chilterns, on the route
of the Ridgeway long-distance trail. Inglenook fireplace and
beams inside. Good choice of dishes with full restaurant
facilities and bar meals.

OXFORD　　　　　　　　　　　Map 06 SP50

Anchor
2 Hayfield Rd, Walton Manor OX2 6TT ☎ 01865 510282
Dir: *A34 Oxford Ring Road(N), exit Peartree Roundabout, 1.5m then R at Polstead Rd, follow rd to bottom, pub on R*
A friendly 1930s pub, once frequented by local resident
Lawrence of Arabia. Wide ranging menus and strong emphasis
on food. In summer there are barbecues and pig roasts in the
garden.

Turf Tavern ♀
4 Bath Place, off Holywell St OX1 3SU ☎ 01865 243235
Situated in the heart of Oxford, approached through hidden
alleyways and winding passages, this famous pub lies in the
shadow of the city wall and the colleges. It is especially popular
in the summer when customers can relax in the sheltered
courtyards. Eleven real ales are served daily, from a choice of
around 500 over a year, along with some typical pub fare.
OPEN: 11-11 (Sun 12-10.30). **BAR MEALS:** L served all week.
D served all week 12-8. Av main course £4.95.
BREWERY/COMPANY: Whitbread. **FACILITIES:** Garden:
Food served outside

The White House
2 Botley Rd OX2 0AB ☎ 01865 242823 ▤ 01865 793331
Dir: *2 minutes walk from rail station*
Set back from a busy road, this pub was once a tollhouse
where people crossed the river to enter Oxford. The menu
may include roast fillet of salmon with roast peppers and fresh
herbs, sauteed calves' liver with onion sauce, pork cutlets
cooked in beer with cabbage and bacon, or wild mushroom
ravioli.　　　　　　　　　　　　　　*continued*

OPEN: 11-11. **BAR MEALS:** L served all week. D served all week
12.30-2 6-7.30. Av main course £4.50. **RESTAURANT:** L served
all week. D served all week 12.30-2 6-9.30. Av 3 course à la carte
£20. **BREWERY/COMPANY:** Punch Taverns.
PRINCIPAL BEERS: Wadworth 6X, Greene King Abbot Ale, Bass,
Fullers London Pride. **FACILITIES:** Garden: Dogs allowed.
NOTES: Parking 15

PISHILL　　　　　　　　　　　Map 04 SU78

Pick of the Pubs

The Crown Inn 🛏 ♀
RG9 6HH ☎ 01491 638364 ▤ 01491 638364
e-mail: jc@carpon.fsnet.co.uk
Dir: *On B480 off A4130, NW of Henley-on-Thames*

A long-standing favourite, close to the magnificent
parkland of Stonor House, a 15th-century brick and flint
coaching inn (with one bedroom!) with origins that may
well date it back to the 11th. At the top of a steep climb for
horse-drawn carriages from Henley into the Chilterns and
on to Oxford, ostlers would water the horses while all else
refreshed themselves: it is arguable that the village was
once spelled with an extra 's' in the middle.
　　In approximately four acres of grounds, its 400-year-old
thatched barn has been renovated to cater to private
functions and weddings. Winter Warmer and Shoot Lunch
fixed-price lunches offer hearty pea and ham broth and
venison sausages or chicken liver parfait and Welsh-style
lamb cawl as they should, while main menus offer greater
variety. Starters of warm mushroom and thyme tartlet
glazed with Stilton or minestrone with shaved Parmesan,
may be followed by veal escalope with sage and Parma
ham, monkfish medallions in a Thai red curry sauce and
fillet of beef with cambazola and garlic mash, with white
chocolate torte for dessert.
OPEN: 11.30-2.30 6-11 (Sun 12-3, 7-10.30). Closed 25-26 Dec
Jan 1. **BAR MEALS:** L served all week. D served all week
12-2 7-9.30. Av main course £7.50. **RESTAURANT:** L served
all week. D served all week 12-2 7-9.30. Av 3 course à la carte
£20. **BREWERY/COMPANY:** Free House.
PRINCIPAL BEERS: Brakspear, Fullers.
FACILITIES: Children welcome Garden: Large beer
garden, food served outdoors Dogs allowed garden only.
NOTES: Parking 60. **ROOMS:** 1 bedrooms 1 en suite
s£85 d£85

　AA inspected hotel accommodation

RAMSDEN   Map 06 SP31

The Royal Oak ⏲

High St OX7 3AU ☎ 01993 868213 ▨ 01993 868864
Dir: *From Witney take B4022 toward Charlbury, then turn R before Hailey, and go through Poffley End.*

17th-century former coaching inn on the route of an old Roman road. Excellent base for walking and handy for Blenheim Palace and the unspoilt Wychwood Forest. The extensively refurbished Royal Oak uses the best local meat, fish and vegetable products, incorporating new and unusual items from its London suppliers. Expect pot-roasted pheasant cooked in red wine and Aberdeen Angus fillet steak au poivre, steamed steak and kidney pudding, and popular Sunday roast lunches. Fresh flowers, daily papers and magazines adorn the comfortable yet simply furnished bar.
OPEN: 11.30-3 6.30-11. Closed Dec 25. **BAR MEALS:** L served all week. D served all week 12-2 7-10. Av main course £6.
RESTAURANT: L served all week. D served all week 12-2 7-10. Av 3 course à la carte £15. **BREWERY/COMPANY:** Free House.
PRINCIPAL BEERS: Hook Norton, Fullers ESB, Adnams Broadside, Archers Golden. **FACILITIES:** Garden: patio, food served outside Dogs allowed Water. **NOTES:** Parking 20.
ROOMS: 4 bedrooms 4 en suite s£35 d£50

ROKE   Map 04 SU69

Home Sweet Home 🍴

OX10 6JD ☎ 01491 838249
Dir: *Just off the B4009 from Benson to Watlington, signed on B4009*
Situated on a quiet country road in the tiny hamlet of Roke, this 15th-century inn was converted from four cottages by a local brewer. Log fires in Inglenook fireplaces warm the bar. Menu choices include chicken chasseur, Somerset pork in cider, a choice of steaks, half roast duck with honey and orange, and salmon supreme with lemon butter. A separate vegetarian menu is available.
OPEN: 11-3 (Sun 12-3) 6-11. Closed Sun eve & Dec 25-26.
BAR MEALS: L served all week. D served Mon-Sat 12-2 6-9. Av main course £7.50. **RESTAURANT:** L served all week. D served Mon-Sat 12-2 7-9. Av 3 course à la carte £15.
BREWERY/COMPANY: Free House.
PRINCIPAL BEERS: Brakspear. **FACILITIES:** Children welcome Children's licence Garden: Patio/terrace, outdoor eating. **NOTES:** Parking 60

The Morse Pub Crawl

If you are a fan of Colin Dexter's legendary sleuth 'Inspector Morse' and you have enough time and stamina, you may like to embark on a tour of the detective's favourite pubs in and around Oxford. Many of them will be familiar to you as they have appeared in the long-running television series over the years. Start off at the delightful Turf Tavern sheltering in the shadow of New College and the Radcliffe Camera at the heart of the city, then make your way along the Thames Path to the Trout Inn at Lower Wolvercote. Morse is seen seated outside on the lovely riverside terrace in several episodes. Finish your pub crawl by leaving the riverbank and heading west to neighbouring Wytham, where you can relax in the comfortable surroundings of the creeper-clad White Hart, another favourite 'Morse' pub.

ROTHERFIELD PEPPARD   Map 04 SU78

Pick of the Pubs

The Greyhound ⏲ NEW

Gallowstree Rd RG9 5HT ☎ 0118 9722227
▨ 0118 97222227
e-mail: tambil:1:@c.s.com
Dir: *4 miles from Henley on Thames*
Picture-postcard pretty brick and timber village inn with a wonky tiled roof and splendid front garden decked with upmarket wooden tables and cotton parasols. Desirée Van Reeuwrik and partner Ray Argyle bought the Greyhound two years ago and in that time have created a stylish dining pub-restaurant that has proved a hit with the well-heeled local foodies.

The classic beamed bar, with its woodblock floor, open brick fireplace and minimal furnishings, remains unspoilt and the domain of local drinkers. The adjacent restaurant is housed in a beautifully converted pitched-roof barn, replete with hop-strewn rafters, tasteful paintings and an eclectic mix of furnishings.

Innovative, well presented dishes range from light lunches - bruschetta with griddled vegetables with dressed leaves, chicken Caesar salad, home-made hamburger - to simply described evening options like rack of lamb, herb crust, mint jus, halibut fillet, spinach, oven-dried tomatoes, crisp puff pastry and mussel jus, or entrecote steak with rocket and chips. Puddings include orange crème brûlée and lemon mousse torte with fresh strawberries.
OPEN: 12-3 5.30-11. Closed Mon & 25-28 Dec.
BAR MEALS: L served Tue-Sun. D served Tue-Sun 12-2.15 (3 Sat & Sun) 7-9.30 (10 Fri & Sat). Av main course £10.
RESTAURANT: L served Tue-Sun. D served Tue-Sun 12-2.15 (3 Sat & Sun) 7-9.30 (10 Fri & Sat). Av 3 course à la carte £16.50. **BREWERY/COMPANY:** Free House.
PRINCIPAL BEERS: Brakspear, Fullers London Pride.
FACILITIES: Children welcome Garden: food served outside Dogs allowed.

SHENINGTON   Map 06 SP34

The Bell

OX15 6NQ ☎ 01295 670274
e-mail: thebell@shenington.co.uk
Dir: *M40 J11 take A422 towards Stratford. Village is signposted 3m N of Wroxton*
Nestling amid mellow stone houses, a classic village green and a church with an impressive Tudor tower, the comfortable and welcoming 300-year-old Bell provides home-cooked food prepared with fresh local ingredients. Expect lamb and lime casserole, pork loin braised in apple, cider and pineapple, and Stilton green bean and walnut lasagne. Plenty of good country walks nearby.
OPEN: 12-2.30 7-11. **BAR MEALS:** L served all week. D served all week 12-2 7-11. **RESTAURANT:** L served all week. D served all week 12-2 7-11. Av 3 course à la carte £12.50. **BREWERY/COMPANY:** Free House.
PRINCIPAL BEERS: Hook Norton, Flowers.
FACILITIES: Children welcome Garden: outdoor eating, Dogs allowed Water. **ROOMS:** 3 bedrooms 1 en suite s£20 d£40

SHIPTON-UNDER-WYCHWOOD — Map 06 SP21

The Lamb Inn 🍺
High St OX7 6DQ ☎ 01993 830465 📠 01993 832025
Dir: *4m N of Burford on the A361*
A delightful old Cotswold-stone inn, in which the rustic beamed bar with its stone walls, wooden floor and sturdy furniture make a fine setting for enjoying a wholesome meal. Interesting dishes on the blackboard menu may include game terrine, calves' liver in Pernod, poached salmon, chargrilled tuna with Mediterranean vegetables, and chocolate truffle torte. **OPEN:** 11-11 (Sun 12-10.30). **BAR MEALS:** L served all week. D served all week 12-2 7-9.30. Av main course £10. **RESTAURANT:** L served Sun. D served Tues-Sat 12-2 7-9.30. Av 3 course à la carte £22.50. **BREWERY/COMPANY:** Old English Inns. **PRINCIPAL BEERS:** Hook Norton. **FACILITIES:** Children welcome Garden Dogs allowed. **NOTES:** Parking 15. **ROOMS:** 5 bedrooms 5 en suite s£65 d£75

Pick of the Pubs

The Shaven Crown Hotel
High St OX7 6BA ☎ 01993 830330 📠 01993 832136
Dir: *On A361, halfway between Burford and Chipping Norton opposite village green and church*
The Shaven Crown is recorded as one of the ten oldest inns and hotels in the country. Originally a late 14th-century hospice for the monks of Bruern Abbey, it became an inn in 1571. The notorious fascist Oswald Mosley was imprisoned here during the last war. It is a lovely building of local honey-coloured stone and visitors never fail to be impressed by its original 14th-century gateway, medieval hall with double-collar braced roof, mullioned windows and central courtyard garden. In places it has the feeling of a baronial hall or a stately home.

Dine in the intimate candlelit restaurant, where the best ingredients are combined to create dishes with an cosmopolitan flair, or make for the Monks Bar which offers a very popular and extensive menu, including steak and kidney pie cooked in ale, half duck served with orange and cinnamon sauce, or four Cotswold lamb cutlets. **OPEN:** 11.30-2.30 5-11. **BAR MEALS:** L served all week. D served all week 12-2 5.30-9.30. Av main course £6.95. **RESTAURANT:** L served Sun. D served all week 12-2 7-9. Av 3 course à la carte £21. Av 3 course fixed price £21. **BREWERY/COMPANY:** Free House. **PRINCIPAL BEERS:** Hook Norton, Greene King Abbot Ale, Fullers London Pride. **FACILITIES:** Children welcome Garden: outdoor eating, patio,. **NOTES:** Parking 15. **ROOMS:** 9 bedrooms 9 en suite s£55 d£75 FR£95-£120

SOUTH MORETON — Map 04 SU58

The Crown Inn 🍷
High St OX11 9AG ☎ 01235 812262
Dir: *From Didcot take A4130 towards Wallingford. Village on R*
Friendly 19th-century pub decorated in a rustic cottage style with antique furnishings. Menu includes steak, kidney and Stilton pie, haddock in beer batter, cauliflower moussaka, salmon hollandaise and a variety of pasta dishes.

continued

OPEN: 11-3 (Sun 12-3) 5.30-11 (Sun 7-10.30). Closed Dec 25-26. **BAR MEALS:** L served all week. D served all week 12-2 7-9.30. Av main course £7.95. **RESTAURANT:** D served all week 12-2 7-9.30. Av 3 course à la carte £12.95. **BREWERY/COMPANY:** Wadworth. **PRINCIPAL BEERS:** Badger Tanglefoot, Adnams, Wadworth 6X & Henrys IPA. **FACILITIES:** Children welcome Garden: food served outdoors Dogs allowed. **NOTES:** Parking 30

SOUTH STOKE — Map 04 SU58

The Perch and Pike 🍷
RG8 0JS ☎ 01491 872415 📠 01491 875852
e-mail: forallthatalesthee@supanet.com
Dir: *Between Goring and Wallingford just off B4009*

Set among acres of farmland, with the Ridgeway Path going past the door and surrounded by the Chilterns, this 18th-century pub is in a lovely location. Choose from a menu that may include pot roast partridge with Toulouse sausage, rump of lamb with truffle mash, chargrilled catfish with avocado or smoked salmon and fresh prawn salad. **OPEN:** 11-3 6-11. **BAR MEALS:** L served all week. D served Mon-Sat 12-2.30 7-9.45. Av main course £10.95. **RESTAURANT:** L served all week. D served Mon-Sat 12-2.30 7-9.45. Av 3 course à la carte £27. Av 3 course fixed price £19.95. **BREWERY/COMPANY:** Brakspear. **PRINCIPAL BEERS:** Brakspear Bitter, Special, Old, Mild. **FACILITIES:** Children welcome Garden: food served outside Dogs allowed. **NOTES:** Parking 30. **ROOMS:** 4 bedrooms 4 en suite d£65

Ploughman's Lunch - a pub classic
Only comparatively recently has pub grub become a important feature of the license trade. Without it, most hostelries would simply go out of business. Food trends come and go and new, imaginatively prepared dishes crop up every day on the specials board. However, there is one favourite item on the menu that remains constant and unchanging and that is the good old ploughman's lunch. The simple but appetising ploughman's is based on the medieval farm labourer's lunchtime snack of bread and cheese and is available in just about every pub in the country. The snack and its ingredients have changed little down the years, though today most pubs complement the ploughman's lunch with a pickled onion and a garnish of salad or a variety of exotic cheeses and cold meats. Home-made pickle is also a popular favourite.

IRISH ELIXIR

'Guinness is Good For You'

was the slogan of one of the most successful campaigns in advertising history. Launched in 1928, with pictures and words by Rex Whistler and Dorothy L Sayers among others, it made a brew of black from Ireland into a household name. The firm originated with Arthur Guinness, who started brewing in Dublin in 1759. Besides fathering some 21 children, he sired Ireland's most famous commercial product and one of the great dynasties of the annals of brewing.

STADHAMPTON   Map 04 SU69

Pick of the Pubs

The Crazy Bear 🍴🍴 ♦♦♦♦ 🛏 ⅋

Bear Ln OX44 7UR ☎ 01865 890714 📠 01865 400481

Dir: M40 J7 L on A329

A rural 16th-century property, just 15 minutes' drive from Oxford, that has undergone flamboyant refurbishment into an unusual small hotel full of surprises. Two separate dining-rooms embrace English fine-dining and Thai-style brasserie menus which are also available in the bar, alongside open Swiss sandwiches and exotic salads.

Such vastness of choice tends to preclude consistency of dishes such as croustade of devilled chicken livers and pork Holstein with garlic potatoes, capers and anchovies from the daily menu, and perhaps lobster Thermidor a la carte. Alternative fish dishes highlight Dover sole with baby potatoes and mildly curried King prawns. To follow, perhaps, a caramelised tarte tatin with home-made vanilla ice cream and decent espresso.

Bedrooms, best described as 'art deco', have recently been supplemented by a range of extravagant suites that might struggle to justify their tariff.

OPEN: 12-11. **BAR MEALS:** L served all week. D served all week 12-10. Av main course £12. **RESTAURANT:** L served all week. D served all week 12-3 7-10. Av 3 course fixed price £15.95. **BREWERY/COMPANY:** Free House. **PRINCIPAL BEERS:** Greene King IPA, Ruddles County & Abbot Ale. **FACILITIES:** Garden: outdoor eating, Jap water garden. **NOTES:** Parking 30. **ROOMS:** 12 bedrooms 12 en suite s£60 d£80

STANDLAKE   Map 06 SP30

Pick of the Pubs

The Bell at Standlake 🛏 ⅋

21 High St OX8 7RH ☎ 01865 300784

Dir: Off the A415

Unpretentious, 300-year-old, half-timbered pub nestling in the heart of pretty Standlake and renowned locally for its innovative food and good wines. The small, simply furnished front bar is the venue for some good, light lunchtime meals prepared from fresh ingredients - everything is make on the premises, except the bread which is sourced from a quality local bakery.

The blackboard menu may list decent 'doorstop' sandwiches, home-made corned beef hash, and organic Welsh goats' cheese pudding with tomato salad and pesto dressing. Locals fill the bar in the evening while dining emphasis shifts to the rear lounge and dining room (booking advisable).

Cooking moves up a gear, the daily menu listing fish from Cornwall and Scotland - Shetland mussels with Thai green curry spices and coconut milk, baked sea bass with roe fritters and Asian pesto - and local estate game like roast partridge with creamy lemon sauce. Choices extend to locally-farmed pork baked with Stilton and leek crust with port gravy and braised oxtail in red wine and root vegetables, and, for pudding, saffron and cardamom rice pudding with fresh mango purée. Sunday roasts; 11 wines by the glass.

OPEN: 12-3 6-11 (Sun 7-10.30). Closed Mon (ex BH) & Dec 25 eve. **BAR MEALS:** L served Tues-Sat (& BH) 12-2.30. Av main course £9. **RESTAURANT:** L served Sun. D served Tues-Sat (& BH) 12-2 6.30-9.30. Av 3 course à la carte £20. Av 3 course fixed price £13.95. **BREWERY/COMPANY:** Greene King. **PRINCIPAL BEERS:** Morland Original, Bass, Flowers Original, Wadworth 6X. **FACILITIES:** Children welcome Garden: outdoor eating Dogs allowed only in non food areas, Water. **NOTES:** Parking 40

STANTON ST JOHN   Map 06 SP50

Star Inn ⅋

Middle Rd OX33 1EX ☎ 01865 351277

Dir: At A40/Oxford ring road rdbt take Stanton exit, follow rd to T junct, R to Stanton, 3rd L, pub on L 50yds

Although the Star is only fifteen minutes drive from the centre of Oxford, it still retains a distinctly 'village' feel. The oldest part of the pub dates from the early 17th century, and in the past, the building has been used as a butcher's shop and an abattoir. The garden is peaceful and secluded. Typical menu features ribeye steak, moussaka, vegetarian cannelloni, and shoulder of lamb.

OPEN: 11-2.30 6.30-11. **BAR MEALS:** L served all week. D served all week 12-2 6.30-9.30. Av main course £6.95. **BREWERY/COMPANY:** Wadworth. **PRINCIPAL BEERS:** Wadworth 6X & Henrys IPA. **FACILITIES:** Children welcome Garden: food served outside Dogs allowed Water bowls. **NOTES:** Parking 50

STANTON ST JOHN continued

Pick of the Pubs

The Talk House 𝖸
Wheatley Rd OX33 1EX ☎ 01865 351648
▤ 01865 351085
e-mail: thetalkhousestantonstjohn.co.uk
Dir: Stanton-St-John signed from the Oxford ring road
Well converted and extended 17th-century inn within easy
reach of Oxford and the A40 and well worth seeking out
since new owners took over in May 2000.

A Gothic-style ambience pervades throughout the
attractive and welcoming bars, where you can sample
moules with lemon and chive cream, smoked seafood
terrine, and chargrilled Mediterranean vegetables for
starters, with baked salmon with red wine glaze, half-
shoulder of lamb with honey, garlic and rosemary sauce,
or game casserole with parsley dumpling for main course.
Four en suite bedrooms lined the attractive rear courtyard.
OPEN: 12-3 5.30-11. **BAR MEALS:** L served all week.
D served all week 12-2 7-10. Av main course £10.
RESTAURANT: L served all week. D served all week 12-2
7-10. Av 3 course à la carte £20.
BREWERY/COMPANY: Free House.
PRINCIPAL BEERS: Hook Norton, Greene King Old
Speckled Hen, Fullers London Pride,. **FACILITIES:** Children
welcome Garden: fountain, Food served outside.
NOTES: Parking 60. **ROOMS:** 4 bedrooms 4 en suite s£40
d£49.50

STEEPLE ASTON   Map 06 SP42

Red Lion 🐑
South Side OX25 4RY ☎ 01869 340225
Dir: Off A4260 between Oxford & Banbury
The art of conversation and the enjoyment of fresh food is
positively encouraged at this traditional pub. The 17th-century
building comprises a bar, separate dining room, library and
floral terrace. Typical dishes include Arbroath smokies en
cocotte, jugged hare with forcemeat balls, and a soufflé of
fresh lime.
OPEN: 11-3 6-11 (Sun 12-3, 7-10.30). **BAR MEALS:** L served
Mon-Sat 12-2. Av main course £4.80. **RESTAURANT:** L served
none. D served Tue-Sat 7.30-9.15. Av 3 course à la carte £23.
BREWERY/COMPANY: Free House.
PRINCIPAL BEERS: Hook Norton. **FACILITIES:** Garden: Floral
terrace Dogs allowed. **NOTES:** Parking 15

STEVENTON   Map 04 SU49

The Cherry Tree
33 High St OX13 6RS ☎ 01235 831222
*Dir: Leave A34 at Milton Interchange, follow signs for Steventon, go
into village, over railway bridge, pub on R*
Inviting roadside tavern, full of old world charm. Home made
specials feature on the varied menu. Wadworth ales.

STOKE ROW   Map 04 SU68

Pick of the Pubs

Crooked Billet 🐑 𝖸
RG9 5PU ☎ 01491 681048   ▤ 01491 682231
*Dir: From Henley to Oxford A4130.Turn L at Nettlebed for Stoke
Row*
Built in 1642 and once the hideout of notorious
highwayman Dick Turpin, this rustic, off-the-beaten-track
cottage epitomises all that a true country pub should be.
Delightfully unspoilt inside with low beams, ancient tiled
floors, open fires and simple furnishings, it is very much a
dining venue attracting well-heeled folk for some first-class
food. An extensive menu offers an adventurous choice of
modern dishes.

Expect starters like foie gras and chicken liver parfait
with caramelised orange and green peppercorn dressing
and Chinese confit duck leg with stir-fried vegetables and
hoi sin. Main course options include fresh fish - sea bass
with baby squid and roast Mediterranean vegetables,
baked red mullet with pesto and anchovy dressing - rack
of lamb with Madeira jus and Thai marinated chicken with
lemon grass broth.

Finish with lemon tart or British farmhouse cheeses.
Meat is smoked on the premises and meat and dairy
produce is local and organic. Global list of wines;
Brakspear Bitter drawn from the barrel in the cellar. 3-acre
garden bordering Chiltern woods.

OPEN: 12-11(Sun 12-10.30). **RESTAURANT:** L
served all week. D served all week 12-2.30 7-10. Av 3 course
à la carte £25. Av 2 course fixed price £11.95.
BREWERY/COMPANY: Brakspear.
PRINCIPAL BEERS: Brakspear. **FACILITIES:** Children
welcome Garden: food served outside. **NOTES:** Parking 50

STRATTON AUDLEY   Map 06 SP62

The Red Lion
Church St OX27 9AG ☎ 01869 277225   ▤ 01869 277225
e-mail: robtalbotcooper@talk21.co.uk
Dir: 2 Miles N of Bicester, just off the Buckingham Road
Charming thatched pub that contains more than you'd think.
Main bar, private dining room, and a restaurant are all served
by a varied menu, and the 60-seater terrace is ideal for eating
out.

SUTTON COURTENAY · Map 04 SU59

Pick of the Pubs

The Fish 🍴 ♟
4 Appleford Rd OX14 4NQ ☎ 01235 848242
📠 01235 848014
e-mail: mike@thefish.co.uk
Dir: From A415 in Abingdon take B4017 then L onto B4016 to village

Unassuming, late 19th-century brick-built pub located a short stroll for the Thames in the heart of this beautiful and historic village - where Asquith and George Orwell are buried. Very much a dining pub-restaurant although drinkers are welcome at the bar. Good value bistro lunches are served in the front bar-cum-dining area and in the attractive garden and patio when fine: dishes are modern versions of classic French and English dishes with a strong emphasis on fresh seafood. Typical choices include pan-seared scallops with chilli vinaigrette, carpaccio of tuna with mooli, mint and black olives, sea bass on a leek and potato sauce with caviar butter, and roast monkfish with chorizo cassoulet and saffron sauce. Further options may be crispy duck confit with tabouleh and sun-dried tomato jam and calves' liver and bacon with shallot confit, with almond tart with vanilla ice cream or dark chocolate marquise with coffee bean syrup to follow. Set-price and à la carte dinners.

OPEN: 12-3.30 6-11 (Sat 6.30-11, Sun 7-10.30). Closed 2 days between Xmas & New Year. **BAR MEALS:** L served Mon-Sat 12-2. Av main course £14. **RESTAURANT:** L served all week. D served all week 12-2 7-9.30. Av 3 course à la carte £25. Av 3 course fixed price £19.95. **BREWERY/COMPANY:** Greene King. **PRINCIPAL BEERS:** Morland Original, Greeen King IPA. **FACILITIES:** Children welcome Garden: patio, outdoor eating Dogs allowed Water. **NOTES:** Parking 30.
ROOMS: 2 bedrooms 2 en suite s£36 d£45

SWALCLIFFE · Map 06 SP33

Stag's Head ♟ NEW
☎ 01295 780232 📠 01295 788977
e-mail: stagsheadswalcliffe@dial.pipes.com
Dir: 6M W of banbury on the B4035

Pretty thatched pub dating back to the late 15th century or even earlier. With its picture postcard look and picturesque village setting, it's not suprising this ancient inn draws a broad range of customers. Among the better dining pubs in Oxfordshire, the Stags Head offers an eclectic range of dishes, from traditional steaks and pot-roasted lamb, to lamb tikka massala and lime and chilli chicken. Vegetarian options might include Stilton and artichoke pasta or roasted peppers and

continued

goats' cheese. Dine or enjoy a decent pint alfresco in the newly landscaped garden.
OPEN: 11.30-2.30. Closed Sun eve in winter & Mon lunch. 6.30-11. **BAR MEALS:** L served all week. D served all week 12-2.15 7-9.30. Av main course £9. **BREWERY/COMPANY:** Free House. **PRINCIPAL BEERS:** Brakspears PA, Hook Norton Best, Vale Black Beauty, Exmoor Stag. **FACILITIES:** Children welcome Garden: food served outside Dogs allowed

SWERFORD · Map 06 SP33

Pick of the Pubs

The Mason's Arms 🍴 NEW
OX7 4AP ☎ 01608 683121 📠 01608 683105
e-mail: masonsarms@swerford.fsbusiness.co.uk
Set in 3 acres overlooking the Swere Valley on the edge of the Cotswolds, the Masons is a lovely, 300-year-old stone pub that has been stylishly redesigned throughout in country-farmhouse style to provide a modern dining venue without destroying the traditional charm of a village inn. In addition to wonderful views and a relaxed, informal atmosphere, fresh produce is sourced locally to create the imaginative, modern pub dishes listed on the eclectic menu available in the bar. From starters like seafood terrine with lime and chilli sour cream and Thai-style salmon and prawn fishcake with coriander and lime aïoli, main course options range from pub favourites - Gloucester sausages on apple and parsnip mash with red onion gravy, beer-battered cod with 'fat' chips and mushy peas - given a modern makeover, to pepper-crusted rack of lamb with red wine jus, grilled mackerel with a lime scented beurre blanc, and pan-fried monkfish with wild mushroom and bacon risotto. Hook Norton Best on tap, a select list of wines, and popular themed evenings.
OPEN: 12-3 6-11. **RESTAURANT:** L served all week. D served all week 12-2 6-10. Av 3 course à la carte £10.
BREWERY/COMPANY: Free House.
PRINCIPAL BEERS: Hook Norton Best,.
FACILITIES: Children welcome Garden: food served outside Dogs allowed. **NOTES:** Parking 50

SWINBROOK · Map 06 SP21

The Swan Inn NEW
OX18 4DY ☎ 01993 822165
Dir: Take the A40 towards Burford & Cheltenham at the end of the dual carriage way is a rdbt, straight over the turn R for Swinbrook the pub can be found over the bridge on the left side

With its flagstone floors, antique furnishings and open fires, the 400-year-old Swan is full of charm and character and has long been associated with the adjoining mill. Step outside and the pub's riverside setting by the Windrush cannot fail to impress. Plenty of scenic walks and popular tourist attractions close by. Choose cottage pie, spaghetti carbonara or mushroom and smoked bacon from the snack menu, followed perhaps by sirloin steak, Norfolk chicken cooked with tarragon or pan-fried trout with dried fruits.
OPEN: 11.30-3 6.30-11. **BAR MEALS:** L served all week. D served all week 12-2 7-9. Av main course £6. **RESTAURANT:** L served all week. D served all week 12-2 7-9. Av 3 course à la carte £16.50. **BREWERY/COMPANY:** Free House.
PRINCIPAL BEERS: Greene King Morland Original, Old Speckled Hen, Wadworth 6X. **FACILITIES:** Children welcome Garden: food served outside Dogs allowed Water.
NOTES: Parking 10

TADMARTON

The Lampet Arms ◆◆◆ ♀
Main St OX15 5TB ☎ 01295 780070 ▤ 01295 780260
e-mail: lampet@compuserve.com
Dir: *take the B4035 from Banbury to Tadmarton for 5m*
Victorian-style building named after Captain Lampet, the local
landowner who built it. The captain mistakenly believed he
could persuade the council to have the local railway line
directed through the village, thereby increasing trade. Breast
of duck, red snapper, grilled lamb chops, thai curry and
vegetable couscous are typical menu choices. Good choice of
sweets. The well equipped bedrooms are located in the former
stable block.
OPEN: 11.30-3 5-11 (Sun 12-3, 7-10.30). **BAR MEALS:** L served
all week. D served all week 12-2 6.30-9.30. Av main course £5.50.
RESTAURANT: L served all week. D served all week 12-2
6.30-9.30. Av 3 course à la carte £12.
BREWERY/COMPANY: Free House.
PRINCIPAL BEERS: Flowers IPA, Boddingtons, Marstons
Pedigree, Fullers London Pride. **FACILITIES:** Children welcome
Garden: terrace, outdoor eating, Dogs allowed except in the
garden. **NOTES:** Parking 18. **ROOMS:** 4 bedrooms 4 en suite
s£39 d£60 FR£70-£80

THAME
Map 06 SP70

The Swan Hotel ♀ NEW
9 Upper Hight St OX9 3ER ☎ 01844 261211
▤ 01844 261954
e-mail: swanthame@hotmail.com
Former coaching inn, dating from the 16th-century,
overlooking the market square in Thame. The Tudor painted
ceiling is a feature of the upstairs restaurant, while downstairs
there is a cosy beamed bar with an open fire. Food options
range from steak sandwich with cheese, onions and chips to
pork tenderloin stuffed with prunes and pistachio nuts, served
with a Cognac and cream sauce.
OPEN: 11-11. Closed 25-26 Dec. **BAR MEALS:** L served all
week. D served all week 12-2 7-9.30. Av main course £5.20.
RESTAURANT: L served all week. D served all week 12-2 7-9.30.
Av 3 course à la carte £18. **BREWERY/COMPANY:** Free House.
PRINCIPAL BEERS: Hook Norton, Timothy Taylor Landlord,
Brakspears, Shepherd Neame Spitfire. **FACILITIES:** Dogs allowed
Water. **NOTES:** Parking 200. **ROOMS:** 7 bedrooms
7 en suite s£50 d£80

TOOT BALDON
Map 06 SP50

The Crown Inn
OX44 9NG ☎ 01865 343240 ▤ 01865 343240
Dir: *Exit Oxford via Cowley, after 2m on the Stadhampton road R for
the Paldons*
Enjoying a pleasant rural location close to Oxford, this
welcoming, 300-year-old village pub is a popular destination
for some honest home cooking and summer barbeques.

WANTAGE
Map 04 SU38

The Hare ♀ NEW
Reading Rd, West Hendred ☎ 01235 833249
Dir: *Situated at West Hendred on A417 Between Wantage (3m W)
and didcot (5m E)*
Good quality home-cooked food is the hallmark of this
recently refurbished pub, close to the charming Vale of the
White Horse. The unusual 'Old Colonial' exterior conceals

traditional wooden floors, beams and an open fireplace. Your
meal might start with a pastry box of field and oyster
mushrooms, followed by Thai fishcakes or pot-roasted guinea
fowl. Round things off with warm chocolate brownies and
mascarpone.

OPEN: 11.30-2.30 5.30-11 (Fri-Sun 11.30-11). Closed 1 Jan.
RESTAURANT: L served all week. D served all week 12-2 7-9.
Av 3 course à la carte £20.50. Av 2 course fixed price £15.
BREWERY/COMPANY: Greene King.
PRINCIPAL BEERS: Greene King Abbot Ale, IPA, Morland
Original. **FACILITIES:** Garden: food served outside Dogs
allowed Water, during the day. **NOTES:** Parking 37

The Star Inn ◆◆◆◆
Watery Ln, Sparsholt OX12 9PL ☎ 01235 751539/751001
▤ 01235 751539
Dir: *Sparsholt is 4m west of Wantage, take the B4507 Wantage to
Ashbury road and turn off R to the village, the Star Inn is signposted*
Situated in horse racing downland country close to the
Ridgeway, this 300-year-old village local is popular with the
local racing fraternity. A sample menu features steak and ale
pie, lasagne, cod or haddock in beer batter, and the filling
bubble-and-squeak topped with bacon and two eggs.
OPEN: 12-3 6-11 (Sat 12-11, Sun 12-10.30). Closed Dec 25.
BAR MEALS: L served Tue-Sun. D served all week 12-2 7-9. Av
main course £7.50. **RESTAURANT:** L served Tue-Sun. D served
all week 12-2 7-9. Av 3 course à la carte £14.95.
BREWERY/COMPANY: Free House.
PRINCIPAL BEERS: Morland Original, Butts.
FACILITIES: Children welcome Garden: large garden, BBQ,
food served outside Dogs allowed. **NOTES:** Parking 20.
ROOMS: 8 bedrooms 8 en suite d£55

WATLINGTON

The Chequers
Love Ln, Watlington OX9 5RA
Attractive, rambling old pub festooned with flowers in
summer. Bustling, relaxed atmosphere in character interior -
low beams, antique oak tables; lovely vine-covered
conservatory. Home-cooked traditional pub food. Splendid
garden for alfresco eating.

WESTCOTT BARTON
Map 06 SP42

The Fox Inn
Enstone Rd OX7 7BN ☎ 01869 340338
e-mail: sarnett@ukonline.co.uk
Original flagstone floors, oak beams and a roaring fire in the
ancient inglenook are among the attractions at this welcoming
17th-century Cotswold village pub. New licensees have
maintained the popular pizza and pasta dishes on the 'Italian

continued

continued

Specials' menu and, in addition to cold platters, salads and traditional bar snacks, have introduced a new restaurant menu. Typical dishes here include medallions of venison and chargrilled steak with pepper and cognac sauce.
OPEN: 12-2.30 5-11 (Sun 12-2.30, 5-10.30). **BAR MEALS:** L served all week. D served all week 12-2 7-9. Av main course £5.50. **RESTAURANT:** L served all week. D served Mon-Sat 12-2 7-9. Av 3 course à la carte £18. **BREWERY/COMPANY:** Enterprise Inns. **PRINCIPAL BEERS:** Hook Norton Best, Theakston XB, Marstons Pedigree,. **FACILITIES:** Children welcome Garden: food served outisde Dogs allowed Water. **NOTES:** Parking 20

WESTON-ON-THE-GREEN
Map 06 SP51

The Chequers ♀
Northampton Rd OX6 8QH ☎ 01869 350319
🖹 01869 350024
e-mail: rchequers@aol.com
Dir: *2M from M40 J9*
17th-century coaching inn built of Cotswold stone. The bar offers a traditional menu (burgers, lasagne, scampi), while the restaurant is devoted to Thai food. The menu includes kwaitiew noodle dishes, pad (stir-fry), kaeng (Thai curry), khoa (rice dishes), and pla (fish and seafood).
OPEN: 11.30-3 6-11. **BAR MEALS:** L served all week. D served all week 12-2.30 7-10.30. Av main course £6.50. **RESTAURANT:** L served all week. D served all week 12-2.30 7-10.30. Av 3 course à la carte £14. Av 2 course fixed price £10. **BREWERY/COMPANY:** Fullers. **PRINCIPAL BEERS:** Fullers London Pride, Fullers ESB. **FACILITIES:** Children welcome Garden: outdoor eating, patio, Dogs allowed Water. **NOTES:** Parking 45

WHEATLEY
Map 06 SP50

Bat & Ball Inn ♦♦♦
28 High St OX44 9HJ ☎ 01865 874379 🖹 01865 873363
Dir: *Pass thru Wheatley towards Garsington, take only L turn, signed Cuddesdon*
In a picturesque village with views over the Chilterns and Berkshire Downs, this old coaching inn is renowned for its collection of cricketing memorabilia. Bedrooms.

WITNEY
Map 06 SP31

The Bell
Standlake Rd, Ducklington OX8 7UP ☎ 01993 702514
Thatched pub by the village. Bells from the beams dominate the decor. Flagstone-floored main bar, promising food, garden and bedrooms.

AA Bed & Breakfast
2002
Bed Breakfast Guide

Britain's best-selling B&B guide featuring over 3500 great places to stay

www.theAA.com

AA Lifestyle Guides

WOODSTOCK
Map 06 SP41

Pick of the Pubs

Kings Head Inn 🏵 ♦♦♦♦ 🕮 ♀
Chapel Hill, Wootton OX20 1DX ☎ 01993 811340
🖹 01993 813131
e-mail: t.fay@kings-head.co.uk
Dir: *On A44 2m N of Woodstock then R to Wootton. Inn near church on Chapel Hill*
Built of warm Cotswold stone, this 16th-century dining pub stands in the centre of sleepy Wootton village 2 miles north of Woodstock. In the beamed bars, a civilised blend of wooden tables, old settles and soft seating all help to create a relaxed, informal atmosphere. Seasonal variety comes with winter log fires, and in summer you can eat out in the peaceful garden. Well-equipped bedrooms are comfortably appointed with pine furniture, making this a good centre for touring Oxfordshire and the Cotswolds. In the non-smoking restaurant, the menu betrays a modern British inclination, with some Mediterranean and New World influences. At lunchtime, home-made soup, Scotch fillet steak, Cantonese braised duck, or cured Scottish salmon are typical dishes. The dinner menu might kick off with seared scallops on samphire, or parfait of foie gras, followed by warm duck salad, chargrilled pork medallions with basil and honey, marinated venison or slow-roasted spiced lamb shank.
OPEN: 11-11 (Closed Sun eve). Closed Dec 25. **BAR MEALS:** L served all week. D served Mon-Sat 12-2 7-9. Av main course £10.95. **RESTAURANT:** L served all week. D served Mon-Sat 12-2 7-9. Av 3 course à la carte £25. **BREWERY/COMPANY:** Free House. **PRINCIPAL BEERS:** Wadworth 6X. **FACILITIES:** Garden: outdoor eating **NOTES:** Parking 8. **ROOMS:** 3 bedrooms 3 en suite s£65 d£75 FR£80-£100

WOOLSTONE
Map 04 SU28

The White Horse ♀
SN7 7QL ☎ 01367 820726 🖹 01367 820566
e-mail: whorseuffington@aol.com

Attractive beamed and thatched 16th-century village inn, just five minutes' walk from the Uffington White Horse and Ancient Monument. Bar food includes salads, ploughman's lunches and freshly cooked cod and chips. In the restaurant expect calves' liver, rack of lamb, steaks, and baked swordfish.
OPEN: 11-3 6-11 (Sun 12-3 7-10.30). **BAR MEALS:** L served all week. D served all week 11-3 6-11. Av main course £5.95. **RESTAURANT:** L served all week. D served all week 12-3 7-10. Av 3 course à la carte £17. Av 3 course fixed price £16.95.

continued

BREWERY/COMPANY: Free House.
PRINCIPAL BEERS: Arkells, Fullers, Hook Norton, Wadworth.
FACILITIES: Children welcome Garden: outdoor eating, patio
Dogs allowed only in garden. **NOTES:** Parking 80.
ROOMS: 6 bedrooms 6 en suite s£50 d£65 FR££65-£75

WYTHAM   Map 06 SP40

White Hart
OX2 8QA ☎ 01865 244372
Dir: Just off A34 NW of Oxford
In the pretty, thatched village of Wytham (owned by Oxford
University), this attractive, creeper-covered pub has flagstone
floors and open fires. It has frequently been used in the
television series Inspector Morse.

RUTLAND

CLIPSHAM   Map 09 SK91

Pick of the Pubs

The Olive Branch 🍴 ♀ NEW
Main St LE15 7SH ☎ 01780 410355 📠 01780 410000
e-mail: olive@work.gb.com
Dir: 2m off A1 at Ram Jam junction, 10m N of Stamford
A traditional village pub, well worth a detour from
Stamford and the nearby A1, that was rescued from
closure by a unique alliance of villagers, friends and the
families of the three local lads, Ben, Marcus and Sean who
now run the place with style and enthusiasm.

An attractive front garden and terrace and an interior
brim-full of locally made furniture and artists' works - all
for sale - engender a community spirit that blends well
with a deserved reputation for fine food. Add open log
fires, mulled wine and chestnuts in winter; barbeques,
Morris dancing and garden skittles in summer and you
have something special.

Dishes using local produce dominate the daily lunch
and dinner menus: bouillabaisse fish soup with rouille and
honey roast confit duck leg (one or two) with smoked
bacon cassoulet alongside pan-fried salmon with spinach
and nutmeg, Lincolnshire sausages with onion gravy and
chargrilled beef fillet with rösti potato and red wine sauce;
followed by bread-and-butter pudding and Strawberry
Eton Mess.

Wholemeal Rearsby bread sandwiches, Stilton cheeses
from Cropwell Bishop and Colston Bassett; real ales from
Oakham's Grainstore brewery and a wide choice of wines
by the glass are further indicative of these new owners'
meticulous attention to detail.
OPEN: 12-3.30 6-11. (Sun 12-6 only, Sat all day June-Aug).
BAR MEALS: L served all week. D served Mon-Sat 12-2
7-9.30 Av main course £9.95. **RESTAURANT:** L served all
week. D served Mon-Sat 12-2 7-9.30. Av 3 course à la carte
£19.50. Av 3 course set lunch £10.50.
BREWERY/COMPANY: Free House.
PRINCIPAL BEERS: Grainstore 1050 & Olive Oil, Fenland,
Brewster's. **FACILITIES:** Children welcome. Garden: terrace,
outdoor eating. **NOTES:** Parking 15

COTTESMORE   Map 09 SK91

The Sun Inn 🍴
25 Main St LE15 7DH ☎ 01572 812321
A new owner has taken the helm of this whitewashed, 17th-
century thatched pub, situated within easy reach of Rutland
Water and historic Oakham. The contemporary decor remains
- rag-washed walls, flagged or wooden floors strewn with rugs,
old pine and sturdy oak tables - in the rambling and civilised
interior. Changed are menus, expect to find sausage and
mustard mash, fish and chips, shoulder of lamb, baked king
prawns in garlic and seafood platter on the blackboard.
Everards and Adnams ales.
OPEN: 11-2.30 6-11.30. **BAR MEALS:** L served all week. D
served Mon-Sat 12-2 7-9.30. Av main course £8.75.
RESTAURANT: L served all week. D served Mon-Sat 12-2 7-9.30.
Av 3 course à la carte £15. **BREWERY/COMPANY:** Everards
Brewery. **PRINCIPAL BEERS:** Adnams, Everards Tiger.
FACILITIES: Garden Dogs allowed. **NOTES:** Parking 15

EMPINGHAM   Map 06 SK90

White Horse Inn ★ ★ ♀
Main St LE15 8PS ☎ 01780 460221 📠 01780 460521
e-mail: info@the-white-horse.co.uk
Dir: From A1 take A606 signed Oakham & Rutland Water
This stone built inn, a former 17th-century farmhouse, is set in
a lovely village on the edge of Rutland Water. Rutland Water
trout is a feature, along with other fish dishes; or Lincolnshire
sausage and mash, home baked ham, or spinach and ricotta
ravioli. Some bedrooms are housed in a converted stable
block across the courtyard.
OPEN: 8-11. **BAR MEALS:** L served all week. D served all week
12-2.15 7.15-9.45. Av main course £7.95. **RESTAURANT:** L served
all week. D served all week 12-2.15 7.15-10. Av 3 course à la carte
£18. **PRINCIPAL BEERS:** Ruddles, Courage Directors, Greene
King Old Speckled Hen. **FACILITIES:** Children welcome
Children's licence Garden: outdoor eating, patio.
NOTES: Parking 60. **ROOMS:** 13 bedrooms 13 en suite s£50
d£63

EXTON

Fox & Hounds
LE15 8AP ☎ 01572 812403
Fine old coaching inn close to Rutland Water and Viking Way.
Pretty lawns. Bedrooms.

The Grainstore
Located in a derelict Victorian grainstore
next to Oakham railway station, Davis'es
Brewing Company was formed in 1995 by Tony
Davis and Mike Davies. Tony had worked at
Ruddles and Mike had been in construction so
between them they built a traditional tower
brewhouse and went into business. Brews
include Cooking (3.6%),
Triple B (4.2%) and
Ten Fifty (5.0%).

LYDDINGTON   Map 06 SP89

Pick of the Pubs

Old White Hart 🐾 ♀
5 Main St LE15 9LR ☎ 01572 821703 🗎 01572 821965
e-mail: theoldwhitehart@supernet.com
Honey-coloured 17th-century stone pub standing by the
green in an attractive village high above the Welland
Valley, close to good walks and Rutland Water. Interesting,
freshly prepared food is served in the cosy main bar, with
its heavy beams, dried flower arrangements, traditional
furnishings and splendid log fire, and in the adjoining
dining areas.
   Good blackboard specials may include warm
salad of smoked bacon, black pudding and cherry
tomatoes topped with grilled Slipcote cheese and balsamic
dressing and grilled sardines with garlic toast for starters,
followed by deep-fried Grimsby haddock, whole Dover
sole, herb-crusted cod with pesto dressing, wild
mushroom and asparagus risotto, home-made Gloucester
Old Spot sausages, and confit neck of lamb on mash.
Ambitious evening carte. Good selection of real ales and
wines by the glass. Flower-filled rear garden with 10
pétanque pitches.
OPEN: 12-3 6.30-11. Closed 25 Dec. **BAR MEALS:** L served
all week. D served all week 12-2 6.30-9. Av main course £10.
RESTAURANT: L served all week. D served all week 12-2
6.30-9. Av 3 course à la carte £17. Av 3 course fixed price
£12.95. **BREWERY/COMPANY:** Free House.
PRINCIPAL BEERS: Greene King IPA & Abbot Ale, Timothy
Taylor Landlord, Black Sheep. **FACILITIES:** Children
welcome Garden: patio, outside eating. **NOTES:** Parking
25. **ROOMS:** 5 bedrooms 5 en suite s£45 d£65 FR£95

MARKET OVERTON   Map 08 SK81

Black Bull 🐾
2 Teigh Rd LE15 7PW ☎ 01572 767677 🗎 01572 767291
Thatched and beamed 15th-century building enjoying a pretty
village setting close to Rutland Water. The focus is on fresh fish
dishes such as Spanish-style black bream, zander fillet, and
seafood casserole, with options of Rutland chicken, sirloin
steak with peppercorn sauce, and lamb and Stilton pie.
OPEN: 11.30-2.30 6-11 (Sun 12-2.30, 7-10.30). **BAR MEALS:** L
served all week. D served all week 12-1.45 6.30-9.45. Av main
course £6.95. **RESTAURANT:** L served all week. D served all
week 12-1.45 6.30-9.45. **BREWERY/COMPANY:** Free House.
PRINCIPAL BEERS: Marstons Pedigree, Hook Norton, Theakston
Black Bull, Ruddles Best. **ROOMS:** 2 bedrooms 2 en suite s£30
d£45

OAKHAM   Map 06 SK80

Barnsdale Lodge Hotel ◉ ★ ★ ★
The Avenue, Rutland Water, North Shore LE15 8AH
☎ 01572 724678 🗎 01572 724961
e-mail: barnsdale.lodge@btconnect.com
Originally a 17th-century farmhouse, this distinctive Edwardian
style hotel overlooks Rutland Water in the heart of picturesque
Rutland. The bar offers real ales, including local brews.
Individually decorated bedrooms are furnished in country
house style.

The Blue Ball
6 Cedar St, Braunston LE15 8QS
☎ 01572 722135 🗎 01572 724169
Dir: From A1 take A606 to Oakham.Village SW of Oakham
Thatched and beamed village inn, formerly called The Globe,
dating from the 1600s, and reputedly Rutland's oldest pub.
The new Italian landlord is planning big things for the pub's
food and personality.

Pick of the Pubs

The Finch's Arms 🐾 ♀
Oakham Rd, Hambleton LE15 8TL ☎ 01572 756575
🗎 01572 771142
Experienced publicans Colin & Celia Crawford have
tastefully refurbished this stone-built 17th-century inn, set
in a sleepy village on a narrow strip of land jutting into
Rutland Water, and offer interesting Mediterranean-style
food in a relaxed atmosphere, and six individually
furnished en suite bedrooms. From the stylish restaurant,
with its cane furnishings and open fires, and the neat
summer terrace, diners can enjoy stunning views across
Rutland Water while tucking into such dishes as confit
pork chump on Puy lentils, Savoy cabbage and fondant
potato, bouillabaisse, pan-seared gurnard with basil broth,
and smoked salmon lasagne. Starter dishes include
chicken liver parfait with red onion marmalade, crab
soufflé and warm Stilton brûlée with wild mushroom
compôte. The comfortable bar area has warm yellow rag-
washed walls, stripped pine, wooded floors and open
fires. Here you will find cask ales, decent wines and decent
coffee from the Gaggia machine.
OPEN: 10.30-3 6-11.30. **BAR MEALS:** L served all week.
D served all week 12-2.30 7-9.30. Av main course £8.95.
RESTAURANT: L served all week. D served all week 12-2.30
7-9.30. Av 3 course à la carte £18. **BREWERY/COMPANY:** Free House.
PRINCIPAL BEERS: Greene King Abbot Ale, Marstons
Pedigree, Theakstons. **FACILITIES:** Children welcome
Garden: Food served outside. **NOTES:** Parking 40.
ROOMS: 6 bedrooms 6 en suite s£55 d£70

The Grainstore Brewery NEW
Station Approach LE15 6RE ☎ 01572 770065
🗎 01572 770068
Founded in 1995, Davis's Brewing Company is housed in the
three-storey Victorian grain store next to Oakham railway
station. Finest quality ingredients and hops are used to make
the beers that can be sampled in the pub's Tap Room. Filled
baguettes and Stilton and pork pie ploughman's are of
secondary importance. Go for the brewery tours and blind
tastings; rustic wooden floors and furniture that attract walkers
by the score.
OPEN: 11-3 5-11 (Fri-Sun all day). **BAR MEALS:** L served all
week 11-3. **BREWERY/COMPANY:** Free House.
PRINCIPAL BEERS: Grainstore Cooking, TripleB, Ten Fifty,
Steaming Billy Bitter. **FACILITIES:** Dogs allowed Water, biscuit.
NOTES: Parking 8 No credit cards

The Old Plough
2 Church St, Braunston LE15 8QY ☎ 01572 722714
🗎 01572 770382
Dir: SW of Oakham
Tastefully modernised village inn, handy for exploring the old
county of Rutland and visiting the lovely Georgian town of
continued

England

Oakham. With light lunches on the terrace and candle-lit dining in the picturesque conservatory a sense of occasion is easily engendered. Newish enthusiastic owners, so expect interesting pub food and some refurbishment to this genteel and very popular country pub.
OPEN: 11-3 6-11 (Sat 11-11, Sun 12-10.30). **BAR MEALS:** L served all week 12-2. Av main course £7. **RESTAURANT:** L served all week. D served all week 12-2 7-10. Av 3 course à la carte £15. **BREWERY/COMPANY:** Free House.
PRINCIPAL BEERS: Grainstore Triple B, Greene King Old Speckled Hen. **FACILITIES:** Children welcome Garden: patio, outdoor eating. **NOTES:** Parking 30. **ROOMS:** 1 bedrooms 1 en suite s£65 d£55 FR£85

STRETTON   Map 09 SK91

Pick of the Pubs

Ram Jam Inn 🌐 ★ ★
The Great North Rd LE15 7QX ☎ 01780 410776
📠 01780 410361
e-mail: rji@rutnet.co.uk
Dir: On A1 northbound carriageway past B1668 turn off, through service station into hotel car park
Sitting beside a lonely stretch of the A1, this delightful roadside inn was originally known as the Winchilsea Arms. Then, sometime during the 18th century, publican Charles Blake put a sign above the front door advertising 'Fine Ram Jam'. Was this the name of Blake's own home-brew? Possibly - but the name has certainly stuck.
Today, an informal but stylish café-bar and bistro welcomes travellers on the long haul to the North, and spacious bedrooms with cheerful soft furnishings and modern en suite bathrooms make this a tempting overnight stop. The imaginative menu offers everything from hot and cold sandwiches to clotted cream teas and three-course meals.
Popular dishes include crispy chicken samosas, Mediterranean pannini, or steamed salmon with ratatouille and new potatoes. For something more substantial, choose Rutland sausage and mash, braised leg of lamb, or Stilton and sage dumplings with roasted celery. All this, plus desserts, hot drinks, cakes, pastries, and a children's menu, too.
OPEN: 7am-11pm. Closed 25 Dec. **BAR MEALS:** L served all week. D served all week 12-9.30. Av main course £6.95. **RESTAURANT:** L served all week. D served all week 12-9.30. Av 3 course à la carte £16.50. **BREWERY/COMPANY:** Free House. **PRINCIPAL BEERS:** Fullers London Pride, John Smiths. **FACILITIES:** Children welcome Garden: patio, outdoor eating, Dogs allowed garden only.
NOTES: Parking 64. **ROOMS:** 7 bedrooms 7 en suite s£46 d£56

All AA listed accommodation can also be found on the AA's internet site **www.theAA.com**

UPPINGHAM   Map 06 SP89

Exeter Arms 🍺
Barrowden LE15 8EQ ☎ 01572 747247
e-mail: info@exeterarms.co.uk
17th-century pub overlooking the Welland valley and the village duck pond in England's smallest county, just 20 miles across. Ideally placed for walking in the Rockingham Forest. Daily changing blackboard menu offers the likes of game pie, lambs liver with onions and tuna steak in citrus sauce, while the bar serves a range of its own Boys beers.
OPEN: 12-2 6-11 (Sun 7-10.30). **BAR MEALS:** L served all week. D served all week 12-2 7-9. Av main course £8. **RESTAURANT:** L served all week. D served all week 12-2 7-9. Av 3 course à la carte £13. **PRINCIPAL BEERS:** Own Beers. **FACILITIES:** Garden: Food served outside Dogs allowed Water. **NOTES:** Parking 15. **ROOMS:** 3 bedrooms 3 en suite

WHITWELL   Map 06 SK90

Noel Arms Inn 🛏️
Main St LE15 8BW ☎ 01780 460334   📠 01780 460531
Dir: From A1 take A606 to Oakham
Country pub near Rutland Water with a cosy lounge in the original thatched building and a more modern bar. Dishes range from bangers and mash at lunchtime, to roast monkfish with saute potatoes, spinach and braised leek, and rack of English lamb with Mediterranean vegetables and rosemary and lentil jus.
OPEN: 11-11 (Breakfast 7.30-9.30). **BAR MEALS:** L served all week. D served all week 12-3 7-9.30. Av main course £7.50. **RESTAURANT:** L served all week. D served all week 12-3 7-9.30. Av 3 course à la carte £18. **BREWERY/COMPANY:** Free House. **PRINCIPAL BEERS:** Marstons Pedigree, Adnams Broadside, Flowers Original. **FACILITIES:** Children welcome Garden: BBQ Dogs allowed. **NOTES:** Parking 60. **ROOMS:** 8 bedrooms 8 en suite s£40 d£65

WING   Map 06 SK80

The Cuckoo Inn
3 Top St LE15 8SE ☎ 01572 737340
Dir: A6003 from Oakham, turn R then L
Four miles from Rutland Water, a part-thatched 17th-century coaching inn noted for unusual guest ales from micro-breweries: the pub has a rose garden and barbeque. Home-cooked food is notably good value: steak and kidney pie; lamb casserole - supplemented ey some authentic Indian dishes such as chicken Madras and lamb rogan josh.
OPEN: 11.30-3 (Sun 12-4, 7-10.30) 6.30-11 (closed Tue lunch). **BAR MEALS:** L served Wed-Mon. D served Wed-Mon 11.30-2.30 7-10. Av main course £6. **BREWERY/COMPANY:** Free House. **PRINCIPAL BEERS:** Marston's Pedigree. **FACILITIES:** Children welcome Garden: BBQ, outdoor eating, floral display Dogs allowed. **NOTES:** Parking 20 No credit cards

Pick of the Pubs

Kings Arms ◆◆◆◆ 🛏️ 🍺
Top St LE15 8SE ☎ 01572 737634   📠 01572 737255
e-mail: enquiries@thekingsarms.co.uk
See Pick of the Pubs on page 365

OPEN: 12-3 6-11 (Fri-Sun 12-12).
BAR MEALS: L served all week.
D served all week 12-2 6.30-9.30.
Av main course £7.50
RESTAURANT: L served all week.
D served all week 12-2 6.30-9.30.
Av 3 course a la carte £15.
BREWERY/COMPANY:
Free House.
PRINCIPAL BEERS: Grainstore
Cooking, two guest beers.
FACILITIES: Children welcome.
Garden: patio outdoor eating.
NOTES: Parking 25.
ROOMS: 8 bedrooms 8 en suite
s£40-£70 d£55-£100 FR£70-£100.

The Kings Arms

◆◆◆ 🐑 ♀

Top Street LE15 8SE
☎ 01572 737634 🖻 01572 737255
e-mail: enquiries@thekingsarms.co.uk
Dir: 1m off A6003 between Oakham
and Uppingham

Built in 1642 from traditional slate and stone, this comfortable old inn stands in a quaint village famous for its maze, just two miles from Rutland Water, benefiting also from the hands-on input of its family owners. Comfortable accommodation and good food make this a fine base for exploring tiny Rutland.

Flagstone floors, low beams, nooks, crannies and warming- winter log fires add to its particular character, while the cottage-style, well-equipped bedrooms, divided between the Old Bakehouse and 'Granny's Cottage', are spacious and relaxing.

Careful purchasing makes optimum use of fresh fish, meat and vegetables, in large part obtained from local suppliers. On the daily specials board, expect to find chicken breasts wrapped in bacon with a local Stilton cheese sauce, sea bass on wild rocket with citrus dressing and monkfish medallions wrapped in Parma ham set on a bed of tomato and garlic sauce. Equally ambitious daily alternatives are likely to include carrot and coriander soup, wild mushroom and Brie tatin with balsamic dressing, honey-glazed duck with caramelised black cherries and pear parfait with calvados and hazelnut praline.

None of this excludes those who would prefer a snack in the bar, where comprehensive choices include filled crusty baguettes served with salad, fresh seasonal soup with crusty bread, old-fashioned steak and kidney pie, chef Neil's fish stew slowly cooked in wine, herbs and tomato, beer-battered haddock with chunky chips, and honey-baked local ham with fried egg and chips.

Great pride is taken in providing the best available ales from local micro-breweries, including nearby Oakham Grainstore Bitter, while the wine selection from an independent supplier in nearby Oundle, though limited, is carefully selected.

SHROPSHIRE

ALBRIGHTON
Map 08 SJ41

The Horns of Boningale NEW
☎ 01902 372347   📠 01902 372970
e-mail: horns@boningale.freeserve.co.uk
Dir: *From Wolverton, follow the A41 to Oken, turn L at traffic lights onto the Holyhead Road towards Shifnal , the Horns is on the L 2miles from Oaken*
This 300 year-old free house was formerly popular as a 'ham and eggery' with Shropshire cattlemen, and the dish is still available. Now completely refurbished as a civilised dining pub, the main bar is divided into three cosy rooms. There's also a large formal restaurant, leading out to landscaped gardens and an ornamental fishpond. Expect, steak and ale pie, Thai curry, savoury bean tartlet, and halibut mornay.
OPEN: 12-3 6-12. **BAR MEALS:** L served all week. D served all week 12-2 6-9.30. Av main course £8. **RESTAURANT:** L served all week. D served all week 12-2 6-9.30. Av 3 course à la carte £15. Av 3 course fixed price £16.25. **PRINCIPAL BEERS:** Hook Norton Old Hooky, Badger Tanglefoot. **FACILITIES:** Children welcome Garden: Food served outside. **NOTES:** Parking 50

BISHOP'S CASTLE
Map 08 SO38

Boars Head ◆◆◆
Church St SY9 5AE ☎ 01588 638521   📠 01588 630126
e-mail: sales@boarsheadhotel.co.uk
Set in largely unspoilt countryside, this 16th-century coaching inn was once in the centre of one of England's most Rotten Boroughs, and was granted its first full license in 1642. The beamed bar is a focus for village life, as well as serving up salmon hollandaise, chicken in cream and sherry sauce, and trout with almonds. Rooms are in a converted stable block now known as 'the Curly Tail'. All have their own entrance and STV.
BAR MEALS: L served all week. D served all week 12-2 6.30-9.30. Av main course £6. **RESTAURANT:** L served all week. D served all week 12-2 6.30-9.30. Av 3 course à la carte £15. **BREWERY/COMPANY:** Free House. **PRINCIPAL BEERS:** Courage Best, Courage Directors, Theakstons Best. **FACILITIES:** Children welcome Children's licence Dogs allowed Bedrooms only. **NOTES:** Parking 20. **ROOMS:** 4 bedrooms 4 en suite s£35 d£60 FR£65-£75

The Castle Hotel
The Square SY9 5BN ☎ 01588 638403   📠 01588 638403
Built on the site of the old castle keep, this 18th-century coaching inn retains its character and includes open fires, a fine example of a Georgian staircase and a garden with lovely views over the town and valley beyond. Strong emphasis on freshly prepared food, a good selection of sweets and a wide choice of malt whiskies.
OPEN: 12-2.30 6.30-11. **BAR MEALS:** L served all week. D served all week 12-1.30 6.30-9. Av main course £7.95. **BREWERY/COMPANY:** Free House. **PRINCIPAL BEERS:** Hobson's, Bass, Black Sheep. **FACILITIES:** Garden: patio. **NOTES:** Parking 30. **ROOMS:** 5 bedrooms 5 en suite s£35 d£60

◆ AA inspected guest accommodation

Micro-Breweries of Shropshire
Shropshire real ale pedigree is impeccable, leading the way in real ale since the 1970s. Salopian Brewery is on the site of an old diary in Shrewsbury; Hanby Ales continues a two century tradition of brewing in Wem; The Wood Brewery was established in Wistanstow in 1980; Corvedale Brewery is the newest addition, built from scratch in Corfton; Munslow Brewhouse is set in a Munslow Tudor coaching inn, and can be seen from the bar; Six Bells Brewery is in a Bishop's Castle pub that has been licensed since 1750; also in Bishop's Castle, Three Tuns Brewery is in an original four storey brew tower; and Hobsons Brewery is in a farmyard in Cleobury

The Three Tuns Inn ♀
Salop St SY9 5BW ☎ 01588 638797   📠 01588 638081
e-mail: info@thethreetunsinn.co.uk
Late 16th-century timbered-framed pub in the centre of the village serving tip-top ales brewed across the courtyard, and home-cooked food prepared from fresh local produce. Expect rich fish soup, beef in Three Tuns ale, seafood pancakes, goats' cheese with red onion marmalade, game pie and decent sandwiches. Added attractions include a small brewing museum and en suite bedrooms in the converted stables.
OPEN: 12-11 (Sun 12-10.30). **BAR MEALS:** L served all week. D served all week 12-2.30 7-9.30. **BREWERY/COMPANY:** Free House. **PRINCIPAL BEERS:** Three Tuns Sexton, Tuns Offa's Ale, & Tuns XXX. **FACILITIES:** Children welcome Garden: patio, outdoor eating Dogs allowed. **NOTES:** Parking 6. **ROOMS:** 4 bedrooms 4 en suite s£45 d£75

BRIDGNORTH
Map 08 SO79

The Bear ♀
Northgate WV16 4ET ☎ 01746 763250
Dir: *From High Street (Bridgnorth) go through Northgate (sandstone archway) and the pub is on the L*
Traditional Grade II listed hostelry in one of the loveliest of the Severn-side towns. The way it clings to the top of a high sandstone cliff gives it an almost continental flavour. A former coaching inn, the award-winning Bear boasts two carpeted bars which are characterised by whisky-water jugs, gas-type wall lamps and wheelback chairs. Good quality, appetising menu offers the likes of ham, egg and chips, braised lamb shank, wild mushroom and spinach risotto, and salmon and herb fishcakes. Daily-changing real ales and a choice of seven malts.
OPEN: 11-3 5-11 (Sun 7-10.30). **BAR MEALS:** L served all week 12-2. Av main course £5. **BREWERY/COMPANY:** Free House. **PRINCIPAL BEERS:** Changing guest ales. **FACILITIES:** Garden: Food served outside. **NOTES:** Parking 18. **ROOMS:** 3 bedrooms 3 en suite s£25 d£45 No credit cards

The Lion O'Morfe
Upper Farmcote WV15 5PS ☎ 01746 710678
Dir: *Off A458(Bridgnorth/Stourbridge) 2.5m from Bridgnorth follow signs for Claverley on L,0.5m up hill on L*
Friendly pub dating from the early 1850s when the owner paid two guineas to Excise for change of use from a Georgian farmhouse to an inn. The name 'Morfe' is derived from the Welsh for 'marsh'. Standard bar food.

Bottle & Glass Inn, Picklescott

BOTTLE & GLASS INN, PICKLESCOTT

SY6 6NR. Tel: 01694 751345
Directions: off A49 at Dorrington between Shrewsbury & Church Stretton *Unspoilt 17th-century stone-built inn tucked away in a peaceful spot below the Long Mynd. Character beamed bars with open log fires and welcoming atmosphere. Tip-top Woods ales, good value food, including home-made pies. Bedrooms.*
Open: 12-2 7-11. Bar Meals: 12-2 7-9 (no food Mon lunch). Children and dogs welcome. Garden/patio. Parking.
(see page 374 for full entry)

A **peaceful walk through rolling Shropshire farming countryside**

At the crossroads outside the pub, turn left and pass Top House before turning right, signed to the church. Take the bridleway right, through a gate, and follow arrows across the field to a further gate. Keep ahead, cross a stream and pass through a waymarked gate onto a track. At a fork, bear left uphill, then beyond a gate, turn right along the road to a left-hand bend. Go through the gate on the right, bear left, then after 100 yards (91m), at a pair of gates, turn right along the hedge to a gate into a field. Continue to a further gate on the right, then head downhill to a bridge over a stream to Old Mill Farm.

Follow the track, turn right to Yew Tree Farm, then at a left-hand bend turn right through a gate. Immediately cross the double stile on your left. Keep the hedge on your left, cross a field to a gate and track and continue through two more gates onto a hard track. Turn left, then right at the road, then right again at the T-junction.

Take the next road left and descend, then climb to take the waymarked footpath right. Cross the field to a stile, then bear left downhill to a bridge over a stream. Cross two stiles, then keep right-handed alongside a fence to pass a white farmhouse (left). Cross two stiles, a stream and another stile, then bear diagonally up a field to a gate. Beyond this and another gate on the left, head diagonally across the field to a gate and road. Turn left, pass Woolstaston church, then turn right along the track just before Pine Cottage. Cross a field, climb a stile, then bear left downhill to a gate.

Turn right down to another gate, cross a stream and ascend to a gate between two oak trees, Turn left, follow the hedge to a gate onto a track and turn left. Pass through a gate onto a metalled track and turn left. At the road, turn right for the pub.

Distance: 5 1/2 miles (8.8km)
Map: OS Landranger 137
Paths: field paths and tracks; some road walking
Terrain: farmland and country lanes
Gradient: undulating; a few fairly steep ascents

Walk submitted by: The Bottle & Glass

England

BURLTON

Pick of the Pubs

The Burlton Inn
SY4 5TB ☎ 01939 270284 ▤ 01939 270204
e-mail: beam@burltoninn.co.uk
Dir: 8M N of Shrewsbury on A528 towards Ellesmere

Six adjacent en-suite bedrooms have been recently added by enterprising owners to this classy 18th-century inn close to the old London to Holyhead coaching route. A quiet pint is promised in neat, well furnished cottagey rooms, free of music and amusement machines, where the best available market produce is listed on daily specials boards. Look for potted Solway shrimps, fresh sea bream with tomato and chilli sauce and pan-seared pears and Parma ham with a balsamic drizzle, as well as vegetarian options. Hot open ciabattas might consist of minute steak with fried red onion and sliced chicken breast with curried mayonnaise. Fresh baguettes then add roast ham with home-made chutney, tuna and spring onion and soft Brie with grapes. More substantial offerings might be venison casserole with port and juniper berries or sesame beef stir-fry with peppers, water-chestnuts and ginger: 10-ounce steaks from the local butcher round off the many options.
OPEN: 11-3 6-11 (Sun 12-3 7-10.30). Closed Dec 25-26 Jan 1. **BAR MEALS:** L served all week. D served all week 12-2 6.30-9.45. Av main course £8. **RESTAURANT:** L served all week. D served all week 12-2 6.30-9.45.
BREWERY/COMPANY: Free House.
PRINCIPAL BEERS: Banks. **FACILITIES:** Children welcome Garden: patio/terrace, outdoor eating, Dogs allowed By arrangement. **NOTES:** Parking 40. **ROOMS:** 6 bedrooms 6 en suite s£45 d£70

CHURCH STRETTON   Map 08 SO49

The Royal Oak
Cardington SY6 7JZ ☎ 01694 771266
Reputedly the oldest pub in Shropshire, dating from 1462, this Grade II listed building retains the atmosphere and character of a traditional hostelry, nestling into the hillside just below the church in this off-the-beaten track village. The low beams, massive walls and big inglenook fireplace make it the perfect setting on bleak winter days. Garden and patio for peaceful summer sipping. Wide range of traditional pub food, although the choice of food may change under the new owners. Reports welcome.
OPEN: 12-3 7-11 (Sun 12-3, 7-10.30). **BAR MEALS:** L served Tue-Sun. D served Tue-Sat 12-2 7.30-8.30. Av main course £4.75.
BREWERY/COMPANY: Free House.   *continued*

PRINCIPAL BEERS: Hobsons Best Bitter, Woods Shropshire Lad, Bass, Marstons Pedigree. **FACILITIES:** Children welcome Children's licence Garden: Patio, outdoor eating Dogs allowed. **NOTES:** Parking 30

CLEOBURY MORTIMER   Map 08 SO67

Pick of the Pubs

The Crown at Hopton ◉ ◆◆◆◆
Hopton Wafers DY14 0NB ☎ 01299 270372
▤ 01299 271127
Dir: On A4117 8m west of Ludlow, 2m east of Cleobury Mortimer
Located in a sleepy hollow, this former coaching inn is surrounded by immaculate gardens and has its own duck pond. The 16th-century free house was once owned by a nearby estate, and the informal Rent Room bar recalls the days when rents were collected here from the local tenants.

The inn, which has been lovingly restored to a high standard, boasts two inglenook fireplaces, exposed timbers and an elegant dining room. Bedrooms are individually furnished to maximum guest comfort and, in addition to occasional period furniture, all offer en suite facilities. Altogether a perfect base for exploring this magnificent area. The chef, Barry Price, creates imaginative dishes using fresh seasonal ingredients. Roast avocado with garlic and bacon, or grilled feta cheese with prosciutto might precede beef Wellington, loin of lamb, chicken en croute, or roast monkfish wrapped in bacon. Leave room for the pastry chef's home-made desserts.
OPEN: 12-3 6-11. **BAR MEALS:** L served all week. D served all week 12-2.30 6-9.30. Av main course £9.95.
RESTAURANT: L served Sun. D served Tue-Sat 12-3 7-9.30. Av 3 course à la carte £21.95. **BREWERY/COMPANY:** Free House. **PRINCIPAL BEERS:** Marstons Pedigree, Timothy Taylor Landlord. **FACILITIES:** Garden: patio area, Food served outside. **NOTES:** Parking 40. **ROOMS:** 7 bedrooms 7 en suite s£44 d£70

The Kings Arms Hotel
DY14 8BS ☎ 01299 270252
Dir: take A456 from Kidderminster the A4117 to Cleobury Mortimer
Beams, oak floors and a fine inglenook fireplace characterise this 15th-century coaching inn which nestles in the heart of this picturesque village. Bar snacks are served all day by friendly staff. Popular choices include devilled whitebait, pigeon breast, game mixed grill, wild boar and swordfish.
OPEN: 11.30-11 (Sun 12-10.30). **BAR MEALS:** L served all week. D served all week 11.30-9.30. Av main course £6.95.
RESTAURANT: L served all week. D served all week 12-2 7-9.30. Av 3 course à la carte £11.95. **PRINCIPAL BEERS:** Hobsons Best, Youngs Special, Greene King Abbot Ale.
FACILITIES: Children welcome. **NOTES:** Parking 4.
ROOMS: 4 bedrooms 4 en suite s£25 d£40

COALPORT   Map 08 SJ60

The Woodbridge Inn & Restaurant
TF2 9NB ☎ 01952 882054
Dir: Off A442 S of Telford
A 16th-century coaching inn overlooking the Severn Gorge by Coalport Bridge. The garden offers riverside seating and a weekend barbecue, weather permitting.

CRAVEN ARMS   Map 08 SO48

The Plough ⟐
Wistanstow SY7 8DG ☎ 01588 673251 📠 01588 672419
e-mail: plough@bartender.net
Home of the Woods Brewery and serving their full range of
beers, this country pub is well worth the short diversion off the
A49. Sample a pint of Woods Special, Shropshire Lad or Parish
in the homely bar with its simple furnishings and roaring log
fires, and tuck into a traditional English bar meal from the
monthly-changing menu. Choices include home-made soups
and terrines, cider-baked ham with parsley sauce, beery beef
stew, liver and bacon casserole and country venison pie. Tours
of the brewery by arrangement.
OPEN: 11.30-2.30 6.30-11. **BAR MEALS:** L served all week. D
served all week 12-2 6.30-9. Av main course £6.95.
PRINCIPAL BEERS: Woods Parish Special, Shropshire Lad..
NOTES: Parking 50

The Sun Inn
Corfton SY7 9DF ☎ 01584 861239 & 861503
e-mail: thesun@corfton.co.uk
Dir: on the B4368 7m N of Ludlow
Dating back to 1613, the Sun has a large busy bar as well as an
extensive patio area. The pub has its own brewery and plays
host to regular beer festivals during Easter and August Bank
Holidays. It was also once the home of the infamous Molly
Morgan, who was transported to Australia in the 1760s. Menu
may include leek and Stilton bake, chicken tikka, lamb
Shrewsbury, or smoked haddock with prawns and pasta. The
Sun is especially welcoming to disabled customers.
OPEN: 11-2.30 6-11. **BAR MEALS:** L served all week. D served
all week 12-2 7-9. Av main course £6.50. **RESTAURANT:** L
served all week. D served all week 12-2 7-9. Av 3 course à la carte
£10. **BREWERY/COMPANY:** Free House.
PRINCIPAL BEERS: Corvedale Normans Pride & Secret Hop.
FACILITIES: Children welcome Children's licence Garden:
outdoor eating, patio Dogs allowed. **NOTES:** Parking 30

CRESSAGE   Map 08 SJ50

Pick of the Pubs

The Cholmondeley Riverside Inn ◆◆◆◆ ⟐
SY5 6AF ☎ 01952 510900 📠 01952 510980
Dir: On A458 Shrewsbury-Bridgnorth rd
In three acres of garden alongside the River Severn, this
extensively refurbished coaching inn offers river view
dining both outdoors and in a modern conservatory. The
single menu serves both dining areas and spacious bar,
furnished and decorated in haphazard country style.
Traditional pub dishes include hot crab pâté and
mushrooms with Shropshire blue cheese, followed by
local lamb noisettes with parsnip chips, and salmon
fishcakes with hollandaise. Exotic alternatives follow the
lines of Peking duck pancakes with hoisin sauce, "Pee-kai"
chicken breasts with satay sauce, and spinach, sorrel and
mozzarella parcels.
OPEN: 11-3 7-11. Closed 25 Dec. **BAR MEALS:** L served all
week. D served all week 12-2.30 7-10. Av main course £7.50.
RESTAURANT: L served all week. D served all week 12-2.30
7-10. **BREWERY/COMPANY:** Free House.
PRINCIPAL BEERS: Marstons Pedigree, Banks.
FACILITIES: Children welcome Garden: patio, outdoor
eating Dogs allowed. **NOTES:** Parking 100.
ROOMS: 7 bedrooms 7 en suite s£50 d£65

HODNET   Map 08 SJ62

The Bear Hotel ★ ★ 🛏
TF9 3NH ☎ 01630 685214 📠 01630 685787
Dir: Junction A53 & A442 on sharp corner in middle of small village
An illuminated cellar garden, once a priest hole, is one of the
more unusual attractions at this 16th-century coaching inn.
Hodnet Hall Gardens are close by. Extensive menu includes bar
snacks and restaurant meals. Fidget pie, chicken goujons and
traditional fish and chips are among the blackboard dishes.
OPEN: 10.30-11 (Sun 12-10.30). **BAR MEALS:** L served all week.
D served all week 12-2 6.30-9.30. Av main course £6.
RESTAURANT: L served all week. D served all week 12-2 7-9.30.
Av 3 course à la carte £16. **BREWERY/COMPANY:** Free House.
PRINCIPAL BEERS: Theakston, John Smiths, Courage Directors.
FACILITIES: Children welcome Garden: outdoor eating.
NOTES: Parking 70. **ROOMS:** 8 bedrooms 8 en suite d£60
FR£70-£100

IRONBRIDGE   Map 08 SJ68

Pick of the Pubs

The Malthouse 🛏 ⟐
The Wharfage TF8 7NH ☎ 01952 433712
📠 01952 433298
e-mail: enquiries@malthousepubs.co.uk
Stylishly refurbished 18th-century ale house at the heart of
this world-famous village renowned for its spectacular
natural beauty and award-winning museums. Located on
the banks of the River Severn it is an obvious refreshment
stop for those tackling the Severn Way, Britain's longest
riverside walk. Traditional colours and textures, low-
beamed ceilings and an assortment of alcoves add to the
charm of the pub. Enjoy live jazz and food in the
Malthouse Bar, savouring its buzzy atmosphere, or dine in
the more sophisticated restaurant where well-presented
dishes might include lamb chump with leek and mustard
crumble on port and caper sauce, whole Brixham plaice
with fried garlic samphire, and lemon and saffron risotto
with fresh mint, pine nuts and Parmesan cheese. The
Malthouse also has six en suite bedrooms and an annexe
of three rooms, two of which are en suite.
OPEN: 11-11 (Sun 12-3 6-10.30). Closed 25-26 Dec.
BAR MEALS: L served all week. D served all week 12-2.30
6-9.30. Av main course £6.50. **RESTAURANT:** L served all
week. D served all week 12-2 6.30-9.45. Av 3 course à la carte
£17. **BREWERY/COMPANY:** Greenalls.
PRINCIPAL BEERS: Flowers Original, Boddingtons, Tetley.
FACILITIES: Children welcome Garden: Patio, food served
outside. **NOTES:** Parking 15. **ROOMS:** 6 bedrooms
6 en suite d£49

 Pubs offering a good choice of
seafood on the menu.

LLANFAIR WATERDINE
Map 08 SO27

Pick of the Pubs

The Waterdine ◉ ◉ NEW
LD7 1TU ☎ 01547 528214 ▤ 01547 529992
Dir: 4m NW of Knighton, just off the Newtown road
An original 16th-century Welsh longhouse and former drovers' inn set in the beautiful upper Teme valley, close to the Offa's Dyke Path, the inn stands in lovely mature gardens overlooking the river below. Bedrooms are individually designed, decorated and furnished, with good facilities and each with its share of the view. Timbered throughout are a comfortable lounge bar with an impressive inglenook and log-burning stove, the heavily-beamed tap-room, a conservatory for fine dining and a Bistro with wonderful views for breakfast and light lunches.

Menus are the brainchild of Master Chef Ken Adams who applies his impeccable pedigree to sourcing the best local produce supplemented by organic vegetables and fruit from the pub garden. Bar food can be as simple as goose confit with bacon salad and omelette Arnold Bennett or well-balanced salmon fishcakes on spinach with watercress sauce or rack of lamb with provençale vegetables. Fixed-price lunches offer duck leg salad with wild mushrooms and poached egg, roast loin of Shropshire lamb with sherry tomato sauce and a seafood rendezvous in light saffron broth. Dinner further extends options of true quality and class that many will travel the extra mile for.

OPEN: 12-2 7-11. Closed 1 wk Winter 1wk Spring.
BAR MEALS: L served Tue-Sun. D served Mon-Sat 12-2 7-9.30. Av main course £10. **RESTAURANT:** L served Tue-Sun. D served Mon-Sat 12-1.45 7-9. Av 3 course à la carte £20. Av 3 course fixed price £18.
BREWERY/COMPANY: Free House.
PRINCIPAL BEERS: Woodhampton Jack Snipe, Woods Shropshire Legends. **FACILITIES:** Garden: outdoor eating.
NOTES: Parking 15. **ROOMS:** 3 bedrooms 3 en suite s£40 d£70

LUDLOW
Map 08 SO57

The Charlton Arms ◆◆◆ ♀ NEW
SY8 1PJ ☎ 01584 872813 ▤ 01584 879120
Dir: Situated on Ludford Bridge on the Hereford road, South exit Ludlow town centre
This family-run free house stands on the outskirts of Ludlow, beside the River Teme. The little town has lots of interesting shops, and it's a good centre for walkers and cyclists. You'll find a nice range of locally-brewed real ales, plus popular snacks, salads and bar meals. Daily specials might include hand-made faggots, lamb cutlets with bramble sauce, or griddled marlin with lime and tomato dressing.
BAR MEALS: L served all week. D served all week 12-2 7-9. Av main course £5.25. **BREWERY/COMPANY:** Free House.
PRINCIPAL BEERS: Hobsons Best Bitter, Wye Vally Butty Bach, Woods Shropshire Lad. **FACILITIES:** Garden: Food served outside. **NOTES:** Parking 40. **ROOMS:** 6 bedrooms 6 en suite s£30 d£45

The Church Inn ◆◆◆
Buttercross SY8 1AW ☎ 01584 872174 ▤ 01584 877146
Dir: Town centre
Occupying one of the oldest sites in Ludlow, going back at least seven centuries, the Church Inn is an ideal base for exploring the beautiful Welsh Marches. Good range of real ales.

Pick of the Pubs

Unicorn Inn ♀
Corve St SY8 1DU ☎ 01584 873555
Dir: A49 to Ludlow
At the very edge of town, by the River Corve, a traditional beamed and panelled inn that was rescued from dereliction by its current owners over a decade ago. No longer offering accommodation, the pub thrives through a combination of local and tourist trade, with open log fires in winter and a riverside summer terrace that have an instant appeal.

At night the dining room is candle-lit and atmospheric, and it is here that the best of the day's offerings can be found. Start perhaps with chicken liver pâté or an Aegean salad, followed by half a roast duck with redcurrant sauce or casseroled lamb shank in scrumpy gravy. Local shopping also provides fresh ingredients for bar food such as parsnip and sweet pepper crumble, farmhouse sausages with bubble-and-squeak and black pudding in cider and mustard sauce. Probably unsung in comparison to some grander neighbours in the town, here is a venue for good food lovers without expense accounts.

OPEN: 12-2.30 6-11 (Sun 12-3.30, 7-10.30). Closed Dec 25.
BAR MEALS: L served all week. D served all week 12-2.15 6-9.15. Av main course £6.50. **RESTAURANT:** L served all week. D served all week 12-2.15 6-9.15. Av 3 course à la carte £16.50. **BREWERY/COMPANY:** Free House.
PRINCIPAL BEERS: Worthington, Bass, Hancocks HB.
FACILITIES: Garden: terrace, outdoor eating Dogs allowed Water. **NOTES:** Parking 3

MADELEY
Map 08 SJ60

The New Inn
Blists Hill Victorian Town, Legges Way TF7 5DU
☎ 01952 588892 ▤ 01952 243447
e-mail: pam@ercallcatering.enta.net
Dir: Between Telford & Broseley
Victorian pub set in the Blists Hill Open Air Museum, part of the complex of Ironbridge Gorge Museums, which celebrate Britain's industrial heritage. The museum recreates the year 1901, right down to the use of old money, which is available at the Bank. The pub was brought from Walsall, and rebuilt on its current site in 1983. (Open 11-5 only)

MINSTERLEY
Map 08 SJ30

The Stables Inn
Drury Ln, Hopesgate SY5 0EP ☎ 01743 891344
Dir: From Shrewsbury A488 turn L at r'about in Minsterley. At Plox Green x-roads turn R. Pub approx 3m.
Built around 1680 to serve the drovers travelling between Montgomery and Shrewsbury markets, this inn is situated in a tiny hamlet of just eight houses. Traditional pub fare is on offer, including a selection of steaks and home-made casseroles, curries, lasagne, and chilli con carne.

continued

OPEN: 12-3 (Sat-Sun) 6-11 (Sat-Mon 7-11). Closed 1 Jan.
BAR MEALS: L served Sat-Sun. D served Sun, Tue-Sat 12-1.45
7-9.30. Av main course £7.50. **RESTAURANT:** L served Sat-Sun.
D served Sun, Tue-Sat 12-1.45 7-9.30.
BREWERY/COMPANY: Free House.
PRINCIPAL BEERS: Worthington, Everard's Tiger Best, Young's
Best Bitter. **FACILITIES:** Children welcome Garden: Beer
Garden: food served outside Dogs allowed In Beer Garden Only.
NOTES: Parking 40 No credit cards

MORVILLE   Map 08 SO69

Acton Arms
WV16 4RJ ☎ 01746 714209
e-mail: aeton-arms@madasfish.com
Dir: On A458, 3m W of Bridgnorth
Believed to be England's most frequently haunted inn, with
three resident spooks, the Acton Arms, a former coaching inn,
is situated close to Upper Cresset Hall.

MUCH WENLOCK   Map 08 SO69

The Feathers
Brockton TF13 6JR ☎ 01746 785202
Stylish dining in beamed, stone-lined rooms with
Mediterranean-style decor and atmosphere; seasonally-
changing menus - reports please!

The George & Dragon ♀
2 High St TF13 6AA ☎ 01952 727312
Dir: on A458 halfway between Shrewsbury & Bridgnorth
Authentic 16th-century pub with a fascinating array of beer
trays, bottle labels, cigarette adverts and pictures. More than
500 water jugs hang from the beams, one of the largest
collections in the country. Attractive Victorian fireplaces and
antique settles. Popular bar food includes rarebits,
ploughman's, jacket potatoes and sandwiches. Specials may
include roast beef and Yorkshire pudding or Thai chicken
curry.
OPEN: 12-2.30 6-11 (Sun 12-2.30, 7-10.30). **BAR MEALS:** L
served all week. D served all week 12-2 6.30-9. Av main course
£7.95. **RESTAURANT:** L served all week. D served all week 12-2
6.30-9. Av 3 course à la carte £13.50.
BREWERY/COMPANY: Free House.
PRINCIPAL BEERS: Hook Norton, Everards Tiger, Salopian
Golden Thread, Hobsons Town Crier. **FACILITIES:** Children
welcome No credit cards

Longville Arms
Longville in the Dale TF13 6DT ☎ 01694 771206
🖷 01694 771742
Dir: From Shrewsbury take A49 to Church Stretton, then B4371 to
Longville
Prettily situated in a scenic corner of Shropshire, ideally placed
for walking and touring, this welcoming country inn has been
carefully restored and now includes a new 60-seat dining
room. Solid elm or cast-iron-framed tables, new oak panelling
and wood-burning stoves are among the features which help
to generate a warm, friendly ambience inside. Favourite dishes
on the wide-ranging bar menu and specials board include beef
and ale pie, gammon steak, Thai chicken curry, battered cod
and carrot and nut loaf with a herby tomato sauce.
OPEN: 12-3 7-11 (Sat-Sun 12-3 6-11). **BAR MEALS:** L served all
week. D served all week 12-2.30 7-9.30. Av main course £7.
RESTAURANT: L served all week. D served all week 12-2.30
7-9.30. Av 3 course à la carte £12.50.
BREWERY/COMPANY: Free House.
PRINCIPAL BEERS: Courage Directors, John Smiths,
Theakstons, Wells Bombardier. **FACILITIES:** Children welcome
Garden: outdoor eating, Dogs allowed Not in garden.
NOTES: Parking 40. **ROOMS:** 5 bedrooms 5 en suite s£30 d£46
FR£50-£70

The Talbot Inn 🐷
High St TF13 6AA ☎ 01952 727077 🖷 01952 728436

Dating from 1360, the Talbot may have been a hostel for
travellers and a centre for alms giving. Delightful courtyard
which was used in the 1949 film Gone to Earth. Daily specials
highlight the varied menu, which may include steak and
kidney pie, fresh salmon, Shropshire pie and cod mornay.
OPEN: 11-3 6.15-11 (Sun 12-3, 7-10.30). Closed 25 Dec.
BAR MEALS: L served all week. D served Sun-Fri 12-2 7-9.30. Av
main course £7. **RESTAURANT:** L served Sun. D served all week
12-2 7-9.30. Av 3 course à la carte £18. Av 3 course fixed price £10.
BREWERY/COMPANY: Free House. **PRINCIPAL BEERS:** Bass.
FACILITIES: Children welcome Garden: floral display, outdoor
eating. **NOTES:** Parking 5. **ROOMS:** 6 bedrooms 6 en suite
s£45 d£90

All AA listed accommodation can also be found on
the AA's internet site **www.theAA.com**

England

MUCH WENLOCK continued

Pick of the Pubs

Wenlock Edge Inn
Hilltop, Wenlock Edge TF13 6DJ ☎ 01746 785678
▤ 01746 785285
e-mail: info@wenlockedgeinn.co.uk
Dir: 4.5m from Much Wenlock on B4371
Beside a quiet road near one of the high points of
Wenlock Edge's dramatic wooded ridge, this row of
original 17th-century quarrymen's cottages has been a
long-standing favourite since its rescue from dereliction by
the Waring family in 1984. The small country-style dining-
room and bars, one with a wood-burning stove, are cosy,
friendly and relaxed: those who prefer privacy to
conversation and jovial banter may not benefit fully from
its unique atmosphere. Hobson's ales provide a suitable
accompaniment to the Shrewsbury lamb, venison or
steak-and-mushroom pies and chicken and apricot quiche
that define the inn's home-cooking. Vegetable-based
soups might be ham with asparagus in spring or an
autumnal cock-a-leekie, with pan-fried fresh fish, local
beef steaks and roast lamb legs to follow. Sponges, tarts
and crumbles are all made on the premises, while a
hearty country breakfast is appreciated by the walking
types who stay overnight.
OPEN: 11.30-2.30 6.30-11. Closed 24-26 Dec.
BAR MEALS: L served Tue-Sun. D served Tue-Sun 12-2 7-9.
Av main course £7.25. **RESTAURANT:** L served Tue-Sun. D
served Tue-Sat 12-2 7-9. Av 3 course à la carte £14.75.
BREWERY/COMPANY: Free House.
PRINCIPAL BEERS: Hobsons Best & Town Crier.
FACILITIES: Garden: outdoor eating, patio Dogs allowed
Water, toys. **NOTES:** Parking 50. **ROOMS:** 3 bedrooms
3 en suite s£41.50 d£67.50

MUNSLOW   Map 08 SO58

The Munslow Inn
SY7 9ET ☎ 01584 841205 ▤ 01584 841255
e-mail: viclandlord@tinyworld.co.uk
Dir: On B4368 between Craven Arms & Much Wenlock
Home-brewed ales and freshly prepared food draw visitors to
this impressive looking Georgian pub, which hides a
welcoming Tudor interior. Chalkboards list traditional bar food,
while the restaurant offers the likes of tom yum soup, beef
olive, coq au vin, and mushroom bovary (in garlic topped with
soft cheese).
OPEN: 12-2.30 7-11. **BAR MEALS:** L served all week. D served
all week 12-2 7-9.30. Av main course £7. **RESTAURANT:** L
served all week. D served all week 12-2 7-9.30. Av 3 course à la
carte £17. **BREWERY/COMPANY:** Free House.
PRINCIPAL BEERS: Butchers Dog (own brew).
FACILITIES: Children welcome Garden: patio.
NOTES: Parking 20. **ROOMS:** 4 bedrooms 4 en suite s£30 d£45

NESSCLIFFE   Map 08 SJ31

The Old Three Pigeons Inn ▤ ♀
SY4 1DB ☎ 01743 741279
e-mail: dillon@threepigeons.fsnet.co.uk
Dir: On A5 London road, 8 Miles W of Shrewsbury
Built of sandstone, ship's timbers, wattle and daub, this 15th-
century inn features a highwayman's carved wooden seat, and
continued

holds a gourmet club evening every month. Characteristic
dishes include sirloin of local beef in a Stilton sauce, whole
pan-fried sea bass, shellfish platter, gammon steak topped
with butter fried eggs, crab, and platter of hand-dived king
scallops, bacon and garlic.
OPEN: 11.30-3 7-11 (closed Mon). **BAR MEALS:** L served Tue-
Sun 11.30-3. Av main course £5. **RESTAURANT:** L served Sun. D
served Tue-Sun 11.30-3 7-10. Av 3 course à la carte £10.
BREWERY/COMPANY: Free House. **PRINCIPAL BEERS:** John
Smiths. **FACILITIES:** Children welcome Garden: Food served
outside Dogs allowed. **NOTES:** Parking 50

NEWPORT   Map 08 SJ71

The Swan at Forton NEW
TF10 8BY ☎ 01925 812169 ▤ 01925 812722
e-mail: mailtheswan@forton.co.uk
A family-run free house in a picturesque village on the border
between Shropshire and Staffordshire. The extensive menus
are served in two large, comfortable bars, as well as in the
non-smoking restaurant. A home-made pie night and a curry
night are amongst the regular special events. Popular dishes
include steak and kidney pie, poacher's chicken, battered cod
or haddock with mushy peas, and the weekend carvery.
OPEN: 12-3 6-11. **BAR MEALS:** L served all week. D served all
week 12-2 6-10. Av main course £6. **RESTAURANT:** L served all
week. D served all week 12-2 6-10. Av 3 course à la carte £8. Av 3
course fixed price £10.95. **PRINCIPAL BEERS:** Bass, Flowers IPA,
Marstons Pedigree, Greene King Old Speckled Hen.
FACILITIES: Children welcome Garden: Food served outside.
NOTES: Parking 67. **ROOMS:** 9 bedrooms 7 en suite s£25 d£40

NORTON   Map 08 SJ70

Pick of the Pubs

Hundred House Hotel ◉ ◉ ★ ★ ▤ ♀
Bridgnorth Rd TF11 9EE ☎ 01952 730353
▤ 01952 730355
e-mail: hphundredhouse@compuserve.com
See Pick of the Pubs on page 373

The Severn Way
Shropshire section
Linking Wales and England, the 210-mile Severn Way traces
the route of Britain's longest river, from its source to the sea. Starting
high in the watery, peat wastelands of Plynlimon, the way traverses a
variety of landscape, including remote moorland, lush valleys and
dense forest, before crossing the English border into Shropshire. By
the time you reach Shrewsbury, you'll want to take a break and this
loveliest of English towns has several classic character inns to cater for
the tired and thirsty walker. Try the historic Armoury overlooking the
Severn, or the Castle Vaults sheltering below Shrewsbury Castle. Fed
and watered, return to the trail and head south-east to historic
Ironbridge, originally one of the major centres of the Industrial
Revolution and now a UNESCO-designated World Heritage Site. The
Malthouse here is ideal for a pint, something to eat or even an
overnight stop. South of Ironbridge, the Severn reaches Bridgnorth, a
delightful old market town perched on a red sandstone ridge. Explore
its quaint streets, take a ride on the cliff railway, which connects the
upper and lower parts of the town, and relax over a drink or a
meal at the Bear, a Grade II listed pub in Northgate. If time
permits, you might also like to take a nostalgic steam
ride on the famous Severn Valley Railway.

PICK OF THE PUBS

OPEN: 11-11 (Sun 11-10.30).
BAR MEALS: L served all week.
D served all week 12-2.30 6-10.
Av main course £8
RESTAURANT: L served all week.
D served all week 12-2.30 6-10.
Av 3 course a la carte £27.50.
BREWERY/COMPANY:
Free House.
PRINCIPAL BEERS: Smiles
Heritage, Wood Shropshire Lad,
Everards Tiger, Charles Wells
Bombardier.
FACILITIES: Children welcome.
Garden: outdoor eating. Dogs
allowed by arrangement.
NOTES: Parking 40.
ROOMS: 10 bedrooms 10 en suite
s£69-£85 d£95-110 FR£110.

Hundred House Hotel

Bridgnorth Rd TF11 9EE
☎ 01952 730353 📠 01952 730355
e-mail: hphundredhouse@messages.co.uk
Dir: On A442 6m N of Bridgnorth

'Magic hotel - a haven of kindness, comfort and service' are typical guest comments that sum up the Hundred House with good cause. A rare all-rounder where staff, interior decor, quality of food and accommodation all stand out, and where years of hard work and dedication have created a great inn.

Though a 14th-century thatched courtyard barn stands here to this day, the main inn, a fine creeper-clad brick building, is of Georgian origin and stands in its own mature orchard and garden. Very individual, beautifully restored and furnished, full of character and professionally run by the Phillips family for the past fourteen years, the Hundred House is a stylish hotel, quality restaurant and informal pub all rolled into one. Expect quarry tiled floors, exposed brick walls, huge fireplaces with log fires, stained-glass windows and a warm, intimate atmosphere throughout the rambling bar and dining areas.

The hotel has its own enclosed herb garden, the produce of which both hangs in the bar and dots the brasserie and restaurant menus. Food is skilfully prepared and competently cooked in items as disparate as steak and kidney pudding braised in stout and hot potato cakes served with tempura onion rings, aïoli, mushroom sauce and rocket. Alternatively, go for Greek salad with feta and olives, followed by Cajun-style chicken with sweet red pepper coulis and perhaps cold rice pudding with an unctuous caramel sauce. From the carte, options regularly include assiette of Hereford duck, potted, poached and confit followed by Shropshire lamb chump with rosemary sauce and macaroni gratin, rounding off with hot treacle tart or Neapolitan ice cream bombe.

Individually styled and well equipped bedrooms have period furniture and attractive soft furnishings.

OSWESTRY   Map 08 SJ22

The Bear Hotel ♦♦♦♦ ♀
Salop Rd SY11 2NR ☎ 01691 652093 ▤ 01691 679996
e-mail: pub@bearhotel.net
Comfortable town-centre 19th-century coaching inn, once a
temperance hotel, that now features a memorable whisky bar
with over 131 single malts. Bar brunches and burgers through
the day are supplemented by regular specials such as
gammon steak, beef stroganoff, salmon with chardonnay
sauce, and lamb with mustard sauce. Other light bites include
jacket potatoes, ploughman's, omelettes, sandwiches, and
triple decker baps. Friendly welcome and nightly a la carte.
OPEN: 11-3 7-11 (Sun 7-11 only). Closed Dec 25, 1 Jan.
BAR MEALS: L served Mon-Sat. D served Mon-Sat 12-2 7-9.30.
Av main course £4. **RESTAURANT:** D served Mon-Sat 7-9.30.
Av 3 course à la carte £15. **PRINCIPAL BEERS:** Marstons
Pedigree. **FACILITIES:** Children welcome Dogs allowed.
NOTES: Parking 25. **ROOMS:** 10 bedrooms 5 en suite s£25
d£60

Pick of the Pubs

The Bradford Arms 🐑 ♀
Llanymynech SY22 6EJ ☎ 01691 830582
▤ 01691-830728
e-mail: info@bradford-arms.com
Dir: On A483 in village centre
Victorianised in 1901, this former coaching inn originally
belonged to the Earl of Bradford Estates. Comfortable
furnishings, soft lighting and an open fire help to generate
an intimate atmosphere. Everything except ice cream is
made on the premises and the inn offers an enterprising
modern English and European menu.
Expect smoked salmon with creamy dill and mustard
dressing and King prawns sautéed in garlic butter with
asparagus and mushrooms among the imaginative
starters, while main courses may feature sautéed breast of
duck with sauce of stock, pear juice, balsamic vinegar and
pear liqueur on a bed of caramelised pear, and grilled
glazed salmon with cannellini bean purée.
Excellent and extensive choice of cheeses, including a
rare blue cheese made from Jersey milk and a rich-tasting,
good smoked Cheddar. Five en suite bedrooms, including
one family room, are an additional new feature of the inn.
OPEN: 12-2 7-11. Closed 2wks Sept, 25-26 Dec, 2 wks Jan.
BAR MEALS: L served Tue-Sun. D served Tue-Sun 12-2 7-10.
Av main course £9.95. **RESTAURANT:** D served Tue-Sun
7-10. Av 3 course à la carte £19.
BREWERY/COMPANY: Free House.
PRINCIPAL BEERS: Greene King Abbot Ale, Shepherd
Neame Bishops Finger. **FACILITIES:** Dogs allowed Guide
dogs only. **NOTES:** Parking 20. **ROOMS:** 5 bedrooms
5 en suite s£35 d£50 FR£70

The Horseshoe
Llanyblodwel SY10 8NQ ☎ 01691 828969
Timbered Tudor inn by the River Tanat on the Powys border,
close to the Offa's Dyke path. Oak-panelled dining room;
varied menus.

Pick of the Pubs

The Old Mill Inn 🐑
Candy SY10 9AZ ☎ 01691 657058 ▤ 01691 680918
e-mail: theoldmill.inn@virgin.net
Dir: from B4579 follow signs for Trefonen, after the Ashfield on R,
take 1st R towards Llansillin, 1st R down hill
Peacefully situated in the Candy Valley, the Old Mill has
been a pub for about 20 years. The famous Offa's Dyke
Path, one of Britain's most popular national trails, is just a
yard or two from the main door and the River Morda runs
beside the inn.
On winter days, the pub's cosy interior is the obvious
place to be, with a spacious conservatory overlooking
extensive gardens, a crackling log fire and a welcoming
ambience enhancing the pleasant surroundings. A wide-
ranging selection of starters, including Bantry Bay mussels
in white wine cream and vegetable spring rolls with sweet
and sour sauce, sets the tone for dinner which varies from
venison pie with red wine, mushrooms and puff pastry, to
seafood Helsinki-style, consisting of crab, hake, crevettes,
mussels, squid and red mullet with lemon, capers, garlic,
chives and gherkin butter.
OPEN: 12-3 (Wed-Thur) (Sun 12-3, 7-10.30) 7-11 (6-11
Fri & Sat). **BAR MEALS:** L served Wed-Sun. D served Wed-
Sun 12-2.30 6-9.30. Av main course £5.95. **RESTAURANT:** L
served Wed-Sun. D served Wed-Sun 12-2.30 6-9.30. Av 3
course à la carte £12. **BREWERY/COMPANY:** Free House.
PRINCIPAL BEERS: Greene King Old Speckled Hen, Tetleys.
FACILITIES: Children welcome Children's licence Garden:
outdoor eating, patio. Dogs allowed Water.
NOTES: Parking 200. **ROOMS:** 5 bedrooms s£17 d£34

The Walls
Welsh Walls SY11 1AW ☎ 01691 670970 ▤ 01691 653820
e-mail: thewalls@pernickety.co.uk
Large busy pub with an almost eccentric atmosphere. Licenced
for civil weddings. Located in a former Victorian church school.

PICKLESCOTT   Map 08 SO49

Bottle & Glass Inn
SY6 6NR ☎ 01694 751345 ▤ 01694 751345
Dir: Turn off A49 at Dorrington between Shrewsbury & Church
Stretton
This traditional country inn serves all kinds of people but
locals always come first. It is situated in beautiful countryside
on the slopes of the Longmynd in the heart of South
Shropshire hill country. The emphasis is on local ales and local
produce. Straightforward dishes including steaks, cod, and
gammon off the bone, and there is a popular Sunday carvery.
OPEN: 12-2 7-12. Closed weekdays in Winter. **BAR MEALS:** L
served Tue, Thur, Sat & Sun. D served Mon-Sat 12-1.45 7-8.45. Av
main course £6.50. **RESTAURANT:** L served Tue-Sun. D served
Mon-Sat 12-2 7-9. Av 3 course à la carte £13.25. Av 4 course fixed
price £14.25. **BREWERY/COMPANY:** Free House.
PRINCIPAL BEERS: Woods Parish, Shropshire Gold Salopians.
FACILITIES: Children welcome Children's licence Garden:
patio Dogs allowed bar only, Water.
NOTES: Parking 20. **ROOMS:** 3 bedrooms 3 en suite s£35 d£50
See Pub Walk on page 367

SHIFNAL
Map 08 SJ70

Odfellows Wine Bar ♀
Market Place TF11 9AU ☎ 01952 461517 📄 01952 463855
e-mail: matt@odley.co.uk
Dir: *3rd exit from Mway rdbt, at next rdbt take 3rd exit, past petrol station, round bend under railway bridge, bar on L*
Speciality coffees, five real ales and over 40 wines from around the world - including many by the glass - are offered at this interesting single room wine bar, with its high ceilings, elevated dining area and conservatory. Dishes represent modern British and world themes - marinated duck breast, rabbit baked with two mustards and cream, and carpaccio of tuna and smoked salmon with orange, tomato and coriander salsa. Live music Sunday evening.
OPEN: 12-2.30 5.30-11 (Sun & Fri open all day). Closed Dec 25-26, Jan 1. **BAR MEALS:** L served all week 12-2. Av main course £10.50. **RESTAURANT:** L served all week. D served all week 12-2 7-10. Av 3 course à la carte £18. **BREWERY/COMPANY:** Free House. **PRINCIPAL BEERS:** Bathams, Timothy Taylor Landlord, Enville, Holdens. **NOTES:** Parking 35. **ROOMS:** 7 bedrooms 7 en suite s£37.50 d£47.50

SHREWSBURY
Map 08 SJ41

Pick of the Pubs

The Armoury ♀
Welsh Bridge, Victoria Quay SY1 1HH
☎ 01743 340525 📄 01743 340526
On the banks of the River Severn near Shrewsbury's Welsh Bridge, the site was granted to the friars of St Augustine by King Henry III in 1255, but its monastery was later destroyed at the Dissolution. The present 1806 armoury building was abandoned in 1882, later re-erected as a bakery and restored to present use in 1995, regaining its historic title.
   All-day opening, a feast of regular guest ales and modern-day food options make it ever more popular today. Ploughman's and granary bread sandwiches form the basis of a standard snack menu; however more jewels are to be found for those with adventurous appetites. Chicken and coconut goujons with curried peach chutney and tomato polenta loaf with olives and balsamic dressing, followed by Thai mussel stew, braised ham hock with honey and mustard glaze and tomato and vegetable penne topped with Mozzarella, raising expectations above the norm, have all met with approval. Rather more conventional puddings such as steamed treacle sponge and roast pineapple with rum and raisin ice cream equally merit approval.
OPEN: 12-11 (Sun 12-10.30). Closed 25-26 Dec. **BAR MEALS:** L served all week. D served all week 12-2.30 6-9.30, (all day wknd). Av main course £8.
BREWERY/COMPANY: Free House.
PRINCIPAL BEERS: Wood Shropshire Lad, Wadworth 6X, Boddingtons.

The Castle Vaults
16 Castle Gates SY1 2AB ☎ 01743 358807
e-mail: george.mitchell@virgin.net
Dir: *From S: M6, M54, A5. From N: M6, A49*
An early 19th-century ale house, the Castle Vaults has a roof garden and nestles beneath the shadow of Shrewsbury Castle. Bedrooms.

The Plume of Feathers
Harley SY5 6LP ☎ 01952 727360 📄 01952 728542
Many original features still survive at this historic inn which started life as a pair of cottages around 1620. The name of the inn was recorded in 1842. Open fires, antique furniture and old beams give the interior a cosy, inviting atmosphere.

White Horse Inn ♀
Pulvierbatch SY5 8DS ☎ 01743 718247
Dir: *7m past the Nuffield Hospital*
Some 8 miles south of Shrewsbury off the A49, a cruck-structured building - reputedly 13th-century - houses this fine old inn hidden down country lanes. If Rob Roy (beef-and-cheese) sandwiches, Arbroath pancakes and Cullen Skink indicate a Scottish bias, home-made curries and beef Stroganoff help restore the balance.
OPEN: 11.30-11. **BAR MEALS:** L served all week. D served all week 12-2 7-9.30. Av main course £5.
BREWERY/COMPANY: Whitbread.
PRINCIPAL BEERS: Flowers Original, Black Sheep, Whitbread Trophy. **FACILITIES:** Children welcome. **NOTES:** Parking 50

TELFORD

The Grove Inn ♦♦♦
10 Wellington Rd, Coalbrookdale TF8 7DX
☎ 01952 432269 📄 01252 433269
e-mail: frog@fat-frog.co.uk
A small corner of France in Coalbrookdale - this former coaching inn, next to the Coalbrookdale Museum in the Ironbridge Gorge, has a French chef/proprietor and a lovely continental-style garden. The Fat Frog restaurant in the basement might offer fillet Rossini, grilled black pudding in brandy, and chicken stuffed with Camembert. There is also a seafood and wine bar.
OPEN: 12-2.30 5.30-11. **BAR MEALS:** L served all week. D served all week 12.30-2 6.30-8.30. Av main course £6.50.
RESTAURANT: L served all week. D served Mon-Sat 12.30-2 7-9.30. Av 3 course à la carte £18.50.
BREWERY/COMPANY: Free House.
PRINCIPAL BEERS: Banks Original, Banks Traditional.
FACILITIES: Garden: patio/terrace, outdoor eating, BBQ.
NOTES: Parking 12. **ROOMS:** 5 bedrooms 5 en suite s£30 d£45 2 family rooms £55-£75

WENTNOR
Map 08 SO39

The Crown Inn
SY9 5EE ☎ 01588 650613 📄 01588 650436
e-mail: crowninn@talk21.com
Dir: *From Shrewsbury A49 to Church Stretton, follow signs over Long Mynd to Asterton, R to Wentnor*
Standing in the shadow of the famous Long Mynd, in an area with vast potential for walking and other outdoor pursuits, the Crown is a traditional, unspoilt 17th-century coaching inn with log fires, beams and horse brasses. Food is served in the bar and non-smoking restaurant and the choice changes daily. Sample one of the interesting dishes, such as pork loin with stilton and apricots, tarragon chicken or noisette of lamb, rounding off with an appetising home-made pudding.
continued

England

OPEN: 12-3 7-11 (Sat 12-3 6-11). Closed Dec 25. **BAR MEALS:** L served all week. D served all week 12-2 7-9. Av main course £7. **RESTAURANT:** L served all week. D served all week 12-2 7-9. Av 3 course à la carte £18. **BREWERY/COMPANY:** Free House. **PRINCIPAL BEERS:** Hobsons, Worthington, Greene King Old Speckled Hen, Wood Shropshire Lad. **FACILITIES:** Children welcome Garden: outdoor eating Dogs allowed garden only. **NOTES:** Parking 20. **ROOMS:** 3 bedrooms 2 en suite s£25 d£30

WESTON HEATH   Map 08 SJ71

Pick of the Pubs

The Countess's Arms ♀

TF11 8RY ☎ 01952 691123   ▤ 01952 691660
Owned by the Earl of Bradford and re-opened in 1998 after extensive refurbishment, this popular rural Shropshire pub sports a spacious, wooden-floored bar and first-floor gallery where customers can look down on the blue glass mosaic tiled bar below. The pub is situated one mile from Weston Park, the family seat of the Earls of Bradford, and a short drive from Boscobel House, where Charles II sought refuge from Cromwell's soldiers after the Battle of Worcester. Interesting menu features honest pub food and among the dishes are traditional beer battered cod, salmon with coriander and chilli, and Thai green chicken curry.
OPEN: 9am-12mdnt. **BAR MEALS:** L served all week. D served all week 11-10.30. Av main course £4.95.
RESTAURANT: L served all week. D served all week 11-10.30. Av 3 course à la carte £12.
BREWERY/COMPANY: Free House.
PRINCIPAL BEERS: Banks's, Boddingtons, Flowers IPA.
FACILITIES: Children welcome Children's licence Garden: outdoor eating, patio. **NOTES:** Parking 100

WHITCHURCH   Map 08 SJ54

The Horse & Jockey

Church St SY13 1LB ☎ 01948 664902   ▤ 01948 664902
e-mail: andy.thelwell@onmail.co.uk
Dir: In town centre next to church
Built in three stages during the 17th, 18th and 19th centuries, the oldest area of this pub is an oak-beamed, three-storey building. A wide-ranging menu offers salmon and prawn gratin, and home-made paté for starters, followed perhaps by chicken chilli, beef Wellington and lemon sole roulade.

continued

OPEN: 11.30-2.30 6-11. **BAR MEALS:** L served all week. D served all week 11.30-2.30 6-10. Av main course £4.95. **RESTAURANT:** L served all week. D served all week 11.30-2.30 6-10. Av 3 course à la carte £14.55. **BREWERY/COMPANY:** Vaux. **PRINCIPAL BEERS:** Worthington, Wadworth 6X, Boddingtons, Courage Directors. **FACILITIES:** Children welcome Garden: patio, outdoor eating, BBQ. **NOTES:** Parking 10

Willey Moor Lock Tavern ♀

Tarporley Rd SY13 4HF ☎ 01948 663274
Dir: 2m N of Whitchurch on A49 (Warrington/Tarporley)
Former lock keeper's cottage idyllically situated beside the Llangollen Canal in rural South Cheshire. Neatly decorated low-beamed rooms with teapot collection, open log fires and a good choice of real ales for the afficionado. Traditional pub food - breaded fillet of plaice, steaks, lasagne or chicken curry. **OPEN:** 12-2.30 6-11 (Sun 12-2.30 7-10.30). **BAR MEALS:** L served all week. D served all week 12-2 6-9.30. Av main course £5. **RESTAURANT:** L served all week. D served all week 12-2 7-9.30. **BREWERY/COMPANY:** Free House. **PRINCIPAL BEERS:** Theakston. **FACILITIES:** Children welcome Garden: Beer garden by the canal, food served outside Dogs allowed Water. **NOTES:** Parking 50 No credit cards

---

WOORE   Map 08 SJ74

Swan at Woore 🛏 ♀

Nantwich Rd CW3 9SA ☎ 01630 647220
Dir: A51 Stone to Nantwich road 10 miles from Nantwich in the village of Woore which is between Stone and Nantwich
Refurbished 19th-century dining inn by the A51 near Stapley Water Gardens. Four separate eating areas lead off from a central servery. Daily specials boards supplement the menu, which might include crispy confit of duck, slow roast knuckle of lamb, roasted salmon on vegetable linguine, or red onion and garlic 'Tarte Tatin'. There's a separate fish menu - grilled red mullet fillets, perhaps, or seared tuna on roasted sweet peppers.
OPEN: 12-3.30 5-11 (all day Sat-Sun). **BAR MEALS:** L served all week. D served all week 12-2.30 6.30-9.30. Av main course £7.50. **RESTAURANT:** L served all week. D served all week 12-3.30 6.30-9.30. Av 3 course à la carte £19. **BREWERY/COMPANY:** Greenalls. **PRINCIPAL BEERS:** Bass, Marstons Pedigree. **FACILITIES:** Children welcome Children's licence Garden: patio, food served outside. **NOTES:** Parking 40

England

WORFIELD
Map 08 SO79

The Dog Inn NEW
Main St WV15 5LF ☎ 01746 716020 📄 01746 716050
e-mail: dogworfield@aol.com
Dir: On the Wolverhampton road turn L opposite the Wheel pub over the bridge and turn R in to the village of Worfield the Dog is on the L
Under the same ownership as the Munslow Arms at Munslow (qv), the Dog is an ancient pub nestling in a picturesque village of handsome houses close to the River Worfe. Spick-and-span with a tiled floor and light pine furnishings inside following major refurbishment, it offers tip-top Butcher's Ales (brewed at the Munslow Arms) and a short menu listing home-cooked dishes. Choose from lunchtime ploughman's and filled baguettes, or crab soup, lemon sole, Thai chilli chicken, pheasant in red wine, or haddock bake from the evening carte and specials board.
OPEN: 12-2.30 7-11. **BAR MEALS:** L served all week. D served all week 12-2 7-9.30. Av main course £6. **RESTAURANT:** L served all week. D served all week 12-2 7-9.30. Av 3 course à la carte £17. Av 3 course fixed price £10.95.
BREWERY/COMPANY: Free House.
PRINCIPAL BEERS: Courage Directors, Wells Bombardier, Butchers Best Bitter, Highgate Best Bitter. **FACILITIES:** Children welcome Garden: food served outside Dogs allowed Please ask Staff before (resident terrier). **NOTES:** Parking 8

SOMERSET

APPLEY
Map 03 ST02

Pick of the Pubs

The Globe Inn 🏠
TA21 0HJ ☎ 01823 672327
Dir: From M5 J6 take A38 towards Exeter. Village signposted in 5m
Rambling, 500-year-old slate and cob-built pub hidden away in a secluded hamlet and reached via tortuous, narrow lanes. Surrounded by rolling, unspoilt countryside, the Globe is a perfect starting point for a relaxing rural ramble. Return to a decent pint of Cotleigh ale and a good pub meal, served throughout the four rustic yet comfortably furnished rooms, each with its own collection: one pictures of magpies and another Titanic memorabilia. Extensive choice of food favouring fresh fish - smoked haddock and bacon chowder, whole lemon sole and pan-fried king prawns in garlic butter. Hearty alternatives include venison pie, Thai vegetable curry, crispy duck with orange and Madeira sauce, and beef Stroganoff. Reliable bar snacks and excellent Sunday lunches - booking advisable.
OPEN: 11-3 6.30-11 (closed Mon). **BAR MEALS:** L served Tue-Sun. D served Tue-Sun 12-2 7-10. Av main course £8.50. **RESTAURANT:** L served Sun. D served Tue-Sat 12-2 7-10. Av 3 course à la carte £16. **BREWERY/COMPANY:** Free House. **PRINCIPAL BEERS:** Cotleigh Tawny, Butcombe Bitter. **FACILITIES:** Children welcome Garden: outdoor eating Dogs allowed garden only. **NOTES:** Parking 30

ASHCOTT
Map 03 ST43

Ring O Bells 🍺
High St TA7 9PZ ☎ 01458 210232 📄 01458 210880
e-mail: info@ringobells.com
Dir: From M5 follow signs A39 & Glastonbury. Turn north off A39 at post office follow signs to church and village hall
Friendly, award-winning pub close to Glastonbury and the Polden Hills. Pleasant blend of original 18th-century building and recently opened function room and skittle alley. The inn uses fresh local ingredients and typical blackboard specials may include lemon chicken, lambs' kidney and sausage ragout, pork chop stuffed with Cheddar and apple, and fresh haddock mornay. Among the interesting ever-changing real ales is one local beer.
OPEN: 12-3 7-11 (Sun 7-10.30). Closed 25 Dec. **BAR MEALS:** L served all week. D served all week 12-2 7-11. Av main course £5.50. **RESTAURANT:** 12 7. Av 3 course à la carte £11.
BREWERY/COMPANY: Free House **FACILITIES:** Children welcome Garden: food served outside. **NOTES:** Parking 25

ASHILL
Map 03 ST31

Square & Compass
Windmill Hill TA19 9NX ☎ 01823 480467
Dir: Turn off A358 at Stewley Cross service station (Ashill) 1M along Wood Road, behind service station
Family-run free house at the heart of rural Somerset. Lovely gardens in summer and wonderful views over the Blackdown Hills. Welcoming bar area has recently been refurbished and includes various hand-made settles and tables. A log fire crackles away on cold winter days. Pleasing mix of traditional English and European dishes includes seafood crêpes, spaghetti Marinara, plaice and prawns in white sauce and scampi. Good range of well-kept West Country ales.
OPEN: 12-3 6.30-11 (Sun 7-11). **BAR MEALS:** L served all week. D served all week 12-3 6.30-10. Av main course £6.50.
RESTAURANT: D served all week. Av 3 course à la carte £12. **BREWERY/COMPANY:** Free House.
PRINCIPAL BEERS: Exmoor Ale, Moor Withycutter, Wadworth 6X, Exmoor Gold. **FACILITIES:** Children welcome Garden: Food served outside Dogs allowed. **NOTES:** Parking 30

AXBRIDGE
Map 03 ST45

Lamb Inn
The Square BS26 2AP ☎ 01934 732253
Rambling town-centre inn on the square, opposite King John's hunting lodge. Comfortable bars with log fires. Good range of Butcombe ales and farm ciders. Skittle alley and large terraced garden.

The Oak House
The Square BS26 2AP ☎ 01934 732444 📄 01934 733112
Dir: From M5 J22, take A38 to Bristol. Turn onto A371 to Cheddar/Wells, then L at Axbridge. Town centre
Parts of this inn date from the 11th century, and much of its historic character is retained in the beams, stone walls, inglenook fireplaces and an ancient well linked to the Cheddar caverns. Bedrooms.

England

BATH
Map 03 ST76

The Olde Green Tree ⚲
12 Green St BA1 2JE ☎ 01225 448259
Dir: Town centre
Three-roomed, oak-panelled pub, loved for its faded
splendour, dim atmosphere and a front room decorated with
World War II Spitfires. Menus include basic pub fare - soup,
bangers and mash, rolls and salads - a popular northern Thai
curry, and daily vegetarian specials. Five real ales are served,
along with German lager, local cider, and an array of malts,
wines and good coffee.
OPEN: 11-11 (Sun 12-10.30). Closed 25-26 Dec, 1 Jan.
BAR MEALS: L served Mon-Sat 12-2.15. Av main course £5.
BREWERY/COMPANY: Phoenix Inns.
PRINCIPAL BEERS: changing guest beers. **FACILITIES:** Dogs
allowed   manager's discretion only No credit cards

Pack Horse Inn
Southstoke Ln, South Stoke BA2 7DU
☎ 01225 832060   🖷 01225 830075
Dir: 2.5m from Bath city centre, via the A367(A37). Turn onto B3110
towards Frome. South Stoke turning on R.
Dating back to 1489, this historic pub was built by monks to
provide shelter for pilgrims and travellers. Views from the
garden over rolling Somerset countryside. Original bar and
inglenook fireplace inside. Well known locally for its traditional
cider, including Taunton Traditional and Thatcher Cheddar
Valley. Light snacks, baguettes and burgers and dishes such as
sherry chicken and steak Diane typify the menu.
OPEN: 11.30-2.30 6-11 (Fri-Sun 11-11). **BAR MEALS:** L served
all week. D served all week 12-2 6-9. Av main course £5.25.
PRINCIPAL BEERS: Ushers Best, Courage Best, Wadworth 6X.
FACILITIES: Children welcome   Children's licence   Garden:
outdoor eating, patio/terrace   Dogs allowed

Richmond Arms ⚲
7 Richmond Place BA1 5PZ ☎ 01225 316725
A mile from the city centre in Georgian Lansdown with a
south-facing garden, the pub has been minimalistically
refurbished. Attention thus turns rapidly to inventive food with
a modern touch: honey and ginger glazed aubergine on Puy
lentils with roasted peppers; kangaroo steak with sweet Thai
chilli sauce; mango and rum cheesecake with strawberry
coulis.
OPEN: 12-3 6-11 (Mon 6-11 only). **BAR MEALS:** L served Tue-
Sun. D served Tue-Sat 12-2 6-8.30 (9 Fri & Sat). Av main course
£9. **PRINCIPAL BEERS:** Bass, Butcombe, Courage Best.
FACILITIES: Garden: outdoor eating   No credit cards

BATHAMPTON
Map 03 ST76

The George Inn
Mill Ln BA2 6TR ☎ 01225 425079   🖷 01225 425079
Dir: M4 J18 onto A46 L at traffic lights & follow signs for Bathampton
A traditional country pub on the Kennet and Avon Canal in a
quiet village location just a mile from Bath. Home-cooked food
using fresh local produce.

For pubs with AA rosette awards for food
see page 10

BECKINGTON
Map 03 ST85

Pick of the Pubs

Woolpack Inn ◉ ★ ★ 🍴
BA3 6SP ☎ 01373 831244   🖷 01373 831223
Dir: Just off A36 near junction with A361
Relaxing 16th-century coaching inn featuring an attractive,
flagstoned bar and various cosy dining areas. Noted locally
for good food, the wide range of freshly prepared dishes
may include pan-fried calamari with almonds and saffron,
crab cakes with red Thai curry sauce, sea bass on squid
with Parma ham, pan-fried pork fillet with roast baby sweet
potatoes and Drambuie reduction, and caramelised pear
millefeuille with coffee and caramel sauce.
OPEN: 11-11 (Sun 12-10.30). **BAR MEALS:** L served
all week. D served all week 12-2.30 6.30-9.30 (9 Sun).
RESTAURANT: L served all week. D served all week 12-2.30
7-9.30. **BREWERY/COMPANY:** Old English Inns.
PRINCIPAL BEERS: Ruddles County, Wadworth 6X,
Courage Best & Directors. **FACILITIES:** Children welcome
Dogs allowed. **ROOMS:** 11 bedrooms 11 en suite s£60 d£80

BLAGDON
Map 03 ST55

The New Inn
Church St BS40 7SB ☎ 01761 462475   🖷 01761 463523
e-mail: the.new-inn@virgin.net
Dir: From Bristol take A38 S then A368 towards Bath
Open fires, traditional home-cooked food, and magnificent
views across fields to Blagdon Lake are among the attractions
at this welcoming 17th-century inn, tucked away near the
church. Trout fishing is available.

BRADFORD-ON-TONE
Map 03 ST12

White Horse Inn ⚲
TA4 1HF ☎ 01823 461239
Dir: N of A38 between Taunton & Wellington
A stone-built country pub, the White Horse is situated in the
centre of the village opposite the church. Expect a friendly
welcome and good value food, including bar snacks, a restaurant
menu (also available in the bar) and daily specials from the
blackboard. Favourites are home-made beer-battered cod,
salmon fishcakes, and half shoulder of lamb.
OPEN: 11.30-3.00 (Sun 12-3.00) 5.30-11 (Sun 7-10.30).
BAR MEALS: L served all week. D served Mon-Sat 12-2
6.30-9.30. Av main course £4. **RESTAURANT:** L served all week.
D served Mon-Sat 12-2 6.30-9.30. Av 3 course à la carte £14.
BREWERY/COMPANY: Enterprise Inns.
PRINCIPAL BEERS: Butcombe, Fuller's London Pride.
FACILITIES: Garden: lawn, Pergola Dogs allowed.
NOTES: Parking 20

BRIDGWATER
Map 03 ST33

Ashcott Inn ⚲
50 Bath Rd, Ashcott TA7 9QH ☎ 01458 210282
🖷 01458 210282
Dir: M5 J23 follow signs for A39 to Bridgwater
Dating back to the 16th century, this former coaching inn has
an attractive bar with beams and stripped stone walls, as well
as quaint old seats and an assortment of oak and elm tables.
Outside is a popular terrace and a delightful walled garden. The
new licensees have introduced a new changing menu, perhaps
continued

offering many Cumberland sausages with caramelised red onions, supreme of salmon with a spinach and rocket salad, swordfish with black pepper and lime, and chargrilled tuna loin. Try one of the interestingly filled wraps or ciabatta rolls. **OPEN:** 11-3 (Easter-end Sept open all day) 5-11. **BAR MEALS:** L served all week. D served all week 12-2.30 7-9.30. Av main course £8. **RESTAURANT:** L served all week. D served all week 12-2.30 7-9.30. Av 3 course à la carte £16.
BREWERY/COMPANY: Heavitree.
PRINCIPAL BEERS: Butcombe, Greene King Old Speckled Hen.
FACILITIES: Children welcome Garden: sheltered, food served outside. **NOTES:** Parking 50

BRUTON

The Claire De Lune ◆◆◆◆ ♀
2-4 High St BA10 0AA ☎ 01749 813395 📠 01749 813395
e-mail: drew.beard@virgin.net
Dir: 6 miles off the A303 on the B3081, situated on the eastern end of Bruton High St
Situated in the heart of this historic Saxon town, the Claire de Lune is a modern bar and bistro housed in a large double jettied building dating from 1500. Comfortable en suite bedrooms are available, and the interesting monthly menu lists fillet of cod with a herb crust, lamb noisette, and aubergine and chevre gateaux. Snacks include filled baguettes and ploughman's lunches.
OPEN: 11-2 7-11. Closed 1 Jan-31 Jan. **RESTAURANT:** L served Tue-Sat. D served Tue-Sat 12-2 7-9. Av 3 course à la carte £17.50. Av 3 course fixed price £14.95. **BREWERY/COMPANY:** Free House **FACILITIES:** Children welcome Children's licence Garden: patio, outdoor eating, BBQ. **ROOMS:** 3 bedrooms 3 en suite s£35 d£47.50

BUTLEIGH
Map 03 ST53

The Rose & Portcullis
Sub Rd BA6 8TQ ☎ 01458 850287 📠 01458 850120

16th-century freehouse just a short drive from the historic towns of Glastonbury and Street. Thatched bars and an inglenook fireplace give the place plenty of warmth and character. The name is associated with the coat of arms of the local lord of the manor. Wholesome pub grub includes cottage pie, mixed grill, ham, egg and chips, golden fried scampi and vegetable lasagne. Light meals include baguettes, burgers, salads, ploughman's, omelettes and jacket potatoes.
OPEN: 12-3 6-11. **BAR MEALS:** L served all week. D served all week 12-2 7-9. Av main course £6. **RESTAURANT:** L served all week. D served all week 12-2 7-9. Av 3 course à la carte £14.
BREWERY/COMPANY: Free House.
PRINCIPAL BEERS: Flowers Original, Butcombe.
FACILITIES: Children welcome Garden: outdoor eating Dogs allowed. **NOTES:** Parking 50

CASTLE CARY
Map 03 ST63

The George Hotel ★ ★ ♀
Market Place BA7 7AH ☎ 01963 350761 📠 01963 350035
Dir: From A303 take A371 at Wincanton, then N to Castle Cary
Built of stone and thatch, this lovely 15th-century inn is under new management. Blending perfectly into this pretty, historic market town, it offers spacious bedrooms and cosy bars. An imaginative range of dishes is available, making good use of fresh local produce, and including, perhaps, a half shoulder of lamb with garlic and mint jus, or crispy duck confit with plum sauce.
OPEN: 11-11. **BAR MEALS:** L served all week. D served all week 12-2 7-9. Av main course £4.95. **RESTAURANT:** L served Sun. D served all week 12-2 7-9. Av 3 course à la carte £5.
BREWERY/COMPANY: Old English Inns.
PRINCIPAL BEERS: Otter, Wadworth 6X. **FACILITIES:** Children welcome Dogs allowed. **NOTES:** Parking 10.
ROOMS: 14 bedrooms 14 en suite s£50 d£75

Horse Pond Inn ◆◆◆ ♀
The Triangle BA7 7BD ☎ 01963 350318 📠 01963 351764
e-mail: horsepondinn@aol.com

Modernised and extended 16th-century inn, with en suite motel-style accommodation, situated in the historic country town of Castle Cary. Comfortable bar offering a range of real ales and an extensive menu of traditional pub food. Expect decent home-made pies - steak and kidney, chicken and mushroom etc - home-cooked ham, steaks, and breaded plaice.
OPEN: 10.30am-11pm (Sun 12-3 7-10.30). **BAR MEALS:** L served all week. D served all week 12-2.15 7-9. Av main course £5.
RESTAURANT: D served all week 7-9.
BREWERY/COMPANY: Free House.
PRINCIPAL BEERS: Courage Best & Directors, John Smiths, Ruddles Best. **FACILITIES:** Children welcome Garden: outdoor eating Dogs allowed. **ROOMS:** 5 bedrooms 5 en suite s£30-£35 d£45-£50

CHARD
Map 03 ST30

The Happy Return
East St TA20 1EP ☎ 01460 63152
Dir: From M5 Taunton, take Ilminster rd then follow signs to Chard, L at junct with A30 into East Street. Pub on R
A friendly local with a warm welcome and straightforward selection of bar food. Be sure to sample the pies. The chef has twice been Steak and Kidney Pie Champion, and also won Pie of the Century in 2000.

Hornsbury Hill
Eleighwater TA20 3AQ ☎ 01460 63317 📠 01460 63317
Dir: A358 to Chard. Pub 2m
More restaurant than pub housed in a 200-year-old corn mill and museum and set in five acres of landscaped water gardens. Good comfortable bar, real ales and bedrooms.

CHEW MAGNA

Pony & Trap 𝄞
Newtown BS40 8TQ ☎ 01275 332627
Refurbished 200-year-old rural pub enjoying a peaceful
hillside location with beautiful views across the Chew Valley
from the rear garden. Good informal pubby atmosphere, a
warm welcome and traditional home-cooked food await in the
bar. Typical dishes range from beef casserole, fish pie and
breaded plaice to salmon in white wine sauce, and fillet steak.
OPEN: 12-11. **BAR MEALS:** L served all week. D served all week
12-2 7-9.30. Av main course £6.50.
BREWERY/COMPANY: Ushers. **PRINCIPAL BEERS:** Ushers
Best, Butcombe Bitter. **FACILITIES:** Children welcome Garden:
patio, outdoor eating Dogs allowed. **NOTES:** Parking 50

CHURCHILL   Map 03 ST45

Pick of the Pubs

Crown Inn
The Batch, Skinners Ln BS25 5PP ☎ 01934 852995
Dir: Take A38 S of Bristol. Turn R at Churchill traffic lights, then
1st L
Totally unspoilt gem of a stone-built pub situated at the
base of the Mendip Hills and close to invigorating local
walks. Originally a coaching stop on the old Bristol to
Exeter route, it once housed the village grocer's and
butcher's shop before real ale became its main
commodity. Today, an ever-changing range of local brews
are tapped straight from the barrel in the two rustic stone-
walled and flagstone-floored bars. Bag a table by the open
fire and sample, perhaps, a pint of RCH PG Steam Bitter
from Weston-super-Mare. Freshly prepared food is served
at lunchtime only, the blackboard listing rare beef
sandwiches, filled jacket potatoes, cauliflower cheeses,
locally-caught trout and popular casseroles. Peaceful front
terrace for summer alfresco sipping.
OPEN: 11.30-11. **BAR MEALS:** L served all week 12-2.30.
BREWERY/COMPANY: Free House.
PRINCIPAL BEERS: Bass, Palmers IPA, guest ales.
FACILITIES: Children welcome Garden: Food served
outside Dogs allowed. **NOTES:** Parking 20 No credit cards

CHURCHINFORD   Map 03 ST21

The York Inn ◆◆◆◆ 🕮
Honiton Rd TA3 7RF ☎ 01823 601333
e-mail: enquiries@the-york-inn.freeserve.co.uk
Dir: Exit M5 J26, towards Wellington for 0.5m, 1st L at rdbt. 1m L onto
Ford St, 2m at top of hill L, 4m phone box, R to Inn
Traditional inn with beams and an inglenook fireplace, dating
from around 1600 and located in an Area of Outstanding
Natural Beauty. There is a lively locals bar serving freshly
prepared snacks and a separate dining room, where the
emphasis is on fresh seafood and locally supplied game.
Options include king scallops with garlic butter, mussels
marinière, and turbot fillets with seafood sauce.
OPEN: 12-3 6-11. **BAR MEALS:** L served Tue-Sun. D served
Mon-Sat 12-3 7-11. Av main course £5.50. **RESTAURANT:** L
served Tue-Sun. D served Mon-Sat 12-3 7-11. Av 3 course à la
carte £22. **BREWERY/COMPANY:** Free House.
PRINCIPAL BEERS: Otter Ale. **FACILITIES:** Garden: flowered
courtyard, Food served outside Dogs allowed. **NOTES:** Parking
12. **ROOMS:** 3 bedrooms 3 en suite s£32 d£48

CLEVEDON

The Black Horse
Clevedon Ln, Clapton-in-Gordano BS20 7RH
☎ 01275 842105
Flagstoned, 14th-century pub, once the village lock-up, tucked
down country lanes close to the M5 (J19). Genuine unspoilt
atmosphere in historic bar. Real ales from the cask; simple bar
food.

COMBE HAY   Map 03 ST75

Pick of the Pubs

The Wheatsheaf ◆◆◆◆ 🕮
BA2 7EG ☎ 01225 833504 🖷 01225 833504
e-mail: Pete@wheatsheaf.co.uk
Dir: Take A369 Exeter rd from Bath to Odd Down, turn L at park
towards Combe Hay. Follow lane for approx 2m to thatched
cottage & turn L

Nestling on a hillside overlooking a peaceful valley, 2
miles south of Bath off the A367, the 17th-century
Wheatsheaf is a pretty, black and white timbered pub,
adorned with flowers in summer, and featuring an
attractively landscaped terraced garden, an ideal spot for
summer imbibing.
New owner, Peter Wilkins, took over in November 2000
and has maintained the unspoilt character of the rambling
bar, complete with massive solid wooden tables, sporting
prints and open log fire. Food on the varied carte features
home-cooked dishes, notably local game in season and
fresh fish. Typical choices may include ploughman's
lunches, terrines, and locally caught trout, in addition to
roast rack of lamb, breast of pheasant stuffed with cream
cheese, mushrooms and garlic, and chicken filled with
crab and prawns and wrapped in bacon. Comfortable
overnight accommodation in a converted stable block.
OPEN: 11-2.30 6-10.30 (Sun 12-3,7-10.30). Closed 25-26 Dec,
Jan 1. **BAR MEALS:** L served all week. D served all week
12-2 6.30-9.30. Av main course £10. **RESTAURANT:** L
served all week. D served all week 12-2 6.30-9.30. Av 3 course
à la carte £17. **BREWERY/COMPANY:** Free House.
PRINCIPAL BEERS: Courage Best, John Smith, Greene King
Old Speckled Hen. **FACILITIES:** Children welcome
Children's licence Garden: pond, outdoor eating, patio,
Dogs allowed on leads. **NOTES:** Parking 100.
ROOMS: 3 bedrooms 3 en suite s£50 d£75 FR£95

COMPTON MARTIN

Ring of Bells
Main St BS40 6JE ☎ 01761 221284
e-mail: roger@ring47.freeserve.co.uk
Village pub with views of the Mendip Hills and the coast.
Family-friendly; good ales (Butcombe); bar food and daily
specials using local produce.

CRANMORE
Map 03 ST64

Strode Arms 🐦 ♀
BA4 4QJ ☎ 01749 880450 📠 01749 880598
Dir: S of A361, 3.5m E of Shepton Mallet, 7.5m W of Frome
Rambling, mostly 15th-century building, a farmhouse
and coaching inn, with a splendid front terrace overlooking the
village duck pond. Spacious bar areas are neatly laid-out with
comfortable country furnishings and warmed by open log
fires. Both the varied printed menu and daily specials draw
local diners and visitors to the nearby East Somerset Railway.
From the board order, perhaps, smoked haddock and cod
fishcakes, peppered rib of beef with a shallot and red wine
sauce, braised lambs' heart with lemon and lime stuffing and,
for pudding, a home-made coconut and orange tart.
OPEN: 11.30-2.30 6.30-11.30. **BAR MEALS:** L served all week. D
served Mon-Sat 12-2 7-9.30. Av main course £8.
RESTAURANT: L served all week. D served Mon-Sat 12-2 7-9.30.
Av 3 course à la carte £13.50. **BREWERY/COMPANY:** Free
House. **PRINCIPAL BEERS:** Flowers IPA, Wadworth 6X,
Marston's Pedigree. **FACILITIES:** Children welcome Garden:
patio, outdoor eating Dogs allowed. **NOTES:** Parking 24

CREWKERNE
Map 03 ST40

The Manor Arms ♦♦♦ ♀
North Perrott TA18 7SG ☎ 01460 72901 📠 01460 72901
*Dir: From A30 (Yeovil/Honiton rd) take A3066 towards Bridport, N
Perrott 1.5m further on*
On the Dorset-Somerset border, this 16th-century Grade II
listed pub and its neighbouring hamstone cottages overlook
the village green. The popular River Parrett trail runs by the
door. The inn has been lovingly restored and an inglenook
fireplace, flagstone floors and oak beams are among the
charming features inside. Bar food includes steak and ale pie,
pork roulade and seafood crumble, while the specials board
might highlight whole plaice, chicken supreme and fillet steak
medallions. Most of the bedrooms are located in a converted
coach house.

OPEN: 11.30-2.30 (Sun 12-2.30 7-10.30) 6.45-11.00.
BAR MEALS: L served all week. D served all week 12-1.45 7-9. Av
main course £5.25. **RESTAURANT:** L served all week. D served
all week 12-1.45 7-9. Av 3 course à la carte £18.
BREWERY/COMPANY: Free House. *continued*

PRINCIPAL BEERS: Butcombe, Otter. **FACILITIES:** Children
welcome Children's licence Garden: outdoor eating.
NOTES: Parking 20. **ROOMS:** 8 bedrooms 8 en suite s£35 d£42
FR£52-£58

CROSCOMBE

The Bull Terrier ♦♦♦
Long St BA5 3QJ ☎ 01749 343658
e-mail: barry.vidler@bullterrierpub.co.uk
Dir: half way between Wells & Shepton Mallet on the A371
One of Somerset's oldest pubs, formerly the Rose & Crown,
first licensed in 1612. The building dates from the late 15th
century, though the fireplace and ceiling in the inglenook bar
were added in the 16th century. One menu is offered
throughout, including snacks, steaks, curry, and home-made
pies.
OPEN: 12-2.30 7-11 (Sun 12-2.30, 7-10.30). **BAR MEALS:** L
served all week. D served all week 12-2 7-9. Av main course £7.25.
RESTAURANT: L served all week. D served all week 12-2 7-9. Av
3 course à la carte £14. **BREWERY/COMPANY:** Free House.
PRINCIPAL BEERS: Butcombe, Courage Directors, Marstons
Pedigree, Greene King Old Speckled Hen. **FACILITIES:** Garden:
patio/terrace, outdoor eating. **NOTES:** Parking 3.
ROOMS: 2 bedrooms 2 en suite s£30 d£48

DINNINGTON
Map 03 ST41

Rose & Crown Inn
TA17 8SX ☎ 01460 52397
Dir: N of A30 between Crewkerne & Chard
Licensed for over 250 years, this traditional village pub is
situated on the old Fosse Way, and has a very relaxed
atmosphere and friendly locals. An ideal location for cycling
and walking. Local beers available.

DITCHEAT
Map 03 ST63

The Manor House Inn ♦♦♦♦ ♀
BA4 6RB ☎ 01749 860276
*Dir: from Shepton Mallet take the Castle Cary road, after 3m R to
Ditcheat*

Over the years since its first appearance as The White Hart,
this red-brick pub has had a number of names, but the current
owners choose to subtitle it "The Heart of Somerset
Hospitality." A typical menu offers grilled tiger prawns, prime
Scottish fillet, roast Somerset duck breast with fig and port
wine sauce, and rack of English lamb. There are also light
luncheons, ciabattas, and specials. Three rooms to let.
continued

England

OPEN: 12-2.30 6.30-11. **BAR MEALS:** L served all week. D served all week 12-2 7-9.30. Av main course £6.95.
RESTAURANT: L served all week. D served all week 12-2 7-9.30. Av 3 course à la carte £22. **BREWERY/COMPANY:** Free House.
PRINCIPAL BEERS: Butcombe, Fullers London Pride, John Smiths. **FACILITIES:** Garden: Food served outside Dogs allowed. **NOTES:** Parking 25. **ROOMS:** 3 bedrooms 3 en suite s£35 d£65 FR£85-£95

EAST COKER
Map 03 ST51

The Helyar Arms ♦♦♦♦
Moor Ln BA22 9JR ☎ 01935 862332 🖃 01935 864129
e-mail: info@helyar-arms.co.uk
Dir: from Yeovil, take A30 or A37, follow signs for East Coker

This Grade II listed inn, parts of which date back to 1460, takes its name from Archdeacon Helyar, once owner of Coker Court and chaplain to Elizabeth I. The village churchyard is the resting place of American poet T.S. Eliot. Somerset chicken, fisherman's pie, pork with a herb crust, or game in season might feature on the imaginative menu. Bedrooms are all en suite and feature many useful facilities.
OPEN: 11.30-3 (Sun 12-3, 6-10.30) 6-11. **BAR MEALS:** L served all week. D served all week 12-2.30 6.30-9.30. Av main course £7.
RESTAURANT: L served all week. D served all week 12-2.30 6.30-9.30. Av 3 course à la carte £15.
BREWERY/COMPANY: Inn Partnership.
PRINCIPAL BEERS: Bass, Flowers Original, Fullers London Pride, Greene King IPA. **FACILITIES:** Garden: outdoor eating, BBQ.
NOTES: Parking 40. **ROOMS:** 6 bedrooms 6 en suite s£59 d£70

Exmoor Ales
'Nectar of the Gods'
William Hancock started brewing at the Golden Hill Brewery in Wiveliscombe in 1807. Hancock's, after merging with Arnolds, was a large concern in the 1920s. In 1955 it was taken over, and then closed four years later. After twenty years of beer-related inactivity Exmoor Ales took over the premises and began producing brews. Within a year the infant operation had won 'Best Bitter' at the 1980 Great British Beer Festival, and things have kept on getting better. The current crop of moorland wildlife-inspired brews includes Exmoor Hart (4.8%), Exmoor Stag (5.2%), Exmoor Wildcat (4.4%) and Exmoor Fox (4.2%).

EXFORD
Map 03 SS83

Pick of the Pubs

The Crown Inn ◎ ◎ ★ ★ ★ 🐾 ♀
TA24 7PP ☎ 01643 831554 🖃 01643 831665
e-mail: bradleyhotelsexmoor@easynet.co.uk
Dir: From M5 J25 follow signs for Taunton. Take A358 then B3224 via Wheddon Cross to Exford

A charming coaching inn dating back to the 16th century situated in the heart of Exmoor National Park, with Exford's village green to the front and a spacious, mature water and terrace garden to the rear where outdoor eating is a pleasure in summer. Hotel bedrooms look out over this pretty moorland village. The cosy bar and a smart dining-room set with crisp white table linen each have their own menus bristling with imaginative ideas and making full use of local produce.
In the bar at lunch or in the evening look for pressed terrine of venison with apple and saffron chutney and flat mushroom, spinach and goats' cheese pithivier before baked halibut with asparagus, spring onions and sage oil, herb-encrusted chicken with ratatouille and olive oil mash and calves' liver with pea purée and pancetta; rounding off with dark chocolate delice or West Country cheeses. More formal dinners and Sunday lunch are served at fixed prices in the restaurant.
OPEN: 11-3 6-11. **BAR MEALS:** L served all week. D served all week 12-2 6.30-9.30. Av main course £10.
RESTAURANT: L served Sun. D served all week 12-2 7-9. Av 3 course à la carte £25. Av 4 course fixed price £32.50.
BREWERY/COMPANY: Free House.
PRINCIPAL BEERS: Exmoor Ale, Fox & Gold, Flowers.
FACILITIES: Children welcome Garden: outdoor eating, patio, Dogs allowed Water. **NOTES:** Parking 20.
ROOMS: 17 bedrooms 17 en suite s£47.50 d£80

FAULKLAND
Map 03 ST75

The Faulkland Inn NEW
BA3 5UX ☎ 01373 834312
e-mail: enquiries@faulkland-inn.co.uk
Dir: On the A366 between Radstock and Trowbridge, 17M from Bristol & the M4/M5
Family-run coaching inn set in a village complete with a green, stocks, standing stones and pond. The style of cooking is unique to the area, with a modern international approach, utilising local fish, game and cheese. Weekly menus range through various platters, pasta, curry and chargrilled steaks in the bar, and restaurant dishes such as noisettes of wild boar, haggis and red onion tart with brandy and peppercorn sauce.

continued

OPEN: 12-3 6-11. **BAR MEALS:** L served all week. D served all week 12-2 7-10. Av main course £5.50. **RESTAURANT:** L served all week. D served all week 12-2 7-9.30. Av 3 course à la carte £18.50. **BREWERY/COMPANY:** Free House. **PRINCIPAL BEERS:** Butcombe, Ruddles, Wells Bombardier. **FACILITIES:** Garden: food served outside. **NOTES:** Parking 30. **ROOMS:** 3 bedrooms 3 en suite d£35

Tuckers Grave
Faulkland BA3 5XF ☎ 01373 834230
Tapped ales and farm cider in Somerset's smallest pub. Tiny atmospheric bar with old settles. Lunchtime sandwiches and ploughman's lunches.

FITZHEAD   Map 03 ST12

Fitzhead Inn
TA4 3JP ☎ 01823 400667
Cosy 250-year-old pub hidden away in the Vale of Taunton. Numerous pictures and plates adorn the walls. Expect a relaxed atmosphere, good real ales including local beer, and appetising home-cooked food. Typical dishes might include rack of lamb, John Dory, shellfish platter or fillet steak.
OPEN: 12-2 7-11. **BAR MEALS:** L served all week. D served all week 12-2 7-9.45. Av main course £6.50. **RESTAURANT:** L served all week. D served all week 12-2 7-9.45. Av 3 course à la carte £16.50. **BREWERY/COMPANY:** Free House. **PRINCIPAL BEERS:** Cotleigh Tawny, Fullers London Pride, Juwards Ales. **FACILITIES:** Children welcome Garden: food served outside Dogs allowed. **ROOMS:** 4 bedrooms 4 en suite No credit cards

---

FRESHFORD   Map 03 ST76

The Inn at Freshford
BA3 6EG ☎ 01225 722250   📠 01225 723887
e-mail: dwillbob32@aol.com
Dir: 1m from A36 between Beckington & Limpley Stoke
Traditional 17th-century inn with log fires, located in the Limpley Valley. The area is ideal walking country, especially down by the Kennet & Avon Canal. Extensive gardens.
OPEN: 11-3 6-11. **BAR MEALS:** L served all week. D served all week 12-2 6-9. **RESTAURANT:** L served all week. D served all week 12-2 6-9. Av 3 course à la carte £14. **BREWERY/COMPANY:** Latona Leisure. **PRINCIPAL BEERS:** Courage Cask, Wadworth 6X, Marstons Pedigree. **FACILITIES:** Children welcome Garden: food served outside. **NOTES:** Parking 60

FROME   Map 03 ST74

The Horse & Groom
East Woodlands BA11 5LY ☎ 01373 462802
📠 01373 462802
e-mail: horse.and.groom@care4free.net
Dir: Just off Frome by-pass (A361 Shepton Mallet/Devizes rd)
You'll find this charming country pub down a narrow lane, opposite a farm, and fronted by five pollarded limes. Pine pews and settles stand on the flagstone floor by a huge inglenook fireplace in the bar, while the carpeted lounge provides easy chairs and a sofa. The new owners offer an interesting range of dishes, from liver and bacon to lemon sole Louisiana, with peppers, banana and garlic.
continued

OPEN: 11.30-2.30 (Sun 12-3, 7-10) 6.30-11. **BAR MEALS:** L served Tue-Sun. D served Tue-Sat 12-2 6.30-9. Av main course £6.50. **RESTAURANT:** L served Tue-Sun. D served Tue-Sat 12-2 6.30-9. Av 3 course à la carte £15. **PRINCIPAL BEERS:** Wadworth 6X, Greene King IPA, Butcombe, Branscombe Branoc. **FACILITIES:** Children welcome Garden: food served outside Dogs allowed Water. **NOTES:** Parking 15

Pick of the Pubs

The Talbot Inn ⊕ ♦♦♦♦
High St, Mells BA11 3PN ☎ 01373 812254
📠 01373 813599
Dir: From A36(T), R onto A361 to Frome, then A362 towards Radstock, 0.5m then L to Mells 2.5m
At the heart of this timeless feudal village with its splendid church, magnificent manor house and unspoilt stone cottages is the Talbot Inn, a rambling, 15th-century coaching inn with an attractive courtyard and a series of friendly bars. Expect terracotta-painted stone walls, old ceiling beams, country prints, excellent real ales, and reliable home-cooked food, the latter including ravioli of wild mushroom with lemon and tarragon sauce, chicken liver parfait, cod with tomato, basil, olive and garlic crust, chargrilled steaks and banana cheesecake. Good light snacks. Well furnished and comfortable en suite accommodation.
OPEN: 12-2.30 6-11. Closed 25-26 Dec. **BAR MEALS:** L served all week. D served all week 12-2.30 7-12. Av main course £5.50. **RESTAURANT:** L served all week. D served all week 12-2.30 7-12. Av 3 course à la carte £20. **BREWERY/COMPANY:** Free House. **PRINCIPAL BEERS:** Bass, Butcombe Bitter. **FACILITIES:** Children welcome Garden: Cottage garden Dogs allowed. **NOTES:** Parking 10. **ROOMS:** 7 bedrooms 7 en suite s£45 d£75

The White Hart
Trudoxhill BA11 5DP ☎ 01373 836324
Home of the Ash Vine Brewery (visits by arrangement). Bustling village pub with open-plan bar, extensive menu, farm cider and country wines.

GLASTONBURY   Map 03 ST53

The Who'd a Thought It Inn
17 Northload St BA6 9JJ ☎ 01458 834460
📠 01458 831039
Dir: Bottom of High St, 100yds from Abbey ruins
18th-century building with lots of local artefacts and interesting memorabilia. One wall is covered in old photographs and there is even an award-winning gents loo. Bedrooms.

HASELBURY PLUCKNETT   Map 03 ST41

Pick of the Pubs

The Haselbury Inn 🕮 ♉
North St TA18 7RJ ☎ 01460 72488 📠 01460 72488
e-mail: howard@hasleburyinn.fsnet.co.uk
Dir: Just off A30 between Crewkerne & Yeovil on B3066

Situated just off the A30 east of Yeovil, this extended
roadside pub enjoys an attractive village setting on the
Dorset/Somerset border. The buildings were originally
used for the manufacture of sails and flax for ships.
Comfortable, open plan bar with plenty of exposed stone
and brickwork, and warming open fires; separate rear
restaurant. From Lyme Bay crab pot, roast rack of lamb on
bubble-and-squeak rösti with redcurrant jus, and good
steaks and grills on the main menu, daily dishes may
include whole plaice with hand-cut chips, venison with rich
Madeira sauce, and stir-fried lamb and vegetables.

OPEN: 11.45-2.30 6-11 (closed Mon). **BAR MEALS:** L
served Tue-Sun. D served Tue-Sun 12-2 6.15-9.30. Av main
course £8.50. **RESTAURANT:** L served Tue-Sun. D served
Tue-Sun 12-2 6.15-9.30. Av 3 course à la carte £8.50. Av 3
course fixed price £8.50. **BREWERY/COMPANY:** Free
House. **PRINCIPAL BEERS:** Palmers IPA, Ringwood True
Glory, Fullers London Pride, Greene King Old Speckled hen.
FACILITIES: Garden: outdoor eating. **NOTES:** Parking 50

HINTON ST GEORGE   Map 03 ST41

The Lord Poulett Arms ♦♦♦♦ 🕮 ♉
High St TA17 8SE ☎ 01460 73149
e-mail: lordpoulett@aol.com
Dir: 2m N of Crewkerne, 1.5m S of A303

17th-century thatched hamstone inn with sunny beer garden
and a roaring fire in the bar during winter months. Facilities
also include a private dining/meeting room and four letting
bedrooms. Regular folk and blues evenings. Strong emphasis
on home-cooked food with seasonal produce incorporated
into the regularly-changing menu and specials board. Dishes
range from rack of lamb and pork tenderloin in a Dijon
mustard sauce to beef chilli and Hinton cod.
OPEN: 11.30-2.30 6.30-11 (Sun 12-2.30, 7-10.30).
BAR MEALS: L served Tue-Sun. D served Tue-Sun 12-2.30 7-11.
Av main course £7.50. **RESTAURANT:** L served Tue-Sun. D
served Tue-Sun 12-2.30 7-10. Av 3 course à la carte £12.50.
BREWERY/COMPANY: Free House.
PRINCIPAL BEERS: Butcombe Bitter, Otter Ale, Wadworth 6X.
FACILITIES: Children welcome Garden: outdoor eating Dogs
allowed Water tap. **NOTES:** Parking 10. **ROOMS:** 4 bedrooms
4 en suite s£25 d£38

ILCHESTER   Map 03 ST52

Ilchester Arms ♉
The Square BA22 8LN ☎ 01935 840220 📠 01935 841353
e-mail: info@ilchesterarmshotel.co.uk
Dir: From A303 take A37 to Ilchester/Yeovil, L towards Ilchester at 2nd
sign marked Ilchester. Hotel 100yds on R

Elegant, ivy-clad Georgian building in the town square,
featuring flagstone floors, oak beams and open fires
throughout its neat interior. The hotel offers brasserie-style
meals in the bar and a more serious menu in the restaurant,
featuring traditional and Caribbean cuisine along with an
extensive wine list.
OPEN: 11-11. **BAR MEALS:** L served all week. D served all week
12-2.30. Av main course £7.50. **RESTAURANT:** D served all
week 7-9.30/10. Av 3 course à la carte £22.50.
BREWERY/COMPANY: Free House.
PRINCIPAL BEERS: Regularly changing guest ales from local
breweries. **FACILITIES:** Children welcome Garden: BBQ Dogs
allowed in garden. **NOTES:** Parking 25. **ROOMS:** 8 bedrooms
8 en suite s£50 d£75

ILMINSTER   Map 03 ST31

New Inn
Dowlish Wake TA19 0NZ ☎ 01460 52413
Dir: From Ilminster follow signs for Kingstone then Dowlish Wake

A 350-year-old stone-built pub tucked away in a quiet village
close to Perry's thatched cider mill. There are two bars with
woodburning stoves, bar billiards and a skittle alley. The menu
features local produce and West Country specialities, including
fish, steaks and home-made pies.
OPEN: 11-3 (Sun 12-3, 7-10.30) 6-11. **BAR MEALS:** L served all
week. D served all week 12-2.30 7-9.30. Av main course £6.50.
BREWERY/COMPANY: Free House.
PRINCIPAL BEERS: Butcombe Bitter and guest beers.
FACILITIES: Children welcome Garden: outdoor eating, Dogs
allowed. **NOTES:** Parking 50

Brewing's Capital
The fame of Burton upon Trent rests on
the hard water of its springs. The monks made
good beer here in the Middle Ages and by the 17th
century Burton beer was being exported to London.
The 18th-century improvement of the River Trent
navigation opened a route through Hull to the Baltic
and Russia, where Catherine the Great was
exceedingly fond of strong, sweet Burton ale, while the
Mersey and Trent Canal led to Liverpool and the
passage to India. The railway's arrival in 1839 spurred
vigorous expansion, led by the Bass dynasty. Other
famous Burton names included Worthington, Allsop,
Marston and Evershed, and firms from London and
the South built Burton breweries to use the local
water. Ind Coope has been there for many years.
Today the Bass Museum of Brewing and the
Heritage Brewery Museum open
windows on the industry's past.

PICK OF THE PUBS

OPEN: 11-3 6-11.
BAR MEALS: L served all week.
D served all week 12-7-9.30
(9 Sun). Av main course £5.50
(lunch), £11 (dinner).
BREWERY/COMPANY:
Free House.
PRINCIPAL BEERS: Cotleigh Barn
Owl, Otter Ale, Cottage Golden
Arrow, Fullers London Pride.
FACILITIES: Children welcome, no
children under 12 after 8pm.
Garden: outdoor eating.
NOTES: Parking 16.

The Kingsdon Inn

♀

TA11 7LG
☎ 01935 840543
Dir: From A303 take A372 towards
Langport, then B3151 towards Street, 1st
R and R again

Picture-postcard pretty thatched cottage located in an equally attractive village, just a few minutes drive from the A303 at Podimore Island. Weary travellers will find it the perfect retreat for a good home-cooked lunch or supper, especially in the summer front garden with peaceful pastoral views.

A flower-edged path leads to the front door of this delightful 300-year-old cottage and into a rambling, equally charming interior. Older original front rooms have low-beamed ceilings, a huge stone inglenook (not used), scrubbed pine and old stripped tables and chairs and a warm decor, while the lower bar has a blazing log fire on a raised hearth on cooler days. Expect a warm welcome and a convivial atmosphere in which to enjoy some good bar food listed on separate short lunch and evening blackboards that change on a daily basis and feature fresh fish and game in season.

At lunchtime, in addition to reliable pub favourites like battered cod, Stilton ploughman's and steak and kidney pie, there may be leek, Stilton and walnut flan, served with a good dressed salad, pork and herb sausages with mash and onion gravy, and pheasant casserole. Evening dishes extend the choice to king prawns in lime and ginger, baked whole sea bass, wild rabbit in Dijon mustard sauce, beef Stroganoff, roast rack of lamb with port and redcurrant sauce, and grilled wild salmon with hollandaise, all accompanied by hearty bowls of freshly cooked vegetables. Round off with sticky ginger pudding with ginger ice cream.

West Country ales - Cotleigh, Otter, Cottage - take pride of place at the bar, alongside 20 malt whiskies and a fair range of wines; six by the glass. All-in-all, a great village local serving enjoyable food and presided over by a welcoming landlord.

KILVE
Map 03 ST14

The Hood Arms ◆◆◆◆
TA5 1EA ☎ 01278 741210 📄 01278 741477
e-mail: Mattbri@tinyworld.co.uk
Dir: Off A39 between Bridgwater & Minehead

Traditional 17th-century coaching inn, set among the Quantock Hills, and a popular watering hole for walkers. Kilve Beach is within a short walking distance, past an old priory thought to have been the haunt of smugglers.

A typical menu includes steak and ale pie, grills, panfried salmon on lattice crisps, trout with apple and almond butter and swordfish with white wine. Accommodation includes two self-catering cottages.

OPEN: 11-3 6-11. **BAR MEALS:** L served all week. D served all week 12-3 6-9.30. Av main course £6.45. **RESTAURANT:** L served Sun. D served Fri-Sun 12-3 6-9.30. Av 3 course à la carte £15. **BREWERY/COMPANY:** Free House. **PRINCIPAL BEERS:** Exmoor Ale, Wadworth 6X, Otter Ale, Exmoor Fox. **FACILITIES:** Children welcome Children's licence Garden: outdoor eating, patio, Dogs allowed Some areas, Water. **NOTES:** Parking 12. **ROOMS:** 6 bedrooms 6 en suite s£38 d£52 FR£62-£75

KINGSDON
Map 03 ST52

Pick of the Pubs

Kingsdon Inn ♀
TA11 7LG ☎ 01935 840543
See Pick of the Pubs on page 385

Horse-brasses
Delightful and attractive as they are, horse-brasses are nothing like as old as is generally believed. The working horse in a harness gleaming with ornamental hanging brasses is a creature of the period since 1850. The brasses were mass-produced folk art, following the earlier precedent of the heraldic badges worn by the carriage horses of aristocratic families. Favourite symbols include the sun, the moon, the stars and such heraldic creatures as the lion, the stag, the unicorn and the eagle, as well as railway locomotives and ships.

KNAPP
Map 03 ST32

The Rising Sun Inn
TA3 6BG ☎ 01823 490436 📄 01823 490436
Dir: M5 J25, A358 then A378 follow signs for North Curry/Knapp
A Grade II listed Somerset longhouse with roots in the 13th century, the building has been put to a multitude of uses over the centuries before finally becoming a pub in the 1960s.

LANGLEY MARSH
Map 03 ST02

The Three Horseshoes 🐑
TA4 2UL ☎ 01984 623763 📄 01984 623763
Dir: M5 J25 take B3227 to Wiveliscombe. From square follow signs for Langley Marsh. 1m
Handsome 300-year-old red sandstone village inn, full of old motoring memorabilia, collections of banknotes, model aeroplanes and beer mats, and sturdy rustic furnishings. Lively locals' bar with traditional games, decent ales and local farmhouse cider. Food is genuinely home made, with vegetables from the garden, and definitely no chips or fried food on the hand-written menu. Hearty dishes include filled baps and potatoes, thick soups, pizzas and good pies, casseroles and steaks. Daily specials feature fresh fish and imaginative vegetarian and vegan meals.
OPEN: 12-2.30 7-11 (closed Mon Oct-Mar). **BAR MEALS:** L served all week. D served all week 12-2 7-9.30. Av main course £4.95. **RESTAURANT:** L served all week. D served all week 12-2.30 7-9.30. **BREWERY/COMPANY:** Free House. **PRINCIPAL BEERS:** Palmers IPA, Otter Ale, Fullers London Pride, Adnams Southwold. **FACILITIES:** Garden: outdoor eating. **NOTES:** Parking 6

LANGPORT
Map 03 ST42

The Halfway House
Pitney TA10 9AB ☎ 01458 252513
Dir: on B3153 between Langport and Somerton
An excellent choice of real ales on tap and bottled Continental beers draws customers to this delightfully old-fashioned rural pub. Three homely rooms boast open fires, books and games; no music or electronic games. Home-cooked meals include soups, sausages, sandwiches and a good selection of curries in the evening.
OPEN: 11.30-3 5.30-11. Closed 25 Dec. **BAR MEALS:** L served Mon-Sat. D served Mon-Sat 12-2 7-9.30. Av main course £3. **BREWERY/COMPANY:** Free House. **PRINCIPAL BEERS:** Butcombe, Teignworthy, Otter, Cotleigh Tawny. **FACILITIES:** Children welcome Garden: outdoor eating, Dogs allowed. **NOTES:** Parking 30

Rose & Crown
Huish Episcopi TA10 9QT ☎ 01458 250494
Boasting a licensee who was actually born on the premises, this thatched pub is a picture of traditional English hospitality which has been in the same family for over 130 years. A great area for walks and story-telling with the locals. The pub has a wide selection of old pub games, and local farm cider and cider-brandy is available. Typical menu includes spinach lasagne, Stilton and broccoli tart, steak and ale pie, and pork, apple and cider cobbler.
OPEN: 11.30-2.30 5.30-11 (Fri-Sat 11.30-11, Sun 12-10.30). **BAR MEALS:** L served all week. D served all week 12-2 6-8.30. Av main course £5.75. **BREWERY/COMPANY:** Free House. **PRINCIPAL BEERS:** Teignworthy Reel Ale, Bass, Hop Back Summer Lightning, Butcombe Bitter. **FACILITIES:** Children welcome Garden: outdoor eating, Dogs allowed Water. **NOTES:** Parking 50 No credit cards

LEIGH-ON-MENDIP

The Bell Inn ♈
BA3 5QQ ☎ 01373 812316 📠 01373 812163
Dir: *head for Bath, then twrds Radstock following the Frome Rd, turn twrds Mells and then Leigh-on-Mendip*
Situated on the old pilgrims' route to Glastonbury, this historic inn has a fireplace dating back to 1687, built by the same stonemasons who constructed the church. Traditional pub grub - snacks, home-made pies, lasagne - are offered alongside some not so traditional dishes, including sticky Chinese chicken, and cod en croute with provençale sauce.
OPEN: 12-3 6.30-11. **BAR MEALS:** L served all week. D served all week 12-2 6.30-9. Av main course £7. **RESTAURANT:** L served all week. D served all week 12-2 6.30-9. Av 3 course à la carte £15. **BREWERY/COMPANY:** Free House.
PRINCIPAL BEERS: Wadworth 6X, Bass, Butcombe.
FACILITIES: Children welcome Garden: patio, outdoor eating.
NOTES: Parking 20

LITTON   Map 03 ST55

The Kings Arms
BA3 4PW ☎ 01761 241301
Full of nooks and crannies, this 15th-century local at the heart of the Mendips has a large garden with a stream running through it, and boasts a separate children's play area and outdoor eating. Menus offer smoked haddock fish pie, homemade chilli, and steak, mushroom and Guinness pie. Kings Arms Platters include Pigman's Platter - jumbo pork Lincolnshire sausage with eggs and chips.

OPEN: 11-2.30 6-11. **BAR MEALS:** L served all week. D served all week 12-2.30 6.30-10. Av main course £6.50.
BREWERY/COMPANY: Free House. **PRINCIPAL BEERS:** Bass, Butcombe, Wadworth 6X. **FACILITIES:** Children welcome Garden: patio, outdoor eating Dogs allowed on lead at all times.
NOTES: Parking 50

The River Parrett Trail
The River Parrett Trail was devised to link the gentle hill country of the Dorset border with the fragile wetlands of the Somerset Levels and Moors. The final stretch follows the winding river towards Bridgwater Bay and the Bristol Channel. Taking you to the heart of this unspoilt corner of England, the 50-mile trail can be completed either as a comfortable walk over three or four days, or as a series of shorter rambles which allow time to discover and explore the varied landscapes en route. Along the way you'll find old mills, medieval churches and historic sites, as well as the withy beds and willow plantations at the heart of Somerset's willow-growing and basket-making industry. Ideally-placed pubs on the route of the trail include the delightful 16th-century Manor Arms at North Perrott, the 400-year-old Royal Oak at Over Stratton, and the cottage-style Rose & Crown at Stoke St Gregory.

LOWER VOBSTER   Map 03 ST74

Vobster Inn 🐑
BA3 5RJ ☎ 01373 812920 📠 01373 812350
e-mail: vobsterinn@bt.com
Set in four acres in rolling countryside close to Bath, the Vobster Inn is a 17th-century Mendip stone building with a large garden featuring a popular summer barbeque and boules pitch. In addition to 'small plates' - fish and chips, cauliflower cheese, beef lasagne - the interesting menu may list lamb steak with rosemary and garlic, steak au poivre and fresh Cornish seafood, perhaps oven-roasted sea bass with rosemary and sea salt, roast cod with Mediterranean vegetables and Fowey mussels with tomato, garlic and white wine.

OPEN: 12-3 7-11. **BAR MEALS:** L served all week. D served all week 12-2 7-10. Av main course £8.50. **RESTAURANT:** L served all week. D served all week 12-2 7-11. Av 3 course à la carte £15. **BREWERY/COMPANY:** Free House.
PRINCIPAL BEERS: Butcombe, Courage Best, Wadworth 6X, JCB. **FACILITIES:** Children welcome Garden: Beer garden, patio, outdoor eating Dogs allowed. **NOTES:** Parking 45

England

Pick of the Pubs

Royal Oak Inn 🐑 ♀
TA23 0SH ☎ 01984 640319 📠 01984 641561
e-mail: royaloakof.luxborough@virgin.net
Dir: From A38 (Taunton/Minehead) at Washford take minor rd S thru Roadwater

Tucked away in a small Brendon Hills hamlet at the edge of Exmoor's National Park, the part-thatched Royal Oak is a truly rural and unspoilt 14th-century inn. New owners have maintained the rustic atmosphere that makes this place so popular, in particular the slate-floored main bar with its low beams, large open fireplace and hatchway bar. Adjoining dining areas are tastefully decorated in deep greens and reds and adorned with hunting prints.

Food ranges from hearty snacks for famished walkers to classic country dishes featuring seasonal game and fresh fish from Scotland, London and Brixham. After home-made soups come a selection of sandwiches and ploughman's feasts, steak and ale pie, and Thai salmon and crab cakes, supplemented at night by red mullet on pesto mash with tomato and lemon nage, duck confit, roast rack of lamb and fillet steak with glazed shallots and red wine sauce.

A peaceful night is assured in comfortable, pine furnished en suite bedrooms. Newly restored garden.

OPEN: 12-2.30 6-11. **BAR MEALS:** L served all week. D served all week 12-2.30 6-9.30. Av main course £5.50. **RESTAURANT:** L served all week. D served all week 12-2.30 6-9.30. Av 3 course à la carte £19.50.
BREWERY/COMPANY: Free House.
PRINCIPAL BEERS: Tawney, Palmers 200, Exmoor Gold, Palmers Dorset Gold. **FACILITIES:** Children welcome Garden: Patio, food served outside Dogs allowed Water. **NOTES:** Parking 18. **ROOMS:** 12 bedrooms 11 en suite s£40 d£55

Pubs offering a good choice of seafood on the menu.

Hope & Anchor 🐑 ♀
BA2 7DD ☎ 01225 832296 📠 01225 832296
Dir: A367 from Bath to Radstock, L onto B3110 to Frome/Midford. Pub on bottom of hill under railway bridge

Unassuming stone pub set hard beside the busy B3110 in the Cam Valley 3 miles south of Bath. Comfortably furnished bar and dining area, with bare board floor, open stone fireplace and a warm decor, is the setting for some enjoyable pub food. In the bar, order fish soup, chicken and prawn paella, salmon fishcakes with tarragon mayonnaise, or the tapas selection, while restaurant fare may include grilled lemon sole and venison with port, thyme and juniper berry sauce. Lemon and lime cheesecake, and baked raspberry flan for pudding.
OPEN: 11.30-2.30 6.30-11. Closed Dec 25. **BAR MEALS:** L served all week. D served all week 12-2 6.30-9.30.
RESTAURANT: L served all week. D served all week 12-2 6.30-9.30. Av 3 course à la carte £20.
BREWERY/COMPANY: Free House.
PRINCIPAL BEERS: Deuchars IPA, Bass. **FACILITIES:** Garden: patio/terrace, outdoor eating. **NOTES:** Parking 30

Old Station
Wells Rd, Hallatrow, nr Paulton ☎ 01761 452228
Eccentic pub full of bric-à-brac and curios, offering a good range of West Country ales, interesting food in both bars and dining room, and en suite bedrooms.

Pick of the Pubs

The Notley Arms ♀
TA4 4JB ☎ 01984 656217
On the very edge of the Brendon Hills and Exmoor, Monksilver boasts a population of some 90 souls whose winter trade contributes largely to the success of the Coach House skittle alley that graces the pub car park. Wood-burning stoves, a collection of old plates and local paintings, and simple furnishings lend a homely feel to the large bar.

The leaseholder - 'and occasional chef'! - discusses and effects changes to the daily menu with each session, ensuring the freshest available produce is used. Lunch dishes of, perhaps, chicken and bacon pudding and filled baguettes and pittas are supplemented at night by local trout and steaks, pork with leeks, ginger and cream and fresh cod with avocado salsa. There is plenty for children from colouring books and skipping ropes to a tractor to sit on outside in the finer weather. Very much a locals' local, other speciality dishes include fresh fish from Lyme Regis, home-made pasta and good vegetarian options. Plenty of real ales and well-chosen wines accompany.
OPEN: 11.30-2.30 6.30-11. Closed Dec 25, 2wks Jan-Feb.
BAR MEALS: L served all week. D served all week 12-2 7-9.30. Av main course £4. **BREWERY/COMPANY:** Unique Pub Co. **PRINCIPAL BEERS:** Exmoor Ale, Wadworth 6X, Smiles Best. **FACILITIES:** Children welcome Garden: Food served outside Dogs allowed On lead. **NOTES:** Parking 26

England

MONTACUTE
Map 03 ST41

Kings Arms Inn ♀
TA15 6UU ☎ 01935 822513 📠 01935 826549
Dir: Turn off A303 at A3088 roundabout signposted Montacute. Hotel
by church in village centre
Delightful 16th-century hamstone inn with mullioned windows,
situated in a beautiful village close to Montacute House
(National Trust). There is a good range of bar food meals,
while an ever-changing menu of fresh-cooked and wholesome
main meals can be enjoyed in the restaurant or bar.
OPEN: 11-11 (Sun 12-10.30). **BAR MEALS:** L served all week. D
served all week 12-2 7-9. Av main course £7. **RESTAURANT:** L
served all week. D served all week 12-2 7-9. Av 3 course à la carte
£25. Av 3 course fixed price £17.95. **BREWERY/COMPANY:** Old
English Inns. **PRINCIPAL BEERS:** Courage Directors.
FACILITIES: Children welcome Garden: outdoor eating
Dogs allowed not dining area. **NOTES:** Parking 12.
ROOMS: 15 bedrooms 15 en suite s£55 d£70

The Phelips Arms
The Borough TA15 6XB ☎ 01935 822557
Dir: From Cartgate roundabout on A303 follow signs for Montacute
Overlooking the village square close to historic Montacute
House (NT), this attractive, 17th-century hamstone building
has a tranquil walled garden and character bars. Used as a
location for the recent film version of Sense and Sensibility.
Reliable bar food. Skittle alley. Bedrooms.

NETHER STOWEY
Map 03 ST13

The Cottage Inn
Keenthorne TA5 1HZ ☎ 01278 732355
Dir: M5 J23 follow A39 signs for Cannington/Minehead. Inn on A39
Dating from the 16th century, the Cottage is an old coaching
inn and traditional cider house where cider was made until
about 15 years ago.

NORTH CURRY
Map 03 ST32

The Bird in Hand
1 Queen Square TA3 6LT ☎ 01823 490248
Friendly 16th-century village inn with large stone inglenook
fireplaces, flagstone floors, exposed beams and studwork.
Fresh food is offered from a short menu using seasonal
produce. Expect hearty soups, local farmhouse cheeses, local
sausages, grilled sirloin steak, and lemon sole with herbs.
OPEN: 12-3 7-11 (Sat 12-4 7-11. Sun 12-5 7-10.30).
BAR MEALS: L served Tue-Sun. D served Fri-Sat 12-2 7-9.
Av main course £5. **BREWERY/COMPANY:** Free House.
PRINCIPAL BEERS: Badger Tanglefoot, Exmoor Gold, Otter Ale,
Cotleigh Barn Owl. **FACILITIES:** Children welcome patio, BBQ,
food served outdoors Dogs allowed. **NOTES:** Parking 20

We endeavour to be as accurate as possible but changes
in personnel and data can occur in establishments after
the guide has gone to press

NORTON ST PHILIP
Map 03 ST75

Pick of the Pubs

George Inn ♀
High St BA3 6LH ☎ 01373 834224 📠 01373 834861
Dir: From Bath take A36 to Warminster, after 6m take A366 on R
to Radstock, village 1m

Few buildings have offered hospitality to travellers for
over six hundred years, but The George is one of them.
Originally built late in the 14th century as a monastic
guesthouse, this spectacular stone and timber-framed
building is now one of the finest surviving medieval inns in
the land. With its galleried courtyard, soaring timber roofs
and 15th-century stair tower, the inn was meticulously
restored to full hotel status in 1998. The eight en suite
bedrooms have been skilfully furnished to provide
modern comforts, whilst still reflecting their authentic
period charm.
    The inn has featured in various films and TV series
including Moll Flanders, and The Remains of the Day. Well
kept Wadworth ales and a decent wine list complement
lunchtime snacks and a full restaurant menu. Expect
home-made soup, game terrine, or vegetables roasted
with basil, followed by steaks, pan fried duck, or lamb
chops with redcurrant and mint. Seafoods include cod in
white wine sauce, and filo-wrapped tiger prawns.
OPEN: 11-2.30 5.30-11 (11-11 summer only).
BAR MEALS: L served all week. D served all week 12-2.30
6.30-9.30. Av main course £6.95. **RESTAURANT:** L served
all week. D served all week 12-2.30 6.30-9.30. Av 3 course à la
carte £20. **BREWERY/COMPANY:** Wadworth.
PRINCIPAL BEERS: Wadworth 6X, Henrys IPA, Old Timer &
Summersault. **FACILITIES:** Garden: Food served outside
Dogs allowed By Arrangement. **NOTES:** Parking 26.
ROOMS: 8 bedrooms 8 en suite d£80

NUNNEY
Map 03 ST74

The George at Nunney ★ ★
Church St BA11 4LW ☎ 01373 836458 📠 01373 836565
Dir: 0.5m N off A361, Frome/Shepton Mallet
Rambling old coaching inn set in an historic conservation
village, opposite a 13th-century castle. Fish features
prominently on the menu.

OTHERY

Rose & Crown
East Lyng TA3 5AU ☎ 01823 698235
e-mail: derek.mason@btinternet.com
Set among the Somerset Levels, this 13th-century coaching inn
serves a range of real ales, and offers a relaxed atmosphere
without electronic entertainment. Extensive bar menu, with
many vegetarian choices.

OVER STRATTON   Map 03 ST41

The Royal Oak 🐑 ♀
TA13 5LQ ☎ 01460 240906 ▤ 01460 242421
Dir: A3088 from Yeovil, L onto A303, Over Stratton on R after S
Petherton
Welcoming thatched pub dating back about 400 years. Savour
the cosy atmosphere of the beamed bar, with its flagstones,
log fires, pews and settles. A pleasant, peaceful garden, a
barbecue and a children's play area are among the inn's
outdoor attractions. An extensive menu Toulouse sausages
with creamy mashed potatoes and onion, home-made beef
lasagne, Thai-style halibut with egg noodles and aromatic
vegetables, and lamb steak marinated in garlic and herbs.
OPEN: 11-3 6-11. **BAR MEALS:** L served all week. D served all
week 12-2.30 7-9.30. Av main course £10. **RESTAURANT:** L
served all week. D served all week 12-2.30 7-9.30. Av 3 course à la
carte £20. **BREWERY/COMPANY:** Woodhouse Inns.
PRINCIPAL BEERS: Badger Best & Tanglefoot.
FACILITIES: Children welcome Children's licence Garden:
Patio, outdoor eating Dogs allowed Water. **NOTES:** Parking 70

PORLOCK   Map 03 SS84

The Ship Inn
High St TA24 8QD ☎ 01643 862507 ▤ 01643 863224
Dir: A358 to Williton, then A39 to Porlock
Set at the foot of Porlock Hill between Exmoor and the sea, the
Ship is one of the oldest inns on Exmoor, with open fires and
flagstone flooring. New licensees.

PRIDDY   Map 03 ST55

New Inn 🐑 ♀
Priddy Green BA5 3BB ☎ 01749 676465 ▤ 01749 679463
Dir: From M4 J18 take A39 R to Priddy 3m before Wells. From J19
through Bristol onto A39. From M5 J21 take A371 to Cheddar, then
B3371
Overlooking the village green high up in the Mendip Hills, this
15th-century former farmhouse is popular among walkers,
riders and pot-holers, and once served beer to the local lead
miners. The Priddy Sheep Fayre is held on the village green, as
it has been since the 14th century. Typical menu features lamb
cutlets in mint butter, cod and chips, spinach and mushroom
lasagne, and a variety of jacket potatoes, omelettes and
toasties.
OPEN: 11.30-2.30 (Sun & Mon 12-2.30) 7-11. **BAR MEALS:** L
served all week. D served all week 12-2 7-9.30. **RESTAURANT:** L
served all week. D served all week 12-2 7-9.30.
BREWERY/COMPANY: Free House. **PRINCIPAL BEERS:** Bass,
Fullers London Pride, Wadworth 6X. **FACILITIES:** Children
welcome Garden: patio, food served outside. **NOTES:** Parking
30. **ROOMS:** 6 bedrooms 2 en suite s£23 d£34

RUDGE   Map 03 ST85

The Full Moon at Rudge 🐑
BA11 2QF ☎ 01373 830936 ▤ 01373 831366
Dir: From A36 (Bath/Warminster rd) follow signs for Rudge
There's been a coaching inn or hostelry on this site, at the
crossroads of the old drovers' routes, since the early 1700s.
The inn retains its small rooms, stone floors and scrubbed
tables. Fresh fish is a feature, ranging from home-made
fishcakes to sea bass with roasted vegetables.
OPEN: 12-3 6-11. **BAR MEALS:** L served Mon-Sat 12-3. Av main
course £5.50. **RESTAURANT:** D served Mon-Sat 6.30-9.30. Av 3
course à la carte £20. **BREWERY/COMPANY:** Free House.
PRINCIPAL BEERS: Butcombe Bitter, Bass, Worthington.
FACILITIES: Children welcome Garden: Dogs allowed.
NOTES: Parking 90. **ROOMS:** 5 bedrooms 5 en suite s£40 d£60

SHEPTON MALLET   Map 03 ST64

Pick of the Pubs

The Three Horseshoes ♀
Batcombe BA4 6HE ☎ 01749 850359 ▤ 01749 850615
e-mail: tony@three-horseshoes.co.uk
Dir: Take A359 from Frome to Bruton. Batcombe signed on R
Honey-coloured stone, 16th-century coaching inn tucked
away in a pretty village in the heart of the very rural
Batcombe Vale. Terracotta painted walls, exposed stripped
beams, attractive stencilling, and a fine stone inglenook
with log fire characterise the long and low-ceilinged main
bar. Tony and Sarah Lethbridge are doing well here,
offering a good range of ales and a varied blackboard
menu of interesting home-cooked dishes that attract
discerning diners from far and wide. In addition to
lunchtime baguettes and hearty soups, expect to find sea
bass with roasted sun-blushed tomatoes, pesto and deep-
fried leeks, salmon on asparagus salad with chive cream
sauce, calves' liver with bacon, onions and red wine jus,
and venison steak with roasted vegetables and Madeira
jus. Lovely rear garden with play area and views of the
parish church.
OPEN: 12-3 6.30-11. **BAR MEALS:** L served all week. D
served all week 12-2 7-9.30. Av main course £6.95.
RESTAURANT: L served all week. D served all week 12-2
6.30-9.30. Av 3 course à la carte £20.
BREWERY/COMPANY: Free House.
PRINCIPAL BEERS: Butcombe Bitter, Wadworth 6X,
Adnams, Bass. **FACILITIES:** Children welcome Garden:
food served outside Dogs allowed Water.
NOTES: Parking 25

Pubs offering a good choice of
seafood on the menu.

The Waggon and Horses

Frome Rd, Doulting Beacon BA4 4LA ☎ 01749 880302
🖹 01749 880602
e-mail: fcardona@onetel.com
Dir: *1.5m N of Shepton Mallet at crossroads with Wells-Frome road*
Dating from about 1790 and situated between the market town of Frome and the cathedral city of Wells, this bustling stone-built pub was originally a coaching inn and is now listed in the Mendip archives as being of architectural and historical interest. Character, atmosphere and spirit make it a popular local, and robust food with lots of flavour characterises the diverse menu which offers popular pub lunches and perennial favourites like escalope of veal in Madeira sauce, lamb stew with seasonal vegetables, and deep-fried cod in paprika and garlic butter.

OPEN: 11-3 6-11.20 (Sun 12-3, 7-11). **BAR MEALS:** L served all week. D served all week 12-2 6.30-10. Av main course £9.50. **RESTAURANT:** L served all week. D served all week 12-2 6.30-10. Av 3 course à la carte £15. **BREWERY/COMPANY:** Ushers. **PRINCIPAL BEERS:** Ushers Best, Founders. **FACILITIES:** Garden: patio, outdoor eating Dogs allowed on lead please. **NOTES:** Parking 40

Smiles

Beginning operations in 1978, Smiles uses the classic tower principle of brewing. This allows gravity to do much of the work of moving the brew around at various stages, and was very widespread during the Victorian and Edwardian eras. Brewery tours include a meal and plenty of ale. Beers include Smiles Original (3.8%), Smiles Best Bitter (4.1%), and a variety of seasonal ales such as Old Tosser (4.3%), April Fuel (4.8%), Maiden Leg Over (3.5%) and Holly Hops (5.0%). Wes' Englun' is Smiles' own cider (5.0%).

Pick of the Pubs

The Montague Inn ♦♦♦♦ 🐾

BA9 8JW ☎ 01749 813213
Dir: *R off A371 between Wincanton & Castle Cary towards Shepton Montague*
Comfortably refurbished, stone-built village inn nestling in rolling unspoilt Somerset countryside on the edge of sleepy Shepton Montague. Following several changes of ownership in recent years, enthusiastic new licensee Pat Elcock is intent on restoring the inn's respected name for offering quality modern pub food.

Tastefully decorated throughout, including the three well appointed rear bedrooms, with the homely bar featuring old dark pine and an open log fire; cosy, terracotta-painted dining-room. Accompany a decent pint of Greene King IPA or Butcombe in the bar with a filled ciabatta or daily pasta dish, while in the restaurant choose from an imaginative short carte and daily specials. Typically, start with chicken liver parfait or Tuscan seafood broth, then follow with rack of lamb on celeriac purée with Madeira jus or monkfish wrapped in bacon on saffron noodles. Good home-made pudding and pleasant, efficient service. Attractive summer terrace with rural views for summer sipping.

OPEN: 12-2.30 6-11 (closed Mon lunch). **BAR MEALS:** L served Tue-Sun 12-2.30. Av main course £6. **RESTAURANT:** L served Sun. D served Tue-Sat 7.30-11. Av 3 course à la carte £25. Av 3 course fixed price £25. **BREWERY/COMPANY:** Free House. **PRINCIPAL BEERS:** Butcombe Bitter, Greene King IPA, Fullers London Pride, Oakhill Best. **FACILITIES:** Children welcome Garden: Dogs allowed. **NOTES:** Parking 30. **ROOMS:** 3 bedrooms 3 en suite s£30 d£45

The Globe

Market Square TA11 7LX ☎ 01458 272474
🖹 01458 274789
Dir: *4m from A303*
Fresh fish at weekends and hearty English cooking draw local diners to this 17th-century former coaching inn in the market square.

Skills and Crafts

Inns with names like the Bricklayers Arms and the Masons Arms hark back to the days when groups of craftsmen and tradesmen met regularly in the local hostelry. The trade union movement originally grew up in pubs in this way and a 'local' can mean either a pub or a union branch. Itinerant craftsmen would expect a welcome at these houses, too, and pick up news of work. The Axe and Compasses is a carpenters' badge, the Three (or more) Horseshoes a device of smiths, the Wheatsheaf of bakers and the Beetle and Wedge of builders, while quite a few pubs display the Oddfellows Arms. The Shoulder of Mutton could signify that the landlord doubled as a butcher.

SPARKFORD   Map 03 ST62

The Sparkford Inn

High St BA22 7JH ☎ 01963 400218 🖳 01963 440358

Dir: just off A303, 400yds from rdbt at Sparkford

Picturesque, 15th-century former coaching inn characterized by its popular garden, beamed bars and fascinating old prints and photographs. Nearby is the Haynes Motor Museum with a vast collection of classic cars and motorbikes. Varied menu offers a selection of grills, beef and Guinness casserole and salmon and spinach pie, while typical specials might include grilled lemon sole, baked pork tenderloin and pan-fried duck with Cointreau and redcurrant sauce. Good lunchtime carvery and large selection of locally-made puddings.

OPEN: 11-3 7-11. **BAR MEALS:** L served all week. D served all week 12-2.15 7-10. Av main course £6.50. **RESTAURANT:** L served all week. D served all week 12-2 7-9.30. Av 3 course à la carte £12. **BREWERY/COMPANY:** Free House. **PRINCIPAL BEERS:** Bass, Otter Ale, Greene King Old Speckled Hen. **FACILITIES:** Children welcome Garden: beer garden , food served outside Dogs allowed. **NOTES:** Parking 40. **ROOMS:** 10 bedrooms 10 en suite s£30 d£45 FR£60

STANTON WICK   Map 03 ST66

Pick of the Pubs

The Carpenters Arms 🐾 ♀

BS39 4BX ☎ 01761 490202 🖳 01761 490763

e-mail: carpenters@dial.pipex.com

Dir: From A37(Bristol/Wells rd) take A368 towards Weston-S-Mare take 1st R

A converted row of honey-stoned miners' cottages in a tiny hamlet overlooking the Chew Valley, converted into a civilised residential inn of great charm and character. Beyond the attractive façade, complete with clambering roses and colourful tubs of flowers, is a comfortable, newly refurbished stone-walled bar with low beams, warming open fire and a chatty, music-free atmosphere. Separate beamed restaurant for more formal dining. The Cooper's Parlour, with its extensive chalkboard, is the focus of imaginative snacks and bar food ranging from unusual sandwiches (poached salmon with watercress and dill dressing), liver and pork terrine with plum and ginger chutney, traditional steak, mushroom and ale pie, Thai chicken curry, and chargrilled steaks. More elaborate restaurant choices may include Cornish mussel, scallop and tiger prawn chowder and roast duck with cranberry and port jus. Twelve immaculate and well appointed cottagey bedrooms have solid pine furnishings and en suite facilities. Splendid dining terrace with a water feature and outdoor heating.

OPEN: 11-11. **BAR MEALS:** L served all week. D served all week 12-2 7-10. Av main course £8.95. **RESTAURANT:** L served Sun. D served all week 12-2 7-10. Av 3 course à la carte £20. **BREWERY/COMPANY:** Buccaneer Holdings. **PRINCIPAL BEERS:** Bass, Butcombe, Courage Best, Wadworth 6X. **FACILITIES:** Children welcome Garden: patio, outdoor eating. **NOTES:** Parking 200. **ROOMS:** 12 bedrooms 12 en suite s£59.50 d£79.50 FR£89.50

STAPLE FITZPANE

The Greyhound Inn ♦♦♦♦ 🐾 ♀

TA3 5SP ☎ 01823 480227 🖳 01823 481117

Dir: From M5, A316 to A303, after 3m R to village

Nestling in a picturesque village, this Grade II listed coaching inn has recently been upgraded to include four en suite bedrooms. Taking its name from men known as Greyhounds, who dispatched news on horseback, the pub is within easy reach of the Devon and Dorset coasts. A series of rambling, connecting rooms, characterised by flagstone floors, old timbers and natural stone walls, greets the visitor, with a good

continued

selection of traditional ales and seasonal, freshly prepared dishes, including home-made fishcakes, vegetable curry, lasagne and sausages and mash with onion gravy. **OPEN:** 12-3 5-11 (Summer open all day). **BAR MEALS:** L served all week. D served all week 12-2 6.30-9.30. Av main course £6.75. **BREWERY/COMPANY:** Free House. **PRINCIPAL BEERS:** Bass. **FACILITIES:** Children welcome Children's licence Garden: BBQ, patio, outdoor eating Dogs allowed on leads. **NOTES:** Parking 60. **ROOMS:** 4 bedrooms 4 en suite s£40 d£70

STOGUMBER

The White Horse
High St TA4 3TA ☎ 01984 656277
Dir: Opposite the church in the centre of the village
Traditional village local tucked away on the edge of the Quantock Hills, offering good food and ale, farm cider, and bedrooms in the adjacent Market House.

STOKE ST GREGORY   Map 03 ST32

Rose & Crown 🐑 ♀
Woodhill TA3 6EW ☎ 01823 490296 🖥 01823 490996
e-mail: ron.browning@virgin.net
Dir: M5 J25, A358/A378 then 1st L through North Curry to Stoke St Gregory church on R. Pub 0.5m on L
Close to the famous Somerset Levels and handy for Wells and Glastonbury, this picturesque cottage-style pub includes a 60-ft well and an attractive dining room recently converted from the inn's old skittle alley. Fresh local produce and fish from Brixham are used and there is a good selection of real ales and guest beers. Grilled skate wings, mixed grill and lamb cutlets are popular in the bar, and restaurant dishes might include ribeye steak, scrumpy chicken and local trout. **OPEN:** 11-3 7-11. **BAR MEALS:** L served all week. D served all week 12.30-2 7-10. Av main course £7.50. **RESTAURANT:** L served all week. D served all week 12.30-2 7-10. Av 3 course à la carte £13.25. **BREWERY/COMPANY:** Free House. **PRINCIPAL BEERS:** Hardy Royal Oak & Hardy Country, Exmoor Ale. **FACILITIES:** Children welcome Garden: Food served outside Dogs allowed. **NOTES:** Parking 20. **ROOMS:** 6 bedrooms 3 en suite s£25 d£38 FR£75

Bottoms Up

As a customer in a 17th-century inn or alehouse, you might find yourself with a pint or quart pot made of wood, horn, leather in your hand. They all had the advantage of not breaking if dropped, though the effect on the beer's taste might not suit today's palates. A cut above these utensils were mugs and tankards of pewter, which some pubs still supply and some drinkers still swear by them. In 19th-century hostelries, however, pewter gradually gave way to china and glass, with the occasional joky china mug made with a frog crouching at the bottom, to give the unwary toper a nasty shock.

TAUNTON   Map 03 ST22

Pick of the Pubs

The Blue Ball 🐑 ♀ NEW
Triscombe, nr Crowcombe TA4 3HE ☎ 01984 618242
Dir: 9M from Taunton on the Minehead A358 road, turn L signposted Triscombe the pub is 1.5M along this road
Unspoilt 18th-century thatched pub hidden away along a narrow lane amid the Quantock Hills, offering imaginative pub food, Somerset ales, decent wines and an informal dining atmosphere to a well heeled and discerning clientele. Carpeted main bar with rustic, country-style furnishings, sporting prints, and daily-changing blackboard menus above the huge inglenook fireplace.
    Locally sourced produce feature in tea-smoked Quantock duck breast with port and redcurrant sauce, pheasant with Calvados and caramelised apples, lamb loin stuffed with apricots and pistachio nuts, and Dunster Beach codling with Puy lentils and salsa verde. Starters may include spicy carrot, coconut and coriander soup and terrine of ham and foie gras, while for pudding try the prune and Armagnac tart or a plate of West Country cheeses. Impressive list of 400 wines; any under £20 available by the glass.
    Super terraced garden with view over the Vale of Taunton. Footpaths lead into the Quantocks and miles of breezy walks. **OPEN:** 12-3 7-11. **BAR MEALS:** L served all week. D served all week 12-1.45 7-9. Av main course £7.50. **BREWERY/COMPANY:** Free House. **PRINCIPAL BEERS:** Cotleigh Tawny, Youngs Special, Hop Back Summer Lightning,. **FACILITIES:** Garden: Food served outside Dogs allowed Water. **NOTES:** Parking 20 No credit cards

Queens Arms
Pitminster TA3 7AZ ☎ 01823 421529
Old country pub on the fringe of the Blackdown Hills, Fish restaurant; seven ales; good wines. Bedrooms.

WAMBROOK   Map 03 ST20

The Cotley Inn
TA20 3EN ☎ 01460 62348 🖥 01460 68833
e-mail: cotley70@freeserve.co.uk
Traditional stone-built inn in an area renowned for local walks and fine country views. A welcoming atmosphere awaits inside and the walls are lined with watercolours, oils and sculptures by local artists. Cosy bar and adjoining dining-room offer a wide range of meals and snacks prepared with fresh produce. 'Small eats' include vegetable and Stilton crumble, breaded trout and chicken and gammon pie, while 'big meaty eats' might feature lamb chops, gammon steak and devilled kidneys. **OPEN:** 11-3 7-11. **BAR MEALS:** L served all week. D served all week 12-3 7-11. Av main course £4. **RESTAURANT:** L served all week. D served all week 12-3 7-11. Av 3 course à la carte £12. **BREWERY/COMPANY:** Free House **FACILITIES:** Children welcome Garden: outdoor eating, Dogs allowed. **NOTES:** Parking 40. **ROOMS:** 2 bedrooms s£35 d£45

WASHFORD Map 03 ST04

The Washford Inn ♦♦♦
TA23 0PP ☎ 01984 640256

The steam railway between Minehead and Bishop's Lydeard near Taunton runs directly behind this pleasant family inn, which is well situated for many enjoyable walking routes and offers home-cooked, locally produced food. Lasagne, prawn platter, 10oz gammon steak, mussels in garlic and roast lamb shank are among the appetising dishes.
OPEN: 12-11 (Winter 12-3, 5-11). **BAR MEALS:** L served all week. D served all week 12-9 12-9. Av main course £4.99.
RESTAURANT: L served all week. D served all week 12-2.30 6-9. Av 3 course à la carte £12. Av 2 course fixed price £6.95.
BREWERY/COMPANY: Free House.
PRINCIPAL BEERS: Butcombe Gold, Courage Directors, Wadworth 6X, Bass. **FACILITIES:** Children welcome Children's licence Garden: outdoor eating, patio Dogs allowed.
NOTES: Parking 40. **ROOMS:** 7 bedrooms 7 en suite s£24 d£48

WATERROW Map 03 ST02

The Rock Inn ♦♦♦
TA4 2AX ☎ 01984 623293 01984 623293
Dir: *From Taunton take B3227. Waterrow approx 14m W*

400-year-old former coaching inn built into the rock face, in a lovely green valley beside the River Tone. Sit in the peaceful bar, with winter log fire and traditional furnishings, and sample the appetising menu. Expect grilled local rainbow trout, game pie and a selection of grills and casseroles. The landlord has recently been voted "Most Miserable Landlord in Somerset", which isn't as bad as it sounds!
OPEN: 7.30-3 6-12. **BAR MEALS:** L served all week. D served all week 11-2.30 6-10.30. Av main course £3.50. **RESTAURANT:** L served all week. D served all week 11-2.30 6-10.30. Av 3 course à la carte £12. **BREWERY/COMPANY:** Free House.
PRINCIPAL BEERS: Cotleigh Tawny, Exmoor Gold.
FACILITIES: Children welcome Dogs allowed.
NOTES: Parking 20. **ROOMS:** 7 bedrooms 7 en suite s£24 d£48

WELLS Map 03 ST54

Pick of the Pubs

The Fountain Inn/Boxers Restaurant
1 St Thomas St BA5 2UU
☎ 01749 672317 01749 670825
e-mail: adrian@finwells.demon.co.uk
See Pick of the Pubs on page 395

The Pheasant Inn
Worth, Wookey BA5 1LQ ☎ 01749 672355
Dir: *W of Wells on the B3139*
Set at the foot of the Mendips with impressive views, this popular country pub includes a traditional public bar where walkers can enjoy a pint of real ale by a welcoming log fire. Comprehensive menu offers freshly made salads, ploughman's lunches, jacket potatoes and open French sticks in the bar, while scampi, sirloin steak and pan-fried veal topped with Parma ham in brandy and Italian herbs might feature as restaurant main courses.
OPEN: 11-3 (Sun 12-3) 6-11 (Sun 7-9). Closed Dec 26, Jan 1.
BAR MEALS: L served all week. D served all week 12-2 6.30-9.30. Av main course £4.95. **RESTAURANT:** L served all week. D served all week 12-2 6.30-9.30. Av 3 course à la carte £12.
BREWERY/COMPANY: Free House.
PRINCIPAL BEERS: Butcombe Gold, Jenning's Cumberland Ale, Timothy Taylor Landlord Ale, Wadworth 6X.
FACILITIES: Children welcome Garden: outdoor eating, BBQ Dogs allowed. **NOTES:** Parking 28

WEST CAMEL Map 03 ST52

The Walnut Tree
Fore St BA22 7QW ☎ 01935 851292 01935 851292
Dir: *Off A303 between Sparkford & Yeovilton Air Base*
Refurbished small hotel located in an peaceful village just a minute's drive from the A303 east of Yeovil. Small carpeted bar offering Butcombe Bitter on tap; extensive front dining areas and thirteen attractively decorated en suite bedrooms in a modern extension. Local specialities and fresh fish on the varied menu, with turbot with mild pepper sauce and guinea fowl with prune and brandy sauce showing the style.
OPEN: 11-3 6.30-11.30. **BAR MEALS:** L served Tue-Sun. D served Mon-Sat 12-2 7-9.30. Av main course £9.95.
RESTAURANT: L served Tue-Sun. D served Mon-Sat 12-2 7-9.30. Av 3 course à la carte £22. **BREWERY/COMPANY:** Free House.
PRINCIPAL BEERS: Butcombe Bitter. **FACILITIES:** Garden: Food served outside. **NOTES:** Parking 40.
ROOMS: 13 bedrooms 13 en suite s£49.50 d£75

Bar Billiards

The ingenious blend of billiards and skittles is a relative newcomer to the pub scene. It was introduced here from Belgium in the 1930s, with support from billiard table manufacturers. The game caught on rapidly, especially in the South and Midlands, and leagues had been organised by the time the Second World War began. Its much more recent rival is pool, which came here from America in the 1960s in the wake of the Paul Newman film The Hustler.

OPEN: 10.30-2.30 6-11 (Sun 12-3 7-10.30). Closed 25-26 Dec.
BAR MEALS: L served all week. D served all week 12-2 6-10. Av main course £6
RESTAURANT: L served all week D served all week 12-2 6-10. Av 3 course a la carte £17.50. Av 3 course lunch £8.50.
BREWERY/COMPANY: Ushers Innspired Inns.
PRINCIPAL BEERS: Butcombe Bitter, Bass, Marston's Pedigree.
FACILITIES: Children welcome.
NOTES: Parking 100.

The Fountain Inn

1 St Thomas Street BA5 2UU
☎ 01749 672317 🖶 01749 670825
e-mail: adrian@finnwells.demon.co.uk
Dir: City centre, at junction of A371 & B3139, 50yds from Wells Cathedral

This popular 15th-century inn is thought to have housed the labourers who helped to build Wells Cathedral, just 50 yards away, and takes its name from the spring that feeds the conduit in Wells. Well deserved reputation for quality food and wine since the present landlords arrived here in 1981.

The Fountain has long been a favourite haunt of the cathedral choir - hardly surprising, since this striking building is just around the corner from Vicars' Close, a street of medieval houses built specially for the Vicars' Choral. The landlord's claim that the pub once housed the cathedral builders is probably a reference to maintenance staff, since the great church was substantially complete by the year 1465. Nowadays there's little doubt about the reasons for the inn's popularity.

Locally brewed Butcombe Bitter is amongst the beers offered in the unpretentious ground floor bar with its winter fires and an extensive menu of home-cooked meals based on fresh local produce. Typical dishes range from deep-fried Brie with tomato and garlic sauce and warm chicken and bacon salad to favourites like speciality sausages and mash with red wine and onion gravy, chargrilled steaks and fruity chicken curry.

In Boxers Restaurant upstairs, expect more imaginative evening dishes with starters like bubble and squeak soup with bacon, Thai fishcake with sweet chilli and ginger relish and main course options such as roasted lamb rump with garlic and rosemary sauce, beef fillet with red wine, garlic and shallot jus, baked monkfish topped with pesto, and orange tilapa fish with crushed new potatoes and a coriander and lime oil setting the cooking style of. Finish with citrus lemon tart, sticky toffee apple pudding, Lovington ice cream or a plate of West Country cheeses.

395

WEST HUNTSPILL   Map 03 ST34

Crossways Inn ♀
Withy Rd TA9 3RA ☎ 01278 783756   🖹 01278 781899
e-mail: crossways.inn@virgin.net
Dir: On A38 3.5m from M5 J22/23
A 17th-century inn with low-ceilinged bars and a relaxed
atmosphere. Bar food dishes may include a choice of steaks,
breaded plaice, a selection of vegetarian meals, and fresh fish
from the specials board. Bistro menu also available. Over
twenty wines.
OPEN: 10.30-3 5.30-11. Closed 25 Dec. **BAR MEALS:** L served
all week. D served all week 12-2 6.30-9. Av main course £5.
RESTAURANT: L served all week. D served all week 12-2 6.30-9.
Av 3 course à la carte £11. Av 3 course fixed price £11.
BREWERY/COMPANY: Free House.
PRINCIPAL BEERS: Hardy Royal Oak, Flowers Original & IPA,
Fullers London Pride, Greene King Abbot Ale.
FACILITIES: Children welcome Garden: outdoor eating, Dogs
allowed. **NOTES:** Parking 60. **ROOMS:** 3 bedrooms 3 en suite
s£24 d£34 FR£34

WHEDDON CROSS

The Rest and Be Thankful Inn ◆◆◆◆
TA24 7DR ☎ 01643 841222   🖹 01643 841813
e-mail: enquiries@restandbethankful.co.uk
Dir: 5m S of Dunster
Located in the highest village in Exmoor, this former coaching
inn has old world charm combined with friendly hospitality. An
ideal spot for those wishing to explore Exmoor and the North
Devon coastline. Some of the bedrooms enjoy views of
Dunkery Beacon, the highest point in Somerset.

WINCANTON   Map 03 ST72

Bull Inn ♀
Hardway, nr Bruton BA10 0LN ☎ 01749 812200
17th-century former coaching inn on the famous Somerset
Levels, close to Bruton, Stourhead Gardens and Wincanton
Racecourse. Frequented by cast members of leading stage
musicals, jockeys and soap stars. Full range of bar meals and
restaurant dishes, including seafood crumble, beef in beer
casserole and pheasant breast in red wine.
OPEN: 11.30-2.30 6-11. **BAR MEALS:** L served all week.
D served all week 12-2 6-10. Av main course £6.95.
RESTAURANT: L served all week. D served all week 12-2 7-9. Av
3 course à la carte £18. **BREWERY/COMPANY:** Free House.
PRINCIPAL BEERS: Butcombe Bitter, Greene King IPA & Old
Speckled Hen, Wadworth 6X. **FACILITIES:** Children welcome
Garden: food served outside Dogs allowed.
NOTES: Parking 30

♀   Pubs offering six or more wines by the glass

WINSFORD   Map 03 SS93

Pick of the Pubs

The Royal Oak Inn ★ ★ ★
TA24 7JE ☎ 01643 851455   🖹 01643 851009
e-mail: enquiries@royaloak-somerset.co.uk
Dir: M5 South, J27, at Tiverton roundabout North on A396.
A charming 12th-century inn with inglenook fireplaces and
oak beams, set in the heart of an Exmoor village. Popular
with locals and the hunting, shooting and fishing set, and
an excellent base for walking on Exmoor. It offers 'country
house' style accommodation and good country cooking in
both the convivial bar and smart dining room. Typical
English dishes use locally sourced, fresh produce. Main
courses may feature steak and kidney pudding, local
pheasant, partridge and venison in season, and other
game or fresh fish.
OPEN: 11-3 6-11. **BAR MEALS:** L served all week. D served
all week 12-2 7-9.30. Av main course £8.50.
RESTAURANT: L served Sun. D served all week 12.15-2.30
7.30-9. **BREWERY/COMPANY:** Free House.
PRINCIPAL BEERS: Cotleigh Barn Owl, Exmoor Ale.
FACILITIES: Children welcome Garden: Dogs allowed.
NOTES: Parking 20. **ROOMS:** 14 bedrooms 14 en suite s£78
d£98

WHICH IS THE OLDEST PUB?
The question has no sure answer. Records are
fragmentary and a building, or part of it, may be far
older than its use as a drinking house. The Old Ferry
Boat Inn at Holywell in the Cambridgeshire fens is
claimed to go back to the 6th century as a monastic
ferry station and the Olde Fighting Cocks in St Albans
to the 8th century as an abbey fishing lodge by the
River Ver. A more believable contender is the Bingley
Arms at Bardsey, West Yorkshire, recorded as the
'priest's inn' in 905, but it was completely rebuilt in
1738. The Ostrich at Colnbrook, Buckinghamshire, is
apparently on the site of a monastic hospice recorded
in 1106 (and its odd name is a pun on 'hospice').
Others claiming a 12th-century origin include the
wonderfully named Olde Trip to Jerusalem in
Nottingham, the Cromwell-linked Royal Oak at
Whatcote in Warwickshire, the venerable Oxenham
Arms at South Zeal in Devon, the half-timbered Pandy
Inn at Dorstone, Herefordshire, the Olde House Inn at
Llangynwyd in South Wales and the Oldes Boar's
Head at Middleton, Greater Manchester. All of them,
of course, have been repeatedly rebuilt and
altered over the centuries.

England

WITHYPOOL
Map 03 SS83

Pick of the Pubs

Royal Oak Inn ⊛ ★ ★ 🍴
TA24 7QP ☎ 01643 831506   🖹 01643 831659
e-mail: enquiries@royaloakwithypool.co.uk
Dir: From M5 thru Taunton on B3224, then B3223 to Withypool

Situated right in the heart of Exmoor, with its walks, rivers and local beauty spots, this inn has a long and colourful history: R.D. Blackmore stayed here whilst writing Lorna Doone. The Rod Room bar is full of fishing memorabilia and in both beamed bars, warmed by open fires, a wealth of good local produce is evident on menus supplemented by a wide range of daily specials. Soups could be curried parsnip or cream of onion, followed by grilled scallops in garlic butter for a light meal or Somerset pork casserole or chicken with peppers, mushroom and cream sauce for a more hearty meal.

Fresh fish, subject to availability, might include poached smoked haddock with parsley sauce and ever-popular fishcakes with fries and salad. Hearty grills include wild boar sausages with pepper sauce and ribeye steak with tomato, mushroom and onions. Walkers can enjoy fresh baguettes, ploughman's and jacket potatoes: residents of newly refreshed bedrooms are offered two- or three-course dinner nightly in the Acorn Restaurant.
OPEN: 11-3.30 6-11. **BAR MEALS:** L served all week. D served all week 12-2 6.30-9.30. Av main course £10. **RESTAURANT:** L served Sun. D served all week 12-2 7-9. Av 3 course à la carte £25. Av 3 course fixed price £25. **BREWERY/COMPANY:** Free House. **PRINCIPAL BEERS:** Exmoor Ale & Fox Bitter, Tetley, Oakhill Yeoman. **FACILITIES:** Children welcome patio, outdoor eating Dogs allowed Kennels if needed. **NOTES:** Parking 20. **ROOMS:** 8 bedrooms 8 en suite s£38 d£76

WOOKEY
Map 03 ST54

The Burcott Inn 🍺
Wells Rd BA5 1NJ ☎ 01749 673874
A convenient stop for visitors to Wells or the Mendip Hills, this stone-built roadside inn is characterised by beams, open fires, pine tables and settles. Freshly prepared food is available in the bars, restaurant and large garden, and over 70 guest beers are served each year. The carte is supported by daily specials such as smoked salmon and prawn bake, Somerset-style lamb cutlets, and crispy duck with black cherry sauce.
OPEN: 11.30-2.30 6-11. Closed 25/26 Dec, 1 Jan. **BAR MEALS:** L

continued

served all week. D served all week 12-2.30 6.30-9.30. Av main course £6. **RESTAURANT:** L served all week. D served all week 12-2.30 6.30-9.30. Av 3 course à la carte £14.50.
BREWERY/COMPANY: Free House.
PRINCIPAL BEERS: Timothy Taylor Landlord, Greene King Abbot Ale, Cotleigh Barn Owl Bitter. **FACILITIES:** Children welcome Garden: patio, outdoor eating. **NOTES:** Parking 30

WOOLVERTON

Red Lion
Bath Rd BA2 7QS ☎ 01373 831050
Dir: On the A36 between Bath & Warminster
Once a court room, this 400-year-old building has a lovely stone floor and an open fire. It is decorated in Elizabethan style and is, of course, haunted. Good home cooking is served, ranging from sandwiches to steaks. Plenty of fish choice. Convenient for Bath, Trowbridge, Frome and Longleat.

STAFFORDSHIRE

ABBOTS BROMLEY
Map 09 SK02

The Royal Oak
Bagot St WS15 3DB ☎ 01283 840117
There is a friendly village atmosphere at this black and white pub, with its open fires, beamed ceilings and oak-panelled restaurant.

ALREWAS
Map 09 SK11

The Old Boat NEW
DE13 7DB ☎ 01283 791468   🖹 01283 791468
Originally built as a watering hole for canal construction workers, the Old Boat is situated on the Trent and Mersey Canal with the beer garden backing on to it. Fresh food in informal surroundings features seafood, with fruits de mer as a 'signature dish' and options like red sea bream and sea bass fillet with herb vinaigrette on braised chicory, or baked best end of lamb with a mustard crust.
OPEN: 11.30-3.30 6.30-11.30 (all day Sun Mar-Sept). Closed 25 Dec, 31Dec. **BAR MEALS:** L served all week. D served all week 12-2.30 7-9.30. Av main course £9.50. **RESTAURANT:** L served all week. D served all week 12-2.30 7-9.30. Av 3 course à la carte £20. **PRINCIPAL BEERS:** Ushers Bitter & Founders Ale. **FACILITIES:** Children welcome Garden: Food served outside Dogs allowed Water. **NOTES:** Parking 40

ALTON
Map 09 SK04

Bulls Head Inn ◆◆◆
High St ST10 4AQ ☎ 01538 702307   🖹 01538 702065
e-mail: janet@alton.freeserve.co.uk
Traditional beers, home cooking and well-equipped accommodation are provided in the heart of Alton, less than a mile from Alton Towers theme park. Oak beams and an inglenook fireplace set the scene for the old world bar, the cosy snug (where children can sit) and the country-style restaurant. Menus offer the likes of sirloin steak, hunters' chicken, and duck with Stilton.
CLOSED: Xmas & New Year. **BAR MEALS:** L served all week. D served all week 12-2 7-9. Av main course £5. **RESTAURANT:** D served all week 7-9. Av 3 course à la carte £10. Av 3 course fixed price £10. **BREWERY/COMPANY:** Free House.
PRINCIPAL BEERS: Bass, Worthington. **FACILITIES:** Children welcome Children's licence. **NOTES:** Parking 15

BURTON UPON TRENT

Burton Bridge Inn
24 Bridge St DE14 1SY ☎ 01283 536596
With its own brewery at the back, this is one of the area's
oldest pubs. An old fashioned interior with oak panelling,
feature fireplaces, and a distinct lack of electronic
entertainment. Full range of Burton Bridge ales.

BUTTERTON   Map 09 SK05

The Black Lion Inn
ST13 7SP ☎ 01538 304232
e-mail: theblacklion@clara.net
Dir: From A52 (between Leek & Ashbourne) take B5053

This charming, 18th-century village inn lies on the edge of the
Manifold valley, in the heart of the Peak District's walking and
cycling country. Winter fires glint on the comfortable clutter of
old brass and china, adding to the pleasure of a well-kept pint.
The popular bar menu includes pies and steaks, as well as
interesting fish dishes. Three upstairs bedrooms provide a
comfortable base from which to explore the National Park.
OPEN: 12-3 (Mon 7-11 only) 7-11 Sunday eve 7-10.30.
BAR MEALS: L served Tue-Sun. D served all week 12-2 7-9. Av
main course £6.50. **RESTAURANT:** L served Sun. D served Fri-
Sat 12-2 7-9.30. Av 3 course à la carte £25.
BREWERY/COMPANY: Free House.
PRINCIPAL BEERS: Theakston Best, Marstons Pedigree,
Hartington IPA & Whim Arbor light, Wells Bombardier.
FACILITIES: Children welcome Children's licence Garden:
patio, outdoor eating Dogs allowed no dogs inside during
mealtimes. **NOTES:** Parking 30. **ROOMS:** 3 bedrooms
3 en suite s£35 d£55

CRESSWELL

Izaak Walton Inn
Cresswell Ln ST11 9RE ☎ 01782 392265 🖷 01782 388340
Dir: Just off A50 SE of Stoke-on-Trent
Appealing, newly refurbished pub/restaurant in the lovely
Staffordshire countryside. Lots of hanging baskets. Wide
ranging menu.

ECCLESHALL

The George
Castle St ST21 6DF ☎ 01785 850300

Former 18th-century coaching inn now a well refurbished,
small town centre hotel with comfortable en suite bedrooms.
Expect a good pubby atmosphere and excellent Slater's ales
brewed in the micro-brewery run by the owners' son. Good
choice of home-made bar food and an interesting range of
dishes listed on the bistro-style restaurant menu.
OPEN: 11-11 (Sun 12-10.30). **BAR MEALS:** L all week. D all week
12-2.30 6-9.45 (12-9.45 Sat & Sun). **RESTAURANT:** L all week
D all week 12-2.30 6-9.45. **BREWERY/COMPANY:** Own Brew.
PRINCIPAL BEERS: Slater's Bitter, Original, Top Totty, Premium,
Seasonal ales. **FACILITIES:** Children welcome Garden: outdoor
eating. **ROOMS:** 9 bedrooms 9 en suite.

HIMLEY

Crooked House
Coppice Mill DY3 4DA ☎ 01384 238583 🖷 01384 214911
Built originally as a farmhouse in 1765, this brick-built pub
suffered from severe subsidence after mine shafts dug in the
1800s collapsed. Having been condemned in the 1940s,
Banks's Brewery restored the pub even though one side is 4ft
lower than the other. Optical illusions abound in the bar -
bottles roll uphill! - and grandfather clocks appear to be falling
over - a unique place, especially after a few pints!!
OPEN: 11.30-11 (Winter times vary, ring for details).
BAR MEALS: L served all week. D served all week 12-2 6-8.30.
Av main course £5. **PRINCIPAL BEERS:** Banks Original/Bitter,
Marstons Pedigree. **FACILITIES:** Children welcome Children's
licence Garden: patio, outdoor eating, Dogs allowed.
NOTES: Parking 50

Ye Olde Royal Oak Inn, Wetton

YE OLDE ROYAL OAK INN, WETTON
DE6 2AF. Tel: 01335 310287
Directions: off Hulme End to Alstonefield road, between B5054 and A515
In an area much favoured by walkers and handy for the Peak District, this 17th-century stone-built inn is well furnished and offers an excellent choice of real ales. Traditional bar food; good Sunday lunches. Moorland garden. Bedrooms.
Open: 12-3 7-11. Bar Meals: 12-2 7-9. Children and dogs welcome. Garden/patio. Parking.
(see page 400 for full entry)

This short yet fairly challenging ramble explores the Manifold Valley, a spectacular limestone gorge, it's steep, wooded slopes around Thor's Cave and upland farmland. Wildlife abounds and the Peak District views are magnificent.

Turn left out of the pub car park and follow signs for Wetton Mill, bearing left and on past the church. Ignore the road for Grindon and take the next left down a rough track, signed to Thor's Cave. In approximately 3/4 mile (1.2km), cross the stile on your right and head across the field towards the rocky outcrop. Cross a stile and take the right-hand path which leads to the mouth of the cave. Take care as the path can be slippery. Excavations of the cave have revealed flint arrowheads, bronze bracelets, pottery and animal bones, indicating that man once lived here thousands of years ago.

Opposite the cave entrance, take the stepping stone path and steeply descend into the Manifold Valley. At the bottom, cross the river and turn right along the broad pathway, fomerly the trackbed of the Manifold Light Railway and now a walk/cycle track. Cross the Wetton to Butterton road and continue until you reach Wetton Mill (National Trust café). Take the waymarked path to the rear of the café between cottages, signed to Wetton.

Climb steeply at first, then follow the well worn path through woodland and into a broad grassy glen between steep-sided hills. Walk through the valley until you reach a restored stone house (Pepper Inn). Go through the gateway and turn right through a squeeze-stile, signposted to Wetton. Head uphill to a stile and go over Wetton Hill, the path leading to a disused small quarry. Go through another squeeze-stile and follow the track to a road. Descend into Wetton, following it back to the inn.

Distance: 4 miles (6.4km)
Map: OS Landranger 119
Paths: field and woodland paths, old railway track
Terrain: National Trust farmland, river valley and wooded hillsides
Gradient: some steep ascents and descents (can be muddy)

Walk submitted by: Ye Olde Royal Oak

The Manifold Valley from Thor's Cave

LEEK
Map 09 SJ95

Ye Olde Royal Oak
Wetton DE6 2AF ☎ 01335 310287 ▤ 01335 310336
e-mail: royaloak2@compuserve.com
Dir: *A515 twrds Buxton, L after 4 miles to Manifold Valley-Alstonfield, follow signs to Wetton village.*

Formerly part of the Chatsworth estate, this welcoming old Peak District inn was first licensed in 1760. The popular Tissington walking and cycling trail is close by, and the pub's moorland garden includes a camper's croft.

Sample the landlord's collection of over forty single malts, then tuck into home-made soups, steak and Guinness pie, or hot chicken salad. There's fresh local trout and pepper-dusted haddock for fish-fanciers. **OPEN:** 12-3 7-11. **BAR MEALS:** L served all week. D served all week 12-2 7-9. Av main course £6. **RESTAURANT:** 12 7. Av 3 course à la carte £10. **BREWERY/COMPANY:** Free House. **PRINCIPAL BEERS:** Marstons Pedigree, Ruddles County, Jennings Cumberland, Black Sheep Special. **FACILITIES:** Children welcome Garden: Beer garden, outdoor eating. **NOTES:** Parking 20. **ROOMS:** 4 bedrooms 4 en suite d£43
See Pub Walk on page 399

NEWCASTLE-UNDER-LYME
Map 08 SJ84

Mainwaring Arms ♀
Whitmore ST5 5HR ☎ 01782 680851 ▤ 01782 680224
A welcoming old creeper-clad inn on the Mainwaring family estate. Crackling log fires set the scene at this very traditional country retreat, where daily blackboard specials support the popular bar menu. Expect freshly-made sandwiches, home-made steak and kidney pie, pork and leek sausages with chive mash, grilled plaice with mustard sauce, or battered cod with chips and mushy peas.
OPEN: 11-11. **BAR MEALS:** L served all week. D served all week 12-3 6-8.30. Av main course £5. **BREWERY/COMPANY:** Free House. **PRINCIPAL BEERS:** Boddingtons, Marstons Pedigree, Bass. **FACILITIES:** Dogs allowed, only when food service is over. **NOTES:** Parking 60

NORBURY JUNCTION
Map 08 SJ72

Junction Country Inn & Restaurant
ST20 0PN ☎ 01785 284288 ▤ 01785 284288
Dir: *From M6 take road for Eccleshall, L at Gt Bridgeford & head for Woodseaves, L there & head for Newport, L for Norb Junct*
Situated near the Shropshire Union Canal, this pub was originally built to tend to the needs of 19th-century canal traffic. It is located at the junction of the Shropshire and now disused Shrewsbury and Newport Canals. Canal boat hire is available. Traditional pub fare with carvery.

ONECOTE
Map 09 SK05

Jervis Arms
ST13 7RU ☎ 01538 304206
Set in the Peak District National Park, this 17th-century inn has a large riverside complete with swings and slides. Decorative china adorns the mantelpiece in the cosy bar, and favourite dishes range from home-cooked ham with egg, chips and peas to lamb in red wine. Home-made pies are also popular. In summer, six to eight guest beers are available.
OPEN: 12-3 7-11 (Sun 12-11). **BAR MEALS:** L served all week. D served all week 12-2 7-10. Av main course £5. **BREWERY/COMPANY:** Free House. **PRINCIPAL BEERS:** Bass, Marston Pedigree, Titanic Premium. **FACILITIES:** Children welcome Children's licence Garden: outdoor eating Dogs allowed Garden only. **NOTES:** Parking 50

ONNELEY

The Wheatsheaf Inn
Barhill Rd CW3 9QF ☎ 01782 751581 ▤ 01782 751499
e-mail: wheatsheaf@pernickety.co.uk
Traditional English inn with solid oak beams, roaring log fires and distinctive furnishings. Wide ranging menu.

STAFFORD
Map 08 SJ92

Pick of the Pubs

The Hollybush Inn 🐶 ♀
Salt ST18 0BX ☎ 01889 508234 ▤ 01889 508058
e-mail: geoff@hollybushinn.co.uk
See Pick of the Pubs on page 401

The Staffordshire Way

The 93-mile Staffordshire Way runs from Mow Cop on the Cheshire border to Kinver Edge at the southern tip of the county. Threading its way through the heart of England's industrial heritage, the trail begins by crossing gritstone hills to the old town of Leek where there is a good choice of pubs, including the Abbey Inn which offers accommodation in converted outbuildings. Beyond Leek, the way makes for the Boat Inn on the Caldon Canal at Cheddleton before reaching the glorious wooded banks and spectacular gorges of the River Churnet - or the 'Staffordshire Rhineland' as this stretch of it is known. Take a break at the 18th-century Bulls Head in Alton before continuing south to the conservation village of Abbots Bromley, noted for its picturesque butter cross. Quench your thirst at the Royal Oak in Bagot Street or the Crown in the Market Place.

OPEN: 12-2.30 6-11
(Sat 12-11 Sun 12-10.30).
BAR MEALS: L served all week.
D served all week 12-2 6-9.30.
Av main course £7.95.
BREWERY/COMPANY:
Free House.
PRINCIPAL BEERS: Boddingtons,
Courage Directors, Bass.
FACILITIES: Children welcome.
Garden: patio, barbeque, outdoor
eating. Dogs allowed.
NOTES: Parking 25.

The Hollybush Inn

Salt ST18 0BX
☎ 01889 508234 📠 01889 506058
e-mail: geoff@hollybushinn.co.uk
Dir: Salt is signed off A51 S of Stone and
off A518 NE of Stafford

Set in open countryside close to the Trent and Mersey Canal and just minutes from Stafford, the immaculately thatched Holly Bush dates back to the 14th century and is Stafford's oldest inn. It was recorded as a hostelry at the time of the Civil War battle at nearby Hopton Heath.

The pub regularly wins awards for its summer flower displays - all grown and planted by the landlady - and in summer the large beer garden plays host to jazz concerts and hog roasts, culminating with a Guy Fawkes Night firework display. Carved heavy beams, open fires, attractive prints and cosy alcoves characterise the comfortably old-fashioned interior.

The pride taken in some very good food is matched only by the warmth of welcome from the licensees and staff. The innovative daily Illustrated menu, allegedly registered at the Post Office as a newspaper (price sixpence), lists green-lip mussels, crab cakes with Thai sauce, baked ciabatta with avocado, tomatoes and Mozzarella and farmhouse pâté, followed by pot-roast venison, the 'favourite' steak and ale pie and poached plaice fillets with white wine and prawn sauce. To follow, ice cream sundaes enough for two, banana split and selected cheeses with water biscuits.

Look out also for the chalkboards listing such specials as black pudding topped with a poached egg, pan-fried duck breast with green peppercorn and brandy sauce, pot-roast rabbit with root vegetables and herb dumplings, and wild mushroom Stroganoff with brown rice; the pastry chef's home-made puddings and pastries round off some memorable eating. Several house wines available by the glass supplement Boddingtons, Bass and Directors cask ales.

Pick of the Pubs

The Moat House ◎ ◎ ★ ★ ★ ★ ♀
Lower Penkridge Rd, Acton Trussell ST17 0RJ
☎ 01785 712217   📠 01785 715344
e-mail: info@moathouse.co.uk
Just a mile from junction 13 of the M6 stands this Grade II
listed property dating back to the 14th century. In addition
to its rural location the moated manor house is noted for
its quality bedrooms, conference facilities and corporate
events.

'Rustic Moaties' feature strongly on the lunchtime
menu - smoked bacon with avocado and basil crème
fraiche and peppered beef sirloin with horseradish and
shallot marmalade typifying the options. Vegetarian and
other pasta alternatives take in salmon ravioli, dill velouté
and Pecorino and fettuccini with tomato fondue,
aubergines and crushed basil.

Evening choices extend to grilled steaks with optional
sauces, preceded by wrapped prawns with Japanese
dressing and home-made desserts or cheese to follow. Upmarket dining in the canal-side conservatory: also licensed
for weddings, with four honeymoon suites.
OPEN: 12-11. Closed Dec 25-26. **BAR MEALS:** L served
Mon-Sat. D served Sun-Fri 12-2.15 6-9.30. **RESTAURANT:** L
served all week. D served all week 12-2 7-10. Av 3 course à la
carte £33. Av 3 course fixed price £16.95.
BREWERY/COMPANY: Free House.
PRINCIPAL BEERS: Bank's Bitter, Marstons Pedigree,
Greene King Old Speckled Hen. **FACILITIES:** Children
welcome Children's licence Garden: outdoor eating, BBQ
Dogs allowed Guide dogs only. **NOTES:** Parking 150.
ROOMS: 32 bedrooms 32 en suite s£105 d£120 FR£110

Yew Tree Inn
Cauldon, Waterhouses ST10 3EJ ☎ 01538 308348
300-year-old pub with plenty of character and lots of
fascinating artefacts, including pianolas, grandfather clocks, a
crank handle telephone and a pub lantern. Interesting and
varied snack menu consists of hand-raised locally-made pork
pies, sandwiches, rolls and quiche. Banana split and home-
made fruit crumble feature among the sweets.
OPEN: 10-2.30 6-11 (Sun 12-3, 7-10.30). **BAR MEALS:** L served
snacks all day. **BREWERY/COMPANY:** Free House.
PRINCIPAL BEERS: Burton Bridge, Titanic Mild, Bass.
FACILITIES: Children welcome Dogs allowed.
NOTES: Parking 50 No credit cards

Horseshoe Inn ♀
Main St DE13 9SD ☎ 01283 564913   📠 01283 511314
Dir: From A38 at Branston follow signs for Tatenhill
Historic pub with much of its original character still intact. In
the winter visitors are warmed by log fires in the bar and
family area. Good local reputation for honest food and a good
pint.

Pick of the Pubs

Ye Olde Dog & Partridge Inn ★ ★ ★ 👁 ♀
High St DE13 9LS ☎ 01283 813030   📠 01283 813178
Dir: On A50 NW of Burton upon Trent (signposted from A50 &
A511)

A resplendent half-timbered inn on the 18th-century
coaching route to London, with parts of its well-restored
interior dating back to the 15th century. Nearby are the
ruins of Tutbury Castle where Mary Queen of Scots
languished in 1658. The brasserie menu features market-
fresh fish - halibut supreme with leeks and grain mustard
or hollandaise sauce and deep-fried haddock with chips
and mushy peas - while Sunday lunches encompass roasts
of Scotch beef, English pork and Derbyshire turkey. Start,
perhaps, with ricotta tortellini or haggis fritters with mint
chutney and round off with traditional apple and rhubarb
crumble or a seasonal berry tart. Warm rustic baguettes
from the carvery are a mid-week feature, along with a
two-course set luncheon and The Dog's celebrated hot
buffet. Adjacent overnight accommodation is both
spacious and well-equipped.
OPEN: 11.45-2 6-11 (Sun 11.45-11). **RESTAURANT:** L
served all week. D served all week 11.45-2 6-9.45.
BREWERY/COMPANY: Free House.
PRINCIPAL BEERS: Marstons Pedigree, Greene King Old
Speckled Hen. **FACILITIES:** Children welcome Garden:
Food served outside Dogs allowed garden only.
NOTES: Parking 100. **ROOMS:** 20 bedrooms 20 en suite
s£35 d£60 FR£95-£107

Ye Olde Crown ♦ ♦
Leek Rd ST10 3HL ☎ 01538 308204
A traditional village local, Ye Olde Crown dates from around
1648 when it was built as a coaching inn. It retains its original
stonework and interior beams, and open fires are lit in winter.
Traditional pub food including full Sunday roast. Homely
accommodation includes adjacent cottage.

The Crown
Main St DE13 8NQ ☎ 01543 472551   📠 01543 473479
Dir: On A515 N of Lichfield
A cosy, friendly village pub with old beams and open fires.
Simple but tasty food is served.

England

Adnams

Taken over by the Adnams family in 1872 the Sole Bay Brewery in Southwold produces traditional beers, using methods steeped in history. It's main beers are Adnams Bitter (3.7%), Broadside (4.7%), Regatta (4.3%), and Fisherman (4.5%). Suffolk Strong (4.5%), the brewery's packaged beer, won a gold medal at Brewing Industry Awards 2000.

SUFFOLK

ALDEBURGH   Map 07 TM45

The Mill Inn 🐑
Market Cross Place IP15 5BJ ☎ 01728 452563
📠 01728 452028
e-mail: tedmillinn@btinternet.com
Dir: Follow Aldeburgh signs from A12 on A1094. Pub last building on L before sea

Occupying a seafront position, this genuine traditional fisherman's inn is frequented by the local lifeboat crew, those visiting the North Warren bird reserve, or walkers from Thorpness and Orford. Opposite is the 17th-century Moot Hall. Good value food ranges from baguettes, crab salads and sandwiches to seafood lasagne and a choice of steaks. The emphasis is very much on locally caught fish.
OPEN: 11-3 6-11. **BAR MEALS:** L served all week. D served all week 12-2 7-9. Av main course £7. **RESTAURANT:** L served all week. D served Fri-Wed 12-2 7-9. Av 3 course à la carte £12.
BREWERY/COMPANY: Adnams.
PRINCIPAL BEERS: Adnams-Bitter, Broadside, Regatta.
ROOMS: 4 bedrooms s£25 d£40

BARNBY   Map 07 TM48

Pick of the Pubs

The Swan Inn 🐑 **NEW**
Swan Ln NR34 7QF ☎ 01520 476646
Dir: Just off the A146 between Lowestoft and Beccles in the village of Barnby
An enterprise bought some 12 years ago by a family of Lowestoft fish wholesalers, it is altogether unsurprising that The Swan has become arguably the county's foremost fish restaurant. Located some five miles inland, the pub comprises a village bar, the hub of local activity, the Fisherman's Cove restaurant and a flower-festooned beer garden where even visitors' dogs are treated to their own low-alcohol 'pet pints' - a large bucket of water.
   Up to 80 different fish dishes appear on the menu, from traditionally smoked local sprats to Scandinavian gravad lax and from locally-landed skate wings in crisp breadcrumbs to prawn and lobster thermidor. Plenty of alternatives for non-lovers of fish encompass egg mayonnaise and Brie wedges with cranberry dip followed by grilled gammon with pineapple and choice rump steak with deep-fried onion rings.
   Self-contained accommodation above the pub is due to be supplemented by further bedrooms in an old outhouse.
OPEN: 11-3 6-12. **BAR MEALS:** L served all week. D served all week 12-2 7-9.30. Av main course £10. **RESTAURANT:** L served all week. D served all week 12-2 7-9.30. Av 3 course à la carte £15. **BREWERY/COMPANY:** Free House.
PRINCIPAL BEERS: Bass, Adnams, Greene King Abbot Ale, IPA. **FACILITIES:** Children welcome Garden: Food served outside Dogs allowed. **NOTES:** Parking 30.

BILDESTON   Map 07 TL94

The Crown Hotel
High St IP7 7EB ☎ 01449 740510 📠 01449 740510
Dir: On B1115 between Hadleigh & Stowmarket
15th-century timber-framed building, formerly a wool merchants house and coaching inn, featuring oak beams, inglenook fireplaces and a two-acre garden. Reputedly the most haunted pub in Britain, it offers traditional snacks alongside daily dishes like vegetable and lentil soup, black olive pate, cod in beer batter, honey-spiced lamb, and whole lemon sole.
OPEN: 11-2.30 6-11. **BAR MEALS:** L served all week. D served all week 12-2 6.30-9.30. Av main course £7. **RESTAURANT:** L served all week. D served all week 12-2 6.30-9.30. Av 3 course à la carte £15. **BREWERY/COMPANY:** Free House.
PRINCIPAL BEERS: Adnams, Nethergate. **FACILITIES:** Children welcome Garden: Dogs allowed. **NOTES:** Parking 30.
ROOMS: 13 bedrooms 13 en suite s£39 d£55

Pubs offering a good choice of seafood on the menu.

THE ANGEL, ◎ ★ ★
LAVENHAM
Market Place CO10 9QZ.
Tel: 01787 247388
Directions: village on A1141
E of A134 between Sudbury
and Bury St Edmunds
*Delightful early 15th-century
inn overlooking the medieval
marketplace and the
magnificent timbered
guildhall. Expect a friendly
welcome, East Anglian ales
and freshly prepared food in
the traditionally furnished
bar. Bedrooms.*
Open: 11-11 (Sun 12-10.30).
Bar Meals: 12-2.15 6.45-9.15.
Children welcome. Garden,
front patio. Parking.
(see page 412 for full entry)

SUFFOLK

*Pub*WALK

The Angel, Lavenham

Combine a fascinating stroll around England's best preserved medieval town, where some 300 listed buildings line its quaint streets, with an excursion into the peaceful countryside to the north of the town.

From the Angel, walk ahead through the Market Square and take the narrow street (Market Lane) in the right-hand corner to reach the High Street. Turn right and walk along the pavement for around 300 yards (274m) to the old railway bridge. Just before the bridge, take the signed path left for the railway walk. Turn left onto the railway cutting at the bottom and follow the old track bed. Cross a road via gates and continue along the course of the old railway.

Pass beneath a bridge and walk up the ramp onto the road. Turn right over the bridge, then take the footpath left in the direction of Lavenham

church. Follow this path until you reach Park Road to the rear of the church and turn left. Bear right at the road junction and look for a footpath on your right by a gap in the wall. Go through a gate, cross a bridge and walk past The Hall. Enter the churchyard via a gate, visit the impressive church with its great square-buttressed flint tower rising to more than 140ft (40m), and exit onto the main road. Turn left downhill into the town.

At The Swan Hotel, turn right along Water Street and then left into Lady Street, opposite Lavenham Priory. Enter Market Place and walk back to the inn. If you wish to explore and learn more about this prosperous medieval wool town, why not hire the audio tour of the town from the pharmacy next to the Swan Hotel.

Distance: 3 miles (4.8km)
Map: OS Landranger 155
Terrain: town streets and farmland
Paths: field paths, disused railway, pavements
Gradient: general level

*Walk submitted by:
The Angel Inn*

Timber framed building in Lavenham

BLYFORD | Map 07 TM47

Queens Head Inn 👻
Southwold Rd IP19 9JY ☎ 01502 478404
Dir: From A12 after Blythburgh take A145, fork L towards Halesworth, Pub on L opp church
Once used by smugglers, with a secret underground passage linking the inn with the nearby church, this 14th-century thatched building is supposedly haunted by the ghosts of seven smugglers shot in the tunnel by excise men.

Varied pub fare includes bar snacks, fish specialities such as Lowestoft cod, or roast Scotch beef and liver and bacon.
OPEN: 11-3 6-11 (Sun 12-3, 7-10.30). **BAR MEALS:** L served Tue-Sun & BH. D served Tue-Sun & BH12-3 6-9. Av main course £6. **BREWERY/COMPANY:** Adnams.
PRINCIPAL BEERS: Adnams - Bitter, Broadside.
FACILITIES: Children welcome Garden: Dogs allowed.
NOTES: Parking 50. **ROOMS:** 2 bedrooms 2 en suite s£20 d£40

BRANDESTON | Map 07 TM26

The Queens Head
The Street IP13 7AD ☎ 01728 685307
Dir: From A14 take A1120 to Earl Soham, then S to Brandeston
Approximately 400 years old, this family-run village pub has wooden panelling, quarry tile floors and open fires, as well as camping facilities at the rear.

Home-cooked traditional English food such as steak, Guinness and mushroom pie, and Phil's giant Yorkshire pudding with sausages, gravy and onions. A range of bar snacks is also served.
OPEN: 11.30-3 6-11 (Sun 12-3, 7-10.30). **BAR MEALS:** L served all week. D served Mon-Sat 12-2.30 7-9.30. Av main course £5.50.
BREWERY/COMPANY: Adnams. **PRINCIPAL BEERS:** Adnams Broadside, Bitter & seasonal ale. **FACILITIES:** Children welcome Garden: paddock for camping Dogs allowed.
NOTES: Parking 30. **ROOMS:** 3 bedrooms s£18 d£36

BROCKLEY GREEN | Map 07 TL74

The Plough Inn 𝑸
CO10 8DT ☎ 01440 786789 📠 01440 786710
e-mail: ploughdave@aol.com
Dir: Take B1061 from A143, approx 1.5m beyond Kedington
Cosy bars with old oak timbers and pine furnishings serve well kept Suffolk ales at this sympathetically extended country pub, and there are wonderful views across the Stour valley.

Dishes range from pot roasted shank of lamb or chilli pancakes in the bar to poached Scotch salmon with tagliatelle or sauteed calves liver in the restaurant.
OPEN: 12-2.30 5-11. **BAR MEALS:** L served all week. D served all week 12-2 7-9.30. Av main course £8. **RESTAURANT:** L served all week. D served all week 12-2 7-9.30. Av 3 course à la carte £20. Av 3 course fixed price £17.50.
BREWERY/COMPANY: Free House.
PRINCIPAL BEERS: Greene King IPA, Adnams Best, Fullers London Pride, Woodforde's Wherry. **FACILITIES:** Children welcome Garden: food served outside Dogs allowed Water bowls. **NOTES:** Parking 50. **ROOMS:** 8 bedrooms 8 en suite s£45 d£65 FR£85

AA inspected hotel accommodation

BROME | Map 07 TM17

Pick of the Pubs

Cornwallis Country Hotel ◉ ◉ ★ ★ ★ 𝑸
IP23 8AJ ☎ 01379 870326 📠 01379 870051
e-mail: info@cornwallis.com
Dir: Just off A140 at Brome
The original Dower House to Brome Hall, dating back to 1561, makes a fine setting for a country hotel of distinction, set in 20 acres of mature gardens complete with yew topiary, water garden and resident heron. The Tudor bar with its 60ft well, three log-burning stoves and mixture of oak and mahogany settles is the informal meeting-and-eating place. No shame here in enjoying a quick bite of curried chicken in turmeric and raisin bread or a white bun of salmon and prawns with tomato and horseradish mayonnaise. Further starters and snacks might be warm Gressingham duck confit with apple chutney or mushroom, red onion and sage risotto with Parmesan curls, while main events add steak and kidney pudding, braised lamb shoulder with sweet red cabbage and deep-fried cod in batter with home-cut chips and mushy minted peas. Restaurant dishes go up a tad in complexity and price, though it remains to the kitchen's credit that such care is taken over ingredients and preparation whichever location you may choose.

OPEN: 11-11. **BAR MEALS:** L served all week. D served all week 12-10. Av main course £9. **RESTAURANT:** L served all week. D served all week 12-2.30 6.30-9.45. Av 3 course à la carte £23. Av 2 course fixed price £20.
BREWERY/COMPANY: Free House.
PRINCIPAL BEERS: Adnams Broadside, St Peters Best.
FACILITIES: Children welcome Garden: patio, BBQ, outdoor eating Dogs allowed. **NOTES:** Parking 400.
ROOMS: 16 bedrooms 16 en suite s£72.50 d£90 FR£100

BURY ST EDMUNDS | Map 07 TL86

Gardeners Arms
Tostock IP30 9PA ☎ 01359 270460
Convenient for the A14, this unspoilt village local close to the green boasts a stone-floored public bar and some imaginative food. Greene King ales; sheltered lawn for summer sipping.

The Linden Tree
7 Out Northgate IP33 1JQ ☎ 01284 754600
Dir: opposite railway station
Busy town pub with a large garden. Suits all ages, swings and see-saw for children. Opposite railway station.

The Nutshell
17 The Traverse IP33 1BJ ☎ 01742 764867
Known as the smallest pub in Britain, this novel thatched inn covers an area of 15ft x 7ft 6 inches and features in the Guinness Book of Records.

Six Bells Inn ♦♦♦♦ 🛏 ♈
The Green, Bardwell IP31 1AW ☎ 01359 250820
▤ 01359 250820
e-mail: sixbellsbardwell@aol.com
Dir: From A143 take turning marked Six Bells & Bardwell Windmill, premises 1m on L just before village green
Low-beamed 16th-century pub which was featured in the classic comedy series 'Dad's Army.' Scenes were filmed here and in the surrounding area and a photograph of the much-loved cast hangs in the bar. An inglenook fireplace and an old Suffolk range are also among the charming pub features, and for those seeking a perfect rural retreat, there is pine-furnished cottage-style accommodation in a converted barn. Freshly prepared food might include sea bass with lemon and parsley, pork fillet in ginger and orange sauce and medallions of duck breast.
OPEN: 12-2 6.30-10.30 (Fri-Sat 6-11). Closed Mon-Wed lunch, 25-26 Dec. **BAR MEALS:** L served Thur-Sun. D served all week 12-1.30 6.45-9.15. **RESTAURANT:** L served Thu-Sun. D served all week 12-1.30 6.45-9.15. Av 3 course à la carte £17.50. Av 3 course fixed price £12.50.
BREWERY/COMPANY: Free House.
PRINCIPAL BEERS: Adnams Best, Fullers London Pride, Batemans Six Bells. **FACILITIES:** Garden: Dogs allowed, garden only. **NOTES:** Parking 40. **ROOMS:** 10 bedrooms
10 en suite s£42.50 d£50 FR£55-£90

CAVENDISH   Map 07 TL84

Bull Inn 🛏
High St CO10 8AX ☎ 01787 280245
Dir: A134 Bury St Edmunds to Long Melford, then R at green, pub 5m on R
The unassuming Victorian façade of this pub, set in one of Suffolk's most beautiful villages, hides a splendid 15th-century beamed interior. Expect a good atmosphere and decent food, the daily-changing blackboard menu listing, perhaps, curries, shank of lamb, fresh fish and shellfish, and a roast on Sundays.
OPEN: 10.30-3 6-11 (Sun 12-3, 7-11). **BAR MEALS:** L served Tue-Sun. D served Tue-Sun 12-2 6-9. Av main course £7. **RESTAURANT:** L served Tue-Sun. D served Tue-Sun 12-2 6-9. Av 3 course à la carte £18 9. **BREWERY/COMPANY:** Adnams. **PRINCIPAL BEERS:** Adnams Bitter & Broadside. **FACILITIES:** Children welcome Garden: patio, BBQ, food served outside Dogs allowed. **NOTES:** Parking 30. **ROOMS:** 3 bedrooms 3 en suite

CHELMONDISTON   Map 07 TM23

Butt & Oyster ♈
Pin Mill Ln IP9 1JW ☎ 01473 780764 ▤ 01473 780764
The role of this 16th century pub on the eerie Suffolk coast has always been to provide sustenance for the local bargees and rivermen whose thirst for beer is near legendary. Today, with its character still thankfully intact, the Butt & Oyster is a favourite haunt of locals, tourists and yachtsmen. A mixture of seafood and traditional dishes characterises the menu, including toad in the hole, steak and kidney pie and scampi and chips. *continued*

OPEN: 11-3 7-11 (wknd and Etr-Sep 11-11). **BAR MEALS:** L served all week. D served all week 12-2 7-9.30. Av main course £5.50. **BREWERY/COMPANY:** Pubmaster.
PRINCIPAL BEERS: Tolly Cobbold. **FACILITIES:** Children welcome Garden: outdoor eating, riverside Dogs allowed in garden only, Water. **NOTES:** Parking 40

CHILLESFORD   Map 07 TM35

The Froize Inn 🛏 ♈
The Street IP12 3PU ☎ 01394 450282
Dir: From the A12 (toward Lowestoft) take B1084, Chillesford 5m

Built on the site of Chillesford Friary, this distinctive red-brick building dates back to around 1490 and stands on today's popular Suffolk coast path. Alistair and Joy Shaw who refurbished the inn and were renowned for offering innovative fish and seafood cooking have leased the pub to a small company. Reports on the new regime please.
OPEN: 12-3 6-11 (all day wknd). Closed Mon, 3wks Feb-Mar, 1wk end Sep. **BAR MEALS:** L served Tues-Sun. D served Tues-Sun 12-3 7-9. Av main course £7.50. **RESTAURANT:** L served Tues-Sun. D served Tues-Sun 12-3 7-9. Av 3 course à la carte £25.
BREWERY/COMPANY: Free House.
PRINCIPAL BEERS: Woodforde's, Adnams, St Peter's, Mauldons.
FACILITIES: Children welcome Garden: patio, children's area, C&C, beer garden with seating Dogs allowed.
NOTES: Parking 70. **ROOMS:** 2 bedrooms 2 en suite s£30 d£50 FR£65-£75 No credit cards

CLARE

The Bell Hotel
Market Hill CO10 8NN
Half-timbered 16th-century posting house with a wealth of carved beams, panelling and open fires. Conservatory dining room; terrace.

COCKFIELD   Map 07 TL95

Three Horseshoes ♈
Stow's Hill IP30 0JB ☎ 01284 828177
e-mail: threehorseshoes@tinyworld.co.uk
Dir: A134 towards Sudbury, then L onto A1141 towards Lavenham & Cockfield
Pink-washed 14th-century thatched inn with beautiful gardens and uninterrupted views of rolling countryside. The restaurant has one of the oldest king posts in Suffolk in its vaulted roof, and the heavily beamed bar offers an impressive array of hand pulled ales. Home-made pies, suet puddings, fresh monster cod, steaks and Superman mixed grill are typical dishes. *continued*

OPEN: 11-3 6-11 Sun 10.30. **BAR MEALS:** L served Wed-Mon.
D served Mon-Sat 12-2 6-9.30. Av main course £6.95.
RESTAURANT: L served Wed-Mon. D served Wed-Mon 12-2
6-9.30. Av 3 course à la carte £13. **BREWERY/COMPANY:** Free
House. **PRINCIPAL BEERS:** Greene King IPA, Adnams,
Nethergate. **FACILITIES:** Children welcome Garden: outdoor
eating, BBQ, fountain Dogs allowed Water. **NOTES:** Parking 40

COTTON   Map 07 TM06

Pick of the Pubs

The Trowel & Hammer Inn 🛏️
Mill Rd IP14 4QL ☎ 01449 781234   📠 01449 781765
Dir: From A14 follow signs to Haughley, then Bacton, then turn
left for Cotton.
Built in 1450 as a hostelry for merchants heading inland
from the east coast, this is now a thriving community
village pub with a succession of beamed rooms to
accommodate all-comers from 'rowdy farmers to retired
colonels', forever plotting the pub's next source of
entertainment.
  This is not, however to decry the output of a dedicated
kitchen whose craftily sourced specialities include fresh
cod and chips, beef carbonnade with mustard croutons, a
casserole of scallops, langoustine, red snapper and
prawns and baked chicken, bacon and garlic in puff pastry
with sage gravy.
  Daily up-dated menus make best use of market
shopping to embrace Norfolk duck, black sea bream, racks
of lamb with redcurrant and mint sauce and mushroom
Stroganoff.
  Well-chosen real ales and guest ales are supplemented
by international wines from a list that includes a fair
selection of half bottles:- all should be fun for customers
and staff.
OPEN: 11.30-3 6-11 (Sat 11.30-11, Sun 12-10.30).
BAR MEALS: L served all week. D served all week 12-2 6-10.
Av main course £7. **RESTAURANT:** L served all week. D
served all week 12-2 6-10. Av 3 course à la carte £14.
BREWERY/COMPANY: Free House.
PRINCIPAL BEERS: Adnams, Greene King IPA & Abbot Ale,
Nethergate. **FACILITIES:** Garden: BBQ, outdoor eating
Dogs allowed, water, biscuits. **NOTES:** Parking 50

DUNWICH   Map 07 TM47

Pick of the Pubs

The Ship Inn 🛏️
St James St IP17 3DT ☎ 01728 648219
📠 01728 648675
Dir: N on A12 from Ipswich thru Yoxford, R signed Dunwich
At one time a medieval port of some size and importance,
the original Dunwich was virtually destroyed by a terrible
storm in 1326. Further storms and erosion followed and
now the place is little more than a small seaside village
beside a shingle beach. Once the haunt of smugglers and
seafarers, the Ship is now a popular dining destination
attracting many locals and visitors.
  Using fresh local produce, especially fish, the inn offers
a varied menu and a good choice of real ales. Choose
perhaps from the simple lunchtime menu, which includes
the likes of cod and chips, macaroni cheese and salad
platter, or sample fish crumble, peppered sirloin steak or
breast of duck with an orange sauce, in the restaurant.
OPEN: 11-3.30 6-11. **BAR MEALS:** L served all week. D
served all week 12-2 7-9.15. Av main course £8.
RESTAURANT: L served all week. D served all week 12-2
7-9.15. **BREWERY/COMPANY:** Free House.
PRINCIPAL BEERS: Adnams. **FACILITIES:** Children
welcome Garden: patio, outdoor eating Dogs allowed.
NOTES: Parking 10. **ROOMS:** 3 bedrooms 3 en suite s£45
d£55

EARL SOHAM   Map 07 TM26

Victoria
The Street IP13 7RL ☎ 01728 685758
Dir: From the A14 at Stowmarket, Earl Soham is on the A1120
Friendly, down-to-earth village pub with its own brewery
attached to the rear of the building. Traditional pub fare on
offer such as corned beef hash, home-made meat and
vegetarian lasagnes, various casseroles, goulash, fish pies, and
cashew nut curry. Home-made desserts include sponge
pudding and treacle and walnut tart.
OPEN: 11.30-3 6-11 (Sun 12-3, 7-10.30). **BAR MEALS:** L served
all week. D served all week 11.30-2 6-10. Av main course £5.50.
BREWERY/COMPANY: Free House. **PRINCIPAL BEERS:** Earl
Soham-Victoria Bitter, Albert Ale, & Gannet Mild (all brewed on
site). **FACILITIES:** Children welcome Garden: Dogs allowed
garden only. **NOTES:** Parking 25 No credit cards

EASTBRIDGE   Map 07 TM46

The Eels Foot Inn
IP16 4SN ☎ 01728 830154   📠 01728 830154
e-mail: theeelesfoot@AOL.com
Dir: From A12 at Yoxford take B1122 (signed Leiston/Sizewell).Turn L
at Theberton
Edge of village pub once the haunt of smugglers and named
after apparatus used by the local cobbler who occupied these
premises. Close to Minsmere Bird Reserve. Most of the food is
home-made, including steak, pork and venison casserole, fish
pies, and vegetable lasagne.   *continued*

OPEN: 11-3 7-11 (July- August 11-11). **BAR MEALS:** L served all week. D served Sun, Tue-Sat (Mon in summer)12-2 7-9. Av main course £5. **BREWERY/COMPANY:** Adnams.
PRINCIPAL BEERS: Adnams-Bitter, Broadside, Old, Regatta.
FACILITIES: Children welcome Garden: large grassed terraces, barbecue Dogs allowed water bowls. **NOTES:** Parking 200.
ROOMS: 1 bedrooms 1 en suite No credit cards

ERWARTON   Map 07 TM23

The Queens Head
The Street IP9 1LN ☎ 01473 787550
Dir: From Ipswich take B1456 to Shotley
Handsome mid 17th-century building in traditional Suffolk style, enjoying fine views of coast and countryside. Low beamed ceilings, exposed timbers and first class meals make this a worthwhile destination. Look out for the fascinating display of navigational maps in the loos. Dishes range from lamb shank in red wine and rosemary sauce, smoked haddock, or pheasant casserole, to roast venison, seafood lasagne, or steak and kidney pud.
OPEN: 11-3 (Sun 12-3) 6.30-11 (Sun 7-10.30). Closed 25 Dec.
BAR MEALS: L served all week. D served all week 12-2.45 7-9.30.
RESTAURANT: L served all week. D served all week 12-2.45 7-9.30. Av 3 course fixed price £15.75.
BREWERY/COMPANY: Free House.
PRINCIPAL BEERS: Adnams Best, Greene King IPA, Adnams Broadside. **FACILITIES:** Children welcome Garden: patio/terrace, outdoor eating **NOTES:** Parking 30

FRAMLINGHAM   Map 07 TM26

The Station Hotel ♀
Station Rd IP13 9EE ☎ 01728 723455
e-mail: neilpascoe@excite.co.uk
Dir: Bypass Ipswich heading toward Lowestoft on the A12
Victorian pub near a former railway station with a large main bar and an intimate snug at the rear. The interior features wooden floors, wooden furniture and real fires. Fresh fish is a speciality at weekends, and other favourites are the home-made soups and both meat and vegetarian lasagne.
OPEN: 12-3 5-11. **BAR MEALS:** L served all week. D served all week 12-2 7-10. Av main course £5. **RESTAURANT:** L served all week. D served all week 12-2 7-10. Av 3 course à la carte £11.
BREWERY/COMPANY: Free House.
PRINCIPAL BEERS: Earl Soham Victoria, Albert & Mild, guest beers. **FACILITIES:** Children welcome Garden: pond, patio, food served outdoors Dogs allowed. **NOTES:** Parking 20

AA The Restaurant Guide 2002

The right choice every time with this invaluable guide for gourmets

AA Lifestyle Guides

www.theAA.com

FRAMSDEN   Map 07 TM15

The Dobermann Inn
The Street IP14 6HG ☎ 01473 890461
Dir: S off A1120(Stowmarket/Yoxford)
A 16th-century thatched freehouse, with beams, open fire and antique furniture. Previously known as the Greyhound, it was re-named by the current owner, a prominent owner, breeder and judge of Dobermanns. Meals range from bar snacks to steak and mushroom pie, venison pie, duck legs stuffed with pork, apple and rosemary, or spicy nut loaf.
OPEN: 12-3 7-11. **BAR MEALS:** L served Tue-Sun. D served Tue-Sun 12-2 7-10. **RESTAURANT:** L served Tue-Sun. D served Tue-Sun 12-2 7-10. **BREWERY/COMPANY:** Free House.
PRINCIPAL BEERS: Adnams Best & Broadside, Greene King Abbot Ale, Maldons Moletrap. **FACILITIES:** Garden: outdoor eating, Dogs allowed garden only. **NOTES:** Parking 27.
ROOMS: 1 bedrooms 1 en suite d£50 No credit cards

GREAT GLEMHAM   Map 07 TM36

The Crown Inn
IP17 2DA ☎ 01728 663693
Dir: A12 Ipswich to Lowestoft, in Stratford-St-Andrew L at Shell garage. Crown 1.5m
Cosy, extensively renovated 17th-century village pub overlooking the Great Glemham Estate and within easy reach of the Suffolk Heritage Coast. Fish dishes include salmon marinated in lime and coriander, and fresh cod or haddock cooked in beer batter. Other options are home-made steak and kidney pie, gammon and lasagne.
OPEN: 11.30-2.30 6.30-11 (closed Mon). **BAR MEALS:** L served Tue-Sun. D served Tue-Sun 11.30-2.30 6.30-10. Av main course £6.95. **BREWERY/COMPANY:** Free House.
PRINCIPAL BEERS: Greene King Old Speckled Hen & IPA.
FACILITIES: Children welcome Garden: Dogs allowed.
NOTES: Parking 20

HADLEIGH   Map 07 TM04

The Marquis of Cornwallis ♀
Upper St, Layham IP7 5JZ ☎ 01473 822051
🖷 01473 822051
e-mail: marquislayham@aol.com
Dir: From Colchester take A12 then B1070 towards Hadleigh. Layham signed on L, last village before Hadleigh
Situated in two acres of garden sloping down to the River Brett, this 17th-century inn is named after a British military commander who was defeated in the American War of Independence. It uses traditional country recipes and specialises in home-made pies. Dishes are prepared from local Suffolk produce, and range from baguettes, and ploughmans' to grilled plaice fillets, pork loin steaks and cidered chicken casserole.
OPEN: 12-3 (Sun 7-10.30) 6-11 (Whit-Aug Sat 12-11, Sun 12-10.30). **BAR MEALS:** L served all week. D served all week 12-2.30 7-9.30. Av main course £5.75. **RESTAURANT:** L served all week. D served all week 12-2.30 7-9.30. Av 3 course à la carte £15. **BREWERY/COMPANY:** Free House.
PRINCIPAL BEERS: Adnams, Greene King IPA & Abbot Ale, Wadworth 6X. **FACILITIES:** Children welcome Garden: food served outdoors Dogs allowed. **NOTES:** Parking 30

HALESWORTH   Map 07 TM37

Pick of the Pubs

The Queen's Head 🐑 ♀
The Street, Bramfield IP19 9HT ☎ 01986 784214
📄 01986 784797
e-mail: qhbfield@aol.com
Dir: 2m from A12 on the A144 towards Halesworth
One of the first pubs outside London to be recognised for
its certified organic menu, this is a traditional Suffolk pub
close to the Heritage Coast and only a few minutes' drive
from Southwold. Most ingredients for their home-
produced meals are collected from local organic farms
and growers or from the fishing boats at Dunwich Beach.
Old favourites such as steak, kidney and Adnams ale pie
preserve a long tradition, while at Sunday lunch expect to
find Red Poll beef, British saddleback pork and rare-breed
Hebridean Hogget lamb on the fixed-price menu. Organic
specialities include eggs in curry sauce with toasted
almonds and roast potato wedges with apples, bacon and
mushrooms, followed by chicken, leek and bacon crumble
and curried nut loaf with spicy tomato sauce. Round off
with bread-and-butter pudding. In the same family
ownership, Southwold Lodge at Wrentham - on the other
side of the A12 - offers comfortable holiday
accommodation, sharing its food philosophy and many of
the same suppliers.
OPEN: 11.45-2.30 (Sun 12-3, 7-10.30) 6.30-11 (7-11 Mon).
Closed 26 Dec. **BAR MEALS:** L served all week. D served all
week 12-2 6.30-10. Av main course £8.95.
BREWERY/COMPANY: Adnams.
PRINCIPAL BEERS: Adnams Bitter & Broadside.
FACILITIES: Children welcome Garden: outdoor eating,
patio Dogs allowed. **NOTES:** Parking 15.
ROOMS: 2 bedrooms 2 en suite s£35 d£50

HARTEST   Map 07 TL85

The Crown 🐑
The Green IP29 4DH ☎ 01284 830250
Dir: On B1066 S of Bury St Edmunds
Once known as Hartest Hall, this heavily beamed 15th-century
building is set on the village green next to the church. One
menu is offered throughout, with the emphasis on an
impressive range of fresh fish from Lowestoft. Special set
meals during the week provide particularly good value.
OPEN: 11-2.30 6-11. **BAR MEALS:** L served all week. D served
all week 12-2 6.30-9.30. Av main course £9. **RESTAURANT:** L
served all week. D served all week 12-2 6.30-9.30. Av 3 course à la
carte £13.50. **BREWERY/COMPANY:** Greene King.
PRINCIPAL BEERS: Greene King Abbot Ale, Old Speckled Hen &
IPA. **FACILITIES:** Children welcome Garden: Dogs allowed.
NOTES: Parking 40

HOLBROOK   Map 07 TM13

The Compasses
Ipswich Rd IP9 2QR ☎ 01473 328332 📄 01473 327403
Dir: From A137 S of Ipswich, take B1456/B1080
Traditional country pub situated on the Shotley peninsula, in
an area of outstanding natural beauty. Due to come under
new management at time of press. Certainly worth a visit, if
only for the location.

HONEY TYE   Map 07 TL93

The Lion ♀
CO6 4NX ☎ 01206 263434 📄 01206 263434
Dir: On A134 between Colchester & Sudbury
Low-beamed ceilings and an open log fire are features of this
traditional country dining pub on the Essex/Suffolk border.
Interesting menu offers a choice of dishes - for example,
baked supreme of salmon, home made steak and real ale pie,
braised gigot leg of lamb steak, or pan seared medallions of
pork tenderloin.
OPEN: 11-3 5.45-11 (Sun 12-10.30). **BAR MEALS:** L served all
week. D served all week 12-2 6-9.30 (all day Sun). Av main course
£8.25. **RESTAURANT:** L served all week. D served all week 12-2
6-9.30. **BREWERY/COMPANY:** Free House.
PRINCIPAL BEERS: Greene King IPA, Adnams Bitter.
FACILITIES: Children welcome Garden: patio area, outdoor
eating. **NOTES:** Parking 40

HORRINGER   Map 07 TL86

Pick of the Pubs

Beehive 🐑 ♀
The Street IP29 5SN ☎ 01284 735260
e-mail: thebeehive@virginnet.co
Dir: From A14, 1st turning for Bury St Edmunds, sign for Westley
& Ickworth Park
In a small village of thatched cottages belonging once to
Ickworth House - now a National Trust property - the
Beehive is built around a Victorian flint stone cottage
divided into cosy dining areas with antique pine tables and
chairs: the picturesque garden has a patio for al fresco
dining in summer. The proprietors have been here for
more than fifteen years.
A typical menu offers bacon and leek risotto, pan-fried
venison liver over red onion mash, grilled Torbay sole with
scallop butter, lobster salad, and roast monkfish tail with
salty capers.
OPEN: 11.30-2.30 7-11. Closed Dec 25-26. **BAR MEALS:** L
served all week. D served Mon-Sat 12-2 7-9.45. Av main
course £6.95. **BREWERY/COMPANY:** Greene King.
PRINCIPAL BEERS: Greene King - IPA, Abbot Ale.
FACILITIES: Children welcome Garden: patio, food served
outside Dogs allowed, garden only.
NOTES: Parking 30

HOXNE

The Swan
Low St IP21 5AS ☎ 01379 668275
A hostelry since 1619, this Grade II listed building was built by
the Bishop of Norwich as guest quarters to his now defunct
summer palace. Walled garden - ideal for summer eating.

Pubs offering a good choice of
seafood on the menu.

OPEN: 12-3 6-11 (Sun 12-3 7-10.30). Closed 25 Dec, 26 Dec eve & 1 Jan eve.
BAR MEALS: L served all week. D served all week 12-2.30 6-10. Av main course £9
RESTAURANT: L served all week D served all week 12-2.30 6-10. Av 3 course a la carte £19.
BREWERY/COMPANY: Greene King.
PRINCIPAL BEERS: Greene King IPA & Abbot Ale.
FACILITIES: Children welcome. Garden: terrace outdoor eating. Dogs allowed.
NOTES: Parking 50.

The Red Lion

The Street IP28 6PS
☎ 01638 717802 📠 01638 515702
e-mail: lizard2020@supanet.com
Dir: On the A1101 between Mildenhall and Bury St Edmunds.

Set back from the A1101 with a neat front lawn and a raised rear terrace overlooking the River Lark and open fields, this attractive, sympathetically restored 16th-century thatched inn is a handy refreshment stop following a visit to West Stow Country Park and the Anglo-Saxon Village.

Full of exposed low beams and warming log fires, rugs on wooden floors, antique furniture and curios, and mellow evening candlelight, the Red Lion is a popular dining destination, in particular for fresh fish delivered daily from Lowestoft. A reliable range of interesting home-cooked food using quality local produce is offered. On the fish menu you will find up to 15 different types of fish and seafood, perhaps including Brancaster mussels in a cream, garlic, celery and white wine sauce, scallops with hazelnut and basil butter, sea bass with chilli butter, skate wing with caramelised onion and bacon, and barracuda fillet with black peppercorn sauce.

Simple and appetising bar food ranges from home-made soups and pâtés, warm chicken and pasta salad and Newmarket sausages, mash and onion and mustard gravy, to a formidable mixed grill, and vegetable curry. On the carte you may find rack of lamb with red wine, mushroom and rosemary sauce, lambs' liver and kidneys in a Dijon mustard and bacon sauce, and Gressingham duck with plum sauce. Typical examples from the seasonal game menu include venison steak with a chive and red pepper butter, an exotic game grill, and partidge with honey and mango sauce. Home-made puddings for chocoholics include rich chocolate pots and chocolate Bailey's cheesecake.

At the bar, choose from well kept Greene King ales, a good range of wines, including country fruit wines, and fruit presses.

411

ICKLINGHAM   Map 07 TL77

Pick of the Pubs

The Red Lion
The Street IP28 6PS ☎ 01638 717802 📠 01638 515702
e-mail: lizard2020@supernet.com
See Pick of the Pubs on page 411

IXWORTH   Map 07 TL97

Pykkerell Inn
38 High St IP31 2HH ☎ 01359 230398 📠 01359 230398
Dir: A14 trunk rd/jct Bury St Edmunds central to A143, towards Diss
15th-century coaching inn with original beams, inglenook
fireplace, wood-panelled library room, and 14th-century barn
enclosing a patio with barbeque. Menu boards highlight fresh
fish, such as sea bass on basil mash with herb dressing,
alongside steak and ale pie, venison with red wine and
mushroom sauce, and beef Stroganoff.
OPEN: 12-3 6-11. **BAR MEALS:** L served Mon-Sat 12-2.30. Av
main course £6. **RESTAURANT:** L served all week. D served
Mon-Sat 12-2.30 6-10. Av 3 course à la carte £18.
BREWERY/COMPANY: Greene King. **PRINCIPAL
BEERS:** Greene King IPA & Abbot Ale. **FACILITIES:** Children
welcome Garden: Dogs allowed. **NOTES:** Parking 30

KERSEY   Map 07 TM04

The Bell Inn
IP7 6DY ☎ 01473 823229
*Dir: Follow A1171 from Bury St Edmunds thru Lavenham, follow signs
for Kersey*
Splendid 14th-century timbered inn in one of Suffolk's most
picturesque villages. The pub has a wealth of old beams,
flagstone floors and log fires, as well as a resident ghost.

KETTLEBURGH   Map 07 TM26

The Chequers Inn
IP13 7JT ☎ 01728 723760 & 724369
*Dir: From Ipswich A12 onto B1116, L onto B1078 then R through
Easton*
The Chequers is set in beautiful countryside on the banks of
the River Deben. The landlord is a fellow of the British Institute
of Innkeepers and serves a wide range of cask ales endorsed
by the Cask Marque. In addition to snack and restaurant
meals, there is a £3 menu in the bar including local sausages
and ham with home-produced free-range eggs.
OPEN: 11-2.30 6-11. **BAR MEALS:** L served all week. D served
all week 12-2 7-9.30. Av main course £3. **RESTAURANT:** L
served all week. D served all week 12-2 7-9.30. Av 3 course à la
carte £15. **BREWERY/COMPANY:** Free House.
PRINCIPAL BEERS: Greene King IPA, Adnams Southwold,
Marstons Pedigree,. **FACILITIES:** Children welcome Garden:
outdoor eating, patio, dogs allowed, as long as under control.
NOTES: Parking 40

LAVENHAM   Map 07 TL94

Pick of the Pubs

Angel Hotel ◉ ★ ★ ♀
Market Place CO10 9QZ ☎ 01787 247388
📠 01787 248344
e-mail: angellav@aol.com
*Dir: From A14 take Bury East/Sudbury turn off A143, after 4m
take A1141 to Lavenham, Angel is off the High Street*
This fine old inn, licensed originally in 1420, stands amidst
some 300 listed buildings in England's best preserved
medieval wool town.
  A popular venue with a great atmosphere, the Angel
assumes a thoroughly modern attitude to food in both bar
and dining-room that consistently attracts a loyal clientele.
Local produce and real ales, along with well-chosen house
wines, appeal to all tastes, balancing its modern ideas,
traditional dishes and well-sourced fresh foodstuffs to
good effect.
  Daily menus rarely miss out on the likes of steak-and-
ale pie and market-fresh fish epitomised by grilled whole
plaice and skate wings with lemon and capers. Oysters
served plain or grilled with garlic, bacon and tarragon and
game terrine with Cumberland sauce are typical
precursors to braised hare with mushrooms and red wine
and chicken breast with Stilton and chives that emanate
from the top drawer of traditional pub cooking. Trendier
options might include cod and tuna fishcakes with parsley
sauce and perhaps tarte tatin of Mediterranean
vegetables.
  Overnight accommodation is top-drawer also for those
who appreciate their creature comforts unsullied by
thought of the cost.

OPEN: 11-11 (Sun 12-10.30). Closed 25-26 Dec.
BAR MEALS: L served all week. D served all week 12-2.15
6.45-9.15. Av main course £8. **RESTAURANT:** L served all
week. D served all week 12-2.15 6.45-9.15. Av 3 course à la
carte £15. **BREWERY/COMPANY:** Free House.
PRINCIPAL BEERS: Adnams, Nethergate, Greene King
IPA/Abbott. **FACILITIES:** Children welcome Children's
licence Garden: patio, outdoor eating, lawns.
NOTES: Parking 105. **ROOMS:** 8 bedrooms 8 en suite s£45
d£70 FR£90

See Pub Walk on page 405

LAXFIELD   Map 07 TM27

Pick of the Pubs

The Kings Head
Gorams Mill Ln IP13 8DW ☎ 01986 798395
Virtually unchanged since Victorian times, this charming
inn is known locally as The Low House.
   Beer is served from the tap room. There is no bar and
customers sit on original high-backed settles and enjoy
traditional Suffolk music on Tuesday lunchtimes. Home-
cooked fare includes game duck and steak and kidney pie.
OPEN: 11-3 (11-11 Tues) 6-11 (Sun 12-3, 7-10.30).
BAR MEALS: L served all week. D served all week 12-2 7-9.
Av main course £5.50. **BREWERY/COMPANY:** Free House.
PRINCIPAL BEERS: Adnams Best & Broadside, Greene King
IPA & Abbot Ale. **FACILITIES:** Children welcome Garden:
Large lawned area Dogs allowed. **NOTES:** Parking 30
No credit cards

LEISTON   Map 07 TM46

Parrot and Punchbowl
Aldringham Ln, Aldringham IP16 4PY
☎ 01728 830221 ▤ 01728 833297
16th-century village pub located a mile from the Suffolk
Heritage Coast - good local walks. Expect plenty of beams and
brass, good ales and a wide-ranging bar menu.

LEVINGTON   Map 07 TM23

The Ship Inn 🐑
Church Ln IP10 0LQ ☎ 01473 659573
Dir: off the A14 towards Felixstowe
Overlooking the River Orwell and neighbouring countryside,
this lovely 14th-century thatched pub is very popular with
walkers, birdwatchers and yachting folk, who seek out the
home-made bar food.
   Expect fisherman's pie, steak and kidney pudding, kippers,
salmon fishcakes, and pheasant in white grape sauce - among
other interesting dishes.
OPEN: 11.30-3 6.30-11. **BAR MEALS:** L served all week.
D served Wed-Sat 12-2 7-9. Av main course £6.50.
RESTAURANT: L served all week. D served Wed-Sat 12-2 7-9. Av
3 course à la carte £11. **BREWERY/COMPANY:** Pubmaster.
PRINCIPAL BEERS: Ship Inn Bitter, Greene King IPA, Adnams
Best, Broadside. **FACILITIES:** Garden: patio, outdoor eating.
NOTES: Parking 70

Mauldons
The story of Mauldons Brewery began as long ago as
1795 when Anna Maria Mauldon started brewing at the
Bull Hotel at Bullingdon near Sudbury. By 1960 the
company consisted of a brewery with 30 tied houses, a
wine and spirit business and a small farm. Apart from a
gap of 22 years, the brewery was run by the Mauldon
family from the late-18th century until March 2000 when
it was acquired by Steve & Alison Sims. As a young
reporter working on the Morning Chronicle, Charles
Dickens came to Sudbury in 1834 to cover a story on local
corruption. The town became Eatanswill in his classic
'Pickwick Papers' and , to celebrate the writer's link with
Sudbury, Mauldons produce a range of beers with a
Dickensian theme. Look out for Dickens (4%), Pickwick
(4.2%) and Peggotty's Porter (4.1%).

LIDGATE   Map 07 TL75

Pick of the Pubs

Star Inn 🐑
The Street CB8 9PP ☎ 01638 500275
Dir: From Newmarket, clocktower in High st, follow signs toward
Clare on B1063. Lidgate 7m from Newmarket
A friendly, relaxed and informal inn that has made its
mark as one of the country's best Spanish eating houses,
in the same hands for over eight years. Pretty and pink-
washed, it is made up - obviously so - of two Elizabethan
cottages with gardens both behind and in front. Two
traditionally furnished bars with heavy oak and pine tables
lead to a small, comparatively plain dining-room. The
landlady's Catalan roots are clearly defined on a menu
that offers Mediterranean fish soup, paella and Spanish
omelettes alongside tomato and goats' cheese salad,
monkfish meunière and roast lamb in garlic and red wine.
Run-of-the-mill alternatives take in such choices as
lasagne, venison sausages and home-made cheesecake. A
short selection of wines is chalked up on a board and real
ale is dispensed, unusually, from horizontal beer handles:
don't pull backwards, but push down!
OPEN: 11-3 5-11. **BAR MEALS:** L served all week. D served
Mon-Sat 12-2 7-10. Av main course £11.50. **RESTAURANT:** L
served all week. D served Mon-Sat 12-2 7-10. Av 3 course à la
carte £19.50. **BREWERY/COMPANY:** Greene King.
PRINCIPAL BEERS: Greene King IPA, Abbot Ale, & Old
Speckled Hen. **FACILITIES:** Children welcome Garden:
BBQ, outdoor eating. **NOTES:** Parking 12

LONG MELFORD   Map 07 TL84

The Crown Hotel
Hall St CO10 9JL ☎ 01787 377666 ▤ 01787 379005
Dir: from Sudbury take A134 to Bury St Edmunds, at 1st rndbt take 1st
L to Long Melford
At the heart of Constable country, Long Melford's pub was
built in 1610 yet retains a Tudor cellar and oak beams.

MARKET WESTON   Map 07 TL97

The Mill Inn 🍺
Bury Rd IP22 2PD ☎ 01359 221018
e-mail: andrew.leasy@talk21.com
Dir: A14 Bury St Edmunds, follow A143 to Great Barton & Stanton, L
on B1111 thru Barningham, next village M Weston
Old Chimneys ales from the nearby micro-brewery boost the
choice of beers at this Victorian manor house, situated at the
centre of the local Windmill Trail. Local produce features in a
varied menu that may include pork divan, steak and stout pie,
aubergine, tomato and mozzarella bake, grilled salmon fillet
with harb and caper butter, escalope of turkey Columbian, or
guinea fowl calvados.
OPEN: 11-3 (Nov-Feb from 12) 7-11 (closed Mon).
BAR MEALS: L served Tue-Sun. D served Tue-Sun 12-2 7-9.30.
Av main course £2.95. **RESTAURANT:** L served Tue-Sun. D
served Tue-Sun 12-2 7-9.30. Av 3 course à la carte £12.50.
BREWERY/COMPANY: Free House.
PRINCIPAL BEERS: Greene King, Adnams Best, Old Chimneys
Great Raft & Military Mild. **FACILITIES:** Children welcome
Garden: outdoor eating. **NOTES:** Parking 30

MELTON   Map 07 TM25

Wilford Bridge
Wilford Bridge Rd IP12 2PA ☎ 01394 386141
Dir: *Head to the coast from the A12, follow signs to Bawdsey &*
Orford, cross railway lines, next pub on L

Busy pub close to Sutton Hoo, the world famous Saxon burial
ship. There is a good range of snacks and light meals, and an
impressive choice of fresh fish and seafood. Other options
might be game in season, chargrilled steaks or chicken, and a
selection of vegetarian dishes.
OPEN: 11-3 6.30-11 (Sun 12-3 7-11). **BAR MEALS:** L served all
week. D served all week 11.30-2 6.30-9.30. Av main course £6.95.
RESTAURANT: L served all week. D served all week 11.30-2
6.30-9.30. Av 3 course à la carte £14. **BREWERY/COMPANY:** Free
House. **PRINCIPAL BEERS:** Adnams Best, Broadside.
FACILITIES: Children welcome Garden: patio, food served
outdoors. **NOTES:** Parking 40

MONKS ELEIGH   Map 07 TL94

Pick of the Pubs

The Swan Inn 🛏 🍸
The Street IP7 7AU ☎ 01449 741391
Dir: *On the B1115 between Sudbury & Hadleigh*
Just across from the village green, this attractive thatched
free house blends easily with Monks Eleigh's colour-
washed cottages, pretty gardens and imposing church.
The village was founded on the prosperous local wool
trade, and the pub dates partly from the 14th century.
Wattle and daub panels were discovered in one room
during renovations, and the dining room boasts a
magnificent beamed ceiling and open fire. Owners Nigel
and Carol Ramsbottom use seasonal local produce to
create menus which change almost daily. Game features
heavily during the winter months, whilst lobsters, fish and
asparagus take pride of place in summer. A typical menu
might start with Orford smoked prawns, steamed mussels,
or home-cured gravlax with dill and mustard mayonnaise.
Move on through pan-fried wild duck, whole roast teal,
creamy smoked haddock pie, or sea bass with a fresh
herb stuffing. Round off the meal with baked apple and
ginger pudding, or coffee, rum and cardamom trifle.
OPEN: 12-3 7-11 (Apr-Sept 6pm opening). **BAR MEALS:** L
served Tue-Sun. D served Tue-Sat 12-2 7-9.30. Av main course
£8.75. **RESTAURANT:** L served Tue-Sun. D served Tue-Sat
12-2 7-9.30. Av 3 course à la carte £16.
BREWERY/COMPANY: Free House.
PRINCIPAL BEERS: Greene King IPA, Adnams Bitter &
Broadside. **FACILITIES:** Children welcome Garden:
outdoor eating. **NOTES:** Parking 10

The Suffolk Coast Path
With its salt marshes and winding river estuaries,
it's hardly surprising Suffolk's delightfully unspoilt
coastline was once the sinister sanctuary of prosperous
smugglers. Even today it has a nerve-tingling air of
mystery. The only way to discover and appreciate this
remote corner of England is on foot, following the 50-
mile Suffolk Coast Path which runs between Felixstowe
and Lowestoft. Near its starting point, the trail visits the
picturesque village Orford, home to two of Suffolk's
most historic coastal pubs - the Jolly Sailor and the
King's Head. Nearby is eerie, mysterious Orford Ness,
once the setting for military research. Beyond Orford,
the trail makes for Snape Maltings, renowned as the
home of the Aldeburgh Festival. If, by now, the walk
has sapped you dry, you'll probably make a beeline for
the Plough & Sail, the Crown or the Golden Key.
Alternatively, you might press on to the Ship at
Dunwich, once a medieval port and now a sleepy
village looking out over the unrelieved emptiness of
the North Sea. The last leg of the trail brings you to
delightful Southwold where you'll find the Crown Hotel
sheltering beneath the town's white-walled lighthouse.
Adnams Brewery is based here and a tour of
Southwold offers the chance to sample a pint
or two of the company's finest ales.

ORFORD   Map 07 TM45

Jolly Sailor Inn 🛏
Quay St IP12 2NU ☎ 01394 450243 🖹 0870 128 7874
e-mail: jollyorf@aol.com
Dir: *On B1084 E of Woodbridge*
Situated on the atmospheric Suffolk Heritage Coast, this
ancient smugglers' inn was built with timbers from ships
wrecked on remote Orford Ness, Europe's largest vegetated
shingle spit. During the 14th and 15th centuries, before the
harbour silted up, the village of Orford was a bustling coastal
port.
    Strong fish emphasis on the varied menu, including Orford
cod and skate and local crab in summer. Home-made lasagne
and chilli con carne also feature among the dishes. Classic
interior with several small flagstoned rooms set around a
central servery.
OPEN: 11.30-2.30 7-11. **BAR MEALS:** L served all week.
D served all week 12-2 7.15-8.45. Av main course £5.
BREWERY/COMPANY: Adnams. **PRINCIPAL BEERS:** Adnams
Bitter & Broadside. **FACILITIES:** Garden: food served outside
Dogs allowed on lead only. **ROOMS:** 3 bedrooms d£35
No credit cards

King's Head
Front St IP12 2LW ☎ 01394 450271
e-mail: ian-thornton@talk21.com
Dir: *From Woodbridge follow signsfor Orford Castle along the B1084*
through Butley and Chillesford onto Orford
Modernised Tudor inn overlooking churchyard. Attractive
dining room; Adnams ales and good wines. En suite
bedrooms.

The Cock Inn, Polstead

THE COCK INN, POLSTEAD
The Green CO6 5AL.
Tel: 01206 263150
Directions: Colchester/A134
towards Sudbury then R
*Attractive 17th-century rural
village pub overlooking the
green. Comfortably furnished
bar, with open fire and East
Anglian ales. Interesting,
freshly-prepared food,
including lunchtime rolls and
more elaborate evening fare.*
Open: 11-3 6-11 (Sun 12-3 6-
10.30), Closed Mon. Bar Meals:
11.30-2.30 6.30-9. Children
welcome. Garden. Parking.
(see page 416 for full entry)

A peaceful and scenic ramble aound Polstead village and along the River Box. Good views across the village and rolling Suffolk countryside from the top of Bell Hill

From the pub car park turn left along Rockalls Road. In 1/4 mile (0.4km), take the arrowed path left and keeping the garden pond on your left, continue along the bridleway to a crossing of tracks by a cottage. Turn left and soon reach the road. Turn left, then in 50 yards (45m), follow the signed footpath right to reach a stile. Ignore the left-hand path and keep ahead along the right-hand hedge, the path soon bearing left to a kissing-gate. Proceed straight on with Sprotts Farm on your right and continue to the road and turn left.

Turn right in 1/4 mile (0.4km) into Homey Bridge Lane and follow the track downhill to the River Box. Cross the ford to a road junction. Here, turn left through the kissing-gate and follow the waymarked path through the field beside the river. Eventually reach Mill Lane and turn left. Pass Polstead Mill, then at the T-junction turn left into Mill Street and cross the river bridge. In 100 yards (91m), take the arrowed path right through a kissing-gate and walk up Bell Hill for 1/2 mile (0.8km) to a stile and junction of paths.

(Short route: Instead of crossing the stile at the top of Bell Hill, take the waymarked path left, downhill to the road. Follow the road straight ahead and turn right, signed to The Cock Inn. Pass the duck pond and climb the hill back to the pub).

Continue ahead and soon turn left along a farm track. At the road, cross the stile opposite and head downhill across a field to a further stile. Soon, as the path bears right, go through the kissing-gate on your left and follow the path (can be muddy) through two further gates (pond right). Head for the far right-hand corner of the field to a stile, then continue between houses to a road. The village green and the pub are just ahead of you to your right.

Distance: 4 1/2 miles (6.4km) or 3 1/2 miles (4.8km)
Map: OS Landranger 155
Paths: field paths, bridleways and tracks
Terrain: farmland, country lanes
Gradient: undulating; one fairly steep climb up Bell Hill

*Walk submitted by:
The Cock Inn*

Flatford Mill on the River Stour

England

Pick of the Pubs

The Cock Inn 🌐 🐑 ♀
The Green CO6 5AL ☎ 01206 263150 📠 01206 263150
e-mail: enquiries@the-cock-inn-polstead.fsbusiness.co.uk
Dir: *Colchester/A134 towards Sudbury then R*

A 17th-century pub with Victorian extensions situated in a peaceful village at the heart of Constable country: it stands at the top of Polstead hill opposite the village green and central to many cycling and rambling routes.

The surroundings are very rustic, with scrubbed tables and quarry-tiled floors, plain painted walls, beams and open fireplaces. Food generally follows a similar theme on a fairly eclectic menu that sees some repetition in basic sauces. Virtually everything bar the bread is home made on a regularly-changing menu that features a fair share of fish dishes based on fresh salmon, sole and sea bass.

A typical main meal might feature winter vegetable soup garnished with crispy smoked bacon, chicken breast stuffed with cream cheese and sun-dried tomatoes and served with assorted sautéed vegetables and steamed cherry pudding with crème anglaise. Families are made particularly welcome, with a large garden to play - and eat - in when the weather is kind.
OPEN: 11-3 (Sun 12-3, 6-10.30) 6-11 (closed Mon).
BAR MEALS: L served Tues-Sun. D served Tues-Sat 11.30-2 6.30-9. Av main course £7.90. **RESTAURANT:** L served Tue-Sun. D served Tues-Sat 11.30-2 6.30-9. Av 3 course à la carte £20. **BREWERY/COMPANY:** Free House.
PRINCIPAL BEERS: Greene King IPA, + Guest Ales.
FACILITIES: Children welcome Children's licence Garden: outdoor eating Dogs allowed Water bowl in garden.
NOTES: Parking 12

See Pub Walk on page 415

  AA inspected guest accommodation

Pick of the Pubs

Ramsholt Arms 🐑 ♀
Dock Rd IP12 3AB ☎ 01394 411229
e-mail: ramsholtarms@tinyworld.co.uk
Dir: *End of lane on beach at Ramsholt, signed off B1083 Woodbridge to Bawdsey*
Enjoying a glorious, unrivalled postion on a tidal beach overlooking the River Deben, this 18th-century, pink-washed former farmhouse, ferryman's cottage and smugglers' inn is the perfect summer evening destination for a pint on the terrace to watch the glorious sunset over the river. Expect a civilised atmosphere, picture windows, Adnams ales, and good home-cooked food, in particular fish and seafood in summer and local game in winter. Blackboard dishes could include cod and chips, local lobster, Cromer crab, whole Dover sole, roast partridge and decent pies. Comfortable bedrooms make the most of the view; rewarding riverside walks.
OPEN: 11.30-3 6.30-11 (summer 11-11, Sun 12-10.30).
Closed 25 Dec. **BAR MEALS:** L served all week. D served all week 12-2 7-9. Av main course £6.95.
BREWERY/COMPANY: Free House.
PRINCIPAL BEERS: Adnams, Greene King
FACILITIES: Children welcome Garden: patio, outdoor eating, Dogs allowed. **NOTES:** Parking 60.
ROOMS: 4 bedrooms s£45 d£90

Brewers Arms
Lower Rd IP30 0RJ ☎ 01449 736377 737059
📠 01449 736377
e-mail: jchamb1045@aol.com
Dir: *From A14 take A1088 toward Woolpit, Rattlesden 2.8m from Woolpit*
Enjoy a decent pint of Abbot Ale and relax in the attractive surroundings of this solid 16th-century village hostelry, situated just a short drive from Bury St Edmunds. The dining area was originally the public bar and the lounge bar has book-lined walls and lots of bric-a-brac. Open fires and an old bread oven add to the charm.

The well-designed and imaginative menu changes weekly and may feature steak pudding, roast hock of ham with a mild mustard gravy, and salmon fishcakes with watercress sauce. Good range of desserts.
OPEN: 12-2.30 6.30-11 (closed Mon). **BAR MEALS:** L served Tue-Sun. D served Tue-Sat 12.30-2.30 7.00-10.30. Av main course £10. **RESTAURANT:** L served Tue-Sun. D served Wed-Sat 12.30-2.30 7-10.30. Av 3 course à la carte £18.
BREWERY/COMPANY: Greene King.
PRINCIPAL BEERS: Greene King IPA & Abbot Ale.
FACILITIES: Children welcome Garden: beer garden , food served outside Dogs allowed in garden & public bar only.
NOTES: Parking 20

St Peter & the Tale of the Fruit Beer

Set in rural Suffolk, in the outbuildings of a medieval hall, St Peter's Brewery produces a wide range of traditional and speciality beers using water drawn from its own deep-water bore hole. The beers come in a distinctive flask-shaped green bottle, modelled on an 18th-century American style, and include Cream Stout (6.5%), Millenium Ale (7.0%) and Organic Ale (4.5%). There are also fruit beers (elderberry, grapefruit), spiced ales (lemon & ginger, cinnamon & apple) and honey porter. St Peter's Hall itself contains a restaurant and bar, and brewery tours are available.

ST PETER SOUTH ELMHAM   Map 07 TM38

Pick of the Pubs

St Peter's Hall ◉ 🛏 ♀
NR35 1NQ ☎ 01986 782322   🖃 01986 782505
e-mail: beers@stpetersbrewery.co.uk
Dir: From A143/A144 between Halesworth and Bungay follow brown and white signs to St Peter's Brewery

A unique bar and restaurant housed in a former medieval monastery of great character dating from 1280, and extended in 1539 using architectural salvage from nearby Flixton Priory. A magnificent moated building that dominates the surrounding farmland. Expect stone floors, lofty ceilings, a huge inglenook fireplace with open fire, a chapel above the porch and furnishings dating from the 17th and 18th centuries.

Menus change weekly and are sensibly short to cater for weekend (Fri-Sun) opening. With fruit, vegetables and herbs from the garden, menus may feature spicy roasted cauliflower soup and ceviche of smoked tuna, salmon and halibut with mango salsa and balsamic vinaigrette for starters, followed by braised lamb fillet on champ with rosemary and redcurrant jus, grilled whole Torbay sole, and sea bass with vanilla and chervil. Finish with Belgian chocolate and rum flan or glazed lemon tart with black cherry compôte. The excellent St Peter's ales on tap are brewed in the outbuildings - well worth a tour!
OPEN: 11-11 (Sun 11-7). **BAR MEALS:** L served Fri-Sun. D served Fri-Sat 12.30-2 7-10. Av main course £12.95.
RESTAURANT: L served Fri-Sun. D served Fri-Sat 12.30 7. Av 3 course à la carte £20. **BREWERY/COMPANY:** St Peters Brewery. **PRINCIPAL BEERS:** St Peters.
FACILITIES: Garden: Moated garden, outdoor eating.
NOTES: Parking 150

REDE   Map 05 TL85

The Plough 🛏
IP29 4BE ☎ 01284 789208
Dir: on the A143 between Bury St Edmonds and Haverhill
Picture-postcard thatched 16th-century pub set beside a pond on the village green. Worth the effort in finding for the freshly prepared food served in rambling low-beamed bars. Blackboard-listed dishes may include monkfish Creole, local rabbit in a tarragon and spring onion sauce, and chicken breast with an orange and kumquat sauce.
OPEN: 11-3 6.30-11. **BAR MEALS:** L served all week. D served Mon-Sat 12-2 7-9. Av main course £7. **RESTAURANT:** L served all week. D served Mon-Sat 12-2 7-9.
BREWERY/COMPANY: Greene King.
PRINCIPAL BEERS: Greene King IPA & Abbot Ale, Ruddles Counrty. **FACILITIES:** Children welcome Garden: outdoor eating. **NOTES:** Parking 60

RISBY   Map 07 TL86

The White Horse Inn ♀
Newmarket Rd IP28 6RD ☎ 01284 810686
🖃 01284 810666
e-mail: whitehorse@lineone.net
Dir: A14 from Bury St Edmunds
Former coaching inn with a colourful history - as a communications centre in World War II in case of invasion, and for the ghostly spectre of a murdered hanging judge occasionally reflected in the restaurant mirror. The pub is otherwise known for its real ales - up to 15 each week - its extensive carte and freshly produced bar food.
OPEN: 12-3 (Fri-Sun all day) 6-11. **BAR MEALS:** L served all week. D served all week 12-2.30 6.30-9.30. Av main course £10. **RESTAURANT:** L served all week. D served all week 12-2.30 6.30-9.30. Av 3 course à la carte £20.
BREWERY/COMPANY: Free House.
PRINCIPAL BEERS: Fullers London Pride, Shepherds Neame Spitfire, Woodfordes Wherry, Wells Bombardier.
FACILITIES: Garden: Food served outside.
NOTES: Parking 100. **ROOMS:** 14 bedrooms 12 en suite d£40

AA Bed & Breakfast 2002
Britain's best-selling B&B guide featuring over 3500 great places to stay
www.theAA.com

AA Lifestyle Guides

SNAPE Map 07 TM35

Pick of the Pubs

The Crown Inn 🐑 ⏻
Bridge Rd IP17 1SL ☎ 01728 688324
Dir: A12 N to Lowestoft, R to Aldeburgh, then R again in Snape at crossroads by church, pub at bottom of hill
There's a wealth of beams and brick floors at this charming, 15th century smugglers' inn, as well as 'the old codgers' - an unusual, semi-circular area of old Suffolk settles clustered around the inglenook fireplace. Lying close to the River Alde with its timeless scenery and tranquil coastal bird reserves, the pub and its sheltered garden provides a refuge from gaming machines, jukeboxes and piped music. And why not? You'll find all the entertainment you need at the nearby Snape Maltings concert venue. The modern, brasserie-style menu is featured on regularly-changing blackboards, and there's a natural emphasis on seafood. Starters include soft herring roes on tapenade toast, or cauliflower and Stilton soup. Move on to whole brill grilled with Montpellier butter, a hearty steak and kidney pudding, or sea bass with roasted Italian vegetables, salsa verde and salads. Finally, round off with home-made sticky toffee pudding, crème brûlée or Calvados apple crêpes.
OPEN: 12-3 6-11. Closed Dec 25. **BAR MEALS:** L served all week. D served all week 12-2 7-9. Av main course £8.95. **RESTAURANT:** L served all week. D served all week 12-2 7-9. Av 3 course à la carte £17.50.
BREWERY/COMPANY: Adnams.
PRINCIPAL BEERS: Adnams Best & Broadside.
FACILITIES: Garden: outdoor eating. **NOTES:** Parking 40.
ROOMS: 3 bedrooms 3 en suite s£45 d£65

The Golden Key
Priory Ln IP17 1SQ ☎ 01728 688510
Recently extended 15th-century cottage-style pub close to Snape Maltings. Home-cooked food; Adnams ales; bedrooms.

Plough & Sail 🐑 ⏻
Snape Maltings IP17 1SR ☎ 01728 688413
🖹 01728 688930
e-mail: enquiries@snapemaltings.co.uk

Part of the Snape Maltings Riverside Centre that incorporates the famous Concert Hall, art gallery and shops, the bustling Plough and Sail is justifiably popular with pre-concert goers. Rambling interior includes a new bar and restaurant, while the large terrace provides welcome alfresco seating in summer. Expect good bar food, perhaps including Suffolk ham and egg ciabatta, seared Aldeburgh cod with tomato and cucumber relish, Thai chicken, and lunchtime sandwiches and ploughman's.

continued

OPEN: 11-5.30 (summer 11-11). **BAR MEALS:** L served all week12-2.30. Av main course £5.95. **RESTAURANT:** L served all week. D served all week 12-2.30 7-9. Av 3 course à la carte £18.
BREWERY/COMPANY: Free House.
PRINCIPAL BEERS: Adnams Broadside, Woodfordes, Adnams Oyster. **FACILITIES:** Children welcome Children's licence Garden: patio/terrace, outdoor eating Dogs allowed.
NOTES: Parking 100. **ROOMS:** 4 bedrooms 4 en suite

SOUTHWOLD Map 07 TM57

The Angel
High St, Wangford NR34 8RL ☎ 01502 578636
🖹 01502 578555
e-mail: enquireis@angelinn.freeserve.co.uk
Set in the heart of pretty Wangford, overlooking the historic parish church, this traditional cream and green-painted inn dates back to the 17th century and has a handsome Georgian façade. Exposed beams and roaring log fires characterise the cosy bar and adjoining dining room. Home-made dishes include steak and kidney pudding, fish and chips, and liver and bacon casserole.
OPEN: 12-11. **BAR MEALS:** L served all week. D served all week 12-2 7-9. Av main course £5.75. **RESTAURANT:** L served all week. D served all week 12-2 7-9. Av 3 course à la carte £16.
BREWERY/COMPANY: Free House.
PRINCIPAL BEERS: Adnams, Woodfordes Wherry, Greene King Abbot Ale. **FACILITIES:** Children welcome Garden: Food served outside Dogs allowed. **NOTES:** Parking 20.
ROOMS: 7 bedrooms 7 en suite s£45 d£59

Pick of the Pubs

Crown Hotel ⊛ ★ ★ 🐑 ⏻
The High St IP18 6DP ☎ 01502 722275
🖹 01502 727263
e-mail: crownreception/adnams@adnams.co.uk
Dir: off A12 take A1094 to Southwold, stay on main road into town centre, hotel on L in High St
Posting house dating from 1750, fulfilling the purposes of pub, wine bar, restaurant and small hotel. As flagship for Adnams brewery, it offers excellent ales and wines, and good food in both the bar and restaurant. Typical imaginative dishes in the bar might be smoked haddock and mussel chowder, deep-fried feta wrapped in Parma ham, pan-fried skate with gremolata butter, and braised lamb shank with pease pudding. In the restaurant look for pork fillet with rosemary polenta and marinated vegetables and glazed lamon tart with chocolate mousse to finish. Bedrooms are attractively decorated with co-ordinated soft furnishings and well equipped.
OPEN: 10.30-3 6-11. **BAR MEALS:** L served all week. D served all week 12.15-2 7-9.30. Av main course £10. **RESTAURANT:** L served all week. D served all week 12.30-1.30 7.30-9.30. Av 3 course à la carte £25.50. Av 3 course fixed price £27. **BREWERY/COMPANY:** Adnams.
PRINCIPAL BEERS: Adnams. **FACILITIES:** Children welcome Patio **NOTES:** Parking 18. **ROOMS:** 14 bedrooms 11 en suite s£57 d£82

 For pubs with AA rosette awards for food see page 10

STOKE-BY-NAYLAND   Map 07 TL93

Pick of the Pubs

The Angel Inn 🏆 ♦♦♦♦ 🍵
CO6 4SA ☎ 01206 263245 📠 01206 263373
Dir: From A12 take Colchester R turn, then A134, 5m to Nayland. From A12 S take B1068

Chesterfields surrounding an open fire and dining areas that include an air-conditioned conservatory, patio and sun terrace are up-to-date features of this former village inn whose original wattle-and-daub panels are clearly pre-16th century. Tables for lunch and dinner may be reserved in The Well Room with its high ceiling open to the rafters, a gallery leading to the residents' accommodation, rough brick and timber studded walls and the well itself, fully 52 feet deep.

Eating in the bar, by comparison, is strictly on a first-come, first served basis. Chalkboard menus change each day according to the seasons and market availability, with first-class fish options and generous portions of salad or fresh vegetables. Dressed crab with home-made mayonnaise and griddled sardines in oregano come before skate wings, fresh haddock and brochette of scallops wrapped in bacon. Mushroom and pistachio pate, ballotine of duck with cassis and roast pork loin with apple mousse redress the balance, rounding off with steamed apple pudding or dark chocolate ganache gateau.

OPEN: 11-2.30 6-11. Closed Dec 25-26, Jan 1.
BAR MEALS: L served all week. D served all week 12-2 6.30-9. Av main course £9.95. **RESTAURANT:** L served all week. D served all week 12-2 6.30-9. Av 3 course à la carte £15. **BREWERY/COMPANY:** Free House.
PRINCIPAL BEERS: Greene King IPA & Abbot Ale, Adnams Best. **FACILITIES:** patio, food served outside.
NOTES: Parking 25. **ROOMS:** 6 bedrooms 6 en suite s£50 d£65

SWILLAND   Map 07 TM15

Moon & Mushroom Inn 🏆
High Rd IP6 9LR ☎ 01473 785320 📠 01473 785320
Dir: 6 miles north of Ipswich taking the Westerfield Rd

A row of former 16th-century village cottages and a pub since 1721; its current name the result of a locals' competition 250 years later. Real ale is sold by gravity only and home cooking prevails. Venison casserole, beef with noodles and halibut mornay are ladelled from tureens with self-served vegetables.
OPEN: 11-2.30 6-11 (Mon 6-11 only). **BAR MEALS:** L served Tue-Sat. D served Tue-Sat 12-2 6.30-8.15. Av main course £6.55.
BREWERY/COMPANY: Free House.
PRINCIPAL BEERS: Adnams Southwold, Woodfordes Wherry, Greenjack Grasshopper. **FACILITIES:** Garden: patio, outdoor eating Dogs allowed. **NOTES:** Parking 47 No credit cards

---

THORNHAM MAGNA   Map 07 TM17

The Four Horseshoes 🏆
Wickham Rd IP23 8HD ☎ 01379 678777 📠 01379 678134
Dir: From Diss on A140 turn R and follow signs for Finningham, 0.5m turn R for Thornham Magna
Thornham Magna is a delightful, unspoilt village, close to Thornham Country Park and the interesting thatched church at Thornham Parva. This fine 12th-century inn, with a splendid thatched roof and timber-framed walls, offers varied bar food - home made steak and ale pie, chicken Kiev, Dover sole, mussels or roasts.
OPEN: 11.30-3 6-11. **BAR MEALS:** L served all week. D served all week 12-2 6.30-9. Av main course £6.95. **RESTAURANT:** D served all week 6.30-9. Av 3 course à la carte £15.
PRINCIPAL BEERS: Adnams, Courage directors.
FACILITIES: Children welcome Garden: Dogs allowed.
NOTES: Parking 80. **ROOMS:** 8 bedrooms 7 en suite s£45 d£55 FR£70

Paradise Restored

The historic Tolly Cobbold brewery in Ipswich, where Thomas Cobbold began brewing in 1746, was opened to the public in 1992, with a new pub called the Brewery Tap established in the former Cobbold family house. The Cobbolds merged with another Suffolk brewing dynasty, the Tollemarches, in 1957, but 20 years later Tolly Cobbold vanished into the maw of a giant multinational. It re-emerged like Jonah from the whale in 1990 and an independent management has set about reviving old beer recipes, such as Cobnut. A new brewery was built in 1995 and the old Victorian brewery tower is now used for guided brewery tours.

WALBERSWICK   Map 07 TM47

Pick of the Pubs

Bell Inn  ♈
Ferry Rd IP18 6TN ☎ 01502 723109 🖹 01502 722728
e-mail: bellinn@btinternet.com
Dir: *From A12 take B1387 to Walberswick*

Reputedly over 600 years old, the Bell lies on Suffolk's
lonely and splendidly atmospheric coast, just to the south
of the picturesque town of Southwold. Nearby is the old
fishing harbour on the River Blyth and between Easter and
September you can be rowed across the water by the local
ferryman. The entire area is a mecca for walkers, artists
and ornithologists and the beautiful church at nearby
Blythburgh, known as the Cathedral of the Marshes, was
used by Cromwell's soldiers to stable their horses. Step
into the Bell and instantly you'll feel its cosy, welcoming
atmosphere.
   Traditional English pub fare and a seasonal menu are
the Bell's hallmarks and among the perennial
favourites are battered cod, fish pie, home-cooked ham,
egg and chips, Cajun chicken with noodles and stir-fry
vegetables, and home-made pie of the day.
OPEN: 11-3 6-11 (end Jul-4 Sep 11-11). **BAR MEALS:** L
served all week. D served Mon-Sat 12-2 6-9 (all day in
summer). Av main course £6.50. **RESTAURANT:** D served
all week 6-9. Av 3 course à la carte £15.
BREWERY/COMPANY: Adnams.
PRINCIPAL BEERS: Adnams - Best, Broadside.
FACILITIES: Children welcome Garden: food served
outside Dogs allowed, on leads only. **NOTES:** Parking 10.
ROOMS: 6 bedrooms 6 en suite s£40 d£70

WESTLETON   Map 07 TM46

The Crown at Westleton 🏵 ★ ★
IP17 3AD ☎ 0800 328 6001 🖹 01728 648239
e-mail: reception@westletoncrown.com
Dir: *Turn off the A12 just past Yoxford Northbound, follow the tourist*
signs for 2 miles
Bustling old coaching inn nestling in a quiet village close to the
coast and bird reserves. Well established and offering genuine
hospitality in a relaxed atmosphere, it also features sound
home cooking and good wines and whiskies. Menu choices
range from interesting salads and ploughmans' through to
roasted rump of lamb with bubble and squeak or slow-roasted
belly of pork.   *continued*

OPEN: 11-3 6-11 (Sun 7-10.30). **BAR MEALS:** L served all week.
D served all week 12-2.15 7-9.30. **RESTAURANT:** L served all
week. D served all week 12-2.15 7-9.30.
BREWERY/COMPANY: Free House.
PRINCIPAL BEERS: Adnams, Greene King IPA.
FACILITIES: Children welcome Garden Dogs allowed.
ROOMS: 19 bedrooms 19 en suite s£59.50 d£69.50

WINGFIELD   Map 07 TM27

Pick of the Pubs

De la Pole Arms
Church Rd IP21 5RA ☎ 01379 384545
🖹 01379 384377
Dir: *Opposite Wingfield College*

Lost down narrow country lanes close to the Norfolk
border and lovingly restored by St Peter's Brewery, the
16th-century De La Pole Arms may be hard to find but the
effort is well worth it! Inside, you will find two charming
bars, each filled with an eclectic mix of stripped wood
tables and chairs, rug-strewn quarry-tiled floors, log-
burning stoves, and a generally civilised dining ambience.
However, the atmosphere is relaxed, the ale excellent -
expect the full range of St Peter's brews - and the food
particularly commendable.
   House specialities include fish and chips (batter made
from St Peter's wheat beer), salmon and prawn pudding,
Sussex stew, seafood platter, wild rabbit casserole, and
caramelised pork steak with sweet and sour sauce and
crispy apple fritters. In the restaurant choose, perhaps,
seared king scallops, followed by rack of lamb with
rosemary and port. Peaceful side terrace overlooking the
historic parish church and Old College.
OPEN: 11-3 6-11 (Sun 12-3, 7-10.30). Closed Mon Nov 1-
Mar 31. **BAR MEALS:** L served Tues-Sun. D served
Tues-Sun 12-2 7-9. Av main course £7.95.
RESTAURANT: L served Tues-Sun. D served Tues-Sun 12-2
7-9. Av 3 course à la carte £22.
BREWERY/COMPANY: St Peters Brewery.
PRINCIPAL BEERS: St Peters Best, Strong Ale, and Fruit
Beer. **NOTES:** Parking 20

All AA listed accommodation can also be found on
the AA's internet site **www.theAA.com**

SURREY

ABINGER
Map 04 TQ14

The Volunteer
Water Ln, Sutton RH5 6PR ☎ 01306 730798
▤ 01306 731621
e-mail: thevolunteer@ukonline.co.uk
Dir: Between Guildford & Dorking, 1m S of A25

Enjoying a peaceful rural setting with views over the Mole Valley, this 17th-century pub is popular among walkers, who regularly fill the charming, low-ceilinged rooms. Typical seafood dishes include Torbay sole, red sea bream, skate, and fresh lobster. The menu also features Jamaican jerk chicken, Chinese beef pitta, Thai chicken wrap, and a good selection of cheeses. **OPEN:** 11-3 5-11 (All day Sat & Sun). **BAR MEALS:** L served all week. D served all week 12-2.30 7-9.30. Av main course £10. **RESTAURANT:** L served all week. D served all week 12-2.30 7-9.30. Av 3 course à la carte £20. **BREWERY/COMPANY:** Woodhouse Inns. **PRINCIPAL BEERS:** Badger: Tanglefoot, Dorset Best, King & Barnes Sussex. **FACILITIES:** Garden: waterfall, terraced lawns, outdoor eating, Dogs allowed, water, biscuits. **NOTES:** Parking 30

ALBURY
Map 04 TQ04

The Drummond Arms Inn ♦♦♦
The Street GU5 9AG ☎ 01483 202039 ▤ 01483 205361
Situated in the pretty village of Albury below the North Downs, this charming old inn has an attractive riverside garden and offers well furnished, comfortable en suite accommodation. Traditional pub food, served in the panelled bars, includes home-made steak and kidney pie, grilled lemon sole, or cold poached salmon salad, as well as burgers, jacket potatoes and filled baguettes. **OPEN:** 11-3 6-11. **BAR MEALS:** L served all week. D served Mon-Sat 12-2 7-9. Av main course £7. **RESTAURANT:** D served Tue-Sat 7-9. Av 3 course à la carte £15. **PRINCIPAL BEERS:** Courage Best, Gales HSB, Brakspears. **FACILITIES:** Garden: patio, BBQ, outdoor eating. **NOTES:** Parking 70. **ROOMS:** 11 bedrooms 11 en suite s£45 d£60

William IV
Little London GU5 9DG ☎ 01483 202685
Dir: just off the A25 between Guildford & Dorking
A stone's throw from Guildford and yet deep in the heart of the Surrey countryside, this quaint country pub is named after William IV who was succeeded by Queen Victoria in 1837. Great for local hikes and very popular with members of the walking fraternity; attractive garden for post-walk relaxation. Wide-ranging choice of real ales and a blackboard menu

continued

which changes daily. Expect pot-roast lamb shank, veal escalope with parsley sauce, tuna steak and pan-fried liver and bacon with onion gravy and leek mash. **OPEN:** 11-3 5.30-11 (Sun 12-3, 7-10.30). **BAR MEALS:** L served all week. D served Tue-Sat 12-2 7-9. Av main course £5.50. **RESTAURANT:** 7-9. Av 3 course à la carte £18. **BREWERY/COMPANY:** Free House. **PRINCIPAL BEERS:** Flowers IPA, Wadworth 6X, Hall & Woodhouse, Pilgrim. **FACILITIES:** Garden: outdoor eating Dogs allowed Water. **NOTES:** Parking 15
See Pub Walk on page 423

BETCHWORTH
Map 05 TQ25

The Red Lion
Old Reigate Rd RH3 7DS ☎ 01737 843336
▤ 01737 843336
e-mail: redlionbetch@aol.com

Set in 18 acres with a cricket ground and rolling countryside views, this award-winning, 200-year-old pub offers an extensive menu. Beyond baguettes and ploughman's lunches the choice includes sole and smoked salmon, Barbary duck breast, aubergine and broccoli fritters, deep-fried plaice and chips, Toulouse sausage and mash, and steak and ale pie. **OPEN:** 11-11 (Sun12-10.30). Closed Dec 31-Jan 2. **BAR MEALS:** L served all week. D served all week 12-3 6-10. Av main course £10. **BREWERY/COMPANY:** Punch Taverns. **PRINCIPAL BEERS:** Fullers London Pride, Youngs, Greene King Old Speckled Hen, Adnams Broadside. **FACILITIES:** Children welcome Garden: outdoor eating, patio. **NOTES:** Parking 50. **ROOMS:** 6 bedrooms 6 en suite s£60 d£80

BLACKBROOK
Map 04 TQ14

The Plough at Blackbrook
RH5 4DS ☎ 01306 886603
Dir: A24 to Dorking, then toward Horsham, 0.75m from Deepdene rdbt L to Blackbrook
Former coaching inn surrounded by idyllic countryside and an ideal base for local walks. Friendly ambience and welcoming atmosphere inside, striking rural views through large windows and a popular cottage garden at the rear. Wide variety of wines and good, well-kept ales complement the varied menus. Lunchtime bar meals and snacks feature toasted 'deli' bagels, local pork sausages and half a roast chicken. Among the specials are moussaka, rack of lamb, seafood Florentine, banana split and sorbet in chocolate cups. **OPEN:** 11-2.30 6-11 (Sun 12-3, 7-10.30). Closed 25-26 Dec, 1 Jan. **BAR MEALS:** L served all week. D served Tue-Sun 12-2 7-9. **BREWERY/COMPANY:** Hall & Woodhouse. **PRINCIPAL BEERS:** King & Barnes Sussex. **FACILITIES:** Garden: outdoor eating, Dogs allowed Water. **NOTES:** Parking 22

The Thames Path
(Surrey section)

Beyond Windsor the Thames Path crosses from Berkshire into neighbouring Surrey and here the river's surroundings become increasingly more urban as the trail heads for London. At Staines you reach the Swan Hotel, located on the south side of the Thames by Staines Bridge. Once the haunt of bargees transporting their cargoes up and down river, the present building is 18th century, though records indicate the original Swan dates back to 1606. Further down stream you come to Thames Court at Shepperton, built for the Dutch Ambassador early in the 20th century and tastefully refurbished in 1997. During the 1950s it became a guesthouse with an exclusive private members club known as Thames Court. The trail's next watering hole is the 1930s-style Fox on the River. Originally known as the Albany, after Lord Darnley who was given the title of Duke of Albany following his marriage to Mary Queen of Scots, the pub attracts many customers to its delightful riverside garden. There is also a ferry service across the river at certain times of the year.

BRAMLEY   Map 04 TQ04

Jolly Farmer Inn 🛏 ♈
High St GU5 0HB ☎ 01483 893355 📠 01483 890484
e-mail: accom@jollyfarmer.co.uk
Dir: Onto A3, then A281, Bramley 3m S of Guildford

Family-run, 350-year-old coaching inn, with a restaurant housed in a beautiful old Sussex barn. The owners pride themselves on their traditional fare and range of cask beers, including two local brews. Food is prepared to order from fresh produce, and dishes range from burgers, pies, curries and lasagne to mature Scottish steaks, chicken supreme, stuffed sea bass, and pan-fried skate wing.
OPEN: 11-3 6-11 (Sun 12-3, 7-10.30). **BAR MEALS:** L served all week. D served all week 12-2 6.30-10. Av main course £9.50. **RESTAURANT:** L served all week. D served all week 12-2 7-9.30. Av 3 course à la carte £18.50. **BREWERY/COMPANY:** Free House. **PRINCIPAL BEERS:** Hogs Back TEA, BadgerBest, Bass, Itchen Valley Godfather. **FACILITIES:** Children welcome Garden: outdoor eating, patio. **NOTES:** Parking 22. **ROOMS:** 10 bedrooms 9 en suite s£40 d£50 FR£60-£140

CHIDDINGFOLD   Map 04 SU93

Pick of the Pubs

The Crown Inn 🛏
The Green GU8 4TX ☎ 01428 682255
📠 01428 685736
Dir: On A283 between Milford & Petworth

Historic inn, dating back over 700 years, with lots of charming features, including ancient panelling, open fires, distinctive carvings and huge beams. Comfortably refurbished by owning brewery Hall and Woodhouse, this striking inn offers individually-styled bedrooms, some with four-poster beds, in a unique setting making it an excellent choice for a relaxing weekend break, especially with Petworth, the famous Devil's Punch Bowl and miles of walking on the scenic South Downs nearby.

Reliable food ranges from sausage and mash with onion gravy, chicken tagliatelle, freshly battered fish and chips, and decent sandwiches, warm salads and ploughman's at lunchtime, to Torbay sole, monkfish and tiger prawns pan-fried with ginger and lime cream sauce and served on tagliatelle, and roast duck with sweet plum sauce on the evening menu.
OPEN: 11-11. **BAR MEALS:** L served all week. D served all week 12-2.30 6.30-9.30. Av main course £8.95. **BREWERY/COMPANY:** Hall & Woodhouse. **PRINCIPAL BEERS:** Badger Dorset Best & Tanglefoot, King & Barnes Sussex Ale. **FACILITIES:** Garden: outdoor eating, patio, BBQ Dogs allowed. **ROOMS:** 8 bedrooms 8 en suite s£57 d£67

CLAYGATE

Swan Inn
Hare Ln KT10 9BT
Village pub with Edwardian interior. Cricket-team HQ overlooking the village green; hearty bar food.

SURREY

**WILLIAM IV,
ALBURY HEATH**

Little London, Albury Heath,
Nr Guildford GU5 9DG.
Tel: 01483 202685
Directions: just off A25
between Guildford & Dorking
*Bustling, old-fashioned
country pub in a popular
walking area below the
North Downs. Cottagey
beamed rooms with
flagstone floors, warming log
fires, rustic furnishings,
choice of real ales, and
home-made food. Great
walkers pub.*
Open: 11-3 5.30-11 (Sun 12-3
7-10.30). Bar Meals: 12-2 7-9
(no food Sun & Mon eve).
Children in eating area only.
Dogs welcome. Garden.
Parking
(see page 421 for full entry)

PubWALK

William IV,
Albury Heath

Taking in the charming village of Shere and beautiful Albury Park, this short walk explores the fine rolling Surrey countryside below the scenic North Downs.

On leaving the pub, turn left uphill through the hamlet of Little London. Take the track on your left and follow it to the road. Cross over and go through the kissing-gate into Albury Park. Follow the fenced path down through an avenue of massive chestnut trees and soon reach a cottage by a ford. Do not cross the stream, but turn right, following the path beside the stream towards Shere.

Walk into the village, go through The Square and continue ahead towards the church. Pass the church and turn right into Church Hill. Where it turns right, go left and take the arrowed footpath right, heading up across fields to the footbridge over the railway cutting. Keep to the footpath until you reach a road (Hook Lane). Turn right and shortly turn left along the waymarked footpath, eventually reaching a lane. Cross straight over and follow the track, signed to Parklands Farm.

Continue to the level crossing. Do not cross it, but turn left past the cottages and follow the path towards Ponds Farm. At the farm, cross the stile and walk up the gravel drive to Brook Lane. Turn right, pass beneath the railway and follow the lane to the pub.

Distance: 3 miles (4.8km)
Map: OS Landranger 186 &187
Terrain: farmland, parkland, country lanes
Paths: field paths, bridleways and green lanes; some road walking
Gradient: undulating

*Walk submitted by:
William IV*

St James's Church, Shere

COBHAM — Map 04 TQ16

The Cricketers

Downside KT11 3NX ☎ 01932 862105 ▤ 01932 868186
e-mail: jamesclifton@msn.com
Dir: From A3 take A245 towards Cobham, 2nd r'about turn R, then 1st R opp Waitrose. Pub 1.5m
Traditional 16th-century pub overlooking the village green, with log fires in winter and candlelit tables. A blackboard menu of hot food complements a daily buffet of freshly carved meats, seafood and raised pies. The restaurant offers formal dining with dishes such as baked sea bass with fennel, leeks and red pepper sauce or pan-fried calves' liver with pancetta.
OPEN: 11-2.30 6-11. Closed 25 Dec. **BAR MEALS:** L served all week. D served all week 12-2 6.30-10. Av main course £7.50. **RESTAURANT:** L served Sun, Tue-Sat. D served Tue-Sat 12.15-1.45 7.15-9.30. Av 3 course à la carte £22. Av 3 course fixed price £16.95. **BREWERY/COMPANY:** Inntrepreneur.
PRINCIPAL BEERS: Wadworth 6X, Youngs Bitter.
FACILITIES: Garden: patio, outdoor eating. **NOTES:** Parking 80

COLDHARBOUR — Map 04 TQ14

The Plough Inn

Coldharbour Ln RH5 6HD ☎ 01306 711793
e-mail: PloughInn@hotmail.com
Dir: M25 J9 - A24 to Dorking. A25 towards Guildford. Coldharbour signposted from the one-way system
Family-run 17th-century pub in the depths of National Trust countryside on Leith Hill. Traditional home-cooked English food accompanies a range of real ales, two of which (Tallywhacker and Crooked Furrow) are brewed on site. Bar food offers snacks, a daily pie, and bangers and mash, while the restaurant menu might have fresh mussels, pan-fried venison with blueberry sauce, and sticky walnut and toffee pudding.
OPEN: 11.30-3 6-11 (Sat-Sun 11.30-11). **BAR MEALS:** L served all week. D served all week 12-2.30 7-9.30. Av main course £7. **RESTAURANT:** L served all week. D served all week 12-2.30 7-9.30. Av 3 course à la carte £19.50.
BREWERY/COMPANY: Free House.
PRINCIPAL BEERS: Crooked Furrow, Leith Hill Tallywhacker, Shepherd Neame Master Brew, Adnams Broadside.
FACILITIES: Garden: food served outside.
ROOMS: 3 bedrooms 3 en suite s£55 d£65

COMPTON — Map 04 SU94

The Harrow Inn

The Street GU3 1EG ☎ 01483 810379 ▤ 01483 813854
Dir: 3m S of Guildford on A3 then B3000 towards Godalming. Compton on R
Beamed and simply furnished pub tucked away in an attractive village just off the A3. Handy refreshment stop - Greene King ales and changing blackboard bar menu. New licensees.
OPEN: 8am-11pm. **BAR MEALS:** L served all week. D served Mon-Sat 12-3 6-10. **RESTAURANT:** L served Sun. D served Mon-Sat 12-3 6-10. Av 3 course à la carte £17.
BREWERY/COMPANY: Punch Taverns.
PRINCIPAL BEERS: Greene King IPA & Abbot Ale, Hogs Back TEA. **FACILITIES:** Children welcome Garden: Patio/food served outside Dogs allowed. **NOTES:** Parking 50.
ROOMS: 4 bedrooms 4 en suite s£50 d£55

The Withies Inn

Withies Ln GU3 1JA ☎ 01483 421158 ▤ 01483 425904
The splendid garden is one of the pub's chief attractions, filled with overhanging weeping willows, apple trees and dazzling flower borders. Inside the atmosphere is friendly and welcoming, with low beams, 17th-century carved panels and an art nouveau settle, while log fires crackle away in the huge inglenook fireplace.
Expect a good choice of bar snacks, filled jacket potatoes and sandwiches, while the restaurant menu offers dishes such as chicken Kiev, fresh salmon salad, and rack of lamb with rosemary.
OPEN: 11-3 6-11 (Sun 12-3, 6-11). **BAR MEALS:** L served all week. D served Mon-Sat 12-2.30 7-10. Av main course £4.75. **RESTAURANT:** L served all week. D served all week 12-2.30 7-10. Av 3 course à la carte £30. **BREWERY/COMPANY:** Free House.
PRINCIPAL BEERS: Greene King IPA, Bass, Fullers London Pride, Sussex. **FACILITIES:** Garden: outdoor eating. Dogs allowed, garden only. **NOTES:** Parking 70

DORKING — Map 04 TQ14

Abinger Hatch

Abinger Ln, Abinger Common RH5 6HZ ☎ 01306 730737
Dir: A25 from Guildford, L to Abinger Common
17th-century pub, situated opposite the church and duck pond, with flagged floors, beamed ceilings, open fires and a welcoming atmosphere. Main dishes include breaded Brie with chutney, vegetable kiev with salsa and cheese sauce, seared salmon, sweet and sour calamari, and the 'Mighty Mixed Grill.'
OPEN: 11.30-2.30 5-11 (all day wknd). **BAR MEALS:** L served all week. D served Tue-Sat 12-2 6-9.30. Av main course £6. **RESTAURANT:** L served all week. D served all week 12-2 6-9.30. Av 3 course à la carte £15. **BREWERY/COMPANY:** Free House.
PRINCIPAL BEERS: Harveys, Fullers London Pride, Badger Tanglefoot. **FACILITIES:** Children welcome Children's licence Garden: outdoor eating Dogs allowed. **NOTES:** Parking 35

The Day of the Hog

Set in converted 18th-century barns located between Farnham and Guildford, the Hogs Back Brewery produces more than 30 different ales of various strengths and styles. These include Hair of the Hog (3.5%), Rip Snorter (5.0%), the Xmas ale Santa's Wobble (7.5%) and T.E.A. (Traditional English Ale) (4.2%). Brewery tours available.

England

Pick of the Pubs

The Stephan Langton ♀
Friday St, Abinger Common RH5 6JR ☎ 01306 730775
Dir: Between Dorking & Guildford leave A25 @ Hollow Lane, W of Wootton. Go S for 1.5m then L into Friday Street
Turn at the pond by Abinger Common to find this lovely brick and timber pub tucked away in a secluded hamlet surrounded by undulating mixed woodland. This fine old inn is named after a 13th-century archbishop of Canterbury and is the perfect retreat after an invigorating walk to the top of nearby Leith Hill. Chef/patron Jonathan Coomb bought the pub in summer 2000 and has been gradually refurbishing the pub to match the style and quality of the food he is now offering here. In addition to home-made bread, pasta and ice cream, expect to find mussels with parsley, garlic and chilli on tagliatelle, bruschetta of goats' cheese with roast tomato and olives, or poached skate with Puy lentils and salsa verde on the bar menu. Equally appealing is the simply described restaurant menu. Follow spiced apple and parsnip soup with herb-crusted baked cod with fennel and tomato fondue or haunch of rabbit with Serrano ham and goats' cheese gnocchi, and finish with vanilla and Bourbon crème brûlée.
OPEN: 11-3 6-11 (Sat-Sun all day). **BAR MEALS:** L served Tues-Sun. D served Tues-Sat 12.30-3 7-10. Av main course £6. **RESTAURANT:** L served Tues-Sun. D served Tues-Sat 12.30-3 7-10. Av 3 course à la carte £18.
BREWERY/COMPANY: Free House.
PRINCIPAL BEERS: Fuller's London Pride, Adnams, Harveys Sussex Bitter,. **FACILITIES:** Children welcome Garden: outdoor eating, patio, BBQ Dogs allowed.
NOTES: Parking 20

DUNSFOLD   Map 04 TQ03

The Sun Inn
The Common GU8 4LE ☎ 01483 200242 ▤ 200113
Dir: A281 thru Shalford & Bramley, take B2130 to Godalming. Dunsfold on L after 2 miles
Heavily timbered coaching inn with open fireplaces and three bar areas, opposite a cricket green. The village boasts seven ponds. Today's menu may include steak and kidney pie, venison sausages, fresh grilled trout and beef Stroganoff.
OPEN: 11-3 (Sun 12-4) 6-11 (Sun 7-10.30). **BAR MEALS:** L served all week. D served all week 12-2.15 7-10. Av main course £8.95. **BREWERY/COMPANY:** Punch Taverns.
PRINCIPAL BEERS: Friary Meux Best, Marstons Pedigree, King & Barnes Sussex. **FACILITIES:** Children welcome Children's licence Garden: outdoor eating, patio/terrace, BBQ Dogs allowed

---

EFFINGHAM   Map 04 TQ15

The Plough ♀
Orestan Ln KT24 5SW ☎ 01372 458121 ▤ 01372 458121
Dir: Between Guildford & Leatherhead on A246
A modern pub with a traditional feel, The Plough provides a peaceful retreat in a rural setting close to Polesden Lacy National Trust House. Home-cooked British dishes include the likes of mushroom and grilled tomato bruschetta, calves' liver mash with carrots and sage butter, and bread and butter pudding. *continued*

OPEN: 11-3 5.30-11. **BAR MEALS:** L served all week. D served all week 12-2.30 7-10. Av main course £7.95. **RESTAURANT:** L served all week. D served all week 12-2.30 7-10. Av 3 course à la carte £16. **BREWERY/COMPANY:** Youngs.
PRINCIPAL BEERS: Youngs IPA, Winter Warmer & Special.
FACILITIES: Garden: patio, outdoor eating. **NOTES:** Parking 40

EGHAM   Map 04 TQ07

The Fox and Hounds 🐾 ♀
Bishopgate Rd, Englefield Green TW20 0XU
☎ 01784 433098 ▤ 01784 438775
Dir: From village green turn L into Castle Hill Rd, then R into Bishops Gate Rd
The Surrey border once ran through the centre of this good English pub, convenient for walkers and riders. Still used by members of the Household Cavalry who tether their horses outside while they refresh themselves inside. There is a range of daily-changing fish specials as well as menu options such as roast half shoulder of lamb, Dutch calves' liver and Barbary duck breast.
OPEN: 11-11 (Sun 12-10.30). **BAR MEALS:** L served all week. D served all week 12-2.30 6.30-10. Av main course £5.95.
RESTAURANT: L served all week. D served all week 12-2.30 6.30-10. Av 3 course à la carte £23.95.
BREWERY/COMPANY: Free House.
PRINCIPAL BEERS: Fullers London Pride, Brakspear.
FACILITIES: Children welcome Garden: beer garden with seating, patio, BBQ Dogs allowed. **NOTES:** Parking 60

ELSTEAD   Map 04 SU94

Pick of the Pubs

The Woolpack ♀
The Green GU8 6HD ☎ 01252 703106
▤ 01252 703106
Dir: Milford exit off A3
There's plenty of atmosphere in this attractive, tile-hung pub, overlooking the village green. Nearby, the River Wey flows beneath the ancient Elstead bridge, and there are some good walks in the local area. The building was originally constructed in the 18th century as a store for woollen bales; weaving shuttles and other wool industry memorabilia now decorate the bar, with its low beams, open fires, and high-backed settles. Just the place, then, to come for a game of crib, dominoes or chess on a cold winter's night. You'll find good, cask conditioned ales, and the large blackboard menus are regularly changed. Starters include home-made soup or pâté, whitebait, breaded Camembert, and smoked trout with horseradish. Moving on, you can expect monkfish, beef casserole, or duck and spicy sausage cassoulet, as well as spinach and cottage cheese lasagne or chilli vegetables with an omelette topping. There's always a large selection of fresh, home-made desserts, too.
OPEN: 11-2.30 6-11 (Sat 11-11, Sun 12-11). Closed 26 Dec.
BAR MEALS: L served all week. D served all week 12-2 7-9.45. Av main course £8.25. **RESTAURANT:** L served all week. D served all week 12-2 7-9.45. Av 3 course à la carte £16. **BREWERY/COMPANY:** Punch Taverns.
PRINCIPAL BEERS: Greene King Abbot Ale, Fullers London Pride, Tetleys. **FACILITIES:** Children welcome Garden: food served outside Dogs allowed. **NOTES:** Parking 15

England

EWHURST   Map 04 TQ04

The Windmill Inn
Pitch Hill GU6 7NN ☎ 01483 277566
Dir: From Cranleigh take B2127, through Ewhurst. At mini rndbt take
Shere road. Pub 1.5m on R
Affording far-reaching views across the Weald to the South
Downs, this welcoming inn was originally the haunt of 18th-
century smugglers. Rebuilt after a fire in 1906. Traditional pub
food. Close to a wealth of good walks.

GUILDFORD   Map 04 SU94

Red Lion ♀
Shamley Green GU5 0UB ☎ 01483 892202
▤ 01483 894055
Attractively situated old pub overlooking the village cricket
pitch, with summer gardens, winter fires and en suite
bedrooms. No less than four varied menus are served in the
cosy bar and large, comfortable restaurant. Steak and
Murphy's pie, folded spinach and mushroom crêpes, salmon
steaks, sea bass, and lasagne al forno are typical dishes.
OPEN: 12-3 7-11 (Sat 8-11pm, Sun 8-10.30pm). **BAR MEALS:** L
served all week. D served all week 12-3 6.30-10. Av main course
£8.95. **RESTAURANT:** L served all week. D served all week 12-3
6.30-10. Av 3 course à la carte £20. **BREWERY/ COMPANY:** Pubmaster. **PRINCIPAL BEERS:** Adnams Broadside, Marstons
Pedigree, Youngs. **FACILITIES:** Garden: food served outside.
NOTES: Parking 30. **ROOMS:** 4 bedrooms 4 en suite s£45 d£55

HASCOMBE   Map 04 TQ03

The White Horse
The Street GU8 4JA ☎ 01483 208258 ▤ 01483 208200
e-mail: jamesb.ward@virgin.net
Dir: from Godalming take B2130. Pub on L 0.5m after Hascombe
Friendly 16th-century pub situated in picturesque countryside.
Noted in summer for its colourful garden, dazzling hanging
baskets and flowers. Restaurant menu and extensive
blackboard specials in the bar may offer calves' liver and
bacon, home-made steak burger, home-made pies and Thai
style salmon and prawn fishcakes.
OPEN: 10-3 5.30-11 (Sat 10-11, Sun 12-10.30). Closed Dec 25.
BAR MEALS: L served all week. D served all week 12-2 7-10.
RESTAURANT: L served all week. D served Mon-Sat 12-2 7-10.
Av 3 course à la carte £25. **BREWERY/COMPANY:** Punch
Taverns. **PRINCIPAL BEERS:** Adnams, Fullers London Pride,
Hall & Woodhouse Millennium. **FACILITIES:** Children welcome
Garden: outdoor eating, patio Dogs allowed.
NOTES: Parking 55

HASLEMERE   Map 04 SU93

The Wheatsheaf Inn ♦♦♦ ♀
Grayswood Rd, Grayswood GU27 2DE ☎ 01428 644440
▤ 01428 641285
Dir: Leave A3 at Milford, A286 to Haslemere. Grayswood approx
1.5m N
Close to Haslemere, Guildford, Petworth and Midhurst, this
Victorian village inn has some of Surrey's loveliest walks right
on its doorstep. Nearby is the magnificent viewpoint at Black
Down where Alfred Lord Tennyson lived for 24 years. Quality,
well-presented fare is freshly prepared and ranges from
mushroom Stroganoff and avocado and prawn salad to duck
breast with cranberry sauce and venison steak with red wine
gravy. Extensive snack menu. Comfortable bedrooms are all
similar in style and furnished to a good standard.
continued

OPEN: 11-3 6-11. **BAR MEALS:** L served all week. D served all
week 12-2 7-10. **RESTAURANT:** L served all week. D served all
week 12-2 7-10. **BREWERY/COMPANY:** Free House.
PRINCIPAL BEERS: Wadworth 6X, Fullers London Pride,
Harveys Sussex Bitter, Timothy Taylor Landlord.
FACILITIES: Garden: food served outside. **NOTES:** Parking 20.
ROOMS: 7 bedrooms 7 en suite s£55 d£75

HINDHEAD   Map 04 SU83

Devil's Punchbowl Inn ♀
London Rd GU26 6AG ☎ 01428 606565 ▤ 01428 605713
Dir: from M25 take A3 to Guildford, from there head toward
Portsmouth
The hotel, which dates from the early 1800s, stands 900ft
above sea level with wonderful views as far as London on a
clear day. The 'punchbowl' is a large natural bowl in the
ground across the road. Food ranges from ploughman's
lunches to sandwiches and 16oz steaks and sizzling hot
platters.
OPEN: 11-11 (Sun 12-10.30). **BAR MEALS:** L served all week. D
served all week 12-10. Av main course £6.95. **RESTAURANT:** L
served all week. D served all week 12-10pm. Av 3 course à la carte
£17. **BREWERY/COMPANY:** Eldridge Pope.
PRINCIPAL BEERS: Bass, Wells Bombardier.
FACILITIES: Children welcome Garden: outdoor eating Dogs
allowed. **NOTES:** Parking 65. **ROOMS:** 34 bedrooms
34 en suite s£69 d£89 FR£110

HOLMBURY ST MARY

The Royal Oak
The Glade RH5 6PF ☎ 01306 730120
Neatly thatched 18th-century inn tucked away in a picturesque
village on the Surrey downs. Cosy, unpretentious bars with
open fires and beams attracting a loyal local trade. Home-
made traditional pub food.

LEIGH   Map 05 TQ24

The Plough ♀
Church Rd RH2 8NJ ☎ 01306 611348
▤ 01306 611299
Welcoming country pub overlooking the village green and
situated opposite St Bartholomew's Church. Varied clientele,
good atmosphere and quaint low beams which are padded!
Comprehensive menu offers an extensive choice of
sandwiches, snacks and more substantial dishes, including
honey-glazed duck, tuna steak and sausage and mash with
onion gravy. Expect pavlova, apple pie and chocolate fudge
cake among the puddings.
continued

OPEN: 11-11 (Sun 12-10.30). **BAR MEALS:** L served all week. D served all week 12-3 7-10. Av main course £7. **RESTAURANT:** L served all week. D served all week 12-3 7-10. Av 3 course à la carte £15. **BREWERY/COMPANY:** Hall & Woodhouse. **PRINCIPAL BEERS:** Badger Best & Tanglefoot. **FACILITIES:** Children welcome Garden: food served outside Dogs allowed Water. **NOTES:** Parking 6

MICKLEHAM   Map 04 TQ15

Pick of the Pubs

King William IV
Byttom Hill RH5 6EL ☎ 01372 372590
Dir: Just off A24 (Leatherhead-Dorking), by partly green painted restaurant, just N of B2289
This popular, family-run freehouse was formerly an ale house for the staff on Lord Beaverbrook's nearby Cherkley estate. There are plenty of good walks on the National Trust's nearby properties at Box Hill and Headley Heath, and the pub itself is perched on a hillside with picturesque views across Norbury Park and the Mole Valley. The building dates from 1790 with some Victorian additions, and a panelled snug complements the larger back bar with its open fire, cast iron tables and grandfather clock. Meals are freshly cooked by the chef/landlord; look out for calves' liver and bacon, pheasant in red wine, shoulder of lamb with mint and garlic, or Thai chicken curry. You'll also find vegetarian options, and seafood dishes like chargrilled swordfish, stuffed haddock, jumbo prawns and New Zealand mussels. There are Sunday roasts, too, and summer barbecues in the attractive terraced garden.
OPEN: 11-3 6-11 (Sun 12-3, 7-10.30). Closed 25 Dec,. **BAR MEALS:** L served all week. D served all week 12-2 7-9.30. Av main course £7.75. **BREWERY/COMPANY:** Free House. **PRINCIPAL BEERS:** Hogs Back TEA & Hop Garden Gold, Badger Best, Adnams Best. **FACILITIES:** Garden: outdoor eating, patio Dogs allowed, garden only

The Running Horses
Old London Rd RH5 6DU ☎ 01372 372279
🖷 01372 363004
e-mail: enqs@therunninghorses.totalserve.co.uk
Dir: Off A24 between Leatherhead & Dorking

Providing sustenance to travellers for more than 400 years, the inn is situated in a pretty village half a mile from Box Hill. The bar features a Highwayman's hideaway and an inglenook fireplace, and these days there are five en suite bedrooms. Dishes range from salmon and crab fishcakes with caper sauce to English lamb in flaky pastry with black pudding, apple chutney and port wine jus.   *continued*

OPEN: 11.30-3 5.30-11 (Sun 12-3.30, 7-10.30). Closed Dec 26. **BAR MEALS:** L served all week 12-2.30 7-9.30. Av main course £13.50. **RESTAURANT:** L served all week. D served Mon-Sat 12-2.30 7-9.30. Av 3 course à la carte £21. **BREWERY/COMPANY:** Vanguard. **PRINCIPAL BEERS:** London Pride, Youngs, Greene King. **ROOMS:** 5 bedrooms 5 en suite s£80 d£90

NEWDIGATE   Map 04 TQ14

The Six Bells
Village St RH5 5DH ☎ 01306 631276   🖷 01306 631793
Dir: 5m S of Dorking (A24), L at Beare Green rdbt, R at T-jct in village

Picturesque timber-framed pub in a quiet village location and reputedly once a smuggler's haunt. Light meals and bar snacks might include the Six Bells club sandwich and a range of baguettes and filled jacket potatoes. Daily-changing blackboard menu may offer rack of lamb and poached salmon.
OPEN: 11-3 6-11 (Sun 12-3, 7-10.30). **BAR MEALS:** L served all week. D served Mon-Sat 12-2.30 7-9.30. Av main course £6. **RESTAURANT:** L served all week. D served Mon-Sat 12-2.30 7-9.30. Av 3 course à la carte £25. Av 3 course fixed price £13.90. **BREWERY/COMPANY:** Free House. **PRINCIPAL BEERS:** Youngs, Fullers London Pride, Greene King Old Speckled Hen, Tetleys. **FACILITIES:** Garden: patio/terrace, outdoor eating Dogs allowed. **NOTES:** Parking 40

The Surrey Oaks
Parkgate Rd RH5 5DZ ☎ 01306 631200   🖷 01306 631200
Dir: turn off either A24 or A25 and follow signs to Newdigate, The Surry Oaks is 1M E of Newdigate Village on the road towards Leigh/Charlwood
The present leaseholders took over this part 16th-century country pub in 1993 and have completely renovated the Georgian bar, now the restaurant. There are also two small bars, one of which has a superb inglenook fireplace and stone-flagged floors. With its variety of ever-changing guest ales, the inn hosts an annual beer festival on August Bank Holiday. Comprehensive restaurant and bar snack menus as well as lunchtime and evening specials. Expect roast beef, leek and Stilton crumble, pheasant supreme in game sauce and lemon sole.
OPEN: 11.30-2.30 (Sat-Sun till 3) 5.30-11. **BAR MEALS:** L served all week. D served Tue-Sat 12-2 7-9.30. Av main course £5.95. **RESTAURANT:** L served all week. D served Tue-Sat 12-2 7-9.30. Av 3 course à la carte £13.95. **BREWERY/COMPANY:** Punch Taverns. **PRINCIPAL BEERS:** Adnams, Fullers London Pride. **FACILITIES:** Children welcome Garden: outdoor eating, patio. **NOTES:** Parking 75

OCKLEY

Map 04 TQ14

Pick of the Pubs

Bryce's at The Old School House @ 🍸
RH5 5TH ☎ 01306 627430 📠 01306 628274
e-mail: bryces.fish@virgin.net
Dir: 8m S of Dorking on A29

The eponymous Bill Bryce purchased this former boys' boarding school in 1982, converting it into a spacious bar and restaurant that is renowned for the finest seafood around. The range of available fish is limited only by market availability, and Bill prides himself both on its freshness and the simplicity of presentation. Seemingly endless bar food options include Bryce's home-cured gravadlax and fish cakes offered with a choice of dressings in addition to smoked and cured fish platter and simple fresh cod in beer batter. If you don't like fish there is no problem, with available options that include herb-crusted Brie fritters, open sandwiches of Charnwood cheese with smoked bacon, calves' liver on garlic and shallot mash and lasagne bolognase with crusty bread. Restaurant specials typified by smoked salmon and prawn papillote and Dover sole with lobster sauce are followed, as in the bar, by home-made desserts posted on the blackboard. Now a free house, beers include Gales real ales and imaginative wines including special cellar vintages.
OPEN: 11-3 6-11 (closed Sun eve). Closed 25-26 Dec, 1 Jan.
BAR MEALS: L served all week. D served all week 12-2.30 6.30-9.30. Av main course £8.50. **RESTAURANT:** L served all week. D served Mon-Sat 12-2.30 7-9.30. Av 3 course à la carte £24. Av 2 course fixed price £15.50.
BREWERY/COMPANY: King & Barnes.
PRINCIPAL BEERS: Gales HSB,GB, Butser.
FACILITIES: Children welcome. Terrace, food served outside Dogs allowed Water. **NOTES:** Parking 25

The Kings Arms Inn 🍺
Stane St RH5 5TP ☎ 01306 711224 📠 01306 711224
Dir: From M25 J9 take A24 through Dorking towards Horsham, A29 to Ockley
Heavily beamed 16th-century village inn with welcoming log fires, a priest hole and friendly ghost all adding to the atmosphere. Home-made food from the same menu is offered in the bar and restaurant, with dishes such as dressed crab salad, fresh grilled cod with Vietnamese sauce, roast lamb with honey and mustard, and pheasant breast stuffed with Stilton and wrapped in bacon.
OPEN: 11-2.30 (Sun 12-3, 7-10.30) 6-11. **BAR MEALS:** L served all week. D served all week 12-2 7-9.30. Av main course £9.
RESTAURANT: L served Tue-Sun. D served Tue-Sat 12-2 7-9.30.
BREWERY/COMPANY: Free House. *continued*

PRINCIPAL BEERS: Whitbread Flowers Original, Eldridge Pope, Greene King Old Speckled Hen, Marstons Pedigree.
FACILITIES: Garden: outdoor eating, patio.
NOTES: Parking 40. **ROOMS:** 6 bedrooms 6 en suite

PIRBRIGHT

Map 04 SU95

The Royal Oak 🍸
Aldershot Rd GU24 0DQ ☎ 01483 232466
Dir: M3 J3 take A322 towards Guildford, then A324 towards Aldershot
Tudor cottage pub with an oak church door, stained glass windows and pew seating. In summer the garden is glorious, while in winter there are welcoming log fires in the rambling bars. Wide choice of real ales, up to nine at any one time. Menu may include salmon and thyme fishcakes, Mediterranean vegetable couscous, moules marinière et frites, steak and ale pie, drunken duck, or Aberdeen Angus rib eye steak.
OPEN: 11-11 (Sun 12-10.30). **BAR MEALS:** L served all week. D served all week 12-2 6.30-9.30 (all day wknds). Av main course £6. **BREWERY/COMPANY:** Whitbread.
PRINCIPAL BEERS: Interbrew Flowers Original & IPA Hogs Back TEA. **FACILITIES:** Garden: outdoor eating Dogs allowed garden only, guide dogs allowed inside. **NOTES:** Parking 50

REDHILL

Map 05 TQ25

William IV 🍺
Little Cotton Ln, Bletchingly RH1 4QF ☎ 01883 743278
Dir: from M25 J6 take A25 towards Redhill. Turn R at top of Bletchingly High Street
Victorian country pub retaining three small rooms - the snug, lounge and dining room. Located down a leafy lane at the end of a row of terrace cottages. Close to the Pilgrims Way which runs over the North Downs. Enjoy a summer drink or eat al fresco in the peaceful garden or sample lambs' liver and bacon, chicken korma or minced beef and vegetable pie from the choice of home-made specials. Wide-ranging menus.
OPEN: 11.30-3 6-11 (Sun 12-4 6.30-10.30). **BAR MEALS:** L served all week. D served all week 12-2.15 6.45-9.30. Av main course £7. **RESTAURANT:** L served all week. D served all week 12-2.15 6.45-9.30. Av 3 course à la carte £14.
BREWERY/COMPANY: Punch Taverns.
PRINCIPAL BEERS: Adnams, Wadworth 6X, Greene King IPA, Youngs Special, Harvey's. **FACILITIES:** Garden: outdoor eating, Dogs allowed On leads. **NOTES:** Parking 10

STAINES

Map 04 TQ07

The Swan Hotel
The Hythe TW18 3JB ☎ 01784 452494 📠 01784 461593
Dir: Just off A308, S of Staines Bridge. 12m from M25, M4 & M3. 5m from Heathrow
The hotel, set on the south bank of the Thames by Staines Bridge, retains its original pub atmosphere and has two large bars and a conservatory overlooking the river terrace.

VIRGINIA WATER

The Wheatsheaf Hotel ★ ★ 🍺 🍸
London Rd GU25 4QF ☎ 01344 842057 📠 01344 842932
e-mail: the.wheatsheaf@virgin.net
The Wheatsheaf dates back to the second half of the 18th century and is beautifully situated overlooking Virginia Water on the edge of Windsor Great Park. Chalkboard menus offer a good range of freshly prepared dishes with fresh fish as a *continued*

speciality. Popular options are beer battered cod and chips, roast queen fish with pesto crust, and braised lamb shank on mustard mash.
OPEN: 11-11. **BAR MEALS:** L served all week. D served all week 12-10. Av main course £9. **RESTAURANT:** L served all week. D served all week 12-10. Av 3 course à la carte £14.
PRINCIPAL BEERS: Courage Best, Directors, Marstons Pedigree, John Smiths. **FACILITIES:** Garden: patio, outdoor eating.
NOTES: Parking 90.
ROOMS: 17 bedrooms 17 en suite s£85 d£90

WALLISWOOD
Map 04 TQ13

The Scarlett Arms
RH5 5RD ☎ 01306 627243
Dir: S on A29 from Dorking, thru Ockley, R for Walliswood/Oakwood Hill
Oak beams, a stone floor and a fine open fireplace give a homely feel to this unspoilt, 400-year-old rural pub. Simple country cooking is the perfect complement to the excellent King & Barnes ales on offer.

WEST END
Map 04 SU96

Pick of the Pubs

The Inn @ West End ♀ NEW
42 Guildford Rd GU24 9PW ☎ 01276 858652
📠 01276 485842
e-mail: greatfood@the-inn.co.uk
Dir: On the A322 towards Guildford 3M from J3 of the M3
Having successfully run the Brickmakers Arms at nearby Windlesham (qv) for some years, Gerry and Ann Price acquired, renamed and totally refurbished this now stylish pub-restaurant on the A322, 3 miles from the M3 (J3).
 Light, modern and airy throughout, the 'Inn' has rapidly become the place to eat in the area, attracting M3 travellers and local 'diners and quaffers' for first-class food and great wines (Gerry is also a wine merchant!), served in a relaxed pub atmosphere.
 From excellent value set lunch and Sunday lunch menus, and regular themed dinners, imaginative monthly-changing menus list an eclectic range of freshly prepared food.
 Expect home-made breads, fresh fish from Portsmouth - roast monkfish with bacon and smoked salmon cream sauce, gurnard with basil pesto - and local estate game alongside starters/light bites like salmon and dill fishcakes with tartare sauce and tomato and basil soup, and such main dishes as beef fillet with wild mushrooms, tomato and red wine jus, or calves' liver with mustard mash and spinach. Good puddings and sandwiches.
OPEN: 12-3 5-11. **BAR MEALS:** L served all week. D served all week 12-2.30 6-9.30. Av main course £9.
RESTAURANT: L served all week. D served all week 12-2.30 6-9.30. Av 3 course à la carte £30. Av 3 course fixed price £15.30. **BREWERY/COMPANY:** Free House.
PRINCIPAL BEERS: Courage Best, Fullers London Pride, Youngs Special. **FACILITIES:** Garden: Food served outside.
NOTES: Parking 35

WEST CLANDON
Map 04 TQ05

Onslow Arms 🛏 ♀
The Street GU4 7TE ☎ 01483 222447 📠 01483 211126
Dir: A3 then A247

Dating from 1623 with an inglenook fireplace and a unique traditional roasting spit, this pub is convenient for both Heathrow and Gatwick airports and has its own helipad! Fish dishes might include Dover sole, halibut, or sea bass, while other main course options are duck breast with black cherry sauce, rib eye steak, and game in season.
OPEN: 11-11 (Sun 12-10.30). **BAR MEALS:** L served all week. D served all week 12.15-2.30 7-10. Av main course £6.50.
RESTAURANT: L served all week. D served all week 12.30-2 7-10. Av 3 course à la carte £26. Av 3 course fixed price £18.95.
BREWERY/COMPANY: Free House.
PRINCIPAL BEERS: Courage, Whitbread, Youngs, King & Barnes.
FACILITIES: Children welcome Garden: Beer garden patio, food served outside Dogs allowed. **NOTES:** Parking 200

Inns, Taverns and Alehouses

As the middle ages wore on, a rough distinction grew up between three types of drinking-house: the inn, the tavern and the alehouse. At the top of the tree, the inn provided lodging, meals and drink for well-to-do travellers. The tavern was more like a wine bar, with no accommodation. Usually in a town, it dispensed wine and sometimes food to prosperous customers. A bunch of evergreen leaves above the door might identify it and it was associated, in puritanical minds at least, with gambling, loose women and disreputable songs.
At the bottom of the ladder and far more numerous, alehouses catered for ordinary people. As their name implies, they were simply dwelling houses where ale was brewed and sold. Often kept by women, they were generally one-room, wattle-and-daub hovels which supplied a take-out service for the neighbours. Inside there was no bar counter, customers and the alewife huddled close, pigs and chickens wandered in and out, and standards of hygiene would horrify patrons today. The quality of the ale was checked by a local official, the ale-conner, and the houses identified themselves with an alestake. This long pole with leaves at the end was the forerunner of today's pub sign.

England

Skittles

Skittles is a far older game than darts or dominoes, on record in London since the 15th century, when it was banned. Henry VIII enjoyed it and had his own skittle alley, but governments kept vainly trying to stop ordinary people playing, because they ought to have been practising their archery and because they gambled so heavily. Even so, the game became popular enough to make 'beer and skittles' proverbial. Basically, three wooden balls are propelled at nine pins to knock them down, but there are sharp variations in the rules between different areas and pubs. Varieties include London or Old English Skittles, West Country Skittles, Long Alley and Aunt Sally, as well as several types of table skittles.

WINDLESHAM   Map 04 SU96

Pick of the Pubs

Brickmakers Arms 🛏 ♀
Chertsey Rd GU20 6HT ☎ 01276 472267 & 451914
🖥 01276 451014
e-mail: brickmakers@theoldmonk.co.uk
Dir: *Take the A30 into Sunningdale turn down Chobham Road, 2M you come to a Rdbt right turn continue for 1M pub on R*
Bought by the Old Monk Company two years ago, this unassuming, Victorian roadside pub lies on the edge of the village and just a few minutes drive from the M3 (J3). Comfortably refurbished bar, with a flagstoned floor, open fire, real ales and good wines by the glass, and neatly appointed dining areas for those wishing to linger longer over 3 courses with wine. Snacks in the bar range from freshly baked Italian breads (smoked ham and spicy chutney, to salmon and dill fishcakes with chive sauce, and steak and ale pie. Style and complexity of dishes move up a gear on the carte, where dishes may include roast shoulder of lamb studded with garlic and rosemary, pepper-crusted beef medallions with whisky and shallot jus, and daily fish specials like monkfish wrapped in Parma ham with crab and dill sauce. Just 5 minutes from the 10th hole of Sunningdale Golf Club.
OPEN: 11-3 5-11 (all day wkds). **BAR MEALS:** L served all week. D served all week 12-2.30 6-10. Av main course £7.
RESTAURANT: L served all week. D served all week 12-2.30 6-10. Av 3 course à la carte £23.
BREWERY/COMPANY: Free House **FACILITIES:** Children welcome Garden: food served outside Dogs allowed, on leads please. **NOTES:** Parking 40

WITLEY   Map 04 SU93

The White Hart
Petworth Rd GU8 5PH ☎ 01428 683695
Dir: *From A3 follow signs to Milford, then A283 towards Petworth. Pub 2m on L*
16th-century coaching inn with illustrious connections. Richard II used the pub as a hunting lodge and George Eliot based characters in her novel Middlemarch on the clientele. Shepherd Neame.

SUSSEX, EAST

ALCISTON   Map 05 TQ50

Pick of the Pubs

Rose Cottage Inn 🛏 ♀
BN26 6UW ☎ 01323 870377 🖥 01323 871440
e-mail: ian@alciston.freeserve.co.uk
Dir: *Off A27 between Eastbourne & Lewes*
A fiercely traditional pub in a cul-de-sac village close to the South Downs that has been in the same family ownership for some 40 years and remains celebrated for traditional home-cooked food that includes locally supplied seasonal fish and game.

Lunchtime bar food takes in hot-smoked mackerel pâté and fried scampi tails with tartare sauce, supplemented in the evenings by the likes of cheesey-topped garlic mussels and roast Sussex duckling with passion fruit and Marsala sauce: round off here with luxury ice creams and sorbets or home-made cheesecake with raspberry sauce. At dinner in the restaurant, expect from a separate menu deep-fried Camembert with port and redcurrant jelly, flamed English pork with apricots, sherry and cream and home-made meringue with seasonal fresh fruits.

Popular walkers' retreat and a venue for locals seeking a peaceful drink, either in the small front garden or in one of the rambling cosy rooms inside.
OPEN: 11.30-3 (Sun 12-3) 6.30-11 (Sun 7-10.30).
BAR MEALS: L served all week. D served all week 12-2 7-9.30. **RESTAURANT:** D served Mon-Sat 7-9. Av 3 course à la carte £17.50. **BREWERY/COMPANY:** Free House.
PRINCIPAL BEERS: Harveys Best. **FACILITIES:** Garden: food served outside No dogs. **NOTES:** Parking 25.
ROOMS: 1 bedrooms 1 en suite d£45

ALFRISTON   Map 05 TQ50

George Inn ♀
High St BN26 5SY ☎ 01323 870319 🖥 01323 871384
e-mail: george_inn@hotmail.com
Grade I listed building first licensed in 1397 in one of the region's loveliest villages and reputed to boast a network of smuggler tunnels. Among the interior features are heavy oak beams and an ancient inglenook fireplace. The menus change regularly, and all ingredients are bought in fresh every day. Try the Sussex baked ham, beef Wellington, 10oz sirloin steak or goats' cheese and frangipane pithivier with a sweet chilli sauce.
OPEN: 11-11 (Winter 12-3, 6-11, Sat 11-11, Sun 12-10.30). Closed Dec 25. **BAR MEALS:** L served all week. D served all week 12-2.30 7-9. Av main course £6. **RESTAURANT:** L served all week. D served all week 12-2.30 7-9. Av 3 course à la carte £18.
PRINCIPAL BEERS: Greene King Old Speckled Hen & Abbot Ale, Ruddles County. **FACILITIES:** Children welcome Garden: food served outside Dogs allowed. **ROOMS:** 7 bedrooms 6 en suite

---

We endeavour to be as accurate as possible but changes in personnel and data can occur in establishments after the guide has gone to press

Ram Inn, Firle

RAM INN, FIRLE
BN8 6NS. Tel: 01273 858222
Directions: off A27 2m E of
Lewes
*Named after the crest of the
Gage family of nearby Firle
Place, the Ram is a rustic and
unspoilt old coaching inn
nestling at the foot of the South
Downs. Daily-changing menu.
Family friendly - children's
menu & room. Walled garden.*
Open: 11.30-11 (Sun 12-10.30).
Bar Meals: 12-9. Cream teas 3-
5.30. Children welcome.
Garden/patio. Parking.

(see page 434 for full entry)

An exhilarating walk from the estate village of Firle to the top of Firle Beacon, then along the top of the South Downs with far-reaching views, returning to Firle via Charleston Farmhouse, the 1920s home of the 'Bloomsbury Group' of artists and writers.

Walk up the village street, passing the shop, and take the bridleway through Place Farm towards the Downs. Follow what is the old coach road along the field edge, gradually ascending to a copse and junction of paths. Turn right through the double gates and climb the track uphill beside woodland to reach a gate. Climb steeply on to the South Downs, joining the South Downs Way at the summit. Savour the spectacular views and walk past the trig point at Firle Beacon.

In 1/2 mile (0.8km), look out for a track on your left and descend off the Downs. Cross the old coach road (track) and continue along the track to Tilton Farm. John Maynard Keynes, the famous British economist lived here early last century. Shortly after the farm

buildings, turn left along a track leading to Charleston Farmhouse. Virginia Woolf, Vanessa Bell and Duncan Grant, among others, used to reside here. The house and gardens are open daily during the summer (tearooms).

Walk past the house and take the footpath ahead alongside a ditch and field. Go through a gate on the left and pass beside a copse (right), then cross the field to a further gate (Firle Tower ahead). Beyond another gate, walk up to the brow of the hill, cross the track to Firle Tower and go through a gate in a small copse. Follow the path across a field and through an iron gate beside the Dower House to a farm road. Go through the gate opposite into Firle Park and follow the oak marker posts across the park (Firle Park open Weds, Thur & Sun pm - cream teas). Exit the park via a kissing-gate and walk past cottages and gardens to the village shop, Turn right back to the inn.

Distance: 4 1/2 miles (7.2km)
Map: OS Landranger 198/199
Paths: field paths, broad tracks, South Downs Way
Terrain: downland, farmland and parkland
Gradient: undulating in places; one steep climb to top of South Downs

*Walk submitted by:
The Ram Inn*

Firle Place

ARLINGTON
Map 05 TQ50

Old Oak Inn
BN26 6SJ ☎ 01323 482072
e-mail: arnllo@yahoo.com
Dir: N of A27 between Polegate & Lewes
Originally the village almshouse, dating from 1733, which became a pub in the early 1900s. Typical bar dishes include filled baguettes and ploughman's, as well as pasta and curries. In the restaurant expect the likes of roast duck, fresh grilled trout, and home made steak, kidney and Guinness pie
OPEN: 11-3 6-11. **BAR MEALS:** L served all week. D served Tue-Sat 12-2 7-9. Av main course £6.25. **RESTAURANT:** L served all week. D served Tue-Sat 12-2 7-9. Av 3 course à la carte £15.
BREWERY/COMPANY: Free House.
PRINCIPAL BEERS: Harveys, Badger, Rother Valley Level Best & guest ales. **FACILITIES:** Children welcome Garden: Outdoor eating Dogs allowed Water provided. **NOTES:** Parking 30

ASHBURNHAM PLACE
Map 05 TQ61

Ash Tree Inn
Brownbread St TN33 9NX ☎ 01424 892104
The Ash Tree is a friendly old pub with three open fires, plenty of beams and a traditional local atmosphere. Bar food includes ploughmans', salads and sandwiches, while the restaurant menu may feature duck breast in cherry sauce, cottage pie or poached salmon.
OPEN: 12-4 7-11. **BAR MEALS:** L served all week. D served all week 12-2 7-9. Av main course £8. **RESTAURANT:** L served all week. D served Tue-Sat 12-2 7-9. Av 3 course à la carte £17.50.
BREWERY/COMPANY: Free House.
PRINCIPAL BEERS: Harveys Best, Greene King Old Speckled Hen, Brakspear & guest ales. **FACILITIES:** Children welcome Garden: Dogs allowed. **NOTES:** Parking 20

BARCOMBE
Map 05 TQ41

The Anchor Inn ♀
Anchor Ln BN8 5BS ☎ 01273 400414 ▤ 01273 401029
Dir: From A26 (Lewes/Uckfield rd)
Fine 18th-century smugglers' inn where you can enjoy a drink on the trim riverside lawn after indulging in some relaxing boating activity on the Ouse. Alternatively, explore the rolling South Downs or visit nearby Brighton and Lewes. The inn, which was originally built for bargees who journeyed upriver from Newhaven, has undergone recent changes and the new owners have added two new bars made of oak from a French priory. Freshly prepared bar and restaurant food ranges from baguettes and ploughman's lunches, to seafood crumble, cod in beer batter and liver and bacon with mustard mash.
OPEN: 11-11 (Sun 12-10.30). **BAR MEALS:** L served all week. D served all week 12-3 6-9. Av main course £7.45.
RESTAURANT: L served all week. D served all week 12-3 6-9. Av 3 course à la carte £14.95. **BREWERY/COMPANY:** Free House.
PRINCIPAL BEERS: Harvey Best, Badger Tanglefoot.
FACILITIES: Garden: Patio, Outdoor eating.
NOTES: Parking 100. **ROOMS:** 4 bedrooms 2 en suite s£40 d£55

For pubs with AA rosette awards for food
see page 10

BERWICK
Map 05 TQ50

Pick of the Pubs

The Cricketers Arms ♀
BN26 6SP ☎ 01323 870469 ▤ 01323 871411
Dir: Off A27 between Polegate & Lewes (follow signs for Berwick Church)

Just off the A27 and a handy watering hole for walkers hiking the South Downs Way, the unspoilt, 500-year-old Cricketers Inn was originally a terrace of flint cottages before becoming an ale house some 200 years ago. Delightfully unpretentious inside, its three charming rooms sporting half-panelled walls, open fires, simple scrubbed tables, and a good chatty atmosphere. Excellent Harveys ales tapped straight from the cask and a short menu listing traditional home-made food, perhaps steaks, honeyed ham, egg and chips and a good selection of fresh local fish. Magnificent cottage garden for summer drinking.
OPEN: 11-3 6-11 (Sun 11-11, summer Sat 11-11). Closed 25 Dec. **BAR MEALS:** L served all week. D served all week 12-2.15 6.30-9. Av main course £6.
BREWERY/COMPANY: Harveys of Lewes.
PRINCIPAL BEERS: Harveys Best, PA & seasonal ales.
FACILITIES: Children welcome Garden: cottage style.
NOTES: Parking 25

BLACKBOYS
Map 05 TQ52

The Blackboys Inn ▤
Lewes Rd TN22 5LG ☎ 01825 890283
Dir: On B2192 between Halland (on A22) and Heathfield
Rambling, black-weatherboarded 14th-century inn set in large gardens overlooking an iris and lily-covered pond. It has a splendid beamed interior, complete with resident ghost. A wide range of fresh home-cooked dishes is served from the bar snack menu, restaurant carte and blackboard specials. Expect the likes of hot seafood platter (for two), Thai lamb salad, and fillet steak with mushroom, cream and brandy sauce.
OPEN: 11-3 6-11 (Sun 12-3, 7-10.30). Closed Jan 1. **BAR MEALS:** L served all week. D served all week 12-3 6.30-10.30. Av main course £6. **RESTAURANT:** L served all week. D served Mon-Sat 12-2.30 7-10. Av 3 course à la carte £20.
BREWERY/COMPANY: Harveys of Lewes.
PRINCIPAL BEERS: Harveys Best, Harveys Pale Bitter, Harveys Old. **FACILITIES:** Children welcome Garden: pond, trees, food served outside Dogs allowed in public bar, Water.
NOTES: Parking 40

BRIGHTON
Map 05 TQ30

The Greys 🍸
105 Southover St BN2 2UA ☎ 01273 680734
e-mail: mike@greyspub.com
A small Brighton bar boasting original live music. The interesting menu might feature roast duckling with myrtle berry and claret sauce, game pie, or grilled Dover sole, with desserts taking in French strawberry flan, chocolate terrine or bread and butter pudding with apricots.
OPEN: 11-3 5.30-11 (Sat-Sun 11-11). **BAR MEALS:** L served Tue-Sun. D served Tue-Thu & Sat 12-2 7-9.30. Av main course £6.95. **BREWERY/COMPANY:** Whitbread.
PRINCIPAL BEERS: Black Sheep. **FACILITIES:** Dogs allowed on leads. **NOTES:** Parking 16 No credit cards

CHIDDINGLY
Map 05 TQ51

The Six Bells ♈
BN8 6HE ☎ 01825 872227
Dir: E of A22 between Hailsham & Uckfield (turn opp Golden Cross PH)
Inglenook fireplaces and plenty of bric-a-brac are to be found at this large character free house which is where various veteran car and motorbike enthusiasts meet on club nights. The jury in the famous onion pie murder trial sat and deliberated in the bar before finding the defendant guilty. Exceptionally good value bar food includes such dishes as shepherds pie, steak and kidney pie, tuna pasta bake, buttered crab with salad and chicken curry with rice.
OPEN: 11-3 6-11. **BAR MEALS:** L served Sun-Sat. D served Sun-Sat 11-2.30 6-10.30. Av main course £4.
BREWERY/COMPANY: Free House.
PRINCIPAL BEERS: Courage Directors, John Smiths, Harveys Best. **FACILITIES:** Children welcome Garden Dogs allowed. **NOTES:** Parking 60

COWBEECH
Map 05 TQ61

Merrie Harriers
BN27 4JQ ☎ 01323 833108 📠 01323 833845
e-mail: merrie.harriers@talk21.com
Dir: Off A271, between Hailsham & Herstmonceux
17th-century clapboarded coaching inn within easy reach of atmospheric Pevensey Levels and the fascinating Herstmonceux Castle and Science Park, the setting for the famous observatory. Inside the pub are low-beamed ceilings, a traditional high-backed settle and open fires. Extensive lunch menu includes steak and ale pie, mixed grill, sausage and mash and rainbow trout, while in the evening expect fresh plaice and prawn Mornay, 8oz sirloin steak and hot chocolate fudge cake with ice cream.
OPEN: 11.30-2.30 6.15-11. **BAR MEALS:** L served all week. D served all week 12-2 6.30-9. Av main course £8.50.
RESTAURANT: L served all week. D served all week 12-2 6.30-9. Av 3 course à la carte £14. **BREWERY/COMPANY:** Free House.
PRINCIPAL BEERS: Harveys Best. **FACILITIES:** Garden: food served outside. **NOTES:** Parking 20

Room prices minimum single and minimum double rates are shown. FR indicates family room

---

DANEHILL
Map 05 TQ42

Pick of the Pubs

The Coach and Horses 🍸
RH17 7JF ☎ 01825 740369
Dir: From E Grinstead travel S through Forest Row on A22 to J with A275 Lewes Road turn R on A275 for 2 M untill Danehill turn L on school lane 1/2 M pub is on the L
19th-century cottagey pub built of local sandstone with former stables now forming part of the restaurant. Homely winter fires and neatly tended gardens add plenty of character and colour to the picturesque surroundings, and half-panelled walls, highly polished wooden floorboards and vaulted beamed ceilings give the place a charming, timeless feel. In an age when many country pubs are closing, the Coach & Horses proves that some classic hostelries can survive in any climate. Food plays a key role in the pub's success, with a selection of lunchtime snacks and a constantly-changing evening menu. Expect grilled skate wing with a lemon and caper butter, pan-fried calves' liver on polenta with roasted beetroot, or lamb meatballs with a tomato and basil sauce on tagliatelle. Leave room for a dessert, perhaps orange and Grand Marnier bread-and-butter-pudding or Salcombe Dairy ice cream.
OPEN: 11.30-3 6-11. **BAR MEALS:** L served all week. D served all week 12-2 7-9. Av main course £8.95.
RESTAURANT: L served all week. D served all week 12-2 7-9. Av 3 course à la carte £18.
BREWERY/COMPANY: Free House.
PRINCIPAL BEERS: Harveys Best, Harveys Old Ale, Hook Norton. **FACILITIES:** Garden: food served outside Dogs allowed Water. **NOTES:** Parking 30

DITCHLING
Map 05 TQ31

The Bull ♈
2 High St BN6 8TA ☎ 01273 843147 📠 01273 857787
Dir: A23 N from Brighton, then A27 E towards Lewes, after 1m turn L following signs to Ditchling
Dating from 1569, with its first known license being given in 1636, The Bull has a long history which includes a stint as a court house. Public areas are heavily beamed and furnished with antiques.

Harveys
The name of this well-established Sussex brewery has long been associated with the supply of beers, wines and spirits within the county. Records of 1794 indicate that deliveries of old red port, sherry and claret were made within a 20-mile radius of the old medieval town of Lewes, the company's home base. Changes and improvements have been made over the years, but Harveys still survives as an independent family brewery. Among its current cask conditioned beers are Sussex Best Bitter (4%), Armada Ale (4.5%) and XX Mild Ale (3%). The choicest Kent and Sussex hops and a yeast that has remained unchanged in the brewery for over three decades play a key role in the success of Harveys quality beers.

England

EAST CHILTINGTON — Map 05 TQ31

Pick of the Pubs

The Jolly Sportsman ♀
Chapel Ln BN7 3BA ☎ 01273 890400
🖩 01273 890400
e-mail: jollysportsman@mistral.co.uk
Dir: From Lewes take Offham/Chailey rd A275, L at Offham onto B2166 towards Plumpton, take Novington Ln, after approx 1m L into Chapel Ln
Sympathetically upgraded to a character Victorian-style dining inn by respected restaurateur Bruce Wass from Thackerays in Tunbridge Wells, this isolated pub enjoys a lovely garden setting on a quiet dead-end road looking out to the South Downs. The nearby Rectory Brewery (run by a vicar) supplies some of the beers drawn from the cask in the small atmospheric bar, with its stripped wooden floor and mix of comfortable furniture. Well sourced food shines on daily-changing menus, served throughout the bar and smart, yet informal restaurant, from a wide range of eclectic disciplines: haggis, neeps and tatties, ciabatta with pesto, tomato and goats' cheese, and a five-cheese ploughman's rub shoulders with poached organic salmon fillet with butter sauce and Cornish mussels, cockles, winkles and clams. Fennel and mustard soup, seared herbed and spiced tuna steak, corn-fed Goosnargh chicken with oyster mushrooms and venison with braised red cabbage develop the theme. Follow with exotic fruit-filled shortbread, hot rice pudding with prunes and port, or a plate of British farmhouse cheeses.
OPEN: 12-2.30 6-11 (Sun 12-4). Closed Sun eve, all Mon (ex BH) & 25/26 Dec. **BAR MEALS:** L served Tue-Sun. D served Tue-Sat 12.30-2.30 7-9. Av main course £9.75. **RESTAURANT:** L served Tue-Sun. D served Tue-Sat 12.30-2.30 7-9. Av 3 course à la carte £20. Av 2 course fixed price £10. **BREWERY/COMPANY:** Free House. **PRINCIPAL BEERS:** Harveys Best. **FACILITIES:** Children welcome Children's licence Garden: patio, outdoor eating Dogs allowed. **NOTES:** Parking 30

EAST DEAN — Map 05 TV59

Pick of the Pubs

The Tiger Inn ♀
BN20 0DA ☎ 01323 423209 🖩 01323 423209
Dir: Signed from A259 heading to the coast
Rose-covered flint-built pub on the village green, popular with walkers for its real ales and home-cooked food - from steak and ale pie to whole lobster. Candle-lit in the evenings, offering an intimate and cosy environment. Quality wines are offered from a blackboard, as many as ten by the glass. In summer you can choose from 20 different ploughmans', featuring 13 English cheeses. Bookings are not taken and it can get very busy.
OPEN: 11-3 6-11 (Sat 11-11, Sun 12-10.30). **BAR MEALS:** L served all week. D served all week 12-2 6.30-9. Av main course £6. **BREWERY/COMPANY:** Free House. **PRINCIPAL BEERS:** Harvey Best, Flowers Original, Timothy Taylor Landlord, Adnams Best. **FACILITIES:** Dogs allowed No credit cards

EWHURST GREEN — Map 05 TQ72

The White Dog Inn
Village St TN32 5TD ☎ 01580 830264
Dir: Between Staplecross & Bodiam off B2165 & B2244
A 16th-century country inn enjoying a quiet village location with splendid views across the Rother Valley to Bodiam Castle. Homely bar and restaurant with polished tiled floors and inglenook fireplace.

EXCEAT — Map 05 TV59

The Golden Galleon
Exceat Bridge BN25 4AB ☎ 01323 892247
Dir: On A259, 1.5m E of Seaford
Real ale on tap at this popular 18th-century inn comes from the pub's own micro-brewery - Cuckmere Haven Brewery. The inn is believed to have inspired Rudyard Kipling's Song of the Smugglers. Wide-ranging menu.

FIRLE — Map 05 TQ40

The Ram Inn ♀
BN8 6NS ☎ 01273 858222
e-mail: michaelwooller@themail.co.uk
Dir: R off A27 3m E of Lewes

Tucked away at the foot of the South Downs, this 17th century coaching inn offers a popular menu in rustic, unpretentious surroundings. Snuggle around the winter fires, and try hot and spicy chicken wings, Cumberland ring sausage and mash, or a traditional Sunday roast. In summer, relax in the large flint-walled garden with a substantial ploughman's, or cool off with locally-made Willett's Farm ice cream. Children's menu and popular afternoon cream teas.
OPEN: 11.30-11 (Sun 12-10.30). **BAR MEALS:** L served all week. D served all week 12-9. **BREWERY/COMPANY:** Free House. **PRINCIPAL BEERS:** Harveys Best. **FACILITIES:** Children welcome Children's licence Garden: beer garden, outdoor eating, Dogs allowed Water. **NOTES:** Parking 10
See Pub Walk on page 431

FLETCHING   Map 05 TQ42

Pick of the Pubs

The Griffin Inn 🐾 ⚐
TN22 3SS ☎ 01825 722890 ▤ 01825 722810
Dir: M23 J10 to East Grinstead then A22 then A275. Village
signed on L. 10m from M23
Close to the Ashdown Forest in an unspoilt country village,
the Griffin's two-acre, west-facing garden claims one of
Sussex's most beautiful views - especially at sunset.
Equally appealing is the sheltered rear terrace of this fine
16th-century building, which is transformed on warm
summer days into an extension of the restaurant - the
perfect setting for alfresco dining. Inside, old beams and
wainscot walls, open log fires and a motley collection of
old pews and wheelback chairs characterise the main bar.
Separate locals' bar and a pretty rear restaurant.
Imaginative menus that change almost with every session
take a modern approach in the use of freshest available
produce, especially local organic meats and vegetables.
Typical dishes range from ham and lentil soup, slow-
cooked lamb shanks with red wine on parsley mash,
bouillabaisse and game pie in the bar, to squid ink risotto
with scallops, roast duck confit with creamed pak choi and
egg noodles, and olive-crusted salmon with herb risotto
and saffron cream in the restaurant. Excellent Sunday
lunches, decent ales and fine wines. Comfortable
bedrooms with smart en suite bathrooms.
OPEN: 12-3 6-11. Closed 25 Dec. **BAR MEALS:** L served all
week. D served all week 12-2.30 7-9.30. Av main course £8.
RESTAURANT: L served all week. D served Mon-Sat
12.15-2.30 7.15-9.30. Av 3 course à la carte £23. Av 3 course
fixed price £18.50. **BREWERY/COMPANY:** Free House.
PRINCIPAL BEERS: Harvey Best, Badger Tanglefoot, Hardys
Country. **FACILITIES:** Children welcome Garden: patio,
BBQ, outdoor eating Dogs allowed overnight by
arrangement. **NOTES:** Parking 20. **ROOMS:** 8 bedrooms
8 en suite s£50 d£75 FR£85

GUN HILL   Map 05 TQ51

The Gun Inn 🐾
TN21 0JU ☎ 01825 872361 ▤ 01825873081
Dir: From A22 London-Eastbourne, Golden Cross (3m N of
Hailsham) L past Esso station, 1.5m down lane on L
Originally a 15th-century farmhouse situated in a tiny hamlet
amid rolling Sussex countryside. Resplendent in summer with
its pretty gardens and flower-adorned façade, it offers fresh
fish, crab in season, steak and kidney pie, Sussex smokie, or
smoked salmon and broccoli pasta, and there is an extensive
vegetarian menu.
OPEN: 11.30-3 6-11. Closed Dec 25-26. **BAR MEALS:** L served
all week. D served all week 12-2 6-9.30. Av main course £6.30.
BREWERY/COMPANY: Free House.
PRINCIPAL BEERS: Wadworth 6X, Adnams Best, Harvey Best.
FACILITIES: Children welcome Children's licence Garden:
outdoor eating Dogs allowed. **NOTES:** Parking 55

HARTFIELD   Map 05 TQ43

Anchor Inn
Church St TN7 4AG ☎ 01892 770424
Dir: On B2110
14th-century pub with stone floors and a large inglenook
fireplace, situated in the heart of Winnie the Pooh country, on
continued

the edge of Ashdown Forest. Bar food ranges from prawn and
crab curry, to fillet of plaice and chips, pork and bacon satay,
or chicken mangetout and mango kebab.
OPEN: 11-11 (Sun 12-10.30). **BAR MEALS:** L served all week.
D served all week 12-2 6-10. Av main course £5.75.
RESTAURANT: L served all week. D served Tue-Sat 12-2
7-9.30. Av 3 course à la carte £20. **BREWERY/COMPANY:** Free
House. **PRINCIPAL BEERS:** Fullers London Pride, Harveys Best,
Flowers IPA & Original, Bass. **FACILITIES:** Children welcome
Garden: Outdoor eating Dogs allowed. **NOTES:** Parking 30.
ROOMS: 2 bedrooms 2 en suite s£35 d£50

Pick of the Pubs

The Hatch Inn ⚐
Coleman's Hatch TN7 4ET ☎ 01342 822363
▤ 01342 822363
e-mail: Nilkad@bigfoot.com
Dir: A22 14 iles, L at Forest Row rdbt, follow for 3 miles until
Colemans Hatch and turn R
Classic 15th-century inn which was originally a row of
three cottages reputed to date back to 1430 and thought
to have been built to house workers at the local water-
driven hammer mill.
    Previously known as the Cock Inn, the Hatch takes its
name from the original coalman's gate leading onto
Ashdown Forest. Frequently seen on television in various
dramas and adverts and possibly a haunt of smugglers at
one time, the inn is only minutes away from the famous,
restored Pooh Bridge, immortalised in A.A. Milne's Winne
the Pooh stories.
    Good quality food includes fresh grilled Dover sole with
lemon and parsley butter, chargrilled ostrich steak with a
timbale of braised red cabbage and wild mushroom
sauce, and home-made steak and kidney pie with
shortcrust pastry.

OPEN: 11.30-3 5.30-11 (all day Sat May-Sept & Sun).
Closed Dec 25. **BAR MEALS:** L served all week. D served
Tue-Sat 12-2.30 7.30-9.15. Av main course £8.
RESTAURANT: L served all week. D served Tue-Sat 12-2.30
7.30-9.15. Av 3 course à la carte £25.
BREWERY/COMPANY: Free House.
PRINCIPAL BEERS: Harveys. **FACILITIES:** Garden: beer
garden, outdoor eating, Dogs allowed Water

HEATHFIELD

Three Cups Inn
Three Cups TN21 9LR ☎ 01435 830252
Unspoilt rural pub dating from 1700. Located on a ridge in the
High Weald, close to many good walks. Bar food.

England

Pick of the Pubs

The Queen's Head 🗺 ♀
Parsonage Ln TN36 4BL ☎ 01424 814552
📠 01424 814766
Dir: Between Hastings & Rye on A259
There's always a warm welcome beneath the high
beamed ceilings of this distinctive, tile-hung pub, which is
renowned for its hearty, home-cooked meals and a good
selection of well-kept real ales. The seventeenth-century
building has been licensed since 1831, and enjoys
spectacular views across the Brede Valley to the historic
town of Rye. Large inglenook fireplaces, church pews and
clutter of old farm implements all add to the relaxed
character of this bustling, independent free house, where
the full menu is served all day at weekends. Look out for
popular soups, and traditional pub favourites like
ploughman's lunches, steak in french bread, or ham, egg
and chips. Specials might include pork in cider, a choice of
fresh market fish, or chicken and Stilton bake, plus lentil
and courgette gratin or spinach, Brie and mushroom
lasagne for vegetarians. Leave room for Bakewell tart,
chocolate fudge cake or a fruit sorbet to finish.
OPEN: 11-11 (Sun 12-10.30). **BAR MEALS:** L served all
week. D served all week 12-2.45 6.15-9.45. Av main course
£6.50. **BREWERY/COMPANY:** Free House.
PRINCIPAL BEERS: Rother Valley Level Best, Greene King
Abbot Ale, Ringwood Old Thumper, Woodfordes Wherry.
FACILITIES: Children welcome Garden: Beer garden, BBQ,
outdoor eating Dogs allowed on a lead.
NOTES: Parking 50

The Juggs ♀
The Street BN7 3NT ☎ 01273 472523   📠 01273 483274
e-mail: admin@juggspub.co.uk
Dir: E of Brighton on A27

Named after the women who walked from Brighton with
baskets of fish for sale, this rambling, tile-hung 15th-century
cottage, tucked beneath the South Downs, offers an interesting
selection of freshly cooked food.
OPEN: 11-3 6-11 (11-11 Apr-Sep). Closed 25 Dec eve, 26 & 31
Dec, 1 Jan. **BAR MEALS:** L served all week. D served all week
12-2 6-9.30. Av main course £7. **RESTAURANT:** L served all
week. D served all week 12-2 6-9.30. Av 3 course à la carte £13.
BREWERY/COMPANY: Free House.
PRINCIPAL BEERS: Harveys, guest ales. **FACILITIES:** Children
welcome Garden: patio, food served outdoors. Dogs allowed, on
leads. **NOTES:** Parking 26.

The Snowdrop
South St BN7 2BU ☎ 01273 471018
Eccentric town centre pub full of bric-à-brac. Good selection of
changing real ales; lunchtime food; garden. Noted for
vegetarian food, live jazz and a friendly atmosphere.

Plough & Harrow 🗺
BN26 5RE ☎ 01323 870632   📠 01323 870632
Dir: S of A27 between Lewes & Polegate
Gloriously situated on the edge of the South Downs, this
Grade II listed thatched building lies in a small village on the
scenic Cuckmere Haven. Only minutes from historic Alfriston
and the Sussex coast. Good, wholesome pub fare includes
ploughmans, home-made pie, fresh cod, quiche, Litlington
beef, steak and swordfish.
OPEN: 11-3 6-11 (Sun 12-3, 7-10.30). **BAR MEALS:** L served all
week. D served all week 12-2.30 6.30-9.30. Av main course £8.95.
RESTAURANT: L served all week. D served all week 12-2.30
6.30-9.30. Av 3 course à la carte £18.
BREWERY/COMPANY: Free House.
PRINCIPAL BEERS: Harveys Best, Badger Best & Tanglefoot.
FACILITIES: Children welcome Garden: outdoor eating Dogs
allowed, not in restaurant. **NOTES:** Parking 50

The Middle House 🗺 ♀
High St TN20 6AB ☎ 01435 872146   📠 01435 873423
Dir: E of A267, S of Tunbridge Wells
Listed Grade I, the Middle House is a fine example of Elizabethan
architecture with a carved oak restaurant and a Grinling Gibbons
fireplace.
An inglenook in the bar provides a weekly spit roast, while
other options include the impressive fresh fish board with dishes
such as roasted sea bass or chargrilled marlin steak. A good
range of real ales is also offered.
OPEN: 11-11. **BAR MEALS:** L served all week. D served all week
12-2 7-9.30. Av main course £8.95. **RESTAURANT:** L served all
week. D served all week 12-2 7-9.30. Av 3 course à la carte £20. Av
3 course fixed price £17.95. **BREWERY/COMPANY:** Free House.
PRINCIPAL BEERS: Harvey Best, Greene King Abbot Ale, Black
Sheep,Theakstons. **FACILITIES:** Children welcome
Garden: food served outside. **NOTES:** Parking 25.
ROOMS: 6 bedrooms 6 en suite s£45 d£55

Rose & Crown Inn 🗺
Fletching St TN20 6TE ☎ 01435 872200   📠 01435 872200
Attractive 16th-century village inn with splendid front patio and
a rambling interior with low beams, open fires and an unspoilt
atmosphere.
Consult the blackboard for the day's selection of fresh fish
or home-made dishes such as fishcakes, shank of lamb or
Thai-style steak. For a lighter snack, try a Sussex Smokie, or an
Italian ciabatta sandwich.
OPEN: 11-3 6-11 (Sat 11-11, Sun 12-10.30). **BAR MEALS:** L
served all week 12-2. Av main course £6.25. **RESTAURANT:** L
served Tue-Sun. D served Tue-Sat 12-2 7-9. Av 3 course à la carte
£15. **BREWERY/COMPANY:** Enterprise Inns.
PRINCIPAL BEERS: Harveys Sussex Best, Greene King Abbot
Ale, Fullers London Pride. **FACILITIES:** Children welcome
Garden: Dogs allowed, not in restaurant. **NOTES:** Parking 15.
ROOMS: 4 bedrooms 4 en suite d£50

OFFHAM   Map 05 TQ14

The Blacksmith's Arms 🐾
London Rd BN7 3QD ☎ 01273 472971
A busy 200-year-old roadside pub with a reputation for good
local produce freshly cooked by its chefs. Country pâté with
Balsamic gooseberry jam; guinea fowl, apricot and plum pot
roast; Stilton, mushrooms and celery baked in filo pastry; wild
sea bass steak roasted with peppers, red onions and
coriander; and grilled lamb chump chops served on parsnip
purée demonstrate the versatility of the kitchen.
OPEN: 12-3 6.30-11. Closed Dec 25-26. **BAR MEALS:** L served
all week. D served Mon-Sat 12-2.30 7-9. Av main course £9.
RESTAURANT: L served all week. D served Mon-Sat 12-2 7-9. Av
3 course à la carte £17.50. **BREWERY/COMPANY:** Free House.
PRINCIPAL BEERS: Harveys Ales. **FACILITIES:** Garden:
patio/terrace, outdoor eating Dogs allowed. **NOTES:** Parking 22

OLD HEATHFIELD   Map 05 TQ52

Pick of the Pubs

Star Inn 🐾
Church St TN21 9AH ☎ 01435 863570
📠 01435 862020
e-mail: heathfieldsstar@c.s.com
Dir: M25-A21
Built as an inn for the stonemasons who constructed the
church in the 14th century, this creeper-clad, honey-stone
building has a wonderful, award-winning summer garden
that abounds with colourful flowers and unusual picnic
benches and affords impressive views across the High
Weald; a view once painted by Turner. Equally appealing is
the atmospheric, low-beamed main bar with its huge
inglenook fireplace and cosy dining ambience. Good bar
food focuses on fresh fish from Billingsgate or direct from
boats in Hastings. Specialities include cod and chips, red
mullet served with squid ink linguini, large cock crabs,
bouillabaisse and mussels in wine, garlic and cream. For
those favouring meat, you will find home-made steak and
kidney pie, marinated duck breast, Highland steaks and
local venison on menu. Generous ploughman's lunches
and excellent Harveys and Shepherd Neame brews on
handpump.
OPEN: 11.30-3 5.30-11. **BAR MEALS:** L served all week.
D served all week 12-2.15 7-9.30. Av main course £7.
RESTAURANT: L served all week. D served all week 12-2.15
7-9.30. Av 3 course à la carte £20.
BREWERY/COMPANY: Free House.
PRINCIPAL BEERS: Harvey Best, Shepherd Neame Master
Brew & Bishops Finger. **FACILITIES:** Garden: picnic
tables, food served outside Dogs allowed. **NOTES:** Parking 20

POYNINGS   Map 05 TQ21

Royal Oak Inn 🍷
The Street BN45 7AQ ☎ 01273 857389 📠 01273 857787
Dir: N on the A23 just outside Brighton, take the A281 (signed for
Henfield & Poynings), then follow signs into Poynings village
Nestling at the foot of the South Downs, close to the famous
Devil's Dyke, this white-painted village pub is popular on
summer weekends for its excellent barbecue facilities. Also
very popular with walkers, it offers good ales and a varied
menu, including the Poynings (pronounced Punnings locally)
continued

grill, bangers and mash, poached fillet of salmon Hollandaise,
chicken, leek and mushroom pie, and a variety of sandwiches,
baked potatoes and ploughmans'.
OPEN: 11-11 (Sun 12-10.30). **BAR MEALS:** L served all week.
D served all week 12-2.30 6-9.30. Av main course £7.50.
BREWERY/COMPANY: Free House.
PRINCIPAL BEERS: Harveys Sussex, Courage Directors, Greene
King Old Speckled Hen. **FACILITIES:** Children welcome Garden:
beer garden , outdoor eating, patio, Dogs allowed.
NOTES: Parking 35

RINGMER   Map 05 TQ41

The Cock 🐾 🍷
Uckfield Rd BN8 5RX ☎ 01273 812040 📠 01273 812040
Dir: On A26 approx 2m N of Lewes (not in Ringmer village)

Local legend has it that Cromwell mustered his troops here
before the siege of Arundel. The 16th-century coaching inn has
original oak beams and an inglenook fireplace. The same
menu is offered throughout, with traditional dishes such as
lamb chops, steak and ale pie, or ham, egg and chips, as well
as trout with sherry and almonds, swordfish provençale, and
smoked haddock.
OPEN: 11-3 6-11. Closed Dec 25. **BAR MEALS:** L served all
week. D served all week 12-2 6.30-9.30. Av main course £7.50.
RESTAURANT: L served all week. D served all week 12-2
6.30-9.30. Av 3 course à la carte £15.
BREWERY/COMPANY: Free House.
PRINCIPAL BEERS: Harveys Best, Ruddles County, Fullers
London Pride, Rother Valley. **FACILITIES:** Children welcome
Garden: Outdoor eating Dogs allowed Dog chews.
NOTES: Parking 20

RUSHLAKE GREEN   Map 05 TQ61

Horse & Groom 🐾 🍷
TN21 9QE ☎ 01435 830320 📠 01435 830320
e-mail: chappellhatpeg@aol.com
Grade II listed building on the village green with pleasant
views from the well cultivated gardens. Dishes are offered
from blackboard menus in the cosy bars. Steak, kidney and
Guinness pudding and smoked salmon with home-made
tagliatelle are favourites, along with the excellent fresh fish
choice - perhaps monkfish in filo with vanilla and ginger or
fresh loin of tuna on Bombay potatoes with lime and
coriander dressing.
OPEN: 11.30-3 5.30-11. **BAR MEALS:** L served all week.
D served all week 12-2.30 7-9.30. Av main course £12.
RESTAURANT: L served all week. D served all week 12-2.30
7-9.30. Av 3 course à la carte £12. **BREWERY/COMPANY:** Free
House. **PRINCIPAL BEERS:** Harveys, Shepherd Neame Spitfire
& Master Brew. **FACILITIES:** Children welcome Garden: Food
served outside Dogs allowed. **NOTES:** Parking 20

England

England

Mermaid Inn ◉ ★ ★ ★ ♀
Mermaid St TN31 7EY ☎ 01797 223065 🖹 01797 225069
e-mail: mermaidinnrye@btclick.com
Destroyed by the French in 1377 and rebuilt in 1420, this
famous smugglers' inn is steeped in history and is now a
beautifully presented hotel. Ancient beams and attractive
stonework abound in the civilised interior, including the cosy
lounge and the well appointed restaurant. Classic old bar to
the rear of the main hotel, complete with vast inglenook and
traditional bar food. Rosetted restaurant carte and antique
furnished bedrooms.
OPEN: 11-11 (Sun 12-11). **BAR MEALS:** L served Mon-Fri.
D served Mon-Fri. Av main course £7.50. **RESTAURANT:** L
served all week. D served all week. Av 3 course à la carte £16.
BREWERY/COMPANY: Free House.
PRINCIPAL BEERS: Greene King Old Speckled Hen, Marstons
Pedigree. **FACILITIES:** Children welcome Garden: patio/terrace,
outdoor eating, fountain Dogs allowed in garden only, water.
NOTES: Parking 26. **ROOMS:** 31 bedrooms 31 en suite
s£70 d£140

Pick of the Pubs

The Ypres Castle Inn ♀
Gun Garden TN31 7HH ☎ 01797 223248
Tucked away near the Ypres Tower, this 18th-century
weatherboarded inn is named after Sir John Ypres, and
was once something of a smuggling centre. New owners
have recently taken over and early indications of the
menu are promising. Expect blackboard menus and dishes
like scallops with sage and lemon, moules marinière, local
pork and sage sausages with mustard mash and onion
gravy, pan-fried sea bass with fresh herbs, and rack of
saltmarsh lamb with redcurrant. Worth seeking out after a
stroll around this famous Cinque Port, especially for a
drink on the lawn or terrace with river, coast and
countryside views. Reports please.
OPEN: 12-11 (Jan-Mar Mon-Fri 12-3, 6-11, Sat 12-4 6-11 Sun
12-4 7-10.30). **BAR MEALS:** L served all week. D served all
week 12-2.30 7-10.30. Av main course £8. **RESTAURANT:** L
served all week. D served all week 12-2.30 7-10.30. Av 3
course à la carte £18. **BREWERY/COMPANY:** Free House.
PRINCIPAL BEERS: Harveys Best, Youngs, Adnams
Broadside, Bass. **FACILITIES:** Children welcome Garden:
food served outside Dogs allowed Water

The Bull
Dunster Mill Ln TN5 7HH ☎ 01580 200586
🖹 01580 201289
*Dir: From M5 exit at Sevenoaks toward Hastings, R at x-rds onto
B2087, R onto B2099 through Ticehurst, R for Three Legged Cross*

In a peaceful hamlet setting, the Bull is a real country pub,
with oak beams and large open fires, based around a Wealden
hall house built around 1385. Food choice ranges from
Shrewsbury lamb and Javanese beef, to venison in red wine,
poached salmon, and harvest vegetable and leek crumble.
OPEN: 11-11. Closed Dec 25 & 26 eve. **BAR MEALS:** L served
all week. D served all week 11-2.30 6.30-9.30. Av main course
£6.51. **RESTAURANT:** L served all week. D served all week
11-2.30 6.30-9.30. Av 3 course à la carte £18.
BREWERY/COMPANY: Free House.
PRINCIPAL BEERS: Harvey's, Bass. **FACILITIES:** Children
welcome Garden: outdoor eating Dogs allowed.
NOTES: Parking 80. **ROOMS:** 3 bedrooms 3 en suite s£30 d£50

The Plough
Coldharbour Rd BN27 3QJ ☎ 01323 844859
Dir: Off A22, W of Hailsham
A 17th-century former farmhouse, which has been a pub since
the late 18th century. The building contains two bars and two
restaurants, and is popular with walkers. There is also a large
beer garden with a play area for children.

The Wealdway

Exploring some of England's prettiest pastoral and downland landscapes, the 82-mile Wealdway
begins at Gravesend on the Thames Estuary and then cuts through Kent's 'Garden of England' to reach the
glorious sandy heathland of the 6000-acre Ashdown Forest -Winnie the Pooh country. AA Milne, the character's
creator, lived nearby. The 14th-century Anchor at Hartfield, on the edge of the forest and only a stone's throw from
the route, will be too tempting to avoid after an arduous trek across country on a hot summer's day. You'll probably
want to pause and lick your wounds when you reach Blackboys too, and the cosy bar of the charming Blackboys Inn
is the perfect setting for rest and relaxation. Further south you can stop off at the Six Bells at Chiddingly and enjoy a
pint at the Old Oak Inn at Arlington, situated close to a popular reservoir and wildlife haunt. Alternatively, make
a worthwhile detour through the lovely Cuckmere Valley to the George Inn at Alfriston or the delightfully
unspoilt Cricketers Arms at neighbouring Berwick. The trail finishes at blustery Beachy Head, one of
Britain's most famous and dramatic coastal landmarks.

PICK OF THE PUBS

OPEN: 11.30-3 5.30-11
(Sun 12-3 7-10.30
BAR MEALS: L served all week.
D served all week 12-2 7.30-9.30.
Av main course £6.50
RESTAURANT: L served all week.
D served all week 12-2 7.30-9.
Av 3 course a la carte £16.50.
BREWERY/COMPANY:
Harveys of Lewes.
PRINCIPAL BEERS: Harveys Best
Bitter, Pale Ale & seasonal beers.
FACILITIES: Garden: patio, tables
on the green, outdoor eating.
NOTES: Parking 20.

The Dorset Arms

TN7 4BD
☎ 01892 770278 🖹 01892 770195
e-mail: jep@dorsetarms.co.uk
Dir: on B2110 between Hartfield and
Groombridge, 4m W of Tunbridge Wells

On the borders of Kent and Sussex close to Ashdown Forest and Royal Tunbridge Wells, this historic, white weatherboarded 15th-century inn takes its name from the arms of the Sackville family, once Earls of Dorset, whose seat at the splendid Buckhurst Park is close by.

Imagine an open-halled farmhouse with soot-covered rafters and an earthen floor, converted in the 18th century into an inn retaining many Tudor features such as the dining-room's massive wall and ceiling beams, the Sussex oak floor and the magnificent log fire in the bar, and an ice-cave built into the hillside behind what is now part of the pub kitchen.

As a family-run concern, attention to detail embraces provision of locally brewed real ales of quality from Harveys Brewery in Lewes and attention to obtaining the best available fresh food from local sources. Served throughout, menus supplemented by exhaustive daily blackboard specials offer great value for money. Hot lunches and light suppers could be baked trout with sauté potatoes, home-roasted ham with eggs and chips or spinach and feta cheese goujons - all suitably garnished. For a treat, though, scour the specials board for rich steak and ale or creamy chicken and mushroom pies with fresh vegetables, griddled fresh Torbay sole with parsley butter, monkfish and prawns in a rich tomato, herb and white wine sauce, and crispy roast duck breast with stuffing and plum sauce. From a lengthy fixed-price menu, choices might include home-made chicken liver pâté, pheasant breasts in whisky and cream sauce and dark chocolate truffle torte.

There remain simple ploughman's lunches and toasted sandwiches at lunchtime and a spacious garden in which to enjoy them with all the family on fine summer days.

England

WARBLETON
Map 05 TQ61

The War bill in Tun Inn
Church Hill TN21 9BD ☎ 01435 830636 🗎 01435 830636
e-mail: warbillintun@ic24.net
An attractive and peacefully situated 15th-century village inn
about which many stories are told: tales of contreband, priest
holes and ghosts. Modernised interior with red plush
furnishings and inglenook fireplace. An ideal stopping place
for walkers and cyclists. The extensive menu runs from
sandwiches, seafood salads and cold meat platters, to fried
fillet of plaice, king prawns in the shell, Cyprus chicken with
grapes and mushrooms, and poached wild salmon steak in a
seafood sauce.
OPEN: 12-3 7-11. **BAR MEALS:** L served all week. D served all
week 12-1.45 7-9.30. Av main course £4.95. **RESTAURANT:** L
served all week. D served all week 12-1.45 7-9.30. Av 3 course à la
carte £12. **BREWERY/COMPANY:** Free House.
PRINCIPAL BEERS: Harveys Best, Crown Inn Ironmaster,
Warbleton Winter Ale. **FACILITIES:** Children welcome Garden:
beer garden Dogs allowed Water. **NOTES:** Parking 20

WINCHELSEA

The New Inn
German St TN36 4EN
Rambling 18th-century inn of some character enjoying a
delightful village setting close to Rye and the Sussex coast.
Georgian decor; fine views; bedrooms.

WITHYHAM
Map 05 TQ43

Pick of the Pubs

The Dorset Arms 🍺
TN7 4BD ☎ 01892 770278 🗎 01892 770195
e-mail: jep@dorset-arms.co.uk
See Pick of the Pubs on page 439

SUSSEX, WEST

AMBERLEY
Map 04 TQ01

Black Horse
High St, Amberley BN18 9NL ☎ 01798 831552
Lively local in charming, historic village in the Arun Valley at
the base of the South Downs - excellent local walks. Good real
ales and traditional pub food.

The Bridge Inn
Houghton Bridge BN18 9LR ☎ 01798 831619
Dir: *5m N of Arundel on B2139*
The original structure of the inn dates from 1420, and the
building has a Grade II listing. Special features are the open
fires and display of original oil and watercolour paintings. The
menu offers a comprehensive fish choice plus dishes such as
roast duck or shoulder of lamb.
OPEN: 11-11 (Sun 12-10.30). **BAR MEALS:** L served all week. D
served all week 12-2.30 7-9.30. Av main course £8.
RESTAURANT: L served all week. D served all week 12-2.30
7-9.30. Av 3 course à la carte £15. Av 3 course fixed price £15.
BREWERY/COMPANY: Free House.
PRINCIPAL BEERS: Flowers Original, Harveys Sussex, Fullers
London Pride, Tanglefoot. **FACILITIES:** Children welcome
Garden: Dogs allowed. **NOTES:** Parking 20

ARDINGLY
Map 07 TQ32

The Gardeners Arms 🍺 🍴
Selsfield Rd RH17 6TJ ☎ 01444 892328 🗎 01444 892331
Dir: *On B2028 between Haywards Heath and Turners Hill, follow
signs to Wakehurst Place*

Believed to date back over 400 years, this character pub was,
reputedly, the home of a magistrate who may have conducted
hangings on the front lawn. Nothing as grisly greets the eye
today, and the interior conveys a relaxed, inviting atmosphere,
with open fires, oak beams and panelling, combined with
antique furniture, fresh flowers and charming nooks and
crannies. Ashdown Forest walks lie right on the doorstep, and
nearby are Wakehurst Place and the famous Bluebell Railway.
Popular choice of straightforward bar meals and blackboard
specials, including Cajun spiced tuna, pasta bolognaise, Torbay
sole and duck with plum and ginger sauce.
OPEN: 11.30-3 6-11. **BAR MEALS:** L served all week. D served
all week 12-2 6.30-9.30. Av main course £8.95. **RESTAURANT:** L
served all week. D served all week 12-2 6.30-9.30. Av 3 course à la
carte £18.50. **BREWERY/COMPANY:** Woodhouse Inns.
PRINCIPAL BEERS: Badger: Best/Tanglefoot/Golden Champion.
FACILITIES: Garden: patio, outdoor eating Dogs allowed
Water. **NOTES:** Parking 60

ASHURST
Map 04 TQ11

The Fountain Inn
BN44 3AP ☎ 01403 710219 🗎 01403 711071
Dir: *On B2135 N of Steyning*
A 16th-century free house located in a peaceful village. Local
resident Laurence Olivier frequented the pub and Paul
McCartney made the video for 'White Christmas' in the bar.
The Fountain has its own 16th-century cider press used for
apple pressing and scrumpy-making. Sample sea bass with dill
and lemon butter, steak, mushroom and ale pie or roasted
vegetables and goats' cheese in filo pastry from the
imaginative menu.
OPEN: 11.30-2.30 6-11 (Sun 12-3, 7-10.30). **BAR MEALS:** L
served all week. D served Tue-Sat 11.30-2 6-9.30. Av main course
£8.95. **BREWERY/COMPANY:** Free House.
PRINCIPAL BEERS: Harveys Sussex, Shepherd Neame Master
Brew, Fullers London Pride Adnams Best. **FACILITIES:** Garden:
patio, Outdoor eating Dogs allowed Water. **NOTES:** Parking 50
No credit cards

Room prices minimum single and minimum double
rates are shown. FR indicates family room

OLD HOUSE AT HOME, SOUTHBOURNE
Cot Lane, Chidham.
Tel: 01243 572477
Directions: turn R (Cot Lane) off A259 at Nutbourne between Emsworth & Bosham
Attractive, 300-year-old brick pub situated in a peaceful village on a low lying peninsula jutting out into Chichester Harbour. Comfortable interior and good range of real ales and home-cooked food. Excellent walking and wildlife.
Open: 11.30-2.30 6-11 (Sun 12-3 7-10.30). Bar Meals 12-2 6-9.30. Children and dogs welcome. Garden. Parking.
(see page 448 for full entry)

*Pub*WALK

Old House at Home, Southbourne

A bracing, mostly flat ramble following a peaceful shoreline path around Cobnor Point with views across Chichester Harbour, an important haven for birdlife.

Turn right out of the inn and follow the lane through the village. Just before the church, bear off right and follow the waymarked path around the left-hand edge of a large field, passing Chidmere Pond on your left to reach a lane. Turn left, pass Elizabethan Chidmere House, then take the narrow path right, between high hedges to another lane.

Turn left and walk to a development called Harbour Way, opposite a large pond. Keep to the footpath which runs down to the foreshore (left of the private road), then turn right along the coastal path. Follow it through the Youth Activity Centre (as signposted) and down past the Cobnor dinghy park. Soon re-join the coast path and proceed round

Cobnor Point, with good views across the harbour and west to the Isle of Wight.

Shortly, descend some timber steps to the beach and head west along the foreshore (access may be difficult during exceptional high tides). The path eventually joins the raised bank above the shore. At a waymarker, turn left inland between poplars and a ditch to reach Cot Lane. Turn right and walk back to the pub.

Distance: 5 miles (8km)
Map: OS Landranger 197
Terrain: farmland, coast, country lanes
Paths: field and shoreline paths, metalled lanes
Gradient: level

Walk submitted by:
Paul Latham

Chichester Harbour at Bosham

BILLINGSHURST
Map 04 TQ02

The Blue Ship
The Haven RH14 9BS ☎ 01403 822709
Victorian brick and tile-hung rural cottage, with 15th-century interior, hidden down a country lane off the A29. King and Barnes ales; delightful cottage garden.

Cricketers Arms ♀
Loxwood Rd, Wisborough Green RH14 0DG
☎ 01403 700369
Traditional village pub dating from the 16th century with oak beams, wooden floors and open fires. It is idyllically located overlooking the village green with views of cricket matches and hot air balloon rides.
    A full bar menu is served, ranging from snacks to three course meals and Sunday roasts. Typical dishes include steak and Guinness pie, steamed mussels, lamb kleftico and Cricketers chicken.
OPEN: 11.30-2.30 5.30-11. **BAR MEALS:** L served all week.
D served all week 12-2 6.30-9. Av main course £6.
RESTAURANT: L served all week. D served all week 12-2 6.30-9.
Av 3 course à la carte £15. **BREWERY/COMPANY:** Whitbread.
PRINCIPAL BEERS: Fullers London Pride, Wadworth 6X, Flowers Original,. **FACILITIES:** Children welcome Garden: food served outside Dogs allowed Water

Ye Olde Six Bells
76 High St RH14 9QS ☎ 01403 782124
Dir: *On the A29 between London & Bognor, 17m from Bognor*

Attractive timbered town pub dating back to 1436 and featuring flagstone floors and an inglenook fireplace. Noted for the legend of a cursed tunnel leading to the nearby church. Good King and Barnes ales, a pretty roadside garden, and traditional pub food including brunch, steak and kidney pudding, gammon steak and home-made cauliflower cheese.
OPEN: 11-2.30 5.30-11 (Sun 12-3, 7-10.30). **BAR MEALS:** L served all week. D served Mon-Sat 12-2 7-9. Av main course £4.50. **BREWERY/COMPANY:** Hall & Woodhouse.
PRINCIPAL BEERS: Badger Tanglefoot & Best, King & Barnes Sussex Ale. **FACILITIES:** Children welcome Garden: play area, patio, outdoor eating, BBQ Dogs allowed on a lead.
NOTES: Parking 15

Pubs offering a good choice of seafood on the menu.

Ballard's Brewery
Ballard's Brewery produced its first pint in 1980, but didn't gain its name until it moved to the Ballard's Pub at Elsted Marsh. Since then the operation has grown within modest limits, and now produces some 1500 gallons of beer a week. The barley is milled on site, and no sugars, colourings or additives (except isinglass) are used. Ballard's beers include Nyewood Gold (5.0%), Midhurst Mild (3.5%), Trotton Bitter (3.6%) and Wassail (6.0%). Brewery tours are available, and a beer walk is held on the first Sunday of each December to celebrate the new 'beer of the year'.

BURPHAM
Map 04 TQ00

Pick of the Pubs

George & Dragon ⊛ ⊙
BN18 9RR ☎ 01903 883131
Dir: *Off A27 1m E of Arundel, signed Burpham, 2.5m pub on L*
An old smuggling inn with a dining emphasis located in a peaceful village at the foot of the South Downs, where there are lovely walks alongside the nearby River Arun. In a setting of beamed ceilings and yellow painted walls hung with a variety of modern prints, informally dressed staff provide casual yet attentive service to a sociable local clientele attracted by menus that evolve with the seasons. Bar lunch and supper menus feature starter-size portions of smoked duck salad, smoked salmon and prawns with lemon and chive mayonnaise and Parma ham with mozzarella and mixed leaves, with blackboard specials adding perhaps steak and Stilton puff pastry pie and pheasant in juniper sauce. More serious dining tempts with starters of langoustine and scallop tortellini and quail and spinach pithivier with white truffle oil, followed by cannon of monkfish with crab and saffron mousse and venison medallions with a bitter chocolate and redcurrant reduction. Time is taken in producing hot mango pastry with coconut ice cream and a grand Marnier and orange soufflé with chocolate sorbet that prove well worth the wait.
OPEN: 11-2.30 6-11 (Sun 12-3, 7-10.30). Closed Sun Eve Oct-Etr, 25 Dec. **BAR MEALS:** L served all week.
D served Mon-Sat 12-2 7-9.30. Av main course £6.20.
RESTAURANT: L served Sun. D served Mon-Sat 12.15-2 7-9.30. Av 3 course à la carte £23.50.
BREWERY/COMPANY: Free House.
PRINCIPAL BEERS: Harvey Best, Brewery-on-Sea Spinnaker Bitter, Fullers London Pride. **FACILITIES:** patio, outdoor eating. **NOTES:** Parking 40

CHILGROVE — Map 04 SU81

Pick of the Pubs

The White Horse at Chilgrove 🐾 ♀
High St PO18 9HX ☎ 01243 535219 📠 01243 535301
Dir: On B2141 between Chichester & Petersfield

Picture if you will a picturesque South Downs hostelry, dating from 1756, with a team of French chefs and a celebrated yet user-friendly wine list in a very British setting conducive to the enjoyment of its understated charm. In essence a gastronomic inn, The White Horse pre-dates a myriad of trendy imitators with style and confidence, many of its long-serving staff greeting the host of regular diners as members of the family.

Today's food styles may have changed, yet in this case the fusion of French cuisine and English hospitality has remained unchanged. Bar lunches do give way to the restaurant's greater clout, yet the selection will still impress; chicken, avocado and bacon salad, Selsey crab and fresh rock oysters, roast young grouse or partridge and braised local hare staying true to the inn's former roots.

Italian-style open sandwiches and a glass of real ale are equally worth the detour for those not wishing to go the whole hog. Chicken liver parfait with apple chutney, confit duck on raspberry jus and strawberry brûlée with tuille biscuit in the restaurant well live up to expectations.

OPEN: 11-3 6-11 (closed Mon). **BAR MEALS:** L served Tue-Sun. D served Tue-Sat 12-2 6-9. **RESTAURANT:** L served Tue-Sun. D served Tue-Sat 12-2 6-9. Av 3 course à la carte £25. **BREWERY/COMPANY:** Free House **FACILITIES:** Children welcome Garden: outdoor eating Dogs allowed. **NOTES:** Parking 100. **ROOMS:** 8 bedrooms 8 en suite

COMPTON — Map 04 SU71

Coach & Horses 🐾
The Square PO18 9HA ☎ 023 92631228
Dir: On B2146 S of Petersfield

Located in the village square beside the B2146, this early 17th-century coaching inn has a lively locals' bar in a Victorian extension and a character lounge-cum-dining-room in the original timber-framed part. Hearty snacks are served in the bar, while in the convivial surroundings of the lounge bar you can order ribeye steak, calves' liver and bacon, local game and fresh fish dishes. Skittle alley and sheltered rear garden.

continued

OPEN: 12-3 6-11. **BAR MEALS:** L served all week. D served all week 12-2 6-9. Av main course £5.60. **RESTAURANT:** L served Sun, Tue-Sat. D served Tue-Sat 12-2 6-9. Av 3 course à la carte £15. **BREWERY/COMPANY:** Free House.
PRINCIPAL BEERS: Fullers ESB, Ballard's Best, Cheriton Diggers Gold. **FACILITIES:** Children welcome Garden: patio, BBQ, outdoor eating Dogs allowed.

COPTHORNE — Map 05 TQ33

Hunters Moon Inn 🐾
Copthorne Bank RH10 3JF ☎ 01342 713309
📠 01342 714399
e-mail: enquiries@huntersmooninn.co.uk
Dir: M23, J10 Copthorne Way to roundabout, 1st L, then R into Copthorne Bank

Once associated with poachers and smugglers, this village pub has comfortable lounges, open log fireplace and a walled patio garden. A varied menu offers grilled smoked haddock on sagaloo with mango coulis, roast lamb rack with couscous, ostrich with port wine sauce, and ragout of wild mushrooms in puff pastry. Good wine list.
OPEN: 11-3 5.30-11 (Sun 12-3, 7-10.30). Closed Dec 26. **RESTAURANT:** L served all week. D served all week 12-2 7-9. **BREWERY/COMPANY:** Free House.
PRINCIPAL BEERS: Badger Best, Fullers London Pride.
FACILITIES: Garden Dogs allowed. **NOTES:** Parking 100. **ROOMS:** 10 bedrooms 10 en suite s£65 d£65 FR£75-£85

DUNCTON — Map 05 SU91

The Cricketers
GU28 0LB ☎ 01798 342473 📠 01799 342473
Attractive white-painted pub situated in spectacular walking country at the western end of the South Downs. Delightful and very popular garden with extensive deck seating and weekend barbecues. Rumoured to be haunted, the inn has changed little over the years. Full range of meat, fish and salad dishes, with main courses including belly of pork, pan-fried salmon, shoulder of lamb, cod and chips and steak and ale pie.
OPEN: 11-3 6-11. **BAR MEALS:** L served all week. D served all week 12-2.30 7-9.30. Av main course £8.50. **RESTAURANT:** L served all week. D served all week 12-3 7-9.30. Av 3 course à la carte £16. **PRINCIPAL BEERS:** Youngs Bitter, Archers Golden,. **FACILITIES:** Garden: food served outside. **NOTES:** Parking 30

EARTHAM — Map 04 SU90

The George Inn
PO18 0LT ☎ 01243 814340 📠 01243 814340
Dir: From A27 at Tangmere r'about follow signs for Crockerhill/Eartham

Built in the 18th century as an ale house for local estate workers, the pub has a candlelit restaurant with an open fire, exposed ships' beams and patio doors leading to a delightful garden.

EAST DEAN — Map 05 TV59

The Hurdlemakers
Main Rd PO18 0JG ☎ 01243 811318 📠 01243 821294
The name of this old village pub, built of traditional Sussex flint, recalls a once-thriving rural craft which employed several men from East Dean. Handy for nearby Goodwood races and the South Downs Way.

ELSTED   Map 04 SU81

Pick of the Pubs

The Elsted Inn 🐑 ♀
Elsted Marsh GU29 0JT ☎ 01730 813662
*Dir: From Midhurst take A272 W. After 4m L signed 'Elsted &
Harting'(NB Elsted Marsh also known as Lower Elsted)*
New owners at this unpretentious Victorian roadside pub
are maintaining the style of cooking that made this rural
retreat so popular. So expect hearty country cooking
based on quality local produce, notably venison, free-
range eggs, hand-made bread and sausages, and locally
grown vegetables. Also expect local Ballard's Best to wash
down Sussex bacon pudding, venison casserole, pork in
cider, whole grilled plaice, delicious home-made soups,
hand-cut sandwiches and ploughman's lunches. For the
sweet-toothed there is bread-and-butter pudding and
home-made ice creams. Homely, wooden-floored bars
with log fires and a pine-furnished rear dining area.
Changing blackboard menus; summer barbeques;
comfortable bedrooms in rear converted coach house.
OPEN: 11.30-3 5.30-11 (Sun 12-3 6-11). **BAR MEALS:** L
served all week. D served all week 12-2 7-9.30. Av main
course £4.95. **RESTAURANT:** L served all week. D served all
week 12-2 7-9.30. Av 3 course à la carte £15.50.
BREWERY/COMPANY: Free House.
PRINCIPAL BEERS: Ballards Trotton, Best & Wassail, Fullers
London Pride, Hopback Summer Lightning.
FACILITIES: Children welcome Garden: patio, BBQ,
outdoor eating Dogs allowed, food and water bowls.
NOTES: Parking 8. **ROOMS:** 4 bedrooms 4 en suite s£35
d£55

Pick of the Pubs

The Three Horseshoes
GU29 0JY ☎ 01730 825746
*Dir: A272 from Midhurst to Petersfield, after 2m L to Harting &
Elsted, after 3m pub on L*
Nestling below the South Downs in a peaceful, out-of-the-
way village, the Three Horseshoes, a 16th-century former
drovers' ale house, is, in many ways, the quintessential
English country pub. Full of rustic rural charm, the unspoilt
cottagey bars feature worn tiled floors, low-beamed
ceilings, latch doors, a vast inglenook with winter log fire,
and a motley mix of wooden furniture. On fine days the
extensive rear garden, complete with roaming chickens
and stunning South Downs views, is a popular attraction.
In addition, tip-top real ales are drawn from the cask and
a daily-changing blackboard menu offers some robust
country cooking. Good hearty dishes may include roasted
red pepper with garlic, basil and anchovies, baked Brie
with cranberry sauce, steak, kidney and Murphy's pie,
braised lamb with apples and apricots, calves' liver and
bacon, crab and lobster in summer, and excellent
ploughman's lunches with unusual cheeses, including the
local Gospel Green cheddar. Equally substantial puddings
such as lemon meringue roulade and bread-and-butter
pudding.
OPEN: 11-2.30 6-11 (Sun 12-3, 7-10.30). **BAR MEALS:** L
served all week. D served all week 12-2 7-9.30. Av main
course £8.95. **BREWERY/COMPANY:** Free House.
PRINCIPAL BEERS: Cheriton Pots Ale, Ballards Best, Fullers
London Pride, Ringwood Fortyniner. **FACILITIES:** Garden:
Outside eating Dogs allowed on leads. **NOTES:** Parking 30

FERNHURST   Map 04 SU82

Pick of the Pubs

The King's Arms 🐑 ♀
Midhurst Rd GU27 3HA ☎ 01428 652005
▤ 01428 658970
*Dir: On A286 between Haslemere and Midhurst, in S of
Fernhurst*
An original 17th-century barn conversion amidst rolling
farmland set in 22 acres of orchard and gardens. The
Sussex stone pub and outbuildings, flower-decked in
summer, comprise a cosy, beamed bar with inglenook to
one side and to the other an informal dining area
decorated with wine memorabilia, leading to a patio
whose pergola supports living vines and ivy. Combining
the best of traditional and modern cooking Michael Hirst
reflects current trends, collecting his own fresh produce
regularly from the markets and taking into account
seasonal changes in ingredients and prices. From there
everything is home made, from pasta and salad dressings
to ice cream and sorbets. Classic pub favourites from local
butchers' sausages and mash and cod in beer batter to
ambitious sea bass fillets with lobster ravioli and tomato
beurre blanc or carpaccio of peppered beef fillet with
Parmesan and truffle oil dressing produce impressive
results. Blackboard additions on any one day might
include Caesar salad with grilled chicken, roast monkfish
with mildly curried aubergine and cinnamon bavarois with
poached pears. Classic real ales and wines by the glass
measure up to a similar standard.

OPEN: 11.30-3 5.30-11 (closed Sunday evenings). Closed 25
Dec, 1st 2 wks in Jan. **BAR MEALS:** L served all week. D
served Mon-Sat 12-2.30 7-9.30. Av main course £22.
RESTAURANT: L served all week. D served Mon-Sat 12-2.30
7-9.30. Av 3 course à la carte £20.
BREWERY/COMPANY: Free House.
PRINCIPAL BEERS: Timothy Taylor Landlord, Otter Bright,
Fullers London Pride, Gales HSB. **FACILITIES:** Children
welcome Garden: patio, outdoor eating Dogs allowed
Water. **NOTES:** Parking 45

The Red Lion 🐑 ♀
The Green GU27 3HY ☎ 01428 653304 ▤ 01428 661120
e-mail: redlionzzz@aol.com
*Dir: From A3 at Hindhead take A287 to Haslemere, then A286 to
Fernhurst*
This 500-year-old building, reputedly the oldest pub in the
village, overlooks the village green and has a striking
sandstone exterior, old oak beams and open fires. Good
varied menu includes an interesting range of fish dishes, as
continued

well as dishes such as spinach and mushroom pancakes, steak and kidney pie, and peppered chicken.
OPEN: 10-3 5-11. Closed 25 Dec. **BAR MEALS:** L served all week. D served all week 12-3 6-11. **RESTAURANT:** L served all week. D served all week 12-3 6-11. Av 3 course à la carte £14.
BREWERY/COMPANY: Free House. **PRINCIPAL BEERS:** King & Barnes Sussex Best, Marstons Pedigree, Flowers Original, Hogs Back TEA. **FACILITIES:** Garden: Food served outside Dogs allowed Water. **NOTES:** Parking 50

HALNAKER
Map 04 SU90

Anglesey Arms
PO18 0NQ ☎ 01243 773474
Dir: 4m E from centre of Chichester on A285 (Petworth Road)
Traditional village inn run by the same landlord for over 30 years. It is close to 'glorious Goodwood', the Downs and Chichester Harbour, and the village itself is famous for its windmill, immortalised in a poem by Hilaire Belloc. The menu has a good choice of steaks, Selsey crab, jumbo bangers, and home-made puddings like apple pie and custard.
OPEN: 11-3 6-11. Closed 25 Dec. **BAR MEALS:** L served all week. D served all week 12-2 7-10. Av main course £8.
RESTAURANT: L served all week. D served all week 12-2 7.30-10. Av 3 course à la carte £15. **BREWERY/COMPANY:** Pubmaster.
PRINCIPAL BEERS: Friary Meux, Greene King IPA, Burton Ale.
FACILITIES: Children welcome Garden: Food served outside Dogs allowed, water. **NOTES:** Parking 50

HAMMERPOT
Map 04 TQ00

The Woodman Arms
BN16 4EU ☎ 01903 871240 📠 01903 871240
Dir: E of Arundel, off the A27
16th-century thatched pub built to accommodate local woodmen. Low beams, award-winning gardens and good, home-cooked food make it a popular country destination. Situated on the edge of the South Downs, the pub is ideally placed for lots of spectacular downland rambles. Free maps are provided and there are guided walks here at weekends during March. Pan-fried duck breast with port and Cumberland sauce, chicken curry, steak with Stilton and port and fresh fish dishes feature on the varied bar menu.
OPEN: 11-3 6-11 (Sun 12-3, 7-10.30). **BAR MEALS:** L served all week. D served Mon-Sat 12-2.15 6.45-9. Av main course £6.
RESTAURANT: L served all week. D served Mon-Sat 12-2.15 6.45-9. Av 3 course à la carte £12.
BREWERY/COMPANY: Gales. **PRINCIPAL BEERS:** Gales HSB, Gales Butser, Gales GB. **FACILITIES:** Children welcome Children's licence Garden: patio/terrace, outdoor eating, BBQ Dogs allowed. **NOTES:** Parking 30

HAYWARDS HEATH
Map 05 TQ32

The Sloop ♀
Sloop Ln, Scaynes Hill RH17 7NP ☎ 01444 831219
e-mail: nigel.cannon@lineone.net
Handy for the Bluebell Railway and the gardens at Sheffield Park, this peacefully located 19th-century pub is close to the tranquil River Ouse, which offers good quality fishing, and the magical Ashdown Forest, superb for scenic walking. Live music to suit all tastes, an impressive wine list and a good selection of well-kept ales add to the attractions here. Maple and mustard chicken, Sussex sausages, whole sea bass and New Hampshire fish stew, a house favourite, feature on the well-designed menu.
continued

OPEN: 12-3 6-11 (Sun 12-10.30). **BAR MEALS:** L served all week. D served all week 12-2.15 6.30-9.15. Av main course £8.50.
RESTAURANT: L served all week. D served all week 12-2.15 6.30-9.15. Av 3 course à la carte £17.50.
PRINCIPAL BEERS: Greene King IPA & Abbot Ale, Ruddles County, XX Dark Mild. **FACILITIES:** Children welcome Garden: Food served outside Dogs allowed (Public bar).
NOTES: Parking 75

HENFIELD

The Royal Oak NEW
BN5 9AY ☎ 01444 881252
This delightful, 14th-century, black and white timbered cottage has been dispensing ale for over 200 years and continues to maintain the traditional, unspoilt character that many village pubs lost long ago. A true ale house, so expect head-cracking low beams, a huge inglenook with winter log fire, wooden and flagged floors, rustic furnishings and real ale straight from the cask. Extensive summer gardens and a limited menu of decent sandwiches, home-made soup and ploughman's.
OPEN: 11-2.30 5.30-11 (Sun 12-3, 7-10.30). **BAR MEALS:** L served all week. D served all week 11-2.30 5.30-11.
BREWERY/COMPANY: Inn Business.
PRINCIPAL BEERS: Harveys Best Bitter, Marstons Pedigree.
FACILITIES: Garden: Food served outside Dogs allowed Water.
No credit cards

HORSHAM
Map 04 TQ02

The Black Jug
31 North St RH12 1RJ ☎ 01403 253526 📠 01403 217821
Dir: 100yrds from Horsham railway station, almost straight opp Horsham Art Centre
Relaxed, light and airy town pub with stripped wood floors, darkwood furnishings, and a spacious rear conservatory. The daily-changing blackboard menu lists an interesting selection of dishes which range from grilled marinated Halloumi cheese on ciabatta or Chinese pancakes with prawn, lime and coriander, to wildboar steak with apple potato cake or pan-fried turkey breast with pine nuts.
OPEN: 11-11 (Sun 12-10.30). **BAR MEALS:** L served all week. D served all week 12-10. Av main course £8. **RESTAURANT:** L served all week. D served all week 12-10. Av 3 course à la carte £15.50. **BREWERY/COMPANY:** Scottish Courage.
PRINCIPAL BEERS: Courage Directors, Marstons Pedigree, Wadworth 6X, Harveys Best. **FACILITIES:** Children welcome.
NOTES: Parking 9

KIRDFORD
Map 04 TQ02

The Half Moon Inn 🐑 ♀
RH14 0LT ☎ 01403 820223 📠 01403 820224
Dir: Off A272 between Billingshurst & Petworth. At Wisborough Green follow signs 'Kirdford'
A sympathetically enlarged 17th-century village inn by the parish church of an unspoilt Sussex village near the River Arun: the mortuary once stood opposite, and coffins were made in one of the outhouses. Fresh fish remains a major draw, and includes dishes such as green lip mussels, squid, king prawn, seafood noodle salad, and spicy seafood soup. Other choices include a range of Thai cuisine. New landlord.
continued

England

The Half Moon Inn

OPEN: 11-3 (Summer Sat-Sun open all day) 6-11 (Sun 12-3 6-10.30). Closed 25 Dec. **BAR MEALS:** L served all week. D served Mon-Sat (Sun in summer)11-2.30 7-9.30. Av main course £6. **RESTAURANT:** L served all week. D served Mon-Sat (Sun in summer)11-2.30 7-9.30. Av 3 course à la carte £15. Av 3 course fixed price £20. **BREWERY/COMPANY:** Whitbread. **PRINCIPAL BEERS:** Arundel, Greene King Abbot Ale, King & Barnes Sussex, Fullers London Pride. **FACILITIES:** Children welcome Garden: Boules pitch, outdoor eating. **NOTES:** Parking 12. **ROOMS:** 1 en suite s£45 d£55

LICKFOLD   Map 04 SU92

Pick of the Pubs

Lickfold Inn 🌐 🐛 ♀
GU28 9EY ☎ 01798 861285 📠 01798 861342
Dir: From A3 take A283, through Chiddingfold, 2m on R signed 'Lurgashall Winery', pub in 1m
A smart, up-market brick and wood fronted inn, dating back to 1460, down quiet country lanes deep in the heart of the South Downs. Popular with the rambling fraternity and handy for Goodwood races and the National Trust's magnificent Petworth House, it is a popular place with its Georgian settles, Tudor oak beams, open fires and moulded panelling: an enormous inglenook fireplace with a spit is the downstairs centrepiece. A serious approach to freshly prepared food promises crispy duck pancake with plum chutney, wild boar and apple sausages on mash, roast duck breast with blackberry and elderberry jus and seared salmon with stir-fried vegetables and noodles in teriyaki marinade. Fish specials include crab and celeriac tart with fennel salsa and squid and scallops with sweet chilli butter alongside the more traditional ale-battered cod with chips and aïoli: for vegetarians perhaps linguine with goats' cheese, hazelnuts, red peppers and basil. Imaginative open sandwiches on home-made bread at lunch only Monday to Friday: desserts such as apple parfait with caramel sauce and poached spiced pears with pomegranate syrup are home-made also.
OPEN: 11-3.30 6-11.30. **BAR MEALS:** L served all week. D served all week 12-2.30 7-9.30. Av main course £12.50. **RESTAURANT:** L served all week. D served all week 12-2.30 7-9.30. Av 3 course à la carte £25.
BREWERY/COMPANY: Free House.
PRINCIPAL BEERS: Ballards Best, Fullers ESB, Hog's Back TEA. **FACILITIES:** Children welcome Children's licence Garden: patio, outdoor eating, BBQ Dogs allowed Water bowl. **NOTES:** Parking 50

LURGASHALL   Map 04 SU92

The Noah's Ark
The Green GU28 9ET ☎ 01428 707346 📠 01428 707742
e-mail: bernarn.wija@which.net
Dir: Off A283 N of Petworth
This charming 16th century inn is the perfect summer grandstand for cricket on the village green. When the nights draw in, settle down by the log fire for a game of cribbage, cards or dominoes. The snack menu includes hot wraps, salads and baked potatoes; expect main courses like guinea fowl, venison steak with apricot and port jus, or swordfish with tomato salsa.
OPEN: 11-3 6-11. Closed Dec 25. **BAR MEALS:** L served all week. D served Tue-Sat 12-2.30 7-10. Av main course £11.50. **RESTAURANT:** L served Mon-Sat. D served Mon-Sat 12-2 7-10. Av 3 course à la carte £20. **BREWERY/COMPANY:** Greene King. **PRINCIPAL BEERS:** Greene King IPA & Old Speckled Hen, Badger Tanglefoot. **FACILITIES:** Children welcome Children's licence Garden: outdoor eating. **NOTES:** Parking 20

MIDHURST   Map 04 SO82

The Angel Hotel
North St GU29 9DN ☎ 01730 812421 📠 01730 815928
Much extended Tudor coaching inn with Georgian frontage close to Cowdray Castle in an attractive small town. New owners and now more civilised hotel and restaurant than inn, although there is a popular bar and bistro.

NUTHURST   Map 04 TQ12

Pick of the Pubs

Black Horse Inn ♀
Nuthurst St RH13 6LH ☎ 01403 891272
📠 01403 891148
Tucked away up a quiet backwater and half-hidden behind its own colourful window boxes, this quintessential Sussex free house probably dates back to the 17th century. Originally built as a row of cottages with a forge in the adjoining barn, the mellow clay tiles and local bricks now shelter a stone-flagged bar with a large inglenook and blazing winter fires. The pub stands close to a babbling little stream; in warmer weather, there's a lovely garden and a host of attractive walks in the surrounding countryside. Food is served in the bar, and in the comfortable dining room, where the basic snacks menu is supplemented by around a dozen daily specials. Expect rib-eye steaks, Sussex herby sausage with colcannon, stuffed plaice, monkfish, and spicy tofu stir-fry.
OPEN: 11-3 6-11 (Sun 12-3, 7-11). **BAR MEALS:** L served all week. D served all week 12-2.30 6-9.30. Av main course £8.95. **RESTAURANT:** L served all week. D served all week 12-2.30 6-9.30. **BREWERY/COMPANY:** Free House.
PRINCIPAL BEERS: Harveys Sussex, Fullers London Pride.
FACILITIES: Children welcome Garden: outdoor eating, patio/terrace, Dogs allowed. **NOTES:** Parking 26

♀   Pubs offering six or more wines by the glass

OVING   Map 04 SU90

The Gribble Inn
PO20 6BP ☎ 01243 786893 ▤ 01243 786893
Dir: From A27 take A259. After 1m L at roundabout, 1st R, 1st L to Oving
A fine thatched 16th-century inn with secluded garden, and two enormous log fires, low wooden beams, and settle seating in the character main bar. Beers are brewed on the premises. The pub was named after Rose Gribble, a local schoolteacher and poetess.

PETWORTH   Map 04 SU92

The Black Horse
Byworth GU28 0HL ☎ 01798 342424
Supposedly built on the site of an old priory in a beautiful village setting, the pub's Georgian, three-storey, brick and stone frontage hides a much older interior dating back to the 14th century. Wooden floors and furniture, half-panelled walls and open fires characterise the three, rustic interconnecting rooms. Good ales and pub meals ranging from steak and kidney pudding and ploughman's lunches, to venison casserole and crab cakes with salad. Busy in summer; lovely terraced gardens with peaceful valley views.
OPEN: 11-2.30 6-11. Closed Dec 26. **BAR MEALS:** L served all week. D served all week 12-2 7-9. Av main course £6.
RESTAURANT: L served all week. D served all week 12-2 7-9. Av 3 course à la carte £14. **PRINCIPAL BEERS:** Fullers London Pride, Arundel Gold, Cheriton Pots Ale. **FACILITIES:** Garden: food served outside Dogs allowed Water. **NOTES:** Parking 24

Pick of the Pubs
The Halfway Bridge Inn
Halfway Bridge GU28 9BP ☎ 01798 861281
▤ 01798 861878
e-mail: mail@thesussexpub.co.uk
Dir: On A272
Set midway between Midhurst and Petworth, this rambling, red-brick inn was originally built as a coaching inn in 1740. Well run by the Hawkins family and locally popular, especially among the polo set, and A272 travellers, for the interesting food served throughout the tastefully furnished interconnecting rooms. After an appetiser of marinated olives, commence your meal with fish soup with rouille, smoked haddock tartare with horseradish dressing, or Parma ham, roasted pepper and shallot salad, moving on to venison, red wine and juniper berry casserole with grain mustard mash, herb-crusted cod fillet, or wild mushroom and Parmesan risotto. Those with room should try the banana toffee pie. Real fires offer a warm welcome in winter; for the summer there are tables out on the lawn and on the sheltered rear patio. Accommodation in eight en suite bedrooms was due to come on line in Summer 2001.
OPEN: 11-3 6-11 (Closed Sun eve in winter). Closed 25 Dec. **BAR MEALS:** L served all week. D served all week 12-2 7-10. Av main course £8. **RESTAURANT:** L served all week. D served all week 12-2 7-10. Av 3 course à la carte £16.50.
BREWERY/COMPANY: Free House.
PRINCIPAL BEERS: Gales HSB, Cheriton Pots Ale, Fullers London Pride, Harveys Best. **FACILITIES:** Garden: patio, outdoor eating Dogs allowed Water. **NOTES:** Parking 20.
ROOMS: 8 bedrooms 8 en suite s£45 d£65

Welldiggers Arms Ⓢ ♈
Pulborough Rd GU28 0HG ☎ 01798 342287
Dir: 1m E of Petworth on the A283
Welldiggers once occupied this rustic, 300-year-old roadside pub which boasts low-beamed bars with open log fires and huge oak tables. Convenient for racing at Goodwood and Fontwell, as well as a visit to Sir Edward Elgar's cottage. Representative dishes include English steaks, seafood royale, steak and kidney pudding, king prawn langoustine, smoked haddock and poached eggs, and fish soup with aïoli.
OPEN: 11-3 6.30. Closed Dec 25. **BAR MEALS:** L served all week. D served Mon-Sat 12-2 6.30-9.30. Av main course £8.50.
RESTAURANT: L served all week. D served Mon-Sat 12-2 6.30-9.30. Av 3 course à la carte £12.50.
BREWERY/COMPANY: Free House.
PRINCIPAL BEERS: Youngs. **FACILITIES:** Children welcome Garden: Food served outside Dogs allowed.
NOTES: Parking 35

ROWHOOK   Map 04 TQ13

The Chequers Inn ⓈⓈ ♈
RH12 3PY ☎ 01403 790480
Dir: Off A29 NW of Horsham
Originally named after the chequer tree in the pub's large garden, a Grade II listed building of great character with a wealth of beams and flagstones, the bars warmed by open fires. Coming under new management at the time this guide went to press. The new licensees have ambitious plans on the food side.
OPEN: 11-3 (Sun 12-3, 7-10.30) 6-11. **BAR MEALS:** L served all week. D served Mon-Sat 12-2 7-9.30. **RESTAURANT:** L served all week. D served Mon-Sat 12-2 7-9.30.
BREWERY/COMPANY: Punch Taverns.
PRINCIPAL BEERS: Harvey's Sussex Ale, Young's Special.
FACILITIES: Garden: patio, outdoor eating, BBQ Dogs allowed.
NOTES: Parking 30

RUDGWICK   Map 04 TQ03

The Fox Inn ⓈⓈ ♈
Guildford Rd, Bucks Green RH12 3JP ☎ 01403 822386
▤ 01403 823950
e-mail: enquiries@foxinn.co.uk
Dir: situated on A281 midway between Horsham and Guildford
Attractive, 16th-century family-run pub on the green, close to the River Arun. Long food hours take in all-day breakfast and afternoon teas; bar meals and speciality fish dishes. Lobster and seafood platter, skate wings and Cajun tuna steak share honours with chicken fajitas, sizzling beef stir-fry and spinach and mushroom Stroganoff.
OPEN: 11-11 (Sun 12-10.30). **BAR MEALS:** L served all week. D served all week 12-10. Av main course £6.95.
BREWERY/COMPANY: Hall & Woodhouse.
PRINCIPAL BEERS: King & Barnes Sussex, Tanglefoot.
FACILITIES: Children welcome Garden: patio, outdoor eating Dogs allowed. **NOTES:** Parking 30

SHIPLEY   Map 04 TQ12

George & Dragon
Dragons Green RH13 7JE ☎ 01403 741320
Signposted off the A272 between Coolham and the A24, this 16th-century tile-hung cottage is the ideal refreshment stop, especially on a summer's evening when the spacious and

continued

peaceful garden is the perfect retreat for weary travellers. Character interior with inglenook fireplace and head-cracking low beams. Freshly prepared food ranges from tomato and basil soup, deep-fried Brie with cranberry sauce and cod in batter with home-made chips to half-shoulder of lamb and lasagne. Shipley is famous for its smock mill, one of the tallest in Sussex.
OPEN: 11-3 6-11 (Sat 11-11, Sun 12-10.30). **BAR MEALS:** L served all week. D served all week 12-2 6.45-9.30. Av main course £4. **RESTAURANT:** L served all week. D served all week 12-2 6.45-9. Av 3 course à la carte £10. Av 3 course fixed price £10.
BREWERY/COMPANY: Hall & Woodhouse.
PRINCIPAL BEERS: Badger Best & Tanglefoot.
FACILITIES: Children welcome Children's licence Garden: outdoor eating, BBQ Dogs allowed. **NOTES:** Parking 20 No credit cards

---

SIDLESHAM
Map 04 SZ89

Crab & Lobster
Mill Ln PO20 7NB ☎ 01243 641233
Dir: Off B2145 between Chichester & Selsey
Well-kept pub situated close to the shores of Pagham Harbour, a noted nature reserve. Popular with walkers and twitchers who fill the cosy bars (open fires) in winter, and the pretty rear garden with mudflat views in summer.

SINGLETON
Map 04 SU81

Pick of the Pubs

The Fox Goes Free ☜ ♀
Charlton PO18 0HU ☎ 01243 811461 📠 01243 811461
Dir: A286 6m from Chichester, towards Midhurst 1m from Goodwood racecourse
Formerly known as the Charlton Fox, this 400 year-old brick and flint pub nestles in a sequestered valley with undisturbed views of the South Downs. The pub was favoured as a hunting lodge by William III, and also hosted the first Women's Institute meeting in 1915.
    With its two huge fireplaces, standing timbers and old pews, the building simply exudes charm and character. But this is an inn for all seasons, and the outdoor bar and barbecue make maximum use of the lovely flint-walled herb garden and listed apple trees. Four welcoming bedrooms make The Fox an ideal country retreat.
    Food served throughout marries traditional and modern styles. Expect venison steak in redcurrant and port, pigeon breast in apple and Calvados, steak and kidney pie, red sea bream with bacon and white wine cream, tuna steak with peppers and pesto, or ratatouille and goats' cheese bake.
OPEN: 11-3 (Sun 12-4, all day in summer) 6-11 (Sat all day). **BAR MEALS:** L served all week. D served all week 12-2.30 6.30-10.30. **RESTAURANT:** L served all week. D served all week 12-2.30 6-10.30. Av 3 course à la carte £15.50.
BREWERY/COMPANY: Free House.
PRINCIPAL BEERS: Ringwood Best, Ballards Best, Fox Bitter, Bass. **FACILITIES:** Garden: Food served outside Dogs allowed Water. **NOTES:** Parking 8. **ROOMS:** 4 bedrooms 2 en suite s£35 d£50

AA inspected hotel accommodation

SOUTHBOURNE
Map 04 SU70

The Old House at Home ☜ ♀
Cot Lane, Chidham PO18 8SU
☎ 01243 572477
Sleepy Chidham is situated on a low lying peninsula jutting out into Chichester Harbour, close to wonderful scenic walks and wildlife-rich marshes. Often filled with walkers and twitchers, the 300-year-old Old House at Home offers a warm welcome, good bar food and four ales on tap, notably guest beers like Cheriton Brewhouse Pots Ale.
    Home-cooked food ranges from ploughman's lunches and sandwiches to local fish - fresh battered cod, tuna with salad Niçoise, whole sea bass baked in herbs, crevettes in chilli sauce -and interesting meat options like slow-roasted lamb shank and duck with orange salad.
OPEN: 11.30-2.30 6-11. **BAR MEALS:** L served all week. D served all week 12-2 6-9.30. Av main course £5.95.
BREWERY/COMPANY: Free House.
PRINCIPAL BEERS: Ringwood Best,. **FACILITIES:** Garden: Food served outside. **NOTES:** Parking 30
See Pub Walk on page 441

SOUTH HARTING
Map 04 SU71

The Ship Inn ☜
GU31 5PZ ☎ 01730 825302
Dir: From Petersfield take B2146 towards Chichester
17th-century inn constructed from a ships timbers, hence its name. Home-made pies are a feature, and other popular dishes include Sussex hotpot, lemon sole, moussaka, venison steaks and a choice of vegetarian options. A range of bar snacks is also available.
OPEN: 11-11 (Sun 12-10.30 Tue-Thu 11-2.30, 6-11).
BAR MEALS: 12-2.30 7-9.30. Av main course £7.95.
BREWERY/COMPANY: Free House.
PRINCIPAL BEERS: Palmers IPA, Cheriton Pots Ale.
FACILITIES: Garden: Dogs allowed. **NOTES:** Parking 5

STEDHAM
Map 04 SU82

Hamilton Arms/Nava Thai Restaurant
School Ln GU29 0NZ ☎ 01730 812555 📠 01730 817459
e-mail: hamiltonarms@hotmail.com
Dir: Off A272 between Midhurst & Petersfield

Located in a delightful village close to the South Downs, this traditional-looking pub is not what it seems. Its range of authentic Thai food sets it apart from other hostelries in the area, though many classic English pub favourites are also available. Named after Nelson's mistress, the pub is renowned for its decor, colourful sunshades and dazzling display of floral baskets. Expect cottage pie and Spanish omelette on the English bar menu. *continued*

OPEN: 11-3 6-11 (closed Mon). Closed 1 wk Jan.
BAR MEALS: L served Sun, Tue-Sat. D served Sun, Tue-Sat 12-2.30 6-10.30. Av main course £6. **RESTAURANT:** L served Sun, Tue-Sat. D served Sun, Tue-Sat 12-2.30 6-10.30. Av 3 course à la carte £18.50. Av 4 course fixed price £20.
BREWERY/COMPANY: Free House.
PRINCIPAL BEERS: Ballards Best, Fullers London Pride,.
FACILITIES: Children welcome Garden: Food served outside Dogs allowed Water. **NOTES:** Parking 40

SUTTON
Map 04 SU91

Pick of the Pubs

White Horse Inn ♦♦♦ 🐾 ♀
The Street RH20 1PS
☎ 01798 869221   🖹 01798 869291
Dir: Turn off A29 at foot of Bury Hill. After 2m pass Roman Villa on R. 1m to Sutton

Pretty Georgian inn tucked away in a sleepy village at the base of the South Downs. Neat bars and dining room, and comfortable en suite accommodation. Expect imaginative food, the daily-changing choice featuring perhaps Stilton and broccoli soup, baked sea bass with lemon basil and tomato, confit of duck, lamb shank with tomatoes and red wine, and French lemon tart.
OPEN: 11-3 6-11. **BAR MEALS:** L served all week. D served all week 12-2 7-9.30. Av main course £5.50.
RESTAURANT: L served all week. D served all week 12-2 7-9.30. Av 3 course à la carte £22.50.
BREWERY/COMPANY: Free House.
PRINCIPAL BEERS: Fullers London Pride, Youngs PA, Shepherd Neame Spitfire, Courage Best.
FACILITIES: Children welcome Garden: Dogs allowed.
NOTES: Parking 10. **ROOMS:** 6 bedrooms 6 en suite s£55 d£65

AA The Restaurant Guide 2002

The right choice every time with this invaluable guide for gourmets

www.theAA.com

AA Lifestyle Guides

TILLINGTON
Map 04 SU92

Pick of the Pubs

The Horse Guards Inn 🐾 ♀
GU28 9AF ☎ 01798 342332   🖹 01798 344351
e-mail: mail@horseguardsinn.co.uk
Dir: On A272 1m W of Petworth. Inn next to church
Until the mid 19th century, this charming 300 year-old free house was known as the New Star Inn. It was renamed after becoming popular with the Horse Guards, who were on security duties in nearby Petworth Park.
The pub was converted from three cottages, and the rambling series of tastefully refurbished rooms features stripped beams, open fires, pine panelling and antique furnishings. The restaurant, and some of the en suite bedrooms, enjoy good views across the Rother Valley to the South Downs; there's a lovely terrace at the front, and a secluded rear garden for summer dining. The pub attracts an upmarket clientele, who appreciate its civilised atmosphere, quality wines, and imaginative well presented food.
Beyond lunchtime sandwiches and hot snacks, the choice may chilled pear and watercress soup, ballotine of foie gras with fruit chutney, whole Dover sole, lobster salad, tian of crab, langoustine with celeriac and avocado remoulade, steaks and local game. Recently taken over by the owners of the White Horse at Sutton (qv)
OPEN: 11-3 6-11. **BAR MEALS:** L served all week. D served all week 12-2 7-10. Av main course £8.50. **RESTAURANT:** L served all week. D served all week 12-2 7-10. Av 3 course à la carte £21. **BREWERY/COMPANY:** Free House.
PRINCIPAL BEERS: Wadworth 6X, Badger Best.
FACILITIES: Children welcome Garden: patio, outdoor eating. **NOTES:** Parking 5. **ROOMS:** 3 bedrooms 3 en suite d£72

WALBERTON
Map 04 SU90

Oaks Bar 🐾 ♀
Yapton Ln BN18 0LS ☎ 01243 552865   🖹 01243 553862
e-mail: reservations@oakslodge.co.uk
Dir: on A27 between Arundel & Fontwell
Converted 18th-century coaching inn conveniently located between Arundel and Chichester, close to the South Downs, two beautiful cathedrals and 'Glorious Goodwood'. Real ales are served in the bar and there is an imaginative brasserie menu. Check out the 'ultimate fish and chips', including cod, monkfish and tiger prawns in beer batter, Oaks beef and wild mushroom sausages, and roasted rack of lamb with brioche crust.
OPEN: 11.30-3 6-11. **BAR MEALS:** L served all week. D served all week 12-3 6-10. Av main course £8. **RESTAURANT:** L served all week 12-3 6-10. Av 3 course à la carte £22.
BREWERY/COMPANY: Free House.
PRINCIPAL BEERS: Badger. **FACILITIES:** Children welcome Garden: outdoor eating, patio/terrace, no dogs ex guide dogs. **NOTES:** Parking 23. **ROOMS:** 4 bedrooms 4 en suite s£40 d£55

All AA listed accommodation can also be found on the AA's internet site **www.theAA.com**

WARNHAM   Map 04 TQ13

The Greets Inn ♀
47 Friday St RH12 3QY
☎ 01403 265047 📠 01403 265047
Dir: Off A24 N of Horsham
Fine Sussex hall house dating from about 1350 and built for
Elias Greet, a local merchant. Magnificent fine inglenook
fireplace and head-crackingly low beams in the flagstone-
floored bar and rambling series of dining areas.
  Interesting range of dishes include pan-fried venison
medallions with Cumberland sauce, chargrilled lamb steak
with garlic and herb butter, fillet of John Dory on provençale
noodles with sauce vierge, and seared tuna with coconut
sauce and scented lime rice. Traditional pub dishes and
summer weekend barbeques.

OPEN: 11-2.30 (Sun 12-2, 7-10.30) 6-11. **BAR MEALS:** L served
all week. D served all week 12-2.15 6.45-9.15. Av main course £5.
RESTAURANT: L served all week. D served all week 12-2.15
6.45-9.15. Av 3 course à la carte £20.
BREWERY/COMPANY: Whitbread.
PRINCIPAL BEERS: Flowers Original, Fullers London Pride,
Harveys Sussex. **FACILITIES:** Children welcome Children's
licence Garden: outdoor eating Dogs allowed Water Provided.
NOTES: Parking 30

WEST HOATHLY   Map 05 TQ33

The Cat Inn ♀
Queen's Square RH19 4PP ☎ 01342 810369
16th-century village inn situated opposite an historic 11th-
century church. Seating outside on the sunny front terrace.
High beamed ceiling and huge inglenook fireplace inside.
  Bar food includes cottage pie and sausage and mash. Try
the vegetarian sweetcorn cake, pan-fried halibut or venison
steak from the wholesome restaurant menu.
OPEN: 11-3 5.30-11 (Sat 11-11, Sun 12-5, 7-10.30).
BAR MEALS: L served all week. D served all week 12-2.30 7-9.30.
Av main course £9.95. **RESTAURANT:** L served all week.
D served all week 12-2.30 7-9.30. **BREWERY/COMPANY:** Free
House. **PRINCIPAL BEERS:** Harveys Best, King & Barnes Sussex.
NOTES: Parking 30

Pubs offering a good choice of
seafood on the menu.

Royal State
The Crown is one of the commonest inn
names, for patriotic reasons and sometimes
because the inn stood on royal land. The Rose and
Crown celebrates Henry VII's achievement in ending
civil war by reconciling the rival roses of York and
Lancaster in the crown. The King's Head, King's Arms
and Queen's Arms are equally familiar, often with
Henry VIII on the sign, roughly after Holbein. Elizabeth
I, the Georges, Queen Victoria and Prince Albert make
their appearances, too, and many pubs are names after
childen of George III or Queen Victoria (the Duke of
York, Duke of Clarence, Duke of Edinburgh, etc). Others
honour the Prince of Wales or his badge of the
Feathers, while the Fleur de Lys recalls the fact that
down to 1801 the kings of England claimed to
be kings of France as well.

TYNE & WEAR

NEWCASTLE UPON TYNE

Cooperage
The Close, Quayside NE1 3RF ☎ 0191 232 8286
Set on the waterfront under the city's famed bridges, the
Cooperage is one of the oldest pubs in the area. Lots of real
ale choice.

Crown Posoda
31 The Side, Dean St NE1 3JE ☎ 0191 232 1269
Complete with Victorian stained glass screens, this friendly old
pub also boasts gilt mirrors and candelabra. Real ale.
Lunchtime pub food. No children.

Shiremoor House Farm
Middle Engine Ln, New York NE29 8DZ ☎ 0191 257 6302
Located in what were once derelict farm buildings, this pub
offers large bars, plenty of ale choice, and tables in the
courtyard. Pub food. Children welcome.

WHITLEY BAY   Map 11 NZ37

The Waterford Arms 🐑 ♀
Collywell Bay Rd, Seaton Sluice NE26 4QZ
☎ 0191 2370450 & 296 5287 📠 0191 2370450
*Dir: From A1 N of Newcastle take A19 at Seaton Burn then follow
signs for A190 to Seaton Sluice*
The building dates back to 1899 and is situated close to the
small local fishing harbour, overlooking the North Sea.
Splendid beaches and sand dunes are within easy reach, and
the pub is very popular with walkers. Seafood dishes are the
speciality, including a whale-sized cod or haddock and chips,
seafood feast, and salmon.
OPEN: 12-11.30 (Sun 12-11). **BAR MEALS:** L served all week.
D served all week 12-11.30 5-11.30. Av main course £4.
RESTAURANT: L served all week. D served all week 12-11.30
5-11.30. **BREWERY/COMPANY:** Pubmaster.
PRINCIPAL BEERS: Marstons Pedigree, Tetleys, Worthington,
John Smith's. **FACILITIES:** Children welcome Food served
outside Dogs allowed. **NOTES:** Parking 90.
ROOMS: 5 bedrooms 5 en suite

WARWICKSHIRE

ALDERMINSTER
Map 04 SP24

Pick of the Pubs

The Bell ♦♦♦♦ ♀
CV37 8NY ☎ 01789 450414 📠 01789 450998
e-mail: thebellald@aol.com
Dir: On A3400 3.5M S of Stratford-upon-Avon

Within easy reach of Stratford-upon-Avon and Warwick Castle, you'll find a relaxed atmosphere at this former coaching inn. Fresh flowers decorate the friendly and welcoming bars, and the spacious conservatory looks out across a charming courtyard garden to the rolling Stour valley countryside.

The regular programme mailed to 'Friends of the Bell' features special events like jazz, Irish nights and carol singing, but drop in any time for a regularly-changing menu and daily blackboard specials. Start with home-made soup, mushroom Stroganoff, or a bowl of mussels in white wine. Freshly prepared main courses might include fisherman's crêpes, chargrilled lamb cutlets, vegetarian bake with salad, or lamb's liver with bubble and squeak. Round off with pears in red wine, steamed pudding and custard, or a chocolate, almond and brandy torte.

The pub is well placed for touring the Cotswolds, and offers accommodation in five individually furnished rooms. All are well equipped, most have en suite facilities and all overlook the garden.

OPEN: 12-2.30 7-11. **BAR MEALS:** L served all week. D served all week 12-2 7-9. Av main course £6.50. **RESTAURANT:** L served all week. D served all week 12-2 7-9. Av 3 course à la carte £16. **BREWERY/COMPANY:** Free House. **PRINCIPAL BEERS:** Greene King IPA & Old Speckled Hen. **FACILITIES:** Children welcome Garden: patio, outdoor eating Dogs allowed on lead, water. **NOTES:** Parking 70. **ROOMS:** 5 bedrooms 3 en suite s£25 d£40 FR£50-£80

ARDENS GRAFTON
Map 03 SP15

Pick of the Pubs

The Golden Cross 🍴 ♀ NEW
B50 4LG ☎ 01789 772420 📠 01789 773697

Nestling in the heart of Shakespeare country west of Stratford, with views across a rolling Warwickshire landscape, the Golden Cross is a stylishly refurbished rural inn offering imaginative, freshly prepared food in an informal pub atmosphere. Relax with a pint in the beamed bar, with its rug-strewn stone floor mellow decor and scrubbed pine tables, or dine in style in the light and airy, high-ceilinged dining-room. Extensive menus successfully blend traditional pub favourites (given a modern twist) with more inventive dishes. Start with confit duck leg with ginger and vanilla-scented rice, cream of roast tomato and rosemary soup or chicken liver parfait with orange and lime confit. To follow, choices include braised lamb shank with celeriac mash and redcurrant sauce, steak, ale and root vegetable pie, and spiced chicken breast with ratatouille couscous and red pepper jus. At lunch accompany a pint of Hook Norton with an avocado and smoked bacon ciabatta or marmalade glazed ham, egg and chips. Home-made puddings.

OPEN: 11-2.30 6-11 (all day Sat-Sun). **BAR MEALS:** L served all week. D served all week 12-2.30 7-9.30. Av main course £7. **RESTAURANT:** L served all week 12-2.30 7-9.30. Av 3 course à la carte £15. Av 3 course fixed price £10.50. **PRINCIPAL BEERS:** Hook Norton, Bass, Flowers IPA. **FACILITIES:** Children welcome Garden: food served outside. **NOTES:** Parking 80 No credit cards

ASTON CANTLOW

Pick of the Pubs

King's Head 🍴 ♀
21 Bearley Rd B95 6HY ☎ 01789 488242 📠 01789 488137

Pretty black and white Tudor pub set in an ancient village deep in the heart of Shakespeare country. Flanked by a huge spreading chestnut tree, and oozing old-world atmosphere, this impressive building has recently been sensitively refurbished in modern style. Tastefully rustic inside, with huge polished flagstones, exposed original beams, old scrubbed pine tables, painted brick walls, open log fires and scatter cushions on pew benches and antique settles; light and airy rear dining-room. Expect a laid-back atmosphere and approach to dining - sit where you want and eat what you want from an innovative modern pub menu - plus piped jazz, first-rate real ales, decent wines and coffee. Begin with rustic bread, roast garlic and extra virgin olive oil or sautéed pigeon breast with roasted red onion and crispy bacon, following on with salmon, cod and chive fishcakes with celeriac tartare, chargrilled venison steak with cranberry jus, the 'famous' duck supper, or one of the 'fishy' specials like baked monkfish with basil pesto and roasted tomatoes. Finish with chocolate bread-and-butter pudding. Smart rear terrace for alfresco summer dining.

OPEN: 12-3 5.30-11 (Summer open all day). **BAR MEALS:** L served all week. D served all week 12-2.30 7-10. Av main course £9.95. **RESTAURANT:** L served all week. D served all week 12-2.30 7-10. Av 3 course à la carte £16.50. **PRINCIPAL BEERS:** Greene King Abbot Ale. **FACILITIES:** Children welcome Garden: food served outside Dogs allowed

BROOM
Map 03 SP05

Broom Tavern
High St B50 4HL ☎ 01789 773656 🖹 01789 772983
e-mail: richard@distinctivepubs.freeserve.co.uk
Dir: N of B439 W of Stratford-upon-Avon

Charming brick and timber 16th-century inn, reputedly haunted by a cavalier killed on the cellar steps. The same menu is offered in the bar and restaurant. 'Tavern Favourites' include home-made steak and kidney pie and the Tavern duck supper, while 'From Around the Globe' there might be seafood fettucine, Chinese stir-fry or the Tavern balti.
OPEN: 11.30-2.30 5-11. **BAR MEALS:** L served all week. D served all week 12-2 6.30-9. Av main course £7.50.
RESTAURANT: D served all week 6.30-9. Av 3 course à la carte £14. **BREWERY/COMPANY:** Greene King.
PRINCIPAL BEERS: Green King IPA. **FACILITIES:** Children welcome Garden: Beer garden, outdoor eating, BBQ Dogs allowed except in garden. **NOTES:** Parking 30

EDGEHILL
Map 04 SP34

The Castle Inn
OX15 6DJ ☎ 01295 670255 🖹 01295 670521
e-mail: castleedghill@msn.com
Dir: M40 then A422. 6m until Upton House, then turn next R 1.5m
Nestling on a beech-clad ridge on the Oxfordshire border with Warwickshire, the Castle Inn is surely one of the most unusual pubs in the country. An 18th-century battlemented folly, built by local architect Sanderson Miller in the 1740s to commemorate the centenary of the Battle of Edgehill , the inn was first licensed back in 1822.
Traditional home-cooked dishes such as mixed grill, lasagne and gammon steak and egg. Daily specials may include chicken curry and pasta twists in tomato and mushroom sauce.
OPEN: 11.15-2.30 6.15-11. **BAR MEALS:** L served all week. D served all week 12-2 6.30-9. Av main course £6.50.
BREWERY/COMPANY: Hook Norton.
PRINCIPAL BEERS: Hook Norton - Best/Old, Old Hooky, Generation, 12 Days & Haymaker. **FACILITIES:** Garden: food served outside Dogs allowed. **NOTES:** Parking 40.
ROOMS: 3 bedrooms 3 en suite s£35 d£55 FR£65

ETTINGTON
Map 04 SP24

Pick of the Pubs

The Chequers Inn & Restaurant 🍴 ♀
CV37 7SR ☎ 01789 740387 🖹 01789 748097
Dir: 5m S of Stratford on A422, 1m S of Jct between A422 & A429, 1/4m from Jct between Fosse Way & A422
Comfortably refurbished 17th-century inn situated in the heart of Warwickshire and well placed for visitors exploring Stratford-upon-Avon and Shakespeare country. Break your tour here and relax in the neat, simply furnished lounge bar and order an imaginative bar meal from the short, daily-changing blackboard menu. Try the trio of sausages on creamy mash with red wine and red onion gravy, hot steamed asparagus with lemon butter, smoked bacon and chicken liver parfait, and oven-roasted shank of lamb on garlic and parsley mash with mint gravy. Those with time may like to explore the imaginative carte and dine in the rear restaurant. Menu choices range from mussel, prawn and coconut milk risotto with chargrilled squid and chilli jam and confit leg of duck to roast supreme of chicken on wilted spinach with lemon and tarragon cream sauce. Come on a Friday and sample the impressive fish menu. Good value list of wines.
OPEN: 12-2.30 7-11. Closed Sun eve and Tue lunch in winter.
BAR MEALS: 12-2 7-9. **RESTAURANT:** L served Wed-Mon. D served Mon-Sat 12-2 7-9. Av 3 course à la carte £22. Av 3 course fixed price £12. **BREWERY/COMPANY:** Free House. **PRINCIPAL BEERS:** Fullers London Pride, Adnams, Hook Norton. **FACILITIES:** Children welcome Garden: Beer garden, patio, BBQ, outdoor eating Dogs allowed (garden only). **NOTES:** Parking 40

The Houndshill
Banbury Rd CV37 7NS ☎ 01789 740267 🖹 01789 740075
Dir: On A422 SE of Stratford-upon-Avon
Attractive traditional family-run inn set in the Heart of England, making it the ideal base for visits to Stratford-upon-Avon and the Cotswolds. The Houndshill has a pleasant tree-lined garden and is very popular with families. Typical dishes include grilled sirloin steak, seared swordfish, pan-fried fillet of salmon, lamb cutlets and haddock kiev. Lots of light bites.

OPEN: 12-3 7-11 (Sun 12-3, 7-10.30). Closed Dec 25-28.
BAR MEALS: L served all week. D served all week 12-2 7-9.30. Av main course £8.50. **BREWERY/COMPANY:** Free House.
PRINCIPAL BEERS: Hook Norton Best, Marstons Pedigree.
FACILITIES: Children welcome Garden: outdoor eating Dogs allowed. **NOTES:** Parking 50. **ROOMS:** 8 bedrooms 8 en suite s£35 d£55 FR£65-80

Howard Arms, Ilmington

From the charming village of Ilmington, set on the northern scarp of the Cotswold Hills, this beautiful walk takes in Foxcote House, an old drovers' road, and magnificent views from the highest point in Warwickshire.

Turn right from the pub and take the waymarked footpath to the left of Vine Cottage. Follow the path to the lane and turn left. Just before the school, go through the kissing-gate and follow the fenced path to a stile. Proceed with the footpath arrows through three meadows via stiles. At the far end of the third meadow, cross the stile close to the right-hand corner and head left up the bank to cross a stile near a pool.

Continue along the left-hand field edge, drop downhill to cross a stile and bear left over a brook. Keep to the path across a further brook and climb the stile into a field. Turn left around the field edge to join a drive. Pass through a gate to Drover's Road and turn left. Ascend to TV masts.

Turn left, opposite the masts, alongside the wall and proceed through the gate in the field corner. Walk to the left of the oak tree to reach a gate and a lane. Turn left, then immediately right along a farm road to reach a lane (views of Foxcote House). Turn left, then in 250 yards (228m) take the arrowed path left. Cross the field to a stile into old quarry meadow and head down the gully to a gate in the far right corner.

Walk down the hedged track, which becomes Grump Street, to reach the village. Proceed downhill to Lower Green and the inn.

Distance: 4 miles (6.4km)
Map: OS Landranger 151
Terrain: downland and farmland
Paths: Field paths and farm tracks
Gradient: undulating with some short steep climbs

Walk submitted by:
Richard Shurey

Ilmington Manor

HOWARD ARMS, ILMINGTON 🏵
Lower Green CV36 4LT.
Tel: 01608 682226
Directions: off A4300 S of Stratford-upon-Avon
Rambling, 17th-century Cotswold stone inn overlooking the village green. Full of period charm and character with stone floors, heavy timbers, open fires and civilised décor. Innovative modern menu, good ales and comfortable accommodation.
Open: 11-3 6-11 Bar Meals: 12-2 7-9 (9.30 Fri & Sat). Children welcome. No dogs inside. Garden & patio. Parking.
(see page 454 for full entry)

GREAT WOLFORD
Map 04 SP23

Fox & Hounds Inn 🛏 🍸
CV36 5NQ ☎ 01608 674220 📠 01608 674220
Dir: Off A44 NE of Moreton-in-Marsh
Exuding old-world charm, with polished flagstone floors, old settles, huge inglenook fireplace, heavy ceiling beams adorned with jugs or festooned with hops, and intimate evening candlelight, this unspoilt, Cotswold stone-built inn dates from the 17th century. Built as a pub to serve the estate workers, it now offers an impressive range of real ales and whiskies, and a good choice of home-made food. From ploughman's lunches, scampi and steaks the menu extends to interesting daily blackboard specials such as venison with red wine sauce, roast shank of lamb game pie, grilled Dover sole and lamb kleftico. Attractive front terrace for summer alfresco drinking.
OPEN: 12-3 7-11 (closed Mon). **BAR MEALS:** L served Tue-Sun. D served Tue-Sun 12-2 7-9. Av main course £9. **RESTAURANT:** L served Tue-Sun 12-2 7-9. Av 3 course à la carte £15. **BREWERY/COMPANY:** Free House.
PRINCIPAL BEERS: Shepherd Neame Spitfire, Hook Norton, Black Sheep, Boddingtons. **FACILITIES:** Children welcome Garden: patio, outdoor eating Dogs allowed managers discretion only. **NOTES:** Parking 20. **ROOMS:** 4 bedrooms 4 en suite d£40 No credit cards

ILMINGTON
Map 04 SP24

Pick of the Pubs

Howard Arms ⊕ 🛏 🍸
Lower Green CV36 4LT ☎ 01608 682226
📠 01608 682226
e-mail: howard.arms@virgin.net
Dir: Off A429 or A34
Pride of place overlooking the village green in this charming village is the rambling, 17th-century Cotswold-stone Howard Arms, an inviting inn linked to nearby Foxcote House and one of England's most illustrious families. Ex-hoteliers, Robert and Gill Greenstock, have successfully created a civilised modern dining pub, full of period charm and character, with stone floors, open fires, heavy timbers and an informal atmosphere. Choose from varied weekly-changing menu of freshly prepared dishes. Begin with guinea fowl and pork terrine with red onion marmalade, chargrilled tuna salad Niçoise, or sesame crumbed chicken cakes with chilli cream dip, moving on to seared Cornish scallops with provençale sauce and couscous, chargrilled venison with parsnip purée with juniper and port sauce, or pan-fried sea bass with caramelised chicory and lemon butter sauce. Finish with a home-made pudding, perhaps glazed lemon tart with orange compôte, or Rocombe Farm organic ice creams. Three comfortable and tastefully appointed upstairs bedrooms.
OPEN: 11-3 6-11. Closed 25 Dec. **BAR MEALS:** L served all week. D served Mon-Sat 12-2 7-9. Av main course £11.50. **BREWERY/COMPANY:** Free House.
PRINCIPAL BEERS: Everards Tiger, Adnams, North Cotswold Brewery Genesis, Greene King Old Speckled Hen. **FACILITIES:** Garden: patio, outdoor eating Guide dogs only. **NOTES:** Parking 25. **ROOMS:** 3 bedrooms 3 en suite s£40 d£74

See Pub Walk on page 453

LAPWORTH
Map 07 SP17

Pick of the Pubs

The Boot 🛏
Old Warwick Rd B94 6JU ☎ 01564 782464
📠 01564 784989
Just 3 miles from the M42 (J4) and located beside the Grand Union Canal in the unspoilt village of Lapworth, the stylish Boot Inn, a 16th-century former coaching inn, is well worth seeking out. Apart from the smartly refurbished interior and lively atmosphere, it is the modern, brasserie-style food and the interesting global list of wines that attracts local diners here. The colourful printed menu lists an interesting choice of Mediterranean inspired dishes, including porcini, spinach and pinenut risotto, Toulouse sausages with spiced onions on champ, chargrilled ribeye steak with puttanesca butter, pot-roasted lamb shank with tomato, fresh herb and red wine sauce, and a good choice of fresh fish on the daily changing chalkboard, perhaps roast cod with Parmesan crust and vine tomatoes on mash. Imaginatively filled sandwiches (salmon with crème fraiche).
OPEN: 11-3 5.30-11 (11-11 summer) . Closed Dec 25.
BAR MEALS: L served all week. D served all week 12-2.30 7-10. Av main course £9. **RESTAURANT:** L served all week. D served all week 12-2.30 7-10. Av 3 course à la carte £18.
BREWERY/COMPANY: Free House.
PRINCIPAL BEERS: Greene King Old Speckled Hen, Wadworth 6X, John Smiths,. **FACILITIES:** Children welcome Children's licence Garden: patio, outdoor eating, BBQ Dogs allowed. **NOTES:** Parking 200

LONG ITCHINGTON

The Two Boats
Southam Rd CV47 8QZ ☎ 01926 812640
Dir: Located on Grand Union canal next to the Coventry to Banbury Rd (A423)
Popular pub located on a beautiful stretch of the Grand Union Canal. Canalside garden, 3 real ales and traditional pub food.

LOWER BRAILES
Map 04 SP33

The George Hotel 🍸
High St OX15 5HN ☎ 01608 685223 📠 01608 685916
Dir: B4035 toward Shipston on Stour

12th-century coaching inn built to house the monks who constructed the local church. Handy base for visiting Banbury and Hidcote Manor and touring the Vale of Evesham. Inglenook fireplaces, mullion windows and beamed ceilings

continued

inside. Frequented by Morris Men and members of the Sealed Knot. Food range includes game in season, pasta, curry, traditional steaks and salad.
OPEN: 11-11 (Sun 12-10.30). **BAR MEALS:** L served all week. D served all week 12-2 7-9.30. Av main course £6.20. **RESTAURANT:** L served all week. D served all week 12-2 7-9.30. Av 3 course à la carte £16. **BREWERY/COMPANY:** Hook Norton. **PRINCIPAL BEERS:** Hook Norton - Generation, Mild, Hooky Best, Old Hooky. **FACILITIES:** Garden: patio, Food served outside Dogs allowed Water. **NOTES:** Parking 60. **ROOMS:** 8 bedrooms 8 en suite d£30

LOWSONFORD
Map 03 SP16

Fleur De Lys ♀
Lapworth St B95 5HJ ☎ 01564 782431 ▯ 01564 782431
Dir: A34 (Birmingham to Stratford)
Converted from three cottages and a mortuary and located alongside the Stratford-upon-Avon Canal, this 17th-century pub boasts a galleried dining-room and atmospheric bars with low beams and real log fires. It was where the original Fleur de Lys pies were made. The style is casual dining with poached halibut, beef Wellington and traditional fish and chips among the wholesome dishes.
OPEN: 11-11 (Sun 12-10.30). **BAR MEALS:** L served all week. D served all week 12-2.30 6-9.30. Av main course £7.95. **BREWERY/COMPANY:** Whitbread. **PRINCIPAL BEERS:** Flowers Original, Wadworth 6X, Marstons Pedigree, Greene King Old Speckled Hen. **FACILITIES:** Children welcome Garden: outdoor eating Dogs allowed Water. **NOTES:** Parking 150

MONKS KIRBY
Map 04 SP48

The Bell Inn ⌂
Bell Ln CV23 0QY ☎ 01788 832352
Dir: Off the Fosseway Intersection with B4455

The Spanish owners of this quaint, timbered inn, originally a priory gatehouse and brewhouse cottage, describe it as 'a corner of Spain in the heart of England.' Not surprisingly, there's a strong emphasis on Mediterranean cuisine here, with an extensive tapas menu. Sample paella Valencia, chilli prawn pasta or chateaubriand Spanish style or perhaps choose from the wide-ranging selection of seafood dishes - grilled sea bass, whole lobster and grilled shark among them.
OPEN: 12-2.30 7-11. Closed 26 Dec, 1 Jan. **BAR MEALS:** L served Tue-Thu. D served Sun-Thu 12-2.30 7-11. Av main course £4.50. **RESTAURANT:** L served Tue-Sun. D served all week 12-2.30 7-11. Av 3 course à la carte £18. **BREWERY/COMPANY:** Free House. **PRINCIPAL BEERS:** Flowers, Boddingtons. **FACILITIES:** Children welcome Garden: food served outside

---

PRINCETHORPE
Map 04 SP47

The Three Horseshoes ♀
Southam Rd CV23 9PR ☎ 01926 632345
Dir: On A423 at X of B4455 & B4453
Traditional coaching inn, built about 1856, on the Fosse Way. It has a large garden with a range of children's play equipment overlooking open countryside. Beams, horse brasses and log fires characterise the bar, where a blackboard menu of home-cooked food is available.

RATLEY
Map 04 SP34

The Rose and Crown
OX15 6DS ☎ 01295 678148
Dir: Follow Edgehill signs
Following the Battle of Edgehill nearby, a Roundhead was discovered in the chimney of this 11th-century pub and beheaded in the hearth. His ghost reputedly haunts the building. Enjoy the peaceful village location and the traditional pub food, perhaps including tuna pasta bake, salmon fillet, chicken curry, cheese-topped sherherd's pie, or braised lamb hock.
OPEN: 12-2.30 6.30-11. **BAR MEALS:** L served all week. D served all week 12-2 7-9. Av main course £5.95. **BREWERY/COMPANY:** Free House. **PRINCIPAL BEERS:** Wells Bombardier & Eagle IPA, Badger Tanglefoot,. **FACILITIES:** Children welcome Garden: patio, outdoor eating Dogs allowed

---

RUGBY
Map 09 SP57

Golden Lion Inn ♦♦♦♦ ♀
Easenhall CV23 0JA ☎ 01788 832265 ▯ 01788 832878
e-mail: goldenlioninn@aol.com
Dir: from Rugby School take A426 towards Leicester

Run by the same family since 1931, this 16th-century inn has a welcoming bar and an old fashioned village setting. A sample menu includes braised mussels in cream and cider, roast breast of Gressingham duck, poached eggs with glazed hollandaise, grilled lamb cutlets and baked fillet of salmon. Rooms are individually styled, and all come with STV. One room has a Chinese four-poster.
OPEN: 11-11. **BAR MEALS:** L served all week. D served all week 12-2 6-9.45. Av main course £6.50. **RESTAURANT:** L served all week. D served all week 12-2 6-9.45. Av 3 course à la carte £18.75. Av 3 course fixed price £21.50. **BREWERY/COMPANY:** Free House. **PRINCIPAL BEERS:** Greene King Abbot Ale, Ruddles Best Bitter, Greene King IPA. **FACILITIES:** Children welcome Garden: outdoor eating, patio. **NOTES:** Parking 80. **ROOMS:** 12 bedrooms 12 en suite s£55 d£65 FR£80

England

SHIPSTON ON STOUR   Map 04 SP24

The Red Lion ◆◆◆◆
Main St, Long Compton CV36 5JS ☎ 01608 684221
📠 01608 684221
e-mail: redlionnot@aol.com
Dir: On A3400 between Shipston on Stour & Chipping Norton
Grade II listed stone-built coaching inn dating from 1748, set in
an area of outstanding natural beauty on the edge of the
Cotswolds. The bar has open fireplaces and cosy corners, and
offers a menu that includes sandwiches, jacket potatoes,
salads, grills and sizzlers. Bedrooms have been individually
designed, and come with all expected facilities.
OPEN: 11-2.30 (Sun 12-3, 7-10.30) 6-11. **BAR MEALS:** L served
all week. D served all week 12-2 7-9. Av main course £7.
RESTAURANT: D served Mon-Sat 7-9. Av 3 course à la carte £20.
BREWERY/COMPANY: Free House.
PRINCIPAL BEERS: Hook Norton, Websters, Theakstons,
Adnams, Courage Directors. **FACILITIES:** Children welcome
Garden: outdoor eating Dogs allowed. **NOTES:** Parking 60.
ROOMS: 5 bedrooms 5 en suite s£30 d£50 FR£70

White Bear Hotel 🛏 ♀
High St CV36 4AJ ☎ 01608 661558   📠 01608 661558
e-mail: inisfallen@aol.com
A fine old coaching inn, partly 16th-century, overlooking the
market place. The two beamed bars, one warmed by a log-
burning stove, are full of character. A typical menu may
include panfried chicken breast, Thai vegetable curry, sweet
and sour pork on sesame oil noodles, or gently grilled plaice
fillet.
OPEN: 11-11 (Sun 12-10.30). **BAR MEALS:** L served all week.
D served Mon-Sat 12-2 6.30-10. Av main course £8.25.
RESTAURANT: L served all week. D served Mon-Sat 12-2
6.30-10. Av 3 course à la carte £15.
BREWERY/COMPANY: Punch Taverns.
PRINCIPAL BEERS: Marstons Pedigree, Bass.
FACILITIES: Children welcome Garden: patio, Food served
outside Dogs allowed Water. **NOTES:** Parking 20.
ROOMS: 10 bedrooms 10 en suite s£25 d£50

STRATFORD-UPON-AVON   Map 03 SP25

The Dirty Duck
Waterside CV37 6BA ☎ 01789 297312   📠 01789 263751
Frequented by members of the Royal Shakespeare Company
from the nearby theatre, this traditional, partly Elizabethan inn
has a splendid front terrace with peaceful views across the
River Avon.

Pick of the Pubs

The Fox and Goose Inn ◉ ♀ **NEW**
Armscote CV37 8DD ☎ 01608 682293
📠 01608 682293
Dir: Off A3400 7m S of Stratford

Having run and sold two thriving food outlets in nearby
Stratford-upon-Avon during the nineties, successful
businesswoman Sue Gray thought she would retire and
take things easy. A year later, in April 2000, she bought
her village local and set about transforming it into a stylish
pub-restaurant with rooms. It may look like a traditional
country pub from the outside, formerly two cottages and a
blacksmith's forge, but inside a buzzy, cosmopolitan
atmosphere fills the deep red-walled bar, brightly painted
dining room, and extends upstairs to the eccentric, luxury
en suite bedrooms. Matching the decor and ambience is a
daily-changing menu listing modern pub food, which has
been drawing discerning diners for miles. Try the
seafood terrine with lemon dressing or lamb kofta with
mint yoghurt for starters, then calves' liver with bubble-
and-squeak and red wine jus, sea bass on linguine with
sweet chilli and lime pickle, or roasted pheasant with
braised lentils and bacon, and finish with dark chocolate
torte or bread-and-butter pudding. Lovely garden with
decked terrace for fine weather dining.
OPEN: 11-3 6-11 (all day in summer if busy). Closed 25-26
Dec. **BAR MEALS:** L served all week. D served all week
12-2.30 7-9.30. Av main course £10. **RESTAURANT:** L
served all week. D served all week 12-2.30 7-9.30. Av 3 course
à la carte £18. **BREWERY/COMPANY:** Free House.
PRINCIPAL BEERS: Hook Norton Old Hooky, Greene King
Old Speckled Hen, Charles Wells Bombardier, Fullers
London Pride. **FACILITIES:** Garden: Food served outside.
NOTES: Parking 20. **ROOMS:** 4 bedrooms 4 en suite s£35
d£70

Pubs with literary connections

Many of Britain's pubs are associated with some of the country's leading literary figures. One or two were regular customers, while
others were occasional callers. Charles Dickens writes about the Waggon & Horses at Beckhampton in Wiltshire in 'Pickwick
Papers', one of Scotland's most famous sons, Robert Burns, was a frequent visitor to the Black Bull at Moffat in Dumfries and
Galloway, while Thomas Hardy refers to the Turf Tavern in Oxford in 'Jude the Obscure.' In London the Jerusalem Tavern, the
Centre Page and Ye Olde Cheshire Cheese are associated with such luminaries as Samuel Johnson, Ernest Hemingway, GK
Chesterton and Arthur Conan Doyle. James Herriot and his wife celebrated their second wedding anniversary at the Wensleydale
Heifer at West Witton in the Yorkshire Dales, and JB Priestley's favourite pub was the George Inn at nearby Hubberholme. One of
Britain's more adventurous literary figures was the French-born writer Hilaire Belloc who spent much of his life in Sussex. In the
autumn of 1902 Belloc walked from Robertsbridge in the east of the county to South Harting in the west, later writing about his
odyssey and his visits to various country inns along the way. Among other pubs in Sussex, he refers to the 14th-century Blackboys
Inn near Uckfield and the Grade II listed Bridge Inn near Amberley.

TEMPLE GRAFTON
Map 04 SP15

The Blue Boar
B49 6NR ☎ 01789 750010 ▤ 01789 750635
e-mail: blueboar@covlink.co.uk
Bustling 16th-century inn with a 35-foot glass-covered well in the restaurant bar. There are welcoming open fires in winter, and in summer a patio garden with views of the Cotswold Hills. The village has links with Shakespeare, and was mentioned in the Domesday Book. All tastes are catered for with specials such as seared tuna with crayfish, char-grilled steak, baked salmon in Thai spices, and tortelloni pasta.
OPEN: 11-11. **BAR MEALS:** L served all week. D served all week 12-2 6-10. Av main course £6.95. **RESTAURANT:** L served all week. D served all week 12-2.30 6-10. Av 3 course à la carte £7.95.
BREWERY/COMPANY: Free House.
PRINCIPAL BEERS: Hook Norton, Morland Old Speckled Hen, Theakston XB. **FACILITIES:** Children welcome Garden: outdoor eating, patio Dogs allowed Guide dogs only.
ROOMS: 15 bedrooms 15 en suite s£42 d£62

WARWICK
Map 04 SP26

The Tilted Wig
11 Market Place CV34 4SA ☎ 01926 410466 & 411534
▤ 01926 495740
Dir: From M40 J15 follow A429 into Warwick, after 1.5m L into Brook St on into Market Place

Overlooking the market square, this attractive pine furnished hostelry combines the atmosphere of a brasserie, wine bar and restaurant all rolled into one. Originally a coaching inn and now a Grade II listed building. The name stems from its proximity to the Crown Court. A wide variety of food includes chicken breast wrapped in bacon with Stilton and mushroom sauce, lasagne verdi, spinach and ricotta tortelloni carbonara, minted lamb steak in red wine and mint sauce, plus a selection of salads, baguettes, sandwiches and jacket potatoes.
OPEN: 11-11 (Sun 12-10.30). Closed Dec 25. **BAR MEALS:** L served all week. D served Mon-Sat 12-3 6-9. Av main course £6.95. **BREWERY/COMPANY:** Punch Taverns.
PRINCIPAL BEERS: Tetley, Adnams Broadside.
FACILITIES: Children welcome Garden: Beer garden & patio, food served outside. **NOTES:** Parking 6. **ROOMS:** 4 bedrooms 4 en suite s£55 d£55

WHATCOTE
Map 04 SP24

Royal Oak
CV36 5EF ☎ 01295 680319
Historic 12th-century inn built for workers building churches in the area. Cromwell reputedly stopped here for a drink after the Battle of Edge Hill. Regularly changing menu.

WITHYBROOK
Map 04 SP48

The Pheasant
Main St CV7 9LT ☎ 01455 220480 ▤ 01455 220633
Dir: Off B4112 NE of Coventry

Charming 17th-century coaching inn located next to the brook from which the village takes its name. The interior is characterised by an inglenook fireplace, farm implements and horse racing photographs. The extensive menu encompasses fish and seafood; steak, chicken and grills; game; omelettes; cold meats; cheeses and sandwiches or rolls. All this plus daily specials on the blackboard.
OPEN: 12-3 6-11 (Sun 12-10.30). Closed 25-26 Dec.
BAR MEALS: L served all week. D served all week 12-2 6.30-10.
BREWERY/COMPANY: Free House.
PRINCIPAL BEERS: Courage Directors, Theakstons Best.
FACILITIES: Children welcome Garden: Dogs allowed in garden only at manager's discretion. **NOTES:** Parking 55

WOOTTON WAWEN
Map 04 SP16

The Bulls Head
Stratford Rd B95 6BD ☎ 01564 792511
Dir: On A3400
There is plenty of atmosphere at this picturesque inn, originally two large cottages. Low beams, flagstones and old pews can be found inside. A variety of dishes is available and the blackboard changes daily. Fillet of plaice on a chive and cheese crust, or Indian spicy lamb and roast aubergine may be on the menu.
OPEN: 12-3 6-11 (Sun 7-10.30 Summer all day). **BAR MEALS:** L served all week. D served all week 12-2.30 7-10. Av main course £11. **RESTAURANT:** L served Sun. D served Fri-Sat 12-2.30 7-10. Av 3 course à la carte £18. **BREWERY/COMPANY:** W'hampton & Dudley. **PRINCIPAL BEERS:** Marstons Pedigree, Banks Bitter, guest ales. **FACILITIES:** Children welcome. **NOTES:** Parking 30

Black Country Best
The Black Country has a reputation for good traditional beer and 'Unspoilt by Progress' is the motto of Banks' and Hanson's, which brew under the umbrella of Wolverhampton and Dudley Breweries. The Banks firm, established in Wolverhampton in 1875, amalgamated with tow other local companies in 1890. One of them was Thompson's of Dudley and Edwin John Thompson became managing director. His great-grandson was the managing director a century later. The firm bought another Dudley brewery, Hanson's, in 1943.

WEST MIDLANDS

BARSTON   Map 09 SP27

Pick of the Pubs

The Malt Shovel 🏨 🛏️ ♟️
Barston Ln B92 0JP ☎ 01675 443223 📠 01675 443223

Handily close to Solihull, a country pub and restaurant that features a welcoming bar with an easy-going atmosphere and a converted barn for more formal eating. The latter features original timbers, peach coloured walls and light green wooden panelling that create a warm, inviting ambience. Cask conditioned ales, imported beers and some fine wines feature in the bar whose choices run to duck spring rolls with chilli dipping sauce and marinated rump of lamb with parsnip chips, spinach and salsa verde. Starter or main dish alternatives include kidneys, bacon and field mushrooms on toast, salmon fishcakes with horseradish crème fraiche and tagliatelli with roasted Mediterranean vegetables and pesto. In the restaurant, add battered cod or rib-eye steak with fat, hand-cut chips and daily fish specials (winner of the Central Region Seafood Pub of the Year in 2001) with chocolate and apricot brioche pudding or panacotta with wild berry compôte to follow. **OPEN:** 12-3 5.30-11 (Sun 12-10.30). **BAR MEALS:** L served all week. D served Mon-Sat 12-2.30 6.30-9.45. **RESTAURANT:** L served Sun. D served Tue-Sat 12-2.30 7-9.45. Av 3 course à la carte £27. **BREWERY/COMPANY:** Free House. **PRINCIPAL BEERS:** Greene King Old Speckled Hen, Bass. **FACILITIES:** Garden: patio/terrace, outdoor eating. **NOTES:** Parking 30

COVENTRY   Map 09 SP37

The Rose and Castle
Ansty CV7 9HZ ☎ 024 76612822
Dir: From junc of M6/M69 at Walsgrave follow signs for Ansty.0.75m to pub
Small canalside pub offering a wide range of bar snacks and light meals, speciality dishes might include Ansty chicken.

NETHERTON   Map 09 SO98

Little Dry Dock
Windmill End DY2 9HU ☎ 01384 235369
Hard to find without a map, the pub is so named as the bar contains a former coal-carrying barge raised from the canal, its engine also immaculately preserved. Broccoli and cheese bake or ricotta and spinach canelloni vie for a place on the

menu with faggot and peas or Desperate Dan's pies, home-baked to a traditional recipe.
OPEN: 12-3 7-11 (Sun 7-10.30). **BAR MEALS:** L served all week. D served all week 12-2.30 6-10. Av main course £7.25. **PRINCIPAL BEERS:** Ushers Best. **FACILITIES:** Children welcome Children's licence Dogs allowed. **NOTES:** Parking 24

OLDBURY   Map 09 SO98

Waggon & Horses
17a Church St B69 3AD ☎ 0121 5525467
A listed back bar, copper ceiling and original tilework are among the character features to be found at this real ale pub. Traditional bar food. Town centre location.

SEDGLEY

Beacon Hotel
129 Bilston St DY3 1JE ☎ 01902 883380
Traditional Victorian pub and brewery dating back some 150 years; brewery tours by arrangement. Unspoilt, authentic atmosphere; large garden.

WEST BROMWICH   Map 08 SP09

The Vine
Roebuck St B70 6RD ☎ 0121 5532866 📠 0121 5255450
e-mail: suki@sukis.co.uk
Traditional Victorian pub, or authentic Indian restaurant? Well, both, actually! Regulars congregate in the cosy front bars to appreciate the quality and range of Suki Patel's real ales, maybe with a cheese ploughman's or double egg and chips. But walk through to the bright veranda restaurant and barbecue kitchen to find great value Indian food, cooked before your eyes. From chicken dupiaza to lamb bhuna or vegetable balti, you won't be disappointed.
OPEN: 11.30-2.30 5-11 (Fri-Sun all day). **BAR MEALS:** L served all week. D served all week 12-2 5-10.30. Av main course £3.75. **RESTAURANT:** D served all week 5-10.30. Av 3 course à la carte £8. **BREWERY/COMPANY:** Free House. **PRINCIPAL BEERS:** 8-12 regularly changing real ales. **FACILITIES:** Children welcome Garden: food served outside

WIGHT, ISLE OF

ARRETON   Map 04 SZ58

Hare and Hounds
Downend Rd PO30 2NU ☎ 01983 523446
📠 01983 523378
Next to Robin Hill Country Park with fine downland views, an old historic thatched pub with a long, colourful history that has been much extended and opened up in recent years. Day-long menus cater for a variety of tastes. Good walking area. Old English Inns.

The White Lion
PO30 3AA ☎ 01983 528479 📠 01983 525479
e-mail: cthewhitelion@aol.com
Popular village pub with a cosy atmosphere and a good, local reputation for well priced, good quality bar food. Garden has a children's play area and an aviary.

continued

BEMBRIDGE
Map 04 SZ68

The Crab & Lobster Inn 🛏 ♀
32 Foreland Fields Rd PO35 5TR ☎ 01983 872244
Clifftop inn with a large patio area affording magnificent views across the Solent and English Channel. Locals and tourists alike seek out the friendly atmosphere in the nautically themed bars. As the name suggests, local seafood is the speciality, with warm hors d'oeuvre of lobster, scallops, shrimps, mussels, prawns and crab, and locally caught lobster served grilled, thermidor or with salad.
OPEN: 11-3 6-11 (summer all day). **BAR MEALS:** L served all week. D served all week 12-2.30 6.30-9.30. Av main course £7.
RESTAURANT: L served all week. D served all week 12-2.30 7-10. Av 3 course à la carte £15. **BREWERY/COMPANY:** Whitbread.
PRINCIPAL BEERS: Flowers Original, Castle Eden Ale, Goddards Fuggle-Dee-Dum. **FACILITIES:** Children welcome Garden: Food served outside Dogs allowed Water. **NOTES:** Parking 40.
ROOMS: 5 bedrooms 5 en suite s£35 d£40

BONCHURCH
Map 04 SZ57

The Bonchurch Inn
Bonchurch Shute PO38 1NU ☎ 01938 852611
📠 01983 856657
e-mail: gillian@bonchurch-inn.co.uk
Dir: South coast of the Island
17th-century coaching inn with cobbled courtyard, located in picturesque island village where Charles Dickens wrote part of David Copperfield. Italian specialities feature heavily on the menu, including costata di bue, anatra all'inglese, and spaghetti bolognese. More traditional dishes are also on the menu, such as ploughman's lunches, grilled fillet steak, breaded plaice, and chicken kiev.
OPEN: 11-3.30 6.30-11. Closed 25 Dec. **BAR MEALS:** L served all week. D served all week 11-2.15 6.30-9. Av main course £6.
RESTAURANT: D served all week 6.30-9.30. Av 3 course à la carte £20. **BREWERY/COMPANY:** Free House.
PRINCIPAL BEERS: Courage Directors & Best.
FACILITIES: Children welcome Food served outside Dogs allowed Water. **NOTES:** Parking 7. **ROOMS:** 2 bedrooms 1 en suite

CHALE
Map 04 SZ47

Clarendon Hotel & Wight Mouse Inn ★ ★ 🛏
PO38 2HA ☎ 01983 730431 📠 01983 730431
e-mail: info@wightmouseinns.co.uk
Dir: On B3399 next to St Andrews church, Chale
This 17th-century coaching inn overlooks West Wight's superb coastline and is handy for Blackgang Chine and lovely sandy beaches. The family-friendly theme is being developed and the 'chilled mouse' self-contained shop unit in the garden is especially popular, while the adjacent pub has log fires, a welcoming atmosphere and over 350 malt whiskies. Straightforward bar menu that might include lemon and herb butterfly chicken breast, T-bone steak, and seafood au gratin.
OPEN: 11-midnight (Sun 12-10.30). **BAR MEALS:** L served all week. D served all week 12-9.30. **RESTAURANT:** L served all week. D served all week 12-3 6-9.30. Av 2 course fixed price £5.
BREWERY/COMPANY: Free House.
PRINCIPAL BEERS: Boddingtons, Wadworth 6X, Gales HSB, Greene King Old Speckled Hen. **FACILITIES:** Children welcome Children's licence Garden: patio, outdoor eating Dogs allowed.
NOTES: Parking 200. **ROOMS:** 12 bedrooms 12 en suite s£39 d£78

COWES
Map 04 SZ49

The Folly ♀
Folly Ln PO32 6NA ☎ 01983 297171 📠 01983 297444
e-mail: Follyinn.whippingham@whitbread.com
Reached by both land and water and very popular with the Solent's boating fraternity, the Folly is one of the island's more unusual pubs. Parts of the building are built of timber which originally came from an old sea-going French barge moored on the River Medina. Wood from the hull can be found in the nautically-themed bar. Extensive specials board menu ranging from minty lamb casserole and beef in ale pie, to mushroom Stroganoff and liver and bacon casserole.
OPEN: 11-11 (Sun 12-10.30). BHs & Cowes Week late opening.
BAR MEALS: L served all week. D served all week 12-9.30. Av main course £6.95. **PRINCIPAL BEERS:** Flowers Original, IPA, Greene King Old Speckled Hen, Gales HSB.
FACILITIES: Children welcome Garden: food served outside Dogs allowed Water. **NOTES:** Parking 30

FRESHWATER
Map 04 SZ38

Pick of the Pubs

The Red Lion 🛏 ♀
Church Place PO40 9BP ☎ 01983 754925
📠 01983 754925
Dir: In Freshwater follow signs for parish church
Tucked away in a picturesque corner of the old village, a stone's throw from All Saints Church and just a short stroll from the tidal River Yar and enjoyable walks, the civilised Red Lion Inn attracts yachting types from nearby Yarmouth, for the interesting range of food on offer - booking advisable. The open-plan bar is comfortably furnished with country-kitchen style tables and chairs, some antique pine and relaxing sofas. Arrive early as the blackboard menu may rapidly shorten as the evening progresses - only so many portions of each dish are prepared daily. Begin with crab au gratin, clam chowder, smoked trout terrine and delicious herring roes on toast, then tackle home-made fishcakes with parsley sauce, sea bass with fennel and Pernod, rack of lamb with redcurrant gravy, sausages and mash with onion gravy or fresh local lobster and whole grilled plaice. Puddings range from bread-and-apricot pudding and citrus cheesecake to home-made ice creams. Unlikely to run out are the four real ales, including the excellent Goddards Best brewed on the island.
OPEN: 11.30-3 (Sun 12-3) 5.30-11 (Sun 7-10.30).
BAR MEALS: L served all week. D served all week 12-2 6.30-9. Av main course £9.
BREWERY/COMPANY: Whitbread.
PRINCIPAL BEERS: Flowers Original, Fullers London Pride, Goddards. **FACILITIES:** Garden: Food served outside Dogs allowed. **NOTES:** Parking 20

NITON
Map 04 SZ57

Buddle Inn ♀
St Catherines Rd PO38 2NE ☎ 01983 730243
e-mail: buddleinn@aol.com
Dir: Take A3055 from Ventnor. In Niton take 1st L signed 'to the lighthouse'
Enjoy the relaxed, unhurried atmosphere of this cliff-top pub, one of the island's oldest hostelries. Popular with walkers and
continued

England

characterised by stone flags, oak beams and a broad fireplace. Once a smugglers' haunt and with a little imagination it's possible to picture wreckers concealing their booty here on dark stormy nights. Wide selection of food includes home-made pies and quiches, curry and home-cooked ham, as well as other pub favourites, grills and seafood specialities. **OPEN:** 11-11 (Sun 12-10.30). **BAR MEALS:** L served all week. D served all week 11.30-2.45 6-9.30. Av main course £10. **BREWERY/COMPANY:** Whitbread. **PRINCIPAL BEERS:** Flowers Original, Bass, Greene King Abbot Ale, Adnams Best. **FACILITIES:** Garden: food served outside Dogs allowed Water. **NOTES:** Parking 50

ROOKLEY

The Chequers
Niton Rd PO38 3NZ ☎ 01983 840314
Overlooking rolling farmland, this family-friendly pub was once a Customs and Excise house, but now comes complete with playhouse, toboggan and pony rides in the garden. For those who want a quiet drink, there is also a child-free area. Food all day. Lunchtime carvery.

The Isle of Wight Coast Path

Following this popular trail is the best way to appreciate the island's coastal scenery and stunning views. Go there in early summer or autumn when the place is a lot less crowded, allow five or six days to complete the 65-mile walk at a leisurely pace and feel the sun on your back and the sea breeze on your face. From Yarmouth, follow the trail in a clockwise direction, calling in at the New Inn in Shalfleet, the clifftop Crab & Lobster Inn at Bembridge and the beach-side Fisherman's Cottage at Shanklin. The island's south coast offers some of the best scenery and here you may like to relax at the Spyglass at Ventnor, the Buddle Inn at Niton, the Clarendon Hotel and Wight Mouse Inn at Chale or the Red Lion at Freshwater.

SEAVIEW   Map 04 SZ69

Pick of the Pubs

Seaview Hotel & Restaurant ◉ ◉ ★ ★ ★ 🕭 ♀
High St PO34 5EX ☎ 01983 612711 🖹 01983 613729
e-mail: reception@seaviewhotel.co.uk
Dir: B3330 Ryde-Seaview rd, turn L via Puckpool along seafront duver road, hotel is situated on left hand side adjacent to the sea
Would that more British seaside inns would aspire to the standards set here for over 20 years. Unpretentious yet highly professional service adds an extra dimension to this small property by Seaview's picturesque sailing village that has become one of the island's best loved. The food, more brasserie than pub, is entirely in keeping with the setting, and a warm welcome is extended to all-comers. Island farmers and fishermen are well supported by a purchasing policy that brings to the table soft herring roes with lemon and capers, a ramekin of local crab, and warm goats' cheese and smoked Island tomato tart amongst the varied starters. Local plaice fillets may then appear with thermidor sauce, breast of chicken with fettucine and roast peppers and local pork loin stuffed with black pudding in cider sauce. Apple pancakes with spiced berries and tipsy roast pears add an extra dimension to dessert. The conservatory is a delight for casual dining, while overnight residents are pampered with exclusive dining and notably comfortable accommodation.
OPEN: 11-2.30 6-11. Closed Dec 24-27. **BAR MEALS:** L served all week. D served all week 12-2 7-9.30. Av main course £6. **RESTAURANT:** L served all week. D served Mon-Sat 12-2 7.30-9.30. Av 3 course à la carte £20. **BREWERY/COMPANY:** Free House. **PRINCIPAL BEERS:** Goddards, Greene King Abbot Ale. **FACILITIES:** Children welcome Garden: Courtyard/patio, food served outside Dogs allowed. **NOTES:** Parking 12. **ROOMS:** 16 bedrooms 16 en suite s£55 d£70

SHALFLEET   Map 04 SZ48

The New Inn 🕭 ♀
Mill Ln PO30 4NS ☎ 01983 531314 🖹 01983 531314
e-mail: martin.bullock@virgin.net
Dating back to 1753 and one of the Isle of Wight's best-known watering holes, the New Inn is conveniently located on the 65-mile coast path, near the National Trust's Newtown River and Nature Reserve. Renowned for its seafood and use of local produce. Expect whole crab salad, local lobster and mackerel and seafood royale, in addition to steak Diane and chicken supreme. Wide-ranging international wine list.
OPEN: 11-3 6-11 (Jul-Aug all day). **BAR MEALS:** L served all week. D served all week 12-2.30 6-10. Av main course £9.95. **RESTAURANT:** L served all week. D served all week 12-2.30 6-10. Av 3 course à la carte £20. **BREWERY/COMPANY:** Free House. **PRINCIPAL BEERS:** Bass, Wadworth 6X, Flowers Original. **FACILITIES:** Garden: food served outside Dogs allowed Water. **NOTES:** Parking 20

SHANKLIN   Map 04 SZ58

Fisherman's Cottage ♀
Shanklin Chine PO37 6BN ☎ 01983 863882
🖹 01983 874215
Beautifully situated right on Appley beach, the thatched cottage was built in 1817 by Shanklin's first operator of covered

continued

'bathing machines'. Inside the low-beamed bar, the pub's history is recorded in the period pictures that line the walls. The simple menu includes sandwiches, salads, jacket potatoes, and popular favourites like battered cod, and jumbo sausage hot dogs. The pub is closed from November to February.
OPEN: Mar-Oct 11-3 7-11. **BAR MEALS:** L served all week. D served all week 11-2 7-9. Av main course £5.
BREWERY/COMPANY: Free House.
PRINCIPAL BEERS: Courage Directors. **FACILITIES:** Children welcome Garden: Large patio area, food served outside Dogs allowed No credit cards

SHORWELL
Map 04 SZ48

The Crown Inn
Walkers Ln PO30 3JZ ☎ 01983 740293 ▤ 01983 740293
Dir: From Newport to Carisbrooke High St, then L at rdbt at top of hill, take B3323 to Shorwell

Opposite the church in the centre of the village, this 17th-century pub is set in award-winning gardens complete with a play area, and a stream, with huge trout and a colony of mallards. Food is offered from a bar menu and specials board with local fish - sea bass with crab sauce - and options such as spiced lamb chops with mango salsa and chicken supreme with apricots and brandy.
OPEN: 10.30-3 6-11. **BAR MEALS:** L served all week. D served all week 12-3 6-10. Av main course £6.95.
BREWERY/COMPANY: Whitbread.
PRINCIPAL BEERS: Whitbread Boddingtons, Wadworth 6X, Flowers Original, Badger Tanglefoot. **FACILITIES:** Children welcome Garden: Dogs allowed, must be on lead.
NOTES: Parking 60

Darts
Although darts is now regarded as the archetypal pub game, its history is shrouded in almost total mystery and it may not have entered the pub scene until well into the 19th century. The original board may have been the end of a barrel, with the doubles ring as its outer ring. The accepted arrangement of numbers round the rim dates from the 1890s, but there are variant types of board in different areas of the country. The Yorkshire board, for instance, has no trebles ring. Nor does the Lancashire or Manchester board, which has a very narrow doubles ring and is customarily kept soaked in beer when not in use.

VENTNOR
Map 04 SZ57

The Spyglass Inn
The Esplanade PO38 1JX ☎ 01983 855338
▤ 01983 855220
Dir: Town centre
The huge collection of seafaring memorabilia fascinates visitors to this popular 19th-century pub, which is located at the western end of Ventnor Esplanade. An extensive terrace overlooking the sea is ideal for summer drinks and meals. Seafood is the speciality, including Ventnor Bay lobsters and crabs. Live music is provided most evenings - country, folk or jazz.

OPEN: 10.30-3 (Sun 12) 6.30-11 (May-Oct 10.30-11, open all day). **BAR MEALS:** L served all week. D served all week 12-2.15 7-9.30. Av main course £5.50. **RESTAURANT:** L served all week. D served all week 12-2.15 7-9.30. **BREWERY/COMPANY:** Free House. **PRINCIPAL BEERS:** Badger Dorset Best & Tanglefoot, Ventnor Golden, Ventor Oyster Stout. **FACILITIES:** Children welcome Garden: Terraces, Food served outside Dogs allowed. **NOTES:** Parking 10. **ROOMS:** 3 bedrooms 3 en suite d£45

WILTSHIRE

ALDERBURY
Map 03 SU12

The Green Dragon
Old Rd SP5 3AR ☎ 01722 710263
Dir: 1m off A36 (Southampton/Salisbury rd)
There are fine views of Salisbury Cathedral from this 14th-century pub. Dickens wrote Martin Chuzzlewit here, and called the pub the Blue Dragon. An interesting and daily changing menu features home-made meat and vegetarian dishes using locally sourced produce.
OPEN: 11.30-2.30 (Sun 12-3, 7-10.30) 6-11. **BAR MEALS:** L served all week. D served all week 12-2 7-9. Av main course £5. **RESTAURANT:** L served Tue-Sun. D served Tue-Sat 12-2 7-9. Av 3 course à la carte £16. **BREWERY/COMPANY:** Hall & Woodhouse. **PRINCIPAL BEERS:** Badger Dorset Best & Tanglefoot, Guinness. **FACILITIES:** Children welcome Garden: BBQ, outdoor eating Dogs allowed outside on lead. **NOTES:** Parking 10

 Pubs offering a good choice of seafood on the menu.

England

ALVEDISTON

Pick of the Pubs

The Crown
SP5 5JY ☎ 01722 780335 🗎 01722 780836
Dir: 2.5m off A30 approx half-way between Salisbury and Shaftesbury

Tastefully extended 15th-century thatched inn tucked away in a tiny hamlet in the tranquil Ebble Valley between Salisbury and Shaftesbury. Recently refurbished under new owners, the Crown maintains an old-world character with head-cracking low beams, two inglenook fireplaces and comfortable old furnishings throughout the three interconnecting rooms. Expect a relaxing atmosphere and freshly prepared food listed on chalkboards in the main bar area. In addition to traditional home-made favourites, look out for seasonal game and fresh fish dishes, perhaps sea bass on crab and chive mash, cod wrapped in Parma ham, salmon fishcakes and whole roasted plaice with lemon and thyme liquor. Four en suite bedrooms. More reports please!
OPEN: 11.30-3 6-11 (Sun 12-3, 7-10.30). **BAR MEALS:** L served all week. D served all week 12-2 6-9.30. Av main course £5. **RESTAURANT:** L served all week. D served all week 12-2 6-9.30. Av 3 course à la carte £18. **BREWERY/COMPANY:** Free House **FACILITIES:** Children welcome Garden: outdoor eating, patio, Dogs allowed Water. **NOTES:** Parking 40. **ROOMS:** 4 bedrooms 4 en suite s£25 d£47.50 FR£70

AXFORD   Map 04 SU27

Red Lion Inn
SN8 2HA ☎ 01672 520271 🗎 01672 520271
Dir: M4 J15, A246 Marlborough centre. Follow signs for Ramsbury. Inn 3m
17th-century brick and flint inn with peaceful views across the unspoilt beauty of the Kennet Valley. Fresh fish and game (in season) feature on the extensive specials blackboard. Typical dishes include lobster thermidor, Dover sole, fillet of beef Portuguaise, roast local pheasant and trout grilled in butter and almonds. Bar snacks and Sunday roasts are also available.
OPEN: 11-3 6.30-11. **BAR MEALS:** L served all week. D served all week 12-2 7-10. Av main course £4.95. **RESTAURANT:** L served all week. D served all week 12-2 7-10. Av 3 course à la carte £20. **BREWERY/COMPANY:** Free House.
PRINCIPAL BEERS: Hook Norton Best, Wadworth 6X, guest beers. **FACILITIES:** Children welcome Garden: outdoor eating, patio. **NOTES:** Parking 30

BARFORD ST MARTIN   Map 03 SU03

Barford Inn
SP3 4AB ☎ 01722 742242 🗎 01722 743606
e-mail: ido@barfordinn.co.uk
Dir: on A30 5m W of Salisbury
Just five miles from Salisbury is this 16th-century former coaching inn with welcoming lounge, lower bar area and intimate snug. During WWII the Wiltshire Yeomanry dedicated a tank to the pub, then known as The Green Dragon. Specials may include chargrilled valentine of pork, pan-fried escalope of veal, whole sea bass or baked aubergine. Friday night is Israeli BBQ night. The bright, well-appointed bedrooms are in an annexe.
OPEN: 11-11. Closed Dec 25. **BAR MEALS:** L served all week. D served all week 12-2.30 7-9.30. Av main course £9. **RESTAURANT:** L served all week. D served all week 12-2.30 7-9.30. Av 3 course à la carte £20. **BREWERY/COMPANY:** Hall & Woodhouse. **PRINCIPAL BEERS:** Badger Dorset Best, Badger Tanglefoot. **FACILITIES:** Children welcome Garden: Food served outside. **NOTES:** Parking 40. **ROOMS:** 4 bedrooms 4 en suite s£40 d£45

BECKHAMPTON   Map 03 SU06

Waggon & Horses
SN8 1QJ ☎ 01672 539418
A beautiful thatched coaching inn dating back 400 years located close to the Avebury Stone circles. It was mentioned in Dickens"Pickwick Papers'.

BOX   Map 03 ST86

The Quarrymans Arms ⚲
Box Hill SN13 8HN ☎ 01225 743569
Dir: Phone the pub for accurate directions
A 300-year-old miners' pub tucked away in the hillside with splendid views over the Colerne Valley - great for walkers, cavers, potholers and cyclists. The snack menu lists burgers, fish and chips and macaroni cheese, while the main menu offers Barbary duck, pork Dijonnaise, and pan-fried tuna steak.
OPEN: 11-3.30 6-11 (Sun 11-3.30, 7-10.30). **BAR MEALS:** L served all week. D served all week 11-3 6.30-10.30. Av main course £7.95. **RESTAURANT:** L served all week. D served all week 11-3 6.30-10.30. Av 3 course à la carte £15.
BREWERY/COMPANY: Free House.
PRINCIPAL BEERS: Butcombe, Wadworth 6X, Moles.
FACILITIES: Children welcome Garden: enclosed, patio, BBQ Dogs allowed. **NOTES:** Parking 25. **ROOMS:** 2 bedrooms s£25 d£45 FR£55

BRADFORD-ON-AVON   Map 03 ST86

The Canal Tavern
49 Frome Rd BA15 1LE ☎ 01225 867426 865232
Dir: From Bath A4 to Bathford roundabout then A363
Kennet and Avon canalside pub displaying all manner of waterways memorabilia.

◆ AA inspected guest accommodation

Hop Pole Inn, Limpley Stoke

Pub**WALK**

WILTSHIRE

HOP POLE INN, LIMPLEY STOKE

Woods Hill, Lower Limpley Stoke BA3 6HS.

Tel: 01225 723134

Directions: off A36 S of Bath

Historic stone-built pub, formerly a monks wine lodge dating from 1580, situated just a short stroll from the Kennet and Avon Canal. Speciality home-made pies and local game in season feature on the wide-ranging menu.

Open: 11-2.30 6-11. Bar Meals: 12-2.15 6.30-9.15. Children welcome. Garden. Parking.

(see page 473 for full entry)

This delightful short walk through the wooded Avon Valley incorporates the peaceful tow path beside the Kennet and Avon Canal, and grand views across Wiltshire and the city of Bath.

On leaving the pub turn left and walk to the B3108. Turn right under the railway bridge watching for traffic, Cross over the River Avon bridge and climb the stile on your right. Walk to the end of the field and join the canal tow path. Turn right along this attractive stretch of canal for a mile to the next bridge, cross it and climb the stile left into the field. Climb the hill, cross the next stile and walk up a steep track, reaching the lane via a flight of steps.

Turn left and continue to a hairpin bend in the road. Turn right up a short but steep section of hill. Deep in the ground under your feet are the tunnels where the limestone was cut to build the canals and aqueducts. Continue past Dorothy House, the local hospice, on the outskirts of Winsley. At the crossroads turn left. Cross over the Winsley by-pass and walk to your left.

At the next junction turn right opposite the entrance to Avon Park Care Centre. (At this point, for a shorter walk, continue down the hill, under the bridge, turn left and back to the Hop Pole).

The longer walk crosses the high limestone plateau. Continue along the lane between well built stone walls, passing Conkwell Grange Farm and Horse Stud. Having passed two houses on your right, after a sharp bend look for a track on your left. Follow the track steeply down through the woods to the canal and Dundas aqueduct below. Join the tow path and cross John Rennie's magnificent edifice high above the river and railway. At Dundas Basin cross the footbridge, note the industrial archaeology, and cross the lifting bridge at the entrance to the Somerset Coal Canal and walk back over the aqueduct on the other side. Continue along the towpath to the main road. Turn right, over the river, under the railway bridge, turn left and walk back to the Hop Pole.

Distance: 4.5 miles (7.2km)
Map: OS Landranger 172
Terrain: farmland, woodland, country lanes
Paths: field and woodland paths, tow path
Gradient: one steep ascent and descent

Walk submitted by:
The Hop Pole Inn

The Kennet and Avon Canal

BRADFORD-ON-AVON continued

The Dandy Lion ♀
35 Market St BA15 1LL ☎ 01225 863433 ▤ 01225 869169
A 17th-century terraced building whose interior decor reflects the town's busy antique trade, and offers both convivial pub dining and exclusivity in an upper restaurant. Light bites and pasta with daily specials - goats' cheese tart, faggots and mash and minted lamb curry - by day. Gravadlax and self-cooked steaks on "hot stones" at night.
OPEN: 10.30-3 6-11 (Sun 11.30-3 7-10.30). **BAR MEALS:** L served all week 12-2.15. Av main course £4.95. **RESTAURANT:** L served Sun. D served all week 12-2.15 7-9.30. Av 3 course à la carte £15.95. **BREWERY/COMPANY:** Wadworth.
PRINCIPAL BEERS: Butcombe, Wadworth 6X, Henrys IPA & Seasonal Ales. **FACILITIES:** Children welcome Children's licence

Pick of the Pubs

The Kings Arms & Chancel Restaurant ♀
Monkton Farleigh BA15 2QQ ☎ 01225 858705
e-mail: nils@kingsarms-bath.org.uk
Dir: Follow A4 from Bath to Bradford, At Bathford join A363, turning L to Monkton Farleigh
Just five minutes' drive from Bradford-on-Avon in the quaint rural village of Monkton Farleigh, this historic Bath stone and pan-tiled building - dating back to the 11th Century - was originally a monks' retreat detached from the nearby monastery. Steeped in history, its many features include stone mullion windows and flagged floor in the Chancel Bar and a vast inglenook in the medieval-style restaurant, hung with old tapestries and pewter plates. Approached by way of an arboreal courtyard, the pub leads through to an enclosed garden with parasolled tables, home in an aviary to golden pheasants, lovebirds and an African long-eared golden owl. Bar food at lunch only includes burgers of beef - with bacon and cheese - tuna, minted lamb and Cajun chicken with melted Mozzarella. Bath bangers with mustard mash and onion gravy and crispy chicken Caesar salad are typical alternatives. Dinner promises chicken liver parfait with brioche, crusted pork loin with braised leeks and peppercorn sauce and rhubarb tarte tatin.
OPEN: 11-11 (Sun 12-10.30). **BAR MEALS:** L served Tue-Sun. D served Tue-Sun 12-3 5.30-10. **RESTAURANT:** L served Tue-Sun. D served Tue-Sun 12-3 5.30-10. Av 3 course à la carte £31. **PRINCIPAL BEERS:** Bass, Wadworth 6X, Butcombe Bitter. **FACILITIES:** Children welcome Children's licence Garden: outdoor eating, patio, Dogs allowed. **NOTES:** Parking 45

AA The Restaurant Guide 2002

The right choice every time with this invaluable guide for gourmets

www.theAA.com

AA Lifestyle Guides

BRINKWORTH   Map 03 SU08

Pick of the Pubs

The Three Crowns 🍽 ♀
SN15 5AF ☎ 01666 510366 ▤ 01666 510303
Dir: A3102 to Wootton Bassett, then B4042, 5m to Brinkworth
At the very edge of Dauntsey Vale by the green of a quiet village between Wootton Bassett and Malmesbury, stands this 200-year-old inn, whose stone-flagged conservatory, newly-added garden room extension and gas-heated summer dining patio are a draw to a food-conscious clientele.
Main meal choices are unusual and often ambitious, including kangaroo, crocodile and ostrich - marinated and griddled - alongside more traditional, upmarket pub food listed on daily-changing blackboards at prices to match. For a lunchtime snack try one of the enormous ploughman's platters, filled jacket potatoes or huge double-decker rolls. A lack of starters leads to stuffed roast guinea fowl with red wine sauce, lamb and mint pie, Somerset wild boar, pan-fried sea bass with raspberry olive oil dressing, tuna en croute with white wine, prawn and cream sauce. Dishes are freshly prepared to order and accompanied by a large dish of six crisply cooked vegetables.
Delicious home-made puddings and an ever-improving list of wines; 10 by the glass. Enjoy a decent pint of Archers Village in the popular bar, now a 'no eating' zone.
OPEN: 10-3 6-11. Closed 25 Dec. **BAR MEALS:** L served all week 12-2. Av main course £14. **RESTAURANT:** L served all week. D served all week 12-2 6-9.30. Av 3 course à la carte £20. **BREWERY/COMPANY:** Whitbread.
PRINCIPAL BEERS: Wadworth 6X, Boddingtons, Castle Eden, Fullers London Pride. **FACILITIES:** Children welcome Children's licence Garden: patio, outdoor eating Dogs allowed garden & bar only. **NOTES:** Parking 40

BROAD CHALKE   Map 03 SU02

The Queens Head Inn ♀
1 North St SP5 5EN ☎ 01722 780344 ▤ 01722 780344
Dir: Take A354 from Salisbury toward Blandford Forum, at Coombe Bissett turn R toward Bishopstone, follow rd for 4m
Attractive 15th-century inn with friendly atmosphere and low-beamed bars, once the village bakehouse. Sample steak pie, home-made chicken and mushroom pie, or Spanish casserole from the appealing menu. Alternatively, try one of the seasonal game dishes, such as pheasant and bacon, jugged hare or rabbit, from the specials board.
OPEN: 11-3 6-11 (Sun 12-3, 7-10.30). **BAR MEALS:** L served all week. D served all week 12-2 7-9. Av main course £6.50. **RESTAURANT:** L served all week. D served all week 12-2 7-9. **BREWERY/COMPANY:** Free House.
PRINCIPAL BEERS: Greene King IPA & Old Speckled Hen, Wadworth 6X. **FACILITIES:** Children welcome Garden: Patio garden, food served outdoors. **NOTES:** Parking 30. **ROOMS:** 4 bedrooms 4 en suite s£30 d£50 FR£65

BROMHAM
Map 03 ST96

The Greyhound Inn
SN15 2HA ☎ 01380 850241
Dir: Chippenham rd from Devizes for 4m. L into Bromham
New proprietors welcome visitors to this 300-year-old pub, which has an inside artesian well, beamed ceilings, and an open fireplace. Large garden and skittle alley.

BURTON
Map 03 ST87

The Old House at Home 🐑 Ⴅ
SN14 7LT ☎ 01454 218227 📠 01454 218865
Dir: On B4039 NW of Chippenham
A soft stone, ivy-clad pub with beautiful landscaped gardens and a waterfall. Inside there are low beams and an open fire. Overseen by the same landlord for over fifteen years. The kitchen offers a good fish choice, vegetarian and pasta dishes, and traditional pub meals. Favourites include lamb cutlets with champ, salmon and asparagus, woodland duck breast with stuffing, and king scallops in Cointreau.
OPEN: 11.30-2.30 7-11 (w/end 11.30-3, Sun 7-10.30) (closed Tue lunch). **BAR MEALS:** L served Wed-Mon. D served all week 12-2 7-10. Av main course £11. **BREWERY/COMPANY:** Free House.
PRINCIPAL BEERS: Wadworth 6X, Smiles Best, Bass.
FACILITIES: Children welcome Garden: BBQ, outdoor eating.
NOTES: Parking 25

CALNE
Map 03 ST97

Lansdowne Arms
Derry Hill SN11 9NS ☎ 01249 812422
Coaching house dating from 1843, close to Bowood House, with scenic views along the Avon Valley to Bath. Home-cooked food; daily specials. Wadworth.

White Horse Inn
Compton Bassett SN11 8RG ☎ 01249 813118
📠 01249 811595
Dating back to the 18th century, the White Horse is a popular watering hole on the Wiltshire tourist trail. Historic towns and villages such as Bath, Marlborough, Lacock and Avebury lie within easy reach. Well-planned, imaginative menu offers the likes of lemon sole, spicy meatballs with spaghetti and tomato sauce, mixed grill and devilled kidneys with garlic croutons. Try one of the popular real ales.
OPEN: 11-3 5-11. **BAR MEALS:** L served all week 12-2 7-9.30. D served all week 12-2 7-9.30. Av main course £10.95. **RESTAURANT:** L served all week. D served all week 12-2 7-9.30. Av 3 course à la carte £25. **BREWERY/COMPANY:** Free House.
PRINCIPAL BEERS: Wadworth 6X, Hook Norton,.
FACILITIES: Garden: food served outside Dogs allowed.
NOTES: Parking 75. **ROOMS:** 7 bedrooms 7 en suite s£39.50 d£59.50

CASTLE COMBE
Map 03 ST87

The White Hart Ⴅ
Castle St SN14 7HS ☎ 01249 782295
Historic, part-timbered 14th century pub in a classic village which film fans will recognise as Puddleby-on-the-Marsh in the movie version of Doctor Doolittle. Many charming features inside the inn, including low ceilings, beams and a cosy log fire. Pleasant patio gardens, sunny conservatory and sheltered courtyard also attract customers. Extensive menu offers the likes of cod and chips, mixed grill and steak and ale pie.
continued

OPEN: 11-3 6-11 (Sun 12-10.30). **BAR MEALS:** L served all week. D served all week 12-2 6.30-9. Av main course £5.95. **RESTAURANT:** L served all week. D served all week 12-2 6.30-9. Av 3 course à la carte £12. **BREWERY/COMPANY:** Wadworth. **PRINCIPAL BEERS:** Wadworth 6X & Henry's Original IPA. **FACILITIES:** Children welcome Garden: outdoor eating Dogs allowed

CHILMARK
Map 03 ST93

The Black Dog 🐑 Ⴅ NEW
SP3 5AH ☎ 01722 716344 📠 01722 716124
Set beside the B3089 west of Salisbury in the pretty village of Chilmark, the 15th-century stone-built Black Dog is a great country pub. First and foremost, it is the village local, yet successfully combines its unspoilt historic charm with an appealing modern decor, tip-top local ales, a warm, friendly welcome, and offers excellent contemporary pub food. Classic main bar with red and black tiled floor, a huge table topped with unusual dried flower arrangements, and a chatty atmosphere; adjoining beamed and cosy dining areas. Good, popular food ranges from Black Dog burger, imaginatively filled baguettes and venison in red wine casserole at lunchtime, to modern, well presented evening dishes listed on the interesting carte. For starters, try lime and basil marinated salmon with hollandaise or smoked chicken and asparagus Caesar salad with Parmesan shavings, followed by grilled Torbay sole, roast monkfish on lightly curried mussels with cream, coconut and lime, or a prime fillet steak with cracked black pepper, Dijon mustard, brandy and cream. Huge rear garden for summer imbibing.
OPEN: 11-3 6-11. **BAR MEALS:** L served all week. D served all week 12-2.30 6-9.30. Av main course £6.25.
RESTAURANT: L served all week. D served all week 12-2.30 6-9.30. Av 3 course à la carte £20.
PRINCIPAL BEERS: Bass, Wadworth 6X.
FACILITIES: Children welcome Garden: Food served outside Dogs allowed. **NOTES:** Parking 30

CHRISTIAN MALFORD
Map 03 ST97

The Rising Sun NEW
Station Rd SN15 4BL ☎ 01249 721571 📠 01249 721571
e-mail: risingsun@tesco.net
Dir: From M4 J 17 take B4122 towards Sutton Benger, turn L on to the B4069, pass through Sutton Benger after 1M you come into Christian Malford, turn R into the village (station road) the pub is the last building on the L
Since taking over this cosy free house in 1999, Colin and Helen Hutchens have created an informal village local with homely furnishings and real fires. Freshly cooked local and organic produce feature on the weekly changing menus, and popular lunchtime bar snacks give place to more adventurous evening fare. Expect pheasant or venison, peppered steak with mustard mash, or rabbit in white wine with bubble-and-squeak.
OPEN: 12-2.30 6.30-11. **BAR MEALS:** L served all week. D served all week 12-2 6.30-10. Av main course £5.
RESTAURANT: L served all week. D served all week 12-2 6.30-10. Av 3 course à la carte £17. **BREWERY/COMPANY:** Free House.
PRINCIPAL BEERS: Hook Norton & guest ale.
FACILITIES: Garden: food served outside Dogs allowed Water.
NOTES: Parking 15

Wadworth & Co Ltd

of Devizes was founded in 1875 by Henry Wadworth and since then has become one of England's finest breweries. Wadworth left no heir, but his partner and brother-in-law did, and his family, the Bartholomews, still own and operate the company. The current HQ is at the Northgate Brewery that was built by the founder in 1885, and some of the original equipment is still in use. The building was constructed to allow gravity to do much of the work, as electricity was then not so readily available. Other traditional procedures remain in the shape of dray horses and one of only eight beer barrel coopers still working in Britain.

COLLINGBOURNE DUCIS   Map 04 SU25

The Shears Inn & Country Hotel

The Cadley Rd SN8 3ED ☎ 01264 850304
🖹 01264 850220
Dir: On A338 NW of Andover & Ludgershall
A traditional thatched country inn with beams and brick floors, the Shears is well situated for both Marlborough and Salisbury.

CORSHAM   Map 03 ST87

Methuen Arms Hotel

2 High St SN13 0HB ☎ 01249 714867 🖹 01249 712004
Dir: Town centre, on A4 between Bath & Chippenham
Part of the building began as a nunnery in the 14th century, and mullioned windows can still be seen in the long bar skittle alley, where Prince Phillip used to play, back in 1947. Built of Cotswold stone with a Georgian facade, the hotel once belonged to Lord Methuen, and now serves a range of daily specials.

CORSLEY HEATH   Map 03 ST84

The Royal Oak Inn

BA12 7PR ☎ 01373 832238
Dir: On A362 between Warminster & Frome
Situated on the edge of the Longleat estate, this 16th-century inn was built on the site of a 15th-century monk's retreat and is owned by the Marquis of Bath.

CORTON   Map 03 ST94

Pick of the Pubs

The Dove Inn 🍺 ♟

BA12 0SZ ☎ 01985 850109 🖹 01985 851041
e-mail: info@thedove.co.uk
Dir: Between Salisbury & Warminster on minor rd (parallel to A36)

Tucked away off the beaten track, this delightful Victorian free house stands in a quiet hamlet in the peaceful Wylye Valley. The pleasantly refurbished bar features an unusual central fireplace, and there's a good range of well kept real ales. Five newly developed en suite bedrooms make The Dove an ideal touring base; Bath, Salisbury and Stonehenge are all within easy reach. Besides a busy local trade, the pub's varied and original menu draws customers from further afield. Popular lunchtime bar meals give way to a full evening carte. Starters like smoked duck with kumquats, oven-baked blue cheese and gooseberries, or home-made gravad lax with beetroot and Drambuie might precede spicy wild venison, veal au gratin, or chicken with haggis, and locally-shot pigeon. Leave room for fruit pies and crumbles, peach crème brûlée, or lemon syllabub with shortbread.
OPEN: 12-3 (Sat-Sun 12-3.30) 6.30-11 (Sat 7-11 Sun 7-10.30).
BAR MEALS: L served all week. D served all week 12-2.30
7-9.30. **RESTAURANT:** L served all week. D served all week
12-3 7-9.30. **BREWERY/COMPANY:** Free House.
PRINCIPAL BEERS: Oakhill Best, Brakspear, Wadworth 6X,
Fullers London Pride. **FACILITIES:** Children welcome
Garden: patio, outdoor eating Dogs allowed Water.
NOTES: Parking 24. **ROOMS:** 4 bedrooms 4 en suite s£50
d£70 FR£90

DEVIZES   Map 03 SU06

The Bear Hotel ★ ★ ★ ♟

The Market Place SN10 1HS ☎ 01380 722444
🖹 01380 722450
e-mail: beardevizes@aol.com
This attractive coaching inn dates from 1599, and now combines modern facilities with old-fashioned hospitality. You'll find old beams, log fires and fresh flowers throughout the hotel's comfortable lounges and bars. Expect an extensive choice of baguettes, bar meals and grills, as well as interesting restaurant fare that includes noisettes of lamb, pheasant with smoked bacon and mushroom duxelle, Dover sole, and leek, mushroom and saffron risotto. The bedrooms vary in size, but all are well equipped and most have refurbished bathrooms.

continued

OPEN: 9.30-11. Closed 25-26 Dec. **BAR MEALS:** L served all week. D served all week 11-2.30 7-9.15. Av main course £6.50. **RESTAURANT:** L served all week. D served all week 12.15-1.45 7-9.15. Av 3 course à la carte £19.50. **BREWERY/COMPANY:** Wadworth. **PRINCIPAL BEERS:** Wadworth 6X. **FACILITIES:** Children welcome Dogs allowed. **ROOMS:** 24 bedrooms 24 en suite s£60 d£88 FR£98

The Elm Tree
Long St SN10 1NJ ☎ 01380 723834
16th-century town centre coaching inn with a sheltered courtyard and a menu specialising in Italian cooking. Wadworth.

Fox & Hounds
Nursteed Rd SN10 3HJ ☎ 01380 723789 ⓘ 01380 723789
Dir: On A342 between Devizes & Andover, 1m from Devizes town boundary
Thatched former farmhouse located near its owning brewery - customers are guaranteed a tip-top pint of Wadworth 6X.

The Raven Inn
Poulshot Rd SN10 1RW ☎ 01380 828271 ⓘ 01380 828271
Dir: Take A361 out of Devizes towards Trowbridge, turn L at sign for Poulshot
Traditional, part timbered, 18th-century Wiltshire inn situated just beyond the northern edge of the spacious village green. Classic Kennet & Avon Canal tow path walking beside the nearby famous Caen Hill locks.

EAST KNOYLE   Map 03 ST83

The Fox and Hounds
The Green SP3 6BN ☎ 01747 830573 ⓘ 01747 830865
Dir: Off A303 onto A350 for 200yds, then R. Pub 1 0.5m on L
Originally three cottages, dating from the late 15th century, this thatched pub overlooks the Blackmore Vale with fine views for up to 20 miles. East Knoyle is the birthplace of Sir Christopher Wren, and was also home to Lady Jayne Seymour.

EBBESBOURNE WAKE   Map 03 ST92

Pick of the Pubs

The Horseshoe
Handley St SP5 5JF ☎ 01722 780474
Nestling in the folds of the Wiltshire Downs, close to the meandering River Ebble, and reflecting the peaceful unspoilt rural charm of the village in which it stands, is the 17th-century Horseshoe Inn, a true country pub that has been run by the Bath family for the past 14 years. Adorned with climbing roses, with a pretty flower-filled garden, it is a homely and traditional local with a central servery dispensing ale from the barrel to two rooms, both filled with simple furniture, old farming implements and country bygones.
Bar food is good value and freshly prepared from local produce. Expect rustic and hearty meals, including liver and bacon casserole, wild boar and apricot pie, locally-made faggots in onion gravy, fish bake, honey-roast duckling with gooseberry sauce, and local estate game on the blackboard menu. Good sandwiches and ploughman's lunches; notable 3-course set Sunday lunch - booking essential.
OPEN: 12-3 6.30-11. **BAR MEALS:** L served all week. D served Tue-Fri, & Sun 12-2 7-9.30. Av main course £8.25. **RESTAURANT:** D served Tue-Sat 12-2 7-9.30. Av 3 course à la carte £15. **BREWERY/COMPANY:** Free House. **PRINCIPAL BEERS:** Wadworth 6X, Ringwood Best, Adnams Broadside, Butcombe Best. **FACILITIES:** Garden: Food served outside. **NOTES:** Parking 20. **ROOMS:** 2 bedrooms 2 en suite d£50

Ⴘ Pubs offering six or more wines by the glass

The Kennet & Avon Canal
Following the towpath of the 87-mile Kennet & Avon Canal is the best way to appreciate its varied wildlife, luxuriant flora and fauna and colourful boating activity, and there is a varied assortment of canalside pubs where you can take a break from the trail. Walking from east to west, you may like to try the Victorian Harrow Inn at Little Bedwyn, the 16th-century Royal Oak at Wootton Rivers, the historic French Horn at Pewsey, and the Bridge Inn at Horton. On reaching Devizes, home of the famous Wadworth Brewery, take a stroll through the town and stop off at the Bear Hotel in the Market Place or the Elm Tree in Long Street. Beyond Devizes, take a detour to the George and Dragon at Rowde before following the towpath to the colourful Barge Inn at Seend and the delightful 16th-century Hop Pole at Limpley Stoke. Along the way you may like to explore the quaint old streets of Bradford-on-Avon, perhaps popping into the Canal Tavern in Frome Road or the terraced Dandy Lion in Market Street. The Georgian delights of Bath await you at the end of the trail, where you might like to relax at the Richmond Arms or the Olde Green Tree.

Pick of the Pubs

The Beckford Arms
SP3 6PX ☎ 01747 870385   ▤ 01747 851496
e-mail: beck.ford@ukonline.co.uk
*Dir: 2m from A303 (Fonthill Bishop turning) halfway between
Hindon & Tisbury at crossroads next to Beckford Estate*

Substantial 18th-century stone-built inn peacefully situated
opposite the Fonthill Estate and providing a good base
from which to explore the unspoilt Nadder Valley. Eddie
and Karen Costello have transformed this rural retreat
since arriving here two years ago. Beyond the basic locals'
bar, you will find a rambling main bar, adjoining dining
area and an airy conservatory all decorated in a tastefully
rustic style, complete with scrubbed plank tables topped
with huge candles, and warm terracotta-painted walls.
Expect a roaring log fire in winter, a relaxed, laid-back
atmosphere, and interesting modern pub menus.

From ciabatta sandwiches, hearty soups, salads, salmon
and prawn fishcakes with basil and lime reduction, or a
Thai curry at lunchtime, the choice of well presented
dishes extends, perhaps, to rack of lamb with tomatoes,
wine and Italian herbs, sautéed medallions of Wiltshire
pork with caramelised apple, Calvados and cider, and
salmon with Vermouth glaze in the evening. Generous
bowls of fresh vegetables, colourful plates and friendly
service all add to the dining experience here.

Sun-trap patio and a delightful garden - perfect for
summer sipping. Good value overnight accommodation.
OPEN: 12-11 (Sun 12-10.30). **BAR MEALS:** L served all
week. D served all week 12-2.30 7-9.30. Av main course
£8.95. **BREWERY/COMPANY:** Free House.
PRINCIPAL BEERS: Hop Back Best, Greene King Abbot Ale,
Timothy Taylor Landlord, Smiles Original.
FACILITIES: Children welcome Garden: food served
outside Dogs allowed. **NOTES:** Parking 40.
ROOMS: 8 bedrooms 5 en suite s£35 d£65

Pick of the Pubs

The White Hart ⊛ ⏝ ♀
SN14 8RP ☎ 01249 782213   ▤ 01249 783075
*Dir: From M4 J17 take A429 then A420, Ford is situated
alongside A420*

In a sleepy village deep in the Bybrook Valley, this 16th-
century coaching inn stands by a babbling trout stream.
Within, it combines a traditional bar food and excellent
real ale section with a more intimate beamed dining-room
with wooden tables candlelit by night. Most of the
bedrooms are in converted stables and hayloft across the
lane, well-fitted with modern appointments with a
peaceful night's rest promised. There is a pleasant relaxed
and friendly atmosphere.

Fixed-price lunch selections include smoked salmon,
braised lamb shank with colcannon and lemon
cheesecake with strawberry ice cream. Alternatives in the
bar might be Thai chicken curry, grilled plaice with lemon
and chive butter and macaroni cheese with mushrooms,
spinach and grain mustard. Further dining options run to
breast of duck with honey, peppercorns and couscous and
fillet of salmon on pasta nero with buttered spinach and
samphire accompanied by a wine list of commendable
variety.

OPEN: 11-3 7-11. **BAR MEALS:** L served all week. D served
all week 12-2 6.30-9.30. Av main course £5.95.
RESTAURANT: L served all week. D served all week 12-2
7-9.30. Av 3 course à la carte £25.50. Av 3 course fixed price
£13.95. **BREWERY/COMPANY:** Lionheart.
PRINCIPAL BEERS: Marstons Pedigree, Wadworth 6X,
Bass, Courage Directors. **FACILITIES:** Children welcome
Garden: outdoor eating, patio, riverside Dogs allowed by
arragement. **NOTES:** Parking 80. **ROOMS:** 11 bedrooms
11 en suite s£64 d£84

Bar Billiards

The ingenious blend of billiards and skittles is a relative newcomer to the pub scene. It was
introduced here from Belgium in the 1930s, with support from billiard table
manufacturers. The game caught on rapidly, especially in the South and Midlands, and
leagues had been organised by the time the Second World War began. Its much more
recent rival is pool, which came here from America in the 1960s in the wake of the Paul
Newman film The Hustler.

England

Pubs on Screen

Next time to you go to a pub, take a close look at your surroundings but don't be surprised if you can't remember exactly where you've seen the place before. It's more than likely that you've spotted it on the large or small screen as many of Britain's hostelries have been used as locations for film and television productions over the years. More often than not the company chooses a classic inn in a picturesque English village and sometimes a few minor cosmetic changes are necessary to meet the demands of the script. For example, modern photographs and electric lighting had to be removed from the Fleece at Bretforton in Worcestershire before this historic pub could appear as the Blue Dragon in the 1994 version of 'Martin Chuzzlewit.' Elsewhere, the back parlour of the Kings Arms at Askrigg in North Yorkshire was converted into the Drovers Arms for the television version of James Herriot's 'All Creatures Great and Small.' The Jolly Sailor at Bursledon near Southampton featured in the sailing soap 'Howards Way' and the George at Norton St Philip in Somerset has appeared in 'Moll Flanders,' 'Tom Jones' and 'The Remains of the Day.' You might also recognise the Castle Inn at Chiddingstone in Kent from 'The Wind in the Willows', 'The Wicked Lady' and 'Room with a View.' One of the most frequently used hostelries is the Stag & Huntsmen at Hambleden in Buckinghamshire. 'Chitty, Chitty, Bang, Bang,' 'Poirot,' 'A Village Affair' and '101 Dalmatians' were filmed here - among many other productions.

GREAT HINTON   Map 03 ST95

Pick of the Pubs

The Linnet ⊛ 🍴 ♀
BA14 6BT ☎ 01380 870354 📠 01380 870354
Dir: Just off the A361 Devizes to Trowbridge rd

A sleepy village local that has been given a new lease of life by its new tenant and chef, Jonathan Furby, is the latest in a line of Wiltshire pubs to have become, almost overnight, a dining pub of repute, with dining chairs and comfortably-spaced tables neatly laid and flower-adorned. Everything is freshly home-made, from a range of breads and pasta to home-made ice cream. Purchasing of fresh ingredients, local where possible, shows on menus that are kept sensibly short and supplemented daily by what is available at market. Single-dish lunches run from broccoli and pepper tart and tagliatelle with chicken, leeks, asparagus and smoked cheese sauce to marinated ribeye steak in shallot and red wine sauce: alternatively a two or three-course lunch is offered at very kind prices. At dinner, go perhaps for duck pancakes on cucumber salsa with plum sauce, pan-fried lemon sole with crab and dill dumpling on langoustine and chive sauce, rounding off perhaps with chocolate and pecan sponge with toffee cream. Presentation is top-class and service pleasantly relaxed and informal.
OPEN: 11-2.30 6.30-11 (Sun 12-3, 7-10.30). Closed Mon.
BAR MEALS: L served Tue-Sun. D served Tue-Sun 12-2 6.30-9.30. Av main course £10. **RESTAURANT:** L served Tue-Sun. D served Tue-Sun 12-2 6.30-9.30. Av 3 course à la carte £18. **BREWERY/COMPANY:** Wadworth.
PRINCIPAL BEERS: Wadworth 6X & Henrys IPA.
FACILITIES: Garden: large patio area, outdoor eating,.
NOTES: Parking 45

GRITTLETON   Map 03 ST88

The Neeld Arms
The Street SN14 6AP ☎ 01249 782470 📠 01249 782358
e-mail: neeldarms@genie.co.uk
This old Cotswold-stone pub stands just 15mins from the M4,

surrounded by Wiltshire countryside. A good range of quality beers is offered at the bar and the small blackboard menu offers a few superbly cooked dishes.

The bedrooms are warmly decorated with soft furnishings and have an individual, extremely comfortable bed in each (one four-poster). At Breakfast, a wide choice is provided, including a full cooked platter.

OPEN: 5.30-11 (Sat 11-3, 5.30-11, Sun 12-3, 6-10.30).
BAR MEALS: L served Sat-Sun. D served all week 11-3 6-9.30. Av main course £8.50. **BREWERY/COMPANY:** Free House.
PRINCIPAL BEERS: Wadworth 6X, Fullers London Pride, Buckleys Best. **FACILITIES:** Children welcome Garden: outdoor eating Dogs allowed. **NOTES:** Parking 12.
ROOMS: 6 bedrooms 6 en suite s£38.50 d£53.50 FR£73.50-£93.50

HEYTESBURY   Map 03 ST94

Pick of the Pubs

The Angel Inn 🍴 ♀
High St BA12 0ED ☎ 01985 840330 📠 01985 840931
e-mail: Angelheytesbury@aol.com
See Pick of the Pubs on page 471

continued

Moles in the Bar

Formed in 1973 to supply soft drinks to the area, Cascade Soft Drinks expanded into real ales in the early 80s when it took on Roger Catte who had been working for Watney's in London. With the purchase of their 'brewery tap' pub, the Rising Sun at Lacock, Cascade began the chain that now has more than ten pubs. Mole ales include Molegrip (4.3%), Barleymole (4.2%) and the seasonal ale Moell! Moel! (6.0%)

Pick of the Pubs

The Lamb at Hindon ◎ ★ ★ 🛏 ♀

High St SP3 6DP ☎ 01747 820573 📠 01747 820605
e-mail: the-lamb@demon.co.uk
Dir: 1m from A303 & B3089 in the centre of the village

HINDON   Map 03 ST93

Pick of the Pubs

Grosvenor Arms ◎ ◎ ★ ★ 🛏 ♀

SP3 6DJ ☎ 01747 820696 📠 01747 820869
Dir: 1.5m from A303, on B3089 towards Salisbury

A particularly attractive and unspoilt Georgian village in the most rural part of Wiltshire. At its heart opposite the parish church stands this handsome coaching inn, set round an enclosed courtyard, that has undergone extensive and sympathetic refurbishment to bedrooms and public areas in a mix of modern styles. Open fires grace the bars and a stylish sitting-room with old beams retained throughout. Totally fresh produce, much of it organic, forms the basis of contemporary brasserie-style dishes that can be as straightforward as Wiltshire sausages with onion mash or as accomplished as double-baked blue cheese soufflé with rocket salad. Similarly, fresh fish ranges from deep-fried cod and chips to roast sea bass with aubergine and garlic purée. Snack on ciabatta and focaccia sandwiches over real ales or decent wines by the glass, and in fine weather treat the dog at the courtyard tables to a bespoke pack that includes a mat, snacks and fresh water.
OPEN: 11-3 7-11. **BAR MEALS:** L served all week. D served all week 12-2 7-9.30. Av main course £10. **RESTAURANT:** L served all week. D served all week 12-2 7-9.30. Av 3 course à la carte £20. Av 2 course fixed price £9.
BREWERY/COMPANY: Free House.
PRINCIPAL BEERS: Wadworth 6X, Bass.
FACILITIES: Children welcome Garden: patio area, food served outside Dogs allowed. **NOTES:** Parking 20.
ROOMS: 7 bedrooms 7 en suite s£45 d£50

Situated in picturesque Hindon, this 17th-century posting inn is a handy refreshment stop for A303 travellers. A weekly market was held here until 1862, with business transactions conducted in the bar.
A relaxing restaurant serves local produce, including game in season, while bar food may feature hearty ploughman's lunches, venison and mushroom casserole, and whole Dover sole.
Cold food is served in the bar until 12.30, tea and scones are served throughout the afternoon too.
OPEN: 11-11 (Sun 12-10.30). **BAR MEALS:** L served all week. D served all week 12-2.30 7-10. Av main course £7.95.
RESTAURANT: L served all week. D served all week 12-1.45 7-9.30. Av 3 course à la carte £19.95. Av 3 course fixed price £19.95. **BREWERY/COMPANY:** Free House.
PRINCIPAL BEERS: Wadworth 6X, Hampshire Ironside and King Alfred, Stonehenge Pigswill, Everards Tiger.
FACILITIES: Children welcome Garden: outdoor eating, patio, beer garden Dogs allowed. **NOTES:** Parking 25.
ROOMS: 14 bedrooms 14 en suite s£35 d£75

The Making of Beer

The traditional ingredients of beer are water, barley malt, hops, yeats and ripe judgement. One traditional brewery's products will taste different from another's because of variations in the blending of the ingredients and the timing of process. It all starts with barley, amlted in a kiln at the malting: the higher the temperature, the darker the beer. The powdered malt is mixed with hot water to make a mash. How the hot mash is and how long it is allowed to stand will affect the taste and in the old days local spring water gave beer a distinctive local flavour. Burton upon Trent's eminent reputation for bitter rested on the gypsum in the town's water.
The liquid from the mash is boiled up with hops - the more hops, the bitterer - and sugar is often added. Next the liquid is cooled and yeast is stirred in to make it ferment. The 'green beer' is eventually run into casks to mature. Keg beer is filtered, sterilised and carbonated, and then stored in sealed containers and taste more like bottled beers, which are put through the same process.

OPEN: 11.30-3 6.30-11.
BAR MEALS: L served all week. D served all week 12-3 7-9. (9.30 Fri & Sat) Av main course £10.
RESTAURANT: L served all week. D served all week 12-3 7-9. (9.30 Fri & Sat) Av 3 course a la carte £20.
BREWERY/COMPANY: Free House.
PRINCIPAL BEERS: Ringwood Best, Marston's Pedigree, Timothy Taylor Landlord.
FACILITIES: Children welcome. Courtyard, outdoor eating. Dogs allowed.
ROOMS: 9 bedrooms 9 en suite S£45-£55 d£55-£70 FR£80.

The Angel Inn

High Street BA12 0ED
☎ 01985 840330 📠 01985 840931
e-mail: angelheytesbury@aol.com
Dir: From A303 take A36 towards Bath, 8m, Heytesbury signed L

One of the new breed of modern dining pubs, this tastefully restored 17th-century coaching inn is tucked away in a tiny village in the tranquil Wylye Valley, just a few minutes drive from Warminster. Well placed for exploring Bath, Salisbury and the neaby Longleat Estate.

There's a reassuringly civilised atmosphere at this welcoming old inn, with its long beamed bar featuring scrubbed pine tables, warm terracotta-painted walls and attractive fireplace with warming woodburner A separate lounge area with squashy sofas and easy chairs leads through to the neatly furnished rear dining room. In summer, guests spill out into the secluded courtyard garden with its hardwood tables and cotton parasols. Newish owners have added a few bedrooms and stylishly refurbished existing rooms, which are proving popular with both business people and tourists.

The relaxed, friendly service makes dining a pleasure. Innovative, seasonally changing menus feature quality ingredients and plenty of imagination. For starters or a 'light bite' choose warm salad of chicken and bacon with balsamic dressing, chicken liver parfait with apple and grape chutney, 'chunky' Caesar salad, or ciabatta bread topped with ham, mustard and melted cheese. More substantial offerings include chargrilled calves' liver with creamy mash and onion marmalade, game and vegetable pie, roast salmon with Parmesan risotto and crispy leeks, double-baked cheese soufflé, and good salmon and plaice fishcakes with a rustic tomato and garlic sauce. For pudding try the lemon tart or the iced strawberry parfait.

Expect a quality list of wines (12 by the glass) with useful tasting notes to complement the food and good real ale on tap, perhaps Ringwood Best and Timothy Taylor Landlord.

England

HOLT   Map 03 ST86

Pick of the Pubs

The Tollgate Inn 🍴 NEW
BA14 6PX ☎ 01225 782326 📠 01225 782805
Dir: On B 3105 between Bradford on Avon and Melksham M4
J18, A46 towards Bath, then A363 to Bradford on Avon then
B3105 Melksham, pub on the R handside

A traditional 16th-century roadside inn with a relaxed
atmosphere of comfy sofas, daily papers and glossy
magazines dotted around a welcoming log fire. Aiming to
provide interesting and original food alongside unusual
fine wines and guest ales, a restaurant has been added on
the first floor in what was originally a chapel for the
weavers who once worked below.

Freshly produced food, with meat, game and poultry
from nearby farms, locally-grown fruit and vegetables and
fish delivered daily from Cornwall signal the pedigree of
new chef/patron Alexander Venables whose results on the
plate live up to their promise. A good showing of fish -
potted kipper with bacon, dill and horseradish; smoked
haddock risotto; Cornish fish stew with aïoli croutes - is
supplemented by fresh grilled lobster and bouillabaisse on
the daily specials board. Salad of confit duck leg, local
'Church Farm' beef Wellington and braised Moroccan-
style lamb shoulder, followed perhaps by caramelised
banana pancakes are indicative of a generally eclectic
style. A short, fixed-price lunch menu offers especially
good value.
OPEN: 11.30-2.30 6.30-11. Closed Mon. **BAR MEALS:** L
served Tue-Sun. D served Tue-Sat 12-2 7-9.30. Av main course
£12.50. **RESTAURANT:** L served Tue-Sun. D served Tue-Sat
12-2 7-9.30. Av 3 course à la carte £20.
BREWERY/COMPANY: Free House.
PRINCIPAL BEERS: Bath Ale Gem, Tisbury Brewery Best,
Abbey Ales Bellringer, Shepherd Neame Spitfire.
FACILITIES: Garden: food served outside.
NOTES: Parking 40

HORNINGSHAM   Map 03 ST84

The Bath Arms ★ ★ ♀
BA12 7LY ☎ 01985 844308 📠 01985 844150
Dir: Off B3092 S of Frome
Purchased from Glastonbury Abbey and converted into a pub
in 1763, the Bath Arms is an impressive, creeper-clad stone inn
occupying a prime position at one of the entrances to Longleat
Estate. Recently acquired by Young's Brewery, it has been
comfortably refurbished and features a fine beamed bar with
settles and old wooden tables, and a terracotta painted dining-
room with open fire.

Promising early menus offer traditional fish and chips, tuna
with mango salsa and herb oil, poussin with bacon and
braised Savoy cabbage, ribeye steak with red wine jus, and
snacks like Longleat ploughman's. New rear terrace.
OPEN: 12-3 6-11 (Closed Sun eve in Winter, May-Oct open all
day). **BAR MEALS:** L served all week. D served Mon-Sat 12-2.30
7-9.30. Av main course £6.50. **RESTAURANT:** L served all week.
D served Mon-Sat 12-2.30 7-9.30. Av 3 course à la carte £10.95.
BREWERY/COMPANY: Youngs. **PRINCIPAL BEERS:** Youngs
Bitter, Special, Triple AAA. **FACILITIES:** Children welcome
Garden: food served outside. **NOTES:** Parking 15.
ROOMS: 9 bedrooms 9 en suite s£45 d£65

HORTON   Map 03 SU06

The Bridge Inn
SN10 2JS ☎ 01380 860273
Dir: A361 from Devizes, R at 3rd roundabout
Spacious renovated pub, with well furnished bars, log fires,
welcoming atmosphere, and a large garden with barbeque.
Situated next to the Kennet and Avon Canal. Wide choice
always displayed on specials blackboards.

KILMINGTON   Map 03 ST73

The Red Lion Inn
Kilmington BA12 6RP ☎ 01985 844263
Dir: B3092 off A303 N towards Frome. Pub 2.5m from A303 on R on
B3092 just after turning to Stourhead Gardens
15th-century inn owned by the National Trust and handy for
Stourhead, Shaftesbury and Salisbury Plain. Two horses were
kept here to make up the team of four required to pull the
stage coach up the nearby hill. Cosy atmosphere and log fires
inside, with window seats and a curved high-backed settle.
Traditional home-cooked food ranges from chicken casserole
and lamb and apricot pie to Cornish pasty and meat and
vegetable lasagnes. Well kept real ales with two guest beers
available.
OPEN: 11.30-2.30 (Sun 12-3) 6.30-11 (Sun 7-10.30).
BAR MEALS: L served all week 12-1.50. Av main course £4.45.
BREWERY/COMPANY: Free House.
PRINCIPAL BEERS: Butcombe. **FACILITIES:** Children welcome
Garden: outdoor eating Dogs allowed (not in bar during food
times). **NOTES:** Parking 25. **ROOMS:** 2 bedrooms s£25 d£35
No credit cards

LACOCK   Map 03 ST96

The George Inn 🍴
4 West St SN15 2LH ☎ 01249 730263
Dir: M4 J17 take A350 S
Situated in a beautiful National Trust village, the George dates
from 1361 and boasts many classic features, including a
medieval fireplace, a low beamed ceiling, mullioned windows,
flagstones and an old treadwheel by which a dog would drive
the spit. Lacock is regularly used as a film and TV location.
Sample home-made lasagne, battered cod, Wiltshire ham or
beef and Guinness pie from the wholesome snack menu.
Overnight accommodation is provided at the owner's
farmhouse nearby - complimentary transport to and from the
pub!
OPEN: 10-2.30 5-11. **BAR MEALS:** L served all week. D served
all week 12-2 6-10. Av main course £6.50. **RESTAURANT:** L
served all week. D served all week 12-2 6-10. Av 3 course à la
carte £12. Av 3 course fixed price £12.50.
BREWERY/COMPANY: Wadworth.
PRINCIPAL BEERS: Wadworth 6X, Henrys IPA, Old Timer &
Farmers Glory. **FACILITIES:** Children welcome Garden: beer
garden patio, BBQ, food served outdoors Dogs allowed, garden
only. **NOTES:** Parking 40. **ROOMS:** 3 bedrooms 3 en suite s£25
d£40

 ★   AA inspected hotel accommodation

Red Lion Inn ♟
1 High St SN15 2LQ ☎ 01249 730456 ▤ 01249 730766
Dir: *just off A350 between Chippenham & Melksham*
Pub dating from from the 1700s, set in a National Trust village. The older part of the building has exposed timbers and a large open fire. The same menu is offered throughout, with the likes of home-made beef and ale pie, and pork and cider casserole. **OPEN:** 11.30-3 6-11 (Ring for details of summer times). **BAR MEALS:** L served all week. D served all week 12-2.30 6-9. Av main course £6.95. **RESTAURANT:** L served all week. D served all week 12-2.30 6-9. Av 3 course à la carte £13. **BREWERY/COMPANY:** Wadworth. **PRINCIPAL BEERS:** Wadworth Henry's IPA & 6X. **FACILITIES:** Children welcome Garden: beer garden with seating, patio Dogs allowed. **NOTES:** Parking 70. **ROOMS:** 5 bedrooms 5 en suite s£45 d£65

LIMPLEY STOKE   Map 03 ST76

The Hop Pole Inn
Woods Hill, Lower Limpley Stoke BA3 6HS
☎ 01225 723134 ▤ 01225 723199
e-mail: latonahop@aol.com
Dir: *Off A36 (Bath to Warminster road)*
The Hop Pole dates from 1580, the name coming from the hop plant that still grows outside the pub. It is set in the Limpley Stoke Valley and offers walkers, cyclists and motorists a tranquil venue in which to enjoy the extensive carte, daily specials, comprehensive wine list and choice of real ales. Traditional home-made pies are popular, along with local trout, beef Wellington and rack of lamb. **OPEN:** 11-2.30 6-11 (Sun 12-3, 7-10.30). Closed 25 Dec. **BAR MEALS:** L served all week. D served all week 12-2.15 6.30-9.15. Av main course £6. **RESTAURANT:** L served all week. D served all week 12-2.15 6.30-9.15. Av 3 course à la carte £16. **BREWERY/COMPANY:** Free House. **PRINCIPAL BEERS:** Courage Best, Butcombe, Bass. **FACILITIES:** Children welcome Garden: patio, outdoor eating Dogs allowed. **NOTES:** Parking 20
See Pub Walk on page 463

LITTLE BEDWYN   Map 04 SU26

Pick of the Pubs

The Harrow Inn ◉ ◉ 🛏 ♟
SN8 3JP ☎ 01672 870871 ▤ 01672 870871
e-mail: dining@harrowinn.co.uk
See Pick of the Pubs on page 475

LITTLE CHEVERELL   Map 03 ST95

The Owl 🛏
Low Rd SN10 4JS ☎ 01380 812263
Dir: *A344 from Stonehenge, then A360, after 10m L onto B3098, R after 0.5m, Owl signposted*
Cosy 19th-century local situated well off-the-beaten-track in a tiny hamlet and surrounded by farmland and views of Salisbury Plain. Since arriving here in April 2000, new landlady - Pia Maria Boast - has repainted the homely and neatly traditional bars, adding fresh flowers, papers and various farming implements. Daily-changing blackboard menus reflect the seasons, the choice of home-made dishes ranging from ploughman's and pasta meals to evening options featuring fresh fish - haddock, skate wing, whole sea bass. Pretty garden that runs down to the Cheverell Brook. **OPEN:** 11.30-2.30 6-11. **BAR MEALS:** L served all week. D served all week 12-2 6-9.30. Av main course £7. **BREWERY/COMPANY:** Free House. **PRINCIPAL BEERS:** Wadworth 6X & Changing real ales. **FACILITIES:** Garden: Food served outside Dogs allowed. **NOTES:** Parking 16

 For pubs with AA rosette awards for food see page 10

National Trust Pubs

The National Trust began in 1895 and secured its first property a year later, paying the princely sum of £10 for it. Today, it is the country's biggest landowner, with over 600,000 acres of countryside, 550 miles of coastline, over 300 historic houses and more than 150 gardens. As a rule, we don't associate the National Trust with Britain's pubs, but this long-established independent charity owns a number of notable hostelries around the country. Among the most famous are the ancient Fleece Inn - originally a medieval farmhouse - at Bretforton in the Cotswolds, the 18th-century Castle Inn in the picturesque Kent village of Chiddingstone, and the historic George at Lacock in Wiltshire. The National Trust's George in London's Borough High Street is the only surviving example of the capital's once numerous galleried coaching inns, while the Spread Eagle at Stourhead, close to the Somerset/Wiltshire border, was acquired by the Trust in 1947. A number of distinguished visitors have passed through its doors over the years, including Horace Walpole and David Niven.

LOWER CHICKSGROVE   Map 03 ST92

Pick of the Pubs

Compasses Inn ♀
SP3 6NB ☎ 01722 714318 🖥 01722 714318
e-mail: thecompassesinn@tinyworld.co.uk
Dir: *A30 W from Salisbury, after 10m R signed Chicksgrove*
A timeless air of peace and tranquillity pervades within this attractive 16th-century thatched inn, set in the unspoilt Nadder Valley. Landlord Jonathan Bold is succeeding here where others before him have failed, that is in attracting people out to this remote rural pub. Imaginative, well presented food is the key.

Diners are now negotiating the narrow lanes and walking down the old cobbled path that leads to the latched door and into the long and low-beamed bar, with its bare stone walls, worn flagstone floors, large inglenook with wood-burning stove, and an assortment of traditional furniture.

In addition to a warm welcome and local real ales, they find an ever-changing blackboard menu, which may feature smoked salmon and sun-dried tomato tart, bouillabaise, pork and chorizo cassoulet, Thai fishcakes, roast duck with balsamic and honey reduction, and grey mullet with fresh tarragon and lemon. Good puddings. Overnight accommodation in four en suite bedrooms; one tucked beneath the heavy thatch.
OPEN: 12-3 6-11 (Sun 12-3, 7-10.30). Closed Mon except BH Mon, then closed Tue. **BAR MEALS:** L served Tue-Sun. served Tue-Sat 7-9. Av main course £9.95.
BREWERY/COMPANY: Free House.
PRINCIPAL BEERS: Bass, Wadworth 6X, Tisbury Stonehenge, Chicksgrove Churl. **FACILITIES:** Children welcome Garden: patio/terrace, outdoor eating Dogs allowed Water. **NOTES:** Parking 30. **ROOMS:** 4 bedrooms 4 en suite s£40 d£55 FR£65-£75

LOWER WOODFORD   Map 03 SU13

The Wheatsheaf
SP4 6NQ ☎ 01722 782203 🖥 01722 782203
Dir: *Take A360 N of Salisbury. Village signposted 1st R*
Beer was brewed at this thriving country pub, formerly a farm, until the beginning of the 20th century. Occupying a charming rural setting close to the Avon, one of its more unusual features is an indoor fish pond and miniature footbridge dividing the dining areas. Expect steak and mushroom pie, Italian meatballs, pan-fried venison with mushrooms, lasagne, and red mullet with pancetta and bean salad on the well-planned menu.

LUDWELL   Map 03 ST92

Grove Arms Inn ♦♦♦♦ NEW
SP7 9ND ☎ 01747 828328 🖥 01747 828960
Dir: *On main A30 Shaftsbury to Salisbury Rd 3 M from Shaftsbury*
Grade II listed thatched inn, completely refurbished and offering well-kept accommodation in six letting rooms. Home-cooked pub food includes fresh pizzas, steaks with all the trimmings, rabbit pie cooked in cider, and favourite puddings like sherry trifle and apple crumble. The owners pride themselves on their Sunday lunch, which always includes topside of beef. *continued*

OPEN: 12-11.30. **BAR MEALS:** L served all week. D served all week 12-2.30 6-9.30. Av main course £8.
BREWERY/COMPANY: Free House.
PRINCIPAL BEERS: Ringwood Best, Ringwood Fortyniner.
FACILITIES: Garden: Food served outside. **NOTES:** Parking 60.
ROOMS: 6 bedrooms 6 en suite s£40 d£50

MALMESBURY   Map 03 ST98

Pick of the Pubs

Horse & Groom 🌸 ♦♦♦♦♦ ♀
The Street, Charlton SN16 9DL ☎ 01666 823904
🖥 01666 823390
Dir: *from M4 head towards Malmesbury, 2nd rdbt go R towards Cricklade on B4040, premises through the village on the left*
A small, relaxed and civilised 16th-century coaching inn set back from the road in a pleasant garden that features with a duck-pond. Sympathetic conversion has brought the three bedrooms and two bars and dining-room up to modern expectations without any detriment to the inn's inherent character: log fires burn in winter and drinks and snacks are served outdoors in fine weather.

Menus appeal to all tastes and pockets with starters or light snacks that include salmon tagliatelle, grilled Brie slices with Cumberland sauce, stuffed toasted mushrooms and fillets of plaice meunière: all is cooked to order and subject to availability of fresh produce. Main dishes balance the traditional beer-battered haddock with home-made chips and beef, Stilton and Guinness pie with more up-to-date interpretations of ballotine of duck with apricots and basil and escalope of monkfish with red pepper sauce. For dessert, lemon shortbread tartlets, blueberry fritters and genuine Cotswolde ice creams. Well-chosen real ales attract a loyal local following.
OPEN: 12-3 7-11 (all day wknds). Closed 25/26 Dec.
BAR MEALS: L served all week. D served all week 12-2 7-10. Av main course £4. **RESTAURANT:** L served all week. D served all week 12-2 7-10. Av 3 course à la carte £25.
BREWERY/COMPANY: Free House.
PRINCIPAL BEERS: Wadworth 6X, Archers Village, Smiles Best, Uley old Spot. **FACILITIES:** Garden: outdoor eating, pond Dogs allowed Water. **NOTES:** Parking 40.
ROOMS: 3 bedrooms 3 en suite s£60 d£80

All AA listed accommodation can also be found on the AA's internet site **www.theAA.com**

OPEN: 12-3 6-11 (Sun 12-3 only). Closed Sun eve & all Mon, 4 weeks Xmas & 4 weeks Aug.
BAR MEALS: L served Tue-Sun. D served Tue-Sat 12-2 7-10. Av main course £16.
RESTAURANT: L served Tue-Sun. D served Tue-Sat 12-2 7-9. Av 3 course a la carte £28. Av 3 course fixed price £35.
BREWERY/COMPANY: Free House.
PRINCIPAL BEERS: Tiger Beer.
FACILITIES: Garden: patio, outdoor eating. Dogs allowed - proprietor's discretion only.
NOTES: Parking - lane only.

The Harrow Inn

SN8 3JP
☎ 01672 870871 📄 01672 870871
e-mail: dining@harrowinn.co.uk
Dir: From M4, A338 to Hungerford, then R A4 to Marlborough. Turn L in 2m

On account of its size, at the heart of a tiny village tucked down country lanes close to the Kennet & Avon Canal, booking is always advisable at this elegantly refurbished Victorian pub. Enthusiasts of inspired modern cooking and fine wines travel from far and wide to dine here.

Visitors are welcome equally to partake of a simple starter as a full meal; to quaff a pint of Tiger or sip some indulgent house wines in totally egalitarian surroundings. Whilst not the most attractive externally, inside lies a surprise of crisply clothed tables, sparkling glassware and striking blue-and-yellow crockery replete with summery motifs.

Food is equally vibrant in flavours and colour and the careful sourcing of produce - in particular the fish selection delivered direct from Brixham - confidently lives up to expectations. At the upper echelon a tasting menu that includes spiced lobster bisque, miniature seafood appetisers, scallop and foie gras terrine and seared sea bass with sweet chilli sauce establishes the kitchen's pedigree - no less in evidence in light meals such as warm leek and Parmesan tart with goat's cheese salad, carpaccio of tuna with ginger and soy dressing or risotto of wild mushrooms. Aberdeen Angus beef, identified by its farm of origin, may have a morel and veal jus; crispy duck more than a hint of Chinese spices and pan-fried calves' sweetbreads an accompaniment of foie gras and black pudding. Typically to follow, expect to encounter a chilled lemon and ginger terrine decorated with fruit coulis for a delicate balance.

Two dining areas are reserved for non-smokers, yet space is allowed for casual drinking at the bar, with umbrella-ed tables in the garden for eating al fresco in fine weather.

MALMESBURY continued

The Smoking Dog
62 The High St SN16 9AT
☎ 01666 825823 📠 01666 829137
Refined 18th-century town centre pub with stone floors and
log fires. Expect daily papers, decent wines, a relaxing
atmosphere, and an interesting range of food.
Choose from home-made burgers and steak ciabatta or,
perhaps, fresh tuna with fresh roast chillies, baked avocado
with Brie, and venison on a bed of braised cabbage.
OPEN: 11.30-11 (Sun 12-10.30). **BAR MEALS:** L served all week.
D served all week 12-2 7-9.30. Av main course £7.50.
RESTAURANT: L served all week. D served all week 12-2 7-9.30.
Av 3 course à la carte £25. **PRINCIPAL BEERS:** Wadworth 6X,
Archers Best, Bass, Brain's Bitter. **FACILITIES:** Children welcome
Garden: Dogs allowed

Pick of the Pubs

The Vine Tree 🐾 🍷
Foxley Rd, Norton SN16 0JP ☎ 01666 837654
📠 01666 838003
e-mail: info@thevinetree.co.uk
See Pick of the Pubs on page 477

MARTEN   Map 04 SU26

Tipsy Miller
SN8 3SH ☎ 01264 731372
Dir: 6m SW of Hungerford om A338
Isolated downland free house close to Wilton Windmill, the
Avebury Stones, the Hungerford Antiques Centre, and
Stonehenge. The restaurant serves a wide range of freshly
prepared dishes including steaks, fresh fish, exotic game, pies
and vegetarian meals - sauces are a speciality.

OPEN: 11-2.30 6.30-11 (Sun 12-3, 7-10.30). **BAR MEALS:** L
served all week. D served all week 12-2.30 6.30-10.
RESTAURANT: L served all week. D served all week 12-2.30
6.30-10. **BREWERY/COMPANY:** Free House.
PRINCIPAL BEERS: Bass, Butts. **FACILITIES:** Children welcome
Garden: outdoor eating Dogs allowed. **NOTES:** Parking 25

AA Hotel Booking Service on 0870 5050505 to book
at AA recognised hotels and B & Bs in the
UK and Ireland, or through our Internet site:
www.theAA.com

Down on the Farm

Cider has been drunk in Britain since before
Roman times and was originally made of fermented
crab apple juice. Farmers made their own, especially in the
West Country, and by the 17th century about 350 varieties of
cider apple tree were cultivated, with names like Redstreak and
Kingston Black, Sweet Coppin and Handsome Maud.
The basic process of cider-making is to crush apples in a press,
run off the juice and leave it to ferment narurally in casks for four
months or so. The Industrial Revolution, however, transferred
cider from the farm to the factory and by the 1960s the major
producers were following the same path as the brewers and
efficiently turning out a standardised product - weak, sweet
and fizzy - that had only a distant resemblance to the
powerful ' rough cider' or 'scrumpy' of earlier days.
Fortunately, a draught cider renaissance has
followed in the wake of the real ale revival, and
one of the Campaign for Real Ale's aim is
to prevent the disappearance of
rough cider and perry.

MELKSHAM   Map 03 ST96

Kings Arms Hotel
Market Place SN12 6EX ☎ 01225 707272 📠 01225 702085
Dir: In the town centre opposite Lloyds Bank
Once an important coaching house on the London to Bath
route, warmth and hospitality are offered by this traditional
market place inn.

MERE   Map 03 ST83

Old Ship Inn
Castle St BA12 6JE ☎ 01747 860258 📠 01747 860501
Dir: W of Stonehenge just off A303
You are assured of a warm welcome at this 16th-century
coaching inn. Architectural features include stone walls,
flagstone floors and an original elm stairway. Home-cooked
dishes are served in the bar, and there is a full carte in the
oak-beamed restaurant.

Talbot Hotel ◆◆◆
The Square BA12 6DR ☎ 01747 860427
e-mail: h.aylett@liimember.net
Dir: follow signs from A303 into village
Expect a friendly welcome at this 16th-century coaching inn.
Many attractions are within easy reach, including Longleat,
Salisbury, Wincanton racecourse and Sherborne Castle.
Charles II stayed here at one point, as he fled Cromwell's
forces in 1651. A sample menu includes greenlipped mussels,
smoked mackerel, Barnsley lamb chops, tikka marsala curry
and grilled trout with almonds. Plenty of snacks are also
available.
OPEN: 11-11 (Mon-Tue 11-3, 6-11 Sun 12-3, 7-10.30).
BAR MEALS: L served all week. D served all week 12-2.30
6.30-9.30. Av main course £6.50. **RESTAURANT:** L served all
week. D served all week 12-2.30 6.30-9.30. Av 3 course à la carte
£12. **BREWERY/COMPANY:** Hall & Woodhouse.
PRINCIPAL BEERS: Badger Dorset Best, Champion Ale & Badger
IPA. **FACILITIES:** Children welcome Garden: Terrace, food
served outside Dogs allowed except in garden.
NOTES: Parking 20. **ROOMS:** 7 bedrooms 7 en suite s£32.50
d£53 FR£65-£77

Open: 11.30-2.30 6-11
(Sun 12-10.30).
Bar Meals: L served all week.
D served all week 12-2.30 7-9.30
(10 Sat, all day Sun).
Av main course £8.
RESTAURANT: L served all week
D served all week 12-2.30 7-9.30
(10 Sat, all day Sun).
£25.**BREWERY/COMPANY:**
Free House.
PRINCIPLE BEERS: Archers
Village, Bass, Wychwood Fiddlers
Elbow.
FACILITIES: Children welcome.
Garden: terrace, outdoor eating,
play area. Dogs allowed.
NOTES: Parking 45+.

The Vine Tree

Foxley Road, Norton SN16 0JP
☎ 01666 837654 🖹 01666 838003
e-mail: info@thevinetree.co.uk
Dir: From B4040 W of Malmesbury take
minor rd L to Foxley, then L for Norton

The essence of a quality village free house in the heart of Wiltshire's countryside, the Vine Tree, a converted 18th-century mill house, is close to Malmesbury, Tetbury and Westonbirt Arboretum. Growing reputation for interesting, modern pub food and memorable summer alfresco dining.

Well worth the 3 mile drive from the M4 (J17) in winter for the log fire in the cosy main bar, the warm welcome from licensee Tiggi Wood and a satisfying meal in one of the pine-furnished dining areas. In summer, head this way for civilised outdoor lunches and suppers on the tranquil sun-trap terrace, complete with fountain, rose beds, trailing vines and large cotton parasols; adjacent two-acre garden with play area for kids to let off steam in. For liquid refreshment try a pint of the locally-brewed Archers Village Bitter, or a large glass of wine, perhaps the house champagne, from the carefully selected list; decent cappuccino and espresso coffee.

A modern British approach is taken to the stylish dishes of local sausages with colcannon mash and thyme gravy, oven-roasted Cotswold lamb with chargrilled vegetables and rosemary jus, and fishy daily specials like roast cod with crab and tiger prawn mousseline and chilli butte, and Thai roasted sea bass with lime and coriander sauce. 'Light' bites and starters include pheasant and pistachio terrine with apple and cider brandy chutney, a bowl of moules marinière with crusty bread, and deep-fried Brie with Thai jelly. Roquefort tart with pine nuts and salsa verde for vegetarians; rich chocolate mousse with crème anglaise to follow. Dishes are freshly prepared using quality ingredients, including local game. Imaginative Sunday lunch menu. Popular summer barbeques.

Plans include converting the stables into en suite bedrooms.

England

NUNTON
Map 03 SU12

The Radnor Arms
SP5 4HS ☎ 01722 329722
Dir: *From Salisbury ring road take A338 to Ringwood. Nunton signposted on R*

A popular pub in the centre of the village dating from around 1750. Bar snacks are supplemented by an extensive fish choice and daily specials, which might include steamed turbot, seared salmon or braised lamb shank, all freshly prepared. Fine summer garden with rural views.
OPEN: 11-3 (Sun 12-3) 6-11 (Sun 7-10.30). **BAR MEALS:** L served all week. D served all week 12-2.30 7-9.30. Av main course £6. **RESTAURANT:** L served all week. D served all week 12-2.30 7-9.30. **BREWERY/COMPANY:** Hall & Woodhouse. **PRINCIPAL BEERS:** Badger Tanglefoot, Best & Golden Champion. **FACILITIES:** Children welcome Children's licence Garden: patio/terrace, outdoor eating, BBQ Dogs allowed. **NOTES:** Parking 40

PEWSEY
Map 03 SU16

The French Horn
Marlborough Rd SN9 5NT ☎ 01672 562443
▤ 01672 562785
Dir: *A338 thru Hungerford, at Burbage take B3087 to Pewsey*
Situated by historic Pewsey Wharf on the Kennet & Avon Canal, this attractive pub is very popular with locals, walkers and cyclists. Napoleonic prisoners of war, building a stretch of the canal, were apparently summoned to the inn to be fed and watered by the sound of a French horn.
Interesting and imaginative menu offers such dishes as slow-braised lamb shank, Oriental marinated chicken and whole-baked American golden trout. Examples of the appetising bar specials include Thai green chicken curry, pan-fried lambs' liver and provençale fish stew.
OPEN: 12-2.30 6.30-11. Closed Dec 25. **BAR MEALS:** L served all week. D served all week 12-2.15 7-9.15. Av main course £6. **RESTAURANT:** L served all week. D served all week 12-2.15 7-9.15. Av 3 course à la carte £18. **BREWERY/COMPANY:** Wadworth. **PRINCIPAL BEERS:** Wadworth 6X, Henry's IPA, Summersault & Old Timer. **FACILITIES:** Children welcome Garden: outdoor eating Dogs allowed Water. **NOTES:** Parking 20

For pubs with AA rosette awards for food
see page 10

Pick of the Pubs

The Seven Stars
Bottlesford SN9 6LU ☎ 01672 851325
▤ 01672 851583
e-mail: sevenstars@dialin.net
Dir: *Off A345*
Thatched and creeper-clad 16th-century building tucked away down narrow lanes in the heart of the Pewsey Vale. Best approached from the A345 at North Newnton (follow signs for Woodborough, then Bottlesford), it is well worth the effort for the splendid 7-acre garden, complete with lake and rural views to the White Horse on Pewsey Down. Delightful rambling interior of beams and black oak panelling in which to sample locally-made cider, West Country real ales and some good food prepared by French chef/patron Philippe Cheminade.
Gallic-inspired dishes such as foie gras terrine with port jelly, Brittany fish soup or seafood platter, cassoulet Toulousain (with ham, confit of duck and sausage), and veal Normande are well executed, as one would expect, but so are more traditional offerings like pan-fried pheasant with wild mushrooms and port sauce, oven-baked perch and roast rib of beef with Yorkshire pudding. Decent sandwiches, filled baguettes and ploughman's lunches for those popping in for just a snack.
OPEN: 12-3 6-11 (closed Sun eve, all Mon & 1 wk after New Year. **BAR MEALS:** L served all week. D served all week 12-2 7-9.30. Av main course £12.75. **RESTAURANT:** L served Tue-Sun. D served Tue-Sat 12-2 7-9.30. Av 3 course à la carte £18. **BREWERY/COMPANY:** Free House. **PRINCIPAL BEERS:** Wadworth 6X, Badger Dorset Best. **FACILITIES:** Children welcome Garden: patio, outdoor eating. **NOTES:** Parking 50

The Woodbridge Inn
North Newnton SN9 6JZ ☎ 01980 630266
▤ 01980 630266
Dir: *2m SW on A345*
Formerly a bakery, toll house, and brewhouse, this 16th-century building is situated amid four acres of riverside meadows. Wadworth ales. New larger play area available in garden.

The Birds of the Air
Pride of place among bird signs is taken by the Swan, often adopted by inns close to a river. The eccentric Swan with Two Necks probably began as a swan with two nicks in its beak. The Cock may be related to cock-fighting or to St Peter. Geese and chickens appear alone or keeping dangerous company with the Fox. The Bird in Hand comes from falconry and the Dog and Duck either from fowling or from the amusement of setting a dog on a pinioned duck. The Eagle is from Heraldry and the Magpie and Stump from the countryside, while rarities include the Parrot and the Peahen.

England

PITTON   Map 04 SU23

Pick of the Pubs

The Silver Plough ♀
White Hill SP5 1DU ☎ 01722 712266 ▤ 01722 712266
Dir: From Salisbury take A30 towards Andover, Pitton signposted (approx 3m)
At the heart of a quiet village full of thatched houses and surrounded by rolling countryside and a peaceful garden, this popular pub was converted from a farmstead only sixty years ago. Handy for visiting the New Forest and within easy reach of many lovely downland and woodland walks. Inside are black beams strung with numerous antique bootwarmers, toby jugs, painted clogs and various other artefacts. Dishes are prepared with the use of local produce and sauces and puddings are home-made. Food is extensive and varied, ranging from fillet of salmon with a prawn sauce and pan-fried venison steak, to sautéed Mediterranean vegetables bound in pesto and encased in a crisp puff-pastry case, and strips of chicken stir-fried in chilli oil with Oriental-style vegetables on a bed of noodles. Good selection of pasta dishes, ploughman's lunches and sandwich platters.
OPEN: 11-3 6-11 (Sun 12-3, 6-10.30). **BAR MEALS:** L served all week. D served all week 12-2.30 7-9.30. Av main course £8. **RESTAURANT:** L served all week. D served all week 12-2.30 7-9.30. Av 3 course à la carte £17.
BREWERY/COMPANY: Hall & Woodhouse.
PRINCIPAL BEERS: Badger Tanglefoot & Dorset Best, King & Barnes Sussex, Badger IPA. **FACILITIES:** Children welcome Garden: Beer garden, outdoor eating Dogs allowed, lounge bar only. **NOTES:** Parking 50

RAMSBURY   Map 04 SU27

Pick of the Pubs

The Bell 🍴 ♀
The Square SN8 2PE ☎ 01672 520230
Refurbished in a light and contemporary style, The Bell is in the centre of Ramsbury and has a pretty garden to the rear. The chef provides a fresh and innovative menu, described as "northern with a southern twist". Strong flavours and imaginative combinations using local produce result in stylish dishes like butter bean soup with asparagus and ham, spiced crab cake with tomato chutney, and fillet of beef with red wine sauce. Good snacks: global list of wines: Newish owners, reports welcome.
OPEN: 12-3 6-11. **RESTAURANT:** L served all week. D served Mon-Sat 12-2.15 7-9.30.
BREWERY/COMPANY: Free House.
PRINCIPAL BEERS: Wadworth 6X, Greene King IPA, guest ales. **FACILITIES:** Children welcome Garden: Dogs allowed. **NOTES:** Parking 20

REDLYNCH   Map 04 SU22

Kings Head
SP5 2JT ☎ 01725 510420
Adorned in summer with hanging baskets, this attractive, cottagey, 17th-century pub is convenient for visitors exploring the Avon valley and the New Forest. Low beams and open
continued

fires add to the charm. Dishes available might include chicken breast stuffed with asparagus and smoked cheese, ham hock glazed with honey and mustard, or tortilla basket filled with stir fried vegetables.
OPEN: 11-4 6-11. **BAR MEALS:** L served all week. D served all week 12-3 6-10. Av main course £6.50.
BREWERY/COMPANY: Ushers. **PRINCIPAL BEERS:** Ushers Best, Spring Fever & Founders. **FACILITIES:** Children welcome Garden: Dogs allowed. **NOTES:** Parking 30

ROWDE   Map 03 ST96

Pick of the Pubs

The George and Dragon ⊛ ⊛ 🍴 ♀
High St SN10 2PN ☎ 01380 723053 ▤ 01380 724738
e-mail: gd-rowde@lineone.net

Although reputedly the pub has stood here since around the 1400s, the present building dates back to 1675 - and still retains its outside gents' loo! A relaxed, informal atmosphere prevails in the panelled bars and dining-room that are seasonally warmed by open log fires. Pristine fresh Cornish fish takes centre stage on Tim Withers's daily menus which have shown great consistency over the years. His lobster bisque - described as superb - is a great curtain-raiser to house specialities such as warm salad of scallops and bacon, Thai fish curry and a celebrated cheese soufflé with Parmesan and cream. Daily alternatives might include mussel and oyster soup, home-made pasta with creamy ham and mushroom sauce and organic Aberdeen Angus steak and kidney pie, followed by pineapple and mango meringue with Jersey cream. Helen Withers behind the bar looks a picture of rosy-cheeked health, adding just that extra dimension to a true dining experience.
OPEN: 12-3 7-11. Closed Mon lunch, 25 Dec, 1 Jan.
BAR MEALS: L served Tue-Sat. D served Tue-Sat 12-2 7-10. Av main course £15. **RESTAURANT:** L served Tue-Sat. D served Tue-Sat 12-2 7-10. Av 3 course à la carte £25. Av 2 course fixed price £10. **BREWERY/COMPANY:** Free House.
PRINCIPAL BEERS: Hop Back Summer Lightning, Butcombe, Milk Street Brewery, Bath Ales.
FACILITIES: Children welcome Garden: food served outside Dogs allowed. Water. **NOTES:** Parking 10

SALISBURY   Map 03 SU12

The Coach & Horses
Winchester St SP1 1HG ☎ 01722 336254 ▤ 01722 414319
Many changes have taken place in its 500-year history, but the black and white timbered facade of Salisbury's oldest inn remains. Slate-floored bar and cobbled courtyard. Bedrooms.

SALISBURY continued

The Old Mill at Harnham 🍴
Town Path, West Harnham SP2 8EU ☎ 01722 327517
🖹 01722 333367
Dir: near city centre, on River Avon
Listed building which became Wiltshire's first papermaking mill in 1550. Tranquil meadow setting with classic views of Salisbury Cathedral. Crystal clear water diverted from the River Nadder cascades through the restaurant. Bedrooms.

SEEND   Map 03 ST96

The Barge Inn 🍴 🍷
Seend Cleeve SN12 6QB ☎ 01380 828230
🖹 01380 828972
Dir: Off A365 between Melksham & Devizes
Delightfully-situated Victorian barge-style pub on the Kennet and Avon Canal between Bath and Devizes. The inn is a converted wharf house once owned by the Duke of Somerset's family who leased it to a brewer in 1857. Note the delicately painted Victorian flowers which adorn the ceilings and upper walls. Extensive choice of wholesome bar food, including open sandwiches, ploughman's lunches, ham and eggs and steak, kidney and ale pie. Thai-style crab cakes, fresh local crayfish and baked salmon fillet feature among the appetising fish dishes.
OPEN: 11-2.30 (Sun 12-4, 7-11) 6-11. **BAR MEALS:** L served all week. D served all week 12-2 7-9.30. Av main course £8.95.
RESTAURANT: L served all week. D served all week 12-2 7-9.30. Av 3 course à la carte £19. **BREWERY/COMPANY:** Wadworth.
PRINCIPAL BEERS: Wadworth 6X & Henry's IPA, Badger Tanglefoot. **FACILITIES:** Children welcome Garden: outdoor eating Dogs allowed Water. **NOTES:** Parking 50

Bell Inn
Bell Hill SN12 6SA ☎ 01380 828338
e-mail: chrisduparcq@hotmail.com
Step back to the time of the Civil War and picture Oliver Cromwell and his troops breakfasting at this inn in September 1645, on their way from Trowbridge to attack Devizes Castle. The inn prides itself on being at the centre of village life and the emphasis here is on good conversation without intrusive music. Large petanque and French boules pitch in the garden. Favourite dishes tend to include fresh sea bass, spicy sausage and beef in ale casserole.
OPEN: 11-3 (Sun 12-3, 7-10.30) 5.30-11. Jan-Apr eve open 6-11.
BAR MEALS: L served all week. D served Tue-Sun 12-2.15 6.15-9.30. Av main course £6.25. **RESTAURANT:** L served all week. D served Tue-Sun 12-2.15 6.15-9.30. Av 3 course à la carte £13.50. **BREWERY/COMPANY:** Wadworth.
PRINCIPAL BEERS: Wadworth 6X & Henry's IPA, Henrys Smooth. **FACILITIES:** Children welcome Garden: outdoor eating. **NOTES:** Parking 30

SHERSTON   Map 03 ST88

The Rattlebone Inn 🍷
Church St SN16 0LR ☎ 01666 840871 🖹 01666 840871
Dir: M4 J18 take A46 towards Stroud, then R onto B4040 through Acton Turville & onto Sherston. Or N from M4 J17 & follow signs
According to legend, this 16th-century village inn stands where local hero John Rattlebone died of his wounds after the Battle

of Sherston in 1016. The pub is due for refurbishment after a recent takeover by Youngs, but the rambling series of beamed rooms will keep their existing character. A good choice of imaginative dishes includes Welsh lamb noisettes, stuffed chicken breasts, and chargrilled swordfish steak.
OPEN: 11-11.20. **BAR MEALS:** L served all week. D served all week 12-2 7-9.30. Av main course £4.50. **RESTAURANT:** L served all week. D served all week 12-2 7-9.30. Av 3 course à la carte £17.50. **BREWERY/COMPANY:** Youngs.
PRINCIPAL BEERS: Youngs Special, Bitter, Smiles Best, Youngs Triple A. **FACILITIES:** Children welcome Garden: Food served outside

---

STAPLEFORD   Map 03 SU03

Pick of the Pubs

The Boot Inn
High St, Berwick St James SP3 4TN ☎ 01722 790243
Dir: Village signed off A36 at Stapleford 7m NW of Salisbury
An attractive, 16th-century stone and flint inn enjoying a sleepy village setting, with an award-winning garden festooned in summer with colourful flower borders and hanging baskets.
   Traditional unspoilt interior with a warm and friendly atmosphere, and a regularly-changing menu listing above average, home-cooked food. Fresh local produce, including herbs and vegetables from the garden are used in starters like seafood medley with lemon and dill mayonnaise, and beef tomato, feta cheese and olives with basil and olive oil dressing.
   For main course, try pan-fried lambs' kidneys on apple rösti with cider jus, beef in Stilton stew, or roulade of Wiltshire pork with green peppercorns. Freshly-made puddings and well kept Wadworth ales. Home to the famous Boot Inn Pumpkin Club.
OPEN: 12-3 6-11. **BAR MEALS:** L served all week. D served all week 12-2.30 6.30-9.30. Av main course £8.95.
PRINCIPAL BEERS: Wadworth 6X, Bass.
FACILITIES: Garden: food served outside Dogs allowed Water. **NOTES:** Parking 18

STOURHEAD   Map 03 ST73

Spread Eagle Inn
BA12 6QE ☎ 01747 840587 🖹 01747 840954
Dir: N of A303 off B3092
Fine 18th-century brick inn peacefully located in the heart of Stourhead Estate (NT), just yards from the magnificent landscaped gardens, enchanting lakes and woodland walks. Popular all day with visitors seeking refreshment, it offers traditional pub food, including lasagne, steak and kidney pie and sandwiches. Cold food is served between 12 and 9.
OPEN: 9-11. **BAR MEALS:** L served all week. D served all week 12-3 6-9. Av main course £5.95. **RESTAURANT:** D served all week 6-9. Av 3 course à la carte £15.
BREWERY/COMPANY: Free House.
PRINCIPAL BEERS: Courage Best. **FACILITIES:** Children welcome Garden:. **NOTES:** Parking 200. **ROOMS:** 5 bedrooms 5 en suite s£60 d£85

TOLLARD ROYAL   Map 03 ST91

King John Inn
SP5 5PS ☎ 01725 516207   🖥 01725 516459
Dir: On B3081 (7m E of Shaftesbury)
A Victorian building, opened in 1859, the King John is a
friendly and relaxing place. Expect an interesting menu - you
won't find chips here. Bedrooms.

UPPER CHUTE   Map 04 SU25

The Cross Keys NEW
SP11 9ER ☎ 01264 730295   🖥 01264 730889
Located in a walkers' paradise on top of the North Wessex
Downs, this welcoming free house enjoys commanding views
from its south-facing terrace and large garden. Traditional pub
favourites like cheese ploughman's or ham, eggs and chips are
supported by home-cooked specials including chicken and
mushroom casserole, steak and ale pie, grilled sea bass, and
Sunday roasts.
OPEN: 11-3 6-11. Closed 26 Dec, 1 Jan. **BAR MEALS:** L served
all week. D served all week 12-2.15 6-9.30. Av main course £7.25.
RESTAURANT: L served all week. D served all week 12-2.15
6-9.30. Av 3 course à la carte £14. **BREWERY/COMPANY:** Free
House. **PRINCIPAL BEERS:** Fullers London Pride, Wadworth
Henrys IPA, Hampshire King Alfred. **FACILITIES:** Children
welcome Garden: Food served outside Dogs allowed.
NOTES: Parking 40

UPTON LOVELL   Map 03 ST94

Prince Leopold 🐑 ♈
BA12 0JP ☎ 01985 850460   🖥 01985 850737
e-mail: Princeleopold@Lineone.net
Dir: S of A36 between Warminster & Salisbury
Village inn with a riverside setting, named after Queen
Victoria's youngest son - a frequent visitor when he lived in
nearby Boyton. The River Wylye runs through the garden that
enjoys some fine views across the valley. The menu offers a
good choice of balti curries, shoulder of lamb, rib eye steak
with Stilton crust and a selection of fish in season.
OPEN: 12-3 7-11. **BAR MEALS:** L served Tue-Sun. D served
Tue-Sun 12-2 7-9.30. Av main course £6.90. **RESTAURANT:** L
served Tue-Sun. D served Tue-Sun 12-2 7-9.30. Av 3 course à la
carte £14. **BREWERY/COMPANY:** Free House.
PRINCIPAL BEERS: Ringwood, John Smith.
FACILITIES: Children welcome Garden: Beer garden, patio..
NOTES: Parking 20. **ROOMS:** 6 bedrooms 6 en suite s£30 d£45

AA The Restaurant Guide 2002

The right choice every time
with this invaluable guide
for gourmets

The Restaurant Guide 2002

www.theAA.com

AA Lifestyle Guides

WARMINSTER   Map 03 ST84

Pick of the Pubs

The Angel Inn ⊛ ♦♦♦♦♦ 🐑 ♈
Upton Scudamore BA12 0AG ☎ 01985 213225
🖥 01985 218182

Comfortably refurbished old whitewashed inn situated in
a small village north of Warminster, offering a relaxed and
unpretentious atmosphere, freshly prepared food and ten
individually furnished bedrooms that are perfect for
businessmen weary of faceless hotel accommodation.
A high beamed ceiling and soft lighting characterise the
main bar, with its scrubbed pine tables, warm decor and
attractive feature fireplaces. In summer, guests spill out
on to the terrace with its hardwood tables and big cotton
parasols.
    Regularly changing menus feature quality
ingredients and plenty of imagination, whilst the decent
wine list offers six or seven selections available by the
glass. Lunchtime choices include rustic bread with roasted
garlic and pickled vegetables, home-made steak and
mushroom pie, smoked haddock fishcakes, or locally
made sausages and mash.
    Evenings bring starters like pheasant and chestnut
terrine, Gressingham duck with peppered pear and
caramel jus, grilled cod and goats' cheese potato cake, hot
pork piri piri with couscous, or asparagus tortillas served
with a chilli bean salad. Blackboard puddings include
profiteroles with ice cream and chocolate sauce.
OPEN: 12-3 6-11. **BAR MEALS:** L served all week. D served
all week 12-2 7-9.30. Av main course £6.95.
RESTAURANT: L served all week. D served all week 12-2
7-9.30. Av 3 course à la carte £20.
BREWERY/COMPANY: Free House.
PRINCIPAL BEERS: Wadworth 6X, Butcombe.
FACILITIES: Children welcome Garden: patio/terrace,
outdoor eating, BBQ Dogs allowed. **NOTES:** Parking 30.
ROOMS: 10 bedrooms 10 en suite s£49.50 d£70 FR£85

The George Inn ♦♦♦♦
BA12 7DG ☎ 01985 840396   🖥 01985 841333
A river runs through the beer garden of this 18th-century
coaching inn. Open fires burn in both bar and restaurant, and
the Sunday lunchtime carvery is very popular locally.
Bedrooms.

England

WESTBURY Map 03 ST85

The Duke of Bratton ♦♦ ♇
Melbourne St, Bratton BA13 4RW
☎ 01380 830242 📄 01380 831239
Dir: *from Westbury follow B3098*

Three cottages were made into the 'new' Duke in 1861 when the original pub next door was pulled down. The bar has a lighter menu offering soup, haddock and chips, cottage pie and baguettes. The restaurant may offer Scottish sirloin, breast of Wiltshire chicken, Wiltshire cooked ham, Applewood smoked trout or Stilton and double cream tagliatelle. A specials board is also available.

OPEN: 11.30-3 7-11 (Sat 11-11 in summer, Sun 12-3, 7-10.30).
BAR MEALS: L served all week. D served all week 12-2 7-9. Av main course £8.75. **RESTAURANT:** L served all week. D served all week 12-2 7-9. Av 3 course à la carte £16.50.
BREWERY/COMPANY: Free House.
PRINCIPAL BEERS: Moles Best, Courage Best, Everards Tiger, Moles Molenium. **FACILITIES:** Garden: outdoor eating, Dogs allowed By arrangement. **NOTES:** Parking 30.
ROOMS: 3 bedrooms s£25 d£40

Pins & Firkins

Brewing has a rich store of technical terms and old-fashioned measures. The conventional container for draught beer - for centuries made of wood, but nowadays of metal - is called a cask. A barrel in brewing terminology is a 36-gallon cask, and a keg is a sealed metal container for beer that has been filtered, sterilised and pressurised before leaving the brewery. British beer in pubs still comes in pints and half-pints and pubs still order their beer using the old-style cask measures, which follow a scale of nine

pin - 4.5 gallons **firkin** - 9 gallons
kilderkin - 18 gallons **barrel** - 36 gallons
hogshead - 54 gallons

Two obsolete cask sizes are the butt of 108 gallons and the tun, which held varying quantities above 200 gallons. A yard of ale is a glass tube 3ft long and containing up to 3 pints, now only use in drinking contests.

WHITLEY Map 03 ST86

Pick of the Pubs

The Pear Tree Inn ⊚ 🐸 ♇
Top Ln SN12 8QX ☎ 01225 709131 📄 01225 702276
Dir: *A365 from Melksham toward Bath, at Shaw R on B3353 into Whitley, 1st L in lane, pub is at end of lane.*

A former working farm dating back to 1750, the building stands in four acres of garden dominated by large oak trees and surrounded by open countryside. It remains very much a local venue, with flagstone floors and open fires, while the dining-room has a rustic feel, decorated in part by old garden implements. The heart of the business lies in the kitchen in production of everything from fresh local ingredients, which is clearly evident from its imaginative lunch and dinner menus. From the former, go for smoked salmon bruschetta with avocado and lemon dressing or creamy wild mushroom risotto with Parmesan tuille and rosemary oil (in either starter or larger portions) and at night splash out on lamb sweetbread and pheasant terrine, followed by corn-fed chicken with tarragon, confit onion, bacon lardons and champ potato. British cheeses with apple and fig chutney or glazed prune and Armagnac tart with Jersey ice cream to follow.
OPEN: 11-3 6-11. **BAR MEALS:** L served all week. D served all week 12-2 6.30-9.30. **RESTAURANT:** L served all week. D served all week 12-2 6.30-9.30.
BREWERY/COMPANY: Free House.
PRINCIPAL BEERS: Wadworth 6X, Bass, Abbey Bellringer, Oakhill Best. **FACILITIES:** Children welcome Garden: patio, outdoor eating. **NOTES:** Parking 60

WINTERBOURNE BASSETT Map 03 SU07

The White Horse Inn NEW
SN4 9QB ☎ 01793 731257
e-mail: ckstone@btinternet.com
Village pub on the Marlborough Downs, just off the main Swindon-Devizes road, two miles north of the Avebury Stone Circle. Food is served in the bar and conservatory restaurant from a wide selection of dishes to suit all tastes and budgets. Dishes are prepared from fresh produce, local where possible, and house specialities include red mullet pastis, lamb Marrakech, Caribbean chicken, and baked vanilla cheesecake.

continued

OPEN: 11-3 7-11. **BAR MEALS:** L served all week. D served all week 12-2.30 7-10. Av main course £5.75. **RESTAURANT:** L served all week. D served all week 12-2.30 7-10.
BREWERY/COMPANY: Wadworth.
PRINCIPAL BEERS: Wadworth 6X, IPA, Hophouse Brews.
FACILITIES: Garden: Food served outside. **NOTES:** Parking 25

WOODFALLS	Map 03 SU12

The Woodfalls Inn ♦♦♦♦
The Ridge SP5 2LN ☎ 01725 513222 ▤ 01725 513220
Dir: B3080 to Woodfalls
Built in 1868 as an ale house and coaching inn on the northern edge of the New Forest, this attractively refurbished inn offers well equipped bedrooms and a good range of food. Fish from local harbours is a speciality.

WOOTTON RIVERS	Map 03 SU16

Royal Oak 🐾 ⵣ
SN8 4NQ ☎ 01672 810322 ▤ 01672 811168
Dir: 3m S from Marlborough off A346

Thatched and timbered 16th-century inn situated 100 yards from the Kennet and Avon Canal in one of Wiltshire's prettiest villages. Heavily beamed bars. A typical menu includes roast beef with horse radish sauce, grilled salmon with chilli and pesto sauce, roast partridge, venison steak and chicken casserole.
OPEN: 10.30-3.30 6-11. **BAR MEALS:** L served all week. D served all week 12-2.30 6-9.30. Av main course £7.
RESTAURANT: L served all week. D served all week 12-2.30 6-9.30. Av 3 course à la carte £12.50.
BREWERY/COMPANY: Free House.
PRINCIPAL BEERS: Wadworth 6X, guest ales.
FACILITIES: Children welcome Garden: patio, outdoor eating. Dogs allowed. **ROOMS:** 5 bedrooms 3 en suite s£20-£40 d£40-£50 FR£60-£90

WYLYE

The Bell Inn ♦♦♦ ⵣ
High St, Wylye BA12 0QP ☎ 01985 248338
▤ 01985 248389
e-mail: LK.thebell@wylye2.freeserve.co.uk
There's a wealth of old oak beams, log fires and an inglenook fireplace at this 14th-century coaching inn, situated in the pretty Wylye Valley.
You can eat in the bar, which offers sandwiches, steaks and smoked Wiltshire ham alongside the regularly changing choice of cask ales, or more formally in the restaurant. Typical dishes are pan-fried trio of pigeon breasts, and roast fillet of beef in Madeira.

OPEN: 11.30-2.30 6-11 (Sun 12-3, 7-10.30). **BAR MEALS:** L served all week. D served all week 12-2 6-9.30. Av main course £7.50. **RESTAURANT:** L served all week. D served all week 12-2 6-9.30. Av 3 course à la carte £25. **BREWERY/COMPANY:** Free House **FACILITIES:** Children's licence Garden: outdoor eating Dogs allowed Water. **NOTES:** Parking 20.
ROOMS: 3 bedrooms 3 en suite

WORCESTERSHIRE

ABBERLEY	Map 03 ST76

Manor Arms Country Inn ♦♦♦ ⵣ
WR6 6BN ☎ 01299 896507 ▤ 01299 896723
e-mail: manorarms@abberley.com
Originally owned by the lord of the manor, this 300-year-old inn is a building of great charm and character, situated in a delightful English village high on the Abberley Hills.
Great area for walkers. Nearby places of interest include West Midland Safari and Leisure Park, Ironbridge and the Severn Valley Railway. Original oak beams, and a log-burning fire enhance the appeal of the place. Expect a varied selection of steaks, pies and soups.
OPEN: 12-3 6-11 (closed Mon lunch in winter). **BAR MEALS:** L served all week. D served all week 12-2 7-9. Av main course £6.50. **RESTAURANT:** D served all week 7-9.30. Av 3 course fixed price £14. **BREWERY/COMPANY:** Enterprise Inns.
PRINCIPAL BEERS: Fullers London Pride, Theakstons Best Bitter.
FACILITIES: Children's licence Garden: patio/terrace, outdoor eating. **NOTES:** Parking 25. **ROOMS:** 10 bedrooms 10 en suite s£38 d£50 2 family rooms £68-75

England

Pick of the Pubs

Horse & Jockey 🛏 ♀
Far Forest DY14 9DX ☎ 01299 266239
▤ 01299 266227
e-mail: suzanne-st@hotmail.com

Fully operational for just three years following restoration this free house, first licensed as a pub in 1807, stands at the heart of a former family estate overlooking the Wyre Forest and Lem Brook Valley. Interior features include old blackened beams, a large inglenook and the original fresh-water well over which now sits a glass-panelled dining table. Regardless of such antiquity, food on offer is full of imaginative modern twists, using freshest available local ingredients to create modern, up-dated interpretations of English pub favourites. Publican pie and home-baked ham with honey, mustard and fried egg rub shoulders with tandoori chicken with mint dip and market-fresh fish that might offer up dressed crab in parsley sauce or roast grey mullet with pineapple and citrus chutney. Venison and beetroot terrine, speciality chilli sausages on mango mash and grilled lemon sole with pine-nut butter precede marbled chocolate mousse and apple and blackberry tart in their turn.
OPEN: 12-3 6-11 (Sun 12-10.30). **BAR MEALS:** L served all week. D served all week 12-2.30 6-9.30. Av main course £6. **RESTAURANT:** D served all week 6-9.30. Av 3 course à la carte £16. **BREWERY/COMPANY:** Free House. **PRINCIPAL BEERS:** Marstons Pedigree, Hobsons Original, Hobsons Town Crier, Greene King Old Speckled Hen. **FACILITIES:** Children welcome Children's licence Garden: outdoor eating, views of Lem Valley Dogs allowed garden only. **NOTES:** Parking 50

Little Pack Horse ♀
31 High St DY12 2DH ☎ 01299 403762 ▤ 01299 403762
e-mail: littlepackhorse@aol.com
Historic timber-framed inn with low beams and an elm timber bar, located in one of the Severn Valley's prettiest towns. The interior is warmed by a cosy woodburning stove and candlelit at night. Expect steak and ale Desperate Dan pie, Cajun roast chicken, scampi and faggots with mash and mushy peas among other dishes.
OPEN: 12-3 6-11 (Sat-Sun 12-11). **BAR MEALS:** L served all week. D served all week 12-2.15 6.30-9.30. Av main course £5. **PRINCIPAL BEERS:** Ushers - Best, Four Seasons,. **FACILITIES:** Children welcome Garden: patio, food served outiside Dogs allowed

The Bear & Ragged Staff 🛏 ♀ **NEW**
Station Rd WR6 5JH ☎ 01886 833399 ▤ 01886 833106
e-mail: bearragged@aol.com
Dir: Off the A4103 (Hereford Road) 3M form the centre of Malvern follow A449 turning L just before Powick village at the signpost for Bransford
Mid-way between Worcester and the Malvern Hills, this smart dining pub has an enviable reputation for its imaginative menus and fresh Cornish fish. Lunchtime bar meals include brunch rolls, Cajun-spiced salmon, and five cheese tortellini. It's wise to book for the restaurant at weekends, when starters like avocado, crab and tomato pancake might precede ribeye steak with shallots and red wine sauce, roast cod on butter bean mash, or grilled haddock with bacon and thyme.
OPEN: 12-2.30 6.30-10.30. **BAR MEALS:** L served all week 12-2. Av main course £6. **RESTAURANT:** L served all week. D served Mon-Sat 12-2 7-9. Av 3 course à la carte £20. **BREWERY/COMPANY:** Free House. **PRINCIPAL BEERS:** Bass, Highgate Special Bitter, Hobsons Best Bitter. **FACILITIES:** Garden: food served outside. **NOTES:** Parking 40

Fox & Hounds Inn 🛏 ♀
Church St GL20 7LA ☎ 01684 772377 ▤ 01684 772373
Dir: M5 J9 into Tewkesbury take B4080 towards Pershore. Bredon 3m
Pretty 16th-century thatched pub, resplendent with colourful, over-flowing hanging baskets in summer, close to the River Avon. There is a wide-ranging menu available throughout, plus blackboard specials and lunchtime bar snacks. Favourite dishes include home-made pies, fresh game in season, crispy duck, and the daily fresh fish selection.
OPEN: 11-3 6-11 (Sun 12-3, 6.30-10.30). **BAR MEALS:** L served all week. D served all week 12-2 6.30-9.30. Av main course £6.95. **RESTAURANT:** L served all week 12-2.30 6.30-9.30. Av 3 course à la carte £12. **BREWERY/COMPANY:** Whitbread. **PRINCIPAL BEERS:** Banks, Marstons Pedigree, Greene King Old Speckled Hen. **FACILITIES:** Children welcome Garden: patio, outdoor eating, BBQ. **NOTES:** Parking 35

Strange Games

Competitiveness and ingenuity have thrown up a rich variety of pub games besides the best-known ones, from lawn billiards to maggot racing to clay pipe smoking contests, where the object is to keep a pipeful of tobacco alight longest. Cribbage and other once popular card games are not seen so often nowadays, but bagatelle is alive and well in Chester and Coventry. In Knur and Spell up North the players hit a small ball (the knur) as far as possible with a bat. Bat and Trap, an odd variety of cricket, has a long history going back at least to the 16th century in Kent. In Sussex the game of Toad in the Hole involves pitching flat discs into a hole in a table and in Lincolnshire they throw pennies into a hole and call it gnurdling. For all the video games and one-arm bandits, older and more convivial pastimes are still alive in British pubs.

BRETFORTON   Map 03 SP04

Pick of the Pubs

The Fleece Inn ♀
The Cross WR11 5JE ☎ 01386 831173
Dir: B4035 from Evesham
Owned by the National Trust, the Fleece is a living
museum that can trace a history back 1200 years.
Converted from working farm to hostelry in 1848, it
houses rooms called the Dugout - once the farm pantry;
the Pewter Room with a world-famous collection
reputedly abandoned by Cromwell; and the Brewhouse
which once produced beer and cider. Mementoes abound
of the former owner, Miss Taplin, who bequeathed it to
the nation - provided potato crisps were never sold! Hot
meals from the kitchen include mixed grills and Sunday
roast lunch. See Morrismen on Bank Holidays; early June
asparagus auctions; July beer festival; and August summer
fête
OPEN: 11-3 6-11. **BAR MEALS:** L served all week. D served
all week 11.45-2 6.30-9. Av main course £4.50.
BREWERY/COMPANY: Free House.
PRINCIPAL BEERS: Uley, Hook Norton, Woods.
FACILITIES: Children welcome Garden: outdoor eating,.
NOTES: Parking 20

DROITWICH   Map 03 SO86

The Chequers
Cutnall Green WR9 0DJ ☎ 01299 851292 ▤ 01299 851131
Well maintained traditional inn with lots of exposed beams
inside. Interesting and varied menu. Cosy atmosphere.

Old Cock Inn
Friar St WR9 8EQ ☎ 01905 774233
Dating from the 17th century, this charming pub has its share
of history. During the Civil War, Roundhead artillery used the
high ground nearby to shell Royalist troops at the church.
Three of the stained-glass windows rescued from the rubble
are now incorporated into the pubs upstairs rooms.

FLADBURY   Map 03 SO94

Chequers Inn ★ ★
Chequers Ln WR10 2PZ ☎ 01386 860276
▤ 01386 861286
e-mail: chequers_inn_fladbury@hotmail.com
Dir: Off A4538 between Evesham and Pershore
14th-century inn tucked away in a pretty village with views of
the glorious Bredon Hills. Inside are lots of old beams and a
cosy fire. Under new management, the Chequers uses fresh
local produce in its home-made dishes and offers a changing
monthly menu in addition to daily specials. Expect rack of
lamb with port wine and redcurrant sauce and sweet and sour
monkfish among other dishes.
OPEN: 11-3 6-11. **BAR MEALS:** L served all week. D served all
week 12-2 6.30-10. Av main course £7. **RESTAURANT:** L served
all week. D served all week 12-2 6.30-10. Av 3 course à la carte
£18. **BREWERY/COMPANY:** Free House.
PRINCIPAL BEERS: Theakstons Best, Courage Directors, Fullers
London Pride, Timothy Taylor Landlord. **FACILITIES:** Garden:
food served outside. **NOTES:** Parking 28.
ROOMS: 8 bedrooms 8 en suite s£49 d£60

FLYFORD FLAVELL   Map 03 SO95

The Boot Inn ♦♦♦♦
Radford Rd WR7 4BS ☎ 01386 462658
*Dir: Take Evesham rd, L at 2nd rdbt onto A422, Flyford Flavell signed
after 3m*
Part 13th-century former coaching inn enjoying a quiet village
location on the Wychavon Way. Well placed for the Cotswolds
and Malvern Hills, it offers en suite accommodation, and
traditional pub meals in the timbered bars. Recently
refurbished, and very popular with the locals. Look to the
specials board for home-made faggots, liver and bacon, cod in
beer batter, or saddle of lamb.
OPEN: 11-2.30 (Sat-Sun 11-3) 6.30-11 (Sat 6-11, Sun 7-11).
BAR MEALS: L served all week. D served 12-2 6.30-10 (no bar
food Sat eve). Av main course £3.95. **RESTAURANT:** L served all
week. D served all week 12-2 6.30-10. Av 3 course à la carte £12.
BREWERY/COMPANY: Free House.
PRINCIPAL BEERS: Boddingtons, Wadworth 6X, Greene King
Old Speckled Hen, Marstons Pedigree. **FACILITIES:** Children
welcome Garden: beer garden with seating, patio, food served in
garden Dogs allowed. **NOTES:** Parking 30.
ROOMS: 1 bedrooms 1 en suite s£45.50 d£55

HONEYBOURNE   Map 03 SP14

The Thatched Tavern ♀
WR11 5PQ ☎ 01386 830454 ▤ 01386 833842
e-mail: pjpubco@fsbdial.co.uk
Dir: 6 miles from Chipping Campden
Good as its name, this charming old 15th-century inn nestles
under a thatched roof. Flagstone floors and open fires add to
the cheerful atmosphere of a genuine village pub. Well kept
ales accompany good value meals that range from bar snacks
to midweek specials and Sunday brunch. Everything from hot
baguettes or steak and kidney pudding to minted lamb steaks,
pan-fried sardines or spinach and red pepper lasagne comes
with the same friendly service.
OPEN: 11-3 6-11. **BAR MEALS:** L served all week. D served all
week 12-2.30 7-10. Av main course £8. **RESTAURANT:** L served
all week. D served all week 12-2.30 7-10. Av 3 course à la carte
£18.50. **BREWERY/COMPANY:** Punch Taverns.
PRINCIPAL BEERS: Adnams Broadside, Bass, Fullers London
Pride, Marstons Pedigree. **FACILITIES:** Garden: Food served
outside. **NOTES:** Parking 25

KEMPSEY · Map 03 SO84

Pick of the Pubs

Walter de Cantelupe Inn 🐑 ♀
Main Rd WR5 3NA ☎ 01905 820572 📠 01905 820572
e-mail: walter.depub@fsbdial.co.uk
Dir: 4m S of Worcester City centre, on A38 in the centre of village

The Georgian façade of this curiously named inn belies its
16th-century origins - and, if you need proof, just take a
look at the exposed remains of the original oak timbering
in the middle of the building.
  The inn, which was originally one of a row of three
cottages, is named after the rebel Bishop of Worcester
who colluded with Baron Simon de Montfort prior to the
nearby battle of Evesham in 1265. Nowadays you'll find a
relaxed, informal atmosphere, with comfortable dining
chairs, an old settle, and a large fireplace. The lounge area
opens onto the walled, south-facing rear garden.
  The inn is noted for well kept, hand pumped real ales,
and a regularly updated blackboard menu featuring local
ingredients and home cooking. Typical dishes might
include ploughman's with local cheeses, steak and
Guinness pie, roast half shoulder of lamb, baked natural
smoked haddock, and fresh crab enchiladas.
OPEN: 12-2 6-11 (Sun 6-10.30). Closed Mon ex BH.
& Dec 25-26. **BAR MEALS:** L served Tue-Sun. D served
Tue-Sat 12-2 6.30-9.30. Av main course £6.50.
RESTAURANT: L served Tue-Sun. D served Tue-Sat 12-2 7-9.
Av 3 course à la carte £16.50. **BREWERY/COMPANY:** Free
House. **PRINCIPAL BEERS:** Marstons Bitter, Timothy
Talyor Landlord, Malvern Hill Black Pear.
FACILITIES: Children welcome Garden: outdoor eating,
patio, Dogs allowed over night by arragement.
NOTES: Parking 24. **ROOMS:** s£23.50 d£37.50
FR£50-£60

KNIGHTWICK · Map 03 SO75

Pick of the Pubs

The Talbot at Knightwick 🐑 ♀
WR6 5PH ☎ 01886 821235 📠 01886 821060
e-mail: temevalley@aol.com
Dir: A44 through Worcester, 8m W turn onto B4197

Entirely home-produced organic foods and home-brewed
ale using local Worcestershire hops mark out the Talbot, at
the heart of the Teme Valley, for special attention. Its
freedom from 'gimmickry and mock old-worldliness' is
another excuse for making a special detour. Family owners
have plied their trade here for 18 years with fervour and
dedication, producing such bar delights as saffron fish
soup with rouille to precede minced lamb pie with cheese
pastry and steamed jam pudding or blackberry fluff to
follow. Set dinner in the small, informal restaurant comes
at fixed prices with an optional course of local cheeses and
fig salami. Look for goose-neck pudding from a traditional
recipe, wild duck with bay leaves and garlic and an exotic
potato pie with grated truffle and olive oil. Then accept the
dare of treacle hollyhog or home-made ice creams in a
brandy-snap basket.
OPEN: 11-11 (Sun 12-10.30). **BAR MEALS:** L served all
week. D served all week 12-2 6.30-9.30. Av main course £7.
RESTAURANT: L served all week. D served all week 12-2
6.30-9.30. Av 3 course fixed price £14.95.
BREWERY/COMPANY: Free House.
PRINCIPAL BEERS: Teme Valley. **FACILITIES:** Children
welcome Garden: patio, food served outdoors Dogs
allowed by arrangement only. **NOTES:** Parking 50.
ROOMS: 10 bedrooms 7 en suite s£38 d£50

MALVERN · Map 03 SO74

Farmers Arms ♀
Birts St, Birtsmorton WR13 6AP ☎ 01684 833308
Dir: On B4208 S of Great Malvern
Expect a friendly welcome at this 15th-century black and white
timbered pub, in a quiet parish close to the Malvern Hills. It
serves decent ales and homely bar food in its low-beamed
rooms, including cottage pie, macaroni cheese, Hereford pie
and a variety of jacket potatoes, Vienna rolls and sandwiches.
OPEN: 11-2.30 6-11 (Sun 12-2.30 7-11). **BAR MEALS:** L served
all week. D served all week 11-2 6-9.30. Av main course £4.
BREWERY/COMPANY: Free House.
PRINCIPAL BEERS: Hook Norton Best & Old Hooky.
FACILITIES: Children welcome Garden: patio, outdoor eating
Dogs allowed. **NOTES:** Parking 30 No credit cards

OMBERSLEY — Map 03 SO86

Pick of the Pubs

Crown & Sandys Arms 🐑 ♀ NEW
Main Rd WR9 0EW ☎ 01905 620252 🖨 01905 620769
e-mail: richardeverton@crownandsandys.co.uk
Local general store owner and wine merchant Richard
Everton bought this impressive, Dutch-gabled, 17th-century
inn, set in pretty village full of ancient timber-framed
cottages, nearly two years ago and has successfully
transformed it into a trendy, modern dining venue. People
travel from miles around to eat either in the large,
flagstoned bar, with its mix of sturdy furnishings and open
fireplaces, or in one of the very stylish bistros, one featuring
zebra-print chairs and marble-topped tables. The draw,
other than the bustling, laid-back atmosphere and the
decent wine list, is the ambitious modern pub cooking,
notably that of fresh fish and seafood. A lengthy main menu
lists Caesar salad with chargrilled chicken, carpaccio of
peppered beef fillet, slow-roasted shank of lamb on bubble-
and-squeak with red wine and rosemary jus, and Malaysian
curry, while daily fish specials may include seafood chowder
and sea bass stuffed with lemon, capers and fresh herbs.
OPEN: 11.30-2.30 5-11 (11.30-11 Sat & Sun).
BAR MEALS: L served all week. D served all week 12-2.30
6-10 (Sun 12-10). Av main course £10. **RESTAURANT:** L
served all week. D served all week 12-2.30 6-10. Av 3 course
à la carte £20. **BREWERY/COMPANY:** Free House.
PRINCIPAL BEERS: Adnams, Marstons Pedigree, Greene
King Abbot Ale, Woods Parish Bitter. **FACILITIES:** Children
welcome Garden: food served outside. **NOTES:** Parking
100. **ROOMS:** 4 bedrooms 4 en suite d£50

Pick of the Pubs

The Kings Arms 🐑 ♀
Main Rd WR9 0EW ☎ 01905 620142 🖨 01905 620142
Dir: Just off A449
Like the rest of the charming village in which it stands, this
wonderful black and white timbered inn oozes history and
character. Dating back to 1411, it was reputedly King
Charles's first stop after fleeing the Battle of Worcester in
1651. Inviting, dimly-lit interior with flagstone floors, thick
oak beams, intimate nooks and crannies and three blazing
log fires in winter. The cosy atmosphere welcomes visitors
tempted by an array of modern pub food - especially fish
fresh from Birmingham market - available on a daily basis.
Expect oysters on ice, snow crab claws with lemon
mayonnaise, paella, and at least 12 fish dishes, perhaps
hake with pesto and walnut crust and plump cod with
home-made chips. In season the fresh seafood platter
takes some beating. Alternative dishes include steak and
kidney pudding, couscous salad with chargrilled vegetables,
beef Wellington and roast lamb shank with dauphinoise
potatoes. Chocolate brownie with warm chocolate sauce
and Stilton cheese with port to finish.
OPEN: 11-3 5.30-11. Closed 25 Dec. **BAR MEALS:** L served
all week. D served Mon-Sat 12-2.15 6-10. Av main course
£8.75. **BREWERY/COMPANY:** Free House.
PRINCIPAL BEERS: Banks's, Marstons Pedigree, Cannon
Royal Arrowhead. **FACILITIES:** Children welcome Garden:
patio, outdoor eating **NOTES:** Parking 60

PENSAX — Map 03 SO76

The Bell Inn
WR6 6AE ☎ 01299 896677
Dir: From Kidderminster A456 to Clows Top, B4202 towards Abberley,
pub 2m on L
Mock Tudor pub built in 1883 by John Joseph Jones who also
built the famous clock tower at Abberley Hall. It offers all the
warmth and charm you'd expect of a country pub, with a
constantly changing selection of guest real ales and home-
cooked food based on fresh local produce. A winter selection
from the blackboard included faggots with mushy peas, liver
and onions, chicken curry, and game pie.
OPEN: 12-2.30 5-11 (Sun 12-10.30; closed Mon lunch).
BAR MEALS: L served Tue-Sun. D served all week 12-2 6-9. Av
main course £6. **RESTAURANT:** L served Tue-Sun. D served all
week 12-2 6-9. **BREWERY/COMPANY:** Free House.
PRINCIPAL BEERS: Enville Best, Archers Golden, Timothy Taylor
Best Bitter, Hobsons Town Crier. **FACILITIES:** Children welcome
Garden: Beer garden, outdoor eating Dogs allowed On leads.
NOTES: Parking 20

POWICK — Map 03 SO85

The Halfway House
Bastonford WR2 4SL ☎ 01905 831098
Dir: From A15 J7 take A4440 then A449
Situated at the foot of the Malvern Hills, midway between
Worcester and Malvern. All dishes are listed on blackboards
and the choice ranges from jumbo baps and Aberdeen Angus
steaks to Black Country faggots and curry. Fresh fish when
available might include seared fillet of mullet and natural oak-
smoked haddock.
OPEN: 12-3 6-11. Closed Mon lunch. **BAR MEALS:** L served
Tue-Sun. D served all week 12-2.30 6-9. Av main course £8.
RESTAURANT: L served Tue-Sun. D served all week 12-2.30 6-9.
Av 3 course à la carte £18.50. **BREWERY/COMPANY:** Free
House. **PRINCIPAL BEERS:** Marstons Pedigree, St Georges,
Eccleshall. **FACILITIES:** Children welcome Garden: Dogs
allowed. **NOTES:** Parking 30. **ROOMS:** 2 bedrooms
2 en suite s£70

SHATTERFORD — Map 08 SO78

The Bellmans Cross 🐑
Bridgnorth Rd DY12 1RN ☎ 01299 861322
🖨 01299 861047
Dir: on A442 5m outside Kidderminster

Mid 19th-century inn, recently completely refurbished and
surrounded by lovely Worcestershire countryside. Menus vary
with the seasons and the food is freshly prepared. There is an

continued

intimate atmosphere in Dominique's Restaurant, which offers cooking in the French style with dishes such as roast salmon with mussel and saffron sauce and prime fillet of Scottish beef with black pudding and truffle sauce. **OPEN:** 11-3 6-11 (all day BHs). **BAR MEALS:** L served all week. D served all week 12-2.15 6-9.30. **RESTAURANT:** L served all week. D served all week 12-2.15 6-9.30.
BREWERY/COMPANY: Free House. **PRINCIPAL BEERS:** Bass, Greene King Old Speckled Hen, Worthington.
FACILITIES: Garden: patio, outdoor eating **NOTES:** Parking 25

Red Lion Inn 🍷
Bridgnorth Rd DY12 1SU ☎ 01299 861221
Dir: N from Kidderminster on the A442
Family-run freehouse set in beautiful countryside, where locals congregate around 'the hottest little coal fire in Shropshire'. The inn offers a choice of real ales, and a range of food from sandwiches to T-bone steaks. The restaurant and one of the bars is no-smoking, and one menu serves all. Local produce features in season, including Arley pheasant, Ludlow venison and fresh fish delivered daily.
OPEN: 11.30-2.30 6.30-11 (Sun 12-3 7-10.30). Closed Dec 25.
BAR MEALS: L served all week. D served all week 11.30-2 6.30-9.30. Av main course £6. **RESTAURANT:** L served all week. D served all week 11.30-2 6.30-9.30. Av 3 course à la carte £15.
BREWERY/COMPANY: Free House.
PRINCIPAL BEERS: Bathams, Banks' Mild, Shropshire Lad, Wye Valley Butty Bach. **FACILITIES:** Children welcome Garden: outdoor eating, patio. **NOTES:** Parking 50

TENBURY WELLS   Map 03 SO56

The Fountain Inn 🍷 NEW
Oldwood, St Michaels WR15 8TR ☎ 01584 810701
🖷 01584 819030
e-mail: miami@fountaininn.freeserve.co.uk
Dir: 1m out of Tenbury Wells on the A4112 Leominster Road
Víctor Meldrew would not believe it - a 17th-century black and white country inn, with a real live shark tank nestling incongruously beside the roaring log fire. Hand-pulled guest beers and the exclusive Fountain Ale complement the short snack menu and daily specials. Main courses like Hunter's chicken, Mediterranean lamb, or wild mushroom strudel satisfy larger appetites, whilst blackened red snapper, garlic swordfish and salted sea bass are typical fish dishes. But please, don't ask for shark!
OPEN: 11-11. **BAR MEALS:** L served all week. D served all week 12-10. Av main course £6.95. **RESTAURANT:** L served all week. D served all week 12-10. Av 3 course à la carte £13.95.
BREWERY/COMPANY: Free House. **PRINCIPAL BEERS:** Bass, Black Sheep. **FACILITIES:** Children welcome Garden: food served outside **NOTES:** Parking 60

Pick of the Pubs

Peacock Inn ⊛ ♦♦♦♦ 👁 🍷
WR15 8LL ☎ 01584 810506 🖷 01584 811236
e-mail: jvidler@fsbdial.co.uk
Dir: A456 from Worcester then A443 to Tenbury Wells. Inn is 1.25m E of Tenbury Wells

Nestling in the Teme Valley, famous for its hopyards and orchards, and with fine views across the river, this 14th-century coaching inn has been sympathetically extended and a wealth of pretty shrubs, hanging baskets and ivy create a superb welcoming exterior. Many of the original features, including oak beams, open log fires, are retained within the relaxing bars and oak-panelled restaurant. Local market produce plays a full part on modern menus, from home-made steak and kidney pudding, game pie, Thai fishcakes with a vegetable sweet and sour sauce and fresh cod in beer batter, to interesting daily specials favouring fresh fish from Birmingham market - roast monkfish with Indian noodles and caramelised shallot sauce and chargrilled tuna with roasted peppers and garlic sauce. Lighter pasta meals and home-made pizzas on the bistro menu. Puddings range from old-fashioned treacle sponge pudding with crème anglaise to iced nougat with raspberry coulis. Quality overnight accommodation in spacious, well equipped and attractive bedrooms; two with four-poster beds.
OPEN: 12.30-3 6-11. **BAR MEALS:** L served all week. D served all week 12-2.30 7-9.30. Av main course £8.95.
RESTAURANT: L served all week. D served all week 12-2.30 7-9.30. Av 3 course à la carte £19.
BREWERY/COMPANY: Free House.
PRINCIPAL BEERS: Burton, Tetley, Hook Norton Old Hooky. **FACILITIES:** Children welcome Garden: outdoor eating, patio Dogs allowed manager's discretion only.
NOTES: Parking 30. **ROOMS:** 3 bedrooms 3 en suite

SHADES & GRADES OF BEER
A distincyion between beer and ale used to be drawn centuries ago. Ale was the old British brew made without hops. Not until the 15th century did the use of hops spread to Britain from the Continent and the suspect, newfangled, bitterer drink was called beer. Ale is no longer made and the two words are now used indiscriminately. Bottled beer is distinguished from draught beer from a cask, keg or tank, but a more useful dividing line may be the one between real ale, which matures in the cask, and keg or bottled beer that does not.
Bitter is the classic British draught beer, brewed with plenty of hops. Mild, less heavily hopped and less sharp in taste, is most often found in the Midlands and the North West of England. Old ale usually means stronger mild, matured longer. Light ale or pale ale is bottled beer of a lightish colour Lager is lighter and blander still, in a bottle or on draught. Brown ale is a darker, richer bottled beer, and porter is richer still. Stout is the blackest and richest of all.Strong ale or barley wine has a higher alcohol content than the others, or should have.

WYRE PIDDLE
Map 03 SO94

The Anchor Inn 👁 ♀
Main St WR10 2JB ☎ 01386 552799 📠 01386 552799
Dir: *From M5 J6 take A4538 S towards Evesham*
Originally boatmen's cottages, this traditional country inn dates from the 17th century, and has lovely garden terraces with tables overlooking the River Avon and the beautiful south Worcestershire countryside. Boats are always welcome and there are large moorings free to customers. Regularly changing seasonal menus are supplemented by daily specials, and options range from sandwich platters to venison sausage, steak and mushroom casserole, or grilled halibut steak with lobster sauce.

OPEN: 11-2.30 (Sat-Sun 12-3) 6-11 (Sun 7-10.30). Closed 26 Dec.
BAR MEALS: L served all week. D served all week 12-2.15 7-9.15.
Av main course £8. **RESTAURANT:** L served all week. D served all week 12-2.15 7-9.15. Av 3 course à la carte £15.
BREWERY/COMPANY: Whitbread.
PRINCIPAL BEERS: Flowers Original, Boddingtons, Marstons Pedigree. **FACILITIES:** Children's licence Garden: Beer garden with seating, outdoor eating. **NOTES:** Parking 10

YORKSHIRE, EAST RIDING OF

BEVERLEY
Map 09 TA03

White Horse Inn
22 Hengate HU17 8BN ☎ 01482 861973 📠 01482 861973
Dir: *A1079 from York to Beverley*
Carefully preserved 16th-century brick inn, more commonly known as 'Nellies', with basic but very atmospheric little rooms huddled around the central bar, mostly with gas lighting, open fires and some old ranges. Simple lunchtime bar food includes mince and onion pie, chilli, roast chicken, vegetable lasagne, and braised steak. Live music includes jazz and folk.
OPEN: 11-11 (Sun 12-10.30). **BAR MEALS:** L served Tue-Sun. 12-2. Av main course £4.25. **BREWERY/COMPANY:** Samuel Smith. **PRINCIPAL BEERS:** Samuel Smith Old Brewery Bitter & Sovereign Bitter. **FACILITIES:** Children welcome Garden: outdoor eating Dogs allowed on leads only, Water. **NOTES:** Parking 30 No credit cards

BRANDESBURTON
Map 09 TA14

The Dacre Arms
Main St YO25 8RL ☎ 01964 542392 📠 01964 542392
This popular village inn is the home of the Franklin Dead Brief. The society was started in 1844 and currently has 300 members. Each one pays 20p on the death of a member and the landlord is always the treasurer. An extensive range of

continued

quality pub food includes large filled Yorkshire puddings, steak and ale pie, lasagne and curries.
OPEN: 11.30-2.30 6-11 (open all day wknds). **BAR MEALS:** L served all week. D served all week 12-2 6-10. Av main course £5.
RESTAURANT: D served Wed-Sun 7-9. Av 3 course à la carte £16. Av 3 course fixed price £11.75.
BREWERY/COMPANY: Free House.
PRINCIPAL BEERS: Black Sheep. **FACILITIES:** Garden: outdoor eating, BBQ. **NOTES:** Parking 60

BREIGHTON
Map 09 SE73

Ye Olde Poachers Inne
Main St YO8 6DH ☎ 01757 288849
Medieval theme nights are among the attractions at this family-run pub and restaurant, complete with medieval rest and armour decorating the walls.

DRIFFIELD
Map 09 TA05

The Bell ★ ★ ★ 👁
46 Market Place YO25 6AN ☎ 01377 256661
📠 01377 253228
e-mail: bell@bestwestern.co.uk
Dir: *Enter town from A164, turn R at traffic lights. Car park 50yrds on L behind black railings*
Delightful 18th-century coaching inn, furnished with antiques, in a Yorkshire market town. The oak panelled bar serves 300 whiskies and cask beers. Food ranges from sandwiches and 'fabulous forkfuls' like steak and kidney pie, to options of whole breast of duck, or salmon en croute, and a specialist steak selection. Bedrooms have modern facilities, and there are suites available.
OPEN: 10-2.30 6-11 (Sun 11-2.30 7-10.30). Closed Dec 25.
BAR MEALS: L served all week. D served all week 12-1.30 7-9.30.
Av main course £8. **RESTAURANT:** L served Sun. D served Mon-Sat 7-9.30. Av 3 course à la carte £20. Av 3 course fixed price £15. **BREWERY/COMPANY:** Free House.
PRINCIPAL BEERS: Daleside Old Ledger & Green Grass.
FACILITIES: Children's licence. **NOTES:** Parking 18.
ROOMS: 16 bedrooms 16 en suite s£76 d£108

FLAMBOROUGH
Map 09 TA27

The Seabirds Inn 👁 ♀
Tower St YO15 1PD ☎ 01262 850242 📠 01262 850242
Dir: *On B1255 E of Bridlington*
Just down the road from the RSPB's spectacular Bempton Cliffs bird sanctuary and the stunning cliffs at Flamborough Head, this aptly-named pub was once a traditional fisherman's local. Today, it has a reputation for fresh fish dishes, including Whitby creel prawns, local crab and haddock, as well as lobsters, salmon and plaice. Daily specials like pork and Stilton sausages, Barnsley chops or roast duck with celeriac mash support an ever-changing selection of real ales.
OPEN: 11-3 (Sun 12-3) 7-11 (Sat 6.30-11, Sun 8-10.30).
BAR MEALS: L served all week. D served Mon-Sat 12-2 7-9.
Av main course £6.50. **RESTAURANT:** L served Mon-Sat. D served Mon-Sat 12-2 7-9. Av 3 course à la carte £14.
BREWERY/COMPANY: Free House. **PRINCIPAL BEERS:** John Smiths. Boddingtons Bitter. **FACILITIES:** Garden: beer garden, outside eating Dogs allowed water. **NOTES:** Parking 20
See Pub Walk on page 491

HOLME UPON SPALDING MOOR   Map 09 SE83

Ye Olde Red Lion Hotel
Old Rd YO43 4AD ☎ 01430 860220 📠 01430 861471
e-mail: benwalsh@redlion.prestel.co.uk
Dir: *off A1079 (York/Hull road).* At Market Weighton take A614
Historic 17th-century coaching inn with a friendly atmosphere,
oak beams and an open fire. Once provided hospitality for
weary travellers guided across the marshes by monks. Good
quality home-cooked bar food might feature bangers and
mash or steak and kidney pie. Restaurant main courses
include roast rack of lamb, Caribbean chicken, or fillet of
halibut.
OPEN: 11.30-2.30 (Sun 12-3) 6-11 (7-10.30). **BAR MEALS:** L
served all week. D served all week 12-1.45 6.45-9.45. Av main
course £10. **RESTAURANT:** L served all week. D served all week
12-1.30 7.15-9.30. **BREWERY/COMPANY:** Free House.
PRINCIPAL BEERS: Tetley, Bass. **FACILITIES:** Children
welcome Garden: Patio, outdoor Eating. **NOTES:** Parking 60.
ROOMS: 8 bedrooms 8 en suite s£34.50 d£56

HUGGATE   Map 09 SE85

The Wolds Inn
YO42 1YH ☎ 01377 288217
e-mail: hudggate@woldsinn.freeserve.co.uk
Dir: *S of A166 between York & Driffield*

Beneath a huddle of tiled roofs and white painted chimneys,
this former coaching inn claims to be the highest on the
Yorkshire Wolds. The cosy panelled bar with its traditional
games is the perfect antidote to a day's walking. Expect home-
cooked ham baguettes and seafood platters in the bar, with
grills, salmon fillets and daily vegetarian specials in the
restaurant.
OPEN: 12-2 6.45-11 (closed Mon, ex BH). **BAR MEALS:** L
served Tue-Sun. D served Sun, Tue-Fri 12-2 7-9.30. Av main course
£5. **RESTAURANT:** L served Sun. D served Sun, Tue-Sat 12-2.30
7-9.30. Av 3 course à la carte £16 9.30.
BREWERY/COMPANY: Free House.
PRINCIPAL BEERS: Tetley, Timothy Taylor Landlord, Greene
King Old speckled hen,. **FACILITIES:** Children welcome Garden:
beer garden,Outdoor eating Dogs allowed Water.
NOTES: Parking 50. **ROOMS:** 3 bedrooms 3 en suite s£22.50
d£35

  Pubs offering six or more wines by
the glass

Horse-brasses
Delightful and attractive as they are,
horse-brasses are nothing like as old as is
generally believed. The working horse in a
harness gleaming with ornamental hanging
brasses is a creature of the period since 1850.
The brasses were mass-produced folk art,
following the earlier precedent of the heraldic
badges worn by the carriage horses of
aristocratic families. Favourite symbols include
the sun, the moon, the stars and such heraldic
creatures as the lion, the stag, the unicorn
and the eagle, as well as railway
locomotives and ships.

HULL   Map 09 TA02

The Minerva Hotel
Nelson St, Victoria Pier HU1 1XE ☎ 01482 326909
📠 01482 326909
Dir: *M62 onto A63, then Castle St, turn R at signpost for Fruit Market
into Queens St at the top of Queens St on R hand side of the pier*
Handsome riverside pub built in 1831 and famous in the area
for its nautical memorabilia, rambling, old-fashioned rooms
and cosy snugs - one of which only has room for three people.
Three beer festivals a year are a permanent fixture here and
the inn offers a good choice of well-kept real ales. Simple but
appetising home-made bar food might include meat and
potato pie, beef cobbler, haddock cooked to a traditional
Minerva recipe, lasagne and curry. Finish off with bread-and-
butter pudding or toffee cream pie.
OPEN: 11-11 (Sun 12-10.30). Closed Dec 25. **BAR MEALS:** L
served Mon-Thur. D served Mon-Thu 12-2 6-9. Av main course
£4.50. **RESTAURANT:** L served Mon-Thur. D served Mon-Thur
12-2 6-9. Av 3 course à la carte £8.50.
BREWERY/COMPANY: Allied Domecq.
PRINCIPAL BEERS: Tetley, Timothy Taylor Landlord, Black
Sheep, Roosters. **FACILITIES:** Children welcome Garden: patio,
Food served outside Dogs allowed garden only

KILHAM

The Old Star NEW
Church St YO25 4RL ☎ 01262 420619 📠 01262 420712
e-mail: jofrend@cwcom.net
Sympathetically restored under new ownership, this village
pub retains its traditional appeal, with a separate restaurant in
a converted stable block. Home-cooked food is served from an
all day menu with the likes of lamb shank or steak and kidney
pie, while the weekend dinner menu might offer chicken
Rossini or beef Stroganoff. Occasional themed food weekends
are held during the year.
OPEN: 11-2 6-11 (Sat 11-11, Sun 11-10.30). **BAR MEALS:** L
served all week. D served all week 12-2 7-9.30. Av main course
£4.95. **RESTAURANT:** L served By appointment. D served all
week 12-2 7-9.30. Av 3 course à la carte £14.95. Av 2 course fixed
price £12.95. **BREWERY/COMPANY:** Free House.
PRINCIPAL BEERS: Theakstons XB, John Smiths.
FACILITIES: Children welcome Garden: food served outside
Dogs allowed. **NOTES:** Parking 5

Seabirds Inn, Flamborough

SEABIRDS INN, FLAMBOROUGH
Tower Street YO15 1PD.
Tel: 01262 850242
Directions: village on B1255 E of Bridlington
Expect a warm welcome, home-made food, and a bar adorned with nautical memorabilia at this homely old fisherman's local, situated in a village close to the chalk cliffs of Flamborough Head.
Open: 11-3 7-11 (Sat from 6.30, Sun 12-3 7-10.30). Closed Mon eve in winter. Bar Meals: 12-2 7-9 (no food Sun eve). Children welcome. Garden. Parking.
(see page 489 for full entry)

An exhilarating cliff-top walk from Flamborough to the lighthouse at Flamborough Head, where massive chalk cliffs provide a haven to seabirds and afford panoramic views across Bridlington Bay

Turn right on leaving the pub and walk down Tower Street. Shortly, cross the road and walk through the churchyard. Turn right along Lily Lane, then left into Butlers Lane and along West Street. In 50 yards (46m), take the path through Beacon Farm, signed to Beacon Hill. Pass outbuildings, cross two stiles, then gently up beside the left-hand hedge, then the wire fence, eventually reaching the cliff top.

Turn left and keep to the cliff-top path, down 80 steps to South Landing (bay). Walk uphill and take waymarked path right and ascend steps. Keep right (circular walk marker), then right again at a fork and keep to the marked cliff path. Cross two gullies via steps and bridges, then on reaching a sign (Lighthouse 1 mile), ignore wooden bridge across a ditch and head inland. Keep to the right-hand hedge across two field boundaries and to reach a lane via steps.

Turn right and continue to the Lighthouse. Take the private road to the right of the Lighthouse towards the Fog Signal Station and take the path on the right, signed 'South Landing 2½ miles'. Gently climb the bank on an indistinct path parallel with the field boundary (on right - not enclosed) and continue across the headland to its south side. Turn right along the cliff-top path and continue to the wooden bridge ignored earlier.

Retrace your steps along the cliff path, crossing the two gullies, until you arrive at the first fork (circular chalk walk) before South Landing is reached. Turn right inland keeping the fence on your left. Keep to the waymarked path past Cliff House Farm, then having zig-zagged downhill, leave the circular walk by crossing a bridge over a stream and enter a copse. Walk along the northern perimeter of the wood to reach a car park. Turn right uphill into Flamborough. Turn left at the crossroads, then right into Tower Street for the pub.

Distance: 6 miles (10km)
Map: OS Landranger 101
Terrain: farmland, clifftop, country lanes
Paths: field and cliff-top paths; some road walking
Gradient: gently undulating; easy gradients; some steps

Walk submitted by:
M Grocutt

Cliffs at Flamborough Head

England

Pick of the Pubs

Wellington Inn 🍴 ♈

19 The Green YO25 9TE ☎ 01377 217294
▤ 01377 217192
Dir: On B1284 NE of Beverley

Opposite the picture-postcard village green, the Wellington is a focal point: completely renovated by the present owners, its clientele is drawn from far afield for decent bar lunches and impressive à la carte dining. Traditional soups and sandwiches supplement a frequently changed lunch menu that offers fresh crab salad and country pâté with crab apple and herb jelly before main courses such as seafood linguini, cassoulet of pork and chorizo, and beef cooked in Guinness with root vegetables and Irish colcannon. At night, expect queen scallop and chorizo tart with red pepper sauce, baked cod fillet on potatoes sautéed with smoked salmon and served with orange and coriander hollandaise, and roasted duck breast with parsnip purée, caramelised apple and Calvados jus. Puddings range from raspberry crème brûlée to three-tier chocolate terrine. Good list of wines with useful tasting notes.
OPEN: 12-3 6.30-11. **BAR MEALS:** L served all week. D served all week 12-2 7-9. Av main course £9.
RESTAURANT: D served all week 7-9.30. Av 3 course à la carte £23. **BREWERY/COMPANY:** Free House.
PRINCIPAL BEERS: Timothy Taylor Landlord & Dark Mild, Black Sheep Best, John Smiths. **FACILITIES:** Garden: Courtyard, food served outside. **NOTES:** Parking 40

The Triton Inn ♦♦♦ ♈

YO25 3XQ ☎ 01377 236644
Dir: leave A166 at Garton on the Wolds, take B1252 to Sledmere
18th-century coaching inn nestling in the shadow of historic Sledmere House. Oak panelled bar contains history of the once-famous Sledmere stud. Neat, comfortable bedrooms make this a good base for exploring the Yorkshire Wolds. Lasagne, lemon chicken, steaks and beef Stroganoff among a variety of dishes.
OPEN: 11.30-2.30 7-11 (Sat 11.30-3 6.30-11, Sun 12-4 7-10.30). Closed Mon 1 Oct-31 Mar. **BAR MEALS:** L served all week. D served all week 12-2 7-9. Av main course £5.75.
RESTAURANT: L served all week. D served all week 12-2 7-9. Av 3 course à la carte £13.30. **BREWERY/COMPANY:** Free House.
PRINCIPAL BEERS: Tetleys, John Smiths. **FACILITIES:** Children welcome Garden: patio/terrace, outdoor eating.
NOTES: Parking 35. **ROOMS:** 5 bedrooms 2 en suite s£24 d£44 1 family room £60-70

YORKSHIRE, NORTH

The Ship Inn

Moor End YO23 2UH ☎ 01904 705609 & 703888
▤ 01904 705971
Dir: from York take A1036 south after Dringhouses take follow signs for Bishopthorpe and then Acaster Malbis
17th-century coaching house with a relaxing riverside garden very pleasant for watching the colourful boats and barges. Acaster Malbis is the site of a Roman fort. Traditional bar food is on offer, including steak in ale pie, and battered haddock fillet. Specials might feature Thai spiced crab cakes or escolar fillet.
OPEN: 11.30-11. **BAR MEALS:** L served all week. D served all week 12-3 5-9. Av main course £5.75. **RESTAURANT:** L served all week. D served all week 12-3 5-9. Av 3 course à la carte £14.95.
BREWERY/COMPANY: Enterprise Inns.
PRINCIPAL BEERS: Marstons Pedigree, Theakstons.
FACILITIES: Children welcome Garden: River Ouse Dogs allowed manager's discretion only. **NOTES:** Parking 60.
ROOMS: 8 bedrooms 7 en suite d£45 FR£60

The Friar's Head

Akebar Park DL8 5LY ☎ 01677 450201 ▤ 01677 450046
Dir: Take A684 from Leeming Bar Motel (on A1). W towards Leyburn for 7m. Friar's Head is in Akebar Park
Originally a farm and stud, where the Cistercian monks of Jervaulx Abbey bred their horses in the 16th century. It is now part of a golf complex with three courses.

The Craven Arms

BD23 6DA ☎ 01756 720270 ▤ 01756 720270
Dir: From Skipton take A59 towards Harrogate, B6160 N. Village signed on R.(Pub just outside village)
Old world Dales pub with beams, a Yorkshire range and log fires, and spectacular views of the River Wharfe and Simon's Seat. Old artefacts and notes are displayed on the bar ceiling. Steak and kidney pie, game pie and Cumberland sausage are among the traditional dishes.
OPEN: 11.30-3 (Sun 12-3 7-10.30) 6.30-11. **BAR MEALS:** L served all week. D served all week 12-2 7-9.30. Av main course £5.50. **BREWERY/COMPANY:** Free House.
PRINCIPAL BEERS: Black Sheep, Tetley, Theakston Old Peculier.
FACILITIES: Children welcome Garden: Beer garden , food served outdoors Dogs allowed Not during meal times.
NOTES: Parking 35

Smuggling and Skulduggery

All round Britain's coast an explosion of smuggling was the 18th-century response to high excise duties on goods imported from abroad. There were villages in Kent where people were said to wash their windows with smuggled gin, it was so cheap. Inns were often involved, because they had cellars where casks and bales could conveniently be hidden and they could sell smuggled drink. Smugglers were nothing like as romantic in real life as they are in fiction. Lawless and violent smuggling gangs could exercise a reign of terror. Other criminal activities were often associated with some of the rougher pubs, where thieves planned operations, the landlord fenced stolen goods and the 'gentlemen of the road' dropped in. Many a pub on the Great North Road claims the famous highwayman Dick Turpin as a habitué.

MALT SHOVEL INN, BREARTON

HG3 3BX. Tel: 01423 862929
Directions: take B6165
towards Knaresborough from
A61 N of Harrogate
*Popular 16th-century inn
peacefully situated in an off-
the-beaten-track village deep
in farming country. Original
oak beams litter the civilised
bars, while heaters warm the
patio. Expect imaginative,
freshly prepared food, micro-
brewery ales, and a warm
welcome.*
Open: 12-2.30 6.45-11.
Closed Mon. Bar Meals: 12-2
7-9. Children welcome.
Garden & patio. Parking.
(see page 497 for full entry)

Pub WALK

Malt Shovel Inn, Brearton

A pleasant rural ramble across rolling farmland to the east of the A61, incorporating peaceful tracks and field paths linking three attractive villages.

From the front of the inn, cross the road and walk up Lillygate Lane. Where it curves right, take the pitted lane left, uphill between hedgerows. Pass a copse and continue alongside a field to a lane (Rake's Lane). Turn right, then in 400 yards (365m), take the track left, downhill through a field to a footbridge across a beck. Pass the Lime Kilns Farm and walk uphill to where a metalled lane merges from the left. Turn left into Burton Leonard, following the road left across the village green and take the lane left at the top of the hill.

Opposite Prospect House, take the arrowed path through a gate (Mountgarret Estates), and keep straight ahead along the right-hand hedge to the next gate and stile. Descend through woodland and across a clearing, ignoring the gate left, aiming slightly downhill to a fence stile (yellow markers). Cross the field diagonally downhill, turning left through double gates to a track. Turn right and follow the track uphill along the left-hand field edge.

At the top, turn right, then almost immediately left along another track (hedge right). Where the track veers left, proceed ahead along the field edge to a stile to the right of a conifer plantation. Follow the field edge to a stile and keep ahead towards the gap in the hedge. Beyond stile (beside gate), continue downhill, passing church to reach a gate and lane. Turn left, then at a sign for Stainley Hall Farm, take the right-hand track over a bridge. Keep straight ahead where the lane forks, downhill towards Brearton. Shortly, turn left, pass Greenwich Farm, then turn left again back along Main Street to the inn.

Distance: 5 1/2 miles (8.8km)
Map: OS Landranger
Terrain: farmland, patches of woodland and village lanes
Paths: field and woodland paths, tracks and lanes
Gradient: undulating; uphill sections are not too strenuous

Walk submitted by: The Malt Shovel

England

ASENBY   Map 09 SE37

Pick of the Pubs

Crab & Lobster 🌐 🌐 🛏 ♀
YO7 3QL ☎ 01845 577286 📠 01845 577109
See Pick of the Pubs on page 495

ASKRIGG   Map 09 SD99

Kings Arms Hotel 🛏 ♀
Market Place DL8 3HQ ☎ 01969 650817 📠 01969 650817
Dir: N off A684 between Hawes & Leyburn
At the heart of the Yorkshire Dales, Askrigg is surrounded by
stunning scenery against a backdrop of Pennine hills: its pub,
built in 1762 as racing stables, was converted to an inn in 1860.
Bar and bistro specialities include lamb and leek casserole,
Cajun chicken, Thai red curry and noodles, and deep fried
haddock. Look to the blackboard for daily changing specials.

OPEN: 11-3 6-11 (Sat 11-11, Sun 12-10.30). **BAR MEALS:** L
served all week. D served all week 12-2 6.30-9. Av main course £7.
RESTAURANT: D served all week 7-9. Av 3 course à la carte £16.
BREWERY/COMPANY: Free House.
PRINCIPAL BEERS: Theakston XB, John Smiths, Black Sheep.
FACILITIES: Children welcome Garden: Stone courtyard, food
served outside Dogs allowed Water

Hambleton Ales
After being made redundant twice
during the early 90s recession, Nick
Stafford hit on the idea of starting a
brewery in the tiny hamlet of Holme-on-
Swale. The result, a decade later, is a
booming brewhouse that employs ten
people, produces around 20,000 pints of
beer a week, and has won numerous beer
festival awards. These beers have a
unique flavour and largely draw on the
local legend of the white horse: Stallion,
Stud, Hambleton, Goldfield and
Nightmare.

AYSGARTH   Map 09 SE08

The George & Dragon NEW
DL8 3AD ☎ 01969 663358 📠 01969 663773

Beautifully situated near Aysgarth Falls in the heart of Herriot
country, the new owners of this attractive 17th century free
house continue the long tradition of Yorkshire hospitality.
Beamed ceilings and open fires set the scene for freshly
cooked daily specials like wild boar steak, pheasant, venison
or monkfish, whilst the standard menu includes pot-roasted
guinea fowl, liver and bacon, and Cumberland sausage and
mash.
OPEN: 11-11. **BAR MEALS:** L served all week. D served all week
12-2 6-9. Av main course £8.50. **RESTAURANT:** L served all
week. D served all week 12-2 6-9. Av 3 course à la carte £8.50. Av
3 course fixed price £10.95. **BREWERY/COMPANY:** Free
House. **PRINCIPAL BEERS:** Black Sheep, John Smiths,
Theakstons Bitter. **FACILITIES:** Children welcome Garden: food
served outside Dogs allowed Water. **NOTES:** Parking 35.
ROOMS: 7 bedrooms 7 en suite s£33.50 d£59

BAINBRIDGE   Map 09 SD99

Rose & Crown Hotel ★ ★
DL8 3EE ☎ 01969 650225 📠 01969 650735
e-mail: stay@theprideofwensleydale.co.uk
Dir: On A684 in centre of village
Overlooking the village green, this traditional 500-year-old
coaching inn is home to the forest horn, blown each evening
from Holy Rood (September 27th) to Shrovetide to guide
travellers safely to the village. Appetising choice of starters and
light snacks, while main courses include chicken breast in
white wine and Stilton, guinea fowl, rack of lamb, or halibut
steak.
OPEN: 11-11 (Sun 12-10.30). **BAR MEALS:** L served all week.
D served all week 12-2 6-9.30. Av main course £6.50.
RESTAURANT: L served Sun. D served all week 12-2.30 7-9.30.
Av 3 course à la carte £18. **BREWERY/COMPANY:** Free House.
PRINCIPAL BEERS: Websters, Black Sheep, John Smiths.
FACILITIES: Children welcome Children's licence Garden:
patio, outdoor eating, BBQ Dogs allowed. **NOTES:** Parking 65.
ROOMS: 12 bedrooms 12 en suite s£26 d£52

BEDALE   Map 09 SE28

Freemasons Arms
Nosterfield DL8 2QP ☎ 01677 470548
Cluttered with curios and memorabilia, this inviting, long and
low whitewashed building, formerly a row of 18th-century
cottages, features English cooking that uses local produce.
Booking is essential.

PICK OF THE PUBS

OPEN: 11.30-3, 6.30-11.
BAR MEALS: L served all week.
D served all week 12-2.30 6.30-10.
Av main course £11.50.
RESTAURANT: L served all week.
D served all week 12-2.30 7-10.
Av 3 course a la carte £25.
Av 4 course fixed price £27.50.
BREWERY/COMPANY:
Free House.
PRINCIPLE BEERS: Black Sheep
Bitter, Theakston Best, Tetley,
Worthington Best.
FACILITIES: Children welcome.
Garden: 7 acres, patio, outdoor
eating. Dogs allowed.
NOTES: Parking 50.
ROOMS: 12 bedrooms 12 en suite
d£120-£150.

The Crab & Lobster

YO7 3QL
☎ 01845 577286 📄 01845 577109
Dir: From A1(M) junction take A168
towards Thirsk, then first L

In an idyllic spot amid seven acres of garden, lake and
streams stands this unique 17th-century thatched pub, chock
full of antiques, bygones and curios, and the equally
individual Crab Manor Hotel. Renowned for quality food,
notably innovative fish dishes, and eccentric accommodation.

A decade on since purchasing this once run-down pub close to the
A1, and eight years since adding the adjacent Crab Manor to the business, enthusiastic owners David and Jackie
Barnard have now realised their dream in creating a thriving food pub and developing a small country house hotel
with opulent and quite unique bedrooms, including three 'beach huts' in the surrounding grounds. In the 'Crab', an
Aladdin's Cave of themed bric-à-brac and antiques, low beams, ledges and window sills in both the cosy bar and
brasserie dining room are covered with pots, pans, parasols and puppets, and old fishing pots and mock crabs.

The menu is less cluttered though and the emphasis is on
imaginative and adventurous fish and seafood dishes, with culinary
influences from France, Italy and some touches from Asia. Virtually
everything is on offer, from the famous fish Club sandwich (lunch
only), bouillabaisse, fresh oysters served on crushed ice, mussels
with black beans and spring onions, and Thai fishcakes to Goan fish
curry, 'posh' fish and chips with mushy peas, mixed fish grill with
garlic and pesto mash, whole roasted sea bass with tropical fruit
salsa, and lemon sole with gingered crab and shellfish cream.

Carnivores are not forgotten however, and can tuck into daube
of beef with horseradish mash and caramelised carrots, or steamed
venison pudding. Finish with lemon and lime crème fraiche tart or a
plate of farmhouse cheeses with home-made bread.

England

BILBROUGH
Map 09 SE54

Pick of the Pubs

The Three Hares Inn & Restaurant ⊛ ⊛ 🐦 ♀
Main St YO23 3PH ☎ 01937 832128 📄 01937 834626
e-mail: info@thethreehares.co.uk
Dir: *Bilbrough can be reached from either direction on the A64, SW of York*

Located in a peaceful village near the historic city of York, an inviting 18th-century dining pub whose restaurant incorporates the old village forge. The end bar with its flagged floor and exposed beams adds further character serving hand-pulled, cask-conditioned beers of note and an extensive wine list with several choices by the glass. Meals available from the blackboards, changed regularly according to market availability, display imagination and attention to detail. Well-made country soups, game and fennel suet pudding, spiced sardine fillets with Tuscan vegetables and roast vegetable and goats' cheese tart well indicate the style of starters; followed by brill fillets with smoked Toulouse sausage and wild mushrooms, roast venison topside with colcannon and breast and thigh of pheasant with roast sweet potatoes and pancetta. Rather more staid restaurant choices may include chicken liver pâté with apple chutney, roast cod with Puy lentils and lamb chump with roast garlic and sweetbreads: potatoes and seasonal vegetables come as extras for two people.
OPEN: 12-3 7-11 (Sun 12-3 only). Closed 3wks in Jan & Feb.
BAR MEALS: L served Tue-Sun. D served Tue-Sat 12-2 7-9.15. Av main course £7.95. **RESTAURANT:** L served Tue-Sun. D served Tue-Sat 12-2 7-9.15. Av 3 course à la carte £20. **BREWERY/COMPANY:** Free House.
PRINCIPAL BEERS: Timothy Taylor Landlord, Black Sheep.
FACILITIES: Garden: outdoor eating, patio.
NOTES: Parking 30

AA The Restaurant Guide 2002

The right choice every time with this invaluable guide for gourmets

www.theAA.com

AA Lifestyle Guides

The Dales Way
(North Yorkshire section)

Linking two of Britain's most beautiful National Parks, the Yorkshire Dales and the Lake District, the 84-mile Dales Way starts officially at Ilkley, in brooding gritstone country, then heads up through Wharfedale towards the spectacular limestone region of the western Dales. Majestic landscapes await you en route, a glorious, constantly-changing backdrop of dramatic high moorland, limestone scars, undiscovered emerald green valleys, dashing rivers and timeless villages, where you'll receive a warm welcome in some of Yorkshire's loveliest classic pubs. Rest those weary limbs at the delightful Craven Arms at Appletreewick, the Fox and Hounds in Starbotton or the Buck Inn in adjacent Buckden before beginning the slow climb to Ribblehead.

BOROUGHBRIDGE
Map 09 SE36

Pick of the Pubs

The Black Bull Inn 🐦 ♀
6 St James Square YO51 9AR ☎ 01423 322413
📄 01423 323915
Dir: *from J48 A1(M) take B6265 for 1mile E*

Grade II listed building, 800 years old in parts and reputedly haunted, which has always been an inn. Typical dishes on the interesting menus range from crab and salmon fishcakes, and mushroom and bacon ragout, to sea bass with pesto butter sauce, venison with shallot and port sauce, and beef in creamy whisky sauce.
OPEN: 11-11 (Sun 12-10.30). **BAR MEALS:** L served all week. D served all week 12-2 6-9.30. Av main course £6.
RESTAURANT: L served all week. D served all week 12-2 7-9.30. Av 3 course à la carte £15.
BREWERY/COMPANY: Free House.
PRINCIPAL BEERS: Black Sheep, John Smiths, guest ale.
FACILITIES: Children welcome. **NOTES:** Parking 4.
ROOMS: 4 bedrooms 4 en suite s£40.50 d£54

England

BREARTON   Map 08 SE36

Pick of the Pubs

Malt Shovel Inn 🍽 ⚲
HG3 3BX ☎ 01423 862929
Dir: *From A61 (Ripon/Harrogate) take B6165 towards Knaresborough. Turn at Brearton - 1.5m.*
The Malt Shovel has been at the heart of this small farming community for nearly five centuries; and, says the landlord, it stands 'on the road to nowhere'. Yet, despite its rural situation, the pub is within ten minutes drive of Harrogate, Knaresborough and Ripon. There's a clutter of beer mugs, horse brasses and hunting scenes in the heavily-beamed rooms leading off from the carved oak bar, and you can enjoy a quiet game of dominoes or shove ha'penny without any electronic intrusions. The blackboard menu caters for all tastes. Meat dishes include steak and ale pie, lamb casserole, or liver, bacon and black pudding with red wine gravy. Fish lovers might expect haddock in beer batter, seafood gratin, or smoked salmon salad, and there's an interesting range of vegetarian options, too. Goats' cheese and leek tart, nut roast, and potato and tomato curry are typical choices.
OPEN: 12-2.30 6.45-11 (Sun 12-2.30, 7-10.30).
BAR MEALS: L served Tue-Sun. D served Tue-Sat 12-2 7-9. Av main course £6. **BREWERY/COMPANY:** Free House.
PRINCIPAL BEERS: Daleside Nightjar, Durham Magus, Black Sheep, Theakston Masham. **FACILITIES:** Children welcome Garden: Patio, Heated garden Dogs allowed garden only. **NOTES:** Parking 20 No credit cards
See Pub Walk on page 493

BROUGHTON   Map 09 SD95

Bull Inn
BD23 3AE ☎ 01756 792065
Dir: *On A59 4m from Skipton coming from M6*
A friendly welcome awaits at this real country pub, resting on the edge of the Yorkshire Dales at the front of Broughton Hall, yet accessibly on the main A59. There's a Junior Menu for children.

BUCKDEN   Map 09 SD97

Pick of the Pubs

The Buck Inn ⊛ ⊛ ★ ★ 🍽 ⚲
BD23 5JA ☎ 01756 760228 📠 01756 760227
e-mail: thebuckinn@yorks.net
Dir: *From Skipton take B6265, then B6160*
Between the extensive bar menu and carte, a wide choice of imaginative dishes is on offer at this traditional Georgian coaching inn nestling in Upper Wharfedale in the Yorkshire Dales. Expect the likes of moules marinière, braised local lamb in filo pastry with thyme jus, and seared tuna loin with salsa.
OPEN: 11-11 (Sun 12-10.30). **BAR MEALS:** L served all week. D served all week 12-2 6.30-9.30 (Sun 12-5 7-8.30). Av main course £8. **RESTAURANT:** D served all week 6.30-9.30. Av 3 course à la carte £25.
BREWERY/COMPANY: Free House.
PRINCIPAL BEERS: Theakston - Bitter, Black Bull, Best, & Old Peculier. **FACILITIES:** Children welcome Garden: Dogs allowed. **NOTES:** Parking 40. **ROOMS:** 14 bedrooms 14 en suite s£36 d£72

BURNSALL   ·   Map 09 SE06

Pick of the Pubs

The Red Lion ⊛ ★ ★ 🍽 ⚲
By the Bridge BD23 6BU ☎ 01756 720204
📠 01756 720292
e-mail: redlion@daelnet.co.uk
Dir: *From Skipton take A59 east take B6160 towards Bolton Abbey, Burnsall 7m*

An old-fashioned 16th-century country inn full of old-world charm on the banks of the River Wharfe at the heart of the Dales. With grounds running down to the river and a cosy interior of old armchairs, sofas and wood-burning stove, this family-run establishment offers something for everyone. Upstairs bedrooms have beams and slanting, low ceilings; those in the annexe are more spacious and have family facilities. Local ingredients play a large part on the seasonal menus that offer Pateley Bridge sausages with black pudding and apple sauce, beef carpaccio with rocket and Parmesan and chargrilled wild salmon with spinach, asparagus and hollandaise. The quality of ingredients is equally evidenced by provençale fish soup, chargrilled beef fillet on potato and carrot galette and soundly made lemon tart served in the restaurant. Lamb from the surrounding fells, game in season and fish fresh from the East Coast ports all play a regular part.
OPEN: 8am-11.30pm (Sun closes 10.30). **BAR MEALS:** L served all week. D served all week 12-2.30 6-9.30. Av main course £9. **RESTAURANT:** L served Sun. D served all week 12-3 7-9.30. Av 3 course à la carte £24.95. Av 3 course fixed price £24.95. **BREWERY/COMPANY:** Free House.
PRINCIPAL BEERS: Theakston Black Bull, Greene King Old Speckled Hen, Timothy Taylor Landlord, John Smiths.
FACILITIES: Children welcome Children's licence Garden: patio, outdoor eating Dogs allowed (not in bedrooms).
NOTES: Parking 70. **ROOMS:** 11 bedrooms 11 en suite s£50 d£100 FR£100-£147

BYLAND ABBEY   Map 09 SE57

Pick of the Pubs

Abbey Inn 🍽 ⚲
YO61 4BD ☎ 01347 868204 📠 01347 868678
e-mail: jane@nordli.freeserve.co.uk
See Pick of the Pubs on page 499

CARLTON   Map 09 SE08

Foresters Arms
DL8 4BB ☎ 01969 640272
Dir: *S of Leyburn off A684 or A6108*
Nestling in beautiful Coverdale, a 16th-century country inn
with flagged floors, beamed ceilings and open fires that have a
special appeal: surrounded by fine scenery, its rear views take
in an ancient burial mound. Under new management.

CARTHORPE   Map 09 SE38

Pick of the Pubs

The Fox & Hounds 🏨 ♀
DL8 2LG ☎ 01845 567433 📠 01845 567155
Dir: *Off A1, signposted on both northbound & southbound
carriageways*
In a peaceful village just off the A1, this neat 200-year-old
pub, formerly the local smithy, retains the old forge as a
feature of the dining-room: old smithy implements and
numerous prints of Victorian Whitby adorn the
comfortably furnished interior. A single menu served
throughout is supplemented by daily fish deliveries
featured separately: choices might be rolled lemon sole
fillets, filled with salmon and prawns, halibut steak with a
grain mustard sauce, or poached Scottish salmon with
hollandaise sauce. Other options include grilled lamb
cutlets with redcurrant gravy, penne pasta with a
mushroom and white wine sauce, or roasted lamb shank
with red cabbage and root vegetable purée. Look out for
the changing blackboard specials.
OPEN: 12-2.30 7-11. Closed Mon & 1st wk Jan.
BAR MEALS: L served Sun, Tue-Sat. D served Sun, Tue-Sat
12-2 7-10. Av main course £9. **RESTAURANT:** L served Sun,
Tue-Sat. D served Sun, Tue-Sat 12-2 7-10. Av 3 course à la
carte £15. Av 3 course fixed price £12.95.
BREWERY/COMPANY: Free House.
PRINCIPAL BEERS: John Smiths. **FACILITIES:** Children
welcome. **NOTES:** Parking 22

Dominoes

Dominoes came to Britain from the Continent at
the end of the 18th century, perhaps brought back
by British soldiers serving in the Napoleonic Wars.
French prisoners-of-war made sets of dominoes,
not only for their own amusement but to sell to
the British. Many different varieties are played in
pubs besides the standard block game, and some
pubs belong to dominoe leagues.

CLAPHAM   Map 08 SD76

New Inn
LA2 8HH ☎ 015242 51203 📠 015242 51496
e-mail: newinn@compuserve.com
Dir: *On A65 in Yorkshire Dales National Park*

Family-run 18th-century coaching inn set in a peaceful Dales
village beneath Ingleborough, one of Yorkshire's most famous
summits. There are good walks from the doorstep, including
one to Ingleborough Show Cave (the inn has strong links with
the caving fraternity). Honest pub food includes Brie crumble,
chilli and rice, and oxtail with baby onions in red wine gravy.
OPEN: 11-11 (Winter 11-3, 6.30- 11). **BAR MEALS:** L served all
week. D served all week 12-2 7-9. Av main course £6.
RESTAURANT: D served all week 7-8.30. Av 3 course à la carte
£16.50. Av 4 course fixed price £16.50.
BREWERY/COMPANY: Free House.
PRINCIPAL BEERS: Fullback, Dent, Black Sheep, Tetleys.
FACILITIES: Children welcome Garden: riverside, waterfall, food
served outside Dogs allowed Water always avalible.
NOTES: Parking 35. **ROOMS:** 19 bedrooms 19 en suite d£50

COXWOLD   Map 09 SE57

The Fauconberg Arms 🏨 ♀
Main St YO61 4AD ☎ 01347 868214 📠 01347 868172
Dir: *Take A19 S from Thirsk, 2m turn L, signposted alternative route
for caravans/heavy vehicles. 5m to village*
The pub's name comes from the Fauconberg family, who were
given the village and estate by Henry V111. It's a traditional
country inn with antiques galore and a fine fire on colder days.
All the food is home-made, including roast beef with Yorkshire
pudding, and butterscotch pudding with custard. New owners
as we went to press.
OPEN: 11-2.30 6.30-11 (Sun 12-2.30, 7-10.30). **BAR MEALS:** L
served all week. D served all week 12-2 7-9. Av main course £6.45.
RESTAURANT: L served all week. D served all week 12-2 7-9.
Av 3 course à la carte £12.95. **BREWERY/COMPANY:** Free
House. **PRINCIPAL BEERS:** Theakston, Tetley, John Smiths,
Greene King Old Speckled Hen. **FACILITIES:** Children welcome
patio. **NOTES:** Parking 25. **ROOMS:** 4 bedrooms 4 en suite
s£35 d£60

OPEN: 11.30-3 6.30-11. Closed Sun eve and Mon lunch.
BAR MEALS: L served Tue-Sun. D served Mon-Sat 12-2 6.30-9. Av main course £9.
RESTAURANT: L served Tue-Sun. D served Mon-Sat 12-2 6.30-9. Av 3 course a la carte £20.
BREWERY/COMPANY: Free House.
PRINCIPAL BEERS: Black Sheep Bitter, Tetley Bitter.
FACILITIES: Children welcome. Garden: patio, outdoor eating
NOTES: Parking 30.
ROOMS: 3 bedrooms 3 en suite s£50-£80 d£70-£110

The Abbey Inn

YO61 4BD
☎ 01347 868204 📠 01347 868678
e-mail: jane@nordli.freeserve.co.uk
Dir: From A19 between York & Thirsk, turn L for Coxwold/Byland Abbey

In an isolated rural position midway between Wass and Coxwold, the rambling, stone-built Abbey Inn stands, as its name suggests, in the shadow of the hauntingly beautiful ruins of Byland Abbey. Worth locating for modern pub food, individual decor and superior pub accommodation.

Built by Benedictine monks from nearby Ampleforth during the 19th-century, the plain, creeper-clad stone façade hides a very individual interior. Four splendid interconnecting rooms are full of charm and atmosphere, each featuring either bare board or flagstone floors strewn with rugs, open fireplaces, and an eclectic mix of furnishings, from huge settles with scatter cushions to Jacobean-style chairs and oak and stripped deal tables topped with large, gothic candlesticks. Fine tapestries, stuffed birds, dried flowers and unusual objets d'arts complete the interesting decor.

Apart from the setting and decor, the attraction here is the enterprising range of modern British food offered on a seasonally changing menu and daily specials board. At lunchtime choose hot bacon and Brie baguette, chicken liver and ginger parfait with apricot compote, beef in Black Sheep ale pie or seared salmon with tomato and coriander butter, while the evening menu may list venison fillet on celeriac purée with black cherry sauce, seared tuna with mango and papaya salsa, or monkfish on herb mash with lemon grass sauce. Traditional puddings include sticky toffee pudding with toffee cream and chocolate and pear cheesecake with warm chocolate sauce. Commendable list of wines; half-bottle bin ends and eight by the glass. Lovely summer terrace and garden.

A peaceful night is assured in beautifully appointed en suite bedrooms which overlook the floodlit Abbey.

CRAY Map 09 S097

The White Lion Inn NEW
Cray BD23 5JB ☎ 01756 760262
Hand-pulled real ales and hearty home cooking are bywords
for this nicely restored drovers' inn, set in the remote upper
reaches of Wharfedale. Original beams, open fires and stone-
flagged floors set the scene, and you can discover the ancient
game of 'Bull 'ook'. Lunchtime brings sandwiches, filled
Yorkshire puddings and hot meals; expect stuffed chicken
breasts, venison casserole, and poached salmon or trout in the
evenings.
OPEN: 11.30-11. **BAR MEALS:** L served all week. D served all
week. Av main course £7.50. **BREWERY/COMPANY:** Free
House. **PRINCIPAL BEERS:** Black Sheep Bitter, Roosters Yankee,
Moorhouse Pendle Witches Brew, Black Cat Mild.
FACILITIES: Children welcome Garden: Food served outside
Dogs allowed Water. **NOTES:** Parking 20.
ROOMS: 9 bedrooms 7 en suite s£30 d£40

CROPTON Map 09 SE78

The New Inn NEW
YO18 8HH ☎ 01751 417330 ▤ 01751 417310
e-mail: newinn@cropton.fsbusiness.co.uk
With the award-winning Cropton micro-brewery in its own
grounds, this family-run free house on the edge of the North
York Moors National Park is popular with locals and visitors
alike. Meals are served in the newly restored village bar, and
in the elegant Victorian restaurant not to mention the
brewery's own visitor centre! Typical dishes include steak and
ale pie, special lamb joint, and salmon Veronique.
OPEN: 11-11 (Jan-Feb 11-2.30, 6-11). **BAR MEALS:** L served all
week. D served all week 12-2 6-9.30. Av main course £6.50.
RESTAURANT: L served all week. D served all week 12-2 6-9.30.
Av 3 course à la carte £15. **BREWERY/COMPANY:** Free House.
PRINCIPAL BEERS: Cropton Two Pints, Monkmans Slaughter &
Backwoods, Thwaites Best Bitter. **FACILITIES:** Children welcome
Garden: Food served outside. **NOTES:** Parking 50.
ROOMS: 9 bedrooms 9 en suite s£31 d£54

DACRE BANKS Map 09 SE16

The Royal Oak Inn 🍺
Oak Ln HG3 4EN ☎ 01423 780200
e-mail: royaloakdacre@aol.com
Dir: From A59(Harrogate/Skipton) take B6451 towards Pateley Bridge

Family-run 18th-century freehouse in Nidderdale - a
designated Area of Outstanding Natural Beauty. It's an ideal
stop for anglers, tourists and walkers from the nearby
Nidderdale Way. Food ranges from snacks, steaks and Cajun
chicken in the bar to rabbit casserole, rack of lamb, and fillet
continued

of turbot with white wine sauce in the restaurant.
OPEN: 11.30-3 5-11 (Sun 11.30-3, 7-10.30). **BAR MEALS:** L
served all week. D served Mon-Sat 11.30-2 6.30-9. Av main course
£7.95. **RESTAURANT:** L served all week. D served all week
11.30-2 6.30-9. Av 3 course à la carte £13.95. Av 3 course fixed
price £9.95. **BREWERY/COMPANY:** Free House.
PRINCIPAL BEERS: Daleside Old Leg Over, Rudgate Yorkshire
Dales, John Smiths. **FACILITIES:** Children welcome Garden:
outdoor eating, patio. **NOTES:** Parking 15.
ROOMS: 3 bedrooms 3 en suite s£30 d£50

DANBY Map 11 NZ70

Duke of Wellington Inn
YO21 2LY ☎ 01287 660351 ▤ 01287 660351
e-mail: landlord@dukeofwellington.freeserve.co.uk
Dir: From A171 between Guisborough & Whitby take rd signed
'Danby & Moors Centre'
Traditional stone-built pub in one of Britain's most popular
outdoor playgrounds. Used as a recruiting post by local
regiments during the Napoleonic Wars, with a cast-iron plaque
of the Duke of Wellington above the fireplace. Relax in the
friendly locals' bar and sample one of the award-winning ales
or malt whiskies. Home-cooked meals are served in the bars
and refurbished restaurant and include salmon fishcakes,
garden vegetable pie, steak and kidney pie and lamb chops
with mustard and herb dressing.
OPEN: 11-3 7-11. **BAR MEALS:** L served all week. D served all
week 12-2 7-9. Av main course £7. **RESTAURANT:** L served Sun.
D served all week 12-2 7-9. Av 3 course à la carte £15.
BREWERY/COMPANY: Free House. **PRINCIPAL BEERS:** John
Smith's Magnet, Cameron's Strongarm. **FACILITIES:** Children
welcome Dogs allowed. **NOTES:** Parking 12.
ROOMS: 8 bedrooms 8 en suite s£28 d£56

Samuel Smith

This firmly established brewery is
the oldest in Yorkshire (established
1758) and is claims to be the only
one in Britain which has its own
coopers making all its own casks. The
brewing process uses no brewing
sugar, and traditional Yorkshire
Squares do the fermenting. Tours
are available.

EAST WITTON
Map 09 SE18

Pick of the Pubs

The Blue Lion 🛏 ♀
DL8 4SN ☎ 01969 624273 ▪ 01969 624189
e-mail: bluelion@breathemail.net

Self-promoted as a "country retreat" and tastefully restored over the years, this 18th-century former coaching inn that once attracted trade from drovers and travellers on their journeys through Wensleydale remains today the focal point of East Witton village. Charming, individually decorated bedrooms are well equipped to meet the expectations of today's more discerning visitors, while the bar with its flagstone floor and open fire and a dining-room that glimmers with soft candle-light of an evening, create a romantic setting for the enjoyment of predominantly local fresh foods cooked with care and not a little enthusiasm.
Bar food is in no way the poor relation, with starters of roast scallops with gruyere and lemon risotto or game bird terrine with romesco sauce and walnut pickle followed by fresh tagliatelli tossed in cep sauce with shaved Parmesan, a sea bass, salmon and cod trio served on a ratatouille tart with tapenade and cassoulet of pork rib, duck and Toulouse sausage served with pancetta and mashed potato. Simpler main dishes might be monkfish fillets with herb crust and langoustine sauce and braised ham hock flavoured with grain mustard, apple and prunes. **OPEN:** 11-11. **BAR MEALS:** L served all week. D served all week 12-2 7-9. **RESTAURANT:** L served Sun. D served all week 12-2 7-9. Av 3 course à la carte £30.
BREWERY/COMPANY: Free House.
PRINCIPAL BEERS: Theakstons, Black Sheep Riggwelter, Theakston Old Peculier. **FACILITIES:** Children welcome Garden: patio, outdoor eating Dogs allowed.
NOTES: Parking 30. **ROOMS:** 12 bedrooms 12 en suite s£53.50 d£69 FR£79-£99

See Pub Walk on page 503

ELSLACK
Map 09 SD94

The Tempest Arms ♀
BD23 3AY ☎ 01282 842450 ▪ 01282 843331
Dir: From Skipton take A59 towards Gisburn. Elslack signed on L on A56
Traditional stone-built inn set amid beautiful dale scenery and named after the Tempest family from nearby Broughton Hall. The classic bar offers cosy corners, wing chairs and log fires, while oak beams, wooden floors and candlelight create an atmospheric setting in the dining room. Typical dishes are
continued

shoulder of lamb cooked with Jennings bitter, salmon hollandaise, and seafood grill.
OPEN: 12-3 7-11pm. **BAR MEALS:** L served all week. D served all week 12-2 6-9.30. Av main course £6. **RESTAURANT:** L served all week. D served all week 12-2 6-9.30. Av 3 course à la carte £14.
BREWERY/COMPANY: Jennings. **PRINCIPAL BEERS:** Jennings - Bitter, Cumberland & Sneck Lifter,. **FACILITIES:** Children's licence Garden: patio, outdoor eating. **NOTES:** Parking 120.
ROOMS: 10 bedrooms 10 en suite s£52 d£65

ESCRICK
Map 09 SE64

Black Bull Inn ♦♦
Main St YO19 6JP ☎ 01904 728245 ▪ 01904 728154
Dir: From York follow the A19 for 5m, enter Escrick, take second L up main street, premises located on the L
Situated in the heart of a quiet village, this 19th-century pub is within easy reach of York racecourse and the historic city centre.

FADMOOR
Map 09 SE68

Pick of the Pubs

The Plough Inn 🛏 ♀
Main St YO62 7HY ☎ 01751 431515
Dir: 1m N of Kirkbymoorside on the A170 Thirsk to Scarborough Rd
Overlooking the green of this tranquil village on the edge of the North Yorkshire Moors with views to the Wolds and Vale of Pickering, this stylishly refurbished country pub with snug little rooms and open fires is a popular local haunt with a reputation for imaginative food. Run in genuinely hospitable fashion, its daily menus list home-made soups, filled baguettes, fresh haddock with chips and traditional suet steak and kidney pudding. Sample starters for dinner list fresh fisherman-style mussels, duck liver and pork terrine and wild mushrooms with bacon before herb-crusted roast cod on leek and cheese mash, lobster thermidor, pork medallions with Parmesan and blue cheese sauce and seasonal local game casserole. Sticky toffee pudding with hot toffee sauce and almond meringue roulade with fruit compôte are typical of home-made puddings; while real Yorkshire ales and an extensive list of well-chosen wines demonstrate similar attention to detail.
OPEN: 12-2.30 6.30-11 (Winter closed Mon & Tue). Closed 25-26th Dec, 1st Jan & BHs. **BAR MEALS:** L served Tue-Sun. D served Tue-Sat 12-2 6.30-8.45 (no food Sun eve in winter). **RESTAURANT:** L served Tue-Sun. D served Tue-Sat 12-2 6.30-8.45. Av 3 course à la carte £16.50. **BREWERY/COMPANY:** Free House.
PRINCIPAL BEERS: Black Sheep, Timothy Taylor Landlord.
FACILITIES: Children welcome Garden: patio, Food served outside. **NOTES:** Parking 20

GIGGLESWICK
Map 08 SD86

Black Horse Hotel ♦♦♦
32 Church St BD24 0BE ☎ 01729 822506
The Black Horse is set in the middle of an attractive village, next to the church and behind the market cross. A good choice of home-cooked meals is served either in the bar or dining room, perhaps lamb hotpot, lasagne (meat or vegetarian), poached salmon, and a selection of pizzas. There are three comfortable en suite bedrooms.
continued

OPEN: 12-2.30 5.30-11 (Sat-Sun all day). **BAR MEALS:** L served all week. D served all week 12-1.45 7-8.45. Av main course £7. **RESTAURANT:** L served Sun. D served all week 12-1.45 7-8.45. Av 3 course à la carte £15. **BREWERY/COMPANY:** Free House. **PRINCIPAL BEERS:** Tetley, Black Sheep, Timothy Taylor Landlord, John Smiths. **FACILITIES:** Garden: outdoor eating, patio. **NOTES:** Parking 16. **ROOMS:** 3 bedrooms 3 en suite s£38 d£54

GOATHLAND
Map 11 NZ80

Birch Hall Inn ♀ NEW
Beckhole ☎ 01947 896245
e-mail: birchhallinn@beckhole.freeserve.co.uk
Remotely situated between the North York Moors steam railway and the Grosmont Rail Trail walk, this extraordinary little free house consists of two very small rooms separated by a confectionery shop. There's an open fire in main bar, and a tiny family room that leads out into a large garden. Well kept real ales wash down home-baked Beck Hole butties and cakes, and locally made pies.
OPEN: 11-3 (Sun 12-3, 7.30-10.30) 7.30-11. **BAR MEALS:** L served all week. D served all week. Av main course £1.90.
BREWERY/COMPANY: Free House.
PRINCIPAL BEERS: Black Sheep, Theakstons Black Bull, Black Dog Scallywag, Rhatus. **FACILITIES:** Children welcome Garden: food served outside Dogs allowed on leads, Water & dog treat. No credit cards

Mallyan Spout ★ ★
The Common YO22 5AN ☎ 01947 896486
🖹 01947 896327
Dir: Off A169 (Whitby/Pickering rd)
Ivy-clad, stone-built Victorian property with mullioned windows, named after the famous waterfall at the rear of the hotel. Fresh fish from Whitby is a feature of both menus. Bedrooms.

GREAT AYTON
Map 11 NZ51

The Royal Oak Hotel ◆◆◆
123 High St TS9 6BW ☎ 01642 722361 🖹 01642 724047
Handy for Roseberry Topping, the Cleveland Hills and the North York Moors, this traditional rural hostelry offers a fine choice of food and ales. Winter log fires, beamed ceilings and lots of character enhance the atmosphere.

GREAT OUSEBURN
Map 09 SE46

The Crown Inn
Main St YO26 9RF ☎ 01423 330430 🖹 01423 331095
The famous Tiller Girls dancing troupe began its career at this cheery pub situated in a picturesque village, and a previous landlord once played for Leeds United. Now under new ownership, the new menus have an imaginative tone.

For pubs with AA rosette awards for food
see page 10

HARROGATE
Map 09 SE35

Pick of the Pubs

The Boars Head Hotel ◉ ◉ ★ ★ ★ 🐦
Ripley Castle Estate HG3 3AY ☎ 01423 771888
🖹 01423 771509
e-mail: reservations@boarsheadripley.co.uk
Dir: On the A61 Harrogate/Ripon road, the Hotel is in the centre of Ripley village

Part of the feudal village of Ripley, adjacent to the Castle, this is a stylish pub whose awards over the last decade are legion. Under the tutelage of Sir Thomas Ingilby, a resident chef/patron supervises classy, daily-changing bar and restaurant menus of which regulars never tire. The range of real ales and well-chosen wines thus comes as an added bonus. Diners are invited to trot along to starters of Spanish chorizo with wild mushrooms and bacon lardons or tossed salad of feta cheese, black olives and tomato, and pig out on seared salmon escalope with couscous or roast breast of duck with sweet potato purée: 'boaring it is not' says the menu. Classier restaurant dishes include seared medallions of monkfish with cherry tomatoes and Parma ham, award-winning venison sausages with grain mustard mash and sticky toffee brûlée with vanilla pod ice cream. Serene courtyard bedrooms offer, at a price, the stuff romantic dreams are made of.
OPEN: 11-11 (Winter Mon-Sat 11-3, 5-11) Sun 12-10.30 (Winter Sun 12-3, 5-10.30). **BAR MEALS:** L served all week. D served all week 12-2.30 6.30-10. Av main course £8.95. **RESTAURANT:** L served all week. D served all week 12-2 7-9.30. **BREWERY/COMPANY:** Free House. **PRINCIPAL BEERS:** Theakston Best, Black Bull, Timothy Taylor Landlord, Old Peculier. **FACILITIES:** Children welcome Garden: outdoor eating, Dogs allowed garden only. **NOTES:** Parking 45. **ROOMS:** 25 bedrooms 25 en suite s£95 d£115

HAWES
Map 09 SD88

Board Hotel ◆◆◆
Market Place DL8 3RD ☎ 01969 667223 🖹 01969 667970
e-mail: theboardhotel1@netscapeonline.co.uk
Dir: M6 J37 - A684 east to Hawes coming down the hill, first public house in your left opposite the market hall
Traditional Dales pub in the heart of Hawes in beautiful Wensleydale. Directly opposite the famous cheese factory. Expect a friendly welcome and hearty traditional pub food.

**THE BLUE LION,
EAST WITTON**
DL8 4SN. Tel: 01969 624273
Directions: on A6108
between Leyburn and Ripon
*Civilised 18th-century
coaching inn overlooking the
village green and classic
estate village, close to
Jervaulx Abbey and beautiful
Dales scenery. Delightful
interior, excellent Black
Sheep ales, upmarket pub
food, and comfortable
accommodation.*
Open: 11-11 (Sun 12-10.30).
Bar Meals: 12-2 7-9. Children
and dogs welcome. Garden
and patio. Parking.
(see page 501 for full entry)

*Pub*WALK

The Blue Lion, East Witton

From the attractive estate village of East Witton, this varied walk climbs steadily to open moorland where you are rewarded with fine views across the Ure Valley to Jervaulx Abbey, and into the Yorkshire Dales.

From the front of the inn, cross the road and turn right, then left along the road past the telephone box. In 200 yards (182m), where the road turns sharp left, fork right up the fell road. Ascend steeply to the top of the hill, then follow the track round to the right to reach a gate on to the moor. Turn left through the gate and walk down to Sowden Beck farmhouse, crossing the beck by the ford or bridge.

Pass in front of the house, and keep to the track up the field to a gate and track. Turn left and pass a small plantation to the entrance to house called Moorcote. Go through the gate beside the cattle grid, walk up the drive, following the waymarker round the buildings to a track. Turn left, cross a bridge to reach a gate and field. Turn half-right and go through a gate into woodland.

Proceed downhill to Hammer Farm. Cross the farm road and take the footpath behind farm buildings. Proceed through two fields, then in a steep field, turn left and follow a sunken path down to a gate. Turn right to a further gate onto a road and bridge over a beck. Pass Thirsting Castle Lodge and continue through Waterloo Farm and past the old churchyard and the former rectory. Shortly, rejoin your outward route, following the road back to the inn.

Distance: 4 1/2 miles (7.2km)
Map: OS Landranger 99
Terrain: farmland, moorland, country lanes
Paths: field and woodland paths, tracks and fell roads
Gradient: undulating; uphill first 1 1/2miles (2km)

*Walk submitted by:
The Blue Lion*

Stone walls and track in Wensleydale

England

HELMSLEY   Map 09 SE68

The Feathers Hotel NEW
YO62 5BT ☎ 01439 770275 🖹 01439 771101
Dir: From A1(M) Jct 168 to Thirsk, then A170 for 14m to Hemsley
Traditional country inn fronting onto the market place. The
beamed Pickwick Bar, located in one of the oldest houses in
Helmsley, is popular with locals, and freshly cooked food is
served in the Feversham dining room and bar with its
Mouseman of Kilburn furniture. Deep-fried whitebait with
salad, Thai garlic and ginger chicken with fragrant rice, and
steamed treacle sponge with custard are typical dishes.
OPEN: 10.30-11. **BAR MEALS:** L served all week. D served all
week 12-2.30 6-9.30. Av main course £8. **RESTAURANT:** L served
all week. D served all week 12-2.30 6-9.30. Av 3 course à la carte
£18. **BREWERY/COMPANY:** Free House **FACILITIES:** Children
welcome Garden: Food served outside. **NOTES:** Parking 24.
ROOMS: 14 bedrooms 14 en suite s£45 d£60

Pick of the Pubs

The Feversham Arms Hotel 🏮 ★ ★ ★ ♀
1 High St YO62 5AG ☎ 01439 770766
🖹 01439 770346
e-mail: fevershams@hotmail.com
*Dir: from the A1(M) jct A168 to Thirsk, then A170 for 14m to
Helmsley*

Built in 1855 on the site of an older hostelry, this civilised
little hotel was completely transformed by its new owners
towards the end of 2000. The extensive refurbishment
created an intimate new dining room, with a redesigned
lounge and bar area. Look, too, for the newly-built brasserie,
which aims for adventurous contemporary cooking in an
informal atmosphere. Meanwhile, the accommodation
hasn't been overlooked; there are seven new suites, and the
seventeen en suite bedrooms have been upgraded and
redecorated. Guests also have access to the hotel's fitness
suite, outdoor swimming pool and tennis court. The menu
starts with spicy smoked haddock soup, duck confit
pancakes, or goats' cheese tart. Main courses include prawn
and fresh pea risotto, seared calves' liver with bacon, mash
and gravy, or haddock and salmon fishcakes, all
complemented by an extensive international wine list.
OPEN: 10-2.30 6-11. **BAR MEALS:** L served all week.
D served all week 12-2 7-9. Av main course £12.
RESTAURANT: L served all week. D served all week 12-2
7-10. Av 3 course à la carte £20.
BREWERY/COMPANY: Free House.
PRINCIPAL BEERS: Theakstons Best, John Smiths.
FACILITIES: Children welcome Garden: Food served
outside Dogs allowed. **NOTES:** Parking 50.
ROOMS: 17 bedrooms 17 en suite s£70 d£90

Pick of the Pubs

The Star Inn 🏮 🏮 🐾 ♀
Harome YO62 5JE ☎ 01439 770397 🖹 01439 771833
*Dir: From Helmsley take A170 towards Kirkbymoorside.
0.5m turn R for Harome*
Truly picturesque, a 14th-century part-thatched inn that
boasts a finely restored cruck-framed longhouse, housing
these days a restaurant of high repute in the former byres.
The separate bar, full of hand-carved oak furniture,
dispenses fine real ales and carefully selected house wines
by the glass. Produce-led food is epitomised by the
dedicated use of home-grown fresh herbs from a fragrant,
lovingly tended garden and seasonal exotica chosen
through a network of hand-picked local suppliers. Flavours
are bold, vibrant and flavourful, in such dishes as Blue
Foot mushrooms with baby spinach and white truffle oil,
North Sea monkfish roast with black truffle mash and
back-in-favour oxtails braised in beer with stockpot carrots
and parsnip purée; accompanied typically with pommes
frites and aïoli or garden herb salad. Caramelised lemon
tart with raspberry coulis and well-chosen regional
farmhouse cheeses exhibit that similar thought and care
carry through right to the end. Al fresco summer dining is
an utter delight, in itself worth the detour, as are the three
tastefully furnished bedrooms, each with their own kitchen
and bathroom, situated in Black Eagle Cottage, a 15th-
century thatched building situated along the peaceful
village lane.
OPEN: 11.30-3 6.30-11 (Sun 12-10.30). Closed Mon lunch
2 wks Jan, 1 wk Nov. **BAR MEALS:** L served Tue-Sun.
D served Tue-Sat 11.30-2 6.30-10 (Sun 12-6 only).
RESTAURANT: L served Tue-Sun. D served Tue-Sat 11.30-2
6.30-10. Av 3 course à la carte £25.
BREWERY/COMPANY: Free House.
PRINCIPAL BEERS: Black Sheep Special, John Smiths,
Theakston Best, Captain Cook's Sunset. **FACILITIES:** Children
welcome Garden: patio, outdoor eating, Dogs allowed in
garden and bedrooms only. **NOTES:** Parking 24
ROOMS: 3 bedrooms 3 en suite s£45 d£90

HETTON   Map 09 SD95

Pick of the Pubs

The Angel 🏮 🏮 🐾 ♀
BD23 6LT ☎ 01756 730263 🖹 01756 730363
AA/Sea Fish Industry Authority National Seafood Pub of
the Year 2002

See Pick of the Pubs on page 505

AA Bed & Breakfast
2002
Britain's best-selling B&B
guide featuring over 3500
great places to stay

AA Bed & Breakfast Guide

www.theAA.com

AA Lifestyle Guides

OPEN: 12-3 6-10.30 (Sat till 11).
BAR MEALS: L served all week.
D served all week 12-2 6-9.
Av main course £8.50.
RESTAURANT: L served Sun
D served Mon-Sat 12-2 6-9.
Av 3 course a la carte £25.
Av 3 course fixed price £29.95.
BREWERY/COMPANY:
Free House.
PRINCIPAL BEERS: Tetley, Black
Sheep Bitter, Timothy Taylor Bitter
& Landlord.
FACILITIES: Children welcome.
Garden: patio, outdoor eating.
Dogs allowed.
NOTES: Parking 56.

AA/Sea Fish Industry Authority National
Seafood Pub of the Year 2002

BD23 6LT
☎ 01756 730263 📄 01756 730363
Dir: In village centre, B6265 (Rylstone)
to Grassington, signedposted from A59
Skipton by-pass

The Angel

Edging towards a 20th year in the same hands, the Angel is an institution in these parts - its reputation for fine food legendary. Remarkably unspoilt, it is a genuine 400-year-old Dales pub, converted originally from a farmhouse that dispensed ale to passing cattle drovers.

Full of nooks and crannies and oak beams, with roaring fires in winter, it stands in beautiful countryside no less than six miles from the nearest shop! An underlying philosophy epitomises what the British pub should be all about; no matter whether your choice is a bowl of soup and a pint of Black Sheep or the full three-course 'works' the intention is to make every visit memorable.

Throughout the Brasserie, Early Bird and à la carte Restaurant menus the emphasis is on thoroughly good food prepared from the freshest, best available ingredients - and it shows. Blackboard specials with a somewhat fishy bias feature the best of the day's shopping, as in Provençale fish soup, queen scallops in garlic butter - in starter or main portions - and smoked haddock with spinach, slow-roast tomatoes and hollandaise sauce. None render the alternatives any less special: Yorkshire Dales lamb racks with pesto crust, or shoulders roasted with root vegetables; preceded by black pudding on Puy lentils, pumpkin and sage risotto or game terrine set in a port wine jelly, and followed by memorable crème brûlée, rich chocolate mousse pot and the definitive sticky toffee pudding. Vacuum pressure facilitates service of over 20 fine wines by the glass.

Summer alfresco lunches can be enjoyed on the rear terrace with views over Rylestone Fell.

HOVINGHAM
Map 09 SE67

The Malt Shovel
Main St YO62 4LF ☎ 01653 628264 🖹 01653 628264
Dir: 18 miles NE of York, 5 miles from Castle Howard
Friendly pub retaining many original features, situated in a
pretty village close to Castle Howard. Unspoilt atmosphere;
good value food.

Pick of the Pubs

The Worsley Arms Hotel ⊛ ⊛ ★ ★ ★ 🖼 ♀
Main St YO62 4LA ☎ 01653 628234 🖹 01653 628130
e-mail: worsleyarms@aol.com
*Dir: From A1 take A64 towards Malton, L onto B1257 signed
Slingsby & Hovingham. 2m to Hovingham*
At the village centre opposite Hovingham Hall, birthplace
of the Duchess of Kent, this historic inn's family
connections are well documented in family portraits that
hang throughout the public areas: its further sporting
association, traditionally played for a century or more on
the adjacent village green between lords and locals, is
featured in the Cricketers' Bar. Overlooking are the bistro
and restaurant whose menus rely on supplies of seasonal
fish and game produced with justifiable confidence and
pride. Good real ales, wines and coffee accompany upmarket food that comes at a fair price: salmon and halibut
fishcakes and local venison sausages with parsnip mash.
Up a step at dinner expect oak-smoked salmon, brill fillets
with Savoy cabbage or honeyed lamb shank with minted
pea mash, followed by dark chocolate marquise with glazed
bananas. Traditional lounges, comfortable bedrooms and a
private garden invite the well-heeled to linger longer.
OPEN: 12-2.30 7-11. **BAR MEALS:** L served all week.
D served all week 12-2 7-10. Av main course £8.50.
RESTAURANT: L served Sun. D served all week 12-2 7-10.
Av 3 course à la carte £25. Av 3 course fixed price £25.
BREWERY/COMPANY: Free House.
PRINCIPAL BEERS: John Smiths, Stallion.
FACILITIES: Children welcome Garden: patio, outdoor
eating Dogs allowed. **NOTES:** Parking 30.
ROOMS: 19 bedrooms 19 en suite s£60 d£70 FR£80-£120

HUBBERHOLME
Map 09 SD97

The George Inn
BD23 5JE ☎ 01756 760223 🖹 01756 760808
Dir: At Buckden on B6160 take turn for Hubberholme

Named after the Viking king Hubba who settled in the area,
the village of Hubberholme has the highest road in Yorkshire
running through it, rising to a height of 1,934 feet. JB Priestley,
continued

who is buried in the local churchyard, regarded the 18th-
century George as his favourite watering hole. Stone walls,
antique plates, mullion windows and an open fire enhance the
pub's character. Good, wholesome food ranges from hot and
cold snacks to more substantial dishes and home-made main
courses. Expect hearty casseroles, halibut steak, vegetarian
moussaka, lamb chops, and chicken, ham and leek pie on the
varied menu.
OPEN: 11.30-3 6.30-11 (Summer 11.30-11). Closed middle 2
weeks in Jan. **BAR MEALS:** L served all week. D served all week
12-2 6.30-8.45. Av main course £8. **BREWERY/COMPANY:** Free
House. **PRINCIPAL BEERS:** Black Sheep, Tetley.
FACILITIES: Garden: patio, food served in garden Dogs allowed
Water and Biscuits Provided. **NOTES:** Parking 20.
ROOMS: 7 bedrooms 4 en suite s£28 d£42 FR£60-£84

HUNTON
Map 09 SE19

New Inn 🖼 ♀ NEW
☎ 01677 450009
Small 100-year-old village pub enjoying open views across
rolling countryside and run by chef/patron Ian Vipond. Cosy
bar with open fire and Theakston ales, and a separate intimate
restaurant in which guests can sample interesting modern pub
food. Begin with crab risotto with pan-fried king scallops or
warm salad of goats' cheese and roast peppers, moving on to
sea bass with spinach and garlic king prawns or beef fillet with
bacon, shallots and red wine sauce.
OPEN: 12-3 7-11. **BAR MEALS:** L served Thur-Sun. D served
Wed-Mon 12-2 7-9. Av main course £7. **RESTAURANT:** L served
Thur-Sun. D served Wed-Mon 12-2 7-9. Av 3 course à la carte £15.
BREWERY/COMPANY: Free House.
PRINCIPAL BEERS: Theakstons Best Bitter, Black Bull, Courage
Directors, John Smiths. **FACILITIES:** Children welcome Garden:
Food served outside. **NOTES:** Parking 20 No credit cards

KELD
Map 11 NY80

Tan Hill Inn NEW
☎ 01833 628246
Dir: Signed off B6270 at Keld in Swaledale, W of Richmond
Set on the Pennine Way in an isolated position, this hospitable
16th-century inn is the highest in England, at 1,732 feet above
sea level. Once at a major trading crossroads, the Tan Hill Inn
is now popular with walkers and motorists enjoying the
austere beauty of the Pennines.
OPEN: 11-11. **BAR MEALS:** L served all week. D served all week
12-2.30 7-9. Av main course £5.95. **BREWERY/COMPANY:** Free
House. **PRINCIPAL BEERS:** Theakstons Best, XB, Old Peculier.
FACILITIES: Children welcome Garden: Food served outside
Dogs allowed. **ROOMS:** 7 bedrooms 7 en suite s£32 d£30
No credit cards

KIRBY HILL
Map 11 NZ10

The Shoulder of Mutton Inn
DL11 7JH ☎ 01748 822772
Dir: 4m N of Richmond, 6m from A1 A66 J at Scotch Corner
200-year-old traditional inn in an elevated village position,
with original beams in the Stable Restaurant. Ideal base for
exploring the Yorkshire countryside. Relax inside and choose
from a straightforward menu characterised by good home
cooking. Favourites might include Kirby cod, steak and
mushroom pie, shoulder of lamb, rabbit pie, and chilli.
continued

The Shoulder of Mutton Inn

OPEN: 12-2 7-11. **BAR MEALS:** L served Mon-Sat. D served all week 12-2 7-9.30. Av main course £7. **RESTAURANT:** L served Sat-Sun. D served all week 12-2 7-9.30. Av 3 course à la carte £9. **BREWERY/COMPANY:** Free House. **PRINCIPAL BEERS:** John Smiths, Jennings Cumberland Ale, Black Sheep. **FACILITIES:** Children welcome Garden: patio, Food served outside. **NOTES:** Parking 28. **ROOMS:** 5 bedrooms 5 en suite s£35 d£45

KIRKBYMOORSIDE   Map 09 SE68

Pick of the Pubs

George & Dragon Hotel ★ ★ 🛏 ⚲
17 Market Place YO62 6AA ☎ 01751 433334
📠 01751 432933
Dir: Just off A170 between Scarborough & Thirsk in centre of the Market Town
A natural stopping place between the old Great North Road and the east coast, this former coaching inn in the centre of town dates from the early 1600s. Now, its location on the edge of the North York Moors National Park makes it a handy touring base, with Helmsley Castle, the North York Moors steam railway and Nunnington Hall all within easy reach.
    Hand-pulled real ales and wines by the glass feature in the cosy beamed bar, with its blazing winter fires, old sporting prints and memorabilia. The recently refurbished Knights' Restaurant in the former brewhouse offers a wide choice of fare, and lunchtime blackboard specials give way to a candlelit à la carte environment in the evening. Choose from starters like moules marinière, tomato, Mozzarella and Parma ham platter, or stuffed mushrooms; main courses include seafood hotpot, beef goulash, stuffed duck breast, or roasted salmon on fresh spinach. After supper, 18 comfortably furnished en suite bedrooms offer a good night's rest.
OPEN: 10-11. **BAR MEALS:** L served all week. D served all week 12-2.15 6.30-9.15. Av main course £5. **RESTAURANT:** L served all week. D served all week 12-2.15 6.30-9.15. Av 3 course à la carte £20. **BREWERY/COMPANY:** Free House. **PRINCIPAL BEERS:** Black Sheep. **FACILITIES:** Children welcome Children's licence Garden: patio, outdoor eating Dogs allowed. **NOTES:** Parking 15. **ROOMS:** 18 bedrooms 18 en suite s£49 d£79

The Lion Inn
Blakey Ridge YO62 7LQ ☎ 01751 417320 📠 01751 417717
Dir: From A170 follow signs 'Hutton le Hole/Castleton'. 6m N of Hutton le Hole.
An isolated moorland location for this, the fourth highest inn in England. Cosy inside with low ceilings, beams and stone walls. Typical dishes are home made steak and mushroom pie in the bar, along with the snacks and sandwiches, and beef wellington, poached trout, or vegetarian Stroganoff in the restaurant.
OPEN: 10-11. **BAR MEALS:** L served all week. D served all week 12-10pm. Av main course £6.50. **RESTAURANT:** L served all week. D served all week 12-10. Av 3 course à la carte £13. **BREWERY/COMPANY:** Free House.
PRINCIPAL BEERS: Theakston Black Bull, Bitter & Old Peculier, John Smiths Bitter, Greene King Old Speckled Hen. **FACILITIES:** Children welcome Garden: Beer garden, Outside Eating Dogs allowed. **NOTES:** Parking 200. **ROOMS:** 10 bedrooms 7 en suite s£17.50 d£25 FR£25-£29pp

KIRKHAM   Map 09 SE76

Pick of the Pubs

Stone Trough Inn ⚲
Kirkham Abbey YO60 7JS ☎ 01653 618713
📠 01653 618819
e-mail: info@stonetroughinn.co.uk
Dir: 1 1/2m off A64, between York & Malton
Isolated beside a narrow lane high above Kirkham Abbey and the River Derwent, and handy for nearby Castle Howard, this traditional stone country inn has been well refurbished by newish licensees.
    A rambling series of beamed and cosy rooms feature welcoming log fires, comfortable furnishings and a relaxed and friendly atmosphere. Having worked in the kitchens at the renowned Winteringham Fields restaurant in Lincolnshire, chef/landlord Adam Richardson offers impressive, modern pub menus. In the bar are choices of home-made soups (tomato and roasted red pepper), chicken liver parfait with Cumberland sauce, and Caesar salad with smoked chicken to start; followed by smoked haddock fishcakes with lemon butter sauce, and honey-glazed duck leg with Oriental salad.
    Dinner choices add seared scallops with saffron risotto, herb lemon oil and crispy Parma ham, pan-fried calves' liver with herb mash, red onion confit and sage sauce, and warm chocolate tart with whisky cream. Chips are home-made - and so too are the petit fours. Traditional Sunday lunch. Alfresco summer seating with fine views.
OPEN: 12-2.30 6-11 (Sun 11.45-10.30). Closed Mon & Dec 25. **BAR MEALS:** L served Tues-Sun. D served Tues-Sun 12-2 6.30-7.30. Av main course £6.95. **RESTAURANT:** L served Sun. D served Tue-Sat 12-2.15 6.45-9.30. Av 3 course à la carte £23. **BREWERY/COMPANY:** Free House. **PRINCIPAL BEERS:** Tetley, Timothy Taylor Landlord, Black Sheep, Guest ales. **FACILITIES:** Children welcome Garden: Food served outside. **NOTES:** Parking 100

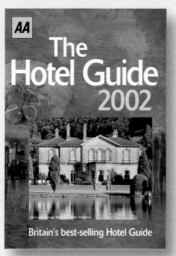
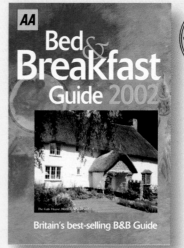
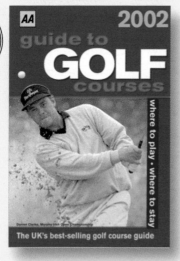
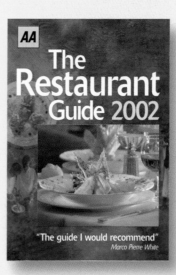

KNARESBOROUGH — Map 09 SE35

Pick of the Pubs

The General Tarleton Inn ◉ ◉ ★ ★ ★ 🛏 ♀
Boroughbridge Rd, Ferrensby HG5 0PZ
☎ 01423 340284   🖪 01423 340288
Dir: On A6055, on crossroads in Ferrensby

Former 18th-century coaching inn within easy reach of the A1, Harrogate and the Yorkshire Dales and under the same ownership as the equally impressive Angel Inn at Hetton (qv). Tastefully refurbished it sports a rambling, low-beamed bar with open fires, a comfortable mix of furnishings, cosy nooks and crannies; ideal for an intimate dinner chosen from the imaginative brasserie-style menu and interesting daily blackboard additions. Alternatively, dine in the light and airy covered courtyard.

Order at the bar; perhaps choosing chicken liver and foie gras parfait, grilled queen scallops with garlic and cheese or provençale fish soup to start, moving on to roast confit duck on braised red cabbage with parsnip crisps and redcurrant jus, pan-fried haddock with black pudding pomme purée and wholegrain mustard sauce, or loin of Dales lamb on garlic mash with a tomato and basil jus. Round off with traditional sticky toffee pudding with caramel sauce or lemon tart with raspberry coulis.

Fixed-price dinner menu in the adjacent restaurant. An impressive wine list complements the menu; 20 by the glass. Fourteen well appointed bedrooms are housed in a modern rear extension.
OPEN: 12-3 6-11. Closed Dec 25. **BAR MEALS:** L served all week. D served all week 12-2.15 6-9.30. Av main course £8.95. **RESTAURANT:** L served Sun. D served Mon-Sat 12-1.30 7-9.30. Av 3 course à la carte £25. Av 3 course fixed price £25. **BREWERY/COMPANY:** Free House.
PRINCIPAL BEERS: Black Sheep, Tetley, Timothy Taylors Landlord. **FACILITIES:** Children welcome Garden: outdoor eating. **NOTES:** Parking 60. **ROOMS:** 14 bedrooms 14 en suite s£75.95 d£84.90

LASTINGHAM — Map 09 SE79

Blacksmiths Arms NEW
☎ 01751 417247   🖪 01751 417247
e-mail: magsmiller2000@hotmail.com
This stone-built inn dating from 1673 was a blacksmith's for many years. It is situated opposite the church in a beautiful village, which is part of a conservation area within the National Park. Furnishings are in keeping with the pub's great age, and good conversation is provided by the rich cross-section of folk in the bar. Food is plentiful, with dishes of fresh cod and chips, honey roast duck, and seafood platter.
OPEN: 11.30-3.30 6.30-11 (Winter 12-3, 7-11). **BAR MEALS:** L served all week. D served all week 12-2.30 7-9.15. Av main course £6.95. **RESTAURANT:** D served all week 7-9.15. Av 3 course à la carte £14. **BREWERY/COMPANY:** Free House.
PRINCIPAL BEERS: Theakstons Best Bitter, Black Sheep, Black Bull Bitter. **FACILITIES:** Garden: Food served outside.
ROOMS: 3 bedrooms 3 en suite d£50

LEYBURN — Map 09 SE19

Pick of the Pubs

Sandpiper Inn ♀
Market Place DL8 5AT ☎ 01969 622206
🖪 01969 625367
e-mail: hsandpiper@aol.com
Dir: From A1 take A684 to Leyburn

The oldest building in Leyburn, dating back to around 1640, has been a pub for just 30 years and an outstanding one since its purchase in 1999 by the Harrison family. With a beautiful summer garden, a bar, snug and dining-room within, it is traditional in style and thoroughly sensible in its approach to food.

In addition to the safer options such as fish and chips in real ale batter and Yorkshire ham with eggs and fried potatoes that proliferate on the bar lunch menu, a modern British menu with a hint of Mediterranean flavours is the ever-increasing draw at dinner. Warm goats' cheese on red onion and tomato salad and seared scallops with Jerusalem artichoke puree amongst the starters are indicative of the care taken over fresh produce and balanced flavours. Further evidence comes in main dishes that include pot-roast rabbit with wild mushrooms, a fresh fish selection sauced with saffron and chives and loin of venison with liquorice sauce. Pasta with wilted greens and feta cheese and rib-eye steaks from the grill are amongst the popular alternatives, followed by raspberry and almond tart or iced lemon meringue terrine. Two smart en suite bedrooms have recently been added.

OPEN: 11.30-3 6.30-11. **BAR MEALS:** L served all week. D served all week 12-2.30 6.30-10. Av main course £6. **RESTAURANT:** L served all week. D served all week 12-2.30 6.30-9. Av 3 course à la carte £20. **BREWERY/COMPANY:** Free House.
PRINCIPAL BEERS: Black Sheep Best & Special, Theakston, Dent Aviator. **FACILITIES:** Garden: Food served outside Dogs allowed. **NOTES:** Parking 6. **ROOMS:** 2 bedrooms 2 en suite s£45 d£55

Wyvill Arms 🛏 ♀
Constable-Burton DL8 5LH ☎ 01677 450581
Situated on the edge of the Yorkshire Dales, this popular inn offers welcoming bars with open fires, beams and flagstones. Takes its name from a local family who converted what was a 1920s farmstead into a pub. Calves liver, fish and chips, Wyvill lamb, cassoulet of chicken and fillet of beef feature on the appetising menu. *continued*

509

Wyvill Arms

OPEN: 11-3 5.30-11. **BAR MEALS:** L served all week. D served all week 11.30-2.15 5.30-9.30. Av main course £6. **RESTAURANT:** D served all week 5.30-9.30. Av 3 course à la carte £20. **BREWERY/COMPANY:** Free House. **PRINCIPAL BEERS:** Theakston, Black Sheep, John Smiths. **FACILITIES:** Children welcome Garden: outdoor eating, patio Dogs allowed. **NOTES:** Parking 40. **ROOMS:** 3 bedrooms 3 en suite s£30 d£56 FR£60

LINTON   Map 07 SD96

The Fountaine Inn
BD23 5HJ ☎ 01756 752210
Dir: From Skipton take B6162 8m turn R for Linton
A very attractive 16th-century inn located in the Yorkshire Dales National Park on the banks of the River Beck. New landlord.

LITTON

Queens Arms
BD23 5QJ ☎ 01756 770208
e-mail: queensarmslitton@mserve.net
Early 16th-century inn located in a remote corner of the Yorkshire Dales, a perfect base for walking and touring. Low ceilings, beams and coal fires give the place a traditional, timeless feel. A good range of food incorporates local produce and international flavours. There's plenty of fish, including fresh halibut with seafood sauce, vegetarian dishes, home-made pies and a generous mixed grill.
OPEN: 11.45-3 6.45-11 (July-Aug Sat-Sun open all day). Closed Mon (ex BHs) and 3 Jan-1Feb. **BAR MEALS:** L served Tue-Sun. D served Tue-Sun 12-2 7-9. Av main course £7. **RESTAURANT:** L served Tue-Sun. D served Tue-Sun 12-2 7-9. Av 3 course à la carte £15. **BREWERY/COMPANY:** Free House. **PRINCIPAL BEERS:** Tetleys. **FACILITIES:** Children welcome Garden: outdoor eating, patio Dogs allowed. **NOTES:** Parking 10. **ROOMS:** 4 bedrooms 4 en suite s£30 d£30 FR£30-£78

LONG PRESTON   Map 08 SD85

Maypole Inn ♀
Maypole Green BD23 4PH ☎ 01729 840219
▤ 01729 840456
e-mail: landlord@maypole.co.uk
Dir: On A65 between Settle and Skipton
Friendly 300-year-old inn, set in a picturesque Yorkshire Dales village, within easy reach of the Forest of Bowland and the Pennines, and offering en suite accommodation and traditional home cooking. After a good moorland walk enjoy

continued

braised lamb and rosemary, ham and eggs, fillet of salmon in asparagus sauce, or mushroom and walnut loaf.
OPEN: 11-3 (Sun 12-10.30) 6-11 (Sat 5-11). **BAR MEALS:** L served all week. D served all week 12-2 6.30-9. Av main course £6.50. **RESTAURANT:** L served all week. D served all week 12-2 6.30-9. Av 3 course à la carte £13 9. **BREWERY/COMPANY:** Whitbread. **PRINCIPAL BEERS:** Timothy Taylor Landlord, Castle Eden. **FACILITIES:** Children welcome Garden: outdoor eating Dogs allowed. **NOTES:** Parking 30. **ROOMS:** 6 bedrooms 6 en suite s£29 d£47 2 family rooms £59

MARTON

The Appletree Country Inn NEW
YO62 6RD ☎ 01751 431457 ▤ 01751 430190
A promising and imaginative menu is served at this modern dining pub, which has recently been taken over by new ambitious management. 3 local cask ales, and more than 8 wines by the glass. Reports welcome.

MASHAM   Map 09 SE28

The Black Sheep Brewery NEW
HG4 4EN ☎ 01765 689227 ▤ 01765 689746
e-mail: helen.broadley@blacksheep.co.uk
Schoolboy humour is on the menu at this popular brewery complex on the edge of the Yorkshire Dales. Besides the 'shepherded' brewery tours, 'ewe' can simply call in to eat and drink in the stylish bistro and 'baa...r'. In just ten years, Black Sheep ales have achieved a national reputation, and dishes like lamb shank in Square Ale sauce make the most of them. Also lunchtime sandwiches, roast local pheasant, poached salmon, or provençale vegetable tartlet.
OPEN: 11-5.30 7-11. Closed 25-26 Dec. **BAR MEALS:** L served all week. D served all week 12-2.30. Av main course £6. **RESTAURANT:** L served all week. D served all week 12-2.30. **PRINCIPAL BEERS:** Black Sheep beers. **FACILITIES:** Children welcome Garden: Food served outside Dogs allowed Guide dogs only. **NOTES:** Parking 25

Kings Head Hotel ★ ★ ♀
Market Place HG4 4EF ☎ 01765 689295 ▤ 01765 689070
e-mail: 6395@snr.co.uk
Overlooking Masham's spacious market square with its cross and maypole, this handsome 18th-century inn was once an excise office. Combines classic Georgian splendour with modern day comforts and is a perfect base for touring the Yorkshire Dales. Expect fish and chips with mushy peas, herb roasted salmon, steak and ale pie, or lamb cobbler. Bedrooms are well decorated and comfortable.
OPEN: 11-11. **BAR MEALS:** L served all week. D served all week 12-9.45 6-10. Av main course £6. **RESTAURANT:** L served all week. D served all week 12-9.45 6-10. Av 3 course à la carte £20. **PRINCIPAL BEERS:** Theakstons Best Bitter, Black Bull, Old Peculier & Cool Cask. **FACILITIES:** Children welcome Garden: patio, outdoor eating. **ROOMS:** 10 bedrooms 10 en suite s£45 d£60

The White Swan Hotel ★ ★  🍽 ♀
Market Place DL8 4PE ☎ 01969 622093 📠 01969 624551
e-mail: whiteswan@easynet.co.uk
Dir: From A1, take A684 toward Leyburn then A6108 to Ripon, 1.5m to Middleton
Traditional Dales coaching inn located on the market square, with beams, flagstone floors and open fires. An ideal place to sit and watch the racehorses riding out in the morning. The emphasis is on quality accommodation and good food. The bar menu offers sausage and bubble and squeak with onion gravy, fillet of salmon on wilted spinach with a tomato and tarragon sauce, and venison and duck terrine served with Cumberland sauce.
OPEN: 12-3 6.30-11. **BAR MEALS:** L served all week. D served all week 12-2 6.30-9. Av main course £6.50. **RESTAURANT:** L served all week. D served all week 12-2 6.30-9. Av 3 course à la carte £12. **BREWERY/COMPANY:** Free House.
PRINCIPAL BEERS: Black Sheep, Hambleton, John Smiths.
FACILITIES: Children welcome Garden: Beer garden, patio, outdoor eating Dogs allowed. **ROOMS:** 11 bedrooms 11 en suite s£38 d£56 FR£80

MIDDLESMOOR   Map 09 SE07

Crown Hotel
HG3 5ST ☎ 01423 755204
Dating back in parts to the 17th century, this village pub offers the chance to enjoy a good pint of local ale by a roaring fire, or in a sunny beer garden. A good spot for those navigating the Nidderdale Way or local potholes.

MOULTON   Map 11 NZ20

Pick of the Pubs

Black Bull Inn 🍽
DL10 6QJ ☎ 01325 377289 📠 01325 377422
Dir: 1m S of Scotch Corner off A1
Well-established favourite among a discerning dining clientele and well placed for famished A1 travellers (1 mile south of Scotch Corner) seeking a civilised retreat. Lunchtime meals are served in the characterful, relaxing bar, warmed by a roaring fire in winter, and in the side dark-panelled Fish Bar. An imaginative, seasonally-changing menu lists light snacks such as seafood pancake, linguine with tomato sauce, pancetta and parmesan, Welsh rarebit and bacon, smoked haddock, walnut and gruyère quiche and various salads and sandwiches. In the evenings, when the pub becomes a fish and seafood restaurant proper, serving shellfish from Scotland and seafood from the east coast of England, dine in one of the original Pullman carriages, vintage 1932, from the Brighton Belle, or in the attractive Conservatory restaurant (complete with huge grapevine). Seasonal game and Aberdeen Angus steaks are the featured alternatives on the extensive carte. The Pagenham family have nurtured the restaurant's reputation, which extends far and wide, for 37 years now.
OPEN: 12-2.30 6-10.30 (Fri-Sat 6-11). Closed 24-26 Dec.
BAR MEALS: L served Mon-Sun 12-2. Av main course £5.75.
RESTAURANT: L served Mon-Fri. D served Mon-Sat 12-2 6.45-10.15. Av 3 course à la carte £25. Av 3 course fixed price £15.50. **BREWERY/COMPANY:** Free House.
PRINCIPAL BEERS: Theakstons Best. **FACILITIES:** Garden: patio, outdoor eating, BBQ. **NOTES:** Parking 80

MUKER   Map 09 SD99

The Farmers Arms
DL11 6QG ☎ 01748 886297
Dir: From Richmond take A6108 towards Leyburn, turn R onto B6270
Traditional village local at the head of beautiful Swaledale; popular with walkers on the Pennine Way and the Coast to Coast route. Sit by the open fire in the simply furnished main bar and accompany a pint of Theakstons with a decent bar meal. Try wild mushroom lasagne, poached salmon, roast chicken or a steak.
OPEN: 11-3 7-11 (from 6.30 Easter-Oct). **BAR MEALS:** L served all week. D served all week 12-2.30 7-8.50. Av main course £6.
BREWERY/COMPANY: Free House.
PRINCIPAL BEERS: Theakston-Best, Old Peculier, John Smiths, Nimmo's XXXX. **FACILITIES:** Children welcome Garden: Patio, food served outdoors Dogs allowed Water Provided.
NOTES: Parking 6 No credit cards

NUNNINGTON   Map 09 SE67

The Royal Oak Inn ♀ NEW
Church St YO62 5US ☎ 01439 748271 📠 01439 748271
Dir: Close to church at the opposite end of the village to Nunnington hall (National Trust)

Solid stone-built pub situated below the parish church in this sleepy rural backwater in the Howardian Hills, a short drive from the North Yorkshire Moors. After visiting Nunnington Hall (NT), enjoy a pint of Theakston ale and lunch in the spick-and-span open-plan bar, furnished with scrubbed pine and decked with farming memorabilia. Long-established landlord offers an extensive range of traditional, home-cooked pub food, alongside decent specials like rack of lamb with port and mint sauce, wild boar sausages with leek and potato mash, and halibut and tiger prawns with soy and star anise dressing.
OPEN: 12-2.30 6.30-9.50. Closed Mon. **BAR MEALS:** L served Tue-Sun. D served Tue-Sun 12-2 6.30-9.50. Av main course £8.50.
RESTAURANT: L served Tue-Sun. D served Tue-Sun 12-2 6.30-9.50. Av 3 course à la carte £16.50.
BREWERY/COMPANY: Free House.
PRINCIPAL BEERS: Theakston Best & Old Peculier.
NOTES: Parking 18

 Pubs offering a good choice of seafood on the menu.

OSMOTHERLEY   Map 09 SE49

Pick of the Pubs

Three Tuns Inn 🏵 ♦♦♦ 🍴 ♈

South End DL6 3BN ☎ 01609 883301
📠 01609 883301
Dir: Off A19

At the edge of the Yorkshire Moors by the Hambleton Way and Lyke Wake Walk, this recently extended village-centre inn stands amongst a row of solid stone 17th-century cottages. Hanging baskets and colourful floral displays grace a frontage ideal for people-watching. To enjoy the views make for the rustic rear garden.

Its new modern interior is designed to create a relaxed atmosphere in which to enjoy food freshly prepared from up-dated seasonal menus offering a wide choice. Amongst starters look for wild boar terrine with cranberry and pineapple syrup, chicken ravioli with stir-fried vegetables and chilli sauce and crab and salmon fishcakes with lemon and chive crème fraiche. Progress through king prawn, mussel and monkfish ragout, roast duck breast with Madeira jus and a vegetarian stuffed aubergine with artichoke tartlet to desserts such as brandy baskets with forest fruits and Tia Maria ice cream. Booking advisable for set-price Sunday lunch.
OPEN: 12-3 6-11. **BAR MEALS:** L served all week. D served Mon-Sat 12-3.30 6-10.30. **RESTAURANT:** L served all week. D served Mon-Sat 12-3.30 6-10.30. Av 3 course à la carte £25.
BREWERY/COMPANY: Free House.
PRINCIPAL BEERS: Theakston BB. **FACILITIES:** Garden: Food served outside. **NOTES:** Parking 4.
ROOMS: 7 bedrooms 7 en suite s£49 d£65

Black Sheep

Founded by Paul Theakston, a member of the fifth generation of the famous brewing family, the Black Sheep brewery was intended as something of a protest against the increasing dominance of the large breweries, hence the name. Since 1992 Black Sheep has gone from strength to strength, and now can safely be called a major independent. The HQ is part of an older brewery that was taken over by Paul's grandfather in 1919. The visitor sent has a shop, a bar and bistro, and guided tours, but this is not the place to go to if you're allergic to 'sheep' humour. Baaa-d puns are much in evidence. Major ales are Best (3.8%), Yorkshire Square Ale (5%) and Riggwelter (5.9%). More amusing than the sheep gags is the Monty Python Holy Grail Ale (4.7%), brewed to commemorate 30 years of Pythonic madness.

PATELEY BRIDGE   Map 09 SE16

Pick of the Pubs

The Sportmans Arms Hotel 🍴 ♈

Wath-in-Nidderdale HG3 5PP ☎ 01423 711306
📠 01423 712524
Dir: A39/B6451, restaurant 2m N of Pateley Bridge
Beloved of sportsmen from far and wide, this special pub and small hotel stands in a conservation village at the heart of one of the most beautiful and least commercialised areas of the Yorkshire Dales. A custom-built kitchen, run by chef/patron Ray Carter for nearly a quarter century, lies at the heart of the operation with Nidderdale trout, local beef, lamb, pork and the finest varieties of game all contributing in turn to his seasonal menus. True to the best pub traditions, real ales and fine wines accompany blackboard dishes served in an informal bar and daily restaurant menus that tempt all-comers to partake of consistently good food. Queen scallops with asparagus and fresh pasta and warm goats' cheese on roasted peppers are typically offered in advance of Scarborough Woof in a tomato and basil crust, chicken breast with risotto and wild mushrooms and sirloin steak in a Stilton and olive sauce. Summer pudding on warm days, sticky toffee on colder ones and a celebrated Wath rarebit with anchovy and capers show that the kitchen has lost none of its flair.
OPEN: 12-2.30 7-11. Closed 25 Dec. **BAR MEALS:** L served all week. D served all week 12-2 7-9. Av main course £9.
RESTAURANT: L served all week. D served all week 12-2 7-9.30. Av 3 course à la carte £23.
BREWERY/COMPANY: Free House.
PRINCIPAL BEERS: Younger, Theakston, John Smiths.
FACILITIES: Garden: outdoor eating. **NOTES:** Parking 30.
ROOMS: 13 bedrooms 12 en suite s£45 d£70

AA The Restaurant Guide 2002

The right choice every time
with this invaluable guide
for gourmets

AA Lifestyle Guides

www.theAA.com

PICKERING   Map 09 SE88

Pick of the Pubs

Fox & Hounds Country Inn ◉ ◆◆◆◆
Sinnington YO62 6SQ ☎ 01751 431577
🖷 01751 432791
e-mail: foxhoundsinn@easynet.co.uk
Dir: 3m W of town, off A170
This inviting stone-built inn stands just off the main A170
in Sinnington village, a peaceful backwater that was by-
passed during the 1930s. An arched bridge over the pretty
River Seven and a broad village green makes this an
attractive location, right on the edge of the North York
Moors National Park.

Inside the former coaching inn, oak-beamed ceilings,
ancient wood panelling and open fires set the scene for a
relaxing meal in the well appointed dining room, or a
longer stay in one of the pub's ten, comfortable en suite
bedrooms. Expect imaginative, well presented modern
cooking, perhaps starting with duck and pistachio pâté,
steamed mussels, or pan-fried black pudding with mustard
sauce.

Main courses might include seared tuna steak, braised
beef with red wine and shallot sauce, or pasta with sweet
leeks, wild mushrooms and Mascarpone. For pudding, try
the rhubarb and honey brûlée, pear and liquorice parfait
or pineapple tarte Tatin.
OPEN: 12-2 6-11. **BAR MEALS:** L served all week. D served
all week 12-2 6.30-9. Av main course £6.95.
RESTAURANT: L served all week. D served all week 12-2
6.30-9. Av 3 course à la carte £15.
BREWERY/COMPANY: Free House.
PRINCIPAL BEERS: Camerons. **FACILITIES:** Children
welcome Garden: outdoor eating Dogs allowed.
NOTES: Parking 30. **ROOMS:** 10 bedrooms 10 en suite s£44
d£50 FR£70-£90

Horseshoe Inn
Main St, Levisham YO18 7NL ☎ 01751 460240
🖷 01751 460240
e-mail: horseshoeinn@levisham.com
16th-century family-run inn with spacious lounge bar and
inviting atmosphere. Situated in a peaceful village, this is an
ideal base for walking and touring in the beautiful North York
Moors National Park.
Very handy for the nearby steam railway which features in
the Heartbeat television series. Extensive menu of traditional
dishes offers home made steak and kidney pie, poached
salmon, Whitby haddock and a good vegetarian selection.
OPEN: 11-3 6-11. Closed 25 Dec. **BAR MEALS:** L served all
week. D served all week 12-2 6.30-9. Av main course £7.
RESTAURANT: L served All. D served All12-2 6.30-9. Av 3 course
à la carte £7. **BREWERY/COMPANY:** Free House.
PRINCIPAL BEERS: Theakstons, John Smiths.
FACILITIES: Children welcome Garden: outdoor eating Dogs
allowed. **NOTES:** Parking 50. **ROOMS:** 6 bedrooms 3 en suite
s£26 d£52 No credit cards

AA inspected guest accommodation

Pick of the Pubs

The White Swan ◉ ★ ★ 🕮 ♀
Market Place YO18 7AA ☎ 01751 472288
🖷 01751 475554
e-mail: welcome@white-swan.co.uk
*Dir: In the market place between the church and the steam
railway station*
Attractive stone-built coaching inn located in the centre of
Pickering, the largest of Ryedale's four market towns and
an ideal base for exploring the riches of the region - the
nearby Dalby Forest, the heather moorland of the glorious
North York Moors and the natural beauty of Yorkshire's
spectacular heritage coastline. Pickering is also served by
the North York Moors steam railway; from here
passengers can begin an 18-mile train ride through the
heart of the National Park. Built as a four-roomed cottage,
the White Swan was once the haunt of salt smugglers.

Interesting, extensive menus offer dishes ranging from
dressed Whitby crab and Thai chicken, to seared pigeon
and pea tart, beef fillet with Parmesan and lemon, crisp
suckling pig with caramelised onion mash and black
pudding. Impressive wine list. Comfortable and appealing
bedrooms.
OPEN: 10-3 6-11 (July-Sep from 5pm). **BAR MEALS:** L
served all week. D served all week 12-2 7-9. Av main course
£7.50. **RESTAURANT:** L served all week. D served all week
12-2 7.30-9. Av 3 course à la carte £23.50.
BREWERY/COMPANY: Free House.
PRINCIPAL BEERS: Black Sheep Best & Special.
FACILITIES: Children welcome Garden: outdoor eating,
patio, Dogs allowed. **NOTES:** Parking 35.
ROOMS: 12 bedrooms 12 en suite s£60 d£90 FR£90-£140

PICKHILL   Map 09 SE38

Pick of the Pubs

Nags Head Country Inn ★ ★ 🕮 ♀
YO7 4JG ☎ 01845 567391 🖷 01845 567212
e-mail: enquiries@nagsheadpickhill.freeserve.co.uk
Dir: 1 E of A1(4m N of A1/A61 junction).W of Thirsk
At the centre of the tiny village of Pickhill near the River
Swale, this former coaching inn with beamed ceilings and
stone flagged floors is at the heart of "Herriot Country".
Bar and restaurant meals are chosen from a single menu
that is constantly up-dated to make best use of available
produce.

Seafood pancake mornay, creamed garlic mushrooms
with bacon and cheese topping and chicken liver pâté with
apple chutney are notable starters. Main dishes range
from cottage pie with leek-and-cheese mash to roast pork
fillet in a herb crust. Fresh fish includes baked Gilt Head
bream; game might be pheasant breast with parsnip rösti
and wild mushrooms.
OPEN: 11-11. **BAR MEALS:** L served all week. D served all
week 12-2 6-9.30. **RESTAURANT:** L served all week. D
served all week 12-2 7-9.30. **BREWERY/COMPANY:** Free
House. **PRINCIPAL BEERS:** Hambleton Best Bitter,
Theakston Black Bull, Black Sheep Bitter.
FACILITIES: Children welcome Garden: outdoor eating,
patio, BBQ, Dogs allowed. **NOTES:** Parking 40.
ROOMS: 17 bedrooms 17 en suite s£40 d£60 FR£80

England

RAMSGILL   Map 09 SE17

Pick of the Pubs

The Yorke Arms ⊛ ⊛ ★ ★ ♈
HG3 5RL ☎ 01423 755243 ▤ 01423 755330
e-mail: enquiries@yorke-arms.co.uk
See Pick of the Pubs on page 515

RICHMOND   Map 11 NZ10

Pick of the Pubs

Charles Bathurst Inn ◆◆◆◆ ⌾
Arkengarthdale DL11 6EN ☎ 01748 884567 & 884265
▤ 01748 884599
e-mail: info@cbinn.co.uk

The 'CB Inn', a tastefully refurbished 18th-century hostelry, lies tucked away in the remote and stunningly beautiful Arkengarthdale in the Yorkshire Dales National Park. Charles Bathurst was the local land and mine owner in the Dale during the 18th century. Inside you will find open fires, wooden floors, a relaxing atmosphere, excellent Yorkshire ales, and freshly cooked food prepared from local produce - perfect following an invigorating walk along the Pennine Way or the Coast-to-Coast Path. Charles and Stacy Cody have established a fine inn, offering innovative food and comfortable accommodation, since arriving here in 1996. Dishes on the ever-changing 'mirror' menu may feature spiced tomato and lentil soup, lime and ham filled guinea fowl with Madeira jus, shank of lamb on lentil cakes with juniper jus, locally-shot game in season, and fresh fish from Whitby - monkfish on noodles with chilli coconut sauce. Puddings include orange bread-and-butter pudding. Lovely views from individually designed en suite bedrooms.
OPEN: 11-11. **BAR MEALS:** L served all week. D served all week 12-2 6.30-9. Av main course £8. **RESTAURANT:** L served all week. D served all week 12-2 6.30-9. Av 3 course à la carte £14.50. **BREWERY/COMPANY:** Free House. **PRINCIPAL BEERS:** Theakstons, John Smiths Bitter, Black Sheep BB. **FACILITIES:** Children welcome Garden: outdoor eating Dogs allowed. **NOTES:** Parking 50. **ROOMS:** 18 bedrooms 18 en suite s£40 d£55

ROBIN HOOD'S BAY   Map 11 NZ90

Laurel Inn ♈
New Rd YO22 4SE ☎ 01947 880400
Picturesque Robin Hood's Bay is the setting for this small, traditional pub which retains lots of character features, including beams and an open fire. The bar is decorated with old photographs, and an international collection of lager bottles. This coastal fishing village was once the haunt of smugglers who used a network of underground tunnels and secret passages to bring the booty ashore. Straightforward simple menu offers wholesome sandwiches and soups.
OPEN: 12-11 (Sun 12-10.30). **BREWERY/COMPANY:** Free House. **PRINCIPAL BEERS:** Theakston's Black Bull, Theakston's Old Peculier, John Smiths. **FACILITIES:** Children welcome Small Patio Dogs allowed No credit cards

---

ROSEDALE ABBEY   Map 09 SE79

Pick of the Pubs

The Milburn Arms Hotel ⊛ ⊛ ★ ★ ⌾ ♈
YO18 8RA ☎ 01751 417312 ▤ 01751 417541
Dir: A170 W from Pickering 3m, R at sign to Rosedale then 7m N
Set in a tiny village in the heart of the North York Moors National Park, this charming country house hotel makes an idyllic retreat from the pressures of 21st-century life. Built in 1776, the family-run hotel now offers eleven beautifully furnished en suite bedrooms, with a cosy bar, soft sofas and log fires in the public rooms.
There's plenty of walking straight from the hotel, which is also well placed for touring. Castle Howard, Rievaulx Abbey, and Helmsley Castle are all within easy reach, and the nearby North Yorkshire Moors steam railway provides a different perspective.
The civilised Priory Restaurant offers a broad range of quality dishes, skilfully prepared to order. Local steamed mussels or pan-fried chicken livers sharpen the palate for marinated venison, magret of duck, or halibut steak with seafood chowder. Caramelised peach parfait or chocolate marque round off a satisfying meal.
OPEN: 11.30-3 6.30-11 (Open all day Sat in Summer). **BAR MEALS:** L served all week. D served all week 12-2.15 6.30-9. Av main course £7.95. **RESTAURANT:** D served all week 7-9. Av 3 course à la carte £20. **BREWERY/COMPANY:** Free House. **PRINCIPAL BEERS:** Black Sheep, Tetleys, John Smiths. **FACILITIES:** Children welcome Garden: Food served outside Dogs allowed. **NOTES:** Parking 60. **ROOMS:** 11 bedrooms 11 en suite s£39.50 d£32

AA Hotel Booking Service on 0870 5050505 to book at AA recognised hotels and B & Bs in the UK and Ireland, or through our Internet site:
www.theAA.com

OPEN: 11-3 6-11
(Sun 12-3 6-10.30).
BAR MEALS: L served all week.
D served all week 12-2 7-9.
Av main course £11
RESTAURANT: L served all week
D served all week 12-2 7-9.
Av 3 course a la carte £24.
BREWERY/COMPANY:
Free House.
PRINCIPAL BEERS: Black Sheep
Special, Theakston Best.
FACILITIES: No children under 12.
Garden: patio outdoor eating.
Dogs allowed.
NOTES: Parking 20.
ROOMS: 13 bedrooms 13 en suite
s£90 d£85-£110. Dinner, Bed &
Breakfast only.

The Yorke Arms

HG3 5RL
☎ 01423 755243 📠 01423 755330
e-mail: enquiries@yorke-arms.co.uk
Dir: Turn off at Pateley Bridge at filling
station on Low Wath rd. Signed to
Ramsgill, continue for 4m.

Creeper-clad 18th-century stone building nestling in a sleepy hamlet in the heart of Upper Nidderdale close to the shores of Gouthwaite Reservoir. Originally a shooting lodge for the Yorke family, it became an inn in the late 19th century and now offers ambitious, skilled cooking for discerning guests .

Bought by former restaurateurs Frances and Gerald Atkins in 1996, this striking building is now more civilised inn and restaurant than cosy country pub, although all are welcome to pop in for morning coffee or a pint of Black Sheep Special at the bar. Most come here to relax in the stone-floored bar or in the attractive lounge with easy chairs and open fires, prior to dining in the bistro or neatly appointed restaurant. It is a comfortable, traditional setting in which to sample Frances's creative modern English cooking which is based on the best local produce available.

From sandwiches made with home-made bread, Yorkshire ham, egg and chips, and fresh pasta dishes at lunchtime, the ecelctic, daily-changing carte may list plump and deliciously sweet seared scallops with crispy vegetables and a well judged coriander aioli, or a beautifully presented and moist smoked venison and foie gras terrine among the starters. Rustic and robust sounding main dishes, like roast saddle of rabbit with braised celery and cranberry relish and dried fruit-crusted lamb with potato rösti, Puy lentils and grilled vegetables, are surprisingly light and subtle in construction yet display real depth of flavours. Fishy alternatives may include roast turbot with spinach and chicken ravioli . Finish with tangy apricot tart or home-made ice creams. Very friendly and attentive staff.

Peaceful overnight accommodation in well furnished and very comfortable bedrooms - dinner, bed & breakfast only.

ROSEDALE ABBEY continued

Pick of the Pubs

White Horse Farm Hotel ★ ★
YO18 8SE ☎ 01751 417239 📠 01751 417781
e-mail: sales@whitehorsefarmhotel.co.uk
Dir: Turn off A170, follow signs to Rosedale for approx 7m, hotel
sign points up steep hill out of village, hotel 300yds on left

Former farmhouse situated in 12 acres high above the
pretty village of Rosedale Abbey with spectacular
moorland views. Licensed since 1702, when one end of the
stone farmhouse was turned into a 'tap room' for local
miners, it has gradually been transformed into a
comfortable inn with over fifteen en suite bedrooms.

Homely, stone-walled interior with open fires farming
memorabilia and a relaxing pubby atmosphere.
Accompany a good pint of Yorkshire ale with a hearty bar
meal, perhaps chicken and ham pie, Whitby haddock pot,
stuffed pheasant with bubble-and-squeak, and speciality
sausages with onion mash and redcurrant jus. Book for
traditional Sunday lunch.
OPEN: 11.30-2.30 (closed Mon-Tue lunch during Nov-Feb)
6.30-11 (Sun 6.30-10.30). **BAR MEALS:** L served all week.
D served Mon-Sat 12-2 6.30-9.30. Av main course £8.
RESTAURANT: L served all week. D served Mon-Sat 12-2
7-12. Av 3 course fixed price £22.95.
BREWERY/COMPANY: Free House.
PRINCIPAL BEERS: Black Sheep - Bitter, Special &
Riggwelter, John Smiths. **FACILITIES:** Children welcome
Garden: Beer garden, Outdoor Eating Dogs allowed Very
dog friendly. **ROOMS:** 15 bedrooms
15 en suite s£33 d£66 FR£66-£130

See Pub Walk on page 517

SAWLEY Map 09 SE26

The Sawley Arms ◆◆◆◆◆
HG4 3EQ ☎ 01765 620642
Dir: A1-Knaresborough-Ripley, or A1-Ripon B6265-Pateley Bridge

Popular, delightfully old-fashioned 200-year-old pub run by
the same welcoming landlady for nearly 30 years. The award-
winning garden is her pride and joy and provides a dazzling
array of colours. Close by are many tourist attractions,
including the renowned Fountains Abbey.

Varied menu supplemented by interesting daily specials,
freshly-cut sandwiches and wholesome snacks or starters.
Steak pie, salmon mousse, chicken in mushroom sauce and
beef salad are among the favourite dishes.
OPEN: 11.30-3 6.30-10.30 (closed Sun-Mon eve in Winter).
BAR MEALS: L served all week. D served all week 12-2.30 6.30-9.
Av main course £6.50. **RESTAURANT:** L served all week.
D served all week 12-2.30 6.30-9. Av 3 course à la carte £17.50.
BREWERY/COMPANY: Free House.
PRINCIPAL BEERS: Theakston, John Smiths.
FACILITIES: Garden: Beer garden, outdoor eating.
NOTES: Parking 50. **ROOMS:** 2 bedrooms 2 en suite d£65

The Cleveland Way

Britain's second oldest long-distance footpath, the horseshoe-shaped
100-mile Cleveland Way divides into two distinct halves. The first part is
open moorland and countryside, the second dramatic coastline and
clifftops. Enjoy a hearty meal at the Feversham Arms Hotel in the
delightful Yorkshire market town of Helmsley, where the walk starts,
then head north across the spectacular heather-clad North York Moors
to the 450-year-old Three Tuns at Osmotherley. Further north still, the
way passes close to Great Ayton where you can relax and rest those
aching limbs at the traditional Royal Oak Hotel. Captain Cook spent
part of his childhood in the village. The trail heads for the coast now,
turning south to visit Whitby, famous for the 18th-century Magpie Café
overlooking the harbour, then on to the Laurel Inn at Robin Hood's Bay.
From here the way follows the scenic Heritage Coast to Filey Brigg.

WHITE HORSE FARM HOTEL, ★★ ROSEDALE ABBEY

YO18 8SE. Tel: 01751 417239

Directions: 7m off A170, 3m NW of Pickering

Former farmhouse situated high up in Rosedale overlooking the moors and village, with spectacular views from the front terrace. Convivial stone-walled bar, hearty Yorkshire cooking and beers from Black Sheep and Theakston. Accommodation.

Open: 11.30-2.30 6.30-11. Closed Mon & Tue lunch Nov-Feb. Bar Meals: 12-2 6.30-9.30 (Sun 12-2 only). Children and dogs welcome. Garden & terrace. Parking.

(see page 516 for full entry)

*Pub*WALK

White Horse Farm Hotel, Rosedale Abbey

Explore Rosedale's 19th-century mining industry and savour magnificent moorland and valley views on this invigorating ramble in the North Yorkshire Moors

From the car park, cross the main road and follow the delightful daleside road to the hamlet of Thorgill. Keep to this quiet country lane, pass some holiday cottages and continue to a track on your left, near an old chapel. Follow this track through a gate and begin climbing past the ruin of Gill Bank Farm. Continue uphill to a stile in a wall, and keep to the footpath to another stile. You are now on the moor that leads up to Sheriff's Pit and ahead of you can see your destination, the former pit manager's house.

Keep to the path uphill to Sheriff's Pit. Note the 280-ft open shaft beyond the wire fence, pause to savour the memorable views, and then set off along the cinder track of the old ironstone railway in a south-south-easterly direction. Enjoy the lovely views of Rosedale Abbey nestling in the valley below and look out for the many moorland birds and wildlife that thrive here. Continue along the former trackbed, passing old mine workings, to Chimney Bank Terminus. Walk to the road, turn left and steeply descend off the moor back to the inn.

Distance: 5 miles (8km)
Map: OS Landranger 94
Terrain: moorland, country lanes
Paths: old railway trackbed and metalled lanes
Gradient: undulating; one fairly steep climb and one steep descent

Walk submitted by: Robert Horseman

SAXTON | Map 09 SE43

Pick of the Pubs

The Plough Inn 🐑 ♀
Headwell Ln LS24 9PX ☎ 01937 557242
▤ 01937 557655
Dir: Off A64 join A162 thru Towton, R onto B1217, Saxton signposted

A white stone, 250-year-old former farmhouse in a historic village surrounded by serene walking country, offering quality food throughout the cosy restaurant and adjoining carpeted bar. At lunchtime only can one enjoy chef/proprietor Simon Treanor's bar snacks, either one of the lunchtime specials (breast of chicken on couscous with wild mushroom sauce), a filled baguette, a ploughman's lunch or a dish from the restaurant menu. The latter may include starters like asparagus and leek soup, seafood parcel with lobster sauce and avocado salad with toasted goats' cheese, with such main course option as pan-fried calves' liver, slow-roast shoulder of lamb on Tuscan beans with balsamic vinegar sauce, beef fillet with green peppercorn sauce, and roast monkfish with red pepper compôte and a beurre blanc sauce. Puddings include a classic lemon tart. Monthly gourmet nights follow seasonal themes, and booking is essential for Sunday lunch. Yorkshire ales on tap and a decent list of wines with useful tasting notes.
OPEN: 12-3 6-11. Closed Mon & 1st 2 wks Jan.
BAR MEALS: L served Tues-Sun 12-3. Av main course £10.95. **RESTAURANT:** L served Tues-Sun. D served Tues-Sat 12-2 6.30-9.30. Av 3 course à la carte £23.
BREWERY/COMPANY: Free House.
PRINCIPAL BEERS: Theakston,Timothy Taylor Landlord, Rudgate Ruby Mild. **FACILITIES:** Children welcome Garden: patio, outdoor eating Dogs allowed (ex guide dogs).
NOTES: Parking 30

The Church's Sway
Inn signs reflecting the past importance of the Church include the Cross, the Mitre, the Adam and Eve, the Angel. The Salutation commemorates the Annunciation to the Virgin Mary. The Anchor is not always a nautical sign, but can be a Christian symbol of hope. The Star may be the one the three kings followed to Bethlehem and the Seven Stars are the Virgin Mary's crown. The Bell is a church bell and names like the Eight Bells and generally related to a notable local peal. Inns near a church dedicated to St Peter may be called the Cross Keys, which are the saint's keys of heaven and hell, or the Cock, for the one that crowed twice. The Lamb and Flag was the badge of the crusading Knights Templar (and was later adopted by the Merchant Tailors). The Catherine Wheel is the Emblem of St Catherine of Alexandria, who was much venerated in the crusading period and according to legend was martyred by being broken on a spiked wheel.

SCAWTON | Map 09 SE58

Pick of the Pubs

The Hare Inn 🐑 ♀
YO7 2HG ☎ 01845 597289 ▤ 01845 597289
Packed with old books, memorabilia and bric-a-brac this quaint 17th-century inn on Sutton Bank and close to Rievaulx Abbey offers an unfailingly warm welcome. Under low-beamed ceilings expect to find flagged floors, antique pine tables, open fires and a wood-burning stove in one of the dining areas. Daily menus are displayed throughout on large blackboards with an impressive variety of choice.

Begin adventurously with crab tartlet with Gruyère and red pepper marmalade or smoked duck and bacon salad, proceeding through roast pork knuckle with cider gravy and apple sauce, fresh Whitby cod with champ potato and parsley sauce or beef Wellington in Madeira sauce, to a range of afters that typically include a trio of chocolate desserts, sticky toffee pudding and hazelnut vacherin with apricot cream. As a general rule, booking is advised: children welcome.
OPEN: 12-3 6.30-11 (Sun 12-3.30, 6.30-11). Closed Mon lunch. **BAR MEALS:** L served Tue-Sun. D served all week 12-2.30 6.30-9.30. Av main course £8.
RESTAURANT: L served Tue-Sun. D served all week 12-2.30 6.30-9.30. Av 3 course à la carte £13.50.
BREWERY/COMPANY: Free House.
PRINCIPAL BEERS: Timothy Taylor Landlord, Theakstons, John Smiths. **FACILITIES:** Children welcome Garden: outdoor eating, herb garden, dove cote Dogs allowed garden only. **NOTES:** Parking 18

SETTLE | Map 08 SD89

Golden Lion Hotel ♦♦♦ ♀
Duke St BD24 9DU ☎ 01729 822203 ▤ 01729 824103
e-mail: bookings@goldenlion.york.net
Dir: in the town centre opposite Barclays Bank
Situated in the heart of Settle's 17th-century market place, the hotel dates back to about 1640. Once a traditional coaching inn, comfortable bedrooms are still available for the weary traveller. Traditional and continental dishes, using only fresh produce, include beef risotto, baby leg of lamb, vegetable tart, and roast Norfolk duck.
OPEN: 11-11. **BAR MEALS:** L served all week. D served all week 12-2.30 6-10. Av main course £6.50. **RESTAURANT:** L served all week. D served all week 12-2.30 6-10. Av 3 course à la carte £14.90. **BREWERY/COMPANY:** Thwaites.
PRINCIPAL BEERS: Thwaites Bitter, Best Mild.
FACILITIES: Children welcome Patio, fish pond.
NOTES: Parking 14. **ROOMS:** 12 bedrooms 10 en suite s£25 d£50

SKIPTON | Map 09 SD95

Devonshire Arms
Grassington Rd, Cracoe BD23 6LA ☎ 01756 730237
▤ 01756 730142
The Rhylstone Ladies WI calendar originated at this pub, a convivial dales inn convenient for the Three Peaks. There's a good atmosphere in the beamed bar and panelled dining room, where the menu features dishes enriched with Jennings ale, such as beer bangers and mash and braised roasted shoulder of lamb. *continued*

England

OPEN: 11.30-11 (Sun 12-10.30). **BAR MEALS:** L served all week. D served all week 12-2.30 6.30-9.30. Av main course £7.95. **RESTAURANT:** L served all week. D served all week 12-2.30 6.30-9.30. Av 3 course à la carte £15. **BREWERY/COMPANY:** Jennings. **PRINCIPAL BEERS:** Jennings Bitter & Cumberland, Theakstons. **FACILITIES:** Children welcome Garden: patio/terrace, outdoor eating Dogs allowed except in garden. **NOTES:** Parking 80. **ROOMS:** 6 bedrooms 6 en suite s£29.50 d£45 FR£57.30

STARBOTTON   Map 09 SD97

Fox & Hounds Inn
BD23 5HY ☎ 01756 760269 ▤ 01756 760862
e-mail: Hilary-Jimmy@Supanet.com
Dir: *on B6160 N of Kettlewell*
Situated in a picturesque limestone village in Upper Wharfedale, this ancient pub was originally built as a private house. Much of its trade comes from the summer influx of tourists and those tackling the long-distance Dales Way nearby. Make for the cosy bar, with its solid furnishings and flagstones, and sample a pint of Black Sheep or Theakston ales while you peruse the extensive blackboard menu which offers interesting main courses and good vegetarian meals. Expect steak and mushroom pie, lamb and mint burger in a bap, scampi, and mixed bean and apple casserole.
OPEN: 11.30-2.30 7-10.30 (BHs open lunch only). Closed Jan-mid Feb. **BAR MEALS:** L served Mon-Sun. D served Mon-Sun 12-2 7-9. Av main course £7.50. **BREWERY/COMPANY:** Free House. **PRINCIPAL BEERS:** Black Sheep, Timothy Taylor Landlord, Theakston Old Peculier & Black Bull. **FACILITIES:** patio. **NOTES:** Parking 15. **ROOMS:** 2 bedrooms 2 en suite d£60

TERRINGTON   Map 09 SE67

Bay Horse Inn
YO60 6PP ☎ 01653 648416
Homely village pub with a good food trade. Game pie, fresh fish and locally produced steaks and roasts are features of the menu, supported by blackboard specials such as pork chop with Madeira and mushrooms, pheasant in red wine, and salmon with capers and prawns.
OPEN: 12-3 6.30-11 (Sun 12-3, 6.30-10.30). **BAR MEALS:** L served all week. D served Mon-Sat 12-2 7-9. Av main course £6. **RESTAURANT:** L served all week. D served Mon-Sat 12-2 7-9. **BREWERY/COMPANY:** Free House. **PRINCIPAL BEERS:** Stones, Black Sheep, Timothy Taylor Landlord. **FACILITIES:** Children welcome Garden: Picnic tables. **NOTES:** Parking 30

Nine Men's Morris

A certain eeriness clings to one of the world's oldest games, which was played in Ancient Egypt 3,000 years ago and in Ireland in prehistoric times. It involves moving pegs or counters to form rows of three on a board or playing surface with 24 holes marked on it in an intricate pattern.

THIRSK

The Carpenters Arms ♀ NEW
Felixkirk YO7 2DP ☎ 01845 537369 ▤ 01845 537889
Dir: *2m outside Thirsk on the A170*
Late 18th-century inn situated in a pretty village just outside the famous market town of Thirsk where the hugely popular writer and vet James Herriot had his surgery for many years. The inn stands on the site of an old carpenter's and blacksmith's premises and the bar includes low beams adorned with old fashioned carpenter's tools and artefacts. Generous snacks and more substantial fare, including popular specials - pressed game terrine with Oxford sauce and toasted fruit bread, and sea bass on aromatic couscous with saffron cream.
OPEN: 11.30-3 6.30-11. **BAR MEALS:** L served all week. D served all week 12-2 7-9. Av main course £9.50. **RESTAURANT:** L served all week. D served all week 12-2 7-9. Av 3 course à la carte £20. **BREWERY/COMPANY:** Free House. **PRINCIPAL BEERS:** Tetley, Marstons Pedigree. **FACILITIES:** Children welcome Food served outside. **NOTES:** Parking 50

THORGANBY   Map 09 TF29

The Jefferson Arms
Main St YO19 6DA ☎ 01904 448316 ▤ 01904 448316
A lovely old inn dating from 1730, in a sleepy village just outside York, that offers speciality Swiss-style cuisine. The popular rosti - from ham and tomato pizzaiolo to ostrich and cranberry "Strauss" - are all freshly made.
OPEN: 12-3 6-11. **BAR MEALS:** L served Tue-Sun. D served Tue-Sun 12-2.30 6-9. Av main course £5.95. **RESTAURANT:** L served Sun. D served Tue-Sun 12-2.30 6-9. Av 3 course à la carte £20. **BREWERY/COMPANY:** Free House. **PRINCIPAL BEERS:** John Smiths, Black Sheep. **FACILITIES:** Garden: outdoor eating, patio. **NOTES:** Parking 55. **ROOMS:** 3 bedrooms 3 en suite s£35 d£55

THORNTON LE DALE

The New Inn ♦♦♦♦ ♀ NEW
Maltongate YO18 7LF ☎ 01751 474226 ▤ 01751 477715
e-mail: newinntld@aol.com
Log fires and old-world charm make this family-run free house the perfect antidote to a day's walking on the moors. With its nicely furnished en suite bedrooms, the New Inn is handy for the North York Moors steam railway and 'Heartbeat' country. Good home cooking characterises the popular menu; expect local seafood, lamb chump steak, pan-fried chicken with peppers and olives, or vegetarian lasagne.
OPEN: 12-2.30 6.30-11. **BAR MEALS:** L served all week. D served all week 12-2.30 6.30-9. Av main course £8.50. **BREWERY/COMPANY:** Free House. **PRINCIPAL BEERS:** Timothy Taylor Landlord, Black Sheep. **NOTES:** Parking 15. **ROOMS:** 6 bedrooms 6 en suite s£37 d£54

Pubs offering a good choice of seafood on the menu.

THORNTON WATLASS — Map 09 SE28

Pick of the Pubs

The Buck Inn ★
HG4 4AH ☎ 01677 422461 🖹 01677 422447
e-mail: buckwatlass@btconnect.com
Dir: From A1 at Leeming Bar take A684 to Bedale, then B6268.
Village 2m on R, hotel by cricket green

The Buck Inn doesn't just overlook the village cricket green; players score four runs for hitting the pub wall, and six if the ball goes over the roof! It's not hard to see why this pleasantly situated old free house is so popular with locals and visitors alike. In winter, a roaring fire warms the cosy bar, and a choice of forty malt whiskies helps to drive out the cold. The traditional bedrooms are comfortable and attractively decorated, and the pub offers fishing, golfing and racing breaks. Meanwhile, walkers can explore the Ure valley, and the Yorkshire Dales National Park is also within easy reach. Lunchtime brings interesting snacks like Masham rarebit or Caesar salad with smoked chicken, whilst the evening menu includes rich venison casserole, spicy duck breast, seafood tagliatelle, or cauliflower and mushroom bake.
OPEN: 11-11 (Sun 12-10.30). **BAR MEALS:** L served all week. D served all week 12-2 6.30-9.30. Av main course £7.50. **RESTAURANT:** L served all week 12-2
6.30-9.30. Av 3 course à la carte £16.50.
BREWERY/COMPANY: Free House.
PRINCIPAL BEERS: Theakston, Tetley, Black Sheep, John Smiths. **FACILITIES:** Children welcome Garden: outdoor eating, patio, Dogs allowed in garden & bedrooms, Water.
NOTES: Parking 40. **ROOMS:** 7 bedrooms 5 en suite s£36 d£55 2 family rooms £75

THRESHFIELD — Map 09 SD96

The Old Hall Inn
BD23 5HB ☎ 01756 752441 🖹 01756 752481
Dir: From Skipton north on B6265
Popular Dales inn which takes its name from the 15th-century hall at the rear, built by monks and reputedly the oldest inhabited building in Wharfedale. Good base for excellent walking. The aviary in the garden houses parrots among others. Interesting blackboard menu with lots of fish dishes.

WASS — Map 09 SE57

Wombwell Arms 🐑 ♀
YO61 4BE ☎ 01347 868280 🖹 01347 868039
Dir: From A1 take A168 to A19 jnct. York exit, then L after 2.5m, L at Coxwold to Ampleforth, Wass 2m
Built in 1621, the Wombwell Arms is a traditional coaching inn with a good local reputation. A series of stylishly decorated and pine-furnished rooms provide the setting for good bistro-style food. A typical menu includes tagliatelle with wild mushrooms, Whitby cod fillet with a crisp and cheese topping, King Prawns, minted lamb, venison with Guinness and port sauce, and 'Scrumpy Rabbit.' New owners.
OPEN: 12-2.30 7-11 (closed Sun eve in winter & all Mon).
BAR MEALS: L served Tue-Sun. D served Tue-Sat 12-2 7-9. Av main course £9. **RESTAURANT:** L served Tue-Sun. D served Tue-Sat 12-2 7-9. Av 3 course à la carte £20.
BREWERY/COMPANY: Free House.
PRINCIPAL BEERS: Black Sheep, Timothy Taylor Landlord, Cropton Two Pints. **FACILITIES:** Children welcome Food served outside Dogs allowed garden only. **NOTES:** Parking 15.
ROOMS: 3 bedrooms 3 en suite s£34 d£49

WEAVERTHORPE — Map 09 SE97

Pick of the Pubs

The Star Country Inn NEW
YO17 8EY ☎ 01944 738273
e-mail: info@starinn.net
Dir: 12m E of Malton to Sherborn Village, traffic lights on A64, turn R at the lights Weaverthorpe 4m Star inn on the Junct facing
In the midst of the Yorkshire Wolds and at the heart of a thriving village community, this ascendant Star has expanded over the years to incorporate adjacent cottages that house an extended dining area and comfortable accommodation for overnight guests who will relish both the abundant peace and quiet and landlady Susan Richardson's consistently good food.
  The rustic facilities of bar and dining-room, with large open fires and a convivial atmosphere are the perfect complement to food that is based on traditional family recipes combined with the best fresh produce of the area - exciting summer salads and game from the moors in winter. Favourite starters include Wold mushrooms with avocado, bacon and onions and both Yorkshire and herb puddings served with onion gravy, then traditional main courses weigh in with pheasant supreme with garlic and Stilton sauce, prime grilled steaks and boned duck breast with noodles and bitter orange sauce. Trendier influences colour the likes of Mexican quesadilla with chargrilled vegetables and a Caesar salad of hot chicken, bacon strips and Parmesan. Sunday lunch and regular special events evenings are particularly popular.
OPEN: 12-3 7-11. **BAR MEALS:** L served Wed-Sun. D served all week 12-2 7-9.30. Av main course £8.50.
RESTAURANT: L served Wed-Sun. D served all week 12-2 7-9.30. Av 3 course à la carte £15.
BREWERY/COMPANY: Free House **FACILITIES:** Garden: Food served outside. **NOTES:** Parking 30.
ROOMS: 3 bedrooms 3 en suite s£26 d£42 FR£70

WEST BURTON   Map 09 SE08

Fox & Hounds
DL8 4JY ☎ 01969 663279 📠 01969 663111
e-mail: alanfish@fox-hounds.demon.co.uk
Close to the heart of beautiful Wensleydale, this 17th-century coaching inn is attractively located by the pretty green in a totally unspoilt village. Traditional pub food is a feature here. Bedrooms.

WEST TANFIELD   Map 09 SE27

Pick of the Pubs

The Bruce Arms ♦♦♦ 🍸
Main St HG4 5JJ ☎ 01677 470325 📠 01677 470796
Dir: On A6108 Ripon/Masham rd, close to A1
Dating from 1820, this ivy-covered stone-built free house is situated close to the River Ure, just a few miles north of Ripon. This is a relaxed, informal venue, with traditional features like exposed beams, log fires, and candle-topped tables to complement the traditional decor. The three en suite bedrooms are comfortable, and provide good facilities for touring. Guests have easy access to the Yorkshire Dales, as well as local attractions like Jervaulx Abbey, Aysgarth Falls, and the Wensleydale cheese centre at Hawes.
   An extensive wine list underscores the bistro atmosphere, with blackboard menus that reflect local and seasonal produce. Warm up your palate with roast goat's cheese in filo pastry, smoked chicken and avocado, or black pudding with poached egg and hollandaise. Then move on to main courses like cod with cherry tomato compôte, roast halibut, sea bass with ginger and couscous, or calves' liver with bacon and mash.
OPEN: 12-2 6.30-11. Closed Dec 31-Jan 1, 1 Wk Feb, June & Nov. **BAR MEALS:** L served Tue-Sun. D served Mon-Sat 12-2 6.30-9.30. Av main course £11.50.
BREWERY/COMPANY: Free House.
PRINCIPAL BEERS: Black Sheep. **FACILITIES:** patio.
NOTES: Parking 15. **ROOMS:** 3 bedrooms 3 en suite s£37.50 d£55

Bottoms Up

As a customer in a 17th-century inn or alehouse, you might find yourself with a pint or quart pot made of wood, horn, leather in your hand. They all had the advantage of not breaking if dropped, though the effect on the beer's taste might not suit today's palates. A cut above these utensils were mugs and tankards of pewter, which some pubs still supply and some drinkers still swear by them. In 19th-century hostelries, however, pewter gradually gave way to china and glass, with the occasional joky china mug made with a frog crouching at the bottom, to give the unwary toper a nasty shock.

WEST WITTON   Map 09 SE08

Pick of the Pubs

The Wensleydale Heifer Inn ⊛ ★ ★ 🍸
DL8 4LS ☎ 01969 622322 📠 01969 624183
e-mail: heifer@daelnet.co.uk
Dir: A684, at West end of village.

This traditional whitewashed free house has been a village landmark since 1631. It still retains much of its original character in the atmospheric bar, and in the cosy lounge with its comfortable armchairs and crackling log fire. Nicely furnished en suite bedrooms are available in three historic buildings; Rose Cottage, the Old Reading Room, and the inn itself.
   Meals are also served in a choice of three venues, with the bar, informal bistro or candlelit restaurant offering choices to suit every mood. The menus are extensive, and vegetarians are well catered for. Starters like goats' cheese and red onion tart, or Whitby seafood pancake make an impressive precursor to raised game pie, trout in filo pastry, or broccoli and cream cheese crêpes. Leave room for home-made desserts such as chocolate mouse with almond tuile in a spun sugar basket.
OPEN: 9-11. **BAR MEALS:** L served all week. D served all week 12-2 6-9. Av main course £8. **RESTAURANT:** D served all week 6-9. Av 3 course à la carte £16.
BREWERY/COMPANY: Free House.
PRINCIPAL BEERS: Theakston, John Smiths, Black Sheep.
FACILITIES: Children welcome Garden: outdoor eating Dogs allowed. **NOTES:** Parking 30. **ROOMS:** 9 bedrooms 9 en suite s£60 d£72

WHITBY   Map 11 NZ81

The Magpie Cafe 🍸
14 Pier Rd YO21 3PU ☎ 01947 602058 📠 01947 601801
e-mail: ian@magpiecafe.co.uk
Combine a visit to this 18th-century former merchant's house with a tour of historic Whitby. Climb the 199 steps to the ruined Abbey and enjoy the magnificent views of the town and coast.
   Built in 1750 as the home of a local merchant, the award-winning Magpie is not really a pub but a licensed restaurant specialising in excellent fresh Whitby fish and seafood. Cod, haddock, lobster thermidor, lemon sole and grilled plaice are perennial favourites. *continued*

England

The Magpie Cafe

OPEN: 11.30-9 (closed Jan). **BAR MEALS:** L served all week. D served all week 11.30-9. Av main course £6. **RESTAURANT:** L served all week. D served all week 11.30-9. Av 3 course à la carte £10. **BREWERY/COMPANY:** Free House. **PRINCIPAL BEERS:** Crompton, Scoresby Bitter, Tetley Bitter. **FACILITIES:** Children welcome

---

WIGGLESWORTH   Map 08 SD85

The Plough Inn
BD23 4RJ ☎ 01729 840243 🖳 01729 840638
e-mail: steve@the-plough-wigglesworth.freeserve.co.uk
Dir: *from A65 between Skipton & Long Preston take B6478 to Wigglesworth*
Set in the spectacular limestone country of the western Dales, this 18th-century inn was originally a working farm and then an RAF billet during the Second World War. Ideally placed for touring and exploring the region. Innovative head chef enhances the quality and presentation of food here, with dishes including steak and venison pie, breast of chicken and delice of salmon.
OPEN: 11-2.30 6.30-11. **BAR MEALS:** L served all week. D served all week 12-2 7-9. Av main course £7. **RESTAURANT:** L served all week. D served all week 12-2 7-9. Av 3 course à la carte £16.50. Av 3 course fixed price £16.50.
BREWERY/COMPANY: Free House.
PRINCIPAL BEERS: Tetley, Black Sheep. **FACILITIES:** Children welcome Garden: outdoor eating. **NOTES:** Parking 70.
ROOMS: 12 bedrooms 12 en suite s£37 d£58

YORKSHIRE, SOUTH

BRADFIELD   Map 09 SK29

The Strines Inn
Bradfield Dale S6 6JE ☎ 0114 2851247
Dir: *off A57 between Sheffield toward Manchester*
The original manor house was built in 1275, but most of the present building dates from the 1550s, and has been an inn since 1771. It is set among grouse moors in the Peak District National Park, overlooking the Strines Reservoir. Real fires burn in all three rooms, where home-made fare, including pies, salmon steak, lasagne and vegetable balti, is served.
OPEN: 10.30-3 6.30-11 (all day wknds & Mar-Sep). Closed Dec 25. **BAR MEALS:** L served all week. D served all week 10.30-2.30 6.30-9. Av main course £5.95.
BREWERY/COMPANY: Free House.
PRINCIPAL BEERS: Greene King Old Speckled Hen, Marston Pedigree, Mansfield Ridings Bitter. **FACILITIES:** Children welcome Garden: patio, food served in garden Dogs allowed Water, Meat on Sundays. **NOTES:** Parking 50.
ROOMS: 3 bedrooms 3 en suite s£40 d£65 FR£75-£100

DONCASTER

Waterfront Inn
Canal Ln, West Stockwith DN10 4ET ☎ 01427 891223
Popular with the boating community, this River Trent canal basin waterside inn has a garden with barbeque. Good value food.

PENISTONE   Map 09 SE20

Cubley Hall ⛾
Mortimer Rd, Cubley S36 9DF ☎ 01226 766086
🖳 01226 767335
e-mail: cubleyhall@ukonline.co.uk

Once a moorland farm on the Pennine packhorse routes, this imposing stone-built inn retains many original features and is renowned for its restaurant, converted from an oak-beamed barn. The menu offers a choice from the chargrill, a range of pasta and pizza dishes, summer salads and fresh fish - grilled halibut steak, and salmon with salsa.
OPEN: 11-11 (Sun 12-10.30). **BAR MEALS:** L served all week. D served all week 12-9.30. Av main course £6. **RESTAURANT:** L served all week. D served all week 12-9.30. Av 3 course à la carte £15. **BREWERY/COMPANY:** Free House.
PRINCIPAL BEERS: Tetley, Burton Ale, Greene King Abbot Ale. **FACILITIES:** Children welcome Garden: Beer garden, patio, food served outdoors. **NOTES:** Parking 100.
ROOMS: 12 bedrooms 12 en suite s£50.50 d£60 FR£60-£75

SHEFFIELD   Map 09 SK38

The Fat Cat
23 Alma St S3 8SA ☎ 0114 249 4801 🖳 0114 249 4803
e-mail: enquiries@thefatcat.co.uk
Built in the 1850s, this fiercely independent pub serves as something of an alternative to the large chains that dominate the area. The Kelham Island Brewery is owned by the Fat Cat, and has its own visitor centre nearby. A wide range of real ales are always available, and vegans and vegetarians are well catered for. A typical menu includes lentil soup, cheddar, tomato and potato bake, mushroom and hazelnut pie, courgette and sunflower crunch, and creamy prawn pasta.
OPEN: 12-3 5.30-11 (Sun 7-10.30). Closed Dec 25-26.
BAR MEALS: L served all week. D served all week 12-2.30 6-7.30. Av main course £2.50. **BREWERY/COMPANY:** Free House.
PRINCIPAL BEERS: Timothy Taylor Landlord, Kelham Island bitter, Pale Rider. **FACILITIES:** Children welcome Garden: outdoor eating, BBQ Dogs allowed No credit cards

The Trout Inn ♀
33 Valley Rd, Barlow S18 5SL ☎ 0114 2890893
🖷 0114 2891284
e-mail: troutinn@trout-inn.freeserve.co.uk
New owners have taken on this traditional country inn which stands beside the B6051 north-west of Chesterfield on the edge of the glorious Peak District. Trout-fishing memorabilia and hand-painted murals adorn the walls, and evening candlelight enhances the relaxing dining atmosphere. Interesting food options range from speciality sandwiches - salmon and Cheddar melt - deep-fried battered cod with 'chunky' chips and minted lamb with red wine and onion gravy at lunch to pan-fried halibut with tomato, basil and white sauce, and roasted duck with redcurrant jus. Regular themed food nights.
OPEN: 12-3 6-11. **RESTAURANT:** L served all week. D served all week 12-2.30 6.30-9.30. Av 3 course à la carte £16.50.
BREWERY/COMPANY: Free House. **PRINCIPAL BEERS:** Bass.
FACILITIES: Garden: Food served outside Dogs allowed Water.
NOTES: Parking 25

YORKSHIRE, WEST

CLIFTON   Map 09 SE12

Black Horse Inn ♀
HD6 4HJ ☎ 01484 713862 🖷 01484 400582
e-mail: mail@blackhorseclifton.co.uk
Dir: N of Brighouse
A 16th-century coaching inn with an unusual past. Once used as a meeting place for the loom-wrecking Luddites, it was later a variety club that played host to Roy Orbison, Showaddywaddy and Shirley Bassey. Interior has oak-beamed rooms and open coal fires. Good home-cooked food has been served here for over 50 years, from sandwiches to pork saltimboca, spinach, ricotta and pinenut lasagne, and venison haunch steak.
OPEN: 11-3 5.30-11 (Sun 12-3, 5.30-10.30). **BAR MEALS:** L served all week. D served all week 12-2.15 5.30-9.30. Av main course £7. **RESTAURANT:** L served Sun-Fri. D served all week 12-2.15 5.30-9.30. Av 3 course à la carte £18.95.
BREWERY/COMPANY: Whitbread.
PRINCIPAL BEERS: Boddingtons, Timothy Taylor Landlord, Greene King Old Speckled Hen. **FACILITIES:** Children welcome Garden: Food served outside. **NOTES:** Parking 50.
ROOMS: 20 bedrooms 20 en suite s£39.50 d£60

Kelham Island
The Kelham Island Brewery was established in 1990, making it the first new independent brewery in Sheffield in the 20th century. The company moved to larger, purpose-built premises at Kelham Island in 1999 and the new site has five times the capacity of the previous one. The brewery's aim is to produce beers of the highest quality from pure brewing ingredients. The current brews include Pride of Sheffield (4.5%), Pale Rider (5.2%) and Cathedral Ale (5%). Visitors are welcome in organised parties of between 10 and 20 people.

DEWSBURY   Map 09 SE22

West Riding Licensed Refreshment Rooms
Dewsbury Railway Station, Wellington Rd WF13 1HF
☎ 01924 459193 🖷 01924 507444

Converted 19th-century railway station building on the Trans-Pennine route. Daily blackboard specials include a range of meat, fish, vegetarian and vegan meals, such as Alaskan fishcakes, walnut escalopes, lamb pasticcio and carrot roulade with water cress filling. An always changing selection of real ales is also available.
OPEN: 11-11 (Sun 12-10.30). Closed 25 Dec. **BAR MEALS:** L served all week. D served Tue-Wed 12-3 6-9.
BREWERY/COMPANY: Free House.
PRINCIPAL BEERS: Taylors Dark Mild, Taylors Landlord, Black Sheep. **FACILITIES:** Children welcome Garden: outdoor eating Dogs allowed. **NOTES:** Parking 600 No credit cards

EAST KESWICK   Map 09 SE34

The Travellers Rest
Harewood Rd, East Keswick LS17 9HL ☎ 01937 572766
Just two miles from Harewood House, this large 17th-century country pub is also handy for Leeds, Harrogate and the Yorkshire Dales. Daily changing specials blackboard.

HALIFAX   Map 09 SE02

The Rock Inn Hotel ★ ★ ★ 🐑 ♀
Holywell Green HX4 9BS ☎ 01422 379721
🖷 01422 379110
e-mail: the rock@dial.pipex.com
Dir: From M62 J24 follow signs for Blackley, L at crossroads, approx 0.5m on L
Substantial modern extensions have transformed this attractive 17th-century wayside inn into a thriving hotel and conference venue in the scenic valley of Holywell Green. All-day dining in the brasserie-style conservatory is truly cosmopolitan; kick off with freshly prepared parsnip and apple soup or crispy duck and seaweed, followed by liver and bacon, Thai-style steamed halibut, chicken piri piri or vegetables jalfrezi.
OPEN: 11-11. **BAR MEALS:** L served all week. D served all week 12-10. Av main course £4.25. **RESTAURANT:** L served all week. D served all week 12-10. Av 3 course à la carte £17.
BREWERY/COMPANY: Free House.
PRINCIPAL BEERS: Black Sheep, Timothy Taylor Landlord.
FACILITIES: Children welcome Garden: outdoor eating, Dogs allowed. **NOTES:** Parking 124. **ROOMS:** 30 bedrooms 30 en suite s£55-£120 d£64-£120 FR£74-£120

England

Pick of the Pubs

Shibden Mill Inn ◉ ◆◆◆◆ ♀
Shibden Mill Fold HX3 7UL ☎ 01422 365840
▤ 01422 362971

Skirted by a stream, this, low, whitewashed 17th-century inn stands in the Shibden Valley overlooking Red Beck. Newly revealed oak beams and rafters imbue much character on the cosy bar and intimate, candlelit restaurant where, along with a heated patio, some imaginative bar food has a truly modern feel. Smoked haddock risotto, twice-baked cheese soufflé, Toulouse sausage with white bean stew and potted ham with new potato salad are substantial starters. Wine suggestions accompany such main courses as salmon with oyster mushroom sauce, beef Rossini with Madeira jus and confit of lamb shoulder with mint and basil pesto jus. If you have room, round off with chocolate tart with raspberry coulis and malteaser ice cream or steamed lemon pudding. En suite bedrooms are tastefully furnished and thoughtfully equipped.
BAR MEALS: L served all week. D served Mon-Sat 12-2 6-9.30. Av main course £7.75. **RESTAURANT:** L served all week. D served Mon-Sat 12-2 6-9.30. Av 3 course à la carte £17. **BREWERY/COMPANY:** Free House.
PRINCIPAL BEERS: John Smiths, Theakston XB, Shibden Mill. **FACILITIES:** Children welcome Garden: outdoor eating, patio/terrace, heated Dogs allowed in garden only. **NOTES:** Parking 200. **ROOMS:** 13 bedrooms 13 en suite s£55 d£67

HAREWOOD
Map 09 SE34

Harewood Arms Hotel ♀
Harrogate Rd LS17 9LH ☎ 0113 2886566
▤ 0113 2886064
e-mail: unwind@theharewoodarmshotel.co.uk
Dir: On A61 S of Harrogate
Built in 1815 this former coaching inn is close to Harewood House, home of the Earl and Countess of Harewood. A good location for those visiting Harrogate, Leeds, York and the Dales. Typical menu includes baked salmon delice, grilled Yorkshire gammon, prime Yorkshire sausages, and nut roast provencale. Lighter meals include salads, sandwiches, baguettes, and omelettes.
OPEN: 11-11. **BAR MEALS:** L served all week. D served all week 12-3 5-10. Av main course £6. **RESTAURANT:** L served all week. D served all week 12-2 7-10. Av 3 course à la carte £21.50.
BREWERY/COMPANY: Samuel Smith **FACILITIES:** Garden: Food served outside Dogs allowed. **NOTES:** Parking 90. **ROOMS:** 24 bedrooms 24 en suite s£60 d£72

HAWORTH
Map 09 SE03

The Old White Lion Hotel ★ ★
Main St BD22 8DU ☎ 01535 642313 ▤ 01535 646222
e-mail: Enquiries@oldwhitelionhotel.com
Dir: Turn off A629 onto B6142, hotel 0.5m past Haworth Station
300-year-old former coaching inn located at the top of a cobbled street, close to the Brontë Museum and Parsonage. Traditionally furnished bars offer a welcome respite from the tourist trail. Theakston ales, and a wide range of generously served snacks and meals. Local pheasant, cassoulette of field mushrooms, or peppered monkfish might feature; and there are bedrooms available, some with lovely views.
OPEN: 11-3 6-11 (all day w/end). **BAR MEALS:** L served all week. D served all week 11.30-2.30 6.30-9.30. **RESTAURANT:** L served Sun. D served all week 7-9.30. Av 3 course à la carte £14.50. **BREWERY/COMPANY:** Free House.
PRINCIPAL BEERS: Theakstons Best/Black Bull, Tetleys, Scottish Courage John Smiths. **FACILITIES:** Children welcome Dogs allowed Guide dogs only. **NOTES:** Parking 9.
ROOMS: 14 bedrooms 14 en suite s£46 d£62 FR£73-£95

HORBURY
Map 09 SE21

Quarry Inn
70 Quarry Hill WF4 5NF ☎ 01924 272523
Dir: On the A642 approx 2.5m from Wakefield
Creeper-clad stone pub built in the 19th-century in the hollow of a disused quarry. Comfortable, split-level interior adorned with brass artefacts, and a traditional range of pub food enhanced by daily specials. Bedrooms.

LEDSHAM
Map 09 SE42

The Chequers Inn
Claypit Ln LS25 5LP ☎ 01977 683135 ▤ 01977 680791
Dir: Between A1 & A656 above Castleford
Quaint creeper-covered inn located in an old estate village in the countryside to the east of Leeds. Unusually, the pub is closed on Sunday because the one-time lady of the manor was offended by drunken farm workers on her way to church more than 160 years ago. Inside are low beams and wooden settles, giving the pub the feel of a traditional village establishment.

England

LEEDS　　　　　　　　　　　　Map 09 SE23

Whitelocks ♀
Turks Head Yard, Briggate LS1 6HB ☎ 0113 2453950
🖥 0113 2423368
Dir: next to Marks & Spencer in Briggate
First licensed in 1715, this wonderfully preserved, city centre
pub was originally known as the Turks Head. Inside are all
manner of classic features, including a long, narrow bar with
polychrome tiles, stained-glass windows and eye-catching
advertising mirrors. Look out for the Dickensian style bar at
the end of the yard. Popular menu offers herb-roasted baby
chicken with garlic mayonnaise, sirloin steak and fish and
chips in beer batter.
OPEN: 11-11 (Sun 12-10.30). Closed Dec 25-26 Jan 1.
BAR MEALS: L served all week 11-8. Av main course £6.
RESTAURANT: L served all week. D served Mon-Sat 12-2.30
5.30-7.30. Av 3 course à la carte £12.
PRINCIPAL BEERS: Greene King Old Speckled Hen, Ruddles
Best, Batemans XB, Theakstons Cool Cask & Old Peculier.
FACILITIES: Children welcome Garden: Outside Eating

LINTON　　　　　　　　　　　Map 09 SE34

The Windmill Inn 🐑 ♀
Main St LS22 4HT ☎ 01937 582209 🖥 01937 582209
Dir: from A1 exit at Tadcaster/Otley junction and follow Otley signs. In
Collingham follow signs for Linton
A coaching inn since 1674, the building actually dates from
1314 and originally housed the owner of the long-disappeared
windmill. Stone walls, antique settles, log fires and oak beams
set the scene in which to enjoy good bar food prepared by
new licensees. Specials include braised shoulder of lamb on
buttered spinach with minty gravy, tuna steak with pepper
butter and beef and Guinness pie.
OPEN: 11.30-3 (From Easter open all day) 5-11 (Sat-Sun
11.30-11). **BAR MEALS:** L served all week. D served Tue-Sat 12-2
5.30-9. Av main course £6. **RESTAURANT:** L served all week. D
served all week 12-2 5.30-9. Av 3 course à la carte £15.
BREWERY/COMPANY: Scottish Courage.
PRINCIPAL BEERS: John Smiths, Theakston Best, Ruddles
County. **FACILITIES:** Children welcome Garden: Food served
outside Dogs allowed Water. **NOTES:** Parking 60

MYTHOLMROYD

Shoulder of Mutton
New Rd HX7 5DZ ☎ 01422 883165
Dir: A646 Halifax to Todmorden, in Mytholmroyd on B6138, opp train
station
Located in a small village set against the rugged Pennines, this
popular pub is used by all the local sporting organisations as a
meeting place. Handy for local walks and the route of the
circular Calderdale Way. The bar features an unusual
collection of material concerning the Crag Coiners, 18th-
century forgers. Straightforward pub food might include steak
and onion pie, filled giant Yorkshire pudding, battered
haddock or beef in ale. Carvery also available.
OPEN: 11.30-3 7-11 (Sat 11.30-11, Sun 12-10.30). **BAR MEALS:** L
served all week. D served Wed-Mon 12-2 7-8. Av main course
£3.99. **BREWERY/COMPANY:** Whitbread.
PRINCIPAL BEERS: Black Sheep, Boddingtons, Flowers, Timothy
Taylor Landlord. **FACILITIES:** Children welcome Garden:
outdoor eating, patio, riverside Dogs allowed Water, Treats.
NOTES: Parking 25 No credit cards

The Green Man
The most uncanny and enigmatic
of inn signs represents a figure of folk
custom from the distant past, the Jack in the
Green who appeared at May Day revels. He was
a man covered with green leaves and branches,
who probably stood for the rebirth of plants,
trees and greenery in the spring. Virile and wild,
part human and part tree, he is often found
carved eerily in churches. A connection grew up
between him and Robin Hood, the forest
outlaw, and this is perpetuated in some Green
Man pub signs, which show an archer or
a forester in Lincoln green.

NEWALL　　　　　　　　　　　Map 09 SE14

The Spite
LS21 2EY ☎ 01943 463063
Traditional village pub which boasts a legend of feuding
landlords, and a vast collection of framed banknotes in the
relaxing bars.

RIPPONDEN　　　　　　　　　Map 09 SE01

Old Bridge Inn ♀
Priest Ln HX6 4DF ☎ 01422 822595 🖥 01422 824810
Dir: 5m from Halifax in village centre by church

Ripponden's cobbled packhorse bridge lies just a few yards
from this restored 14th-century inn located in a picturesque
conservation village once visited by Daniel Defoe. Award-
winning window boxes and hanging baskets brighten the
exterior and inside are thick stone walls, ancient beams and
antique oak tables. Food is freshly prepared on the premises,
up to a dozen wines are served by the glass and the inn offers
an impressive choice of about 30 malt whiskies. Dishes range
from Italian shepherds pie and mushroom, lentil and Stilton
lasagne, to meat and potato pie and venison sausages with
red wine gravy.
OPEN: 12-3 5.30-11 (Sat 12-11, Sun 12-10.30). **BAR MEALS:** L
served all week. D served Mon-Fri 12-2 6.30-9.30. Av main course
£5. **BREWERY/COMPANY:** Free House.
PRINCIPAL BEERS: Timothy Taylor Landlord & Golden Best,
Black Sheep Best, Moorhouses Premier. **FACILITIES:** Children
welcome Garden: Beer garden, outdoor eating.
NOTES: Parking 40

ROYDHOUSE   Map 09 SE21

Pick of the Pubs

The Three Acres Inn 🐾 ♀
HD8 8LR ☎ 01484 602606 🖹 01484 608411
e-mail: 3acres@globalnet.co.uk
See Pick of the Pubs on page 527

SHELF   Map 09 SE12

Duke of York
West St, Stone Chair HX3 7LN ☎ 01422 202056
🖹 01422 206618
Dir: M62 J25 to Brighouse.Take A644 N. Inn 500yds on R after Stone Chair r'about
There's a vast array of brassware and bric-a-brac at this 17th-century former coaching inn, and the atmosphere is lively. Traditional pub food is served along with a wide range of cask conditioned ales. Bedrooms include two in converted weavers' cottages.

From Gin Shop to Gin Palace

As the alehouses moved further up in the world in the 18th century, new drinking-houses filled the vacant space at the foot of the social ladder. These were the gin shops (or dram shops, for brandy). Gin was cheap and strong, it was adulterated with anything from turpentine to sulphuric acid, and in the slums of London and other towns the poor could get 'drunk for a penny, dead drunk for twopence' as the slogan went, in squalid cellars, hovels and back alleys. The scenes of drunkenness and degradation - vividly depicted in Hogarth's 'Gin Lane' - were so appalling that Parliament moved decisively in the 1750s to make spirits more expensive.

Following the sharp rise in beer prices at the end of the century, gin made a comeback in the industrial slums and from the 1820s on the distillers made a bid for working-class custom by opening gin palaces of ostentatious grandeur. The brewers followed this lead, hence the creation of magnificent Victorian and Edwardian pubs opulently provided with mahogany panelling, tiles and gilt, engraved mirrors and decorated glass, ornate gas lamps and richly elaborate ceilings. A few of them survive as reminders of vanished splendour.

SOWERBY BRIDGE   Map 09 SE02

Pick of the Pubs

The Millbank at Millbank NEW
HX6 3DY ☎ 01422 825588 🖹 01422 822080
e-mail: millbankph@ukonline.co.uk
Dir: A58 from Sowerby Bridge to Ripponden turn R at Triange
A traditional stone pub and restaurant in a delightful village location with contemporary architect-designed interiors and a burgeoning reputation for the quality of its food.

A cosy Tap Room has stone-flagged floors - and top-of-the-range real ales; the main wooden-floored bar has a contemporary wine bar feel and the light and airy dining-room has French windows opening on to a raised terrace with stunning views out to the gardens and valley beyond.

Food here has a predominantly British/European bias with emphasis on local fresh produce cooked simply enough to bring out its goodness and flavour. Favourites include chicken liver parfait with fig chutney and smoked chicken salad with goats' cheese and sun-blushed tomatoes, followed by confit of Barbary duck leg with pancetta mash and plum sauce and monkfish fillets wrapped in Parma ham with mustard leeks and new potatoes.

Alternative light meals might be gratin of queen scallops with garlic or spinach, walnut and gorgonzola tart with, to follow, warm chocolate and almond cake or rice pudding with toffee ice cream and caramel sauce. An enjoyable dining and drinking experience in suitably informal surroundings.
OPEN: 12-3 6-11 (Sat & Sun 12-11). Closed Mon.
BAR MEALS: L served Tue-Sun. D served Tues-Sat 12-2 6.30-9.30. Av main course £6.95. **RESTAURANT:** L served Tue-Sun. D served Tues-Sat 12-2 6.30-9.30. Av 3 course à la carte £19. Av 2 course fixed price £10.95.
BREWERY/COMPANY: Free House.
PRINCIPAL BEERS: Black Sheep, Timothy Taylor Landlord.
FACILITIES: Children welcome Garden: Food served outside Dogs allowed

PICK OF THE PUBS

OPEN: 12-3 7-11 (Sat 7-11 only). Closed 25 Dec.
BAR MEALS: L served Sun-Fri. D served all week 12-2 7-9.45. Av main course £9
RESTAURANT: L served Sun-Fri D served all week 12-2 7-9.45. Av 3 course a la carte £27. Av 3 course lunch £17.95.
BREWERY/COMPANY: Free House.
PRINCIPAL BEERS: Timothy Taylor Landlord, Morland Old Speckled Hen, Mansfield Riding Bitter, Marston's Pedigree.
FACILITIES: Children welcome. Garden: terrace.
NOTES: Parking 100.
ROOMS: 20 bedrooms 20 en suite s£55 d£75.

Three Acres Inn

Shelley HD8 8LR
☎ 01484 602606 ▤ 01484 608411
e-mail: 3acres@globalnet.co.uk
Dir: From Huddersfield take A629 then B6116 and take L turn for village.

Another long-standing Yorkshire favourite, in the same hands for over thirty years, that commands an imposing Pennine position above Huddersfield close to Emley Moor's TV mast. Just ten minutes from the M1 (J38), the inn is noted for its commendable food and warm hospitality.

In addition to first-class accommodation in twenty individually decorated bedrooms, dotted around the spacious car park, guests are invited to sample the delights of 'The Grocer', Truelove and Orme's much-acclaimed delicatessen offering for sale the very best British regional produce. On an impeccable bar menu the 'little notes' say it all: freshly-prepared food cooked to order may result in some delay at busy periods, 'not to be disturbed by cigarette smoke, mobile phones or any other annoying gadgets'. Enjoy instead some fine house wines, Adnams Bitter or Old Speckled Hen and simple, congenial conversation.

Whilst much of what emerges is purely traditional it will nonetheless delight. From a Scottish salmon, cumber and dill mayonnaise baguette to individual steak, kidney and mushroom pie under herb and mustard short-crust pastry this epitomises traditional pub fare. Yet other surprises in store can include crispy Japanese chicken on wok-fried greens with sweet chilli sauce, confit lamb shoulder with white beans and sage and pea and mint mash, aubergine cannelloni with Mozzarella and pine-nut stuffing and a pineapple carpaccio marinated in spices and dressed with a mango sorbet. Choices are legion, with no diminution in quality; meat-and-drink to regular diners and a delight to the uninitiated.

The stunning views across the rolling Pennine countryside are best appreciated from the front terrace on warm summer days.

England

THORNTON | Map 09 SE03

Pick of the Pubs

Ring O'Bells 🐷 ♀
212 Hilltop Rd BD13 3QL ☎ 01274 832296
📠 01274 831707
e-mail: ringobells@btinternet.com
Dir: *From M62 take A58 for 5m, R at crossroads onto A644, after 4.5m follow signs for Denholme, on to Well Head Rd into Hilltop Rd*

Situated high in the hills near the Brontë village of Haworth, this pub offers dramatic views of the surrounding Pennines - on clear days up to 30 miles. Formerly a 19th-century Wesleyan chapel (hence the name) and two mill workers' cottages, the interior is unique and retains many original features, including allegedly the ghost of a former priest.

Quality dishes, both traditional and innovative, share daily menus in both bar and restaurant, featuring perhaps spicy fish Mediterranean-style bisque, local game hotpot in red wine and rosemary, Chilean sea bass steak with crab and spring onion couscous and pies and pasta of the day, maybe 'mock goose' with black pudding and onions and chicken and vegetable ratatouille.

A la carte choices are voluminous and jokily titled; as in Italian Job pork meatballs and Asian Encounter spiced minced lamb to start and Dogger Bank fresh haddock dishes and a Bonanza of steaks in many guises. Home-made desserts include School Pud suet roly-poly and a sinful chocolate assiette known as Pauline's Treasures.
OPEN: 11.30-3.30 5.30-11 (Sun 12-4.30, 6.30-10.30). Closed Dec 25. **BAR MEALS:** L served all week. D served all week 12-2 5.30-9.30. Av main course £8. **RESTAURANT:** L served all week. D served all week 12-2 7-9.30. Av 3 course à la carte £18. **BREWERY/COMPANY:** Free House.
PRINCIPAL BEERS: John Smiths, Black Sheep Bitter & Special. **FACILITIES:** Children welcome.
NOTES: Parking 25

TODMORDEN | Map 09 SD92

Staff of Life ♦♦♦
550 Burnley Rd OL14 8JF ☎ 01706 812929
📠 01706 813773
e-mail: staff.of.life@Talk21.com
Dir: *on A646 between Halifax & Burnley*
Situated amidst dramatic Pennine scenery, this quaint stone-built inn dates back to 1838 and was once the centre of a thriving mill community. Well known for its wide range of curries. The basic menu is augmented by daily specials and typical dishes include steaks, rack of lamb, Cumberland sausage with egg and chips, or broccoli and cream cheese bake. The pleasant, attractively decorated bedrooms offer value for money accommodation.
OPEN: 7-11 (Sat 12-11, Sun 12-4, 7-10.30). **BAR MEALS:** L served Sat-Sun. D served Tue-Sun 12-2.45 7-9.30.
BREWERY/COMPANY: Free House.
PRINCIPAL BEERS: Timothy Taylor Landlord, Golden Best, Best Bitter. **FACILITIES:** Children welcome Garden: Dogs allowed.
NOTES: Parking 26. **ROOMS:** 3 bedrooms 3 en suite s£24 d£36

WAKEFIELD | Map 09 SE32

Kaye Arms Inn & Brasserie 🐷 ♀
29 Wakefield Rd, Grange Moor WF4 4BG ☎ 01924 848385
📠 01924 848977
e-mail: niccola@kayearms.fsbusiness.co.uk
Dir: *from M1 follow signs for mining museum, 3m further on (A642)*
Established, family-run dining pub within easy reach of the popular National Coal Mining Museum. Imaginative bar food and impressive wine list. Expect such dishes as salmon and prawn fishcake, smoked haddock with poached egg, confit of duck leg with white turnip gratin, garlic and rosemary, and gammon steak with fresh pineapple, egg and chips.
OPEN: 11.30-3 7-11. Closed Mon lunch & Dec 25- Jan 2.
BAR MEALS: L served Tue-Sun. D served Tue-Sun 12-2 7.15-9.30. Av main course £10. **RESTAURANT:** L served Tue-Sun. D served Tue-Sat 12-2 7.15-9.30. Av 3 course à la carte £18.
BREWERY/COMPANY: Free House. **PRINCIPAL BEERS:** John Smiths, Theakstons Best. **NOTES:** Parking 50

The Spindle Tree
467 Aberford Rd WF3 4AJ ☎ 01924 824810
Dir: *from M62 Eastbound, R at rdbt to Stanley, pub 1m down on R*
Traditional pub close to Wakefield town centre serving a varied, good quality pub menu throughout the unpretentious interior. Open all day weekends. Pubmaster.

WIDDOP | Map 09 SD93

Pack Horse Inn
HX7 7AT ☎ 01422 842803 📠 01422 842803
Dir: *Off A646 & A6033*
A converted laithe farmhouse dating from the 1600s, 300 yards from the Pennine Way and popular with walkers. Bedrooms.

Scotland

Pub of the Year for Scotland

The Wheatsheaf at Swinton,
Scottish Borders

Scotland

SCOTLAND

ABERDEEN CITY

ABERDEEN   Map 13 NJ90

Old Blackfriars
52 Castle Gate AB11 5BB ☎ 01224 581922
Traditional city centre pub with many fascinating features,
including stone and wooden interior and original stained glass
window display. Built on the site of property owned by
Blackfriars Dominican monks. Battered haddock, home-made
beefburgers and mixed grills feature among the popular bar
meals. Breakfasts, toasted sandwiches and freshly prepared
daily specials.
OPEN: 11-12 (Sun 12.30-11). Closed Dec 25 & Jan 1.
BAR MEALS: L served all week. D served all week 11-9. Av main
course £5. **BREWERY/COMPANY:** Belhaven.
PRINCIPAL BEERS: Belhaven 80/-, Belhaven St Andrews,
Caledonian IPA, Caledonian 80/-. **FACILITIES:** Children welcome
Children's licence

Prince of Wales
7 St Nicholas Ln AB10 1HF ☎ 01224 640597
Dir: city centre
Historic city centre pub, dating back to 1850 and boasting the
longest bar in Aberdeen, extending to 60 feet. Originally
known as the Café Royal, the pub was renamed in 1856. Wide
range of real ales, a selection of freshly made soups, filled
baguettes and baked potatoes, and home-cooked food that
might include breaded haddock, chicken pie, baked potatoes,
roast pork with apricot stuffing and local turbot.
OPEN: 11am-midnight (Sunday 12.30-11). **BAR MEALS:** L
served all week. D served all week 11.30-2. Av main course £4.
BREWERY/COMPANY: Free House.
PRINCIPAL BEERS: Theakstons Old Peculier, Bass, Caledonian
80/-,Timothy Taylor Landlord.

ABERDEENSHIRE

MARYCULTER   Map 13 NO89

Old Mill Inn
South Deeside Rd AB12 5FX ☎ 01224 733212
▤ 01224 732884
e-mail: Info@oldmillinn.co.uk
Dir: 5m W of Aberdeen on B9077
A 200-year-old country inn on the edge of the River Dee, just
10 minutes' from Aberdeen city centre. Fresh local produce is
a feature of the menu, with interesting dishes such as sirloin
steak chasseur, supreme of chicken Rob Roy, king prawn
jambolaya, or leek and cheese parcels.
OPEN: 11-11. **BAR MEALS:** L served all week. D served all week
12-2, 5.30-9.30. Av main course £5.50. **RESTAURANT:** L served
all week. D served all week 12-2 5.30-9.30. Av 3 course à la carte
£15.50. Av 2 course fixed price £5. **BREWERY/COMPANY:** Free
House. **PRINCIPAL BEERS:** Bass, Deuchers IPA.
FACILITIES: Children welcome Garden: patio Outdoor eating.
NOTES: Parking 100. **ROOMS:** 7 bedrooms 7 en suite s£40
d£50 FR£60-£65

Ⴘ   Pubs offering six or more wines by the glass

NETHERLEY   Map 13 NO89

Pick of the Pubs

Lairhillock Inn and Restaurant 🏠 Ⴘ
AB39 3QS ☎ 01569 730001 ▤ 01569 731175
e-mail: lairhillock@dreathemail.net
Dir: From Aberdeen take A90 turn R at Durris turning
200-year-old coaching inn situated in the heart of
magnificent Deeside, a region of Scotland much loved by
Queen Victoria. This regal landscape has changed little
over the centuries and there are numerous opportunities
for sightseeing and walking. Plenty of old world charm
inside the Lairhillock, with its bar, dining areas and
recently-added conservatory. Whatever the season there
are lovely countryside views. Wide-ranging daily specials
may feature breast of chicken, escalopes of venison,
braised lamb shank, baked duo of fish, wild mushroom
risotto and monkfish and crayfish stir-fry. Jazz and blues
nights are a regular fixture, as are speciality food evenings.
Good choice of well-kept real ales.

OPEN: 11-2.30 5-11 (Sat 11-12, Sun 12-11). Closed 26 Dec,
1-2 Jan. **BAR MEALS:** L served all week. D served all week
12-2 6-9.30. Av main course £8.95. **RESTAURANT:** L served
Sun only. D served Wed-Mon 12 7-11. Av 3 course à la carte
£25. **BREWERY/COMPANY:** Free House.
PRINCIPAL BEERS: Timothy Taylor Landlord, Marstons
Pedigree, Fullers London Pride. **FACILITIES:** Children
welcome Garden: paved eating area, Food served outside
Dogs allowed. **NOTES:** Parking 100

OLDMELDRUM   Map 13 NJ82

The Redgarth Ⴘ
Kirk Brae AB51 0DJ ☎ 01651 872353
Dir: On A947
There are magnificent views of Bennachie and the surrounding
countryside from this friendly establishment, which serves a
range of cask conditioned ales along with dishes prepared on the
premises using fresh local produce. Examples are Cajun salmon,
roast Aberdeen Angus with Yorkshire pudding, mixed game pie,
spinach and ricotta parcel, and poached haddock mornay.
OPEN: 11-2.30 5-11 (Fri-Sat till 12pm). Closed Dec 25-26 Jan 1-3.
BAR MEALS: L served all week. D served all week 12-2 5-9. Av
main course £5. **RESTAURANT:** L served all week. D served all
week 12-2 5-9. Av 3 course à la carte £15.
BREWERY/COMPANY: Free House.
PRINCIPAL BEERS: Inveralmond Thrappledouser, Caledonian
Deuchers IPA, Timothy Taylor Landlord, Burton Ale.
FACILITIES: Children welcome Children's licence Garden: Beer
garden,Outdoor eating Dogs allowed garden only Water
provided. **NOTES:** Parking 60. **ROOMS:** 3 bedrooms 3 en suite
s£40 d£50

Scotland

Tudor & Stuart Hostelries

After the closing down of the monasteries, prosperity and increasing travel brought a rise in the number and standards of inns. By Elizabeth I's time there were hostelries big enough to lodge 300 people and their horses. Inns were commercial centres for local merchants and traders, some were 'posthouses' for the developing mail service and in the 17th century smart shops appeared in the largest inns.

The introduction of hops was stoutly resisted. Henry VIII would drink only hopless ale and the brewers were castigated for ruining the traditional drink. Beer brewed with hops kept better for longer, however, which stimulated the development of large-scale breweries and both inns and alehouses gradually gave up brewing their own.

Alehouses were growing steadily less primitive. The main drinking room might still be the kitchen, for warmth. Furniture would be simple - a few trestle tables, benches and stools. As the number of people on the roads grew, alehouses began to offer a night's lodging, though in the poorer ones the traveller might sleep on the kitchen table or in bed with the landlord and his wife. Games were played just outside the house - quoits, skittles, bowls - and customers relieved themselves there too.

STONEHAVEN   Map 13 NO88

Marine Hotel 🛏 🍷
9/10 Shorehead AB39 2JY ☎ 01569 762155
🖃 01569 766691
Dir: *15m south of Aberdeen on A90*
Ironically, this harbour-side bar was built as a temperance hotel in the 19th century. It is thought that some of the remains from Dunnottar Castle were used to build the pub, as a number of gargoyles are visible on the front. Good variety of beers available, including Dunnottar Ale, especially brewed for this establishment. Regularly changing specials include plenty of seafood and local game.
OPEN: 11-12. Closed 25 Dec, 1 Jan. **BAR MEALS:** L served all week. D served all week 12-2 5-9. Av main course £6.95.
RESTAURANT: L served all week. D served all week 12-2 5-9. Av 3 course fixed price £7.50. **BREWERY/COMPANY:** Free House.
PRINCIPAL BEERS: Timothy Taylor Landlord, Deuchars IPA, Fullers London Pride, Moorhouses Black Cat.
FACILITIES: Children welcome   Children's licence

ANGUS

GLENISLA   Map 13 NO26

Pick of the Pubs

The Glenisla Hotel
PH11 8PH ☎ 01575 582223   🖃 01575 582223
e-mail: glenislahotel@sol.co.uk
Dir: *On B954*

New owners Ian and Anne Kemp continue the tradition of warm Scottish hospitality at this attractive, whitewashed 17th-century coaching inn, with its six cosy en suite bedrooms. The hotel stands in a magnificent glen on the former route from Perth to Braemar, where the nearby River Isla makes its way down towards the falls at Reekie Linn.

Visitors mingle with locals around a roaring log fire in the convivial, oak-beamed bar, where Inveralmond ales and hearty meals are served on plain wooden tables. There's a complete change of style in the civilised dining room, where pretty, full-length curtains complement the neatly-laid tables with their elegant napery and candlesticks. The daily changing menu might include lamb cutlets with marmalade and mustard, local venison, Orkney herrings, or pasta in tomato and basil sauce.
OPEN: 11-11 (Fri-Sat midnight). Closed Dec 25-26.
BAR MEALS: L served all week. D served all week 12-2.30 6.30-8.30 (12-8 Sun). Av main course £9.95.
RESTAURANT: L served all week. D served all week 12-2.30 6.30-8.30 (12-8 Sun). Av 3 course à la carte £18.
BREWERY/COMPANY: Free House.
PRINCIPAL BEERS: Inveralmond Independence, Thrappledowser & Liafail. **FACILITIES:** Children welcome Garden: Barbeque, food served outside Dogs allowed Outside kennels available if required. **NOTES:** Parking 20.
ROOMS: 6 bedrooms 6 en suite s£28 d£50

ARGYLL & BUTE

ARDENTINNY   Map 10 NS18

Ardentinny Hotel
Loch Long PA23 8TR ☎ 01369 810209   🖃 01369 810241
One of the West Coast of Scotland's most enchanting old droving inns, dating back to the early 1700s. Local produce is sourced from the surrounding hills and lochs. Expect some changes from the new management.

Scotland

ARDFERN | Map 10 NM80

The Gallery of Lorne Inn
PA31 8QN ☎ 01852 500284 🖹 01852 500284
Dir: 25 S of Oban. A816 then B8002
Beautifully located on the shores of Loch Craignish, this 18th-century droving inn is surrounded by stunning scenery and is popular with the fishing and sailing communities. Seafood figures prominently on both the bar and restaurant menus, with moules marinière, fresh sole, local langoustines, and Loch Etive salmon. Other favourites are coq au vin, ragout of venison with mushrooms, and leek and Stilton pasta. Finish with home-made sticky ginger pudding with toffee sauce.
OPEN: 11-2.30 5-10. Closed Dec 25. **BAR MEALS:** L served all week. D served all week 12-2 6-9. Av main course £6.95.
RESTAURANT: D served all week 6.30-9.15. Av 3 course à la carte £16. **BREWERY/COMPANY:** Free House.
FACILITIES: Children welcome Garden: patio, outdoor eating, Dogs allowed. **NOTES:** Parking 50. **ROOMS:** 7 bedrooms 7 en suite s£33.50 d£67

ARDUAINE | Map 10 NM71

Pick of the Pubs

Loch Melfort Hotel ◉ ◉ ★ ★ ★
PA34 4XG ☎ 01852 200233 🖹 01852 200214
e-mail: LMhotel@aol.com
Dir: on the A816 20m south of Oban
In a stunning loch-side location with views across Asknish Bay and the Sound of Jura, with a panorama of mountains in the background, this is a long-standing favourite of visitors to the West Coast whether by land or sea. The hotel has its own moorings at the loch's edge and Arduaine Gardens (National Trust) are literally next door, a delight to visit in summer.

The new Skerry bistro, specialising in local seafood, does a fine line in crumbed fillets of cod, hand-dived Mull scallops, salmon and prawn fishcakes and lobsters from Luing either cold in the shell or split and grilled with herb or garlic butter. In addition to sandwiches and meals for smaller persons, there is a good alternative selection ranging from home-made Highland beef-burgers and pasta carbonara to cassoulet of Scottish and French sausages and cutlets of Speyside lamb with caper wine gravy. In the restaurant, at dinner only, similar fine ingredients are promised in more elaborate guises with a spectacular seafood buffet on Sundays.
OPEN: 10.30-11.30. Closed mid-Jan to mid-Feb.
BAR MEALS: L served all week. D served all week 12-2.30 6-9. Av main course £6. **RESTAURANT:** D served all week 7.30-9. Av 5 course fixed price £30.
BREWERY/COMPANY: Free House **FACILITIES:** Children welcome Garden: Food served outside Dogs allowed Water. **NOTES:** Parking 50. **ROOMS:** 26 bedrooms 26 en suite s£80 d£70

Pubs offering a good choice of seafood on the menu.

CLACHAN-SEIL | Map 10 NM71

Pick of the Pubs

Tigh an Truish Inn
PA34 4QZ ☎ 01852 300242
Dir: 14m S of Oban, take A816, 12m turn off B844 toward Atlantic Bridge
Roughly translated, Tigh an Truish is Gaelic for 'house of trousers'. After the Battle of Culloden in 1746, the wearing of kilts was outlawed and anyone caught wearing one faced execution. Many Seil islanders defied this ruling and it was at this historic, white-painted inn that they swapped their kilts for trousers before travelling to the mainland.

Handy for good walks and lovely gardens and especially popular with tourists and yachting folk, the Tigh an Truish Inn offers a good appetising menu based on the best local produce.

Daily soups, smoked salmon and sweet pickled herring feature among the starters, while steak and ale pie, home-made chicken curry, venison in pepper cream and Drambuie sauce, and seafood pie are offered as main courses. Try one of the inn's puddings, perhaps apple crumble or syrup sponge.
OPEN: 11-3 5-11. Closed 25 Dec & Jan 1. **BAR MEALS:** L served all week. D served all week 12-2 6-8.30. Av main course £5.50. **RESTAURANT:** L served all week. D served all week 12-2 6-8.30. **BREWERY/COMPANY:** Free House.
PRINCIPAL BEERS: McEwans 80/-. **FACILITIES:** Children welcome Children's licence Garden: outdoor eating Dogs allowed. **NOTES:** Parking 35. **ROOMS:** 2 bedrooms 2 en suite s£40 d£40 No credit cards

---

CRINAN | Map 10 NR79

Pick of the Pubs

Crinan Hotel NEW
PA31 8SR ☎ 01546 830261 🖹 01546 830292
e-mail: nryan@crinanhotel.com
Very smart, large white 19th-century building in the Scottish baronial style set beside the harbourside and the Crinan Canal in a tiny fishing village, with magnificent views across the Loch Fyne to the hills beyond.

Famous for its top-floor seafood restaurant (Lock 16) and individually furnished bedrooms, but worth visiting for its civilised café-bar where excellent light meals using the same quality ingredients can be savoured.

Typical dishes include home-made soups, Loch Etive mussels with garlic and cream, prime Aberdeen Angus steaks with hand-cut chips and first-rate fish - roast Jura monkfish with ragout of mussels, basil and garlic on olive oil mash. Splendid paved terrace with sea and canal views.
OPEN: 11-12. **BAR MEALS:** L served all week. D served all week 12.30-2.30 6.30-8.30. Av main course £8.50.
RESTAURANT: D served all week 7-9.
BREWERY/COMPANY: Free House **FACILITIES:** Children welcome Garden: Food served outside Dogs allowed.
NOTES: Parking 30. **ROOMS:** 20 bedrooms 20 en suite s£70 d£140

Scotland

Coylet Inn 🍴 Ⓨ
Loch Eck PA23 8SG ☎ 01369 840426 📠 01369 840426
e-mail: coylet@btinternet.com
Comfortable 17th-century coaching inn located on the shores of Loch Eck at the heart of the Argyll Forest Park. Newly renovated in a traditional style that has left its character largely unaltered. Fishing, water-skiing, sailing and speed-boating are available on the Loch. Local produce forms a major part of a hearty menu that may include beef, venison, lamb, poultry, oysters, lobsters and other various seafood.
OPEN: 11-2.30 5-12. Closed 25 Dec. **BAR MEALS:** L served all week. D served all week 12-3 5.30-9.30. Av main course £12.
RESTAURANT: L served all week. D served all week 12-3 5.30-9.30. Av 3 course à la carte £18.
BREWERY/COMPANY: Free House.
PRINCIPAL BEERS: McEwans 80/-, Deuchars IPA.
FACILITIES: Children welcome Garden: outdoor eating, patio, Dogs allowed rooms/garden only. **NOTES:** Parking 40.
ROOMS: 4 bedrooms 4 en suite s£30 d£40

Pick of the Pubs

Kilberry Inn
PA29 6YD ☎ 01880 770223
e-mail: relax@killberryinn.com
Dir: From Lochgilphead take A83 south. Take B8024 signposted Kilberry
Miles from nowhere by a coastal loop of single track road, the Kilberry was converted from a "bat 'n' ben" cottage that housed this tiny hamlet's post office some 17 years ago. Today it is an established eating-house of fine repute with letting bedrooms which, though on the modest side, are as tranquil and comfortable - with fabulous panoramic views - as can be found on this stretch of the coast.
For customers to travel this far out of the way, the food has to be special; and it is. A simply furnished dining-room of stone walls, beams and open fires is warmly welcoming and family friendly. Meanwhile, despite (or because of) its remote location, everything from bread and cakes to preserves and chutneys is home-made. Menu favourites include smoked haddock and prawn chowder, oven-baked salmon with anchovies and green beans, country sausage pie and lamb fillets with garlic and rosemary, followed perhaps by walnut tart with nutmeg ice cream.
The inn has been under new ownership since last year, yet early indications are that future success looks as assured as ever it was.
OPEN: 11-2 5-10. Closed Oct-end of March. **BAR MEALS:** L served Mon-Sat. D served Mon-Sat. 12.15-2 6.30-9. Av main course £8. **RESTAURANT:** L served Mon-Sat. D served Mon-Sat 12.15-2 6.30-9. Av 3 course à la carte £15. Av 2 course fixed price £10. **BREWERY/COMPANY:** Free House.
PRINCIPAL BEERS: Selection of Scottish bottled beers.
FACILITIES: Children welcome Dogs allowed. Water.
NOTES: Parking 8. **ROOMS:** 3 bedrooms 3 en suite s£30 d£60

Kilfinan Hotel Bistro Bar
PA21 2EP ☎ 01700 821201 📠 01700 821205
Set on the shores of Loch Fyne, this comfortable, 18th-century coaching inn is a haven for country pursuits, and offers excellent food.

Pick of the Pubs

Cairnbaan Hotel & Restaurant ⊛ ★ ★ ★ 🍴 Ⓨ
Cairnbaan PA31 8SJ ☎ 01546 603668
📠 01546 606045
e-mail: cairnbaan.hotel@virgin.net
Dir: 2m N, take A816 from Lochgilphead, hotel off B841
Late 18th-century coaching inn overlooking Lock 5 on the Crinan Canal - the perfect place to watch the world go by. Fresh seafood, including scallops and langoustines, and game feature on the menu, along with a daily curry, venison burger, steaks, and well loved traditional puddings.
OPEN: 11-11. **BAR MEALS:** L served all week. D served all week 12-2.30 6-9.30. Av main course £8. **RESTAURANT:** D served all week 6-9.30. Av 3 course à la carte £23.
BREWERY/COMPANY: Free House.
PRINCIPAL BEERS: Bass. **FACILITIES:** Garden: patio, outdoor eating, beer garden. **NOTES:** Parking 50.
ROOMS: 12 bedrooms 12 en suite s£50 d£80

Pick of the Pubs

Pierhouse Hotel & Restaurant 🍴
PA38 4DE ☎ 01631 730302 📠 01631 730400
e-mail: pierhouse@btinternet.com
By the water's edge of Loch Linnhe, looking out over Lismore Island towards Mull, the Pierhouse started life as the Pier Master's residence when the cargo and passenger vessels that traversed the loch would moor at the nearby pier.
Since conversion into a purpose-built hotel in 1992, the demand for good seafood led to extension of the restaurant some five years later. Its reputation is based today on the quality of local lobsters, prawns, scallops and salmon caught by local fishermen within sight of the hotel terrace. Lismore oysters, clam chowder, cracked crab claws and Pierhouse salmon cake extend the options, followed by fisherman's pie, langoustine thermidor and a peerless Giant Platter sufficient for two.
Among non-fish alternatives are home-made chicken liver pâté, mushroom Stroganoff, beef or chicken stir-fry and fillets of Scottish beef and local pork with creamy peppercorn sauce and fresh vegetables.
OPEN: 11.30-11.30 (Sun 12-11). Closed Dec 25.
BAR MEALS: L served all week 12.30-2.30 6.30-9.30. Av main course £12.95. **RESTAURANT:** L served all week. D served all week 12.30-2.30 6.30-9.30. Av 3 course à la carte £19.50. **BREWERY/COMPANY:** Free House.
PRINCIPAL BEERS: Calders Cream, Calders 70/-, Tetley.
FACILITIES: Children welcome Garden: Dogs allowed.
NOTES: Parking 20. **ROOMS:** 12 bedrooms 12 en suite s£45 d£60

Scotland

STRACHUR   Map 10 NN00

Pick of the Pubs

Creggans Inn ◉ ★ ★ ★
PA27 8BX ☎ 01369 860279 🖹 01369 860637
e-mail: info@creggans-inn.co.uk
Dir: A82 from Glasgow, at Tarbet take A83 to Cairndow, then A815 down coast to Strachur
Standing at the very lip of Loch Fyne, Creggans has been a coaching inn since Mary Queen of Scots' day and today is a comfortable small hotel that has recently enjoyed considerable refurbishment. Views from the hills above take in vistas across the Mull of Kintyre to the Western Isles. The new bar, MacPhunns, pays tribute to a laird of ancient lineage who fell on hard times and took to stealing sheep. Use of local produce, more legally obtained, plays its full part in preparing menus that include Loch Fyne oysters, king scallops and local wild game, venison and hill lamb. Perennial favourites include moules marinière, steak and ale pie, fillet of salmon with roast vegetables, fresh cod from Tarbert - used in the ever-popular fish and chips - and chocolate terrine.
OPEN: 11-11 (11-1am summer) (12-11 winter Sun, 12-1am summer Sun). **BAR MEALS:** L served all week. D served all week 12-2.30 6-8. Av main course £6.50. **RESTAURANT:** D served all week 7-9. Av 3 course à la carte £26.50. Av 3 course fixed price £26.50. **BREWERY/COMPANY:** Free House. **PRINCIPAL BEERS:** Flowers IPA, Coniston, Bluebird Bitter, Courage Directors. **FACILITIES:** Children welcome Garden: patio, outdoor eating. **NOTES:** Parking 36. **ROOMS:** 14 bedrooms 14 en suite s£55 d£110

TARBERT LOCH FYNE   Map 10 NR86

Victoria Hotel ◆ ◆ ◆ 🖤 NEW
Barmore Rd PA29 6TW ☎ 01880 820236
🖹 01880 820638
e-mail: victoria.hotel@lineone.net
Centrally situated in a picturesque fishing village on the Kintyre peninsula, the Victoria was built as a hotel in the late 18th century. As well as good food, log fires and friendly atmosphere, the hotel is renowned for its recently created restaurant, which enjoys romantic views over Loch Fyne. Stuffed roast pheasant, seafood cluster, chargrilled salmon, or vegetable ragout are just a taste of the hotel's extensive menus.
OPEN: 11-12 (Sun 12-12) (Closed 3-5.30 in winter). Closed 25 Dec. **BAR MEALS:** L served all week. D served all week 12-2 6-9.30. Av main course £10. **RESTAURANT:** D served all week 6.30-9.30. Av 3 course à la carte £25. Av 3 course fixed price £25. **BREWERY/COMPANY:** Free House. **PRINCIPAL BEERS:** Boddingtons Bitter. **FACILITIES:** Children welcome Dogs allowed Water. **ROOMS:** 5 bedrooms 5 en suite s£27 d£54

TAYNUILT   Map 10 NN03

Polfearn Hotel ★ ★ 🖤
PA35 1JQ ☎ 01866 822251 🖹 01866 822251
Dir: turn off A85, continue 1.5m through village down to loch shore
Friendly family-run hotel at the foot of Ben Cruachen, close to the shores of Loch Etive, with stunning all-round views. Whether you're working, walking, cycling, riding, shooting or fishing in the area, the proprietors will store things, dry things,
continued

feed, water and warm you with little formality. Dishes are cooked to order from fresh local produce, notably seafood and steak from the local butcher.
OPEN: 12-2 5.30-11. Closed 25-26 Dec. **BAR MEALS:** L served all week. D served all week 12-1.45 5.30-8.45. Av main course £8. **RESTAURANT:** L served all week. D served all week 12-1.45 5.30-8.45. **BREWERY/COMPANY:** Free House. **PRINCIPAL BEERS:** weekly changing guest ale. **FACILITIES:** Children welcome Garden: Food served outside Dogs allowed. **NOTES:** Parking 50. **ROOMS:** 14 bedrooms 14 en suite s£20 d£40

TAYVALLICH   Map 10 NR78

Pick of the Pubs

Tayvallich Inn 🐑
PA31 8PL ☎ 01546 870282 🖹 01546 870333
e-mail: tayvallich.inn@virgin.net
See Pick of the Pubs on page 535

CITY OF EDINBURGH

EDINBURGH   Map 11 NT27

Bennets Bar
8 Leven St EH3 9LG ☎ 0131 229 5143
Opened in 1839 and taken over by Dougie Bennet in the early 20th century, this mirrored and tiled bar has close connections with the King's Theatre and often plays host to thirsty actors. Over 100 malt whiskies available.

The Bow Bar
80 The West Bow EH1 2HH ☎ 0131 2267667
Offering 160 malt whiskies, 10 rums and a gantry made from part of an old church, The Bow Bar is a fine example of the traditional Scottish old town pub. No music, no machines, only good conversation.

Isle of Skye Brewery
Established by two local teachers in 1995, the award-winning Isle of Skye Brewery prides itself on its success and growing reputation for high quality cask-conditioned ales and bottled beer. When the company started, the Skye ales were only available locally and in the central belt of Scotland. Today, they can be bought in most parts of Britain. Among the five main ales are Hebridean Gold (4.3%) - a unique Skye ale brewed with porridge oats to give it an exceptional smoothness, and Black Cullin (4.5%), a dark ale brewed with stout ingredients, rolled roast oats and Scottish heather honey. Brewery tours are available by prior arrangement.

OPEN: Winter: 11-2.30 6-11
(Fri-Sat 5pm-1am, Sun 5pm-12).
Summer: 11-12 (Fri-Sat till 1am).
Closed 25-26 Dec & 1-2 Jan.
BAR MEALS: L served all week.
D served all week 12-2 6-8.
Av main course £7
RESTAURANT: D served all week
7-9. Av 3 course a la carte £23.
BREWERY/COMPANY:
Free House.
PRINCIPAL BEERS: Calders 70/- &
80/-.
FACILITIES: Children welcome
Garden: patio, BBQ, outdoor
eating. Dogs allowed.
NOTES: Parking 20.

The Tayvallich Inn

PA31 8PL
☎ 01546 870282 📠 01546 870333
e-mail: tayvallich.inn@virgin.net
Dir: From Lochgilphead take A816 then
B841/B8025 for 11 miles

Converted from an old bus garage in 1971, Andrew and Anne Wilson's 'house in the pass' as it translates, stands by a natural harbour at the head of Loch Sween with stunning views over the anchorage, especially from the picnic tables that front the inn in summer.

The cosy bar with a yachting theme and the more formal dining-room feature original works by local artists and large picture windows from which to gaze out over the village and across Tayvallich Bay.

Unsurprisingly the main speciality here is fresh seafood, marked up daily on chalk boards, though all the food is sourced locally including meat, poultry, game and vegetables. Bar food is simple, straightforward and unpretentious, while many of the same ingredients appear on the restaurant menus cooked in more ambitious ways. Mussels, hot-smoked salmon, Loch Sween oysters and Sound of Jura scallops are regular features, the specials board adding perhaps poached River Add salmon, pan-fried halibut with wild mushroom sauce and monkfish sautéed with green peppercorns.

Home-made burgers with chips and salad, venison sausages with mustard mash, Caesar salad with grilled chicken and fish and chips appear in the bar; in the restaurant expect baked goat's cheese with roasted peppers, chicken breasts wrapped in Parma ham and spinach with a tarragon and mustard dressing, beef Stroganoff and prime Scottish steaks either sauced or plain with fresh vegetables and potatoes. Look out also for the mammoth Tayvallich seafood platter: but try to leave room also for home-made sweets such as apple and bramble crumble, cranachan and lemon posset with shortcake biscuits.

EDINBURGH continued

Doric Tavern ♀
15-16 Market St EH1 1DE ☎ 0131 225 1084
▤ 0131 220 0894
Bustling pub and bistro close to the Castle in the heart of one of Britain's most beautiful cities. Building dates back to 1816. The menu changes daily but expect haggis, venison in brioche, steamed halibut and pasta dishes among the main courses. All fresh produce. Simple snacks in the bar include soup, pies and rolls.
OPEN: 12-1. Closed Dec 25-26, Jan 1. **BAR MEALS:** L served Mon-Sat. D served Mon-Sat. Av main course £3.50.
RESTAURANT: L served all week. D served all week. Av 3 course à la carte £14. Av 3 course fixed price £19.75.
BREWERY/COMPANY: Free House.
PRINCIPAL BEERS: Deuchars IPA, Caledonian 80/-.

Royal Ettrick Hotel
13 Ettrick Rd EH10 5BJ ☎ 0131 2286413
▤ 0131 229 7330
Dir: From W end of street follow Lothian road, turn R onto Gilmor place for 0.75m, Hotel on R behind Bowling Green
Period mansion, now a hotel, situated in a residential suburb west of the city. Classic lounge bar with a two-tiered conservatory extension serving a popular menu, all day, every day. Bedrooms.

The Ship on the Shore 🍴
24/26 The Shore, Leith EH6 6QN ☎ 0131 555 0409
A short distance from the Royal Yacht Britannia, now moored permanently in the historic port of Leith, this cosy, atmospheric bistro is situated in a bustling, cosmopolitan area of Edinburgh. Small bar and panelled dining room inside with a nautical theme reflecting the history of the local docks. Seafood is the speciality, plus an assortment of meat and vegetarian dishes. Expect sole with a creamy seafood sauce, crab and gruyère tart and monkfish tail with a cherry, tomato, olive and garlic compôte.
OPEN: 12-1. Closed Dec 25-26, 1-2 Jan. **BAR MEALS:** L served all week. D served all week 12-2.30 6-8.30. Av main course £4.50.
RESTAURANT: L served all week. D served all week 12-2.30 6-10. Av 3 course à la carte £20. Av 3 course fixed price £16.95. **BREWERY/COMPANY:** Free House.
PRINCIPAL BEERS: Deuchars IPA, 80/-, 70/-.

The Starbank Inn
64 Laverockbank Rd EH5 3BZ ☎ 0131 552 4141
▤ 0131 552 4141

Tastefully renovated stone pub situated on the waterfront of North Edinburgh, affording splendid views over the Firth of Forth to the Fife coast. The bar menu typically offers roast
continued

lamb with mint sauce, poached salmon, mince and tatties, a vegetarian dish of the day, and chicken with tarragon cream sauce.
OPEN: 11-11 (Thu-Sat 11-12, Sun 12.30-11). **BAR MEALS:** L served all week. D served all week 12-2.30 6-9.30 (12-9.30 wkends). Av main course £5. **RESTAURANT:** L served all week. D served all week 12-2.30 6-9.30. **BREWERY/COMPANY:** Free House. **PRINCIPAL BEERS:** Belhaven 80/-, Belhaven Sandy Hunters Traditional, Belhaven St Andrews/IPA, Timothy Taylor Landlord & guests. **FACILITIES:** Children welcome Dogs allowed (on leads)

RATHO   Map 11 NT17

Pick of the Pubs

The Bridge Inn
27 Baird Rd EH28 8RA ☎ 0131 333 1320
▤ 0131 333 3480
e-mail: info@bridgeinn.com
Dir: From Newbridge interchange B7030, follow signs for Ratho

A former farmhouse built in the mid-1700s, the inn became a renowned staging-post and watering-hole during construction of the Union Canal around 1822. Today as the base for Edinburgh's Canal Centre, with its vintage fleet of restaurant boats and sightseeing launches, it has become a destination pub with loads of attractions - and menus - for all the family. Fresh local produce, freshly prepared and freshly served, is the ethic that has lived on for 30 years under its present ownership.
    Representative of this are dishes such as warm chicken and bacon salad served with smooth cheese cream, Ratho haggis fillet steak with cream and mushroom sauce, Thai-spiced salmon goujons in tumeric butter and the celebrated Scottish cranachan, incorporating West Craigie farm raspberries, oatmeal, Drambuie and cream. For fish lovers, a seasonal Scottish seafood platter, monkfish baked in lemon and tarragon yoghurt and smoked salmon and prawn potato cakes rolled in oatmeal. A coming attraction is the scheduled re-opening in 2002 of the canal itself, closed since 1965.
OPEN: 12-11 (Sat 11-12, Sun 12.30-11). **BAR MEALS:** L served all week 12-9. Av main course £6.75.
RESTAURANT: L served all week. D served all week 12-2 6.30-9. Av 3 course à la carte £20.
BREWERY/COMPANY: Free House.
PRINCIPAL BEERS: Bellhaven 80/-, Bellhaven best,.
FACILITIES: Children welcome Children's licence Garden: outdoor eating, patio **NOTES:** Parking 60
See Pub Walk on page 537

See Pub Walk on page 537

Scotland

BRIDGE INN, RATHO
27 Baird Road EH28 8RA.
Tel: 0131 333 1320
Directions: from Newbridge interchange B7030, follow signs for Ratho
Formerly a farmhouse and later a staging post for boats on the Union Canal, this historic inn was built in about 1750. Well stocked bars, adorned with canal memorabilia, good food, welcoming atmosphere, and canal boat trips.
Open: 12-11 (Sat 11-12, Sun 12.30-11). Bar Meals 12-9. Children & dogs welcome. Garden & patio. Parking.
(see page 536 for full entry)

Pub WALK

Bridge Inn, Ratho

With much to see along the way, this interesting walk climbs to the top of South Plat Hill for far-reaching view across the Firth of Forth, returning to the inn via a level tow path beside the Union Canal.

Leave the pub car park, cross the canal bridge and walk to church. Although much renovated, it dates from 1243 and is well worth a closer look. Passing the church, take the opening on the left at the top of the rise by a lodge for Ratho Hall. Walk up the lane passing a line of trees off to your right, known locally as Jeans Brae and the original road into Ratho.

Continue to the top of the hill, passing the trig point and the new National Rock Climbing Centre housed in an old quarry. Enjoy the far-reaching views across the Forth Bridges to the coast of Fife and the hills of Stirling and Perthshire, as far as Ben Lomond. Walk downhill past the entrance to the climbing centre and, at the bottom, turn left onto the canal tow path.

Follow the canal between two disused quarries. The canal once transported the quarried stone to Edinburgh before the coming of the railway. Coming out of the trees, look over the wall on your left to see a white wall, all that remains of the original Pop Inn. The walled gardens belong to Ratho Hall. The next building you see was built as a distillery and the white house behind housed the distillery manager. It was the scene of a brutal murder. The culprit was the son of the then owner of the Bridge Inn, who was the last man to be hanged in public in Edinburgh. The full story is on display in the pub.

Keep to the tow path and pass under the bridge by the inn, turning left up onto the pavement to cross the bridge back to the inn. From April to September you can walk west along the canal tow path to the Almond Aqueduct and return to the inn by boat.

Distance: 4 miles (6.4km)
Map: OS Landranger 65
Terrain: canal tow path and country lanes
Paths: well surfaced tow path and metalled lanes
Gradient: fairly level; one gentle climb up South Plat Hill.

Walk submitted by:
Ron Day, The Bridge Inn

CITY OF GLASGOW

GLASGOW
Map 10 NS56

Auctioneers
6 North Court, Vincent St G1 2DP ☎ 0141 229 5851
▤ 0141 229 5852
Once an auction room known as McTears, this city centre pub is the ideal place to catch a big televised sporting event, or try to catch a glimpse of a harmless Victorian ghost.

Buttery ◔ ♈
652 Argyle St G3 8UF ☎ 0141 221 8188 ▤ 0141 204 4639
Dir: Town centre
Thriving restaurant and oyster bar housed in a former tenement building, with a rich, wood-panelled Victorian interior, sparkling crystal and starched white linen. Dishes range around the globe with fillets of red snapper on wilted pak-choi with honey, soya and ginger dressing, and fillet of Scottish beef topped with chicken and wild mushroom ravioli, with creamed shallots and lemon thyme sauce.
OPEN: 12-2.30 7-10.30. Closed Sun, 25-26 Dec, 1-2 Jan.
BAR MEALS: L served all week. D served all week12-2.30
7-10.30. Av main course £15. **RESTAURANT:** D served all week
12-2.30 7-10.30. Av 3 course à la carte £35. Av 3 course fixed price
£16.85. **PRINCIPAL BEERS:** Calders 80/-. **NOTES:** Parking 20

Rab Ha's ◔
53 Hutchieson St G1 1SH ☎ 0141 572 0400
Dir: City centre
Victorian building, recently refurbished, housing a pub, restaurant and bedrooms. Expect a traditional pub atmosphere and some innovative cooking. Choices include fajitas, tempura, Thai curries and organic beef burger in the bar. The restaurant offers fusion cooking with dishes from the ocean, the earth and from home.
OPEN: 11-12. **BAR MEALS:** L served all week. D served all week
12-10. Av main course £6. **RESTAURANT:** L served all week. D
served all week. Av 3 course à la carte £25. Av 2 course fixed price
£10.95. **BREWERY/COMPANY:** Free House.
PRINCIPAL BEERS: McEwans 70/- & 80/-.
FACILITIES: Children welcome Dogs allowed.
ROOMS: 4 bedrooms 4 en suite s£50 d£70

For pubs with AA rosette awards for food
see page 10

Pick of the Pubs

Ubiquitous Chip ◉ ◉ ◔ ♈
12 Ashton Ln G12 8SJ ☎ 0141 334 5007
▤ 0141 337 1302
Situated on a cobbled lane, just off Byres Road, the 'Chip' centres on a traditional bar with an open coal fire and the original byres tastefully incorporated. It continues to buzz, as it has since 1971, and remains unafraid of innovation. Traditional draught beers, selected malt whiskies and first-class wines by the glass supplement a menu that is full of refreshingly bright ideas. Organic Orkney salmon is marinated in honey, tamarind and ginger and served with mash and spinach sauce; free-range belly pork, lightly spiced, is served with mixed greens and mash; and there is even a vegetarian haggis on offer, served with bashed neeps. Regular starters include a creamy chicken velouté with truffle oil, and to follow the spiced apple purée in a crispy tartlet is a minor masterpiece. The main dining area in a lofty covered courtyard sports plenty of live greenery, while upstairs is a brasserie-style eating area offering wholesome Scottish produce at more modest prices.
OPEN: 12-12. Closed 25 Dec, 1 Jan. **BAR MEALS:** L served all week. D served all week 12-2.30 5.30-11.
Av main course £8.95. **BREWERY/COMPANY:** Free House.
PRINCIPAL BEERS: Caledonian 80/-, & Deuchars IPA.
FACILITIES: Children welcome

DUMFRIES & GALLOWAY

AULDGIRTH
Map 10 NX98

Auldgirth Inn
DG2 0XG ☎ 01387 740250 ▤ 01387 740694
Dir: 8m NE of Dumfries on A76 Kilmarnock Rd
This 500-year-old inn was originally a stopping off place for monks and pilgrims walking across Scotland, and in later times became Robert Burns' local. It has a large central chimneystack with a cross on it, and the River Nith runs past the front door. Queen scallops and king prawns are a popular choice, along with local salmon, venison haggis or noisettes of Dumfriesshire lamb.
OPEN: 11.30-2.30 5.30-11. **BAR MEALS:** L served all week. D served all week 12-2 6-9. Av main course £7. **RESTAURANT:** L served all week. D served all week 12-2 6-9.
BREWERY/COMPANY: Free House.
PRINCIPAL BEERS: Belhavens Best. **FACILITIES:** Children welcome Garden: patio/terrace, picnic benches, outdoor eating
Dogs allowed. **ROOMS:** 5 bedrooms 5 en suite s£30 d£50

SHADES & GRADES OF BEER
A distinction between beer and ale used to be drawn centuries ago. Ale was the old British brew made without hops. Not until the 15th century did the use of hops spread to Britain from the Continent and the suspect, newfangled, bitterer drink was called beer. Ale is no longer made and the two words are now used indiscriminately. Bottled beer is distinguished from draught beer from a cask, keg or tank, but a more useful dividing line may be the one between real ale, which matures in the cask, and keg or bottled beer that does not.
Bitter is the classic British draught beer, brewed with plenty of hops. Mild, less heavily hopped and less sharp in taste, is most often found in the Midlands and the North West of England. Old ale usually means stronger mild, matured longer. Light ale or pale ale is bottled beer of a lightish colour Lager is lighter and blander still, in a bottle or on draught. Brown ale is a darker, richer bottled beer, and porter is richer still. Stout is the blackest and richest of all. Strong ale or barley wine has a higher alcohol content than the others, or should have.

CANONBIE
Map 11 NY37

Pick of the Pubs

Riverside Inn 🐾 ⅋
DG14 0UX ☎ 013873 71512 & 71295 📠 013873 71866
e-mail: information@theriversideinn.fsbusiness.co.uk
Dir: *Just across Scottish border on A7, 1st R is Canonbie*

A traditional white-painted inn overlooking the River Esk just within the Scottish borders. Accommodation and residents' lounge are cosy and comfortable while food is offered both in the bar and dining room. In front of a log fire in the bar choose from the blackboard menu a variety of seasonal fish and game, free-range organic poultry and Buccleuch estate beef. Simpler options include Cumbrian air-dried ham, Scottish smoked salmon and vegetarian homity pie, or more adventurously try the Aga-roast cod with cheese and red onions, stuffed pheasant breast with cream and sun-dried tomato sauce or Goosnargh chicken with lemon and rosemary. Three-course menus at fixed prices promise carrot and orange soup or Stilton puffs with cranberry sauce to begin, sea bass with cider and cream sauce or chargrilled Scottish ribeye steak to follow and date sponge with toffee sauce, meringues with chocolate sauce or a plate of Scottish cheeses for afters. **OPEN:** 12.30-2.30 6.30-11. **BAR MEALS:** L served all week. D served all week 12.30-2 7-9. Av main course £8.50. **RESTAURANT:** D served all week 7-9. Av 3 course à la carte £19.50. Av 3 course fixed price £19.50. **BREWERY/COMPANY:** Free House. **PRINCIPAL BEERS:** Yates, Caledonian Deuchars IPA. **FACILITIES:** Children welcome Children's licence Garden: Food served outside. **NOTES:** Parking 20. **ROOMS:** 7 bedrooms 7 en suite s£55 d£70

CASTLE DOUGLAS
Map 10 NX76

Douglas Arms Hotel ★ ★
King St DG7 1DB ☎ 01556 502231 📠 01556 504000
e-mail: doughot@aol.com
Modernised 18th-century coaching inn, one of the oldest buildings in town, where welcoming open fires are lit in the winter months. Chicken curry and fresh haddock in batter are typical bar dishes, while the restaurant might offer supreme of salmon, or medallions of beef in whisky and mustard sauce. **OPEN:** 11-12. **BAR MEALS:** L served all week D served all week 12-9. Av main course £6.50. **RESTAURANT:** L served Sun. D served all week 12-2.15 6-10. Av 3 course à la carte £16. Av 3 course fixed price £13.50. **BREWERY/COMPANY:** Free House. **PRINCIPAL BEERS:** Sulwath, Orkney, Caledonian, Broughton. **FACILITIES:** Children welcome Children's licence Dogs allowed. **NOTES:** Parking 18. **ROOMS:** 24 bedrooms 24 en suite s£37.50 d£68.50 FR£78.50

DALBEATTIE
Map 10 NX86

Anchor Hotel ♦♦♦
Main St, Kippford DG5 4LN ☎ 01556 620205
📠 01556 620205
Dir: *A711 to Dalbeattie. follow Solway Coast sign to Kippford*
This family-run small hotel overlooks the Marina and Urr Water estuary, and its Seafarers' Bar is a yachtmens' haven. The area is also ideal for walkers and bird watchers. The menu has a definite seafaring theme, and includes such specialities as swordfish steaks, chicken citron, 'Trawlerman's Burgers', 'Captain's Nibbles' and a selection of vegetarian dishes. Most bedrooms are en suite, and some overlook the Marina. **OPEN:** 11-3 5-12. Closed 25 Dec. **BAR MEALS:** L served all week. D served all week 12-2.30 5.30-9.30. Av main course £6.50. **RESTAURANT:** L served all week. D served all week 12-2 5.30-9.30. **BREWERY/COMPANY:** Free House. **PRINCIPAL BEERS:** Theakstons, Boddingtons, Marstons, Pedigree. **FACILITIES:** Children welcome Children's licence. **ROOMS:** 4 bedrooms 4 en suite s£28 d£55 FR£55.00 + £5 per child

EAGLESFIELD
Map 11 NY27

The Courtyard Restaurant
DG11 3PQ ☎ 01461 500215
Dir: *8m N of Gretna*
Former drapers shop built in 1914 and converted into a bar/restaurant in the mid-1980s. Popular with travellers heading for the Highlands, it offers good home cooking. Enjoy lasagne, fruity chicken curry, or steak and chips in the bar, or baked cod with cheese and mustard or venison with cranberry in the rear restaurant. **OPEN:** 12-2.30 6.30-12. **BAR MEALS:** L served Tue-Sun. D served Tue-Fri, Sun12-2 6.30-9. Av main course £5.95. **RESTAURANT:** L served Sun. D served Tue-Sun 12-2 7-9. Av 3 course à la carte £16. **BREWERY/COMPANY:** Free House **FACILITIES:** Children welcome Garden: Dogs allowed. **NOTES:** Parking 20. **ROOMS:** 3 bedrooms 3 en suite s£21 d£36

ISLE OF WHITHORN
Map 10 NX43

The Steam Packet Inn 🐾
Harbour Row DG8 8LL ☎ 01988 500334
📠 01988 500627
e-mail: Steampacketinn@btconnect.com
Dir: *From Newton Stewart take A714, then A746 to Whithorn, then Isle of Whithorn*
Picture windows in the attractively modernised bar of this 18th-century inn afford delightful harbour views. A varying choice of guest ales is served and an impressive selection of malt whiskies. Seafood is prominent on the menu, bought directly from boats landing in the village, and the best Scottish steaks are sourced from a single estate in the Borders. Dishes include lobster bisque, and seared scallops with black pudding and sauce vierge. **OPEN:** 11-11 (Winter 11-2.30, 6.30-11). Closed Dec 25. **BAR MEALS:** L served all week. D served all week 12-2 7-9.30. Av main course £7. **RESTAURANT:** L served all week. D served all week 12-2 7-9.30. **BREWERY/COMPANY:** Free House. **PRINCIPAL BEERS:** Theakston XB, Deuchars IPA - Caledonian, Black Sheep Best. **FACILITIES:** Children welcome Garden: sheltered, Food served outside Dogs allowed. **NOTES:** Parking 4. **ROOMS:** 7 bedrooms 7 en suite s£22.50 d£45

Scotland

The George and Dragon

As England's patron saint, St George figures frequently on inn signs, often with the dragon whose defeat was his most celebrated exploit. According to the legend, he killed it to save a beautiful princess who would otherwise have been given to the monster. Alternatively, the George is the jewel of the Order of the Garter, England's premier order of knighthood, which was founded by King Edward III in the 14th century. An allied name is the Star and Garter, which also refers to the order's insignia. Or again, the George can mean any of the six kings of that name since the Hanoverian dynasty succeeded to the throne.

KIRKCUDBRIGHT

Selkirk Arms Hotel

Old High St DE6 4JG ☎ 01557 330402 ▤ 01557 331639
Traditional white-painted pub on street corner. Nice gardens to rear. Has associations with Scottish poet, Robert Burns.

MOFFAT   Map 10 NT00

Black Bull Inn

Churchgate DG10 9EG ☎ 01683 220206 ▤ 01683 220483
e-mail: hotel@blackbullmoffat.co.uk
The main building dates from the 16th century and was used by Graham of Claverhouse as his headquarters. Scottish bard Robert Burns was a frequent visitor around 1790. Traditional fare includes steak and ale pie, jugged hare, salmon fillet with various sauces, and a unique prawn steak sizzler.
OPEN: 11-11 (Thu-Sat 11-12). **BAR MEALS:** L served all week. D served all week 11.30-2.15 6-9.15. Av main course £5.50.
RESTAURANT: L served all week. D served all week 11.30-2.15 6-9.30. Av 3 course à la carte £10. **BREWERY/COMPANY:** Free House. **PRINCIPAL BEERS:** McEwans, Theakston.
FACILITIES: Children welcome Beer garden, food served outside Dogs allowed. **ROOMS:** 7 bedrooms 7 en suite s£35 d£26.50

NEW ABBEY   Map 10 NX96

Criffel Inn

2 The Square DG2 8BX ☎ 01387 850305
▤ 01556 850305
Dir: M/A74 leave at Gretna, A75 to Dumfries, A710 S to New Abbey
Situated in an historic conservation village close to 13th-century Sweetheart Abbey, this small, unassuming hotel has an attractive garden perfect for relaxation and summer sipping. Unchanged for many years, it offers appetising dishes such as Solway salmon, char-grilled halibut steak, chicken with wild mushrooms and tagliatelle, and a home made vegetarian dish of the day.
OPEN: 12-2.30 5-11. **BAR MEALS:** L served all week. D served all week 12-2 5-8. Av main course £5.95. **RESTAURANT:** L served all week. D served all week 12-2 5-8. Av 3 course à la carte £15. **BREWERY/COMPANY:** Free House.
PRINCIPAL BEERS: Belhaven IPA, Deuchars IPA, Flowers Original, Timothy Taylor Landlord. **FACILITIES:** Children welcome Garden: Food served outside Dogs allowed Water. **NOTES:** Parking 8. **ROOMS:** 5 bedrooms 3 en suite s£23.50 d£47

NEWTON STEWART   Map 10 NX46

Pick of the Pubs

Creebridge House Hotel ★ ★

Minnigaff DG8 6NP ☎ 01671 402121 ▤ 01671 403258
e-mail: info@creebridge.co.uk
Dir: From A75 into Newton Stewart, turn right over river bridge, hotel 200yds on left.
Standing in three acres of grounds with fish pond, croquet lawn and herb garden, the house dates from 1760 with many interior features of the period. Frequented by golfers, fishermen, shooters, walkers and families. In the cosy beamed bar and brasserie Galloway lamb, Solway salmon and Kirkcudbright scallops take pride of place; the lamb in filo parcels on an onion confit having been a Scottish national award-winner. For a starter or snack try the scallops seared on fettucine with asparagus and saffron cream; for main course the salmon on herb noodles with basil oil.
OPEN: 12-2.30 6-11. **BAR MEALS:** L served all week. D served all week 12-2 6-9. Av main course £7.50.
RESTAURANT: D served all week 7-9. Av 3 course à la carte £22. Av 4 course fixed price £19.
BREWERY/COMPANY: Free House.
PRINCIPAL BEERS: Orkney Dark Island, Black Sheep, Fullers London Pride. **FACILITIES:** Children welcome Children's licence Garden: 3 Acres, outdoor eating, Dogs allowed Kennels. **NOTES:** Parking 40.
ROOMS: 19 bedrooms 19 en suite s£49 d£60 FR£60-£98

PORTPATRICK   Map 10 NW95

Crown Hotel 🛏 ♀

9 North Crescent DG9 8SX ☎ 01776 810261
▤ 01776 810551
Bustling harbourside hotel created from former fishermen's cottages with fine views across the Irish Sea. There is a great atmosphere in the rambling old bar with its open fire and seafaring displays. Extensive menus are based on fresh local produce with an emphasis on seafood - seafood platter, roast monkfish tails, Galloway scallops, Crown lobster, and whole sea bass among the options.
OPEN: 11-11.30. **BAR MEALS:** L served all week. D served all week 12-10. **RESTAURANT:** L served all week. D served all week 12-10. **BREWERY/COMPANY:** Free House
FACILITIES: Children welcome Garden: Dogs allowed.
ROOMS: 12 bedrooms 12 en suite s£38 d£36 FR£80.00

DUNDEE CITY

BROUGHTY FERRY   Map 11 NO43

Fisherman's Tavern ♀

10-16 Fort St DD5 2AD ☎ 01382 775941 ▤ 01382 477466
e-mail: fishermans@sol.co.uk
Dir: From Dundee City centre follow A930 to Broughty Ferry, take a right at Scottish Tourist Board, road sign for Fishermans Tavern hotel.
Listed 17th-century fisherman's cottage converted to a pub in 1827. Combines a picturesque coastal setting with award-winning hospitality and acclaimed bar food. The inn also offers new, tastefully decorated en suite rooms. Popular, well-planned menu ranges from light snacks to traditional wholesome fare and international favourites. After a stroll along the sands, try butterfly grilled chicken, Tay salmon with parsley butter and lemon or pan-fried lambs liver with bacon and onions.   *continued*
continued

OPEN: 11-12. **BAR MEALS:** L served all week 11.30-2.30. Av main course £5. **BREWERY/COMPANY:** Free House. **PRINCIPAL BEERS:** Belhaven, Inveralmond Ossian's. **FACILITIES:** Children welcome Garden: outdoor eating, Dogs allowed Water, Biscuits. **ROOMS:** 14 bedrooms 7 en suite s£19 d£36

The Royal Arch Bar ♀ NEW
285 Brook St DD5 2DS ☎ 01382 779741
Dating from 1856, this friendly free house has attracted many colourful characters. Look up their caricatures in the traditional public bar, or relax amongst elegant female statues in the comfortable art deco lounge. Snacks include burgers and jacket potatoes, and meals like beef Highlander, full rack ribs, seafood platter, or mushroom and nut fettuccine are served throughout the pub.
OPEN: 11-12 (Sun 12.30-12). Closed 1 Jan. **BAR MEALS:** L served all week. D served all week 11.30-3 4.30-8. Av main course £4.75. **BREWERY/COMPANY:** Free House. **PRINCIPAL BEERS:** McEwans 80/-, Belhaven Best. **FACILITIES:** Children welcome Dogs allowed Public bar only

DUNDEE   Map 11 NO43

Mercantile Bar
100/108 Commercial St DD1 2AJ ☎ 01382 225500
🗎 01382 224650
Dir: Town centre
Busy town centre pub serving McEwans ales and traditional bar snacks. Pub supports Dundee's musical talents with a songwriting club. Upstairs restaurant.

EAST AYRSHIRE

DALRYMPLE   Map 10 NS31

The Kirkton Inn ♦♦♦
1 Main St KA6 6DF ☎ 01292 560241 🗎 01292 560835
e-mail: kirkton@cqm.co.uk
Dir: Between A77 & A713 approx 5m from Ayr signed from both roads

Village centre inn situated a short stroll from the River Doon. Robert Burns was reputed to have drunk here. Well situated for a visit to the Burns Centre and Cottage, the beach at Ayr or Blairquhan Castle. Popular pub food features steaks, grills, wild Doon salmon, roast breast of chicken and bacon, and seasonal vegetable tagliatelle.
OPEN: 11am-midnight (Sun 12.30-11). **BAR MEALS:** L served all week. D served all week 11-9. Av main course £3. **RESTAURANT:** L served all week. D served all week 11-9. Av 3 course à la carte £14. Av 3 course fixed price £10.
BREWERY/COMPANY: Free House.   *continued*

PRINCIPAL BEERS: McEwans 60/-. **FACILITIES:** Children welcome Garden: patio, outdoor eating Dogs allowed Water. **NOTES:** Parking 50. **ROOMS:** 11 bedrooms 11 en suite s£22 d£35 FR£40-£55

GATEHEAD   Map 10 NS33

The Cochrane Inn
45 Main Rd KA2 0AP ☎ 01563 570122
Dir: from Glasgow A77 to Kilmarnock, then A759 to Gatehead
The emphasis is on contemporary British food at this village centre pub, just a short drive from the Ayrshire coast. Friendly, bustling atmosphere inside. Good choice of starters may include soused herring and grilled goat's cheese, while main courses might feature stuffed pancake, pan-fried trio of seafood with tiger prawns, or smoked haddock risotto.
OPEN: 11-3 5-12. Closed 1 Jan. **BAR MEALS:** L served all week. D served all week 12-2 6-9. Av main course £7.25.
RESTAURANT: L served all week. D served all week 12-2 6-9. **BREWERY/COMPANY:** Free House **FACILITIES:** Children welcome Garden. **NOTES:** Parking 30

EAST LOTHIAN

EAST LINTON   Map 11 NT57

Pick of the Pubs

Drovers Inn 🍸
5 Bridge St EH40 3AG ☎ 01620 860298
Dir: Off A1 5m past Haddington, follow rd under railway bridge, then L
Close to the River Tyne and Linn Falls, a pubby old coaching inn that once was a watering hole for sheep and cattle hersdmen traversing north and south. The bar's wooden floors, beamed ceilings and half-panelled walls provide a nostalgic atmosphere for a beer by the fire, while the scene in the upstairs dining room is altogether more sumptuous, with antique furniture and rich, warm colours.

Bistro menus offer the simpler choices of feta cheese salad with black olives, venison casserole in red wine sauce and cheese tartlet of ratatouille Niçoise that supplement chef's daily creations of seasonal local produce widely used in sizzling honey and ginger pie, and rack of Borders lamb with mint and onion marmalade. Fresh salads of lobster and crab and Scottish salmon fillet with prawn, lemon and chilli butter bolster the aquatic options.

At dinner, perhaps saddle of rabbit with apricot and pepper mash followed by old-fashioned baked rice and sultana pudding; at any time a relaxed atmosphere with emphasis on friendly Scottish hospitality.
OPEN: 11.30-11 (Fri & Sat till 12, Sun 11.30-11). Closed 25 Dec, 1 Jan. **BAR MEALS:** L served all week. D served Sun-Fri 11.30-2 6-9.30. Av main course £7.50. **RESTAURANT:** L served all week. D served all week 11.30-2 6-9.30. Av 3 course à la carte £20. **BREWERY/COMPANY:** Free House. **PRINCIPAL BEERS:** Adnams Broadside, Caledonian 80/-, Fullers ESB, Wadworth 6X. **FACILITIES:** Children welcome Garden: Food served outside

GIFFORD
Map 11 NT56

Goblin Ha' Hotel ♀
EH41 4QH ☎ 01620 810244 ▤ 01620 810718
Dir: *On A846, 100yrds from main village square on shore side of the road*
Traditional hotel with a good atmosphere located by the village square and green. A varied range of home-cooked food is offered in the bar and adjoining conservatory. Dishes include home-made burgers, steaks, fresh mussel and saffron stew, and lamb Caledonian with Drambuie sauce.

OPEN: 11-2.30 5-11. **BAR MEALS:** L served all week. D served all week 12.30-2 6.30-9. Av main course £6.95.
BREWERY/COMPANY: Free House.
PRINCIPAL BEERS: Hopback Summer Lightning, Marstons Pedigree, Bellhaven, Timothy Taylor Landlord.
FACILITIES: Children welcome Children's licence Garden: outdoor eating, patio, pets corner Dogs allowed.
ROOMS: 7 bedrooms 6 en suite s£20 d£50

GULLANE
Map 11 NT48

The Golf Inn ♀ NEW
Main St EH31 2AB ☎ 01620 843259 ▤ 01620 842066
e-mail: info@golfinn.co.uk
The inn has 12 golf courses in its vicinity, including the Muirfield Golf Course, host for the 2002 British Open Championship, which is just 500 yards away. Golf is the theme in the public bar with a full-length wall display of trophies and memorabilia. Fish features prominently with dishes such as mussels marinière, gravad lax, fishcakes, and roast monkfish tails with onion and garlic confit. There's also an impressive choice of single malt whiskies.
OPEN: 11-11. **BAR MEALS:** L served all week. D served all week 12-2.30 6.30-9.30. Av main course £7.50. **RESTAURANT:** L served all week. D served all week 12-2.30 6.30-9.30. Av 3 course à la carte £20. **BREWERY/COMPANY:** Free House.
PRINCIPAL BEERS: McEwans 70/-, Belhaven Best.
FACILITIES: Children welcome Garden: Food served outside Dogs allowed. **ROOMS:** 14 bedrooms 14 en suite s£40 d£60

FALKIRK

CASTLECARY
Map 10 NS77

Castlecary House Hotel ♀
Main St G68 0HD ☎ 01324 840233 ▤ 01324 841608
Dir: *Off A80 N of Cumbernauld*
Friendly hotel complex much of which is a 19th-century coaching inn. Close to historic Antonine Wall and Forth & Clyde Canal. Recent developments include Cameron's Restaurant, with 120 covers, and fifteen new bedrooms. From traditional pub food and home-made burgers, the varied menus include assorted pasta dishes, roast loin of pork in mushroom sauce, venison in red cherry sauce, Scottish haddock and gingered fillet of pork.
OPEN: 11-11 (Thur- Sat 11-11.30, Sun 12.30-11). **BAR MEALS:** L served all week. D served all week 12-2 6-9. Av main course £5.
RESTAURANT: L served all week. D served all week 12-2 6-9. Av 3 course à la carte £17. **BREWERY/COMPANY:** Free House.
PRINCIPAL BEERS: Arran Dark, Belhaven 80/-, Sandy Hunter, Stones Bitter. **FACILITIES:** Children welcome Children's licence Garden: outdoor eating, patio Dogs allowed garden only.
ROOMS: 70 bedrooms 65 en suite s£55 d£43

FIFE

ANSTRUTHER
Map 11 NO50

The Dreel Tavern
16 High St West KY10 3DL ☎ 01333 310727
▤ 01333 311401
There's plenty of atmosphere at this 16th-century inn, with its oak beams, open fire and stone walls - three foot thick in some places. A conservatory extension overlooks the beer garden and Dreel Burn. Home-cooked food and cask-conditioned ales are served. Dishes range from baguettes and bangers in the bar to steak pie, battered haddock and pan-fried chicken fillet in the restaurant.
OPEN: 11-12 (Sun 12.30-12). **BAR MEALS:** L served all week. D served all week 12-2 5.30-9. Av main course £5.95.
RESTAURANT: L served all week. D served all week 12-2 5.30-9. Av 3 course à la carte £11. **BREWERY/COMPANY:** Free House.
PRINCIPAL BEERS: Orkney Dark Island, Timothy Taylor Landlord, Harviestoun Bitter & Twisted, Greene King Abbot Ale.
FACILITIES: Children welcome Children's licence Garden: Beer garden, outdoor eating Dogs allowed Water, Biscuits.
NOTES: Parking 3

AUCHTERMUCHTY

Forest Hills Hotel ♦♦♦
23 High St KY14 7AN ☎ 01337 828318 ▤ 01337 828318
e-mail: lomond-foresthotels@hotmail.com
Popular inn located in the village square, with an oak-beamed bar, Flemish murals, a cosy lounge, and en suite bedrooms. Traditional pub food.

BURNTISLAND

Burntisland Sands Hotel ♦♦♦
Lochie Rd KY3 9JX ☎ 01592 872230
Small, family-run hotel situated just yards from a sandy beach with view across the bay. Popular with families. Good range of traditional pub food.
continued

OPEN: 11-12. **BAR MEALS:** L served all week. D served all week 12-2.30 6-8.30. Av main course £4.95. **RESTAURANT:** L served all week. D served all week 12-2.30 6-8.30.
BREWERY/COMPANY: Free House **FACILITIES:** Children welcome Children's licence Garden: patio/terrace, BBQ, rabbit hutch Dogs allowed. **NOTES:** Parking 20.
ROOMS: 4 bedrooms 4 en suite s£25 d£45 1 family room £50-£64

CRAIL   Map 11 NO60

The Golf Hotel
4 High St KY10 3TD ☎ 01333 450206 ▤ 01333 450795
e-mail: thegolfhotel@allglobal.net
With roots in the 14th-century, this is the site of one of Scotland's oldest coaching inns, although the current building dates from the 18th century. The name comes from the inn's connection with the Crail Golfing Society, formed here in 1786. The nearby harbour has been much photographed over the years. A typical lunch menu features lamb and mint casserole, chicken curry and fresh haddock fillet. Other options include sandwiches, baguettes, salads, baked potatoes and burgers.
OPEN: 11-11 (Sun 12-11). Closed Jan 1. **BAR MEALS:** L served all week. D served all week 12-9. Av main course £5.50.
RESTAURANT: L served all week. D served all week 12-9. Av 3 course à la carte £12. **BREWERY/COMPANY:** Free House.
PRINCIPAL BEERS: McEwans 70, John Smiths.
FACILITIES: Children welcome Garden: Beer Garden, Outdoor Eating Dogs allowed. **NOTES:** Parking 10.
ROOMS: 5 bedrooms 5 en suite s£25 d£21

DUNFERMLINE

The Hideaway Lodge & Restaurant ★ ★ 🛏 ♀
Kingseat Rd, Halbeath KY12 0UB ☎ 01383 725474
▤ 01383 622821
e-mail: enquiries@thehideaway.co.uk

Pleasant country inn enjoying a rural setting on the outskirts of Dunfermline, close to the M90 (J3). Each room is named after a Scottish loch. Extensive menu featuring fresh local produce. May include roast fillet of cod with a roast pepper crust, seared king scallops with a cheesy herb crust, penne pasta with smoked salmon and dill, and a variety of steaks.
OPEN: 12-3 5-11 (Sun 12.30-9.30). **BAR MEALS:** L served all week. D served all week 12-2 5-9.30. **RESTAURANT:** L served all week. D served all week 12-2 5-9.30. Av 3 course à la carte £12.50.
BREWERY/COMPANY: Free House.
PRINCIPAL BEERS: Calders 70/-. **FACILITIES:** Children welcome Garden: outdoor eating Dogs allowed garden only.
NOTES: Parking 35. **ROOMS:** 8 bedrooms 8 en suite s£45 d£45

ELIE   Map 11 NO40

Pick of the Pubs

The Ship Inn
The Toft KY9 1DT ☎ 01333 330246 ▤ 01333 330864
e-mail: shipinnelie@aol.com
Dir: Follow A915 & A917 to Elie. Follow signs from High St to Watersport Centre to the Toft.
There's always lots going on at this lively free house, right on the waterfront at Elie Bay. The pub's own cricket club plays on the beach; there are wine evenings, summer barbecues, and a winter curry club, not to mention the annual rugby match on the beach against Edinburgh Academicals. And, if that's not enough, this 19th-century hostelry with its open fires and upstairs restaurant is just a stone's throw from one of Scotland's finest watersports centres. There's even a telescope on the restaurant balcony, for close-up views of the beach! Traditional home-made fare with fresh, local ingredients characterises the menu, which changes twice each day. Hearty lunchtime sandwiches include Cheddar and apple, or ribeye steak, with hot dishes like bangers and mash in 80/- gravy, steak and Guinness pie, or chicken piri piri appearing as regular favourites. Fish dishes also feature strongly; expect haddock and chips, sea bass, and an interesting combination of smoked haddock with smoked salmon and prawns.
OPEN: 11-11 (Summer 11-midnight/Sun from 12.30). Closed 25 Dec. **BAR MEALS:** L served all week. D served all week 12-2 6-9. **RESTAURANT:** L served all week. D served all week 12-2 6-9. **BREWERY/COMPANY:** Free House.
PRINCIPAL BEERS: Theakstons Best, McEwan's 80/-.
FACILITIES: Children welcome Children's licence Garden: outdoor eating, patio,

---

The Fife Coastal Walk

One of Scotland's lesser-known regions and once the home of the country's kings and saints, Fife is a 20-mile-wide peninsula between the Firth of Forth and the Tay. A great way to blend coast and countryside is by following the 94-mile Fife Coastal Walk, which explores a beautiful stretch of the Scottish coastline between Inverkeithing, just north of the Forth Bridge, and Newburgh, near Perth. Discover Fife's fascinating legacy of caves, castles and ancient fishing ports en route and expect a warm welcome at a variety of coastal pubs and waterfront hostelries along the way, including the Georgian Old Rectory Inn at Dysart, the Crusoe Hotel on the sea wall at Lower Largo, the 19th-century Ship Inn at Elie, the Dreel Tavern at Anstruther, and the historic Golf Hotel at Crail, reputed to be one of Scotland's oldest coaching inns.

Scotland

KIRKCALDY   Map 11 NT29

Pick of the Pubs

The Old Rectory Inn ⚑
West Quality St, Dysart KY1 2TE ☎ 01592 651211
📠 01592 655221
Dir: From Edinburgh take A92 to Kirkcaldy, then A907, A955 to Dysart R at Nat Trust sign

Built by a prominent Dysart merchant in 1771, this delightful old inn sports a splendid walled garden perched above the harbour. It remains today, after several changes of use and ownership, a destination for lovers of the local produce that is a feature of both bar and restaurant menus. Pride of place goes to seafood dishes such as haddock fillets in prawn and cheese sauce and the stew of salmon, prawns, mussels, scallops and mussels in light fish stock.

Alternatively, start with Stilton mousse or a Caesar salad followed by 'three tenors' tortellini, chicken, ham and mushroom vol-au-vent or fillet steaks of any size cut to order. Equally tempting and delicious are the hot sticky toffee pudding and banana split with raspberry sauce and whipped cream.

A further blackboard menu lists the long-serving chef's daily recommendations, ranging from baby black pudding fritters, through braised pheasant to green pea and carrot loaf with vegetable gravy. **OPEN:** 12-3 6.45-12 (Sun 12.30-4 only). Closed 1wk Jan & 2wks mid-Oct 2 wks early July. **BAR MEALS:** L served Tue-Sun. D served Tue-Sat 12-2 7-9.30. Av main course £7. **RESTAURANT:** L served Tue-Sun. D served Tue-Sat 12-3 6.45-12. Av 3 course à la carte £22.50.
BREWERY/COMPANY: Free House. **PRINCIPAL BEERS:** Calders Cream Ale. **FACILITIES:** Garden: Food served outside **NOTES:** Parking 12

LOWER LARGO   Map 11 NO40

Crusoe Hotel 🐄 ⚑
2 Main St KY8 6BT ☎ 01333 320759 📠 01333 320865
e-mail: relax@crusoe-hotel.co.uk
Dir: A92 to Kirkcaldy East, A915 to Lundin Links, then R to Lower Largo
This historic inn is located on the sea wall in Lower Largo, birthplace of Alexander Selkirk, the real-life castaway immortalised by Daniel Defoe in his novel, Robinson Crusoe. The area was also at the heart of the once-thriving herring fishing industry. A wide selection of home-cooked local fare is served, including a variety of steaks and seafood in season, perhaps lobster, moules marinière or sea bass.

continued

OPEN: 11-12 (Fri 11-1, Sun 12.30-12) (food available 12.30-3, 6-9). **BAR MEALS:** L served all week. D served all week 12-3 6-9. Av main course £4. **RESTAURANT:** L served all week. D served all week 12-3 6.30-9. Av 3 course à la carte £20.
BREWERY/COMPANY: Free House **FACILITIES:** Children welcome Dogs allowed. **NOTES:** Parking 30.
ROOMS: 17 bedrooms 17 en suite s£35 d£60 FR£80-£120

MARKINCH   Map 11 NO20

Town House Hotel ♦♦♦
1 High St KY7 6DQ ☎ 01592 758459 📠 01592 755039
Dir: Off A92(Dundee/Kirkcaldy rd) Hotel opp. rail station
Family-run 17th-century coaching inn situated in the heart of town. It offers a fixed-price lunch menu of two or three courses, and a supper carte of imaginative dishes, such as steak Madagascar, Drunken Bull pie, Cajun style chicken, grilled Gressingham duck breast, and pasta arrabbiata.
OPEN: 12-2.30 6-11. Closed 25/26 Dec, 1/2 Jan. **BAR MEALS:** L served Mon-Sat. D served all week 12-2 6-9. Av main course £7.95. **RESTAURANT:** L served Mon-Sat. D served all week 12-2 6-9. Av 3 course à la carte £15. Av 3 course fixed price £8.50.
BREWERY/COMPANY: Free House **FACILITIES:** Children welcome. **ROOMS:** 4 bedrooms 3 en suite s£30 d£50

ST MONANS   Map 12 NO50

Pick of the Pubs

Seafood Bar & Restaurant ◉ ◉ 🐄 ⚑
16 West End KY10 2BX ☎ 01333 730327
📠 01333 730327
e-mail: theseafood.restaurant@virginnet.co.uk
Dir: Take A595 from St Andrews to Anstruther, then W on A917 through Pittenweem. At St Monans harbour turn R
This stunning little restaurant is perched so close to the harbour's edge that you half expect the seafood to come strolling into the kitchen, instead of hanging around waiting to be caught. Here the waves crash on acres of pungent seaweed, so al fresco meals on the terrace are best reserved for calmer days.

In the restaurant, you'll need to book early to get a table near the huge plate glass windows, with their panoramic views across the mussel beds to the Isle of May and Bass Rock. The sophisticated menu focuses strongly on local seafood of unimpeachable quality. Expect Kilbrandon oysters, kiln-roasted smoked salmon, or lobster ravioli to start, followed by grilled Dover sole, Cajun spiced monkfish, or turbot with sautéed spinach and fennel. Meat eaters may find the odd token dish; seared fillet of beef on herb risotto, perhaps, or roast breast of guinea fowl.
OPEN: 12-3 6-11. Closed Sun eve & all Mon Sep-Apr, 1 Dec-31 Jan. **BAR MEALS:** L served Tue-Sun. D served Tue-Sun 12-3 7-9.30. Av main course £10.50. **RESTAURANT:** L served Tue-Sun. D served Tue-Sun 12-3 7-9.30. Av 3 course à la carte £18. Av 3 course fixed price £18.
BREWERY/COMPANY: Free House.
PRINCIPAL BEERS: Belhaven 80/-, Belhaven Best.
FACILITIES: Garden: Food served outside.
NOTES: Parking 10

HIGHLAND

ACHILTIBUIE — Map 12 NC00

Summer Isles Hotel & Bar
IV26 2YG ☎ 01854 622282 🖹 01854 622251
Dir: *take A835 N from Ullapool for 10m, Achiltibuie signed on L, 15m to village, hotel 1m on L*
At the end of a long and twisting single track road, skirting lochs Lurgain, Badagyle and Oscaig, is this village hotel and bar overlooking the Summer Isles bay. The emphasis is on locally caught and home produced food - seafood platters, smoked salmon steaks, venison and freshly baked brown bread. In the restaurant a five course dinner is served at 8pm, and it pays to book ahead for a table.
OPEN: 12-11 (4-11 in winter). Closed Dec 25, Jan 1.
BAR MEALS: L served all week. D served all week 12-2.30 6.30-8.30. Av main course £10. **RESTAURANT:** L served all week. D served all week 12.30-2 6.30-8.30. Av 5 course fixed price £40. **BREWERY/COMPANY:** Free House
FACILITIES: Children welcome **NOTES:** Parking 20.
ROOMS: 13 bedrooms 13 en suite s£52 d£104

ALTNAHARRA — Map 13 NC53

Altnaharra Hotel 👁
IV27 4UE ☎ 01549 411222 🖹 01549 411222
e-mail: altnaharra@btinternet.com
Dir: *A9 to Bonar Bridge, A336 to Lairg & Tongue*
Traditional Highland hotel with a major focus on fishing, set in the middle of fantastic scenery. Lunch and dinner are available on pre-booking, the set-price menus featuring local venison, lamb and fish from Scrabster. Dishes might include smoked trout with pink grapefruit, and duck breast in plum sauce.
OPEN: 12-2.30 5-11. **RESTAURANT:** L served Sun. D served all week 12-2 6-9. Av 3 course à la carte £26.25. Av 2 course fixed price £22. **BREWERY/COMPANY:** Free House.
FACILITIES: Children welcome Garden: Dogs allowed garden only. **NOTES:** Parking 60. **ROOMS:** 15 bedrooms 15 en suite s£69 d£138

Country Matters

Country occupations and pursuits provide many inns with their names. The Wheatsheaf, the Barley Mow, the Haywain, the Dun Cow, the Heifer, the Plough (sometimes the constellation) and the Harrow recall the farming year's immemorial round. Horses, long essential to agriculture, communications and sport, figure frequently - the Black Horse, the Nag's Head, the Grey Mare and many more. The Bull and the Bear are often related to the once popular sport of baiting the animals with dogs. The dog is usually a sporting dog and hunting has supplied many names, from the Fox and Hounds and the Hare and Hounds to numerous deer (also from heraldry), including the Stag and Hounds, the White Hart and the Roebuck. There are signs related to angling, too, such as the Angler and the Trout, and there are Jolly Cricketers and even Jolly Farmers.

Pick of the Pubs

Applecross Inn 👁 ⚲
Shore St IV54 8LR ☎ 01520 744262 🖹 01520 744400
Dir: *From Lochcarron to Kishorn then L onto unclassifed rd to Applecross over 'Bealach Na Ba'*
Situated on the shore of beautiful Applecross Bay, with views out towards Skye, this is a spectacular location with its private beer garden stretching down to a sandy cove. Traditional decor and a wood-burning stove grace the bar, whose light bites and snacks include home-made soup such as smoked haddock chowder, deep-fried mushrooms stuffed with haggis, and Stornaway black pudding with apple mash.

The signature seafood special includes queen scallops, monkfish and squat lobster in creamy prawn sauce, while prime Scottish steaks come with sauces that include peppercorn, Chasseur and caper varieties. Local venison, featuring amongst the choice of burgers, is also casseroled with whole-grain mustard and red cabbage and pan-fried in medallions with port and red wine sauce.

Diners who have left room can round off with raspberry Cranachan, 'boozy' bread-and-butter pudding with cream or a selection of cheeses from the nearby West Highland Dairy. Bedrooms have good facilities with magnificent sea views.

OPEN: 11-11 (Sun 12.30-11) (Dec-Jan Closed Sun 7pm).
BAR MEALS: L served all week. D served all week 12-9.
Av main course £5.75. **RESTAURANT:** L served by appointment. D served all week 6-9. Av 3 course à la carte £20. Av 3 course fixed price £20.
BREWERY/COMPANY: Free House **FACILITIES:** Children welcome Children's licence Garden: outdoor eating, patio, Dogs allowed Water. **NOTES:** Parking 30. **ROOMS:** 7 bedrooms 3 en suite s£25 d£25

See Pub Walk on page 547

We endeavour to be as accurate as possible but changes in personnel and data can occur in establishments after the guide has gone to press

Scotland

AVIEMORE   Map 13 NH81

The Old Bridge Inn ♀
Dalfaber Rd PH22 1PU ☎ 01479 811137 ▤ 01479 811372
e-mail: oldbridgeinn@freeserve.co.uk
Dir: Exit A9 to Aviemore, 1st L to 'Ski road' then 1st L again - 200m
Cosy and friendly Highland pub overlooking the River Spey.
Dine in the relaxing bars or in the attractive riverside garden.
Look out for venison steaks and casserole, Forfar chicken
supreme, grilled Spey salmon, mussels in white wine garlic
sauce, and traditional haggis, neeps and tatties.

OPEN: 11-11 (Thur-Sat 11-1, Sun 12.30-12) Times may vary please
ring for details. **BAR MEALS:** L served all week. D served all
week 12-2 6-9. Av main course £6.95. **RESTAURANT:** L served
all week. D served all week 12 6-9. Av 3 course à la carte £15.50.
Av 3 course fixed price £12.95. **BREWERY/COMPANY:** Free
House. **PRINCIPAL BEERS:** Tomintoul Wild Cat.
FACILITIES: Children welcome Garden: Food served outside.
NOTES: Parking 24

CARBOST

The Old Inn
IV47 8SR ☎ 01478 640205 ▤ 01478 640450
e-mail: oldinn@carbost.f9.co.uk
Once a croft house, this Highland inn is a perfect base for hill
walkers and climbers. Rents used to be collected here and a
local dentist pulled teeth in one of the upstairs rooms! The
patio offers splendid views of the loch and the Cuillins, while
inside is a charming mix of wooden floors and original stone
walls. Traditional bar food includes the likes of vegetarian
platter, pizzas and sausages while stews, curries, local venison
and haggis feature among the specials.
OPEN: 11-12 (hours change in winter please ring).
BAR MEALS: L served all week. D served all week 12-2 6.30-10.
Av main course £6.50. **BREWERY/COMPANY:** Free House
FACILITIES: Children welcome Children's licence Garden:
Outdoor eating, patio Dogs allowed. **NOTES:** Parking 20.
ROOMS: 6 bedrooms 6 en suite s£28 d£46

CARRBRIDGE   Map 13 NH92

Dalrachney Lodge Hotel ★ ★ ★
PH23 3AT ☎ 01479 841252 ▤ 01479 841383
e-mail: stay@dalrachney.co.uk
Dir: A9 onto A938 for 1.5m, through village, pub on R
Sympathetically restored Victorian shooting lodge, with log
fires and period furniture, set in 14 acres of mature grounds.
Local ingredients, notably Aberdeen Angus beef and Scottish
lamb, feature in a varied range of dishes. Choices include
casserole of shellfish, medallions of wild venison, grilled
rainbow trout and breast of duckling.
continued

OPEN: 12-2 5.30-11. **BAR MEALS:** L served all week. D served
all week 12-2 5.30-11. Av main course £6.50. **RESTAURANT:** D
served all week 7-8.30. Av 3 course à la carte £25.
BREWERY/COMPANY: Free House **FACILITIES:** Children
welcome Garden: Food served outside Dogs allowed.
NOTES: Parking 40. **ROOMS:** 16 bedrooms 16 en suite

CAWDOR   Map 13 NH85

Pick of the Pubs

Cawdor Tavern ☜ ♀
The Lane IV12 5XP ☎ 01667 404777 ▤ 01667 404777
e-mail: Cawdort@aol.com
Dir: from A96 (Inverness-Aberdeen) take B9006 & follow signs
for Cawdor Castle. Tavern in village centre.

With more than 100 malt whiskies, three Scottish ales,
including Dark Island Ale from Orkney, and a strong
Scottish flavour to the menu, it's hardly surprising this
refurbished pub, formerly the joiner's workshop for
Cawdor Estate, draws discerning diners from far and wide.
Old oak panelling from Cawdor castle and roaring log fires
provide a cosy atmosphere on long winter nights and the
garden patio is ideal for al fresco dining in summer.
Typical dishes range from beer-battered scampi and
grilled Ayrshire steak to fillet of Shetland salmon and pot-
roasted Speyside pheasant.
OPEN: 11-3 5-11 (May-Oct 11-11). Closed 25 Dec, 1 Jan.
BAR MEALS: L served all week. D served all week 12-2 5.30-9.
Av main course £7.95. **RESTAURANT:** L served all week.
D served Tue-Sat (all summer)12-2 6.30-9. Av 3 course à la
carte £19.50. **BREWERY/COMPANY:** Free House.
PRINCIPAL BEERS: Tennents 80/-, Deuchars IPA, Isle of Skye
Red Cullin, Orkney Dark Island. **FACILITIES:** Children
welcome Garden: Food served outside Dogs allowed Water.
NOTES: Parking 60

HIGHLAND

THE APPLECROSS INN, APPLECROSS
Shore Street IV54 8LR.
Tel: 01520 744262
Directions: off A896, 18m W
of Loch Carron, over Bealach
na Ba, the highest mountain
pass in Britain.
*Overlooking Raasay and the
Isle of Skye, this popular
village inn is situated on the
shore of beautiful Applecross
Bay. Wide selection of all-day
bar food using local produce
and specialising in seafood.
Bedrooms.*
Open: 11-11 (Sun 12.30-11
till 7 Dec & Jan). Bar Meals
12-9. Children and dogs
welcome. Garden. Parking.
(see page 545 for full entry)

*Pub*WALK

Applecross Inn, Applecross

Enjoy stunning views across Applecross Bay to the Isle of Skye, and look out for otters, seals, pine marten and eagles on this varied and interesting walk from an isolated inn.

From the inn turn right and follow the coast road or walk along the beach for a mile (1.6km). On approaching the bridge over Applecross River, take the footpath right and follow it upstream for 1/4 mile (0.4km). (To visit the Applecross Heritage Centre, cross the river bridge and follow the road for 1/4 mile (0.4km) and return to the bridge).

On reaching a wooden road bridge, go through a gate on the right-hand side and follow a woodland path beside the river. Walk through a field and keep to the path beside a tributary stream for about 1/2 mile (0.8km). Shortly, follow the obvious path that doubles back through a tunnel of rhododendrons on the right-hand side of a slope (narrow in places) to reach a lane opposite the Gamekeepers Cottage.

Bear left uphill, pass quarry workings and Keppoch House, then cross the road (Bealach na Ba road) and go through a gate into forest. Shortly, on your right, a track leads deep into the forest for 1/4 mile (0.4km) to reach steps down to the Old Forge and a road.

Here, either gently descend to the shore and inn. Or, continue on the waymarked path through the campsite, passing the tearoom, to reach the stile on the far side of the campsite. Walk through a small wood to a high stile (deer fence) and follow the steep path down to the road in Milltown. Turn right along the shore back to the inn.

Distance: 4 miles (6.4km)
Map: OS Landranger 24
Terrain: coast & woodland
Paths: woodland, field and riverside paths, beach and metalled lanes
Gradient: fairly easy; gentle slopes

*Walk submitted by:
The Applecross Inn*

Over the sea to Skye

CONTIN   Map 13 NH45

Achilty Hotel ★ ★ 🛏️
IV14 9EG ☎ 01997 421355 📠 01997 421923
Dir: *On A835, at the northern edge of Contin*
Well-converted 300-year-old farm steadings, situated near a
fast-flowing mountain river, created this former coaching inn
on the village edge. Traditional Scottish dishes highlight the
menu, in particular haggis with whisky and cream, venison
with port and cranberries, Highland beef, and fresh local
seafood.
OPEN: 11-11. **BAR MEALS:** L served all week. D served all
week. Av main course £9.95. **RESTAURANT:** L served all week.
D served all week 12-2.30 5.30-9.30. Av 3 course à la carte £16.
BREWERY/COMPANY: Free House.
PRINCIPAL BEERS: Calders Cream, Calders 70/-.
FACILITIES: Children welcome Garden: Dogs allowed.
NOTES: Parking 80. **ROOMS:** 12 bedrooms 12 en suite s£30
d£48

DORNOCH   Map 13 NH78

Mallin House Hotel 🐑
Church St IV25 3LP ☎ 01862 810335 📠 01862 810810
e-mail: mallin.house.hotel@zetnet.co.uk
Dir: *from Tain (on A9) take A836 to Bonar Bridge, then turn left onto
A949 in direction of Dornoch (approx 10m)*

Mallin House is a modern hotel just 200 yards from the Royal
Dornoch Golf Course. The area is also ideal for angling,
ponytrekking and birdwatching.
A single menu, strong on Scottish cooking is offered
throughout, with an emphasis on fresh seafood, including
deep fried haddock, cullen skink, king scallops with crab claws.
OPEN: 11-2.30 5-11. **BAR MEALS:** L served all week. D served
all week 12.30-2 6.30-9. Av main course £6.25. **RESTAURANT:** L
served all week. D served all week 12.30-2 6.30-9. Av 3 course à la
carte £25. **BREWERY/COMPANY:** Free House.
PRINCIPAL BEERS: John Smiths. **FACILITIES:** Children
welcome Garden: Dogs allowed Not in bar.
NOTES: Parking 22. **ROOMS:** 10 bedrooms 10 en suite s£35
d£58

Pubs offering a good choice of
seafood on the menu.

Skills and Crafts

Inns with names like the Bricklayers Arms
and the Masons Arms hark back to the days
when groups of craftsmen and tradesmen met
regularly in the local hostelry. The trade union
movement originally grew up in pubs in this way
and a 'local' can mean either a pub or a union
branch. Itinerant craftsmen would expect a
welcome at these houses, too, and pick up news of
work. The Axe and Compasses is a carpenters'
badge, the Three (or more) Horseshoes a device
of smiths, the Wheatsheaf of bakers and the Beetle
and Wedge of builders, while quite a few pubs
display the Oddfellows Arms. The Shoulder
of Mutton could signify that the
landlord doubled as a butcher.

DUNDONNELL   Map 12 NH08

Pick of the Pubs

Dundonnell House 🏵️ 🏵️ ★ ★ ★ 🛏️ 🍷
IV23 2QR ☎ 01854 633204 📠 01854 633366
e-mail: selbie@dundonnellhotel.co.uk
Dir: *From Inverness W on the A835, at Braemore junct take A382
for Gairloch*
Sheltering beneath the massive Al Teallach mountain
range, with superb views down Little Loch Broom, this
much-extended former drovers' inn boasted just four
bedrooms when acquired by the Florence family some
forty years ago. Today, in one of Scotland's finest holiday
areas, their acclaimed hotel is a magnet for visitors to
Wester Ross.
The Broom Beg ('little broom') bar and bistro
provide a casual atmosphere in which to relax after a day
exploring and enjoy good food, beers and an extensive
range of malt whiskies. It is a long way to the shops, so
local produce plays a full part on a menu providing batter-
crisp haddock fillets, with chips and tartare sauce, local
salmon with prawn, chervil and citrus butter, chicken fillets
and prime Angus steaks from their own Aberdeenshire
butcher.
Lunchtime snacks can be as simple as Orkney
Cheddar cheese and apple open sandwiches, beef- or
veggie-burgers and local oak-smoked salmon with dill
sauce and brown bread. Dinner in the spacious restaurant
continues to be a key attraction for residents.
OPEN: 11-11 (Reduced Hrs Nov-Mar please phone).
BAR MEALS: L served all week. D served all week 12-2
6-8.30. Av main course £7.95. **RESTAURANT:** D served all
week 7-8.30. Av 3 course à la carte £24.50.
BREWERY/COMPANY: Free House.
PRINCIPAL BEERS: John Smiths. **FACILITIES:** Children
welcome Children's licence Dogs allowed.
NOTES: Parking 60. **ROOMS:** 28 bedrooms 28 en suite
s£37.50 d£37.50

The Old Inn, Gairloch

THE OLD INN, GAIRLOCH
IV21 2BD.
Tel: 01445 712006
Directions: off main A832,
near harbour at S end of village
*Traditional Highland coaching
inn, specialising in real ales, real
food, real fires and real
Highland hospitality. Good
value bar food and bistro menu
specialising in fresh seafood.
Bedrooms and walkers' lodge
accommodation.*
Open: 11-11. Bar Meals: 12-
2.30 6-9. Children and dogs
welcome. Garden. Parking.
(see page 551 for full entry)

A glorious walk through Flowerdale Glen, noted for its historical, natural and architectural interest, to two waterfalls on the upper reaches of the valley. Magnificent mountain and coastal views. Walk information leaflets available from the inn.

Leave the inn, cross the old footbridge and turn right up the tarmac 'Private Road' (restricted vehicle access; walkers welcome - Red Walk). Walk up the valley, passing two lochans on the right and the ice house on the left. Continue past the white mansion of Flowerdale House, the ancient seat of the Mackenzies of Gairloch. Looking down the old drive from the house you can see a raised circular plot of land about 23 yards (21m) across. Known as the the 'Island of Justice', it was where the laird presided over the trials of local criminals. The track soon bears left by the old stable block. Built in 1730, it is considered to be the earliest dated barn in Scotland. Proceed past The Temple House and veer right past the sawmill. Continue along the track to Flowerdale Mains Farm and the end of the tarmac.

Pass the farm gate and follow the firm farm track. Walk through a devastated forest area, pass a junction and small wooden bridge on your right (return route), and continue up the glen. On reaching a fork in the stream, cross the wooden bridge to the right and and walk up to the waterfall known as 'Eas Dubh' (Black Falls). Ascend path to the left of the waterfall and proceed to the new wooden footbridge over the stream. Follow the path round and down the opposite side of the valley back to the first wooden bridge encountered.

Either cross the bridge and retrace outward route back to the inn, or follow forest track south (Blue Walk). Ascend to the highest point and savour spectacular views over the glen and out to Gairloch Bay, Skye and the Outer Isles. Follow the track down and over the footbridge on the right. The route leads you through farmland and over Cherry Hill. Soon you join the Old Road (former route to Gairloch before 1846), that leads down through the valley back to the car park of the Old Inn.

Distance: 3 miles (4km) or 3½ miles (4.8km)
Map: OS Landranger 19
Paths: farm tracks, forest paths and single track road
Terrain: woodland, farmland, heather moorland
Gradient: modest ascents and descents; short steep climb to waterfall

*Walk submitted by:
The Old Inn*

The village of Gairloch

FORT AUGUSTUS
Map 12 NH30

Pick of the Pubs

The Lock Inn 🐑 ♀
Canalside PH32 4AU ☎ 01320 366302
Dir: *On the banks of Caledonian Canal in Fort Augustus*
Built in 1820, this former bank and post office building,
replete with flagstone floors and original beams, stands on
the banks of the Caledonian Canal close to Loch Ness.

Food standards were set to improve following
development of a new state-of-the-art kitchen in 2001 that
has already been recognised by the Scottish Beef Guild
Society for its use of local produce. A thousand Celtic
welcomes are extended to regulars and visitors who come
to enjoy the regular Scottish folk music evenings when a
special dinner features brandied seafood bisque and Loch
an Ora whisky- flavoured game pâté, followed by seared
calves' liver and Angus sirloin steaks.

House specials include Nessie's Dragon hot-pot pie,
Cajun salmon fillets and Glenlivet venison casserole. Start
perhaps with Thai salmon cakes and round off with Loch
Ness mud pie.
OPEN: 11-11 (Summer 11-midnight). Closed 25 Dec, 1 Jan.
BAR MEALS: L served all week. D served all week 12-3 6-10.
Av main course £6.50. **RESTAURANT:** L served all week.
D served all week 12-3 6-10. Av 3 course à la carte £15.
BREWERY/COMPANY: Free House.
PRINCIPAL BEERS: Caledonian 80/-, Orkney Dark Island,
Black Isle. **FACILITIES:** Children welcome Children's licence
Garden: outdoor eating, patio

Drays and Horses

A few breweries still engagingly use Shire
horses and old-style drays to deliver their as in
days of yore. The older 18th-century drays were
two-wheeled wagons drawn by a pair of horses in
tandem, with the driver sitting on one of the
barrels. From this developed the more familiar
four-wheeled dray, drawn by two horses abreast,
with the driver perched up on a high seat. Some of
them had open sides, other rails or low boards,
while some had iron stanchions supporting chains.
Strong, hardy and weighing in at about a ton, Shire
horses trace their ancestry from the vast, tank-like
warhorses of the Middle Ages, which rumbled into
battle at a ground-shaking trot. Their descendants
today rumble through the streets on more
peaceful and merciful errands.

FORT WILLIAM
Map 12 NN17

Pick of the Pubs

Moorings Hotel ◉ ★ ★ ★
Banavie PH33 7LY ☎ 01397 772797 📠 01397 772441
e-mail: reservations@moorings-fortwilliam.co.uk
Dir: *from A82 in Fort William follow signs for Mallaig, then L
onto A830 for 1m. Cross canal bridge then 1st R signposted
Banavie*

A modern hotel west of town that stands beside Neptune's
Staircase on the Caledonian Canal, with panoramic views
on clear days towards Ben Nevis and the surrounding
mountains. Bedrooms have fresh decor and good facilities,
as do the Upper Deck lounge and popular Mariners' Bar
that share a nautical theme.

Daily bar food has a strong inclination towards local fish
such as West Coast haddock and lochy salmon, Angus
beef, Grampian chicken and, of course, haggis served with
clapshot and Drambuie sauce. Moorings bangers and
burgers make up the numbers along with Caesar salad,
pasta carbonara and a varied sandwich selection.

Afternoon tea, available throughout the day, includes a
selection of the chef's cakes: alternative desserts include
Dutch apple pie and traditional Scottish cranachan. A la
carte and set-price dinners in the Jacobean-style dining-
room feature much of the local produce for which the
Highlands are so justly famous.
OPEN: 12-11.45. **BAR MEALS:** L served all week. D served
all week 12-9.30. Av main course £7.50. **RESTAURANT:** D
served all week 7-9.30. Av 3 course à la carte £23. Av 4 course
fixed price £26. **BREWERY/COMPANY:** Free House
FACILITIES: Children welcome Children's licence Garden:
small patio, outdoor eating, Dogs allowed Water.
NOTES: Parking 80. **ROOMS:** 21 bedrooms 21 en suite
s£35 d£60 FR£80-£116

GAIRLOCH
Map 12 NG87

The Old Inn  ♉
IV21 2BD ☎ 01445 712006 ▤ 01445 712445
e-mail: nomadscot@lineone.net
Dir: just off main A832, near harbour at S end of village
The oldest hostelry in Gairloch was built by the estate in 1750, originally as a changing house for horses. The inn's site, at the foot of Flowerdale Glen by the harbour, has inspired many artists.

Another attraction these days is the range of real ales and seafood specialities. Favourite dishes include bouillabaisse, crab platter, locally landed langoustine, grilled wild venison steak and home-made lamb and rosemary pie.

OPEN: 11-12. **BAR MEALS:** L served all week. D served all week 12-2.30 6-9. Av main course £6.50. **RESTAURANT:** L served all week. D served all week 12-2.30 6-9. Av 3 course à la carte £15.
BREWERY/COMPANY: Free House.
PRINCIPAL BEERS: Greene King Old Speckled Hen, Courage Directors, Isle of Skye Red Cullin, Isle of Skye Blind Piper, Bellhaven St Andrews Ale. **FACILITIES:** Children welcome Children's licence Garden: Beer garden, Outdoor eating Dogs allowed Rugs. **NOTES:** Parking 20. **ROOMS:** 14 bedrooms 14 en suite s£25 d£40 FR£50-£75
See Pub Walk on page 549

GARVE
Map 12 NH36

Inchbae Lodge Hotel
IV23 2PH ☎ 01997 455269 ▤ 01997 455207
Dir: On A835, hotel 6m W of Garve
19th-century hunting lodge situated on the banks of the River Blackwater, with a new dining conservatory offering panoramic views. Haggis is served traditionally with neeps and tatties. A vegetarian haggis is also provided. Other options are seafood platter, local smoked salmon, and wood pigeon braised in red wine and Marsala with bacon, mushroom, celery and shallots.
OPEN: 11-11. **BAR MEALS:** L served all week. D served all week 12-2.30 5-8.30. Av main course £6.50. **RESTAURANT:** L served Sun. D served all week 12-2 7-8. Av 3 course fixed price £19.95.
BREWERY/COMPANY: Free House.
PRINCIPAL BEERS: Belhaven, guest Scottish ale.
FACILITIES: Children welcome Garden: 7 Acres inc island on river Dogs allowed. **NOTES:** Parking 30.
ROOMS: 15 bedrooms 15 en suite s£28 d£56

GLENCOE
Map 12 NN15

Clachaig Inn
PH49 4HX ☎ 01855 811252 ▤ 01855 811679
e-mail: inn@clachaig.com
Dir: In the heart of Glen Coe itself, just off the A82, 20m S of Fort William and 2m E of Glencoe village
Situated at the very heart of Glencoe, this inn has provided hospitality for over 300 years. It is a short forest walk from Signal Rock, where the signal was given for the infamous massacre of 1692.

More recently Clachaig has become perhaps the centre of Scottish mountaineering, renowned for its real ales and some 120 malt whiskies. Haggis, neeps and tatties, and venison casserole are typical of the robust fare.
OPEN: 11-11 (Fri 11-12, Sat 11-11.30). **BAR MEALS:** L served all week. D served all week 12-9. Av main course £7.50.
BREWERY/COMPANY: Free House. **PRINCIPAL BEERS:** Isle of Skye Red Cullin, Orkney Dark Island, Heather Fraoch Heather Ale, Houston St Peter's Well. **FACILITIES:** Children welcome Garden: outdoor eating, patio/terrace. **NOTES:** Parking 40.
ROOMS: 20 bedrooms 17 en suite s£30 d£24 FR£32-£36

GLENELG
Map 12 NG81

Pick of the Pubs

Glenelg Inn
IV40 8JR ☎ 01599 522273 ▤ 01599 522283
e-mail: christophermain@glenelg-inn.com
Dir: From Shiel Bridge (A87) take unclassified road to Glenelg
Very much a 'home from home' this characterful 150-year-old village inn commands stunning views across the Glenelg Bay to Skye beyond from its splendid waterside garden.

Local produce lies at the heart of daily menus that feature, for example, Loch Hourn scallops and Loch Onich salmon in any guise that takes the fancy. To start, Scottish Camembert and Brie are served with a basil crust and onion marmalade on mixed leaves, whilst to follow there might be Scottish beef fillet on crushed celeriac with red wine and thyme sauce or West Coast cod with crusted pecorino and pesto dressing.

Follow that with bitter chocolate cake with crème fraiche and local strawberries or a caramelised pineapple and ginger meringue.

A truly romantic place to stay, Glenelg remains virtually undiscovered - and many are of the opinion that it should stay so.
OPEN: 12-11. Closed End Oct-Etr (ex by arrangement).
BAR MEALS: L served all week. D served Mon-Sat 12.30-2 6-9.30. Av main course £7. **RESTAURANT:** 12.30-2 7.30-9. Av 3 course à la carte £25. **BREWERY/COMPANY:** Free House **FACILITIES:** Children welcome Garden: large, with trees, Food served outside Dogs allowed. **ROOMS:** 6 bedrooms 6 en suite

KYLESKU

Map 12 NC23

Kylesku Hotel
IV27 4HW ☎ 01971 502231 📄 01971 502313
e-mail: kylesku.hotel@excite.co.uk
Dir: *35m N of Ullapool on the A838, turn into Kylesku, hotel is at the end of the road at Old Ferry Pier*

This coaching inn on the old ferry slipway between Loch Glencoul and Loch Glendhu in the Highlands of Sutherland is an ideal location for birdwatchers, wildlife enthusiasts, climbers and walkers. Both bar and restaurant menus specialise in locally caught seafood and venison in season. Options include lobster, grilled langoustines with garlic mayonnaise, and pan-fried Lochinver haddock with lemon butter.
OPEN: 11-11 (Mon-Thur 10-11.30, Fri 10-12, Sat 10-11 Sun 12.30-11). Closed 1 Nov-28 Feb. **BAR MEALS:** L served all week. D served all week 12-2.30 6-9.30. Av main course £7.
RESTAURANT: L served all week. D served all week 12-2.30 7-9.30. Av 3 course à la carte £21.95. Av 2 course fixed price £18.95.
BREWERY/COMPANY: Free House **FACILITIES:** Children welcome Children's licence Garden: outdoor eating, patio/terrace, good views Dogs allowed Always welcome.
NOTES: Parking 50. **ROOMS:** 8 bedrooms 6 en suite s£30 d£55 FR£75-£85

LYBSTER

Map 13 ND23

The Portland Arms Hotel
KW3 6BS ☎ 01593 721721 📄 01593 721722
e-mail: portland.arms@btconnect.com
Dir: *Beside the main A9 road, when travelling from Inverness to Wick, hotel situated on the left hand side of the road, 200 yrds from the Lybster sign*
Long a favoured stop-off point between Wick and Thurso, the Portland Arms dates from the 19th century. Dishes include pan-fried lamb chop on a garlic mash with a rosemary jus, and chicken supreme wrapped in bacon, stuffed with Haggis and served with a whisky cream sauce.
OPEN: 7.30-11. Closed Dec 31-Jan 3. **BAR MEALS:** L served all week. D served all week 11.30-3 5-9. Av main course £7.50.
RESTAURANT: L served all week. D served all week 11.30-3 5-9. Av 3 course à la carte £15. **BREWERY/COMPANY:** Free House.
PRINCIPAL BEERS: Tennent 70/-. **FACILITIES:** Children welcome **NOTES:** Parking 20. **ROOMS:** 22 bedrooms 22 en suite s£45 d£68

NORTH BALLACHULISH

Map 12 NN06

Loch Leven Hotel
Old Ferry Rd, Onich PH33 6SA ☎ 01855 821236
📄 01855 821550
Dir: *off the main A82 at N of Ballachulish Bridge*
Situated on the northern shore of Loch Leven, this 17th-century coaching inn is ideally placed for touring the Great Glen and Western Highlands.
Steak and mushroom pie, vegetarian haggis, fresh battered haddock, venison sausages in red wine, and farmhouse chicken feature on the bar menu. Good range of Oriental and seafood dishes.
OPEN: 11am-midnight (Thur-Sat 11-1am). **BAR MEALS:** L served all week. D served all week 11-9. Av main course £6.50.
BREWERY/COMPANY: Free House. **PRINCIPAL BEERS:** John Smiths, McEwan 80/-. **FACILITIES:** Children welcome Garden.
NOTES: Parking 50. **ROOMS:** 10 bedrooms 10 en suite s£25 d£50

ONICH

Map 12 NN06

Pick of the Pubs

Onich Hotel 🏵 ★ ★ ★
PH33 6RY ☎ 01855 821214 📄 01855 821484
e-mail: reservations@onich-fortwilliam.co.uk
Dir: *Beside A82, 2m N of Ballachulish Bridge*

Beautifully located hotel on the shores of Loch Linnhe with spectacular views across to Glencoe and Morvern. Light meals and hearty bar suppers are served in the garden lounge, main bar or out on the terrace, alongside a wide selection of draught beers and malt whiskies. Typical dishes are ballontine of pheasant and haggis, breaded Mallaig haddock, and venison casserole.
OPEN: 11-11. **BAR MEALS:** L served all week. D served all week 12-10. Av main course £7. **RESTAURANT:** D served all week 7-9. Av 4 course fixed price £26.
BREWERY/COMPANY: Free House.
PRINCIPAL BEERS: Tetleys, Calders, Alloa.
FACILITIES: Children welcome Children's licence Garden: Beer garden, Outdoor eating Dogs allowed.
NOTES: Parking 50. **ROOMS:** 25 bedrooms 25 en suite

SHEILDAIG BAR, SHIELDAIG

IV54 8XN. Tel: 01520 755251

Directions: village off A896 Lochcarron to Gairloch road

Popular small bar adjacent to a comfortable hotel and located in a picturesque fishing village overlooking Shieldaig Island and Loch Torridon. Expect to find fresh seafood, landed by local boats, alongside traditional dishes on the short menu. Bedrooms.

Open: 11-11 (Sun 12.30-10.30) Winter: Mon-Fri 11-2.30 5-11, Sat 11-11, closed Sun. Bar Meals: 12-2.30 6-8.30. Children and dogs welcome. Front courtyard. Parking.

(see page 554 for full entry)

HIGHLAND

Pub WALK

Shieldaig Bar, Shieldaig

A beautiful low-level walk offering panoramic views of Shieldaig Island, the Outer Hebrides (on a clear day), and the spectacular Torridon mountain range.

Turn right on leaving the pub and walk along the seafront, looking out for seals and otters in the rock pools at low tide. Head uphill and where the road turns right continue up the rough track passing the village school on your left. At the playing fields, turn left and where the track forks, keep right, the track soon leading you to the clifftop.

Walk along the clear path, passing several shingle beaches below and enjoy excellent views of the Isle of Pines, Skye and, to your right, upper Loch Torridon. At a fork (by a cairn), take the left path which becomes a little indistinct as it climbs over rocks. Go to the top of the rocks to pick up the path again. Just before reaching the end of the headland, branch off left by a small house to a small grassy knoll for excellent all-round views back to the village, out to sea and to the magnificent Torridon Mountains. If time allows, explore the small harbour and, at low tide, the tip of the headland.

Retrace steps to the small house and scramble up the rocky ledge behind it. At the top, pick up the path again and follow it through a silver birch copse and across the grassy clearing beyond. Turn right at the white house, heading away from the sea, and walk to the top of the grass where you will re-locate the path. Continue ahead, keeping the fish farm to your left, the path eventually leading you back to the fork of paths at the small cairn. Retrace your steps back to the inn.

Distance: 3 miles (4.8km)
Map: OS Landranger 24
Terrain: clifftop, rocky shoreline, village lane
Paths: rough grassy coast path (marshy in places); metalled lane
Gradient: mainly level; one ot two easy scrambles

*Walk submitted by:
The Shieldaig Bar*

Looking towards the Torridon Mountains

Pick of the Pubs

The Plockton Hotel 🛏
Harbour St IV52 8TN ☎ 01599 544274
🖷 01599 544475
e-mail: sales@plocktonhotel.co.uk
Dir: On A87 to Kyle of Lochalsh take turn at Balmacara. Plockton 7m N.
AA/Sea Fish Authority
Seafood Pub of the Year for Scotland 2002
In a National Trust village that is described as idyllic, the hotel stretches right along the waterfront on the shores of Loch Carron. Recent developments have included expansion of modern en suite bedrooms into the next door cottage and a new garden restaurant opening to a rear courtyard and thence to the gardens. Local produce from all around - both water and dry land - forms the basis for cooking whose philosophy is to keep it simple and do it well. Plockton prawns, Loch Carron salmon and local queen scallops are landed by mid-afternoon down by the harbour; other fresh fish being landed at Gairloch or Kinlochbervie. Beef from locally raised stock and Highland venison play a full part on the seasonal menus. House specialities include Plockton Smokies - baked layers of locally smoked mackerel and Achmore cheese - salad of pickled sweet herring and prawns, turbot fillet grilled with an orange butter and the ever-popular platter of freshly caught seafood and smoked fish. Haggis and whisky starters and iced cranachan parfait round off a dinner that is mindfully true to the tastes of the Highlands.
OPEN: 11-11.45 (Sun 12.30-11). **BAR MEALS:** L served all week. D served all week 12-2.15 6-9.15. **RESTAURANT:** L served all week. D served all week 12-2.15 6-9.15. Av 3 course à la carte £20. **BREWERY/COMPANY:** Free House.
PRINCIPAL BEERS: Caledonian Deuchars IPA.
FACILITIES: Children welcome Children's licence Garden: outdoor eating Dogs allowed. **ROOMS:** 15 bedrooms 15 en suite s£40 d£60

Shove Halfpenny

The game is still played with pre-decimal halfpennies, lovingly preserved, but is not as popular and widespread in pubs as it used to be. It is a scaled-down version of shuffleboard, which involved propelling flat metal discs along a smooth wooden table up to 30ft long. Down to the First World War a playing area was often drawn in chalk on the bar or a tabletop, but today a special wooden or slate board is used, 24 inches long by 15 inches wide. As usual, the house rules vary in detail from one pub to another.

Pick of the Pubs

Plockton Inn & Seafood Restaurant 🛏
Innes St IV52 8TW ☎ 01599 544222 🖷 01599 544487
e-mail: plocktoninn@plocktoninn.freeserve.co.uk
Dir: On A87 to Kyle of Lochalsh take turn at Balmacara. Plockton 7m N
This attractive, stone-built free house stands just 50 metres from the sea, at the heart of the picturesque fishing village that formed the setting for the Hamish Macbeth TV series. Formerly a church manse, the Plockton Inn is now run by a local family. The atmosphere is relaxed and friendly; there are winter fires in both bars, and the prettily decorated en suite bedrooms are comfortable and well-equipped. Local produce takes pride of place on the menu, and locally caught fish and shellfish are prepared in the family's purpose-built smoke house behind the hotel. Expect freshly-made sandwiches, home-made fish soup, and hot dishes like haggis and clapshot, steamed Loch Leven mussels, or garlic langoustines. The daily-changing black-boards might feature stuffed sardines, king scallops with bacon, sea bass with lime and coriander, or pheasant with redcurrant and port. Vegetarian options include chick pea patties, stuffed mushrooms, or lentil and mushroom moussaka.
OPEN: 11-1am (Sat 11-11.30, Sun 12.30-11). **BAR MEALS:** L served all week. D served all week 12-2.30 5.30-8. Av main course £9. **RESTAURANT:** L served all week. D served all week 12-2.30 5.30-8. Av 3 course à la carte £16.45.
BREWERY/COMPANY: Free House.
PRINCIPAL BEERS: Greene King Abbot Ale & Old Speckled Hen, Fullers London Pride, Isle Of Skye Blaven.
FACILITIES: Children welcome Garden: Food served outside Dogs allowed. **NOTES:** Parking 6.
ROOMS: 6 bedrooms 5 en suite s£25 d£58

Pick of the Pubs

Shieldaig Bar 🛏 ♀
IV54 8XN ☎ 01520 755251 🖷 01520 755321
e-mail: tighane.lechotel@shieldaig.fsnet.co.uk
Expect a warm welcome and stunning views from picture windows across Loch Torridon to the sea beyond at this popular small bar, set in the heart of a charming fishing village. Due to space the Field's cannot provide a wide variety of beers in the neat little bar, but they do a fine job in offering fresh local seafood delivered straight from the village boats. Enjoy delicious fish and chips, langoustines with garlic mayonnaise, dressed crab, locally smoked salmon, and Kinlochbervie lemon sole duglere. Comfortable and well maintained bedrooms in the adjacent Tigh an Eilean Hotel, also owned by the Field's.
OPEN: 11-11 (Sun 12.30-10) (Winter Closed Mon-Fri 3-5). Closed Dec 25 & Jan 1. **BAR MEALS:** L served all week. D served all week 12-2.30 6-8.30. Av main course £6.
RESTAURANT: D served all week 7-8.30. Av 3 course à la carte £27. Av 3 course fixed price £27.
BREWERY/COMPANY: Free House **FACILITIES:** Children welcome Children's licence Courtyard, Food served outside Dogs allowed Water. **ROOMS:** 11 bedrooms 11 en suite s£49.50 d£110

See Pub Walk on page 553

ULLAPOOL   Map 12 NH19

The Argyll Hotel
Argyll St IV26 2UB ☎ 01854 612422 ▤ 01854 612522
Traditional family-run hotel just a short stroll from the shores of Loch Broom. Timeless public bar and comfortable main bar, both with open fires and a good choice of malt whiskies to choose from. West coast scallops and halibut, chicken supreme, venison medallions, and haggis, neeps and tatties feature on the varied menus.
OPEN: 11-11.30 (Sun 12-11). **BAR MEALS:** L served all week. D served all week 12-1.30 5.30-9. Av main course £7.50.
RESTAURANT: D served all week 5.30-9.
BREWERY/COMPANY: Free House.
PRINCIPAL BEERS: Calders 70/-, 2 Scottish guest ales.
FACILITIES: Children welcome. **NOTES:** Parking 20.
ROOMS: 8 bedrooms 6 en suite s£25 d£40

Pick of the Pubs

The Ceilidh Place
14 West Argyle St IV26 2TY ☎ 01854 612103
▤ 01854 612886
e-mail: reception@ceilidh.demon.co.uk
Dir: On entering Ullapool, along Shore St, pass pier and take 1st R. Hotel is straight ahead at top of hill

Simply a unique place and an Ullapool institution for fully 30 years, set back from the port whence the ferry crosses to Lewis. Under one roof are an all-day bar, informal dining area, bookshop and abundant local art that visitors are encouraged to peruse at their leisure. Bedrooms in the hotel and bunk-house are comfortably furnished, if somewhat basic, yet the friendly welcome and an abundance of real ales and malt whiskies more than compensate. At the simpler end of the various menus are crab cakes with avocado salad and smoked lamb with honey and mint dressing; more substantially smoked haddock fish pie in parsley sauce and T-bone steak and chips. Locally-landed fish is always available in specials such as monkfish and halibut brochettes with tarragon and dill sauce, while in season look for the Highland venison with red wine and juniper jus, followed for benefit of the sweet-toothed by profiteroles with white chocolate and Grand Marnier.
OPEN: 11-11 (Sun 12.30-11). Closed 2nd Wk in Jan for 2 Wks. **BAR MEALS:** L served all week. D served all week 12 6-9. Av main course £9. **RESTAURANT:** D served all week 7-9.30. Av 3 course à la carte £26.
BREWERY/COMPANY: Free House.
PRINCIPAL BEERS: Belhaven Best. **FACILITIES:** Children's licence Garden: patio, fruit trees & herbs Dogs allowed garden only. **NOTES:** Parking 20. **ROOMS:** 13 bedrooms 10 en suite s£35 d£70 FR£80-£130

Morefield Hotel & Mariners Restaurant
North Rd IV26 2TQ ☎ 01854 612161 ▤ 01854 612171
Popular bar and seafood restaurant, also known for its large selection of malt whiskies and ports. Possible dishes include lobster royale, seafood Thermidor, or Achiltibuie salmon and roast scallop terrine. If you're not feeling fishy try Aberdeen Angus prime sirloin, pork fillet Stilton, or something from the vegetarian menu.
OPEN: 11-2.30 5-11 (11-11 summer). **BAR MEALS:** L served all week. D served all week 2 5.30-9.30. Av main course £9.
RESTAURANT: D served all week 6.30-9.30. Av 3 course à la carte £20. **BREWERY/COMPANY:** Free House.
PRINCIPAL BEERS: Belhaven, Tennent, 2 guest ales.
FACILITIES: Children welcome Small beer garden
NOTES: Parking 50. **ROOMS:** 10 bedrooms 10 en suite s£25 d£40

MIDLOTHIAN

PENICUIK   Map 11 NT25

Howgate Restaurant ♀
Howgate EH26 8PY ☎ 01968 670000 ▤ 01968 670000
Dir: On A6094, 3m SE of Penicuik
A varied range of dishes is available at this successful, efficiently-run restaurant and bistro, built as stables in the 18th century. The menus change with the seasons to ensure the freshest produce is used. Log fires in winter and the glow of candlelight ensure a relaxing, welcoming atmosphere. Try steak and mushroom pie, Scottish salmon on stir-fried beans with chilli and Kumquat marmalade or lamb shank with roasted root vegetables and chive mash. Choice of good grills and home-made puddings.
OPEN: 12-2.30 6-11. Closed Dec 25-26, 1-2 Jan. **BAR MEALS:** L served all week. D served all week 12-2.30 6-9.30.
RESTAURANT: L served all week. D served all week 12-2.30 6-9.30. Av 3 course à la carte £25. **BREWERY/COMPANY:** Free House. **PRINCIPAL BEERS:** Belhaven Best.
FACILITIES: Children welcome Children's licence Garden: outdoor eating, BBQ. **NOTES:** Parking 45

MORAY

FOCHABERS   Map 13 NJ35

Gordon Arms Hotel
80 High St IV32 7DH ☎ 01343 820508 ▤ 01343 820300
e-mail: info@gordonarmshotel.com
Former coaching inn, where good food and comfortable accommodation have been provided for over 200 years. Public rooms retain much of their original character, and fine local ingredients are a feature of the menus.

PERTH & KINROSS

ABERFELDY   Map 13 NN84

Ailean Chraggan Hotel ♀
Weem PH15 2LD ☎ 01887 820346 ▤ 01887 829009
Dir: A9 N to jct at Ballinluig then A827 onto Aberfeldy, R onto B846
Small hotel in the heart of Scotland, with views over the River Tay to the hills beyond. Quality local produce is a feature of the menus, notably salmon from the Tay, beef, and game in season. Expect the likes of fresh seafood platter with Loch Etive prawns, mussels, oysters, smoked salmon pâté, smoked trout, scallops in bacon and queenie scallops in garlic.

continued

Scotland

OPEN: 12-2 6.30-9.30 (8.30 in winter). Closed 25-26 Dec, 1-2 Jan.
BAR MEALS: L served all week. D served all week 12-2 6.30-9.30.
RESTAURANT: L served all week. D served all week 12-2
6.30-9.30. **BREWERY/COMPANY:** Free House.
FACILITIES: Children welcome Garden: Food served outside
Dogs allowed. **NOTES:** Parking 40. **ROOMS:** 5 bedrooms 5 en
suite s£42.50 d£85

ALMONDBANK   Map 10 NO02

Almondbank Inn
31 Main St PH1 3NJ ☎ 01738 583242
Dir: *From Perth take A85 towards Crieff. 3m to Almondbank*
Enjoying fine views over the River Almond from its neat rear
garden, this Victorian village inn specialises in imaginative pub
grub. The new landlord is an ex-football manager, and has
introduced something of a footballing theme to the pub. River
bank walk from pub garden.

BURRELTON   Map 13 NO23

The Burrelton Park Inn
High St PH13 9NX ☎ 01828 670206
Ideally situated for touring the Highlands, this long roadside
inn is characterised by its typical Scottish vernacular style.
Spacious lounge bar and conservatory offering steamed
mussels, braised lambs' liver and farmhouse mixed grill, and a
well appointed restaurant featuring stuffed supreme of chicken
and vension fillet - among other more elaborate dishes. Fresh
catch of the day and special high teas served.
OPEN: 11-11 (Sat-Sun 11.30-11.45). **BAR MEALS:** L served all
week. D served all week 12-8.30 (Sat 12-9, Sun 12-8). Av main
course £6.95. **RESTAURANT:** L served all week. D served all
week 12-8.30 (Sat 12-9, Sun 12-8). Av 3 course à la carte £18.
BREWERY/COMPANY: Free House **FACILITIES:** Children
welcome Dogs allowed. **NOTES:** Parking 30. **ROOMS:** 5
bedrooms 5 en suite s£30 d£45

CLEISH   Map 10 NT09

Nivingston House ★ ★ ★
KY13 0LS ☎ 01577 850216 ▤ 01577 850238
e-mail: nivingstonhouse@breathemail.net
Dir: *2m W of M90 J5*
17th-century converted farmhouse in 14 acres of landscaped
grounds. Wonderful views of the Cleish Hills. Lunch and
dinner menus change daily and the ingredients used are
market fresh every day. Expect grilled Tay salmon with shallot
and chive cream sauce, Ma Bruce's Stovie cake with whisky
sauce, and curried chicken in filo pastry among the
imaginatively devised dishes.
OPEN: 12-2.30 5.30-11. **BAR MEALS:** L served all week. D
served all week 12-2 7-9. Av main course £6. **RESTAURANT:** L
served all week. D served all week 12-2 7-9. Av 3 course à la carte
£16.50. Av 4 course fixed price £27.50.
BREWERY/COMPANY: Free House.
PRINCIPAL BEERS: Calders. **FACILITIES:** Children welcome
Garden: BBQ, outdoor eating Dogs allowed garden only.
NOTES: Parking 40. **ROOMS:** 17 bedrooms 17 en suite s£70
d£100 FR£100-£120

GLENDEVON   Map 10 NN90

Pick of the Pubs

Tormaukin Hotel 🐷 ♀
FK14 7JY ☎ 01259 781252 ▤ 01259 781526
e-mail: enquiries@tormaukin.co.uk
Dir: *On A823 between M90 & A9*

Surrounded by the Ochil Hills this 18th-century former
drovers' inn has an idyllic setting in the middle of
nowhere; yet hill walks, loch and river fishing and golf
courses are all within easy reach.
Sympathetic refurbishment has retained many original
features - stone walls, exposed beams and natural timbers
- that lend such character to the main building, though
some of the bedrooms are in an adjacent converted stable
block.
Bar lunches and suppers, served by blazing log fires in
the cosy lounge and bars, cover a range of snacks,
children's choices and daily blackboard specials. Smoked
haddock fishcakes on coriander cream sauce, peppered
goats' cheese on ciabatta, shank of lamb in red wine sauce
and local hare and venison pie may feature. Mussel, onion
and potato chowder, pork and apple sausages and fillet
steak on haggis with Glayva sauce all appear on the
regular menu, along with desserts such as steamed
chocolate pudding and Scotch pancakes with caramelised
apples. Restaurant dinners are à la carte.
OPEN: 11-11 (Sun 12-11). Closed 25 Dec. **BAR MEALS:** L
served all week. D served all week 12-2 5.30-9.30. Av main
course £8.50. **RESTAURANT:** D served all week 6.30-9.30.
Av 3 course à la carte £25. **BREWERY/COMPANY:** Free
House. **PRINCIPAL BEERS:** Harviestoun Bitter &
Twisted/Original, Timothy Taylor Landlord.
FACILITIES: Children welcome patio Dogs allowed By
arrangement in certain areas. **NOTES:** Parking 50.
ROOMS: 10 bedrooms 10 en suite

Room prices minimum single and minimum double
rates are shown. FR indicates family room

GLENFARG	Map 11 NO11

The Bein Inn ♈
PH2 9PY ☎ 01577 830216 📠 01577 830211
e-mail: enquiries@beininn.com

Dating from 1863, this historic inn is a stone's throw from Balvaird Castle which featured in the 1995 film Rob Roy. Open log fires and a cosy lounge add to the charm and the basement bar is decorated with authentic rock music memorabilia from the 60s and 70s; live music programme featuring international artists.

Daily-changing specials board listing dishes like collops of monkfish and scampi, sirloin steak with mushroom and Drambuie sauce, and aubergine, tomato and Mozzarella stack with basil cream sauce.
OPEN: 11-2.30 5-11. **BAR MEALS:** L served all week. D served all week 12-2 5-9. Av main course £8. **RESTAURANT:** L served all week. D served all week 12-2 7-9. Av 3 course à la carte £22.
BREWERY/COMPANY: Free House.
PRINCIPAL BEERS: Belhaven Best,. **FACILITIES:** Dogs allowed.
NOTES: Parking 30. **ROOMS:** 11 bedrooms 11 en suite s£25 d£50

Glenfarg Hotel ★ ★
Main St PH2 9NU ☎ 01577 830241 📠 01577 830665
e-mail: info@glenfarghotel.co.uk
Distinctive castellated Victorian hotel, with a turret, set on the edge of the Ochil hills. It has been completely refurbished to provide a choice of bars serving international dishes, including pizza, fajitas, curries, and pies. The restaurant menu features local produce, notably Scottish beef and salmon.
OPEN: 11.30-11 (11.30-11.30 Sat-Sun). **BAR MEALS:** L served all week. D served all week 12-2 6-9. Av main course £7.
RESTAURANT: L served all week. D served all week 12-2 6.30-9. Av 3 course fixed price £15.95. **BREWERY/COMPANY:** Free House. **PRINCIPAL BEERS:** Timothy Taylor Landlord.
FACILITIES: Children's licence Garden: outdoor eating, patio, BBQ. **NOTES:** Parking 20. **ROOMS:** 17 bedrooms 17 en suite s£30 d£50 FR£67-£98

> AA Hotel Booking Service on 0870 5050505 to book
> at AA recognised hotels and B & Bs in the
> UK and Ireland, or through our Internet site:
> **www.theAA.com**

KILLIECRANKIE	Map 13 NN96

Pick of the Pubs

The Killiecrankie Hotel ◎ ◎ ★ ★
PH16 5LG ☎ 01796 473220 📠 01796 472451
e-mail: enquiries@killiecrankiehotel.co.uk
Dir: Turn off A9 at Killiecrankie. Hotel 3m N on B8079 on R

Good food together with genuine hospitality and a high level of personal attention are the hallmarks of this charming holiday hotel set in mature gardens at the northern end of the National Trust's Killiecrankie Pass. Well-presented day rooms include a relaxing lounge and cosy well-stocked bar with an adjacent conservatory for informal eating. Indigenous Scottish produce is a notable feature of menus here that promise sweet-cured Orkney herrings, local lamb gigot steaks, home-made steak burgers and poached salmon in mayonnaise with salad and new potatoes. With vegetable and bean cassoulet and numerous Sunday roasts, there is something for all tastes; the more sweet-toothed will enjoy the syrup pudding with cream or spiced apple crumble with vanilla ice, while the Scottish Cheddar comes with celery and grapes. An elegant dining-room with striking table appointments, lit candles and fresh flowers adds a more special location for fixed-price dinners that allow similarly fine ingredients to speak for themselves. Bright airy bedrooms are furnished in pine and well equipped with a wide range of amenities.
OPEN: 11-2.30 5.30-11. Closed All Jan, Mon-Tue in Feb, Mar & Dec. **BAR MEALS:** L served all week. D served all week 12.30-2 6.30-9.30. Av main course £7.
RESTAURANT: D served all week 7-8.30. Av 4 course fixed price £32.50. **BREWERY/COMPANY:** Free House
FACILITIES: Children welcome Children's licence Garden: patio, herb and veg garden Dogs allowed. **NOTES:** Parking 15. **ROOMS:** 10 bedrooms 10 en suite s£69 d£138

KILMAHOG	

The Lade Inn
FK17 8HD ☎ 01877 330152 📠 01877 331878
e-mail: paul@theladeinnscotland.freeserve.co.uk
Detached white-painted building set in its own grounds on the Leny Estate west of Callander. Cosy bar with open fire and collection of brasses, and separate dining area offering real Scottish cooking. Expect haggis, neeps and tatties, roast haunch of venison with red wine gravy, game casserole and local trout, alongside sandwiches and traditional pub meals.
continued

OPEN: 12-3 5.30-10.30 (12.30-10 Sun). Closed 1 Jan.
BAR MEALS: L served all week. D served all week 12-2.30
5.30-9.30 (12.30-9.30 Sun). Av main course £7.85.
BREWERY/COMPANY: Free House.
PRINCIPAL BEERS: Courage Directors, Orkney Red MacGregor,
Broughton Greenmantle Ale. **FACILITIES:** Children welcome
Garden: outdoor eating, patio, ponds Dogs allowed.
NOTES: Parking 40

KINNESSWOOD   Map 11 NN10

Pick of the Pubs

Lomond Country Inn 🏵 ★ ★ ♀
KY13 9HN ☎ 01592 840253 🖷 01592 840693
e-mail: enquiries@lomondcountryinn.com
*Dir: M90 J5, follow signs for Glenrothes then Scotlandwell,
Kinnesswood next village*
A privately-owned small hotel on the slopes of the
Lomond Hills that has been entertaining and sheltering
guests for more than 100 years. All the en suite bedrooms
are furnished to a high standard, four in the main house
and the remainder in a nearby annexe. Cosy public areas
sport log fires and a friendly atmosphere: the bar serves
real ales and offers a fine collection of single malts, while
the recently refurbished dining-room has the best views
over Loch Leven. Bar meals begin with smooth chicken
liver pâté with onion chutney or smoked chicken and
mango salad before pies of seafood or beef and ale,
traditional sausages on mustard mash and fishcakes with
tomato and avocado salsa. Round off with white peach
mousse, pear Bakewell tart or selected Highland and
Island cheeses. Restaurant dishes such as baby black
pudding and onion chutney, tuna steak Teriyaki and
chargrilled Scottish steaks show a good eye for local
produce and innovation in preparation and presentation.
OPEN: 11-11 (Fri-Sat 11-11.45). **BAR MEALS:** L served all
week. D served all week 12-2.30 6-9.30. Av main course £7.75.
RESTAURANT: L served all week. D served all week 12-2.30
6-10. Av 3 course à la carte £17.50. Av 2 course fixed price
£15.50. **BREWERY/COMPANY:** Free House.
PRINCIPAL BEERS: Deuchers IPA, Calders Cream, Tetleys,
Orkney Dark Island. **FACILITIES:** Children welcome
Children's licence Garden: beer garden , food served
outdoors Dogs allowed Kennels. **NOTES:** Parking 50.
ROOMS: 12 bedrooms 12 en suite s£40 d£64

KINROSS   Map 10 NO10

The Muirs Inn Kinross ◆ ◆ ◆
49 Muirs KY13 8AU ☎ 01577 862270 🖷 01577 862270
e-mail: themuirsinn@aol.com
*Dir: from M90 J6 take A922 to T-junction. Inn diagonally opposite
on R*
Dating back to the 1800s, this listed building was once a
farmhouse where the local blacksmith lodged. The Muirs Inn
later became a small hotel and drinks were served through the
side window to mounted horse riders. The word 'Muirs' is old
Scottish for moorland. Menu includes venison sausages,
haggis and puff pastry parcel, deep-fried haddock and
tagliatelle carbonara served with fried ham. Impressive
selection of beers and malt whiskies.

continued

OPEN: 12-11. **BAR MEALS:** L served all week. D served all week
12-2 5-9.30. Av main course £5.95. **RESTAURANT:** L served all
week. D served all week 12-2 5-9.30. Av 3 course à la carte £11.95.
BREWERY/COMPANY: Free House.
PRINCIPAL BEERS: Belhaven 80/-, Orkney Dark Island.
FACILITIES: Children welcome Children's licence Garden: Beer
garden, patio, food served outside. **NOTES:** Parking 8.
ROOMS: 5 bedrooms 5 en suite s£35 d£70 FR£55

PITLOCHRY   Map 13 NN95

Pick of the Pubs

Moulin Hotel ★ ★ ♀
11-13 Kirkmichael Rd, Moulin PH16 5EW
☎ 01796 472196 🖷 01796 474098
e-mail: hotel@moulin.u-net.com
Dir: From A9 at Pitlochry take A923. Moulin 0.75m
Half a century before the Jacobite rebellion of 1745, the
Moulin Hotel was established at the foot of 2,757ft Ben
Vrackie, on the old drove road from Dunkeld to Kingussie.
The modern road runs through nearby Pitlochry, leaving
Moulin as an ideal base for walking and touring.
  The large, white painted pub with its summer courtyard
garden is popular with tourists and locals alike, whilst in
winter, two blazing log fires set the scene for a game of
cards, dominoes or bar billiards. Well kept real ales come
from the pub's own micro-brewery, and there's plenty of
Gaelic fare on the big all-day menu.
  Start with potted hough and oatcakes, or Skye mussels
with garlic, before moving on to venison Braveheart,
haggis and neeps, or a game casserole McDuff. There's
haddock or salmon too, and vegetarians can expect
sautéed mushroom pancakes, stuffed peppers, and
vegetable goulash. Bedrooms vary in size and style, with
on-going refurbishment steadily improving standards of
comfort and facilities.
OPEN: 12-11 (Fri-Sat 12-11.45). **BAR MEALS:** L served all
week. D served all week 12-9.30. Av main course £7.
RESTAURANT: D served all week 6-9. Av 3 course à la carte
£17.95. Av 4 course fixed price £18.95.
BREWERY/COMPANY: Free House.
PRINCIPAL BEERS: Moulin - Braveheart, Old Remedial, Ale
of Atholl, Moulin Light. **FACILITIES:** Children welcome
Garden: Dogs allowed. **NOTES:** Parking 40. **ROOMS:** 15
bedrooms 15 en suite s£30 d£40

POWMILL

Map 10 NT09

Gartwhinzean Hotel ★ ★ ★ ♀
FK14 7NW ☎ 01577 840595 ▤ 01577 840779
Dir: *A977 to Kincardine Bridge road, for approx 7m to the vilage of Powmill, hotel at the end of village*
Located between two of Scotland's finest cities, Edinburgh and Perth, and handy for exploring the nearby Ochil and Cleish Hills, this attractive hotel overlooks Perthshire's picturesque countryside. A large selection of malt whiskies and a cosy open fire add to the attractions. Traditional steak pie, lightly grilled fillet of salmon and noisettes of lamb feature among the dishes on the interesting, regularly changing menu.
OPEN: 11.30-11. **BAR MEALS:** L served all week. D served all week 12-2.30 6.30-9.30. Av main course £6.95. **RESTAURANT:** L served all week. D served all week 12-2.30 6.30-9.30. Av 3 course à la carte £17.50. Av 3 course fixed price £17.50. **BREWERY/COMPANY:** Free House. **PRINCIPAL BEERS:** Maclay 70/, Calders 70. **FACILITIES:** Children welcome Garden: Food served outside Dogs allowed Water. **NOTES:** Parking 150. **ROOMS:** 23 bedrooms 23 en suite s£50 d£60

RENFREWSHIRE

HOUSTON

Map 10 NS46

Fox & Hounds ♀
South St PA6 7EN ☎ 01505 612448 & 612991
▤ 01505 614133
Dir: *M8 - Glasgow Airport. A737- Houston*
The horse tack decorating the first-floor Huntsman's bar gives this popular, well-kept village inn a somewhat English atmosphere. But the extensive, freshly-prepared menu tells a different story; look for local haggis and neeps, seared fillet of salmon , or Scotch pie and chips. What's more, you can wash down dishes like braised lamb shank, grilled West Coast crayfish, or home-made aubergine bake with award-winning ales from the on-site Houston Brewery.
OPEN: 11-11. **BAR MEALS:** L served all week. D served all week 12-2.30 5.30-10. Av main course £7.75. **RESTAURANT:** L served all week. D served all week 12-2.30 5.30-10. Av 3 course à la carte £20. **BREWERY/COMPANY:** Free House. **PRINCIPAL BEERS:** St Peters Well, Killelan, Barochan. **FACILITIES:** Children welcome Children's licence Dogs allowed. **NOTES:** Parking 40

SCOTTISH BORDERS

EDDLESTON

Map 11 NT24

Horse Shoe Inn ♀
EH45 8QP ☎ 01721 730225 & 730306 ▤ 01721 730268
e-mail: horseshoe.inn@ladon.co.uk
Dir: *On A703 S of Edinburgh. From M74 to Biggar, then A72 to Peebles & A703 N to Eddleston*
Situated in glorious Border country near historic Peebles and cosmopolitan Edinburgh, this former village smithy was once a coffee shop and a garage. The doors and wooden panelling come from a church. Impressive menu offers such dishes as braised lamb shank, cod in beer batter, venison casserole and Aberdeen Angus beef and ale pie. Interesting selection of lighter bites and puddings, including chilled caramelised apple tart and traditional cranachan. Wide-ranging wine list.
continued

OPEN: 11-3 (all day summer 5.30-12). **BAR MEALS:** L served all week. D served all week 12.30-2.30 6.30-9.30. Av main course £6.45. **RESTAURANT:** L served all week. D served all week 12.30-2.30 6.30-9.30. Av 3 course à la carte £18. **BREWERY/COMPANY:** Free House. **PRINCIPAL BEERS:** McEwans 70/-. **FACILITIES:** Children's licence. **NOTES:** Parking 35. **ROOMS:** 7 bedrooms 7 en suite s£25 d£40 FR£70

ETTRICK

Map 11 NT31

Tushielaw Inn
TD7 5HT ☎ 01750 62205 ▤ 01750 62205
e-mail: Gordon.Harrison@Virgin.net
Dir: *At junction of B709 & B711(W of Hawick)*

On the banks of Ettrick Water, surrounded by the Border hills, is this 18th-century former coaching inn and drovers' halt. Free trout fishing is provided to residents on the loch, and fishing permits are available. The inn appeals to walkers and cyclists with its welcoming open fire and wholesome meals, including pheasant casserole and venison pie in season, local lamb, Aberdeen Angus steaks and, of course, local trout.
OPEN: 12-2.30 6-11 (Sun 12-2.30 7-11). Closed 25 Dec & Jan 1. **BAR MEALS:** L served all week. D served all week 12-2.15 7-9. Av main course £6.50. **RESTAURANT:** L served all week. D served all week 12-2.15 7-9. Av 3 course à la carte £13. **BREWERY/COMPANY:** Free House **FACILITIES:** Children welcome Children's licence Garden: patio, food served outside Dogs allowed. **NOTES:** Parking 8. **ROOMS:** 3 bedrooms 3 en suite s£30 d£46 FR£62

GALASHIELS

Map 11 NT43

Abbotsford Arms ★ ★ 🐑
63 Stirling St TD1 1BY ☎ 01896 752517 ▤ 01896 750744
e-mail: abb2517@aol.com
Dir: *Turn off A7 down Ladhope Vale, turn L opposite the Bus Station*
Ideal for local golf courses and touring the beautiful Borders countryside, this family-run, stone-built hotel offers comfortable accommodation and traditional bar food. The menu includes steaks, lasagne, sea bass, salmon and chicken dishes.
OPEN: 11-11. Closed 25 Dec, 2 Jan. **BAR MEALS:** L served all week. D served all week 12-9. Av main course £5.50. **RESTAURANT:** L served all week. D served all week 12-9. Av 3 course à la carte £12. **BREWERY/COMPANY:** Free House **FACILITIES:** Children welcome Children's licence Garden: outdoor eating. **NOTES:** Parking 10. **ROOMS:** 14 bedrooms 14 en suite s£40 d£60

GALASHIELS continued

Kingsknowles ★ ★ ★ 🛏️
1 Selkirk Rd TD1 3HY ☎ 01896 758375 🖹 01896 750377
e-mail: enquiries@kingsknowes.co.uk
Dir: *Off A7 at Galashiels/Selkirk rdbt*
Baronial mansion, dating from 1869, with idiosyncratic French
Gothic and early Renaissance detail. It is set in extensive
grounds, complete with a play park, looking onto the Eildon
Hills. Speciality dishes include Three Sisters of Eildon - a lamb,
pork and beef kebab with pepper sauce - and the Auld
Alliance - Eyemouth haddock filled with smoked haddock
mousseline and cheese.
OPEN: 11.45-11 Sun-Wed 11.45-12 Thurs-Sat . **BAR MEALS:** L
served all week. D served all week 11.45-2
5.45-9.30. Av main course £6.50. **RESTAURANT:** L served all
week. D served all week 11.45-2 5.45-9.30. Av 5 course fixed price
£19.95. **BREWERY/COMPANY:** Free House
FACILITIES: Children welcome Garden: 3.5 acres of private land
Dogs allowed. **NOTES:** Parking 60. **ROOMS:** 11 bedrooms
11 en suite s£49 d£74

INNERLEITHEN Map 11 NT33

Traquair Arms Hotel ♦ ♦ ♦
Traquair Rd EH44 6PD ☎ 01896 830229
🖹 01896 830260
e-mail: traquair.arms@scotborders.com
Dir: *6m E of Peebles on A72. Hotel 100metres from junc with B709*
New owners the Johnsons have taken over this traditional
stone-built inn. It has a village setting close to the River Tweed
surrounded by lovely Borders countryside and offers 10 en
suite bedrooms, a dining room and cosy bar. Real ales include
Traquair Ale from nearby Traquair House, and the food has a
distinctive Scottish flavour with dishes of Finnan savoury, and
roast pheasant with rowanberry jelly.
OPEN: 11-11.30. **BAR MEALS:** L served all week. D served all
week 12-9. Av main course £5.50. **RESTAURANT:** L served all
week. D served all week 12-9. **BREWERY/COMPANY:** Free
House. **PRINCIPAL BEERS:** Traquair Bear, Broughton
Greenmantle & Black Douglas. **FACILITIES:** Children welcome
Garden: secluded Dogs allowed. **NOTES:** Parking 18.
ROOMS: 10 bedrooms
10 en suite s£45 d£58

KELSO Map 11 NT73

Queens Head Hotel ★ ★
Bridge St TD5 7JD ☎ 01573 224636 🖹 01573 224459
Situated between the cobbled square and Rennie's Bridge over
the Tweed, this 18th-century Georgian coaching inn has
historical connections with Kelso Abbey and Bonnie Prince
Charlie. Home-cooked food, served in the comfortable lounge
and restaurant, includes lambs' liver and onion, pan-fried
monkfish and bacon, and Dover sole.
OPEN: 11-2.45 4.45-11. **BAR MEALS:** L served all week. D
served all week 12-2 6-9. Av main course £5.50.
RESTAURANT: L served all week. D served all week 12-2 6-9.
Av 3 course à la carte £15. **BREWERY/COMPANY:** Free House.
PRINCIPAL BEERS: Firkin IPA. **FACILITIES:** Children welcome.
NOTES: Parking 4. **ROOMS:** 11 bedrooms 10 en suite s£37
d£50

LAUDER Map 11 NT54

Lauderdale Hotel ★ ★
1 Edinburgh Rd TD2 6TW ☎ 01578 722231
🖹 01578 718642
e-mail: Enquiries@lauderdale-hotel.co.uk
Dir: *on the main A68 25m S of Edinburgh*
Imposing Edwardian building standing in its own extensive
grounds. A cheerful lounge bar and a good range of
generously served food. Abundant floral displays during
summer. Dishes include deep-fried chicken fillets, rich beef
gylas, apricot stuffed roast loin of pork, and roast of the day.
Regularly changing specials blackboard.
OPEN: 11-11 (Thu-Sat 11-12). **BAR MEALS:** L served all week.
D served all week 12-2 5-9.30. Av main course £5.75.
RESTAURANT: L served all week. D served all week 12-2
6.30-9.30. Av 3 course à la carte £15.50.
BREWERY/COMPANY: Free House.
PRINCIPAL BEERS: Deuchars IPA. **FACILITIES:** Children
welcome Children's licence Garden: Beer garden with seating,
food served outdoors. **NOTES:** Parking 50.
ROOMS: 10 bedrooms 10 en suite s£37 d£58 FR£65-£90

MELROSE Map 11 NT53

Pick of the Pubs

Burts Hotel ◉ ◉ ★ ★ ★
Market Square TD6 9PN ☎ 01896 822285
🖹 01896 822870
e-mail: burtshotel@aol.com
Dir: *A6091, 2m from A68 3m South of Earlsdon*
Family-owned and run for over 30 years, Burts, built in
1722 for a local dignitary, stands on the picturesque
market square of this interesting Borders town. A hunting
and shooting theme extends through the busy bars and
restaurant warmed by winter log fires, where classic
Scottish ales and over 100 malt whiskies are on dispense.
Lunch and bar suppers change in response to market
availability of local produce and come in well-planned and
executed combinations. To start, escabèche of hake with
Niçoise salad and avocado and basil salsa or a filo tartlet
of Stilton, roast red peppers and cherry tomato; followed
by marinated chicken supreme in Thai red curry with
spiced onion and cucumber yoghurt or sole paupiettes on
marinated brocolli and spinach cream. Scotch Border
lamb cutlets, home-made beef-burgers and Aberdeen
Angus steaks for heartier appetites, with warm treacle tart
or Selkirk Bannock pudding and caramel sauce to follow.
Fixed-price restaurant lunches and dinner offer similar
quality ingredients in more elaborate guises, accompanied
by interesting house wines.
OPEN: 11-2.30 5-11. **BAR MEALS:** L served all week. D
served all week 12-2 6-9.30. Av main course £7.
RESTAURANT: L served all week. D served all week 12-2
7-9. Av 3 course fixed price £27.75.
BREWERY/COMPANY: Free House.
PRINCIPAL BEERS: Caledonian 80/-, Deuchars IPA, Timothy
Taylor Landlord. **FACILITIES:** Children welcome Children's
licence Garden: outdoor eating Dogs allowed.
NOTES: Parking 40. **ROOMS:** 20 bedrooms 20 en suite
s£46 d£80 FR£100

ST BOSWELLS Map 11 NT53

Buccleuch Arms Hotel ★ ★

The Green TD6 0EW ☎ 01835 822243 ▤ 01835 823965

e-mail: bucchotel@aol.com

Dir: on A68, 8m N of Jedburgh

Perfectly situated at the heart of the Scottish Borders, this 16th-century inn offers a varied menu to suit every palate. Food options include topside of beef stuffed with haggis, deep-fried Whitby scampi tails with home-made tartare sauce, grilled sole, breaded haddock and a range of changing specials. Hill walking, clay pigeon shooting, and fishing activities can be arranged. Comfortable well equipped bedrooms.

OPEN: 7.30am-11. Closed 25 Dec. **BAR MEALS:** L served all week. D served all week 12-2 6-9. Av main course £6.50. **RESTAURANT:** L served all week. D served all week 12-3 6-9. Av 3 course à la carte £21.95. Av 2 course fixed price £18.95. **BREWERY/COMPANY:** Free House. **PRINCIPAL BEERS:** Calders70/-,80/-, Claders Cream Ale, Greenmantle. **FACILITIES:** Children welcome Garden: Food served outside Dogs allowed. **NOTES:** Parking 60. **ROOMS:** 19 bedrooms 19 en suite s£40 d£70

Broughton & Traquair

Deep in the beautiful Scottish Borders lies the home of Broughton Ales. The brewery produces a range of popular beers whose names recall the colour and romance of this glorious region of the country. Greenmantle Ale (3.9%) takes its name the classic adventure by John Buchan, while Black Douglas (5.2%) is named after Lord James Douglas, a member of one of Scotland's most famous families. His swarthy good looks earned him the name 'Black Douglas' A staunch supporter of Robert the Bruce, Douglas and the King of Scots were pursued across country by Edward I's army. Evening tours by arrangement.

Oak Production from Traquair

Although there was a working brewery here from the 16th to the 18th centuries, the current wave of beers flowing from Traquair House began in 1965, when the late Peter Maxwell Stuart took over. Three beers are currently produced by the only British brewhouse to ferment its total production in oak: Traquair House Ale (7.2%), Traquair Bear Ale (5%) and Traquair Jacobite Ale (8%). The last of these was brewed to celebrate the Jacobite Rebellion in 1745, and is spiced with coriander. Brewery tours are available.

SWINTON Map 11 NT84

Pick of the Pubs

Wheatsheaf Hotel 🏵 🏵 ♦♦♦♦ 🐑 ♀

Main St TD11 3JJ ☎ 01890 860257 ▤ 01890 860688

e-mail: reception@wheatsheaf-swinton.co.uk

Dir: 6m N of Duns on A6112

AA Pub of the Year for Scotland 2002.

The Wheatsheaf has been in the same hands for 15 years, fronted by a chef/patron who is passionate about his use of local produce. Not only does he cook it, he hunts and fishes it too; salmon from the Tweed, game from the Borders and seafood from the Berwickshire coast. In addition to up-graded bedrooms with modern en suite facilities he has also added a rod-and-boot room true to the area's sporting roots. Light lunches and snacks, washed down with best Scottish ale, are no less pivotal to this success, with an impressive list of choices offering the finest tastes of Scotland. Classy dishes such as wood-pigeon breast with black pudding on Madeira sauce and aubergine and tomato melanzane glazed with Parmesan may come in small or large portions, with heartier dishes that include braised oxtails on a real ale sauce and pork, apple and leek meatballs in cider gravy with bubble-and-squeak. A la carte dinners featuring seared salmon fillets and roast loin of Highland venison are followed by steamed lemon sponge pudding, vanilla pod brûlée and Scottish cheeses with oatcakes.

OPEN: 11-2.30 6-11. Closed Mon, Sun eve in winter. Last 2 wks Jan, 1 Wk July. **BAR MEALS:** L served Tue-Sun. D served Tue-Sun 11.45-2.15 6.30-9.30. Av main course £8. **RESTAURANT:** L served Tue-Sun. D served Tue-Sun 1 1.45-2.15 6-9.30. Av 3 course à la carte £20. **BREWERY/COMPANY:** Free House. **PRINCIPAL BEERS:** Caledonian 80/- & Deuchers IPA, Broughton Greenmantle Ale. **FACILITIES:** Children welcome Children's licence Garden: outdoor eating, patio, Dogs allowed. **NOTES:** Parking 8. **ROOMS:** 7 bedrooms 7 en suite s£50 d£80

Pubs offering a good choice of seafood on the menu.

Scotland

TIBBIE SHIELS INN   Map 11 NT22

Pick of the Pubs

Tibbie Shiels Inn ◆◆◆
St Mary's Loch TD7 5LH ☎ 01750 42231
Dir: From Moffat take A708. Inn is 14m on R
Situated on the isthmus between St Mary's Loch and Loch of the Lowes, by the scenic Southern Upland Way, the inn is named after the fine lady who first opened it in 1826 and prospered there for fully 50 years. Its spirit is unchanged, in low-ceilinged, cosy bars full of character and old-world charm, frequented by ramblers and rodsmen - residents fish free of charge. Menus reflect the seasons with winter game and fresh fish, as well as more exotic dishes. A typical menu includes Holy Mole chilli rice, steak and ale pie, and the Tibbie mixed grill. The comfortable bedrooms are all en suite.
OPEN: 11-11 (Sun 12.30-11). **BAR MEALS:** L served all week. D served all week 12-8.30. Av main course £5.25. **RESTAURANT:** L served all week. D served all week 12-8.30. Av 3 course à la carte £9.75.
BREWERY/COMPANY: Free House.
PRINCIPAL BEERS: Broughton Greenmantle Ale, Belhaven 80/-. **FACILITIES:** Children welcome Children's licence Garden: patio, lochside location **NOTES:** Parking 50.
ROOMS: 5 bedrooms 5 en suite s£30 d£52

TWEEDSMUIR   Map 10 NT12

The Crook Inn
ML12 6QN ☎ 01899 880272   🖹 01899 880294
e-mail: thecrookinn@btinternet.com
Scotland's oldest licensed coaching inn, frequented by Robbie Burns, the Crook dates from the 16th century and is located in the lovely Tweed Valley. In the 30s it was refurbished in art deco style, and many of these features remain. Bar meals and dinner menus offer dishes such as sirloin steak with Drambuie cream sauce and herb-crusted fillet of salmon.
OPEN: 9am-12midnight. Closed Dec 25. **BAR MEALS:** L served all week. D served all week 12-9.30. Av main course £7.
RESTAURANT: L served all week. D served all week 12-9.30. Av 4 course fixed price £19.50. **BREWERY/COMPANY:** Free House.
PRINCIPAL BEERS: Broughton Greenmantle.
FACILITIES: Children welcome Children's licence Garden: patio, outdoor eating Dogs allowed. **NOTES:** Parking 60.
ROOMS: 8 bedrooms 8 en suite s£28.50 d£48

SHETLAND

BRAE

Busta House Hotel
Busta ZE2 9QN ☎ 01806 522506   🖹 01806 522588
Built in 1588, this is the oldest occupied building on Shetland. The hotel also has some of the few trees on Shetland in its garden. Seaside location.

SOUTH AYRSHIRE

SYMINGTON   Map 10 NS33

Wheatsheaf Inn 🐑
Main St KA1 5QB ☎ 01563 830307   🖹 01563 830307
A lovely village setting for this 17th-century inn, where log fires burn in every room and local artists' work is displayed on the

continued

walls. Fresh fish highlights the menu with options like fillet of salmon with lemon and basil cream, or baked sea bass with ginger and lime. Alternatively, try haggis, neeps and tatties with Drambuie and onion cream.
OPEN: 11-12. Closed 25 Dec, 1 Jan. **BAR MEALS:** L served all week. D served all week 12-9.30. Av main course £7.
RESTAURANT: L served all week. D served all week 12-9.30. Av 3 course à la carte £13. **BREWERY/COMPANY:** Belhaven.
PRINCIPAL BEERS: Belhaven Best,. **FACILITIES:** Children welcome Garden: Outside eating. **NOTES:** Parking 20

STIRLING

BRIG O'TURK   Map 10 NN50

The Byre Inn 🐑
FK17 8HT ☎ 01877 376292   🖹 01877 376357
e-mail: Meder@connectfree.co.uk
Converted from a cattle shed, this old stone building with beams and log fires is located on the edge of the Queen Elizabeth Forest in the heart of the Trossachs. Enjoy a meal by the fire in the bar after a day's hiking, or dine more formally in the restaurant. Interesting dishes include venison tournados on wild mushrooms and port jus, and braised turbot with tagliatelle and Champagne beurre blanc.
OPEN: 12-3 6-11 (closed Mon). **BAR MEALS:** L served Tues-Sun. D served Tues-Sun 12-2 6-9.30. Av main course £9.50.
RESTAURANT: L served Wed-Mon. D served Wed-Mon 12-2 6-9.30. Av 3 course à la carte £22. **BREWERY/COMPANY:** Free House. **PRINCIPAL BEERS:** Heathers Ale.
FACILITIES: Children welcome Garden: Beer Garden: Outdoor eating Dogs allowed garden only. **NOTES:** Parking 30

CRIANLARICH

Ben More Lodge Hotel ◆◆◆
FK20 8QS ☎ 01838 300210   🖹 01838 300218
e-mail: info@ben-more.co.uk
Dir: From Glasgow take A82 to Crianlarich, turn R at T Junc in village in direction of Stirling

Hotel in a beautiful setting at the foot of Ben More (3800 ft) on the road to the North West Highlands, offering accommodation in timber-built lodges. Both bar and restaurant menus feature local salmon and trout and a good selection of steaks and chops.
OPEN: 11-12. Closed Mon-Fri early Nov-mid March.
BAR MEALS: L served all week. D served all week 12-2.30 6-8.45. Av main course £6. **RESTAURANT:** L served all week. D served all week 12-2.30 6-8.45. Av 3 course à la carte £16.
BREWERY/COMPANY: Free House **FACILITIES:** Children welcome Garden: outdoor eating, patio/terrace Dogs allowed.
NOTES: Parking 50. **ROOMS:** 11 bedrooms 11 en suite s£40 d£50 family room £65-£94

Scotland

DRYMEN
Map 10 NS48

Clachan Inn
2 Main St G63 0BP ☎ 01360 660824 ▤ 01360 660751
Quaint, white-painted cottage, believed to be the oldest
licensed pub in Scotland, situated in a small village on the
West Highland Way. Locate the appealing lounge bar for
freshly-made food, the varied menus listing filled baked
potatoes, salads, chicken and mushroom pasta bake, fish and
chips, sirloin steak with bacon and Roquefort sauce, and good
daily specials.
OPEN: 11-12. **BAR MEALS:** L served all week. D served all week
12-4 6-10. Av main course £5.85. **RESTAURANT:** L served all
week. D served all week 12-4 6-10. Av 3 course à la carte £15.
BREWERY/COMPANY: Free House.
PRINCIPAL BEERS: Caledonian Deuchars IPA, Belhaven.
FACILITIES: Children welcome Dogs allowed.
ROOMS: 3 bedrooms s£22 d£44

KIPPEN
Map 10 NS69

Cross Keys Hotel
Main St FK8 3DN ☎ 01786 870293 ▤ 01786 870293
e-mail: crosskeys@kippen70.fsnet.co.uk
The village of Kippen, situated in the Fintry Hills overlooking
the Forth Valley, has strong associations with Rob Roy. The pub
dates from 1703, retains its original stone walls, and enjoys
real fires in winter. Home-made beefsteak pie is a popular
option, along with Craigellachie smoked salmon platter, from
a menu that serves both bar and restaurant.
OPEN: 12-2.30 (Fri-Sat 5.30-1am, Sun 12.30-11 Apr-Sep all day
Sat-Sun 5.30-12). Closed 1 Jan. **BAR MEALS:** L served all week.
D served all week 12-2 5.30-9.30. Av main course £6.
BREWERY/COMPANY: Free House.
PRINCIPAL BEERS: Belhaven Best, IPA, 80/-, Harviestoun Bitter
& Twisted. **FACILITIES:** Children welcome Garden: outdoor
eating Dogs allowed Water. **NOTES:** Parking 5.
ROOMS: 2 bedrooms 1 en suite d£45

STRATHBLANE
Map 10 NS57

Kirkhouse Inn
Glasgow Rd G3 9AA ☎ 01360 771771 ▤ 01360 771771
Dir: A81 Aberfoyce rd from Glasgow city centre through Bearsden &
Milngavie, Strathblane on junct with A891
17th-century coaching inn nestling beneath the jagged scarp of
the Campsie Fells, a rolling patchwork of green volcanic hills
and picturesque villages. Interesting menu offers international
cuisine as well as traditional British dishes.
OPEN: 10-midnight (Fri-Sat 10-1am). **BAR MEALS:** L served all
week 12-5. Av main course £7. **RESTAURANT:** L served all week.
D served all week 12-5 5-10. **PRINCIPAL BEERS:** Belhaven.
BREWERY/COMPANY: Cawley Hotels. **NOTES:** Parking 300.
ROOMS: 16 bedrooms
16 en suite s£49.50 d£70

THORNHILL
Map 11 NN60

Lion & Unicorn
FK8 3PJ ☎ 01786 850204
Dir: On A873 Blair Drummond to Aberfoyle
Droving inn dating from 1635, once frequented by Rob Roy
MacGregor. These days it has a games room and and the most
recent addition, three en suite letting rooms, which were
under construction as the guide went to press. Home-cooked
dishes range from roast beef and Yorkshire pudding in the bar
to rack of Persian lamb with apricots and rosemary in the
continued

restaurant.
OPEN: 12-12 (Fri-Sat 12-1). **BAR MEALS:** L served all week. D
served all week 12-9. Av main course £5.50. **RESTAURANT:** L
served all week. D served all week 12-9. Av 3 course à la carte £20.
BREWERY/COMPANY: Free House **FACILITIES:** Children
welcome Garden: Dogs allowed. **NOTES:** Parking 25

WEST LOTHIAN

LINLITHGOW
Map 10 NS97

Pick of the Pubs

Champany Inn ◉ ◉
Champany EH49 7LU ☎ 01506 834532
▤ 01506 834302
e-mail: reception@champany.com
The road to Champany Inn and its 16th-century
association with Linlithgow Castle are full of anecdote and
fond recollections. The Davidsons' long-standing pub and
restaurant, said to be the home of perfectly prepared
Aberdeen Angus beef, is almost an institution. For
dedicated pub-goers, the Chop and Ale House menu
offers choices for all, from the burgers and sausages made
in-house through pickled cod in curry and onion sauce to
speciality fish and chips and cold buffets of sirloin ham or
spit-roast chicken. From T-bone and sirloin to rib-eye, rib-
loin and heart-of-rump, the steaks are unparalleled and
served with healthy home-cut chips, coleslaw and salad.
Cullen Skink and best end Scottish spring lamb chops will
be found on the menu along with seasonal lobster,
salmon and local game in the rather more formal,
traditional restaurant. Hand-picked wines, including many
champagnes, encompass the old and new worlds; perhaps
just that added incentive to indulge in a restful overnight
stay and hearty Scottish breakfast.
OPEN: 12-2 (all day w/end) 6.30-11. Closed 25/26 Dec, 1/2
Jan. **BAR MEALS:** L served all week. D served all week 12-2
6.30-11. Av main course £8.95. **RESTAURANT:** L served
Mon-Fri. D served Mon-Sat 12.30-2 7-11. Av 3 course à la
carte £40. **BREWERY/COMPANY:** Free House.
PRINCIPAL BEERS: Belhaven. **FACILITIES:** Children
welcome Garden: patio, outdoor eating.
NOTES: Parking 50. **ROOMS:** 16 bedrooms 16 en suite
s£105 d£105 FR£125

WESTERN ISLES

ISLAY, ISLE OF

BALLYGRANT
Map 10 NR36

Ballygrant Inn ⌂
PA45 7QR ☎ 01496 840277 ▤ 01496 840277
e-mail: ballygrant-inn@isle-of-islay.freeserve.co.uk
Dir: NE of Isle of Islay, 3m from ferry terminal at Port Askaig
Situated in two and a half acres of grounds, this converted
farmhouse offers a warm welcome to tourists, walkers and
fishermen alike. Local ales and malt whiskies are served in the
bar, along with bar meals that include venison casserole,
grilled local scallops, and sirloin steaks. The restaurant menu
features crab, lamb cutlets, salmon and grilled trout among
others. Many of the ingredients used are locally produced.
Occasional folk or blues music.
continued

OPEN: 11-11 (Wkds 11-1am). **BAR MEALS:** L served all week. D served all week. Av main course £6.50. **RESTAURANT:** L served all week. D served all week. Av 3 course fixed price £16.
BREWERY/COMPANY: Free House **FACILITIES:** Children welcome Children's licence Garden: outdoor eating, patio Dogs allowed. **NOTES:** Parking 35. **ROOMS:** 3 bedrooms 3 en suite s£23.50 d£45 FR£55-£70

BOWMORE   Map 10 NR35

Pick of the Pubs

The Harbour Inn 🌑 🌑 🐑 ♀
The Square PA43 7JR ☎ 01496 810330
📧 01496 810990
e-mail: harbour@harbour-inn.com
This unpretentious little gem of an inn, wedged between the square and harbour of the island's capital, has undergone recent extensions of restaurant and conservatory that now look out from the water's edge across Lochindaal to the peaks of Jura beyond. Bedroom accommodation has also been up-graded to match, as business just keeps on growing and dinner reservations are virtually essential.
   The bar and lounge extend a warm winter welcome with an open peat fire and a bistro menu - at lunch only - that remains a showcase for chef/patron Scott Chances dedication to natural Scottish cooking. All the beef, lamb and game come from Islay and Jura and shellfish is collected directly from the quayside. Alongside freshly baked jumbo rolls and simply grilled steaks and lamb cutlets with home-made chips are Islay seafood chowder, crab fishcakes with tartare sauce and fresh Loch Gruinart oysters to start, followed by loin of local hare on a slice of haggis and stir-fried Lagavulin scallops and monkfish with soy and honey sauce. To round off, a Bavarois cream laced with 17-year-old Bowmore whisky comes with dark chocolate ice cream.
OPEN: 11-1am. **BAR MEALS:** L served Mon-Sat 12-2.30. Av main course £6.50. **RESTAURANT:** L served Mon-Sat. D served all week 12-2.30 6-9. Av 3 course à la carte £25.
BREWERY/COMPANY: Free House.
PRINCIPAL BEERS: McEwan 70/- & 80/-.
FACILITIES: Garden: Dogs allowed. **ROOMS:** 7 bedrooms 7 en suite s£42 d£70

AA inspected hotel accommodation

NORTH UIST

CARINISH   Map 12 NF86

Carinish Inn 🐑 **NEW**
☎ 01876 580673 📧 01876 580665
e-mail: carinishinn@macinnesbros.co.uk
Modern-style refurbished inn at Carinish, North Uist, convenient for the RSPB Balranald Nature Reserve and local archaeological sites. Fish features prominently on the set-price menu, including roast fillet of West Coast salmon, stuffed monkfish tail wrapped in bacon with stewed tomatoes and polenta, and seafood casserole in a creamy wine and herb sauce. Local artists perform every Saturday night.

OPEN: 11-11 (Thur-Sat 11-1am, Sun 12.30-11). **BAR MEALS:** L served all week. D served all week 12-2.30 6.30-9.30. Av main course £7.50. **RESTAURANT:** L served all week. D served all week 12-2.30 6.30-9.30. Av 3 course à la carte £15.
BREWERY/COMPANY: Free House **FACILITIES:** Children welcome. **NOTES:** Parking 50. **ROOMS:** 8 bedrooms 8 en suite s£45 d£65

SKYE, ISLE OF

ARDVASAR   Map 12 NG60

Ardvasar Hotel ★ ★ ♀
IV45 8RS ☎ 01471 844223 📧 01471 844495
Dir: From ferry terminal, 50yds & turn L

The second oldest inn on Skye, this well-appointed white-painted cottage-style hotel offers a warm, friendly welcome and acts as an ideal base for exploring the island, spotting the wildlife and enjoying the stunning scenery. Overlooking the Sound of Sleat, the Ardvasar is within walking distance of the Clan Donald Centre and the ferry at Armadale. Popular menus offers freshly-caught seafood, as well as baked venison in peppers and port wine pie, lamb and leek potato hotpot and savoury vegetable crumble. Straightforward basket meals are a perennial favourite.   *continued*

OPEN: 11-11. **BAR MEALS:** L served all week. D served all week 12-2.30 5.30-9.30. Av main course £10.50. **RESTAURANT:** D served all week 7.30-9. Av 3 course à la carte £24.50.
BREWERY/COMPANY: Free House. **PRINCIPAL BEERS:** 80/-.
FACILITIES: Children welcome Garden: Food served outside Dogs allowed. **NOTES:** Parking 30. **ROOMS:** 10 bedrooms 10 en suite s£50 d£80

ISLE ORNSAY
Map 12 NG71

Pick of the Pubs

Hotel Eilean Iarmain 🥄 🥄 ★ ★ 🐑
IV43 8QR ☎ 01471 833332 📠 01471 833275
e-mail: hotel@eilean-iarmain.co.uk
Dir: A851, A852 right to Isle Ornsay harbour front

A very special, 19th-century award-winning Hebridean hotel overlooking Isle Ornsay harbour - well-known to fans of Flora MacDonald - that enjoys spectacular sea views. Poets and artists are drawn here by its unique heritage and the Celtic heritage typified by the Celtic-speaking staff.

Morag Mac Donald claims that her guests will leave with their lives enriched: they will undoubtedly depart with well-satisfied appetites! Look first to the specials board for the likes of brandied crab and lobster bisque, roast monkfish tails with mushroom duxelle and tomato salsa and tian of raspberry tuilles served on a wild berry coulis.

Bar meals can be as simple as peppered mackerel with creamed horseradish, roast baby chicken with red wine and onion jus and hot apple sponge crumble with rum and raisin ice cream.
OPEN: 12-12 (12-2.30, 5-12 in winter).
BAR MEALS: L served all week. D served all week 12.30-2.30 6.30-9.30. Av main course £8. **RESTAURANT:** L served all week. D served all week 12.30-2 7.30-9. Av 3 course à la carte £25. Av 5 course fixed price £31.
BREWERY/COMPANY: Free House.
PRINCIPAL BEERS: McEwans 80/-. **FACILITIES:** Children welcome Garden: Food served outside Dogs allowed.
NOTES: Parking 30. **ROOMS:** 12 bedrooms 12 en suite s£90 d£120 FR£160-£190

🐑 Pubs offering a good choice of seafood on the menu.

SOUTH UIST

LOCHBOISDALE
Map 12 NF71

Polochar Inn 🐑
Polochar HS8 5TT ☎ 01878 700215 📠 01878 700768
Dir: From Lochboisdale travel W & take B888. Hotel at end of road
Overlooking the sea towards the islands of Eriskay and Barra, this superbly situated 18th-century inn enjoys beautiful sunsets. The bar menu offers fresh seafood dishes and steaks with various sauces, while restaurant fare includes venison, fresh scallops or steak pie.

OPEN: 11-11 (Fri 11-1, Sat 11-11.30, Sun 12.30-11).
BAR MEALS: L served all week. D served all week 12.30-2.30 6-9. Av main course £8. **RESTAURANT:** L served all week. D served all week 12-2.30 6-9. Av 3 course à la carte £15.
BREWERY/COMPANY: Free House. **FACILITIES:** Children welcome Garden: barbecue. **NOTES:** Parking 40. **ROOMS:** 11 bedrooms 11 en suite s£35 d£55

Jugs
Toby jugs grin cheerfully from their vantage points in many a pub interior. They were first made in the Staffordshire Potteries in the 18th century and the standard figure wears a black tricorn hat, holds a foaming jug of beer and sits in a chair whose sides are covered by the skirts of his ample topcoat. This is the Ordinary Toby, but connoisseurs distinguish between the Long Face, the Sharp Face and the Roman Nose variations. Numerous variants include the Sailor, the Squire, the Tipsy Man and the Drunken Parson. Other jugs represent famous figures of history or literature, from Nelson and Mr Gladstone to Falstaff and John Bull, while modern examples include Winston Churchill and Clark Gable. There are a few female Tobies, but essentially the jugs depict the jovial male toper, benevolent and beery.

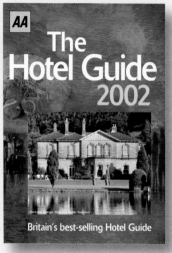

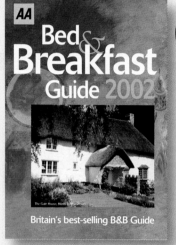

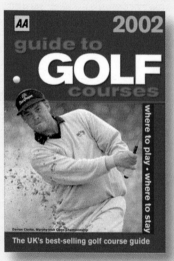
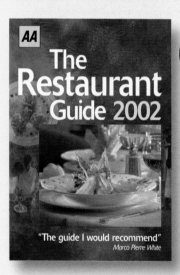

Wales

Pub of the Year for Wales

The Bear Hotel,
Crickhowell, Powys

WALES

BRIDGEND

KENFIG Map 03 SS88

Prince of Wales Inn ♀
CF33 4PR ☎ 01656 740356
Dir: M4 J37 into North Cornelly & follow signs for nature reserve, Kenfig
Dating from 1440, this stone-built inn has been many things in its time including a school, guildhall and courtroom. Why not sup some real cask ale in the bar by an inviting log fire? Typical menu includes steak and onion pie, lasagne, chicken and mushroom pie, and a variety of fish dishes. Look out for today's specials on the blackboard.
OPEN: 11-4 6-11 (Fri, Sat & Sun all day). **BAR MEALS:** L served all week. D served all week 12-2.30 7-9.30. Av main course £5.50.
RESTAURANT: 12-2.30 7-9.30. Av 3 course à la carte £14.
BREWERY/COMPANY: Free House. **PRINCIPAL BEERS:** Bass Triangle, Worthington Best, Brains, Thomas Watkin OSB.
FACILITIES: Children welcome Garden: Food served outside Dogs allowed Water, toys. **NOTES:** Parking 30

MAESTEG Map 03 SS89

Old House Inn 🐾 ♀
Llangynwyd CF34 9SB ☎ 01656 733310 ▤ 01656 737337
One of the oldest pubs in Wales, dating back to 1147, the Old House has a thatched roof, huge beams and walls over 3 feet thick. Lots of antiques and bric-à-brac illustrate the early days of the Welsh valleys. The fresh fish menu features trout, hake, cod and salmon. Other menu choices include grills, baked jacket potatoes, steak and ale pie, chicken curry, aubergine lasagne, and spinach and canneloni. Blackboard specials change every day.

OPEN: 11-11. **BAR MEALS:** L served all week. D served all week 11-2.30 6-10. Av main course £5. **RESTAURANT:** L served all week. D served all week 11-2.30 6-10. Av 3 course à la carte £14.
BREWERY/COMPANY: Whitbread.
PRINCIPAL BEERS: Flowers Original, Flowers IPA, Brains.
FACILITIES: Children welcome Children's licence Garden: outdoor eating, patio Dogs allowed. **NOTES:** Parking 150

CARDIFF

CARDIFF Map 03 ST17

Buff's Wine Bar & Restaurant
8 Mount Stuart Square CF10 5EE ☎ 029 20464628
▤ 029 20480715
Housed in a listed building at the heart of the former docklands - now being restored as Cardiff Bay's *continued*

commercial centre - business executives here lunch on game terrine with Cumberland sauce, deep-fried chevre with onion marmalade, and fish cakes in mild curry sauce. A la carte lunches above and evening dinner parties by arrangement.
OPEN: 11-11. Closed BHs. **BAR MEALS:** L served Mon-Fri 11.30-3.30. Av main course £5. **RESTAURANT:** L served Mon-Fri 12-2. Av 3 course à la carte £18. **BREWERY/COMPANY:** Free House **FACILITIES:** Garden: patio, outdoor eating

Cayo Arms NEW
36 Cathedral Rd CF11 9HL ☎ 02920 391910
e-mail: Manager@cayocardiff.plus.com
Dir: From Cardiff take Kingsway West turn R into Cathedral Road
Wales's newest brewery company has moved into Cardiff at this nationally-known bi-lingual pub on a leafy thoroughfare leading to the new stadium and city centre. In front is a large patio garden with umbrella-ed tables and patio heaters that add to the draw on Match Days of Tomos Watkins's ales. The same brew is used in a steak and ale pie and the batter for their celebrated fish and chips. Bedroom accommodation, though modest, is useful to know in the area.
OPEN: 12-11. **BAR MEALS:** L served all week. D served all week 12-6. Av main course £4.95. **BREWERY/COMPANY:** Tomos Watkin & Sons. **PRINCIPAL BEERS:** Watkins Brewery Bitter, OSB, Whoosh, Merlin Stout. **FACILITIES:** Garden: Food served outside. **NOTES:** Parking 30. **ROOMS:** 6 bedrooms 6 en suite s£29.50 d£29.50

CREIGIAU Map 03 ST08

Pick of the Pubs

Caesars Arms ◉ 🐾 ♀
Cardiff Rd CF15 9NN ☎ 029 20890486
▤ 029 20892176
Dir: 1m from M4 J34
Among the select band of offshoots of a successful central Cardiff enterprise, Caesar's is situated some ten miles out of town yet just a mile or so down winding lanes from the M4 (J34). A terrace overlooking the gardens and ubiquitous BMWs - and shaded by large umbrellas in summer - adds extra dining space to this ever-popular outlet.
Its basic formula is now well-known in these parts with fabulous fresh fish and meats displayed in shaved-ice counters, to be accompanied by breads, good hand-cut chips and self-served salads. From a vast choice, also highlighted on rarely-changing blackboards, select from crawfish tails in garlic butter and dressed local crab, followed by sea bass baked in rock salt and grilled lobster - charged according to weight.
The many alternatives include crispy honeyed duckling and fillet of beef Alicia, to be enjoyed at leisure with traditional ale or an impressive collection of French, Spanish and New World wines.
OPEN: 12-4.30 7-12. Closed 25 Dec. **BAR MEALS:** L served all week.D served all week 12-2.30 (3.30 Sun) 7-10.30. Av main course £5. **RESTAURANT:** L served all week. D served Mon-Sat 12-2.30 7-10.30. Av 3 course à la carte £17.50. **BREWERY/COMPANY:** Free House. **PRINCIPAL BEERS:** Hancocks. **FACILITIES:** Children welcome Garden: Food served outside. **NOTES:** Parking 100

ABERGORLECH
Map 02 SN53

The Black Lion
SA32 7SN ☎ 01558 685271
Dir: From Carmarthen take A40 eastwards, then B4310 signposted Brechfa & Abergorlech
Small 16th-century black and white inn with beams and flagstone floors situated on the banks of the River Cothi on the edge of the Brechfa Forest.

BRECHFA
Map 02 SN53

Forest Arms
SA32 7RA ☎ 01267 202339
Stone-built, early 19th-century inn nestling in a pretty village in the beautiful Cothi Valley. Fishing mementos adorn the unspoilt, traditional bars.

LLANARTHNE
Map 02 SN52

Golden Grove Arms ♀
SA32 8JU ☎ 01558 668551 ▤ 01558 668069
Dir: From end M4 take A48 towards Carmarthen, then R at Pantyeynon, 2 or 3m to Llanarthne
Visitors to the Towy Valley and Wales's National Botanic Garden will find Llanarthne mid-way between Carmarthen and Llandeilo. Up-to-date country accommodation and facilities in a natural rural setting draw the crowds to both bars and restaurant for home-cooked traditional and vegetarian cuisine. Extensive choices encompass local fish and butchers meats, various pasta options and a speciality range of curries, followed by numerous home-made desserts. Lots in the garden to occupy the children - and their own menu.
OPEN: 11-11. **BAR MEALS:** L served all week. D served all week. Av main course £6. **RESTAURANT:** L served all week. D served all week. Av 3 course à la carte £12.
BREWERY/COMPANY: Free House.
PRINCIPAL BEERS: Brains Buckleys Best, & Reverend James Original Ale. **FACILITIES:** Children welcome Garden: outdoor eating, patio. **NOTES:** Parking 40. **ROOMS:** 8 bedrooms 8 en suite s£35 d£45 FR£65-£70

LLANDDAROG
Map 02 SN51

White Hart Inn
SA32 8NT ☎ 01267 275395 ▤ 01267 275395
Dir: 6m E of Carmarthen towards Swansea, just off A48 on B4310, signed Llanddarog
Built in 1371, this thatched, stone pub originally housed the stone masons who built their first church next door. Heavy beams, stone fireplaces, and a wide-ranging menu. Cole's Family Brewery provides some of the ales.
OPEN: 11.30-3 6.30-11 (Sun 12-3 7-10.30). Closed Dec 25.
BAR MEALS: L served all week. D served all week 11.30-2 6.30-10. Av main course £5. **RESTAURANT:** L served all week. D served all week 11.30-2 6.30-10. Av 3 course à la carte £15.
BREWERY/COMPANY: Free House.
PRINCIPAL BEERS: Cwrw Blasus. **FACILITIES:** Children welcome Garden: patio/terrace, outdoor eating, BBQ, floral displays **NOTES:** Parking 50

LLANDEILO
Map 03 SN62

The Angel Inn ▥ ♀
Salem SA19 7LY ☎ 01558 823394 ▤ 01558 823371
Dir: A40 then B4302, turn L 1m after leaving A40 then turn R at T.Junct and travel 0.25m to Angel Inn. Located on the right hand side
Beamed ceilings and a large collection of interesting artefacts and pictures characterise this village pub, which comprises two bars and a 100-seater restaurant. There is popular bar food, a children's menu, a selection of vegetarian dishes and daily specials such as local sea trout and Cajun chicken.
OPEN: 5.30-12 (Sun 12-4). Closed 26 Dec-1 Jan. **BAR MEALS:** L served Sun. D served Mon-Sat 12-2 6.30-10. Av main course £5.
RESTAURANT: L served Sun. D served Mon-Sat 12-2 6.30-10. Av 3 course à la carte £12.50. **BREWERY/COMPANY:** Free House.
PRINCIPAL BEERS: Worthington, Highgate Dark Mild.
FACILITIES: Children welcome Garden: beer garden with seating, food served outside Dogs allowed. **NOTES:** Parking 60.
ROOMS: 3 bedrooms 3 en suite s£25 d£40 FR£50-£60

The Castle Brewery
113 Rhosmaen St SA19 6EN ☎ 01558 823446
e-mail: Simon@llandeilo.plus.com
19th-century Edwardian-style hotel within easy reach of Dinefwr Castle and wonderful walks through classic parkland. Charming tiled and partly green-painted back bar attracts plenty of locals, while the front bar and side area offers smart furnishings and the chance to relax in comfort over a drink. Enclosed rear courtyard is the venue for musical and artistic talents throughout the year.
    Extensive range of award-winning Tomas Watkins ales are available and good quality bar and restaurant food prepared with the finest of fresh local ingredients. Expect hearty dishes such as stout and beef casserole, fillet of lamb and plaice on the bone.
OPEN: 12-11 (Sun 12-10.30). **BAR MEALS:** L served all week. D served all week 12-2.30 6.30-9. Av main course £4.50.
RESTAURANT: D served Mon-Sat 7-9. Av 3 course à la carte £12.
BREWERY/COMPANY: Tomos Watkin & Sons.
PRINCIPAL BEERS: Watkins Best, OSB, Whoosh & Merlins Stout.
FACILITIES: Children welcome Garden: Enclosed courtyard, food served outside

The Cottage Inn ▥ ♀
Pentrefelin SA19 6SD ☎ 01558 822890 ▤ 01558 823309
Dir: On main A40 between Brecon & Carmarthen, 1.5 miles W of Llandeilo
Formerly the Nags Head Inn, this timbered coaching inn is now under new ownership. It is just 1.5 miles from Aberglasney Gardens and six miles from the National Botanical Gardens. Choose from the extensive bar menu or the à la carte selection, including the good range of fish.
OPEN: 12-3 6-12.30. Closed Dec 25. **BAR MEALS:** L served all week. D served all week 12-2.30 6-10. Av main course £6.
RESTAURANT: L served all week. D served all week 12-2.30 6-10. Av 3 course à la carte £16. **BREWERY/COMPANY:** Free House.
PRINCIPAL BEERS: Thomos Watkins, Boddingtons, Wadworth 6X, Felinfoel Double Dragon. **FACILITIES:** Children welcome Garden: Food served outside. **NOTES:** Parking 60.
ROOMS: 5 bedrooms 5 en suite

Wales

Wales

LLANDOVERY   Map 02 SN73

Neuadd Fawr Arms ♀ NEW
Cilycwm SA20 0ST ☎ 01550 721644
Dir: On the A40 take the A483 Builth Wells Rd, after 300 metres turn L at the crossroads continue along this rd for 3m and take 2nd l over river Bridge, continue to Cilycwm pub is on R
Traditional pub with slate floors, quarry tiles and oak boards among various character features. Peacefully situated in a picturesque village which lies on the route of an old drovers' trail, the inn is handy for exploring the Towy Valley and the Cambrian Mountains. Don't be surprised to see red kites swooping over the hills. Good range of real ales and wines, and a varied menu offering dishes made with freshly cooked ingredients and local produce. Expect wild mushroom tagliatelle, breast of duck, crab salad, and ratatouille au gratin.
BAR MEALS: L served all week. D served all week 12-2.30 6.30-9. Av main course £5.50. **RESTAURANT:** L served all week. D served all week 12-2.30 6.30-9. Av 3 course à la carte £14.
BREWERY/COMPANY: Free House.
PRINCIPAL BEERS: Tomos Watkin Whoosh, Brains Reverand James, Felinfoel Double Dragon. **FACILITIES:** Children welcome Garden: Food served outside. **NOTES:** Parking 15.
ROOMS: 2 bedrooms 2 en suite s£27.50 d£50

LLANDYBIE   Map 02 SN61

The Red Lion Inn NEW
SA18 3JB ☎ 01269 851202
Almost 300 years old, this historic inn retains the atmosphere and feel of the original pub. Several fireplaces and other original features remain to generate a friendly, welcoming environment in which to relax and enjoy good food and well kept real ales. The menu is created by a team of enthusiastic and professional chefs who have many years' experience between them. Dishes range from fillet of salmon with roast potato and spinach, to breast of chicken stuffed with Mozzarella and wrapped in Parma ham.
OPEN: 12-3 6-11. **BAR MEALS:** L served all week. D served all week 12-2 6-9.30. Av main course £9.
BREWERY/COMPANY: Bass. **PRINCIPAL BEERS:** Bass, Hancocks HB, Greene King IPA. **FACILITIES:** Children welcome Garden: Food served outside. **NOTES:** Parking 50

Brains Crown Buckley
Brains, the Cardiff-based brewery, has been in the Brain family since Samuel Brain and his uncle acquired the Old Brewery in the 1880s. In the spring of 1997 the company took over Crown Buckley to become the largest independent brewery in Wales. Among the popular brews are Brains Bitter (3.7%), Buckley's Dark Mild (3.4%) and Brains SA Best Bitter (4.2%). Brains also launched Dylan's beer several years ago. This premium smooth ale has a distinctive palate and is named after the poet Dylan Thomas. Brewery tours are planned for the future.

PONT-AR-GOTHI   Map 02 SN52

Pick of the Pubs

The Salutation Inn
SA32 7NH ☎ 01267 290336
Dir: On A40 between Carmarthen & Llandeilo
The 'Sal' as it is affectionately known to the locals, has long been pulling them in from as far away as Swansea and Llanelli. Partly, this can be put down to the lure of the Towy valley, with its lush farmland and excellent fishing, but the Salutation has always had its own attractions, not least a reputation for food that has strengthened under the stewardship of Richard and Sera Porter. It's a pub with history, character and a loyal following of colourful locals who congregate around the bar where Felinfoel Double Dragon is the preferred ale. Stripped floors, bare tables and candles are the defining features of both bar and restaurant areas where generous blackboards, offer a selection of broadly modern British dishes. In robust style, starters can include roast belly of pork with oriental stir fry and chicken liver feuillete with braised leeks whilst mains have included braised lamb shank with Colcannon mash or pan-fried halibut with salt cod dauphinoise potatoes.
OPEN: 12-3 6-12. **BAR MEALS:** L served all week. D served all week 12-2 6-9.30. Av main course £5.50.
RESTAURANT: L served Sun. D served all week 12-2 6-9.30. Av 3 course à la carte £17.50. **BREWERY/ COMPANY:** Felinfoel. **PRINCIPAL BEERS:** Felinfoel - Double Dragon, Dragon Bitter, Dragon Dark. **FACILITIES:** Children welcome Garden: Food served outside. **NOTES:** Parking 15

RHANDIRMWYN   Map 03 SN74

The Royal Oak Inn ♦♦♦
SA20 0NY ☎ 01550 760201 🖳 01550 760332
e-mail: royaloak@rhandirmwyn.com

Attractive 17th-century hillside inn, formerly Earl Cawdor's hunting lodge, in the hamlet of Rhandirmwyn, due north of Llandovery, and famed for its fine views over the upper Towy Valley. The Dinas bird reserve is literally on the doorstep. Stone interiors warmed by log fires, half-a-dozen real ales, home-cooked bar meals and beer garden. A typical menu includes lemon and tarragon turkey fillet, Welsh rump steak, veggieburger and chips, or grilled trout.
OPEN: 11.30-3 6-11. **BAR MEALS:** L served all week. D served all week 12-2.30 6-9.30. Av main course £6.50. **RESTAURANT:** L served all week. D served all week 12-2 6-9.30. **BREWERY/ COMPANY:** Free House. **PRINCIPAL BEERS:** Greene King Abbot Ale, Wadworth 6X, Burton. **FACILITIES:** Children welcome Garden: patio, outdoor eating Dogs allowed. **NOTES:** Parking 20. **ROOMS:** 5 bedrooms 3 en suite s£22.50 d£25

RHOS   Map 02 SN33

Lamb of Rhos ♈
SA44 5EE ☎ 01559 370055
Country inn with flagstone floors, beamed ceilings and open fires - as well as its own jail and the 'seat to nowhere'. A menu of traditional pub fare includes steaks, chops, mixed grill, vegetarian and vegan dishes all cooked on the premises.
OPEN: 12-11. **BAR MEALS:** L served all week. D served all week 12-2 6-9. **RESTAURANT:** L served Sun. D served Fri-Sat 12-2 7-9. **BREWERY/COMPANY:** Free House.
PRINCIPAL BEERS: Banks Original. **FACILITIES:** Children welcome Garden: outdoor eating, patio Dogs allowed garden only. **NOTES:** Parking 50.
ROOMS: 4 bedrooms 4 en suite s£25 d£35 No credit cards

CEREDIGION

CARDIGAN   Map 02 SN14

Black Lion Hotel NEW
High St SA43 1HJ ☎ 01239 612532
e-mail: manager@blacklion.plus.com
Dir: On the A487 through Cardigan, 20 miles north of Fishguard
Once a 'one-room grog-shop' dating back to 1105, the Black Lion lays claim to being one of Wales's oldest coaching inns. Today, in the hands of the country's youngest brewery it offers comfortable town-centre accommodation - opposite the historic castle - in an evocative atmosphere. Tomos Watkins's ale beefs up the steak and ale pie and fresh locally-landed crab, lobster and sewin fill out a seasonal menu of well-tried specialities: in the bar creamy garlic mussels, vegetable curry and lasagne verdi and on the restaurant menu Welsh laverbread with cockles, pork chops with black pudding and generous steaks with optional extra sauces.
BAR MEALS: L served all week. D served all week 12-2.30 6-9. Av main course £4.95. **RESTAURANT:** L served all week. D served all week 12-2.30 6-9. Av 3 course à la carte £15.
BREWERY/COMPANY: Tomos Watkin & Sons.
PRINCIPAL BEERS: Watkins Woosh, Brewery Bitter, OSB & Dark.
FACILITIES: Children welcome. **NOTES:** Parking 20.
ROOMS: 14 bedrooms 14 en suite s£30 d£40 FR£40

Webley Hotel ◆◆◆
Poppit Sands SA43 3LN ☎ 01239 612085
Dir: A484 from Carmarthen to Cardigan, then to St Dogmaels, turn R in village centre to Poppit Sands

Located on the coastal path, and within walking distance of Poppit Sands, this hotel overlooks the Teifi Estuary and Cardigan Island. Bar food ranges from haddock and trout, to daily specials like pork with lemongrass and ginger, chicken in cream and mustard sauce, or beef barolo.   *continued*

OPEN: 11.30-3 6.30-11.30. Closed 25 Dec. **BAR MEALS:** L served all week. D served all week 11.30-2 6.30-9. Av main course £5.80. **BREWERY/COMPANY:** Free House.
PRINCIPAL BEERS: Bass, Brains Buckleys Bitter.
FACILITIES: Children welcome Garden: Food served outside Dogs allowed garden only. **NOTES:** Parking 60.
ROOMS: 8 bedrooms 5 en suite s£21 d£42 No credit cards

LLWYNDAFYDD   Map 02 SN35

Crown Inn
SA44 6BU ☎ 01545 560396   ▤ 01545 560857
e-mail: anthony.amss@virgin.net
Dir: Off A487 NE of Cardigan
Traditional 18th-century Welsh longhouse with original beams and open fireplaces, close to Cardigan Bay. The delightful, award-winning garden is one of the pub's main attractions, its tree-sheltered setting, pond and colourful flowers attracting many customers.
From the inn it's an easy walk down the lane to a cove where there are caves and National Trust cliffs. Plenty to choose from among the bar specials, including beef steak braised in red wine and mushrooms and grilled whole lemon sole with a anchovy, caper and lemon butter. Extensive bar menu and wine list.
OPEN: 12-3 6-11. **BAR MEALS:** L served all week. D served all week 12-2 6-9. Av main course £7.50. **RESTAURANT:** L served By appointment only. D served all week 12-2.30 6.30-9. Av 3 course à la carte £19. **BREWERY/COMPANY:** Free House.
PRINCIPAL BEERS: Flowers Original & IPA, Wadworth 6X, Courage Directors, Tomos Watkins OSB. **FACILITIES:** Children welcome Garden: Food served outside Dogs allowed, Garden only, water. **NOTES:** Parking 80

CONWY

ABERGELE   Map 08 SH97

Pick of the Pubs

Kinmel Arms ◉ 🍴
St George LL22 9BP ☎ 01745 832207   ▤ 01745 832207
Dir: from Bodelwyddan towards Abergele take slip road at St George. Take 1st L and Kinmel Arms is on L at top of hill
In a village conservation area on the edge of Kinmel Estate, a civilised dining pub that nonetheless remains a true local. Daily bar meals, listed on blackboards, are taken in the lounge bar and conservatory - a great summer draw.
Choices range from the simplest cod in beer batter and steak and ale pie to Cajun-spiced salmon, vegetable moussaka and chargrilled chicken Caesar salad. Dining room menus with an accent on local fish include home-smoked salmon, sea bass with vierge dressing and skate wing with caper butter. Alternatives include Kinmel venison with local elderberry sauce. Round off with lemon tart served with lemon mousse. Sunday lunch.
OPEN: 12-3 7-11. **BAR MEALS:** L served all week. D served all week 12-2 7-9. Av main course £6.25. **RESTAURANT:** L served all week. D served all week 12-2 7-9. Av 3 course à la carte £14.50. Av 3 course fixed price £13.95.
BREWERY/COMPANY: Free House.
PRINCIPAL BEERS: Marstons Bitter & Pedigree, Thwaites.
FACILITIES: Children welcome Garden: outdoor eating, patio, BBQ Dogs allowed. **NOTES:** Parking 40

BETWS-Y-COED Map 08 SH75

Ty Gwyn Hotel ◆◆◆◆ 🛏️
LL24 0SG ☎ 01690 710383 710787 📠 01690 710383
Dir: At Juction of A5/A470, 100 yards S of Waterloo Bridge.
Former coaching inn with old world characteristics situated
overlooking the River Conwy amid marvellous mountain
scenery. Good home-cooked food includes local pheasant and
fresh salmon in the bar, and in the restaurant perhaps
marinated fillet of kangaroo, chargrilled sea bass, and lobster
thermidor.
OPEN: 12-2 7-11.30. **BAR MEALS:** L served all week. D served
all week 12-2 7-9. Av main course £5.95. **RESTAURANT:** L
served Sun. D served all week 12-2 7-9. Av 3 course à la carte
£17.95. **BREWERY/COMPANY:** Free House.
PRINCIPAL BEERS: Wadworth 6X, Boddingtons.
FACILITIES: Children welcome. **NOTES:** Parking 12.
ROOMS: 12 bedrooms 9 en suite s£20 d£34

CAPEL CURIG Map 08 SH75

Cobdens Hotel ★ ★ 🍷
LL24 0EE ☎ 01690 720243 📠 01690 720354
e-mail: info@cobdens.co.uk
Dir: On A5, 4m N of Betws-Y-Coed
Situated at the foot of Moel Siabod in the heart of Snowdonia,
this 250-year-old inn is a popular centre for outdoor pursuits.
The emphasis is on wholesome food prepared from fresh local
ingredients. The evening menu might offer roast leg of lamb
stuffed with apricots, root vegetable curry with coconut, and
baked chicken breast with pomme fondant and white wine
and tarragon cream sauce.
OPEN: 11-11 (Sun 12-10.30). **BAR MEALS:** L served all week.
D served all week 12-2.30 6.30-9. Av main course £7.50.
RESTAURANT: L served all week. D served all week 12-2.30
6.30-9. **BREWERY/COMPANY:** Free House.
PRINCIPAL BEERS: Greene King Old Speckled Hen.
FACILITIES: Children welcome Garden: outdoor eating, patio
Dogs allowed. **NOTES:** Parking 35. **ROOMS:** 16 bedrooms
16 en suite s£29.50 d£59 FR£71-£83

CONWY Map 08 SH77

The Groes Inn ★ ★ ★ 🛏️
LL32 8TN ☎ 01492 650545 📠 01492 650855
*Dir: Off A55 to Conwy, L at mini r'about by Conwy castle onto B5106,
2 1/2m inn on R*
Built around 500 years ago in the River Conwy Valley, the
Groes Inn gained its licence in 1573, reputedly making it the
first Licenced House in Wales. The focus is on local fish - try
the popular seafood platter and finish with one of the
delicious home-made ice creams. Home-made bread is also a
popular feature of the menu
OPEN: 12-3 6.30-11. **BAR MEALS:** L served all week. D served
all week 12-2.15 6.30-9. Av main course £8. **RESTAURANT:** L
served all week. D served all week 12-2.15 6.30-9. Av 3 course
fixed price £25. **BREWERY/COMPANY:** Free House.
PRINCIPAL BEERS: Tetley, Burton Ale. **FACILITIES:** Children
welcome Garden: **NOTES:** Parking 90. **ROOMS:** 14 bedrooms
14 en suite s£64 d£81

GWYTHERIN Map 08 SH86

Lion Inn 🍷
LL22 8UU ☎ 01745 860244
Dir: 3m off A548 (Llanrwst/Abergele rd) on B5384
The original inn dates back some 300 years, but has been
gradually extended over the last century. It is located in a
historic village surrounded by beautiful countryside.
Food ranges from snacks and beer-battered cod in the bar,
to Anglesey eggs and fillet steak in the restaurant.
OPEN: 12-3 7-11 (Times may vary ring for details).
BAR MEALS: L served Tue-Sun. D served Tue-Sun 12-2 7-9. Av
main course £5. **RESTAURANT:** L served Tue-Sun. D served
Tue-Sun 12-2 7-9. Av 3 course à la carte £12. Av 3 course fixed
price £12. **BREWERY/COMPANY:** Free House.
PRINCIPAL BEERS: Marstons Pedigree. **FACILITIES:** Children
welcome Children's licence Garden: patio, outdoor eating,
Dogs allowed basket, food, water, blankets. **NOTES:** Parking 15.
ROOMS: 6 bedrooms 6 en suite s£27 d£40 FR£45

LLANDUDNO JUNCTION Map 08 SH87

Pick of the Pubs

The Queens Head 🛏️ 🍷
Glanwydden LL31 9JP ☎ 01492 546570
📠 01492 546487
*Dir: Take A470 from A55 towards Llandudno, at 3rd roundabout
R towards Penrhyn Bay, then 2nd R into Glanwydden, pub on L*
A short drive inland from the sea-front, the Curetons'
celebrated pub is well worth seeking out for its range of
good food that relies in large part on local Welsh produce
served in imaginative guises.
Daily fish dishes relying on Conwy salmon, fresh local
mussels and scallops are some of the highlights of a
lengthy menu that also includes braised Welsh Black beef,
possibly in a wild mushroom and Madeira sauce, and
grilled venison sausages with red wine and onion gravy.
Open 'tasty baps' and steak rolls with sautéed onions are
a lunchtime feature, supplemented by pasta, salads and
vegetarian dishes - typically asparagus and mushroom
pancakes with Napoli sauce.
The speciality seafood platter of smoked and fresh
seafood comes in single or double portions with dipping
sauce and new potatoes. In addition to home-made
chocolate brandy trifle and hot cherry Bakewell tart,
cheeses include local goats' and smoked Cheddar from
Llanrwst in the Conwy valley.
OPEN: 11-3 6-11 (Sun 11-10.30). Closed 25 Dec.
BAR MEALS: L served all week. D served all week 12-2.15
6-9. **RESTAURANT:** L served all week. D served all week
12-2.15 6-9. **BREWERY/COMPANY:** Vanguard.
PRINCIPAL BEERS: Tetley, Burton. **FACILITIES:** Patio, food
served outside **NOTES:** Parking 20

LLANNEFYDD Map 08 SH97

The Hawk & Buckle Inn
LL16 5ED ☎ 01745 540249 📠 01745 540316
e-mail: hawkandbuckle@btinternet.com
Situated 200m up in the hills, this 17th-century coaching inn
affords wonderful views over rolling fields to the sea beyond.
Menus offer a good choice of food based on local produce.

LLANRWST

Map 08 SH86

White Horse Inn ♦♦♦♦ ⬚
Capel Garmon LL26 0RW ☎ 01690 710271
⬚ 01690 710721
e-mail: whitehorse@supanet.com
A striking collection of Victorian pottery and china hangs from the beamed ceiling of this 400-year-old inn. Bar meals are served every evening and traditional roasts for Sunday lunch. Restaurant dishes include fillet steak in a Stilton and cream sauce, or the chef's special lamb. Bedrooms come with the expected facilities.
OPEN: 12-3 6-11 (Sun 12-2.30 6-10.30). **BAR MEALS:** L served Wed, Sat-Sun. D served all week 12-2 6.30-9.30. Av main course £6.50. **RESTAURANT:** D served Wed-Sun 7-9.30. Av 3 course à la carte £18. **BREWERY/COMPANY:** Free House. **PRINCIPAL BEERS:** Bass, Black Sheep. **FACILITIES:** Children welcome Garden: outdoor eating, patio Dogs allowed not overnight, water. **NOTES:** Parking 30. **ROOMS:** 6 bedrooms 6 en suite s£30 d£56

DENBIGHSHIRE

BODFARI

Map 08 SJ07

The Dinorben Arms ⬚ ⬚
LL16 4DA ☎ 01745 710309 ⬚ 01745 710580
e-mail: info@dinorbenarms.com
Dir: Come off A55 onto B5122 through Caerwys, R onto A541, R after 2.5m in Bodfari. Pub 100yrds of B541 next to church
Heavily beamed 17th-century inn with tiered patios and hillside gardens. The inn has its own private wine cellar and an extensive range of malt whiskies, including many from long closed distilleries. Food options encompass Scandinavian-style smörgasbord, farmhouse buffets, a weekend carvery, children's menu and traditional bar food. Steaks, Welsh lamb and fresh local salmon all feature in the home-made dishes.
OPEN: 12-3 6-11.30 (Sun 12-11). **BAR MEALS:** L served all week. D served all week 12-3 6-10.30. Av main course £6. **RESTAURANT:** L served all week. D served all week 12-3 6-10.30. **BREWERY/COMPANY:** Free House. **PRINCIPAL BEERS:** Tetley, Batemans, Greene King Old Speckled Hen. **FACILITIES:** Children welcome Garden: patio, outdoor eating Dogs allowed Garden only. **NOTES:** Parking 120

LLANGOLLEN

Map 08 SJ24

The Famous Britannia Inn
Horseshoe Pass LL20 8DW ☎ 01978 860144
⬚ 01978 860144
e-mail: brit@globalnet.co.uk
Dir: From Llangollen take A542 N 2m
14th-century coaching inn set in its own award-winning gardens with beautiful views of the Vale of Llangollen. Situated at the foot of the famous Horseshoe Pass.

LLANYNYS

Map 08 SJ16

Cerrigllwydion Arms
LL16 4PA ☎ 01745 890247 ⬚ 01745 890247
Dir: A525 towards Denbigh, R after 1.5m, then L and 1m to pub
Rambling inn built in about 1400 by Edward Edwards, attorney of Cerrigllwydion Hall, for the benefit of his churchgoers. Atmospheric rooms and a pleasant garden with views of the Clwydian Hills. Typical menu includes grills, steak kidney and ale pie, lamb cutlets in honey and mustard, duck on the bone and salmon fillet in prawn and cream sauce. Bar menu also available.
continued

OPEN: 12-3 7-11 (closed Mon). **BAR MEALS:** L served Tue-Sun 12-2. Av main course £5.50. **RESTAURANT:** L served Tue-Sun. D served Tue-Sun 12-2 7-9. Av 3 course à la carte £12.
BREWERY/COMPANY: Free House. **PRINCIPAL BEERS:** Bass, Tetley. **FACILITIES:** Children welcome Garden: lawned with picnic tables. **NOTES:** Parking 50

RUTHIN

Map 08 SJ15

Pick of the Pubs

Ye Olde Anchor Inn
2 Rhos St LL15 1DY ☎ 01824 702813 ⬚ 01824 703050
e-mail: hotel@anchorinn.co.uk
Dir: at jct of A525 and A494
In the originally mediaeval town of Ruthin, the Anchor stands out as a base for touring the Conwy coast, Preseli hills and Snowdonia: Chester, Shrewsbury, Llangollen and Caernarfon are all within an easy drive. A relaxed atmosphere permeates the bar and restaurant whose food output is clearly home made. Chicken satay and mushrooms stuffed with spinach and cream cheese are typical starters, followed by scallops with black pudding, chicken breast in Boursin sauce and carpet-bag or Chateaubriand steaks. Crème brûlée, crepes Suzette and bananas in rum and toffee sauce are typical desserts. Recently extended accommodation offers up-to-date facilities at competitive prices with a hearty breakfast to set overnight guests happily on their way.
OPEN: 11-11 (till 10.30 Sun). **BAR MEALS:** L served all week 12-2.30. Av main course £7. **RESTAURANT:** D served all week 7-10. Av 3 course à la carte £16.80.
BREWERY/COMPANY: Free House.
PRINCIPAL BEERS: Bass. **FACILITIES:** Children welcome Children's licence Dogs allowed. **NOTES:** Parking 20.
ROOMS: 26 bedrooms 26 en suite s£34.50 d£49 FR£65

Pick of the Pubs

White Horse Inn
Hendrerwydd LL16 4LL ☎ 01824 790218
Mid-way between Ruthin and Denbigh turn up narrow, winding lanes in the foothills of the Clwydian Range to happen upon this straggly old inn that looks something and nothing from the outside. Such a delight then to enjoy such a warm welcome from landlord Vit and competent modern European and Celtic cooking by his wife Ruth Vintr, a happy London emigré. Simple home-baked ham with two eggs and chips or warm chicken and bacon salad are served in style, though a more special lunch might consist of mushroom and tarragon pâté, lamb skewers with roast garlic dip and banana crêpe with ice cream. Ruth's cooking comes into its own by night when dining room menus proceed enticingly to spicy chicken cakes with Thai red curry, fresh provençale sea bass or Welsh ribeye steak with creamy Stilton sauce, followed by a host of desserts (Mr Jones's chocolate mousse and the ever-popular Eton Mess) or a commendable platter of natural Welsh cheeses.
OPEN: 12-2.30 6-11. **BAR MEALS:** L served all week. D served all week. Av main course £4.50. **RESTAURANT:** L served all week. D served all week. Av 3 course à la carte £20.
PRINCIPAL BEERS: Changing guest ales.
FACILITIES: Children welcome Garden: Food served outside Dogs allowed. **NOTES:** Parking 50 No credit cards

Wales

Wales

ST ASAPH   Map 08 SJ07

Pick of the Pubs

The Plough Inn 🍽 🍷
The Roe LL17 0LU ☎ 01745 585080 🖹 01745 585363
Dir: Rhyl/St Asaph turning from A55, L at rdbt, pub 200yds on L

Unparallelled in the country, the development of this 18th-century former coaching inn over the past two years has been remarkable, and now comprises a real ale bar, up-market bistro, an Italian-themed art deco restaurant and a wine shop. Standing just out of town on the original Holyhead-to-London road, it buzzes with activity throughout the day and has become a notable dining venue by night - winner of the Welsh Seafood Pub of the Year in 2001. Taking horseracing as its principal theme, the Paddock Bar offers a quick bite menu to accompany beers principally from local micro-breweries while the Racecourse Bistro, with its mural of Chester racecourse, features a fresh fish display, assorted steaks from the chargrill and house specialities from cod in beer batter with real chips to braised shank of Welsh lamb with roasted vegetables and crushed garlic potatoes. An entirely separate menu in Graffiti Italiano offers pizzas and pasta in many guises, in addition to such dishes as veal medallions with mushrooms, cream and herb risotto.
OPEN: 10-11. **BAR MEALS:** L served all week. D served all week 12-3 6-10. Av main course £6.95. **RESTAURANT:** L served all week. D served all week 12-3 6-10. Av 3 course à la carte £10.95. Av 2 course fixed price £9.95. **BREWERY/COMPANY:** Free House. **PRINCIPAL BEERS:** Greene King Old Speckled Hen, Shepherd Neame Spitfire,. **FACILITIES:** Children welcome Garden: outdoor eating, patio, BBQ Dogs allowed. **NOTES:** Parking 200

FLINTSHIRE

BABELL   Map 08 SN83

Black Lion Inn
CH8 8PZ ☎ 01352 720239
Dir: From Holywell take B5121 towards A541 (Mold to Denbigh road) & take 2nd R to Babell
Once used as a retreat for drovers, this grade II listed, 13th-century former farmhouse has been run by the present management since 1966. The restaurant and bar menus change constantly and might feature crispy roast duckling with black cherry sauce, fillet steak en croute, tenderloin of pork or sweet and sour chicken. Pheasant and wild salmon are available in season.
OPEN: 7pm-11pm (Open morning 1st Sun each month). **BAR MEALS:** D served Fri-Sat 7.30-9.30. Av main course £8.50.
continued

RESTAURANT: D served Fri-Sat 7.15-9.30. Av 3 course à la carte £17.50. **BREWERY/COMPANY:** Free House.
PRINCIPAL BEERS: Boddingtons. **NOTES:** Parking 80.
ROOMS: 2 bedrooms 2 en suite s£25 d£30

CILCAIN   Map 08 SJ16

White Horse Inn
CH7 5NN ☎ 01352 740142 🖹 01352 740142
e-mail: cjeory@packardbell.org
Dir: From Mold take A541 towards Denbigh. After approx 6m turn L
Situated in a lovely hillside village, the inn is several hundred years old and very popular with walkers, cyclists, horse-riders and people out for a drive in the beautiful surrounding countryside. The dishes are home-made by the landlord's wife using only the best quality ingredients - local wherever possible - including steak and kidney pie, ham and eggs, lamb tajine and various curries.
OPEN: 12-3 6.30-11 (Sat-Sun 12-11). **BAR MEALS:** L served all week. D served all week 12-2 7-9. Av main course £6.
BREWERY/COMPANY: Free House.
PRINCIPAL BEERS: Marstons Pedigree, Banks Bitter, Greene King Abbot Ale. **FACILITIES:** Garden: patio, food served outdoors Dogs allowed. **NOTES:** Parking 12

HALKYN   Map 08 SJ27

Britannia Inn
Pentre Rd CH8 8BS ☎ 01352 780272
e-mail: sarah.pollitt@britanniainn.freeserve.co.uk
Dir: Off A55 on B5123
500-year-old stone pub on an old coach route between Chester and Holyhead, with views over the Dee estuary and Wirral. It features a family farm with chickens, ducks and donkeys. Typical dishes are honey lamb steak, poached salmon fillet, Cumberland sausage, and gammon steak.
OPEN: 11-11 (Sun 12-10.30). **BAR MEALS:** L served all week. D served all week 12-2.30 6.30-9. Av main course £6.
RESTAURANT: L served all week. D served all week 12-2.30 6.30-9. Av 3 course à la carte £10. **BREWERY/COMPANY:** J W Lees. **PRINCIPAL BEERS:** Lees Bitter, GM Mild & Moonraker. **FACILITIES:** Children welcome Garden: outdoor eating, patio. **NOTES:** Parking 40

LIXWM   Map 08 SJ17

The Crown Inn
CH8 8NQ ☎ 01352 781112
Dir: Off the B5121 S of Holywell
Early 17th-century inn enjoying a pretty village setting near the Clwydian Mountains and the Offa's Dyke Path. Coming under new management at the time of going to press.

MOLD   Map 08 SJ26

The Druid Inn
Ruthin Rd, Llanferres CH7 5SN ☎ 01352 810225
Dir: A494 from Mold, Druid 4 1/2m along road on R
At this 17th-century coaching inn, overlooking the Alyn Valley and the Craig Harris mountains, a daily blackboard menu features decent home-cooked food such as braised shoulder of lamb in red wine, salmon wrapped in bacon with hollandaise, steak, ale and mushroom pie, and imaginatively-filled granary baps.
OPEN: 11.30-3 5.30-11 (Sat, Sun & BH 11.30-11). **BAR MEALS:** L served all week. D served all week 12-3 6-10 (12-10 Sat, Sun & BH). Av main course £8.25. **RESTAURANT:** L served all week.
continued

D served all week 12-3 6-10. Av 3 course à la carte £14.
BREWERY/COMPANY: Burtonwood. **PRINCIPAL BEERS:** Burtonwood Best Bitter & changing guest ale. **FACILITIES:** Children welcome Garden: Dogs allowed. **NOTES:** Parking 40.
ROOMS: 5 bedrooms 1 en suite s£30 d£38.50

NORTHOP Map 08 SJ26

Pick of the Pubs

Stables Bar Restaurant 🛏 ♀
Soughton Hall CH7 6AB ☎ 01352 840577
📠 01352 840382
Dir: from A55, take A5119 through Northop village

A purpose-built destination pub in the Grade I listed stables of the former Bishop of Chester's Palace that delivers all that it promises. The ground floor contains a real ale bar with an impressive variety of bar food available, whereas upstairs diners will find an open-plan kitchen and an adjacent, fully-stocked wine shop. Point out your chosen fresh fish, seafood or steaks and they will be cooked to order, accompanied by fresh breads, hand-cut chips and a self-served salad. Roast vegetables and red wine jus grace the roast shanks of lamb and with whole sea bass come wilted greens, a medley of carrot and courgettes and a fish-scented champagne cream sauce. Literally next door is the Hall itself, a magnificent pile offering splendid country-house bedrooms; particularly popular for weddings and special events in a unique setting.
OPEN: 11-3 6-11.30. **BAR MEALS:** L served all week. D served all week 12-2.30 7-10. Av main course £5.
RESTAURANT: L served all week. D served all week 12-2.30 7-10. Av 3 course à la carte £25. **BREWERY/COMPANY:** Free House. **PRINCIPAL BEERS:** Shepherd Neame Spitfire, Coach House Dick turpin. **FACILITIES:** Children welcome Garden: outdoor eating, patio, Dogs allowed.
ROOMS: 15 bedrooms 15 en suite s£80 d£100 FR£150

On the Inside

The earliest pubs were people's homes and were furnished and decorated accordingly. It was not until the 1820s that the bar-counter made its appearance, but already a distinction had grown up between the taproom for labourers and poorer customers, and the parlour began to sport carpets, pictures of the royal family and cases of butterflies or stuffed birds. The Victorian gin palaces introduced an altogether plushier style.

The big brewing chains have intruded a fake and regimental note into pub decor, but many pubs still nostalgically display Toby jugs or horse-brasses, agricultural bygones, ornamental brass plates or gleaming copper pans.

Some maintain their individuality with collections of oddities that have taken the landlord's fancy - police equipment or cigarette cards, neckties or man traps, or even fossilised hot cross buns.

Wales

GWYNEDD

ABERDYFI Map 08 SN69

Dovey Inn 🛏 ♀
Seaview Ter LL35 0EF ☎ 01654 767332 📠 01654 767996
e-mail: doveyinn@aol.com
Historic inn on the estuary of the River Dovey, only 20 yards from the sea and the fine sandy beach. The village clings to the hills above the estuary, once a major slate port and now a sailing centre. An extensive seafood menu varies from mussels and clams on bruschetta to chargrilled monkfish. There is also a good choice of snacks, meat and vegetarian options.

OPEN: 11-11 (Sun 12-10.30). **BAR MEALS:** L served all week. D served all week 12-2.30 6-9.30. Av main course £7.25.
BREWERY/COMPANY: Free House. **PRINCIPAL BEERS:** Hancocks HB, Bass. **FACILITIES:** Children welcome Children's licence Patio, food served outside Dogs allowed. **ROOMS:** 8 bedrooms 8 en suite s£79 d£59

Pick of the Pubs

Penhelig Arms Hotel ★ ★ ♀
Terrace Rd LL35 0LT ☎ 01654 767215 ▤ 01654 767690
e-mail: penheligarms@saqnet.co.uk
Dir: On A493 (coastal rd) W of Machynlleth

A studiedly informal family-run hotel and restaurant, formerly voted Welsh Seafood Pub of the Year, this is a jewel on the north-west Wales coastline, enjoying spectacular views across the tidal Dyfi estuary.

Guests, many returning times over, enjoy a warm and relaxed atmosphere in the bar with its unique central hearth or lounge in fine weather on the sea wall opposite awaiting delivery of ever-enticing food.

Fresh fish, lobster and crabs arrive literally from the quay and solid reliance on local produce is evidenced by menus that are up-dated twice daily. There might be mullet fillets grilled with a chilli, ginger and garlic butter, fillet of cod with spinach mash and prawn sauce or seared salmon fillets with linguini and red pesto dressing. Pwdin (Welsh puddings) embrace fresh fruit meringue with raspberry sauce and apricot frangipane tart.

Robert Hughes's monthly house wine list never disappoints: start in the dining-room with a chilled glass of champagne, though 'Dim Ysmygu' relates to this area's restrictions on nicotine abuse. Beautifully furnished en suite bedrooms are comfortable and well maintained; all but one share the estuary views.
OPEN: 11.30-3.30 5.30-11 (Sun 12-3.30, 6-10.30). Closed Dec 25-26. **BAR MEALS:** L served all week. D served all week 12-2.30 6.30-9.30. Av main course £7.95. **RESTAURANT:** L served all week. D served all week 12-2.30 7-9.30. Av 3 course à la carte £21. Av 3 course fixed price £22.
BREWERY/COMPANY: Free House.
PRINCIPAL BEERS: Tetley, Brains SA, Greene King Abbot Ale, Adnams Broadside. **FACILITIES:** Children welcome Children's licence Garden: outdoor eating, patio, seaside seating area Dogs allowed. **NOTES:** Parking 12.
ROOMS: 14 bedrooms 14 en suite s£42 d£70 FR£70-£88 + 10 child per night

See Pub Walk on page 577

St Tudwal's Inn ♀
High St LL53 7DS ☎ 01758 712539 ▤ 01758 713701
Dir: take A499 from Pwllheli, follow one way system, pub on R
A Victorian building, now converted to provide two bars and a restaurant, believed to be haunted by a Victorian lady. Steaks are a popular option, alongside dishes such as sea bass poached in sherry with julienne peppers, duck with port, cream and mushroom sauce, and lamb cutlets with wine gravy.
OPEN: 11-11 (Sun 12-10.30). **BAR MEALS:** L served all week. D served all week 12-2.30 6-9. Av main course £6.25.
RESTAURANT: D served all week 6-9. Av 3 course à la carte £17.50. **PRINCIPAL BEERS:** Robinsons Best, Hatters Mild.
FACILITIES: Children welcome Garden: outdoor eating, patio Dogs allowed. **NOTES:** Parking 20.
ROOMS: 6 bedrooms 5 en suite s£25 d£45 FR£60

The Miners Arms
Llechwedd Slate Caverns LL41 3NB ☎ 01766 830306
▤ 01766 831260
Dir: Blaenau Ffestiniog is 25 miles from Llandudno on the N Wales coast, situated on the A4 to main N-S Trunk Rd
On the site of one of Wales's leading tourist attractions - Llechwedd Slate Caverns - this pub was originally two miners cottages. Expect slate floors, open fires and staff in Victorian costume.
OPEN: 11am-5.30pm only. Closed Nov, Jan, Feb.
BREWERY/COMPANY: Free House **FACILITIES:** Children welcome Garden: outdoor eating, patio Dogs allowed

The Halfway House
LL40 2UE ☎ 01341 430635
Dir: On A436 between Dolgellau & Barmouth
Dating back to 1700, the Halfway House has recently changed hands and, among other refurbishment work, the new licensees have installed mellow pine chapel pews and reopened the fireplaces, giving the place a welcoming, cosy atmosphere. Situated near the Mawddach estuary, much loved by Wordsworth, the pub is directly on the route of several popular local walks. Good range of cask conditioned ales, several of which are from local breweries, and an impressive range of specials, including Cape Cod chicken, pork ribs and local lamb chops with a leek and Stilton sauce.
OPEN: 11-11 (Sun 12-10.30). Closed Dec 25. **BAR MEALS:** L served all week. D served all week 12-2.30 6-9.30. Av main course £7. **RESTAURANT:** L served all week. D served all week 12-2.30 6-9.30. **BREWERY/COMPANY:** Free House.
PRINCIPAL BEERS: Courage Directors, Wye Valley Dorothy Goodbody's, Brain's, Flannery's. **FACILITIES:** Children welcome Garden: outdoor eating, patio/terrace, BBQ Dogs allowed.
NOTES: Parking 30

Wales

*Pub*WALK

Penhelig Arms, Aberdyfi

PENHELIG ARMS,
ABERDYFI ⊛ ★ ★
Terrace Road LL35 0LT.
Tel: 01654 767215
Directions: on A493 (coast
road) W of Machynlleth
*In a wonderful location just
metres from the Dyfi estuary
with a fine backdrop of
mountains, this 1650s inn is a
delight. Character bar, alfresco
eating by the sea wall, and
menus specialising in local fish
and seafood. Bedrooms.*
Open: 11.30-3.30 5.30-11 (Sun
12-3.30 6-10.30). Bar Meals: 12-
2.30 6.30-9.30. Children and
dogs welcome. Patio. Parking.
(see page 576 for full entry)

A beautiful walk along the coast, followed by a short steep climb and stunning views across Cardigan Bay, returning to Aberdyfi via peaceful woodland paths.

On leaving the pub, cross the road and follow the river to a gate. If the tide is low or falling, go through another gate and follow the old Roman Road (can be wet & slippery) to Picnic Island. If unsure, you can follow the main road to a layby where the island is clearly signed. Cross the railway bridge to admire the views from Picnic Island and return to the road.

From Picnic Island turn right and follow main road for 100 yards (91m). Cross over stile on left and take left footpath beside stream. Cross footbridge and latter stile. Continue past Outward Bound buildings and bear left through gate. Continue uphill past a green shed, cross track way, and continue uphill. Keep ahead where the track veers left and continue towards trees through a small gate. Descend steeply through the woods to a ladder stile at the bottom left-hand corner of the woods.

Turn left along the lane and continue to Trefrifawr Farm, where you have the option of following the waymarked farm trail. Enter the yard, keep right of the house to a stile and proceed uphill (stream right) to a ladder stile. Follow the track which veers right, cross a farm track and continue to a lane.

Turn left, with views encompassing Cardigan Bay and, on a clear day, the Lleyn Peninsula and Bardsey Island, and walk downhill. Go through a gate, then turn right through double gates and bear half-right downhill towards waymarker post. Go through gap in hedge, turn right and cross a stile and stream. Turn left downhill beside the stream to a stile and head downhill towards stream and trees.

Gently climb to a stile and keep to the path, passing marker post, and descend to a stile. Continue to steps beside houses to a road. Turn right, then immediately left and continue downhill to a road and turn left. Pass beneath the railway back to the inn.

Distance: 4 miles (6.4km)
Map: OS Landranger 135
Terrain: coast, woodland, farmland, country lanes
Paths: coast path, tracks, woodland and field paths (optional farm trail)
Gradient: undulating; some steep ascents and descents

Walk submitted by:
The Penhelig Arms

DOLGELLAU
Map 08 SH71

Pick of the Pubs

George III Hotel ★ ★ 🍺
Penmaenpool LL40 1YD ☎ 01341 422525
📠 01341 423565
Dir: 2m West of A493 beyond RSPB Centre
The hotel stands at the water's edge of the magnificent
Mawddach Estuary, with splendid views across to
Snowdonia. A good touring base, it stands next to an RSPB
sanctuary, with six bedrooms converted from the former
railway station and waiting room that closed in 1964.

The Cellar Bar right by the water is ideal for families,
cyclists and walkers, while the upper level Dresser Bar and
dining-rooms are rather more genteel. Noted for local
salmon and sea trout, pheasant, wild duck and venison in
season, meals are home cooked and fresh with many well-
tried favourites to choose from.

At their simplest these include home-baked ham,
traditional Welsh rarebit and a smoked fish platter with
horseradish: crab and salmon fishcakes, minted leg of
Welsh lamb steak and Cumberland sausage with onion
gravy are popular alternatives. A la carte in the
recently extended restaurant, expect to find prawn and
mushroom pancakes with Parmesan, honey-glazed
duckling breast in orange sauce and hot black cherries
with maraschino liqueur and vanilla ice.
OPEN: 11-11. **BAR MEALS:** L served all week. D served all
week 12-2.30 6.30-9.30. Av main course £7.50.
RESTAURANT: L served Sun. D served all week 12-2 7-9. Av
3 course à la carte £25. **BREWERY/COMPANY:** Free
House. **PRINCIPAL BEERS:** Ruddles Best, John Smiths.
FACILITIES: Children welcome Children's licence Garden:
outdoor eating, Dogs allowed. **NOTES:** Parking 60.
ROOMS: 11 bedrooms 11 en suite s£45 d£80

LLANDWROG
Map 08 SN45

The Harp Inn 🍺
Tyn'llan LL54 5SY ☎ 01286 831071 📠 01286 830239
e-mail: management@theharp.globalnet.co.uk
Dir: A55 from Chester bypass, signed off A487 Pwllhelli rd
A long established haven for travellers, the inn is located in the
historic home village of the nearby Glynllifon Estate, between
the mountains of Snowdonia and the beautiful beaches of
Dinas Dinlle. Food options include the 'Friday Fiver' curry or
steak, budget lunches and candlelit dinners. Favourites include
local seafood, Aberdeen Angus beef, and Welsh lamb, with
'afters' like spotted dick with custard.
OPEN: 12-3 6-11 (Mon 6pm-11pm Sat 12-11, Sun12-3, 7-10.30).
Closed Mon lunch, all Mon Oct-Mar & Jan 1. **BAR MEALS:** L
served Tue-Sun. D served Tue-Sun 12-2 6.30-8.30. Av main course
£6.95. **RESTAURANT:** L served Sun. D served Tue-Sun 12-2
6.30-8.30. Av 3 course à la carte £15.
BREWERY/COMPANY: Free House. **PRINCIPAL BEERS:** Bass,
Black Sheep. **FACILITIES:** Children welcome Garden: resident
parrot, outdoor eating,patio. **NOTES:** Parking 20.
ROOMS: 4 bedrooms 1 en suite s£24 d£36 FRE70
See Pub Walk on page 579

LLANENGAN
Map 08 SH22

The Sun Inn
LL53 7LG ☎ 01758 712660
Dir: From Pwllheli take A499 S to Abersoch.Then 1.5m towards Hells
Mouth Beach
Friendly and welcoming pub, reputedly haunted, with a
wishing well in the garden, and where the locals are likely to
burst into song. The changing menu of home-cooked dishes
includes steaks, lasagne and chicken breast.
OPEN: 12-3 6-11 (open all day Sat). **BAR MEALS:** L served all
week. D served all week 12-3 6-9. Av main course £6.95.
PRINCIPAL BEERS: Robinson Best & Old Stockport Bitter.
FACILITIES: Children welcome Garden: **NOTES:** Parking 70

MAENTWROG
Map 08 SH64

Grapes Hotel
LL41 4HN ☎ 01766 590365 & 590365 📠 01766 590654
Dir: A5 thru Corwen to Bala, A487 to Maentwrog, onto A496, pub
100yrds in RH side
Grade II listed 17th-century coaching inn with an ancient cellar
dating back even further. As well as being located at the heart
of the Snowdonia National Park, the Grapes is also renowned
for its famous visitors over the years. Lloyd George was a
regular customer at the inn and Lillie Langtry took tea here.
Pitch-pine pews and bars and roaring log fires are among the
character features inside. Fresh home-cooked meals and daily
specials include ham and leek bake, lamb chops, beef Madras
and pork ribs.

OPEN: 11-11 (Sun 12-10.30). Closed Dec 25. **BAR MEALS:** L
served all week. D served all week 12-2.15 6-9.30. Av main course
£7.50. **BREWERY/COMPANY:** Free House.
PRINCIPAL BEERS: Marstons Pedigree, Greene King Old
Speckled Hen & IPA, Wye Valley Butty Bach.
FACILITIES: Children welcome Garden: Food served outside
Dogs allowed Public bar only. **NOTES:** Parking 36.
ROOMS: 8 bedrooms 8 en suite s£30 d£60

Wales

HARP INN, LLANDWROG
Tyn'llan LL54 5SY.
Tel: 01286 831071
Directions: off A499 S of
Caernarvon
*Close to Dinas Dinlle beach
and handy for Snowdonia,
this family-run inn offers
interesting menus and good
real ale in its welcoming
lounge bar. Look to the
board for the daily fish
specials. Cottagey bedrooms.*
Open: 12-3 6-11 (Sat 12-11,
Sun 12-3 7-10.30, closed Sun
eve Oct-Mar & Mon lunch).
Bar Meals: 12-2 6.30-8.30 (no
food all Mon). Children
welcome. Garden. Parking.
(see page 578 for full entry)

GWYNEDD

*Pub*WALK

Harp Inn, Llandwrog

Easy and breezy, this flat and enjoyable peninsula walk explores the fine beach at Dinas Dinlle and Foryd Bay, noted for its birdlife. Panoramic views extend from the mountains of Snowdonia to the Lleyn Peninsula.

Turn left from the front of the inn and walk along the road for 1/2 mile (0.8km) to a T-junction. Turn right and follow the road down to Dinas Dinlle beach, a fine stretch of sand running the whole length of the peninsula. Turn right along the promenade and enjoy views across the Menai Straits to the Isle of Anglesey on your right.

At the end of the promenade, keep to the seaward side of the public toilets and follow the path through the dunes, or if the tide is out walk along the beach. On nearing Fort Belan, cut inland away from the sea and pick up the grassy bank (old railway line) to reach a bird hide. Pause here for a moment to watch the birdlife in Foryd Bay.

With the sea to your left, follow the path south beside Foryd Bay and soon pass Morfa Lodge Caravan Site. Continue for about 1/2 mile (0.8km) and cross the footbridge over the river. Follow what can be an overgrown path to the road, passing Chatham Farm on your left. Turn right along the road and follow it for nearly 1 1/4 miles (2km) back to the village and the pub.

Distance: 6 miles (10km)
Map: OS Landranger 115
Terrain: beach, dunes, estuary, farmland
Paths: promenade, tracks, coast and estuary path
Gradient: mainly level

*Walk submitted by:
The Harp Inn*

The Lleyn Peninsula

Wales

NANTGWYNANT   Map 08 SH56

Pen-Y-Gwryd
LL55 4NT ☎ 01286 870211
Dir: 6m S of Llanberis at head of Gwryd river, close to junction of A4086 & A498
Situated in the magnificent Snowdonia National Park, this cosy climber's pub is the home of British mountaineering. The 1953 Everest team used it as a training base and scrawled their signatures on the ceiling. As well as being an inn, offering shelter and hospitality against a rugged backdrop, it also doubles as a mountain rescue post. Wholesome fare from the daily-changing menu might feature roast Welsh sirloin of beef, roast duck, and lamb in red wine and paprika.
OPEN: 11-11. **BAR MEALS:** L served all week 12-2.
RESTAURANT: D served all week 7.30-8. Av 3 course à la carte £17. Av 5 course fixed price £17. **BREWERY/COMPANY:** Free House. **PRINCIPAL BEERS:** Bass. **FACILITIES:** Children welcome Garden: outdoor eating, swimming pool, sauna Dogs allowed. **NOTES:** Parking 25. **ROOMS:** 16 bedrooms 5 en suite s£23 d£46 No credit cards

---

PORTHMADOG   Map 08 SH53

The Ship 🍴 ♀
Lombard St LL49 9AP ☎ 01766 512990
Dir: From A55 take A470 S towards the coast
The oldest pub still operating in Porthmadog, The Ship is located close to the harbour and is mentioned in many maritime books on the area. One menu serves all, with plenty of fresh fish - black bream and mussels in season, whole sea bass and salmon fillet in herb crust. Other options include chicken dijonaise, lamb shank, and parsnip and leek crumble.
OPEN: 11-11 (Sun 12-10.30). Closed Dec 25. **BAR MEALS:** L served all week. D served Mon-Sat 12-2 6.30-9.
BREWERY/COMPANY: Punch Taverns.
PRINCIPAL BEERS: Greene King Old Speckled Hen and IPA, Tetley Bitter, Dark Mild. **FACILITIES:** Children's licence Dogs allowed

---

TUDWEILIOG   Map 08 SH23

Lion Hotel
LL53 8ND ☎ 01758 770244   🖩 01758 770244
e-mail: andrewlee@claramail.com
Dir: A499 from Caernarfon, B4417 Tudweiliog
Village inn with a large garden and play area, and plenty of parking. Dishes range from bar snacks to home-made dishes such as curry and casseroles. Popular options are local steaks and gammon, haddock, steak and kidney pie, or chicken and leeks with ginger.
OPEN: 11.30-11 (Winter 12-2, 7-11, all day Sat). **BAR MEALS:** L served all week. D served Mon-Sat 12-2 6-9. Av main course £5.50. **BREWERY/COMPANY:** Free House.
PRINCIPAL BEERS: Marstons Pedigree, Boddingtons, Theakston.
FACILITIES: Children welcome Garden: Food served outside Dogs allowed garden only. **NOTES:** Parking 40.
ROOMS: 4 bedrooms 4 en suite s£26 d£40

ISLE OF ANGLESEY

ANGLESEY, ISLE OF

BEAUMARIS   Map 08 SH67

The Liverpool Arms Hotel ♀
Castle St LL58 8BA ☎ 01248 810362   🖩 01248 811135
Dir: A5 across the Menai Straits, R onto A545 through Menai Bridge
Historic inn dating back to 1706 when there was a busy trade between Liverpool and Beaumaris - hence the name. Strong nautical theme with timbers from HMS Victory, Nelson's flagship. Popular, daily-changing blackboard menus and a summer salad bar. Expect a choice of fish dishes, as well as scrumpy pork hock in cider sauce, home made steak pie, or spinach and ricotta cannelloni.
OPEN: 11.30-11.30. **BAR MEALS:** L served all week. D served all week 12-2 6-9. Av main course £7. **BREWERY/COMPANY:** Free House. **PRINCIPAL BEERS:** Greene King Old Speckled Hen, Tetley, Brains S.A. & Best Bitter. **FACILITIES:** Children welcome. **NOTES:** Parking 12. **ROOMS:** 10 bedrooms 10 en suite s£35 d£55 FR£65

BEAUMARIS   Map 08 SH67

Pick of the Pubs

Ye Olde Bulls Head Inn ◉ ◉ ★ ★ 🍴 ♀
Castle St LL58 8AP ☎ 01248 810329   🖩 01248 811294
e-mail: info@bullsheadinn.co.uk
Dir: From Brittania Road Bridge follow A545
AA/Sea Fish Industry Authority
Seafood Pub of The Year 2002.
A celebrated watering-hole set just back from the Menai Straits and a stone's throw from Beaumaris Castle that has been popular since the days of Charles Dickens and centuries before that. Bedrooms take their name from Dickens characters and an interior full of period memorabilia, including the town's old ducking stool, are all evocative of days gone by.
All the more surprising, therefore, has been the success of the new brasserie that is all harlequin tiles, local stone and old beams that looks out across the old coach yard. Roast fresh asparagus with grilled goats' cheese and pappardelle pasta with bolognese sauce and fresh basil chiffonade rub shoulders with ploughman's salads of farmhouse Penbryn or Shropshire Blue cheese and braised lamb on potato and spinach hash.
The fresh seafood selection, earning the Bull's Head our Welsh Seafood Pub of the Year award, includes classic seafood chowder with garlic rouille, pave of salmon on crab and fennel risotto and seared tuna on Parmesan polenta and salsa verde. The newly-furnished first floor restaurant offers more formal dinners that never compromise on quality, backed by a wine list that is a connoisseur's delight.
OPEN: 11-11. **BAR MEALS:** L served Mon-Sat. D served all week 12-2 6-9.30. Av main course £6.50.
RESTAURANT: D served all week 7-9.30. Av 3 course à la carte £29.75. **BREWERY/COMPANY:** Free House.
PRINCIPAL BEERS: Bass, Hancocks, Worthington.
FACILITIES: Children welcome. **NOTES:** Parking 10.
ROOMS: 13 bedrooms 13 en suite s£60 d£87

LLANFACHRAETH   Map 08 SH38

Holland Hotel ◆◆◆ ♀
LL65 4UH ☎ 01407 740252 🖷 01407 471344
e-mail: info@holland-hotel.co.uk
A friendly 18th-century inn within easy reach of the Anglesey
Heritage coastline and Holyhead ferry port. Also convenient
for stunning scenery, safe sandy beaches, and a championship
golf course. Local produce forms the mainstay of menus that
include steak in stout, salads, Indian dishes, a vegetarian
selection, dressed crab and seafood platter.
OPEN: 11-11. **BAR MEALS:** L served all week. D served all week
12-3 6-9. Av main course £5.50. **RESTAURANT:** 12-3 6-9. Av 3
course à la carte £10. **BREWERY/COMPANY:** J W Lees.
PRINCIPAL BEERS: J W Lees. **FACILITIES:** Children welcome
Garden: outdoor eating Dogs allowed water provided.
NOTES: Parking 40. **ROOMS:** 4 bedrooms 4 en suite s£32 d£59
FR£59-£71

RED WHARF BAY   Map 08 SH58

Pick of the Pubs

The Ship Inn 🍴 ♀
LL75 8RJ ☎ 01248 852568 🖷 01248 851013
Dating back to the 18th century, when this bay was a
thriving port for the import of coal and fertilisers, the old
Quay Inn used to serve ale to landing sailors from 6am
onwards. In the same hands now for some 30 years, the
'newly-named' Ship rightly claims to be a purveyor of
quality food, fine wines and real ales.
    Turn up after high tide to witness delivery of the
freshest Conwy Bay fish and seafood, as used in crispy
crab ravioli with chillies and spring onions and sea bass
fillets served on noodles with a Thai-scented sauce. In
winter, find cosy fireside tables at which to enjoy hot
bacon baguettes with avocado, or beef sirloin strips with
peppercorns flamed in cognac - followed perhaps by bara
brith and butter pudding or Anglesey ice cream.
    In season the ever-popular waterside beer garden
comes into its own and a more extensive dinner menu is
offered upstairs: food served all day on Sunday and Bank
Holidays.
OPEN: 11-3.30 (Sat 11-11, Sun 12-10.30) 6.30-11 (Summer
11-11 daily). **BAR MEALS:** L served all week. D served all
week 12-2.30 6.30-9. Av main course £6.50.
RESTAURANT: D served all week 7-10. Av 3 course à la
carte £20. **BREWERY/COMPANY:** Free House.
PRINCIPAL BEERS: Friary Meux, Burton Ale, Tetley,
Marstons Pedigree. **FACILITIES:** Children welcome Garden:
patio, outdoor eating Dogs allowed garden only, Water.
NOTES: Parking 45

ABERGAVENNY   Map 03 SO21

Pick of the Pubs

Clytha Arms 🍴 ♀
Clytha NP7 9BW ☎ 01873 840206 🖷 01873 840206
Dir: From A449/A40 junction (E of Abergavenny) follow signs for
'Old Road Abergavenny/Clytha'
Set in its own grounds alongside the old Abergavenny
road (B4598) just three miles from Raglan's famous 15th-
century castle, this former dower house is surrounded by
green lawns and interesting gardens not far from the River
Usk. Four en suite bedrooms, individually styled and full of
character, offer dinner, bed and breakfast on request with
a full Welsh breakfast and vegetarian alternatives.
    Simple yet imaginative bar snacks such as faggots and
peas in beer and onion gravy, home-made wild boar
sausages with potato pancakes and leek and laverbread
rissoles suitably soak up some of South Wales's finest ales,
while to accompany the monthly dining menus is a hand-
picked wine list with many options by the glass.
    The daily set menu might offer crab rissoles with
coriander sauce, lambs' kidneys with tomato and basil or
Cajun-spiced turkey steak with salsa and wild rice,
followed by chocolate and Armagnac mousse or a
selection of Welsh farmhouse cheeses.
OPEN: 12-3.30 6-11. Closed 25 Dec. **BAR MEALS:** L served
Tue-Sun. D served all week 12.30-2.30 7-9.30. Av main course
£6. **RESTAURANT:** L served all week. D served Tue-Sat
12.30-2.30 7-9. Av 3 course à la carte £25. Av 3 course fixed
price £15.95. **BREWERY/COMPANY:** Free House.
PRINCIPAL BEERS: Caledonian Deuchers IPA, Bass,
Felinfoel Double Dragon. **FACILITIES:** Children welcome
Children's licence Garden: outdoor eating, **NOTES:** Parking
100. **ROOMS:** 4 bedrooms 4 en suite s£45 d£60

Pantrhiwgoch Hotel ◉ ★ ★
Brecon Rd NP8 1EP ☎ 01873 810550 🖷 01873 811880
e-mail: info@pantrhiwgoch.co.uk
Dir: On A40 between Abergavenny & Crickhowell
This part-16th-century inn and restaurant perches on a high
bank of the River Usk with splendid views of the valley and
Blorenge Mountain beyond. In addition to two bars,
conservatory and dining room serving the same menu, there is
a fine summer terrace looking down over the river. A sample
lunchtime menu includes hake with chips and salad, sirloin
steak, local sausages with mash and onion gravy, chicken
curry, and falafel fritters with provençale sauce.
OPEN: 11-11. **BAR MEALS:** L served all week. D served all week
12-2.30 6.30-9.30. Av main course £10.95. **RESTAURANT:** L
served all week. D served all week 12-2.30 6.30-9.30. Av 3 course
à la carte £25. **BREWERY/COMPANY:** Free House.
PRINCIPAL BEERS: Felinfoel Double Dragon. **FACILITIES:**
Garden: Terrace overlooking river, outdoor eating. **NOTES:**
Parking 80. **ROOMS:** 18 bedrooms 18 en suite s£63 d£63

Wales

ABERGAVENNY continued

The Skirrid Mountain Inn
Lanvihangel Crucorney NP7 8DH ☎ 01873 890258
Ancient, mainly Tudor stone inn, reputedly the oldest inn in
Wales and a courthouse between 1110 and the 17th century.
Nearly 200 people were hanged here and a beam above the
foot of the stairs served as a scaffold. Appetising bar and
restaurant menu offers the likes of local lamb chops, Welsh
Champion sausages and home-made vegetarian Skirrid loaf.
OPEN: 12-3 6-11 (11-11 Jul-Sep, Sat 12-11, Sun 12-10.30).
BAR MEALS: L served all week. D served Mon-Sun 12-2.30 7-9.
Av main course £7.95. **RESTAURANT:** L served all week. D
served Mon-Sat 12-2.30 7-9. **PRINCIPAL BEERS:** Ushers Best,
Ushers Founders, Ushers Four Seasons, Bass.
FACILITIES: Children welcome Garden: patio/terrace, BBQ,
floral displays Dogs allowed. **NOTES:** Parking 20.
ROOMS: 2 bedrooms 2 en suite s£40 d£69 No credit cards

Pick of the Pubs

Walnut Tree Inn 🏅 🏅 🌿
Llandewi Skirrid NP7 8AW ☎ 01873 852797
🖥 01873 859764
e-mail: stephenandfrancesco@thewalnuttree.co.uk
Dir: 3m NE of Abergavenny on B4521
Synonymous with the very origins of country dining in the
humble surroundings of a 'pub' some 40 years ago, the
landmark Walnut Tree has changed hands; and a brave
man is former Marco Pierre White protégé, Stephen Terry,
to assume the mantle. Unsurprisingly, given his pedigree,
the take-over appears apparently seamless: credit cards
are now taken, yet unavoidably the toilets remain out-of-
doors. The menu stays true to tradition, with many of the
Old Master's dishes retained as in Vicisgrassi Maceratese
and suckling pig porchetta still retained, though a more
up-to-date awareness of today's trends is clearly making
itself felt. Not a local for the casual passer-by, best buys at
the bar come less from beer pumps than from a wine list
that remains peerless, to accompany food worth travelling
miles for. Sourcing of ingredients remains as diligent as
ever: Lady Llanover's salt duck and divers' scallops with
trevisano and pancetta to start, followed by monkfish
saltimbocca with broad beans, cannellini beans and chick
peas or confit shoulder of Welsh lamb and potatoes. This
is serious food: don't drop in for a quick sandwich!
OPEN: 12-4 6.30-12 (Sun & BH Mon 12-4only). Closed Sun
eve, allMon (ex BH) & 1 wk at Xmas,. **RESTAURANT:** L
served Tue-Sun. D served Tue-Sat 12-3 6.30-11.
BREWERY/COMPANY: Free House.
PRINCIPAL BEERS: no real ale. **FACILITIES:** Children
welcome. **NOTES:** Parking 50

BETTWS-NEWYDD   Map 03 SO30

Pick of the Pubs

Black Bear Inn 🌿
NP15 1JN ☎ 01873 880701 🖥 01873 881198
Dir: Off B4598 N of Usk
Surrounded by rolling Monmouthshire countryside in a
tiny hamlet, 'cooking by Molineux' here is as spontaneous
as it gets. The bar's oak beams, flagstone floor and open
fire have been left as original as possible with supplies
from local micro-breweries always on tap.
   Local produce is used almost entirely in the dining-
rooms: salmon and brown trout are landed from the River
Usk less than a quarter mile away and farmed venison,
lamb, beef and seasonal game are ever in plentiful supply.
   The greatest fun for dinner is to choose 'whatever
comes from the kitchen' that could be crispy duck salad
with raspberry vinaigrette, fresh turbot with white wine,
mushrooms and cream, followed by Bailey's Irish Cream
cheesecake. Smaller feasts might include tasty home-
made fishcakes, beef medallions in Madeira sauce and
chocolate-and-orange terrine, all served with minimal
formality.
OPEN: 12-2 6-12 (Sun 12-10.30) Closed Mon lunch.
BAR MEALS: L served Tue-Sun. D served all week 12-2 6-10.
Av main course £5.90. **RESTAURANT:** L served Tue-Sun. D
served Mon-Sat 12-2 6-10. Av 3 course à la carte £20.
BREWERY/COMPANY: Free House.
PRINCIPAL BEERS: Freeminers Speculation, Bath Gem,
Fullers London Pride, Timothy Taylor Landlord.
FACILITIES: Children welcome Garden: outdoor eating,
patio, Dogs allowed Water tap. **NOTES:** Parking 20.
ROOMS: 4 bedrooms s£25 d£50 FR£60 No credit cards

WHICH IS THE OLDEST PUB?
The question has no sure answer. Records are
fragmentary and a building, or part of it, may be far
older than its use as a drinking house. The Old Ferry
Boat Inn at Holywell in the Cambridgeshire fens is
claimed to go back to the 6th century as a monastic
ferry station and the Olde Fighting Cocks in St Albans
to the 8th century as an abbey fishing lodge by the
River Ver. A more believable contender is the Bingley
Arms at Bardsey, West Yorkshire, recorded as the
'priest's inn' in 905, but it was completely rebuilt in
1738. The Ostrich at Colnbrook, Buckinghamshire, is
apparently on the site of a monastic hospice recorded
in 1106 (and its odd name is a pun on 'hospice').
Others claiming a 12th-century origin include the
wonderfully named Olde Trip to Jerusalem in
Nottingham, the Cromwell-linked Royal Oak at
Whatcote in Warwickshire, the venerable Oxenham
Arms at South Zeal in Devon, the half-timbered Pandy
Inn at Dorstone, Herefordshire, the Olde House Inn at
Llangynwyd in South Wales and the Oldes Boar's
Head at Middleton, Greater Manchester. All of them,
of course, have been repeatedly rebuilt and
altered over the centuries.

OPEN: 12-3 6-11.
Closed Sun & Mon eve
BAR MEALS: L served all week.
D served Tue-Sat 12-2.30 7-9.30
(10 wknd). Av main course £13.50.
RESTAURANT: L served all week.
D served Tue-Sat 12-2.30 7-9.30
(10 wknd). Av 3 course a la carte
£25.
BREWERY/COMPANY:
Free House.
PRINCIPLE BEERS: Hancocks HB,
Bass, Buckleys Reverend St James,
guest beer.
FACILITIES: Children welcome.
Garden: patio, outdoor eating.
NOTES: Parking 50.

The Newbridge Inn

♀ NEW

NP15 1LY
☎ 01633 451000 🖨 01633 451001
e-mail: themanager@the-newbridge-com
Dir: From M4 (j26), take Caerleon to Usk rd.
In Llandybi, opposite Cwrt Bleddyn Hotel,
follow lane through Tredunhock to riverside

On the southern bank of the river by the 'new' 17th-century stone bridge, this classic old pub stands alone at the heart of the Vale of Usk. A warm, friendly welcome on entering indicates the arrival of enthusiastic new owners who have transformed this well-known pub.

The waterside garden and terrace make a perfect spot for salmon watching while dramatic new interior design features lemon-washed walls, exposed brickwork, bare boards, pine-clad bar and informal dining on three levels with a spiral staircase leading to the top-most floor. Contemporary displays of Irish artist Graham Knuttel's striking paintings adorn the walls and hand-decorated blackboards promote future special events. Unclothed tables and some modern jazz (not always in the background) create a suitably informal atmosphere in which the best of the day's dishes display a passion for good, fresh produce. Simple lunchtime fare includes Club and steak sandwiches alongside Breton-style fish soup, confit of duck leg with plum sauce and roast chicken breast with creamed leeks, rösti potato and red wine sauce: substantial alternatives might be roast cod with shellfish sauce and chargrilled peppered fillet steak with a turret of precisely hand-cut chips.

Under its high rafters the whole place, shimmering with candlelight, is reflected in the river to create a romantic dinner setting. Snail, bacon and quails' egg salad, Welsh lamb knuckle with bean cassoulet or asparagus and wild mushroom risotto with Parmesan crisps, followed by apple and cinnamon tartlet with Calvados ice cream are accompanied by some dozen wines by the glass, including champagne.

Pick of the Pubs

The Boat Inn ♀
The Back NP16 5HH ☎ 01291 628192
▤ 01291 628193
e-mail: boatinn.co.uk

Dating originally from 1795, The Boat stands on the banks of the River Wye, with a front terrace, barbeque and tables in the first floor restaurant that look out upon the ever-changing scene. Salmon fisheries were once sited virtually next door: the shop boats moored in the tide with deep nets stretched across the tidal flow below Brunel's tubular railway bridge.

Today's revitalised pub combines the virtues of a popular local with an honest approach to providing good bar and restaurant food. Lunch daily need not be a complicated affair, with fresh soup and filled baguettes an acceptable alternative to fish and chips in the bar.

A longer dining menu adds to traditional starters of smooth liver parfait and beer-battered mushrooms a varied selection of main dishes that is likely to include shank of lamb with red wine jus, grilled sea bass with shellfish sauce and steaks with various complementary sauces. Diners may choose between seasonal vegetables and potato, or opt for chips and salad, followed by mostly cold desserts; and enjoy Sunday lunch well into the afternoon.
OPEN: 11-11 (12-10.30 Sun). **BAR MEALS:** L served all week. D served all week 12-3 6.30-10. Av main course £4.50. **RESTAURANT:** L served all week. D served all week 12-3 6.30-10. Av 3 course à la carte £12.
BREWERY/COMPANY: Unique Pub Co.
PRINCIPAL BEERS: Bass, Smiles, Wadworth 6X,.
FACILITIES: Children welcome Children's licence Garden: patio/terrace, outdoor eating Dogs allowed except in garden. **NOTES:** Parking 20

AA Hotel Booking Service on 0870 5050505 to book
at AA recognised hotels and B & Bs in the
UK and Ireland, or through our Internet site:
www.theAA.com

Castle View Hotel
16 Bridge St NP16 5EZ ☎ 01291 620349 ▤ 01291 627397
e-mail: mart@castview.demon.co.uk
Dir: Opposite Chepstow Castle
Built as a private house some 300 years ago, its solid walls up to five feet thick in places, this hotel is situated opposite the castle, alongside the River Wye. The regularly changing menu might offer steaks, breast of chicken stuffed with Stilton, and cod in beer batter.

OPEN: 12-2.30 6-11. **BAR MEALS:** L served all week. D served Mon-Sat 12-2 6.30-9.30. Av main course £4.50. **RESTAURANT:** L served Sun. D served Mon-Sat 12-2 6.30-9.30. Av 3 course à la carte £15. **BREWERY/COMPANY:** Free House.
PRINCIPAL BEERS: Tetley. **FACILITIES:** Children welcome Garden: Outdoor eating Dogs allowed. **NOTES:** Parking 200.
ROOMS: 13 bedrooms 13 en suite s£39 d£50 FR£50-£70

LLANDOGO

The Sloop Inn ♦♦♦
NP25 4TW ☎ 01594 530291 ▤ 01594 530935
Overlooking the River Wye just north of Tintern Abbey, this traditional hostelry offers well maintained accommodation and wide range of bar meals.

LLANTRISANT   Map 03 ST39

Greyhound Inn ♀
NP15 1LE ☎ 01291 672505 & 673447 ▤ 01291 673255
e-mail: enquiry@greyhound-inn.com
Dir: From M4 take A449 towards Monmouth, 1st jct to Usk, L into Usk Sq. Take 2nd L signed Llantrisant. 2.5m to inn
17th-century Welsh longhouse which became a country inn in 1845 and is perfectly situated for exploring miles of stunning Welsh countryside. Award-winning gardens, open log fires and a stone stable block converted to en suite letting rooms add to the charm and character of the place. Good range of home-cooked dishes and tempting daily specials. Try the pheasant in port and redcurrant sauce, Welsh venison and ale pie, chicken chasseur or the delicious local salmon.
OPEN: 11-11. Closed 25 Dec. **BAR MEALS:** L served all week. D served Mon-Sat 11.45-2.15 6-10.30. Av main course £7.
RESTAURANT: L served all week. D served Mon-Sat 11.45-2.15 6-10.30. Av 3 course à la carte £13. **BREWERY/COMPANY:** Free House. **PRINCIPAL BEERS:** Flowers Original, Marstons Pedigree, Wadworth 6X, Greene King Abbot Ale.
FACILITIES: Children welcome Garden: pond with fountain, food served outside Dogs allowed. **NOTES:** Parking 60.
ROOMS: 10 bedrooms 10 en suite s£45 d£60

LLANVAIR DISCOED   Map 03 ST49

Pick of the Pubs

The Woodland Restaurant & Bar ⏻
NP16 6LX ☎ 01633 400313
Close to the Roman fortress town of Caerwent, just minutes' drive away, and Wentwood's forest and reservoir, this historic old inn has recently undergone major redevelopment to accommodate an increasing number of diners attracted by its warm welcome and carefully prepared, imaginative food. It remains at heart a friendly village local, with simple bistro food along the lines of beef Madras, chicken stir-fry and meatballs with Napoli sauce all readily available. It is on the dining-room menu, though, that quality cooking shines through, starting perhaps with salmon, sorrel and spinach filo parcels and proceeding to chicken roulade Princess, rack of Welsh lamb and individual beef Wellington. A strong showing of market-fresh fish includes sea bass roast in rock salt and roulade of lemon sole filled with ginger-scented prawns and mushrooms. Round off with bread-and-butter pudding or glazed lemon tart: then plan to return for the ever-popular Sunday lunch.
OPEN: 11-3 6-11 (Sun 12-3, 7-10.30). **BAR MEALS:** L served all week. D served Mon-Sat 12-2 6.30-10. Av main course £5.95. **RESTAURANT:** L served all week. D served Mon-Sat 12-2 6.30-9. Av 3 course à la carte £20. **BREWERY/COMPANY:** Free House. **PRINCIPAL BEERS:** Buckleys IPA. **FACILITIES:** Children welcome Garden: patio/terrace, outdoor eating Dogs allowed. **NOTES:** Parking 30

LLANVAPLEY   Map 03 SO31

Red Hart Inn
NP7 8SN ☎ 01600 780227   🖹 01600 780279
e-mail: enquiries@redhartinn.co.uk
Dir: On B4233 E of Abergavenny
A typically old-fashioned rural public house, opposite the 12th-century village church and close by Offa's Dyke Path: an extensive garden looks out over open country. The menu has an international flavour.

PENALLT   Map 03 SO51

The Boat Inn
Lone Ln NP25 4AJ ☎ 01600 712615
Dir: From Monmouth take A466.In Redbrook the pub car park is signposted. Park & walk across rail bridge over R Wye
Dating back over 350 years, this riverside pub has served as a hostelry for quarry, mill, paper and tin mine workers, and even had a landlord operating a ferry across the Wye at shift times. Excellent real ales.

SHIRENEWTON   Map 03 ST49

The Carpenters Arms
Usk Rd NP16 6BU ☎ 01291 641231
Dir: M48 J2 take A48 to Chepstow then A4661, B4235.Village 3m on L
A 400-year-old hostelry, formerly a smithy and carpenter's shop, with flagstone floors, open fires and a pleasant wooded valley location near the Wye and Usk valleys. It is now furnished with antiques, and offers straightforward bar food. A typical menu includes steak and mushroom pie, guinea fowl in orange sauce, pheasant casserole, and chicken in leek and Stilton sauce. *continued*

OPEN: 11-2.30 6-11. **BAR MEALS:** L served all week. D served Mon-Sat 12-2 7-9.30. Av main course £5. **BREWERY/COMPANY:** Free House. **PRINCIPAL BEERS:** Fullers London Pride, Wadworth 6X, Marstons Pedigree,Theakstons Old Peculier. **FACILITIES:** Dogs allowed. **NOTES:** Parking 20 No credit cards

TAL-Y-COED   Map 03 SO41

The Halfway House Inn
NP7 8TL ☎ 01600 780269   🖹 01600 780269
Dir: On B4233 (between Abergavenny & Monmouth)
Originally a drovers' inn dating from the 17th century, this handsome, wisteria-clad inn is situated in tranquil countryside within easy reach of the Wye Valley and the Brecon Beacons.

TREDUNHOCK   Map 03 ST39

Pick of the Pubs

The Newbridge Inn 🍴 ⏻ NEW
NP15 1LY ☎ 01633 451000   🖹 01633 541001
e-mail: themanager@the-newbridge.com
See Pick of the Pubs on page 583

TRELLECK   Map 03 SO50

The Lion Inn
NP25 4PA ☎ 01600 860322   🖹 01600 860060
e-mail: lion@web-fanatics.co.uk
Dir: From A40 just south of Monmouth take B4293 and follow signs for Trelleck
Located opposite the church and reputedly haunted, this former brew and coach house offers traditional pub food. Choices range from South African mixed grill and ostrich steak to home-made cottage pie and chicken tikka masala served with rice. There are also ploughman's lunches, omelettes and various fish dishes.
OPEN: 12-3 6-11 (Mon 7-11; closed Sun eve). **BAR MEALS:** L served all week. D served Mon-Sat 12-2 7-9.30. Av main course £6. **RESTAURANT:** L served all week. D served Mon-Sat 12-2 7-9.30. Av 3 course à la carte £13. Av 3 course fixed price £12.95. **BREWERY/COMPANY:** Free House. **PRINCIPAL BEERS:** Bath Ales, SP Sporting Ales, Wadworth 6X, Fullers London Pride. **FACILITIES:** Children welcome Garden: patio/terrace, outdoor eating Dogs allowed. **NOTES:** Parking 30

◆   AA inspected guest accommodation

Wales

USK   Map 03 SO30

The Nags Head Inn ♀
Twyn Square NP15 1BH ☎ 01291 672820
🖥 01291 672720
Dir: On A472
Flower-adorned 15th-century inn overlooking the town square,
just a short stroll from the River Usk. The village itself has won
Wales in Bloom for the last 17 years, and the same family have
run the inn for over thirty years. Local game in season,
including pheasant cooked in port, and wild Usk salmon are
specialities on the menu. Regular dishes include steak pie,
ham platter and chicken in red wine, followed by home-made
apple pie.
OPEN: 10-3 5.30-11. Closed Dec 25. **BAR MEALS:** L served all
week. D served all week 10-3 5.30-10.30. Av main course £8.
RESTAURANT: L served all week. D served all week 11.30-3
5.30-10.30. Av 3 course à la carte £13.
BREWERY/COMPANY: Free House.
PRINCIPAL BEERS: Brains-Bitter, Dark, Buckleys Best &
Reverend James. **FACILITIES:** Children welcome Garden: Beer
garden, outdoor eating

PEMBROKESHIRE

AMROTH   Map 02 SN10

The New Inn 🐑
SA67 8NW ☎ 01834 812368
Dir: A48 to Carmarthen, A40 to St Clears, A477 to Llanteg then L
A 400-year-old inn, originally a farmhouse, belonging to
Amroth Castle Estate. It has old world charm with beamed
ceilings, a Flemish chimney, a flagstone floor and an inglenook
fireplace. It is close to the beach, and local lobster and crab
are a feature, along with a popular choice of home-made
dishes including steak and kidney pie, soup and curry.
OPEN: 11.30-3 5.30-11. Closed Nov-Mar. **BAR MEALS:** L served
all week. D served all week 12-2 6-9. **RESTAURANT:** L served all
week. D served all week 12-2 6-9. **BREWERY/COMPANY:** Free
House. **PRINCIPAL BEERS:** Burton, Tetley.
FACILITIES: Children welcome Garden: beer garden, food
served outdoors Dogs allowed. **NOTES:** Parking 100 No credit
cards

CAREW   Map 02 SN00

Carew Inn
SA70 8SL ☎ 01646 651267
e-mail: mandy@carewinn.co.uk
Dir: From A477 take A4075. Inn 400yds opp castle & Celtic cross
A traditional stone-built country inn situated opposite the
Carew Celtic cross and Norman castle, which is a regular
venue for activities by The Sealed Knot. A typical menu
included roast leg of lamb with redcurrant mint and orange
sauce, baked cod with a fennel and herb crust, seafood pie,
and tagliatelle with a Stilton sauce. Live music every Thursday
night under the marquee.
OPEN: 11.30-2.30 4.30-11 (Summer & wknd 11-11). Closed
Dec 25. **BAR MEALS:** L served all week. D served all week
11.30-2.30 6-9. Av main course £7. **RESTAURANT:** L served all
week. D served all week 12-2 6-9. Av 3 course fixed price £15.
BREWERY/COMPANY: Free House.
PRINCIPAL BEERS: Worthington Best, Brains SA & Reverend
James. **FACILITIES:** Children welcome Garden
NOTES: Parking 20

Inns, Taverns and Alehouses

As the middle ages wore on, a rough distinction grew
up between three types of drinking-house: the inn,
the tavern and the alehouse. At the top of the tree, the
inn provided lodging, meals and drink for well-to-do
travellers. The tavern was more like a wine bar, with
no accommodation. Usually in a town, it dispensed
wine and sometimes food to prosperous customers.
A bunch of evergreen leaves above the door might
identify it and it was associated, in puritanical minds
at least, with gambling, loose women and
disreputable songs.
At the bottom of the ladder and far more numerous,
alehouses catered for ordinary people. As there
name implies, they were simply dwelling houses
where ale was brewed and sold. Often kept by
women, they were generally one-room, wattle-and-
daub hovels which supplied a take-out service for the
neighbours. Inside there was no bar counter,
customers and the alewife huddled close, pigs and
chickens wandered in and out, and standards of
hygiene would horrify patrons today. The quality of
the ale was checked by a local official, the ale-conner,
and the houses identified themselves with an
alestake. This long pole with leaves at the end was the
forerunner of today's pub sign.

CILGERRAN   Map 02 SN14

Pendre Inn
Pendre SA43 2SL ☎ 01239 614223
e-mail: warmak@pendre.fsnet.co.uk
Dir: Off A478 south of Cardigan
Fronted by an ancient ash tree growing through the pavement,
a white stone, thick-walled building that dates back to the 14th
century, full of curiosities and memorabilia inside. Freshly-
made meals impress with their variety and value: home-made
soups and pâté followed by Maltese liver and bacon, Mexican
chicken stir-fry and a 'coupelle' of vegetable korma. Home-
made desserts and ices.
OPEN: 12-3. 6-11.30. **BAR MEALS:** L served all week.
D served all week. Av main course £4. **RESTAURANT:** L served
Mon-Sat. D served all week. Av 3 course à la carte £8.95.
BREWERY/COMPANY: Free House.
PRINCIPAL BEERS: Thomas Watkins. **FACILITIES:** Children
welcome Children's licence Garden: outdoor eating, patio,.
NOTES: Parking 6. **ROOMS:** 3 bedrooms 1 en suite s£15 d£25
No credit cards

HAVERFORDWEST   Map 02 SM91

Pick of the Pubs

Georges Bar 🐑 ♀
24 Market St SA61 1NH ☎ 01437 766683
🖥 01437 779090
e-mail: llewis6140@aol.com
See Pick of the Pubs on page 589

ARMSTRONG ARMS, STACKPOLE

SA71 5DF. Tel: 01646 672324
Directions: from Pembroke (B4319); signs for Stackpole
Set in the National Trust's Stackpole Estate, and close to Pembrokeshire's coastal path, this 17th-century stone cottage was once the post office. Cosy interior with log-burning stove and slate floors. Good food using fresh local produce.
Open: 11-3 6-11 (7 winter). Closed Sun eve & Mon in Jan & Feb). Bar Meals: 12-2.30 (2 winter) 7-9.30 (9 winter). Children and dogs welcome. Garden. Parking.
(see page 591 for full entry)

Pub**WALK**

Armstrong Arms, Stackpole

A varied and most enjoyable walk through the beautiful Stackpole Estate, incorporating the famous, wildlife-rich Lily Ponds, superb cliff scenery, magnificent sandy beaches, and a tiny working quay.

Turn right out of the pub car park and head downhill through the village. Continue steeply downhill, cross the stone bridge and take the first footpath left into woodland. Keep to the path, bearing right on nearing the lake, and soon turn left over a bridge at the top end of the lake. Proceed for a mile (1.6km) along this tranquil lakeside path, looking out for otters and the amazing birdlife, including kingfishers, that live here.

Cross the second stone bridge over the lake and make for the beach visible ahead. Where the sandy path forks, keep left of the beach and head up the path through dunes on to the headland (Saddle Point). Admire the beautiful beach (Broad Haven) below and follow the cliff-top path for a mile (1.6km), with spectacular views along the South Pembrokeshire coast and Caldey Island.

Continue round Stackpole Head and proceed to Barafundle Bay, arguably Pembrokeshire's most stunning beach. Either take the flatter route along the top of the beach, or the low route close to the beach (steep access and exit points). Beyond, keep to the coast path and descend steps to tiny Stackpole Quay (café). Head inland from the quay, through the NT car park and follow the permissive footpath across fields. Descend to cross the stone eight-arch bridge across the lake (passed earlier), and turn right on the far side. Retrace your steps back to Stackpole and the pub.

Distance: 5 1/2 miles (8.8km)
Map: OS Landranger 158
Terrain: clifftop, beaches, woodland and lakes
Paths: woodland & field paths, lakeside & coast path
Gradient: gently rolling; steep climb in and out of Stackpole

Walk submitted by: The Armstrong Arms

Point St John on the Pembrokeshire coast

Pick of the Pubs

The Dial Inn 🐑 ♈
Ridgeway Rd SA71 5NU ☎ 01646 672426
📠 01646 672426
Dir: *Just off A4139 (Tenby to Pembroke rd)*

Built in 1830 as the Dower House for nearby Lamphey
Court, The Dial was converted into a pub in 1966,
immediately establishing itself as a popular village local.
Further more recent additions have included new
bedrooms in 2000 and extension of the dining areas.
Every effort is made to use as much fresh local produce as
possible and the daily specials board reflects current
availability. Seasonal selections will likely include sea bass
fillets wrapped around fresh asparagus and oven-baked
cod fillet topped with tomato and melted cheese.
Lamphey lamb is braised with apricots, leeks and
rosemary and pan-fried fillet steak, filled with tomatoes
and Stilton, is accompanied by a pink peppercorn sauce.
The separate 'and also' menu lists horseshoe gammon
steaks, pasta, curries and vegetarian dishes - Glamorgan
sausages with plum chutney perhaps - salads, a pudding
list and Welsh cheese menu. Family room, cards,
dominoes and pool.
OPEN: 11-3 6-11 (Sun 12-3 7-10.30). **BAR MEALS:** L
served all week. D served all week 12-2.30 6.30-9.30.
RESTAURANT: L served all week. D served all week 12-2.30
6.30-9.30. Av 3 course à la carte £15.50.
BREWERY/COMPANY: Free House.
PRINCIPAL BEERS: Hancocks, Bass, Worthington.
FACILITIES: Children welcome Children's licence Garden:
Food served outisde Dogs allowed except in garden.
NOTES: Parking 50. **ROOMS:** 4 bedrooms s£25 d£40

The Stanley Arms ♈
SA67 8BE ☎ 01834 891227
Dir: *Off A40 at Canaston Bridge onto A4075, R at Cross Hands*

Admire the views of Picton Castle and the Cleddau Estuary
from the garden of this 250-year-old building, with its summer
flower-adorned facade, and original flagstone floor in the
public bar. Popular with the sailing community. Home-cooked
pub food includes 'chilli non carne' (meat-free chilli!), deep-
fried plaice, lasagne verdi, ham and mushroom tagliatelle, and
peppered mackerel.
OPEN: 12-3 (all day Fri-Sun May-Sept) 6-11 (Sun 7-10.30). Closed
25 Dec. **BAR MEALS:** L served Tue-Sun. D served all week 12-
2.30 6-9.30. Av main course £6.25. **RESTAURANT:** L served Tue-
Sun. D served all week 12-2.30 6-9.30. Av 3 course à la carte £11.
BREWERY/COMPANY: Free House. **PRINCIPAL BEERS:** Bass
IPA, Worthington. **FACILITIES:** Children welcome Children's
licence Garden: outdoor eating Dogs allowed Water.
NOTES: Parking 20

The Harp Inn 🐑
31 Haverfordwest Rd SA62 5UA ☎ 01348 840061
📠 01348 840812
Dir: *Located on main A40*
Following major refurbishment, the pub's restaurant has
doubled in size, and there is a new function room. The bar
menu is extensive and the restaurant, with its lovely inglenook,
has an impressive range of fresh fish. Other options may
include venison, steaks, and goose breast with port and pear
sauce.
OPEN: 11-3 6-11. **BAR MEALS:** L served all week. D served all
week 12-2.30 6-9.30. Av main course £5.95. **RESTAURANT:** L
served all week. D served all week 12-2.30 6.30-9.30. Av 3 course
à la carte £15. **BREWERY/COMPANY:** Free House
FACILITIES: Children welcome Garden Dogs allowed.
NOTES: Parking 50

Skittles

Skittles is a far older game than darts or dominoes, on record in London since the 15th century, when it was
banned. Henry VIII enjoyed it and had his own skittle alley, but governments kept vainly trying to stop
ordinary people playing, because they ought to have been practising their archery and because they
gambled so heavily. Even so, the game became popular enough to make 'beer and skittles' proverbial.
Basically, three wooden balls are propelled at nine pins to knock them down, but there are sharp variations
in the rules between different areas and pubs. Varieties include London or Old English Skittles, West Country
Skittles, Long Alley and Aunt Sally, as well as several types of table skittles.

Wales

OPEN: 10.30am-11pm. Closed Sun, 25 Dec & 1 Jan
BAR MEALS: L served Mon-Sat. D served Mon-Sat 12-9.45. Av main course £5.
RESTAURANT: L served Mon-Sat D served Mon-Sat 12-9.45. Av 3 course a la carte £15.
BREWERY/COMPANY: Free House.
PRINCIPAL BEERS: Marston's Pedigree, Wye Valley Bitter, guest beer.
FACILITIES: Garden: patio, outdoor eating.

George's Bar

24 Market Street SA61 1NH
☎ 01437 766683 📠 01437 779090
e-mail: llewis6140@aol.com
Dir: on the A40 in the town centre overlooking the castle

Built on the site of the former George's Brewery, this remarkable 18th-century building incorporates many original features in the restoration of its vaulted wine cellar, numerous eating areas and delightful walled garden that boasts spectacular views over Haverfordwest Castle.

Genuine local character is a feature of the all-day café bar and cellar bistro that stays loyal to Welsh tradition with its local produce, freshly prepared food and sheer enthusiasm setting it apart from the norm. In keeping with its brewing heritage, you will find Wye Valley Bitter, Marston's Pedigree and a frequently-changing guest ale on tap, plus a short, global list of wines and monthly wine specials. Including daily specials meal choices must exceed 40 at any one time, from home-made scones and cakes to fish from the Pembrokeshire coast, locally-sourced meats and vegetables, and fresh herbs from the garden - a minor triumph given its locality.

Daily specials featuring real local character might include smoked honey-glazed duck breast salad, goujons of local hake with lime mayonnaise, local seafood chowder with garlic bread, Welsh lamb stew topped with crispy potatoes, and George's turkey, gammon, leek and wild mushroom pie. Amongst possibly a dozen vegetarian options are cheese-topped nut and seed roast in filo pastry, wild mushroom pasta and a hot-and-spicy spinach dahl.

Some wicked desserts include crêpes Suzette, chocolate nut pavlova, old-fashioned treacle tart, and luxury Belgian ice cream sundaes; all contributing to a unique experience that awaits both newcomers and those in the know. For that all important business meeting, there's an airy, fully-equipped private room; free if ten or more are dining in the restaurant.

NEVERN
Map 02 SN04

Trewern Arms ★ ★
SA42 0NB ☎ 01239 820395 ☐ 01239 802173
Dir: On the A487 between Cardigan and Fishguard

Ivy-clad 16th-century inn set in attractive grounds astride the River Nevern. The Brew House bar is a popular local, with flagstone floors and old settles. Speciality dishes include Trewern surf 'n' turf (local sirloin steak stuffed with seafood in cream and brandy sauce), knuckle of lamb and Normandy pork fillet.
OPEN: 11-3 6-11 (Sun 12-3 7-10.30). **BAR MEALS:** L served all week. D served all week 12-2 6-9. Av main course £5.95.
RESTAURANT: L served Sun. D served Thu-Sat 12-1.45 7-9. Av 3 course à la carte £19.50.
BREWERY/COMPANY: Free House.
PRINCIPAL BEERS: Flowers Original, Whitbread Castle Eden Ale, Wadworth 6X. **FACILITIES:** Children welcome Garden: outdoor eating, patio. **NOTES:** Parking 80.
ROOMS: 10 bedrooms 10 en suite FR£60

PEMBROKE DOCK
Map 02 SM90

Ferry Inn 🏠
Pembroke Ferry SA72 6UD ☎ 01646 682947
Dir: A477, off A48, R at garage, signs for Cleddau Bridge, L at roundabout
Creeper-clad 16th-century riverside inn situated under Cleddau Bridge, with splendid views across the estuary from the nautical themed bar and waterside terrace. Expect good fresh local fish and seafood, perhaps deep fried wholetail scampi, poached salmon fillet, or seafood platter. Other options include loin of pork valentine, Cumberland sausage with onion gravy and mashed potatoes, or steak and kidney suet pudding.
OPEN: 11.30-2.45 7-11. Closed 25-26 Dec. **BAR MEALS:** L served all week. D served all week 12-2 7-10. Av main course £5.95. **BREWERY/COMPANY:** Free House.
PRINCIPAL BEERS: Hancocks HB, Bass. **FACILITIES:** Children welcome Garden: riverside terrace Dogs allowed Garden only water provided. **NOTES:** Parking 12

PORTHGAIN
Map 02 SM83

Pick of the Pubs

The Sloop Inn
SA62 5BN ☎ 01348 831449 ☐ 01348 831338
e-mail: Matthew@sloop-inn.freeserve.co.uk
If location were everything, The Sloop would rank amongst Pembrokeshire's best, located by the harbour of a picturesque fishing village that was once the home of a granite quarry and brick factory. The coastal path drops steeply to the harbour-side, where the pub's south-facing patio makes an ideal spot for drinks or lunch in fine weather. The row of former workers' cottages, though small on the outside, has been extended within to house a succession of eating areas with a unifying shipping theme. Porthgain scallops, local cod and sea bass are delivered to the door and feature on a regularly up-dated specials board alongside generously-cut Welsh ribeye beef steaks, chicken and leek suet pudding with Pembrokeshire potatoes and vegetable nut roast with pepper sauce. Lighter single dishes include macaroni and seafood bake, Llangloffan ploughman's and the famous Angry Dog burger. Salads come from a self-service counter and desserts such as white chocolate and raspberry cake mostly from the fridge.
OPEN: 11-11 (Sun 12-4 5.30-10.30). **BAR MEALS:** L served all week. D served all week 12-2.30 6-9.30. Av main course £6.90. **RESTAURANT:** L served all week. D served all week 12 6-9.30. Av 3 course à la carte £18 9.30.
BREWERY/COMPANY: Free House.
PRINCIPAL BEERS: Felinfoel, Worthington, Brains SA, Greene King Old Speckled Hen. **FACILITIES:** Children welcome Children's licence Garden: patio, outdoor eating, BBQ. **NOTES:** Parking 50

SOLVA
Map 02 SM82

The Cambrian Inn 🏠
Main St SA62 6UU ☎ 01437 721210
Dir: 13m from Haverfordwest on the St David's Rd
Something of an institution in this pretty fishing village (but park down by the estuary) is a white-painted Grade II listed 17th-century inn that attracts local and returning visitors alike. Fish fresh from the jetty alongside local duck breast in Cointreau and Welsh lamb shank with rosemary are staple dining choices; bar meals inclining more towards prawn and mushroom pancakes, ploughman's and vegetable lasagne.
OPEN: 11-3 6.30-11 (Winter 12-2.30, 7-11). Closed Dec 25-26.
BAR MEALS: L served all week. D served all week 12-2 7-9.30. Av main course £5.50. **RESTAURANT:** L served all week. D served all week 12-2 7-9.30. Av 3 course à la carte £17.50.
BREWERY/COMPANY: Free House.
PRINCIPAL BEERS: Worthington Best, Marstons Pedigree, Tetley. **FACILITIES:** Children welcome Garden: patio, outdoor eating Dogs allowed garden only. **NOTES:** Parking 12 No credit cards

The Birds of the Air

Pride of place among bird signs is taken by the Swan, often adopted by inns close to a river. The eccentric Swan with Two Necks probably began as a swan with two nicks in its beak. The Cock may be related to cock-fighting or to St Peter. Geese and chickens appear alone or keeping dangerous company with the Fox. The Bird in Hand comes from falconry and the Dog and Duck either from fowling or from the amusement of setting a dog on a pinioned duck. The Eagle is from Heraldry and the Magpie and Stump from the countryside, while rarities include the Parrot and the Peahen.

STACKPOLE   Map 02 SR99

Pick of the Pubs

Armstrong Arms
SA71 5DF ☎ 01646 672324
Dir: From Pembroke take B4319 & follow signs for Stackpole
Close to Pembrokeshire's coastal path, this 17th-century stone cottage at the heart of the National Trust's Stackpole Estate was once the village post office, its original posting box still set in the wall. Exposed ash ceilings, slate floors and bar tops, a log burner and old bread ovens stay true to this legacy. Alongside Buckley's real ales, local produce plays its full part on the menu, with lunch options such as crepes of spinach, red pepper and leek or smoked haddock with tomato and fennel, topped with mature Welsh Cheddar, and Welsh beef braised with ale and mushrooms. More complex dishes at night include smoked trout pâté with orange compote and pasta spirals with mushrooms and broccoli, followed perhaps by monkfish with basil and tomato sauce or baked John Dory with onion cream and rack of Welsh lamb with a sage crust or Welsh Black beef fillet sauced with Madeira and wild mushrooms. For vegetarians, filo parcels of cambozola, beef tomato and spinach and, to follow, a selection of home-made desserts listed on the blackboards.
OPEN: 11-3 6-11. **BAR MEALS:** L served all week. D served all week 12-2 7-9. **RESTAURANT:** L served all week. D served all week 12-2 7-9. Av 3 course à la carte £14.
BREWERY/COMPANY: Free House.
PRINCIPAL BEERS: Buckleys Reverend James & Buckleys Best, Wadworth 6X. **FACILITIES:** Children welcome Garden: outdoor eating Dogs allowed Water.
NOTES: Parking 25
See Pub Walk on page 587

WOLF'S CASTLE   Map 02 SM92

Pick of the Pubs

The Wolfe Inn
SA62 5LS ☎ 01437 741662 📠 01437 741676
Dir: On A40 between Haverfordwest and Fishguard
Successive alterations and improvements to this classic old inn close to the Preseli hills - and hard by the A40 - have assured its success under new ownership. Its secret lies in true dedication to good food, wine and beers served in a genial and relaxed atmosphere. The daily bar menu features 'butcher's bangers' with mash and onion gravy and Glamorgan cheese sausages with provencale sauce, with Welsh fries and a side salad as optional extras. Finer dining embraces terrine of pork liver, chicken, duck and apricots with port and orange sauce and chicken supreme filled with Boursin cheese on a wild mushroom and tarragon sauce. Locally landed crab and lobsters feature regularly on the chef's daily blackboard alongside the ever-popular fisherman's pie and Welsh Black sirloin and fillet steaks.
OPEN: 11-3 6-11 (Sun 11-3 only). **BAR MEALS:** L served all week. D served Mon-Sat 12-2 7-9. **RESTAURANT:** L served all week. D served Mon-Sat 12-2 7-9. Av 3 course à la carte £24. **BREWERY/COMPANY:** Free House.
PRINCIPAL BEERS: Worthington. **FACILITIES:** Garden: outdoor eating, patio, BBQ, rockery, Dogs allowed.
NOTES: Parking 15. **ROOMS:** 3 bedrooms 1 en suite s£35 d£55

POWYS

BERRIEW   Map 08 SJ10

Lion Hotel
SY21 8PQ ☎ 01686 640452 📠 01686 640604
Dir: 5m from Welshpool on A483, R to Berriew. Centre of village next to church.
Expect a friendly family welcome at this 17th-century timbered black and white inn situated in a pretty village setting. From traditional bar snacks, the bistro menu, supplemented by daily fish options and chef's specials, may offer slow-roasted shoulder of Welsh lamb, pan-fried salmon steak, or lamb and rosemary pie.
OPEN: 11.30-3 (Jan-Apr 11.30-2.30) 5.30-11. Closed Dec 25-26.
BAR MEALS: L served all week. D served all week 12-2 7-9. Av main course £8.95. **RESTAURANT:** L served all week. D served all week 12-2 7-9. Av 3 course à la carte £12.50.
BREWERY/COMPANY: Free House. **PRINCIPAL BEERS:** Bass, Worthington, Greene King Old Speckled Hen, Shepherd Neame Spitfire. **FACILITIES:** Children welcome Garden: patio, Outdoor eating. **NOTES:** Parking 6. **ROOMS:** 7 bedrooms 7 en suite s£60 d£80 FR£100

Wales

Pick of the Pubs

The Usk Inn ◆◆◆◆ 🏠 ♀
Talybont-on-Usk LD3 7JE ☎ 01874 676251
📠 676392
e-mail: stay@uskinn.co.uk
Dir: *6m E of Brecon, just off the A40 towards Abergavenny & Crickhowell, if coming through Talybont turn onto Station Rd alongside the railway bridge were 500 yds on the R*

This recently refurbished free house has long been welcoming weary travellers with a good range of real ales. The open fire and flagstone floors remain, but now the inn offers just a little more style. There's a civilised restaurant, with crisp white napery and candlelit tables, and cheerful en suite guest bedrooms featuring locally-made pine furniture and patchwork quilts. Food is taken seriously, with imaginative menus that make good use of fresh local produce. Lunchtime brings home-made soup and a decent selection of sandwiches and baguettes, in addition to a full range of cooked dishes. Expect home-made burgers, local venison, gammon with bubble-and-squeak, or smoked haddock on spinach. Vegetarian choices include sweet potato and leek casserole, or couscous with peppers, artichoke and grilled haloumi.
OPEN: 8am-11pm. Closed Dec 25-26. **BAR MEALS:** L served all week. D served all week 12-3 6.30-10. Av main course £7.95. **RESTAURANT:** L served all week. D served all week 12-2 7-9.30. Av 3 course à la carte £25. Av 3 course fixed price £19.95. **BREWERY/COMPANY:** Free House.
PRINCIPAL BEERS: Brains SA Best, Brains Reverend James, Tomos Watkin OSB, Brains Buckley's Best.
FACILITIES: Children welcome Garden: patio, outdoor eating, Dogs allowed Water, Not in bedrooms.
NOTES: Parking 35. **ROOMS:** 11 bedrooms 11 en suite s£29.50 d£50

Pick of the Pubs

White Swan Inn
Llanfrynach LD3 7BZ ☎ 01874 665276
See Pick of the Pubs on page 595

Pick of the Pubs

The Talkhouse ◆◆◆◆◆◆ ♀ NEW
Pontdolgoch SY17 5JE ☎ 01686 688919
📠 01686 689134
Dir: *From Newtown A487 about 5M towards Machynlleth & Dolgellau, turn R onto A470 just before level crossing into Caersws carry on about 1 M on A470 inn on the L*
If you're hungry or need a break, do not drive past this unassuming, stone pub, set hard beside the A470. Why? Because Colin and Melanie Dawson have refurbished the place from top to bottom. Expect to find a beautifully furnished lounge area, complete with soft sofas, and a relaxing bar with a blazing log fire, wooden settles and piped classical music. The adjoining civilised dining room features a good mix of tables topped with candles. In addition, an ever-changing blackboard menu lists an imaginative range of freshly prepared dishes. Follow nibbles on the bar - home-made parsnip crisps - with Roquefort soufflé or tomato, celery and leek soup, accompanied by half loaf of bread with a choice of butters - try the garlic and chilli butter! Move on, perhaps, with chargrilled rib of Welsh black beef with horseradish mash or tuna with wok-fried Mediterranean vegetables and pesto. If you have room, round off with Lakeland pudding with hot caramel sauce. Well chosen list of wines from Tanners; 10 by the glass. Three smartly decorated and well appointed en suite bedrooms upstairs, so why not indulge a little and stay overnight.

OPEN: 12-2.30 6-11. Closed 25-26 Dec, last Wk Mar, last Wk Sept. **BAR MEALS:** L served Tue-Sat. D served Mon-Sat 12-1.30 6-9. Av main course £10. **RESTAURANT:** L served Tue-Sat. D served Mon-Sat 12-1.30 6-9. Av 3 course à la carte £20. **BREWERY/COMPANY:** Free House.
PRINCIPAL BEERS: Greene King, Bass.
FACILITIES: Garden: Food served outside.
NOTES: Parking 30. **ROOMS:** 3 bedrooms 3 en suite d£65

All AA listed accommodation can also be found on the AA's internet site **www.theAA.com**

CAIN VALLEY HOTEL, LLANFYLLIN ★ ★
High Street SY22 5AQ.
Tel: 01691 648366
Directions: on A490 between Welshpool and Lake Vyrnwy
Character 17th-century coaching inn with many period features and a Jacobean staircase situated in a small rural town close to Lake Vyrnwy. Choice of real ales and a wide range of traditional bar food. Bedrooms.
Open: 11.30-11 (Sun 12-10.30). Bar Meals: 12-2 7-9. Children welcome. Parking.
(see page 598 for full entry)

POWYS

*Pub*WALK

Cain Valley Hotel, Llanfyllin

A short walk across farmland and through John Adams Wood, with fine views of the Berwyn Mountains.

From the front of the hotel, cross the High Street and walk up Market Street. At the top, turn left at Moriah Chapel, then immediately right into New Road. At the end of Bronygaer housing estate on your right, turn left with the footpath sign and cross the bridge to a stile on the right. Cross the field, making for the gate in the corner by woodland.

Follow the well defined path through John Adams Woods. Head across the field to the mid-point of the hedge opposite and continue to a gate in the next field. Maintain direction acros the next field to a stile in the hedge, with excellent views of the Berwyn Mountains to your right.

Turn right along Bachie Road, following it left to a fork with a farm road. Bear left along the farm road, pass through a gate, then climb an old gate on your left into a field. Follow the left-hand boundary to the bottom of the field and go over the wooden fence. Pass through the gateway immediately on your left and continue downhill with the hedge to your right to a gate. Turn left along the road for nearly a mile (1.6km) and turn left back into the town centre for the inn.

View from Tan-y-Pystall, Berwyn Mountains

Distance: 3 1/2 miles (5.6km)
Map: OS Landranger 125
Terrain: farmland, woodland, country lanes
Paths: field and woodland paths, tracks, metalled lanes
Gradient: gently undulating; no steep climbs

Walk submitted by: The Cain Valley Hotel

CARNO   Map 08 SN99

Aleppo Merchant Inn
SY17 5LL ☎ 01686 420210 🗎 01686 420296
e-mail: reception@thealeppo.co.uk
Dir: From Newtown, A489 and A470
Named after his ship by a retired sea captain, this stone-built inn is located in spectacular Welsh countryside between the Snowdonia and Brecon Beacons National Parks. There is a modernised bar with an open fire and straightforward pub food. The menu offers grills, fish and a good choice of vegetarian dishes. Specialities include beef carbonnade, Thai chicken, and vegetarian chilli.
OPEN: 11.30-2.30 7-11. **BAR MEALS:** L served all week. D served all week 12-2 7-9. Av main course £6. **RESTAURANT:** L served all week. D served all week 12-2 7-9. Av 3 course à la carte £12. **BREWERY/COMPANY:** Free House.
PRINCIPAL BEERS: Boddingtons. **FACILITIES:** Garden: food served outdoors. **NOTES:** Parking 50. **ROOMS:** 6 bedrooms 2 en suite s£30 d£45

COEDWAY   Map 08 SJ31

Ye Old Hand and Diamond
SY5 9AR ☎ 01743 884379 🗎 01743 884267
e-mail: oldhanddiamond@btconnect.com
Close to the Shropshire border and the River Severn, this 19th-century inn still retains much of its original character. Large open log fires burn in the winter and autumn. Typical menu includes chicken in mushroom and Stilton cream sauce, pork chops with cider and apple sauce, fresh sea bass, roast beef and Yorkshire pudding, and vegetable cannelloni.

OPEN: 11-11. **BAR MEALS:** L served all week. D served all week. Av main course £9. **RESTAURANT:** L served all week. D served all week. Av 3 course à la carte £15.
BREWERY/COMPANY: Free House. **PRINCIPAL BEERS:** Bass, Worthington. **FACILITIES:** Children welcome Garden: Food served outside **NOTES:** Parking 90. **ROOMS:** 5 bedrooms 5 en suite s£35 d£50 FR£65

CRICKHOWELL   Map 03 SO21

Pick of the Pubs

The Bear ◎ ◎ ★ ★ ★ 🐑 ♀
Brecon Rd NP8 1BW ☎ 01873 810408
🗎 01873 811696
e-mail: bearhotel@aol.com
Dir: On A40 between Abergavenny & Brecon

AA Pub of the Year for Wales 2002
In the same family hands for a quarter century, The Bear just goes on and on: so popular has it been both locally and country-wide that every available nook and cranny has been put to good use as bar, bistro or restaurant space. Add to this the bedrooms, divided between the main 15th-century inn and coach house rooms facing the cobbled courtyard, and its fully deserved reputation becomes clear. A slightly laid-back eccentricity is explained by the owners' regard of the whole house as their own home, treating all-comers with genuine hospitality and supervising the operation with seemingly boundless enthusiasm. Food choices are vast, from bistro specials of fresh linguine with crabmeat and coriander, local lamb noisettes in Vermouth sauce and baked fillet of cod 'Cymreig' on a bed of spinach, to modern European-inspired fine dining menus. Light bar meals run from Welsh rarebit with bacon on toasted olive bread, through prawn cakes with chilli dip and pickled ginger to burgers of local venison on leek and parsnip mash. Super desserts and puddings are all home-made and a peerless Welsh cheeseboard is complemented by a generously-priced range of ports.
OPEN: 10-3 6-11. **BAR MEALS:** L served all week. D served all week 12-2 6-10. Av main course £8. **RESTAURANT:** L served all week. D served Mon-Sat 12-2 7-9.30. Av 3 course à la carte £25. **BREWERY/COMPANY:** Free House.
PRINCIPAL BEERS: Bass, Greene King Old Speckled Hen, Hancocks HB. **FACILITIES:** Children's licence Garden: patio, outdoor eating Dogs allowed.
NOTES: Parking 60. **ROOMS:** 35 bedrooms 35 en suite s£52 d£68 FR£78-£126

Open: 12-3 6-10.30 (Sat till 11).
Bar Meals: L served all week.
D served all week 12-2 6-9. Av
main course £8.50.
RESTAURANT: L served Sun
D Mon-Sat 12-2 6-9. Av 3 course a
la carte £25. Av 3 course fixed
price £29.95.
BREWERY/COMPANY:
Free House.
PRINCIPLE BEERS: Tetley, Black
Sheep Bitter, Timothy Taylor Bitter
& Landlord.
FACILITIES: Children welcome.
Garden: patio, outdoor eating
dogs allowed.
NOTES: Parking 56.

The White Swan Inn

Llanfrynach CD3 7BZ
☎ 01874 665276 🖹 01874
Dir: 2m east of Brecon off the A40

In the heart of the Beacons National Park and tucked off the A40 just three miles east of Brecon stands this typically picturesque village whose low, unassuming inn stands opposite the churchyard. A handily-placed escape from the frenetic pace of Brecon, especially during Jazz Festival week.

Long a renowned local for reasonable pub food, the premises have undergone an impressive make-over under new ownership and kitchen production has gone up a gear also. Entry is by way of an attractive rear patio of stone-topped tables under a straggling trellis: within are retained the polished flagstones, exposed oak beams and vast inglenook that give it so much character. In food terms traditional fuses with modern and east meets west in carefully balanced combinations that make best use of local produce and careful shopping.

Blackboard specials with a fishy bias might include moules marinière and langoustines in garlic butter, followed by cod fillet with Parmesan and red pepper mash or roast monkfish tail with sweet potato, Mediterranean vegetables, rosemary and garlic. Lunch snacks range from Cajun spiced salmon strips with bacon, sour cream and chives to Lincoln sausages with bubble-and-squeak and onion gravy. Open sandwiches include toasted Caprese of tomato, basil and buffalo mozzarella and spicy chargrilled chicken: follow with glazed lemon tart or banana and rum parfait with caramel sauce. At dinner, noteworthy wines accompany foil-baked sea bass, honey-glazed lamb shank with home-dried beetroot and Thai-style wild boar with jasmine rice.. The White Swan is especially popular in summer with walkers and cyclists: trout fishing on the River Usk and the Brecon Canal are both nearby.

Pick of the Pubs

Gliffaes Country House Hotel 🏵 🏵 ★ ★ ★
NP8 1RH ☎ 01874 730371 📱 01874 730463
e-mail: calls@gliffaeshotel.com
Dir: 1m off the A40, 2.5m W of Crickhowell
In the same hands for over 50 years, family commitment
here has now extended to a third generation with no
discernible diminution of standards. The location, in
mature woodland overlooking the River Usk - with some
two miles of private fishing a particularly popular option -
is little short of spectacular. Popular bar lunches of lambs'
liver and bacon with grain mustard mash or a simple
Caesar salad with chargrilled chicken entice gentle
relaxation in the conservatory or on a lofty riverside
terrace. Daily dinner menus command fixed prices for
specialities such as spinach saccottino stuffed with
Gorgonzola, pan-roasted Cornish cod with brandade
potato and fennel and home-made ice creams, or perhaps
rich dark chocolate torte with mango sorbet. Farmhouse
cheeses are picked from the best available English,
Scottish, Irish and - naturally - Welsh sources. Attractively
furnished bedrooms provide good levels of equipment
and comfort.
OPEN: 12-3 6-11. **BAR MEALS:** L served all week 12-2.30.
Av main course £6.50. **RESTAURANT:** D served all week
12.30-2.30 7.30-9.15. Av 3 course fixed price £23.30.
BREWERY/COMPANY: Free House. **PRINCIPAL BEERS:**
John Smiths, Felinfoel Double Dragon Ale. **FACILITIES:**
Children welcome Garden: Food served outside Dogs
allowed in garden, Kennels Water. **NOTES:** Parking 30.
ROOMS: 22 bedrooms 22 en suite s£55 d£67

Pick of the Pubs

Nantyffin Cider Mill 🏵 🐫 ♀
Brecon Rd NP8 1SG ☎ 01873 810775 📱 01873 810775
e-mail: Nantyffin@aol.com
Dir: At junction of A40 & A479, 1.5m west of Crickhowell
A genuine all-rounder of quality pub and restaurant
standing in a picturesque garden just across the road from
the River Usk. The original cider mill, fully working until
the 1960s, has been tastefully incorporated into the main
dining-room, while the bars are full of character and offer
a wide range of real ales and interesting, mainly New
World, wines. Locally grown produce, much of it organic,
forms the basis of imaginative seasonal menus that are
supplemented by daily specials that feature fine market-
fresh fish. Kick off perhaps with Pembrokeshire mussels
steamed with cider and leeks and follow with a mixed fish
and shellfish casserole with linguine, tomato and fennel.
Meatier alternatives might be grilled local black pudding
with Calvados apple purée and salt marsh lamb with herb
crust and garlic-infused rosemary sauce. A comprehensive
dessert list takes in bread-and-butter pudding and classic
tarte au citron, with an alternative choice of traditional
Welsh cheeses with oatcakes and chutney.
OPEN: 12-2.30 6-9.30. Closed Mon, 1 wk Nov, 1wk Jan.
BAR MEALS: L served Tues-Sun. D served Tues-Sat 12-2.30
6.30-9.30. Av main course £10. **RESTAURANT:** L served
Tues-Sun. D served Tues-Sat 12-2.30 7-9.30. Av 3 course à la
carte £21. **BREWERY/COMPANY:** Free House.
PRINCIPAL BEERS: Greene King Old Speckled Hen, Uleys
Old Spot, Tomos Watkins, Felinfoel, Marstons Pedigree.
FACILITIES: Children welcome Garden: outdoor eating,
overlooking River Usk **NOTES:** Parking 40

CWMDU Map 03 SO12

Pick of the Pubs

The Farmers Arms 🐫
NP8 1RU ☎ 01874 730464 📱 01874 730464
e-mail: cwmdu@aol.com
*Dir: From A40 take A479 signed Builth Wells, Cwmdu is 3m
along this road*

Located in the Brecon Beacons National Park, just on the
edge of the Black Mountains, this tiny hamlet stands
tucked away in a typically quiet valley of great natural
beauty. A friendly welcome is assured in a village bar of
traditional character complete with cast iron log-burning
stove. In the dining-room beyond, a wide selection of
dishes maximises the abundance of local ingredients,
catering for all appetites and special needs on request.
A commendable selection of real ales accompanies dishes
such as braised shank of lamb with root vegetables and
rosemary and pan-roast duck breast with stir-fried Thai-
style vegetables. Regularly delivered fresh fish adds brill
fillet with tomato and basil butter sauce and fresh scallops
on cauliflower purée with coriander hollandaise. Tangy
lemon tart arrives on raspberry coulis with lemon curd ice
cream: for the less sweet-toothed fine Welsh cheeses with
celery, grapes and toasted walnuts. Still a proper pub with
comfortable country bedrooms and hands-on, caring
owners.
OPEN: 12-2.30 6.30-11 (Mon 6.30-11 only, except BH Mon
when open all day). **BAR MEALS:** L served Tue-Sun. D
served all week 12-2.15 7-9.30. Av main course £6.50.
RESTAURANT: L served Tue-Sun. D served all week 12-2.15
7-9.30. Av 3 course à la carte £18. Av 3 course fixed price £15.
BREWERY/COMPANY: Free House.
PRINCIPAL BEERS: Uley Old Spot Prize Ale, Tomos Watkin
OSB, Brains Buckley's Reverend James, Hancocks HB.
FACILITIES: Children welcome Garden: outdoor eating
Dogs allowed Water. **NOTES:** Parking 30.
ROOMS: 3 bedrooms 2 en suite s£15 d£30
FR£40-£55

AA Hotel Booking Service on 0870 5050505 to book
at AA recognised hotels and B & Bs in the
UK and Ireland, or through our Internet site:
www.theAA.com

DYLIFE
Map 08 SH89

Star Inn ◆◆◆ ♀
SY19 7BW ☎ 01650 521345 ▤ 01650 521345
Dir: *Between Llanidloes & Machynlleth on mountain Rd*
An air of rustic, rural charm pervades the area in which this popular pub is located - a favourite haunt of Dylan Thomas and Wynford Vaughn Thomas. Red kites swoop overhead and close by is magnificent Clywedog reservoir. Varied choice of straightforward, wholesome pub fare includes curry, steak and kidney pie, gammon and plaice.
OPEN: 12-2.30 6-11 (closed Tue in winter). **BAR MEALS:** L served all week. D served all week 12-2.30 7-11. Av main course £7.50. **BREWERY/COMPANY:** Free House
FACILITIES: Children welcome Garden: patio, outdoor eating, BBQ Dogs allowed on lead at all times. **NOTES:** Parking 60.
ROOMS: 6 bedrooms 2 en suite s£18 d£36 FR£40

ELAN VILLAGE
Map 03 SN96

Elan Valley Hotel 🐾
LD6 5HN ☎ 01597 810448 ▤ 01597 810448
e-mail: Hotel@Elanvalley.demon.co.uk
Dir: *A44 to Rhayader then B4518 for 2m*
Situated below the last of the four reservoirs in the Elan Valley, this rejuvenated hotel, formerly a Victorian fishing lodge, stands in the heart of stunning mid-Wales scenery and is justifiably a popular refreshment stop among visitors to the area. From snacks like ploughman's lunches, hot toasted baguettes and home-baked ham, eggs and chips in the bar, the dining-room menu may offer slow-baked Welsh lamb with aubergine, ginger and peppers, spiced prawn curry and Moroccan chicken with aromatic couscous.
OPEN: 6-11 (weekends 11.30-3.30, 6-11) (Etr-Nov & 1/2 term, 11.30-3.30 Tue-Sun). Closed 25 Dec. **BAR MEALS:** L served Sun-Mon, Wed-Sat (summer only). D served Mon-Sat 12-2.30 7-9.30. **RESTAURANT:** D served all week 7-9. Av 3 course à la carte £17. **BREWERY/COMPANY:** Free House.
PRINCIPAL BEERS: Hancocks HB, Brains Buckley Reverand James, Greene King Old Speckled Hen, Tomos Watkin OSB.
FACILITIES: Children welcome Garden: Outdoor eating Dogs allowed. **NOTES:** Parking 30. **ROOMS:** 11 bedrooms 11 en suite s£35 d£58

♀ Pubs offering six or more wines by the glass

HAY-ON-WYE
Map 03 SO24

Pick of the Pubs

The Famous Old Black Lion ★ ★
HR3 5AD ☎ 01497 820841
Dir: *Town centre*

Perched above the river, close to what was the Lion Gate entrance to the old walled town, this 17th-century coaching inn is said to contain parts dating back to the 13th. An interior full of character includes the comfortable King Richard Bar with candlelit scrubbed pine tables where a jar of the pub's eponymous real ale and informal meals are served in a congenial atmosphere. The restaurant is named after Oliver Cromwell who lodged here while the Roundheads were laying siege to the Royalists in Hay Castle. A diverse bar menu includes Thai fishcakes, Glamorgan sausages of breadcrumbed Caerphilly cheese and duck liver pâté to start, followed by sweet and sour vegetables on soft noodles, scrumpy pork braised in cider, Moroccan lamb served on a bed of couscous and chicken tikka masala with rice. Seasonal additions include Wye salmon, perhaps with spinach and vermouth butter sauce, wild boar steaks and casseroled pheasant. Dinner (only) in the restaurant is rather more formally à la carte.
OPEN: 11-11 (Sun 12-10.30). **BAR MEALS:** L served all week. D served all week 12-2.30 7-9.30. Av main course £8.75. **RESTAURANT:** D served all week 7-9.30. Av 3 course à la carte £23. **BREWERY/COMPANY:** Free House.
PRINCIPAL BEERS: Old Black Lion Ale, Wye Valley.
FACILITIES: Children welcome Garden: Patio, outdoor eating. **NOTES:** Parking 20. **ROOMS:** 10 bedrooms 10 en suite s£32.50 d£58 FR£70-£110

Quoits

Throwing a ring over a low post in the ground is the basis of a pastime which was repeatedly forbidden by law from the 14th century on and at some unknown date became a popular pub game. Clubs were competing in Scotland and the North of England before 1850. The game has always been especially strong in the North East, where a standard throwing distance of 11 yards emerged, but 18 yards is the pitch length in East Anglia. The game is subtler and more elaborate than might be supposed, as is the allied pastime of throwing horseshoes.

HAY-ON-WYE continued

Kilverts Inn 🍴 ♀
The Bullring HR3 5AG ☎ 01497 821042
🖹 01497 821580
e-mail: thekilverts@barbox.net
Dir: From A50 take A49, then L onto B4348 into Hay-on-Wye. In town centre near Butter Market
At the heart of Wales's 'bookshop capital' near the Butter Market - though access and parking can be a little tricky - the hotel derives its name from a noted 19th-century cleric well commemorated in the town. A core menu appears to access local produce, though on the bar menu pizzas, pasta and other pub favourites have a strong presence. Restaurant dinners show rather more imagination: spicy lamb kofta kebabs, grilled trout fillets with coriander butter and local venison haunch steaks.
OPEN: 11-11 (Sun 12-10.30). Closed 25 Dec.
BAR MEALS: L served all week. D served all week 12-2 7-9.30. Av main course £8.95. **RESTAURANT:** D served all week 7-9.30. Av 3 course à la carte £18.75.
BREWERY/COMPANY: Free House.
PRINCIPAL BEERS: Hancock's HB, Bass, Greene King IPA.
FACILITIES: Children welcome Garden: outdoor eating, patio Dogs allowed before 7pm, water provided if requested. **NOTES:** Parking 15. **ROOMS:** 11 bedrooms 11 en suite d£70 FR£80

LLANDINAM   Map 08 SO08

The Lion Hotel
SY17 5BY ☎ 01686 688233 🖹 01686 689124
Dir: on the A470 midway between Newton and Llanidloes
Llandinam is perhaps best known as the home of the first electric light in Wales. The Lion itself is a centre for international para and hang-gliding. It also occupies an attractive riverside setting.

LLANDRINDOD WELLS   Map 03 SO06

The Bell Country Inn
Llanyre LD1 6DY ☎ 01597 823959 🖹 01597 825899
Dir: 1 1/2m NW of Llandrindod Wells on the A4081
Standing in the hills above Llandrindod Wells, and within easy reach of the Elan and Upper Wye valleys, this former 18th-century drovers' inn offers comfortable accommodation and a varied menu. Look to the specials board for the likes of grilled Welsh black fillet steak, poached salmon papillote, roast Usk valley turkey, and mushroom and spinach pie.
OPEN: 11-3 (Sun 12-4) 6-11 (Sun 7-10.30). **BAR MEALS:** L served all week. D served all week 12-2 6.30-9.30. Av main course £6.50. **RESTAURANT:** L served all week. D served all week 12-2 6.30-9.30. **BREWERY/COMPANY:** Free House.
PRINCIPAL BEERS: Worthington, Bass, Hancock's HB.
FACILITIES: Children welcome Garden: outdoor eating, BBQ, herb garden. **NOTES:** Parking 20. **ROOMS:** 9 bedrooms 9 en suite s£35 d£59.50 1 family room £60-£70

LLANFYLLIN   Map 08 SJ11

Cain Valley Hotel ★ ★
High St SY22 5AQ ☎ 01691 648366 🖹 01691 648307
Dir: from Shrewsbury & Oswestry follow signs for Lake Vyrnwy & onto A490 to Llanfyllin. Hotel on R
Grade II 17th-century coaching inn with many period features and a Jacobean staircase. Attractive restaurant with original beams and brickwork. Sample home-made steak and
continued

mushroom pie with Guinness in the bar. Alternatively, choose gammon with cumberland sauce, spicy vegetable roast or swordfish steak from the restaurant menu.
OPEN: 11.30-11 (Sun 12-10.30). Closed 25 Dec. **BAR MEALS:** L served all week. D served all week 12-2 7-9. Av main course £6.50.
RESTAURANT: D served all week 7-9. Av 3 course à la carte £20. **BREWERY/COMPANY:** Free House.
PRINCIPAL BEERS: Worthington, Ansells.
FACILITIES: Children welcome Dogs allowed guests bedrooms only. **NOTES:** Parking 12. **ROOMS:** 12 bedrooms 12 en suite s£37 d£60

See Pub Walk on page 591

The Stumble Inn 🍴
Bwlch-y-Cibau SY22 5LL ☎ 01691 648860
🖹 01691 648955
Dir: A458 to Welshpool, B4393 to Four Crosses and Llansantffraid, A495 Melford, A490 to Bwlch-y-Cibau
Standing opposite the church in a rural farming hamlet in unspoilt mid-Wales countryside close to Lake Vyrnwy, this popular stone-built inn offers a traditional pub atmosphere and food. The menu changes monthly and might feature Thai monkfish, beef goulash, Welsh lamb steak and hake fillet with saffron and prawn cream sauce.
OPEN: 11-3 6-12 (closed Mon). **BAR MEALS:** L served Tue-Sun. D served Tue-Sun 12-2 6-9. Av main course £15.
RESTAURANT: L served Tue-Sun. D served Tue-Sun 12-2 6-10. Av 3 course à la carte £20. Av 2 course fixed price £8.50.
BREWERY/COMPANY: Free House.
PRINCIPAL BEERS: Tetley and regularly changing guest ale.
FACILITIES: Children welcome Garden: old Massey tractor, patio, BBQ. **NOTES:** Parking 40

LLANGATTOCK   Map 03 SO21

The Vine Tree Inn 🍴
The Legar NP8 1HG ☎ 01873 810514 🖹 01873 811299
e-mail: s.lennox@virgin.net
Dir: Take A40 W from Abergavenny then A4077 from Crickhowell
Situated in the beautiful Usk Valley overlooking the medieval bridge, the Vine Tree is predominantly a dining pub. Freshly prepared food includes Vine Tree chicken breast stuffed with prawns and wrapped in bacon, Chicken Cymru, lamb kidneys in sherry sauce, salmon surprise, or trout in chive sauce.
OPEN: 12-3 6-11 (Sun 12-3 7-10.30). **BAR MEALS:** L served all week. D served all week 12-3 6-10. Av main course £7.50.
RESTAURANT: L served all week. D served all week 12-3 6-10. Av 3 course à la carte £21. **BREWERY/COMPANY:** Free House.
PRINCIPAL BEERS: Fullers London Pride, Castle Eden.
FACILITIES: Children welcome. **NOTES:** Parking 27

LLOWES   Map 03 SO14

The Radnor Arms 🍴
HR3 5JA ☎ 01497 847460 🖹 01497 847460
Dir: A438 Brecon-Hereford Rd between Glasbury & Clyro
Fine 400-year-old stone building, formerly a drovers' inn, enjoying stunning views of the Wye Valley and Black Mountains. Freshly-cooked food is served in the small bar with its open fire, friendly atmosphere and blackboard menu. Typical dishes include cod and chips, lemon sole, marinated venison, and various filled rolls and ploughman's.
continued

OPEN: 11-3 6.30-11 (Sun 12-3 7-10.30). Closed Mon.
BAR MEALS: L served Tue-Sun. D served Tue-Sun 12-3 6.30-11.
Av main course £7.50. **RESTAURANT:** L served Tue-Sun. D
served Tue-Sun 12-3 6.30-11. Av 3 course à la carte £12.50.
BREWERY/COMPANY: Free House.
PRINCIPAL BEERS: Felinfoel. **FACILITIES:** Children welcome
Garden: beer garden with seating, food served outside.
NOTES: Parking 50

LLYSWEN   Map 03 SO13

Pick of the Pubs

The Griffin Inn ◎ ♀
LD3 0UR ☎ 01874 754241 📄 01874 754592
e-mail: info@griffin-inn.freeserve.co.uk
Dir: On A470 (Brecon to Builth Wells rd)
A family-run favourite for some 17 years that provides a
friendly, relaxed atmosphere, traditional comforts and all
the sporting benefits of a stay in the glorious upper Wye
Valley. A hub of the local community, guests may find
themselves engaged in conversation with the local
poacher, the preacher, the publicans themselves and even
the village bobby. Wye salmon, fresh trout, seasonal
game, fruit and vegetables all play their part: the rage
these days is 'Tiffin in the Griffin' - plates and bowls of
locally sourced, often organic, dishes sent out one at a
time to share with a partner or more. Greek-style house
salad, duck or chicken liver pâtés, wild mushroom
Stroganoff with rice and seared salmon on tagliatelle are
typical choices for a single-course lunch. At dinner, add
Welsh Black beef daube with red wine and herbs and
slow-roast crispy duck with cherry sauce. Sunday lunch at
a fixed price is as popular as ever: hot-smoked salmon
with Glanwye sauce, roast Herefordshire rib of beef and
fresh fruit crumble or chocolate and brandy biscuit cake.
OPEN: 10.30-3 7-11. Closed 25-26 Dec. **BAR MEALS:** L
served Mon-Sat. D served Mon-Sat 12-2 7-9. Av main course
£12. **RESTAURANT:** L served Sun. D served Mon-Sat 1-2.30
7-9. Av 3 course à la carte £20 9.
BREWERY/COMPANY: Free House.
PRINCIPAL BEERS: Tomos Watkin, Flowers IPA, Robinsons,
Brains Buckley Reverend James. **FACILITIES:** Children
welcome Children's licence Dogs allowed.
NOTES: Parking 20. **ROOMS:** 7 bedrooms 7 en suite
s£40 d£70

MACHYNLLETH   Map 08 SH70

Dolbrodmaeth Inn
Dinas Mawddwy SY20 9LP ☎ 01650 531333
📄 01650 531339
Dir: A54 to A458, W to jct with A470, R for 0.5m, edge of Dinas
Mawddwy on L between road & river
Much restored late 19th-century inn set in the tranquil Dovey
Valley amid spectacular mountain scenery. The inn is popular
with anglers and has its own fishing club.

Pick of the Pubs

Wynnstay Arms
Maengwyn Street SY20 8AE ☎ 01654 702941
📄 01654 703884
e-mail: info@wynnstay-hotel.com
Dir: In town centre at junction of A487/A489
Handsome 18th-century former coaching inn standing in
the heart of this small market town. Very much the focal
point of the town, it also attracts a discerning local dining
clientele for Gareth John's imaginative bar and restaurant
menus which utilise as much fresh local produce as
possible. Relax in the welcoming bar with a pint of Brains
and order a Welsh cheese ploughman's, a casserole of
West Coast seafood, pan-seared salmon with rosemary
butter or Gareth's famous peppered duck. In the
restaurant expect tian of fresh Aberystwyth crab with
avocado and tomato for starters, followed by fillet of sole
with chive velouté, and sticky toffee sponge with
butterscotch sauce for pudding. Good real ales and a well
chosen wine list. Complete refurbishment for bedrooms
and public areas is underway.
OPEN: 11-11. **BAR MEALS:** L served Tue-Sun. D served all
week 12-2 6.30-9. Av main course £7.95.
RESTAURANT: D served all week 7-9. Av 3 course à la carte
£21. **BREWERY/COMPANY:** Free House.
PRINCIPAL BEERS: Flowers IPA, Timothy Taylor Landlord,
Brains Bitter & SA. **FACILITIES:** Children welcome Garden:
outdoor eating. Dogs allowed. **NOTES:** Parking 40.
ROOMS: 23 bedrooms 23 en suite s£45-£55 d£70-£100
FR£70-84

Wales

Top of the Tree

Pubs called the Royal Oak were originally named in loyal remembrance of the day in
1651 when the youthful King Charles II hid in an oak tree at Boscobel in Shropshire, while
Roundhead soldiers unsuccessfully searched the woods for him. The Royal Oak sign often shows
simply the oak tree, or the king is shown perched among the branches - in plain view from all
directions, but conventionally accepted as invisible to the purblind Parliamentarian troops.
Sometimes, more subtly, the tree has a large crown among the foliage. Rarer variants
include the king holding an oak spray with acorns, or acorns below a crown.

Pick of the Pubs

The Bricklayers Arms 🌸 🐾 **NEW**
Chirbury Rd SY15 6QQ ☎ 01686 668177
e-mail: robjennings6@hotmail.com
*Dir: On entering Montgomery, turn L at the first war memorial
300 yds on L handside*

The cobbled square of this historic market town stands
close to the Castle ruins and Offa's Dyke Path: at its
northern edge the old Bricklayers, a former drovers' inn,
dates back to the 13th century. Throughout the bar and
first floor dining-room original rafters, cottage-style
furnishings and abundant bric-a-brac are enhanced by
real open fires and sturdy old floorboards.

Predominantly modern British dishes with distinctly
Welsh intonation mark out Rob Jennings's carefully
chosen menus, while his wife Sue attentively manages the
front of house in an informal and efficient manner. There
is a short but adequate wine list and interesting real ales
including Reverend James, now brewed by Brains in
Cardiff.

On the weekly menu, starters might include seafood
mille fuille with baby leaves and balsamic dressing and
salad of home-cured Welsh bacon with olives and
Parmesan shavings, followed by prime Welsh rib-eye with
leek fondue and Shropshire Blue cream and goats' cheese
topped with sweet potato and aubergine ratatouille. In
winter look for marinated game with rich gravy encased in
pastry; in summer perhaps monkfish tail with dill mash
and tomato salsa.
OPEN: 12-2 6-11. Closed Mon, 2 Wks Feb, 1 wk Sept.
BAR MEALS: L served Tue-Sun. D served Tue-Sun 12-2
7-9.30. Av main course £9.50. **RESTAURANT:** L served
Tue-Sun. D served Tues-Sun 12-2 7-9.30.
BREWERY/COMPANY: Free House.
PRINCIPAL BEERS: Marstons Pedigree, Shepherd Neame
Spitfire, Greene King Old Speckled Hen.
FACILITIES: Children welcome Dogs allowed Water.
NOTES: Parking 15

  For pubs with AA rosette awards for food
see page 10

Pick of the Pubs

Dragon Hotel 🌸 ★ ★
SY15 6PA ☎ 01686 668359 ▤ 01686 668287
e-mail: reception@dragonhotel.com
*Dir: A483 toward Welshpool, R onto B4386 then B4385, Behind
the town hall*

With its black-and white timbered frontage and parts of
the interior dating back to the mid-1600s, there is plenty to
please the eye at this friendly, family-run old coaching inn.
Daily specials on large blackboards feature the best
available local beef and lamb and extensive vegetarian
options. Expect fried haloumi cheese with capers and
dressed leaves, tagliatelle carbonara and a combination
platter, sufficient for two, that includes breaded prawns,
chicken wings, cheese-topped tortilla chips and assorted
dim sum. Freshly prepared restaurant dinners are best
illustrated by starters of sliced partridge breast, followed
by seared venison loin with warm lime and raspberry
couscous or local salmon on an organic spinach and
bacon nest; then a paw-paw brûlée.
OPEN: 11-11. **BAR MEALS:** L served all week. D served all
week 12-2 7-9. Av main course £8. **RESTAURANT:** L served
all week. D served all week 12-2 7-9. Av 3 course à la carte
£23.50. Av 3 course fixed price £18.50.
BREWERY/COMPANY: Free House.
PRINCIPAL BEERS: Wood Special, Boddingtons.
FACILITIES: Children welcome Children's licence Garden:
patio, outdoor eating Dogs allowed not in bar.
NOTES: Parking 20. **ROOMS:** 20 bedrooms 20 en suite
s£45 d£75 FR£80

Red Lion Inn 🐾
Llanfihangel-nant-Melan LD8 2TN ☎ 01544 350220
▤ 01544 350220
e-mail: enquiries@theredlioninn.net
Dir: A483 to Crossgates then R onto A44
Llanfihangel-nant-Melan is a bit of a mouthful, but easy to find
beside the A44 three miles west of New Radnor: its late 16th-
century drovers' inn has been dispensing shelter and
sustenance for centuries. Bar and dining-room mouthfuls,
frequently up-dated to accommodate the best of local fresh
produce, sustain a Welsh accent with toasted Pencarreg goats'
cheese, roast Swansea hake with Penclawdd cockles and
samphire and Welsh black beef fillet with Anna potatoes.

continued

OPEN: 12-2.30 6-11. **BAR MEALS:** 12-2.15 6.30-9.45.
RESTAURANT: D served Wed-Mon 12-2.15 6.30-9.45. Av 3
course à la carte £15. **BREWERY/COMPANY:** Free House.
PRINCIPAL BEERS: Hook Norton. **FACILITIES:** Children
welcome Garden: outdoor eating Dogs allowed.
NOTES: Parking 30. **ROOMS:** 5 bedrooms 5 en suite s£25 d£40
FR£50

OLD RADNOR
Map 03 SO25

Harp Inn
LD8 2RH ☎ 01544 350655 📠 01544 350655
Dir: A44 from Leominster to Gore, then L to Old Radnor
Set on a hillside close to St Stephen's church, this restored
15th-century pub still retains its slate-flagged floor, exposed
stone walls and ancient bread oven. Open fires in winter give
place to spectacular summer views from the pub garden; but,
whatever the season, the bar menu offers plenty of pub
favourites. Restaurant choices include Hereford steaks, ginger
chicken, lamb shank in wine and rosemary, or salmon with dill
and mustard sauce.Please check opening times.
OPEN: 6-11 (Sat-Sun 12-3, 6-10.30). **BAR MEALS:** L served Sat
& Sun. D served Tue-Sun 12-2 6-9. Av main course £6.50.
RESTAURANT: L served Sat. D served Tue-Sun 12-2 7-9.
Av 3 course à la carte £17. **BREWERY/COMPANY:** Free House.
PRINCIPAL BEERS: Shepherd Neame. **FACILITIES:** Children
welcome Garden: outdoor eating, Dogs allowed Not in Rooms.
NOTES: Parking 18. **ROOMS:** 5 bedrooms 2 en suite s£25 d£48
FR£80-£90

PWLLGLOYW
Map 03 SO03

Pick of the Pubs

Seland Newydd 🏆 🏆 🏆
LD3 9PY ☎ 01874 690282
*Dir: 4m N of Brecon on B4520 to Builth Wells, 1m before
Lower Chapel*
Formerly the Camden Arms and renamed 'Seland
Newydd', the Welsh translation of New Zealand, by former
antipodean owners, this refurbished 17th-century
coaching inn enjoys a peaceful village setting in the
Brecon Beacons National Park. Homely and informal bar
and lounge areas with log fire; separate rear restaurant.
Seasonal dining menus are supplemented by a specials
board offering hot Welsh beef & horseradish baguette,
pan-fried chicken livers and smoked bacon with hot
balsamic and redcurrant dressing, and salmon tagliatelle
carbonara among the choice of satisfying lighter dishes.
Restaurant menu options (also available in the bar) may
include braised turbot with celeriac and fennel mash and
vanilla fish cream and roast pheasant with fondant
potatoes, wild mushrooms and game sauce. For pudding,
try the 'creamy, dreamy' bread-and-butter pudding.
Alfresco patio and woodland walk to the River Honduu
where the inn has fishing rights.
OPEN: 12-3 6-11 (11-11 Summer Sat). **BAR MEALS:** L
served Tue-Sun. D served Mon-Sat 12-2 7-9. (9.30 Thu-Sat)
Av main course £8.50. **RESTAURANT:** L served Tue-Sun.
D served Mon-Sat 12-2 7-9. Av 3 course à la carte £20.
BREWERY/COMPANY: Free House.
PRINCIPAL BEERS: Buckeys, Wye Valley Bitter,.
FACILITIES: Children welcome Garden: food served
outside. **NOTES:** Parking 30. **ROOMS:** 3 bedrooms
3 en suite s£37 d£50

TALGARTH
Map 03 so13

Castle Inn ♦♦♦
Pengenffordd LD3 0EP ☎ 01874 711353 📠 01874 711353
e-mail: castlepen@aol.com
Dir: 4m S of Talgarth on the A479
Located within the Brecon Beacons National Park, this former
drovers inn is popular with mountain walkers and outdoor
enthusiasts. The pub, which is 1,000 ft above sea level, takes its
name from an ancient castle and hillfort. Camping and bunk
barn facilities available. Substantial pub food includes beef in
red wine, cottage pie, rump steak and Caribbean curry.
OPEN: 12-3 7-11 (Mon 7-11 only, Sat 12-4, 7-11). Closed Dec 25.
BAR MEALS: L served Tue-Sun. D served all week 12-2 7-9. Av
main course £6. **BREWERY/COMPANY:** Free House.
PRINCIPAL BEERS: 2 or 3 regularly changing ales.
FACILITIES: Children welcome Garden: outdoor eating, small
pond, camping field Dogs allowed except in the garden.
NOTES: Parking 60. **ROOMS:** 5 bedrooms 2 en suite s£20 d£40
1 family room £50.50-£59.50

TALYBONT-ON-USK
Map 03 SN12

Star Inn
LD3 7YX ☎ 01874 676635
e-mail: joanstar@freenetname.co.uk
Traditional 200-year-old village inn situated in a pretty village
within the Brecon Beacons National Park. Garden adjoins river
and picturesque canal. Excellent centre for walking and
outdoor pursuits. Quiz night on Monday, live music on
Wednesday. Hearty bar food with dishes such as lamb's liver
casserole, spinach, leek and pasta bake, grilled trout, or
Hungarian pork goulash.
OPEN: 11-3 6-11 (Sat 11-11). **BAR MEALS:** L served all week.
D served all week 12-2.15 6.30-9.30. Av main course £5.
BREWERY/COMPANY: Free House.
PRINCIPAL BEERS: Felinfoel Double Dragon, Theakston Old
Peculier, Freeminer Best, Bullmastiff Best. **FACILITIES:** Children
welcome Garden: Outdoor eating Dogs allowed.
ROOMS: 2 bedrooms d£45

The Making of Beer

The traditional ingredients of beer are water, barley malt,
hops, yeats and ripe judgement. One traditional
brewery's products will taste different from another's
because of variations in the blending of the ingredients
and the timing of process. It all starts with barley, amlted
in a kiln at the malting: the higher the temperature, the
darker the beer. The powdered malt is mixed with hot
water to make a mash. How the hot mash is and how
long it is allowed to stand will affect the taste and in the
old days local spring water gave beer a distinctive local
flavour. Burton upon Trent's eminent reputation for bitter
rested on the gypsum in the town's water.
The liquid from the mash is boiled up with hops - the
more hops, the bitterer - and sugar is often added. Next
the liquid is cooled and yeast is stirred in to make it
ferment. The 'green beer' is eventually run into casks to
mature. Keg beer is filtered, sterilised and carbonated,
and then stored in sealed containers and taste more like
bottled beers, which are put through the same process.

Wales

Wales

TRECASTLE   Map 03 SN82

Pick of the Pubs

Castle Coaching Inn ♀
LD3 8UH ☎ 01874 636354   🖥 01874 636457
e-mail: hotel.reservation@btinternet.com
Dir: On A40 W of Brecon
A Georgian 300-year-old former coaching inn right by the
main A40 trunk route that boasts a remarkable bow-
fronted bar window, smart bedrooms and a garden totally
remodelled over the years by dedicated family owners.
Bryn Chamberlain masterminds a shopping list paramount
in the use of locally available produce, from which his
culinary skills are put to good use in both bar and dining-
room (always book for the latter).
'From the Ocean' come breadcrumbed goujons of
lemon sole and paupiettes of salmon with tomato and
basil cream sauce, whilst steak and kidney puff pastry pie
and lasagne Liguria are delivered straight from a steaming
hot oven. Traditional grills of Welsh butchers' meats and
tempting vegetarian dishes such as a goats' cheese,
spinach and ricotta cannelloni are representative of a wide
range of alternatives, with tempting afters exemplified by
French apple galette, triple chocolate truffle tart and
peerless Welsh farmhouse cheeses.
OPEN: 12-3 6-11. Closed 25 Dec. **BAR MEALS:** L served all
week. D served all week 12-2 6.30-9.30. Av main course
£6.50. **RESTAURANT:** D served all week 7-9. Av 3 course à
la carte £22. **BREWERY/COMPANY:** Free House.
PRINCIPAL BEERS: Fuller's London Pride, Shepherd Neame
Spitfire, Greene King Triumph Ale, Youngs Special.
FACILITIES: Children welcome Children's licence Garden:
outdoor eating, patio Dogs allowed. **NOTES:** Parking 25.
ROOMS: 10 bedrooms 10 en suite s£45 d£50
FR£60-£70

UPPER CWMTWRCH   Map 03 SN71

George VI Inn NEW
SA9 2XH ☎ 01639 830441   🖥 01639 830411
e-mail: marcusrcoles@aol.com
Dir: 2 M from Ystalyfera Rdbt at Upper Cwmtwrch is the George IV
inn next to the river
Traditional family-owned pub and restaurant, occupying a
scenic riverside location at the foot of the Black Mountains.
The inn boasts a colourful garden and patio which is ideal for
summer al fresco dining. Alternatively, relax by the cosy
woodburner on a cold winter's day and watch the chefs
preparing your meal.
The pub brews its own beers and offers wholesome fare
made from Welsh produce. Home-made pies, including
chicken and steak and kidney, fresh local trout, lobster and
crab and popular roasts feature on the extensive menu.
OPEN: 11.30-3 6.30-11 (Sun 12-3, 7-10.30). Closed Jan.
BAR MEALS: L served Wed-Mon. D served Wed-Mon 11.30-2.30
6.30-10. Av main course £6.50. **RESTAURANT:** L served Wed-
Mon. D served Wed-Mon 11.30-2.30 6.30-10. Av 3 course à la
carte £15. **BREWERY/COMPANY:** Free House
FACILITIES: Children welcome Garden: Food served outside
Dogs allowed Outside only. **NOTES:** Parking 40

SWANSEA

LLANSAMLET   Map 03 SS69

Plough and Harrow
57 Church St SA7 9RL ☎ 01792 772263
e-mail: ploughharrow@llansamlet.plus.com
Dir: 2 M from Junct 44 of M4, 5 M from the centre of Swansea near
the Enterprise Park
Sitting in a quiet Swansea suburb next to a church, this Tomos
Watkin pub has a roaring log fire and some say, a resident
ghost. Cosy relaxed atmosphere with a good local reputation
for its food.

PONTARDDULAIS   Map 02 SN50

The Fountain Inn 🕲
111 Bologoed Rd SA4 1JP ☎ 01792 882501
🖥 01792 885340
e-mail: bookings@fountaininn.com
Dir: A48 from M4 to Pontlliw then on to Pontarddulais, inn on R

This carefully modernised old free house is full of memorabilia
of Swansea's industrial past. The chef uses fresh local produce
to produce an extensive and interesting range of dishes.
Broccoli and Stilton soup, or a warm scallop and bacon salad
might precede chicken stuffed with leeks and Caerphilly
cheese, braised pheasant, or sea bass with lime and rosemary.
Plum crumble or Ameretto and chocolate cake round off the
meal.
OPEN: 12-2 5.30-11.30. **BAR MEALS:** L served all week. D
served all week 12-2 5.30-8.30. Av main course £4.95.
RESTAURANT: L served all week. D served all week 12-2.30
5.30-9.30. Av 3 course à la carte £14.95. Av 3 course fixed price
£8.99. **BREWERY/COMPANY:** Free House.
PRINCIPAL BEERS: Greene King Old Speckled Hen, Fullers
London Pride, Batemans XXXX. **FACILITIES:** Children welcome
Garden: outdoor eating. **NOTES:** Parking 30. **ROOMS:** 9
bedrooms 9 en suite s£37.50 d£42.50 FR£52.50

REYNOLDSTON   Map 02 SS48

King Arthur Hotel 🕲
Higher Green SA3 1AD ☎ 01792 390775   🖥 01792 391075
e-mail: info@kingarthurhotel.co.uk
Dir: Just N of A4118 SW of Swansea
In the heart of the Gower Peninsula, Britain's first designated
Area of Outstanding Natural Beauty, this 18th-century country
inn is ideally located for all outdoor pursuits. The varied menu
ranges from snacks and salads to steaks and home-made pies.
Fresh fish, game and local specialities are offered from the
blackboard. Themed eating nights are popular, including a
monthly fish night.

continued

OPEN: 11-11. Closed 25 Dec. **BAR MEALS:** L served all week. D served all week 12-2.30 6-9.30. Av main course £5.25. **RESTAURANT:** L served all week. D served all week 12-2.30 6-9.30. Av 3 course à la carte £11. Av 3 course fixed price £8.95. **BREWERY/COMPANY:** Free House. **PRINCIPAL BEERS:** Felinfoel Double Dragon, Worthington, Bass. **FACILITIES:** Children welcome Garden: Food served outside. **NOTES:** Parking 80. **ROOMS:** 7 bedrooms 7 en suite s£30 d£40 FR£50-£60

VALE OF GLAMORGAN

EAST ABERTHAW   Map 03 ST06

Pick of the Pubs

Blue Anchor Inn
CF62 3DD ☎ 01446 750329 📠 01446 750077

Rumour has it that this 1380s pub still retains a secret passage down to the shore, where wreckers and smugglers formerly roamed the wild coastline that looks out across the Bristol Channel. Hanging baskets and flower tubs grace the frontage in summer, when the standard choice of daily fare is available. In the inter-linked bars a wide range of real ales accompanies jacket potatoes and sandwiches, traditional Welsh faggots with mash and mushy peas and chicken curry with coconut. Dinner and Sunday lunch menus in the restaurant add devilled whitebait, roast Glamorgan Vale leg of pork, wild rabbit in Parma ham with a mustard and brandy cream and lemon Bakewell tart or chocolate and Tia Maria crème brûlée. **OPEN:** 11-11 (Sun 12-10.30). **BAR MEALS:** L served Mon-Fri. D served Mon-Fri 12-2 6-8. **RESTAURANT:** L served Sun. D served Mon-Sat 12-2.30 7-9.30. **BREWERY/COMPANY:** Free House. **PRINCIPAL BEERS:** Brains Buckleys Best, Theakston Old Peculier, Wadworth 6X, Boddingtons. **FACILITIES:** Children welcome Garden: **NOTES:** Parking 70

MONKNASH   Map 03 SS97

The Plough & Harrow ♈ NEW
CF71 7QQ ☎ 01656 890209
e-mail: pugs@publive.com
In a peaceful country setting, on the edge of a small village with views across the fields to the Bristol Channel, this low, state-roofed building was originally built as the chapter house of a monastery, although it has been a pub for 500 of its 600-year existence. Expect an atmospheric interior, open fires, an excellent choice of real ale on tap, and home-cooked food using fresh local ingredients.
OPEN: 12-12. **BAR MEALS:** L served all week 12-2. Av main course £5. **RESTAURANT:** D served all week 6-9. Av 3 course à la carte £10. **BREWERY/COMPANY:** Free House. **PRINCIPAL BEERS:** Hancocks HB, Shepherd Neame Spitfire, Timothy Taylor Landlord, Bass. **FACILITIES:** Garden: Food served outside Dogs allowed Not during meal times. **NOTES:** Parking 30

PENMARK   Map 03 ST06

Six Bells Inn
CF62 3BP ☎ 01446 710229 📠 01446 710671
Dir: M4 J33 take A4045, follow signs for 'Cardiff Wales Airport' then 'Penmark'
Dating from 1623, this pub has a distinctive Norman archway and takes its name from the bells in the church opposite. Ideally located for Cardiff Wales Airport.

ST HILARY   Map 03 ST07

The Bush Inn
CF71 7DP ☎ 01446 772745
Dir: S of A48, E of Cowbridge
Lovely stone and thatch pub, dating from the 16th-century, with flagstone floors, an inglenook fireplace and spiral staircase. There is a sunny aspect to the front, where tables are set out with views of the old church, and to the rear there is a garden. Dishes range from laverbread and bacon, lasagne and fresh plaice in the bar, to boeuf Calvados and rack of Welsh lamb in the restaurant. **OPEN:** 11.30-11 (Sun 12-10.30). **BAR MEALS:** L served all week. D served Mon-Sat 12-2.30 6.45-9.30. Av main course £4.95. **RESTAURANT:** L served all week. D served Mon-Sat 12-2.30 6.45-9.30. Av 3 course à la carte £16. Av 3 course fixed price £10.95. **BREWERY/COMPANY:** Punch Taverns. **PRINCIPAL BEERS:** Hancocks HB, Bass, Greene King Old Speckled Hen, Worthington. **FACILITIES:** Children welcome Garden: Beer garden, outdoor eating, Dogs allowed garden only water provided. **NOTES:** Parking 60

SIGINGSTONE   Map 03 SS97

Victoria Inn
CF71 7LP ☎ 01446 773943
e-mail: mail@victoriainn.plus.com
Dir: Off the B4270 between Llantwit Major and Cowbridge
With an upstairs restaurant and a downstairs lounge, this quiet village inn is decorated with old photographs and prints, and stocked with a fine selection of malt whiskies and good Welsh ales.

Wales

WREXHAM

HANMER
Map 08 SJ43

Hanmer Arms
SY13 3DE ☎ 01948 830532 🖷 01948 830740
e-mail: enquiries@thehamnerarms.co.uk
Dir: Between Wrexham & Whitchurch on A539, off A525
In the shadow of St Chad's church, this comfortable 16th-century inn commands views of the Berwyn Mountains and northwards to the Cheshire Plain. Food options include grills, steaks, and vegetarian choices. Under new management.

LLANARMON DYFFRYN CEIRIOG
Map 08 SJ13

Pick of the Pubs

The West Arms Hotel 🏵 ★ ★
LL20 7LD ☎ 01691 600665 🖷 01691 600622
e-mail: gowestarms@aol.com
Dir: Leave A483 at Chirk, follow signs for Ceiriog Valley B4500, hotel is 11m from Chirk

A 16th-century shooting inn at the head of the long, winding Ceiriog Valley with the Berwyn Hills as a backdrop. The old-world atmosphere of stone-flagged floors and inglenook fireplaces is matched by the warmth of welcome: touring, hill walking and fishing on the hotel's private stretch of river are among its popular pastimes. Selections of seasonal soups, salads and pasta are supplemented in the bar by braised shoulder of Welsh lamb, grilled fresh Ceiriog trout, sirloin steak and wild mushroom strudel, followed by steamed chocolate pudding and lemon tart. Sunday lunch adds avocado and bacon salad, traditional beef topside, poached salmon hollandaise and warm apple pie. Dinner in the intimate and cosy dining-room is a more involved affair of four courses at fixed prices: here the kitchen comes into its own with a short nightly menu of enjoyable, freshly-cooked dishes that might include watercress pancakes filled with saffron-scented crab and crayfish and local wild duck breast with plum purée.
OPEN: 8am-11pm. **BAR MEALS:** L served all week. D served all week 12-2 7-9. Av main course £6.95. **RESTAURANT:** L served Sun. D served all week 12-2 7-9. Av 3 course fixed price £21.90. **BREWERY/COMPANY:** Free House.
PRINCIPAL BEERS: Whitbread Trophy Bitter, Flowers IPA,.
FACILITIES: Children welcome Garden: outdoor eating, BBQ, Dogs allowed Water, 3 Kennels. **NOTES:** Parking 30.
ROOMS: 15 bedrooms 15 en suite s£46.50 d£97 FR£105.75

MARFORD
Map 08 SJ35

Trevor Arms Hotel 🐑 ♀
LL12 8TA ☎ 01244 570436 🖷 01244 570273
e-mail: mrtnbn@aol.com
Dir: off A483 onto B5102 then R onto B5445 into Marford
Haunted 17th-century coaching inn, that was once the scene of public hangings. Takes its name from Lord Trevor of Trevallin, who was killed in a duel. This grisly past notwithstanding, the Trevor Arms is a charming inn, offering a varied menu. This may include seared tuna steak with hot salad, deep-fried battered black pudding on a bacon and onion mash, grilled supreme of chicken on a casserole of sweet potatoes and mushrooms, poached fillet of salmon with roasted cherry tomatoes and asparagus, or a range of specials from the changing blackboard.
OPEN: 11-11. **BAR MEALS:** L served all week. D served all week 12-10. Av main course £6. **RESTAURANT:** L served all week. D served all week 12-10. Av 3 course à la carte £15. Av 3 course fixed price £7.75. **BREWERY/COMPANY:** Scottish Courage.
PRINCIPAL BEERS: Greenalls, Boddingtons, Theakstons Old Peculier, Greene King Old Speckled Hen. **FACILITIES:** Children welcome Garden: patio, Food served outside. **NOTES:** Parking 70. **ROOMS:** 29 bedrooms 29 en suite s£38 d£39.50 FR£44-£52

Pilgrims, Shrines and Inns

All through the Middle Ages hospitality to strangers was considered a fundamental Christian duty and travellers could stay overnight free at monasteries or bed down with the servants in a nobleman's hall. Gradually, however, with growing prosperity and burgeoning trade, more people began to travel. Among them were pilgrims making their way to the shrines of saints, to acquire religious merit or be cured of sickness. The two most popular pilgrimage centres were the tomb of St Thomas ‡ Becket at Canterbury and the Virgin Mary's shrine at Walsingham in Norfolk, but many other churches possessed wonder-working relics of great sanctity.

Monasteries put poor pilgrims up free in wooden sheds with rush-strewn floors, a brazier for warmth and a few benches, but with mounting affluence better-off pilgrims were ready to pay for greater comfort, a decent meal and congenial company. Scenting a profit, monasteries built inns to meet the demand and others were opened by local landowners and town merchants. Most of Britain's oldest inns go back to these beginnings.

Wales

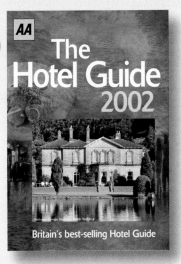
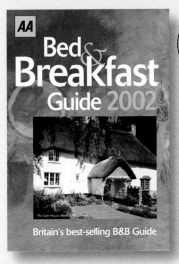

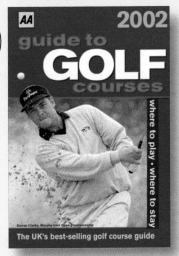
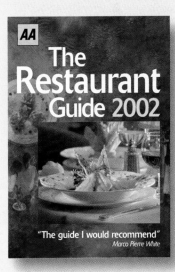

Pick of the Pubs

This is a list of around 500 of the top pubs in Britain, which have been selected by the editor and highlighted in the guide with longer descriptions and a tinted background.

Bedfordshire

Knife & Cleaver, BEDFORD
The Five Bells, STANBRIDGE

Berkshire

The Bell Inn, ALDWORTH
The Crown, BURCHETT'S GREEN
Bel and The Dragon, COOKHAM
Chequers Inn Brasserie, COOKHAM DEAN
The Inn on the Green, COOKHAM DEAN
The Horns, CRAZIES HILL
The Pot Kiln, FRILSHAM
The Swan Inn, INKPEN
The Dundas Arms, KINTBURY
Bird In Hand Country Inn, KNOWL HILL
The Red House, MARSH BENHAM
The Yew Tree Inn, NEWBURY
The George & Dragon, SWALLOWFIELD
The Bladebone Inn, THATCHAM
Harrow Inn, WEST ILSLEY
Rose & Crown, WINKFIELD
The Winterbourne Arms, WINTERBOURNE
The Royal Oak Hotel, YATTENDON

Buckinghamshire

Bottle & Glass, AYLESBURY
Crooked Billet, BLETCHLEY
The Ivy House, CHALFONT ST GILES
The Crown, CUDDINGTON
The Walnut Tree, FAWLEY
The Rising Sun, GREAT MISSENDEN
The Polecat Inn, GREAT MISSENDEN
The Stag & Huntsman Inn, HAMBLEDEN
Mole & Chicken, LONG CRENDON
The Angel Inn, LONG CRENDON
The White Hart, PRESTON BISSETT
The Bull & Butcher, TURVILLE
The Five Arrows Hotel, WADDESDON
Chequers Inn, WOOBURN COMMON

Cambridgeshire

The White Hart, BYTHORN
The Anchor Inn, ELY
The Chequers, FOWLMERE
Crown & Punchbowl, HORNINGSEA
The Old Bridge Hotel, HUNTINGDON
The Pheasant Inn, KEYSTON
The Three Horseshoes, MADINGLEY
The Queen's Head, NEWTON
The Bell Inn, STILTON

Cheshire

The Grosvenor Arms, ALDFORD
The Bhurtpore Inn, ASTON
The Dysart Arms, BUNBURY
The Pheasant Inn, BURWARDSLEY
The Cholmondeley Arms, CHOLMONDELEY

Plough Inn, CONGLETON
The Dog Inn, KNUTSFORD
The Swettenham Arms, SWETTENHAM

Cornwall & Isles of Scilly

The Maltsters Arms, CHAPEL AMBLE
Trengilly Wartha Inn, CONSTANTINE
The Halzephron Inn, GUNWALLOE
Shipwright Arms, HELFORD
The Halfway House Inn, KINGSAND
Royal Oak Inn, LOSTWITHIEL
The Bush Inn, MORWENSTOW
The Old Coastguard Hotel, MOUSEHOLE
The Pandora Inn, MYLOR BRIDGE
The Roseland Inn, PHILLEIGH
Port Gaverne Hotel, PORT GAVERNE
The Sloop Inn, ST IVES
The Rising Sun, ST MAWES
The Victory Inn, ST MAWES
The Springer Spaniel, TREBURLEY
The New Inn, TRESCO
The Gurnards Head Hotel, ZENNOR

Cumbria

The Royal Oak Inn,
   APPLEBY-IN-WESTMORLAND
Tufton Arms Hotel,
   APPLEBY-IN-WESTMORLAND
The Wheatsheaf at Beetham, BEETHAM
The Cavendish Arms, CARTMEL
Masons Arms, CARTMEL
The Punch Bowl Inn, CROSTHWAITE
The Britannia Inn, ELTERWATER
Bower House Inn, ESKDALE GREEN
The Kings Head, KESWICK
The Horse & Farrier Inn, KESWICK
Pheasant Inn, KIRKBY LONSDALE
Snooty Fox, Tavern KIRKBY LONSDALE
Three Shires Inn, LITTLE LANGDALE
Black Swan Hotel, RAVENSTONEDALE
Queens Head Inn, TIRRIL
Queens Head Hotel, TROUTBECK
The Yanwath Gate Inn, YANWATH

Derbyshire

The Lathkil Hotel, BAKEWELL
The Monsal Head, Hotel BAKEWELL
The Chequers Inn, BAKEWELL
Yorkshire Bridge Inn, BAMFORD
The Devonshire Arms, BEELEY
The Waltzing Weasel Inn, BIRCH VALE
The Druid Inn, BIRCHOVER
The Maynard Arms, GRINDLEFORD
The Red Lion Inn, HOGNASTON

Devon

The Rising Sun, ASHBURTON
The Masons Arms, BRANSCOMBE
Drewe Arms, BROADHEMBURY
The Five Bells, Inn CLYST HYDON
The New Inn, CREDITON
The Tuckers Arms, DALWOOD
Royal Castle Hotel, DARTMOUTH
The Nobody Inn, DODDISCOMBSLEIGH
The Union Inn, DOLTON
The Drewe Arms, DREWSTEIGNTON
The Rock Inn, HAYTOR VALE
Hoops Country Inn & Hotel, HORN'S CROSS
Masons Arms Inn, KNOWSTONE
The Arundell Arms, LIFTON
Castle Inn & Hotel, LYDFORD
Dartmoor Inn, LYDFORD
Rising Sun Hotel, LYNMOUTH
The Peter Tavy Inn, PETER TAVY
Jack in the Green Inn, ROCKBEARE
The Tower Inn, SLAPTON
The Sea Trout, STAVERTON
Kings Arms Inn, STOCKLAND
Trademan's Arms, STOKENHAM
Start Bay Inn, TORCROSS
The Watermans Arms, TOTNES
The Durant Arms, TOTNES
The White Hart Bar, DARTINGTON
The Maltsters Arms, TUCKENHAY
The Rising Sun Inn, UMBERLEIGH
The Duke of York, WINKLEIGH

Dorset

Shave Cross Inn, BRIDPORT
The Anchor Inn, BRIDPORT
The Fox Inn, CORSCOMBE
The Cock & Bottle, EAST MORDEN
The Acorn Inn, EVERSHOT
The Museum Arms, FARNHAM
The Bottle Inn, MARSHWOOD

Co Durham

The Morritt Arms Hotel, BARNARD CASTLE
Seven Stars Inn, DURHAM
Rose and Crown, ROMALDKIRK

Essex

Axe & Compasses, ARKESDEN
The Bull Inn, BLACKMORE END
The Green Dragon at Young's End, BRAINTREE
The Cricketers, CLAVERING
The White Hart, GREAT YELDHAM
Bell Inn & Hill House, HORNDON ON THE HILL

Gloucestershire

The Kilkeney Inn, ANDOVERSFORD
The Queens Arms, ASHLEWORTH
The Village Pub, BARNSLEY
Kings Head Inn, BLEDINGTON
The Crown Inn, CHALFORD
The Eight Bells Inn, CHIPPING CAMPDEN
The Churchill Arms, PAXFORD

The Noel Arms Hotel, CHIPPING CAMPDEN
The Crown of Crucis, AMPNEY CRUCIS
Wyndham Arms, CLEARWELL
The New Inn at Coln, COLN ST-ALDWYNS
The Green Dragon Inn, COWLEY
The Kings Arms, DIDMARTON
The Wild Duck, EWEN
Fossebridge Inn, FOSSEBRIDGE
The Fox, LOWER ODDINGTON
Egypt Mill, NAILSWORTH
The Yew Tree, NEWENT
The Eagle and Child, STOW-ON-THE-WOLD
Rose & Crown Inn, STROUD
Bear of Rodborough Hotel, STROUD
Halfway Inn, STROUD
Trouble House Inn, TETBURY
Gumstool Inn, TETBURY

Greater Manchester

White Hart Inn, OLDHAM

Hampshire

Globe on the Lake, ALRESFORD
The Sun Inn, BENTWORTH
The Bell Inn, BROOK
The Master Builders House Hotel, BUCKLERS HARD
The Flower Pots Inn, CHERITON
The East End Arms, EAST END
Star Inn, EAST TYTHERLEY
The Three Lions, FORDINGBRIDGE
The Rose & Thistle, ROCKBOURNE
The Plough Inn, SPARSHOLT
Harrow Inn, STEEP
The Peat Spade, STOCKBRIDGE
The Tichborne Arms, TICHBORNE
The Red House Inn, WHITCHURCH
The Wykeham Arms, WINCHESTER

Herefordshire

Riverside Inn, AYMESTREY
The Roebuck Inn, BRIMFIELD
The Ancient Camp Inn, HEREFORD
Stockton Cross Inn, KIMBOLTON
The Stagg Inn & Restaurant, KINGTON
The Feathers Hotel, LEDBURY
The Lough Pool Inn, SELLACK
Three Crowns Inn, ULLINGSWICK
The Salutation Inn, WEOBLEY
The Sun Inn, WINFORTON

Hertfordshire

The Brocket Arms, WELWYN GARDEN CITY
Alford Arms, BERKHAMSTED

Kent

The Three Chimneys, BIDDENDEN
The Dove Inn, CANTERBURY
Castle Inn, CHIDDINGSTONE
The Albion Tavern, FAVERSHAM
Green Cross Inn, GOUDHURST
Red Lion, HERNHILL
The Harrow Inn, IGHTHAM
The Plough, IVY HATCH

Pick of the Pubs

King William IV, LITTLEBOURNE
The Ringlestone Inn, MAIDSTONE
The George Inn, NEWNHAM
The Dering Arms, PLUCKLEY
The Chequers Inn, SMARDEN
The Bottle House Inn, PENSHURST
The Spotted Dog, SMARTS HILL
Sankeys, ROYAL TUNBRIDGE WELLS
Royal Wells Inn, ROYAL TUNBRIDGE WELLS
The Sportsman, WHITSTABLE

Lancashire

Millstone Hotel, BLACKBURN
The Assheton Arms, CLITHEROE
The Bay Horse Inn, FORTON
The Eagle & Child, BISPHAM GREEN
The Spread Eagle, SAWLEY
The Inn At Whitewell, WHITEWELL
The Mulberry Tree, WRIGHTINGTON

Leicestershire

The Nag's Head, CASTLE DONINGTON
The Bell Inn, EAST LANGTON
Old Barn Inn, GLOOSTON
The Bewicke Arms, HALLATON
The Salisbury Arms, HALSTEAD
The Sun Inn, MARKET HARBOROUGH
The Crown Inn, OLD DALBY
Peacock Inn, REDMILE
The Cock Inn, SIBSON
The Bakers Arms, THORPE LANGTON
The Berkeley Arms, WYMONDHAM

Lincolnshire

The Black Horse Inn, BOURNE
Wig & Mitre, LINCOLN
The George at Stamford, STAMFORD

London

The Grapes, E14
The Crown, E3
The Peasant, EC1
The Eagle, EC1
The Jerusalem Tavern, EC1
The Leopard, EC1
The Bleeding Heart Tavern, EC1
The Duke of Cambridge, N1
St Johns, N19
The Lansdowne, NW1
The Chapel, NW1
The Engineer, NW1
The Vine, NW5
The Salt House, NW8
The Fire Station Restaurant & Bar, SE1
North Pole Bar & Restaurant, SE10
The Chelsea Ram, SW10
The Battersea Boathouse, SW11
The Alma Tavern, SW18
The Cross Keys, SW3
The Coopers of Flood Street, SW3
The White Horse, SW6
The Atlas, SW6
Swag and Tails, SW7
The Artesian Well, SW8
Paradise by Way of Kensal Green, W10

The Ladbroke Arms, W11
The Havelock Tavern, W14
The Cow, W2
Anglesea Arms, W6

Norfolk

White Horse Hotel, BLAKENEY
The Buckinghamshire Arms, BLICKLING
The White Horse, BRANCASTER
The Hoste Arms, BURNHAM MARKET
The Lord Nelson, BURNHAM THORPE
Kings Head, COLTISHALL
Ratcatchers Inn, EASTGATE
Saracen's Head, ERPINGHAM
The Rose & Crown, SNETTISHAM
Stiffkey Red Lion, STIFFKEY
The Wildebeest Arms, STOKE HOLY CROSS
The Hare Arms, STOW BARDOLPH
Chequers Inn, THOMPSON
Lifeboat Inn, THORNHAM
Titchwell Manor Hotel, TITCHWELL
Three Horseshoes, WARHAM ALL SAINTS
Bird in Hand, WRENINGHAM

Northamptonshire

The Queen's Head BULWICK
George and Dragon CHACOMBE
The Falcon Inn FOTHERINGHAY
The King's Head WADENHOE

Northumberland

Victoria Hotel, BAMBURGH
The Manor House Inn, CARTERWAY HEADS
Queens Head Inn, GREAT WHITTINGTON
The Feathers Inn, HEDLEY ON THE HILL
Dipton Mill Inn, HEXHAM
Warenford Lodge, WARENFORD

Nottinghamshire

Victoria Hotel, BEESTON
Martins Arms Inn, COLSTON BASSETT
Robin Hood Inn, ELKESLEY

Oxfordshire

The Boars Head, ARDINGTON
Wyckham Arms, BANBURY
The Boot Inn, BARNARD GATE
Blewbury Inn, BLEWBURY
The Lord Nelson Inn,
   BRIGHTWELL BALDWIN
The Goose, BRITWELL SALOME
The Lamb Inn, BURFORD
The Red Lion Inn, CHALGROVE
The Bull Inn, CHARLBURY
The Highwayman, CHECKENDON
Sir Charles Napier, CHINNOR
The Falkland Arms, CHIPPING NORTON
The Hand & Shears,
   CHURCH HANBOROUGH
The Plough Inn, CLIFTON HAMPDEN
Deddington Arms, DEDDINGTON
The George, DORCHESTER-ON-THAMES
The White Hart, DORCHESTER-ON-THAMES
The Lamb at Buckland, FARINGDON

The Trout at Tadpole Bridge, FARINGDON
Bird in Hand, HAILEY
The Five Horseshoes, HENLEY-ON-THAMES
The Jersey Arms, MIDDLETON STONEY
The Crown Inn, PISHILL
The Greyhound, ROTHERFIELD PEPPARD
The Shaven Crown Hotel,
    SHIPTON-UNDER-WYCHWOOD
The Crazy Bear, STADHAMPTON
The Bell at Standlake, STANDLAKE
The Talk House, STANTON ST JOHN
Crooked Billet, STOKE ROW
The Fish, SUTTON COURTENAY
The Mason's Arms, SWERFORD
Kings Head Inn, WOODSTOCK

Rutland

The Olive Branch, CLIPSHAM
Old White Hart, LYDDINGTON
The Finch's Arms, OAKHAM
Ram Jam Inn, STRETTON
Kings Arms, WING

Shropshire

The Burlton Inn, BURLTON
The Crown Inn, CLEOBURY MORTIMER
The Cholmondeley Riverside Inn, CRESSAGE
The Malthouse, IRONBRIDGE
The Waterdine, LLANFAIR WATERDINE
Unicorn Inn, LUDLOW
Wenlock Edge Inn, MUCH WENLOCK
The Hundred House Hotel, NORTON
The Bradford Arms Restaurant, OSWESTRY
The Old Mill Inn, OSWESTRY
The Armoury, SHREWSBURY
The Countess's Arms, WESTON HEATH

Somerset

The Globe Inn, APPLEY
Woolpack Inn, BECKINGTON
Crown Inn, CHURCHILL
The Wheatsheaf Inn, COMBE HAY
The Crown Hotel, EXFORD
The Talbot Coaching Inn, FROME
The Haselbury Inn, HASELBURY
    PLUCKNETT
Royal Oak of Luxborough, LUXBOROUGH
The Notley Arms, MONKSILVER
George Inn, NORTON ST PHILIP
The Three Horseshoes, SHEPTON MALLET
The Montague Inn, CASTLE CARY
The Carpenters Arms, STANTON WICK
The Blue Ball, TAUNTON
The Royal Oak Inn, WINSFORD
Royal Oak Inn, WITHYPOOL

Staffordshire

The Moat House STAFFORD
The Hollybush Inn STAFFORD
Ye Olde Dog & Partridge Inn TUTBURY

Suffolk

The Swan Inn, BARNBY
Cornwallis Country Hotel, BROME
The Trowel & Hammer Inn, COTTON
The Ship Inn, DUNWICH
The Queen's Head, HALESWORTH
Beehive, HORRINGER
The Red Lion, ICKLINGHAM
Angel Hotel, LAVENHAM
The Kings Head, LAXFIELD
The Star Inn, LIDGATE
The Swan Inn, MONKS ELEIGH
The Cock Inn, POLSTEAD
Ramsholt Arms, RAMSHOLT
The Crown Inn, SNAPE
Crown Hotel, SOUTHWOLD
St Peter's Hall, ST PETER SOUTH ELMHAM
The Angel Inn, STOKE-BY-NAYLAND
Bell Inn, WALBERSWICK
De la Pole Arms, WINGFIELD

Surrey

The Crown Inn, CHIDDINGFOLD
The Stephan Langton, DORKING
The Woolpack, ELSTEAD
King William IV, MICKLEHAM
Bryce's at The Old School House, OCKLEY
The Inn @ West End, WEST END
Brickmakers Arms, WINDLESHAM

Sussex, East

Rose Cottage Inn, ALCISTON
The Cricketers Arms, BERWICK
The Coach and Horses, DANEHILL
The Jolly Sportsman, EAST CHILTINGTON
The Tiger Inn, EAST DEAN
The Griffin Inn, FLETCHING
The Hatch Inn, HARTFIELD
The Queen's Head, ICKLESHAM
Star Inn, OLD HEATHFIELD
The Ypres Castle, RYE
The Dorset Arms, WITHYHAM

Sussex, West

George & Dragon, BURPHAM
The White Horse, CHILGROVE
The Elsted Inn, ELSTED
The Three Horseshoes, ELSTED
The King's Arms, FERNHURST
Lickfold Inn, LICKFOLD
Black Horse Inn, NUTHURST
The Halfway Bridge Inn, PETWORTH
The Fox Goes Free, SINGLETON
White Horse Inn, SUTTON
The Horse Guards Inn, TILLINGTON

Warwickshire

The Bell, ALDERMINSTER
The Golden Cross, ARDENS GRAFTON
King's Head, ASTON CANTLOW
The Chequers Inn & Restaurant, ETTINGTON
The Howard Arms, ILMINGTON
The Boot, LAPWORTH
The Fox and Goose Inn, STRATFORD-UPON-
    AVON

Pick of the Pubs

West Midlands
The Malt Shovel, BARSTON

Wight, Isle of
The Red Lion, FRESHWATER
Seaview Hotel, SEAVIEW

Wiltshire
The Crown, ALVEDISTON
The Kings Arms & Chancel Restaurant,
 BRADFORD-ON-AVON
The Three Crowns, BRINKWORTH
The Black Dog, CHILMARK
The Dove Inn, CORTON
The Horseshoe, EBBESBOURNE WAKE
The Beckford Arms, FONTHILL GIFFORD
The White Hart, FORD
The Linnet, GREAT HINTON
The Angel Inn, HEYTESBURY
The Lamb at Hindon, HINDON
Grosvenor Arms, HINDON
The Tollgate Inn, HOLT
The Harrow Inn, LITTLE BEDWYN
Compasses Inn, LOWER CHICKSGROVE
Horse & Groom, MALMESBURY
The Vine Tree, MALMESBURY
The Seven Stars, PEWSEY
The Silver Plough, PITTON
The Bell, RAMSBURY
The George and Dragon, ROWDE
The Boot Inn, STAPLEFORD
The Angel Inn, WARMINSTER
The Pear Tree Inn, WHITLEY

Worcestershire
Horse & Jockey, BEWDLEY
The Fleece Inn, BRETFORTON
Walter de Cantelupe Inn, KEMPSEY
The Talbot, KNIGHTWICK
The Kings Arms, OMBERSLEY
Crown & Sandys Arms, OMBERSLEY
Peacock Inn, TENBURY WELLS

Yorkshire, East Riding of
Wellington Inn, LUND

Yorkshire, North
Crab & Lobster, ASENBY
The Three Hares Country Inn, BILBROUGH
The Black Bull Inn, BOROUGHBRIDGE
Malt Shovel Inn, BREARTON
The Buck Inn, BUCKDEN
The Red Lion, BURNSALL
Abbey Inn, BYLAND ABBEY
The Fox & Hounds, CARTHORPE
The Blue Lion, EAST WITTON
The Plough Inn, FADMOOR
The Boars Head Hotel, HARROGATE
The Feversham Arms Hotel, HELMSLEY
The Angel, HETTON
The Worsley Arms Hotel, HOVINGHAM
George & Dragon Hotel, KIRKBYMOORSIDE
Stone Trough Inn, KIRKHAM

The General Tarleton Inn,
 KNARESBOROUGH
Sandpiper Inn, LEYBURN
Black Bull Inn, MOULTON
Three Tuns Inn, OSMOTHERLEY
The Sportsmans Arms, PATELEY BRIDGE
The White Swan, PICKERING
Fox & Hounds Country Inn, PICKERING
Nags Head Country Inn, PICKHILL
The Yorke Arms, RAMSGILL
Charles Bathurst Inn, RICHMOND
The Milburn Arms Hotel, ROSEDALE ABBEY
White Horse Farm Hotel, ROSEDALE ABBEY
The Plough Inn, SAXTON
The Hare Inn, SCAWTON
The Buck Inn, THORNTON WATLASS
The Star Country Inn, WEAVERTHORPE
The Bruce Arms, WEST TANFIELD
The Wensleydale Heifer Inn, WEST WITTON

Yorkshire, West
Shinden Mill Inn, HALIFAX
The Three Acres Inn, ROYDHOUSE
The Millbank at Millbank, SOWERBY BRIDGE
Ring O'Bells, THORNTON

SCOTLAND

Aberdeenshire
Lairhillock Inn, NETHERLEY

Angus
Glenisla Hotel, GLENISLA

Argyll & Bute
Loch Melfort Hotel, ARDUAINE
The Harbour Inn, BOWMORE
Tigh an Truish Inn, CLACHAN-SEIL
Crinan Hotel, CRINAN
Kilberry Inn, KILBERRY
Cairnbaan Hotel & Restaurant,
 LOCHGILPHEAD
Pierhouse Hotel & Restaurant, PORT APPIN
Creggans Inn, STRACHUR
Tayvallich Inn, TAYVALLICH

City of Edinburgh
Bridge Inn, RATHO

City of Glasgow
Ubiquitous Chip, GLASGOW

Dumfries & Galloway
Riverside Inn, CANONBIE
Creebridge House Hotel, NEWTON
 STEWART

East Lothian
Drovers Inn, EAST LINTON

Fife
Ship Inn, ELIE
Old Rectory Inn, KIRKCALDY
Seafood Bar & Restaurant, ST MONANS

Highland
Applecross Inn, APPLECROSS
Cawdor Tavern, CAWDOR
Dundonnell House, DUNDONNELL
The Lock Inn, FORT AUGUSTUS
Moorings Hotel, FORT WILLIAM
Glenelg Inn, GLENELG
Hotel Eilean Iarmain, ISLE ORNSAY
Onich Hotel, ONICH
Plockton Inn & Seafood Restaurant,
  PLOCKTON
The Plockton Hotel, PLOCKTON
Shieldaig Bar, SHIELDAIG
The Ceilidh Place, ULLAPOOL

Perth & Kinross
Tormaukin Hotel, GLENDEVON
Killiecrankie Hotel, KILLIECRANKIE
Lomond Country Inn, KINNESSWOOD
Moulin Hotel, PITLOCHRY

Scottish Borders
Burts Hotel, MELROSE
Wheatsheaf Hotel, SWINTON
Tibbie Shiels Inn, TIBBIE SHIELS INN

West Lothian
Champany Inn, LINLITHGOW

WALES

Cardiff
Caesars Arms, CREIGIAU

Carmarthenshire
The Salutation Inn, PONT-AR-GOTHI

Conwy
Kinmel Arms, ABERGELE
Queens Head, LLANDUDNO JUNCTION

Denbighshire
Ye Olde Anchor Inn, RUTHIN
White Horse Inn, RUTHIN
Plough Inn, ST ASAPH

Flintshire
Stables Bar & Restaurant, NORTHROP

Gwynedd
Penhelig Arms Hotel, ABERDYFI
George III Hotel, DOLGELLAU

Isle of Anglesey
Ye Olde Bulls Head, BEAUMARIS
Ship Inn, RED WHARF BAY

Monmouthshire
Clytha Arms, ABERGAVENNY
Walnut Tree Inn, ABERGAVENNY
Black Bear Inn, BETTWS NEWYDD
Boat Inn, CHEPSTOW
Woodland Bar & Restaurant,
  LLANVAIR DISCOED
The Newbridge Inn, TREDUNHOCK

Pembrokeshire
George's Bar, HAVERFORDWEST
Dial Inn, LAMPHEY
Sloop Inn, PORTHGAIN
Armstrong Arms, STACKPOLE
Wolfe Inn, WOLF'S CASTLE

Powys
The Usk Inn, BRECON
The White Swan Inn, BRECON
The Talkhouse, CAERSWS
The Bear, CRICKHOWELL
Gliffaes Country House Hotel,
  CRICKHOWELL
Nantyffin Cider Mill, CRICKHOWELL
Farmers Arms, CWMDU
Famous Old Black Lion, HAY-ON-WYE
Griffin Inn , LLYSWEN
Wynnstay Arms, MACHYNLLETH
The Bricklayers Arms, MONTGOMERY
Dragon Hotel, MONTGOMERY
Seland Newydd, PWLLGLOYW
Castle Coaching Inn, TRECASTLE

Vale of Glamorgan
Blue Anchor Inn, EAST ABERTHAW

Wrexham
West Arms Hotel,
  LLANARMON DYFFRYN CEIRIOG

Seafood Pubs

This is a list of all the pubs in the guide which are recognised by the Sea Fish Industry Authority. Their gazetteer entries are indicated by the blue Sea Fish symbol.

ENGLAND

BEDFORDSHIRE
Knife & Cleaver, BEDFORD
The Five Bells, STANBRIDGE

BERKSHIRE
Chequers Inn Brasserie, COOKHAM DEAN
The Inn on the Green, COOKHAM DEAN
The Horns, CRAZIES HILL
The Rising Sun, HURLEY
The Dundas Arms, KINTBURY
Bird In Hand Country Inn, KNOWL HILL
The Red House, MARSH BENHAM
The Bladebone, Inn THATCHAM

BUCKINGHAMSHIRE
The Hit or Miss, AMERSHAM
The Oak, ASTON CLINTON
Bottle & Glass, AYLESBURY
The Greyhound, BEACONSFIELD
The Black Horse, Inn CHESHAM
The Dinton Hermit, FORD
The Polecat Inn, GREAT MISSENDEN
The Rising Sun, GREAT MISSENDEN
The Green Dragon, HADDENHAM
Mole & Chicken, LONG CRENDON
The Angel Inn, LONG CRENDON
The Carrington Arms, MOULSOE
The Frog, SKIRMETT
King William IV, SPEEN
The Bull & Butcher, TURVILLE
The Five Arrows Hotel, WADDESDON
Chequers Inn, WOOBURN COMMON

CAMBRIDGESHIRE
The Fitzwilliam Arms, CASTOR
The George & Dragon, ELSWORTH
The Black Horse, ELTON
The Anchor Inn, ELY
Ancient Shepherds, FEN DITTON
King William IV, FENSTANTON
White Pheasant, FORDHAM
The Chequers, FOWLMERE
Black Bull, GODMANCHESTER
Crown & Punchbowl, HORNINGSEA
The Old Bridge Hotel, HUNTINGDON
The New Sun Inn, KIMBOLTON
The Three Horseshoes, MADINGLEY

CHESHIRE
The Grosvenor Arms, ALDFORD
The Pheasant Inn, BURWARDSLEY
The Cholmondeley Arms, CHOLMONDELEY
The Badger Inn, CHURCH MINSHULL

Plough Inn, CONGLETON
The Calveley Arms, HANDLEY
The Dog Inn, KNUTSFORD
The Smoker, PLUMLEY
The Swettenham Arms, SWETTENHAM
The Boot Inn, TARPORLEY
The Ship Inn, WINCLE

CO DURHAM
Seven Stars Inn, DURHAM
The Teesdale Hotel, MIDDLETON-IN-TEESDALE
Rose and Crown, ROMALDKIRK

CORNWALL & ISLES OF SCILLY
The Maltsters Arms, CHAPEL AMBLE
Trengilly Wartha Inn, CONSTANTINE
The Smuggler's Den Inn, CUBERT
Ye Olde Plough House Inn, DULOE
The Halzephron Inn, GUNWALLOE
The Halfway House Inn, KINGSAND
The Badger Inn, LELANT
Royal Oak Inn, LOSTWITHIEL
Ship Inn, LOSTWITHIEL
Ship Inn, MOUSEHOLE
The Old Coastguard Hotel, MOUSEHOLE
The Pandora Inn, MYLOR BRIDGE
The Cornish Arms, PENDOGGETT
The Turks Head Inn, PENZANCE
The Roseland Inn, PHILLEIGH
Driftwood Spars Hotel, ST AGNES
The Sloop Inn, ST IVES
The Rising Sun, ST MAWES
The Victory Inn, ST MAWES
The Port William, TINTAGEL
The Springer Spaniel, TREBURLEY
The New Inn, TRESCO
The Wig & Pen Inn & Olivers Restaurant, TRURO
The Quarryman Inn, WADEBRIDGE

CUMBRIA
Drunken Duck Inn, AMBLESIDE
The Cavendish Arms, CARTMEL
The Punch Bowl Inn, CROSTHWAITE
The Travellers Rest Inn, GRASMERE
Queens Head Hotel, HAWKSHEAD
The Kings Head, KESWICK
Pheasant Inn KIRKBY, LONSDALE
The Shepherds Inn, MELMERBY
Black Swan Hotel, RAVENSTONEDALE
Queens Head Inn, TIRRIL
Brackenrigg Inn, WATERMILLOCK

DERBYSHIRE
The Chequers Inn, BAKEWELL
The Monsal Head Hotel, BAKEWELL

The Devonshire Arms, BEELEY
The Druid Inn, BIRCHOVER
The Bulls Head Inn, FOOLOW
The Maynard Arms, GRINDLEFORD
Scotsmans Pack Inn, HATHERSAGE
The Red Lion Inn, HOGNASTON

DEVON
The Rising Sun, ASHBURTON
The Avon Inn, AVONWICK
The Ship Inn, AXMOUTH
Sloop Inn, BANTHAM
The Anchor Inn, BEER
The Old Plough Inn, BERE FERRERS
The Masons Arms, BRANSCOMBE
Drewe Arms, BROADHEMBURY
The George Inn, CHARDSTOCK
The Five Bells Inn, CLYST HYDON
The Anchor Inn, COCKWOOD
Hunters Lodge Inn, CORNWORTHY
The New Inn, CREDITON
The Tuckers Arms, DALWOOD
Cott Inn, DARTINGTON
Royal Castle Hotel, DARTMOUTH
The Cherub Inn, DARTMOUTH
The Union Inn, DOLTON
The Drewe Arms, DREWSTEIGNTON
Red Lion Inn, EXETER
The Rock Inn, HAYTOR VALE
Hoops Country Inn & Hotel, HORN'S CROSS
Old Rydon Inn, KINGSTEIGNTON
Tally Ho Inn, LITTLEHEMPSTON
The Manor Inn, LOWER ASHTON
Dartmoor Inn, LYDFORD
Rising Sun Hotel, LYNMOUTH
The Linny Inn & Hayloft Dining Area NEWTON
    ABBOT
The Wild Goose Inn, NEWTON ABBOT
Jack in the Green Inn, ROCKBEARE
The Tower Inn, SLAPTON
The Millbrook Inn, SOUTH POOL
Kings Arms Inn, STOCKLAND
Trademan's Arms, STOKENHAM
The Village Inn, THURLESTONE
The Lighter Inn, TOPSHAM
Start Bay Inn, TORCROSS
The Durant Arms, TOTNES
The Watermans Arms, TOTNES
Cridford Inn, TRUSHAM
The Maltsters Arms, TUCKENHAY
The Rising Sun Inn, UMBERLEIGH
The Duke of York, WINKLEIGH
The Yarcombe Inn, YARCOMBE

DORSET
The Cricketers, BLANDFORD FORUM
Shave Cross Inn, BRIDPORT
The Anchor Inn, BRIDPORT
The George Hotel, BRIDPORT
The Anchor Inn, BURTON BRADSTOCK
The George Inn, CHIDEOCK
The Ship In Distress, CHRISTCHURCH

The New Inn, CHURCH KNOWLE
The Greyhound Inn, CORFE CASTLE
The Fox Inn, CORSCOMBE
The Sailors Return, EAST CHALDON
The Cock & Bottle, EAST MORDEN
The Acorn Inn, EVERSHOT
The Hambro Arms, MILTON ABBAS
The Coppleridge Inn, MOTCOMBE
Marquis of Lorne, NETTLECOMBE
The Thimble Inn, PIDDLEHINTON
Piddle Inn, PIDDLETRENTHIDE
Brace of Pheasants, PLUSH
Skippers Inn, SHERBORNE
Saxon Arms, STRATTON
The Bankes Arms Hotel, STUDLAND
Rose & Crown Inn, TRENT
The Manor Hotel, WEST BEXINGTON

ESSEX
Axe & Compasses, ARKESDEN
The Swan Inn, CHAPPEL
The Cricketers, CLAVERING
Rose & Crown Hotel, COLCHESTER
The Whalebone, COLCHESTER
The Crown, ELSENHAM
The White Hart, GREAT YELDHAM
Bell Inn & Hill House,
    HORNDON ON THE HILL
The Shepherd and Dog, LANGHAM
Plough & Sail, PAGLESHAM
The Compasses Inn, PATTISWICK
The Plough Inn, RADWINTER
The Cricketers Arms, SAFFRON WALDEN
Cap & Feathers Inn, TILLINGHAM
The Black Buoy Inn, WIVENHOE

GLOUCESTERSHIRE
The Kilkeney Inn, ANDOVERSFORD
The Royal Oak Inn, ANDOVERSFORD
The Queens Arms, ASHLEWORTH
The Crown Inn & Hotel, BLOCKLEY
Wyndham Arms, CLEARWELL
The New Inn at Coln, COLN ST-ALDWYNS
The Kings Arms, DIDMARTON
The Wild Duck, EWEN
Fossebridge Inn, FOSSEBRIDGE
The Farmers Arms, LOWER APPERLEY
Egypt Mill, NAILSWORTH
The Britannia, NAILSWORTH
The Falcon Inn, PAINSWICK
The Churchill Arms, PAXFORD
Rose & Crown, REDMARLEY
The Butchers Arms, SHEEPSCOMBE
The Swan at Southrop, SOUTHROP
The Eagle and, Child STOW-ON-THE-WOLD
Gumstool Inn, TETBURY

GREATER MANCHESTER
Green Ash Hotel, DELPH
The Oddfellows Arms, MELLOR

HAMPSHIRE
The Fox Inn, ALRESFORD

Seafood Pubs

The Bull Inn, BENTLEY
The Red Lion Inn, BOLDRE
The Bell Inn, BROOK
The Five Bells, BURITON
The Burley Inn, BURLEY
The White Hart, CADNAM
The Red Lion, CHALTON
The Compasses Inn, DAMERHAM
The East End Arms, EAST END
Star Inn, EAST TYTHERLEY
The Chestnut Horse, EASTON
The Sussex Brewery, EMSWORTH
The Trooper Inn, FROXFIELD GREEN
New Forest Inn, LYNDHURST
The Trusty Servant, LYNDHURST
The Fleur de Lys, PILLEY
The Rose & Thistle, ROCKBOURNE
The Dukes Head, ROMSEY
The Hatchet Inn, SHERFIELD ENGLISH
The Plough Inn, SPARSHOLT
The Peat Spade, STOCKBRIDGE
The Red House Inn, WHITCHURCH

HEREFORDSHIRE
Riverside Inn, AYMESTREY
The Roebuck Inn, BRIMFIELD
The Nags Head Inn, CANON PYON
Bulls Head, CRASWALL
Yew Tree Inn, DORMINGTON
The Bunch of Carrots, HAMPTON BISHOP
The Crown & Anchor, HEREFORD
Stockton Cross Inn, KIMBOLTON
The Stagg Inn & Restaurant, KINGTON
The Farmers Arms, LEDBURY
The Feathers Hotel, LEDBURY
The Scrumpy House Bar & Restaurant,
   MUCH MARCLE
The Lough Pool Inn, SELLACK
The New Inn, ST OWEN'S CROSS
Three Crowns Inn, ULLINGSWICK
The Salutation Inn, WEOBLEY
Rhydspence Inn, WHITNEY-ON-WYE
The Sun Inn, WINFORTON

HERTFORDSHIRE
Three Horseshoes, HINXWORTH
The Greyhound, HITCHIN
The Nags Head, LITTLE HADHAM

KENT
The Dove Inn, CANTERBURY
The Duke William, CANTERBURY
Griffins Head, CHILLENDEN
The Wheatsheaf, EDENBRIDGE
Malt Shovel Inn, EYNSFORD
The Albion Tavern, FAVERSHAM
Chafford Arms, FORDCOMBE
Green Cross Inn, GOUDHURST
The Harrow Inn, IGHTHAM
The Plough IVY, HATCH
The Bottle House Inn, PENSHURST
The Dering Arms, PLUCKLEY

Royal Wells Inn, ROYAL TUNBRIDGE WELLS
Sankeys, ROYAL TUNBRIDGE WELLS
The Beacon, ROYAL TUNBRIDGE WELLS
The Hare on Langton Green, ROYAL
   TUNBRIDGE WELLS
The Chequers Inn, SMARDEN
The Spotted Dog, SMARTS HILL
The Plough Inn, STALISFIELD GREEN
The Sportsman, WHITSTABLE

LANCASHIRE
The Eagle & Child, BISPHAM GREEN
Dutton Arms, CARNFORTH
The Assheton Arms, CLITHEROE
Hest Bank Hotel, HEST BANK
The Spread Eagle, SAWLEY
The Inn At Whitewell, WHITEWELL
The Mulberry Tree, WRIGHTINGTON

LEICESTERSHIRE
The Nag's Head, CASTLE DONINGTON
Old Barn Inn, GLOOSTON
The Bewicke Arms, HALLATON
The Sun Inn, MARKET HARBOROUGH
The Crown Inn, OLD DALBY
Peacock Inn, REDMILE
The White Swan, SILEBY
Stilton Cheese Inn, SOMERBY
The Bakers Arms, THORPE LANGTON
The Wheatsheaf Inn, WOODHOUSE EAVES

LINCOLNSHIRE
The Black Horse Inn, BOURNE
The Chequers, GEDNEY DYKE
The Ship Inn, SPALDING
The Blue Bell Inn, STAMFORD
The George at Stamford, STAMFORD

LONDON
The Grapes, LONDON E14
The Centre Page, LONDON EC4
The Engineer, LONDON NW1
The Chelsea Ram, LONDON SW10
The Alma Tavern, LONDON SW18
The Ship Inn, LONDON SW18
The Cross Keys, LONDON SW3
The Atlas, LONDON SW6
Swag and Tails, LONDON SW7
The Artesian Well, LONDON SW8
The Cow, LONDON W2
Anglesea Arms, LONDON W6

NORFOLK
Kings Head, BAWBURGH
The Kings Arms, BLAKENEY
White Horse Hotel, BLAKENEY
The White Horse, BRANCASTER
The Hoste Arms, BURNHAM MARKET
George & Dragon Hotel, CLEY NEXT THE SEA
The Crown, COLKIRK
Kings Head, COLTISHALL
Duke of York, DITCHINGHAM
Pilgrims Reach, DOCKING

Ratcatchers Inn, EASTGATE
Red Lion Inn, EATON
Saracen's Head, ERPINGHAM
The Reedham Ferry Inn, REEDHAM
Stiffkey Red Lion, STIFFKEY
The Wildebeest Arms, STOKE HOLY CROSS
The Hare Arms, STOW BARDOLPH
Chequers Inn, THOMPSON
Lifeboat Inn, THORNHAM
Titchwell Manor Hotel, TITCHWELL
The Old Ram Coaching Inn,
   TIVETSHALL ST MARY
The Red Lion Inn, UPPER SHERINGHAM
Three Horseshoes, WARHAM ALL SAINTS
The Dukes Head, WEST RUDHAM
Bird in Hand, WRENINGHAM

NORTHAMPTONSHIRE
The Olde Coach House Inn,
   ASHBY ST LEDGERS
George and Dragon, CHACOMBE
The Exeter Arms, EASTON-ON-THE-HILL
The Kings Arms, FARTHINGSTONE
Tollemache Arms, HARRINGTON

NORTHUMBERLAND
Victoria Hotel, BAMBURGH
Blue Bell Inn, BELFORD
The Highlander, BELSAY
The Rob Roy, BERWICK-UPON-TWEED
The Manor House Inn, CARTERWAY HEADS
The Angel Inn, CORBRIDGE
Tankerville Arms, EGLINGHAM
Queens Head Inn, GREAT WHITTINGTON
Cook and Barker Inn,
   NEWTON ON THE MOOR
The Olde Ship Hotel, SEAHOUSES
Warenford Lodge, WARENFORD

NOTTINGHAMSHIRE
Caunton Beck, CAUNTON
The Martins Arms Inn, COLSTON BASSETT
Robin Hood Inn, ELKESLEY
The Mussel & Crab, TUXFORD

OXFORDSHIRE
The Boars Head, ARDINGTON
The Maytime Inn, ASTHALL
Wyckham Arms, BANBURY
The Inn for All Seasons, BURFORD
The Lamb Inn, BURFORD
The Red Lion Inn, CHALGROVE
The Bull Inn, CHARLBURY
Sir Charles Napier, CHINNOR
Coach And Horses Inn, CHISLEHAMPTON
The Hand & Shears, CHURCH HANBOROUGH
Duke of Cumberland's Head, CLIFTON
Bear & Ragged Staff, CUMNOR
The Vine Inn, CUMNOR
Deddington Arms, DEDDINGTON
The George, DORCHESTER-ON-THAMES
The Lamb at Buckland, FARINGDON
Bird in Hand, HAILEY

The Five Horseshoes, HENLEY-ON-THAMES
The Little Angel, HENLEY-ON-THAMES
The Blowing Stone Inn, KINGSTON LISLE
The Crown Inn, PISHILL
Home Sweet Home, ROKE
The Lamb Inn,
   SHIPTON-UNDER-WYCHWOOD
The Crazy Bear, STADHAMPTON
The Bell at Standlake, STANDLAKE
Red Lion, STEEPLE ASTON
Crooked Billet, STOKE ROW
The Fish, SUTTON COURTENAY
The Mason's Arms, SWERFORD
Kings Head Inn, WOODSTOCK

RUTLAND
The Sun Inn, COTTESMORE
Old White Hart, LYDDINGTON
Black Bull, MARKET OVERTON
The Finch's Arms, OAKHAM
Noel Arms Inn, WHITWELL
Kings Arms, WING

SHROPSHIRE
The Burlton Inn, BURLTON
The Bear Hotel, HODNET
The Malthouse, IRONBRIDGE
The Talbot Inn, MUCH WENLOCK
The Old Three Pigeons Inn, NESSCLIFFE
The Hundred House Hotel, NORTON
The Bradford Arms Restaurant, OSWESTRY
The Old Mill Inn, OSWESTRY
Swan at Woore, WOORE

SOMERSET
The Globe Inn, APPLEY
The Oak House, AXBRIDGE
Woolpack Inn, BECKINGTON
The Montague Inn, CASTLE CARY
The York Inn, CHURCHINFORD
The Wheatsheaf Inn, COMBE HAY
Strode Arms, CRANMORE
The Crown Hotel, EXFORD
Fitzhead Inn, FITZHEAD
The Horse & Groom, FROME
The Talbot 15th-Century Coaching Inn, FROME
The Haselbury Inn, HASELBURY PLUCKNETT
The Lord Poulett Arms, HINTON ST GEORGE
Kingsdon Inn, KINGSDON
The Rising Sun, Inn KNAPP
The Three Horseshoes, LANGLEY MARSH
Vobster Inn, LOWER VOBSTER
Royal Oak of Luxborough, LUXBOROUGH
Hope & Anchor, MIDFORD
The Royal Oak, OVER STRATTON
New Inn, PRIDDY
The Full Moon at Rudge, RUDGE
The Waggon and Horses, SHEPTON MALLET
The Carpenters Arms, STANTON WICK
The Greyhound Inn, STAPLE FITZPAINE
Rose & Crown, STOKE ST GREGORY
The Blue Ball, TAUNTON
The Fountain Inn, WELLS

Seafood Pubs

The Walnut Tree, WEST CAMEL
Royal Oak Inn, WITHYPOOL

STAFFORDSHIRE
The Hollybush Inn, STAFFORD
Ye Olde Dog & Partridge Inn, TUTBURY

SUFFOLK
The Mill Inn, ALDEBURGH
The Swan Inn, BARNBY
The Queens Head Inn, BLYFORD
The Six Bells, BURY ST EDMUNDS
Bull Inn, CAVENDISH
The Froize Inn, CHILLESFORD
The Trowel & Hammer Inn, COTTON
The Ship Inn, DUNWICH
The Queens Head, ERWARTON
The Crown Inn, GREAT GLEMHAM
The Queen's Head, HALESWORTH
The Crown, HARTEST
Beehive, HORRINGER
The Red Lion, ICKLINGHAM
Pykkerell Inn, IXWORTH
The Bell Inn, KERSEY
The Ship Inn, LEVINGTON
The Star Inn, LIDGATE
Wilford Bridge, MELTON
The Swan Inn, MONKS ELEIGH
Jolly Sailor Inn, ORFORD
The Cock Inn, POLSTEAD
Ramsholt Arms, RAMSHOLT
The Plough, REDE
Plough & Sail, SNAPE
The Crown Inn, SNAPE
Crown Hotel, SOUTHWOLD
St Peter's Hall, ST PETER SOUTH ELMHAM
The Rose & Crown, STANTON
The Angel Inn, STOKE-BY-NAYLAND
Bell Inn, WALBERSWICK
De la Pole Arms, WINGFIELD

SURREY
The Volunteer, ABINGER
The Plough, BLACKBROOK
Jolly Farmer Inn, BRAMLEY
The Crown Inn, CHIDDINGFOLD
The Cricketers, COBHAM
The Plough Inn, COLDHARBOUR
The Fox and Hounds, EGHAM
The Running Horses, MICKLEHAM
Bryce's at The Old School House, OCKLEY
The Kings Arms Inn, OCKLEY
William IV Country Pub, REDHILL
The Wheatsheaf Hotel, VIRGINIA WATER
Onslow Arms, WEST CLANDON
Brickmakers Arms, WINDLESHAM

SUSSEX, EAST
Rose Cottage Inn, ALCISTON
The Blackboys Inn, BLACKBOYS
The Greys, BRIGHTON
The Coach and Horses, DANEHILL
The Griffin Inn, FLETCHING

The Gun Inn, GUN HILL
The Queen's Head, ICKLESHAM
Plough & Harrow, LITLINGTON
Rose & Crown Inn, MAYFIELD
The Middle House, MAYFIELD
The Blacksmith's Arms, OFFHAM
Star Inn, OLD HEATHFIELD
The Cock, RINGMER
Horse & Groom, RUSHLAKE GREEN
The Dorset Arms, WITHYHAM

SUSSEX, WEST
The Gardeners Arms, ARDINGLY
George & Dragon, BURPHAM
The White Horse, CHILGROVE
Coach & Horses, COMPTON
Hunters Moon Inn, COPTHORNE
The Elsted Inn, ELSTED
The King's Arms, FERNHURST
The Red Lion, FERNHURST
The Half Moon Inn, KIRDFORD
Lickfold Inn, LICKFOLD
Jeremy's at the Crabtree, LOWER BEEDING
The Halfway Bridge Inn, PETWORTH
Welldiggers Arms, PETWORTH
The Fox Inn, RUDGWICK
The Fox Goes Free, SINGLETON
The Ship Inn, SOUTH HARTING
The Old House at Home, SOUTHBOURNE
White Horse Inn, SUTTON
The Horse Guards Inn, TILLINGTON
Oaks Bar Brasserie & Lodge, WALBERTON

TYNE & WEAR
The Waterford Arms, WHITLEY BAY

WARWICKSHIRE
The Golden Cross, ARDENS GRAFTON
King's Head, ASTON CANTLOW
The Chequers Inn & Restaurant, ETTINGTON
Fox & Hounds Inn, GREAT WOLFORD
The Howard Arms, ILMINGTON
The Boot, LAPWORTH
The Bell Inn, MONKS KIRBY
White Bear Hotel, SHIPSTON ON STOUR
The Bulls Head, WOOTTON WAWEN

WEST MIDLANDS
The Malt Shovel, BARSTON

WIGHT, ISLE OF
The Crab & Lobster Inn, BEMBRIDGE
Clarendon Hotel & Wight Mouse Inn, CHALE
The Red Lion, FRESHWATER
Seaview Hotel, SEAVIEW
The New Inn, SHALFLEET

WILTSHIRE
The Green Dragon, ALDERBURY
The Crown, ALVEDISTON
Red Lion Inn, AXFORD
The Canal Tavern, BRADFORD-ON-AVON
The Three Crowns, BRINKWORTH
The Greyhound Inn, BROMHAM

Seafood Pubs

The Old House at Home, BURTON
The Black Dog, CHILMARK
The Dove Inn, CORTON
The White Hart, FORD
The Linnet, GREAT HINTON
The Angel Inn, HEYTESBURY
Grosvenor Arms, HINDON
The Lamb at Hindon, HINDON
The Tollgate Inn, HOLT
The George Inn, LACOCK
The Harrow Inn, LITTLE BEDWYN
The Owl, LITTLE CHEVERELL
The Radnor Arms, NUNTON
The French Horn, PEWSEY
The Seven Stars, PEWSEY
The Woodbridge Inn, PEWSEY
The Bell, RAMSBURY
The George and Dragon, ROWDE
The Old Mill at Harnham, SALISBURY
The Barge Inn, SEEND
Prince Leopold, UPTON LOVELL
The Angel Inn, WARMINSTER
The Pear Tree Inn, WHITLEY
The Woodfalls Inn, WOODFALLS
Royal Oak, WOOTTON RIVERS

WORCESTERSHIRE
Horse & Jockey, BEWDLEY
Little Pack Horse, BEWDLEY
The Bear & Ragged Staff, BRANSFORD
Fox & Hounds Inn & Restaurant, BREDON
Walter de Cantelupe Inn, KEMPSEY
The Talbot, KNIGHTWICK
Crown & Sandys Arms, OMBERSLEY
The Kings Arms, OMBERSLEY
The Bellmans Cross, SHATTERFORD
Peacock Inn, TENBURY WELLS
The Anchor Inn, WYRE PIDDLE

YORKSHIRE, EAST RIDING OF
The Bell, DRIFFIELD
The Seabirds Inn, FLAMBOROUGH
The Wellington Inn, LUND

YORKSHIRE, NORTH
The Friar's Head, AKEBAR
Crab & Lobster, ASENBY
Kings Arms Hotel, ASKRIGG
The Three Hares Country Inn, BILBROUGH
The Black Bull Inn, BOROUGHBRIDGE
Malt Shovel Inn, BREARTON
The Buck Inn, BUCKDEN
The Red Lion, BURNSALL
Foresters Arms, CARLTON
The Fox & Hounds, CARTHORPE
The Fauconberg Arms, COXWOLD
The Royal Oak Inn, DACRE BANKS
The Blue Lion, EAST WITTON
The Plough Inn, FADMOOR
Mallyan Spout, GOATHLAND
The Boars Head Hotel, HARROGATE
The Star Inn, HELMSLEY
The Angel, HETTON

The Worsley Arms Hotel, HOVINGHAM
New Inn, HUNTON
George & Dragon Hotel, KIRKBYMOORSIDE
The General Tarleton Inn, KNARESBOROUGH
Wyvill Arms, LEYBURN
The White Swan Hotel, MIDDLEHAM
Black Bull Inn, MOULTON
Three Tuns Inn, OSMOTHERLEY
The Sportsmans Arms, PATELEY BRIDGE
The White Swan, PICKERING
Nags Head Country Inn, PICKHILL
Charles Bathurst Inn, RICHMOND
The Milburn Arms Hotel, ROSEDALE ABBEY
The Plough Inn, SAXTON
The Hare Inn, SCAWTON
Rose & Crown, SUTTON-ON-THE-FOREST
The Old Hall Inn, THRESHFIELD
Wombwell Arms, WASS
The Bruce Arms , WEST TANFIELD
The Wensleydale, Heifer Inn WEST WITTON
The Magpie Cafe, WHITBY

YORKSHIRE, WEST
The Rock Inn Hotel, HALIFAX
The Windmill Inn, LINTON
The Three Acres Inn, ROYDHOUSE
Ring O'Bells, THORNTON
Kaye Arms Inn & Brasserie, WAKEFIELD

SCOTLAND

ABERDEENSHIRE
Lairhillock Inn, NETHERLEY
Marine Hotel, STONEHAVEN

ARGYLL & BUTE
The Galley of Lorne Inn, ARDFERN
Loch Melfort Hotel, ARDUAINE
Ballygrant Inn, BALLYGRANT
The Harbour Inn, BOWMORE
Tigh an Truish Inn, CLACHAN-SEIL
Crinan Hotel, CRINAN
Coylet Inn, DUNOON
Cairnbaan Hotel & Restaurant LOCHGILPHEAD
Pierhouse Hotel & Restaurant, PORT APPIN
Victoria Hotel, TARBERT
Polfearn Hotel, TAYNUILT
Tayvallich Inn, TAYVALLICH

CITY OF EDINBURGH
The Ship on the Shore, EDINBURGH

CITY OF GLASGOW
Buttery, GLASGOW
Rab Ha's, GLASGOW
Ubiquitous Chip, GLASGOW

DUMFRIES & GALLOWAY
Riverside Inn, CANONBIE
The Steam Packet Inn, ISLE OF WHITHORN
Crown Hotel, PORTPATRICK
EAST LOTHIAN
The Drovers Inn, LINTON

Seafood Pubs

FIFE
The Hideaway Lodge & Restaurant
  DUNFERMLINE
The Crusoe Hotel, LOWER LARGO
The Seafood Bar & Restaurant, ST MONANS

HIGHLAND
Summer Isles Hotel & Bar, ACHILTIBUIE
Altnaharra Hotel, ALTNAHARRA
Applecross Inn, APPLECROSS
Cawdor Tavern, CAWDOR
Achilty Hotel, CONTIN
Mallin House Hotel, DORNOCH
Dundonnell House, DUNDONNELL
The Lock Inn, FORT AUGUSTUS
The Old Inn, GAIRLOCH
Glenelg Inn, GLENELG
Hotel Eilean Iarmain, ISLE ORNSAY
Kylesku Hotel, KYLESKU
Loch Leven Hotel, NORTH BALLACHULISH
Plockton Inn & Seafood Restaurant, PLOCKTON
The Plockton Hotel, PLOCKTON
Shieldaig Bar, SHIELDAIG
Morefield Motel/Mariners Restaurant
  ULLAPOOL
The Argyll Hotel, ULLAPOOL
The Ceilidh Place, ULLAPOOL

MIDLOTHIAN
The Howgate, PENICUIK

PERTH & KINROSS
Ailean Chraggan Hotel, ABERFELDY
The Almondbank Inn, ALMONDBANK
The Burrelton Park Inn, BURRELTON
Tormaukin Hotel, GLEN

SCOTTISH BORDERS
Abbotsford Arms Hotel, GALASHIELS
Kingsknowes Hotel, GALASHIELS
Wheatsheaf Hotel, SWINTON

SOUTH AYRSHIRE
Wheatsheaf Inn, SYMINGTON

STIRLING
The Byre Inn, BRIG O'TURK

WESTERN ISLES
Carinish Inn, CARINISH
The Polochar Inn, LOCHBOISDALE

WALES

BRIDGEND
Old House Inn, MAESTEG

CARDIFF
Caesars Arms, CREIGIAU

CARMARTHENSHIRE
The Angel Inn, LLANDEILO
The Cottage Inn, LLANDEILO

CONWY
Kinmel Arms, ABERGELE
Ty Gwyn Hotel, BETWS-Y-COED
The Groes Inn, CONWY
The Queens Head, LLANDUDNO JUNCTION

DENBIGHSHIRE
The Dinorben Arms, BODFARI
The Plough Inn, ST ASAPH

FLINTSHIRE
Stables Bar Restaurant, NORTHOP

GWYNEDD
Dovey Inn, ABERDYFI
Penhelig Arms Hotel, ABERDYFI
The Halfway House, BONTDDU
George III Hotel, DOLGELLAU
The Harp Inn, LLANDWROG
The Ship, PORTHMADOG

ISLE OF ANGLESEY
Ye Olde Bulls Head Inn, BEAUMARIS
The Ship Inn, RED WHARF BAY

MONMOUTHSHIRE
Clytha Arms, ABERGAVENNY
Walnut Tree Inn, ABERGAVENNY
Black Bear Inn, BETTWS-NEWYDD
The Boat Inn, CHEPSTOW

PEMBROKESHIRE
The New Inn, AMROTH
The Georges Restaurant/Cafe Bar, HAVERFORD
The Dial Inn, LAMPHEY
The Harp Inn, LETTERSTON
Ferry Inn, PEMBROKE DOCK
The Cambrian Inn, SOLVA
Armstrong Arms, STACKPOLE
The Wolfe Inn, WOLF'S CASTLE

POWYS
The Usk Inn, BRECON
Nantyffin Cider Mill, CRICKHOWELL
The Bear, CRICKHOWELL
The Farmers Arms, CWMDU
Elan Valley Hotel, ELAN VILLAGE
Kilverts Hotel, HAY-ON-WYE
The Stumble Inn, LLANFYLLIN
The Vine Tree Inn, LLANGATTOCK
The Radnor Arms, LLOWES
The Bricklayers Arms, MONTGOMERY
Red Lion Inn, NEW RADNOR
Seland Newydd, PWLLGLOYW

SWANSEA
The Fountain Inn, PONTARDDULAIS
King Arthur Hotel, REYNOLDSTON

VALE OF GLAMORGAN
The Six Bells Inn, PENMARK

WREXHAM
Trevor Arms Hotel, MARFORD

Index of Pub Walks

★ Pubs with Stars ★

Pubs with Stars

This is a list of the pubs in this guide which also have AA Star ratings for accommodation. A full listing of AA hotel accommodation can be found in The AA Hotel Guide, and at www.theAA.com/getaway

Pubs with Stars

◆ Pubs with Diamonds ◆

This is a list of the pubs in this guide which also have AA Diamond ratings for accommodation. 1 to 5 Diamonds are awarded for quality. A full listing of AA B&B accommodation can be found in The AA Bed & Breakfast Guide, or at www.theAA.com/getaway

Pubs with Diamonds

Pubs with Diamonds

How to Find a Pub in the Atlas Section

Pubs are located in the gazetteer under the name of the nearest pub or village. If a pub is in a small village or rural area, it may appear under a town within five miles of its actual location. The black dots and town names shown in the atlas refer to the gazetteer location in the guide. Please use the directions in the pub entry to find the pub on foot or by car. If directions are not given, or are not clear, please telephone the pub for details.

Key to County Map

The county map shown here will help you identify the counties within each country. You can look up each county in the guide using the county names at the top of each page. Towns featured in the guide use the atlas pages and index following this map.

England

1 Bedfordshire
2 Berkshire
3 Bristol
4 Buckinghamshire
5 Cambridgeshire
6 Greater Manchester
7 Herefordshire
8 Hertfordshire
9 Leicestershire
10 Northamptonshire
11 Nottinghamshire
12 Rutland
13 Staffordshire
14 Warwickshire
15 West Midlands
16 Worcestershire

Scotland

17 City of Glasgow
18 Clackmannanshire
19 East Ayrshire
20 East Dunbartonshire
21 East Renfrewshire
22 Perth & Kinross
23 Renfrewshire
24 South Lanarkshire
25 West Dunbartonshire

Wales

26 Blaenau Gwent
27 Bridgend
28 Caerphilly
29 Denbighshire
30 Flintshire
31 Merthyr Tydfil
32 Monmouthshire
33 Neath Port Talbot
34 Newport
35 Rhondda Cynon Ta
36 Torfaen
37 Vale of Glamorgan
38 Wrexham

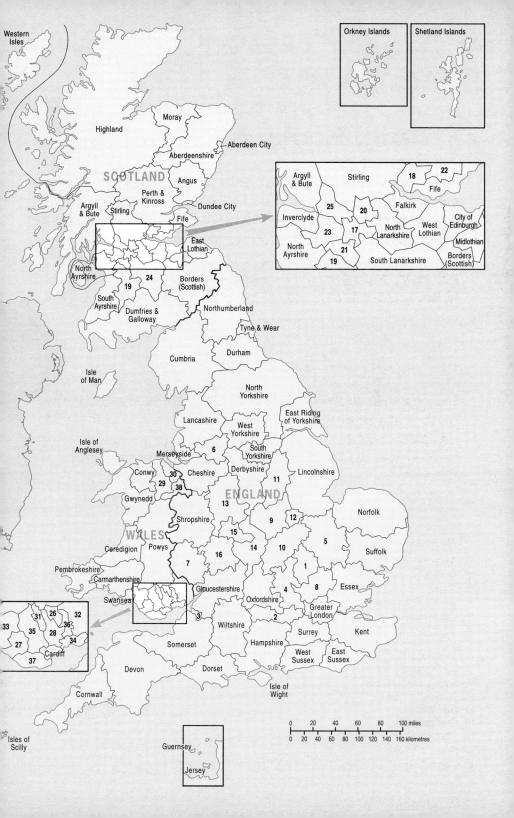

AA Hotel Booking Service

Telephone: 0870 5050505
e-mail: accommodation@aabookings.com
24 hours a day 7 days a week

www.theAA.com/hotels

Tell us where you want to go and we'll help you find a place to stay.

From a rustic farm cottage to a smart city centre hotel even a cosy weekend for two – we can accommodate you.

www.theAA.com/latebeds

Latebeds, a new online service that offers you reduced-price late deals on hotels and B&Bs.

You can find a last-minute place to stay and then book it online in an instant.

Choose from 8,000 quality-rated hotels and B&Bs in the UK and Ireland.
Why not book on-line at www.theAA.com/hotels

KEY TO ATLAS

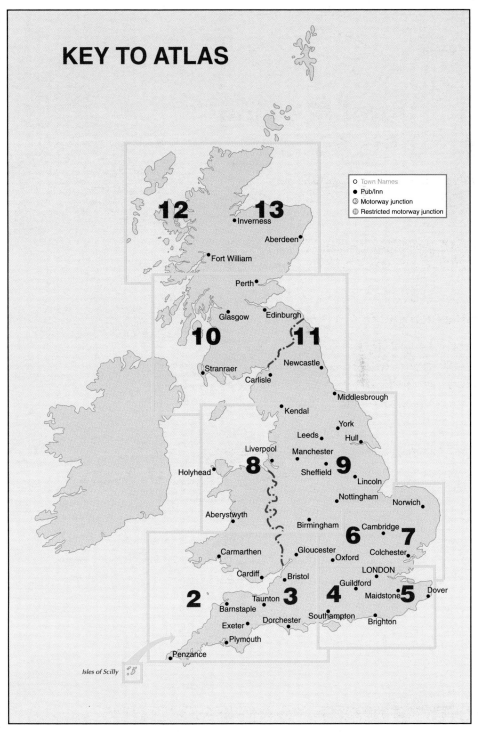

Town Names ○
Pub/Inn ●
Motorway junction
Restricted motorway junction

© Automobile Association Developments Limited 2001

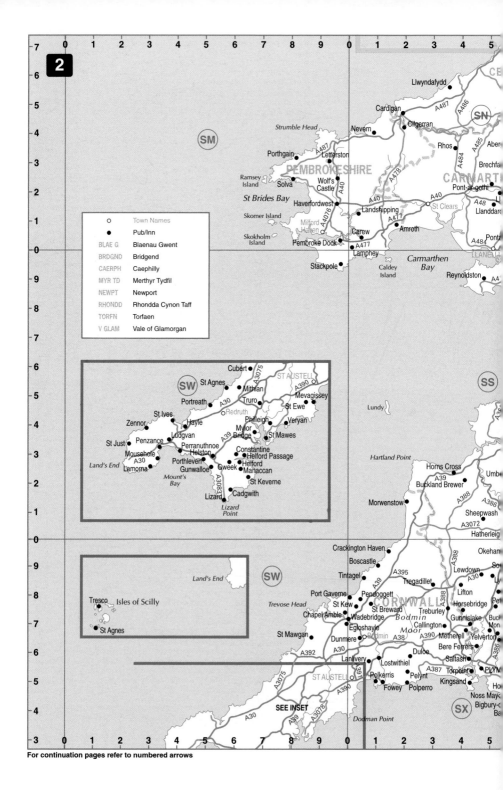

2

○	Town Names
●	Pub/Inn
BLAE G	Blaenau Gwent
BRDGND	Bridgend
CAERPH	Caephilly
MYR TD	Merthyr Tydfil
NEWPT	Newport
RHONDD	Rhondda Cynon Taff
TORFN	Torfaen
V GLAM	Vale of Glamorgan

Llwyndafydd

Cardigan
Cilgerran
SN
Nevern
Strumble Head
Rhos
Aber
Porthgain
Letterston
Brechfa
PEMBROKESHIRE
CARMART
Ramsey
Island
Solva
Wolf's
Castle
Pont-ar-gothi
St Brides Bay
Haverfordwest
Landshipping
St Clears
Llanddar
Skomer Island
Milford
Haven
Carew
Amroth
Skokholm
Island
Pembroke Dock
Lamphey
Ponta
LLANEL

Stackpole
Caldey
Island
Carmarthen
Bay
Reynoldston
A4

SM

CE

SS

Lundy

Hartland Point
Horns Cross
Umb
Buckland Brewer
Morwenstow
Sheepwash
A3072
Hatherle

Cubert
ST AUSTELL
St Agnes
SW
Mithian
Mevagissey
Portreath
Truro
St Ewe
St Ives
Hayle
Phileigh
Veryan
Zennor
Ludgvan
Mylor
Bridge
St Mawes
St Just
Penzance
Perranuthnoe
Constantine
Mousehole
Helston
Helford Passage
Land's End
Porthleven
Helford
Lamorna
Gunwalloe
Gweek
Manaccan
Mount's
Bay
St Keverne
Lizard
Cadgwith
Lizard
Point

Crackington Haven
Boscastle
Okehan
Lewdown
Tintagel
A395
Tregadillet
Lifton
Land's End
SW
Port Gaverne
Pendoggett
Horsebridge
Tresco
Isles of Scilly
Trevose Head
St Kew
Treburley
Gunnislake
Buck
Chapel Amble
Wadebridge
Bodmin
Callington
St Agnes
Egloshayle
Moor
Metherell
Yelverton
St Mawgan
Bodmin
A38
Bere Ferrers
Dunmere
A30
Duloe
Saltash
Lanlivery
Lostwithiel
Torpoint
PLYM
ST AUSTELL
Polkerris
Pelynt
Kingsand
Ho
Fowey
Polperro
Noss May
SEE INSET
SX
Bigbury-
Ba
Dodman Point

For continuation pages refer to numbered arrows

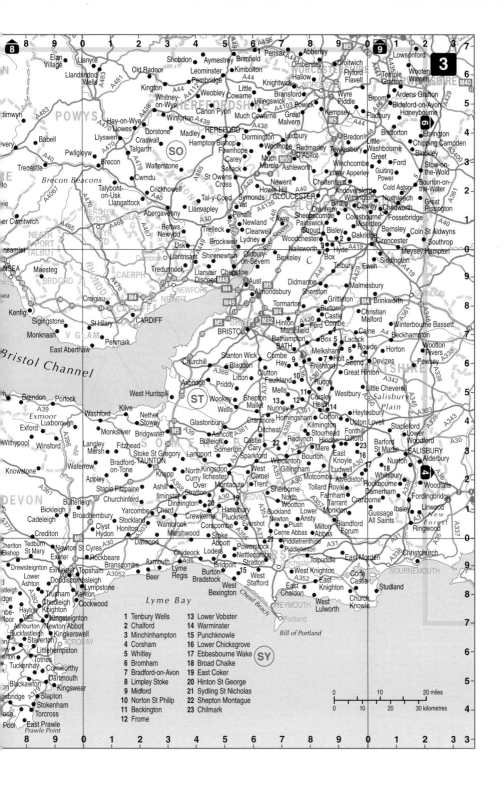

3

N

Elan Village
Llanyre
Llandrindod Wells
Shobdon
Aymestrey
Brimfield
Pensax
Abberley
Ombersley
Droitwich
Flyford
Flavell
Lowsonford
Wooten Wawen

POWYS
Old Radnor
Leominster
Kimbolton
Pembridge
Kington
Whitney-on-Wye
Weobley
Little Cowarne
Knightwick
Hallow
Bransford
Powick
Wyre Piddle
Broom
Temple Grafton
Ardens Grafton
Bidford-on-Avon
Honeybourne

Hay-on-Wye
Dorstone
Llowes
Madley
Winforton
Canon Pyon
Much Cowarne
Ullingswick
Kempsey
Fladbury

Babell
Llyswen
Craswall
HEREFORD
Dormington
Ledbury
Bredon
Little Washbourne
Bretforton
Ebrington

Pwllgloyw
Talgarth
Hampton Bishop
Woolhope
Redmarley D'Abitot
Tewkesbury
Greet
Chipping Campden
Blockley

Brecon
Walterstone
Fownhope
Carey
Much Marcle
Ashleworth
Winchcombe
Ford
Stow-on-the-Wold

Trecastle
Talybont-on-Usk
Cwmdu
Crickhowell
St Owens Cross
Sellack
Newent
Howle Hill
Cheltenham
Lower Apperley
Guiting Power
Bourton-on-the-Water

Brecon Beacons
Llangattock
Tal-y-Coed
Symonds Yat
GLOUCESTER
Andoversford
Withington
Cold Aston
Northleach
Great Rissington

Abergavenny
Llanvapley
Penallt
Cranham
Birdlip
Cowley
Chedworth
Fossebridge

Bettws Newydd
Trelleck
Newland
Clearwell
Aylburton
Stroud
Bisley
Oakridge
Colesbourne
Miserden
Barnsley
Coln St Aldwyns

Usk
Brockweir
Lydney
Woodchester
Nailsworth
Hyde
Cirencester
Southrop

Cwmbran
Llantrisant
Shirenewton
Oldbury-on-Severn
Berkeley
Box
Meysey Hampton

Tredunnock
Llanvair Discoed
Chepstow
Aust
Didmarton
Tetbury
Ewen
Siddington

Crelgiau
M4
NEWPORT
M48
Almondsbury
Sherston
Malmesbury
SWINDON

Kenfig
Sigingstone
M5
M49
Tormarton
Burton
Christian Malford
Brinkworth
Winterbourne Bassett

St Hilary
CARDIFF
BRISTOL
M32
Hinton
Ford
Combe
Calne
Beckhampton
Wootton Rivers

East Aberthaw
Penmark
Churchill
BATH
Box
Lacock
Rowde
Horton
Pewsey

V GLAM
Stanton Wick
Blagdon
Combe Hay
Melksham
Holt
Seend
Devizes
Great Hinton

Axbridge
Litton
Glutton
Faulkland
Rudge
Westbury
Little Cheverell

Salisbury Plain

West Huntspill
Wookey
Priddy
Mells
Corsley
Heath
Heytesbury

Washford
Kilve
Nether Stowey
Glastonbury
Wells
Shepton Mallet
Nunney
Horningsham
Corton
Upton Lovell
Stapleford

Exmoor
Luxborough
Monksilver
Bridgwater
Ashcott
Ditcheat
Cranmore
Kilmington
Stourhead
Hindon
Fonthill Gifford
Barford St Martin
SALISBURY

Exford
Winsford
Langley Marsh
Fitzhead
Butleigh
Castle Cary
Somerton
Redlynch
Mere
East Knoyle
Nunton
Alderbury

Knowstone
Waterrow
Stoke St Gregory
Langport
Sparkford
Wincanton
Bourton
Ludwell
Whitsbury
Woodfalls

Appley
Staple Fitzpaine
Knapp
North Curry
Kingsdon
Ilchester
West Camel
Gillingham
Motcombe
Alvediston
Rockbourne
Woodfalls

DEVON
Bickleigh
Churchinford
Ashill
Over Stratton
Montacute
Trent
Sherborne
Tollard Royal
Damerham
Fordingbridge

Butterleigh
Broadhembury
Yarcombe
Chard
Crewkerne
Plucknett
Buckland Newton
Cerne Abbas
Anstey
Gussage All Saints
Ibsley
Linwood

Cadeleigh
Stockland
Honiton
Wambrook
Corscombe
Evershot
Plush
Milton
Blandford Forum
Ringwood

Crediton
Clyst Hydon
Dalwood
Stoke Abbott
Piddletrenthide
Piddlehinton
A31
Christchurch

Cheriton Bishop
Tedburn St Mary
Newton St Cyres
Rockbeare
Chideock
Loders
Powerstock
Nettlecombe
Tolpuddle
East Morden

Drewsteignton
Exminster
Topsham
Branscombe
Axmouth
Lyme Regis
Bridport
Stratton
Dorchester
West Knighton
Corfe Castle
BOURNEMOUTH

Lower Ashton
Doddiscombsleigh
Kenton
Beer
Burton Bradstock
West Stafford
East Knighton
Studland

Trusham
Lympstone
Cockwood
West Bexington
Chesil Beach
East Chaldon
Church Knowle

Chudleigh
Knighton
Lyme Bay
WEYMOUTH
West Lulworth

Hayton Vale
Kingsteignton
Portland
Bill of Portland

Ashburton
Newton Abbot
Kingskerswell

Buckfastleigh
Staverton
TORQUAY
SY

Littlehempston
Totnes

Tuckenhay
Cornworthy
Dartmouth

Blackawton
Dittisham

Slapton
Stokenham
Torcross

East Prawle
Prawle Point

1 Tenbury Wells	13 Lower Vobster
2 Chalford	14 Warminster
3 Minchinhampton	15 Punchknowle
4 Corsham	16 Lower Chicksgrove
5 Whitley	17 Ebbesbourne Wake
6 Bromham	18 Broad Chalke
7 Bradford-on-Avon	19 East Coker
8 Limpley Stoke	20 Hinton St George
9 Midford	21 Sydling St Nicholas
10 Norton St Philip	22 Shepton Montague
11 Beckington	23 Chilmark
12 Frome	

0   10   20 miles
0   10   20   30 kilometres

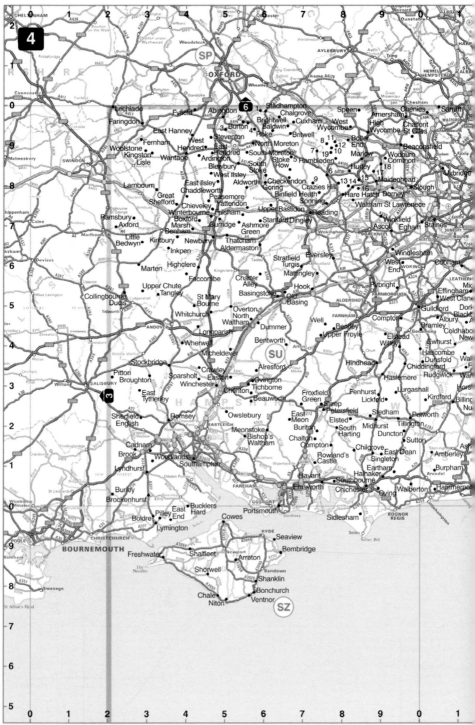

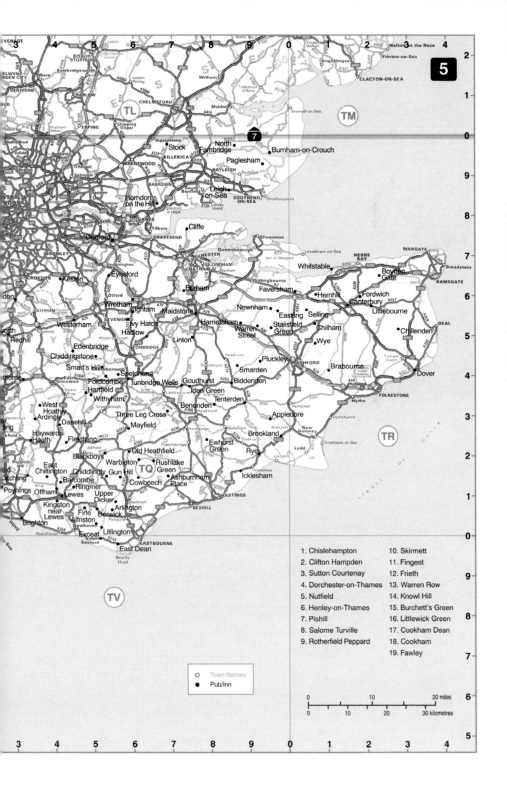

5

1. Chislehampton
2. Clifton Hampden
3. Sutton Courtenay
4. Dorchester-on-Thames
5. Nutfield
6. Henley-on-Thames
7. Pishill
8. Salome Turville
9. Rotherfield Peppard
10. Skirmett
11. Fingest
12. Frieth
13. Warren Row
14. Knowl Hill
15. Burchett's Green
16. Littlewick Green
17. Cookham Dean
18. Cookham
19. Fawley

○ Town Names
● Pub/Inn

| 0 | | 10 | | 20 miles |
| 0 | 10 | 20 | 30 kilometres |

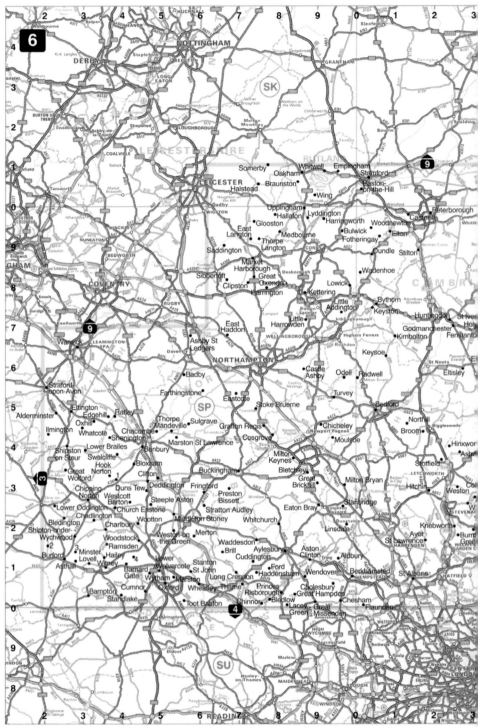

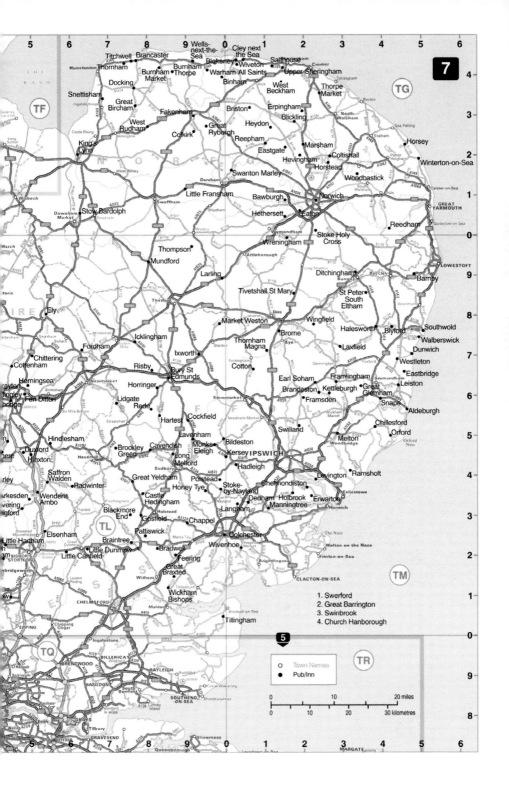

7

TG

TF

5 6 7 8 9 0 1 2 3 4 5 6

Titchwell Brancaster Wells-next-the-Sea Cley next the Sea
Hunstanton Thornham Blakeney Wiveton Salthouse Cromer
Burnham Market Burnham Thorpe Warham All Saints Upper Sheringham
Docking Binham West Beckham Thorpe Market
Snettisham West Beckham Thorpe Market
Great Bircham Fakenham Briston Erpingham North Walsham
West Rudham Heydon Blickling
Colkirk Great Ryburgh Reepham Marsham Horsey
King's Lynn Eastgate Coltishall Winterton-on-Sea
Swanton Marley Hevingham Horstead
Stow Bardolph Little Fransham Bawburgh Woodbastick
Downham Market Hethersett Norwich GREAT YARMOUTH
Eaton Reedham
Thompson Stoke Holy Cross
Mundford Wreningham
Larling Attleborough LOWESTOFT
Ditchingham Barnby
Tivetshall St Mary St Peter South Eltham
Thetford Market Weston Wingfield SOUTHWOLD
Ely Brome Halesworth Blyford Walberswick
Icklingham Thornham Magna Eye Dunwich
Fordham Ixworth Laxfield Westleton
Chittering Cotton Eastbridge
Cottenham Risby Bury St Edmunds Earl Soham Framlingham Leiston
Horningsea Horringer Brandeston Kettleburgh Great Glemham Snape
Fen Ditton Lidgate Rede Framsden Aldeburgh
Hartest Cockfield Swilland Chillesford
Hindlesham Lavenham Bildeston Melton Woodbridge Orford
Duxford Brockley Green Cavendish Monks Eleigh Kersey IPSWICH
Hinxton Long Melford Hadleigh Levington Ramsholt
Saffron Walden Great Yeldham Polstead Chelmondiston Felixstowe
Radwinter Honey Tye Stoke-by-Nayland Dedham Holbrook Erwarton
Wendens Ambo Castle Hedingham Langham Manningtree
Blackmore End Gosfield Halstead Chappel
Elsenham Pattiswick Colchester
Little Hadham Braintree Bradwell Wivenhoe Walton on the Naze
Little Canfield Little Dunmow Feering Frinton-on-Sea
Great Braxted The Naze
Wickham Bishops Brightlingsea
CHELMSFORD Tillingham CLACTON-ON-SEA

TL S E TM

TQ TR BRENTWOOD BILLERICA RAYLEIGH BASILDON SOUTHEND-ON-SEA

1. Swerford
2. Great Barrington
3. Swinbrook
4. Church Hanborough

5

○ Town Names
● Pub/Inn

0 10 20 miles
0 10 20 30 kilometres

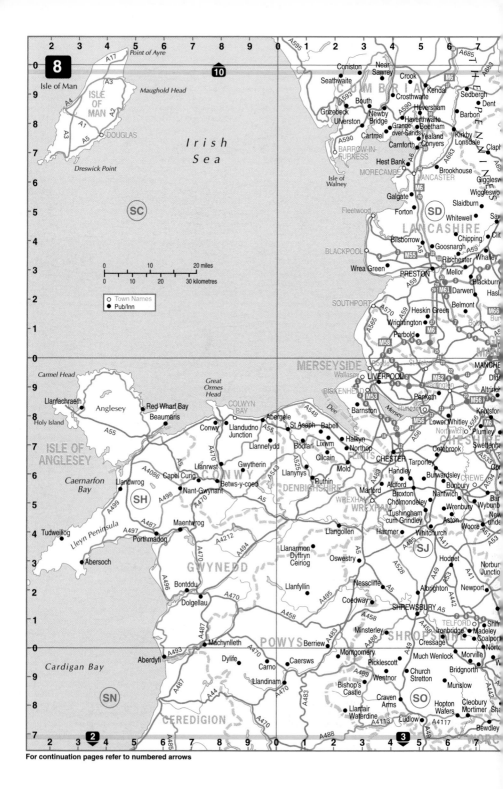

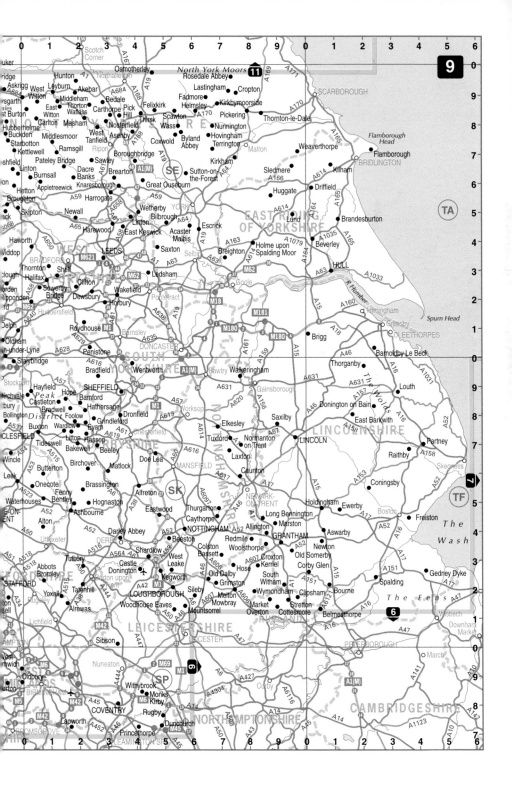

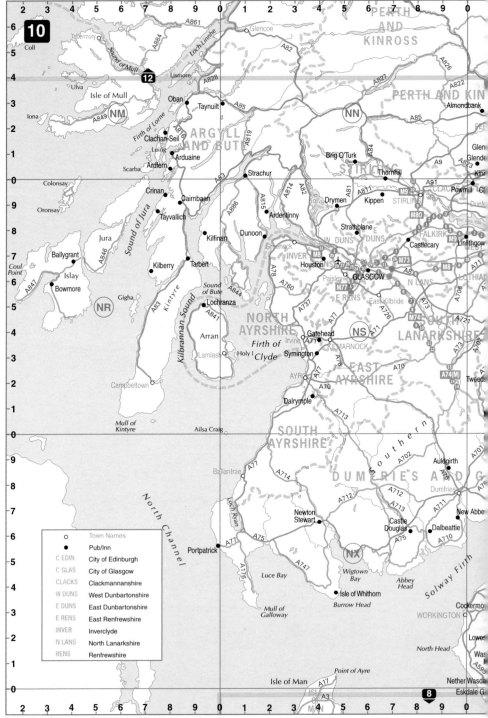

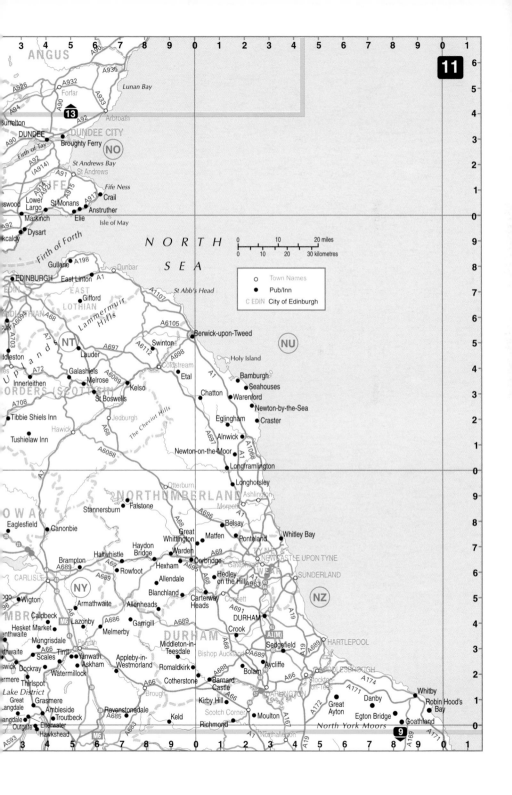

8 5 6 7 8 9 0 1 2 3 4 5 6 7 8 9 0 1 2 3

Cape Wrath

- 7 -

○ Town Names
● Pub/Inn

Rudha Rhobhanais
(Butt of Lewis)

Handa Island

A838

- 6 -

A857

- 5 -

0   10   20 miles
0   10   20   30 kilometres

NB

Tolsta Head

Point of
Stoer

A894

A838

Kylesku

- 4 -

Gallan
Head

Steornabhagh
(Stornoway)

Broad Bay

A866   Eye Peninsula

A858

A837

- 3 -

NA

Scarp

A859

Isle of
Lewis

The Minch

Summer
Isles

Achiltibuie

A835   A837

- 2 -

WESTERN
ISLES

Taransay

Tairbeart
(Tarbert)

Greenstone
Point

Ullapool

- 1 -

Toe Head

Shiant
Islands

The Minch

- 0 -

Pabbay

Harris

Rudha
Reidh

Dundonnell

A832

- 9 -

Uibhist a Tuath
(North Uist)

Sound of Harris

Gairloch

Highlands

- 8 -

Lochnam Madadh
(Lochmaddy)

A867

Carnish

Dunvegan
Head

A87(A856)

NG

Rona

A896

A832   A832   Gan

A835

- 7 -

Beinn na Faoghla
(Benbecula)

NF

The Little Minch

Sound of Raasay

Inner Sound

Applecross

A890

HIGHLAND

- 6 -

- 5 -

Portree

Raasay

Plockton

- 4 -

Uibhist a Deas
(South Uist)

A865

Rudha Hallagro

Carbost

A863

Sconser

Scalpay

Kyle of Lochalsh

North West Highlands

- 3 -

Loch Baghasdail
(Lochboisdale)

Isle
of
Skye

A87
(A850)

Dornie

A887

- 2 -

Sound of Barra

Eriskay

Canna

Cuillin

Isleornsay

A851

Glenelg

A87

Fort
Augustus

- 1 -

Barra

A888

Rum

Sound

Ardvasar

Sound of Sleet

A87

- 0 -

Mingulay

Eigg

Mallaig

- 9 -

Sound of Arisaig

- 8 -

Muck

A830

A82

Fort William

- 7 -

NL

Inner Hebrides

NM

A861

Onich

North Ballachulish

- 6 -

Tobermory

Coll

Dervaig

A884

Loch Linnhe

Glencoe

A82

- 5 -

Tiree

Sound of Mull

Port
Appin

- 4 -

Ulva

10

Lismore

A828

- 3 -

Iona

Isle of Mull

A849

ARGYLL
AND BUT

A85

- 2 -

Firth of Lorne

A816

A819

- 1 -

Luing

5 6 7 8 9 0 1 2 3 4 5 6 7 8 9 0 1 2 3

Scarba

Central London

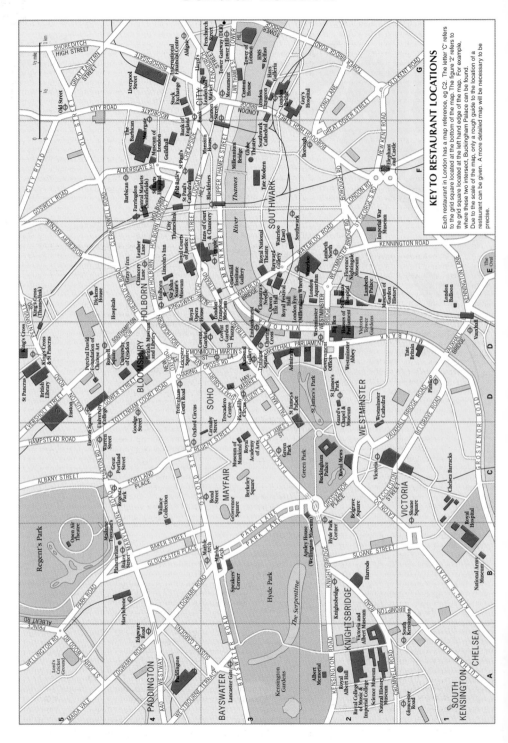

Index

Index

Index

Index

Index

Index

O

Index

Index

Index

Please send this form to:
    Editor, The Pub Guide,
    Lifestyle Guides,
    The Automobile Association,
    Fanum House,
    Basingstoke RG21 4EA

or fax: 01256 491647
or e-mail: lifestyleguides@theAA.com

Please use this form to tell us about any pub or inn you have visited, whether it is in the guide or not currently listed. We are interested in the quality of food, the selection of beers and the overall ambience of the establishment.

Feedback from readers helps us to keep our guide accurate and up to date. Please note, however, that if you have a complaint to make during a visit, we do recommend that you discuss the matter with the pub management there and then so that they have a chance to put things right before your visit is spoilt.

Please note that the AA does not undertake to arbitrate between you and the pub management, or to obtain compensation or engage in protracted correspondence.

Date:

Your name (block capitals)

Your address (block capitals)

....

....

....

.... e-mail address:

Comments

....

....

....

....

....

....

....

(please attach a separate sheet if necessary)

Please tick here if you DO NOT wish to recieve details of AA offers or products ☐

PTO

Readers' Report Form

About The Pub Guide

Have you bought this guide before?

YES ☐ NO ☐

Have you bought any other pub, accommodation or food guides recently? If yes, which ones?

....

....

What do you find most useful about The AA Pub Guide?

....

....

....

....

....

....

....

Is there any other information you would like to see added to this guide?

....

....

....

....

....

What are your main reasons for visiting pubs (tick all that apply)

food ☐   business ☐   accommodation ☐

beer ☐   celebrations ☐   entertainment ☐

atmosphere ☐   leisure ☐   other ....

How often do you visit a pub for a meal?

more than once a week ☐

one a week ☐

once a fortnight ☐

once a month ☐

once in six months ☐

Please send this form to:
    Editor, The Pub Guide,
    Lifestyle Guides,
    The Automobile Association,
    Fanum House,
    Basingstoke RG21 4EA

Readers' Report Form

or fax: 01256 491647
or e-mail: lifestyleguides@theAA.com

Please use this form to tell us about any pub or inn you have visited, whether it is in the guide or not currently listed. We are interested in the quality of food, the selection of beers and the overall ambience of the establishment.

Feedback from readers helps us to keep our guide accurate and up to date. Please note, however, that if you have a complaint to make during a visit, we do recommend that you discuss the matter with the pub management there and then so that they have a chance to put things right before your visit is spoilt.

Please note that the AA does not undertake to arbitrate between you and the pub management, or to obtain compensation or engage in protracted correspondence.

Date:

Your name (block capitals)

Your address (block capitals)

....

....

....

.... e-mail address:

Comments

....

....

....

....

....

....

....

(please attach a separate sheet if necessary)

Please tick here if you DO NOT wish to recieve details of AA offers or products ☐

PTO

Readers' Report Form

About The Pub Guide

YES   NO

Have you bought this guide before? ☐ ☐

Have you bought any other pub, accommodation or food guides recently? If yes, which ones?

....

....

What do you find most useful about The AA Pub Guide?

....

....

....

....

....

....

....

Is there any other information you would like to see added to this guide?

....

....

....

....

....

What are your main reasons for visiting pubs (tick all that apply)

food ☐   business ☐   accommodation ☐

beer ☐   celebrations ☐   entertainment ☐

atmosphere ☐   leisure ☐   other ....

How often do you visit a pub for a meal?

more than once a week ☐

one a week ☐

once a fortnight ☐

once a month ☐

once in six months ☐

Please send this form to:
Editor, The Pub Guide,
Lifestyle Guides,
The Automobile Association,
Fanum House,
Basingstoke RG21 4EA

or fax: 01256 491647
or e-mail: lifestyleguides@theAA.com

Please use this form to tell us about any pub or inn you have visited, whether it is in the guide or not currently listed. We are interested in the quality of food, the selection of beers and the overall ambience of the establishment.

Feedback from readers helps us to keep our guide accurate and up to date. Please note, however, that if you have a complaint to make during a visit, we do recommend that you discuss the matter with the pub management there and then so that they have a chance to put things right before your visit is spoilt.

Please note that the AA does not undertake to arbitrate between you and the pub management, or to obtain compensation or engage in protracted correspondence.

Date:

Your name (block capitals)

Your address (block capitals)

....

....

....

.... e-mail address:

Comments

....

....

....

....

....

....

....

(please attach a separate sheet if necessary)

Please tick here if you DO NOT wish to recieve details of AA offers or products ☐

PTO

Readers' Report Form

About The Pub Guide

Have you bought this guide before?   YES ☐   NO ☐

Have you bought any other pub, accommodation or food guides recently? If yes, which ones?

....

....

What do you find most useful about The AA Pub Guide?

....

....

....

....

....

....

....

Is there any other information you would like to see added to this guide?

....

....

....

....

....

What are your main reasons for visiting pubs (tick all that apply)

food ☐   business ☐   accommodation ☐

beer ☐   celebrations ☐   entertainment ☐

atmosphere ☐   leisure ☐   other ....

How often do you visit a pub for a meal?

more than once a week   ☐
one a week   ☐
once a fortnight   ☐
once a month   ☐
once in six months   ☐